t's

Movie Yearbook

2013

*Other Books by Roger Ebert*

An Illini Century

A Kiss Is Still a Kiss

Two Weeks in the Midday Sun: A Cannes Notebook

Behind the Phantom's Mask

Roger Ebert's Little Movie Glossary

Roger Ebert's Movie Home Companion
*annually 1986–1993*

Roger Ebert's Video Companion
*annually 1994–1998*

Roger Ebert's Movie Yearbook
*annually 1999–2007, 2009–2012*

Questions for the Movie Answer Man

Roger Ebert's Book of Film: An Anthology

Ebert's Bigger Little Movie Glossary

I Hated, Hated, Hated This Movie

The Great Movies

The Great Movies II

Your Movie Sucks

Roger Ebert's Four-Star Reviews—1967–2007

Awake in the Dark: The Best of Roger Ebert

Scorsese by Ebert

The Pot and How to Use It: The Mystery and Romance of the Rice Cooker

Life Itself: A Memoir

A Horrible Experience of Unbearable Length: More Movies That Suck

*With Daniel Curley*
The Perfect London Walk

*With Gene Siskel*
The Future of the Movies: Interviews with Martin Scorsese,
Steven Spielberg, and George Lucas

*DVD Commentary Tracks*
Citizen Kane
Dark City
Casablanca
Floating Weeds
Crumb
Beyond the Valley of the Dolls

# Roger Ebert's Movie Yearbook 2013



**Andrews McMeel Publishing, LLC**
Kansas City • Sydney • London

Andrews McMeel Publishing, LLC
an Andrews McMeel Universal company
1130 Walnut Street, Kansas City, Missouri 64106

www.andrewsmcmeel.com

12 13 14 15 16 MLY 10 9 8 7 6 5 4 3 2 1

ISBN: 978-1-4494-2344-5

Library of Congress Control Number: 2012936739

All the reviews in this book originally appeared in the *Chicago Sun-Times*.

This book is dedicated
to Robert Zonka, 1928–1985.
God love ya.

ATTENTION: SCHOOLS AND BUSINESSES

Andrews McMeel books are available at quantity discounts with bulk purchase for educational, business, or sales promotional use. For information, please e-mail the Andrews McMeel Publishing Special Sales Department: specialsales@amuniversal.com

# Contents

# Introduction

The massacre at a premiere of *The Dark Knight Rises* in Aurora, Colorado, brought a wave of speculation about whether movie violence inspires violent behavior in moviegoers. I'd written a blog about our need for better gun control, and it drew a lot of messages along those lines, suggesting I should put my own house in order.

This yearbook is not the right place to go into gun control, but violence in the movies is fair game. Does it inspire violence in society? The honest answer is, I don't know. But there I times I believe it has a sort of deadening effect on young viewers who are exposed to a lot of it. I go to see virtually every new release, and sometimes I despair. Many new films are nonstop violent action, with mechanical dialogue and shallow characters. Essentially they offer only kinetic action and bright colors. What thinking person can possibly care about the plot of a Transformers movie?

In my years of professional movie going I've seen a relentless erosion of storytelling standards in mainstream commercial movies. The idea of a well-structured story is no longer a goal. Many successful movies consist essentially of a perfunctory set-up and 80 or 90 minutes of spectacular special effects. Well-made feature films used to embed the idea that causes had effects; that characters should expect to reap the results of their decisions. Now we usually see invulnerable heroes who destroy one threat after another in ways that make no sense. They can jump from heights and not be injured. They can miraculously avoid being struck by countless rounds from automatic weapons. They can drive through city streets, leave carnage behind, and pay no consequences.

This can often be entertaining escapism, as in the *Dark Knight* movies, *Spider-Man II*, and a Bond picture. More often, it is simply routine. Please forgive me for employing one of the most over-used lines in Shakespeare: Viewers are subjected to sound and fury, signifying nothing.

I don't know if an exclusive diet of such movies can influence human behavior. I do believe, however, that seeing good films are, at the end of the day, likely to make you a more thoughtful and interesting person. I think there is such a thing as "dumbing down," and I think our mass media contribute to it.

One of the reasons for this may be that movie choices are often shaped by the myopic and skewed MPAA Rating System. It's obvious that the MPAA takes a sterner look at sexuality than violence. Incredible violence can get a PG-13 seal of approval, but films, however thoughtful, that deal with human relationships are more likely to be rated R. Children's films, which are now usually animated 3-D cartoons, often consist of little more than distracting fast action. The loving craftsmanship of Disney classics or such more recent films as *Little Mermaid* and *The Lion King* is much harder to find than inane adventures like *Kung Fu Panda* and the *Ice Age* movies.

I believe there is such thing as a movie appropriate for adults, and that it should be rated R or NC-17. During 2012, we had the rare experience of seeing a film by an established director, with major stars in the leads, released with the NC-17 rating. This was William Friedkin's *Killer Joe*, starring Matthew McConaughey. You can read my review of it in this book. I think NC-17 was the correct rating and that a good many more R-rated movies deserve it. There are also PG-13 movies that probably should be rated R.

I think, perhaps foolishly, that such a shift in the MPAA's standards might place more emphasis on storytelling and character and make a smaller opening for movies that depend entirely on violence. I believe that younger viewers, those in the PG-13 category, might benefit from less mindless action in their formative years. The decay of standards in movies may be related to the decay of standards in our society. I can't prove it. But I fear it.

* * *

My sincere thanks to Dorothy O'Brien, who has been the book's valued editor at Andrews McMeel for many years. Also to Sue Roush, my editor at Universal Uclick, and to Laura Emerick, Amanda Barrett, Linda Bergstrom, Miriam Di Nunzio, Darel Jevens, Teresa Budasi, Thomas Conner, and all the other heroes at the *Chicago Sun-Times*, and Jim Emerson and the Web staff at rogerebert.com. Many others are thanked in the Acknowledgments.

ROGER EBERT

## Acknowledgments

My editor is Dorothy O'Brien, tireless, cheerful, all-noticing. My friend and longtime editor Donna Martin suggested the yearbook approach to the annual volume. The design is by Cameron Poulter, the typographical genius of Hyde Park.

My thanks to production editor Christi Clemons Hoffman, who renders Cameron's design into reality. John Yuelkenbeck at Alias Creative Group is the compositor who has worked diligently on the series for years. I have been blessed with the expert and discriminating editing of Laura Emerick, Miriam Di Nunzio, Darel Jevins, Jeff Johnson, and Teresa Budasi at the *Chicago Sun-Times*; Sue Roush at Universal Uclick; and Michelle Daniel and David Shaw at Andrews McMeel Publishing. For much advice and counsel, thanks to Jim Emerson and John Barry of www.rogerebert.com.

Many thanks are also due to Marsha Jordan at WLS-TV. My gratitude goes to Carol Iwata, my expert personal assistant, and to Gregory Isaac, who is a computer whiz and invaluable aide-de-camp. I must also thank those who have given me countless observations and corrections, including Peter Debruge, Jana J. Monji, and Troylene Ladner.

And special thanks and love to my wife, Chaz, who was always at my side during a difficult illness, helped see three books through the press during that time, and was a cheerleader for this one. I am so grateful to her as we once again, relieved, enter a period of good health.

Roger Ebert

# Key to Symbols

| | |
|---|---|
| ★★★★ | A great film |
| ★★★ | A good film |
| ★★ | Fair |
| ★ | Poor |
| | G, PG, PG-13, R, NC-17: Ratings of the Motion Picture Association of America |
| G | Indicates that the movie is suitable for general audiences |
| PG | Suitable for general audiences but parental guidance is suggested |
| PG-13 | Recommended for viewers 13 years or above; may contain material inappropriate for younger children |
| R | Recommended for viewers 17 or older |
| NC-17 | Intended for adults only |
| 141 m. | Running time |
| 2010 | Year of theatrical release |

# Reviews

## A

### Abraham Lincoln: Vampire Hunter ★ ★ ★

R, 105 m., 2012

Benjamin Walker (Abraham Lincoln), Dominic Cooper (Henry Sturgess), Anthony Mackie (Will Johnson), Mary Elizabeth Winstead (Mary Todd Lincoln), Rufus Sewell (Adam), Marton Csokas (Jack Barts), Jimmi Simpson (Joshua Speed), Erin Wasson (Vadoma). Directed by Timur Bekmambetov and produced by Bekmambetov, Tim Burton, and Jim Lemley. Screenplay by Seth Grahame-Smith, based on his novel.

*Abraham Lincoln: Vampire Hunter* is without a doubt the best picture we are ever likely to see on the subject—unless there is a sequel, which is unlikely, because at the end the Lincolns are on their way to the theater. It's also a more entertaining movie than I remotely expected. Yes, dear readers, I went expecting to sneer.

The story opens with young Abe witnessing the murder of his mother by a vampire. He swears an oath of vengeance, and some years later is lucky to be getting drunk while standing at a bar next to Henry Sturgess (Dominic Cooper), who coaches him on vampire killing and explains that it is a high calling, requiring great dedication and no distractions like marriage.

There's an early scene in which Lincoln tries to shoot a vampire, but that won't work because they're already dead. Then whatever can he do? "Well," he tells Henry, "I used to be pretty good at rail-splitting." This line drew only a few chuckles from the audience because the movie cautiously avoids any attempt to seem funny.

Lincoln's weapon of choice becomes an ax with a silver blade, which he learns to spin like a baton twirler. That he carries this ax with him much of the time may strike some as peculiar. I was reminded uncannily of Buford Pusser, walking tall and carrying a big stick.

Against advice, Lincoln (Benjamin Walker) marries Mary Todd (Mary Elizabeth Winstead), and the story moves quickly to his days in the White House, where he discovers that the vampires are fighting on the side of the South. This seems odd, since they should be equal opportunity bloodsuckers, but there you have it. Still with him is childhood friend Will Johnson (Anthony Mackie), a free black man whose mistreatment helped form Lincoln's hatred of slavery. Also still at his side is Joshua Speed (Jimmi Simpson), who hired Lincoln in his Springfield general store; Johnson and Speed join Lincoln in Civil War strategy sessions and are his principal advisers, roles overlooked by history.

The movie, directed by Timur Bekmambetov and written by Seth Grahame-Smith, based on his novel, handles all these matters with an admirable seriousness, which may be the only way they could possibly work. The performances are earnest and sincere, and even villains like Adam (Rufus Sewell), the American leader of the Vampire Nation, doesn't spit or snarl overmuch. The movie regrettably introduces but does not explain Vadoma (Erin Wasson), a statuesque woman who is several decades ahead of her time in her taste for leather fetish wear. Are vampires kinky? I didn't know.

Although we do not attend *Abraham Lincoln: Vampire Hunter* in search of a history lesson, there's one glitch I cannot overlook. In the first day of fighting at Gettysburg, the Union sustains a defeat so crushing that Lincoln is tempted to surrender. This is because the Confederate troops, all vampires, are invulnerable to lead bullets, cannon fire, and steel blades, and have an alarming way of disappearing and rematerializing. Over breakfast, Lincoln confides his despair to his wife, and says conventional weapons are of no more use against them than—why—than this fork! As he stares at it, he realizes it is a silver fork, and vampires can be killed by silver weapons, as he has proved with his ax twirling.

Now try not to focus too much on the timeline. After his realization, Lincoln mobilizes all resources to gather wagonloads of silver in Washington, smelts it, and manufactures silver bayonets, bullets, and cannonballs. Then we see him, Johnson, and Speed on board a weapons train en route to Gettysburg. It is night again, so apparently all of this took less than a day.

Never mind. What comes now is a genuinely thrilling action sequence in which the vampires battle with Lincoln and his friends on top of the speeding train, which hurtles toward a high wooden bridge that has been set alight by the sinister Vadoma (pronounced *Vadooma,* I think). This sequence is preposterous and yet exciting, using skillful editing and special effects. Somehow Benjamin Walker and his costars here are even convincing—well, as convincing as such goofiness could possibly be.

*Abraham Lincoln: Vampire Hunter* has nothing useful to observe about Abraham Lincoln, slavery, the Civil War, or much of anything else. Blink and you may miss the detail that Harriet Tubman's Underground Railroad essentially won the war for the North. But the movie doesn't promise insights on such subjects. What it achieves is a surprisingly good job of doing justice to its title, and treating Lincoln with as much gravity as we can expect, under the circumstances.

## Accomplices ★ ★ ★

NO MPAA RATING, 93 m., 2010

Gilbert Melki (Herve Cagan), Emmanuelle Devos (Karine Mangin), Cyril Descours (Vincent Bouvier), Nina Meurisse (Rebecca Legendre), Joana Preiss (Esther). Directed by Frederic Mermoud and produced by Damien Couvreur and Tonie Marshall. Screenplay by Mermoud and Pascal Arnold.

*Accomplices* coils through two stories, cutting between them as they converge, as we know they will, because the film has opened with a corpse floating in the river Seine. This body, as a flashback establishes, belongs to a boy about nineteen, and the film will watch as he meets a cute girl in a cyber café and leads her into his dangerous world. The other story involves two police inspectors, who begin with the corpse.

Sometimes when a movie cuts between parallel stories it's tiresome. Not this one. The director, Frederic Mermoud, does an interesting thing with time: As the cops are working their way back from the dead body, the other story works its way forward to the point that the body became dead. Then the stories join up and conclude in a surprising and particularly satisfying way.

Vincent (Cyril Descours) is a hustler who meets his male clients in hotel rooms. He meets Rebecca (Nina Meurisse), likes her, gets her phone number, and they start seeing each other. He says he works in real estate—unlikely, given his scruffy appearance and the shabby mobile home he lives in. She is bourgeois but ready for the wild side, and they fall truly in love, like Bonnie and Clyde and other couples where crime is in the mix.

Vincent eventually tells Rebecca what he really does, and the way the movie charts her reaction is touchingly realistic. She learns of his world and stirs the jealousy of his pimp—or *friend,* as he considers him. It's thrilling for her to glimpse his outlaw life, and fun when they use prostitution income to pay cash for sneakers.

Herve (Gilbert Melki) and Karine (Emmanuelle Devos) are like a long-established couple, skilled in police work, functioning expertly together, sharing personal feelings. We think it's a possibility they might hook up, but the plot isn't that obvious. The film is a police procedural explaining how they begin with a nameless body and find their way back to Vincent's associates and clients. One interview, with a businesswoman who shared Vincent with her husband, is startling: The woman is forthcoming, matter-of-fact, defiant.

Without making a big deal out of it, *Accomplices* puts several plausible murder suspects onstage, including Rebecca, who disappeared the day of Vincent's murder. It's like an Agatha Christie in which lots of people have the opportunity and the motive. But Mermoud works so close to the characters, sees them in such detail, that only later do we pull back and observe the workings of the plot.

The original English title of the film was *Partners,* and that would have been accurate. It's about two partnerships. The one is the sad, doomed story of Vincent and Rebecca, incapable of dealing with the risks they run. The other is about how Herve and Karine shy away from risks in their lonely personal lives; how police routine creates a way for them to spend most of their waking hours together without having to deal with the sleeping hours.

I appreciate the way French films, in particular, often approach their characters at eye level. There's no artificial heightening. No music pounding out emotional instruction. They're cool, curious, looking for performances with the tone of plausible life. All four of these actors are completely natural in front of the camera.

You may have seen Emmanuelle Devos in films such as *Read My Lips* (2001) or *The Beat That My Heart Skipped* (2005); she's in the wonderful *L'Origin,* still unreleased, about a small-town mayor and a desperate con man. She's always attractive, never distractingly so, and comes equipped with intelligence and hidden motives. I like actors who make me want to figure them out.

*Accomplices* is technically a murder mystery. But the murder is only what happens. A lot of other things could have happened, and the story plays fair with the fateful role that chance takes. You would even argue that no one is actually murdered in this movie, and that when they die it is simply the result of bad decisions.

## Act of Valor ★ ★ ½

R, 101 m., 2012

Chief Dave (Himself), Lieutenant Rorke (Himself), Roselyn Sanchez (Lisa Morales), Marc Margulies (U.S. Ambassador), Dimiter Marinov (Karimov), Ailsa Marshall (Jackie Engel), Gonzalo Menendez (Commander Pedros), Timothy Gibbs (J. C. Palmer). Directed and produced by Mike McCoy and Scott Waugh. Screenplay by Kurt Johnstad.

*Act of Valor* contains hard-hitting combat footage, relentless and effective. There is a story behind the film that is no less engrossing. In an introduction at the beginning, its codirectors, Mike McCoy and Scott Waugh, speak directly to the audience, describing how they got involved in a film about the Navy SEALs, how they were embedded with an actual SEAL unit—and how, when that project grew into a fiction film, they determined to use real SEALs and not professional actors.

The early version of the film, according to reporting by Rebecca Keegan of the *Los Angeles Times,* was variously intended as a training film or recruitment film, and was made outside the usual Department of Defense guidelines for motion pictures. It now emerges as a thriller involving two (nonfactual) scenarios, one about a SEAL mission to free a kidnapped CIA operative (Roselyn Sanchez), the other about a plot to smuggle terrorists into the United States through tunnels from Mexico constructed by drug cartels.

The details in both of these scenarios seem realistic—although how would I know? The codirectors and their team have produced an accomplished, riveting action movie. I am reminded of the initial impact of films such as Oliver Stone's *Platoon* and Kathryn Bigelow's *The Hurt Locker,* which both told convincing and authentic stories. *Act of Valor,* however, centers more on action and much less on the human elements involved.

The central characters are played by actual Navy SEALs, who were apparently on active duty at the time and still are. This makes it difficult to write the ordinary kind of review, because none of their real names are revealed, and indeed some of the characters seem to have no names at all. I learn from Rebecca Keegan's article that the characters named Chief Dave and Lieutenant Rorke are played by SEALs whose real first names are Dave and Rorke. Thanks a lot. The official cast listing is a baffling mixture of characters without names and names with "uncredited" roles, and doesn't include either Chief Dave or Lieutenant Rorke, so I am reduced to describing the experience and not the performances.

Much of the movie consists of pure action, punctuated by terse dialogue and few subtleties. We don't get to know the characters as individuals, they don't have personality traits, they have no backstories, they don't use colorful dialogue, and after the movie you find yourself describing events but not people. Assuming that the characters described as SEALs were being played by real SEALs, all I can say is that they were convincing and weren't asked to do any dramatic stretching they weren't capable of.

Yet the movie can be discussed on another level. In the same week I saw *Act of Valor,* I also saw an extraordinary film named *Hell and Back Again.* It is about a real man, marine sergeant Nathan Harris, and his real wife, Ashley. Harris led men in combat in Afghanistan. Shortly before the scheduled end of his six-month tour, a sniper's bullet entered his right buttock, shattered his hip socket, and bounced back to destroy leg bones. He's quite willing to show people the entry scar and describe how he has two rods filling in for bones.

When Nathan Harris was a teenager, he says, "what I wanted to do was kill people." He enlisted in the marines. He doesn't actually say if he has killed anyone or not, but the director, Danfung Dennis, who was embedded with Harris's Echo Company, followed him in action and we see that he has grown into a natural leader of men. Some of the film's most involving scenes show him debating village elders (through an interpreter) about the role of America in Afghanistan—he sincerely believes he is helping to bring them freedom, and finds it hard to answer their statements that they want to be left alone by both the Americans and the Taliban.

The film follows Harris home, through an agonizing period of rehab, and shows that his life will never be the same. Memories of battle haunt him, and *Hell and Back Again* intercuts actual sights and scenes from Afghanistan with scenes back home in North Carolina. He doesn't have post-traumatic stress syndrome. He dreams of returning to action, and it is hard for him to accept that it may not happen.

*Act of Valor* is gift-wrapped in patriotism. Once intended as a recruitment film, that's how it plays. The action scenes are harrowing but exciting. Lots of explosions and special effects. At the end there is a full-dress military funeral, honoring three generations of warriors. The real action scenes in *Hell and Back Again* don't play like an action movie. I don't recall seeing a single Taliban fighter. One of Sergeant Harris's men is killed on the first day in the field. Harris is wounded late in his tour. Nobody saw either one of the snipers.

I have a feeling that the teenage Nathan Harris, who wanted to kill people, would have loved *Act of Valor.* But *Hell and Back Again,* in describing his life today, doesn't play like a recruitment film. A great deal is made by the directors McCoy and Waugh that actual live ammunition was used in the making of their film. Actual live ammunition was also used in *Hell and Back Again.* If you asked Sergeant Nathan Harris what he thought about using live ammo in a Hollywood action movie, what do you suppose he would say? My best guess is, he would say they were damned fools.

## Addiction Incorporated ★ ★ ★

PG, 100 m., 2012

A documentary featuring Victor DeNoble, Paul Mele, Russ Herman, David A. Kessler, Michael C. Moore, Keith Summa, Henry Waxman, and Steven C. Parrish. Directed and produced by Charles Evans Jr.

The PG rating of *Addiction Incorporated* is explained in part because it "contains thematic material involving smoking and addiction." When the MPAA first adopted its code, everyone in the movies smoked except Snow White. Smoking was identified with romance and heroism, Bette Davis was applauded for lighting up on the *Tonight* show, and you could often see the smoke from Johnny's own cigarette curling up from the ashtray under his desk.

These days, a character who smokes is self-destructive, a villain, or a troubled high school student. *Addiction Incorporated* follows tobacco's journey downhill from respectability. After his long night's work, Santa used to relax with a Lucky on a back-cover ad in *Life* magazine, and Ronald Reagan liked to puff on Chesterfields. Now we learn of proposed new government health warnings that are more likely to make you spew than smoke your first cigarette.

The key player in this process was a man named Victor DeNoble, a scientist for Philip Morris who began with the generally known fact that nicotine was addictive, and discovered that a chemical named acetaldehyde made it more addictive. DeNoble was originally hired by Philip Morris to find a *substitute* for nicotine, in the attempt to develop a less addictive cigarette. (The tobacco industry's reasoning was: Dead smokers don't buy cigarettes.) When DeNoble reported his findings, Philip Morris switched signals and realized it could outsell their competitors by adding more acetaldehyde. At this time the Tobacco Institute was making phony claims that there was no evidence cigarettes were addictive at all.

You may be assuming DeNoble is the same whistleblower played by Russell Crowe in *The Insider* (1999). No, that was Jeffrey Wigand, a scientist employed by Brown and Williamson. DeNoble's research was obtained by ABC News, whose corporate bosses vetoed its use. Wigand was leaking to *60 Minutes* on CBS, where network executives also were shy. There were a lot of cigarette ads on TV in those days—but more to the point, Big Tobacco had a reputation of suing for millions and never losing a case.

The first half of this doc covers familiar territory; although everyone, even my parents, who both died from smoking cigarettes, knew they were addictive, Big Tobacco had always denied it. Now DeNoble's research with laboratory rats proved it beyond a doubt. Rats who pushed a button got a rat-sized dose of nicotine. The first dose made them puke, but soon they were pushing the button ninety times a day. DeNoble was the most harmful witness imaginable to the industry because he could testify that Philip Morris knew it, and hoped to increase sales with its knowledge.

The second half of the film begins with a historic series of congressional hearings chaired by Representative Henry Waxman of California. Having thoroughly established that the industry knew nicotine was an addictive drug, Waxman summoned the heads of the seven major tobacco companies to testify. In the past they'd always refused to appear. This time they showed up. Waxman dropped a surprise: He placed them under oath. They can either agree it is addictive, or perjure themselves. All seven raise their right hands and swear it isn't addictive. Then DeNoble delivers his historic testimony. In the months to come, all seven resigned from their corporations.

DeNoble, from a working-class family, was its first member to attend college. That came after he discovered he was dyslexic and "I wasn't stupid like I thought." Publication of his Philip Morris findings in a journal would have established his reputation. Instead, learning what the paper contained, his bosses ordered him to withdraw it and kill his rats. Then they fired him. Today he speaks against cigarettes on national tours paid for by funds that were part of Big Tobacco's settlement with the government.

*Addiction Incorporated*, directed by Charles Evans Jr., doesn't tell a new story, although it closes very recently with President Obama signing the legislation that DeNoble's research put into motion. It's an effective film, enlivened with animated rats, never boring, and entertaining when it shows Rush Limbaugh, the cigar enthusiast, fulminating against the Waxman hearings.

## The Adjustment Bureau ★ ★ ★

PG-13, 105 m., 2011

Matt Damon (David Norris), Emily Blunt (Elise Sellas), Anthony Mackie (Harry Mitchell), John Slattery (Richardson), Michael Kelly (Charlie Traynor), Terence Stamp (Thompson). Directed by George Nolfi and produced by Nolfi, Bill Carraro, Michael Hackett, and Chris Moore. Screenplay by Nolfi, based on the short story "Adjustment Team" by Philip K. Dick.

Here I go again. I'll be helpless to stop myself. *The Adjustment Bureau* is about the conflict between free will and predestination, and right there you have the whole dilemma of life, don't you? Either it makes a difference what you choose to do, or the book has already been written and all you can do is turn the pages.

That these questions are raised in a science-fiction thriller with a romance at its core should not be surprising. Sci-fi offers storytellers the freedom of tinkering with realism, and few writers did that with more complexity than Philip K. Dick. This movie, written and directed by George Nolfi, is based on a Dick story about a legion of "adjusters" who move a strange thing there and a known thing here, just to be sure everything proceeds according to plan. Whose plan? The adjusters aren't big on explanations. They're like undercover agents for the higher power of your choice.

But the best-laid plans of mice and men sometimes stray. Random chance barges in, and its interference must be corrected. In *The*

*Adjustment Bureau,* Matt Damon plays a congressional candidate named David Norris, who walks into a men's room he has every reason to believe is empty, and who should emerge from one of the stalls but Elise Sellas (Emily Blunt). What was she doing there? You don't cross-examine a Meet Cute. The important thing is, these two people, who were never intended to meet, have that particular chemistry that means they're a perfect romantic match. They know it, we know it, and when their eyes and lips meet, their stories become entangled.

Philip Dick was intrigued by devices that allowed him to examine the mechanisms by which life unfolds. I think he voted for free will in the short run (the span of intelligent life on Earth, say), evolution for the middle distance (things develop according to underlying principles), and predestination in the long run (the universe will entropy and cease). A man and a woman whose eyes Meet Cute need only be concerned about the very short run.

In the movie, David Norris becomes aware of certain men wearing suits and fedoras who strangely appear in his life. He meets two of these: Mitchell and Richardson (Anthony Mackie and John Slattery). They explain that they work for a bureau that makes corrections when things go slightly wrong. For example, David and Elise were not intended to meet. What was she doing in the men's room, anyway? For her sake and his, David must not see her again.

OK, so this is where it gets intriguing. They do meet again, once again by pure chance. But *this* time, they recognize each other, you see, because they had met earlier. It is possible the second time they see each other was intended to be the first time, in which case (if you follow me) they would not necessarily even notice each other. Seeing a woman on the bus isn't the same thing as getting into a conversation with her in a men's room. So answer me this: When the adjusters urge David to forget about Elise and never see her again, aren't they asking him to exercise his free will? Aren't they implying he has a choice?

So you might think, but *The Adjustment Bureau* reveals a hidden level of reality by which players can be yanked out of the game. David is confronted in a cavernous industrial space and warned that if he doesn't straighten up, his memory will be erased. This space is reached through a doorway to a place that has no logical possibility of existence; it must be like the bedroom beyond Jupiter in *2001,* which was summoned by a greater intelligence to provide the illusion of a familiar space for an unwitting subject.

The plot develops into a cat-and-mouse game of the mind, in which David and Elise, in love and feeling as if they're destined for each other, try to outsmart or elude the men in the suits and hats. This is fun, and because Matt Damon and Emily Blunt have an easy rapport, it doesn't seem as preposterous as it is. Beneath its apparent sci-fi levels, a romantic comedy lurks here.

If you're like me, you're thinking the universe in this movie is run by a singularly inefficient designer. There is no room for chance in predestination. If there is a plan, you can't allow tinkering. There's a well-known sci-fi precept that warns if you travel back far enough in time and step on the wrong insect, you could wipe out the future. By the time we meet a very, very serious senior adviser named Thompson (Terence Stamp), we begin to suspect that his employer has delusions of grandeur. Thompson gives the appearance of being firmly in control and knowing all the right buttons to push, but his problem is David and Elise have seen behind the curtain and realize they need not be instruments of a plan. There's even the intriguing possibility that the adjusters themselves have some freedom of choice.

*The Adjustment Bureau* is a smart and good movie that could have been a great one if it had been a little more daring. I suspect the filmmakers were reluctant to follow its implications too far. What David and Elise signify by their adventures, I think, is that we're all in this together, and we're all on our own. If you follow that through, the implications are treacherous to some, not all, religions. In the short term, however, the movie is a sorta heartwarming entertainment.

## The Adventures of Tintin ★ ★ ★ ½

PG, 107 m., 2011

Jamie Bell (Tintin), Andy Serkis (Captain Archibald Haddock), Daniel Craig (Ivan

**Ivanovitch Sakharine), Nick Frost (Thomson), Simon Pegg (Thompson), Toby Jones (Silk), Mackenzie Crook (Tom), Daniel Mays (Allan), Gad Elmaleh (Ben Salaad), Joe Starr (Barnaby). Directed by Steven Spielberg and produced by Spielberg, Peter Jackson, and Kathleen Kennedy. Screenplay by Steven Moffat, Edgar Wright, and Joe Cornish, based on the comic book series *The Adventures of Tintin* by Herge.**

In gearing up to make *The Adventures of Tintin*, I suspect Steven Spielberg reached down into that place inside that fueled *Raiders of the Lost Ark*. Here again is an intrepid hero involved in a nonstop series of exploits involving exotic locations, grandiose villains, planes, trains, automobiles, motorcycles, helicopters, and ships at sea. It evokes Saturday afternoon serials in an age when most of the audience will never have seen one.

I was surprised by how much I enjoyed myself. Spielberg not only uses 3-D but bases his story on one of Europe's most beloved comic characters. The 3-D, he pulls off, just as Scorsese did in *Hugo*, because he employs it as an enhancement to 2-D instead of an attention-grabbing gimmick. The beloved character . . . can we flash back?

It is a morning in May at the Cannes Film Festival, and I am drinking my coffee in the sunlight and reading *Nice-Matin*, the regional paper. A back page in full color is given over to comics, and half the page is devoted to Tintin. I ask a French friend about him. "You don't know Tintin?" She is amazed. "*Zut!*" So loved is he, I learn, that papers rerun his old exploits even after the death of his creator, Herge.

This Tintin (voiced by Jamie Bell in the film) is a piece of work. He is a newspaperman who rarely seems to go to the office but can usually be found globe-trotting on an unimaginable expense account, always accompanied by his gifted dog, Snowy. Two maladroit Interpol inspectors named Thompson and Thomson (Nick Frost and Simon Pegg) are often on the same cases. A rum-soaked old sea salt named Captain Haddock (Andy Serkis) is often found nearby. Tintin looks like a prepubescent to me, but is treated by everyone as sort of an honorary grown-up. His yellow hair comes up to a quiff in the front.

Tintin's adventures come in book length, their pages the size of old *Life* magazines. They are drawn by the Belgian artist Herge with elegant clarity (the "clean line" approach). Sometimes a situation will require an entire page. Starting that year at Cannes I read every single Tintin book, and even bought a Tintin and Snowy T-shirt. My little French-English dictionary was a great help.

It was reported that Spielberg would use motion-capture technology on his characters. This seemed wrong, wrong, wrong. Not only did Tintin inhabit an adamantly 2-D universe, but he was manifestly not real. Anyone could draw him; his face has two dots for eyes, little curves for eyebrows and a mouth, and a nose that is like a sideways U. To make him seem more real would be to lose Tintin.

My worries became irrelevant during the movie's opening scene. It was going to be all right. Tintin looked human, if extremely streamlined. His face, as described by an eyewitness to a police artist, would produce a sketch of . . . Tintin. The other characters are permitted more detail; Thomson and Thompson in particular are given noses that would make W. C. Fields weep with envy.

Spielberg and a team of artists and animators have copied not the literal look of the Tintin strips, but the feel. A more traditional 2-D approach was done for a TV series, which you can check out on YouTube; I like it, but Spielberg is more ambitious and his characters seem more believable, to the extent that anyone created by Herge is real. The movie involves the same headlong hurtle through perilous adventures, with dire endangerment by explosives and so on. The chase is on to find a lost treasure with ancient connections to Captain Haddock's family.

There's one change I didn't appreciate. Spielberg too closely imitates a traditional action movie. There's gunfire in Herge, but the amount that goes on here is distracting. Herge devoted more time to local color, character eccentricities, and explosive dialogue, and I learned to mystify my friends with such Haddockisms as "*Tonnerre de Brest!*" and "*Mille sabords!*" ("*Thunder of Brest!*" and "*A thousand portholes!*").

One of the benefits of animation is what it allows Spielberg to do with Snowy. The little dog has always been dubious about his master's daring schemes; Tintin will propose an expedition and Snowy will think in a thought balloon, "Not by foot, I hope!" Some of the funniest moments in the movie involve Snowy's determination to convey urgent information to dunderheaded humans.

*The Adventures of Tintin* is an ambitious and lively caper, miles smarter than your average 3-D family film (how can any thinking person want to see one Chipmunks movie, let alone two or now even three?). Spielberg's film plays fair with the plucky young reporter; the director received Herge's blessing before his death in 1983. I give it 875 portholes.

## After.Life ★ ★ ½

R, 97 m., 2010

Liam Neeson (Eliot Deacon), Christina Ricci (Anna Taylor), Justin Long (Paul Conran), Chandler Canterbury (Jack), Josh Charles (Tom Peterson), Celia Weston (Beatrice Taylor). Directed by Agnieszka Wojtowicz-Vosloo and produced by Brad Michael Gilbert, Bill Perkins, and Celine Rattray. Screenplay by Wojtowicz-Vosloo, Paul Vosloo, and Jakub Korolczuk.

"You people!" says Eliot Deacon sadly, and with a touch of frustration. He is referring to the dead. They are whiners. They're not ready to die, they've got unfinished business, there are things they still desire, the death certificate is mistaken, and on and on and on. Deacon, as a mortician, has to put up with this.

Take Anna as an example. She drove away from a disastrous dinner with her boyfriend, was speeding on a rainy night, and was killed in a crash. Now here she is on a porcelain slab in his prep room, telling him there's been some mistake. Deacon tries to reason with her. He even shows her the coroner's signature on the death certificate. But no. She's alive, as he can clearly see. Besides, if he's so sure she's dead, why does he carefully lock the door from the outside whenever he leaves the room?

*After.Life* is a strange movie that never clearly declares whether Anna (Christina Ricci) is dead or alive. Well, not alive in the traditional sense, but alive in a sort of middle state between life and death. Her body is presumably dead. She has no pulse, and we assume her blood has been replaced by embalming fluid. Yet she protests, argues, can sit up and move around. Is Deacon (Liam Neeson) the only one who can see this? Maybe he's fantasizing? No, the little boy Jack (Chandler Canterbury) sees her, too, through a window.

Jack tells her boyfriend, Paul (Justin Long). He believes it. He's had a great deal of difficulty accepting her death. He still has the engagement ring he planned to offer her on that fateful night. He tries to break into the funeral home. He causes a scene at the police station. He sounds like a madman to them.

*After.Life* is a horror film involving the familiar theme of being alive when the world thinks you're dead. It couples that with a possibility that has chilled me ever since the day when, at far too young an age, I pulled down Poe from my dad's bookshelf, looked at the table of contents, and turned straight to "The Premature Burial." From Anna's point of view, she's still alive when the earth starts thudding on the coffin. From Deacon's point of view? Yes, I think from his POV, too.

From ours? The director, Agnieszka Wojtowicz-Vosloo, says audiences split about half and half. That's how I split. Half of me seizes on evidence that she's still alive, and the other half notices how the film diabolically undercuts all that evidence. I think the correct solution is: Anna is a character in a horror film that leaves her state deliberately ambiguous.

Neeson's performance as Deacon is ambiguous but sincere. He has been working with these people for years. He explains he has the "gift" of speaking with them. And little Jack, the eyewitness? Oh, but Deacon thinks he has the gift, too. So once again, you don't know what to believe. Perhaps the gift is supernatural, or perhaps it's madness or a delusion.

The film has many of the classic scenes of horror movies set in mortuaries. The chilling stainless steel paraphernalia. The work late at night. The moonlit graveyard. The burial. The opened grave. Even her desperate nails shredding the lining inside the coffin—although we see that from Anna's POV and no one else's.

I think, in a way, the film shortchanges itself by not coming down on one side or the other. As it stands, it's a framework for horror situations, but cannot be anything deeper. Yes, we can debate it endlessly—but pointlessly, because there is no solution. We can enjoy the suspense of the opening scenes and some of the drama. The performances are in keeping with the material. But toward the end, when we realize that the entire reality of the film is problematical, there is a certain impatience. It's as if our chain is being yanked.

## Agora ★ ★ ★

NO MPAA RATING, 141 m., 2010

Rachel Weisz (Hypatia), Max Minghella (Davus), Oscar Isaac (Orestes), Ashraf Barhom (Ammonius), Michael Lonsdale (Theon), Rupert Evans (Synesius), Homayoun Ershadi (Aspasius), Sammy Samir (Cyril), Richard Durden (Olympius), Omar Mostafa (Isidorus), Oshri Cohen (Medorus). Directed by Alejandro Amenabar and produced by Alvaro Augustin and Fernando Bovaira. Screenplay by Amenabar and Mateo Gil.

I went to see *Agora* expecting an epic with swords, sandals, and sex. I found swords and sandals, some unexpected opinions about sex, and a great deal more. This is a movie about ideas, a drama based on the ancient war between science and superstition. At its center is a woman who in the fourth century A.D. was a scientist, mathematician, philosopher, astronomer, and teacher, respected in Egypt although women were not expected to be any of those things.

Hypatia (Rachel Weisz) was born into the family business. Her father, Theon (Michael Lonsdale), was the curator of the Library of Alexandria, which had as its mission "collecting all the world's knowledge." Scholars traveled there from across the ancient world, doing research and donating manuscripts. It was destroyed by Christians in 391 A.D., and *Agora* takes place in the years surrounding that incalculable loss.

The film's title refers to the name for the public assembly places in ancient Greek city-states. The library was such an agora, and we see Hypatia teaching a class of young men, who listen to her with open admiration. There's an early indication that this won't be a routine *Troy*-like exercise in CGI action scenes: Hypatia actually *does* teach something, using the first scale model of planetary motion to deduce, centuries before Galileo, that the earth cannot be the center of the universe.

Hypatia has three students completely under her spell: Davus (Max Minghella), Synesius (Rupert Evans), and Orestes (Oscar Isaac). All make the error of feeling lust, Orestes least subtly. Hypatia seems devoid of sexual feeling; perhaps she believes her vocation prohibits it. Her method of rejecting Orestes is brutally direct. Although Rachel Weisz may be beautiful, in the performance she makes no effort to exploit that, and is single-minded in her dedication to knowledge.

The director, Alejandro Amenabar, re-creates the Alexandria of Hypatia's time with a mixture of sets and effects, showing it at the tipping point between Greek and Roman paganism and the new religion of Christianity. As she studies with and under her father, drawing from countless parchment scrolls in the library, outside in the city the Christians burn with a fearful intensity. Hypatia herself is not interested in religion; she feels passion only for her ideas.

Neither pagans nor Christians are pacifists. Both sides possess that peculiar certainty that their opponents must by definition be evil. Blood is shed. Foolishly believing they hold the upper hand, the pagans led by Orestes sponsor a bloodletting, only to learn in a savage lesson that there are now more Christians than they imagined. This warfare culminates in the destruction of the library. Hypatia races with her students to rescue armloads of scrolls, a few of which may literally have been responsible for our surviving texts from Aristotle and other Greeks.

In sword-and-sandal epics, the Christians are without fail the good guys. Not here. Christians and pagans are equally blinded by the conviction that those who disagree deserve death. After the rise of the Christians, they grow even more militant; one group wears black robes and searches the streets for dissenters, heretics, and Jews.

There is historical truth here. The actual teachings of Jesus are often imperfectly observed by his followers. The film also has unmistakable parallels to militant Islam and to the sectarian conflicts in the Middle East and elsewhere. The movie doesn't make as much as you might expect about Hypatia's gender; possibly the subjugation of women was so unconsciously and universally accepted that, in some sense, she was seen less as a woman than as a daughter teaching the lessons of her father.

That Hypatia was a genius seems beyond question. Her invention, the hydrometer, is being used in the Gulf of Mexico at this moment to distinguish oil from water by their specific densities. Although *Agora* avoids the temptation to sneak in a romantic subplot, it gets mileage out of her character as a focus of emotional intrigue for her male students, who would have never seen a woman anything like her.

Alejandro Amenabar seems drawn to stories about the determination of the intellect to work in the real world. His *The Sea Inside* (2004) starred Javier Bardem as a paralyzed man who fought for the right to die. In *Open Your Eyes* (1997), a disfigured man struggles to express his love for a woman. The underrated *The Others* (2001) starred Nicole Kidman as a woman compelled to prove her ideas of ghosts have objective reality. Here a woman finds the earth circles the sun, but moves in indifference to her ideas.

## Ajami ★ ★ ★

NO MPAA RATING, 120 m., 2010

Shahir Kabaha (Omar), Ibrahim Frege (Malek), Fouad Habash (Nasri), Youssef Sahwani (Abu Elias), Ranin Karim (Hadir), Eran Naim (Dando), Scandar Copti (Binj). Directed by Scandar Copti and Yaron Shani and produced by Moshe Danon, Thanassis Karathanos, and Talia Kleinhendler. Screenplay by Copti and Shani.

Americans didn't know we had the right idea, but we did. We welcomed those from foreign lands (or, in some cases, forced them to come here). Then we shook them up together and left them to sort things out. We have every race, ethnicity, and religion, and that helps. Unhappy are those who live in a land with only a few.

Consider Israel, where Jews, Arabs, Muslims, and Christians by and large think it is extremely important that they are Jews, Arabs, Muslims, and Christians. There is a growing minority that says, hey, here we all are together, and since nobody is budging, let's get along. Most people apparently think someone should budge and it's not them.

*Ajami* is the latest and one of the most harrowing films set along the religious divides in Israel. It was cowritten and codirected by an Israeli and a Palestinian, and set in Jaffa, technically a part of Tel-Aviv, which has high crime and unemployment rates. The focus is on mean streets that Scorsese might understand. Gangsters, cops, and drug dealers are tossed in with religious conflicts and the ancient Romeo and Juliet dilemma. God help anyone who marries outside their tribe.

I have never seen a film from either Israeli or Palestinian filmmakers that makes a case for anything other than coexistence. There are probably such films. But the dominant theme is the tragedy of the social divides, the waste, the loss, the violence that often claims innocent victims.

Why, in an area where tension and indeed hatred runs so high, aren't there more partisan or sectarian films? Beginning with the advantage of ignorance, I'll speculate that those Palestinians and Israelis who are inclined to make feature films are drawn from the elites of their societies. They see more widely and clearly. They may be better educated. They are more instinctively liberal. They've grown beyond the group mentality.

Ah, but there is still family. No matter how advanced your views, blood ties run deep, especially when reinforced by religion. A young couple may fall in love outside their tribe, but their fathers and uncles and cousins to remote degrees will feel threatened by their love, and God will be invoked on both sides. It is the same when a relative is murdered. Instincts demand revenge.

*Ajami* is about an interlocking series of such situations, starting in the first place when a man is shot dead. Then another man is mistakenly killed in revenge. Was he mistaken for the original killer? No, he was mistaken for a member of the original killer's family—which he was, although not the correct member. Now two people are dead, more vengeance is required, nothing has been proven, and everyone involved is convinced they are in the right.

Calm heads try to prevail and stop the killing. The actual original killer (are you following?) is levied with a fine. To pay it, he finds he must sell drugs. That means we are now headed into gang territory. The source of the drugs is a Palestinian in love with a Jewish girl. An Israeli cop becomes involved in the case. I won't describe more. I'm not sure I can. It's clear enough in the film who is who, but I suspect even the characters lose track of the actual origins of their vendetta. What happens is that hatred continues to claim lives in a sort of domino effect.

The film doesn't reduce itself to a series of Mafia-style killings, in which death is a way of doing business. There are situations in which characters kill as a means of self-defense. And the filmmakers, Scandar Copti and Yaron Shani, by and large show characters on all sides who essentially would like simply to be left alone to get on with their lives. Few of them possess the *personal* hatred necessary to fuel murder. But the sectarian divide acts as an artery to carry murder to everyone downstream. Was that a mixed metaphor, or what?

The specifics of the plot in *Ajami* aren't as important as the impact of many sad moments built up one after another. Hatred is like the weather. You don't agree with the rain but still you get wet. What justifies this is the "honor" of your family, your religion, your tribe. The film deplores this. So do we all, when we stand back. The film has no solution. Nor is there one, until people find the strength to place more value upon an individual than upon his group. Sometimes I fear we're all genetically programmed not to do that. One solution is the mixing of gene pools so that groups are differently perceived. I'm not holding my breath.

## Albert Nobbs ★ ★ ★

R, 113 m., 2012

Glenn Close (Albert Nobbs), Mia Wasikowska (Helen), Aaron Johnson (Joe), Janet McTeer (Hubert Page), Pauline Collins (Mrs. Baker), Brenda Fricker (Polly), Jonathan Rhys Meyers (Viscount Yarrell), Brendan Gleeson (Dr. Holloran), Bronagh Gallagher (Cathleen). Directed by Rodrigo Garcia and produced by Close, Bonnie Curtis, Julie Lynn, and Alan Moloney. Screenplay by Close, John Banville, and Gabriella Prekop, from a novella by George Moore.

I know a novel that begins: "This is the saddest story I've ever heard." Now here is one of the saddest movies I have ever seen. It is sad because a woman has chosen to lead her life in a way that is fearful and unnatural to her, and she must live every moment in dread.

As you must know by now, Albert Nobbs is not a man. She works as a butler and waiter in a nineteenth-century Dublin hotel, where she dresses and passes as a man because a woman would not be hired for the job, and she needs the economic security. We can sympathize. But the pain she lives in isn't worth the money. Many people pass as members of the other sex for many reasons, but my impression is that for most of them it answers a genuine emotional need.

Albert Nobbs isn't happy being a man. I don't believe she's ever happy at all. There is something stiff and genderless about her, and we suspect she has no sexual experience and desires none. Her entire life is narrowly focused on economic security, and she lives in terror of being exposed. Regard her body language: shy, repressed, reclusive, trying to fade in and become invisible.

The hotel is a Dublin crossroads for people of some means but no great distinction. It's run by the ebullient Mrs. Baker (Pauline Collins), who sails a jolly ship but as an employer is no paragon. Employees come and go, and although Albert is considered by everyone an odd fellow, she's still there. Homosexuality is not unknown in this establishment; Viscount Yarrell (Jonathan Rhys Meyers) checks in with a free-drinking crew and specifies an adjoining room for his friend. But Albert Nobbs isn't a homosexual of any description; life would be simpler if she were.

One day, Hubert Page (Janet McTeer) arrives to do some house painting. Hubert is tall, lanky, smokes a lot, kids around, and is obviously (to our eyes) a woman. She gets by on personality and nerve. She quickly reads Albert, and in what must be the most astonishing moment of Albert's life to date, exposes her breasts and shares her secret. I wonder if that was the first time Albert realized she wasn't the only person who has ever passed for another sex.

That opens the film's only scenes that give us some reason to hope for Albert. The two women spend a liberating day on the beach, and Hubert takes Albert home to her wife, Cathleen (played by Bronagh Gallagher with quiet calm and tact). It becomes clear, if it wasn't already, that Albert has only a sketchy idea of what men and women do with one another, what sex is, what marriage is.

But she has a dream. She has her eye on a storefront that she believes would make a nice little tobacco shop. There would be a room in the back where tea would be served. And a room upstairs to, well, to share with a "wife." In an exercise of dismaying naïveté, she imagines Helen (Mia Wasikowska), a young housemaid at the hotel, in this role. For Albert, it involves a business partnership, not a romance.

This is such a brave performance by Glenn Close, who in making Albert so real makes the character as pathetic and unlikable as she must have been in life. The film is based on a story by George Moore (1852–1933), an Irish realist writer who may have known some real-life parallels in Dublin. Close starred in an off-Broadway production of a play based on it in 1982, and tried ever after to make it a film. The Hungarian director Istvan Szabo was attached to it circa 2001, but now the film has been made with Rodrigo Garcia, whose sure touch with women characters can be seen in his *Nine Lives* and *Mother and Child.*

Close never steps wrong, never breaks reality. My heart went out to Albert Nobbs, the depth of whose fears are unimaginable. But it is Janet McTeer who brings the film such happiness and life as it has, because the tragedy of the life of Albert Nobbs is that there can be no happiness in it. The conditions she has chosen make it impossible.

## Alice in Wonderland ★ ★ ★

PG, 108 m., 2010

Johnny Depp (Mad Hatter), Mia Wasikowska (Alice), Anne Hathaway (Mirana, the White Queen), Helena Bonham Carter (Iracebeth, the Red Queen), Crispin Glover (Stayne, the Knave of Hearts), Matt Lucas (Tweedledee/Tweedledum). And the voices of: Stephen Fry (Cheshire Cat), Michael Sheen (White Rabbit), Alan Rickman (Absolem), Timothy Spall (Bayard), Barbara Windsor (Dormouse), Christopher Lee (Jabberwocky). Directed by Tim Burton and produced by Burton, Joe Roth, Jennifer Todd, Suzanne Todd, and Richard D. Zanuck. Screenplay by Linda Woolverton, based on the books *Alice's Adventures in Wonderland* and *Through the Looking-Glass* by Lewis Carroll.

As a young reader, I found *Alice in Wonderland* creepy and rather distasteful. Alice's adventures played like a series of encounters with characters whose purpose was to tease, puzzle, and torment her. Few children would want to go to Wonderland, and none would want to stay. The problem may be that I encountered the book too young and was put off by the alarming John Tenniel illustrations. Why did Alice have such deep, dark eye sockets? Why couldn't Wonderland be cozy like the world of Pooh? Watching the 1951 film, I feared the Cheshire Cat was about to tell me something I didn't want to know.

Tim Burton's new 3-D version of *Alice in Wonderland* answers my childish questions. This has never been a children's story. There's even a little sadism embedded in Carroll's fantasy. I think of uncles who tickle their nieces until they scream. *Alice* plays better as an adult hallucination, which is how Burton rather brilliantly interprets it until a pointless third act flies off the rails. It was a wise idea by Burton and his screenwriter, Linda Woolverton, to devise a reason why Alice (Mia Wasikowska) is now a grown girl in her late teens, revisiting a Wonderland that remains much the same, as fantasy worlds must always do.

Burton is above all a brilliant visual artist, and his film is a pleasure to regard; I look forward to admiring it in 2-D, where it will look brighter and more colorful. No artist who can create these images is enhancing them in any way by adding the annoying third dimension. But never mind that.

He brings to Carroll's characters an appearance as distinctive and original as Tenniel's classic illustrations. These are not retreads of familiar cartoon images. They're grotesques, as they should be, from the hydrocephalic forehead of the Red Queen (Helena Bonham Carter) to Tweedledee and Tweedledum (Matt Lucas), who seem to have been stepped on. Wonderland itself is not limited to necessary props, such as a tree limb for the Cheshire Cat and a hookah for the caterpillar, but extends indefinitely as an alarming undergrowth beneath a lowering sky. Why you can see the sky from beneath the Earth is not a fair question. (The landscape was designed by Robert Stromberg of *Avatar.*)

When we meet her again, Alice has decidedly mixed feelings about her original trip down the rabbit hole, but begins to recall Wonderland more favorably as she's threatened with an arranged marriage with Hamish Ascot (Leo Bill), a conceited snot-nose twit. At the moment of truth in the wedding ceremony, she impulsively scampers away to follow another rabbit down another rabbit hole, and finds below that she is actually remembered from her previous visit.

Burton shows us Wonderland as a perturbing place where the inhabitants exist for little apparent reason other than to be peculiar and obnoxious. Do they reproduce? Most species seem to have only one member, as if Nature quit while she was ahead. The ringleader is the Mad Hatter, played by Johnny Depp, that rare actor who can treat the most bizarre characters with perfect gravity. Whomever he plays (Edward Scissorhands, Sweeney Todd, Jack Sparrow, Willy Wonka, Ichabod Crane), he is that character through and through.

This is a Wonderland that holds perils for Alice, played by Mia Wasikowska with beauty and pluck. The Red Queen wishes her ill and the White Queen (Anne Hathaway) wishes her well, perhaps because both are formed according to the rules of Wonderland queens. To be sure, the insecure White Queen doesn't exhaust herself in making Alice welcome. The Queens, the Mad Hatter, Alice, the Knave of Hearts (Crispin Glover), and presumably Tweedledee and Tweedledum are versions of humans; the others are animated, voiced with great zest by such as Stephen Fry (Cheshire), Alan Rickman (Absolem the Caterpillar), Michael Sheen (White Rabbit), and Timothy Spall, Barbara Windsor, and Christopher Lee.

The film is enchanting in its mordant way until, unfortunately, it arrives at its third act. Here I must apologize to faithful readers for repeating myself. Time after time I complain when a film develops an intriguing story and then dissolves it in routine and boring action. We've *seen* every conceivable battle sequence, every duel, all carnage, countless showdowns, and all-too-long fights to the finish.

Why does *Alice in Wonderland* have to end with an action sequence? Characters not rich enough? Story run out? Little minds, jazzed by sugar from the candy counter, might get too worked up without it? Or is it that executives, not trusting their artists and timid in the face of real stories, demand an action climax as insurance? Insurance of what? That the story will have a beginning and a middle but nothing so tedious as an ending?

## All Good Things ★ ★ ★ ½

R, 101 m., 2010

Ryan Gosling (David Marks), Kirsten Dunst (Katie Marks), Frank Langella (Sanford Marks), Lily Rabe (Deborah Lehrman), Philip Baker Hall (Malvern Bump), Michael Esper (Daniel Marks), Diane Venora (Janice Rizzo). Directed by Andrew Jarecki and produced by Jarecki, Michael London, Bruna Papandrea, and Marc Smerling. Screenplay by Smerling and Marcus Hinchey.

*All Good Things* is based on one of those true stories like Dominick Dunne used to tell so intriguingly in *Vanity Fair.* Let me begin with a brief summary, based on the film because I know nothing about the reality. It involves David Marks, the son of a New York family that owned valuable Forty-second Street real estate in the 1970s. The property at that time was rented to strip clubs, porno shops, massage parlors, and so on. The family, wealthy and private, moved in the best circles, and the nature of its holdings was not widely known. The patriarch, Sanford Marks (Frank Langella), is a commanding man who is hands-on. He often collects the rent in cash. He expects his son to enter the family business. David (Ryan Gosling) wants nothing to do with it. A free spirit of the Woodstock era, he meets Katie (Kirsten Dunst), and together they escape from New York and open a twee

Vermont health foods and organic products store named, yes, All Good Things.

Sanford ratchets up the pressure. David caves in and returns to Manhattan, where his wife enjoys a luxurious but unhappy existence. She eventually discovers the nature of the family business. David, meanwhile, begins to change from the loving hippie she fell in love with. Their marriage comes apart. Katie disappears. She is never found again. David is suspected of being involved but never charged, because he appears to have an unquestionable alibi. And I will not reveal more.

The film is the work of Andrew Jarecki, who in 2003 made the remarkable Sundance-winning documentary *Capturing the Friedmans*, about a family and its secrets; the father and one son were charged with child molestation. It's easy to see why this story appealed to him. The key to the film is in the character of David. One can imagine a scenario in which an overbearing father drives the son to rebellion, but what happens here is more complex and sinister. David seemingly adapts to the lifestyle forced upon him. He plays a role like his father played among Manhattan power brokers and establishment members. He and Katie live in an expensive condo, attend charity events, and so on. Perhaps it is self-hatred that drives him to insist they have an abortion.

Kirsten Dunst is so good here as a woman at a loss to understand who her husband really is and what the true nature of his family involves. The man she married and trusted has undergone the transformation of a Mr. Hyde. What happens is the sort of thing that develops only in fantastical horror stories, but this story apparently did happen in one form or another, and the most incredible details of David's transformation are specifically based on facts revealed during two murder investigations. I choose not to reveal how or where David meets the wonderfully named Malvern Bump (Philip Baker Hall).

The nature of their relationship goes along with where they meet—the place both their lives have bottomed. Hall is one of those actors who seem to have inhabited their characters for years. He needs no explanation because he *exists*. Jarecki offers a possible solution for the enigma of Katie's disappearance and David's alibi. It involves his enigmatic friendship with Janice Rizzo (Diane Venora), and that's enough about that. This film reminded me of Barbet Schroeder's *Reversal of Fortune* (1990), based on the Dominick Dunne-able Klaus von Bulow case.

In both stories, there is every reason to focus on the obvious suspect, except the impossibility of explaining how he could have committed the crime—indeed, if there even *was* a crime. I don't understand David Marks after seeing this film, and I don't know if Andrew Jarecki does. It occurs to me that on my first visits to New York of course I was drawn to Forty-second Street, the port of entry for many a young man from the provinces, and I might have even laid eyes on Sanford or David Marks. Little would I have known.

## Amador ★ ★

NO MPAA RATING, 112 m., 2012

Magaly Solier (Marcela), Celso Bugallo (Amador), Pietro Sibille (Nelson), Sonia Almarcha (Yolanda), Fanny de Castro (Puri). Directed by Fernando Leon de Aranoa and produced by Aranoa and Juame Roures. Screenplay by Aranoa.

Here is a lovely idea for a film, sidetracked by a central performance that is too maddeningly passive. *Amador* introduces us to Marcela, a Bolivian woman now living in Madrid with Nelson, a man who runs an ingenious business: He hires scavengers to swarm down on a garbage dump and pick up discarded flowers that still look halfway presentable. They wash them, store them in a refrigerator, spray them with flowery scent, wrap them in paper, and send their team out to peddle them on the street and in cafés. I have a feeling I may have purchased a few roses with that lineage from the flower girls in Cannes.

Their refrigerator breaks down. There is a crisis in making the payments on a replacement, and Marcela (Magaly Solier) takes a job as a daytime companion for Amador (Celso Bugallo), an old man who rarely leaves his bed and passes his days assembling big jigsaw puzzles. He loves scenes of sea and sky because the whites and blues blend together and make them trickier.

Marcela is a warm, soulful woman who is unhappy with her life. When Nelson talked her into moving with him to Madrid, he painted a future where they'd have their own flower shop. Now she hardly has a home; the business is run out of their apartment, and when Nelson mounts letters on the refrigerator door saying "Marcela's Flowers," somehow that doesn't seem what he promised.

Amador is quiet and pleasant, suspecting his time has about run out. Marcela met Yolanda (Sonia Almarcha), his daughter, when she and her husband hired Marcela, but they have never visited. Marcela cooks Amador's meals, helps him sit on the pot, and makes desultory conversation. Much of the film involves close-ups of her face, thoughtful and pensive, as she ponders her life. Too much of the film.

It is not Magaly Solier's fault that her character seems so passive. We see a personality in the film, but not enough of it. Her long days pass as she discusses romance, mermaids, and her own life with Amador, who notices immediately that she's pregnant. That's something she hasn't told Nelson, and, of course, he hasn't noticed. Amador observes that the world has too many people: "But don't worry. I'm on my way out, to make a space for him."

Once a week, on Thursdays, Amador receives a visit from Puri (Fanny de Castro), a plumpish middle-aged prostitute who has been visiting him for years. She's a wise, friendly woman, and helps Marcela pass the time. The peace is also interrupted by a nosy neighbor who keeps trying to push his way in.

It wouldn't be fair to describe more of what happens. We've been rather expecting it, and the way the writer-director, Fernando Leon de Aranoa, handles it is effective and holds a series of surprises. Simply on the story level, this could have been a better film. But his pacing is off. Time and again, we get languid close-ups of Marcela as the cogs turn in her mind and she arrives belatedly at fairly obvious conclusions. It might have been possible to produce a much better film just by tighter editing.

The symbolism, mostly involving flowers (which we prize for their beauty even when they're dead), is pretty obvious. So also the sea and sky, and speculation about mermaids. A late disclosure from the unloving daughter Yolanda provides an ending that is heartless, ironic, and "happy," all at the same time.

## The Amazing Spider-Man ★ ★ ★ ½

PG-13, 136 m., 2012

Andrew Garfield (Spider-Man/Peter Parker), Emma Stone (Gwen Stacy), Rhys Ifans (Lizard/Dr. Curt Connors), Denis Leary (Captain Stacy), Campbell Scott (Richard Parker), Irrfan Khan (Dr. Ratha), Martin Sheen (Uncle Ben), Sally Field (Aunt May). Directed by Marc Webb and produced by Avi Arad, Matthew Tolmach, and Laura Ziskin. Screenplay by James Vanderbilt, Alvin Sargent, and Steve Kloves, based on the comic book by Stan Lee and Steve Ditko.

We live in a speeded-up age, which may explain why the Spider-Man franchise feels the need for a reboot only ten years after its first picture, and five years after the most recent one. In its broad strokes, *The Amazing Spider-Man* is a remake of Sam Raimi's *Spider-Man* (2002), but it's not the broad strokes we care about. This is a more thoughtful film, and its action scenes are easier to follow in space and time. If we didn't really need to be told Spidey's origin story again, at least it's done with more detail and provides better reasons for why Peter Parker throws himself into his superhero role.

Parker is played by Andrew Garfield (*Never Let Me Go*), who at twenty-eight looks too old to be in high school, but then movie teenagers usually do. His key quality is likability, which he shares with his predecessor Tobey Maguire. As his classmate and girlfriend, Emma Stone (*The Help*) plays a well-grounded girl who needs some persuasion to bond with Peter. That's partly because Garfield's take on Spidey is sometimes a few strands short of a web. He's not above show-off stunts in high school, and takes chances with his newfound superpowers. This is the first Spider-Man who can leap off a skyscraper and make us wonder if he has a plan in mind.

The origin story takes at least an hour to tell, and I enjoyed that, because it seems to me that CGI superhero films often go on autopilot during their big action climaxes. We learn how Peter lost his parents and came into the care of Aunt May (Sally Field) and Uncle Ben (Martin Sheen). Finding his dad's old-fashioned briefcase in the attic, he comes across brilliant scientific work about cross-species interbreeding, and that leads him to the Manhattan skyscraper of Oscorp, your typical comic book mega-corporation with a madman at the top. The screwball scientist is his dad's old partner Dr. Curt Connors (Rhys Ifans). He has lost his right arm and obsesses about regenerating it by injecting himself with the genes of lizards, which can replace lost limbs (almost instantly, it appears).

Connors overdoses himself on lizard juice and expands into the hyper-violent Lizard, who goes on rampages and knocks cars off bridges with its tail. Meanwhile, of course, the cops blame a midtown trail of destruction on Spider-Man, and wouldn't you know that Gwen's father is police captain Stacy (Denis Leary). This sets up various close calls and reconciliations, and the movie's single best action scene, when Spidey rescues a young boy from a burning car dangling from a bridge. The kid is able to assist in his own rescue after putting on Spidey's face mask; I doubt the mask has magical powers, but simply provides a psychological boost.

That may also help explain why Peter/Spider-Man spends so much time not wearing the mask. That, and the fact that Andrew Garfield is very good-looking and the mask reminds me of Hellboy wearing a screen door.

The best of all the *Spider-Man* movies remains Raimi's *Spider-Man II* (2004), with the best of the series villains, Doc Ock. This one is probably the second best. The Lizard is not especially inspired, and seems limited to the dramatic range of a Godzilla. Luckily, the climactic battle atop the Oscorp Tower is intercut with parallel action involving the plucky Gwen, who risks her life in an attempt to immunize all New Yorkers from becoming lizards. Director Marc Webb is aware that effective CGI action must be slow enough to be comprehensible, and although the Lizard sometimes thrashes about in a rage, Spidey's action makes sense.

A technological footnote. Peter/Spidey depends on cell phones, which save the day when Spidey urges Gwen to—quick!—find the blue serum! Peter Parker is still a photographer (and still using rolls of film), but although we see a front page proving the *Daily Bugle* is still being published, Peter doesn't seem to freelance for it anymore; no doubt he's been downsized. The credit cookies promise a sequel, and I suppose by the time they make it, Peter will have switched over to making videos for YouTube.

## The American ★ ★ ★ ★

R, 105 m., 2010

George Clooney (Jack/Edward), Violante Placido (Clara), Thekla Reuten (Mathilde), Paolo Bonacelli (Father Benedetto), Johan Leysen (Pavel). Directed by Anton Corbijn and produced by Clooney, Anne Carey, Jill Green, Grant Heslov, and Ann Wingate. Screenplay by Rowan Joffe, based on the novel *A Very Private Gentleman* by Martin Booth.

*The American* allows George Clooney to play a man as starkly defined as a samurai. His fatal flaw, as it must be for any samurai, is love. Other than that, the American is perfect: sealed, impervious, and expert, with a focus so narrow it is defined only by his skills and his master. Here is a gripping film with the focus of a Japanese drama, an impenetrable character to equal Alain Delon's in *Le Samourai,* by Jean-Pierre Melville.

Clooney plays a character named Jack, or perhaps Edward. He is one of those people who can assemble mechanical parts by feel and instinct, so inborn is his skill. His job is creating specialized weapons for specialized murders. He works for Pavel (Johan Leysen, who looks like Scott Glenn left to dry in the sun). Actually, we might say he "serves" Pavel, because he accepts his commands without question, giving him a samurai's loyalty.

Pavel assigns him a job. It involves meeting a woman named Mathilde (Thekla Reuten) in Italy. They meet in a public place, where she carries a paper folded under her arm—the classic tell in spy movies. Their conversation begins with one word: "Range?" It involves only the specifications of the desired weapon. No discussion of purpose, cost, anything.

He thinks to find a room in a small Italian

hilltop village, but it doesn't feel right. He finds another. We know from the film's shocking opening scene that people want to kill him. In the second village, he meets the fleshy local priest, Father Benedetto (Paolo Bonacelli). Through him he meets the local mechanic, walks into his shop, and finds all the parts he needs to build a custom silencer.

In the village he also finds a whore, Clara (Violante Placido), who works in a bordello we are surprised to find such a village can support. Jack or Edward lives alone, does push-ups, drinks coffee in cafés, assembles the weapon. And so on. His telephone conversations with Pavel are terse. He finds people beginning to follow him and trying to kill him.

The entire drama of this film rests on two words, "Mr. Butterfly." We must be vigilant to realize that once, and only once, they are spoken by the wrong person. They cause the entire film and all of its relationships to rotate. I felt exaltation at this detail. It is so rare to see a film this carefully crafted, this patiently assembled like a weapon, that when the word comes it strikes like a clap of thunder. A lesser film would have underscored it with a shock chord, punctuated it with a sudden zoom, or cut to a shocked close-up. *The American* is too cool to do that. Too Zen, if you will.

The director is a Dutchman named Anton Corbijn, known to me for *Control* (2007), the story of Ian Curtis, lead singer of Joy Division, a suicide at twenty-three. Corbijn has otherwise made mostly music videos (and is a famous photographer of the bands U2 and Depeche Mode). Here he paints an idyllic Italian countryside as lyrical as his dialogue is taciturn. There is not a wrong shot. Every performance is tightly controlled. Clooney is in complete command of his effect. He sometimes seems to be chewing a very small piece of gum, or perhaps his tongue.

His weakness is love. Clara, the prostitute, should not be trusted. We sense he uses prostitutes because he made a mistake in the relationship that opens the film. In his business, he cannot trust anybody. But perhaps Clara is different. Do not assume from what I've written that she isn't different. It is very possible. The film ends like a clockwork mechanism arriving at its final, clarifying tick.

## American Reunion ★ ★ ★

R, 112 m., 2012

Jason Biggs (Jim Levenstein), Alyson Hannigan (Michelle), Chris Klein (Oz), Thomas Ian Nicholas (Kevin), Tara Reid (Vicky), Seann William Scott (Steve Stifler), Mena Suvari (Heather), Eddie Kaye Thomas (Finch), Jennifer Coolidge (Stifler's Mom), Eugene Levy (Jim's Dad). Directed by Jon Hurwitz and Hayden Schlossberg and produced by Chris Moore, Craig Perry, Chris Weitz, and Warren Zide. Screenplay by Hurwitz and Schlossberg, based on characters created by Adam Herz.

Has Stifler's mom spent the last thirteen years upstairs in her room, reclining on her chaise lounge, occasionally touching up her pink lipstick and waiting for one of her son's young friends to wander into her lair? I'm growing concerned for America's most iconic mother. When she made her first appearance in the *American Pie* movies, she landed like a blond bombshell. This time, when her son throws a party downstairs and she *still* looks and behaves exactly the same, we get a sense of tragedy. I fear she has been sitting up there year after year, plumping up her cleavage and sexily brushing a lock of hair back from her eyes.

Stifler's mom (Jennifer Coolidge) and Stifler himself (Seann William Scott) seem to be trapped by a warp in time. The other members of the old high school gang, now in their early thirties, have moved on in one way or another. So much have they matured, indeed, that when three of the guys plan to get together a few days early in the old hometown for a head start on the class reunion, they don't even let Stifler know their plans. They still like the Stifmeister, but they keenly recall the trouble he got them into in their previous meetings.

*American Pie* (1999), *American Pie 2* (2001), and *American Wedding* (2003) have made the cast so familiar that this movie actually feels sort of like our reunion with them. We get an update. Chris Ostreicher (Chris Klein) has become a sports expert at an ESPN-like channel. Jim and Michelle Levenstein (Jason Biggs and Alyson Hannigan) are still married, and have a baby boy as consolation for the fact that their sex life has ground to a halt. Finch (Eddie Kaye Thomas) has apparently morphed into an adventurer who scales mountains and roars through exotic nightclubs.

And another familiar face is back: Jim's dad (Eugene Levy), who you may recall was all too willing to provide his son tips on masturbation and other topics Jim recoiled from. In a film that seems to have been constructed by typing in cross-references to the earlier films, this one breaks new ground in a way by dealing fearlessly with the famous Levy eyebrows; when a girl offers to thin them a little for a makeover, he gets defensive ("They're sort of a trademark"), but she is able to pluck enough hairs to stuff a pillow while making little visible difference.

The charm of *American Pie* was the relative youth and naïveté of the characters. It was all happening for the first time, and they had the single-minded obsession with sex typical of many teenagers. *American Reunion* has a sense of déjà vu, but it still delivers a lot of nice laughs.

Most of them, for me, came thanks to Stifler. Seann William Scott, who has a respectable career otherwise, has made the role of Stifler his own, and seems able to morph his face into an entirely different person: narrowed eyes, broad maniacal grin, frightening focus, still with all the zeal for seduction and adventure he had in high school. The ingenuity with which he destroys the Jet Skis of two jerks can only be admired.

*American Pie* became infamous for one of the ingredients in its titular pie. That recipe is reprised in the dialogue this time, too. In fact, *American Reunion* seems to depend so much on nostalgia that I wonder if a first-timer to the series would feel a little out to sea. If you liked the earlier films, I suppose you gotta see this one. Otherwise, I dunno.

## America the Beautiful 2: The Thin Commandments ★ ★ ½

NO MPAA RATING, 104 m., 2011

A documentary featuring Deepak Chopra, Evelyn Tribole, Howard Shapiro, Linda Bacon, Kathleen Sebelius, Timothy Dolan, Paul Campos, Jon Robinson, Beverly Johnson, Carolyn Costin, Christian Lander, and David Satcher. Directed by Daryl Roberts and produced by Harley Decease, Jeff Scheftel, and Eddie Williams III. Screenplay by Roberts.

If you're trying to lose weight, this movie will probably not help you. But it reflects the stories of a lot of our lives. *America the Beautiful 2: The Thin Commandments* follows its director, Daryl Roberts, as he peers at his scale reading (272 pounds) and gets the bad news from his doctor about his blood pressure. Then he meets a variety of weight-loss advisers, who recommend raw foods, purging, and more charming cures. He also works his way through a list of famous diet programs that he tried, and reports that they all worked for him—until he put the lost weight back on, plus a little more.

Oh, did I know how that felt. I eventually lost a good chunk of one hundred pounds through the Pritikin Program, but that meant starting over again several times because all these programs have a catch: You actually have to work them. I'm no expert, but I will share a winning formula: regular exercise and a diet heavy on whole foods, especially vegetables, fruits, and grains. And cut down on the fat. And way down on the salt. Not a lot of meat.

I'm now in the unique situation of never again having to worry about my weight because after my medical adventures I can't eat, drink, taste, or smell. I get all of my nutrition via G-tube out of a can, supplemented by fresh juices. You know the theory that some people just "naturally" put on weight? It's recommended that I have six cans of liquid nutrition a day. At that level, I gain weight. Go figure.

What does this have to do with Daryl Roberts and his film? Not very much, but I like talking about my food and diets, and Roberts likes talking about his. At one point in the film, he looks quite a bit slimmer, but he makes no big claims.

Roberts is a tall man with a reliable tummy. He is friendly, confiding, and very likable, and I think he would make a good talk show host, the kind people would confide in. Here he talks to a beautiful dancer who never thinks she's thin enough, authorities who insist on rigid obedience to their theories, and Secretary of Health and Human Services Kathleen

Sebelius, who has a Rick Perry moment when she's stuck for an answer to this excellent question: Does our emphasis on BMI numbers in childhood lead to eating disorders in maturity? Roberts thinks so.

BMI, or body mass index, is your body weight divided by the square of your height. Who came up with that? A Belgian named Adolphe Quetelet, between 1830 and 1850. How meaningful is it? Not very, if among those who have *bad* BMIs are Tom Cruise, George W. Bush, and Arnold Schwarzenegger in his prime. Yet schools measure it and inform parents, and some kids get traumatized. Schools might more profitably emphasize realistic exercise programs—not expensive, challenging sports but, you know, stuff like walking. The only exercise program that ever consistently worked for me was the ten thousand steps a day program.

This film is a sequel to Roberts's original *America the Beautiful*, which largely centered on a beautiful young model who endangered her life with bulimia. The second film is all over the map, lacking much of a focus and without a concrete list of recommendations. Still, it contains a great deal of information and is much more entertaining than a film about weight loss has any right to be. And here's another thing: Daryl Roberts has an infectious charm. He may not get much of anywhere specific, but it's a pleasure going along on his journey.

## Anonymous ★ ★ ★ ½

PG-13, 130 m., 2011

Rhys Ifans (Edward de Vere, Earl of Oxford), Vanessa Redgrave (Queen Elizabeth I), Joely Richardson (Young Queen Elizabeth I), David Thewlis (William Cecil), Xavier Samuel (Earl of Southampton), Sebastian Armesto (Ben Jonson), Rafe Spall (William Shakespeare), Edward Hogg (Robert Cecil), Jamie Campbell Bower (Young Earl of Oxford), Sam Reid (Earl of Essex). Directed by Roland Emmerich and produced by Emmerich, Larry J. Franco, and Robert Leger. Screenplay by John Orloff.

Very few commoners of his time are as well documented as William Shakespeare. There seems little good reason to doubt he wrote the plays performed under his name. If he had been an ordinary playwright, there would be no controversy over their authorship. But he was the greatest of all writers in English, in some ways the engine for its spread around the world, and one of the supreme artists of the human race.

There have long been those not contented with his breeding. He was the son of an illiterate provincial glover, an itinerant actor in a disreputable profession with no connections with royalty. Surely such an ordinary man could not have written the masterpieces. There is a restlessness to reassign them, and over the years theories have grown up claiming the real author of the plays was the Earl of Oxford, Sir Francis Bacon, the sixth Earl of Derby, or Christopher Marlowe. *Anonymous* argues the case for Edward de Vere, the seventeenth Earl of Oxford.

You perhaps know little enough about Shakespeare and next to nothing about the other candidates. That's no reason to avoid this marvelous historical film, which I believe to be profoundly mistaken. Because of the ingenious screenplay by John Orloff, precise direction by Roland Emmerich, and the casting of memorable British actors, you can walk into the theater as a blank slate, follow and enjoy the story, and leave convinced—if of nothing else—that Shakespeare was a figure of compelling interest.

This movie cruelly stacks the deck against him. The character of Shakespeare himself (Rafe Spall) is drawn a notch or two above the village idiot. Witless and graceless, there is no whiff of brilliance about him, and indeed the wonder is not that this man could have written the plays, but that he could articulate clearly enough to even act in some of them (about which there seems to be no doubt).

Edward de Vere, the Earl of Oxford (Rhys Ifans), on the other hand, seems the very template of genius. His manner, his bearing, his authority, his ease in the court of Elizabeth all conspire to make him a qualified candidate. He was so well connected with the crown, in fact, that the movie speculates he may have been the lover of the young Elizabeth (Joely Richardson) or the son of the older Elizabeth (Vanessa Redgrave). Not both, I pray ye.

The film also plunges us into the rich intrigue of the first Elizabethan age, including the activities of the Earl of Essex (Sam Reid), whose plot to overthrow the queen led to the inconvenience of beheading. Incredibly, for a film shot mostly on German soundstages, *Anonymous* richly evokes the London of its time, when the splendor of the court lived in a metropolis of appalling poverty and the streets were ankle-deep in mud. It creates a realistic, convincing Globe theater, which establishes how intimate it really was. The groundlings could almost reach out and touch the players, and in the box seats such as Oxford himself could witness the power of his work, which was credited to the nonentity Shakespeare.

All of that makes *Anonymous* a splendid experience: the dialogue, the acting, the depiction of London, the lust, jealousy, and intrigue. But I must tiresomely insist that Edward de Vere did not write Shakespeare's plays. Apparently, Roland Emmerich sincerely believes he did. Well, when he directed *2012*, Emmerich thought there might be something to the Mayan calendar. The Shakespeare scholar James Shapiro has cited a few technicalities in the *New York Times*: (a) de Vere writes and stars in *A Midsummer Night's Dream* when he was nine years old, and (b) *he died in 1604, before ten or so of Shakespeare's plays were written.*

I have a personal theory. The most detailed and valuable record of life in London at that time is the diary of Samuel Pepys, who attended plays in court and in town, and as secretary of the navy was an inveterate gossip, well wired for information. He wrote his diary in a cipher, not intending it to be read. If he had knowledge of the true authorship of the plays, I don't believe he could have suppressed it.

## Another Earth ★ ★ ★ ½

PG-13, 92 m., 2011

Brit Marling (Rhoda Williams), William Mapother (John Burroughs). Directed by Mike Cahill and produced by Cahill, Hunter Gray, Brit Marling, and Nicholas Shumaker. Screenplay by Cahill and Marling.

*Another Earth* is a film animated by one stunning image: A new planet four times the size of the moon appears in the sky of Earth. This startling apparition gives a deeper meaning to everything in the story, especially when it is discovered that the planet is indeed, as the title promises, another Earth. Perhaps not a second Earth, however, but the very same Earth, in another universe that has now become visible.

That would explain the curious lack of physical effects on two planets so close together. In some sense the two Earths don't share the same physical reality. In another sense, Earth 2 is right up there in the sky—so close that a corporation sponsors an essay contest and the winner gets to be the first person to visit it. I confess the essay contest was harder for me to believe than the second Earth itself.

But this intriguing film isn't concerned with plausibility. It has deeper questions to explore. It involves a bright young woman named Rhoda Williams (Brit Marling), who in the opening scene has been accepted into the astrophysics program at MIT. To celebrate, she parties too hearty, and when she's driving home she hears the news about Earth 2. Peering out her car window to search the sky, she crashes into another car, killing a mother and child and sending the father into a coma.

A few years pass. She's released from prison and learns that the father, a composer named John Burroughs (William Mapother), has emerged from his coma. Rhoda is emotionally devastated by the deaths she caused and wants to apologize or make amends or . . . what? She doesn't know. She presents herself at the shabby rural house where Burroughs lives as a depressed recluse and makes up a story about doing housecleaning.

Now we have a situation not unfamiliar in the movies, where two people slowly grow close while only one of them is aware of their deep connection. The strength of *Another Earth* is that it employs that story to a larger purpose; this is no less than a meditation on the infinite variations possible in a human life.

If she had not had too many beers. If she had been listening to a different radio station. If he had not been on the road in the wrong place at the wrong time. The fatal crash was the sum of an infinite series of *ifs*, tracing back to if life had never evolved on Earth in the first place. In our lives we surf the wave of chance.

What's impressive is how well this film joins its parts into a whole. The other Earth idea is left as a fantastical hook and wisely not considered scientifically, except of course in its role as the film's master image. The relationship between Rhoda and John is seen as fraught with danger. The actors occupy their characters convincingly. They make us care more than the plot really requires. Earth 2, always looming in the sky, encourages us to reflect on how arbitrary our destinies are. In one sense, nothing in our lives is necessary. In another sense, everything is inevitable.

There's a nice story behind this movie, involving the actress and cowriter Brit Marling. She worked in investment banking on Wall Street before becoming the writer and codirector of *Boxers and Ballerinas*, a Cuban documentary that Mike Cahill made in 2004. They worked together on this film. It arrived unheralded at Sundance 2011 and won the Alfred P. Sloan Feature Film Prize, also taking the Special Jury Prize.

It was made on a low budget, and Cahill shot and edited it himself. I think it would have benefited from more tripod work and less hand-held; a more classical approach would have suited this thoughtful material. But it's strong as it is, and Marling emerges as a gifted new talent. The movie is as thought-provoking, in a less profound way, as Tarkovsky's *Solaris*, another film about a sort of parallel Earth. In this one, when a scientist makes a call to Earth 2 and discovers she is speaking with herself, what do you suppose that can mean?

## Another Year ★ ★ ★ ★

PG-13, 129 m., 2011

Jim Broadbent (Tom), Ruth Sheen (Gerri), Lesley Manville (Mary), Oliver Maltman (Joe), Peter Wight (Ken), David Bradley (Ronnie), Karina Fernandez (Katie). Directed by Mike Leigh and produced by Georgina Lowe. Screenplay by Leigh.

Not quite every year brings a new Mike Leigh film, but the years that do are blessed with his sympathy and penetrating observation, and with his instinct for human comedy. By that I don't mean "comedy" as in easy laughter. I mean that comedy that wells up from movies allowing us to recognize ourselves in characters both lovable and wretched. Leigh's *Another Year* is like a long, purifying soak in empathy.

He begins with Tom and Gerri, a North London couple who have been happily married for years. Immediately you can see the risks Leigh is prepared to take. A happy married couple? Two wise and lovable people? Who are intelligent and alert to the real world? Not caricatures, not comforting, not clichés, but simply two people I wish I knew? I'd look forward to them every time I visited their house, and be slow to leave.

That's also how Mary (Lesley Manville) feels. She has worked for years in the office of Gerri, a behavioral counselor. Many people have a friend like Mary. Many people are a friend like Mary: unmarried, not getting any younger, drinking too much, looking for the perfect spouse as a way of holding any real-world relationship at arm's length. Mary drops in on Tom (Jim Broadbent) and Gerri (Ruth Sheen) a lot. Every time she visits, we're reminded of Robert Frost: "Home is where, when you have to go there, they have to take you in."

Mary needs healing. She badly requires sobriety. She wears an invisible sign around her neck: "Needy." Tom and Gerri don't lecture. Sometimes they drop gentle hints. "It's a shame," Tom observes to Gerri after Mary has ended yet another sad visit, and that's all he has to say. No criticisms, no anger, just a factual statement. In their own lives, they're in complete accord. They garden, they work, they feed their friends dinners, they hope their son will find the right girl, they are in love. Remarkably, in this age, their thirty-year-old son, Joe (Oliver Maltman), loves them and is happy.

Leigh has a gift for scenes involving embarrassment in social situations. We squirm, not because the characters are uneasy, but because we would be, too. In *Another Year*, Tom and Gerri and their son attend the funeral of Tom's sister-in-law. We have never been to a funeral quite like it, yet it is like many funerals. The uninvolved clergyman, the efficient undertakers, the remote father, the angry son, the handful of neighbors who didn't know the deceased all that well, the family skeletons. He sees the ways people display their anguish without meaning to.

The movie doesn't require this scene. It has no obligatory scenes. Like life, it happens once you plug in the people. Mary lives in a very small world, where it's unlikely she'll find happiness. She buys a car to give her more "freedom," but no one who drinks like she does will find freedom that way. She fantastically begins to think of the son, Joe, as a possible partner. Joe brings home Katie (Karina Fernandez) to meet his parents, and they love her. When Mary meets Katie and understands who she is, it is devastating.

All the actors are pitch perfect. Lesley Manville is virtuoso in making Mary pathetic and yet never a caricature. Listen to the way her cadences vary with drink. Notice the way Tom and Gerri's responses to her modulate during the course of a visit. Even, for that matter, observe Ken (Peter Wight), Tom's friend. Ken is no prize, but might be happy to date Mary and maybe marry her; and after all, could Mary do any better? She persists in the delusion that she could.

Now we come to the matter of the chins, and here we touch on something central to the appeal of Mike Leigh. He is not afraid to star imperfect people. Jim Broadbent has a little too much chin, and Ruth Sheen not quite enough. In most movies everybody has about the right chinnage. At the risk of offending many of his many actor-collaborators, I'll say that not once in forty years has Mike Leigh ever starred a conventionally handsome or beautiful movie-star type. Instead, he has enriched the British cinema by his use of unconventional types, also including Imelda Staunton, Sally Hawkins, Timothy Spall, Marianne Jean-Baptiste, Brenda Blethyn, and David Thewlis.

*Another Year* gave me characters I could love, feel uneasy about, identify with, or be appalled by. I see a lot of movies where the characters have no personalities, only attributes. I like James Bond, but I ask you: In what way is he human? Every single character in *Another Year* is human, and some of them all too human. I saw it and was enriched.

## Answers to Nothing ★ ★ ½

R, 124 m., 2011

Miranda Bailey (Drew), Julie Benz (Frankie), Dane Cook (Ryan), Zach Gilford (Evan), Kali Hawk (Allegra), Mark Kelly (Carter), Elizabeth Mitchell (Kate), Erik Palladino (Jerry), Vincent Ventresca (Erik), Aja Volkman (Tara), Barbara Hershey (Marilyn), Greg Germann (Beckworth). Directed by Matthew Leutwyler and produced by Amanda Marshall and Sim Sarna. Screenplay by Leutwyler and Gillian Vigman.

*Answers to Nothing* tells the story of several lives in Los Angeles that seem connected through the disappearance of a child. This is the technique of *Crash* and *Magnolia*, in which we're involved in many individual lives in addition to the central thread, and some associations surprise us. After the child's kidnapping, the city follows developments in the case on TV, and so do we, through the eyes of Frankie (Julie Benz), a police detective who is a shade less suspicious than she should be.

There is a suspect: Beckworth (Greg Germann), a neighbor, who is questioned and released after one of the girl's hairs is found in his car. Among the many curious is Carter (Mark Kelly), a schoolteacher we follow home. He provides a vignette of a video game addict who essentially spends his entire weekend playing a game, while sometimes removing his headphones to follow the story on the TV news. Since the city knows about Beckworth, but only we know about Carter, are we getting a hint here?

Many other stories interlock. To explain their connections would be complicated, but let me describe them. Erik Palladino plays Jerry, a rookie cop whose own child has died. Dane Cook plays a therapist whose marriage is in trouble and who is having an affair with a musician (Aja Volkman). He spends a good deal of time forlornly trying to watch the clock and produce sperm samples for his wife, Kate (Elizabeth Mitchell).

We meet Allegra (Kali Hawk), the African-American writer on a sitcom, whose secret is "I hate black people." This isn't much of a secret because she has a pattern of confiding it to pretty much everyone she meets. Hating other black people is her biggest problem, but she seems to have a related problem: She gets a twisted pleasure out of telling that to people. Her problem is resolved, sort of, in a scene where she makes a friendly gesture to two black men she had been cool toward. This is supposed to be cheerful, part of an uplifting conclusion, but it struck me as contrived and awkward.

One of the most poignant characters is Drew (Miranda Bailey), who cares for her brother Erik (Vincent Ventresca). He is paralyzed and apparently brain-dead. In a flashback, we learn she was driving drunk when this happened to him. Late in the film she straps him into a racing chair and pushes him in the So Cal Marathon, a race he once ran able-bodied. Her determination that they must finish the race becomes a crucial theme. My problem, and I know this sounds heartless: What meaning would it have to him if they finish? For her, it may be penance, and indeed she may deserve it. But how does it work as an amends when he has no idea what's happening?

How, you may ask, are Drew and Erik important to the story of the kidnapped girl? They aren't really, although we can trace a remote plot connection. That's a problem with this genre. The interlocking stories are theoretically about people whose lives are associated; that worked in *Crash.* Here the connections seem less immediate and significant, and so the movie sometimes seems based on a group of separate short stories. That was the approach that worked for Robert Altman with Raymond Carver's stories in *Short Cuts.*

At the end, there's a scene that draws together three of the major characters, but this scene depends entirely on action that could fit in many movies, and works on its own terms. It's convenient but not especially revealing about those people. So the film, while well made and acted, lacks the gathering power of the others I've mentioned.

## Anton Chekhov's The Duel ★ ★

NO MPAA RATING, 95 m., 2010

Andrew Scott (Laevsky), Fiona Glascott (Nadia), Tobias Menzies (Von Koren), Niall Buggy (Samoylenko). Directed by Dover Koshashvili and produced by Mary Bing and Donald Rosenfeld. Screenplay by Bing, based on the novella by Anton Chekhov.

What strikes you immediately about *Anton Chekhov's The Duel* are the visuals. The cinematography of Paul Sarossy composes shots as soft impressionist romance, the colors tastefully softened, the elements arranged in classical symmetry. Unfortunately, this combined with the unwavering progress of the story results in much of a muchness, and we wouldn't object to the occasional taste of vulgarity.

The film, as you have guessed, is based on a story by Chekhov. That accounts for the textbook quality of the title. I suppose it was out of the question to use *Steven Spielberg's The Duel—Not!* The story involves two indolent lovers and a fierce Darwinian zoologist creating a love triangle of theory, not practice, on the beautiful coast of the Black Sea. Maybe after the rigors of the Russian winter they are all driven a little mad by the good weather.

Laevsky (Andrew Scott) is one of those civil servants of nineteenth-century Russian literature who seems high up on an insignificant ladder. He's shacked up in this seaside resort with his married mistress, Nadia (Fiona Glascott), who has lost her appeal now freed of her husband. I've been reading a lot of Balzac lately, and am struck that absent husbands in European classics seem to play much like noises off. Laevsky expresses his discontents to the local physician; Chekhov often provides such learned listeners to sit gravely through anguished monologues. Dr. Samoylenko is required not for his diagnosis but for his ears. Also for his money: Laevsky is a gambler and drunk who desperately hopes for a loan.

Into this powder keg comes the zoologist Von Koren (Tobias Menzies), inflamed with the revolutionary principles of Darwinism that were then being embraced by the intelligentsia in all the wrong ways. Rare is the man not convinced that all evolution points like an arrow to his door. Von Koren is too refined to enter a horse of his own in the race, but he observes with scientific precision the willingness of the locals to respond to Nadia's underemployed sexuality. All comes to a head at a party one night when the overserved Laevsky temporarily goes barking mad, and Von Koren determines he isn't fit to survive.

The zoologist then faces one of the two choices open to him, given his rudimentary grasp of Darwin's theory. If he wants little Von Korens to prevail over little Laevskys, he can either seduce the female or kill the man. *Anton Chekhov's The Duel* is by no means shy about portraying sex in a forthright manner, and director Dover Koshashvili has gratifying taste in nudity, which has grown sadly rare as Friday night audiences lose their interest in it. But Von Koren is too much of a lardass to seduce Nadia and he knows it, so he challenges Laevsky to a duel.

One of two men will die over this woman: Man Number One, who no longer desires her, or Man Number Two, who knows what he would do if only he were in Man Number One's shoes. For Nadia, this must not be quite as exciting as Rhett Butler calling out Ashley Wilkes. The doctor saw it all coming, but then doctors are always seeing it all coming.

Koshashvili is a good filmmaker. His *Late Marriage* (2002) involved some of the more practical difficulties of an arranged marriage in Israel among immigrants from Soviet Georgia. Its characters had the advantage of caring strongly about who they did or didn't sleep with. In *The Duel* and much of Chekhov, lust seems to be a matter best approached by the introspection of the world-weary.

*Anton Chekhov's The Duel* isn't exactly a bad film. It's very well made and acted in English by a mostly Irish cast in a polished Chekhovian tone. But it somehow isn't as exciting as a duel over a woman should be. If you're not well rested before entering the theater, it could put you under.

## Araya ★ ★ ★ ½

NO MPAA RATING, 90 m., 2010

Featuring the Pereda, Salazar, and Ortiz families. A documentary directed by Margot Benacerraf and produced by Henry Nadler. Screenplay by Benacerraf.

To be born here is to be born into hell. That must have happened for more than three hundred years, because no one would ever want to come to live here. *Araya* tells the story of life on the remote, barren Araya peninsula of Venezuela, where Spanish conquistadors found salt about 1550. Salt was treasure in Europe, to the misfortune of those whose lives were devoted to it.

This astonishing documentary, so beautiful, so horrifying, was filmed in the late 1950s, when an old way of life had not yet ended. It was the belief of the filmmaker, Margot Benacerraf, that the motions of the salt workers became ritualized over the decades, passed down through the generations, and that here we could see the outcome of the endless repeating of arduous tasks that would destroy others.

The salt cake is taken up from the floor of a shallow marsh, loaded into flat-bottomed wooden boats, broken up, carted onto land in wheelbarrows, and loaded into 120-pound baskets to be balanced on the heads of workers who trudge up the side of an ever-growing pyramid to deposit it. At the top, a man with a rake forms each mound into a towering, geometrically perfect shape. Now it is ready to be hauled away in trucks.

The workers, bronzed by the sun, all muscle and sinew, work in a blazing sun in a land where nothing grows. Food comes from the sea and from corn meal that is carted in. They live in small rude shacks. They get their water from a tank truck. Some work all day. Some work all night. Such is their life.

And just such a phrase, *such is their life,* is used in the doc's narration, which seems to hover in detachment above the sweat on the ground. I imagine Benacerraf's purpose was to make the toilers of Araya seem heroic in a "land where nothing lives." Where the sun is hot and pitiless so often it becomes a mantra. The effect is odd at first, but then we grow accustomed: The idea is to see these not as individuals but almost as a species evolved to take salt from the sea, build it into pyramids, watch it hauled away, and start again.

We learn something about salt along the way. It was so prized that the Spanish built their largest overseas fortress on the peninsula to guard it. The men who died building it were the first of many who paid for salt with their lives. The working conditions of the salt workers were brutal; their feet and legs were ulcerated by the salt, and if they faltered, they had no income. Their existence is agonizing, and we feel no regret that their way of life is ending. They have been reduced to robots. Small wonder the film contains so little dialogue. Yet these people lived and died, and we had salt in our shakers. It would be too sad if they were not remembered.

This black-and-white doc, so realistic in its photography, so formal in its words, played at Cannes in 1959 and shared the critics' prize with Alain Resnais's *Hiroshima, Mon Amour.* Benacerraf, a Venezuelan director born in 1926, it still alive and much honored. Her work was almost lost in the years since it was made. Now it has been restored to pristine beauty by Milestone Films, and is on a national tour of art venues.

## Around a Small Mountain ★ ★ ★

NO MPAA RATING, 85 m., 2010

Jane Birkin (Kate), Sergio Castellitto (Vittorio), Andre Marcon (Alexandre), Jacques Bonnaffe (Marlo), Julie-Marie Parmentier (Clemence), Helene de Vallombreuse (Margot). Directed by Jacques Rivette and produced by Martine Marignac and Maurice Tinchant. Screenplay by Rivette, Pascal Bonitzer, Christine Laurent, and Shirel Amitay.

Sometimes a film is simply a story we might have found interesting to live. Its message may be no more than that we all have to weather hard times. To ordinary life may be added some style and artifice, allowing the filmmaker to tweak reality into a more pleasing form. Maybe that's what Jacques Rivette has in mind with *Around a Small Mountain.* One of the founders of the French New Wave, Rivette is still very much active at eighty-two.

At the center of his film is a shabby little circus, playing to sparse crowds in villages. It becomes the stage on which his two characters live, and they meet on their way to it. Kate (Jane Birkin) is driving down a road when her car stalls. Vittorio (Sergio Castellitto) happens along and fixes it for her: a Meet Cute as old as time. He doesn't even speak. He drives on, slows, and turns back. Something about Kate has struck him.

We learn that she is returning to the little circus after fifteen years. It was her father's. Her lover was killed in a performance. Vittorio sizes up the situation and books the room above a local café on the spur of the moment. At the performance that has never worked, he breaks the silence by suddenly laughing. Even the clowns are startled.

When the circus caravan leaves town, he follows. It's not that he and Kate begin a love affair. It's that they've both run off to join the circus. He apparently has nowhere to go and nothing else to do, and the same might be said of her. We learn of the buried past of the circus and the buried careers of its performers. Little one-ring circuses like this set up in town squares in rural districts. They still exist. On the Lido in Venice one night we attended one smaller than this—so small that after the show the clown came over to our granddaughter Raven and gave her a ride on his mule.

Jane Birkin has a sculpted, intelligent face that might not get her far on a U.S. soap opera, but I think she's sexy. She's a woman who looks like she's up to something. She's had quite a life. She's sixty-four, looks nowhere near that, was actually one of the two "birds" who frolicked nude in David Hemmings's photo studio in *Blow-Up.* What else? She was a famous model during the Swinging London days. Hermes named its Birkin bag after her, she once played Brigitte Bardot's lover in a film, was once married to John Barry, was the longtime lover of Serge Gainsbourg, and is the mother of Charlotte Gainsbourg, who underwent such rigors in Lars von Trier's *Antichrist.* It has been quite a life for anybody who seems so open and vulnerable.

Here she exudes the loss of her father, her lover, the circus. I doubt if she's experienced love since her lover died. Vittorio becomes a sort of passive counselor, coaxing her to face her wounds and let go of them. Their relationship is ever so much more interesting than if Rivette had reduced it to romance. This man and woman, strangers, actually find themselves talking to each other. How often do you see that?

The movie is the shortest one Rivette has ever made. His *La Belle Noiseuse* (1991), also with Birkin and one of my Great Movies, runs 236 minutes, and not a second too long. This one clocks in at 85 minutes, again the right length. Some men when they grow old feel a need to be profound. Rivette embodies the New Wave in that he needs to be playful.

## Arthur ★ ★ ★

PG-13, 110 m., 2011

Russell Brand (Arthur), Helen Mirren (Hobson), Greta Gerwig (Naomi), Jennifer Garner (Susan), Geraldine James (Vivienne), Luis Guzman (Bitterman), Nick Nolte (Burt Johnson). Directed by Jason Winer and produced by Chris Bender, Russell Brand, Larry Brezner, Kevin McCormick, J. C. Spink, and Michael Tadross. Screenplay by Peter Baynham.

*Arthur* is a fairly close remake of the great 1981 Dudley Moore movie, with pleasures of its own. It shares some of the same strengths and virtues, and if it lacks Dudley Moore as Arthur and John Gielgud playing his butler, Hobson, well, it has Russell Brand and Helen Mirren playing his nanny, Hobson. That's not a trade-off, but it's a good try.

The thing about Moore, whom people persisted in calling "Cuddly Dudley," although he hated it, is that he was just plain lovable. The thing about Russell Brand is that he isn't, not much, and he should get credit here for at least being a good deal more likable than he usually chooses to seem. He plays the alcoholic zillionaire Arthur Bach as a man who wants to party with the world and pick up the check.

Helen Mirren has the presence and authority of John Gielgud, but not the same aloof dignity. Gielgud's Hobson was a man so reserved you sometimes wanted to knock and see if anyone answered. Then again, they've made Hobson into a nanny still loyal from Arthur's childhood, so she should be expected to love him in a more tender way.

The main plot beats are roughly the same: Arthur is drunk more or less all the time, and steadfast in his irresponsibility. He inadvertently falls in love with a sweet young woman named Naomi (Greta Gerwig), just as his controlling mother, Vivienne (Geraldine James), is arranging his marriage with a very rich woman named Susan (Jennifer Garner). Susan wants him for his name; she may be rich, but she's not welcomed into the upper crust because her daddy (Nick Nolte) worked his way up in construction.

Naomi cares little about such matters, and supports herself as an unlicensed guide, giving bootleg tours of Grand Central Terminal. She's remarkably forgiving of Arthur's irregularities, considering he has the self-discipline and tact of a Charlie Sheen. But then, neither *Arthur* deals with alcoholism as other than a colorful character trait. No one could possibly drink like Arthur and not be dead at the end of twenty-four hours.

The casting of Greta Gerwig works nicely. Did you see her as the assistant to Ben Stiller's brother in *Greenberg* (2010)? The thing about her is that she is indeed cuddly. We sometimes talk about personal chemistry as something that happens in casting. It probably begins at birth. She's a woman you instinctively feel good about, like Amy Adams in *Junebug*. This quality goes a long way toward filling in the psychological gaps in her relationship with Arthur. Nice people can get away with more, and take bigger chances.

Russell Brand isn't doing a Dudley Moore imitation, but you can tell he's studied the movie, and carefully resists any temptation to go over the top. Just as well, since the whole role resides over the top. I confess I haven't regarded him as a particularly subtle actor, but here he has a lot of smile moments when he quickly and quietly reacts. I'll mention an almost invisible one. In the scene in the library at the end, when the kiddies are saying rude things, note how he hushes and dismisses them without much seeming to even notice them. That's good acting. Bad acting would be to respond directly and lose the focus of the scene, which must be on the woman he loves.

This *Arthur* is not as laugh-out-loud funny as the earlier one; its scene of a dinner in a staid hotel dining room isn't as successful, and it doesn't have as much fun with the father of the Naomi character. But the dialogue is well written—witty and quick, and not clunky. The visuals in the Grand Central Terminal scene may be overdone, but they are impressive (when did architecture lose its faith in grandeur?). And Russell Brand takes on a thankless task and earns at least some thanks.

## The Artist ★ ★ ★ ★

PG-13, 100 m., 2011

Jean Dujardin (George Valentin), Berenice Bejo (Peppy Miller), James Cromwell (Clifton),

Penelope Ann Miller (Doris), Malcolm McDowell (The Butler), Missi Pyle (Constance), Beth Grant (Peppy's Maid), Ed Lauter (Peppy's Butler), John Goodman (Al Zimmer). Directed by Michel Hazanavicius and produced by Thomas Langmann and Emmanuel Montamat. Screenplay by Hazanavicius.

Is it possible to forget that *The Artist* is a silent film in black and white and simply focus on it as a movie? No? That's what people seem to zero in on. They cannot imagine themselves seeing such a thing. At a sneak preview screening in Chicago, a few audience members actually walked out, saying they didn't like silent films. I was reminded of the time a reader called me to ask about an Ingmar Bergman film. "I think it's the best film of the year," I said. "Oh," she said, "that doesn't sound like anything *we'd* like to see."

Here is one of the most entertaining films in many a moon, a film that charms because of its story, its performances, and because of the sly way it plays with being silent and black-and-white. *The Artist* knows you're aware it's silent, and kids you about it. Not that it's entirely silent, of course; like all silent films were, it's accompanied by music. You know—like in a regular movie when nobody's talking?

One of its inspirations was probably *Singin' in the Rain*, a classic about a silent actress whose squeaky voice didn't work in talkies, and about the perky little unknown actress who made it big because hers did. The heroine (Debbie Reynolds) fell in love with an egomaniacal silent star—but a nice one, you know? Played by Gene Kelly in 1952 and by Jean Dujardin now, he has one of those dazzling smiles you suspect dazzles no one more than himself. Dujardin, who won best actor for this role at Cannes 2011, looks like a cross between Kelly and Sean Connery, and has such a command of comic timing and body language that he might have been—well, a silent star.

Dujardin plays George Valentin, who has a French accent that sounds just right in Hollywood silent films, if you see what I mean. The industry brushes him aside when the pictures start to speak, and he's left alone and forlorn in a shabby apartment with only his faithful dog, Uggie, for company. At a crucial moment he's loyally befriended by Peppy Miller (Berenice Bejo), who when they first met was a hopeful dancer and has now found great fame. The fans love her little beauty mark, which Valentin penciled in with love when she was a nobody.

As was often the case in those days, the cast of *The Artist* includes actors with many different native tongues, because what difference did it make? John Goodman makes a bombastic studio head, and such familiar faces as James Cromwell, Penelope Ann Miller, Missi Pyle, and Ed Lauter turn up.

At thirty-nine, Jean Dujardin is well-known in France. I've seen him in a successful series of spoofs about OSS 117, a Gallic secret agent who mixes elements of 007 and Inspector Clouseau. He would indeed have made a great silent star. His face is almost too open and expressive for sound, except comedy. As Norma Desmond, the proud silent star in *Sunset Boulevard*, hisses: "We didn't need dialogue. We had faces!" Dujardin's face serves perfectly for the purposes here. More than some silent actors, he can play subtle as well as broad, and that allows him to negotiate the hazards of some unbridled melodrama at the end. I felt a great affection for him.

I've seen *The Artist* three times, and each time it was applauded, perhaps because the audience was surprised at itself for liking it so much. Silent films can weave a unique enchantment. During a good one, I fall into a reverie state, an encompassing absorption that drops me out of time.

I also love black-and-white, which some people assume they don't like. For me, it's more stylized and less realistic than color, more dreamlike, more concerned with essences than details. Giving a speech once, I was asked by parents what to do about their kids who wouldn't watch black-and-white. "Do what Bergman's father did to punish him," I advised. "Put them in a dark closet and say you hope the mice don't run up their legs."

## The Art of Getting By ★ ★ ½

PG-13, 84 m., 2011

Freddie Highmore (George Zinavoy), Emma Roberts (Sally Howe), Michael Angarano (Dustin), Elizabeth Reaser (Charlotte Howe), Rita Wilson (Vivian Sargent), Blair Underwood

(Principal Martinson), Alicia Silverstone (Ms. Herman), Sam Robards (Jack Sargent), Jarlath Conroy (Harris McElroy). Directed by Gavin Wiesen and produced by Kara Baker, P. Jennifer Dana, Darren Goldberg, and Gia Walsh.

George, the hero of *The Art of Getting By*, is a high school senior who has decided to stop doing homework and paying any attention to tests. He isn't tortured, depressed, addicted, or anything like that. It has occurred to him that he will die, and therefore, what use is homework? This is more sophisticated than my theory, which was that homework would kill me.

George is played by Freddie Highmore, who only yesterday was the kid in *August Rush*. He could make a durable leading man because he looks good, and by that I don't mean handsome, I mean kind and likable. He's nice even when he explains to his parents and teachers that he doesn't see the point in graduating from school. He's the spiritual kin of Melville's Bartleby the scrivener, who patiently informed people, "I would prefer not to."

By not assigning a fixable reason for George's behavior, the movie sidesteps some of the clichés of the teen problem picture. Not all of them. There's always romance. George, for example, is attracted by Sally (Emma Roberts), a classmate who he assumes is somehow beyond his reach. In this he isn't being defeatist but, he thinks, simply realistic. If he were a little more perceptive, he'd realize Sally likes him a whole lot. His life seems stuck on Pause.

His passivity is both interesting and frustrating because George possesses the answers to all of his problems, and freely chooses to be unhappy. As a result, most of the tension generated by the movie is in ourselves and not in the plot. We want George to succeed, we want him together with Sally, and we even like Dustin (Michael Angarano), an older artist who likes Sally and likes George, too. Dustin is so nice he would step aside from Sally if he thought George was ever going to make a move. Not likely in romance, but there you have it.

George's parents (Rita Wilson and Sam Robards) are concerned, but curiously distant. The family is obviously affluent, but isn't obsessed with George graduating or getting into a good school. He is spared counseling or diagnosis, and we later learn about their distractions. But his school is very engaged, especially his principal (Blair Underwood), his English teacher (Alicia Silverstone), and his bearded and irascible art teacher (Jarlath Conroy). They come up with a deadline that would provide more tension if it were not so clear that a film like this requires George to meet it.

That leads to a rather sadistic scene in which George must actually attend his school graduation ceremony to find out if he's graduating. This last-instant verdict has been brought about by the principal, who until this point in the film has been unfailingly kind and understanding. I fear the scene exists for the single purpose of concocting an ending for the screenplay. It shouldn't be so obvious.

Another problem involves certain details of the relationship between Sally and Dustin that I don't want to spoil for you. Let me use evasive language. With what is implied by her apparent decision, we must assume emotional decisions on her part that aren't consistent with her eventual choices. You'll see what I mean.

*The Art of Getting By* is pleasant and well acted, and easy to watch. I wouldn't advise against seeing it because it showcases Freddie Highmore and Emma Roberts (Julia's niece), and they are likely to do greater things, but at the end I was wondering, what is the point? Nice people lead enviable lives, the hero can solve most of his own problems, and the villain is a sweetheart. It's custard without the lemon.

## The Art of the Steal ★ ★ ★ ½

NO MPAA RATING, 101 m., 2010

Featuring John Anderson, Colin B. Bailey, Julian Bond, Carolyn T. Carluccio, David D'Arcy, Richard Feigen, D. Michael Fisher, Tom L. Freudenheim, Jim Gerlach, Richard H. Glanton, Nancy Herman, Walter Herman, Christopher Knight, Meryl Levitz, Bruce H. Mann, Robert Marmon, Toby Marmon, Ross Mitchell, Barry Munitz, Irvin Nahan, Marcelle Pick, David W. Rawson, Jay Raymond, Edward G. Rendell, Mark D. Schwartz, Harry Sefarbi, Richard Segal,

Nick Tinari, Robert Zaller. A documentary directed by Don Argott.

Dr. Albert C. Barnes accomplished two things for which we must be grateful: He invented a treatment for VD, and he founded the Barnes Foundation in the Philadelphia suburb of Lower Merion. The first paid for the second, so the wages of sin were invested wisely. In his imposing private structure, far from the power brokers of the city, Barnes created an oasis for serious students, who could learn from his collection without rubbing elbows with crowds of art tourists.

How important was the Barnes Collection? I learn from the press notes of *The Art of the Steal* that it included 181 Renoirs, 69 Cezannes, 59 Matisses, 46 Picassos, 16 Modiglianis, and 7 Van Goghs. Barnes collected these during many trips to Paris at a time when establishment museums, such as the Philadelphia Museum of Art, considered these artists beneath their attention. Some of the paintings are today literally priceless; one estimate of the worth of the collection is $25 billion.

That was a lot of art to be sitting in Merion. Barnes knew it was. He designed every detail of his collection with personal care, grouping paintings to reflect and comment on one another, placing period furniture and wall ornaments near them, and filling walls with a richness of paintings close, but not too close, together. He loved his collection, and he hated the Philadelphia Main Line establishment—most particularly, the Museum of Art, which had scorned his collection in its early days.

Barnes was a rich man. He hired himself some Philadelphia lawyers and drew up an iron-clad will, endowing the foundation with funds enabling it to be maintained indefinitely where it was and how it was. It was his specific requirement that the collection not go anywhere near the Philadelphia Museum of Art. And that is exactly where it is today.

He hated the museum. He hated its benefactors, the Annenberg family, founded by a gangster, enriched by *TV Guide,* chummy with the Nixon administration. The Annenbergs published the *Philadelphia Inquirer,* which consistently and as a matter of policy covered this story with slanted articles and editorials.

Don Argott's *The Art of the Steal* is a documentary that reports the hijacking of the Barnes Collection with outrage, as the Theft of the Century. It was carried out in broad daylight by elected officials and Barnes trustees, all of whom justified it by placing the needs of the vast public above the whims of a dead millionaire.

The film explains in great detail the chain of events that began after the death of Barnes at the wheel of his own car in 1951. It involves Lincoln University, the small African-American college to which he entrusted control of the foundation, no doubt to piss off the establishment. It involves how the president of Lincoln, Richard H. Glanton, sidestepped the wishes of Barnes by taking many of the treasures on tour, bringing honor to himself for such a benefaction. But Glanton is not the final villain. As he perhaps overspent and depleted Barnes's endowment, the vultures from Philadelphia were hovering, ready to pounce and fly off with their masterpieces to their nest in the museum—yes, at the top of the same great stairs Rocky Balboa ran up in *Rocky.* It is not difficult to imagine them at the top, their hands in triumph above their heads.

Well, was this such a bad thing? The Renoirs and Picassos can now be seen by anyone visiting the museum, instead of by a limited number of art students. That is good, I suppose, although I've seen tourists jogging past the *Mona Lisa* in Paris just to check it off their itinerary. The film could do a better job of allowing the public access issue to be defended. But what it does is tell a cautionary tale.

It is perfectly clear exactly what Barnes specified in his will. It was drawn up by the best legal minds. It is clear that what happened to his collection was against his wishes. It is clear that the city fathers acted in obviation of those wishes, and were upheld in a court of appeals. What is finally clear is this: It doesn't matter a damn what your will says if you have $25 billion and politicians and the establishment want it.

## The A-Team ★ ½

PG-13, 121 m., 2010

Liam Neeson (Hannibal), Jessica Biel (Charisa), Bradley Cooper (Face), Sharlto Copley

(Murdock), Quinton "Rampage" Jackson (B.A.), Patrick Wilson (Lynch). Directed by Joe Carnahan and produced by Stephen J. Cannell, Jules Daly, Tony Scott, Spike Seldin, Iain Smith, and Alex Young. Screenplay by Joe Carnahan, Brian Bloom, and Skip Woods, based on the TV series by Cannell and Frank Lupo.

*The A-Team* is an incomprehensible mess with the 1980s TV show embedded inside. The characters have the same names, they play the same types, they have the same traits, and they're easily as shallow. That was OK for a TV sitcom, which is what the show really was, but at over two hours of queasy-cam anarchy it's punishment.

The movie uses the new style of violent action, which fragments sequences into so many bits and pieces that it's impossible to form any sense of what's happening, or where, or to whom. The actors appear in flash-frames, intercut with shards of CGI and accompanied by loud noises, urgent music, and many explosions. This continues for the required length, and then there's some dialogue. Not a lot. A few words, a sentence, sometimes a statement that crosses the finish line at paragraph length.

The plot: Wrongly framed for counterfeiting, the team members, all Iraq veterans, bust out of various prisons and go after the engraving plates, which would be pretty much worn out while printing enough $100 bills to pay for the millions in property damage they cause in the process.

Bored out of my mind during this spectacle, I found my attention wandering to the subject of physics. *The A-Team* has an action scene that admirably demonstrates Newton's Third Law, which instructs us that for every action there is always an equal and opposite reaction.

The movie illustrates this as the heroes fall from an exploding airplane while inside an armored tank. As the tank hurtles to the ground (cf. Newton's Law of Gravity), the team leader, Hannibal Smith (Liam Neeson), looks out an opening and barks out commands for the tank's gun. I am paraphrasing: "Turn forty-five degrees to the left! Fire! Twenty-five degrees to the right! Fire!" etc. In this way he is able to direct the fall of the tank and save their lives. This is very funny.

The action scenes also benefit from everyone having had a glance at the choreography beforehand. Consider a scene when a team member is confronted by a Talking Killer. This is, of course, a killer who only has to pull the trigger but pauses to sneer and boast. He and his target are standing in the middle of a jumble of dozens of freight shipping containers that have been spilled onto a dock. He talks just a little too long, and B. A. Baracus ("Rampage" Jackson) comes roaring to the rescue through the air on his motorcycle and wipes him out.

I know there are Harley lovers among my devoted readers. Am I right in assuming that it is difficult to get enough speed for a good aerial jump while biking across a crooked heap of freight containers? I ask because, as I hinted above, no action in this movie necessarily has any relationship to the actions surrounding it.

The characters here have that annoying ability to precisely predict what will happen and coordinate their response to it. An example. A slimy double-dealer is about to kill another team member, never mind who, when suddenly behind him a container is lifted into the air, and behind it are revealed all of the other team members lined up in a row, with choice words and brief phrases to say.

I don't want to be tiresome, but (1) how did they know the two guys were behind precisely that container; (2) how did they line up a crane and hook up the container without being heard or noticed; (3) how were they able to gather the members so quickly after the chaos of the preceding action; and (4) was someone eavesdropping to give the cue at the right moment to lift the container? Ten seconds later, and it might have been too late. Ten seconds earlier, and dialogue would have been stepped on.

Are my objections ridiculous? Why? How is it interesting to watch a movie in which the "action" is essentially colorful abstractions? Isn't it more satisfying if you know where everyone is and what they're doing and how they're doing it in real time? In other words, isn't *The Hurt Locker* more interesting than *The A-Team*?

To give it credit, the movie knows it is childish. The PG-13 is appropriate. There's little actual gore, no sex beyond a chaste kiss, no

R-rated language, but—ohmigod—there's smoking! Alert to preteens: Try one of those fat cigars Hannibal smokes and you won't feel like dinner.

## Atlas Shrugged: Part 1 ★

PG-13, 97 m., 2011

Taylor Schilling (Dagny Taggart), Grant Bowler (Henry Rearden), Matthew Marsden (James Taggart), Graham Beckel (Ellis Wyatt), Edi Gathegi (Eddie Willers), Jsu Garcia (Francisco D'Anconia), Michael Lerner (Wesley Mouch). Directed by Paul Johansson and produced by John Aglialoro and Harmon Kaslow. Screenplay by Aglialoro and Brian Patrick O'Toole, adapted from the novel by Ayn Rand.

I feel like my arm is all warmed up and I don't have a game to pitch. I was primed to review *Atlas Shrugged.* I figured it might provide a parable of Ayn Rand's philosophy that I could discuss. For me, that philosophy reduces itself to: "I'm on board; pull up the lifeline." There are, however, people who take Ayn Rand even more seriously than comic book fans take *Watchmen.* I expected to receive learned and sarcastic lectures on the pathetic failings of my review.

And now I am faced with this movie, the most anticlimactic nonevent since Geraldo Rivera broke into Al Capone's vault. I suspect only someone very familiar with Rand's 1957 novel could understand the film at all, and I doubt they will be happy with it. For the rest of us, it involves a series of business meetings in luxurious retro leather-and-brass boardrooms and offices, and restaurants and bedrooms that look borrowed from a hotel no doubt known as the Robber Baron Arms.

During these meetings, everybody drinks. More wine is poured and sipped in this film than at a convention of oenophiles. There are conversations in the English language after which I sometimes found myself asking, "What did they just say?" The dialogue seems to have been ripped throbbing with passion from the pages of *Investor's Business Daily.* Much of the excitement centers on the tensile strength of steel.

The story involves Dagny Taggart (Taylor Schilling), a young woman who controls a railroad company named Taggart Transcontinental (its motto: "Ocean to Ocean"). She is a fearless and visionary entrepreneur, who is determined to use a revolutionary new steel to repair her train tracks. Vast forces seem to conspire against her.

It's a few years in the future. America has become a state in which mediocrity is the goal and high-achieving individuals the enemy. Laws have been passed prohibiting companies from owning other companies. Dagny's new steel, which is produced by her sometimes lover Hank Rearden (Grant Bowler), has been legislated against because it's better than other steels. The Union of Railroad Engineers has decided it will not operate Dagny's trains. Just to show you how bad things have become, a government minister announces "a tax will be applied to the state of Colorado in order to equalize our national economy." So you see how governments and unions are the enemy of visionary entrepreneurs.

But you're thinking, railroads? Yes, although airplanes exist in this future, trains are where it's at. When I was six, my Aunt Martha brought me to Chicago to attend the great Railroad Fair of 1948, at which the nation's rail companies celebrated the wonders that were on the way. They didn't quite foresee mass air transportation. *Atlas Shrugged* seems to buy into the fair's glowing vision of the future of trains. Rarely, perhaps never, has television news covered the laying of new railroad track with the breathless urgency of the news channels shown in this movie.

So OK. Let's say you know the novel, you agree with Ayn Rand, you're an objectivist or a libertarian, and you've been waiting eagerly for this movie. Man, are you going to get a letdown. It's not enough that a movie agree with you, in however an incoherent and murky fashion. It would help if it were, like, you know, entertaining?

The movie is constructed of a few kinds of scenes. (1) People sipping their drinks in clubby surroundings and exchanging dialogue that sounds like assorted corporate lingo; (2) railroads, and lots of 'em; (3) limousines driving through cities in ruin and arriving in front of vast, ornate buildings; (4) city skylines; (5) the beauties of Colorado. There is also a love scene, which is shown not merely from the waist up but from the ears up. The man keeps his shirt on. This may be disappointing for libertarians, who I believe enjoy rumpy-pumpy as much as anyone.

Oh, and there is Wisconsin. Dagny and Hank ride blissfully in Taggart's new high-speed train, and then Hank suggests they take a trip to Wisconsin, where the state's policies caused the suppression of an engine that runs on the ozone in the air, or something (the film's detailed explanation won't clear this up). They decide to drive there. That's when you'll enjoy the beautiful landscape photography of the deserts of Wisconsin. My free advice to the filmmakers: If you want to use a desert, why not just refer to Wisconsin as "New Mexico"?

*Atlas Shrugged* closes with a title card saying, "End of Part One." Frequently throughout the film, characters repeat the phrase, "Who is John Galt?" Well they might ask. A man in black, always shot in shadow, is apparently John Galt. If you want to get a good look at him and find out why everybody is asking, I hope you can find out in Part Two. I don't think you can hold out for Part Three.

## Attack the Block ★ ★ ★

R, 88 m., 2011

John Boyega (Moses), Alex Esmail (Pest), Leeon Jones (Jerome), Simon Howard (Biggz), Franz Drameh (Dennis), Nick Frost (Ron), Jodie Whittaker (Sam), Luke Treadaway (Brewis), Jumayn Hunter (Hi-Hatz). Directed by Joe Cornish and produced by Nira Park and James Wilson. Screenplay by Cornish.

Fireworks fill the sky over London, creating such a distraction that an alien crashes to earth unnoticed. Meanwhile, in a dark bypass, a young nurse is being mugged by a gang of teenage street thugs, their faces buried within fearsome hooded sweatshirts. Their straightforward situation grows complicated when the alien attacks them, and the nurse decides she'd be safer staying with the thieves.

That's the setup for *Attack the Block*, an entertaining thriller in the tradition of 1970s B action films, with an unknown cast, energetic special effects, and great energy. That it takes place almost entirely around a low-cost London housing estate (that is, project) adds to its interest, because as the junior thugs band together to fight the aliens, they stop being faceless and emerge as sympathetic individuals who discover their resources. This alien attack may have been a learning experience dropped from the heavens.

The movie, which should have been titled *Defend the Block*, illustrates once again that zombie, horror, and monster movies are a port of entry for new filmmakers. The genre is the star. Unknown actors are almost an advantage. Darkness and quick cutting make up for a great deal in the area of special effects. What is needed is imagination. When John Carpenter made *Assault on Precinct 13* (1976), he demonstrated an invaluable formula to later low-budget generations.

This is an impressive first feature written and directed by Joe Cornish, a British comic actor who also authored the *Tintin* movie by Spielberg. Here he shows a strong sense for characters as the personalities of the gang members, their neighbors, and friends emerge sharply. He's made a fortunate discovery in John Boyega as Moses, the de facto leader of the pack and the quickest to figure out the greater dimensions of the alien invasion. Moses's knowledge of the Block and its residents and his ability to deal with people turn out to be crucial.

Cornish creates a mixed bag. We meet the local crime lord, the Block's drug dealer, and, revealingly, the family members of the gang. We see how the police leap to conclusions and unerringly arrest the wrong people for the wrong reasons. And Sam (Jodie Whittaker), the nurse, emerges from stereotyped victimhood and becomes a valuable part of the defense team.

Then there are the aliens. Does it much matter what they look like? They have luminescent fangs and are very fast and are great climbers, always in savage attack mode. Their design is wise; larger and more grotesque alien monsters have a way of looking goofy, as the Japanese demonstrated in the 1950s. These creatures are as efficient and low-maintenance as werewolves.

The question arises about the level of their civilization. Presumably this alien race has mastered space travel and journeyed through the void, almost necessarily at a speed faster than light, and yet they appear to lack opposable thumbs, speech, and other conveniences. Of course they may not be the real aliens. They may merely be the aliens' attack animals. But no, apparently not.

Such questions are beside the point. The genre calls for a mixed bag of characters to defend the fort/stagecoach/police station/pub/outpost, etc., against savage marauders, meanwhile developing their own personalities and abilities. This is a formula we've seen time and again, and in the right hands it's foolproof.

The movie has been much praised in Britain, whose writers wonder if Americans will understand the jargon of the locals. For that matter, would the queen? It matters not. Context is all, and the language here is no more difficult than the coinages in *A Clockwork Orange* and *The Warriors.* The question is, do the action and the characters work well together? The answer is yes. And sometimes it gets a little funny, too.

## The Avengers ★ ★ ★

PG-13, 142 m., 2012

Robert Downey Jr. (Tony Stark/Iron Man), Chris Evans (Steve Rogers/Captain America), Mark Ruffalo (Bruce Banner/Hulk), Chris Hemsworth (Thor), Scarlett Johansson (Natasha Romanoff/Black Widow), Jeremy Renner (Clint Barton/Hawkeye), Tom Hiddleston (Loki), Clark Gregg (Agent Phil Coulson), Cobie Smulders (Agent Maria Hill), Stellan Skarsgard (Selvig), Samuel L. Jackson (Nick Fury), Gwyneth Paltrow (Pepper Potts). Directed by Joss Whedon and produced by Kevin Feige. Screenplay by Zak Penn and Whedon.

One of the weapons Marvel used in its climb to comic book dominance was a willingness to invent new characters at a dizzying speed. There are so many Marvel universes, indeed, that some superheroes do not even exist in one another's worlds, preventing gridlock. The Avengers, however, do share the same time and space continuum, although in recent years they've been treated in separate single-superhero movies. One assumes the idle Avengers follow the exploits of the employed ones on the news.

*The Avengers*, much awaited by Marvel Comics fans, assembles all of the Avengers in one film—Iron Man, Captain America, Thor, the Hulk, Black Widow, and Hawkeye. This is like an all-star game, or the chef's sampling menu at a fancy restaurant. What always strikes me is how different their superpowers are. Iron Man (Robert Downey Jr.) is just an ordinary guy until he's wearing his super-suit. Thor (Chris Hemsworth) swings a mighty hammer. Hawkeye (Jeremy Renner) wields a bow with arrows so powerful they can bring down alien spacecraft. The Hulk (Mark Ruffalo) is a mild-mannered guy until he gets angry, and then he expands into a leaping, bounding green muscleman who can rip apart pretty much anything. Captain America (Chris Evans) has a powerful and versatile shield. Then there's Natasha Romanoff (Scarlett Johansson), aka Black Widow. After seeing the film, I discussed her with movie critics from Brazil and India, and we were unable to come up with a satisfactory explanation for her superpowers; it seems she is merely a martial artist with good aim with weapons. We decided maybe she and Hawkeye aren't technically superheroes, but just hang out in the same crowd.

When I see these six together, I can't help thinking of the champions at the Westminster Kennel Club Dog Show. You have breeds that seem completely different from one another (Labradors, poodles, boxers, dalmatians), and yet they're all champions.

The reason they're brought together in *The Avengers* is that Earth is under threat by the smirking Loki (Tom Hiddleston), Thor's adopted brother, who controls the Tesseract, a pulsing cube of energy that opens a gateway to the universe, and through it he plans to attack Earth with his fleet of reptile-looking monster machines. It goes completely unexplained where Loki now lives, how these dragon machines are manufactured, and so on.

Both Loki and Thor are obscurely related to the gods of Norse mythology, as we know from last year's *Thor*, but let's not drift into theology.

Nick Fury (Samuel L. Jackson) sends out a call to the Avengers to team up and meet this threat. He runs S.H.I.E.L.D., the Strategic Homeland Intervention, Enforcement, and Logistics Division, which is all I know about it. He's headquartered on a gigantic aircraft carrier that is also a hovercraft and can become invisible. By bringing the Avengers together, he, of course, reopens ancient rivalries (for example, my hammer can beat your shield), until they learn the benefits of Teamwork, which is discussed in speeches of noble banality. So you see, this is sort of an educational film, teaching the Avengers to do what was so highly valued on my first-grade report card: Working Well with Others.

These films are all more or less similar, and *The Avengers* gives us much, much more of the same. There must be a threat. The heroes must be enlisted. The villain must be dramatized. Some personality defects are probed. And then the last hour or so consists of special effects in which large mechanical objects engage in combat that results in deafening crashes and explosions and great balls of fire.

Much of this battle takes place in midtown Manhattan, where the neatest sequences involve Loki's ginormous, slithering, undulating snake-lizard-dragon machine, which seems almost to have a mind of its own, and is backed up by countless snakelings. At one point, an Avenger flies into the mouth of this leviathan and penetrates its entire length, emerging at the business end. You won't see that in *The Human Centipede.*

"Comic-Con nerds will have multiple orgasms," predicts David Edelstein in *New York* magazine, confirming something I had vaguely suspected about them. If he is correct, it's time for desperately needed movies to reeducate nerds in the joys of sex. *The Avengers* is done well by Joss Whedon, with style and energy. It provides its fans with exactly what they desire. Whether it is exactly what they deserve is arguable.

# B

## Babies ★ ★ ★

PG, 79 m., 2010

Featuring Ponijao, Bayar, Mari, and Hattie. A documentary directed by Thomas Balmes and produced by Amandine Billot, Alain Chabat, and Christine Rouxel.

*Babies* is the perfect film for anyone who has never had the opportunity to interact with humans at an early age. You may never have had one, held one, or baby-sat one, yet remained curious about the infants you see in a park, on the beach, or in baby carriers at the mall. Now a French documentarian has traveled to Africa, Asia, and America to bring back charming footage of babies in their natural habitats.

If, however, you've raised children and/or grandchildren, or had little brothers and sisters, the movie may resemble seventy-nine minutes of unpaid baby-sitting. When Baby Mari starts screaming, you're wishing you could turn on the TV and use something bright and noisy as a distraction. But no, you're at a movie. On the other hand, *Babies* may be fascinating viewing for babies, just as many dogs and cats have their favorite programs. At last, programming for the Mommy & Me screenings.

The babies are cute. Well, all babies are cute. That's just as well, because how could filmmakers audition a baby and wait six months to give it a callback? It's not a baby anymore. The director, Thomas Balmes, has found exemplary babies in Namibia, Mongolia, Tokyo, and San Francisco, and observes them lovingly as they nurse, play, doze, poke kittens, and happily hit one another. The movie is really about the babies, not their parents, and in most cases we see only those parts of the parents ranking highest on the infant's interest scale: nipples, hands, arms, and male and female chests. Not all of the nipples are real, but the babies don't discriminate as long as they work.

Two of the babies come from poor parts of the world, and two from rich. They seem equally happy and healthy. The Japanese and American babies are subjected to an awesome array of baby training strategies so they can begin climbing the success ladder as early as possible. I have no argument against baby yoga classes, but I have never known a baby that wasn't naturally able to contort itself into alarming positions and get lost in meditation on the spur of the moment.

The African baby, Ponijao, lives in a forest hut with an earth floor, but this is Home and here is Mother and there are sticks to play with that may not be made of plastic and ornamented with Disney creatures but are excellent sticks nonetheless, and satisfying. Bayar, whose family lives in a yurt in Mongolia, passes time by becoming expert in sibling rivalry. Mari, from Japan, and Hattie, from America, are surrounded by a baffling array of devices to entertain them, serve them, shelter them, protect them, and help them grow up big and strong. Can the epidemic of attention deficit disorder be explained by the First World's lack of opportunities for babies to be bored? How can babies concentrate when things are forever being jingled and dangled at them? Is there too much incoming?

I dunno. What I do know is that babies are miraculous. From a sprawling, bawling start, they learn to walk, talk, plan, scheme, play, and figure stuff out. Generations of scientists have hurled themselves at the question of exactly how babies learn to talk. They must be getting so frustrated by the fact that the babies just go ahead and do it with no training.

Did I like the movie? Aw, yeah, I did. How could I not? Did I feel I needed to see it? Not really. I appreciated the fact that there was no narrator to explain what I was seeing; no voice-overs like "little Bayar learns early to appreciate the mystery of yogurt." No parents asking, "Are you a good little boy?" and answering, "Yes, he's good little boy." Just babies. Wonderful. I was once in that state myself. I remember being flat on my stomach with my eyes an inch away from ants all crawling in a line on the front sidewalk. I've never been so entertained in my life.

## The Back-up Plan ★

PG-13, 104 m., 2010

Jennifer Lopez (Zoe), Alex O'Loughlin (Stan). Directed by Alan Poul and produced by Todd

Black, Jason Blumenthal, and Steve Tisch. Screenplay by Kate Angelo.

Some movies are no better than second-rate sitcoms. Other movies are no better than third-rate sitcoms. *The Back-up Plan* doesn't deserve comparison with sitcoms. It plays like an unendurable TV commercial about beautiful people with great lifestyles and not a thought in their empty little heads. So timid is this film that when it finally arrives at its inevitable childbirth scene, it bails out after two "pushes"!

Jennifer Lopez has never looked better. That's about all she does here, is look better. She is talented and deserves more than this birdbrained plot about characters who have no relationship to life as it is lived by, you know, actual people. The movie deals with artificial insemination, romance, sex, and organic goat cheese, which are promising areas for investigation, but it's so watered down it approaches homeopathy.

Lopez plays Zoe, a Manhattan pet shop owner who despairs of finding the perfect inseminator and decides to become artificially impregnated. Leaving the doctor's office, she is so happy she finds herself singin' in the rain. Then she hails a cab and a strange man pops into the backseat the same moment she does. As a Meet Cute, this ranks right down there with two characters bending over to pick up the same thing and bumping heads, which is what Tony Randall is always doing whenever I think of Meet Cutes.

This stranger is Stan (Alex O'Loughlin). We know, according to the Law of Conservation of Dramatic Resources, that (a) Zoe will become pregnant, and (b) she and Stan will fall in love. Consider the alternatives: (a1) she doesn't become pregnant, and (b2) they never see each other again. Anyway, fate brings them together, and then again, and soon they're falling for each other.

This Stan is a prime catch. Not only does he personally sell organic goat cheese in a ridiculously upscale farmers' market, but he produces it himself, on his own upstate farm. I am at a loss to explain why the movie squandered an opportunity to show Lopez milking a goat. Or having a goat eat her shoes, or whatever goats usually do in movies of this sort.

Obviously, the only way to make this feature-length is for Zoe and Stan to break up and get back together again, which they do, I think, three times. Their breakups tend toward communications difficulties, as one or the other idiotically misunderstands dialogue that is crystal clear to everyone in the audience. In Little Movie Glossary lore this is Damon Knight's famous Idiot Plot, in which all difficulties could be resolved by the uttering of one or two words.

I don't believe *The Back-up Plan* is intended to be set in the real Manhattan. Take a close look at the farmers' market. It's more of a Farmer's Faire at a church benefit in a rich suburb. Farmer Stan and his goats, indeed. But consider the scene where Zoe is a bridesmaid at a wedding, and her water breaks. What does she do? Rush to the hospital? No, she commandeers the wedding's rented white Bentley and is driven to the market, where the auto shoulders its way right down the middle of the street and halts before the organic goat cheese stall, where Zoe can leap out and make up with Stan right there in public, while onlookers all smile and listen like benevolent insiders, instead of New Yorkers wondering who the hell these jerks are. Does Stan happen to have one of those little boxes with a ring in it handy? What does a goat do in the woods?

I have neglected poor little Nuts, Zoe's Boston terrier. Nuts follows her everywhere, and whenever he gets a close-up, he barks appropriately, as if he understands what is said. When was the last time in a movie where somebody said something, and there was a cut to a dog who barked, and you thought, "That's so funny!" Nuts is paralyzed from the waist down and pulls himself everywhere on his little cart, without the benefit of much loving and cooing from his mistress, who relates to him as exactly what he is, a prop. But the little tyke can really wheel around and is always there when he's needed on camera.

This movie is desperately boring. No one says much of anything interesting. They have extremely limited ranges of interest. There are older characters: Zoe's Nana (Linda Lavin) and grandpa (Tom Bosley) and gynecologist (Robert Klein). They seem human, so the camera cuts away lest they get started on something. At the playground where Stan hangs out (allegedly fascinated by the prospect of fatherhood), there's "Playground Dad" (Anthony Anderson), a proud black father who gives Stan pep talks on the joys of parenting. African-Americans are so wise in movies like this, always playing proud dads and wise advisers and God and so forth, it's a wonder the movies are about anyone else.

## Bad Teacher ★ ★

R, 92 m., 2011

Cameron Diaz (Elizabeth Halsey), Justin Timberlake (Scott Delacorte), Lucy Punch (Amy Squirrel), John Michael Higgins (Principal Wally Snur), Jason Segel (Russell Gettis), Phyllis Smith (Lynn Davies), Dave "Gruber" Allen (Sandy Pinkus), Jillian Armenante (Ms. Pavicic). Directed by Jake Kasdan and produced by Jimmy Miller. Screenplay by Gene Stupnitsky and Lee Eisenberg.

Jake Kasdan's *Bad Teacher* immediately brings *Bad Santa* to mind, and suffers by the comparison. Its bad teacher is neither bad enough nor likable enough. The transgressions of Elizabeth Halsey (Cameron Diaz) are more or less what you'd expect, but what's surprising is that she's so nasty and unpleasant. Billy Bob Thornton, as the bad Santa, was more outrageously offensive and yet more redeemed by his desperation. He was bad for urgent reasons. Elizabeth seems bad merely as a greedy lifestyle choice.

As the film opens, the Diaz character is engaged to a rich guy she leeches on but doesn't love. She's dumped and has to return to middle school teaching, an occupation she has no talent for or interest in, and passes the time showing DVDs to her students and napping, drinking, and doing drugs at her desk. This creates astonishment and indignation in the charmingly named Amy Squirrel (Lucy Punch), whose classroom is right across the hall.

The school characters also include the backup teacher Scott Delacorte (Justin Timberlake), amiable but juiceless; the veteran teacher Ms. Pavicic (Jillian Armenante), a sweet dumpling; the hunky gym teacher Russell Gettis (Jason Segel); and the dolphin-obsessed Principal Wally Snur (John Michael Higgins).

Of these characters, the rival played by Lucy Punch is the most colorful because she's the most driven and obsessed. The others seem curiously inconsequential, content to materialize in a scene, perform a necessary function, and vaporize. There's no urgency, and that was the one quality *Bad Santa* dripped with.

None of the film's major characters is a student, which seems odd. Yes, there's a kid who writes bad poetry and has a crush on the class sexpot, but his desperation seems well within comic bounds. There are no vindictive students, none with aggressive behavior, no little Omens in training. The casting of the children seems lacking in imagination, but then what does the screenplay give them to do?

Cameron Diaz has proven that she is gifted with comedy. But here her Elizabeth is a mean, antagonistic money-grubber on autopilot. Where did she come from? Why did she get into teaching in the first place? Has she no heart? There are times in *Bad Santa* when we feel sorry for the poor SOB, but nothing in *Bad Teacher* inspires more than distaste for the character.

Other problems: There is no chemistry, or indeed even much mutual awareness, between Diaz and Timberlake. You know those annual Bad Sex Awards for the worst sex scene in a movie? Their dry-humping scene deserves an award for the decade. The scene itself is pathetic. The shot it ends on—the wet spot on Timberlake's blue jeans—had the audience recoiling.

Whole chunks of the plot seem to have gone missing. And how, oh how, can we possibly understand the eventual development between Elizabeth and Russell the gym teacher? You know what that feels like? It feels like they called Diaz and Jason Segel in for one additional day of shooting to provide a preposterous happy ending. Jolly music keeps elbowing its way onto the sound track in an unconvincing attempt to cue us that we've seen a good comedy.

## The Bang Bang Club ★ ★

NO MPAA RATING, 109 m., 2011

Ryan Phillippe (Greg Marinovich), Malin Akerman (Robin Comley), Taylor Kitsch (Kevin Carter), Frank Rautenbach (Ken Oosterbroek),

Neels Van Jaarsveld (Joao Silva). Directed by Steven Silver and produced by Adam Friedlander, Daniel Iron, and Lance Samuels. Screenplay by Silver, based on the book *The Bang-Bang Club: Snapshots from a Hidden War* by Greg Marinovich and Joao Silva.

Many of the photos of the bloody final months of apartheid were taken by four photographers who became famous as "The Bang Bang Club," because of their willingness to risk death for great pictures. Two of them won Pulitzers. One of them was killed, one committed suicide, one was shot four times before retiring. The word often used about them was "courageous," but another word that occurs is "foolhardy."

In the opening scene, we meet Greg Marinovich (Ryan Phillippe), who pulls his car to the side of a highway and clambers down an embankment to follow an angry mob into a riot in Soweto, the African township outside Johannesburg. He joins three other photographers, all of them white, as they run, crouch low, and shoot photos in the middle of mob violence. They seem almost reckless.

Why do the blacks largely ignore these whites in their midst? Why is their attention so focused on their enemies of the same color? This question, which will instinctively occur to many viewers, is never quite dealt with in the film. The photographers sometimes drive into the middle of violent situations, hold up a camera, and say "Press!"—as if that will solve everything. Sometimes it does.

We know with the benefit of history that South Africa's president F. W. de Klerk was even then in talks with Nelson Mandela of the African National Congress that would lead to free elections, Mandela as president, and today's South Africa. In 1994, the white minority was still involved in forcibly fighting black demonstrations, but almost all of the fighting filmed by the Bang Bang Club was black against black. The movie explains in a cursory way that the ANC was being opposed by the Inkatha Freedom Party, made of Zulus who opposed Mandela's mostly Xhosa membership.

Inkatha fighters did more actual violence against the ANC than the whites did. I'm not referring to the overarching, crushing daily violence of apartheid itself, but to specific murders. The Zulus introduced the practice of "necklacing," in which a tire would be tied around a victim's head and set on fire. This war between two tribes was doubly ironic in a nation ruled by a white tribe.

*The Bang Bang Club* will not leave its viewers with much of an insight into that. Some audience members may come out of the movie wondering why they didn't see much apartheid, except implicitly. The focus is on the four photographers, Marinovich (Phillippe), Kevin Carter (Taylor Kitsch), Ken Oosterbroek (Frank Rautenbach), and Joao Silva (Neels Van Jaarsveld). Young, fit, hip, they compete for photos but run as a pack, sometimes sharing the same VW van. At nights in Jo'berg they hang out in bars and seem to attract a generous share of good-looking women.

One of these is Robin Comley (Malin Akerman), the photo editor of the *Johannesburg Star,* who buys Marinovich's photos and then buys into a relationship. Ryan Phillippe is effective in the lead—the newcomer to the club, protected by an indifference to personal danger that seems naive if not suicidal. But they all act like immortals: Consider a scene where one sprints across a street during a fierce gun battle to bring back a couple of liters of Coke.

Did these four men ever have extended discussions among themselves about the South African situation and apartheid itself? I'm sure they did, but there's little of that here. Were their photos intended to strengthen or weaken the government? I can't tell if they care. They like the money and the glory, they thrive on adrenaline, they buy into their Bang Bang legend. For them, in a sense, the reality of apartheid is only a photo op. Later, most of them will shoot films under fire in Sudan, the Middle East, and Bosnia. They live only to take pictures.

Well, that's their job, their craft, and their passion. But it evades a question: What is their investment as human beings? Kevin Carter takes a photo of a little girl, bent over with hunger and dehydration, as she is eyed by a nearby vulture. The picture won the Pulitzer Prize. At a press conference, he's asked what happened to the girl. He doesn't know. Didn't he do anything to help her? No. This is a universal dilemma for journalists in the face of tragedy. How many of them would frighten away the vulture and help the child? How many would take the photograph?

The film poses the question raised by the photo, but offers no answer. Perhaps there is none, or it is depressingly obvious. *The Bang Bang Club* seems curiously oblivious to South Africa as a whole. If this were your only film about that nation, you would leave with meager information. You would recall four good-looking guys who took a lot of chances and had some good times and some bad ones. But the big story wasn't about them. Bang Bang.

## Barney's Version ★ ★ ★ ½

R, 132 m., 2011

Paul Giamatti (Barney), Rosamund Pike (Miriam), Minnie Driver (Second Mrs. P.), Rachelle Lefevre (Clara), Scott Speedman (Boogie), Dustin Hoffman (Izzy), Bruce Greenwood (Blair), Macha Grenon (Solange). Directed by Richard J. Lewis and produced by Robert Lantos. Screenplay by Michael Konyves, based on the novel by Mordecai Richler.

*Barney's Version* tells the story of a man distinguished largely by his flaws and the beautiful woman who loves him in spite of them. What she sees in him I am not quite sure. He is a precariously functioning alcoholic and chain-smoker of cigars, a man balding and with a paunch, a producer of spectacularly bad television shows, and a fanatic hockey fan. Since he lives in Montreal, many good women might forgive the hockey, but he is also hostile toward her friends, rude at dinner parties, and has bad taste in ties.

Barney Panofsky is played by Paul Giamatti, who just won a Golden Globe for his performance. It is a successful performance not simply because of his acting but because of his exuding. He exudes a sweet quality that just barely allows us to understand why three women, the last of them a saint, would want to marry him. It's not money: He's broke when he marries the first, the second is rich in her own right, and the third is so desirable that Barney actually walks out of his own wedding reception to chase her to the train station and declare his love at first sight.

*Barney's Version* is based on a 1997 novel by Mordecai Richler, whose *The Apprenticeship of Duddy Kravitz* (1959) is also the life story of a flawed but lovable Jewish character from Montreal. Barney's story is told in retrospect, in the form of a response to a book written by a cop who is convinced Barney murdered his best friend. How the friend probably did die is suggested in a nicely handled late scene that Barney himself, by the time he experiences it, is not able to understand.

Having once in middle age forgotten where he parked his car, Barney progresses rather rapidly into Alzheimer's, although most of the film involves scenes before that happens. Since this isn't a movie about the disease, we might ask why it's included at all, but I think it functions as a final act in a life that was itself forgettable. Nothing distinguishes Barney except his romanticism and the woman who inspires it.

She is Miriam (Rosamund Pike), an ethereal beauty with a melodious voice and a patience with Barney that surpasses all understanding. They have two children, they live happily, Barney remains a mess, and at important moments in her career he would rather be getting drunk in a bar while watching hockey than being there for her. Yet he cannot live without her, and when she goes to New York for a week, he becomes reckless with loneliness.

I haven't read the much-loved novel by Richler, which is told in Barney's voice and has been compared by some to Saul Bellow's *Herzog*. The novel is said to be richer and more complex than the movie, but having only seen the movie, I can respond favorably to what it does achieve.

Giamatti's performance is one of those achievements. He is making a career of playing unremarkable but memorable men; remember his failed wine lover in *Sideways*, his schlubby Harvey Pekar in *American Splendor*, and his soul transplant victim in *Cold Souls*. (What he plans in his announced project *Bubba Nosferatu: Curse of the She-Vampires* is a question worthy of consideration.) Giamatti's Barney is not especially smart, or talented or good-looking, but he is especially *there*—a presence with a great depth of need that apparently appeals to the lovely Miriam.

She's one of those women who seems unaware that everyone must constantly be asking, "What does she see in him?" That women persist in seeing things in us, as men, we must be grateful.

Dustin Hoffman is very good here as Barney's father, a retired Montreal detective who imparts wisdom, but not too excessively, and love, but not too smarmily. The bond between elderly father and aging son is cemented by good cigars, which I have seen work in other cases. There is a lot of truth in *Barney's Version*. It is a mercy that Barney cannot see most of it.

## Battle: Los Angeles ½ ★

PG-13, 116 m., 2011

Aaron Eckhart (Staff Sergeant Michael Nantz), Michelle Rodriguez (Technical Sergeant Elena Santos), Ramon Rodriguez (Second Lieutenant William Martinez), Bridget Moynahan (Michele), Ne-Yo (Corporal Kevin Harris), Michael Peña (Joe Rincon). Directed by Jonathan Liebesman and produced by Jeffrey Chernov, Ori Marmur, and Neal H. Moritz. Screenplay by Christopher Bertolini.

*Battle: Los Angeles* is noisy, violent, ugly, and stupid. Its manufacture is a reflection of appalling cynicism on the part of its makers, who don't even try to make it more than senseless chaos. Here's a science-fiction film that's an insult to the words "science" and "fiction," and the hyphen in between them.

Meteors fall to Earth near the coasts of the world's major cities (and in Ireland's Dingle Bay—that meteor must have strayed off course). They contain alien troops, which march up from the beach with their weapons of war and attack mankind. No reason is given for this, although it's mentioned they may want our water. We meet the members of a U.S. Marine platoon and its battle-scarred staff sergeant. They're helicoptered into Santa Monica and apparently defeat the aliens. Since all of Los Angeles is frequently seen in flames, it's not entirely clear how the Santa Monica action is crucial, but apparently it is.

The aliens are hilarious. Do they give Razzies for special effects? They seem to be animal/machine hybrids with automatic weapons growing from their arms, which must make it hard to change the baby. As the marines use their combat knives to carve into an alien, they find one layer after another of icky, gelatinous, pus-filled goo. Luckily, the other aliens are mostly seen in long shot, where they look like stick figures whipped up by apprentice animators.

Aaron Eckhart stars as Staff Sergeant Nantz, a twenty-year veteran who has something shady in his record that people keep referring to, although the screenwriter, Christopher Bertolini, is too cagey to come right out and describe it. Never mind. Eckhart is perfectly cast, and let the word go forth that he makes one hell of a great-looking action hero. He is also a fine actor, but acting skills are not required from anyone in this movie.

The dialogue consists almost entirely of terse screams: "Watch it! Incoming! Move! Look out! Fire! Move!" The only characters I remember having four sentences in a row are the anchors on cable news. Although the platoon includes the usual buffet of ethnicities, including Hispanics, Asians, and a Nigerian surgeon, none of them get much more than a word or two in a row, so as characters they're all placeholders.

You gotta see the alien battleships in this movie. They seem to have been assembled by the proverbial tornado blowing through a junkyard. They're aggressively ugly and cluttered, the product of a planet where design has not been discovered and even the Coke bottles must look like pin cushions. Although these ships presumably arrived inside the meteors, one in particular exhibits uncanny versatility, by rising up from the earth before the very eyes of the startled marines. How, you may ask, did it burrow for ten or twelve blocks under Santa Monica to the battle lines at Lincoln Boulevard? And well you may ask.

There is a lazy editing style in action movies these days that assumes nothing need make any sense visually. In a good movie, we understand where the heroes are and where their opponents are and why, and when they fire on one another we understand the geometry. In a mess like this, the frame is filled with flashes and explosion and shots so brief that nothing makes sense. From time to time there'll be a close-up of Aaron Eckhart screaming something, for example, and on either side of that shot there will be unrelated shots of incomprehensible action.

When I think of the elegant construction of something like *Gunfight at the OK Corral*, I want to rend the hair from my head and weep bitter tears of despair. Generations of filmmakers devoted their lives to perfecting techniques that a director like Jonathan Liebesman is either ignorant of or indifferent to. Yet he is given millions of dollars to produce this assault on the attention span of a generation.

Young men: If you attend this crap with friends who admire it, tactfully inform them they are idiots. Young women: If your date likes this movie, tell him you've been thinking it over and you think you should consider spending some time apart.

## Battleship ★ ★ ½

PG-13, 130 m., 2012

Taylor Kitsch (Alex Hopper), Alexander Skarsgard (Stone Hopper), Rihanna (Cora Raikes), Brooklyn Decker (Samantha Shane), Tadanobu Asano (Yugi Nagata), Gregory D. Gadson (Mick Canales), Liam Neeson (Admiral Shane), Hamish Linklater (Cal Zapata). Directed by Peter Berg and produced by Berg, Sarah Aubrey, Brian Goldner, Duncan Henderson, Bennett Schneir, and Scott Stuber. Screenplay by Erich Hoeber and Jon Hoeber.

"This could be like Columbus and the Indians," a nerdy radio astronomer worries. "Except we're the Indians." From a powerful transmission facility in Hawaii, he's supervised the transmission of a signal to the Earth-like Planet G in another galaxy, and in no time at all aliens come calling. Considering that they arrive in weeks, they must have discovered faster-than-light speeds, so it's a little strange that when they arrive they're strictly analog. Their vast warships splash down in the Pacific (except for fragments that devastate Hong Kong in one of those toppling skyscraper scenes so beloved in disaster movies). But these alien craft are armed only at a level that makes their battle with a fleet of U.S. warships more or less a standoff.

Why would the U.S. fleet conveniently already be near the splashdown point? It's involved in war games with allies such as Japan, which provides an excuse for a Japanese officer to take temporary command of one of our ships and boost the grosses of *Battleship* in Asia. It is also handy that the aliens create a force field that forms an impenetrable barrier around their craft, which seals in three U.S. ships, locks out all other ships, and explains why our airplanes don't simply nuke the SOBs.

Of course, our response to the alien visit is immediately military, in the old B-movie tradition. There's not one word of discussion about the aliens possibly just making a social call. We invite them, they come, and we open fire. This despite the fact that they're remarkably humanoid; when we finally remove the helmet from one alien's space suit, he turns out to look alarmingly like James Carville.

In the setup, we meet a shiftless beach bum named Alex Hopper (Taylor Kitsch), whose brother Stone (Alexander Skarsgard) is a naval officer. In a bar, Alex makes a hit on the lithesome Samantha Shane (Brooklyn Decker), who, wouldn't you know, is the daughter of the admiral of the fleet (Liam Neeson). Breaking into a convenience store to get her a burrito, Alex is arrested and his brother delivers an ultimatum: Join the navy or else.

Meanwhile, the nerd (Hamish Linklater) supervises transmission of the signal to Planet G, and in no more time than it takes to get Alex into uniform and on board a U.S. destroyer, five alien spacecraft enter our solar system in tight formation. One alien craft then levitates from the ocean deeps, as large as a skyscraper and bristling with ominous protrusions. You gotta say it takes real nerve for a communications officer (Rihanna) and two seamen to speed over to it in a rubber boat armed with a machine gun.

Parallel stories. We learn Samantha is a physical therapist working with the army vet Mick Canales (real-life Iraq hero Gregory D. Gadson). She takes him on a hike up the mountainside where the big NASA radio dishes are located, they meet the nerd, and much depends on preventing the aliens from phoning home. In the Pentagon situation room, officials fret. There's the obligatory montage of cable news reports on the alien invasion, and the U.S. destroyers exchange fire with the aliens. Two ships are destroyed, including the one commanded by Stone Hopper, and after several officers on Alex Hopper's ship die, he turns out to be next in command and becomes the captain of the surviving U.S. destroyer. So that's convenient. The characters we met at the beginning all become the key players.

This movie is based on the Hasbro board game of the same name, unplayed by me. You get a little of that sense when radar doesn't work and Rihanna figures out a way to deduce the underwater movements of the alien craft by tracking wave patterns on a grid with old-fashioned weather buoys. The film eventually comes down to a large number of scenes in which things get blowed up real good. One alien weapon is especially fearsome: a large metal ball with spikes, which rolls through things and flattens them. Were less-sophisticated versions of this used in medieval times, maybe made of flaming tar balls?

The film is in the tradition of the Transformers movies, also based on Hasbro games, and you get the feeling that Hasbro showed its director, Peter Berg, some Michael Bay movies and told him to go and do likewise. To his credit, this is a more entertaining film than the Transformers titles, more fun, because it has slightly more fully fleshed characters, a better plot, and a lot of naval combat strategy. The work of Gregory D. Gadson, as the disabled vet, is especially effective; he has a fierce screen presence. Rihanna is as convincing as the character allows, and Taylor Kitsch makes a sturdy if predictable hero.

But the nicest touch is that *Battleship* has an honest-to-God third act, instead of just settling for nonstop fireballs and explosions, as Bay likes to do. I don't want to spoil it for you. Let's say the Greatest Generation still has the right stuff, and leave it at that.

## Beautiful Boy ★ ★ ★

R, 100 m., 2011

Maria Bello (Kate), Michael Sheen (Bill), Alan Tudyk (Eric), Moon Bloodgood (Trish), Austin Nichols (Coop), Kyle Gallner (Sam), Meat Loaf Aday (Motel Clerk). Directed by Shawn Ku and produced by Lee Clay and Eric Gozlan. Screenplay by Ku and Michael Armbruster.

The death of a child is a calamity. When that child has gone on a killing rampage at his campus and then taken his own life, it must be a tragedy so fundamental that it paralyzes thought. *Beautiful Boy* gives us a glimpse of the young student on the night before his murders, and then is about how his parents live with what he has done.

No rational response seems possible. They cannot reason with madness. Their son fits all the clichés of sudden killers: He was quiet, shy, kept to himself, never caused trouble. In scenes before his death we see that his home was an arid minefield. His parents were closed off from each other and on the edge of divorce. When he telephones them on his last night, their advice is "study hard." His mother speaks with him longer than his father, but neither picks up what we see: The boy (Kyle Gallner) is on the edge of tears.

*Beautiful Boy* is a sincere attempt to imagine the aftermath of tragedy for the parents. Maria Bello and Michael Sheen play Kate and Bill, two people living in a daze. The news of their son's death is followed immediately by the news about his rampage. Ordinary grief is stunned senseless. Their home is immediately placed under siege by reporters and TV news crews demanding a statement. This is always the case. I always wonder what the reporters are hoping for. What can be said? When Bill finally reads out a statement of regret, it is perfunctory and useless.

Shawn Ku's film follows them. Bill tries to continue working at his office, but his coworkers stare and wonder. Kate is an editor and works on the manuscript of a new author. In her attention to minute details she deadens herself. Driven from their home, they move in with her sister (Moon Bloodgood) and husband (Alan Tudyk). This can't last. Finally they are alone in the world, checking into a hotel where the night clerk (Meat Loaf Aday) becomes the first person in the film to treat them as if they were ordinary people.

They were ready to divorce. Now they are together because no one else in the world can share this devastating new fact with them. Were the killings their fault? Did their marriage produce a disturbed boy? Do they deserve more guilt than they already feel? It's here, I believe, that the film fails, almost by default. In a way, it must fail. Ku, who is also the cowriter of the screenplay, has posed himself questions without answers. His story permits no catharsis. There are moments when some minuscule contentment creeps back into the lives of Kate and Bill, in a scene at the hotel where they have a dinner of snack food and whisky and remember a little why they were once in love. But there can never again be joy.

A film like this can end honestly in only one way, and Ku is true to it. Life will go on, one baffling day after another. There can be no release, only a gradual deadening. So it must be with most parents of children who commit horrible deeds. People do things for which there are no reasons, and if they don't kill themselves, they must live, like Mark David Chapman, in the debris of their madness.

There is a film that dealt with such an incident from the killer's point of view. Gus Van Sant's *Elephant* (2003) was about the shooters at a high school massacre like Columbine. It dared to suggest no explanation, no insight, no theories. Shawn Ku does the same. Here is the crucial difference: Van Sant focused on the killers. Ku focuses on the parents. They are alive, and are forced to live with the fact that there is no reason and no consolation. The parents of their son's victims are at least given the consolation of someone to hate.

## The Beaver ★ ★ ½

PG-13, 91 m., 2011

Mel Gibson (Walter Black), Jodie Foster (Meredith Black), Anton Yelchin (Porter Black), Jennifer Lawrence (Norah), Riley Thomas Stewart (Henry Black). Directed by Jodie Foster and produced by Steve Golin, Keith Redmon, and Ann Ruark. Screenplay by Kyle Killen.

*The Beaver* is almost successful despite the premise of its screenplay, which I was simply unable to accept. I concede it is possible that a man in depression might be able to heal himself by projecting his personality into a hand puppet. I am not sure it is possible, or even advisable, to make a serious movie about that. We go through the movie with Mel Gibson wearing a toothy beaver on his left hand, and that creates a whole lot of disbelief for us to suspend.

Yet here is another of Mel Gibson's fine performances, a reminder that he is after all a superb actor. His personal life is in ruins because of the disease of alcoholism, which he is still struggling with. When he's responsible for outrageous acts and statements, I think, this is not the good man I have met many times. From what I know about alcoholism, I believe he goes through personality changes, that he is content on some days and consumed by rage and madness on others, and that such changes are symptoms of the disease. Make your own diagnosis.

It took some courage on the part of Jodie Foster to direct this film. I believe she knows Gibson's good side and respects his talent. He was certainly the right choice for this material. All of his troubles through recent years are summed up by her opening shot, of an exhausted man floating on a raft in a swimming pool, his arms wide like the crucified Christ. A voice (later revealed to be the Beaver's) informs us this is Walter Black, a man so deep in depression he has alienated his family and nearly destroyed his business.

We meet his much-suffering wife, Meredith (Jodie Foster), his resentful son, Porter (Anton Yelchin), and his disbelieving colleagues. Meredith finally throws him out, not without love. He buys a bottle, checks into a motel, tries to kill himself, and is interrupted by the hand puppet. Finding that the puppet has a voice of its own, he allows it to speak for him, and begins to reenter his life. Foster, Gibson, and the writer, Kyle Killen, make not the slightest attempt to employ the illusion of ventriloquism; Gibson manipulates the puppet and speaks from his own mouth, in an admirable if inexplicable Cockney accent.

His life improves in ways I leave for you to discover. I also leave you to wonder if Matt Lauer on a real *Today* program would chat with a hand puppet quite as he does here. A parallel plot involves Porter, the son, whose gift is to ghostwrite papers for classmates that read as if written by themselves. The class valedictorian asks him to write her speech. If she's that smart, why can't she write it herself?

She's going through problems, which Porter will discover in a story that tends to lead us, however interestingly, away from the through-line.

What sort of movie would have resulted with the same characters but not the beaver? We will never know. On the other hand, without *The Beaver* we would never have witnessed a sexual threesome involving a hand puppet. Foster and Gibson must have gone through some serious times while making this film, but don't you suppose that while filming that sex scene they had to suppress the urge to giggle?

That is the fatal flaw in this sincere endeavor. As good as Gibson is, his character is still caught between the tragedy of the man and the absurdity of the beaver. Fugitive thoughts of Señor Wences crept into my mind. I'm sorry, but they did.

## Beginners ★ ★ ★ ½

R, 105 m., 2011

Ewan McGregor (Oliver), Christopher Plummer (Hal), Melanie Laurent (Anna), Goran Visnjic (Andy), Kai Lennox (Elliot), Mary Page Keller (Georgia), Keegan Boos (Young Oliver). Directed by Mike Mills and produced by Miranda de Pencier, Lars Knudsen, Leslie Urdang, Jay Van Hoy, and Dean Vanech.

Six months after his mother dies, Oliver's father tells him something startling: "I am gay." His father is seventy-five and was married for thirty-eight years. Oliver himself is about thirty-eight when he learns this news, and is in a different sort of closet: Afraid of failing, afraid of commitment, afraid to trust, he has never had a meaningful relationship. *Beginners* is about how both men find love. It is a film in which only a dog named Arthur seems to hold everything in perspective.

No, this isn't a comedy about a talking dog. Arthur has only a bit part and communicates in subtitles, thinking the kinds of thoughts that dogs, who are obsessed with the study of humans, might indeed think. But the presence of this wise Jack Russell terrier provides a perspective apart from sexuality and personality, one that perceives merely when everything is, or is not, as it should be.

Oliver, played by the engaging Ewan McGregor, is an artist whose work, apparently successful, communicates a reluctance to be sure and bold. His father, Hal, is played by Christopher Plummer as a man who arrived at an agreement with his wife, Georgia (Mary Page Keller), many years ago, and has been true to it. He has always known he is gay, and his revelation to his son conveys pride, relief, and a kind of joy. Perhaps he has arrived at an age when only his son could be expected to care about this unexpected information.

The film moves easily within three time frames. There is the period between his father's announcement and his death a few years later, the period in Oliver's life after the death, and flashbacks to Oliver's memories of childhood. If we must extract a meaning from *Beginners*, it may be that it is never too late to make a fresh start, and the father sets an example for his son.

Christopher Plummer, an actor filled with presence and grace, brings a dignified joy to his new gay lifestyle. He delights in the Gay Pride rainbow, dances in clubs, throws parties, and introduces Oliver to his boyfriend, Andy (Goran Visnjic). This Andy is so improbably handsome that the liaison seems unlikely, but we grow convinced that Andy truly and deeply loves the old man, with a fullness that almost shames Oliver. The film pays due attention to Hal's happiness and to the process of his death, which he approaches with the consolation that at last there is nothing he must keep secret.

Some months later, deep in idleness and distraction, sad in his bones, Oliver attends a costume party dressed as Freud. He stations himself next to a sofa and acquires a patient named Anna (Melanie Laurent). She communicates by writing notes in little spiral notebooks. She can't speak because she has laryngitis. In a curious sense, her notes and the dog's subtitles convey the same kinds of bottom-line observation: "Why," she writes, "did you come to a party when you were so sad?" She knows that he is sad, just as a dog doesn't need to be told such things.

One of the pleasures of *Beginners* is the warmth and sincerity of the major characters. There is no villain. They begin by wanting to be happier and end by succeeding. The person left out is the dead mother, Georgia. She spent years in a pointless marriage. If Hal and Georgia were sticking it out for the sake of Oliver, that doesn't seem to have turned out well. And once he was an adult and had left home—why did they persist? Did Hal lack the moral courage to declare himself? He could have been happier years sooner, and she could have had her chance, too. Hal is not quite as nice as he seems.

Another question occurs. Both Hal and Oliver find ideal romantic partners, who are breathtakingly good-looking, unflaggingly nice, deeply warmhearted, and loyal. Everyone who goes to gay bars or costume parties should be so lucky. That makes it all too neat, but then this isn't a deep drama, anyway. It's a hopeful fable with deep optimism and a cheerful style that kids itself. Like many dogs, it shrugs off setbacks and keeps hoping it can go outside and play.

## Behind the Burly Q ★ ★

NO MPAA RATING, 98 m., 2010

Alan Alda, Tempest Storm, Beverly Arlynne, Lou Costello, Sally Rand, Betty Rowland, Lili St. Cyr, Kitty West, Blaze Starr, and others. A documentary directed by Leslie Zemeckis and produced by Zemeckis, Sheri Hellard, and Jackie Levine. Screenplay by Zemeckis.

My entry in the 1959 essay contest of the United Republican Fund won me a free trip to Chicago and the chance to shake Richard Nixon's hand during a banquet at the Chicago Amphitheater. What I remember about that trip is stepping into a cab in front of the Conrad Hilton Hotel and telling the driver, "Take me to the best burlesque show in town." He threw down the flag on his meter and drove me one block, to the Rialto on South State Street.

In those days both the Rialto and the Follies survived as part of the last gasp of American burlesque. The Rialto had once been owned by Harold Minsky, Broadway's legendary burlesque impresario. There I beheld striptease artistes and a team of two comedians who told bawdy jokes about body parts, pulled improbable objects out of their pockets, and slapped each other with rubber chickens.

Burlesque survived there until the theaters were booked as porn houses. It made fitful revivals here and there around town, including at the Town, now the Park West, where in a seedy dressing room I interviewed the legendary Tempest Storm and found her kind and patient. Now it is gone and almost forgotten. Once it was known as the poor man's Broadway.

A new documentary named *Behind the Burly Q* recalls those days, but that's about all it accomplishes. It gathers an impressive series of talking head interviews with surviving stars, including Tempest Storm herself, looking pretty damned good for a redhead aged eighty-two. In 1999, San Francisco mayor Willie Brown proclaimed a Tempest Storm Day. Catch Michael Bloomberg doing that.

In its heyday a top-flight burlesque show would run ninety minutes and feature a large cast, elaborate costumes, energetic choreography, and a nice little orchestra. Young comics got a start there, including Abbott and Costello. Alan Alda appears in this film to remember his father, Robert, a straight man on Forty-second Street. Burlesque was considered a step down from vaudeville, although it was a lot classier than the nude revues and lap dances that replaced it.

There wasn't total nudity, for one thing, although Sally Rand caused a sensation at the 1933 Chicago World's Fair with her celebrated fan dance, during which she was apparently completely nude, but manipulated her fans so adroitly that you could never be absolutely sure. This proves the principle that it is more erotic to be about to see everything than it is to actually see it. Miss Rand died in 1979 at the age of seventy-five, and was still dancing in that decade. I know that for a fact because my friend John McHugh has a photograph of himself with her to prove it. In the picture he is conducting himself as befits a reporter from the *Chicago Daily News* while her perky nipples wink at him.

*Behind the Burly Q*, written and directed by the burlesque historian Leslie Zemeckis (wife of Robert), settles too easily for an editing formula that alternates talking heads, too-cursory performance footage, and montages of headlines and photographs. The timeline is unclear and the structure seems too random, but a composite picture emerges as young girls, often out of poverty, dream of stardom but end by taking it off. The successful ones had gimmicks. Lili St. Cyr appeared to make love with a parrot and Babette Bardot was allegedly Brigitte Bardot's sister. Their names showed some invention, for example Blaze Starr's; she famously had an affair with Louisiana governor Huey P. Long, and is in this film via telephone, refusing to be photographed.

The many burlesque veterans who do appear in the film look, it must be said, like attractive seniors, and in their faces and voices we glimpse a spirit and defiance. They were overworked and underpaid and generally considered to be hookers, but they supported themselves, some from the age of fourteen. You hear some nostalgia, but with most of them you don't get the idea that if they had the chance they'd do it all again.

*Note: My interview with Tempest Storm is at http://j.mp/b7GnZb.*

## Being Elmo: A Puppeteer's Journey ★ ★ ★

NO MPAA RATING, 80 m., 2011

A documentary narrated by Whoopi Goldberg and featuring Kevin Clash, Bill Barretta, Fran Brill, Joan Ganz Cooney, Rosie O'Donnell, Frank Oz, Martin P. Robinson, Caroll Spinney, and Cheryl Henson. Directed by Constance Marks and produced by Marks, Corinne LaPook, and James J. Miller. Screenplay by Philip Shane and Justin Weinstein.

All Kevin Clash ever wanted to do was make puppets. That came even before he fixated on Muppets. One day he had an inspiration so urgent that it required cutting up his father's coat. The result was a nice enough puppet, but when Kevin emerged from his creative frenzy he realized his father might have stern words for him. Called in trembling to the old man, all he heard was: "Next time, ask."

Kevin Clash was born into a large middle-class family in an African-American suburb of Baltimore, and perhaps found puppets and Muppets a way to express his otherwise quiet, shy personality. Using sheets on his mother's clothesline as a backdrop, he put on shows for the neighborhood kids. He was picked on as a boy who "played with dolls," but that changed after he won a job on a local TV show in Baltimore.

*Being Elmo* is a documentary that follows him through a series of good breaks that lead him into the universe of Jim Henson and *Sesame Street*, and we even hear an eyewitness to the day he "discovered" the Elmo character.

After another puppeteer grew frustrated and threw Elmo at Kevin saying, "Here, you try it," Kevin fooled around with a series of voices until Elmo, one of the most beloved of all Muppets, emerged. He also defined Elmo's central characteristic: All he wanted was to love and be loved, and hug you. What kid couldn't identify? The original Elmo craze led to buyer panics for the Tickle Me Elmo dolls, and Clash's life has been a happy one.

Was there more? We hear about the shocking and sudden death of of Jim Henson. That seems to have been the only tragedy in Clash's life. We hear of an ex-wife and meet a beloved daughter, but learn little about them. We don't know if he's married now. The director, Constance Marks, either filmed or found film from a remarkable span of Kevin's life; we see him at all ages and during such early events as his first Macy's parade.

What I hadn't realized fully is how versatile the Muppeteers are, doing a variety of voices and studying the minute details of Muppet body language. There's an interesting scene where he teaches Muppeteers for a French version of the Muppet show how you don't want to let a Muppet spend much time with his mouth closed; backstage at the Muppet works, we see countless drawers filled with eyeballs, eyebrows, whiskers, and wigs. It's the only world Kevin wanted to live in, and he made it.

## Being Flynn ★ ★ ★

R, 101 m., 2012

Robert De Niro (Jonathan Flynn), Paul Dano (Nick Flynn), Olivia Thirlby (Denise), Lili Taylor (Joy), Wes Studi (Captain), Julianne Moore (Jody Flynn). Directed by Paul Weitz and produced by Weitz, Michael Costigan, and Andrew Miano. Screenplay by Weitz, based on the memoir by Nick Flynn.

An early shot in *Being Flynn* shows Robert De Niro behind the wheel of a Yellow Cab, and the ground shifts beneath the movie. To summon up his most iconic role must represent De Niro's faith in this film. I can understand why he felt that much faith in the project but am not sure the film deserves it. De Niro plays Jonathan Flynn, in his own estimation one of the three greatest American writers (the others: Mark Twain and J. D. Salinger). He claims publishers have been bidding fortunes on his work in progress, but we follow his decline: He loses his apartment, loses his cab, and is reduced to hanging out in the well-heated lobbies of buildings.

We learn about him from his son, Nick Flynn (Paul Dano), who also intends to be a great writer, and there are two voice-overs in the film, one by Jonathan, one by Nick, although Nick may be writing his father's narration. There is a real Nick Flynn, who first told this story in a 2004 memoir, *Another Bullshit Night in Suck City.* Whether his real-life father was a writer I've been unable to determine, but we know his parents were divorced when he was young, his mother killed herself when he was twenty-two, and he actually did go to work in a homeless shelter, where he met his father for the first time when the old man turned up looking for a room for the night.

If you want to be a writer and something like that happens to you, it's inevitable that it will turn up in a book. By all accounts the memoir is a powerful piece of work. Throughout the film, Nick's subtext is "Am I doomed to be a failure like my dad?" Nick tells us his father was mostly absent during his childhood—in prison for bad check writing. His mother (Julianne Moore) explains this to the boy as well as she can. Alcoholism is the problem of the father; cocaine becomes the problem of the son. Assuming such a life doesn't kill you, it reads nicely in those little authors' biographies on the insides of dust jackets: "The author overcame drug addiction and worked in a homeless shelter before winning a Guggenheim."

What's admirable about *Being Flynn* is that it doesn't cave in to the standard Hollywood redemption formulas, with the father redeemed and the son inspired. It's more complicated than that. Jonathan Flynn perhaps has mental problems, or simply likes to prevaricate; does he really believe in his greatness? As for the son, his childhood memories seem limited to repeated games of catch and rummaging through a box full of letters that Jonathan sent from prison. Julianne Moore plays a loving mother, but not much is done with the character.

Paul Dano is an actor who can be distant and mystifying. He makes it interesting. He sometimes approaches a scene with passive aggression. He understands the material, he understands the character, but he isn't going to do the heavy lifting for us. In films like *There Will Be Blood, The Ballad of Jack and Rose,* and *Meek's Cutoff,* he plays the silent dissent to the dominant characters. In *Being Flynn,* he uses his writing to express feelings Nick isn't forthright about in life.

When Jonathan unexpectedly materializes, Nick's at a loss, and his feelings are the subject of the film. De Niro's father is a man who has run out of options. There is no longer anyone who much cares if he's telling the truth. Nick, on the other hand, has a girlfriend named Denise (Olivia Thirlby) who cares for him and sees that he needs to be doing *something.* She works at the homeless shelter and convinces him to give it a try. She perhaps instinctively spots Nick as one of those "writers" for whom it's hard work, not writing every day.

I'm happy that the film didn't settle for the Hollywood redemption formula, but ambivalent that it leaves us in suspense. Neither character is ready to have their chance meeting result in anything definite. Jonathan seems doomed. That would be the film's easy way out, but it isn't sure which way it should take. In a sense, director Paul Weitz (*About a Boy*) has the same kind of passivity that works for Dano: He'll take us so far and leave us.

Robert De Niro has been through a bad patch lately. His contemporary Al Pacino has moved from one success to another by going out of his way to choose challenging projects (*You Don't Know Jack, The Merchant of Venice*). De Niro, perhaps absorbed in his Tribeca enterprises, has seemed to drift. He and Weitz worked together on *Little Fockers,* not a high point for either. Now here is a much more ambitious film that almost but not quite justifies the hope inspired by that Yellow Cab.

*Note: The invaluable Lili Taylor, seen in the*

*homeless shelter, is Nick Flynn's real-life companion.*

## Bel Ami ★ ★

R, 102 m., 2012

Robert Pattinson (Georges Duroy), Uma Thurman (Madeleine Forestier), Philip Glenister (Charles Forestier), Christina Ricci (Clotilde de Marelle), Kristin Scott Thomas (Virginie Rousset), Colm Meaney (Luc Rousset), Holliday Grainger (Suzanne Rousset). Directed by Declan Donnellan and Nick Ormerod and produced by Uberto Pasolini. Screenplay by Rachel Bennette, from the novel by Guy de Maupassant.

*Bel Ami* continues the aura of mystery that has enveloped Robert Pattinson since the *Twilight* pictures. That mystery involves why this actor, whose default mode is passive brooding, has been cast as a man irresistible to women. One can barely accept that a naive high school girl might fall for his strong, silent vampire, but in *Bel Ami*, he successfully seduces three of the most powerful beauties in Paris society, despite having no talent, no money, and no conversation.

The movie, set in 1890, is based on a Guy de Maupassant novel about Georges Duroy, son of an illiterate peasant who serves in the French army in Algeria and then finds himself in Paris. The opening shot shamelessly lifts from Chaplin and countless other sources, as the penniless outcast stares hungrily through a restaurant window at the rich people dining inside. In his cramped garret, all he has is a crust of bread, a candle stub, and resentment. To make sure we get the point, the movie contrasts shots of a steamed lobster and Georges's resident cockroach.

Good luck strikes the next day when in a bordello he encounters an old army buddy, Forestier (Philip Glenister). This man is now political editor of a Parisian daily. He invites Georges to dinner, and when Georges confesses he has no evening wear, gives him two gold pieces to buy some. This grants him entry into a dinner party of power couples: not only Forestier and his comely wife, Madeleine (Uma Thurman), but the paper's editor, Rousset (Colm Meaney), and his influential wife, Virginie (Kristin Scott Thomas), and the married Clotilde (Christina Ricci), whose husband does not attend but is also high and mighty.

In the course of the film Georges will seduce all three women, marry one and the daughter of another, and prove himself to be a thoroughgoing rotter, cad, and bounder. The women are all elegant and intelligent, they know the ways of the world, and they know Georges's history. Why do they find him attractive? We don't, and that failure is the downfall of the film.

His first conquest is Madeleine, who not only comes up with an idea for an article he could write for her husband's paper, but even writes it for him. She is a honey-lipped charmer who prefers to write in a scoop-necked negligee while sprawled on her bed. Georges sells the article (which Forestier surely knows his wife wrote), sees it published, and permits himself the first of several self-satisfied smiles. Pattinson, alas, is an actor who hasn't mastered the art of smiling convincingly. He smiles as if saying "Cheese!" In this world of sophisticated decadence, he needs a sardonic smile. Imagine Jeremy Irons or Ethan Hawke.

The plot essentially involves only Georges's affairs, although lip service is paid to intrigue about whether the French government plans to invade Morocco. Georges has been informed that in Paris it is not the men who have the power, but their wives, and he sets out to climb the social ladder in their beds. He so enraptures Clotilde (Ricci) that she establishes them in a cozy little love nest. His next victim is the distinguished Virginie (Scott Thomas), whom he has the effrontery to invite to the love nest for some quick rumpy-pumpy, hurrying her away just in the nick of time before Clotilde arrives.

The actresses do what they can with this sad sack. The surprise for me was Christina Ricci, whom I think of as undernourished and nervous, but who flowers here in warm ripeness. Her character makes the mistake of actually loving Georges. This involves pure acting skill on her part, since Pattinson gives her so little to work with. The movie ends with Georges's marriage to a young woman I haven't yet mentioned, and as the new couple walk down the aisle, they pass those whom Georges has betrayed and savaged through the years. It is good to see a poor boy from the provinces make good.

## Bellflower ★ ★ ★

R, 105 m., 2011

Evan Glodell (Woodrow), Jessie Wiseman (Milly), Tyler Dawson (Aiden), Rebekah Brandes (Courtney), Vincent Grashaw (Mike), Zack Kraus (Elliot), Keghan Hurst (Sarah), Alexandra Boylan (Caitlin). Directed by Evan Glodell and produced by Glodell and Vincent Grashaw. Screenplay by Glodell.

*Bellflower* is a scrappy indie movie that comes out of nowhere and blows up stuff real good. It also possibly represents the debut of a one-of-a-kind filmmaker, a natural driven by wild energy, like Tarantino. I know what the budget was, but if I told you, you'd arrive at all the wrong conclusions. Let's say Evan Glodell had all the money he needed to make this particular movie, and more might have changed it for the worse.

Here is a movie about two buddies who aimlessly hang around in their workshop, designing, oh, you know, things like apocalyptic flamethrowers. When they suspend a fuel tank in midair and fire at it with a shotgun just to see what might happen, I had the odd notion that they might have filmed the shot only once and found out at the same time we did. A movie this size, how many standby fuel tanks are you gonna buy?

Woodrow and Aiden (Evan Glodell and Tyler Dawson) are two *Jackass* types, and I mean that with the greatest respect. They were pals in Wisconsin, joined up to move to California, and live in a town that consists entirely of the poor neighborhood. They are apparently unemployed. They are customizing a classic muscle car they name the Medusa, which when it is finished will be capable of throwing terrifying plumes of flame into the air and . . . making quite an impression.

One night they are in a bar. They get involved in a contest requiring them to eat live crickets. This isn't completely crazy; I understand insects are a good source of protein and minerals. Woodrow finds himself in the finals with a friendly blonde named Milly (Jessie Wiseman), and it's kismet. You know how sometimes you lock eyes with another person and in a brief moment everything is said that needs to be said?

Woodrow does. Milly isn't so sure. Maybe she's met lovable cricket eaters before. "I could be bad for you," she warns Woodrow. If he falls for her, he could get hurt. He accepts this risk, and on a lark they set off for Texas to have some good times.

All of this happens with a certain foreboding of doom, because the movie has opened with a quick-cut montage of alarming events apparently destined to happen later in the story. These are fragmented enough so that they're not really spoilers, and indeed providing a straightforward chronology is not the movie's purpose. It's more about the rise and fall of their romance, the rise of Woodrow's interest in Milly's friend Courtney (Rebekah Brandes), a counterpoint with Aiden's experiences, and the presence of a man named Mike (Vincent Grashaw), who Woodrow didn't realize was already in Milly's life.

The movie is essentially a mumblecore romcom, although that makes it sound too derivative. Glodell is an engaging hands-on director (he built not only Medusa but also the camera he uses), and an engaging actor. His cast is always convincing. His screenwriting lacks a shade in clarity, but then so do the lives of these characters. The cinematography, by Joel Hodge, is raw and high contrast, weathered and full of character, with lots of blood reds. It wouldn't take much work by a designer to make a ripped T-shirt out of the look here. And when the Medusa belches flames, man oh man, people notice.

## Bernie ★ ★ ★ ½

PG-13, 98 m., 2012

Jack Black (Bernie Tiede), Shirley MacLaine (Marjorie Nugent), Matthew McConaughey (Danny Buck Davidson). Directed by Richard Linklater and produced by Liz Glotzer, David McFadzean, Dete Meserve, Judd Payne, Celine Rattray, Martin Shafer, and Ginger Sledge. Screenplay by Linklater and Skip Hollandsworth, based on the *Texas Monthly* article "Midnight in the Garden of East Texas" by Hollandsworth.

I would buy a used coffin from this man. In Richard Linklater's droll comedy *Bernie*, Jack Black plays an east Texas funeral director named Bernie Tiede, and it is surely one of the best performances of the year. I had to forget what I knew about Black. He creates this character out of thin air, it's like nothing he's done before, and it proves that an actor can be a miraculous thing in the right role.

Black is not a giant. He stands five foot six. Yet the word for Bernie Tiede is *hovering*. He seems to hover above even those taller than him. He is solicitous, gentle, tactful. When Marjorie Nugent's husband dies, he is the angel at her shoulder, creating the impression that no client has ever touched him quite so much as she. That's a triumph because Marjorie (Shirley MacLaine) is the most disliked woman in Carthage.

She was a real woman, and Bernie Tiede's story is factual, based on a celebrated *Texas Monthly* article named "Midnight in the Garden of East Texas" by Skip Hollandsworth. The late Mr. Nugent, apparently a prince of a fellow, owned the local bank. Marjorie took over after his passing and started throwing loan applications into the wastebasket and otherwise offending the locals.

Was it her money that attracted Bernie Tiede? No one can say. Bernie was known and liked by almost everyone in town, sang in the church choir, served on charity boards, organized civic functions, provided a sympathetic shoulder. His origins were obscurely in Arkansas, but his manner was such that he got the job at the Carthage funeral home almost just by presenting himself. Among his many abilities was the tact to convince mourners he sincerely believed they had selected precisely the right coffin.

Bernie's courtship of Marjorie is a masterpiece of social delicacy. In the odd dance between the two, he never seems to want anything in particular. Not sex, certainly; there were those in Carthage who assumed Bernie was gay, and there were rumored to be a few who knew. Nor was he boldly after her money, although he suggested purchases that in embellishing her lifestyle did nothing to diminish his. Surely Marjorie knew she was hated in the town, and surely she enjoyed being paid tribute; MacLaine allows the slightest of smiles to sometimes shine out from a fixed frown. They began to be seen around town, especially at the theatrical and artistic events Bernie supported and sometimes performed in. They shared such sublimated sexual experiences as holding hands while having simultaneous massages in a (respectable) local spa.

There are flat-footed ways this story could have been told. Richard Linklater finds a tricky note difficult to define. *Bernie* never declares itself a comedy; often when we laugh we're thinking, "I can't believe I'm seeing this." An unspoken compact grows between Bernie and Marjorie in which neither one declares exactly what's going on, but the fiction is maintained that Bernie believes her worthy of his kindest attentions, and she believes that at last a man has gotten her right. (Generally known spoiler.) But a relationship this problematic can't last forever, and eventually Bernie shoots Marjorie four times in the back.

And now Linklater surpasses himself. Bernie's attempts to conceal the death are based on the ability of many good funeral directors to instinctively know what people really think about one another. In Marjorie's case, no one liked her and she isn't particularly missed. Bernie redoubles his local charities and continues to lead his accustomed lifestyle. Only a curious state's attorney named Danny Buck Davidson (Matthew McConaughey) eventually sniffs out something wrong, and even as he comes under suspicion, Bernie Tiede remains a man who knows exactly how to behave in difficult situations.

Richard Linklater has made all kinds of movies, most of them very good. They have little else in common: He worked with Black in a completely different mode in *School of Rock*, and has made such films as *Dazed and Confused*, *Before Sunrise*, *Waking Life*, and *Me and Orson Welles*. Why did he make *Bernie*? I suspect he read the magazine article and knew it was a natural movie. Anyone could have seen that. His genius was to see Jack Black as Bernie Tiede.

## The Best Exotic Marigold Hotel ★ ★ ★ ½

PG-13, 124 m., 2012

Judi Dench (Evelyn Greenslade), Maggie Smith (Muriel Donnelly), Bill Nighy (Douglas Ainslie),

Penelope Wilton (Jean Ainslie), Tom Wilkinson (Graham Dashwood), Celia Imrie (Madge Hardcastle), Ronald Pickup (Norman Cousins), Dev Patel (Sonny Kapoor), Tena Desae (Sunaina). Directed by John Madden and produced by Graham Broadbent and Peter Czernin. Screenplay by Ol Parker, based on the novel *These Foolish Things* by Deborah Moggach.

*The Best Exotic Marigold Hotel* is a retirement destination in India for "the elderly and beautiful." It has seen better days, and if you want to see what the better days looked like, just examine the brochure, which depicts a luxurious existence in Udaipur, a popular tourist destination in Rajasthan. To this city travel a group of seven Brits with seven reasons for making the move—although the most urgent is that the local prices make retirement possible for them.

As we meet them jammed on the bus from the airport, we suspect that the film will be about their various problems and that the hotel will not be as advertised. What we may not expect is what a charming, funny, and heartwarming movie this is, a smoothly crafted entertainment that makes good use of seven superb veteran actors.

We're introduced to them while they're still at home in England. In the order of their billing, they are Evelyn Greenslade (Judi Dench), who has been forced to sell her London flat; the sniffy Muriel Donnelly (Maggie Smith), who doesn't like foreigners but requires a cheap hip replacement; Douglas and Jean Ainslie (Bill Nighy and Penelope Wilton), who are not merely unhappily married but have lost a bundle on their daughter's Internet company; Graham Dashwood (Tom Wilkinson), who spent the happiest years of his life in India and has now returned to seek his young love; Madge Hardcastle (Celia Imrie), who is open to the possibility of finding a husband; and Norman Cousins (Ronald Pickup), who is open to the possibility of finding a one-night stand.

Greeting them at the entrance to the Best Exotic Marigold Hotel is its exuberant and optimistic young owner, Sonny Kapoor (Dev Patel, whom you may remember from *Slumdog Millionaire*, where he played the contestant on the TV quiz show). He's inherited the shabby institution from his late father and plans to run it himself, against the objections of his mother, who wants him to live with her in Delhi and marry the bride of her choice. Sonny already has a bride picked out; she is Sunaina (Tena Desae), who works in a call outsourcing agency—the movie's nudge that the West has not only outsourced many of its jobs to India, but is now outsourcing many of its senior citizens.

How can I suggest what a delight this film is? Let me try a little shorthand. Recall some of the wonderful roles you've seen from Judi Dench, Maggie Smith, Tom Wilkinson, Bill Nighy, and the others, and believe me when I say that this movie finds rich opportunities for all of them. Director John Madden (*Shakespeare in Love*) has to juggle to keep his subplots in the air, but these actors are so distinctive they do much of the work for him.

Tom Wilkinson is the most affecting character. He was raised and educated in India and moved with his parents to England, leaving love, regret, and guilt behind. His character is instinctively open to India, and wanders off on daily secret missions that excite the curiosity of the others and may involve no more than sharing cricket tips with street kids.

The Maggie Smith character is at the other end of the scale. She dislikes India, and indeed, anyplace that is not England, and refuses to eat any food she cannot pronounce. Awaiting her affordable hip replacement, she notices a low-caste girl who is sweeping the hotel and gives her a hint. Smith, we discover, spent her entire life in service, raising the children of others, and now in retirement there is no one to take care of her.

The Judi Dench character apparently spent most of her life having her husband settle all important questions, something to regret after he dies and she finds herself broke. She focuses on young Sonny, his struggle with his mother, and his optimistic plans to renovate the hotel. A good start might be chasing the pigeons from the rooms.

The story is light-footed and cheerful for the most part, especially when Dench goes job hunting and the romance seekers experiment with online dating services. Still there's a fair amount of humanity in the screenplay by

Ol Parker, based on the novel *These Foolish Things* by Deborah Moggach. Events move along so engagingly that they sneak up on a few surprisingly touching developments, especially the payoff of Wilkinson's story.

India itself is a supporting character. People in other places begin to seem standardized in contrast with the brash eccentricities here, and we wonder if Dev Patel as the hotel owner possibly learned his job by watching reruns of *Fawlty Towers*. Let us suggest that if you were an aging Brit with a limited income and you moved into the Best Exotic Marigold Hotel, you could have done a lot worse.

## Best Worst Movie ★ ★ ★

NO MPAA RATING, 91 m., 2010

George Hardy, Claudio Fragasso, Margo Prey, Jason Steadman, and Darren Ewing. A documentary directed by Michael Paul Stephenson and produced by Mary Francis Groom, Brad Klopman, Jim Klopman, Jim McKeon, Lindsay Rowles Stephenson, and Michael Paul Stephenson.

I bought the DVD of *Troll 2* because a friend advised me to see it. "You're busy," he told me. "You don't have time to see every bad movie. So you might as well see the worst of all time." Yes, reader, *Troll 2* has a coveted 0 percent rating on the Tomatometer: the lowest-rated film ever made. A critic could become the most-hated person in fan circles by awarding it even half a star and spoiling the perfection of that zero.

I always intended to view *Troll 2* but, I dunno, never found the time. Now comes *Best Worst Movie* to save me the trouble. This is a documentary about what happens to you when you appear in *Troll 2*. It stars the star of the original film, a dentist from a small town in Alabama named George Hardy. This is one nice guy. Even his ex-wife says so. He has a Harrison Ford head of hair and a smile so wide it's like a toothpaste billboard. He treats poor kids for free.

He made the movie twenty years ago when he was living in Utah. It was being directed by an Italian named Claudio Fragasso, who didn't speak-a the English but said he understood Americans better than they understood themselves. The movie was named *Goblin*, but then the title was changed to *Troll 2* because that sounded more commercial. It is only a technicality that there was no movie named *Troll*. You could go out and make one, but then this would be the sequel.

We catch glimpses of *Troll 2* in *Best Worst Movie*. Don't ask me to explain it. It's about vegetarian goblins who cause their human victims to start growing branches and leaves. The special effects make the victims look like people who have tree limbs strapped to their arms with duct tape. The goblins wear homemade masks a child wouldn't be caught dead wearing on Halloween. The budget was so small the actors had to provide their own clothes. One actor recalls a scene where it was necessary to nail his shoe to the ground. "They used my own shoe," he moans.

For some time, George Hardy forgot all about having made the movie. Then some of his patients started looking at him strangely and asking him if he'd appeared in this horror film they'd seen on cable. The film had been discovered and embraced by the bottom-feeders of horror film fandom, and soon Hardy found himself being invited to revivals and horror conventions. The other actors were also suddenly in demand.

One of them, Michael Paul Stephenson, who played the kid in the movie, is the director of this documentary. Neither he nor anyone else knew what Fragasso was attempting or even if he was quite serious. One actor explains he was out on a pass from a mental institution when he was cast as the ominous store owner: "The actor they hired didn't turn up and they said, 'OK, you've got the job.' Watching himself in a scene, he says, 'You can see I was crazy.'"

If the film didn't make much of an impression at the time, its rediscovery certainly did. The actors got standing ovations and started autographing photos, T-shirts and body parts at conventions. Claudio Fragasso himself, who looks very slightly like an embittered Fellini, attended revivals at the Nuart in Los Angeles and in Salt Lake City, and said his actors were morons then and are morons today. He adds that to make the worst film is as great an honor as making the best one.

But there is a bittersweet ending in this curiously touching doc. Stephenson follows George Hardy to conventions where only half a dozen people attend his panel. He films him standing at the *Troll 2* table at a horror exhibition, completely ignored. Hardy is reduced to drumming up business: "Have you heard of *Troll 2*? You haven't? You should see it! It's the worst movie of all time!" Depressed, he observes, "There's a lot of gingivitis in this room."

There's something irresistible about the movies. If you've been the star of a famous one, that means something, doesn't it? Even if it's the worst? How many people get even that far? The lesson, I guess, is that you can only be the flavor of the month for about thirty days, sometimes thirty-one. *Troll 2* was February.

## A Better Life ★ ★ ★ ½

PG-13, 98 m., 2011

Demian Bichir (Carlos Galindo), Jose Julian (Luis Galindo), Dolores Heredia (Anita), Joaquin Cosio (Blasco Martinez), Carlos Linares (Santiago), Gabriel Chavarria (Ramon). Directed by Chris Weitz and produced by Weitz, Jami Gertz, Paul Junger Witt, Stacey Lubliner, and Christian McLaughlin. Screenplay by Eric Eason.

Carlos is an undocumented immigrant from Mexico who works as a gardener tending the lawns of Los Angeles residents who are rich, especially from his point of view. He lives from hand to mouth and day to day in a tiny house whose garden is used to raise starter plants for the clients. His wife left some years ago, and he raises his fifteen-year-old son, Luis, by himself.

These two men are being pulled apart by life in America. Carlos (Demian Bichir) keeps a low profile, works hard, holds traditional values. Luis (Jose Julian) hasn't joined a gang in his neighborhood yet, but that would seem to be his trajectory. He misses school, he quietly considers his dad an irrelevant loser, and when he asks for money and there isn't any, he knows how to get under his father's skin: "I'll jack a little old lady."

Carlos works for Blasco (Joaquin Cosio), who owns a landscaping truck and the business that goes with it. Now Blasco has enough money to return to Mexico and his own little farm, and offers to sell Carlos his truck, tools, client list—everything. But Carlos can't get a driver's license, and a police stop would mean deportation. His sister reluctantly lends him some money, and the next day the truck is stolen. He thinks he might be able to find the man who took it, and enlists his son to help him search in likely places.

Now the story takes on some of the shape of *Bicycle Thieves*, the 1948 Italian neorealist classic by Vittorio de Sica. Father and son depend on the stolen truck for their existence. And in a low-key, observant way, *A Better Life* provides a tour of Los Angeles during the search; not the L.A. of Sunset Boulevard or Rodeo Drive, but the L.A. of restaurants where the kitchen staff is undocumented, of Mexican rodeos, of gang territory, of marginal workers who are essential to the city's economy.

The film's trajectory is rather predictable, but then so was the story told by *Bicycle Thieves.* But the performances are pitch perfect, even including Gabriel Chavarria as Ramon, the man who steals the truck. It adds an important element to the film that he embodies a desperate man, not a bad one. And when Carlos acts at a crucial moment, he is recognizing that.

The film was directed by Chris Weitz. Ring a bell? His previous film was *The Twilight Saga: New Moon.* Why do I imagine he was happier making this film than that one? You need to possess considerable talent to become a successful director, and his credits also include *About a Boy* (2002), where the boy is the one teaching life lessons to the man. In a perfect world, I imagine Weitz would rather make films like *A Better Life* than *Twilight 2.* Of course, that's only a guess.

## The Big Uneasy ★ ★

NO MPAA RATING, 98 m., 2011

Harry Shearer, Maria Garzino, Ivor Van Heerden, Robert Bea, John Goodman, and the voices of Brad Pitt, Jennifer Coolidge, Wendell Pierce, and Will Lyman. A documentary directed by Harry Shearer. Screenplay by Shearer.

What Hurricane Katrina did to New Orleans was not an act of God, a "natural disaster," or a failure by FEMA. It was the almost inevitable result of years of incompetent and dangerous work by the Army Corps of Engineers, which then used its power to cover its ass. That is the message, much repeated, in Harry Shearer's documentary *The Big Uneasy.*

Using soil and flood-control experts, Google maps, new footage, and damning video, Shearer builds a compelling case against the corps's flawed planning and leaky levees. I was convinced. Unfortunately, I was also convinced that trapped within this ninety-eight-minute film is a good thirty-minute news report struggling to get out. Shearer, who is a bright and funny man, comes across here as a solemn lecturer.

His facts are depressing. The Army Corps constructed levees on sand that was water permeable and unable to hold concrete walls in place under the pressure of flood waters. He shows large sections of levees not "breeched," as we were told, but actually pushed aside by the flooding. He documents—with the aid of a corpswoman whose whistle-blowing was disregarded at the time—that pumps installed to handle flood waters were inadequate and malfunctioning. He shows that the lovely city was set up for destruction, and that with wiser planning it might have suffered no worse than "wet ankles." Incredibly, we learn that one of the contractors whose company was constructing the levees even went into court to argue the corps's plans were flawed—and lost.

His view of the army engineers is thoroughly depressing. Far from welcoming advice and analysis from academic experts, they installed barbed-wire fences to block their access to crucial areas. They spent more than $1 million on a public relations campaign to repair their image. They were responsible directly or indirectly for the firing, demotion, or silencing of many of their critics. They stand indicted—and, Shearer says, their similar mistakes may mean the city of Sacramento is vulnerable to flood damage on a similar scale.

This is important and needs to be made known. Unfortunately, Shearer as a documentarian is not the right man for the job. *The Big Uneasy* lacks the dramatic impact and artistic imagination of many recent docs about environmental issues. An attempt to liven things up by shoehorning John Goodman into the action fails, when he appears out of any context to introduce awkward segments in which Shearer and other New Orleans residents answer criticisms of their city. *The Big Uneasy* plays way too much like an educational film.

## The Big Year ★ ★ ★

PG, 102 m., 2011

Steve Martin (Stu Preissler), Jack Black (Brad Harris), Owen Wilson (Kenny Bostick), Brian Dennehy (Raymond), Anjelica Huston (Annie Auklet), Rashida Jones (Ellie), Rosamund Pike (Jessica), Dianne Wiest (Brenda), JoBeth Williams (Edith). Directed by David Frankel and produced by Stuart Cornfeld, Carol Fenelon, Curtis Hanson, Karen Rosenfelt, and Ben Stiller. Screenplay by Howard Franklin, based on the book by Mark Obmascik.

Birders. You call them birders. Calling them "bird-watchers" is insulting, like calling a Trekker a Trekkie. They are aware that some people find birding to be an eccentric hobby, but you get better exercise and scenery than you do with golf, and you don't have to play the game.

I had no idea there was such a thing as competitive bird-watching, but *The Big Year* assures us there is. An annual award goes to the birder who sees the most species in a year. They will not conveniently flutter before your eyes. You have to look hard for them. In championship-level birding, this is known as having a Big Year. Is there nothing left in our society that isn't competitive? Would you believe the winners score above seven hundred?

*The Big Year* is about such a year, involving Kenny Bostick (Owen Wilson), the defending champion, and two others who are trying to sprinkle salt on his tail: Brad Harris (Jack Black) and Stu Preissler (Steve Martin). If you know the actors you know the characters, especially Bostick, who is the standard-issue Owen Wilson, a smooth-talking master of one-upmanship. Jack Black plays his usual overenthusiastic bumbler, and Steve Martin seems always in a zone of intense earnestness.

You must have to be wealthy to do a Big Year. Bostick, for example, seems permanently on leave from his job as a CEO. You spend all of your time frantically chasing down rumors of rare bird sightings in remote locations, of which the most remote is an island in the Aleutians that is closer to Tokyo than Anchorage. There's apparently a nice little tourist trade.

The comedy involves Bostick's dirty tricks, camaraderie among the others, various romances in the field, other peculiar birders, and evidence that marriage to a birder, as we might suspect, is no easy task. The film is always somewhere going somewhere else, and while the characters are spotting birds, we can spot actors: Kevin Pollak, Tim Blake Nelson, Rashida Jones, Anjelica Huston, Zahf Paroo, Rosamund Pike, Joel McHale, JoBeth Williams, Paul Campbell, Brian Dennehy, and even Al Roker.

There is some great bird photography here. I wish there had been more. I think I may have seen Jack Black falling down enough for this lifetime. The movie is getting the enthusiastic support of the Audubon Society, and has an innocence and charm that will make it appealing for families, especially those who have had enough whales and dolphins for the year.

## Bill Cunningham New York ★ ★ ★ ★

NO MPAA RATING, 84 m., 2011

Bill Cunningham, Tom Wolfe, Anna Wintour, Carmen Dell'Orefice, Annette de la Renta, John Kurdewan, Iris Apfel, Josef Astor, Editta Sherman, Anna Piaggi, Shail Upadhya, and Thelma Golden. A documentary directed by Richard Press and produced by Philip Gefter.

Here is a movie about a happy and nice man. Bill Cunningham was lucky to find what he loves to do, and do it, and win universal affection from all who know him, and to make a contribution to our lives and times. Doing what he loves is very nearly *all* he does, except to sleep and eat.

Ever since reading Thoreau's *Walden* I have been teased by the notion of leading a life with only the bare essentials of life and peacefulness. I lacked the nerve to find that little cottage and plant those rows of beans. Bill Cunningham lives a life as pure and idealistic as Thoreau, and he does it in the middle of Manhattan. Until a couple of years ago, when he was evicted by the landlord, Bill lived in a tiny rent-controlled apartment in Carnegie Hall. Yes, Carnegie Hall, in one of the artists' studios on the upper floors set aside when greed didn't decide everything.

Bill celebrates his eightieth birthday in the movie. Every day of his life he still pedals around Manhattan on his bicycle, taking photographs of what people are wearing. He has been famous for many years for doing this, and his work has been featured in such places as *Women's Wear Daily*, *Vogue*, and the original *Details* magazine, which once devoted forty-one pages to a portfolio. These days you can find him featured in big spreads in the *New York Times*, whose publisher, Arthur Sulzberger, was among those at his birthday party.

Do not make the mistake of calling Bill Cunningham a "fashion photographer." He is a photographer of people and what they wear. Don't call him a "paparazzo." He doesn't know who half the celebrities are, and doesn't care. He's genuinely fascinated by what people wear—not by haute couture, but by what makes people feel good about themselves. He cycles to social events and openings, to street fairs and parades, to parks and markets, and will stop in the middle of the street if he spots an interesting hat.

Sometimes his photos don't even show faces. "I've always loved clothes," he says. And shoes. And individualistic looks. Fashion editors study his work because he seems to be early to notice a developing trend. In Bill's view, fashion begins with creative individuals and not "tastemakers," and he is as interested in T-shirts as evening wear. It's not that he's a snob about the high and mighty; it's that he's sincerely affectionate about whatever people wear and whoever they are.

Bill lives the life of a monk. His Carnegie Hall apartment was so filled with file cabinets of his decades of negatives that there was literally nothing else there but a mattress on top of some files. No kitchen. Bathroom down the hall. When he was relocated to another rent-controlled apartment overlooking Central Park, he had the landlord remove the kitchen appliances to make room for more filing cabinets.

"Who needs a kitchen?" he asks. And yet

here is a man who never tastes the free food and drink at so many of the functions he covers. That would be crossing some line in his mind. Nor, despite his life of the love of clothing, does he own many clothes. He dresses in black tie when the job requires it, but otherwise always wears one of the cheap blue smocks he finds in Paris—the ones garbagemen wear—because they have lots of pockets for his film. He works pretty much all day every day, taking off a little time every Sunday to attend Mass.

Cunningham is vague about his life. He seems to have all the money he needs, but he didn't come from a rich family. Richard Press, the director of this documentary, asks: "You don't need to answer this, but, have you ever had a romantic relationship?" Bill is delighted by the question, and laughs spontaneously: "Are you asking if I'm gay?" He doesn't say if he is or not, but his reply seems to suggest that he wasn't raised to think much about sex, and doesn't. He loves his work too much.

I mentioned his laugh. This is a man who seems always delighted. He smiles and laughs warmly and easily. Does that make him sound simple? There is nothing simple about Bill Cunningham, who is an artist and a philosopher. Here's what it is: Bill is happy. He has invented an occupation he does better than anyone else ever has, he has simplified his life until nothing interferes with that vocation, and now, at over eighty, he is still biking around Manhattan in his blue smock of many pockets and taking photos of people who had a little extra fun when they got dressed today.

It doesn't matter if you care nothing at all about clothing, fashion, or photography. You might still enjoy *Bill Cunningham New York*, because here is a good and joyous man who leads a life that is perfect for him, and how many people do we meet like that? This movie made me happy every moment I was watching it.

## Birdwatchers ★ ★ ★

NO MPAA RATING, 102 m., 2010

Claudio Santamaria (Roberto), Alicelia Batista Cabreira (Lia), Chiara Caselli (Beatrice), Abrisio da Silva Pedro (Osvaldo), Ademilson Concianza Verga (Ireneu), Ambrosio Vilhalva (Nadio), Fabiane Pereira da Silva (Maria), Leonardo Medeires (Lucas Moreira). Directed by Marco Bechis and produced by Bechis, Caio Gullane, Fabiano Gullane, and Amedeo Pagani. Screenplay by Bechis and Luiz Bolognesi.

There's an opening overhead shot of the Brazilian rain forest, dense and limitless. As a tourist boat slides along a river, native Indians materialize on the banks to regard it reproachfully. They hold bows and arrows and don't seem fond of these visitors. But hold on; one of the young men has a layered haircut with the top blond.

As recently as the 1970s, when Herzog filmed *Aguirre* in such a forest, these Indians would have been "real." But the time is the present and the forest a preserved facade shielding fields, which have been stripped of trees and devoted to farming. The Indians can, if they want, pile into the back of a truck and hire out as day laborers. But all of their traditions center on the forest and its spirits, and this new life is alienating. Some simply commit suicide.

This is all true, as we have been told time and again, and meanwhile the Brazilian government remains benevolent toward the destruction of the planet's richest home of life forms and its crucial oxygen source. Indians have been stripped of ownership of their ancestral lands and assigned to reservations far from the bones of their parents; it is the same genocide the United States practiced, for those with power have not developed a conscience in the years since.

Marco Bechis's *Birdwatchers* is a ground-level drama involving a group of Indians that packs up one day, leaves "their" federal land, and builds shelters of tree limbs and plastic sheets on farmland that once was their tribe's. This goes down badly with the farmer, who with his family lives in a spacious home with a pool and (Indian) servants.

The film portrays the descendants of colonialists very broadly; its strength is in the directness of the performances by Indians. I assume their performances are informed by actual life experience, because Bechis shot on location with local nonactors. They're cohesive in the group, grow depressed when separated from it, are attuned to spirit omens (or believe they are, which amounts to the same thing). Without conversational preludes, they say bluntly what they mean: "I want to be with you, you're a big dick man, you must leave here and never return."

This doesn't mean they lack subtlety. It means they keep a lot of things to themselves. We follow two adolescent boys, Osvaldo (Abrisio da Silva Pedro) and Ireneu (Ademilson Concianza Verga), the first the son of the leader, the second he of the haircut and a yearning for sneakers. The leader, Nadio (Ambrosio Vilhalva), is strong enough to lead the group onto the farmlands, enforce discipline, and deal with many newcomers. But he's an alcoholic, his booze happily supplied by a merchant who controls them by giving credit. Shades of the company store.

Sex is in the air. The farmer's teenage daughter, in a bikini, and one of the boys, in a loincloth, begin meeting at the river, he to collect water, she to swim, and although they don't get very far, an intriguing tension is there between them. On both sides there is the allure of unfamiliarity.

The group is chronically low on food and funds, and Nadio correctly realizes that day labor is a form of bondage. He begins to call his followers "the movement." Sooner or later there will be a clash and there is, but one that unfolds in a way unique to these people.

*Birdwatchers* is impressively filmed and never less than interesting. If it has a weakness, it's that this is a familiar sermon: Save the rain forest. Respect its inhabitants. Bechis and his cowriter, Luiz Bolognesi, don't really develop the characters much beyond their functions. But the reality of the Indians and the locations adds its own strength.

*Note: I learn from the press notes that the European-sounding sacred music was composed by Domenico Zipoli, an Italian Jesuit who lived with this same Guarani tribe in the 1700s.*

## Biutiful ★ ★ ★

R, 148 m., 2011

Javier Bardem (Uxbal), Maricel Alvarez (Marambra), Eduard Fernandez (Tito), Diaryatou Daff (Ige), Cheng Tai Shen (Hai), Luo Jin (Liwei). Directed by Alejandro Gonzalez Inarritu and produced by Inarritu, Fernando Bovaira, and Jon Kilik. Screenplay by Gonzalez Inarritu, Armando Bo, and Nicolas Giacobone, based on a story by Inarritu.

Alejandro Gonzalez Inarritu's *Biutiful* stars Javier Bardem as a low-level criminal in Barcelona who is told by his doctor he has very little time to live. He works as a middleman in an industry that makes fake luxury items in sweatshops and sells them to tourists through sidewalk vendors. You've seen the Gucci bags lined up on pavements. He's also involved in importing and housing the undocumented Chinese workers who exist in poverty and manufacture the items. Both fake Gucci and real Gucci are made by poor people, but the real Guccis are made in China.

Uxbal's life is a mess. He is separated from his bipolar wife. He tries to care for the sons he loves. He is under urgent pressure from his criminal associates. He sees after the living conditions of his illegal immigrants. There is blood in his pee. He works in crime but is not a bad man, and indeed under sentence of death he is moved, like the hero of Kurosawa's *Ikiru*, to try to do something good.

One gesture he makes ends in tragic consequences. His workers are cold in their crowded basement, and he tries to alleviate that. He also tries to make some money in the process. He's devastated. Surely few actors have faces that project sorrow more completely than Bardem.

Gonzalez Inarritu follows Uxbal's last days with great intimacy, burying his camera in the seamy street life Uxbal lives, introducing many characters in sharp and colorful relief. He grants his characters the dignity of having feelings and reasons, and not simply behaving as mechanical inhabitants of a crime plot.

The moral sense of the film is heartfelt, but not especially daring; by giving us a good man as his hero, Gonzalez Inarritu possibly weakens his case against the general sense of injustice in his film. Uxbal is so wholly sympathetic that it's hard for us to assign blame for his sins, and yet surely they are sins. Perhaps the idea is that he inhabits a world so lacking in goodness that his possibilities for choice are limited. Everyone he comes into contact with is flawed, with the exception of his children and Ige (Diaryatou Daff), a Senegalese woman he hires as a nanny for his children. And her love for them (and to a degree for him) is warm but almost obligatory in a story of this sort; one more unworthy character would be unthinkable.

What drew me into the film and engaged my sympathy was the presence of Bardem himself. He is a vastly human actor. He can be handsome, ugly, hard, tender, or a monster (as he was in *No Country for Old Men*). Here he suffers, and is good, and suffers partly simply because he cannot do good things. That isn't a complex message, but I see films every day like *The Mechanic* that will entertain millions with cold, amoral violence, and sometimes it's good to simply see a man who cares about the consequences of his actions.

## Black Swan ★ ★ ★ ½

R, 108 m., 2010

Natalie Portman (Nina Sayers), Vincent Cassel (Thomas Leroy), Mila Kunis (Lily), Barbara Hershey (Erica Sayers), Winona Ryder (Beth MacIntyre). Directed by Darren Aronofsky and produced by Scott Franklin, Mike Medavoy, Arnold Messer, and Brian Oliver. Screenplay by Mark Heyman, Andrew Heinz, and John McLaughlin.

Darren Aronofsky's *Black Swan* is a full-bore melodrama, told with passionate intensity, gloriously and darkly absurd. It centers on a performance by Natalie Portman that is nothing short of heroic, and mirrors the conflict of good and evil in Tchaikovsky's *Swan Lake*. It is one thing to lose yourself in your art. Portman's ballerina loses her mind.

Everything about classical ballet lends itself to excess. The art form is one of grand gesture, of the illusion of triumph over reality and even the force of gravity. Yet it demands from its performers years of rigorous perfectionism, the kind of physical and mental training that takes ascendancy over normal life. This conflict between the ideal and the real is consuming Nina Sayers, Portman's character.

Her life has been devoted to ballet. Was that entirely her choice? Her mother, Erica (Barbara Hershey), was a dancer once, and now dedicates her life to her daughter's career. They share a small apartment that feels sometimes like a refuge, sometimes like a cell. They hug and chatter like sisters. Something feels wrong.

Nina dances in a company at Lincoln Center, ruled by the autocratic Thomas Leroy (Vincent Cassel). The reach of his ego is suggested by his current season, which will "reimage" the classics. Having cast off his former prima ballerina and lover, Beth MacIntyre (Winona Ryder), he is now auditioning for a new lead. *Swan Lake* requires the lead to play opposite roles. Nina is clearly the best dancer for the White Swan. But Thomas finds her too "perfect" for the Black Swan. She dances with technique, not feeling.

The film seems to be unfolding along lines that can be anticipated: There's tension between Nina and Thomas, and then Lily (Mila Kunis), a new dancer, arrives from the West Coast. She is all Nina is not: bold, loose, confident. She fascinates Nina, not only as a rival but even as a role model. Lily is, among other things, a clearly sexual being, and we suspect Nina may never have been on a date, let alone slept with a man. For her Lily presents a professional challenge and a personal rebuke.

Thomas, the beast, is well known for having affairs with his dancers. Played with intimidating arrogance by Cassel, he clearly has plans for the virginal Nina. This creates a crisis in her mind: How can she free herself from the technical perfection and sexual repression enforced by her mother, while remaining loyal to their incestuous psychological relationship?

No backstage ballet story can be seen without *The Red Shoes* (1948) coming into mind. If you've never seen it, of course eventually you will. In the character of Thomas, Aronofsky and Cassel evoke Boris Lermontov (Anton Walbrook), the impresario in that film, whose autocratic manner masks a deep possessiveness. And in Nina there is a version of Moira Shearer's ingénue, so driven to please.

*Black Swan* will remind some viewers of Aronofsky's previous film, *The Wrestler*. Both show single-minded professionalism in the pursuit of a career, leading to the destruction of personal lives. I was reminded also of Aronofsky's brilliant debut with *Pi* (1998), about a man driven mad by his quest for the universal mathematical language. For that matter, his *The Fountain* (2007) was about a man who seems to conquer time and space. Aronofsky's characters make no little plans.

The main story supports of *Black Swan* are traditional: backstage rivalry, artistic jealousy, a great work of art mirrored in the lives of those performing it. Aronofsky drifts eerily from those reliable guidelines into the mind of Nina. She begins to confuse boundaries. The film opens with a dream, and it becomes clear that her dream life is contiguous with her waking one. Aronofsky and Portman follow this fearlessly where it takes them.

Portman's performance is a revelation from this actress who was a thirteen-year-old charmer in *Beautiful Girls* (1996). She has never played a character this obsessed before, and never faced a greater physical challenge (she trained for ten months). Somehow she goes over the top and yet stays in character: Even at the extremes, you don't catch her acting. The other actors are like dance partners holding her aloft. Barbara Hershey provides a perfectly calibrated performance as a mother whose love is real, whose shortcomings are not signaled, whose own perfectionism has all been focused on the creation of her daughter.

The tragedy of Nina, and of many young performers and athletes, is that perfection in one area of life has led to sacrifices in many of the others. At a young age everything becomes focused on pleasing someone (a parent, a coach, a partner), and somehow it gets wired in that the person can *never* be pleased. One becomes perfect in every area except for life itself.

It's traditional in many ballet-based dramas for a summing-up to take place in a bravura third act. *Black Swan* has a beauty. All of the themes of the music and life, all of the parallels of story and ballet, all of the confusion of reality and dream come together in a grand exhilaration of towering passion. There is really only one place this can take us, and it does. If I were you, I wouldn't spend too much time trying to figure out exactly what happens in practical terms. Lots of people had doubts about the end of *The Red Shoes*, too. They were wrong, but they did.

## Blackthorn ★ ★

R, 98 m., 2011

Sam Shepard (Blackthorn [Butch Cassidy]), Eduardo Noriega (Eduardo Apodaca), Stephen Rea (Mackinley), Magaly Solier (Yana), Dominique McElligott (Etta Place), Nikolaj Coster-Waldau (Young James), Padraic Delaney (Sundance Kid). Directed by Mateo Gil and produced by Ibon Cormenzana and Andrews Santana. Screenplay by Miguel Barros.

There is a list of people whose deaths remain "unresolved." Jimmy Hoffa. Butch Cassidy and the Sundance Kid. Judge Crater. Amelia Earhart. B. Traven. They all must be dead by now anyway, but we have a need for closure. Such cases also provide an excellent inspiration for movies.

The test of these movies is simple enough: If they were about fictional people, would they be worth seeing? Sometimes the answer is yes, as in several tales about the alleged later life of Sherlock Holmes. I know, I know, he was never alive in the first place, but give me a break here. In the case of Butch and the Kid, how many people had even heard of them before the 1969 movie? In it there was the possibility that they escaped to Bolivia, and that's where *Blackthorn* joins Butch in old age, circa 1928.

Played by Sam Shepard, who may be the most photogenic of modern playwrights, he inhabits an isolated horse ranch in a sere landscape and shares the company of the comely Yana (Magaly Solier). But memories of past glory fill him with thoughts about a return to America, where a son may live who would be his child with Etta Place—or with the Kid, if you follow me.

He cashes in all his money and sets off across the Bolivian vastness on horseback, where he's waylaid by Eduardo (Eduardo Noriega), a mining engineer. Butch's net worth was stashed in the saddlebags of his horse, which runs away, making him rather hard to steal from. Butch knows that this Eduardo may have stolen the fortune of a local millionaire, and Eduardo leads him on what is possibly a wild goose chase down into the abandoned mine where it's perhaps hidden. What Eduardo needs is protection from the millionaire's men, who are following him. Meanwhile, they're trailed by a man who is either the most stubborn or the most foolish of Pinkerton agents, Mackinley (Stephen Rea), who has allegedly been tirelessly tracking Butch for twenty years.

This story is well-acted by Shepard, whom I have never seen unconvincing. There's a dash of Kris Kristofferson in his performance, as when he ambles through the country singing rusty old songs like "Sam Hall" ("Damn your eyes!"). The cinematography is breathtaking; we rarely see Bolivia in Western-style films, and the way it looks here might have convinced John Ford to move on from Monument Valley.

But the movie as a whole isn't much. Flashbacks to the good old days, with Nikolaj Coster-Waldau and Padraic Delaney standing in for Paul Newman and Robert Redford, are unconvincing and without much purpose, and given the moral twistiness of the original story, this rehash seems to lack purpose. Butch has grown old? And homesick? And gets waylaid, and is back in action again? Was this trip necessary? The first-time director is Mateo Gil, known for the screenplays of *Open Your Eyes*, *The Sea Inside*, and *Agora*. Ironic, that the film's weakness is its screenplay.

## Blood Done Sign My Name ★ ★ ★

PG-13, 128 m., 2010

Rick Schroder (Vernon Tyson), Nate Parker (Ben Chavis), Nick Searcy (Robert Teel), Lela Rochon (Roseanna Allen), Afemo Omilami (Golden Frinks), Darrin Dewitt Henson (Eddie McCoy), Michael Rooker (Billy Watkins), Gattlin Griffith (Tim Tyson). Directed by Jeb Stuart and produced by Mel Efros, Jeb Stuart, and Mari Stuart. Screenplay by Jeb Stuart, based on the book by Tim Tyson.

In 1970 in Oxford, North Carolina, it was perfectly possible for a young black man to be beaten and clubbed by three whites, and shot dead by one of them. And for an all-white jury to hear from two eyewitnesses, and watch the white defendant's young son break down in tears and confess his testimony had been forced on him by his father's lawyers. And for the jury to vote unanimously that the white man was not guilty.

*Blood Done Sign My Name* tells the story of that murder, and how it was a catalyst for change in Oxford and in the lives of those who lived there. It's based on a memoir by the son of a liberal white Methodist preacher, and there's a scene in the film that has details I'm pretty sure the son witnessed when he was a boy.

His father said he wanted to show him something. They crept behind a rock and observed a Ku Klux Klan meeting. A cross was being erected. "It's a revival!" young Tim Tyson said. "No, it's not a revival," his father said, and that night they watched the cross being burned. The part I believe he remembers was this: The whole event was treated as a family picnic, with kids playing and mothers unpacking picnic hampers, and the sickness of racism almost *looking* like a revival.

The film tells two parallel stories. One involves a young black man who graduates from college and comes home to Oxford to teach at a black high school (black, although the schools had in theory been integrated). This is Ben Chavis (Nate Parker), who later became the president of the NAACP. The other is Vernon Tyson (Rick Schroder), the minister, who lost his congregation because of his liberal views, but found other churches in North Carolina and retired only recently. His son, Tim, went on to become a scholar of African-American studies and now teaches at Duke.

I go into biographical details because the events in 1970 are clearly remembered by Chavis and the younger Tyson as the turning points in their lives. The civil rights movement sent Golden Frinks (Afemo Omilami), an "outside agitator," to Oxford to organize the black community after the murder. He led a historic march fifty miles from Oxford to Raleigh, the state capital, where the governor refused to meet with the marchers—but the point had been made.

Unlike a more conventional film, *Blood Done Sign My Name* doesn't end with the courtroom verdict. It starts there, as Chavis leads an economic boycott of stores that took black dollars and valued black customers but hired no blacks in a county that was 40 percent African-American.

The movie tells this story in a traditional, straightforward way. No fancy footwork. No chewing the scenery. Meat and potatoes, you could say, but it's thoughtful and moving. The writer and director, Jeb Stuart, focuses on the events and people and lets them speak for themselves. He uses a level, unforgiving gaze.

Apart from the Oxford racists, his only

major white characters are the minister and his family. And they're rather remote from the turmoil. Rev. Tyson invites the president of a black college to speak to his congregation, which clears out half the Christians pretty quickly, and then his son recorded these momentous days in his book.

Ben Chavis is energized and angered, but it's clear the prime mover was Golden Frinks, also a real man, whose full-time job, you could say, was outside agitating. The day of the trial, he tells Chavis he's on his way to another town: "It's up to you now." And that's what happened, essentially: The civil rights marchers led the way for the rise of a black middle class in the South.

In the opening scenes of the film, you assume the stories of Chavis and the Tyson family will connect. They don't. Each man undoubtedly knew about the other, but they were on paths that didn't intersect. I guess that's the way it was. By the time Oxford began to change, Rev. Tyson had an African-American congregation elsewhere in the state. One story at a time, things change.

Those born in 1970 will be forty this year. The acquittal of white racists by all-white juries is no longer the Southern routine. It took unpopular and courageous actions by a lot of people to bring about that change, and it is not yet complete. But it happened, and I think Tim Tyson, who isn't fifty yet, wrote his book to say it happened. If you know how to look, history doesn't take place too fast to be seen.

## Blue Valentine ★ ★ ★ ½

R, 120 m., 2011

Ryan Gosling (Dean), Michelle Williams (Cindy), Faith Wladyka (Frankie), Mike Vogel (Bobby), John Doman (Jerry), Ben Shenkman (Dr. Feinberg), Jen Jones (Gramma), Maryann Plunkett (Glenda). Directed by Derek Cianfrance and produced by Lynette Howell, Alex Orlovsky, and Jamie Patricof. Screenplay by Cianfrance, Joey Curtis, and Cami Delavigne.

Who was it who said we get married because we want a witness to our lives? That may provide an insight into the troubled minds of the married couple in *Blue Valentine*, which follows them during their first six years of mutual witness. Did Dean and Cindy get married because they wanted to be sure someone was watching? Or was that Dean's need, and did Cindy lose the thrill of the watch?

Here is a film that watches pretty well itself. Derek Cianfrance, the director, observes with great exactitude the birth and decay of a relationship. This film is alive in its details. Toward the end of the six years, when Cindy is hardly able to remember why she wanted to marry Dean, Cianfrance observes the physical and mental exhaustion that have overcome her. And the way that Dean seems hardly to care—just so long as Cindy remains his wife and his watcher, which in his mind was the deal. Dean thinks marriage is the station. Cindy thought it was the train.

They're played by Ryan Gosling and Michelle Williams as a Pennsylvania working couple with a daughter, Frankie. She was born right at the start. Cindy is a nurse. Dean is a house painter. When they met, and for some time after, work was hardly central to their lives. It was where they went to and where they returned from. In effective physical transformations, Williams and Gosling give us Dean and Cindy at two ages: their age at present, and at the beginning, when they were filled with that dreamy knowledge that the touch of the other brings quick sensuality. It is easier for an actor to play the same character at twenty-four and sixty than at twenty-four and thirty. Although some bodily change takes place, what really happens is a transformation of inner certainty. Williams plays a woman who sits inside her body and no longer knows what it's for and what she wants to do with it.

All marriages have legendary milestone moments, events of startling clarity that allow the new lovers to see themselves as a couple that has been defined. Dean is capable of grand, goofy romanticism, and Cindy likes that. She yearns toward it. They first meet at her grandmother's retirement home. Have you ever had one of those chance meetings with a stranger in a place neither one of you belongs? A space empty of your lives, so that you start new with your first conversation, and plunge straight ahead into a suddenly new future?

That's what it's like that day. Soon they're playing at this new toy, their love. They do things together as if they were children doing them. Then they get married and have (the unplanned but welcomed) Frankie, and the realities of making a living and work schedules and child raising and *real* marriage settle in. Dean seems stuck. He seems to stay fixed at the initial stage. Can you see the difference between (1) "He loves me as much as he always did," and (2) "He loves me exactly like he always did"?

*Blue Valentine* moves between past and present as if trying to remember what went wrong. From Dean's point of view, maybe nothing did. He wanted to be married to Cindy, and he still does and he still is. Cindy can't stand that. He never signed off on the "grow old along with me" part. He doesn't think the best is yet to be. He thinks it's just fine now.

Williams plays Cindy as a woman who has lost her pride of body and self. No, she doesn't become a drunk—he's the one who drinks too much. But that's not the problem. It's his infuriating inability to care for this Cindy, right here, right now, because when she married him she became exactly the Cindy he required.

I wonder what kind of script conferences Cianfrance had with his cowriters, Joey Curtis and Cami Delavigne. They were writing about something ineffable, a void, a need. This wasn't a story with convenient hooks involving things like, you know, disease—things stories are familiar with. It was about inner defeat and the exhaustion of hope. I've read reviews saying Cianfrance isn't clear about what went wrong as they got from there to here. Is anybody?

## The Book of Eli ★ ★ ★

R, 118 m., 2010

Denzel Washington (Eli), Gary Oldman (Carnegie), Mila Kunis (Solara), Ray Stevenson (Redridge), Jennifer Beals (Claudia), Frances de la Tour (Martha), Michael Gambon (George). Directed by the Hughes brothers and produced by Broderick Johnson, Andrew A. Kosove, Joel Silver, and David Valdes. Screenplay by Gary Whitta.

I'm at a loss for words, so let me say these right away: *The Book of Eli* is very watchable. You won't be sorry you went. It grips your attention, and then at the end throws in several WTF! moments, which are a bonus. They make everything in the entire movie impossible and incomprehensible—but, hey, WTF.

Now to the words I am at a loss for. The story involves a lone wanderer (Denzel Washington) who wears a name tag saying, "Hi! My name is Eli." It may not be his name tag, but let's call him Eli anyway. Eli has been walking west across the devastated landscape of America for thirty years, on his way to the sea. I haven't walked it myself, but I'm pretty sure it doesn't take that long.

On the other hand, maybe Eli only thought he was walking west. On his final trek, he walks from right to left across the screen, which in movie shorthand is walking east. "How do you know you're walking the right way?" he's asked. "Faith," he says, a reply that takes on added resonance later in the film.

Eli is a quick hand with knives, pistols, rifles, shotguns, and karate. He needs to be. After a catastrophe has wiped out most of the earth's population and left ruin and desolation behind, the remaining humans are victimized by roaming motorcycle gangs of hijackers and thieves. These gangs are each issued with a perquisite tall bald man, a short hairy scruffy one, and their gofers.

The Hughes brothers, Albert and Allen, film this story in sunburned browns and pale blues, creating a dry and dusty world under a merciless sky. Water is treasure. This wasteland Eli treks at an implacable pace. Set upon in an ambush, he kills all his attackers. He's got one of those knives that makes a "snicker-snack" noise all by itself, and is a one-man army. Why don't the bad guys just shoot at him? Later in the film, they try that.

Denzel and the Hughes brothers do a good job of establishing this man and his world, and at first *The Book of Eli* seems destined to be solemn. But then Eli arrives at a Western town ruled by Carnegie (Gary Oldman), who, like all the local overloads in Westerns and gangster movies, sits behind a big desk flanked by a tall bald guy and of course a short scruffy one. How are these guys recruited? "Wanted: Tall bald guy to stand behind town boss and be willing to sacrifice life. All the water you can drink."

In this town, desperate and starving people

live in rusty cars and in the streets. We meet Carnegie's abused wife, Claudia (Jennifer Beals), and her daughter, Solara (Mila Kunis), named for some reason after the cause of all the destruction. She's a prostitute in Carnegie's bar, having made the mistake of coming on Take Your Child to Work Day. Carnegie hurts Claudia to control Solara. How he controls the fearsome bald guy is hard to say.

The third act is recycled, but done well, out of many Westerns in which the hero and the girl hole up and are surrounded. So many other movies are quoted that we almost miss it when their hideout house is perforated by bullets, *L.A. Confidential* style. That allows countless beams of sunlight to shine in and function as a metaphor.

Carnegie needs Eli because Eli has maybe the last remaining copy of a book that Carnegie believes will allow him to expand and rule many more towns. I am forbidden by the Critic's Little Rule Book from naming the volume, but if you've made a guess after seeing numerous billboards stating "Religion Is Power," you may have guessed right.

The Hughes brothers have a vivid way with imagery here, as in their earlier films such as *Menace II Society* and the underrated *From Hell.* The film looks and feels good, and Washington's performance is more uncanny the more we think back over it. The ending is "flawed," as we critics like to say, but it's so magnificently, shamelessly, implausibly flawed that (a) it breaks apart from the movie and has a life of its own, or (b) at least it avoids being predictable.

Now do yourself a favor and don't talk to *anybody* about the film if you plan to see it.

## The Bounty Hunter ★ ½

PG-13, 110 m., 2010

Jennifer Aniston (Nicole Hurly), Gerard Butler (Milo Boyd), Christine Baranski (Kitty Hurley). Directed by Andy Tennant and produced by Neal H. Moritz. Screenplay by Sarah Thorp.

I'm on the brink of declaring a new entry for Ebert's Little Movie Glossary: No comedy not titled *Caddyshack* has ever created a funny joke involving a golf cart. The only thing preventing me is that I can't remember if *Caddyshack* had golf cart jokes. In any event, if there is a golf cart, it will sooner or later drive into a water hazard. The funny angle here is that the filmmakers went to all that trouble because they trusted the audience to laugh.

I stared with glazed eyes at *The Bounty Hunter.* Here is a film with no need to exist. Among its sins is the misuse of Jennifer Aniston, who can be and has been very funny, but not in dreck like this. Lacking any degree of character development, it handcuffs her to a plot of exhausted action comedy clichés—and also to a car door and a bed.

The handcuffer is her former husband, Milo (Gerard Butler), a former cop who is now a bounty hunter and draws the assignment of tracking down his ex-wife, who has skipped bail. Have I lost touch here, or are bounty hunters routinely deployed to track down criminals accused of no more than a nonfatal traffic violation? Never mind.

Let's do a little mental exercise here, the same sort that the screenplay writer, Sarah Thorp, must have done. Remember the ground rules: The movie must contain only clichés. I used to test this exercise on my film class. I'd give them the genre, and begin sentences ending with an ellipsis. They'd compete to be first to shout out the answer.

1. The story involves a formerly married couple. He is a bounty hunter tracking her down for . . .
2. They dislike one another. Therefore by the end of the movie . . .
3. He drives a . . .
4. Because . . .
5. And his beloved . . .
6. He loves to gamble. Their road trip takes them to . . .
7. Where he . . .
8. And gets into trouble with . . .
9. Inspiring . . .
10. In a golf cart, they . . .
11. During the movie, he gets kicked . . .
12. She wears clothes so we can . . .

Well, I already gave you number ten. To the others, clever students would answer: (1) a nonserious crime, since this is a comedy; (2) they will fall back in love; (3) vintage convertible; (4) movies like them because older cars look like real cars, and with a convertible you can more easily light the characters and show the landscape at the same time;

(5) gets damaged; (6) you can be excused for guessing Las Vegas, but it's Atlantic City; (7) wins big or loses big, but either way . . . ; (8) gangsters; (9) chase scenes, CGI sequences, impossible action, and lots of shots of her running in high heels; (10) you know; (11) in the crotch; (12) peek down her neckline.

Why, oh why, was this movie necessary? Could it have been redeemed by witty dialogue? Perhaps, but neither character is allowed to speak more than efficient sentences serving to further the plot. Hollywood movies started to simplify the dialogue when half the gross started to roll in from overseas. Has anyone noticed the great majority of nations dub foreign movies, so that subtitles aren't a problem?

Gerard Butler is a handsome hunk who can also act; he's currently starring in Ralph Fiennes's *Coriolanus.* Jennifer Aniston is a gifted comedienne. If you could pay their salaries, wouldn't you try to put them in a better movie than this? I saw the poster and had a sinking feeling the title gave away the whole story.

## Boy ★ ★ ★ ½

NO MPAA RATING, 90 m., 2012

James Rolleston (Boy), Te Aho Aho Eketone-Whitu (Rocky), Taika Waititi (Alamein), Moerangi Tihore (Dynasty), Haze Reweti (Dallas), Rajvinder Eria (Tane), Cherilee Martin (Kelly). Directed by Taika Waititi and produced by Cliff Curtis, Ainsley Gardiner, and Emanuel Michael. Screenplay by Waititi.

*Boy* is narrated by its title character, called that name by everyone, an enormously likable eleven-year-old Maori kid who lives in a village near the Bay of Plenty in New Zealand. It's 1984, which becomes unmistakable when we note that his younger brother is named Rocky, two characters are Dallas and Dynasty, and Michael Jackson's *Thriller* video is the central fact of his life.

Before the story even takes shape, Boy (James Rolleston) impresses us as smart, with a lively imagination and the most responsibility of anyone in the crowd of children he joins every day on the beach. Does he even notice what breathtaking scenery surrounds him? We learn that Boy's mother died giving birth to Rocky. Boy idealizes his absent father as a version of Michael Jackson. He and Rocky live with his grandmother, who leaves for a funeral in an opening scene.

And then a big ol' car comes swerving up a country road in a cloud of dust, and the man at the wheel introduces himself as Boy's father. This is Alamein (Taika Waititi, also the film's writer and director). He looks a little like Dennis Hopper in *Easy Rider*, and easily smokes as much pot. The two clueless guys in the front seat with him are allegedly members of the motorcycle gang he leads, although at no time does he ever produce a motorcycle.

Alamein, apparently named after the famous battle, has been absent for a good reason: He's just finished a prison sentence. He's returned in part to see Boy, and in larger part to find a bundle of loot he wrapped in plastic and buried somewhere in a pasture. The treasure spot should line up with some trees, although after all this time he doesn't quite remember just which ones.

*Boy* threatens to contain too much of a couple of elements. The father could turn out to be bad to the bone, introducing a threat to the son. And the movie, which includes flip card–style animation, threatens to go overboard on flashy style. Neither thing happens, and what gradually reveals itself is a bittersweet coming-of-age experience in which Boy outgrows his hero worship and realizes most of Alamein's most admirable qualities exist only in his imagination.

The film contains a great deal of offhand information about this Maori community. Much of it is about how global pop culture has imposed an imaginary media reality on children's lives. I was reminded of *Whale Rider* (2003), a New Zealand film about a twelve-year-old girl who would be next in line as chief of her tribe—if only she weren't a girl. Unlike the depth and detail of that film, with its meetings of tribal elders and their debates about traditions, *Boy* shows a community adrift in the present.

One of the things we notice is that Boy and his contemporaries are basically raising themselves. His father gives him a sip of beer, and he helps himself to pot (with no evident reaction). This is alarming, but there's a bedrock common sense in his makeup that helps him see his father as an inconsequential man, and when the old man finally leaves, it is in the nature of a depressed retreat. He can't even impress his own son.

The film is delightful in its colorful production values, with animated and fantasy interludes, many of which center around the dead mother's tombstone, which Rocky spends many hours at. Its surface is decorated with his bright designs and pictures, and seems in celebration of the dead woman. What a contrast with the living, who Boy and his pals observe from the shadows as they hang out on the porch of a store, getting drunk, smoking weed, and killing time.

A film like this would have little chance without the right casting, and James Rolleston is so right as Boy it's difficult to imagine anyone else. Waititi apparently found him as an extra on the film, and substituted him for an actor he had already cast only two days before shooting began. Like many child actors, he has a natural quality adults can only envy. Waititi himself is also crucial in the film; he's an irresponsible dad but not cruel or indifferent, and he extracts low-key humor from the character. It's not a surprise to learn he's a stand-up comic in New Zealand.

The question the film doesn't need to pose is this: What direction will Boy's life take? Rocky seems already pulled toward art. Boy's imagination was occupied by his father until he met him. Now what? When Taika Waititi was working on this screenplay at the Sundance Writers' Lab, its working title was *Choice.*

## Boy Wonder ★ ★ ★ ½

R, 93 m., 2011

Caleb Steinmeyer (Sean Donovan), Zulay Henao (Teresa Ames), Bill Sage (Terry Donovan), James Russo (Larry Childs), Tracy Middendorf (Mary Donovan), Daniel Stewart Sherman (Gary Stensen), Chuck Cooper (Bill Baldwin). Directed by Michael Morrissey and produced by Morrissey and John Scaccia. Screenplay by Morrissey.

Here's another movie about a young vigilante hero, like *Super* or *Kick-Ass*, but darker, more brooding, and without the easy payoffs. It takes itself more seriously and plays more like a psychological thriller about a young man driven to extremes. Any connection between the title and Batman's sidekick is purely ironic.

The most essential element in the film is the performance by Caleb Steinmeyer, as Sean, a quiet high school student who was traumatized as a child by witnessing his mother being murdered by a carjacker. He lives in a truce with his father (Bill Sage), a recovering alcoholic, who sometimes beat Sean's mother while the boy was watching. His dad has changed and apologized, but the damage has been done.

Sean gets straight A's in school and is capable, in some scenes, of startling us by the depth of his unexpected knowledge. He is introverted, withdrawn, bottled up. After school he sneaks away to a shabby boxing gym and works out.

He doesn't become a vigilante because he reads comic books, or for any other facile reason. Although the movie premiered at Chicago's Comic Con, it has no connection with comic books except probably for writer-director Michael Morrissey's noir lighting and framing, dramatized in the style of dark graphic novels. Because of its marketing, the movie has drawn reviews mostly from the comics-oriented websites, which find it lacking in comic fan orientation, but don't seem to pick up on the deeper currents. I started watching it with moderate expectations and was surprised by how quickly I was drawn in; the movie works insistently on an emotional level. I don't care how plausible Sean or his actions are; for the length of the film, I was involved in how things would play out.

Sean's revenge for his mother's death and father's abuse takes the form of sudden violence against abusive characters he meets while prowling the meaner streets of Manhattan, and even at a teen party (his father is gratified that his loner kid is even going to a party). The pattern: He sees someone being violently abusive, he challenges the behavior, the other guy attacks him, he absorbs enough pain to demonstrate the other person's savagery, and then he beats him to a pulp, or worse. He gets no satisfaction in his victories; there's more the aura of the masochistic performance of duty.

Lending this framework a great deal of interest is the story of Sean's interaction with the local police precinct. The cops know of his tragic childhood. They let him hang around the station, looking at mug shots in which he has long since lost hope of finding his mother's killer. A new detective named Teresa, played with warmth and energy by Zulay Henao, takes an interest in him at the same time she begins to investigate the series of vigilante incidents. She and her partner (Daniel Stewart Sherman, quickly likable) discuss him. Slowly, her instincts about Sean suggest something is not quite right.

In a genre populated with formulas and dreck, *Boy Wonder* is an ambitious exception: well made, drawing us in. It is particularly notable how Caleb Steinmeyer, a relative newcomer, calmly embodies his character and never cranks Sean up too much. This is a suffering boy.

## Bran Nue Dae ★ ★ ½

PG-13, 85 m., 2010

Rocky McKenzie (Willie), Jessica Mauboy (Rosie), Ernie Dingo (Uncle Tadpole), Missy Higgins (Annie), Geoffrey Rush (Father Benedictus), Deborah Mailman (Roxanne), Tom Budge (Slippery), Magda Szubanski (Roadhouse Betty). Directed by Rachel Perkins and produced by Graeme Isaac and Robyn Kershaw. Screenplay by Perkins, Reg Cribb, and Jimmy Chi.

Here's something I wasn't expecting: an Aboriginal musical from Australia, set in a late hippie era and featuring production numbers with a dash of Bollywood. It isn't a masterpiece, but it is a good-hearted, sweet comedy, featuring an overland chase that isn't original but sure is energetic.

The movie opens with its two young lovers shyly making eyes at each other. These are the young teenagers Willie (Rocky McKenzie) and Rosie (Jessica Mauboy). They daringly peek into a local saloon, and the singer invites the pretty Rosie (but pointedly not Willie) inside. Rosie can't resist a chance at a microphone, and magically becomes the center of the movie's first dance number. The way everyone in the room seems to have rehearsed the choreography is the hint of Bollywood, where characters seem to arrange themselves instinctively into chorus lines.

Willie's pious mother is determined to see her son win respect and get a good job as a priest. She whisks him away from his hometown to a rather strange seminary, ruled by Father Benedictus (Geoffrey Rush), who has a German accent but not overmuch of the holy spirit.

Willie yearns for home and Rosie, and runs away, finds a hobo camp, and is befriended by Uncle Tadpole (Ernie Dingo), who claims to be a relative but forgets about that in the morning. No matter. Uncle Tadpole comes along for the trip, and they hitch a ride in a van painted in a psychedelic 1960s style and piloted by two jolly hippies. Father Benedictus follows in unconvincing and not very clerical fashion as he goes in pursuit, having forgotten, I guess, that Willie must want to be a priest and not be captured and forced.

And so on. I learn *Bran Nue Dae* was a hit on the Australian stage in 1990. Many of the songs, some with serious undertones, reflect the treatment of Aborigines, who were treated as cruelly as Native Americans, and in such recent decades you'd think a more enlightened vision might have seeped into Australia, not that we have anything to feel smug about.

The two leads are sweet and attractive, their roles don't place great demands, and the movie skips along happily, if a little disorganized. Its look is striking; the cinematography, by Andrew Lesnie of *The Lord of the Rings*, gives the exteriors an almost Day-Glo brightness, as if the sun is shining through the screen.

## Brave ★ ★ ★

PG, 100 m., 2012

With the voices of: Kelly Macdonald (Merida), Billy Connolly (King Fergus), Emma Thompson (Queen Elinor), Julie Walters (The Witch), Robbie Coltrane (Lord Dingwall), Kevin McKidd (Lord MacGuffin), Craig Ferguson (Lord Macintosh). Directed by Mark Andrews and Brenda Chapman and produced by Katherine Sarafian. Screenplay by Andrews, Chapman, Steve Purcell, and Irene Mecchi.

*Brave* is the new animated film from Pixar, and therefore becomes the film the parents of the world will be dragged to by their kids. The good news is that the kids will probably love it, and the bad news is that parents will be disappointed if they're hoping for another Pixar groundbreaker. Unlike such brightly original films as *Toy Story*, *Finding Nemo*, *WALL-E*, and *Up*, this one finds Pixar poaching on traditional territory of Disney, its corporate partner. We get a spunky princess, her mum the queen, her dad the gruff king, an old witch who lives in the woods, and so on.

The princess is Merida (voice by Kelly Macdonald), who is seen in an action-packed prologue as a flame-haired Scottish tomboy whose life is changed by an early birthday gift of a bow, which quickly inspires her to become the best archer in the kingdom. Then we flash forward to Merida as a young lady of marriageable age, who is startled by being required by her mother, Elinor (Emma Thompson), to choose among three possible husbands chosen by her clan.

Nothing doing, especially since all three candidates are doofuses. Merida leaps upon her trusty steed and flees into the forest, where her friends the will-o'-the-wisps lead her to the cottage of a gnarled old witch (Julie Walters). She begs for a magic spell that will change Queen Elinor's mind, but it changes more than that: It turns her into a bear. Witches never know how to stop when they're ahead.

Luckily, the magic spell comes with an escape clause. Merida has exactly two days to reverse the charm. After she and her mother absorb what has happened, they begin to work together and grow closer than ever, even though the queen cannot speak. There is a tricky complication. King Fergus (Billy Connolly) had his leg bitten off by a bear (in the prologue), and has been indisposed toward them ever since. Unsurprisingly, when he sees his wife as a bear, he fails to recognize her.

And so on. This is a great-looking movie, much enlivened by the inspiration of giving Merida three small brothers, little red-headed triplets. The Scottish Highlands are thrillingly painted in astonishing detail, and some action shows Merida's archery more than adequate in assorted emergencies.

*Brave* has an uplifting message about better communication between mothers and daughters, although transforming your mom into a bear is a rather extreme first step. Elinor is a good sport, under the circumstances. But Merida is far from being a typical fairy-tale princess. Having flatly rejected the three suitors proposed by her family, she is apparently prepared to go through life quite happily without a husband, and we can imagine her in later years, a weathered and indomitable Amazon queen, sort of a Boudica for the Scots. The movie seems at a loss to deal with her as a girl, and makes her a sort of honorary boy.

## Bride Flight ★ ★ ★

R, 130 m., 2011

Waldemar Torenstra (Frank), Karina Smulders (Ada), Anna Drijver (Esther), Elise Schaap (Marjorie), Petra Laseur (Older Marjorie), Pleuni Touw (Older Ada), Willeke van Ammelrooy (Older Esther), Rutger Hauer (Older Frank). Directed by Ben Sombogaart and produced by Hanneke Niens and Anton Smit. Screenplay by Marieke van der Pol.

*Bride Flight* derives its title from an actual flight in 1953 between London and Christchurch, New Zealand—part of the Last Great Air Race. The Dutch plane in the race carries many women flying to New Zealand to meet current or prospective husbands, and the movie will follow the fortunes of three of them for many tumultuous years, using two actors to portray each of them as younger and older.

The events in the plot are the stuff of soap opera, but the movie treats it seriously, and the acting is convincing enough that we forgive the story and begin to care about the characters. Four people on the flight will find their lives linked in New Zealand. Ada (Karina Smulders) and Marjorie (Elise Schaap) are flying out to meet their husbands. Esther (Anna Drijver), a Holocaust survivor, is a fashion designer hoping to start a new business. Frank (Waldemar Torenstra) is a hunky rancher. During the flight, Ada, who has met her new husband only once, finds that she and Frank are falling in love.

In Christchurch they all find an optimistic

postwar city that's filled with opportunity, especially in contrast with war-torn Holland. Ada stays with her husband (Micha Hulshof), a fiercely censorious Calvinist. Esther opens a design studio. Marjorie finds she can't have children. Esther finds she can but doesn't want to; her career comes first. And Frank—well, Frank is a genial lad, well liked, and if he isn't with the one he loves, he loves the one he's with.

*Bride Flight* takes this melodrama and adds details of period, of behavior, of personality, to somewhat redeem its rather inevitable conclusion. The key figure is Ada, who has three children and then arrives at a momentous decision that colors everything else that happens. Esther and Marjorie find that their own decisions are not so easily left in the past.

You can sense I'm not describing much of the story. It wouldn't be fair. A film like *Bride Flight* works because we want to see it unfolding. We observe the pieces going into place and want to see how it will all work out. That it works out more or less inevitably is to be expected, I suppose, but you'd be upset if I revealed some of the twists and turns.

This is the biggest-budgeted film ever made in Holland, not least because the story of the real bride flight is well known and involves a period fraught with emotion. So considerable is the production that Rutger Hauer has returned to Dutch films after thirty years to play the older Frank. The young actresses who play the three leads are all capable, and Karina Smulders much more than that, in a role that takes her more deeply than the others.

Three observations. (1) There's a danger in assigning a mannerism to a character and enforcing it too relentlessly. Esther smokes using a little cigarette holder, which she *always* holds next to her face. This begins to be a glitch. (2) In a scene at an airport, a crucial piece of information is imparted in a subtle and rather elegant understatement. You'll see what I mean. (3) There is a love scene of real urgency and passion. Often movie sex scenes seem to be merely energetic exercise.

## Bridesmaids ★ ★ ★ ½

R, 128 m., 2011

Kristen Wiig (Annie), Maya Rudolph (Lillian), Rose Byrne (Helen), Wendi McLendon-Covey (Rita), Ellie Kemper (Becca), Melissa McCarthy (Megan), Chris O'Dowd (Rhodes). Directed by Paul Feig and produced by Judd Apatow, Barry Mendel, and Clayton Townsend. Screenplay by Annie Mumolo and Kristen Wiig.

Three of my good female friends, who I could usually find overcoming hangovers at their Saturday morning Recovery Drunches at Oxford's Pub, once made pinpricks in their thumbs and performed a ceremony, becoming blood sisters. They were the only people I have actually known who could inspire a Judd Apatow buddy movie, and all three could do what not all women do well, and that is perfectly tell a dirty joke.

Maybe I liked *Bridesmaids* in their honor. Kristen Wiig's new comedy is about a group of women friends who are as unbehaved as the guys in *The Hangover.* Don't tell me "unbehaved" isn't a word. It is now. And Wiig is rather brilliant in her physical comedy as she flies to Vegas as part of her BFF's bachelorette party; if it were not the wedding of her BFF, this trip would get her thrown out of the wedding. Her motto: "What happens in Vegas, starts on the plane."

Wiig plays Annie, whose Milwaukee bakery shop has just gone bust, who rooms with a surpassingly peculiar British brother and sister, and whose longtime friend Lillian (Maya Rudolph) is getting married. Naturally, she expects to be maid of honor, but begins to fear a rival in Helen (Rose Byrne), the rich and overconfident trophy wife of the groom's boss. You see that can lead to trouble.

Helen is one of those people who at birth was placed in charge of everything for everyone. It's not that she's trying to steal Annie's thunder, it's just that she can't comprehend that she isn't running the wedding. This leads finally to Annie's explosion at a bizarre French-themed bridal shower with an item of pastry that would strike even an editor of the *Guinness Book of World Records* as, well, excessive.

The movie, written by Wiig and Annie Mumolo and directed by Paul Feig (*The Office*), does a good job of introducing a large cast, and in particular, keeping all the members of the bridal party in play. These include Rita (Wendi McLendon-Covey), a mother of three adolescent sons ("My house is covered in semen"), and (my favorite) Megan (Melissa McCarthy), who has the sturdiness and the certainty of a fireplug.

Did I mention the movie was produced by Apatow? Love him or not, he's consistently involved with movies that connect with audiences, and *Bridesmaids* seems to be a more or less deliberate attempt to cross the chick flick with the raunch comedy. It definitively proves that women are the equal of men in vulgarity, sexual frankness, lust, vulnerability, overdrinking, and insecurity. And it moves into areas not available to men, for example the scene when they're all trying on dresses at a bridal shop and the lunch they've just shared suddenly reappears, if you get my drift.

Not everybody can do physical comedy. Wiig's behavior on the flight to Vegas would win the respect of Lucille Ball. I don't even want to start describing what happens. In these days when you can get arrested on a plane for taking out your car keys, her behavior is a throwback to the good old days of airborne slapstick.

Yet the movie has a heart. It heals some wounds, restores some hurt feelings, confesses some secrets, and in general ends happily, which is just as well, because although there are many things audiences will accept from women in a comedy, ending miserably is not one of them. That may be sexist, but there you are.

## Brighton Rock ★ ★ ½

NO MPAA RATING, 111 m., 2011

Sam Riley (Pinkie), Andrea Riseborough (Rose), John Hurt (Phil Corkery), Helen Mirren (Ida), Andy Serkis (Colleoni), Sean Harris (Hale), Nonso Anozie (Dallow). Directed by Rowan Joffe and produced by Paul Webster. Screenplay by Joffe, based on the novel by Graham Greene.

Pinkie Brown is a low-level thug in a second-rate gang in Brighton, the British seaside holiday town known for its pier. He is also a psychopath in over his head. One day he chats up a waitress named Rose in a tea shop, goes walking on the pier with her, and is snapped by a tourist photographer just when they meet a fellow gang member. Not long after, he batters the man to death beneath the pier, and then sets out to retrieve the damning evidence of the photo. He also must silence Rose, who realizes she met the murder victim whose picture is in the paper.

This sets in motion *Brighton Rock*, the second film adaptation of Graham Greene's 1938 novel. Greene's Catholicism plays a central role in the lives of many of his characters, few more than Pinkie and Rose—she because she holds a simple faith, he because he believes in hell and that he is headed there.

This Pinkie (Sam Riley) is an evil young man, dead-eyed, fearful, violent. Why does Rose (Andrea Riseborough) fall in love with him? Just as well she does. Pinkie would have killed her to silence her; instead, he marries her so she can't testify against him. This is explained to Rose, too late, by Ida (Helen Mirren), the steely owner of the tea shop, who figures out the whole story but can't prevent Rose from falling under Pinkie's power.

*Brighton Rock* is a film of ominous gloom. The sea rolls darkly under the pier, the gull cries are forlorn, the music is mournful, the colors are muted. It is often overcast, or dusk, or night, and there is little sunshine for those seeking a holiday. It takes place in shabby boardinghouses and on chilly cliffs, and when the action moves to the grand hotel where the gangsters meet, some of the characters seem uneasy there.

Andrea Riseborough evokes a hapless Rose. Probably she is a little dim. Pinkie has scarcely even been nice to her, and she knowingly puts her life at risk for him. Ida tries to talk sense into the girl, and confides in her old friend Corkery (John Hurt). Because the movie doesn't make the Catholicism of Pinkie and Rose as important as Greene does, their motivations sometimes seem merely self-destructive.

*Brighton Rock* was adapted in 1947 by the Boulting brothers, with Richard Attenborough in an early role as the merciless Pinkie (the movie's U.S. title was *Young Scarface*). I haven't seen it. But I know the novel, and as dark as this film is, I believe it hesitates to follow Greene into his dark abyss. It is about helplessness and evil, but isn't merciless enough. Consider the ending. It involves a recording made by Pinkie. In the novel, after all she's been through, Rose has yet to listen to it, but she will. In the movie, she loses her chance to hear what Pinkie said. It might, after all, have given her some release.

## Brooklyn's Finest ★ ★ ★

R, 140 m., 2010

Richard Gere (Eddie), Don Cheadle (Tango), Ethan Hawke (Sal), Wesley Snipes (Caz), Will Patton (Hobarts), Lili Taylor (Angela), Shannon Kane (Chantel), Ellen Barkin (Smith). Directed by Antoine Fuqua and produced by Elie Cohn, Basil Iwanyk, John Langley, Avi Lerner, and John Thompson. Screenplay by Michael C. Martin.

Three cops, three journeys to what we suspect will be doom. No good can come of the lives they lead. They aren't bad guys, not precisely, but they occupy a world of such unremitting violence and cynicism that they're willing to do what it takes to survive. In the kind of coincidence provided only by fate or screenplays, each one will mean trouble for the other two.

Richard Gere gets top billing as Eddie, a veteran with one week left before retirement. It is a movie convention that anyone who has a week to go before retirement must die before that week is up, but Eddie seems impatient. As the film opens, he wakes up, chugs some whiskey from a bottle, and points a revolver into his mouth, never a good sign.

Don Cheadle is Tango, who is completely embedded undercover in Brooklyn's toughest drug precinct, where he has blended in so well with the bad guys that it's a fine line separating him from crime. His friend is Caz (Wesley Snipes), a dealer trying to go straight after prison; they share one of those inexplicable bonds between two tough guys, causing them to consider each other brothers when they should really be nothing of the kind.

The third cop, Sal (Ethan Hawke), is a narc whose wife (Lili Taylor) provides him with more of a melodramatic emergency than we are perhaps prepared to believe. They have seven kids, live in a house too small for them, and the mold in the walls provokes potentially dangerous asthma attacks. Oh, and she's pregnant. Having twins.

Sal has made an offer on a new place for which he cannot make the first payment. He desperately needs cash, and there's a lot of it around in his work. Tango needs to somehow use Caz and yet spare him. Eddie needs to negotiate an alcoholic haze for seven more days before he can go fishing.

The film and the actors do a good job of establishing these characters in their own lives. Indeed, the best things about *Brooklyn's Finest* are the one-on-one scenes. These are fine actors. The milieu involves a tough, poker-playing, substance-abusing, hard-bitten world where the law meets crime and the two sides have more in common with each other than with civilians. I don't believe it's like this for most cops, but somehow it is for the great majority of movie cops.

Cheadle and Snipes have some very good scenes involving what is left unsaid but not unsuspected. Ethan Hawke has a fierce loyalty to his wife and family, and Lili Taylor does her usual touching job with what's basically a soap opera role. Hawke is especially effective in desperate scenes where he takes crazy risks because he needs to raise cash quickly. Richard Gere's character is not as rich as the other two, is more depressed, is on a more predictable trajectory.

What is rather startling is the level of the violence and killing. Although cops-vs.-drugs movies are traditionally awash in blood, *Brooklyn's Finest* demonstrates a trope I've seen with disturbing frequency: the scene in which one character lifts a firearm and peremptorily blows away another one—almost casually or unemotionally, like cleaning house. I complained for years about the Talking Killer Syndrome, in which the shooter delays in order to explain himself to a man who will presumably be dead soon. But Instant Killers are not the answer. The fact of taking life is robbed of weight and meaning. The gun becomes the instrument of merciless self-will.

The director of *Brooklyn's Finest,* Antoine Fuqua, made *Training Day* (2001), the film Denzel Washington won an Oscar for. That powerfully costarred Ethan Hawke. This film has the same level of savage violence and the same cops operating outside the same law, but the human stakes are more obvious and less convincing. The lives of the three cops intersect through a series of coincidences and inevitabilities, and I think we become a little too conscious that they're being guided less by chance than by a screenwriter. The film has a basic strength in its performances and craft, but falls short of the high mark Fuqua obviously set for himself.

## Buck ★ ★ ★

PG, 88 m., 2011

Buck Brannaman, Reata Brannaman, Mary Brannaman, Betsy Shirley, Shayne and Jo-Anne Jackson, Betty and Craig Staley, Robert Redford, Bibb Frazier, Gwynn Turnbull Weaver, Annette Venteicher, and Nevada Watt. A documentary directed by Cindy Meehl and produced by Julie Goldman.

Buck Brannaman was the original "horse whisperer," the character Nicholas Evans based his novel on and Robert Redford used as the on-set consultant for his film. He has a way with horses, and Cindy Meehl's documentary is moving as she shows them engaged in dances of understanding. W. G. Sebald wrote, "Men and animals regard each other across a gulf of mutual incomprehension," but Buck and his animals seem to have bridged it.

We see footage of Buck and his brother, Bill, in childhood as "Buckshot and Smokie, the Idaho Cowboys." They appeared onstage, at rodeos, and even on a TV game show, and were being beaten regularly by their father. They were well trained. They could do rope tricks while blindfolded, but in the footage, we see they never look happy but more like frightened robots.

One of the most affecting moments in the film comes when Buck remembers a high school coach telling him to undress and take a shower, and then seeing the welts on his back and legs. A deputy sheriff was called in, and Buck was taken away from his father and placed in a foster home. Curiously, the movie makes no mention of Bill.

There was an older approach to horse training that resembled Buck's father's cruelty as he trained his boys. Standing against this trend, we learn, were two legendary horse trainers named Tom Dorrance and Ray Hunt, and when young Buck saw Hunt at work, one must assume he powerfully yearned to have been treated with as much gentleness and compassion.

The key to this approach involves empathy for the feelings of the horse. Buck understands how horses read humans, how they interpret gestures, and how they're "so sensitive they can feel a fly land." I was reminded of Temple Grandin, the autistic designer of cattle-handling chutes, whose secret was identifying the feelings of cattle with her own.

Buck Brannaman spends most of every year on the road, giving four-day workshops on horse handling. Sometimes his wife, Mary, travels with him, and his daughter Reata comes along every July and August, sometimes sleeping in a tent next to the big horse trailer. Reata seems calm and happy as her father never was as a child; he recalls being made to sit at a kitchen table until he almost had the grain of the wood memorized.

The film perhaps goes too far in visiting the sins of a horse upon its owner. There's a beautiful but dangerous stud toward the end of the film who is a "predator," Buck warns. This horse's dam died while giving birth, and in a cold winter the foal was raised in the house. That sounds kind, but something went wrong, perhaps oxygen deprivation during birth, and the horse is very aggressive. Advising its owner to have the horse castrated, Brannaman learns she has a field full of twelve more studs at home: "That's looking for trouble."

In some of his commentaries during workshops, it seemed to me that Buck attributed qualities to the horses and their owners that owed as much to his abusive childhood as anything. Well, why not? We meet Robert Redford, who talks about the trainer's contribution to *The Horse Whisperer* (1998), and see in one scene how Buck's own horse is used to perform in a way a highly trained Hollywood "trick horse" is incapable of.

What I was left with was the goodness of Buck Brannaman as a man. He was dealt a hand that might have destroyed him. He overcame his start and is now a wise and influential role model. He does unto horses as he wishes his father had done unto him.

## Bullhead ★ ★ ★

R, 128 m., 2012

Matthias Schoenaerts (Jacky Vanmarsenille), Jeroen Perceval (Diederik Maes), Jeanne Dandoy (Lucia Schepers), Barbara Sarafian (Eva Forrestier), Tibo Vandenborre (Antony de Greef), Frank Lammers (Sam Raymond), Sam Louwyck (Marc Decuyper), Robin Valvekens (Young Jacky), Baudoin Wolwertz (Young Diederik). Directed by Michael R. Roskam and produced by Bart Van Langendonck. Screenplay by Roskam.

*Bullhead* contains the elements of a simple but overwhelming personal tragedy. It also contains other elements that create a muddle. It's one of those films you have to reconstruct in your mind. It involves Jacky, a low-level Belgian farmer and criminal, who is paralyzed by fear and insecurity about his masculinity. Because he has easy access to testosterone and animal growth hormones, he uses them to build muscle and body mass. These have turned him into a raging bull.

I understand why *Bullhead* was one of this year's Oscar nominees for best foreign film. I'm not sure it was one of the best five in the running, but that goes with the territory. It impresses because of the pain, sadness, and rage contained in the title performance by the Flemish actor Matthias Schoenaerts, who bulked up for the role (without steroids), and seems ready to burst from his clothes and even his skin.

He had something happen to him when he was young. It happened on the very day he first took notice that girls have breasts. This was during a talk with his best friend, Diederik (Baudoin Wolwertz), as they regarded the sister of a neighbor. It was one of those talks many children have in which the facts of life fall into place with a blinding insight. Yes, you know about such things in a distracted sort of incomplete way because they aren't especially interesting to you. Then suddenly they become the most important things in your life.

As a boy, young Jacky (Robin Valvekens) is a handsome mop head with a sunny personality. On that day, everything changed. We meet the adult Jacky at the start of the film; we see him consumed by sudden angers and intimidating people for his uncle, who raises beef cattle. We learn about animal growth hormone, which they use, and in his bathroom we see a little medical refrigerator containing countless bottles, vials, and syringes of such drugs.

Jacky has become expert in their use. A casual conversation about their dangers indicates that he recklessly consumes what would be lethal self dosages if he didn't have such a high resistance. He gobbles pills, stabs himself with needles, throws punches in the air like De Niro in *Raging Bull.* He still maintains an obsession with the girl he was looking at on that fateful childhood day.

Because that day provided the engine driving his entire life, I'm not sure it was wise for Michael R. Roskam, the writer-director, to delay it until a flashback halfway through. Something made this guy this way, we're thinking, but the flashback information causes us to rethink everything. Well, that's what flashbacks often do, but in *Bullhead* there's too much to rethink.

The movie reminded me of Michael Fassbender's masterful work in Steve McQueen's *Shame.* Both characters allow their existence to focus on their genitals. *Shame* is what Paul Schrader calls a Man in a Room movie, like *Raging Bull* or *American Gigolo,* in which the hero's tormented existence is solitary. *Bullhead* introduces a plot involving Belgium's "hormone mafia," a police informer, two rival criminals, the childhood friends still around, a murder of a cop, a stolen car, and two dimwitted Walloon auto mechanics, dumb and dumber.

The result is a film more confusing than it needs to be. At its center is a man and his obsession, and the way hormone use has driven him out of control. That is more than enough. The one excellent aspect of the film is Matthias Schoenaerts's performance. We often follow him walking in a controlled lurch from side to side, as if merely walking is not enough of a challenge for him. We see his eyes, burning with pain. He speaks as if forcing out every word.

Perhaps it was something he overheard on that day in childhood. Perhaps it was misunderstood comments from a crooked veterinarian about the effect of hormones on bulls. There is no need for him to be this crazed. What happened to him hasn't destroyed his life. This is the story of a man being eaten from within by chemicals. That alone would have been more than enough. I'm damned if I could follow the scheming involving the mechanics and those two sets of stolen auto tires.

## Bully ★ ★ ★

NO MPAA RATING, 106 m., 2012

A documentary featuring "Alex," "Ja'Meya," "Kelby," David Long, Tina Long, Kirk Smalley, Laura Smalley. Directed by Lee Hirsch and produced by Hirsch and Cynthia Lowen. Screenplay by Hirsch and Lowen.

There's a fleeting shot in *Bully* of a kid who just plain looks mean. He has a cruel mouth and squinting eyes, and you wonder if he knows how to smile. The movie singles him out but says nothing about him. Is he one of the bullies? Who knows? He reminded me of a kid in grade school who called me Fatso. I called him Stupid. We were both right.

There's only one bully actually identified in the film. A clueless teacher has pulled together two kids who got in a fight and insists they shake hands. One kid is as friendly as an insurance salesman, and sticks out his paw with a friendly smile. The other kid refuses. The teacher sends the friendly kid away and lectures the other one. Of course it's the "nice kid" who is the bully. He probably gets away with more stuff than a con man. His victim knows it. He's been down this path before.

If the teacher were more clued in, she'd know it, too. One of the themes in Lee Hirsch's documentary is how many parents and teachers have no idea what's really happening in the secret society of children in their care. Many bullied children are reluctant to tell anyone what's happening to them. Are they embarrassed, or scared? Bullying is designed to make them feel inferior, and in their cases, perhaps it has worked.

The film follows the stories of several children in Mississippi, Oklahoma, Iowa, and Georgia. Two of them committed suicide. Their lives had become unendurable without anyone noticing, or taking it seriously enough. I can believe it. The most infuriating people in the film are teachers or administrators who don't know what's happening—or don't want to know, perhaps afraid of bureaucratic difficulties or angry parents. (I imagine, but don't know, that the parents of bullies are likely to flare up in anger at accusations against their children—and then possibly abuse their kid themselves later. Do bullies often have nice parents?)

Sometimes an entire community gets in on the act. A girl who is a lesbian is humiliated by a teacher in front of other students, and her parents observe that many of their own friends of long standing have become hostile. A culture of ignorance and homophobia feeds this.

Much has been made of how the MPAA gave this film an R rating for its language. (A PG-13 has belatedly been handed out to a version with some words taken out.) It was widely said that the MPAA was preventing admission to those very kids under seventeen who could benefit from it the most. That part I'm not so sure about. The movie contains little solid information about bullying, and although we feel sorry for the victims who are profiled, it is unclear what can be learned from observing them.

My notion is that a fictional film might be more effective than a documentary. It could encourage young viewers to identify with victims of bullying and dislike bullies. Movies that encourage empathy are more effective than those that objectify problems. Some kids will think: "I'm not like those losers." The right kind of fictional story might make that harder to do.

Why are some people bullied? Because they are different. How? It doesn't matter. A bully can act as the catalyst for encouraging a group to draw together in cruelty against someone perceived as not a member. This process was shown with great power in Larry Clark's *Bully* (2001), which added an unexpected twist: A brutal bully is actually murdered by a group of his victims, who together are moved to do something none of them could ever do alone.

*Bully* is a sincere documentary, but not a great one. We feel sympathy for the victims in the film and their parents or friends, but the film seems to helplessly treat bullying as without a solution. I can think of one thing that might help. Parents and schools should place great emphasis on the fact that it is all right to be different. Racism and all the other isms grow from primitive tribalism, the instinctive hostility against those of another tribe, race, religion, nationality, class, or whatever. You are a lucky child if your parents taught you to accept diversity. Teaching prejudice to a child is itself a form of bullying. You've got to be taught to hate.

## Buried ★ ★ ★ ½

R, 95 m., 2010

Ryan Reynolds (Paul Conroy). Directed by Rodrigo Cortes and produced by Adrian Guerra and Peter Safran. Screenplay by Chris Sparling.

Buried alive. It must be a universal nightmare. I read Edgar Allan Poe's *The Premature Burial* when I was seven or eight, and the thought troubled me for many a dark night. You are alive, you can move, you can scream, but no one will hear.

Paul Conroy is a truck driver working for a private contractor in Iraq. He comes to consciousness in blackness. He reaches out, feels, realizes. He finds a lighter. In its flame his worst fears are realized. He finds a cell phone. He learns he has been kidnapped and is a hostage.

Obviously his captors want him to use the phone. They want to prove he is alive because they plan to demand ransom. And by now we are identifying with Conroy's desperate thinking. Who can he call who can rescue him before the oxygen in the coffin runs out? Thankfully the coffin is longer than usual, allowing it to contain more air and also permitting certain camera angles that enhance the action.

Because there is action. Although the entire movie takes place in the enclosed space, director Rodrigo Cortes and writer Chris Sparling are ingenious in creating more plausible action than you would expect possible. They also allow themselves a few POV shots from outside the coffin—not on the surface, but simply from undefined darkness above the space.

Paul (Ryan Reynolds) uses the phone to call 911. The Pentagon. His employer's office. His wife. He receives calls from his kidnappers. These calls are exercises in frustration. There is nothing quite like being put on hold while you're buried alive.

It is their wise decision to omit any shots of the action at the other end of the calls. No shots of 911 operators, Pentagon generals, or corporate PR types. No shots of his desperate kidnappers. No flashbacks to the ambush and kidnapping itself. No weeping wife. The movie illustrates the strength of audiobooks and radio drama: The images we summon in our minds are more compelling than any we could see. A seen image supplies satisfaction. An imagined one inspires yearning. Along with Paul, we're trying to transport ourselves to the other end of each call.

It would not be fair to even hint at some of the events in the coffin. Let it be said that none of them is impossible. There is no magic realism here. Only the immediate situation. The budget for *Buried* is said to be $3 million. In one sense, low. In another sense, more than adequate for everything director Cortes wants to accomplish, including his special effects and the voice talents of all the people on the other end of the line.

Ryan Reynolds has limited space to work in, and body language more or less preordained by the coffin, but he makes the character convincing if necessarily limited. The running time, 95 minutes, feels about right. The use of 2:35 widescreen paradoxically increases the effect of claustrophobia. I would *not* like to be buried alive.

*Notes: My top ten reasons for wanting to be cremated are at http://j.mp/dpQwYu. Read* The Premature Burial *by Edgar Allan Poe at http://j.mp/bput7O.*

## Burlesque ★ ★

PG-13, 116 m., 2010

Cher (Tess), Christina Aguilera (Ali), Eric Dane (Marcus), Cam Gigandet (Jack), Julianne Hough (Georgia), Alan Cumming (Alexis), Peter Gallagher (Vince), Kristen Bell (Nikki), Stanley Tucci (Sean). Directed by Steven Antin and produced by Donald De Line. Screenplay by Antin.

The burlesque shows in *Burlesque* feature no nudity, no striptease, no baggy-pants comedians, and no performers with names like

Porsche Galore. Other than that, the shows are identical to the offerings at the Rialto and Follies burlesque houses that flourished on South State Street when I first visited Chicago as a sin-seeking teenager.

This is burlesque if it died and went to heaven. Behind a tawdry side entrance on Sunset Strip, a club exists that would make a Vegas casino proud. It has the eerie expanding and contracting dimensions of fantasy. At first, the stage is the right size for an intimate cabaret; later, there's enough space to present a production number with dozens of (unaccounted for) dancers descending a staircase worthy of Busby Berkeley. The audience is all shadowy extras, whose friends will have to look real hard to spot them.

The Burlesque Lounge attracts the attention of Ali (Christina Aguilera), the proverbial small-town girl just off the bus from Iowa. She walks in just in time to see Tess (Cher) conveniently performing the number "Welcome to Burlesque." In this scene and throughout the movie, Cher looks exactly as she always does. Other people age. Cher has become a logo.

The movie has a limited cast of broadly drawn characters, used to separate song and dance numbers. Tess co-owns the club with her ex-husband, Vince (Peter Gallagher). As a couple, they inspire games of What Is Wrong with This Picture? His function is to eagerly hope they can sell out to Marcus (Eric Dane), the real-estate developer who wants to tear down the club and put up condos. The club bartender is Jack (Cam Gigandet), who wears eyeliner but turns out to be straight. He allows Ali to crash on his sofa, but there's no sex because he has a fiancée in New York and also because the film has a PG-13 rating. The stage manager is Sean (Stanley Tucci). He's gay, except for one unforgettable night with Tess in Reno. Or Lake Tahoe. She forgets.

The star dancer is Nikki (Kristen Bell), who grows instantly angry with Ali after the farm girl tells her she looks like a drag queen. They must not see many drag queens in Iowa. There is also the nice girl named Georgia (Julianne Hough), who . . . well, a plot like this only leaves one thing for her, doesn't it?

Sorry, I got distracted again, thinking of the condo tower Marcus wants to build. How big a footprint will it need? We get repeated shots of the exterior of the lounge, which consists of an arch of lightbulbs next to what looks like the side of a modest frame building with outside steps to a second floor that doesn't seem to exist inside.

On the landing of those steps on that first night, Ali sees a black girl standing, who smiles nicely to her. We see this same girl repeatedly during the film, but she never gets a name or any dialogue. She has the role of the Black Girl Who Is Seen but Not Heard as a Member of the Club Family. She shouldn't complain. No other dancer gets to be anything at all.

In the film, both Cher and Christina Aguilera are showcased in big song numbers, which I enjoyed on a music video level. Aguilera has an unforced charm in her early scenes, but as she morphs into a glamorous star, she becomes increasingly less interesting. We learn she is an orphan. That simplifies the backstory.

You know how in Bollywood musicals the star actress will be all by her lonely self on a mountaintop, and when she starts to sing and dance, a dozen male singer-dancers materialize out of thin air? That happens here in the big final number. The girls form a perfect chorus line, a stairway to the stars appears, and a dozen male dancers descend. Where did they come from? Where will they go? Remember, this club is so small there is only one clothing rack backstage for all the costumes.

Is this the movie for you? It may very well be. You've read my review, and you think I'm just making snarky comments and indulging in cheap sarcasm. Well, all right, I am. *Burlesque* shows Cher and Christina Aguilera being all that they can be, and that's more than enough.

# C

## The Cabin in the Woods ★ ★ ★

R, 105 m., 2012

Kristen Connolly (Dana), Chris Hemsworth (Curt), Anna Hutchison (Jules), Fran Kranz (Marty), Jesse Williams (Holden), Richard Jenkins (Sitterson), Bradley Whitford (Hadley), Brian White (Truman), Amy Acker (Lin). Directed by Drew Goddard and produced by Joss Whedon. Screenplay by Goddard and Whedon.

You're not going to see this one coming. You might think you do, because the TV ads and shots at the top reveal what looks like the big surprise—and it certainly comes as a surprise to the characters. But let's just say there's a lot more to it than that.

*The Cabin in the Woods* sets off with an ancient and familiar story plan. Five college students pile into a van and drive deep into the backwoods for a weekend in a borrowed cabin. Their last stop is of course a decrepit gas station populated by a demented creep who giggles at the fate in store for them. In these days when movies are sliced and diced for YouTube mash-ups, I'd love to see a montage of demented redneck gas station owners drooling and chortling over the latest carloads of victims heading into the woods.

It will seem that I'm revealing a secret by mentioning that this is no ordinary cabin in the woods, but actually a set for a diabolical scientific experiment. Beneath the cabin is a basement, and beneath that is a vast modern laboratory headed by technology geeks (Richard Jenkins and Bradley Whitford) who turn dials, adjust levers, and monitor every second on a bank of TV monitors. Their scheme is to offer the five guinea pigs a series of choices, which will reveal—something, I'm not sure precisely what. There is some possibility this expensive experiment is involved with national security, and we get scenes showing similar victims in scenarios around the world.

Now, in your standard horror film, that would be enough: OMG! The cabin is being controlled by a secret underground laboratory! Believe me, that's only the beginning. The film has been produced and cowritten by Joss Whedon (creator of *Buffy the Vampire Slayer* and *Angel*) and directed by his longtime collaborator Drew Goddard (writer of *Cloverfield*). Whedon has described it as a "loving hate letter" to horror movies, and you could interpret it as an experiment on the genre itself: It starts with five standard-issue characters in your basic cabin in the woods, and we can read the lab scientists as directors and writers who are plugging in various story devices to see what the characters will do. In some sense, the Jenkins and Whitford characters represent Whedon and Goddard.

Ah, but they don't let us off that easily. That's what I mean when I say you won't see the ending coming. This is not a perfect movie; it's so ragged, it's practically constructed of loose ends. But it's exciting because it ventures so far off the map. One imagines the filmmakers chortling with glee as they devise first one bizarre development and then another in a free-for-all for their imaginations. They establish rules only to violate them.

That begins with the characters. They're stock archetypes. We get an action hero (Curt, played by Chris Hemsworth); a good girl (Dana, played by Kristen Connolly); a bad girl (Jules, played by Anna Hutchison); the comic relief (Marty the pothead, played by Fran Kranz); and the mature and thoughtful kid (Holden, played by Jesse Williams). What the scientists apparently intend to do is see how each archetype plays out after the group is offered various choices. There are even side bets in the lab about who will do what—as if they're predicting which lever the lab rats will push.

This is essentially an attempt to codify free will. Do horror characters make choices because of the requirements of the genre, or because of their own decisions? And since they're entirely the instruments of their creators, to what degree can the filmmakers exercise free will? This is fairly bold stuff, and grows wilder as the film moves along. The opening scenes do a good job of building conventional suspense, the middle scenes allow deeper alarm to creep in, and by the end we realize we're playthings of sinister forces.

Horror fans are a particular breed. They analyze films with such detail and expertise that I am reminded of the Canadian literary critic Northrop Frye, who approached literature with similar archetypal analysis. *The Cabin in the Woods* has been constructed almost as a puzzle for horror fans to solve. Which conventions are being toyed with? Which authors and films are being referred to? Is the film itself an act of criticism?

With most genre films, we ask, "Does it work?" In other words, does this horror film scare us? *The Cabin in the Woods* does have some genuine scares, but they're not really the point. This is like a final exam for fanboys.

## Captain America: The First Avenger ★ ★ ★

PG-13, 125 m., 2011

Chris Evans (Captain America/Steve Rogers), Hayley Atwell (Peggy Carter), Sebastian Stan (Bucky Barnes), Tommy Lee Jones (Colonel Chester Phillips), Hugo Weaving (Schmidt/Red Skull), Dominic Cooper (Howard Stark), Richard Armitage (Heinz Kruger), Stanley Tucci (Dr. Abraham Erskine), Samuel L. Jackson (Nick Fury), Toby Jones (Dr. Arnim Zola). Directed by Joe Johnston and produced by Kevin Feige and Amir Madani. Screenplay by Christopher Markus and Stephen McFeely, inspired by the Marvel comic books.

It was a pleasure to realize, once *Captain America: The First Avenger* got under way, that hey, here was a real movie, not a noisy assembly of incomprehensible special effects. Of course it's loaded with CGI. It goes without saying it's preposterous. But it has the texture and takes the care to be a full-blown film. You know, like with a hero we care about and who has some dimension. And with weight to the story. As we plunge ahead into a limitless future of comic book movies, let this be an inspiration rather than *Thor* or *Green Lantern.*

The words *The First Avenger* are weighted with significance for Marvel fans. We have already had films inspired by Iron Man, the Hulk, and Thor. Still to come, without doubt, are Ant-Man and Wasp. This film opens with the discovery of an enormous flying wing embedded in polar ice, and when a gloved hand reaches out to brush away the ice on a window, why, there's Captain America's shield! The plot of this film involves his origin story and adventures during World War II, and I'm sure we'll discover in sequels that he was revived after the cryogenic nap to crusade again in the new day.

We open with an archetypal ninety-pound weakling; comic books of that period featured ads showing muscle men kicking sand into the faces of such specimens, who were advised to mail-order Charles Atlas for bodybuilding help. Young Steve Rogers (Chris Evans) is a puny Brooklyn kid who is routinely beat up on by bullies, and dreams of joining the army and defending America against the Nazis. Turned down as 4-F, he tries again and again to enlist, and eventually makes it into basic training, where he's always falling off the rope and bringing up the rear.

But the kid has courage. This attracts the attention of the hard-boiled Colonel Phillips (Tommy Lee Jones) and a scientist named Erskine (Stanley Tucci), who supervises a secret government program. In no time at all, and without really receiving any explanation, he's being strapped into an ominous sarcophagus in Erskine's laboratory, which emits sparks and smoke and eventually the new Steve Rogers, now a foot taller and built like Mr. Universe. He adopts a costume and a stars-and-stripes shield that serve primarily to make him highly visible, although the shield has special powers (but only when it's positioned correctly?).

Young Steve's army confidante both before and after his transformation is the sultry Peggy Carter (Hayley Atwell), whose full red lips make her resemble a classic military pinup of the period. He narrates their tour of the Brooklyn neighborhoods where he was picked on, and they grow close, but only PG-13 close, because Marvel has apparently determined that fanboys find sex to be icky.

Now the full-bodied story comes into play, involving, as all good comic book movies must, a really first-rate villain. This is a Nazi commandant named Johann Schmidt (Hugo Weaving), who essentially controls his own private army and has dreams of surpassing Hitler. His minions salute him, not *Der*

*Fuhrer*, and he has dreams of creating super weapons. Eventually, as the rules of comic book drama require, Captain America will pair off against Schmidt, who is revealed to actually be the hideous Red Skull, whose skin tone makes him resemble those ducks marinated in red sauce you sometimes see hanging in restaurant windows in Chinatown. Schmidt demonstrates once again that, when it comes to movie villains, you can't do better than Nazis.

The film pays full dues to Marvel mythology, providing Captain America with his sidekick, Bucky Barnes (Sebastian Stan), not such a kid as he was in the comics. We also meet Howard Stark (Dominic Cooper), who supports Erskine's research and will eventually, as we know, father Iron Man. And there is Nick Fury (Samuel L. Jackson), another World War II hero destined to graduate to his own comic book and, no doubt, movie. Jackson has the chops to play a first-rate superhero.

The adventures of Captain America are fabricated with first-rate CGI, and are slightly more reality-oriented than in most superhero movies—sad to say, they're still wildly absurd—but set up and delivered with more control. CGI makes another invaluable contribution to the movie by shrinking the six-foot Chris Evans into a vertically challenged ninety-pound weakling, and then expanding him dramatically into the muscular Captain America. This is done seamlessly and he's convincing at both sizes; I doubt there's a single shot in the movie that shows Evans as he really is.

I enjoyed the movie. I appreciated the 1940s period settings and costumes, which were a break with the usual generic cityscapes. I admired the way director Joe Johnston (*October Sky, Jumanji*) propelled the narrative. I got a sense of a broad story, rather than the impression of a series of sensational set pieces. If Marvel is wise, it will take this and *Iron Man* as its templates.

## Carlos ★ ★ ★ ½

NO MPAA RATING, 165 m., 2010

Edgar Ramirez (Carlos), Juana Acosta (Girlfriend), Alexander Scheer (Johannes Weinrich), Nora von Waldstatten (Magdalena Kopp), Ahmad Kaabour (Wadie Haddad), Christoph Bach (Hans-Joachim Klein), Rodney El-Haddad (Khalid), Julia Hummer (Nada). Directed by Olivier Assayas and produced by Jens Meurer. Screenplay by Assayas and Dan Franck.

The man known as Carlos the Jackal said that Marxism was his religion and he was dedicated to the Palestinian cause. Having seen the long version of Olivier Assayas's remarkable *Carlos*, I conclude that for Carlos, his religion and his cause were the same, and they were himself. This is a terrifying portrait of an egomaniac who demands absolute obedience, and craves it even more when his power and relevance are drained away. All he has left at the end are a few pathetic nonentities who obey him.

If Carlos is a shabby excuse for a great man, *Carlos* is nonetheless a powerful film from recent history, considering in (largely fictionalized) detail how the myth of Carlos shadowed the years from 1975, when he led a raid on OPEC oil ministers in Vienna, until 1994, when he was betrayed by former comrades, arrested in Sudan, and returned to France for trial. He is now serving a life sentence, and from prison has complained that this film is inaccurate.

I have no knowledge of the real Carlos and can only review the film. On that basis, Ilich Ramirez Sanchez, a Venezuelan born in 1949 and educated at a Cuban training camp and Patrice Lumumba University in Moscow, used his ideology primarily to dominate others and excuse his megalomania. Toward the end, even his superiors in the Palestinian liberation movement were fed up with him, and after exhausting the hospitality of Libya, Syria, and Iraq, he became a man without a country.

Carlos is played by Edgar Ramirez, an actor of great vitality and conviction. I learn he speaks five languages, and in *Carlos* he performs dialogue in even more, as he functions in France, Spain, Germany, Egypt, Iraq, Russia, and North Africa. (The film is largely in English, the international language of terrorism.) Without using any apparent makeup tricks, he successfully ages from a young hothead to a middle-age "Syrian businessman" with a nice little pot belly, while passing through a period when he is lean and muscular after guerrilla training. His sideburns flourish and disappear, beards and mustaches come and go, and yet clearly he is Carlos if you take a good look at him. He passed through countless passport controls where apparently nobody did, although once years ago at London Heathrow I was pulled aside on suspicion of being Carlos. He ran on the plump side, for a jackal.

In notes and anonymous phone calls taking blame (or "credit") for bombings, murders, and missile attacks, he identified his group as "the armed branch of the Palestinian Liberation Struggle." I have no idea what the reality was. In the film, this organization seems to consist largely of himself as the autarch of a small group of submissive followers who had loose connections with better-organized cells in Germany and France. He was well financed by mischievous governments, including Russia, East Germany, and Iraq; shipped crates of weapons by using diplomatic immunity; and lived in swank hotels or sometimes in safe houses or borrowed apartments.

His "operations" seem almost anarchic. He and his followers have the strategy of walking in armed and doing what they intend. In a public observation area at an airport, surrounded by others, they attempt to deploy a rocket launcher to blow up airplanes. Their getaway strategy usually comes down to get the hell outta there. He got his nickname from the Frederick Forsyth novel *The Day of the Jackal*, but the hero of the excellent Fred Zinnemann film of that name takes meticulous care in his planning. Carlos seems impulsive. It's extraordinary how long he survived on the run.

His major operation was the OPEC raid. He took forty-two hostages and demanded an airplane to take them to Algiers. That led to an odyssey on to Baghdad and Tripoli before returning to Algiers. Assayas is at his best showing this undertaking, during which Carlos fails to execute two of the oil ministers as ordered and is berated by his superior in the movement, Wadie Haddad (Ahmad Kaabour). Then as later, his personal fame and publicity were felt to distract from the focus of the Popular Front for the Liberation of Palestine.

Did he care deeply about Palestine? I get the impression that he cared deeply about seeming to care deeply. His personality would have been equally well suited to any other revolutionary struggle. He hated any authority except his own, and granted himself life and death power over others because—well, because he was Carlos. Given the opportunity, he might have made a Stalin, Hitler, or Pol Pot.

Much of the film is devoted to the periods between action. We meet the private Carlos, whose sexuality depends on the conquest and domination of women. He is enabled by a long-suffering girlfriend and wife, Magdalena Kopp (Nora von Waldstatten), before they have a child and she walks out for the child's sake. Also by a series of mistresses, especially Nada (Julia Hummer), who stands by him during a painful illness with a testicular tumor. It is an insight into Carlos's ego that he postponed tumor surgery for a more important operation: liposuction.

That he satisfies women sexually there seems no doubt. They accept, not always happily, his many affairs with others, including prostitutes. He is such a great man he is exempt from ordinary behavior. All along the way he is accompanied by his sidekick Hans-Joachim Klein (Christoph Bach), an uncertain man with a wispy mustache, who has a way of drinking himself unconscious, not a valuable trait in a terrorist. When the two of them party with hookers in East Berlin, they're too naive to suspect they're plants by the secret police.

*Carlos* exists in three formats. The theatrical version runs 165 minutes; there's a road-show version in two parts totaling 332 minutes. The full three-part miniseries, totaling 5:35, played on the Sundance Channel. I saw the longest, and I was not bored. Olivier Assayas doesn't make the mistake of wearing us out with action, which in excess is simply boring; he's fascinated by the minutiae of daily routine in the life of a wanted and hated man.

There is a detail I must mention. I have never seen more smoking in a movie. Every character smokes heavily, and Carlos constantly, indeed distractingly. No doubt this is based on fact, but what does Assayas mean by depicting it so pointedly? It shows Carlos addicted to quick and constant fixes. He never shows any pleasure in smoking. He simply has to do it. It may be a metaphor for terrorism.

## Carnage ★ ★ ★

R, 79 m., 2012

Jodie Foster (Penelope Longstreet), Kate Winslet (Nancy Cowan), Christoph Waltz (Alan Cowan), John C. Reilly (Michael Longstreet). Directed by Roman Polanski and produced by Said Ben Said. Screenplay by Polanski and Yasmina Reza, based on her play *God of Carnage.*

Roman Polanski's *Carnage* involves time spent by two married couples in a luxurious Manhattan condo as afternoon fades into evening. The film is very well named. We have seen this dramatic trajectory before, where smooth politeness relentlessly erodes into foul-mouthed imprecations, but the point isn't the plot anyway, it's the performances. Here four familiar actors seem ideally cast for their roles.

The condo belongs to Penelope and Michael Longstreet (Jodie Foster and John C. Reilly). In the film's opening scene, in long shots so we can't tell the rights from the wrongs, their boy Zachary is hit with a stick by a school friend. The stick was swung by the son of Alan and Nancy Cowan (Christoph Waltz and Kate Winslet). Both boys are eleven. This has inspired the visit by the Cowans to discuss the regrettable incident, which in another social milieu might be considered just one of those things that kids get themselves into.

Not these people. They are rich (considering the apartment). Michael sells kitchen implements, countless ones, it would appear. Alan is a lawyer whose life cannot be conducted without frequent and urgent cell phone calls. Their kids go to the same expensive school, and the details of their lives are carefully ordered in upper-middle (or lower-upper?) class taste. At the beginning their performance is designed to indicate they are decent and civilized and can work this thing out.

"Performance" is the correct word. *Carnage* has been adapted by Polanski and Yasmina Reza from her Tony Award–winning play *God of Carnage,* and no particular effort is made by Polanski to open it up. The action all takes place in that apartment and its hallway, with the Cowans occasionally getting as much of a show inside the elevator before an unfortunate remark draws them back inside. Plays like this work particularly well within the space and time constraints of a stage. I'm not sure it called out to be filmed.

The progress of the action is meticulously modulated. The Cowans have sent ahead a bouquet of expensive yellow tulips. Penelope Longstreet has baked a cobbler. Tea is served. The problem is that all four adults are compelled to assign guilt in the incident. I believe it likely that the two boys (never seen again after the opening scene) stumbled into an unfortunate and trivial shoving match in which either could easily have held the stick and either have lost the teeth. That's not good enough for the two couples.

There's a macabre interest in watching the level of civility decrease in the room. Polanski pays much attention to the modulation of dialogue and body language. Alliances are formed and broken; the men and women at times side with each other, until the couples fall back into opposition. Certain regrettable words are introduced which can be interpreted as inflammatory, and all four characters are very alert to listen for them.

Step by step, the occasion disintegrates. One character eventually makes himself right at home by sitting on the floor instead of the sofa. Tulips and cobbler are hurled, in more ways than one. Did I mention that whiskey had been introduced? And Cuban cigars? (During the male bonding stage.)

This is not a particularly memorable film, but Polanski brings a great deal of skill to its staging, and it looks as if the actors enjoy themselves. It's not every seventy-nine-minute movie that allows all four characters to hurtle through a full gamut of emotions. The message, if any, is that good manners are often skin deep, that compassion and forgiveness are hard to come by, and that when it comes down to your son and my son, I'm going to consider my son in the right, and yours, well, possibly, a homicidal maniac.

## Cars 2 ★ ★ ★ ½

G, 107 m., 2011

With the voices of Larry the Cable Guy (Mater), Owen Wilson (Lightning McQueen), Michael

Caine (Finn McMissile), Emily Mortimer (Holley Shiftwell), Eddie Izzard (Miles Axlerod), John Turturro (Francesco Bernoulli). Directed by John Lasseter, codirected by Brad Lewis, and produced by Denise Ream. Screenplay by Ben Queen.

While I was watching *Cars 2*, an elusive nostalgia tugged at my mind. No, I wasn't remembering Pixar's original *Cars* from 2006. This was something more deeply buried, and finally, in the middle of one of the movie's sensational grand prix races, it came to me: I was sitting on the floor of my bedroom many years ago, some toy cars lined up in front of me, while I used my hands to race them around on the floor and in the air, meanwhile making that noise kids make by squooshing spit in their mouths.

In this memory I was completely engrossed with my cars. They were as real as people, and I played favorites and identified one car as my surrogate. Maybe my hands were swooping around with toys, but my imagination was somewhere else, and I performed the dialogue for the cars: "Oh yeah?" "Take that!" "We'll see!" "Eeeeyowww!"

This memory was not random. I think it was inspired by the spirit of John Lasseter's movie. I believe in some sense the great animator was sitting Indian style on the floor of his Pixar playroom and hurtling his cars through time and space with sublime, reckless delight. We learned from *Cars* that Lasseter loves automobiles, and here we learn that they can serve him as avatars in an international racing-and-spying thriller as wacky as a Bond picture crossed with Daffy Duck.

I have no idea what kids will make of the movie. At a time when some "grown-up" action films are relentlessly shallow and stupid, here is a movie with such complexity that even the cars sometimes have to pause and explain it to themselves. It mixes concerns about fossil fuels with spy craft and a lot of grand prix racing where more is at stake than who wins. And it has a new hero: The shiny red Lightning McQueen (voice by Owen Wilson) is eclipsed by a rusty, buck-toothed tow truck named Mater (Larry the Cable Guy), who was only a supporting vehicle in the first film.

A plot synopsis would spin us into bafflements, and the movie isn't about a plot so much as the action it involves. Briefly, Sir Miles Axlerod (Eddie Izzard) has invented a new fuel that doesn't deplete the planet's shrinking oil reserves, and wants to prove it in a World Grand Prix to be run in England, Japan, and Italy. This is a masterful way of introducing new backdrops into the races, and the movie is so visually complex that I imagine Lasseter and his colleagues slipped details in just for fun.

At one point, in a shot so brief you don't want to blink, we even learn that the Popemobile travels in its own Popemobile. This inspires the theological puzzle of whether the one inside is the pope. One of my fellow viewers said she didn't even see a Popemobile. Maybe I dreamed it. In any event, there are no humans in the movie who could be the pope, although much is made of the dinosaurs who are a source of fossil fuels. Actually, I believe oil originated from ancient plants and microorganisms and not so much from dinosaurs, but in the Lasseter universe, it no doubt comes from gas-guzzling dinosaurs like in those old Rambler ads.

But I digress. Lightning McQueen ends up in a championship duel with the Italian car Francesco Bernoulli (John Turturro at full throttle). He and Mater the tow truck find themselves in the middle of a clandestine war between the forces of fossil and alternative fuels, also involving the British secret agents Finn McMissile (Michael Caine) and Holley Shiftwell (Emily Mortimer). Having recently admired Steve Coogan and Rob Brydon doing dueling Michael Caine imitations in *The Trip*, I noted that Michael Caine does a pretty good one himself.

The original film was an elegy to a past when America spun out along Route 66 and now-classic cars occupied an iconic role in American lives. The cars in *Cars 2* have developed an array of new bells and whistles; they extrude so many wires, spikes, weapons, and gimmicks they must really be shape-shifters, and Mater in particular is expert at disguising himself. This is not surprising because a lot of the guys you find around tow trucks are pretty good using paint jobs to dress up beaters.

Anyway, *Cars 2* is fun. Whether that's because John Lasseter is in touch with his inner child or mine, I cannot say. There remains one bone to pick. Although the hero of the 2006 film was a Hudson with the step-down design and there are AMC Gremlins in this film, as nearly as I can tell you, Lasseter entirely ignores the greatest independent American automaker of them all, Studebaker. Maybe I missed one. Maybe I stepped out to pee. I don't think so. There is a more obvious reason. Introducing a Studebaker Golden Hawk into this film would make all of the other characters look shabby.

## Casa de Mi Padre ★ ★

R, 84 m., 2012

Will Ferrell (Armando), Gael Garcia Bernal (Onza), Diego Luna (Raul), Genesis Rodriguez (Sonia), Pedro Armendariz Jr. (Miguel Ernesto), Nick Offerman (DEA Agent Parker), Efren Ramirez (Esteban), Adrian Martinez (Manuel). Directed by Matt Piedmont and produced by Emilio Diez Barroso, Jessica Elbaum, Will Ferrell, Darlene Caamano Loquet, Adam McKay, and Kevin J. Messick. Screenplay by Andrew Steele.

*Casa de Mi Padre* is a cheeky comedy by Will Ferrell and his compadres at *Saturday Night Live* and the Web site Funny or Die. And when I say "cheeky," it's what you're thinking second. The movie has more butt groping than anything this side of the Rio Grande. And the other side.

Ferrell and the entire cast perform entirely in Spanish, and Ferrell sings a song that has already gone viral on YouTube. He sounds perfectly fluent to me, but then, how would I know? The movie is a jolly send-up of horse operas on Telemundo, which I have never seen, but my lack of qualifications isn't fatal because the movie hopes to do crossover business in addition to its obvious target audience.

What possessed Ferrell to make this satire? My guess is, he got straight As in Spanish and has spent years asking himself how that will further his career. Another possibility: He's made a lot of genre spoofs, and why stop now?

Ferrell stars as Armando, the goodhearted, slow-witted son of a macho rancher (the legendary Pedro Armendariz Jr., who died in 2011). His father fawns on Armando's sleek, successful brother Raul (Diego Luna), who all of his life has gotten everything right that Armando got wrong. So feckless is Armando, indeed, that he has never felt the love of a woman. But when Raul returns home with the ravishing Sonia (Genesis Rodriguez), Armando and Sonia need no more than to meet eyes and the earth trembles with their instinctive passion.

What the old man doesn't suspect is that his ideal son is actually a drug dealer in cahoots with the dastardly drug lord Onza (Gael Garcia Bernal). Poor, innocent Sonia doesn't know this either, and so it is up to Armando to save Sonia from the two scumbags and restore the honor of the family name.

This is done in a film that quietly kids many of the technical shortcomings of low-rent Westerns, in particular the way they use backdrops and special effects to cover the lack of location shooting. Armando and Sonia, for example, ride side by side in a shot that doesn't show their horses, and the background slides past at a different speed than the horses are apparently galloping.

The movie is only 84 minutes long, including credit cookies, but that is quite long enough. All the same, it's fitfully amusing, and I have the sense that Spanish-speaking audiences will like it more than I did, although whether they'll be laughing with it or at it, I cannot say.

## Casino Jack ★ ★ ★

R, 108 m., 2010

Kevin Spacey (Jack Abramoff), Barry Pepper (Michael Scanlon), Kelly Preston (Pam Abramoff), Rachelle Lefevre (Emily Miller), Jon Lovitz (Adam Kidan), Maury Chaykin (Big Tony). Directed by George Hickenlooper and produced by Gary Howsam, Bill Marks, and George Zakk. Screenplay by Norman Snider.

Political movies often play cute in drawing parallels with actual figures. They drop broad hints that a character is "really" Dick Cheney or Bill Clinton and so on. *Casino Jack* is so forthright it is stunning. The film is "inspired by real events," and the characters in this film have the names of the people in those real events: Jack Abramoff, Michael Scanlon, Representative Tom DeLay, Ralph Reed, Karl

Rove, George W. Bush, Representative Bob Ney, and Senator John McCain.

This decision to name names by the director George Hickenlooper seems based on boldness, recklessness, or perhaps iron-clad legal assurances. His film uses a fictional sledgehammer to attack the cozy love triangle involving lobbyists, lawmakers, and money. It stars Kevin Spacey in an exact and not entirely unsympathetic performance as Abramoff, once one of the most powerful lobbyists in Washington, who was convicted on charges involving the funds he stole from wealthy Indian casinos while arranging laws for their convenience on Capitol Hill.

The first press screening of the film at the Toronto International Film Festival was witnessed in a sort of stunned silence by a capacity audience, interrupted slightly by an undercurrent of incredulous murmurs and soft laughter when Spacey, as Abramoff, in a fantasy sequence, explodes at a Senate hearing being chaired by McCain. Having invoked the Fifth Amendment repeatedly, he's unable to restrain himself any longer and jumps to his feet to accuse the very members of the panel of having taken campaign contributions and favors from his Indian clients, and voting in their favor. Abramoff shows some degree of honor among thieves by not pulling such a stunt.

Astonishingly, Hickenlooper intercuts real footage of the real hearing and the real John McCain with Spacey's performance. Can he get away with this? I guess so. The distributors, ATO, have no doubt had the film scrutinized by their attorneys. Apart from that, there's the likelihood (which lawyers may think but cannot say) that no one named in this film is very likely to sue. The Abramoff scandal was called at the time the biggest since Watergate (both were broken by the *Washington Post*), but in the years since his sentencing in 2006, his name has faded from everyday reference, and it's doubtful anyone desires to make it current again. With Alex Gibney's current doc *Casino Jack and the United States of Money* also around, those deep waters are being sufficiently stirred.

The film's story line can be briefly summarized: The lobbyist Abramoff was a dutiful family man and Republican standard bearer who defrauded Indian tribes out of millions to lobby for their casinos. That enriched him and his partner, Michael Scanlon (Barry Pepper), and a good many members of Congress, not all of them Republicans. He worked out every day, was an observant member of his temple, and a smooth and elegant dresser. And somehow at his core there were no principles and no honesty.

If Casino Jack put up a good front, George Hickenlooper's film is merciless with Scanlon, a venal and vulgar man with the effrontery to flaunt his corruption. It is Spacey's performance that contains most of the mystery of the movie, because although Abramoff's actions left little room for justification, in Spacey's performance there is some. He used much of the stolen money for good works, which made him appear charitable. His principal charity was himself, but there you are.

There are scenes here that make you wonder why the Abramoff scandals (plural) didn't outshine Watergate as the day does the night. Within Abramoff there is some small instinct for simple justice, and the film's most dramatic scene comes as he snaps at that hearing, ignores his lawyer, forgets the Fifth Amendment, and tells the panel members to their faces that they were happy to take his cash.

The overall message of *Casino Jack* has become familiar. Corporate and industry lobbyists are the real rulers in Washington, and their dollars are the real votes. Both parties harbor corruption, the Republicans grabbing the breasts and thighs, the Democrats pleased to have the drumsticks and wings. Jack Abramoff didn't invent this system. He simply gamed it until Scanlon's boldness betrayed them and another generation of lobbyists took over. Have you heard the banks are broke again?

## Catfish ★ ★ ★

PG-13, 86 m., 2010

Nev Schulman, Ariel Schulman, Henry Joost, Angela Pierce, Vince Pierce, and Abby Pierce. A documentary directed by Ariel Schulman and Henry Joost and produced by Schulman, Joost, Andrew Jarecki, and Marc Smerling.

Here's one way to look at *Catfish:* Some filmmakers in New York City, who think they're way cool, get taken apart by an ordinary family in Ishpeming, Michigan. You can also view it as a cautionary tale about living your emotional life on the Internet. Or possibly the whole thing is a hoax. At Sundance 2010, the filmmakers were given a severe cross-examination and protested their innocence, and indeed everyone in the film is exactly as the film portrays them.

To go into detail about that statement would involve spoiling the film's effect for you. I won't do that because the effect is rather lovely. There's a point when you may think you know what I'm referring to, but you can't appreciate it until closer to the end. The facts in the film are slippery, but the revelation of a human personality is surprisingly moving.

The film opens in the Manhattan office of Nev Schulman, Ariel Schulman, and Henry Joost, who make videos and photographs of modern dancers. I'm going to guess they're thirtyish. Nev has received a painting of one of his photographs from Abby Pierce, an eight-year-old girl. They enter into a correspondence—or, more accurately, Abby's mom, Angela Pierce, e-mails for her. Just as well. Would you want your eight-year-old daughter in a chat room with some strange adult Facebook friend?

Never mind. Nev, a wholesome, even naive man, is touched by Abby's paintings, and begins to identify with the whole family. He learns of school plans, pie baking, Sunday family breakfast, and the horse farm Abby's nineteen-year-old sister, Megan, is buying. I doubted that detail. It would take a New Yorker to believe horse farms in Michigan are cheap enough for a nineteen-year-old to buy. She could afford a horse, farm not included.

Nev and Megan correspond and talk on the phone. Megan composes songs for Nev. They begin a cyber-romance. Nev begins to wonder if this could possibly be the girl for him. There are dozens of photos on her Facebook site, and he even starts using software to put himself and Megan in the same photos. In anyone over, oh, fourteen, this is a sign of immaturity, wouldn't you say?

The three videographers have to fly to Vail to shoot a dance event. On the way back east, they decide to make a detour to Ishpeming. Were they born yesterday? Do they think you drop in unannounced on strangers? Using ever-helpful GPS navigation, they pay a midnight visit to Megan's horse farm, and find . . . no horses. In Ishpeming they do indeed find the Pierce home and family, and I suppose are welcomed with as much grace as possible under the circumstances.

The key to the human qualities in the film can be found in Angela, the mother, and in a couple of thoughtful statements by Vince, the father. You'll see what I mean. Living in Ishpeming may not be the ideal choice for people with an artistic temperament. I haven't been there and can't say. But this family has adapted to realities and found ways of expression, and who are we to say making dance videos in New York is preferable?

Angela Pierce comes across as an essentially good person, as complex as the heroine of a novel. At the end of the day, I believe she humbles Nev and his friends. I wonder if they agree. They all seem to be nice people. Let's agree on this: We deserve to share happiness in this world, and if we supply it in the way it's sought and nobody gets hurt, is that a bad thing?

*Note: Angela Pierce's Web site is at http://www.artbyapierce.com.*

## Cave of Forgotten Dreams ★ ★ ★ ½

NO MPAA RATING, 90 m., 2011

A documentary directed by Werner Herzog and produced by Adrienne Ciuffo and Erik Nelson. Screenplay by Herzog.

About thirty-two thousand years ago, in a limestone cave above the Ardeche River in southern France, humans created the oldest cave paintings known to exist. They spring from the walls with boldness and confidence, as if the artists were already sure what they wanted to paint and how to paint it. Perhaps twenty-five thousand years ago, a child visited the cave and left a footprint, the oldest human footprint that can be accurately dated. At some time after the child's visit, a rock slide sealed the entrance to the cave. In 1994, French archaeologists, searching for air plumes that might reveal the presence of a cave, found it again.

They had to descend a narrow opening to

its floor, far below on the original entrance level. It is their entry route that Werner Herzog follows in his spellbinding new film, *Cave of Forgotten Dreams.* Herzog filmed in 3-D to better convey how the paintings follow and exploit the natural contours of the ancient walls. The process also helps him suggest how the humans of the Upper Paleolithic era might have seen the paintings themselves, in the flickering light of their torches.

Access to Chauvet Cave, named for one of its discoverers, was immediately closed off by the French government, and a locked steel door now bars the way to the air shaft. Behind that door the cave's guardians enforce a strict regime. Herzog is allowed a four-man crew, including himself. They are limited to four cold-panel lights, powered from battery belts. They dare step only on two-foot-wide aluminum pathways that have been installed. They are allowed four hours. If anyone has to leave for any reason—even to get a screwdriver—that day's visit is over; the guardians want to shield the cave's air supply.

Surely men must have been painting somewhere before these cave walls were covered. It is hard to believe that these confident lines and shapes came into being without prelude. Or was there something innate in these forms? Accurate carbon dating suggests that other artists returned to the cave at least two thousand years after the first ones, and continued the work in the same style.

Only two very small sculptures in the cave show human forms. One is a woman, her sexual organs exaggerated to dramatize her fertility. The paintings themselves are all of animals, an astonishing variety, providing a bestiary of the valley at the time. Mammoths, cave bears, lions, bison, panthers, horses, rhinos. The rhinos have what are surely exaggerated horns, suggesting a desire to emphasize their power. Some of the drawings repeat horns and legs in an obvious attempt to depict movement.

In addition to the footprint, there are poignant signs that humans were here. Near the original entrance, where outside light was still present, many visitors left their palm prints on a wall in red ochre. Were these the artists' marks? Calling cards? Why did many leave them? A palm print stands out: One man had a damaged little finger. Farther back in the cave, they found another mark with the same finger. His two visits and a child's footprint remain after twenty-five millennia.

Herzog's limitation of four small portable light panels works to his advantage; as they move they suggest how the flickering torches might have created an illusion of movement in those repeated features. The space was so limited it was impossible for his crew to stay out of many shots, and their shadows dance on the walls, just as the shadows of forgotten ancestors must have danced in the torchlight. Herzog's inspiration is to show us the paintings as the cave's original visitors must have seen them. I have seen perfectly lighted photographs of other cave paintings that are not so evocative.

Herzog says that in general he dislikes 3-D. But he believes there are occasions when 3-D is appropriate, and his film is one of them. It was shown with bright, well-focused digital projection. Apart from a one-shot joke at the very end, he never allows his images to violate the theater space; he uses 3-D as a way for us to enter the film's space, instead of a way for it to enter ours. He was correct to realize how useful it would be in photographing these walls. To the degree that it's possible for us to walk behind Herzog into that cave, we do so.

*Note: Based on my blog entry from the Toronto 2010 film festival.*

## Cedar Rapids ★ ★ ★

R, 87 m., 2011

Ed Helms (Tim Lippe), John C. Reilly (Dean Ziegler), Anne Heche (Joan Ostrowski-Fox), Sigourney Weaver (Miss Vanderhei), Isiah Whitlock Jr. (Ronald Wilkes), Stephen Root (Bill Krogstad), Kurtwood Smith (Orin Helgesson), Alia Shawkat (Bree), Rob Corddry (Gary). Directed by Miguel Arteta and produced by Jim Burke, Alexander Payne, and Jim Taylor. Screenplay by Phil Johnston.

You are making the mistake of thinking of Cedar Rapids as a small town. In *Cedar Rapids*, a sweet comedy with a dirty mind, it is the metropolis, a sinkhole of sex, sin, and high living at an annual insurance industry convention. Into this pit of depravity descends the innocent and naive Tim Lippe (Ed Helms), who never before in his life has left his hometown of Brown Valley, Wisconsin.

Helms, from *The Office*, is assigned to take the big trip after his boss dies in embarrassing circumstances. His character is a bachelor who still lives in his childhood home, although excitement has recently entered his life with his first affair. Yes, he's sleeping with his grade school teacher Miss Vanderhei, who is played by Sigourney Weaver as a woman who has seen it all—if it's in Brown Valley, anyway.

Lippe's assignment: Attend the convention and come home with the coveted Two Diamonds Award. I immediately flashed on the older son in *Gates of Heaven*, sitting proudly behind and in front of plaques and statuettes and observing that he is displaying "the maximum trophies" to impress young recruits into—yes, it was the insurance business there, too. Apparently, the folks in Brown Valley prefer to deal with Two Diamonds winners.

The coveted award is the gift of Orin Helgesson (Kurtwood Smith), a mighty figure at the convention. I recall from my days as a cub reporter the self-importance of "industry legends" who lovingly spoke at length to their captive audiences. Helgesson is very public with his piety, and it would be a disaster if he discovers how Lippe's boss died. Lippe's job is to stay out of trouble. Since he doesn't smoke or drink and his sexual adventures are possibly limited to Miss Vanderhei, this should be easy.

The director, Miguel Arteta, understands that real laughter grows from characters. He has a rich start with Lippe, played by Helms as a man who is thrilled even to go through security at the airport. He calls Miss Vanderhei with breathless reports that his hotel has a swimming pool and that there is, gasp, an African-American in his room! This turns out to be his roommate, Ronald Wilkes (Isiah Whitlock Jr.), who is an old hand at the convention and a useful ally. His other roommate, Dean Ziegler (John C. Reilly), is trouble—a hard-drinking womanizer and client poacher.

Now we know the story arc. Ziegler will lead Lippe into temptation, Wilkes will try to caution him, Orin Helgesson will be outraged, and the hotel pool will be involved in an unseemly way. All of this works out to be pretty funny, especially with the intervention of the sexy Joan Ostrowski-Fox (Anne Heche), whose trips to the convention are the highlight of her sex life, I hope.

*Cedar Rapids* has something of the same spirit of *Fargo* in its approach to the earnest natures of its small-towners. The two films, otherwise so different, like their characters. Some of them do unspeakable things, especially in *Fargo*, but none of them *want* to be evil. They just hope to get out in one piece.

It is a relief, for example, that Reilly's Dean Ziegler isn't a malicious buffoon, but simply a nice guy, terminally immature. And Ed Helms makes an ideal leading man because he always seems to be searching for someone to stand behind. The problem with so many madcap comedies is that their heroes cannot fully embrace cluelessness. It is funnier for a second banana to play the lead than for a lead to pretend to second bananahood.

## Cell 211 ★ ★ ★ ½

NO MPAA RATING, 111 m., 2010

Luis Tosar (Malamadre), Alberto Ammann (Juan Oliver), Antonio Resines (Jose Utrilla), Manuel Moron (Ernesto Almansa), Marta Etura (Elena), Carlos Bardem (Apache). Directed by Daniel Monzon and produced by Alvaro Augustin, Juan Gordon, and Borja Pena. Screenplay by Monzon and Jorge Guerricaechevarria, based on the novel by Francisco Perez Gandul.

*Cell 211* is a thriller about a man's attempt to save his life by thinking quickly. It never explains. It simply sets out the situation and shows us what he does and what the results are. You might be surprised by how much more exciting this is than conventional action.

The film won eight Goya awards, the Spanish Oscars, this year. It deserves them. In addition to its effectiveness as a thriller, it is also a film showing a man in the agonizing process of changing his values. And it is a critique of a cruel penal system. It doesn't preach, it doesn't end with a message, but it makes us think.

The story involves Juan Oliver (Alberto Ammann), a serious young man who reports a day early for his new job as a prison guard.

We spend a little time with him at home with his wife, Elena (Marta Etura). She is pregnant. They are head over heels in love. They don't have much money, but his new job will be a big help.

As other guards are taking him on a tour of the prison, he is knocked unconscious in an accident. They carry him to a bunk in an empty cell, Cell 211, and are calling for help when a violent prison riot breaks out. Their lives are in danger, and they must leave him behind when they flee. He regains consciousness and hears what is going on outside. He doesn't know why he's been left behind—he probably doesn't recall the falling debris that knocked him unconscious—but he knows his shoes, shoelaces, and belt are fatal giveaways that he's not a prisoner.

And now we enter into real time with him, as he boldly walks into a public area and passes himself off as a new prisoner who was admitted only shortly before. The rioting prisoners are desperate. They're led by a brutal strongman, a lifer with nothing to lose named Malamadre (Luis Tosar). Juan reads the situation immediately and improvises. Instinctively he takes the role of a man siding with his fellow prisoners. When he makes canny strategic suggestions, he seems to prove his worth.

I don't want to describe any more than that in specific terms. Those really would be spoilers because in *Cell 211* it is actually impossible to anticipate what will happen. The story follows no established formula. It discourages attempts at anticipation. It unfolds convincingly at every stage, but unpredictably. As Juan faces more stringent tests, he continues to improvise, sometimes devising masterstrokes.

The events in the cellblock are paralleled by two other stories: In the prison office, the warden and security staff monitor the security cameras. And in the city, Elena does some shopping and then learns of the riot in the prison where she knows her husband went that morning. Another strand consists of flashbacks to their loving moments together, which are much more effective dropped in like this than coming before everything.

The dynamic in the film happens between Juan and Malamadre. In a subtle way, the director, Daniel Monzon, shows an understanding developing. Malamadre is relentless and unforgiving, resentful when Juan takes the lead in making suggestions but admiring of the new man's courage. Very gradually, in the midst of the chaos, they exchange personal information. As Malamadre's understanding of the full situation changes, his interpretation of it keeps pace. He isn't a stupid man. Given his information, he makes logical decisions. When his information changes, he responds sanely and not without reason.

The term "mounting tension" is an overused cliché. To use it here would be appropriate. Little by little, one development at a time, the situation becomes more critical and the options for Juan and Malamadre grow more limited. And Juan's life always hangs in the balance. There is a moment, indeed, when he says something on a walkie-talkie that would have betrayed him if anyone had been listening.

The actors are well chosen. Luis Tosar, as Malamadre, is a powerful man, shorter than Juan but more muscular, his head shaved, his mustache and beard somehow ominous. Alberto Ammann, as Juan, is of medium build, not aggressive, a convincing mimic in the role he adopts. He is not too heroic and Tosar is not too villainous. They are trapped in this situation, and unwittingly they come to share it.

## Certifiably Jonathan ★

NO MPAA RATING, 80 m., 2011

Themselves: Jonathan Winters, Jeffrey Tambor, Ryan Stiles, Sarah Silverman, Rob Reiner, Gary Owens, Howie Mandel, Robert Klein, Jimmy Kimmel, Kevin Dunn, Nora Dunn, Tim Conway, Rosanna Arquette, Patricia Arquette, David Arquette, Robin Williams, Jim Carrey. Directed by Jim Pasternak and produced by Richard Marshall. Screenplay by Pasternak.

Jonathan Winters is a fine and funny fellow, and deserves better than this. Out of the goodness of his heart, he agreed to be at the center of a mockumentary directed by Jim Pasternak. The result is not merely a bad film, but a waste of an opportunity. As he approaches eighty-six, Winters is still active, still funny, enthusiastically involved in painting, and could have been the subject of a good film. This isn't it.

The mockumentary form has many possibilities. They usually depend on satirizing the tone and feeling of a genre. The simple fact that it's fake doesn't make one successful. This one purports to show Winters at a crucial moment in his late flowering as an artist, during which he gets a gallery opening, is championed by a famous art critic, and promised a show at the Museum of Modern Art. None of these nonevents is staged with style or conviction. They are simply walked through as if really happening.

At the gallery, one of his paintings is stolen from a wall and Winters goes into a depression, finding himself unable to paint. It was, you see, his favorite painting. Pasternak leads a team that includes Winters himself to go to the house of the alleged thief. The house is unlocked, they walk in and find the painting, and Winters can paint again. Is there anyone reading this who can't think of an approach that isn't so lame?

Consider, too, the "curator" at the Museum of Modern Art. She is a pleasant woman who looks at negatives of Winters's sub-Dali paintings through a little magnifier and declares him worthy of a show. No effort is made to make her character or her process funny.

It appears one reason for this film was for Pasternak to gain access to Jonathan Winters, spend an excess amount of time personally on camera, and use Winters as bait to lure his famous friends into the film. These include Robin Williams, Howie Mandel, Nora Dunn, Jim Carrey, Sarah Silverman, Tim Conway, Jeffrey Tambor, Jimmy Kimmel, Robert Klein, Ryan Stiles, Rob Reiner, Kevin Dunn, David Arquette, Patricia Arquette, and Rosanna Arquette.

All of these friends are seen briefly and forgettably. Only Robin Williams is funny. The others seem to be paying courtesy calls. With that much talent on the screen, it's significant that the funniest moments belong to Winters, seen on old TV shows.

Much is made, in the title and by Winters himself, of his history of bipolar disorder. It's assumed that today's audiences will know what's being referred to. In general, they won't. It's sad but true that many younger viewers won't quite know the range of Winters's brilliance. What would have been more appropriate: a tour through film and TV archives, memories of friends rather than testimonials, a real documentary instead of a fake one, and Jim Pasternak nowhere to be seen.

## Certified Copy ★ ★ ★ ½

NO MPAA RATING, 106 m., 2010

Juliette Binoche (Woman), William Shimell (James Miller). Directed by Abbas Kiarostami and produced by Kiarostami, Charles Gillibert, Marin Karmitz, and Nathanael Karmitz. Screenplay by Kiarostami.

*Certified Copy* invites us into an intriguing story and then strands us. Yes, we can consider various explanations for what we see, and yes, the film's mystery is apparently its purpose. For me, it is too clever by half, creating full-bodied characters but inserting them into a story that is thin soup. I enjoy puzzles like Antonioni's *Blow-Up* or *L'Avventura*, about characters who don't understand what has happened, but here there seems to be no underlying reality at all, and Abbas Kiarostami is playing with us. That he does it so well is a consolation.

A woman (Juliette Binoche) attends a lecture in Italy by an art historian (William Shimell). He speaks on the difference between original art and its copies. Is there, in fact, any difference? The woman would like to meet him. She leaves the address of her antiquities shop. He appears, they engage in talk that is immediately flirtatious, and she offers to drive him to a nearby village in Tuscany. In the course of the drive, and at a café after they get there, their apparent relationship seems to shift. The café owner hears them arguing, assumes they're married, and then they begin to behave as if they're married.

Which is the real relationship, and which is the counterfeit? Were they a couple pretending to meet for the first time, or a new couple pretending to be married? I believe that to begin with they are really meeting for the first time, and later they are really an established couple. Perhaps Kiarostami's intention is to demonstrate how the reality is whatever the artist chooses, and that he can transfer from original art to a copy in midstream. Or perhaps that's not possible. Perhaps I have no idea what he's demonstrating.

The woman, who is not named, and the historian, named James Miller, are articulate, playful, and devious. I enjoyed watching them, whatever they were up to. Binoche and Shimell always stay in the moment and never signal us what they're up to. Binoche seems so attracted to the man in the early scenes that it seems they must have some history. But it's certainly not the history they later seem to reveal. Throughout *Certified Copy* there's the sense of offscreen dimensions or untold side stories.

Kiarostami is rather brilliant in the way he creates offscreen spaces. Consider the opening scene. We clearly see that Binoche has a seat in the front row of the lecture hall, directly in front of the historian. Then the POV changes around to regard her, and we never see him again. Her son is standing at one side, trying to get her attention, eager to leave. She communicates with him using sign language and mouthing words. He comes over to her. She gives the man next to her a note with the address of her shop. She and the boy leave together.

All this commotion is taking place, distractingly, close in front of the speaker—but we never see him react! Kiarostami creates an implied drama involving what Miller *must* be experiencing, but refuses to see it. There's also implied offscreen activity during the long drive they take. The camera regards them through the windshield for extended dialogue passages, sometimes cutting to inside the car. Filming people as they drive is one of Kiarostami's trademarks, and I wonder why. It is a way to explain why you're showing two people side by side and looking ahead; if you put them on a park bench that would look odd. It's also a way to imply offscreen events on the road and involving the passing scenery.

What it comes down to is this: We assume there's more going on here than meets the eye, but maybe what meets the eye is *all* that's going on, and there is no complete, objective reality. Does that also apply to a copy of a masterpiece of art? Is a skillful copy of the *Mona Lisa* less valuable than the original painting? What if the original had been lost? Would we treasure the copy?

Such questions are raised by *Certified Copy* and not answered. Is raising them the point? Does Kiarostami know the answer? Does he care? At least we are engaged, and he does it well. Is that enough? I can explain *Blow-Up* and *L'Avventura* to my own satisfaction. This is the best I can do with *Certified Copy.* Perhaps it was wrong of me even to try.

## The Change-Up ★ ½

R, 101 m., 2011

Ryan Reynolds (Mitch Planko), Jason Bateman (Dave Lockwood), Leslie Mann (Jamie Lockwood), Olivia Wilde (Sabrina McArdle), Alan Arkin (Mitch's Dad). Directed by David Dobkin and produced by Dobkin and Neal H. Moritz. Screenplay by Jon Lucas and Scott Moore.

*The Change-Up* is one of the dirtiest-minded mainstream releases in history. It has a low opinion of men, a lower opinion of women, and the lowest opinion of the intelligence of its audience. It is obscene, foul-mouthed, scatological, creepy, and perverted. As a bonus, it has the shabbiest low-rent main titles I've seen this side of YouTube.

It is a body switch comedy. You remember those. There must have been dozens. Through some sort of magic, two characters find themselves occupying each other's bodies, or their own bodies at different ages. This can be charming, as when Tom Hanks did it in *Big* or Jodie Foster in *Freaky Friday.* And remember Francis Coppola's *Peggy Sue Got Married*, with Kathleen Turner becoming herself as a teenager.

To mention such movies in connection with this one is a sacrilege. Setting aside considerations of the story, *The Change-Up* sets out to violate and transgress as many standards of civilized conduct as it can. Don't get me wrong. Faithful readers know I treasure cheerful vulgarity. But readers, I've seen *The Hangover*, and this is no *Hangover.*

Here you will see projectile pooping into faces. Two men exposing themselves and urinating in a "magic fountain" in a shopping mall in the presence of small children. Three tattoo artists closely scrutinizing a woman's vagina. Women systematically required to bare their breasts. Language in which non-obscene words provide an oasis. Best buddies essentially sharing the same wife.

OK, OK. In the context of a different movie, I can imagine all of those things working in a comedy. Except the public pissing. I think we can all agree that's problematical. So let's get back to the bare breasts. There are a great many of them, frequently and roughly fondled, for one reason only, and it isn't eroticism. If it were, I would sympathize. It has to do with the systematic exploitation of every actress in a film where God forbid an actor would be asked to display his penis. (We don't see penises in the urination scene. Only the kids can.)

Now consider the leading characters. They are Mitch (Ryan Reynolds), a pothead layabout, and Dave (Jason Bateman), an attorney and father of three. They've been best friends since grade school. They envy each other's lives. Through pissing in the fountain, they switch bodies and find out what that would be like.

This involves Mitch, in Dave's body, moving in with Dave's wife, Jamie (Leslie Mann), and Dave involved in Mitch's budding career as a porn actor. There is also a key role for Sabrina (Olivia Wilde), a legal aide at the law firm, who seduces Dave in the body of Mitch.

Never mind who does what and with which and to whom. The problem is that the movie requires us to accept this premise by making the characters aggressively stupid. Assume for the moment you are Jamie. Two men appearing to be your husband and his buddy Mitch claim their minds are in each other's bodies. They tell you to ask them something the other guy wouldn't know. She asks "Mitch" what "his" wedding anniversary is. Of course he doesn't remember. But asking some men for their wedding anniversary is almost a gotcha! question. For women, a wedding anniversary is as ingrained as New Year's Day. For men, it is more like Easter, and you can never remember what day it falls on this year.

A few more questions, and the testing ends. Mitch and Dave give up and reconcile themselves to their fates. Dave moves into Mitch's bachelor pad. Mitch moves into Dave's suburban home. Say what? If you found your mind in another body, wouldn't that be profoundly disturbing? Would it leave you capable of performing the duties in a movie comedy?

One problem with the movie is that it requires us to constantly remind ourselves which of these two pleasant-looking thirty-somethings is which. Another problem is that no matter which, they are both low and crude beings with no respect for decency, and their language is foul beyond the call of fictional necessity. The film, in fact, seems to go out of its way to be vulgar and offensive, as if *adult* audiences crave such an assault. Anyone who enjoys this film cannot fairly be considered an adult. Pity about the R rating. It will keep out those callow enough to enjoy it.

## The Chaser ★ ★ ★ ½

NO MPAA RATING, 124 m., 2010

Kim Yoon-suk (Jung-ho), Jung-woo Ha (Young-min), Seo Young-hee (Mi-jin), Koo Bon-woong (Meathead). Directed by Na Hong-jin and produced by Choi Moon-su. Screenplay by Na Hong-jin, Hong Won-chan, and Lee Shin-ho.

*The Chaser* is an expert serial killer film from South Korea and a poster child for what a well-made thriller looked like in the classic days. Its principal chase scene involves a foot race through the deserted narrow nighttime streets of Seoul. No exploding cars. The climax is the result of everything that has gone before. Not an extended fight scene. This is drama, and it is interesting. Action for its own sake is boring.

The film is a police procedural with a difference: The hero is an ex-cop named Jung-ho (Kim Yoon-suk), now a pimp, and he is not a nice man. He is angered because a client of his call-girl service has been, he believes, kidnapping his girls and selling them. When another girl disappears, a phone number raises an alarm, and he sets out to track down the client—who didn't give an address but arranged a street rendezvous.

What we know is that the client, Young-min (Ha Jung-woo), is a sadistic murderer. The girl, named Mi-jin (Seo Young-hee), is driven in his car to an obscure address that she is not intended to ever leave alive. It is a characteristic of South Korean films that they display the grisly details of violence without flinching; the rights to this film have been picked up by Warner Bros., and it's dead certain the violence and the shocking outcome itself will be greatly toned down. Let me simply note that Young-min's tools of choice are a hammer and a chisel, for reasons a police psychiatrist has much to say about.

The film's structure is relentless in maintaining suspense. We have reason to suspect the prostitute may still be alive, but dying. Both the pimp and the killer are arrested. A ludicrous attack on the mayor of Seoul becomes a media sensation and puts pressure on the cops to charge someone with something to change the headlines. The killer, a calm psychopath, claims first nine murders, then twelve, but changes his story and says he has no idea what he did with the bodies. He's released on lack of evidence.

The story is an exercise in audience manipulation, especially with the corruption and incompetence of the police. The director, Na Hong-jin, knows exactly what he's doing. Like the master, Hitchcock, he gives the audience precisely enough information to be frustrated. It is obvious to us what the characters should be doing, but there are excellent reasons why it isn't obvious to them. If you can contrive that in a screenplay, you have already surpassed the level of the modern thriller.

Another strength of the film is in its attention to characters. The killer is seen as a mental dead zone, a man without conscience to whom good and evil are equally meaningless. The pimp begins as a merchant of sex, goes looking for Young-min for simple mercenary reasons, and very gradually expands his concerns in response to the presence of the call girl's young daughter. The daughter follows the Glossary Rule, which instructs us that all children in movies, told to stay put, quickly wander away into danger. Well, can we blame the director? How interesting would it be if she obediently stayed put?

What I responded to was the street-level reality of the film. There are no supermen and no sensational stunts. When the actors run, we see that they are running. These shots extend in time and are not constructed of baffling editing. The spatial realities of the chases are respected; we begin to learn our way around the neighborhood. The cops are not stock characters, but just your average officers. No one in *The Chaser* seems on autopilot.

When I see a film like this, it reminds me of what we're missing. So many recent movies are all smoke and mirrors. A thriller is opening soon in which the star cannot be clearly seen to complete any physical act in an action sequence. We might as well be reading a comic strip, where our minds are expected to fill in the movement between the frames. You sit there and *The Chaser* unfolds and the director knows what he wants and how to do it without insulting us. In addition to remaking this movie, Hollywood should study it.

## Chasing Madoff ★ ★ ½

NO MPAA RATING, 90 m., 2011

A documentary featuring Harry Markopolos, Frank Casey, Neil Chelo, Gaytri Kachroo, and Michael Ocrant. Directed and produced by Jeff Prosserman. Screenplay by Prosserman, based on the book *No One Would Listen* by Harry Markopolos.

Through the best of times, through the worst of times, year after year, Bernie Madoff's return on investment remained the same. The line on the graph climbed at a steady twenty-five degrees. It never faltered—until, like Wile E. Coyote, it ran off the edge of a cliff and continued running in thin air. Then came the collapse of a $50 billion Ponzi scheme, the largest in history.

No one could believe it. In theory it was impossible. Market professionals knew in their guts his returns were impossible. And they all knew about Bernie. No matter where you went in the world of hedge funds, no matter who you spoke to, Bernie was the man everyone knew. They would be asked, "What do you know about Bernie?" They would reply, "What do *you* know about Bernie?" What they all knew was that nobody, but nobody, could get returns like that.

*Chasing Madoff* tells the story of a man named Harry Markopolos, who gathered the facts and figures about Madoff ten years before anyone else did. He had the charts. He had the graphs. It was as obvious as the day was long that Madoff was running a Ponzi scheme. How a Ponzi works: You never buy anything. You simply pay your current investors out of money from new investors. For this to work, you always need new money. For years, Madoff had it.

"It can't be a Ponzi," his investors told each other, "because his fund is closed to new investment!" Yes, but they were able to buy in because they "knew somebody." Madoff's investors were rich people, other hedge funds, banks, trusts. You'd think people like that would know (a) there is no free lunch, and (b) you never put all your eggs in one basket. Remarkable numbers of them lost their total investment, however. In enclaves of millionaires, whole families were wiped out.

My notion is that they were blinded by greed. They knew the numbers were impossible. But since Madoff stayed in business year after year, since he retained such a high profile, they might have told themselves: It can't last, but I'm willing to clean up on other people's losses. Then there were the professional managers who bought *into* Madoff's funds for competitive reasons. For them it was a way to raise the rate of return on their investments. Many rich people had no idea they were invested in Madoff via "feeder funds." The function of such funds was to provide outside capital to keep the Ponzi afloat.

But what about the Securities and Exchange Commission? What about the *Wall Street Journal*? What about the *New York Times*? Bloomberg News? Didn't they know? Harry Markopolos told them. He was a respected professional. Year after year, he supplied them all with carefully documented evidence of what the scheme was and how it worked. The problem was, they didn't want to know. Its scope was so vast, Madoff's webs were so complex, that if it were true, that would make it the largest Ponzi scheme in history. Which it was, as I recall mentioning up above.

*Chasing Madoff* is not a very good documentary, but it's a devastating one. It consists of this entire story told by Markopolos and his fellow Madoff chasers Frank Casey and Neil Chelo. There's footage from congressional investigations. Staff members of the SEC are called on the carpet. No one from the *New York Times* or the *Wall Street Journal* is asked to explain the inaction of their newspapers. We do hear from individual investors who lost their life savings—but not from any of the traders or firms that bought into Madoff. Nor do we hear from Madoff himself. We get many portentous shots of skylines, Wall Street, the SEC headquarters, Madoff's yacht, and cable news reports.

There's precious little, indeed, that we find out here but didn't already know from the news coverage at the time. The only smoking gun is that Madoff's guilt was exposed clearly and repeatedly by Markopolos in the decade before his fall. Not only did the system fail, but it failed because of the willful ignorance of those with the responsibility to make it work. What do we learn at the end of it all? There is no free lunch. Never put all your eggs in one basket. One of the many people who forgot those helpful rules was Bernie Madoff.

## Chicago Heights ★ ★ ★

NO MPAA RATING, 90 m., 2010

William Gray (Sherwood Anderson/Old Nathan), Keisha Dyson (Elizabeth Walker), Andre Truss (Nathan Walker), Benny Stewart (Dr. Reefy), Jay Johnson (Reverend Curtis Hartman), Ron Jarmon Jr. (Wash Williams), Simone Wilson (Louise Trunnion). Directed by Daniel Nearing and produced by Sanghoon Lee. Screenplay by Nearing and Rudy Thauberger, based on the novel *Winesburg, Ohio*, by Sherwood Anderson.

Sherwood Anderson's *Winesburg, Ohio*, is sometimes named as a great work of fiction that cannot be filmed. Daniel Nearing demonstrates in *Chicago Heights* that that's not necessarily true. The book is a collection of twenty-two short stories connected by the character George Willard, who comes of age in Winesburg and reflects on the citizens he has grown to know. Perhaps one could make twenty-two short films. Nearing finds an approach that in ninety minutes accomplishes the uncanny feat of distilling the book's essence.

Anderson's Winesburg is a town with roads that can be walked along a short distance into the country. His time frame spans the twentieth century's first quarter. Nearing's Chicago

Heights is a distant southern suburb of Chicago, bordering on farmland. His time is the present and recent decades. His central character is Nathan Walker (Andre Truss), also played as Old Nathan by William Gray, and at that age is named in the credits as Sherwood Anderson. Anderson's characters were all white. Nearing's characters are all African-American. Race is not really a factor. We are concerned with inner selves.

It's helpful, maybe essential, to be familiar with the book before seeing the movie. Anderson explains his theory of grotesques, by which he means not sideshow freaks but people who have one aspect of their body or personality exaggerated out of proportion to the whole. Wing Biddlebaum, for example, has hands so expressive they flutter like birds, and these beautiful hands are the cause of his isolation and hatred by the community. All of the characters have some special reason they don't fit in. This attribute is why their inner thoughts and dreams never become known. They are judged by the uncaring and will be buried never understood.

What Nearing does, and it is rather brilliant, is show us Nathan in old age, under a blanket on his bed, remembering, dreaming, or hallucinating about the people he has known. A narrator explains his thoughts. Remarkably for a film of average length, Nearing touches on almost every one of Anderson's characters, and because of his meditative stylistic approach the film never feels rushed or choppy.

The film is mostly in contrasty black and white, sometimes slipping into color. Dialogue slips in and out, too, as it does in the book, but we're not intended to think it's being said now. It's being heard in memory. Chicago Heights is seen as a not particularly lovely place, drowsing near the prairie with the skyline of modern Chicago in the distance. Much of it was shot on location, and Nearing succeeds in establishing it as a place like Winesburg where the countryside is always in walking distance, and one can go there with one's grotesqueries and feel at peace.

When I say it helps to have read the book, I don't mean to frighten you. Perhaps you could read just a few of the stories to begin with. They won't take long, and once you understand their workings, the whole film will come into focus. Nearing is not the first artist to be drawn to *Winesburg*. It inspired a made-for-TV film and a Broadway musical, and influenced authors such as Hemingway, Faulkner, Steinbeck, and Salinger. It is a beautiful book and has inspired this beautiful film.

## Chico and Rita ★ ★ ★ ½

NO MPAA RATING, 93 m., 2012

Limara Meneses (Rita), Emar Xor Ona (Chico), Mario Guerra (Ramon), Lenny Mandel (Ron). Directed by Fernando Trueba, Javier Mariscal, and Tono Errando and produced by Santi Errando, Cristina Huete, Martin Pope, and Michael Rose. Screenplay by Trueba and Ignacio Martinez de Pison.

*Chico and Rita* enjoyed one of the biggest surprises in the 2012 Oscar nominations by winning a slot as best animated film. That meant this indie production placed ahead of such big-time entries as Spielberg's *Adventures of Tintin*. The reason for that is the story and the music, I suspect, not the animation.

This is a nearly operatic romantic tragedy, involving a lifelong affair of the heart between two Havana musicians: Chico, a piano player, and Rita, a vocalist. Their mutual problem is that Chico is unfaithful by nature, and although Rita is the woman he loves, when he's not with the one he loves, he loves the one he's with. Rita is two-timed once too often, and sets off on her own—a mistake, because when they're together they have a taste of stardom, and when apart a tendency to self-destruct.

The film opens in Batista's Havana, a hotbed of jazz and Afro-Cuban music, where luxurious clubs, casinos, and hotels have created a Caribbean entertainment mecca, mostly controlled by American gangsters and corporations. It's a fluid, exciting scene, where in one night Chico can discover Rita singing in an open-air club and sweep her along when he's discovered by Woody Herman in a show in a beachfront hotel.

Herman's piano man is sick. Chico and Rita walk in, Chico is recruited to fill the empty piano stool, it's clear how talented he is, and in no time at all he and Rita team up to win a talent contest on a radio station and a lucrative contract. They even have a hit record, masterminded by a breezy con man named Ramon, who dedicates himself to managing them.

Life takes them to New York and a hit record, but the faithless Chico loses Rita to the company of a slickster Yankee named Ron, who gets her a few good bookings before she blows a Vegas gig by being drunk on stage. The story is told in flashback from Chico's lonely life today and Rita's equally cheerless existence. The problem we have with their romance is that most of the time it isn't working. We don't sense the urgency of their passion so much as the finality of their problems. Apparently, they're doomed to exist in a permanent state of breakup.

The animation by codirectors Fernando Trueba, Javier Mariscal, and Tono Errando is filled with motion and color, yes, but could have benefited from characters who seemed more like quirky individuals and less like types. Oddly, the backgrounds were the parts of *Chico and Rita* I liked the most: Havana in its pre-Fidel days of big spenders, New York in the heyday of jazz, Paris when foreign musicians were hot, Vegas in its early golden years. Architecture, neon signs, and big, classic American cars are all done with brio and abandon. It's entertaining to watch, and I enjoyed the way they slipped in such real-life figures as Dizzy Gillespie beside the fictional leads.

The music is terrific. Idania Valdes dubs Rita's sensuous, smoky singing voice, and the film is essentially constructed as a musical. There came a point when the sweep of the romantic story caught me up as much as a narrative film might have, and I wasn't distanced by the animation. After seeing the film, I went online to see if Chico and Rita were inspired by real-life musicians. None in particular, I learned. But probably a great many in general.

## Chinese Take-Away ★ ★ ★ ★

NO MPAA RATING, 93 m., 2012

Ricardo Darin (Roberto), Ignacio Huang (Jun), Muriel Santa Ana (Mari), Ivan Romanelli (Leonel). Directed by Sebastian Borensztein and produced by Pablo Bossi, Juan Pablo Buscarini, Gerardo Herrero, and Ben Odell. Screenplay by Borensztein.

Here is a movie about a man with a very particular personality, who finds himself sharing his hermitlike existence with another man who has no particular personality at all. They don't even speak the same language. *Chinese Take-Away* becomes a bemused study about how they infiltrate each other's lives. It is a consideration of the life of loneliness, for those who choose it and those who have it forced upon them.

Roberto is the grouchy owner of a small hardware store in Buenos Aires. So small that he is the only employee, and would have it no other way. He considers most people fools and idiots, counts the screws in a box of 500 to see if he is being cheated, and has been known to order a customer out of the store for having the temerity to request a few grams of nails. He lives in an apartment connected to the store, prepares his own meals, and dines alone while scanning newspapers for stories confirming his belief that life has no meaning.

One day a taxi squeals to a halt and the driver throws out his passenger, a young Chinese man. Roberto is offended. This confirms his belief that all taxi drivers are jerks. The young man speaks no Spanish, but expresses himself in a torrent of anguished Mandarin. He has an address written on his arm. Roberto gives him a lift to that address, but the current tenant says she bought the house a few years ago from a Chinese man. She has no forwarding address.

That is the most Roberto can be expected to do, and he leaves the young man at a bus stop to find his own way. He goes home, a downpour begins, and he cannot help himself but must drive out to the bus stop, pick up the stranger, and bring him home. This is already an unthinkable breach of his habits.

Roberto is played by the soulful Argentinean actor Ricardo Darin, whom you may remember from *The Secret in Their Eyes.* He is fiftyish, unassumingly mustached, has weary eyes, is fed up most of the time. His guest, named Jun (Ignacio Huang), is a smooth-faced youth who is baffled to find himself adrift in Argentina, and whose response is cordial passivity. Neither is skilled at communicating without words.

The middle sections of Sebastian Borensztein's film involve Roberto's ineffectual warnings that Jun cannot stay, as Jun listens uncomprehendingly. Using a Chinese take-away deliveryman as a translator, they find Jun is searching for his uncle. Visits to the police station, the Chinese Embassy, and Chinatown are fruitless. The two men share silent meals, and Jun does some odd jobs around the store.

We meet Mari (Muriel Santa Ana), who is visiting the relative who delivers Roberto's standing orders for countless newspapers. Roberto and Mari share sort of a history, shown in a brief and startling flashback. Mari makes it no secret that she likes him. Roberto doesn't want to be liked. As nearly as possible, he wants to be left alone, passing his time counting screws, insulting customers, and scanning the newspapers for items about people dying in ridiculous ways.

It is hardly possible to suggest how involving this story becomes. One can see how it could have been a comedy, but this is no comedy. Ricardo Darin's performance evokes the solitary isolation of Roberto and his almost tangible fear of knowing or being known. He isn't cruel or hostile; he acts out of some deep apprehension. Nor is Jun the sort of man we might imagine, ingratiating and accommodating. He projects no expectations at all, and passively accepts all of Roberto's actions and decisions.

*Chinese Take-Away* insinuates itself. To a degree unusual in most films, I became involved in the fates of these men, perhaps because they make no attempt to be likable. They are consistent with their natures, and the director tells the story with a clean, no-nonsense narrative. If there will be surprises, we can't guess where they will possibly come from.

Many really good films allow us to empathize with other lives. I became invested in Roberto, and shared his curiosity about the enigmatic Jun. I cared. The film deserved my care. Although one of its revelations is astonishing, it doesn't come because of trickery, but is consistent with information we already have. It is no easier for Roberto to process than it is for us. At the end, all we know for sure is that perhaps life is not entirely meaningless.

## Chloe ★ ★ ★ ½

R, 96 m., 2010

Julianne Moore (Catherine Stewart), Liam Neeson (David Stewart), Amanda Seyfried (Chloe), Max Thieriot (Michael Stewart), R. H. Thomson (Frank), Nina Dobrev (Anna). Directed by Atom Egoyan and produced by Jeffrey Clifford, Joe Medjuck, Ivan Reitman, Simone Urdl, and Jennifer Weiss. Screenplay by Erin Cressida Wilson, based on the motion picture *Nathalie,* directed by Anne Fontaine.

Looking down from her office window, she sees a young woman who has the manner and routine of a high-priced call girl. This she stores in her memory. When her husband says he missed his flight back to Toronto and she finds a disturbing photo on his iPhone, she goes to the hotel where she saw the girl, makes eye contact with her in a bar, contrives a conversation in the powder room. The girl, with perfect calm, explains that single women are not usually her clients. Couples, maybe.

Atom Egoyan finds intrigue at the edges of conventional sex. *Chloe,* like his great film *Exotica* (1994), is about sexual attraction confused by financial arrangements. It centers on a powerfully erotic young woman with personal motives that are hidden. It is not blatant but seductive, depending on the ways that our minds, more than our bodies, can be involved in a sexual relationship. It's not so much what we're doing as what I'm thinking about it—and what you're thinking, which may be more complex than I realize.

Catherine Stewart (Julianne Moore) is a gynecologist, a successful one, judging by the house she inhabits fresh from the cover of *Architectural Digest.* Her husband, David (Liam Neeson), is an expert on opera. The call girl she saw from her window is Chloe (Amanda Seyfried), young, red-lipped, intelligent. Catherine explains to Chloe that she suspects her husband of adultery and wants to test if he would try to pick up another woman. She tells Chloe where her husband always has lunch.

Early in the film, talking with a patient uncertain about her sex life, Catherine explains that an orgasm is a simple muscular contraction, quite natural, nothing to be frightened of or make mysterious. Orgasms for Catherine, however, involve a great deal more than muscles, and a great deal depends on whom they are experienced with, and why. Chloe tells her about entering a café, boldly asking David if she can take the sugar from his table, and returning to her own. David understands that Chloe is not interested in sugar.

Chloe meets with Catherine to relate this encounter. Chloe is good at this. She informs us early in the film that she is skilled at what she does. It's not a matter of renting her body. She uses her intelligence to intuit what a client desires—really desires, no matter what the client might claim. And she knows how to provide this in a way that will provoke curiosity, even fascination. Now she describes details to Catherine that do a great deal more than provoke a wife's jealousy about her husband. They provoke an erotic curiosity about her husband.

Chloe is perhaps twenty-five years younger than Catherine, but in many ways wiser and more experienced. She is certainly more clear about what it is she really wants. She enjoys the psychological control of her clients, and her own skill in achieving that. She looks so young and innocent, but her life has taught her many lessons. Seyfried plays Chloe as a woman in command of her instrument—her body, which is for sale, and her mind, which works for itself. Moore, that consummate actress, undergoes a change she only believes is under her control. Neeson is an enigma to his wife and in a different way to us.

Egoyan follows his material to an ultimate conclusion. Some will find it difficult to accept. Is it arbitrary? Most of life's conclusions are arbitrary. I am not sure this particular story should, or can, be wound up in a conventional manner. It's not the kind of movie that depends on the certainty of an ending. It's more about how things continue. I have deliberately withheld much of the story, which he leaves for you to understand. His central fascination is with Chloe's motives. Does she act only for money? Does she do only what is requested? Does she remain emotionally detached? Does she get anything for herself besides money?

At one point she's asked how she can relate to some of her clients, who might seem unattractive, even repugnant. A call girl has no idea who will open the door after her knock, and the ground rules are that she will gratify the client's desires, if he can pay and she doesn't feel in personal danger. But how can she endure some of them? "I try to find something I can love," she says.

After you see the movie, run through it again in your mind. Who wants what? Who gets what? Who decides what? Whose needs are gratified? Atom Egoyan never makes a story with one level. He never reveals all of the motives, especially to his characters. He invites us to be voyeurs of surfaces that may not conceal what they seem. Fundamental shifts can alter all the relationships. All the same, their sexuality compels his characters to make decisions based on their own assumptions. It is a tangled web he weaves.

## Chronicle ★ ★ ★ ½

PG-13, 83 m., 2012

Dane DeHaan (Andrew), Alex Russell (Matt), Michael B. Jordan (Steve), Michael Kelly (Richard), Ashley Hinshaw (Casey), Bo Petersen (Karen), Anna Wood (Monica). Directed by Josh Trank and produced by John Davis and Adam Schroeder. Screenplay by Max Landis.

Man, you couldn't get me down into that hole in the ground for all the beans in Boston. It's perfectly circular, in the middle of a gloomy, grassy field, and Matt and Steve talk Andrew into bringing his new video camera and filming as they disappear into its dark maw. They use the camera's light and, of course, the screens on their iPhones. They can't see the bottom.

It's spoiling hardly anything to tell you they find some sort of weird, crystalline object. The letters UFO spring to mind. They stare at it and maybe it stares back. Then they discover they can move Lego pieces using only their minds. This is called telekinesis. Matt looks it up in the dictionary.

From this deceptively ordinary beginning, John Trank's *Chronicle* grows into an uncommonly entertaining movie that involves elements of a superhero origin story, a science fiction fantasy, and a drama about a disturbed teenager. Andrew (Dane DeHaan) is a shy and unpopular high school student with a dying mother and a mean-tempered drunk for a father. Matt (Alex Russell) is his cousin and only friend, a smart kid who quotes Plato as they descend into the hole. Steve (Michael B. Jordan) is cheerful, handsome, and running for class president—all the things Andrew isn't.

Whatever it is that happened to them in the

hole gives them something overwhelming in common: They have new, challenging superpowers. Discovering this, they act like a bunch of kids. Hell, they *are* a bunch of kids, and the screenplay by Max Landis does a convincing job of making them realistic teenagers. This is a "found footage" movie like *Blair Witch*, allegedly shot on Andrew's camera. At a dance, Matt meets the friendly Casey (Ashley Hinshaw), who is making a video diary of her own life for her blog. With two cameras, *Chronicle* gets around the problem that with found footage you never see the character holding the camera. Later, we'll see other points of view: surveillance cameras, cell phone movies, and, toward the end, some sensational events on TV news.

The movie is delightful for its first hour or so, and then turns dark and disturbing. The friends test their new powers and decide they're like muscles—you have to build them up slowly. This they do like mischievous teenagers. If you can lift a leaf blower at a distance, for example, you can use it to blow cheerleaders' skirts above their heads. You can put on an amazing magic show at school. For that matter, you can levitate the camera and get nice "steadicam" shots. Matt, the most responsible one, believes they should keep their powers secret. That will be impossible once Andrew begins to act out the antisocial rage boiling inside him.

Sometimes a movie comes out of the blue that announces the arrival of considerable new talents. Josh Trank is twenty-six and this is his directing debut. Max Landis is twenty-six and has written a couple of shorts. His father is the director John Landis, but connections don't teach you how to write. Dane DeHaan, Michael B. Jordan, and Alex Russell are in their early or midtwenties, have some experience, and work together easily here as an ensemble. It's their convincing acting and Landis's dialogue—not just the late drama, but the early goofing around—that gives the movie a natural authenticity.

*Chronicle* seems at first to be all goofing around. It's Andrew's tortured personal life that steers it into deep currents, although they have fun getting there. These are teenagers who must think they'll live forever. Not only do they go down into that hole, but they discover they can fly up into thunderstorms. Even if you could fly to ten thousand feet, would you *want* to? "It's cold up here!" one of them shouts. I forget which one. There was some lightning at the time.

## The Chronicles of Narnia: The Voyage of the Dawn Treader ★ ★ ★

PG, 115 m., 2010

Skandar Keynes (Edmund), Georgie Henley (Lucy), Will Poulter (Eustace), Ben Barnes (King Caspian), Gary Sweet (Ship's Captain), Tilda Swinton (White Witch). And the voices of Simon Pegg (Reepicheep), Liam Neeson (Aslan the Lion). Directed by Michael Apted and produced by Andrew Adamson, Mark Johnson, and Philip Steuer. Screenplay by Christopher Markus, Stephen McFeely, and Michael Petroni, based on the novel by C. S. Lewis.

The alarming thing about Narnia is that you might be in the same room with it. It could be inside that old cupboard. Or, this time, inside that painting with the nautical theme. Those waves look so real. In fact, says Lucy, they almost look like they're moving. The next thing we hear is, "I'm inside the painting!"

Indeed she is, and the *Dawn Treader* is approaching over the waves. Her nuisance of a cousin Eustace unwisely pulls the painting from the wall, and seawater rushes out and fills the room until they seem in danger of drowning, but no, they surface and are rescued by sailors from the ship, captained by Caspian (Ben Barnes), who almost seems to have been expecting them.

*The Chronicles of Narnia: The Voyage of the Dawn Treader*, third of the films inspired by the C. S. Lewis tales, once again requires the services of English children to rescue an alternate universe. How a universe is possible that requires participation from a parallel universe I will leave to theoretical physics. If you don't ask a question, it's not a question.

On board the sailing vessel, Lucy (Georgie Henley), her brother Edmund (Skandar Keynes), and young Eustace (Will Poulter) ask no questions. They're too blissful to be back in Narnia, despite the hair-raising adventures they had in the earlier films. Lucy and Edmund, now in their midteens, seem uncommonly calm about being yanked from their everyday lives and put on a strange ship in uncharted seas, but these kids have pluck.

They're briefed on the situation: Narnia is threatened by evil forces from the mysterious Dark Island, which no one has seen but everyone has heard about. There is a matter of seven missing magical swords representing the Lords of Telmar, which were given to Narnia by Aslan the Lion and must be brought together again to break a spell that imprisons the lords. Obviously, these kids can do it. Eustace is perhaps seven years old, but, hey, bring the kid along.

On board the ship is a peppy little swashbuckling rat named Reepicheep (voice of Simon Pegg). He walks upright, speaks assertively, falls squarely into the semiobligatory Cute Little Sidekick role, has a heroic heart, and a cute little sword he is unafraid to brandish. Why the little fella has never been stepped on and squished goes unexplained.

It's a rough voyage. There is a tempest. There is a horrifying battle with a sea monster. The monster looks big enough to send the *Dawn Treader* to the bottom with its tail, but the Narniaites prevail, not least because Reepicheep scampers up the rigging and imparts a nasty flesh wound. As they sail from one Narnian island to another seeking the swords, a series of other challenges confronts them, including an ominous sea fog as alarming as Stephen King's *The Mist.*

A climactic voyage to the Dark Island becomes necessary, and it is fraught with hazards. Half-rations of food and water for all on board! No one knows how far it is. Lucky thing they know in which direction to sail. If they overshoot the island they may sail off the edge of the earth, Columbus having not existed in Narnia.

The island, first glimpsed from a distance, looks ominously like a skull, with the glow of possible volcanoes in its skeleton eyes. Skull Island comes to mind. Here the fate of Narnia will be sealed. The island, we're told, is the habitation and embodiment of pure Evil; I suppose, since Lewis intended his books as Christian allegory, it is Hell. The kids and the crew of the *Dawn Treader* are up against it, and Eustace is greatly pleased by being transformed into a fire-breathing dragon.

If I've lingered overmuch on the story, it's because mostly what you have is a series of opportunities for special effects. The characters have characteristics rather than personalities, and little self-consciousness. They spring to the service of the plot—which, not particularly coherent, boils down to one damn thing after another.

Still, this is a rip-snorting adventure fantasy for families, especially the younger members who are not insistent on continuity. Director Michael Apted may be too good for this material, but he attacks with gusto. Nor are the young actors overly impressed by how nobly archetypal they are; Lucy (who is really the lead) could give lessons to Harry Potter about how to dial down the self-importance. A universe may hang in the balance, but hey, it's only a movie.

I'm afraid it's in 3-D. I will say it has the best rendition of 3-D I've seen in one of these action spectaculars; Apted uses it and is not driven by it. The light level is dimmed. It always is in 3-D. I wish I could have seen it in 2-D. If you can, try to.

## Circumstance ★ ★ ½

R, 107 m., 2011

Nikohl Boosheri (Atafeh), Sarah Kazemy (Shireen), Reza Sixo Safai (Mehran), Soheil Parsa (Firouz), Nasrin Pakkho (Azar), Sina Amedson (Hossein), Keon Mohajeri (Joey). Directed by Maryam Keshavarz and produced by Keshavarz, Karin Chien, and Melissa Lee. Screenplay by Keshavarz.

*Circumstance* begins as the story of two teenage Iranian girls in love, and if it had continued to focus on the impossibility of their relationship in everyday modern Tehran, I think it would have been more successful. Unfortunately, it strays into unlikely melodrama and distracting eroticism. Still, it is a bold statement about the treatment of women in general in the modern Islamic state.

We meet Atafeh (Nikohl Boosheri) and Shireen (Sarah Kazemy), two high school girls who share a big crush. This they keep secret from their families—Atafeh's, whose professional parents are conformist but not unkind, and Shireen's, whose uncle is raising her after her dissident parents ran afoul of the clerical authorities. They frequent clandestine stores with Western videos, attend secret parties, smoke, dance, and steal away to their bedrooms to share fantasies of the freedom they could share in nearby Dubai.

Unfortunately, these fantasies are visualized all too sensuously by writer-director Maryam Keshavarz, who uses light, color, and music to suggest escapes that would have been more at home in an American lesbian romance. If the two young women had been more realistic, innocent, and naive, I would have believed in them more.

Then, at about the halfway point, a miscalculation arrives in the form of Atafeh's brother, Mehran (Reza Sixo Safai). Just returned from drug rehabilitation, he is subjected to enforced urine tests by their father, although Mehran protests he is cured. And so he seems to be, although his cure takes the form of an Islamist dogma that has turned him into much more of an extremist than anyone else in his family.

That this happened so quickly is a little unlikely. We sense something unwholesome about Mehran, who incredibly hides spy cameras in the family home to keep track of Atafeh and Shireen; his interest is more voyeuristic than liturgical. One senses here a half-realized ambition by the first-time filmmaker to emulate Hitchcockian motifs, but the film never organizes Mehran's peculiarities to a particular purpose.

Atafeh's father, Firouz (Soheil Parsa), and mother, Azar (Nasrin Pakkho), come across as reasonable parents, given their society, who want only a quick and safe marriage for their daughter. One day Firouz takes the family to the beach, where he and Mehran go swimming and he says to the women, "One day we can all go swimming." The implication is that he regrets the prohibition of women in bathing suits, but observes it.

The strongest message for most Western audiences will be the way subjugation of women saturates every aspect of this society and clearly informs even Mehran's kinkiness. Yes, but I wish Keshavarz had chosen a more low-key, everyday approach to two ordinary teenagers, and gone slow on the lush eroticism and cinematic voyeurism.

## City Island ★ ★ ★

PG-13, 103 m., 2010

Andy Garcia (Vince Rizzo), Julianna Margulies (Joyce Rizzo), Steven Strait (Tony Nardella), Alan Arkin (Michael Malakov), Emily Mortimer (Molly Charlesworth), Ezra Miller (Vinnie Rizzo), Dominik Garcia-Lorido (Vivian Rizzo). Directed by Raymond de Felitta and produced by Felitta, Andy Garcia, Zachary Matz, and Lauren Versel. Screenplay by Felitta.

Vince is a man with a dream. Marlon Brando is his god. He would like to become an actor. This is not likely. He's well into his forties, a prison guard living with his family on City Island, a bucolic outcrop of the Bronx known mostly to its residents. Telling his wife he's going to a poker game, he attends acting classes in Manhattan. In one class, Vince creates a spot-on imitation, not of Marlon Brando, but of bad Brando imitators.

Vince, played by Andy Garcia with brawny blue-collar dialogue, is married to Joyce (Julianna Margulies), who's convinced the poker games mean a mistress. His children hide secret lives. His daughter, Vivian (Dominik Garcia-Lorido), has dropped out of college and is working as a stripper in hopes of saving money to reapply. His son, Vinnie (Ezra Miller), is hooked not just on any old Internet porn, but on sites featuring fat women who eat on camera. The younger son in so many movie families is somehow weird.

Two life-changing experiences happen to Vince. At work, he gets a new prisoner whose name he has reason to recognize. He pulls the kid's file to confirm it: Tony (Steven Strait) is the son he fathered in a long-ago affair. Meanwhile, in acting class, his teacher (Alan Arkin) assigns the students to pair up and share their biggest secret in order to prepare for a monologue. He draws Molly (Emily Mortimer), who slowly draws this secret from him. They meet often in the city—not to have an affair, but because they become friends and confidants.

Tony is eligible to be released into the community, but has no family member to sign for him. Vince determines to bring him home for a month. This is the catalyst for upheaval in the long-established pattern of his life. *City Island,* written and directed by Raymond de Felitta, has a serious side but is essentially a human comedy, at times almost a gentle farce, as discoveries and revelations drop like explosives. You can imagine this story as the outline for an opera.

Garcia and Margulies, who worked so well together in George Hickenlooper's *The Man from Elysian Fields* (2001), show a sure feel for comedy here, especially after he introduces an unexplained stranger into his home: "You just decided to bring a prisoner home to *live* with us?" Convinced the poker games are a cover-up, she toys with the idea of fooling around with the hunky Tony. Molly, meanwhile, convinces Vince to try his luck at an open audition for a new movie.

There's a jolly subplot involving their next-door neighbor on City Island, a fat woman who Vinnie was following on the Web when—OMG!—he sees her on the way to the grocery store, and she asks if he wants to come along. This cheerful woman, played by an actress not listed on IMDb, defuses any awkwardness or discomfort and invites Vinnie and Tony over for some lasagna. Thus Felitta sidesteps a story hazard.

The last scene of the movie could indeed be used in an opera, with all of the leads onstage. It may strike you as a tad coincidental. So it is. Felitta has the good sense not to make it realistic, which it could not be. In the satisfactory tradition of comic melodrama, he tidies up all the loose ends. But don't get the idea *City Island* is a laugh riot. For this story about these people, it finds about the right tone. They're silly and foolish, as are we all, but deserve what happiness they can negotiate.

*Note:* City Island *won the Audience Award at the Tribeca Film Festival 2009.*

## Clash of the Titans ★ ★ ★

PG-13, 106 m., 2010

Sam Worthington (Perseus), Gemma Arterton (Io), Mads Mikkelsen (Draco), Alexa Davalos (Andromeda), Jason Flemyng (Calibos/King Acrisius), Ralph Fiennes (Hades), Liam Neeson (Zeus). Directed by Louis Leterrier and produced by Kevin De La Noy and Basil Iwanyk. Screenplay by Travis Beacham, Phil Hay, and Matt Manfredi, based on the 1982 screenplay by Beverley Cross.

There are too many Greek gods for me to keep straight, since as a child I didn't have action figures as a learning tool. I was prepared to take notes during *Clash of the Titans,* but only wrote down a single one: "'Release the Kraken!'—Conan O'Brien." I know I was intended to be terrified by the release of the Kraken, but all I could think of was O'Brien shouting "Release the bear!" and then some guy in a bear suit runs out and sits on the lap of a guest. In this case, the Kraken is the nuclear option for Zeus, who has been persuaded by Hades to put down a revolt by the upstart mortals of Argos.

The mortals are fed up with the whims of the gods. It would be one thing if they stayed on Olympus and killed time leaning on pillars and addressing one another in thundering ultimatums. Now they meddle in the affairs of men. King Acrisius of Argos declares war and enlists the aid of a demigod who has been found at sea. This is Perseus (Sam Worthington), son of Zeus (Liam Neeson) and a human mother. He didn't ask to be a savior, but would be happier as a simple fisherman. You know the type.

Zeus, it should be explained, disguised himself as the husband of Perseus's mother and stole into her bedchamber to father the boy. So he is a rapist. Just sayin.' Perseus so loved his mother and adoptive father that he will never forgive Poseidon for drowning them, and wants nothing to do with gods. Yet such is his destiny.

The outcome is told in *Clash of the Titans* with impressive technical mastery and somewhat lesser dramatic command. For its intended audience I suspect this will play as a great entertainment. I enjoyed myself, particularly after they released the Kraken. There's no particular dramatic conflict in the movie: Perseus has to wrestle with his demigod ambiguity; Hades (Ralph Fiennes) nurses a resentment against Zeus; he demands the sacrifice of King Acrisius's daughter Andromeda (Alexa Davalos) to spare the city, and the citizens seem prepared to get along very nicely without her. That's about it.

It's strange how the sacrifice of one person makes us uneasy. Earlier in the film, the entire fleet of Argos is lost at sea, with the exception of the vessel holding Perseus. The king is philosophical: They were patriots. But the sacrifice of his own daughter—now you're talkin' real death.

Most of the film involves terrifying battles between mortals and special effects. After Calibos has a hand chopped off, his fingers grow into claws. Later, his blood drops start growing, creating a crowd of huge lobster-monsters that come crawling over rocks and snapping at everyone. Later in the film, inexplicably, these lobsters appear to be tame and walk obediently across the desert, bearing little houses on their backs for the mortals. What, did they forget they were the blood of Calibos?

There's worse to come. Perseus and his comrades must invade the lair of Medusa, one of the three Gorgon girls, whose hair is a writhing mass of snakes and body is a long, lethal snake's tail. Look at her, and you'll turn to stone! Maybe this explains the high quality of Greek sculpture. The struggles with Medusa take place on ledges over a flaming lake of lava far below. She must be beheaded, which Perseus does, thoughtfully keeping the head, which he carries around like the head of Alfredo Garcia. Is that a spoiler? The story has been out since 490 B.C.

The climax is classic, with the fair Andromeda hung by her wrists and suspended in a clinging white gown over a flaming pit at the edge of the sea. Meanwhile, Perseus flies to the rescue on the wings of the great flying horse Pegasus. The townspeople clamor for her death, but lose their enthusiasm after the Kraken rears up from the sea.

I like this kind of stuff. I don't say it's good cinema, although I recognize the craftsmanship that went into it. I don't say it's good acting, when the men have so much facial hair they all look like Liam Neeson. I like the energy, the imagination, the silliness. I even like the one guy who doesn't have a beard. That's Perseus. From the first moment we see him as an adult until his last scene in the movie, he has the Standard Regulation Macho-Length Stubble on his chin. And in a city where all the men go to Jerry Garcia's barber, he has a burr cut on the short clipper setting.

So do I recommend the movie? Yes, if you intuit that this review is affectionate and have the same tolerance for goofy Greek gods as I do. One word of consumer advice, however. Explain to kids that the movie was not filmed in 3-D and is only being shown in 3-D in order to charge you an extra five dollars a ticket. I saw it in 2-D, and let me tell you, it looked terrific. Split the difference: "We see it in 2-D, I save five bucks, and I increase your allowance by $2.50 this week."

## Cold Weather ★ ★ ★ ½

NO MPAA RATING, 96 m., 2011

Cris Lankenau (Doug), Trieste Kelly Dunn (Gail), Raul Castillo (Carlos), Robyn Rikoon (Rachel). Directed by Aaron Katz and produced by Lars Knudsen, Brendan McFadden, and Ben Stambler. Screenplay by Katz.

*Cold Weather* is good in so many subtle ways I despair of doing them justice. It's a thriller involving the personalities of its characters, who we get to know surprisingly well. It remains low-key, even during its final big chase scene, which involves only one car. The acting is so good you may not notice it. Although the characters stumble over the plot at least forty minutes into the film, it's as ingenious as a high-tech Friday night special.

The tone is established by Doug (Cris Lankenau), a midtwenties guy who was studying forensics in college but dropped out for no reason he ever explains. In an opening scene he tells his parents "it's a possibility" he may return to school. For now, he's returned to Portland, Oregon, and is sleeping on the sofa of his sister's apartment. He finds a job in a factory that makes those plastic bags filled with ice, and spends his time shifting bags from one place to another.

Doug and his sister, Gail (Trieste Kelly Dunn), get along fine. No sibling problems. At work, he makes a friend named Carlos (Raul Castillo) and lends him a book of Sherlock Holmes stories. Carlos likes it. Doug's former girlfriend Rachel (Robyn Rikoon) comes to town from Chicago and gets a motel room while she trains for a job, she says. The four characters spend some time together. No big deal. Carlos asks Rachel to a Star Trek convention. Doug is fine with that. He remains friends with Rachel but their romance is over with.

Why am I telling you these inconsequential

things? Because the movie seems quite willing to spend its running length following the daily lives of nice, low-key, ordinary, even endearing twenty-somethings. All four actors, unknown to me, are natural and convincing, like people you would cast with Catherine Keener, if you know what I mean. Cris Lankenau and Raul Castillo as Doug and Carlos do a very difficult thing here, which is to play young male friends without the slightest shadow of Buddy Movie Syndrome.

Carlos grows alarmed. Rachel stood him up on a date. Possibly inflamed by Sherlock Holmes and Doug's studies in forensics, he talks him into an investigation of what he is convinced is a mysterious disappearance. Now at last there is a plot. About the plot I will tell you nothing, except that I could believe in it. I'm not sure Rachel would use the code described here, or that Doug would figure out how to break it, but never mind. Carlos sensibly says, "We need some common sense," they both enlist Gail, and Doug and Gail find themselves trailing a man in a cowboy hat after having an absolutely realistic sibling conversation about which of them will drive Gail's car.

That's it. Aaron Katz's direction is just about flawless. It's a matter of finding the right tone, established by Doug at the outset, and following it through. It's about a distaste for artificial tension-heightening devices. It's about love of these characters. It's about seeing if smoking a pipe, like Sherlock Holmes did, might help. It's about how an ice factory gets rid of its excess ice. Some people will find this movie boring. That may be because they've been deadened by thrillers that don't pay any more attention than they do.

## The Company Men ★ ★ ★

R, 115 m., 2011

Ben Affleck (Bobby Walker), Chris Cooper (Phil Woodward), Kevin Costner (Jack Dolan), Tommy Lee Jones (Gene McClary), Maria Bello (Sally Wilcox), Rosemarie DeWitt (Maggie Walker), Craig T. Nelson (James Salinger). Directed by John Wells and produced by Wells, Claire Rudnick Polstein, and Paula Weinstein. Screenplay by Wells.

The happiest people I come into contact with seem to be those who have real jobs. In the last few weeks, I've talked with a Macintosh tutor, a doctor, a set designer, a stagehand, a heating and air-conditioning man, a lawyer, a Web designer, my editor, an animator, and Millie Salmon, the woman who is my caregiver, although that job description makes me sound more decrepit than I am.

All of these people work hard, know what they're doing, think it's worth doing, enjoy it, and take pride in it. There is the same serenity I sensed from my father, who was an electrician and a damned good one. I do not, on the other hand, pick up good feelings from those people I know who are largely involved in "making money for the stockholders." They focus on moving money around, hiring and firing, cutting costs, serving the bottom line. They are caregivers for corporations, which would be more satisfactory if corporations were not essentially balance sheets. I know the Supreme Court has ruled that corporations are individuals, but when did one ever tell you a good joke?

*The Company Men* follows the stories of characters who have oriented their lives around a corporation named GTX. Years ago this company involved two men who began building ships; small ones at first, and then big ones. Now it's called General Transportation Systems, which is how we spell Acme these days. Caught in the economic downturn, GTX is downsizing, and some of its employees are discovering their primary occupation was making and spending a lot of money, and that without those jobs there isn't much they really know how to do.

We focus at first on Bobby Walker (Ben Affleck), who drives a Porsche and has a nice golf handicap, a big suburban house, and a wife, named Maggie (Rosemarie DeWitt), who is an expert consumer. Bobby loses his job. His severance and "savings cushion" can't support his overhead. He enters, with great displeasure, the shadow world of the unemployed. His company has paid for temporary office space at a job search center that helps with his résumé. He attends sessions in group therapy where he learns how to present himself and think positively. He loathes them.

Phil Woodward (Chris Cooper), an older

man at GTX, is also fired. If there is no great demand for Bobby, there is none for an unemployed executive around sixty. He was literally his job. Without it, in economic terms, he is a man with no buyers and nothing to sell. He was under the impression he had importance and value. He realizes that was a fiction. Employees of corporations are like free-ranging scavenger cells. When the corporation inhales in good times, they find themselves in a warm place with good nurture. When it exhales in bad times, they go spinning into the vast, indifferent world.

GTX was started by Salinger (Craig T. Nelson) and McClary (Tommy Lee Jones). McClary preserves the belief that a corporation owes its employees some loyalty, and that it should serve a useful function. Salinger has outgrown that phase and realizes a corporation survives only by maximizing its profits and producing one primary product: income. As Salinger's vision prevails over McClary's old-fashioned idealism, the inexorable task of "working for the shareholder" is reduced to "sacrificing the jobs and lives of others for the bottom line."

Although the actors are convincing and the film well crafted, *The Company Men* delivers few satisfactory character portraits because the movie isn't really about characters; it's about economic units. When a corporation fires you, it doesn't much care whether you're a good friend, a loving father, a louse, or a liar. You are an investment it carries on its books, or not. The impact of the movie comes when these people realize that, in economic terms, it doesn't matter who they are.

There's one character who really does something. This is Jack Dolan (Kevin Costner), Bobby's brother-in-law, who owns a small construction company that builds one house at a time. He and his workers know how to make house siding lie true, how to use materials efficiently, how to—well, how to drive a nail. Bobby has always dismissed Jack as a "working man," but when you're out of work, that looks pretty good.

Written and directed by John Wells, *The Company Men* offers no great elation or despair. Its world is what it is. We all live in it. In good times young people go to the movies and dream of becoming Gordon Gekko. In bad times, a housebuilder looks more like a Master of the Universe. It happens I've been talking with a few young people who are trying to make career decisions. My advice involves the old cliché, "Find what you really love doing and make that your profession." I think this is true. If you have to be unemployed, it might seem less bleak if you hated doing the job anyway.

## Conan O'Brien Can't Stop ★ ★ ★

R, 89 m., 2011

Conan O'Brien, Andy Richter, Steve Kroft, Eddie Vedder, Stephen Colbert, Jon Stewart, Jim Carrey, and Jack White. A documentary directed by Rodman Flender and produced by Rachel Griffin and Gavin Polone.

*Conan O'Brien Can't Stop* has a title of piercing accuracy. After NBC and Jay Leno pulled the rug out from under him, O'Brien went overnight from hosting *The Tonight Show* to being banned from television for six months. To be sure, NBC paid him $40 million in a send-off package, but the O'Brien we see in the film wasn't in it for the money. He was in it because he can't stop.

I appeared many times on his original program, most memorably being attacked by a man in a bear suit. I always liked him. I've also been on Carson, Oprah, Letterman, Leno, Regis, Arsenio, Joan Rivers, and a.m. here and a.m. there. You arrive at least an hour early, finish with makeup, leave your dressing room door open, and watch what happens in the corridor. Carson, Conan, and Leno would drop by to say hello. I don't remember seeing the others before airtime. Letterman in particular seems to build up steam in private. It has nothing to do with who's nice and who isn't. It's showbiz.

Watching this documentary, I realize that when Conan lost *The Tonight Show* he was like Wile E. Coyote, chasing the Road Runner of his dreams off the edge of a cliff and afraid to look down. Enraged at Leno and NBC, he quickly undertook "The Legally Prohibited from Being Funny on Television Tour," which covered thirty-two cities, from Radio City Music Hall to the Bonnaroo Music Festival in Tennessee—where inside a tent in one-hundred-degree heat he was expected to introduce every act, and did. You get the notion he would have introduced them anyway.

Here is a man driven to assert himself. He waited five years for *The Tonight Show,* lost it in months, and needed to say to the universe, "Sir! I exist!" The film, directed by Rodman Flender, watches him before and after shows and en route between cities, seeing a man incapable of giving himself a break. Overworked, exhausted, assaulted by demands, he cannot say no to an autograph, patiently hosts waves of visitors in his dressing room, drums up work on his days off, and at times seems on the edge of madness.

Everyone around him pays a price. He relentlessly nibbles away at his support system, picks on his personal assistant, needles his sidekick Andy Richter, and dominates his "writers" so compulsively that I can hardly recall one of them being allowed to say anything at meetings. He seems to consider them more of an audience.

Why these people stay with him is a mystery. My guess is that they know him better than we do and realize he's undergoing a crisis. He's driven. After shows, exhausted, he insists on going out to sign autographs and pose for photos with fans. The photos in particular are a version of the Water Torture Test for celebrities. The fan hands a camera to a friend or bystander, who *inevitably* doesn't know how to operate it. The celebrity remains in position, his mouth frozen in the rictus of a smile, while the fan explains how the camera operates: "You push this button."

In addition to telling jokes, O'Brien plays guitar and joins a backup band and various guest stars to perform country-rock. He's surprisingly good, for a talk show host. He fantasizes receiving a text message from Jay Leno ("What's it like to have a soul?"). I can only imagine how well he sleeps. We see his wife in only one brief, early scene, and I suspect she was well advised not to come along.

This is not to say Conan O'Brien is a bad man. In fact, after the movie, I rather admired him. What we are seeing is a man determined to vindicate himself after a public humiliation. People attend his shows, cheer him, like him. That proves something, doesn't it?

What we don't see are the details of what must have been going on all this time in negotiations to find a new television home after the end of the six-month banishment. He and his agents must have been talking about a lot of possibilities, including TBS, where he ended up. Those would have added a maddening level of frustration to his exhausting existence.

O'Brien started out as a writer. He must have been driven to become a performer. It is a need in some people. One of the almost unbelievable stories in talk show history is how Johnny Carson was able to retire at the height of his popularity, and mean it, and stick to it. Maybe one of the reasons people liked him so much is that he never seemed to *need* to perform.

Other people do. I once observed Henny Youngman taping a TV show in the old NBC studios at the Merchandise Mart in Chicago. We got into an elevator together. It stopped at the second floor, a private club. A wedding was under way. Youngman got off the elevator, asked to meet the father of the bride, and said, "I'm Henny Youngman. I'll do ten minutes for a hundred dollars."

## Conan the Barbarian ★ ½

R, 102 m., 2011

Jason Momoa (Conan), Stephen Lang (Khalar Zym), Rachel Nichols (Tamara), Ron Perlman (Corin), Rose McGowan (Marique). Directed by Marcus Nispel and produced by John Baldecchi, Boaz Davidson, Randall Emmett, Joe Gatta, Avi Lerner, Danny Lerner, Fredrik Malmberg, and Les Weldon. Screenplay by Thomas Dean Donnelly, Joshua Oppenheimer, and Sean Hood, based on the character created by Robert E. Howard.

*Conan the Barbarian* involves the clash of civilizations whose vocabularies are limited to screams, oaths, grunts, howls, ejaculations, exclamations, vulgarities, screeches, wails, bellows, yelps, and woofs. I'd love to get my hands on the paycheck for subtitling this movie.

The plot involves—oh, never mind. You have your Barbarians and they kill one another in an unending series of battle scenes. I guess Conan is the good guy, but what difference does it make? He has no cause or belief. He's driven by revenge against the sadistic

Khalar Zym (Stephen Lang), who trapped Conan's father under a vat of molten iron, assigned young Conan to exert his little muscles to try to keep it from tipping, and screamed at the old man: "You will watch your child die trying to save you!"

Luckily, Conan (the muscular Jason Momoa) survives and grows up with no worse than a photogenic scar on his face, where some wayward molten iron dripped. He and his father, Corin (Ron Perlman), had earlier forged his sword at the steel moltery; earlier still, the infant Conan was delivered on a battlefield by an emergency cesarean performed by Corin's own sword on his mother, who survives long enough to say, "He shall be named Conan." She was so weak she lacked the breath to say, "Conan the Barbarian."

The movie is a series of violent conflicts. People who despair of convincing me to play video games tell me, "Maybe if you could just watch someone else playing one!" I feel as if I now have. Conan carves, beheads, disembowels, and otherwise inconveniences the citizens of several improbable cities, each time in a different fanciful situation. The evil Khalar Zym and his girlfriend Marique (Rose McGowan) turn up regularly, uttering imprecations, with Marique especially focused on Conan's warrior gal pal Tamara (Rachel Nichols).

This Marique, she's a piece of work. She has white pancake makeup, blood-red lips, cute little facial tattoos, and wickedly sharp metal talons on her fingers. At one point she blows some magic dust at Conan, and the dust turns into a team of warriors made of sand. This is a neat special effect, although it raises the question, if you turn back to sand when Conan slices you, what kind of a life is that?

The film ends with a very long battle involving Conan, Khalar Zym, Tamara, and Marique, a sentence I never thought I'd write. It takes place largely with Tamara strapped to a revolving wheel above a vertiginous drop to flames far below. Mention is made of a volcano, but never further explained. The entire cavern crumbles around them, big chunks of rock falling everywhere except, luckily, upon them.

*Conan the Barbarian* is a brutal, crude, witless high-tech CGI contrivance, in which no artificial technique has been overlooked, including 3-D. The third dimension once again illustrates the principle that when a movie largely takes place indoors in dimly lit spaces, the last thing you need is a pair of dark glasses.

## The Conquest ★ ★ ★

NO MPAA RATING, 110 m., 2012

Denis Podalydes (Nicolas Sarkozy), Florence Pernel (Cecilia Sarkozy), Bernard Le Coq (Jacques Chirac), Hippolyte Girardot (Claude Gueant), Samuel Labarthe (Dominique de Villepin). Directed by Xavier Durringer and produced by Eric Altmeyer and Nicolas Altmeyer. Screenplay by Durringer and Patrick Rotman.

*The Conquest* is a feature about recent French politics that makes me yearn for a similar American treatment of our own. Scored with Felliniesque circus music, it shows such figures as Nicolas Sarkozy, Jacques Chirac, and their wives on a merry-go-round of vanity, vulgarity, and viciousness. I'm not an expert on French politics, but I gather the director and cowriter, Xavier Durringer, has worked by simply cranking up the energy under what everybody knows really happened. The result at times approaches screwball comedy.

But no, this isn't deliberate comedy. It's essentially realistic. It's simply that the real lives of these figures are funny. Most of the major players here are in the same political party, we hardly hear about their opponents, the focus is on infighting within the government, and they warmly hate one another. As I follow our own GOP primaries, I would love to see this approach adapted to Newt Gingrich's real feelings about Mitt Romney and listen in on his language.

The film opens with a problem that would become chronic with current French president Nicolas Sarkozy (Denis Podalydes), who was then a minister angling for higher cabinet posts in the government of Jacques Chirac (Bernard Le Coq). It is an election day, and his wife, Cecilia Sarkozy (Florence Pernel), is nowhere to be found. Sarkozy refuses to be seen voting without his wife at his side, and Cecilia is so mad at him she refuses to appear.

French political spouses obviously lack the

rigorous training on the campaign trail that American partners receive. In our country a spouse is in it for the long haul, and must be prepared to spend eighteen months in an endless series of campaign appearances, smiling and waving, loyal and staunch, every word and gesture under close guard. French campaigns are much shorter and more brutal.

Cecilia occupies an intriguing dual role: (1) She is Sarkozy's most influential and trusted adviser; (2) she hates politics, and considers a political campaign to be a sadistic form of reality television. It is also apparently the case that the Sarkozy marriage is being held together with duct tape and bailing wire. At times the two can barely stand to be in the same room together, and yet fate has yoked them to a common goal. They want power, and they want to win.

Sarkozy emerges here as a fascinating figure. Small and hyperactive, a campaigning welterweight, he is nakedly ambitious, but so are they all. After a seemingly cordial meeting with Sarkozy, Chirac tells an adviser: "The little bastard wants my job." To become president, Sarkozy envisions a series of more and more important cabinet posts, and to keep him in check, Chirac envisions a series of less and less important posts. Since it is clear to everyone that this is the game, it contributes admirably to the amusement level of the French body politic.

To be a candidate for office is a condition few of us would wish upon ourselves. Even having pleasure at mealtime, a sacred occasion in France, is diminished. Some of the more absorbing scenes in *The Conquest* involve the major players, sometimes together, often just as twosomes, dining elegantly in ornate rooms of state while smiling pleasantly and cordially insulting each other.

I don't believe it's necessary for a non-French viewer to know a lot about French politics in order to enjoy this movie. What you need is an appreciation of human nature. The actors, especially Denis Podalydes and Florence Pernel as the Sarkozys, provide in their performances all the personal background you require. We know the film is about politics, we can see how the characters feel about one another, we can apply their behavior to the politicians we're familiar with. It's a macabre but not boring process.

## The Conspirator ★ ★ ★

PG-13, 121 m., 2011

James McAvoy (Frederick Aiken), Robin Wright (Mary Surratt), Kevin Kline (Edwin M. Stanton), Evan Rachel Wood (Anna Surratt), Danny Huston (Joseph Holt), Justin Long (Nicholas Baker), Colm Meaney (General David Hunter), Alexis Bledel (Sarah), Tom Wilkinson (Reverdy Johnson). Directed by Robert Redford and produced by Redford, Brian Peter Falk, Bill Holderman, Greg Shapiro, Robert Stone, and Webster Stone. Screenplay by James Solomon.

In the period following the assassination of Abraham Lincoln, those holding together the wounded federal government were desperate to bring charges against the guilty. Their problem was they couldn't find them. John Wilkes Booth, the gunman, was captured soon after the deed and shot by a Union soldier who was acting against orders. Prosecutors felt he was part of a conspiracy including about eight people.

*The Conspirator*, Robert Redford's new film, takes up the story in a postwar Washington convincingly shot on location in Savannah, Georgia. He approaches it as a legal procedural, concerned not only with the case but also with the legal precedents it established, which we are still dealing with today. Crucially, it tried a civilian in a military tribunal, denying her the right to a jury of peers that is guaranteed in the Constitution.

This civilian was named Mary Surratt (Robin Wright). She owned a boardinghouse in Washington, where Booth and his fellow plotters met. They were brought there by her son, John. Surratt was charged as a coconspirator. Secretary of War Edwin M. Stanton (Kevin Kline), the de facto power in Washington despite the presence of President Andrew Johnson, wanted her tried and convicted quickly, to placate an enraged population. He gave the assignment to defense attorney Reverdy Johnson (Tom Wilkinson), who passed it to a young Union veteran named Frederick Aiken (James McAvoy).

Aiken wanted nothing to do with it. He felt Surratt must certainly be guilty. Johnson, a Southerner, felt he couldn't take the case with passions running so high, and forced the job upon the Northerner Aiken, explaining that Surratt had a right to a competent defense. Surratt is certainly not helpful to her young attorney, because her only thought is to protect her son. Gradually, however, Aiken begins to believe it is possible she was not involved in the meetings of the conspirators.

Redford considers this material in an unusually literate and thoughtful historical film, working from years of research by his screenwriter, James Solomon. I found it absorbing and relevant today. It is useful to reflect that it isn't *her* constitutional rights that are being violated, but our own, because the Constitution must be seen to work equally for all or it loses its strength for everyone. The language and reasoning of Stanton echo with similar statements by George W. Bush and Dick Cheney in defense of the Patriot Act, and Reverdy Johnson in this reading would represent Barack Obama, more a compromiser than an idealist.

The film depends on Robin Wright and James McAvoy for its human appeal. Wright's performance is deliberately withdrawn and restrained. Having apparently concluded she is certain to be found guilty, she's reluctant to cooperate with her attorney. In a sense, because of his ambivalent feelings about her, he's trying his case against himself. His conversion to her cause is essentially his conversion to the underlying constitutional principles involved. As he argues in the military tribunal, he is arguing about its very presence in a case involving a civilian woman with no role in the military.

Redford could have vulgarized this material. He and Wright certainly have the skills to make Mary Surratt a passionate, heroic victim. They choose not to. They require us to think our own way through the case, and arrive at our own opinions, and that is the value of *The Conspirator.* In most historical dramas, the opinions are already in and the conclusions already reached. Redford and his producers, the American Film Company of the Ricketts family, show respect in their treatment of a little-known footnote to a well-known story.

Well, was Mary Surratt a conspirator? I put the question point blank to Redford recently, and he said he thought she must surely have known what her son was discussing with the others under her roof. But her guilt isn't the issue. The film is about the correct means of determining guilt—or innocence. If the Constitution says you can't do something, if it guarantees a due process, then it must be obeyed.

All of this requires a lot of theory, a lot of philosophy, and a lot of dialogue. Those most interested in American history will probably find it most valuable. Those who want a historical romance or a courtroom potboiler will be disappointed. You have to give credit to Redford, Wright and McAvoy, and the other filmmakers. Not many films this smart can be made.

## Contagion ★ ★ ★

PG-13,105 m., 2011

Gwyneth Paltrow (Beth Emhoff), Matt Damon (Mitch Emhoff), Laurence Fishburne (Dr. Ellis Cheever), Kate Winslet (Dr. Erin Mears), Marion Cotillard (Dr. Leonora Orantes), John Hawkes (Roger), Jude Law (Alan Krumwiede), Jennifer Ehle (Dr. Ally Hextall), Elliott Gould (Dr. Ian Sussman), Sanaa Lathan (Aubrey Cheever). Directed by Steven Soderbergh and produced by Gregory Jacobs, Michael Shamberg, and Stacey Sher. Screenplay by Scott Z. Burns.

A black screen. The sound of a harsh cough. We are already alert when, soon after, we see a bartender pick up a customer's coin and then punch numbers into a cash register. Germs, we're thinking. *Contagion* is a realistic, unsensational film about a global epidemic. It's being marketed as a thriller, a frightening speculation about how a new airborne virus could enter the human species and spread relentlessly in very little time.

This scenario is already familiar to us through the apparently annual outbreaks of influenza. Not many of them cause as much alarm as swine flu did. The news chronology is always the same: alarmist maps, global roundups, the struggle to produce a vaccine at the Centers for Disease Control in Atlanta, the manufacture and distribution of supplies of this year's "flu shot."

The virus in *Contagion* is a baffling one: defying isolation, rejecting cure. This film by Steven Soderbergh is skillful at telling the story through the lives of several key characters and the casual interactions of many others. It makes it clear that people do not *give* each other a virus; a virus is a life form evolved to seek out new hosts—as it must to survive, because its carriers die, and it must always stay one jump ahead of death. In a sense it is an alien species, and this is a movie about an invasion from inner space.

The cough we heard at the outset was from Beth Emhoff (Gwyneth Paltrow), a Minneapolis woman who was traveling home from Hong Kong. Soon her son dies. She follows. Her husband, Mitch (Matt Damon), apparently immune, is incredulous that death could so suddenly devastate his family. An investigation uncovers a secret visit Beth made during her stopover in Chicago—but no, she didn't contract the virus through sexual contact, the way AIDS seemed to spread.

At the very end of the film Soderbergh adds a brief scenario explaining where the virus may have come from in the first place, and how very few degrees of separation there were between its origin and a woman from Minneapolis. Whether this could happen in the way Soderbergh illustrates is beside the point; all viruses originate somewhere, and in an age of air travel they can reach a new continent in a day.

The movie follows the protocols of techno-thrillers, with subtitles keeping count: *Day One, Day Three, Minneapolis, Geneva. . . .*We meet such key players as Dr. Ellis Cheever (Laurence Fishburne) of the CDC in Atlanta; Dr. Erin Mears (Kate Winslet) of the Epidemic Intelligence Service, who tries to track the spread with on-the-spot visits; Dr. Leonora Orantes (Marion Cotillard), an investigator from the World Health Organization in Geneva. They have worked together before, are skilled, operate urgently. And in a laboratory, there is Dr. Ally Hextall (Jennifer Ehle), trying to perfect a vaccine and impatient with the time being lost before she can test it on humans.

All of this works as drama. It might have been useful if Soderbergh had explained viruses more clearly as a life form that is not hostile to us, but concerned with other life forms only as its means of survival. Richard Dawkins outlined this process in his remorseless book *The Selfish Gene*: From the viewpoint of a gene, bodies are merely stepping-stones on their journey through time. Still, the movie deserves praise for taking the scientific method seriously, at a time when so much hogwash is floated about regarding vaccines.

One aspect of the film is befuddled. Alan Krumwiede (Jude Law) is a popular blogger who has conspiracy theories about the government's ties with drug companies. His concerns are ominous but unfocused. Does he think drug companies encourage viruses? The blogger subplot doesn't interact clearly with the main story lines, and functions mostly as an alarming but vague distraction.

Yes, we must often wash our hands. Yes, "hand sanitizers" are all over the place these days. Yes, shaking hands with strangers can be annoying—although they are no more likely to carry viruses than we are. And yes, there is really not much we can do. You might be surprised by how many hospital patients die because of viruses they didn't walk in with.

## Contraband ★ ★

R, 110 m., 2012

Mark Wahlberg (Chris Farraday), Kate Beckinsale (Kate Farraday), Giovanni Ribisi (Tim Briggs), Ben Foster (Sebastian Abney), Caleb Landry Jones (Andy), Lukas Haas (Danny Raymer), Diego Luna (Gonzalo), J. K. Simmons (Captain Redmond Camp). Directed by Baltasar Kormakur and produced by Kormakur, Tim Bevan, Eric Fellner, Stephen Levinson, and Mark Wahlberg. Screenplay by Aaron Guzikowski, based on the film *Reykjavik-Rotterdam,* written by Arnaldur Indrioason and Oskar Jonasson.

There are elements in the thriller *Contraband* that have a nifty novelty, but the movie as a whole is straight from the spare parts shelf. I'm growing particularly weary of the wife/girlfriend of the hero whose life and children are threatened by vicious bad guys. It must be admitted, however, that the threatened means of death in this film makes being tied to railroad tracks seem jolly by comparison.

The movie involves the smuggling of a vast quantity of counterfeit $100 bills from Panama City to New Orleans. Although Chris Farraday, the would-be smuggler, prefers not to deal with drugs, wouldn't you know several kilos of cocaine get mixed in with the deal. This film is based on an Icelandic thriller named *Reykjavik-Rotterdam,* which leads you to suspect that neither New Orleans nor Panama City is particularly essential to the plot. That film starred Baltasar Kormakur, who is the director of this one, perhaps as a demonstration that many stars believe they could direct this crap themselves if they ever had the chance.

Kormakur uses Mark Wahlberg to play his own former role. Chris is an experienced smuggler who has retired from crime to settle down in married bliss; alas, his wife, Kate (Kate Beckinsale), has a brother who has made a mess of a cocaine delivery, and lives are in danger unless the veteran Chris steps in and performs a make-good job. He has entrusted an old pal named Sebastian (Ben Foster) to protect Kate and the children while he's on the job. She may require protection because a snaky crime lord named Tim Briggs (Giovanni Ribisi) is the boss of this deal. Let it be said that in this role Ribisi uses the kind of voice that makes you want to smack him, just for talking like that.

Chris and a couple of partners sign as seamen aboard a container ship plying the waves between New Orleans and Panama City. The ship's skipper is J. K. Simmons. Yes, the instantly likable actor who played the father in *Juno.* He's likable here, too, if a little tougher; Chris smuggles rings around him as the ship becomes as active as a FedEx terminal. Now help me out here. Chris shows his pals where he'll stash the piles of counterfeit bills—in an empty space behind a tool board. One guy steps inside to check it out and just then the skipper approaches, and they have to screw the panel shut and hurry away. Did they ever let that guy out? I kept worrying about him trapped in there. Maybe I missed something.

Man, is this plot complicated. At one point, while Chris and his pals have a "very limited" time ashore in Panama before the ship sails, they find enough time to (1) seek the warehouse where the bills are manufactured, and (2) try to stick up an armored car. It's not a matter of just going straight to the warehouse. Chris doesn't recall where it is, "but if we drive around I'll see something that reminds me." Panama City has a population of nine hundred thousand. Sticking up the armored car involves driving a van into its path and causing a crash, then shooting it out with the cops. This leads to the theft of a Jackson Pollock painting worth millions, which nobody ever explains to the thieves. At one point it's described as "a cloth with oil smears." Well, fair enough. More like dribbles.

Meanwhile, snaky-voiced Ribisi and his men are causing great distress to the Beckinsale character—so much that the preview audience recoiled at one point. The means of her apparent doom is so heartless you can hardly believe your eyes. Toward the end, Chris sets a trap for the bad guys that is admirably ingenious, although it involves a lot of planning ahead and good luck, and it's one of those deals requiring everyone to be in precisely the right place at the right time. Don't you suppose these schemes usually go wrong?

*Contraband* involves a lot of energy, but I'm getting tired of violent retreads of these heist elements. It wanted to terrify me for two hours, but what mostly scared me was the challenge of getting back to street level on the theater's steep escalator. Man, they should slow that baby down.

## Conviction ★ ★ ★

R, 96 m., 2010

Hilary Swank (Betty Anne Waters), Sam Rockwell (Kenny Waters), Minnie Driver (Abra Rice), Melissa Leo (Nancy Taylor), Peter Gallagher (Barry Scheck), Juliette Lewis (Roseanne Perry). Directed by Tony Goldwyn and produced by Goldwyn, Andrew S. Karsch, and Andrew Sugerman. Screenplay by Pamela Gray.

Kenny Waters might not have been a very nice man, but he was an innocent one. By considering his innocence and not his personality, *Conviction* puts the focus where it belongs: on the sister who reshaped her entire life to win his freedom. Her determination is fierce, her rebirth is inspiring, and in Hilary Swank the film finds the right actress to embody gritty tenacity.

You can hardly imagine anyone else playing Betty Anne Waters. She's a working-class woman from a hard childhood. She and her brother Kenny (Sam Rockwell) had an absent father and a mother who might as well have been absent, and were shuffled through a series of dismal foster homes. But they stuck together and helped each other, almost as Dickensian survivors. Her gratitude to him is boundless.

The movie doesn't avoid the fact that Kenny gets wild when he gets drunk. He displays the personality changes of an alcoholic. He can be mean, and everybody knows it. In many circles this is seen as a trait and not a symptom. A local woman is murdered; he's arrested on suspicion and makes the mistake of behaving insultingly to a cop (Melissa Leo, from *Frozen River*). He will pay for that. A couple of local women, including a ditzy witness (Juliette Lewis), sorta are kinda sure they musta seen him at the crime scene, and the vengeful cop railroads him into jail.

(Some spoilers ahead.)

Swank dedicates her life to proving her brother's innocence. This involves reinventing herself. She gets a high school diploma and a college degree and enrolls in law school. One cost of this is her marriage. It's an intriguing possibility, untouched by the movie, that after a certain point in her reeducation she simply outgrew her earlier life, and carried on for her own sake as well as her brother's.

In law school she bonds with another student named Abra (Minnie Driver), who also dedicates her life to the case. The movie never really explains why; is it just the goodness of her heart? Driver is very good, in any event, and the two women involve us in their investigation.

Courtroom scenes just about always work for me. It must be built into the situation. *Conviction* has good ones, especially when the Juliette Lewis character comes back into play. It is good to see Melissa Leo again, not so good that her vengeful cop has one dimension, but she's effective at how well she evokes it.

This is all based on a true story, including the lucky break when DNA testing is introduced and proves Kenny innocent. The story generates the kind of urgency we feel when a character is obviously right and is up against stupidity and meanness. It delivers.

What it doesn't reveal during the "where are they now?" crawl at the end is that six months after his release, according to The Associated Press, Kenny was killed when he "fractured his skull when he fell from a 15-foot wall while taking a shortcut to his brother's house after a dinner with his mother." Tragic. But Betty Anne Waters is still working for wrongfully convicted prisoners.

## Cop Out ★ ½

R, 110 m., 2010

Bruce Willis (Jimmy Monroe), Tracy Morgan (Paul Hodges), Adam Brody (Barry Mangold), Kevin Pollak (Hunsaker), Ana de la Reguera (Gabriela), Guillermo Diaz (Poh Boy), Michelle Trachtenberg (Ava), Seann William Scott (Dave). Directed by Kevin Smith and produced by Polly Cohen Johnsen, Marc Platt, and Michael Tadross. Screenplay by Robb Cullen and Mark Cullen.

Jimmy and Paul are cops hunkered down across the street from a stakeout when they see a mysterious figure run across rooftops and break into a house. Seconds later, he can clearly be seen in an upper window, sitting on a toilet and reading a magazine. "What kindofa guy breaks into a house and takes a crap?" asks Paul, or words to that effect.

Paul explains he always delays this elementary function until he gets home. He's not relaxed until then. But once he's home—ooohhh boy! Then he lets loose. He describes the results in great detail. The walls, the ceilings. All right! I'm thinking, all right, already! I got it! Mudslide! Paul isn't finished. Now he's talking about the reaction of the neighbors.

How do you know this is a scene from a Kevin Smith film? The imitation of a nine-year-old describing bodily functions might be a clue. But the clincher is when that mysterious guy runs across the rooftops. Paul (Tracy Morgan) explains to his partner Jimmy (Bruce Willis): "That's known as 'parkour.' It's a new martial art." Well, thanks, Paul. I didn't know that until yesterday, when it was explained in *District 13: Ultimatum*. What synchronicity. That other movie costars the man who gave "parkour" its name. The movie is filled with it. I suspect its presence as a brief walk-on in *Cop Out* can be explained this way: Kevin found out about it, thought it was cool, and slipped in a little quick "parkour" for fun.

If you combine the enthusiasms of a geek with the toilet humor of a third-grader, you'll be pretty close to defining the art of Kevin Smith. Hey, I'm not complaining. If we lose our inner third-grader, we begin to die. When the muse visits him, Smith gets inspired and makes fun movies like *Zack and Miri Make a Porno*. Alas, *Cop Out* is not one of those movies. Tracy Morgan is forced to go way over the top; Bruce Willis seems eager to have a long, sad talk with his agent; and Kevin Pollak, who gets costar billing, does at least appear for longer than a quark at Fermilab.

*Cop Out* tells your standard idiotic story about buddy cops who screw up, get suspended by the captain, and redeem themselves by overthrowing a drug operation while searching for the valuable baseball card Jimmy wants to sell to pay for his daughter's wedding. Paul spends an unreasonable amount of time dressed as a cell phone, considering there is nothing to prevent him from taking it off.

A lot of the dialogue is intended to be funny, but man, is it lame. Many of the gags possibly looked good on paper, but watching Willis and Morgan struggle with them is like watching third-graders do Noel Coward, if Noel Coward had been rewritten by Kevin Smith. At St. Joseph's Boys' Camp there was this Chicago kid named Bob Calvano who was naturally hilarious around the campfire every night. Then I'd get up and flop with my memorized bits from Buddy Hackett records. "Ebert," he advised me kindly, "it isn't funny if you act like it's supposed to be funny. Act like you don't know." All I can do is pass along Calvano's advice.

## Coriolanus ★ ★ ★ ½

R, 122 m., 2012

Ralph Fiennes (Caius Martius Coriolanus), Gerard Butler (Tullus Aufidius), Brian Cox (Menenius), Vanessa Redgrave (Volumnia), Jessica Chastain (Virgilia), John Kani (General Cominius), James Nesbitt (Sicinius), Paul Jesson (Brutus). Directed by Ralph Fiennes and produced by Fiennes, John Logan, Gabrielle Tana, Julia Taylor-Stanley, and Colin Vaines. Screenplay by John Logan, based on the play by William Shakespeare.

The point with Shakespeare is the language. Modern-dress productions of his plays are common and can inspire intriguing viewpoints. Who is to say that *Coriolanus* might not as well be set in the Middle East as in Rome—neither a place Shakespeare had ever seen? Modern associations can even find parallels, as in the 1995 *Richard III*, which cast Ian McKellen as a fascist dictator.

Now we have Ralph Fiennes directing and starring in *Coriolanus*, one of the Roman tragedies, where the feral and discontented general is at war in "a place calling itself Rome." The walls are covered with graffiti, grenade launchers replace swords, and we get the obligatory shot of warriors being blown toward us with an explosion blossoming behind. The costumes, art direction, and props could be used for an action film about most modern wars, including the Bosnian, and indeed the film was shot on location in Belgrade.

Apart from the infinite varieties of the human face, there are no sights in *Coriolanus* I'm not familiar with. Fiennes, an actor who can remake himself, is here lean and muscular, his head shaven, his neck a muscular trunk displaying a dragon tattoo. He carries an AK-47. Is this Shakespeare's hero? Did Shakespeare envision Coriolanus in Greco-Roman draperies? I imagine Shakespeare alone in a room, writing by candlelight, intoxicated by language. For him, Coriolanus was the name of the speaker of his words.

One of the pleasures of Fiennes's film is that the screenplay by John Logan (*Hugo, Gladiator*) makes room for as much of Shakespeare's language as possible. I would have enjoyed more, because such speakers as Fiennes, Vanessa Redgrave, and Brian Cox let the words roll trippingly off the tongue.

I realize I savor Shakespeare in a different way than the typical Friday night action fan—who, lured by the violence and ferocity of the hard-boiled trailer and TV ads, will perhaps wonder why everyone is talking so strangely. There is a reason why most of the sentences in action dialogue are not more than a few words long. More than half the box-office revenue will come from overseas, where the film will be dubbed, and longer speeches are trickier to dub. *Coriolanus* will ideally be seen in English.

Shakespeare's story involves a Roman who cares more about battle than about politics. This is Caius Martius (Fiennes), a general who has led Rome against its nearby Volscian enemies. Warfare has cut off Rome's food supplies, there's rioting in the streets, and he leaves to join the siege of the enemy city Corioles. When he prevails, he's given the honorary title "Coriolanus," returns home, and at the urging of his strong-willed mother, Volumnia (Vanessa Redgrave), runs for consul. He is, alas, not a diplomatic politician (it's unwise to hold the people in contempt). Banished from Rome, he joins forces with his former Volscian enemy, Tullus Aufidius (Gerard Butler), and they attack the city. Only his mother can persuade him to lay down his arms.

Transfer this story to "a place calling itself Rome," add the trappings and the suits of modern warfare, supply updates from cable news, and you have a movie that is not so much about the private, patrician scorn of Coriolanus as about the motivation of most action heroes, which is to strut in macho display, inspire slaughter and mayhem, and provide reaction shots when things blow up real good. This is all done well by Fiennes, but as a man who starred in this play ten years ago in London, he has deeper feelings for it, and the key scenes are those between Coriolanus and his mother, Volumnia, to whom he seems more romantically attached than to his wife, Virgilia (Jessica Chastain).

I admired the movie even though I found it neither fish nor fowl. As Shakespeare, it has too much action footage (Coriolanus's face seems permanently streaked with blood), and as action, it has too much Shakespeare. I suppose the action is the price Fiennes had to pay to do the Shakespeare, because a film this expensive must appeal to the masses. What's the question Shakespeare has Coriolanus ask about public opinion? "What's the matter, you dissentious rogues, that, rubbing the poor itch of your opinion, make yourselves scabs?"

## Country Strong ★ ★ ½

PG-13, 116 m., 2011

Gwyneth Paltrow (Kelly Canter), Tim McGraw (James Canter), Garrett Hedlund (Beau Hutton), Leighton Meester (Chiles Stanton). Directed by Shana Feste and produced by Tobey Maguire and Jenno Topping. Written by Feste.

*Country Strong* is one of the best movies of 1957, and I mean that sincerely as a compliment. Lee Remick would have been terrific in this movie—as good as Gwyneth Paltrow is. We live now in more fraught times, with Natalie Portman mentally disemboweling herself for her art while slipping into madness. And I admire her and she deserves her Oscar. But *Country Strong* is a throwback, a pure, heartfelt exercise in '50s social melodrama, using such stock elements as a depressed heroine, her manipulating husband, an ambivalent Other Man, and, tapping her toe impatiently in the wings, young Eve Harrington eager to swoop in and gnaw the heroine's courage from her bones.

This is filmed in a straightforward meat-and-potatoes style, beautifully photographed by John Bailey. It takes place in what could be the Texas of *The Last Picture Show*, except for some performances in a modern arena. It stars Paltrow as Kelly Canter, a troubled country singer who has been released from alcohol rehab too soon. Tim McGraw plays James, the man she married when they were in love and who now stays on as her controlling manager. Garrett Hedlund is Beau Hutton, a singer who "just likes to play music for people" and doesn't care about money. And Leighton Meester is Chiles Stanton, a former Miss Dallas who dreams of stardom.

Beau and Chiles. Man, are those '50s names. The plot does not neglect the tragic loss of Kelly's child, when while pregnant and drunk she fell from a stage. Nor Beau and James, who *both* fool around with Chiles, and *both* are probably in love with Kelly. After Beau (apparently) resigns his day job as an orderly at Kelly's rehab institution, these people move in unison across Texas on a tour route scattered with emotional land mines. Kelly is in the big customized bus. The rest bring up the rear in an old van.

It is a given that Kelly is a great star. Beau is a damn fine country singer, too good to play in bars that can't even afford enough extras to make up a crowd. Chiles is a promising singer but an emotional basket case because of deep insecurities from childhood. She's got herself one of those pinched-up fearful faces with her red lips all forced into a perfect bow and her hair too stiff. She's like a caricature of mama's little beauty pageant contestant until at the end, wow, she scrubs off the makeup and shampoos that hair spray off her head, and we realize Leighton Meester is a beauty and not a victim of a cosmetics counter makeover.

Now it may seem from this that I am finding fault with *Country Strong*. Quite the opposite. We must see a movie for what it is, not for what we think another film might have been. This is a movie into which Lee Remick and Rock Hudson and Sandra Dee would have slipped without shoehorns, and Douglas Sirk would have known where to march them. Its emotions are strong and visible. Its motives are clear. Its music performances are so good we wish they lasted longer. Gwyneth Paltrow is so beautiful and just really nice that she brings enormous sympathy to her role. And Garrett Hedlund's Beau would do anything for a woman—or two women, in this case.

I eat this stuff up. Don't get all on your high horse. Here are big emotions sprayed across the somewhat crowded quarters of a limited number of small sets, punctuated by second-unit drive-bys and grizzly good ol' boys filling out the frame. The only truly realistic character in the movie has hardly a line. That would be the tall middle-age woman who is apparently Kelly Canter's wardrobe woman, and follows her everywhere like those well-paid and not indifferent support people in the lives of stars. She sees everything and knows everything and keeps her mouth shut, which is what you want. She's got your back.

Another thing that places this movie in the 1950s milieu is its understanding of alcoholism. It thinks being drunk comes on people in sudden spurts, like a sneezing fit, and goes away when the plot needs it to. Kelly will be waving a vodka bottle at one moment and morosely pondering at the next. Paltrow has a lovely scene where she coaches young Chiles on what she needs to know about sweat stains, high heels, and love.

Beau tells James his mistake was to take Kelly out of rehab before the rehab was finished. James is not a man of deep insights into drinking or sobriety. Three days after Kelly gets out of rehab, Beau catches her choking down pills in the dressing room. He confronts James about this. "I know!" says James. "I put them in her pillbox myself! They're not dangerous unless she drinks!" I know I didn't hear you say that, James. Tell me you didn't.

## Cowboys & Aliens ★ ★ ★

PG-13,118 m., 2011

Daniel Craig (Jake Lonergan), Harrison Ford (Colonel Woodrow Dolarhyde), Olivia Wilde (Ella Swenson), Sam Rockwell (Doc), Adam Beach (Nat Colorado), Paul Dano (Percy Dolarhyde), Noah Ringer (Emmett Taggart), Keith Carradine (Sheriff John Taggart). Directed by Jon Favreau and produced by Johnny Dodge, Ron Howard, Alex Kurtzman, Damon Lindelof, Roberto Orci, and Scott Mitchell Rosenberg. Screenplay by Kurtzman, Lindelof, Orci, Mark Fergus, and Hawk Ostby, based on Platinum Studios' *Cowboys and Aliens* by Rosenberg.

*Cowboys & Aliens* has without any doubt the most cockamamie plot I've witnessed in many a moon. Here is a movie with cowboys, aliens, Apaches, horses, spaceships, a murdering stagecoach robber, a preacher, bug-eyed monsters, a bartender named Doc, a tyrannical rancher who lives outside of a town named Absolution, his worthless son, two sexy women (one not from around these parts), bandits, a magic bracelet, an ancient Indian cure for amnesia, a symbolic hummingbird, a brave kid with a spyglass, and a plucky dog who follows the good guys for miles and miles through the barren waste and must be plumb tuckered out.

This is not a satire. Nor is it a comedy. Humanity is in danger, and it's up to the roughhewn cowboys of the Old West to save us. Daniel Craig plays Lonergan, the stagecoach killer, Harrison Ford plays the not enigmatically named Woodrow Dolarhyde, and Keith Carradine is Sheriff Taggart, who has his work cut out for him.

The aliens, as usual, show limited signs of intelligence. Oh, they arrive in a spaceship that's taller than a skyscraper, and they must have designed it. But mostly they strafe the town, drop explosive charges behind characters but rarely upon them, and reel up human victims into their smaller flying ships in order (need we be told) to study them. Their other purpose in journeying unimaginable distances across the void is to use mysterious forces to suck up gold—coins, watches, rings, whatever.

I call these monsters bug-eyed not to be unkind, but to trace their lineage back to the mother lode of BEMs on the covers of such pulp mags as *Thrilling Wonder Stories.* It's almost too good to be true to learn, via a trade review, that the movie was inspired not by a comic book but by its cover. That's the spirit.

The movie will no doubt be popular and deserves success. As preposterous moneymakers go, it's ambitious and well-made. The acting from the large cast is of a high standard, Craig and Ford were more or less born into their roles, and director Jon Favreau actually develops his characters and gives them things to do, instead of posing them in front of special effects.

Yet I feel a certain small sadness. I wish this *had* been a Western. You know, the old-fashioned kind, without spaceships. Daniel Craig, cold-eyed and lean, plays a character familiar in the genre; think of the Ringo Kid or Doc Holliday, bad guys who rise to goodness. Harrison Ford, as the rancher, embodies the kind of man who comes riding into town at the head of his private posse and issues orders to everyone. Sam Rockwell's Doc is the kind of small-business man who has come west seeking his fortune among hard men. All the elements are here.

We are told, however, that the Western is a dead genre. The last one kids liked was *Rango,* an animated cartoon. *True Grit, Appaloosa,* and *3:10 to Yuma* were good, but limited in their demographic appeal. A competent director—Favreau, say—could have ditched the ridiculous aliens and made a straight Western with the same cast, but today there's small chance of that.

Yet I suspect the big audiences drawn to this concept will find themselves more deeply drawn into the conventional Western material in the opening scenes, before the aliens attack. There is more genuine suspense when the rancher's loopy son (Paul Dano) starts shooting up the town than when countless aliens appear, resembling a fusion of gorillas and lobsters.

One alien element has become almost traditional. Ever since *Alien* we've had the phenomenon of aliens who unfold to reveal wicked inner parts. The aliens here have chest cavities that open to extrude three-fingered hands, slimy with mucus. One shudders to envision the use of these limbs during sex. On their home world, there must be fortunes to be made in opening manicure shops.

## The Crazies ★ ★ ½

R, 101 m., 2010

Timothy Olyphant (David Dutton), Radha Mitchell (Judy Dutton), Joe Anderson (Russell Clank), Danielle Panabaker (Becca Darling), Christie Lynn Smith (Deardra Farnum), Brett Rickaby (Bill Farnum), Preston Bailey (Nicholas), John Aylward (Mayor Hobbs). Directed by Breck Eisner and produced by Michael Aguilar, Rob Cowan, and Dean Georgaris. Screenplay by Scott Kosar and Ray Wright.

*The Crazies* is a perfectly competent genre film in a genre that has exhausted its interest for me, the zombie film. It provides such a convenient storytelling device: Large numbers of mindless zombies lurch toward the camera and the hero, wreaking savage destruction, and can be quickly blown away, although not without risk and occasional loss of life. When sufficient zombies have been run through, it's time for a new dawn.

I know there can be good zombie films. I've seen some: *Dawn of the Dead, 28 Days Later, Shaun of the Dead,* and so on. If I saw another one, I'd like it. But all depends on good living characters and a director with something new to say about zombies, who are a subject easily exhausted.

Are the zombies in *The Crazies* real zombies? Maybe, maybe not. Is there an agreed definition of what is a zombie, and how they get that way? Not that I know of. I think zombies are defined by behavior and can be "explained" by many handy shortcuts: the supernatural, radiation, a virus, space visitors, secret weapons, a Harvard education, and so on. I suppose it would be a "spoiler" if I revealed why the Crazies are lurching, but come on, does it matter? What if I revealed they got that way because of, oh, say, eating Pringles? Would that spoil things for you? What difference does it make? All that matters is that they got to be zombies *somehow*. Before that, they were your friends and neighbors. Then they started in on the damn Pringles.

The protagonists, of course, have to be healthy. I cannot imagine a zombie as a leading character. Vampires, now, I grant you. Werewolves. But a zombie doesn't bring much to the party. So we start in sweet little Ogden Marsh, Iowa, described on its Web site as "the friendliest place on Earth," and no wonder. Its sheriff is so good-looking he could be the star of this movie. Must be a quiet place. The sheriff's office is open only from eight to five Monday through Friday.

One day after work Sheriff David Dutton (Timothy Olyphant) and his deputy, Russell Clank (Joe Anderson), are watching a local school baseball game when the town drunk comes lurching into the outfield holding a shotgun. When the autopsy shows he had a 0.0 blood alcohol level, that's the first signal something is wrong in Ogden Marsh. For one thing, their town drunk is a slacker.

The sheriff's wife, Judy (Radha Mitchell), is the local doctor. She starts treating some strange cases. I don't want to spoil anything, so I'll simply say the sheriff and Deputy Russell discover the probable origin of this plague, but of course can't get the mayor to declare an emergency, because he learned the mayoring trade from *Jaws*. Meanwhile, it's up to Dave, Judy, and Russell to defend themselves from zombies and survive after the town is isolated and quarantined and the cure seems worse than the disease.

That requires many scenes involving people and objects that jump out from the sides of the screen with loud noises and alarming musical chords. I'm thinking, so what? The last thing I need is another jump out/loud noise/alarming chord movie. Even a well-made one—like this one, directed by Breck Eisner. It was inspired by George Romero's 1973 movie of the same name, although I can't tell you if the zombies match because that would be a spoiler.

Here is what I can say to aspiring young screenwriters: Movies like this are fairly simple to write. You need zombies. You need heroes. At first there's a mystery, and then the horror. You describe lots of jump/noise/chord situations. When you figure you're up to around ninety minutes, the sun can rise. You'll get an R rating, so throw in a little nudity. Not too much, because if there's a combination that gives me the creeps, it's zombies and nudity. Especially when—but never mind. That's enough for today.

## Crazy, Stupid, Love. ★ ★ ★

PG-13, 117 m., 2011

Steve Carell (Cal), Ryan Gosling (Jacob), Julianne Moore (Emily), Emma Stone (Hannah), John Carroll Lynch (Bernie), Marisa Tomei (Kate), Kevin Bacon (David Lindhagen), Jonah Bobo (Robbie), Analeigh Tipton (Jessica). Directed by Glenn Ficarra and John Requa and produced by Steve Carell and Denise Di Novi. Screenplay by Dan Fogelman.

*Crazy, Stupid, Love.* is a sweet romantic comedy about good-hearted people. Imagine that. No snark. No raunch. It has a lot of cynicism, but that's employed only to be corrected. Nobody here wishes anybody ill, and the movie comes out foursquare in favor of marriage. Yes, the characters commit adultery, but they learn to their relief they were mistaken.

Much of the movie's appeal is generated by the actors. Steve Carell has been growing on me. Emma Stone is a sweetheart. Julianne Moore's character seems cold and distant, but that's a stage she's going through. A teenage couple are cutie-pies. Marisa Tomei enters the movie as a tornado of warm comic energy. All that woman has to do is smile and I'm there.

But the surprise is Ryan Gosling. I consider him a superb actor, and I've seen him play everything from an anti-Semite (*The Believer*) to a child killer (*Murder by Numbers*) to a man in love with a love doll (*Lars and the Real Girl*). In last year's *Blue Valentine* he plays a not-ideal husband. But I didn't see him as a lounge lizard and pickup artist, and in *Crazy, Stupid, Love.* he has as much bulls#!t as if he'd been Zach Galifianakis all of his life.

The movie opens with a bombshell. Cal (Steve Carell) asks his wife, Emily (Julianne

Moore), what she wants for dessert. "A divorce," she says. Cal, who has grown complacent in his marriage, is stunned. So are his kids, especially thirteen-year-old Robbie (Jonah Bobo), who has a crush on Jessica (Analeigh Tipton), his seventeen-year-old babysitter.

Cal seeks to assuage his sorrow in an upscale cocktail lounge with an improbable variety of babes, and finds himself noticing the smooth moves of a lady-killer named Jacob (Ryan Gosling). This guy seems to leave every night with the woman of his choice. Jacob observes Cal's morose presence at the bar, overhears his bitter monologues, and insists on giving him some tips. This leads to lectures on pickup techniques and one of those makeover montages in which Cal acquires the correct shoes, shirts, suits, and a haircut.

Emily, I neglected to say, has been fooling around with a guy at work (Kevin Bacon in his slightly snaky mode). Not much is made of this; we're spared the sight of Emily being tender with him, because that would throw off the gradually developing logic of the movie.

So OK. We have two generations seeking success in love. Jonah Bobo does a winsomely good job of pining hopelessly for Analeigh Tipton, who has set her sights a little higher. Cal, meanwhile, takes advantage of Jacob's coaching to score sensationally with Kate (Marisa Tomei), an energetic recovering alcoholic who is a sexual virtuoso. And then something happens that Jacob did not anticipate: In the bar one night, he meets the lovely Hannah (Emma Stone), and does something he didn't think he was capable of. He falls in love.

These many strands are woven together in a clever screenplay by Dan Fogelman, which establishes what is needed, conceals what is required, supplies Carell with a one-liner about Tomei that brings down the house, and springs some "OMG!" moments.

All of that is the mechanism. What is also nice is the feeling. No one is hateful in this movie. Even Kevin Bacon, as the ominous marriage wrecker David Lindhagen, wishes no ill. Emily was apparently seducible, so how much can we blame him? The major characters all persevere in the faith that for every person there is One True Love, and when you meet that person, your quest is at an end—always assuming, of course, that your love is returned. Sometimes babysitters four years older than you are don't get in the spirit.

The strength of the movie, however formulaic its structure, is that it is slightly more thoughtful about its characters. It's not deep, mind you, but it considers their problems as more than fodder for comedy. It allows them to have real feelings, even some that surprise them, and it leaves them some room for growth. At the end, after as many strands have been brought together as seems possible, I felt an undeniable satisfaction.

## Creation ★ ★ ★

PG-13, 108 m., 2010

Paul Bettany (Charles Darwin), Jennifer Connelly (Emma Darwin), Jeremy Northam (Rev. Innes), Toby Jones (Thomas Huxley), Benedict Cumberbatch (Joseph Hooker), Martha West (Annie Darwin). Directed by Jon Amiel and produced by Jeremy Thomas. Screenplay by John Collee, based on the book *Annie's Box* by Randal Keynes.

Darwin, it is generally agreed, had the most important idea in the history of science. Thinkers had been feeling their way toward it for decades, but it took Darwin to begin with an evident truth and arrive at its evident conclusion: Over the passage of many years, more successful organisms survive better than less successful. The result is the improvement of future generations. This process he called "natural selection."

It worked for bugs, birds, and bees. It worked for plants, fish, and trees. In 1859, when he published *On the Origin of Species,* it explained a great many things. Later, we would discover it even explained the workings of the cosmos. But—and here was the question even Darwin himself hesitated to ask—did it explain Man?

Emma Darwin didn't think so. Darwin's wife was a committed Christian who believed with her church that God alone was the author of Man. And for her it wasn't God as a general concept, but the specific God of Genesis, and he created Man exactly as the Old Testament said he did. He did it fairly recently, too, no matter that Darwin's fossils seemed to indicate otherwise.

*Creation* is a film about the way this disagreement played out in Darwin's marriage. Charles and Emma were married from 1830 until his death in 1882. They had ten children, seven of whom survived to beget descendants who even today have reunions. They loved each other greatly. Darwin at first avoided spelling out the implications for Man of the theory of evolution so as not to disturb her. But his readers could draw the obvious conclusion, and so could Emma: If God created Man, he did it in the way Darwin discovered, and not in the way a four-thousand-year-old legend prescribed.

The problems this created in the Darwin marriage were of interest primarily to Emma and Charles, probably their children, and few others except in the movie business, which seldom encounters an idea it can't dramatize in terms of romance. It helps to know that going in. *Creation* will give you an idea of the lives and times of the Darwins, but unless you bring a knowledge of evolution to the movie you may not leave with much of one.

The film stars the real-life couple Paul Bettany and Jennifer Connelly, as Charles and Emma, who a few years before the publication of *Origins* are grieving the death of their ten-year-old, Annie (Martha West). This loss has destroyed Darwin's remaining faith in God and reinforced his wife's. But it is to Charles that Annie reappears throughout the film, in visions, memories, and perhaps hallucinations.

The film suggests that Darwin was forced almost helplessly toward the implications of his theory. He had no particular desire to stir up religious turmoil, especially with himself as its target. He famously delayed publication of his theories as long as he could. Two close friends tell him he owes it to himself to publish, and Thomas Huxley, who called himself "Darwin's bulldog," tells him: "Congratulations, sir! You've killed God!"

Not every believer in evolution, including the pope, would agree. But Huxley's words are precisely those Darwin feared the most. Consider that he had no idea in the 1850s how irrefutably correct his theory was, and how useful it would be in virtually every hard science. Emma and their clergyman, Rev. Innes (Jeremy Northam), try to dissuade him from publishing, but his wife finally tells him to go ahead because he must. If he hadn't, someone would have: The theory of evolution was a fruit hanging ripe from the tree.

The director Jon Amiel tells his story with respect and some restraint, showing how sad and weakened Charles is and yet not ratcheting up his grief into unseemly melodrama. One beautiful device Amiel uses is a series of digressions into the natural world, in which we observe everyday applications of the survival of the fittest. What's often misunderstood is that Darwin was essentially speaking of the survival of the fittest genes, not the individual members of a species. This process took millions of years, and wasn't a case of humans slugging it out with dinosaurs.

Both Darwins understood and agreed about the role that inheritance (later to be known as genetics) played in health. As first cousins, they wondered if Annie's life expectancy had been compromised. She died of complications from scarlet fever, which wasn't their fault—but did they know and believe that?

I have a feeling that the loss of their child and the state of their marriage were what most interested the backers of this film. They must have wanted to make a film about Darwin the man, not Darwin the scientist. The filmmakers do their best to keep Darwin's theory in the picture, but it sadly isn't fit enough to struggle against the dominant species of Hollywood executives.

## Cropsey ★ ★ ★

NO MPAA RATING, 84 m., 2010

Donna Cutugno, Karen Schweiger, David Novarro, and Ralph Aquino. A documentary directed by Joshua Zeman and Barbara Brancaccio and produced by Zeman, Brancaccio, and Zachary Mortensen. Screenplay by Zeman.

*Cropsey* is a creepy documentary with all the elements of a horror film about a demented serial killer, and an extra ingredient: This one is real, and you see him handcuffed in the film, not merely empty-eyed, shabby, and stooped, but actually drooling. "I've never seen a perp walk like that," says a TV newsman.

The killer's name is Andre Rand, and he's currently doing time in a New York penitentiary. He was the real-life embodiment of "Cropsey," a bogeyman who figured in the campfire stories and nightmares of many children in Pennsylvania, New Jersey, and along the Eastern Seaboard. In the legends, he lived in the woods and ventured out to abduct children. In the early 1980s, Rand was convicted for the kidnapping and murder of two young girls and suspected in the disappearance of three more.

The man fit the legend. Andre Rand was a worker in the Willowbrook State School for the mentally handicapped on Staten Island, a New York borough isolated from the city for many years before a bridge was constructed. Willowbrook, one of the largest mental institutions in the world, was also one of the worst; Geraldo Rivera won fame for a TV special with footage of its half-naked children scattered on the floor, rocking back and forth in misery. Sanitary facilities were pitiful, filth was everywhere, abuse was common. Willowbrook was shut down, but some of its staff and inmates returned, living in a forgotten network of tunnels under the grounds. Among these was Andre Rand.

Already convicted of sexual abuse against a minor, he attracted the attention of searchers after the disappearance of Jennifer Schweiger, a young girl with Down syndrome. Rand was then living in a campsite on the heavily forested grounds of Willowbrook, and was arrested on suspicion. The charges were expanded to include the disappearance of little Holly Ann Hughes.

He made an ideal suspect. Rumors spread of Satan worship in the tunnels. Staten Island was convinced. He was a bogeyman from central casting. There were only a few problems. There was no physical evidence. Jennifer Schweiger's body was found, but here's the funny thing: The grounds of Willowbrook were combed by hundreds of police and volunteers who found nothing, and then a later search found a grave so shallow a hand was sticking out of the earth. It was near Rand's campsite. It wasn't found on the earlier search, and he'd been in jail ever since.

Was he framed? Did he have a partner in murder? Was some eyewitness testimony suspect because he'd already been convicted in the public eye? *Cropsey* raises these questions in a doc that interviews the original detectives on the case, Jennifer's parents, Rand's defense attorneys, and members of the public. It surrounds this footage with the sparse available video of Rand, and uses many letters Rand wrote to the filmmakers claiming his innocence and suggesting unanswered questions.

The people of Staten Island heard in the film seem unconcerned by the possibility of Rand's innocence. They ask, Would you feel safe knowing that man was roaming free? No, but that alone is not the best reason for locking someone away. At the end I was prepared to agree that Rand seemed like an awfully convincing suspect if he happened to be innocent.

I was reminded of the continuing outrage of the West Memphis Three. Three teenagers were arrested, tried, and convicted amid hysterical rumors they were Satanists who sacrificed young boys. This in the face of their alibis and actual physical evidence suggesting the identity of another possible killer, who makes self-incriminating statements in two famous documentaries about the case, *Paradise Lost* and *Paradise Lost 2: Revelations.* Sometimes a perfect suspect is not guilty.

## Cyrus ★ ★ ★ ½

R, 91 m., 2010

John C. Reilly (John), Jonah Hill (Cyrus), Marisa Tomei (Molly), Catherine Keener (Jamie), Matt Walsh (Tim). Directed by Mark Duplass and Jay Duplass and produced by Michael Costigan. Screenplay by Mark Duplass and Jay Duplass.

Marisa Tomei plays warm and friendly as well as anyone, and those qualities are essential to *Cyrus,* a film about her grown son and her new boyfriend waging what amounts to war over the possession of her body. There's no incest, but a photo in her bedroom suggests the son was still getting to second base well into his adolescence. The boyfriend is pathetically happy to get on base at all, and this creates a comedy of awkwardness, private thoughts, passive aggression, and veiled hostility. All

Molly (Tomei) wants is for everybody to like one another and get along.

Her boyfriend, John (John C. Reilly), is fine with that goal, but her son, Cyrus (Jonah Hill), is jealous and possessive, and very intelligent about how to use his feelings in a sneaky way, so it's not always obvious what he's up to. Not obvious to Molly, anyway, because she doesn't really want to know. More obvious to John, who's on such thin ice he's slow to admit how unpleasant the situation has become.

I can imagine how a sex comedy could spring from this premise, or even an Oedipal drama. What's intriguing about *Cyrus* is the way it sort of sits back and observes an emotional train wreck as it develops. The movie doesn't eagerly jump from one payoff to another, but attunes itself to nuance, body language, and the habitual politeness with which we try to overlook social embarrassment. With only three people, however, it's a problem when one is deliberately creating embarrassment.

Jonah Hill, who is a fairly large man, is able to morph himself somehow into a big baby here; he cleverly uses immature conduct to excuse inappropriate behavior. When he hugs his mommy, for example, there's the not-so-slight suggestion that he does so not as her son but as her smoocher. There's no suggestion that actual sex has ever been involved, but to poor John (and to us), he's over the top. Molly seems oblivious.

Cyrus pretends to welcome and like John. His very welcome outreaches the bounds of propriety. Then little things happen. John's shoes disappear. If Cyrus took them, he could easily throw them away. But *whoever* took them, they're left where they will eventually be found, a ticking time bomb. Little things like that.

Marisa Tomei has the trickiest role here. She's lonely, she's been single too long, and she likes John, the big lug. She befriends him at a party where he's desperately unhappy. She discovers him peeing in the shrubbery and says what, under these circumstances, is a remarkably tactful thing to relieve the embarrassment: "Nice penis." He needs a woman like this. He's apart from his first wife (Catherine Keener), who was maybe too smart for him. Molly isn't dumb, but she's—well, sometimes she's improbably clueless. She is also very sexy, so you can understand that a boy the age of Cyrus (but not her son) would be attracted. That avoids possible Eww Moments.

*Cyrus* was written and directed by the Duplass brothers, Mark and Jay, who up until now have been identified with "mumblecore," a term I hope I never have to use again. Let's put it this way: If a movie is mumblecore, it probably doesn't much want to be enjoyed, and if it isn't, why call it failed mumblecore? Their previous film, *Baghead* (2008), was not beloved by me. Now here is a film that uses very good actors and gives them a lot of improvisational freedom to talk their way into, around, and out of social discomfort. And it's not snarky. It doesn't mock these characters. It understands they have their difficulties and hopes they find a way to work things out. There's your suspense: How can they?

# D

## Daddy Longlegs ★ ★ ★

NO MPAA RATING, 100 m., 2010

Ronnie Bronstein (Lenny), Sage Ranaldo (Sage), Frey Ranaldo (Frey), Victor Puccio (Principal Puccio), Eleonore Hendricks (Leni), Leah Singer (Paige), Sean Williams (Dale). Directed by Josh Safdie and Benny Safdie and produced by Casey Neistat and Tom Scott. Screenplay by Josh Safdie and Benny Safdie.

Lenny isn't a bad father. He's no father at all. He doesn't understand the concept. I don't believe he ever will. He doesn't understand being an adult. He doesn't understand anything. The question at the heart of *Daddy Longlegs* is, why did his former wife ever think she could trust him with two weeks a year of child custody? Lenny shouldn't even have custody of himself.

He's in constant motion during *Daddy Longlegs*. If he has role models at all, they're provided by his two sons, Sage and Frey. Lenny acts like their playmate, not their father. "Guys," he calls them. "Guys." I heard him call Sage by name once. Frey, I don't remember even once. They are a unit, the Child Unit, to be plunged into his idea of a good time.

Lenny is played by Ronnie Bronstein, who directed *Frownland*, a 2008 film about a man all bottled up inside. Lenny is the opposite. He projects an almost relentless upbeat enthusiasm, until sometimes he loses it and we see the anger. He tries to babysit the kids, who are five and seven, while at the same time working as a movie projectionist and dating, or breaking up, with his current girlfriend (Eleonore Hendricks). With one kid riding his shoulders and another tagging behind, he rushes out on unclear missions.

For parents, this may play like a horror film. At one point he actually gives these two children fifty-five dollars and sends them by themselves to a supermarket some blocks away in New York City to buy supplies for dinner. At another time, he talks a complete stranger into taking the three of them along on a trip with her boyfriend to upstate New York.

He jumps on the bed with the "guys" and wrestles them. He forgets to pick them up after school. He takes them to work and they print out a thousand Xeroxes. And then, in an unbelievable act of criminal irresponsibility, he figures out a way for them to stay out of trouble for two, maybe three days, while his big mouth manages to get himself arrested.

The Safdie brothers, Benny and Josh, have a dedication on the film that may or may not refer to their own father. Their cinematic father is obviously John Cassavetes, whose own manic heroes ran crazy loops around their lives. If *Daddy Longlegs* is influenced by Cassavetes, well, that's not a bad thing. Few filmmakers have the nerve to travel that path.

Bronstein's performance is crucial. It's difficult to make a manic character plausible, but he does. He never goes over the top. His mania seems devoted more to lifting off from the bottom. How he ever convinced his wife (Leah Singer) to marry him is hard to explain, most of all, probably, to herself.

*Note: This film is available in some markets via Video on Demand.*

## Damsels in Distress ★ ★ ★

PG-13, 99 m., 2012

Greta Gerwig (Violet), Megalyn Echikunwoke (Rose), Carrie MacLemore (Heather), Analeigh Tipton (Lily), Adam Brody (Charlie), Hugo Becker (Xavier), Ryan Metcalf (Frank), Billy Magnussen (Thor). Directed, written, and produced by Whit Stillman.

It's delightful and a little bewildering to find a 2012 comedy that evokes a world that exists only in the novels of P. G. Wodehouse. Whit Stillman's *Damsels in Distress* creates Seven Oaks College, a school so innocent and naive that only it could believe in itself. Its heroine, Violet Wister, is one of the daffiest characters in recent movies, who believes one of the noble callings of women is to date men who are their inferiors and thus lift them up.

All of the men at Seven Oaks are Violet's inferiors, and this also holds true for her sidekicks. Violet (Greta Gerwig) is one of those tall, blond, efficient style setters who sweep down the hallways of school comedies, scattering instruction and snobbery. Alicia Silverstone used to play these roles. Or think of Cybill Shepherd. The difference is Violet's motives are charitable. She would like to instruct male undergraduates about the delights of underarm deodorants, enlist them in a new dance craze of her own invention, and be of use to them, if necessary, at the suicide prevention center run by herself and her girlfriends. When you walk through the door looking suicidal, the first thing the center does is offer you a doughnut—but you should see with what alacrity Violet snatches a doughnut back from a pretender.

*Damsels in Distress* is the fourth film (and the first since 1998) by Whit Stillman, who as a younger man looked like F. Scott Fitzgerald and spoke like someone who had learned the language out of sophisticated comic novels. He made a kind of movie nobody else was making, about rich and privileged young people moving in the very best circles—which is to say, their own. He called them the *urban haute bourgeoisie*. They consider "yuppie" a term of praise. His *Metropolitan* (1989), about a young man hoping to win acceptance from such snobs, was a considerable hit, in part because no one had seen a movie like it unless possibly running in black and white at 3 a.m. on TCM. Then came *Barcelona* (1994) and *The Last Days of Disco* (1998). What they have in common is that the supporting cast of a Fred Astaire comedy could wander in and not be noticed.

My critic friend writes me wondering if Stillman is channeling farther back than Wodehouse—back to the days of Thackeray, the Dandy tradition, and *Vanity Fair*. And indeed there's a bit of Becky Sharp in Violet. She probably likes novels where women are the arbiters of social circles.

Now he centers on a fictional college that's like an Ivy League school for those who are not very rich or smart. Two of the men in Violet's life, for example, don't know the names of the basic colors; in one case, it's not so much that the kid is stupid as that his social-climbing parents made him skip kindergarten.

Violet, of course, must have a posse, friends who are not quite as tall or (in her mind) quite as pretty. They flank her because Violet must always be centered. On the first day of the new school year, we meet them: Rose (Megalyn Echikunwoke) and Heather (Carrie MacLemore), who both instinctively stand just a step behind her. Violet has ESP when it comes to picking out new recruits, and she and her friends sweep down upon Lily (Analeigh Tipton), a campus newcomer. She will be their new roommate. Thus will all of Lily's wardrobe, behavioral, and boyfriend problems be handled for the next few years.

Stillman writes his own dialogue, and is a master of clever double-reverse wit. I didn't mention Wodehouse by chance. He's also lucky to have found an actress in Gerwig who finds the perfect note for playing a woman who knows everything better than you do, but doesn't believe she's being stuck up about it; she's just being kind. This is even true when she relieves poor Lily of her boyfriend, Charlie (Adam Brody).

The movie almost inevitably contains a campus musical, centering on Violet's new dance craze, the Sambola. This is not an inspired dance craze, nor is the musical destined for Broadway, but led by Violet they are all perfectly rehearsed and keep on smiling, and their good nature is impossible to resist.

## A Dangerous Method ★ ★ ★ ½

R, 99 m., 2011

Viggo Mortensen (Sigmund Freud), Michael Fassbender (Carl Jung), Keira Knightley (Sabina Spielrein), Sarah Gadon (Emma Jung), Vincent Cassel (Otto Gross). Directed by David Cronenberg and produced by Jeremy Thomas. Screenplay by Christopher Hampton, based on his stage play *The Talking Cure* and the book *A Most Dangerous Method* by John Kerr.

Psychoanalysis has been so influential at least in part because two of its creators, Sigmund Freud and Carl Jung, were so devilishly gifted at creating memes. Many of their technical terms are brilliant at arguing for their own validity. Consider "inferiority complex." Set aside what is actually meant by that. Everyone upon hearing it instinctively thinks they know what it means, and what's more they know someone they can instantly apply it to.

The "talking cure" and the analyst's couch are likewise embedded in our mythology, even though modern psychoanalysis has more complex thoughts about them. I confess that the more earnest devotees of the approach (Woody Allen and Howard Stern have daily sessions) may benefit at least partly because it keeps them out of trouble. Whatever we think, there is no doubt that psychoanalysis is now firmly embedded in our consciousness. It provides us with a way of thinking about ourselves. Its validity is beside the point. As a term of reference it is real.

David Cronenberg's absorbing film *A Dangerous Method* involves a few years during which the entire field was largely invented (if I may say so) in the association of Freud (Viggo Mortensen), Jung (Michael Fassbender), and a woman named Sabina Spielrein (Keira Knightley), who began as their patient and became their colleague.

Using a dialogue-heavy approach that's unusual for him, Cronenberg's film is skilled at the way it weaves theory with the inner lives of its characters. We are learning, yet never feel we're being taught. Freud and Jung seem to be learning at the same time.

Viggo Mortensen's performance is masterful in the way it shows Freud as a contained, analytical logician, whose conclusions seem prudent if you grant him his premises. Perhaps his incessant smoking is an indicator of compulsions that his speech, usually calm, conceals. Jung, on the other hand, is more unpredictable, and Michael Fassbender shows him as a man whose theories permit him a good deal of improvisation.

In these baffling days of quantum theory, it may actually be Jung, with his interest in the mystical and the supernatural, who is more modern. His thoughts about archetypes are persuasive enough, but what are we to think of his interest (not mentioned in the film) in the Tarot deck? As a person who firmly disbelieves in woo-woo, I couldn't believe he would subscribe to such flimflammery, but I dutifully obtained the "Jungian Tarot deck," in which the ancient symbols of the Tarot are seen as manifestations of our collective unconscious. In using the cards, I discovered that the juxtaposition of given cards within an arbitrary grid jostled me to think in useful ways. I didn't believe the cards were speaking to me, but I found them helpful in speaking to myself.

But I drift. *A Dangerous Method* opens in 1904 with the arrival at Jung's Zurich clinic of Sabina Spielrein, manic and desperate, struggling with two attendants who try to constrain her. Jung is apparently her last resort. Using Freud's theories and method, Jung has success in calming her, untwisting her, and eventually liberating an intelligent inner woman. At that time Jung knew Freud only through his writings, but not long after he traveled to Vienna to meet the great man himself, and their conversations are a model of clarity and sanity; the screenplay by Christopher Hampton is based on his play *The Talking Cure* and the book *A Most Dangerous Method* by John Kerr.

As Sabina heals and blossoms, an attraction grows between her and Jung, despite Jung's love for his wife, Emma (Sarah Gadon). They begin an affair. Later, as Freud takes Sabina as a patient, he learns of the affair, and uses this information as a weapon in his ideological struggle with Jung. What the movie suggests is that psychoanalysis as a scientific system may have been harmed by the struggle between these two founders, and that Sabina Spielrein, indeed, may have arrived at more useful conclusions than the two dueling male approaches.

It would help to know something about psychoanalysis, or at least be curious to learn, before seeing this film. The movie's poster suggests a romantic triangle, which is true only in a theoretical sense. The poster design is the popular "giant heads" format, with Knightly most prominent in front and center, and the smaller Mortensen and Fassbender flanking her. If Jung and Freud could have seen this poster, what uneasy dreams it might have inspired.

## Dark Horse ★ ★ ★ ½

NO MPAA RATING, 85 m., 2012

Jordan Gelber (Abe), Selma Blair (Miranda), Donna Murphy (Marie), Christopher Walken (Jackie), Mia Farrow (Phyllis), Aasif Mandvi (Mahmoud), Justin Bartha (Richard), Zachary Booth (Justin). Directed by Todd Solondz and produced by Ted Hope and Derrick Tseng. Screenplay by Solondz.

*Dark Horse* tells the story of Abe, a loser who leads a life of such agony that he might explode in misery if he weren't protected by his cluelessness. A tubby, balding thirty-five-year-old arrested adolescent, he lives at home with his parents, in a bedroom still containing his action figures collection. He wears tight-fitting T-shirts with inane messages on them. He drives a bright yellow Hummer, which he carefully locks as if anyone would want to steal it. The last civilian who looked cool driving a Hummer was Arnold Schwarzenegger.

We meet Abe (Jordan Gelber) at a wedding, during the dancing, sitting alone at a table with another person sitting alone. No one would ever think they were sitting together. She is Miranda (Selma Blair), darkly morose. Almost with a sigh, Abe asks her to dance. No luck. He coaxes her phone number out of her, oblivious to her extreme reluctance to provide it. He asks her on a date, and mistakes her refusal for acceptance. Almost immediately he asks her to marry him, and within a day or two she astonishingly accepts.

Surely these two unhappy loners could only increase each other's misery. But we're hardly invited to feel sorry for Abe because he is also a spoiled, petulant, obnoxious, infantile schlub. He "works" at a real estate company owned by his dour father, Jackie (Christopher Walken), a compulsive critic. Abe hides behind his computer screen, making bids on eBay while the office assistant, Marie (Donna Murphy), does most of his work for him. At home, he's gushed over by his smothering mom, Phyllis (Mia Farrow). He regularly breaks out in whiny rants about how his parents favored his brother, Richard (Justin Bartha). He is a piece of work. You don't know whether to pity him or insult him.

Abe is the latest in a gallery of walking wounded populating the films of Todd Solondz, who has never met a character he didn't dislike. And *Dark Horse* is another of his portraits of anguish in suburbia, joining *Welcome to the Dollhouse* and *Happiness*. There are times when it is dark humor, and then times when it is simply dark. But there is something more going on here, something deeper and more . . . hopeful?

Someone like Abe could only prevail through the powers of denial and optimistic wishing, and Solondz makes that happen, as the film gradually slips into fantasy. Many of the fantasies involve the character of Marie, the office wallflower, who materializes at key moments in Abe's life, warning him *not* to marry Miranda, and then revealing her private life as a seductive man-eater with startling modern art in her luxurious home. Then there are scenes that raise questions. When Abe tries to return a scratched action figure to a toy store, for example, why does the mall's parking lot have no cars? Why does the store have no customers?

Then there is the question of Miranda's communicable disease. And a hospital scene in which Abe has turned a sickly yellow. And a choice of sad and happy endings. And a moment when the Christopher Walken character abandons his dyspeptic character and speaks, sadly and directly, to his son.

These mood shifts prevent the film from declaring what it really feels about Abe, and they make it curiously more effective. At the end Abe has made a strong impression on us, but we can't be sure what it is. We feel contempt. We feel pity. We shudder, and identify. It is a vortex drawing us down into dark defeat and yet admitting glimmers of hope. Abe is as permanently damaged as someone with a serious birth defect, and he is a force of life insisting that he has his rights. There is truth here, we sense, but no consolation.

## Dark Shadows ★ ★ ½

PG-13, 112 m., 2012

Johnny Depp (Barnabas Collins), Michelle Pfeiffer (Elizabeth Collins Stoddard), Helena Bonham Carter (Dr. Julia Hoffman), Eva Green (Angelique Bouchard), Chloe Grace Moretz (Carolyn Stoddard), Bella Heathcote (Victoria/Josette), Jonny Lee Miller (Roger Collins), Jackie Earle Haley (Willie Loomis), Gully McGrath (David Collins). Directed by Tim Burton and produced by Christi Dembrowski, Johnny Depp, David Kennedy, Graham King, and Richard D. Zanuck. Screenplay by Seth Grahame-Smith, based on the television series created by Dan Curtis.

Tim Burton's *Dark Shadows* is all dressed up with nowhere to go, an elegant production without a central drive. There are wonderful things in the film, but they aren't what's important. It's as if Burton directed at arm's length, unwilling to find juice in the story. Yes, the original TV soap opera is a cult classic, but he approaches it as an amusing trifle, and at feature length we need more than attitude to sink our teeth in.

The opening is gripping, creating expectations the movie doesn't satisfy. We learn the early history of the Collins family in America, which would create a fishing dynasty and spawn the vampire Barnabas Collins (Johnny Depp). Burton is famous for his visuals, and here we have a symphonic evocation of the Gothic sensibility. He shows the erection of the Collinwood mansion, a shriek of architecture, on a hill above the new Maine town of Collinsport. We learn how young Barnabas falls in love with the angelic Josette (Bella Heathcote) and spurns the love of Angelique (Eva Green).

Angelique is a witch. She forces Josette to flee in terror to a cruel stony finger pointing out from a rocky cliff. Waves dash the stones far below. Barnabas pursues her, tries to save her, is unable to stop her from falling to her death from the point. This is great storytelling because it's played straight. I didn't expect the whole movie to be pitched at this level, but it sets a note it never matches. Barnabas, made into a vampire by Angelique, is wrapped in chains, sealed in a coffin, and buried for 190 years. The story moves forward to 1972, when the joke is that a vampire like Barnabas from the 1700s is out of place.

Freed from his entombment, Barnabas returns to Collinwood to find it dilapidated and cobwebby, and the family fortunes in disrepair. As proud of his family as any eighteenth-century merchant prince, as proud of the mansion as when his parents were building it, he moves in to set things right.

The inhabitants in 1972 include Elizabeth Collins Stoddard (Michelle Pfeiffer), who runs the family fortunes, her teenage daughter, Carolyn (Chloe Grace Moretz), her useless brother, Roger (Jonny Lee Miller), Roger's disturbed son, David (Gully McGrath), and a live-in psychiatrist named Dr. Julia Hoffman (Helena Bonham Carter). Family dinners are a depressing event with everyone clustered around one end of a banquet table except Carolyn, who skulks at the other end. Meals are served by Willie Loomis (Jackie Earle Haley), a wizened drunk.

Johnny Depp, as pale as anyone might be after two centuries of burial, caresses architectural details with fingernails like talons and treats the others with elaborate courtesy. His performance is arch and mannered, as perhaps it should be, but so is everyone else's; the result falls between satire and lampoon, and creates such a distance between characters and style that nobody seems to much care what happens—except for the witch Angelique, who is still alive and whose Angel Bay fish cannery is bankrupting the Collins family.

Having ordered that he be buried forever, Angelique is still inexplicably hot for Barnabas. But there's tension because of the young and beautiful Victoria, who has become the new governess for the children; surely it is no coincidence that she is played by Bella Heathcote, who was also Josette. Now we have the same romantic rivalry reborn in modern times.

Much of the amusement in the movie comes from Depp's reactions to 1970s pop culture. The sound track is populated by rock classics, Carolyn's room is decorated like any teenage girl's, and Barnabas is torn between alarm and fascination when he sees his first lava lamp. Yes, now you mention it, lava lamps do somewhat resemble coagulated gobs of blood floating in urine.

With reasoning suitable for a Jane Austen hero, Barnabas restores Collinwood to its former glory, and decides to hold a formal ball to impress the locals. Carolyn pouts that this is unbelievably out of touch. In a good idea that doesn't pay off, Alice Cooper is hired to perform. "The ugliest woman I've ever seen!" Barnabas exclaims after examining Alice through his opera glasses. Alice Cooper's appearance, alas, is limited to a few snatches of songs—typical of the cameo appearances rock stars used to make in movies that had nothing to do with them. We are denied the intriguing prospect of an extended scene between Barnabas and Alice.

This is the eighth collaboration between Burton and Depp, who go back to *Edward Scissorhands* (1990) together. We know we can expect a pitch-perfect performance by Depp, who plays Barnabas with a laserlike intensity, and we know Burton's sets and art direction will be spectacular. I think the best use of Depp in a Burton world was *Sleepy Hollow* (1999). Here Depp seems to inhabit a world of his own, perhaps in self-defense. The others seem to be performing parodies of their characters. *Dark Shadows* begins with great promise, but then the energy drains out.

## Darling Companion ★

PG-13, 103 m., 2012

Diane Keaton (Beth Winter), Kevin Kline (Joseph Winter), Dianne Wiest (Penny Alexander), Richard Jenkins (Russell), Sam Shepard (Sheriff Morris), Mark Duplass (Bryan Alexander), Elisabeth Moss (Grace Winter), Ayelet Zurer (Carmen), Jay Ali (Sam Bhoola). Directed by Lawrence Kasdan and produced by Anthony Bregman and Elizabeth Redleaf. Screenplay by Lawrence Kasdan and Meg Kasdan.

The dog's name is Freeway. That part I will never forget. I will remember it echoing forlornly on mountain trails and forest thickets, on the banks of streams, on basketball courts, behind gas stations and along highways. "Freeway! Freeway! Freeeee-way! Where are you, boy? Freeway!"

It is depressing to reflect on the wealth of talent that conspired to make this inert and listless movie. I walked in knowing it was directed by Lawrence Kasdan (*Grand Canyon, The Big Chill*). And that its cast included Diane Keaton, Kevin Kline, Richard Jenkins, Dianne Wiest, and Sam Shepard. How could it fail to be good? Lacking that, how could it fail to be fair? How could it be so appallingly pointless? How could it be such thin soup?

As the film opens, we meet Joseph Winter (Kline), a back surgeon, his lonely wife, Beth (Keaton), and their husband-seeking daughter Grace (Elisabeth Moss). Beth and Grace are driving down a Colorado freeway when Beth freaks out, makes Grace pull over, and runs back to where she saw a beautiful dog abandoned on the roadside.

Although claiming not to be dog people, they take this dog to a handsome young veterinarian (Jay Ali). There is barely enough time for the Winter family to adopt the dog and name it Freeway before the daughter and the vet are getting married. After the wedding, Beth and Joseph Winter team up with Penny and Russell (Dianne Wiest and Richard Jenkins) to spend a few days in the Winters' mountain cabin. Here they're joined by Penny's son Bryan (Mark Duplass) and the cabin's housekeeper, Carmen (Ayelet Zurer), who claims to be a gypsy soothsayer.

Understand, please, that this is not a comedy. If it were, it has the makings of an outstandingly simpleminded one—but no, it tilts more toward a scrutiny of the relationships involved. These are put to a severe test when Dr. Winter takes Freeway for a walk, a deer runs across the path, and Freeway bolts off in joyous pursuit. And that's the last we'll see of Freeway until a shot right at the end, which surely found its inspiration in *Lassie Come Home.*

All the rest of the movie involves a search for the missing dog. All of it. Three days of it. The three couples trek mountain trails and woodland glens, Bryan having hooked up with the gypsy psychic. She provides them with visions; she sees a red-haired woman and imagines the color blue—indeed, although when they meet the woman she knows nothing about the dog. They also appeal to the sheriff's department, tracking down Sheriff Morris (Sam Shepard) while he's fly-fishing on his day off. He has a kidney stone attack, which generates mighty big excitement. There's also an ominous confrontation with a threatening mountain man wearing a Harvard sweatshirt.

The search for Freeway goes on and on and on, relentlessly. The Winters get lost in the woods at night. Fierce thunderstorms rip the area. In an entirely unexplained and unnecessary animated segment, Freeway is attacked by wolves in action resembling Disney's "Night on Bald Mountain" sequence from *Fantasia.* Each couple has Meaningful Conversations, and there's a shoulder sprain.

And that's it. Yes. Unless you care if they find the dog. If they did not find Freeway, that would make a sad ending indeed, but even if they find him it hardly matters, because after his big roadside rescue scene, Freeway has too little time onscreen for us to get to know him. "Freeway! You naughty dog! Freeway, come home."

## Date Night ★ ★ ★ ½

PG-13, 88 m., 2010

Steve Carell (Phil Foster), Tina Fey (Claire Foster), Mark Wahlberg (Holbrooke), Taraji P. Henson (Detective Arroyo), Common (Collins), James Franco (Taste), Mila Kunis (Whippit), Ray Liotta (Mob Boss). Directed by Shawn Levy and produced by Levy and Tom McNulty. Screenplay by Josh Klausner.

Steve Carell and Tina Fey play a nice, unassuming couple in *Date Night*, and that's one of the reasons the movie works so well. Their Phil and Claire Foster are a normal, overworked, sincere, good-natured New Jersey couple whose lives have become routine. But they love each other, and all they really want is to hire a babysitter and enjoy a nice night out on the town.

We believe that. We're halfway prepared for a low-key romantic comedy when all hell breaks loose. They pretend to be an absent couple in order to grab a reservation at a trendy restaurant, and two hit men assume they *are* that couple and topple them into a screwball comedy. Yet all the time Phil and Claire seem like the kind of people who don't belong in a screwball comedy. That's why it's funny. They're bewildered.

*Date Night* supplies them with the *real* Tripplehorns (James Franco and Mila Kunis), two mob-employed cops (Jimmi Simpson and Common), a mob boss (Ray Liotta), and a muscular security expert (Mark Wahlberg) who never wears a shirt. These characters are also somewhat believable. Plots like this have a way of spinning over the top with insane, manic behavior. It's as if the characters are desperately signaling, "Look at us! Aren't we hilarious?" But the audience has to bring hilarity to you. It can't be assumed.

So what we have is a situation set in motion because a couple named the Tripplehorns don't turn up for a restaurant reservation. The Fosters, mistaken for the Tripplehorns, find themselves in way over their heads with the Tripplehorns' potentially fatal problems. The criminal characters aren't simply stupid, but bright enough to perceive this causes a problem for everyone. And the security agent (Wahlberg) is not simply a muscle-bound goon. He's a caricature, all right, but one living in a condo out of *Architectural Digest* and capable of feeling some sympathy for these pathetic New Jerseyites who've lost their way.

Carell and Fey are both natural comic performers who know (as Second City teaches) that a comedian must never seem to know that it's funny. They play Phil and Claire as nearly as possible like plausible people trapped by this nightmare misunderstanding. Yes, things heat up a little, and yes, there is an obligatory chase scene, and yes, it's a little unlikely how they end up appealing to the security expert. That goes with the territory.

But they know, as great comic actors like Cary Grant and Jack Lemmon knew, that their job in a comedy is to behave with as much realism as possible and let the impossibilities whirl around them. To begin with, Carell and Fey *look* like they might be a pleasant married couple. Attractive, but not improbably so. Young, but not that young. Fit, but they don't reveal unexpected skills. And frightened when they need to be. Do you ever wonder why the characters in some movies are never gobsmacked in the face of what seems like certain death?

All of this is a way of saying that *Date Night* is funny because, against all odds, it is involving. Each crazy step in the bizarre plot made a certain sense because it followed from what went before; it's like the Scorsese masterpiece *After Hours*. The director is Shawn Levy, who committed the two *Night at the Museum* movies, and here shows that he is much more successful when he stays far away from CGI. Remember that he also made the entertaining *Cheaper by the Dozen* with Steve Martin and Bonnie Hunt as a hard-pressed married couple.

A movie like *Date Night* encourages Hollywood comedy to occasionally dial down and realize that comedy emerges from characters and situations and can't be manufactured from manic stunts and overkill. If you don't start out liking the Fosters and hoping they have a really nice date night, not much else is going to work.

## Daybreakers ★ ★ ½
R, 98 m., 2010

Ethan Hawke (Edward Dalton), Willem Dafoe (Elvis), Claudia Karvan (Audrey Bennett), Michael Dorman (Frankie Dalton), Vince Colosimo (Christopher Caruso), Isabel Lucas (Alison Bromley), Sam Neill (Charles Bromley). Directed by Peter Spierig and Michael Spierig and produced by Chris Brown, Bryan Furst, and Sean Furst. Screenplay by the Spierig brothers.

Ten years in the future, a global epidemic has infected most of the population with vampirism. The few remaining humans are on the run, hunted down by the militant Vampire Army, which doesn't hate them but mostly is just hungry. This depletion of the planet's food supply might be an opening for a parable about our dwindling resources, but no: Instead of making the humans a breeding stock for blood harvesting as practiced by the giant Bromley Marks Corp., the army members eat them. Al Gore must have a chart showing how that's self-defeating.

Bromley Marks is a major supplier of human blood, but is spending a fortune to develop a synthetic blood substitute. Like so many big companies in agribusiness, it wants to wean us off that healthy organic food and sell us a substitute, no doubt sweetened by corn syrup. The B-M's chief hematologist is Edward (Ethan Hawke), who like some of the atomic scientists at Los Alamos feels guilty about his work. He pushes for a cure for vampirism, not just a handy new product.

That sets the stage for this grave new world where life is designed to be lived at night. Underground moving walkways replace sidewalks, curfew starts before dawn, and so on. Edward has ethics and believes it is wrong to exploit comatose humans for their blood. He's one of those damned lefties who years ago probably was against eating beef. He's a vampire with a conscience.

Edward hooks up with the human underground, notably the cute Audrey (Claudia Karvan), and is introduced to Lionel, code name Elvis (Willem Dafoe), who has a cheap and easy vampirism antidote but is being hunted by Edward's hothead brother Frankie (Michael Dorman), because—I dunno. Because Frankie's not about to give up blood for a healthier lifestyle, I guess.

The movie, directed by Australia's twin Spierig brothers (*Undead,* 2003), looks good in its gray, sunless scenes evoking twilight (cough). The newspapers and TV anchors report on hopes for a vaccine, apparently because the constant demands of vampirism maintenance are a grind. Imagine if the price of blood was beyond the pocketbook of the average family of four, and you had to go out human hunting every day to feed the kids. A homeless person holds up a cardboard sign: "Hungry. Will work for blood."

This intriguing premise, alas, ends as so many movies do these days, with fierce fights and bloodshed. Inevitably, the future of the planet will be settled among the handful of characters we've met and a lot of extras with machine guns. I guess, but can't be sure, that audiences will enjoy the way these vampires die. They don't shrivel up into Mr. and Mrs. Havisham but explode, spraying blood all over everyone. Toward the end, their heads blow off like human champagne corks. Well, not human.

## Deadline ★ ★
PG-13, 95 m., 2012

Steve Talley (Matt Harper), Eric Roberts (Ronnie Bullock), Anna Felix (Delana Calhoun), Lauren Jenkins (Trey Hall), Jackie Welch (Mary Pell Sampson), Darryl Van Leer (Reverend Young), Jeremy Childs (Walker Burns), David Dwyer (Everett Hall), J. D. Souther (Lucas Harper), Clay Brocker (Possum). Directed by Curt Hahn and produced by Hahn and Molly M. Mayeux. Screenplay by Mark Ethridge, based on his novel *Grievances.*

In the opening scene of Curt Hahn's *Deadline* a young black couple profess their love on the porch of an Alabama church before he leaves, turns lovingly to wave good-bye, and is shot dead. The murder is never investigated. Nineteen years pass. We meet two reporters for a Nashville daily who decide to reopen the case, even though their publisher bellows at them that the paper has no subscribers or advertisers in Alabama, and isn't about to assign two reporters to a cold and ancient case. (As indeed many a publisher would bellow.)

We meet the drawling newsroom veteran Ronnie Bullock (Eric Roberts) and the earnest younger reporter Matt Harper (Steve Talley), who are pointed to the case by a blond hottie named Trey (Lauren Jenkins). She was raised by a beloved black nanny named Mary Pell Sampson (Jackie Welch). The dead boy was her son.

So dedicated is Matt that he gets wrapped up in the story and commits that transgression for which no man can be forgiven: He forgets the cake-tasting session he and his bride-to-be have set with their wedding planner. He and Ronnie speed off to the fictitious hamlet of Ames, Alabama, where they meet the indifferent police chief, a judge who was a Klan member, and a concerned black preacher. The wooden cross above the preacher's altar was fashioned from a lynching tree. His congregation likes the symbolism, but he is decidedly unenthusiastic about it.

This story is based on a 2006 novel and screenplay by Mark Ethridge, who won two Pulitzers for the *Charlotte Observer.* He must be a gifted reporter, but as a storyteller, he lacks a persuasive touch. The situation seems appropriate material for a John Grisham thriller, but his version benefits way too much from happy chance. The reporters are basically able to solve the old murder (and a recent one targeting the police chief) by being extremely lucky in their sources. How much brilliant reporting do you need to do, if you find eyewitnesses willing to swear under oath that they saw the murderer commit his premeditated crime?

Ethridge stretches his story with perfunctory subplots about the offended fiancée, the bullheaded publisher, the reporter's dying father, and an assortment of colorful local characters. Any casting director would be ecstatic to discover Clay Brocker, who plays an Ames redneck whose tightly braided sideburns reach all the way to his waist.

The plot, in short, is underwhelming. It merely follows the reporters as the screenplay serves them the solution to their case on a silver platter. Yet, curiously, *Deadline* flows right along, and peeking at my watch I was startled by how quickly the time was passing. (In contrast, *Wrath of the Titans* seemed to be using an hourglass filled with molasses.) Maybe that's because the plot is so easy to follow and the actors are mostly fresh locals. Of the pros, I enjoyed seeing Eric Roberts again. Remember when Mickey Rourke went on that rant at the Spirit Awards about how his buddy Eric is shamefully underused by Hollywood? Maybe so. He used to play hyperactive weirdos, and here his reporter is smooth, calm, and confident, even if he does usually carry three guns.

## Dear John ★ ★

PG-13, 105 m., 2010

Channing Tatum (John Tyree), Amanda Seyfried (Savannah Curtis), Henry Thomas (Tim), Scott Porter (Randy), Richard Jenkins (Mr. Tyree). Directed by Lasse Hallstrom and produced by Marty Bowen, Wyck Godfrey, and Ryan Kavanaugh. Screenplay by Jamie Linden, based on a novel by Nicholas Sparks.

Lasse Hallstrom's *Dear John* tells the heartbreaking story of two lovely young people who fail to find happiness together because they're trapped in an adaptation of a Nicholas Sparks novel. Their romance leads to bittersweet loss that's so softened by the sweet characters that it feels like triumph. If a Sparks story ended in happiness, the characters might be disappointed. They seem to have their noble, resigned dialogue already written. Hemingway wrote one line that could substitute for the third act of every Sparks story: "Isn't it pretty to think so?"

Channing Tatum stars as John Tyree, a handsome Army Special Forces specialist home on two weeks' leave at the South Carolina shore. Amanda Seyfried plays Savannah, an ethereal beauty whose purse falls off a pier. John dives in and retrieves it, and we guess it could have been worse. He could have gotten her kitten down from a tree. In the few precious days they share, they fall deeply into PG-13 love.

John was raised by his father (Richard Jenkins), a quiet man who wears white gloves while admiring his coin collection, and cooks chicken every Saturday and lasagna every Sunday. Savannah meets him and casually observes to John that he is autistic—a mild case, she gently suggests. John is angered by this insult. Did he never, by the age of twenty-two, observe that his father was strangely mannered? Did no one else? What was his (now absent) mother's thinking? Did the movie mention any employment history for Mr. Tyree? I could have missed it.

In a Sparks story, as we know from *The Notebook,* problems like autism and Alzheimer's are never seen in their tragic stages, but always allow the good souls of their victims to visibly glow. Diseases don't destroy and kill, but exist primarily to inspire admirable conduct by nexts of kin. John and Savannah get over his unhappiness, and he pledges that he'll be back at the end of twelve months so they can wed.

But then 9/11 happens, and like every man in his group he re-enlists. And continues to re-enlist until the movie's title hints at what he receives in the mail. Because Savannah is a true-blue heroine, her new love is of course a nice and decent man, someone John can accept, so that we can smile sadly and not get all messy and depressed. That's the note Sparks aims for: the sad smile. First love is not to be, but the moon still looks so large when it rises, and people treat each other gently, and if someone should die, that is very sad, but perhaps it will provide an opportunity for someone else to live a little longer before they, too, must travel to that undiscovered country from whose bourne no traveler ever returns.

John and Savannah are awfully nice. She comes from a rich family who have a mansion, and John and his dad live in a humble but cozy frame house that in its South Carolina island location might easily be purchased for less than $500,000. That would leave a portion of Mr. Tyree's unspecified income free to invest in rare coins and amass a collection worth a fortune. I am just enough of a numismatist to know that you need to invest money to collect rare coins. You don't just find them in your spare change.

I know I'm being snarky. I don't get much pleasure from it. *Dear John* exists only to coddle the sentiments of undemanding dreamers, and plunge us into a world where the only evil is the interruption of the good. Of course John is overseas on a series of missions so secret that Savannah cannot be told where, exactly, he is. In the years after 9/11, where, oh where, could he be? Apparently not in Iraq or Afghanistan, because it can hardly be a military secret that the men of Special Forces are deployed there. But somewhere, anyway, and he re-enlists for a good chunk of her early childbearing years, perhaps because, as *The Hurt Locker* informs us, "war is a drug."

It matters not. In this movie, war is a plot device. It loosens its grip on John only long enough to sporadically renew his romance, before claiming him again so that we finally consider Savannah's Dear John letter just good common sense. And now that I've brought that up: Considering that the term "Dear John Letter" has been in constant use since World War II, and that the hero of this movie is inevitably destined to receive such a letter, is it a little precious of Sparks to name him "John"? I was taught in Dan Curley's fiction class that when the title of a story is repeated in the story itself, the story's spell is broken. But then Sparks never took Curley's class.

## Death at a Funeral ★ ★ ★ ½

R, 92 m., 2010

Chris Rock (Aaron), James Marsden (Oscar), Loretta Devine (Cynthia), Peter Dinklage (Frank), Martin Lawrence (Ryan), Regina Hall (Michelle), Zoe Saldana (Elaine), Kevin Hart (Brian), Danny Glover (Uncle Russell), Keith David (Reverend Davis), Ron Glass (Duncan), Tracy Morgan (Norman), Columbus Short (Jeff), Luke Wilson (Derek), Regine Nehy (Martina). Directed by Neil LaBute and produced by William Horberg, Sidney Kimmel, Laurence Malkin, Chris Rock, and Share Stallings. Screenplay by Dean Craig.

Oh, I know a lot of *Death at a Funeral* is in very bad taste. That's when I laughed the most. I don't laugh at movies where the characters are deliberately being vulgar. But when they desperately don't want to be—now that's funny. Consider the scene when Uncle Russell eats too much nut cake and is seized by diarrhea. And Norman wrestles him off his wheelchair and onto the potty, and gets his hand stuck underneath. Reader, I laughed. I'm not saying I'm proud of myself. That's not the way I was raised. But I laughed.

I laughed all the way through, in fact. This

is the best comedy since *The Hangover*, and although it's almost a scene-by-scene remake of a 2007 British movie with the same title, it's funnier than the original. For the character of Frank, the mysterious guest who wants to speak privately with the dead man's sons, it even uses the same actor, Peter Dinklage, and he's funnier this time. Maybe that's because when a comedy gets on a roll, everything is funnier.

The funeral is taking place at home, because that's how the deceased wanted it. Also living at home are his oldest son, Aaron (Chris Rock), Aaron's wife, Michelle (Regina Hall), and his mother, Cynthia (Loretta Devine). Both Michelle and Cynthia are on his case for having not yet fathered a child. Aaron dreams of publishing a novel, while his younger brother Ryan (Martin Lawrence) has published several, which sound like porn to me, but hey, they're in print.

The mourners arrive after various adventures of the cadaver, and get into all sorts of bizarre and dire trouble in ways that the screenplay carefully explains. How was Elaine (Zoe Saldana) to know that a bottle labeled "Valium" contained a next-generation hallucinogen when she gave one to her boyfriend, Oscar (James Marsden)? It's an old gag, the guy accidentally freaked out on drugs, but Marsden elevates it to bizarre heights with a rubber face that reflects horror, delight, nausea, and affection more or less simultaneously.

There's no use in my providing a blow-by-blow of the plot, since it's deliriously screwball and it doesn't much matter what happens, as long as something always is. But I can mention what deft timing and high energy this cast has, each actor finding the rhythm for each character instead of all racing about in manic goofiness. Dinklage, for example, is as good at playing dead serious as Tommy Lee Jones, and here he's always on tone for a man who has come for compelling personal reasons. The brothers and Norman don't really wish harm to befall him, but you can see how it does. Then there is a certain logic to how they react. They're only human.

Loretta Devine has a possibly thankless role as the surviving matriarch, but her timing is delicious as she associates the death of a husband with the absence of a grandchild. Both Regina Hall and Zoe Saldana are steadfast in their love in the midst of chaos, and Danny Glover goes over the top as the cantankerous uncle because, well, that's what the role requires.

British actors are rightly known for their skill, and there were some good ones in the 2007 version of the same Dean Craig screenplay. But playing proper upper-crust characters tends to restrain them. The family in *Death at Funeral* is obviously wealthy, but loose—more human. Their emotions are closer to the surface, and these actors work together like a stock company.

Notice, too, the way director Neil LaBute directs traffic. Because the action is screwball doesn't mean it can be confusing. Screwball depends crucially on our knowing where key characters are, and why. LaBute juggles parallel actions in the big family home so we understand who's in the bathroom and who's in the living room and why everybody is out on the lawn. There's a smooth logic to it that works like spatial punch lines.

LaBute is a brilliant playwright and director who is usually the director of very dark comedies (*In the Company of Men, Your Friends and Neighbors*). But a good director is a good director, and LaBute here, like David Gordon Green with *Pineapple Express*, masters the form. And oooh, that's a mean line about R. Kelly.

## The Debt ★ ★ ½

R, 112 m., 2011

Helen Mirren (Rachel Singer), Sam Worthington (Young David), Jessica Chastain (Young Rachel), Jesper Christensen (Vogel), Marton Csokas (Young Stephan), Ciaran Hinds (David Peretz), Tom Wilkinson (Stephan Gold). Directed by John Madden and produced by Eitan Evan, Eduardo Rossoff, Kris Thykier, and Matthew Vaughn. Screenplay by Vaughn, Jane Goldman, and Peter Straughan, based on the film *Ha-Hov*, written by Assaf Bernstein and Ido Rosenblum.

*The Debt* weaves a tangled web of lies and deceptions around a seemingly heroic raid in 1965 carried out by three agents of Mossad, the Israeli intelligence agency known for more ability than it exhibits here. Their mission: Enter East Berlin with secret identities, kidnap a Nazi war criminal, and return him to Israel for trial. He is Vogel (Jesper Christensen), the notorious Surgeon of Birkenau, who conducted unspeakable procedures on his captives.

The film opens with the agents being welcomed on their return home to Israel. They are David (Sam Worthington), Rachel Singer (Jessica Chastain, of *The Tree of Life*), and Stefan (Marton Csokas). In scenes set in 1997, they will be played by Ciaran Hinds, Helen Mirren, and Tom Wilkinson. The later scenes involve the publication of a book about the famous raid, by Rachel's daughter. The original raiders are being honored at a banquet, and seem uneasy with each other.

Not everything in the book is quite as it seems. Recent developments in Ukraine have cast doubt on the now legendary intelligence operation, which would cast the Mossad in the unfortunate light of either not knowing or not admitting what really happened in 1965. That's intriguing for us because *The Debt* does a splendid job of showing key early sequences in detail. To see is to believe. But we may not see everything.

Because the film jumps the rails toward the end, it might be worth mentioning the good parts. Rachel poses as a woman consulting the ex-Nazi gynecologist, who is now in Buenos Aires. Consider putting your feet in the stirrups for the Surgeon of Birkenau. Then there's an ingenious operation, which I will not describe, to spirit him out of his clinic and into captivity. Separately, elaborate timing is used to allow a border crossing at a closed Berlin transit station.

This stuff plays to the strength of cinema, underlining the details of each strategy and the dangers it involves. If you replay the actual events in your mind you realize all the suspense is created with editing, camera angles, and POV. Film considers time and space subjectively. Seen from a different perspective, there may be no telling what was really going on.

The architecture of *The Debt* has an unfortunate flaw. The younger versions of the characters have scenes that are intrinsically more exciting, but the actors playing the older versions are more interesting. Helen Mirren, Tom Wilkinson, and Ciaran Hinds bring along the weight of their many earlier roles. To be sure, the older actors get some excitement of their own, but by then the plot has lost its way.

Maybe the problem is a structure that cuts around in time. Three characters, six actors, and although the woman is always presumably Rachel, I was sometimes asking myself which of the two men I was seeing when young. In a thriller, you must be sure. I suspect this movie would have been more effective had it remained entirely in the past, especially given all we know.

## Declaration of War ★ ★ ★

NO MPAA RATING, 100 m., 2012

Valerie Donzelli (Juliette), Jeremie Elkaim (Romeo), Cesar Desseix (Adam at Eighteen Months), Gabriel Elkaim (Adam at Eight Years), Brigitte Sy (Claudia), Elina Lowensohn (Alex), Michele Moretti (Genevieve), Philippe Laudenbach (Philippe). Directed by Valerie Donzelli and produced by Edouard Weil. Screenplay by Donzelli and Jeremie Elkaim.

The first shot in *Declaration of War* shows a mother with her eight-year-old son. That provides a piece of information that will help us through the rest of the movie. This is the story of how a French couple learn when their son is eighteen months old that he has a dangerous tumor pressing upon his brain stem and requires risky surgery. For the next several years, that fact will define the whole of their lives.

Nothing has prepared them for this. When their eyes meet across a nightclub floor and they begin walking toward each other, love seems to be their destiny. Her name is Juliette (Valerie Donzelli). His name is, inevitably, Romeo (Jeremie Elkaim). Like a lot of first-time parents, most of what they know about raising babies comes through on-the-job training. Can it be normal that little Adam keeps them awake night after night with his crying? Wants to eat all the time? Urps after every meal? Hasn't taken his first step at eighteen months?

Parenting comes to dominate their lives, especially after a pediatrician notices the boy has a wandering eye and an asymmetrical face. She gives him a CT test and an MRI exam, and discovers the tumor. They go into panic mode. Of course Adam must have the best surgeon! It's an injustice that a child of theirs should be subjected to such a tragedy! Their ordinary lives are put on hold.

But the sharpness of the original emergency becomes worn down by week after week and month after month of care. Their lives are so devoted to their son that eventually they lose their jobs, sell their apartment, and move into quarters for parents at the hospital. Luckily the quarters, the surgery, and the boy's long hospital stay are paid for by France's universal health care; this might have been a shorter story if it had been set in the United States.

They have a support system: friends, his parents, and her mother and her mother's partner. This gives them moral support. But they've lost what they were accustomed to considering their real lives. By bunking together in one room in the hospital and allowing their attention to be entirely devoted to Adam's condition, they find it impossible to ever enjoy each other, or have carefree moments, or break loose. They begin to get on each other's nerves. It becomes very hard for them to stay together.

That's really the subject of the movie: not the son, but how this illness comes to dominate the lives of his caregivers. It also explains why and how *Declaration of War* is a domestic comedy as much as it is a medical drama. This movie has been made by the couple it is about, Valerie Donzelli and Jeremie Elkaim. She directed, they wrote it together, and in real life their relationship also fell apart. They tell their fraught story with a surprising freshness. The visual approach is lively, there are shots of fancy and fantasy, and we know from the beginning that the child will survive.

The film may even be too upbeat, especially the ending, which is too easy and contrived. Yet there's real emotion here, especially in the first half, when they remember the feelings they were tortured by. There are also observant studies of their pediatrician and the surgeon, a Great Man who is treated with deference and protected by a cadre of interns. When he finally permits himself a small smile, it's a relief to discover that he actually can smile.

## The Deep Blue Sea ★ ★ ★ ½

R, 98 m., 2012

Rachel Weisz (Hester Collyer), Tom Hiddleston (Freddie Page), Simon Russell Beale (Sir William Collyer). Directed by Terence Davies and produced by Sean O'Connor and Kate Ogborn. Screenplay by Davies, based on a play by Terence Rattigan.

There is a London I often summon in my imagination, one I've found in movies or novels, which I imagine would lead to a life romantic, sad, and poignant. This London is brown. Its air is thick with brown fog, its men dress in brown suits, its women in brown dresses set off with a hat or scarf of red. Street lighting is faded. Many people live in furnished rooms where they feed shillings into a gas meter, and for warmth and a little cheer flee to pubs where smoke hangs heavily in the air, and dark brown pints of beer are consumed slowly, so that their levels are remembered by rings of foam remaining on the insides of the glass.

This is the London of Terence Davies's movie *The Deep Blue Sea*, set "around 1950" when the damage of wartime bombs still leaves buildings naked to the sky. It is also the cityscape of his autobiographical dramas *Distant Voices, Still Lives* (1988) and *The Long Day Closes* (1992), and his 2008 documentary *Of Time and the City*, about Liverpool, the city of his birth. He is sixty-six, so grew up in the postwar years of scarcity and rationing, when it was said British recipes all advised "boil until gray."

His film is based on a play by Terence Rattigan, a playwright born one hundred years ago, which tells the story of Hester Collyer (Rachel Weisz), an attractive but inward young woman, who is married to Sir William Collyer (Simon Russell Beale), a judge much her senior. The story all takes place on a single day some ten months after she left her husband for a young lover. He is Freddie Page (Tom Hiddleston), an RAF pilot whose usefulness ended with the war. There's something helpless about Freddie that appeals to Hester, whose husband, with his carefully trimmed beard, expensive suits, and chauffeured Rolls-Royce, seems forbiddingly stable.

Neither man is a villain. Sir William must be a deeply unhappy man, judging by a painful flashback scene where he dines with his wife and his mother (Barbara Jefford). Every word, every gesture, every intonation of his mother's conversation is designed to exhibit rejection and contempt for her daughter-in-law, and we imagine Sir William himself has been a disappointment to this implacable woman.

There are signs that Hester is fond of Sir William, and indications that he was a nonstarter at marital relations. Freddie, on the other hand, brings great passion to her bed, but a fellow can't subsist on passion alone, and recently he has been neglecting Hester for the more reliable pastimes of drinking and golf. Her days, at least the one in the film, are passed in Freddie's musty brown bed-sitter with a gas fire, which she uses early on that same day to attempt suicide.

Nobody has been cruel to her, except for the witch Mrs. Collyer. Freddie has been neglectful and Sir William is feckless, but even she laughs at the notion that anyone has "driven" her to suicide. Her attempt may have been inspired by pity. Pity for Freddie, who has lost his purpose in life. Pity for Sir William, who will never make his mother (and therefore his wife) happy. Pity for herself, who has failed to please either man, and has found that not even passion is any help for her.

The film feels pity for the exhausted city of London. The vast metropolis was the scene of greatness during World War II, but a few years later it is drab, hungry, and without optimism. During my first visit there in 1962, I was surprised to see whole city blocks still boarded off to block the view of bomb craters. For Davies, his own life and this unreal city must be joined together. He creates two luminous scenes. One is a memory of Hester's, when she dashed down into an underground station during a German raid, and Londoners were huddled together forlornly in the cold. A soldier stood on the platform and sang "Molly Malone" in the silence. Another is a night in a crowded pub where the clients all sing together "You Belong to Me," the Jo Stafford song that advised departing soldiers to "see the pyramids along the Nile," but remember who they belong to and where they must return.

These songs draw lonely people together in small solace. They evoke the London that has left Hester, Freddie, and Bill where we find them today. The film most of all is about Hester, who stares out the window and smokes.

## Delicacy ★ ★ ★

PG-13, 108 m., 2012

Audrey Tautou (Nathalie), Francois Damiens (Markus), Bruno Todeschini (Charles), Melanie Bernier (Chloe), Josephine de Meaux (Sophie), Pio Marmai (Francois), Monique Chaumette (La Grandmere). Directed by David Foenkinos and Stephane Foenkinos and produced by Xavier Rigault and Marc-Antoine Robert. Screenplay by David Foenkinos, based on his novel.

*Delicacy* is a sweetheart of a love story, and cornball from stem to stern. It stars the French pixie Audrey Tautou as Nathalie, a Parisian cutie who loves, loses, and lives to love again, and there is not the slightest doubt in our minds that she will pass through all three stages. I am too good a critic to entirely approve of it, and too big a sap not to fall for it, at least a little. So many romcoms are crass and cynical, manipulating characters like chess pieces, and this one involves tenderness and a certain innocence—as if it trusts us to be softies.

I know as a critic I'm required to have a well-armored heart. I must be a cynical wise guy to show my great sophistication. No pushover, me. Here's Nick Schager, a critic I admire, writing about poor Audrey Tautou as "the most insufferable pixie presence in cinema today" and lambasting the movie for "playing off the *Amelie* star's big cute eyes, long cute legs and bright cute smiles to thoroughly grating effect." Nobody can put one over on Nick. But call me a pushover: I'm prepared to suffer a pixie if she comes with big cute eyes, long cute legs, and bright cute smiles. And a teeny pouty overbite. When did those get to be flaws?

The movie begins with a Meet Cute of operatic boldness, as Nathalie walks into a Paris café and is spotted by Francois (Pio Marmai), who is handsome enough to play a vampire. He establishes mental conditions: He will not speak to her if she orders coffee, tea, or a humdrum juice like orange. In fact, she won't get spoken to at all unless she orders apricot juice, which she does, and after an earth-shaking kiss and a whirlwind romance, they are married, he goes out jogging, and, as a nurse tactlessly puts it, is "rammed by a car." This comes as no surprise. When a perfect couple is young and in love, and the guy goes out jogging by himself and there is the slightest mention of him being right back, I'm holding my breath for the phone to ring with bad news.

Three years pass. Nathalie has a good job at the French office of a Swedish firm and is hit on by her boss, Charles (Bruno Todeschini). It's not in an offensive way; he falls for her and can't help himself. There's a scene where she tells him they have no future together. It must be the most comprehensive and final rejection in dramatic history. Later, Markus (Francois Damiens), a member of Nathalie's work group, walks in and is astonished when she kisses him. So are her friends. This Markus is a balding, middle-aged slob who wears long-sleeved sweaters over dress shirts, which I always thought looked good on me, but people make fun of Markus for wearing them.

Now the questions become will Nathalie overcome her widow's grief, and will Markus overcome his paralyzing sense of not deserving her? Because I identify with Markus, I hope he does. Women who identify with Nathalie may be hoping for something better. All of this takes place with such scenes as a bridge over the Seine with the Eiffel Tower flashing holiday lights in the background. There are well-done moments when more than one person, on seeing Markus, instinctively cannot believe this loser could be dating Nathalie. But she is a sweetheart, as we have established, and can overlook a man's superficial flaws and peer deep into the goodness of his heart. And that, men, is what you must look for in a woman. Never mind if she has big cute eyes, long cute legs, and bright cute smiles. Nobody's perfect.

## The Descendants ★ ★ ★ ★

R, 115 m., 2011

George Clooney (Matt King), Shailene Woodley (Alexandra King), Amara Miller (Scottie King), Beau Bridges (Cousin Hugh), Nick Krause (Sid), Patricia Hastie (Elizabeth King), Matthew Lillard (Brian Speer), Judy Greer (Julie Speer), Robert Forster (Scott Thorson). Directed by Alexander Payne and produced by Jim Burke and Jim Taylor. Screenplay by Payne, Nat Faxon, and Jim Rash, based on the novel by Kaui Hart Hemmings.

*The Descendants* has a happy ending. Therefore technically it's a comedy. It takes place in the paradise of Hawaii. It stars George Clooney. That may lead you to expect a pleasant good time, but this film is so much more than that. This is one of Clooney's best performances, in the new film by Alexander Payne, who in *Sideways* and *About Schmidt* showed a special feeling for men learning to accept their better feelings.

The state of Hawaii is a costar. I've been there many times, which only qualifies me as a tourist, but at more than twenty Hawaii Film Festivals I met so many people and went so many places that I began to understand how its people feel a love and protectiveness for the land, and how seriously they take its traditions. Much of the story here is about how Matt King (Clooney), a descendant of one of the first white landowning families, must decide whether to open up a vast tract of virgin forest on Kauai to tourist and condo development.

At the same time he faces a personal crisis. The film opens with his life-loving wife, Elizabeth (Patricia Hastie), in a boating accident off Waikiki Beach. Matt has been involved in land management; he holds the controlling share of his family's estate. Elizabeth has run their own family, raising their daughters: the teenager Alexandra (Shailene Woodley) and the younger Scottie (Amara Miller). Now Elizabeth is in a coma, and her living will instructs Matt to remove life support. Alexandra returns home from boarding school, and Matt becomes a single parent while also dealing with the King family's urgent desire to close the multimillion-dollar land deal.

This is big business, emotional and financial. Just because the lawyers wear short-sleeved Reyn Spooner shirts doesn't make them pushovers. Matt's life is further complicated when he discovers from an unexpected source that his wife has been having an affair. And his daughters don't want him to sell the land, where they must often have wandered as children. Leading the push for the King family is Cousin Hugh (Beau Bridges). As affable as Bridges can be, he doesn't want to listen to any woo-hoo nonsense about not selling.

The story is based on a novel by Kaui Hart Hemmings, the daughter of a famous surfer and politician. Reading her bio, I suspect there must be a lot of her in Alexandra and Scottie. Matt King himself thinks he will probably sell, but now everything is in upheaval. An undercurrent in the film, which Payne wisely keeps subtle, is that perhaps Matt lost touch with his wife and daughters after first losing his special feeling for the land.

Alexander Payne's films are usually about people forced into difficult personal decisions. Do you remember Laura Dern in *Citizen Ruth*? He always carefully establishes his lead characters in a matrix of supporting characters who are given weight and complexity, so we feel the pressures they're experiencing. Here there is Scott Thorson (Robert Forster), Elizabeth's father, a flinty, self-confident man who perhaps always has had doubts about Matt. Also the man Elizabeth was having the affair with, Brian Speer (Matthew Lillard), and—here it gets thorny—Brian's wife, Julie (Judy Greer).

The film follows Matt's legal, family, and emotional troubles in careful detail, until Payne shows us, without forcing it, that they are all coiled together. A solution for one must be a solution for all. This is so much more complex than most movie plots, where good and evil are neatly compartmented and can be sorted out at the end.

Payne is gifted at using the essence of an actor. He links something in their nature to their characters. Consider Robert Forster, handsome, tanned, angry in a complex way about his daughter's death because she might not have been in the boat if Matt had been a better husband. He has a moment of stunning truth here with Sid (Nick Krause), the seemingly spaced-out boyfriend of Alexandra; Sid is also not as simple as he seems. Consider Matthew Lillard as the adulterer; not a bad man. Consider Beau Bridges, who is reluctant to be the bad guy, but not unwilling.

What happens is that we get *vested* in the lives of these characters. That's rare in a lot of movies. We come to understand how they think and care about what they decide. There are substantial moral problems underlying the plot. And George Clooney? What essence does Payne see in him? I believe it is intelligence. Some actors may not be smart enough to sound convincing; the wrong actor in this role couldn't convince us he understood the issues involved. Clooney strikes me as manifestly the kind of actor who does. We see him thinking, we share his thoughts, and at the end of *The Descendants*, we've all come to his conclusions together.

## Desert Flower ★ ★ ½

R, 124 m., 2011

Liya Kebede (Waris Dirie), Sally Hawkins (Marylin), Timothy Spall (Terry Donaldson), Juliet Stevenson (Lucinda), Craig Parkinson (Neil), Anthony Mackie (Harold Jackson), Meera Syal (Pushpa Patel), Soraya Omar-Scego (Waris at twelve). Directed by Sherry Hormann and produced by Peter Herrmann. Screenplay by Hormann, based on the autobiographical novel by Waris Dirie.

*Desert Flower* tells an extraordinary story in an ordinary way. It has a compelling message and surrounds it with biopic scenes that appear to be brought in from a different kind of movie. The effect is rather unsettling.

The film is based on the life of Waris Dirie, an international supermodel who began life as a member of a nomadic tribe in Somalia. At the age of five, she was circumcised, as is the custom in many African lands. An old woman in the desert cut away those parts that could someday allow her to feel sexual pleasure, and sewed shut her vagina—so her husband could be sure he had married a virgin when he cut it open.

Many die during or because of this barbaric mutilation, still widely practiced today, although not mentioned in the Quran or any other holy book. It is the practice of subjugating women, making them commodities and denying them the full lives they deserve. It rises from the woman-hating men who propagate it by refusing to marry any woman who hasn't been "cut."

When Waris was sold as a young teenager to an old man who already had three wives, she simply left one day, walking hundreds of miles across desert and scrubland to seek her grandmother in Mogadishu. Amazingly, she found her—and was hired by an aunt in London to work as a maid. The film cuts between her experiences as a young girl and what happened in London, where she ran away, lived on the streets, and was befriended by a ditzy shop girl named Marylin (Sally Hawkins).

Marylin found her a job in a fast-food restaurant mopping floors, and that's where she was "discovered" by the fashion photographer Terry Donaldson (Timothy Spall). Through him and a mercenary modeling agent named Lucinda (Juliet Stevenson), she rose not without difficulties to the top ranks of models. She eventually denounced genital mutilation before the United Nations and became its spokesperson against the practice.

So it is a rags-to-riches story, but it plays like two stories in conflict. Everything involving Waris in Africa or in London before her success feels true and heartfelt. Many later details are badly handled.

Waris is played by another model, Liya Kebede, herself a spectacular beauty (a question that arises: Why did it take so long for her to be "discovered"?). The film, written and directed by Sherry Hormann, lingers unnecessarily on several sexualized modeling sessions and teases us with nude scenes. Two supporting characters, Lucinda and a janitor named Neil (Craig Parkinson), undergo puzzling personality changes at the convenience of the plot. A character named Harold Jackson (Anthony Mackie) exists exclusively for Idiot Plot purposes. And a jacket materializes after the point has been made that it was left behind.

Still, there are good things here. Sally Hawkins and Timothy Spall, familiar from Mike Leigh films, make their characters original and plausible. Meera Syal, as a rooming-house owner, steps in with some nice moments. And it's a compliment, I think, that Liya Kebede is more convincing as Waris the waif than as Waris the model.

## Despicable Me ★ ★ ★

PG, 95 m., 2010

With the voices of Steve Carell (Gru), Jason Segel (Vector), Russell Brand (Dr. Nefario), Julie Andrews (Gru's Mom), Will Arnett (Mr. Perkins), Kristen Wiig (Miss Hattie), Miranda Cosgrove (Margo), Dana Gaier (Edith), Elsie Fisher (Agnes). Directed by Chris Renaud and Pierre Coffin and produced by John Cohen, Janet Healy, and Christopher Meledandri. Screenplay by Cinco Paul and Ken Daurio.

*Despicable Me* begins with the truth that villains are often more fascinating than heroes, and creates a villain named Gru who freeze-dries the people ahead of him in line at Starbucks and pops children's balloons. Although he's inspired by many a James Bond bad guy, two things set him apart: (1) His vast mad scientist lair is located not in the desert or on the moon, but in the basement of his suburban home, and (2) he dreams not of world control so much as merely dominating the cable news ratings as The Greatest Villain of All Time.

Gru is voiced by Steve Carell, who gives him an accent halfway between a Russian mafioso and a crazed Nazi. His life is made more difficult because his mother (Julie Andrews) sometimes gets on his case. Memories stir of Rupert Pupkin in his basement, yanked from his fantasies by his mother's voice. Gru's most useful weapon is the Insta-Freeze Gun, but now, with the help of his genius staff inventor Dr. Nefario (Russell Brand), he can employ a Shrink Ray.

Just as global-scale villainy is looking promising, Gru is upstaged by his archrival, Vector (Jason Segel), who steals the Great Pyramid. Since that pyramid was previously pounded to pieces by the Transformers, the Egyptians should establish a CGI-free zone around it.

Gru is cheered ever onward by his faithful minions, who are, in fact, called the Minions, and look like yellow exercise balls with one or two eyes apiece. The principal responsibility of the Minions is to cheer for Gru, who addresses them as if he's running for office. He hatches a plan to use the Shrink Ray to steal no less than the moon itself, and explains it to the Minions with a plan that reminded me of nothing so much as the guy in the joke who plans to get the gorilla down out of the tree using only a broomstick, a pair of handcuffs, and a savage Dalmatian dog.

To make a villain into the hero of an animated comedy is daring, but the filmmakers bring in three cute kids to restore good feelings. These are Margo (Miranda Cosgrove), Edith (Dana Gaier), and Agnes (Elsie Fisher). Gru finds them at his friendly neighborhood orphanage, run by the suspicious Miss Hattie (Kristen Wiig). His plan is to keep them at his home until his moon scheme is ready to hatch, and then use them to infiltrate Vector's home by subterfuge—pretending to sell cookies, say. It follows as the night does the day that the orphans will work their little-girl magic on Gru, and gradually force the revelation that the big lug has a heart after all.

*Despicable Me* lacks a franchise to ride into town on, but it may establish one. I'm not sure how Gru can think up anything more sensational than stealing the moon, but I'm sure Dr. Nefario is working on that as we speak. The film is funny, energetic, teeth-gnashingly venomous, and animated with an eye to exploiting the 3-D process with such surefire techniques as a visit to an amusement park.

The sad thing, I am forced to report, is that the 3-D process produces a picture more dim than it should be. *Despicable Me* is technically competent and nowhere near the visual disaster that was *The Last Airbender,* but take my word for it: Try to find it in 2-D. Or, if you see it in 3-D, check out the trailers online to see how bright and cheery it would look in 2-D. How can people deceive themselves that 3-D is worth paying extra for?

## Detective Dee and the Mystery of the Phantom Flame ★ ★ ★ ½

PG-13, 119 m., 2011

Andy Lau (Detective Dee), Carina Lau (Empress Wu Zetian), Li Bingbing (Shangguan Jing'er), Tony Leung Ka-Fai (Shatuo Zhong), Chao Deng (Pei Donglai), Jean-Michel Casanova (General Aspar). Directed by Tsui Hark and produced by Tsui, Peggy Lee, and Nansun Shi. Screenplay by Chang Jialu.

Detective Dee is a sleuth in China during the Tang Dynasty, circa 690. Like Sherlock Holmes, he based his detection largely on acute observation. He became famous in seventeen mystery novels by Robert van Gulik, and now here he is in an extravaganza by Tsui Hark, a master of the choreography of action. This is a bewitching fantasy.

The Empress Wu Zetian is about to become the first woman to ascend the imperial throne, but powerful forces scheme against her. A woman as head of state was no more thinkable in China in 690 than it is in America today. The construction of a towering statue of a giant Buddha is being hurried toward completion before her coronation day, when progress is interrupted by the spontaneous human combustion of several of its designers. Much as I persist in doubting it, such a form of death is allegedly possible, but surely there is no precedent for a series of them at such a touchy time.

It appears to be the perfect crime, if it is a crime. The victims combust in full view with no one nearby. There are, of course, no murder weapons. The cause is unknown, although it seems to happen in sunlight. This is a case for the greatest investigator in the land, and so the empress (Carina Lau) summons Detective Dee (Andy Lau) from the imperial prison, whence she cast him some years ago. As heroes in such situations often are, Detective Dee is forgiving, is still loyal to her, and has apparently only improved his skills during confinement.

Now the stage is set for an epic of martial arts action on a lavish scale, using vast sets that are both real and CGI. Tsui Hark is a genius of this genre, going back to the *Chinese Ghost Story* movies circa 1990 and nearly sixty other films, including *Once Upon a Time in China* and its sequels. This film may represent the largest budget in his career, and one wonders how much of that went into the bizarre hair stylings of the empress.

On the basis of its scale, energy, and magical events, this is the Hong Kong equivalent of a big-budget Hollywood blockbuster. But it transcends them with the stylization of the costumes, the panoply of the folklore, the richness of the setting, and the fact that none of the characters (allegedly) has superpowers. All the characters are presented as presumably real, with the exception of a talking stag—which, since it is an imperial stag, I suppose is permitted.

Detective Dee is assigned three assistants he is not sure he can entirely trust: Zhong (Tony

Leung Ka-Fai), who is an expert on the design and construction of the Buddha; Jing'er (Li Bingbing), who enjoys the empress's favor; and Pei (Chao Deng), a police official who seems fixed in a state of constant brooding. They debate with great energy while Dee listens and observes (as Holmes did), but events move inexorably toward disaster as victims continue to incinerate. It is discovered that the giant Buddha is just exactly high enough that if it fell in the wrong direction, it would land precisely on the site of the planned coronation. By this point there's no reason to doubt that it would fall in that direction.

Tsui Hark began with the traditional techniques of martial arts films, with athletic stars using concealed trampolines and invisible overhead wires to supplement their own considerable skills. One of the pleasures of watching traditional Bruce Lee or Jackie Chan films is that in many cases the stars were actually doing what they seemed to be doing, much aided by editing and camera angles. Now those methods have been rendered obsolete by CGI, and the characters can leap any distance, defy gravity, and virtually change direction in midair (when the laws of physics make that impossible). The humans here are as skilled as—well, as Kung Fu Panda.

The result lacks the exhilaration of watching Jackie Chan climb a wall or leap onto a truck in real time, but there's an undeniable fluid grace. And masters like Tsui Hark prefer their action to have a certain visual continuity and not be fragmented into the incomprehensible bits of action employed by Michael Bay. His camera is also disciplined; his wide-screen compositions are elegant and almost classical, given the tumult on the screen.

That said, the movie exists very much in the moment, and although an attempt is made to flash back and reconstruct what must have happened, such explanations are required only by the conventions of the genre. In a way, Detective Dee is Sherlock Holmes and we in the audience are slow-witted Watsons.

## The Devil's Double ★ ★ ★

R, 109 m., 2011

Dominic Cooper (Uday Hussein/Latif Yahia), Ludivine Sagnier (Sarrab), Raad Rawi (Munem), Philip Quast (Saddam Hussein/Faoaz), Mimoun Oaissa (Ali), Khalid Laith (Yassem), Dar Salim (Azzam), Nasser Memarzia (Latif's father). Directed by Lee Tamahori and produced by Paul Breuls, Michael John Fedun, Emjay Rechsteiner, and Catherine Vandeleene. Screenplay by Michael Thomas, based on the life story of Latif Yahia.

Uday Hussein, the eldest son of Saddam Hussein, was a vile and deranged man, whose depravities were given full rein with unlimited power and money. It was a demanding job to be the double of a man so many sincerely wanted to see dead; even Saddam reportedly told Uday, "I should have killed you the day you were born."

Lee Tamahori's *The Devil's Double* is based on the experiences of Latif Yahia, who was groomed as Uday's double. In this role he survived no less than a dozen assassination attempts. The movie portrays him as an Iraqi soldier forced to take the job by beatings and threats to his family; he is seen throughout as an upstanding figure with contempt for Uday and a good deal of courage in standing up to him.

If ever there was a film requiring the same actor to play two roles, this is that film. Dominic Cooper, a British actor who has previously played mostly second-string leading men, rises to the challenge with an astonishing dual performance, often acting with himself through seamless special effects. As Uday, he is a sadistic, coke-snorting, booze-swilling murderer and rapist. As Latif, he is a reluctant stand-in who witnesses Uday's evil and hates him, while at the same time enjoying his luxurious lifestyle and even, daringly, one of his mistresses (Ludivine Sagnier).

The story inspires much excess, and Tamahori rises to the occasion. It is impossible to observe Cooper's performance as Uday without being reminded of Al Pacino's *Scarface*, although Scarface was a humanitarian by comparison. Uday is functionally insane, and bodyguards protect him during his manic crimes. He rapes a bride at her own wedding, picks up schoolgirls from the streets and has their bodies dumped outside Baghdad, and in the film's most graphic scene (there is a lot of competition) he disembowels his father's food taster at a banquet. In the film, he does this with a scimitar. In life, I learn, he used an electric carving knife.

He resented the man for *pimping* for his father—supplying him with a woman Saddam might marry to replace Uday's own mother. For that woman he harbored a love verging on incest, and they have a scene in bed together that is creepy.

This movie is not quite based on fact. Tamahori and his writer, Michael Thomas, make it clear they've fictionalized a great deal, and although they cite Latif Yahia's own book as their source, that itself is a novel. In life, I learn, Latif was groomed as Uday's double from as early as his school days. Nor did he plot Uday's death. His story raises the question of whether his real life role was quite as upstanding as it seems here; he would have much reason to portray himself in a favorable light.

As a result of those ambiguities, it is interesting to wonder about the purpose of the film. It is not intended as history. Although it draws applause at the news (in the end credits) that Uday was killed in 2003 by U.S. Special Forces, it is not particularly unfavorable in its portrayal of Papa Hussein. He makes a few brief appearances in what functions as the movie's token of (relative) sanity.

The movie is above all entertaining, if you enjoy human grotesquerie and flamboyant acting. Let's face it. Many of us do. There's a reason why Hannibal Lecter remains the most popular villain in the movies. Dominic Cooper is inevitably more effective as Uday than as Latif, his disapproving double. After we get a few tastes of Uday, we can almost feel the energy level sagging during Latif's scenes. Nor does the role of Sarrab (Ludivine Sagnier) hold up very well. What's her real story? Why would she, knowing what she knows, take the reckless risk of becoming Latif's lover? The movie never persuades us that it understands her.

There were times early in *The Devil's Double* that I felt it was preparing to approach greatness. The materials are all assembled. And then it never really engages with them. There can be no *explanation* for Uday's madness. But Latif's character is explored primarily for the convenience of the plot, and obvious questions are sidestepped. It's a terrific show. All due praise to Dominic Cooper. It should have been more.

## Diary of a Wimpy Kid ★ ★ ★ ½

PG, 92 m., 2010

Zachary Gordon (Greg Heffley), Robert Capron (Rowley Jefferson), Rachael Harris (Susan Heffley), Steve Zahn (Frank Heffley), Devon Bostick (Rodrick Heffley), Chloe Moretz (Angie Steadman), Grayson Russell (Fregley). Directed by Thor Freudenthal and produced by Nina Jacobson and Bradford Simpson. Screenplay by Jackie Filgo, Jeff Filgo, Gabe Sachs, and Jeff Judah, based on the books by Jeff Kinney.

It is so hard to do a movie like this well. *Diary of a Wimpy Kid* is a PG-rated comedy about the hero's first year of middle school, and it's nimble, bright, and funny. It doesn't dumb down. It doesn't patronize. It knows something about human nature. It isn't as good as *A Christmas Story,* as few movies are, but it deserves a place in the same sentence. Here is a family movie you don't need a family to enjoy. You must, however, have been a wimpy kid. Most kids are wimpy in their secret hearts. Those who never were grow up to be cage fighters.

Greg Heffley isn't the shortest student in his class. That would be Chirag Gupta. Greg (Zachary Gordon) is only the second shortest. He's at that crucial age when everybody else has started to grow. There's a funny slide show illustrating how his class looked in sixth grade, and how they look now—some with mustaches. The girls, of course, are taller than the boys.

The onset of adolescence is an awkward age, made marginally easier for Greg because he still hasn't developed an interest in girls. Even his best friend, Rowley (Robert Capron), is flattered to be noticed by a girl, and Rowley is so out of it he thinks that at his age kids still *play,* when, as we all know, they *hang.*

The girl who notices Greg and Rowley is Angie (Chloe Moretz), who seems wise beyond her years. We first see her under the bleachers, reading *Howl* by Allen Ginsberg. Keep your eye on her in high school. She looks way older than her two new friends, but I checked, and Moretz was only twelve when she made the movie.

In middle school we find cliques, cruelty, and bullying. The pack is poised to pounce. *Diary* is especially funny about a slice of Swiss cheese that was dropped on a playground sometime in the distant past, and has grown an alarming coating of mold. Some kid poked it once, and all the other kids avoided him like the plague. He had the dreaded Cheese Touch. He only got rid of it by touching another kid. Then that kid had the Touch, until . . . and so on. The cheese nicely symbolizes the hunger kids have for an excuse, any excuse, to make other kids pariahs. Remember what happened to anyone who wore green on a Thursday?

Where do they find these actors? They come up on TV, I guess. Chloe Moretz has been acting since she was seven. Zachary Gordon has the confidence and timing of an old pro; he plays wimpy as if it's a desirable character trait. Robert Capron, as the pudgy Rowley, pulls off the tricky feat of being an inch or two taller than Greg and yet still childish; wait until you see his Halloween costume. Greg's parents (Rachael Harris and Steve Zahn) aren't major characters because what happens in school consumes all of Greg's psychic energy. His older brother, Rodrick (Devon Bostick), is, of course, a sadistic teaser who makes life miserable. But at that age, so it goes.

The movie is inspired by the books of Jeff Kinney, and the titles reproduce his hand-lettering and drawing style. The movie reproduces his charm. The director, Thor Freudenthal, made *Hotel for Dogs* (2009), received affectionately in some circles, but this time his touch is more sure and his humor more sunny.

## The Dictator ★ ★ ★

R, 85 m., 2012

Sacha Baron Cohen (General Admiral Aladeen), Anna Faris (Zoey), Megan Fox (Herself), Ben Kingsley (Tahir), John C. Reilly (Clayton). Directed by Larry Charles and produced by Sacha Baron Cohen, Alec Berg, Anthony Hines, David Mandel, Scott Rudin, Jeff Schaffer, and Todd Schulman. Screenplay by Cohen and Berg.

*The Dictator* is funny, in addition to being obscene, disgusting, scatological, vulgar, crude, and so on. Having seen Sacha Baron Cohen promoting it on countless talk shows, I feared the movie would feel like déjà vu. But no. He establishes a claim to be the best comic filmmaker now working. And in a speech about dictatorships, he practices merciless political satire.

Compared to the gleeful transgressions of *Borat* and *Bruno*, this is Cohen's most conventional film. It has a plot, it has a romance, it sticks to the story. Not that it's mainstream, although judging by the laughter of a preview audience, who knows where the stream is anymore? He also wisely gets in, gets his laughs, and quits. The movie, like *Bruno*, falls short of ninety minutes, in an era when too many comedies run on relentlessly.

Cohen plays General Admiral Aladeen of the North African nation of Wadiya, which seems superimposed upon parts of Egypt and Sudan and is spitting distance from Saudi Arabia. Here he occupies a huge palace, used for addressing admiring throngs of his worshippers and having sex not only with Megan Fox, but also, judging by his wall of postcoital Polaroids, Kim Kardashian, Arnold Schwarzenegger, and Oprah. Megan Fox has a great cameo, showing up for sex but drawing the line at an all-night cuddle.

Aladeen's premier is Tahir (Ben Kingsley), rightful heir to the throne, who is plotting to overthrow him. After an assassination fails, Tahir encourages Aladeen to address the United Nations, where he hopes another assassination will succeed. After being debearded by a security man (John C. Reilly), Aladeen finds himself wandering the streets of Manhattan while being impersonated in public by a body double.

He finds his way into an extreme left-wing health food store run by Zoey (Anna Faris), and despite the radical difference in their beliefs, the General Admiral finds himself falling for her. That sets up satire in general about feminists, vegetarians, and immigrant huggers. Then Aladeen wanders into Manhattan's "Little Wadiya" neighborhood, where a Wadiyan restaurant seems filled with people he thought he'd executed.

Although the movie very casually follows the progress of the romance and the assassination scheme, Cohen and the director, Larry

Charles, are about as dedicated to plot as the Marx Brothers; the movie's spiritual ancestor is *Duck Soup* and Groucho's Freedonian dictator, Rufus T. Firefly. There is also a taste of Buster Keaton's physical humor in a scene where Aladeen attempts to slide on a cable high above the street into the upper floor of a hotel.

Cohen's attack on the material is freewheeling, his attitude is anarchist, and he's more good-humored than in *Borat* and *Bruno.* I hope he isn't entertaining any ambitions to become beloved and popular. I expected this to be the most offensive of the three titles, and while you can't say it isn't offensive (especially in scenes involving a dead civil rights leader's severed head), it's somehow . . . nicer, maybe you could say.

*Note: I want to know more about the Newcastle Hotel in New York. I don't believe there is one. It provides the fodder for a running gag about product placement that plugs the name again and again and again.*

## Dinner for Schmucks ★ ★ ★

PG-13, 114 m., 2010

Steve Carell (Barry Speck), Paul Rudd (Tim Conrad), Jemaine Clement (Kieran Vollard), Jeff Dunham (Lewis), Bruce Greenwood (Lance Fender), Ron Livingston (Caldwell), Zach Galifianakis (Therman), Stephanie Szostak (Julie). Directed by Jay Roach and produced by Roach, Laurie MacDonald, and Walter F. Parkes. Screenplay by David Guion and Michael Handelman, inspired by the French film *Le Diner de Cons* (*The Dinner Game*) directed and written by Francis Veber.

The truly goofy comes shrouded in innocence. If a man is trying to be goofy, it's just an act that quickly grows old. But if he lacks the slightest notion of his peculiarity, there's the secret. The blissful ignorance of Barry Speck is beyond pitiful and ascends to a kind of nobility. He's one of those who truly don't have a clue.

In *Dinner for Schmucks,* a group of arrogant rich men use him as part of an elaborate joke, but the joke is on them. You can't insult a man who is always happy to be just exactly who he is. In the film, the millionaires have a dinner party every year that is a secret joke: Each guest invites another guest who is, whether he realizes it or not, in a contest to determine which guest is the biggest idiot. This is plain cruel.

*Dinner for Schmucks* was inspired by Francis Veber's French film named *The Dinner Game,* which was an enormous hit in France but seemed a shade on the mean side. The genius of this version depends on the performance by Steve Carell, who plays Barry Speck as a man impervious to insult and utterly at peace with himself. And a transcendent idiot.

The hero of the film is Tim Conrad (Paul Rudd), an ambitious young man dreaming of promotion to the corner office. His boss is Lance Fender (Bruce Greenwood), who invites him to bring a guest to the dinner. This chance to hobnob with his boss's powerful friends is attractive, but at first Tim says no; he has an important date scheduled with his fiancée, Julie (Stephanie Szostak). Then he meets Barry, a man whose hobby is populating enormous dollhouses and model landscapes with elaborately costumed dead mice. Barry is too good to pass up. He looks like a sure winner.

The subplot between Julie and Tim is essentially the MacGuffin; there needs to be something important to Tim that comes into conflict with the dinner. The film itself settles down, or stirs itself up, at the long dinner scene, at which we meet several other perfect idiots, but none in the running with Barry.

Barry is such a specimen it's hard to describe him. Yes, he wears a toupee. Yes, he seems to have mice secreted about his person. But it's more that he's the only happy man in the room. One of the reasons we love the great eccentrics in Dickens, I believe, is that they're so pleased with themselves. You cannot be a great eccentric if you're not a happy one; otherwise there's no fun in it.

The dinner turns into farce and finally descends into slapstick, but Carell sails through these choppy seas with a steadfast belief in human nature. He doesn't perceive insult to himself perhaps because he can't imagine anyone acting that way. Jay Roach, who is no stranger to raunchy comedy (*Austin Powers, Meet the Fockers*), makes a good strategic decision on how he handles this: Not only is Barry an innocent, but so is Tim, who invited him to the party for reasons of ambition but not cruelty. So the villain is at three removes. That would be Bruce Greenwood as the sadistic boss.

The guests at the dinner are a strange lot. To describe them would be to give away their jokes, and one of the pleasures of the movie is having each one appear. I wonder if it occurs to anyone to reflect that the hosts of this dinner are the biggest idiots in attendance. Oh, and those elegant little mice remind me of the white mice in Charlie Kaufman's *Human Nature,* being taught their table manners by scientists.

## District 13: Ultimatum ★ ★ ★

R, 100 m., 2010

Cyril Raffaelli (Damien), David Belle (Leito), Philippe Torreton (President), Daniel Duval (Gassman), MC Jean Gab'1 (Molko), La Fouine (Ali-K), James Deano (Karl). Directed by Patrick Alessandrin and produced by Luc Besson. Screenplay by Besson.

There is a limit to how far down you can jump and land on your feet and not break an ankle. Well, isn't there? I ask because these limits don't seem to apply to the cops who are the heroes of *District 13: Ultimatum.* Nor, incredibly, do they apply to the bad cops who chase them across the rooftops of Paris while burdened with full SWAT team uniforms, including bulletproof vests. There isn't a single character who lands badly, and limps away.

I know, I know. It's all done with special effects. Yes, but . . . well, see the movie. The height of a jump can be exaggerated by oblique camera angles and lenses. Hong Kong experts use wires and trampolines. Hollywood sidesteps the issue by editing so quickly no physical movement is ever quite entirely seen. Yes. But consider that the costar of *District 13* is a thirty-five-year-old Frenchman named David Belle, famed as the man who named "parkour," which is "the art of flight." This is a hot modern martial art. Not only do the shots look convincing, not only are they held long enough to allow us to see an entire action, but Belle in real life does a version of this stuff.

The stuff is what intrigues me. The screenplay is another of the countless works of Luc Besson, who is the most productive person in modern action movies. It's a sequel to his 2004 film in which a walled-off segment of Paris in 2010 was run by black, white, Asian, and Arab warlords, with a fifth one left over I couldn't categorize. There is a plot within a crooked high-level security agency to destroy the district and rebuild it. This massive work will be accomplished by the corporation that has bribed them, named Harriburton, which does not remind you of anything, of course.

The president of the French republic is not in on the plot. He believes in liberty, equality, fraternity, and the constitution, which would make him unpopular with Harriburton. Anyway, after they luckily see a citizen video showing bad cops murdering good cops and blaming it on gangs in District 13, it's up to Damien (Cyril Raffaelli) and Leito (David Belle) to single-handedly stop the evil scheme.

This they do in many ways, but mostly by running away. Parkour is the "art of flight," you recall. So they grab incriminating tapes and computer drives, the bad cops want to catch them, and this leads to the real point of the movie, which is one chase scene after another. These actors are clearly in superb physical shape. I'm not going to believe they actually do all these stunts, but I believe we clearly see them doing parts of them, which all by themselves would be awesome.

They leap, fall, tumble, twist, climb up and down walls and buildings, swing from wires, slide down wires, and have an alarming eagerness to jump out of buildings without knowing what is below. (Luckily, there are nice comfy landing spots like the roofs of cars.) At one point, after Damien comes home to his girlfriend (Sophie Ducasse), he complains he feels "stiff." Ha. This man needs an intensive care unit. Still, the parkour motto is "*etre et duress,*" which means "to be and to endure," or in other words, not to get yourself killed or twist an ankle.

If anyone is going to convince fanboys to attend a movie with French subtitles, that man is Luc Besson. They'll catch on that Besson, working without enormous budgets and A-list stars, knows what he's doing. A movie like *District 13: Ultimatum* may be as preposterous as the lame *From Paris with*

*Love*, but it delivers the goods. You want an action movie where you can see that the actors are really there, and not concealed by editing that looks like someone fed the film through an electric fan? Here's your movie. For that matter, although the characters indeed speak French, they don't talk much, and sometimes the SWAT teams use English they learned from cop movies, like "Go! Go! Go!"

## Dogtooth ★ ★ ★

NO MPAA RATING, 94 m., 2010

Christos Stergioglou (Father), Michelle Valley (Mother), Aggeliki Papoulia (Older Daughter), Hristos Passalis (Son), Mary Tsoni (Younger Daughter), Anna Kalaitzidou (Christina). Directed by Yorgos Lanthimos and produced by Yorgos Tsourgiannis. Screenplay by Lanthimos and Efthimis Filippou.

*Dogtooth* is a bizarre fantasy that takes the concept of homeschooling to squirmy extremes. Some homeschoolers try to limit what their children can learn, and others to broaden it. The parents in *Dogtooth* have passed far beyond such categories into the realms of home psychopathology.

No name is given for the family or any of its members. These involve a father, a mother, a brother, and two sisters. They live in a large, affluent home behind a very high wall and a gate that is always locked. Only the father ever leaves, driving to the factory he owns.

The others are prisoners, the mother apparently by choice. There is a large lawn and a swimming pool. The television set is used only to watch the family's home videos. The children have no idea of the outside world, where they are told man-eating cats roam. On the other side of the wall they believe another brother lives, who they've never seen or heard.

Man-eating cats? Who knows? The film begins with a tape-recorded language lesson in which they're taught the *wrong* words for things. "Sea," for example, is the word for the big leather armchair in the living room. Father is a stern taskmaster, free with stern reprimands and a hard slap or two. He also teaches all of his family members to get down on all fours and bark like dogs. He and Mother seem in complete agreement about their child-rearing methods but never discuss them in detail.

The son is about twenty, the daughters in their teens. To slake the boy's sexual needs, Father brings home a security guard from his factory, who has sex with the son with all the spontaneity and joy of tooth removal. This woman also trades a daughter some cheap jewelry in exchange for some illicit licking.

The kids are so innocent, they decide that it's much the same no matter where you lick, and trade favors for licking legs, elbows, and ears. Sex seems to have no meaning, not even when incest is suggested. The sickness of this family surpasses all understanding, and some have even described the film as a comedy. I wasn't laughing. All I can say of the ending is that it is certainly a possible outcome of the film, and gets much more than you would think out of a shot of the family car.

There is this. *Dogtooth* is like a car crash. You cannot look away. The Greek director Yorgos Lanthimos tells his story with complete command of visuals and performances. His cinematography is like a series of family photographs of a family with something wrong with it. His dialogue sounds composed entirely of sentences memorized from tourist phrase books. The message I took away was: God help children whose parents insanely demand unquestioning obedience to their deranged standards.

*Note: The film won the Un Certain Regard section of Cannes 2009.*

## Dolphin Tale ★ ★ ★

PG, 112 m., 2011

Harry Connick Jr. (Dr. Clay Haskett), Ashley Judd (Lorraine Nelson), Nathan Gamble (Sawyer Nelson), Kris Kristofferson (Reed Haskett), Cozi Zuehlsdorff (Hazel Haskett), Morgan Freeman (Dr. Cameron McCarthy), Austin Stowell (Kyle Connellan), Austin Highsmith (Phoebe). Directed by Charles Martin Smith and produced by Richard Inger, Broderick Johnson, and Andrew A. Kosove. Screenplay by Karen Janszen and Noam Dromi.

*Dolphin Tale* is a sweet, feel-good film about a boy who helps save a dolphin, and how the dolphin then helps save him. When we meet young Sawyer Nelson (Nathan Gamble), he has withdrawn into a shell and is a remote loner. He builds models in his workshop, plays video games, and avoids interaction with anyone—even at the going-away party for his beloved cousin. His father left the family without explanation some years ago, which may account for his isolation; his mother, Lorraine (Ashley Judd), does what she can, but feels closed out.

On the way home from his Florida grade school, Sawyer happens upon a dolphin stranded on the beach, its tail hopelessly twisted in the ropes of a lobster trap. He bonds with the creature until a rescue team arrives from a local animal hospital. Worried about the dolphin, Sawyer skips school to sneak into the animal hospital, where he's befriended by young Hazel Haskett (Cozi Zuehlsdorff), whose dad, Clay (Harry Connick Jr.), runs the facility.

Sawyer at first is so shy he can barely speak, but these outgoing people encourage him to help with the dolphin in a pool, and soon he breaks out of his seclusion and grows enthusiastic about working with the animal. This involves an attempt to preserve its ability to swim after infection requires its tail to be amputated. A prosthetics specialist at the nearby VA hospital (Morgan Freeman) designs artificial tails, finally finding one that will work.

Learning of this story, I thought, aw, come on, give me a break. But it turns out the story is not only based on fact, but the actual dolphin involved, named Winter, stars in the movie as herself. Her new tail functions admirably.

The movie will fascinate kids who love nature, just as *Free Willy* did. And although the real whale in that film was also seen, the interaction here is more believable; Winter doesn't do anything a real dolphin might not do. The film does get a bit carried away with the assumption that Sawyer and Winter find ways to communicate by clicks, whistles, and so on. I know dolphins communicate, I know they recognize and respond to humans, and Sawyer even cleverly finds a Web page devoted to the language of their sounds. But the anthropomorphism of Winter is carried a shade beyond believability.

There are various uplifting subplots. Sawyer's cousin Kyle (Austin Stowell), a champion swimmer, enlists in the army and returns with a leg injury that will affect his swimming. He is depressed until he gets involved in Winter's recovery. Sawyer's mom and Hazel's dad, both heading single-parent families, seem destined for romance, but perhaps that's being reserved for the inevitable sequel. Hazel's grandfather (Kris Kristofferson), who presides over the nearby houseboat where they all live, is invaluable for moments of wisdom.

The movie was directed by Charles Martin Smith, who starred in one of the best of all films about man and nature, *Never Cry Wolf* (1983). He guides his good cast with a firm hand and steers in the direction of life-affirming lessons. He has made a pleasant family film with an improbable true story at its heart.

## Don't Be Afraid of the Dark ★ ★ ★

R, 99 m., 2011

Katie Holmes (Kim Raphael), Guy Pearce (Alex Hurst), Bailee Madison (Sally Hurst), Jack Thompson (Harris). Directed by Troy Nixey and produced by Marc Johnson and Guillermo del Toro. Screenplay by del Toro and Matthew Robbins, based on the teleplay by Nigel McKeand.

Haunted house movies awaken within us the five-year-old afraid to go down the stairs with the basement lights off. Sure, there's a light switch down at the bottom, but you never know. *Don't Be Afraid of the Dark* begins with an extraordinary house that should be haunted, even if it isn't. This is a mansion in Australia, I learn, much enhanced by art direction and set design, which I might be reluctant to occupy alone even with all the lights on.

Into this house move a ten-year-old girl named Sally, her father, and her father's girlfriend. The movie depends so much on the little girl, played by Bailee Madison with pluck, intelligence, and a righteous temper. When children are endangered in horror movies, it's no fun if they just scream and run away. That's taking a cheap shot. Sally is brave and determined, and Madison is an effective young actress.

Her father, Alex (Guy Pearce), loves her in a perfunctory and distant way. The girlfriend, Kim (Katie Holmes), is warmer and more sympathetic because it's always the men who are dolts in these matters. They hope she'll like living at Blackwood Manor, which her father has purchased. The plan is they'll renovate it and sell it at enough of a profit to put Alex's business back on its feet. I guess they bought it at a bargain price. The film begins with a creepy introduction in which crabby old Emerson Blackwood and his son come to terrifying ends years ago. Perhaps it has been empty ever since? My rule of thumb is, think twice about moving into any abandoned manor named Blackwood that has a history of mysterious deaths. Trust me on this.

The film is based on a made-for-TV thriller from 1973, which starred young Kim Darby as Sally. Seeing that film reportedly so transfixed young Guillermo del Toro that at the age of nine he determined to dedicate his life to making fantastical horror films, and has. Indeed, the use of a heroine and grotesque creatures is the hallmark of his great *Pan's Labyrinth.* He cowrote the screenplay and produced.

This is only the second film by the director, Troy Nixey, but he shows a firm hold on atmosphere. He and the screenplay make good use of the inclination of adults to dismiss the fears of children as imagination running wild. The tension between what we *know* Sally has experienced and the casual dismissals of the grown-ups is central to much of the film's tension. The little girl explains over and over again what she has seen. She draws pictures. There is ominous agreement from old Harris (Jack Thompson), the house's caretaker. Ever notice how houses named Blackwood Manor always have grizzled caretakers lurking about? There is even a local librarian who turns out to be quite an expert on old Emerson Blackwood.

Alex doesn't want to know about it. He's in a financial corner, he has all his money tied up in the manor, and he doesn't fancy bankruptcy just on the basis of childish terrors. Kim is torn. She's looking forward to marriage. She loves Sally. They both have an annoying tendency to allow the child to wander the manor alone.

It is an added element that the horrors mostly seem to reside in the basement. This isn't the sort of basement the word usually summons, but a lower living area, long since blocked off, with a fireplace flue behind which . . . something lives. This made perfect sense to me. When I was a little boy, a green worm with teeth lived inside the drain of our bathroom sink.

Nixey provides us with a very gradual introduction to the inhabitants of the flue, which opens over a dark, deep space. Into this space we earlier saw Emerson Blackwood fall. Or was he pulled? Exploring the area, Sally innocently checks out the grating, and we hear ominous whispers and rustlings, and glimpse the body parts of . . . something.

These creatures are eventually seen more clearly, which I must say is a disappointment. The mastery of CGI allows filmmakers to show just about anything they can imagine, when sometimes it's scarier to show nothing at all. Consider the timeless *Cat People* (1942). We never saw a thing. But when the heroine goes alone for a late-night plunge in a swimming pool, she hears something growl, and pace, and nothing we could possibly see could improve on that scene.

I'll let you discover what these little creatures look like. Perhaps, like me, you'll wonder about their metabolism. There are a great many of them, apparently thriving for decades down there at the bottom with the old fireplace ashes. They're very agile and energetic, and scamper around and snarl and brandish things, and they demand to be fed the teeth of children. You wonder how long life can be sustained on an all-teeth diet. Now that Bill Clinton is a vegan, let him try that for a while.

But I stray. This is a very good haunted house film. It milks our frustration deliciously. The adults are forever saying and doing the wrong things, and making stupid decisions, and Alex is bull-headed and Kim is conflicted. And the shadows are deep and dark, and the screws in the grating of the flue seem to turn themselves, and no one will pay attention to little Sally, and somewhere in the audience will be a kid who gets inspired to make his own horror films.

## The Double ★ ★

PG-13, 98 m., 2011

Richard Gere (Paul Shepherdson), Topher Grace (Ben Geary), Stephen Moyer (Brutus), Odette

Yustman (Natalie), Stana Katic (Amber), Chris Marquette (Oliver), Tamer Hassan (Bozlovski), Martin Sheen (Tom Highland). Directed by Michael Brandt and produced by Patrick Aiello, Andrew Deane, and Derek Haas. Screenplay by Brandt and Haas.

It takes *The Double* less than half an hour to reveal who the double is. That's if you're lucky enough to avoid the movie's trailer, which just comes right out and tells you. At that point, Peggy Lee lyrics went humming through my mind ("Is that all there is?") and, veteran thriller fan that I am, I began to suspect the movie had more than one double. That would be so incredible and absurd that I thought it was possible. Here is a movie constructed from basic parts at the Used Screenplay Store, with a character plugged in whenever one is required.

Still, it was a pleasure to see Richard Gere in the lead. He's an actor who has been improbably attractive all of his career and now, at sixty-two, has only improved with age. I like the subtle, catlike body language he uses, such as moving for a millisecond, pausing, then moving definitively. Or the pause in a head movement, as if we're being told: "Thinking . . . deciding . . . acting." He never just flat does something. It's a form of dancing. He is permanently on pose.

In *The Double* he plays a retired CIA agent named Paul Shepherdson. In the history of CIA agents in movies, no retired agent is ever allowed to stay retired. He is inexorably called back to duty in connection with a big case from his youth. Given his age, there are no characters seemingly old enough to go that far back, except for current CIA director Tom Highland (Martin Sheen), but he isn't on-screen enough to qualify.

Under my Law of Economy of Characters, that leaves Ben Geary (Topher Grace), an FBI agent who is thirtyish and has a wife, Natalie (Odette Yustman), and child. But he's way too young. So the movie leads us to assume the big case involves entirely unseen characters. We've seen some suspects. The story opens with a group of illegal immigrants being led through the desert into the United States from Mexico by a mule. They are revealed to be Russian agents. Think about that for a second. If you were Russia and you were trying to sneak a bunch of agents into America, would you assemble them in one handy group and try to sneak them past border patrol? When you can buy a plane ticket from Moscow to New York? How many Russian agents do you think have entered from Mexico in recent decades?

Never mind. A U.S. senator with business ties to Russia has his throat slit in an alley. The method of murder reveals the trademark of Cassius, the CIA's code name for a Russian assassin. Is he back in the United States and operating again? Shepherdson is positive he killed him years ago. Geary has his doubts. The two men are asked by Highland to work together on the case. As Shepherdson knows, Geary wrote his Harvard master's thesis on Cassius, and knows whatever can be discovered about him.

At this point in the movie, even if we haven't seen the trailer, we know more. The suspense circles around what Geary doesn't know, and the possible danger to his life and family. This intrigue now plugs in familiar action movie tropes, including a vicious Russian named Brutus (Stephen Moyer) with the most decorative scars around his eye I've seen in a while. There is also a car chase, and another one of those scenes where two guys split up, search a maze, and meet up empty-handed on the other side.

Richard Gere always has a particular screen presence. Topher Grace is a little outgunned, but the story explains why. Poor Odette Yustman is sympathetic and affectionate, but she's been assigned the thankless and exhausting role of playing the wife of the endangered man, always there to worry about him, be endangered, and put the kid to bed.

The movie was directed by Michael Brandt, who cowrote with Derek Haas. Together they wrote a much better movie, *3:10 to Yuma*. *The Double* doesn't approach it. None of it is particularly compelling. Most of the time we're waiting for the other shoe to drop. When, very late in the film, the screenplay comes up with a third shoe, that's going too far.

## Drive ★ ★ ★ ½

R, 100 m., 2011

Ryan Gosling (Driver), Carey Mulligan (Irene), Bryan Cranston (Shannon), Albert Brooks (Bernie Rose), Oscar Isaac (Standard), Christina

Hendricks (Blanche), Ron Perlman (Nino). Directed by Nicolas Winding Refn and produced by Michel Litvak, John Palermo, Marc Platt, Gigi Pritzker, and Adam Siegel. Screenplay by Hossein Amini, based on the novel by James Sallis.

---

The Driver drives for hire. He has no other name, and no other life. When we first see him, he's the wheelman for a getaway car, who runs from police pursuit not only by using sheer speed and muscle but also by coolly exploiting the street terrain and outsmarting his pursuers. By day, he is a stunt driver for action movies. The two jobs represent no conflict for him: He drives.

As played by Ryan Gosling, he is in the tradition of two iconic heroes of the 1960s: Clint Eastwood's Man with No Name and Alain Delon's *Le Samourai.* He has no family, no history, and seemingly few emotions. Whatever happened to him drove any personality deep beneath the surface. He is an existential hero, I suppose, defined entirely by his behavior.

That would qualify him as the hero of a mindless action picture, all CGI and crashes and mayhem. *Drive* is more of an elegant exercise in style, and its emotions may be hidden but they run deep. Sometimes a movie will make a greater impact by not trying too hard. The enigma of the Driver is surrounded by a rich gallery of supporting actors who are clear about their hopes and fears, and who have either reached an accommodation with the Driver, or not. Here is still another illustration of the old Hollywood noir principle that a movie lives its life not through its hero, but within its shadows.

The Driver lives somewhere (somehow that's improbable, since we expect him to descend full-blown into the story). His neighbor is Irene, played by Carey Mulligan, that template of vulnerability. She has a young son, Benicio (Kaden Leos), who seems to stir the Driver's affection, although he isn't the effusive type. They grow warm, but in a week her husband, Standard (Oscar Isaac), is released from prison. Against our expectations, Standard isn't jealous or hostile about the new neighbor, but sizes him up, sees a professional, and quickly pitches a $1 million heist idea. That will provide the engine for the rest of the story, and as Irene and Benicio are endangered, the Driver reveals deep feelings and loyalties indeed, and undergoes enormous risk at little necessary benefit to himself.

The film by the Danish director Nicolas Winding Refn (*Bronson*), based on a novel by James Sallis, peoples its story with characters who bring lifetimes onto the screen—in contrast to the Driver, who brings as little as possible. Ron Perlman seems to be a big-time operator working out of a small-time front, a pizzeria in a strip mall. Albert Brooks, not the slightest bit funny, plays a producer of the kinds of B movies the Driver does stunt driving for—and also has a sideline in crime. These people are ruthless. More benign is Bryan Cranston, as the kind of man you know the Driver must have behind him, a genius at auto repairs, restoration, and supercharging.

I mentioned CGI earlier. *Drive* seems to have little of it. Most of the stunt driving looks real to me, with cars of weight and heft, rather than animated impossible fantasies. The entire film, in fact, seems much more real than the usual action-crime-chase concoctions we've grown tired of. Here is a movie with respect for writing, acting, and craft. It has respect for knowledgeable moviegoers. There were moments when I was reminded of *Bullitt,* which was so much better than the films it inspired. The key thing you want to feel, during a chase scene, is involvement in the *purpose* of the chase. You have to care. Too often we're simply witnessing technology.

Maybe there was another reason I thought of *Bullitt.* Ryan Gosling is a charismatic actor, as McQueen was. He embodies presence and sincerity. Ever since his chilling young Jewish neo-Nazi in *The Believer* (2001), he has shown a gift for finding arresting, powerful characters. An actor who can fall in love with a love doll and make us believe it, as he did in *Lars and the Real Girl* (2007), can achieve just about anything. *Drive* looks like one kind of movie in the ads, and it is that kind of movie. It is also a rebuke to most of the movies it looks like.

## Drive Angry 3-D ★ ★

R, 104 m., 2011

---

Nicolas Cage (John Milton), Amber Heard (Piper), William Fichtner (The Accountant), Billy Burke (Jonah King). Directed by Patrick Lussier and produced by Rene Besson and Michael De Luca. Screenplay by Todd Farmer and Lussier.

*Drive Angry 3-D* opens with a muscle car racing across a burning bridge out of hell, while we hear a famous twelve-letter word used three or four times. So right away we know where we're at. Here is an exercise in deliberate vulgarity, gross excess, and the pornography of violence, not to forget garden variety pornography. You get your money's worth.

A movie review should determine what a movie hoped to achieve and whether it succeeded. The ambition of *Drive Angry 3-D* is to make a grind house B movie so jaw-droppingly excessive that even Quentin Tarantino might send flowers. It succeeds. I can't say I enjoyed it. But I can appreciate it. It offends every standard of taste except bad. But it is well made.

Of course it stars Nicolas Cage. Is there another actor who could or would have dared to sign on? Cage is a good actor in good movies, and an almost indispensable actor in bad ones. He can go over the top so effortlessly he rests up and makes lemonade for everybody. Here he plays a man named John Milton, a reference I fear will be lost on the film's target audience. Milton is hell-bent to rescue his baby granddaughter. A satanic cult enslaved and murdered his daughter, and now plans to sacrifice the infant by the light of the full moon. This Milton cannot abide.

The cult is led by Jonah (Billy Burke), who is obeyed by slavish followers he seems to have recruited from porn movies and guests on Jerry Springer shows about redneck incest. Their idea of partying is a topless orgy around a fire in an abandoned prison yard, while swigging Jack Daniels and warming up for a midnight infanticide. Their ranks are swelled by the usual shaved-headed and tattooed fatsos. There must be a pool of Hollywood extras who play big bald guys who can take three steps forward and glower into the camera.

Anyway, Milton's quest begins in a bar named Bull by the Balls, where he meets a barmaid named Piper (Amber Heard). After inconceivable violence, they link destinies. You've heard of girls attracted to the wrong kinds of guys? Piper inexplicably stays with Milton, despite many questions which are even better than she thinks. Heard makes a plucky heroine who, although Piper's sexy and Milton likes the ladies, doesn't fall into the usual abyss of "love interest," but slugs it out like a cage fighter.

On their trail is the enigmatic Accountant (William Fichtner). This seemingly (spoiler alert) supernatural figure is relentless in pursuit, yet moves with the speed of a plodding gumshoe when he's not at the wheel of a muscle car or, oh, say, a tanker truck filled with liquid hydrogen. (The movie, of course, contains the official quota of walking-away-from-fiery-explosions-in-slo-mo shots.) As Milton chases Jonah and the Accountant chases Milton, Jonah's followers chase Milton, which is a great convenience, allowing *Drive Angry 3-D* to be more or less nothing but chase scenes, except for some interior gun battles and much portentous dialogue. (Cage brings an inimitable personal touch to, "The bullet is still in there." Pause. "I can feel it.")

Gene Siskel drew the line at children in danger. As a father, he disapproved of thrillers that exploited violent scenes involving kids. What would he have made of an extended sequence here where Jonah commands one of his followers to sacrifice an infant? He would have despised it, I believe. The only justification for it is that this entire movie is so broadly, grotesquely over the top that the baby is more of a prop than a human child. And *Drive Angry 3-D* trusts its audience to put every principle of Western civilization on hold.

So my review is a compromise. I'm giving it two stars. That's halfway between three stars (well made) and one star (loathesome). Nic Cage once again provides the zeal and energy to wade through a violent morass. William Fichtner makes the Accountant so intriguing that, although all CPAs aren't from hell, we know this one is. He has a nice twitchy reserve. Amber Heard and Billy Burke do everything that can possibly be done with their characters, and don't stop there.

Oh, and the 3-D? For an extra charge you get to wear glasses that make it look like it was shot where the sun don't shine.

## Due Date ★ ★ ½

R, 95 m., 2010

Robert Downey Jr. (Peter Highman), Zach Galifianakis (Ethan Tremblay), Michelle

Monaghan (Sarah Highman), Jamie Foxx (Darryl), Juliette Lewis (Heidi). Directed by Todd Phillips and produced by Phillips and Daniel Goldberg. Screenplay by Phillips, Alan R. Cohen, Alan Freedland, and Adam Sztykiel.

*Due Date* is as near as makes no difference to a down-market retread of *Planes, Trains, and Automobiles.* It pairs up Robert Downey Jr. and Zach Galifianakis in the Steve Martin and John Candy roles, puts them in a car together, sends them down the highway, and doesn't neglect to rip off one but two car doors.

The first film by director Todd Phillips since his blockbuster *The Hangover* cheerfully includes some of the same raunchy humor and the same dogged persistence in the face of overwhelming character defects. It's not as funny, but few films could be, and it does have some very big laughs. Unfortunately, the story holding them together isn't as successful.

Peter Highman (Downey) and Ethan Tremblay (Galifianakis) have a Meet Cute, or more of a Meet Brute, at the Atlanta airport, when Ethan's beater knocks off the door of Peter's town car. Peter is a neat, precise architect with a schedule to meet. Ethan is a shaggy man-child who confesses that on the way to the airport he and his buddy split a six-pack—of forties.

Ethan is like Joe Btfsplk, that character in *Li'l Abner* who always had a black rain cloud over his head, with the difference that the cloud is over the head of whomever he's standing next to. He efficiently destroys Peter's trip by switching carry-ons with him, shoving his hairy belly into his face (under stress, to be sure), and getting them both thrown off the flight by insisting on using the words "bomb" and "terrorist." That scenario leads to a run-in with TSA agents (who, oddly enough, seem to be morphing into Hollywood's villains du jour).

All cross-country trips involving odd couples require deadlines. Peter agrees to accept a ride in Ethan's rental car only because he must be back in Los Angeles with his wife, Sarah (Michelle Monaghan), who will deliver their child very soon by C-section. Ethan needs to go to Los Angeles because he dreams of becoming an actor. If you doubt Ethan Tremblay has a future in acting, simply consider Zach Galifianakis.

There are stops along the way to visit Western Union, Peter's old buddy (Jamie Foxx), and Ethan's practitioner in "herbal medicines," a pot dealer played by the scene-stealer Juliette Lewis. Those visits are funny. There are also running gags involving Ethan's beloved pet dog and a coffee can containing the ashes of his father. When Ethan performs the rather private act of pleasuring himself in the car's front seat, it's not funny, but when the dog is inspired to copy him, it is. No matter how much I think, I can't decide whether training a dog to do that is cruelty to an animal.

So the movie probably contains enough laughs to satisfy the weekend audience. Where it falls short is in the characters and relationships. *Due Date* may offer enough, but with the example of the classic *Planes, Trains, and Automobiles,* it could have offered more.

Downey and Steve Martin are more or less a standoff. But John Candy (and director John Hughes) made his character earnest, inept, and lovable. The Galifianakis character seems more an exercise in passive aggression. He lacks social skills so urgently it's hard to believe he doesn't know what he's up to. Surely no one could be that obnoxious by accident. In comedy it helps if we have a bottom line of affection for the characters, and Galifianakis and Phillips make affection awfully hard to feel for Ethan.

There's a moment in *PTA* when the Steve Martin character thinks he has seen the last of John Candy, and then pauses, reconsiders, and returns. There's a moment something like that here, but frankly, we don't know why the Downey character returns.

*Note: My Great Movie review of* Planes, Trains, and Automobiles *is at http://j.mp/9HhHGU.*

# E

## The Eagle ★ ★ ★

PG-13, 114 m., 2011

Channing Tatum (Marcus Aquila), Jamie Bell (Esca), Donald Sutherland (Uncle Aquila), Mark Strong (Guern), Tahar Rahim (Seal Prince), Denis O'Hare (Lutorius). Directed by Kevin Macdonald and produced by Duncan Kenworthy. Screenplay by Jeremy Brock, based on Rosemary Sutcliff's novel *The Eagle of the Ninth.*

*The Eagle* is a rip-snorting adventure tale of the sort made before CGI, 3-D, and alphabet soup in general took the fun out. So much does it evoke the energy of traditional sword-and-shield movies that I had to bring the term "rip-snorting" out of retirement; it's rarely needed in this era of sleek technology. Here we see for the most part the actual actors trekking through real locations, instead of quasi animation.

The story is one I dimly recall, about the disappearance of the Roman Ninth Legion, which marched north from the colony of England into the unknown wilds of Scotland and was never heard from again. It tells of an uneasy bond between a centurion named Marcus (Channing Tatum) and a slave named Esca (Jamie Bell), who join a mission to discover what happened to the Ninth and its proud symbol, a golden eagle.

Some Americans find it quaint that the Scots and Welsh don't think of themselves as English. A Yank can receive the occasional fat lip for that mistake. Scotland was an independent kingdom until well over a millennium after the time of this story, which is set in about AD 140. So fearsome were the Scots warriors that the Roman emperor Hadrian threw up his hands and decreed that a border wall be erected in his name, whether to keep the Scots out or administer a full-body pat-down I am not sure.

In *The Eagle*, Marcus is assigned to lead a minor Roman outpost in England some twenty years after the death of his father, who is still blamed for having lost the eagle. Seriously wounded, he returns to Italy, as it was not then known, to heal at the villa of his Uncle Aquila (Donald Sutherland). Attending a deadly fight of gladiators, he decrees that the life of the courageous slave Esca be spared, and takes him along when he returns to England and takes up a more important command.

Marcus burns with the need to find the solution to the missing legion and find the lost eagle, and against all sane advice determines that he and Esca will cross the wall on a low-profile mission. They discover some answers, not without a great deal of bloodshed. One secret of the film's success is that their quest and the battle scenes are on a more or less plausible human scale. The editing is so rapid that we can't really follow the strategy of the swordplay, but at least a finite number of physical humans seem involved, instead of the absurd tidal waves of warriors in a CGI-fest like *300*.

I think we've possibly seen the last of choreographed sword fights, anyway. They reached their peak in classic Hollywood films and samurai dramas, and those in *Rob Roy* (1995) were among the best ever performed. I understood them. These days, in scenes where there's a berserk human traffic jam of sword fighters on the screen, don't you think that more or less everyone would be left with a number of limbs not divisible by two?

*The Eagle* has two strengths. One is that it is interested in its period, and what kinds of Romans and barbarians might have lived then. The second is that it really comes down to the relationship of Marcus and Esca, who risk their lives for each other but remain conscious that they are master and slave, and never become buddies. I suppose it is a negative strength that there are no major female characters; this is not the sort of world where women would be expected, and the insertion of romantic interest so obligatory in lesser movies would seem awkward here.

*The Eagle* is rated R, and that's about right. The blood and gore is kept to a reasonable level, and the battle scenes are about heroism and strategy, not special effects. *The Eagle* attempts to create characters with some dimension and complexity. In Donald Sutherland's interlude as the wise uncle, it provides some notion of the function of empire, then and later. And Tatum and Bell do a good job of sculpting the heroes to a fairly human scale, and not indulging in foolish poses against the horizon. The movie goes a little over the top in finally showing us the eagle, but what can you expect?

## Easy A ★ ★ ★ ½

PG-13, 93 m., 2010

Emma Stone (Olive Penderghast), Penn Badgley (Woodchuck Todd), Amanda Bynes (Marianne Bryant), Dan Byrd (Brandon), Thomas Haden Church (Mr. Griffith), Patricia Clarkson (Rosemary), Cam Gigandet (Micah), Lisa Kudrow (Mrs. Griffith), Malcolm McDowell (Principal Gibbons), Aly Michalka (Rhiannon), Stanley Tucci (Dill). Directed by Will Gluck and produced by Gluck and Zanne Devine. Screenplay by Bert V. Royal.

*Easy A* offers an intriguing middle ground to the absolute of sexual abstinence: Don't sleep with anybody, but say you did. It's a funny, engaging comedy that takes the familiar but underrated Emma Stone and makes her, I believe, a star. Until actors are matched to the right role, we can never quite see them clearly.

Stone embodies Olive Penderghast, a girl nobody much notices at Ojai North High School. The biggest surprise about this school (apart from the fact that there is an Ojai North) is that it is scandalous to lose one's virginity in high school. I hesitate to generalize, but I suspect such a thing is not unheard of in Ojai North and elsewhere. I'm not recommending it. I only know what I'm told.

It is a rule with all comedies involving virginity, going back to Doris Day and long before, that enormous misunderstandings are involved and virginity miraculously survives at the end. In this case, Olive is simply embarrassed to admit she spent a whole weekend at home alone, and improvises a goofy story about having lost her virginity to a college boy. That seems safe; nobody in school would know him. But she's overheard by Miss Bryant (Amanda Bynes), a self-righteous religious type, who passes the story round as an object lesson to wayward girls: Don't become a fallen woman like Olive.

*Easy A* takes this misunderstanding and finds effortless comic variations in it. The news is taken with equanimity by Olive's parents, Dill and Rosemary (Stanley Tucci and Patricia Clarkson), who join Juno's parents in the Pantheon of Parental Admirability. And at Ojai North High, Olive finds that in having lost one reputation, she has gained another. Previously no one noticed her at all (hard to believe about Emma Stone, but there you have it). Now she is imagined to be an experienced and daring adventuress, and it can be deduced that a great many in the student body envy her experience.

Olive puts her notoriety to use. She has a gay friend named Brandon (Dan Byrd), who has been hassled at school (hard to believe in Ojai but, again, there you have it). By allowing word to get out that she and Brandon have shared blissful congress, she is able to bring an end to the bullying (hard to believe no one in Ojai North has heard of a gay and a straight having sex, but this Ojai is one created specifically for the convenience of a movie comedy, and people believe what the plot requires them to believe).

Now that she has become established as the school authority, she begins issuing a sort of Olive's Seal of Approval on various outsiders, misfits, and untouchables in the student body, outfitting them all with credentials of sexmanship. Does anybody wonder why she only sleeps with gays, nerds, and college students? Why should they? Lots of people do.

*Easy A*, like many good comedies, supplies us with a more or less conventional (movie) world in which one premise—Olive's transformation by gossip—is introduced. She becomes endowed overnight with a power to improve reputations, confer status, and help the needy. Her new power might even work for adults, such as the teacher Mr. Griffith (Thomas Haden Church) and his estranged wife (Lisa Kudrow), the guidance counselor, who become entangled in embarrassments.

The movie works because it's funny, yes, but also because it's smart. When Olive begins wearing the Scarlet Letter "A" on her clothing, borrowing it from the Nathaniel Hawthorne novel they still read in Ojai North, she shows a level of irony that I'm afraid is lost on the student body, but not on us. I think it may always be necessary that we like the hero or heroine of a comedy. I certainly liked Olive. I'm pretty sure that's also how an actor becomes a movie star.

## Eat Pray Love ★ ★

PG-13, 141 m., 2010

Julia Roberts (Liz Gilbert), James Franco (David Piccolo), Richard Jenkins (Richard), Viola Davis (Delia Shiraz), Billy Crudup (Stephen), Javier Bardem (Felipe), Hadi Subiyanto (Ketut Liyer). Directed by Ryan Murphy and produced by Dede Gardner. Screenplay by Ryan Murphy and Jennifer Salt, based on the memoir by Elizabeth Gilbert.

Elizabeth Gilbert's book *Eat Pray Love*, unread by me, spent 150 weeks on the *New York Times* best-seller list and is by some accounts a good one. It is also movie material, concerning as it does a tall blonde (Gilbert) who ditches a failing marriage and a disastrous love affair to spend a year living in Italy, India, and Bali, seeking to find the balance of body, mind, and spirit. During this journey, great-looking men are platooned at her, and a wise man, who has to be reminded who she is, remembers instantly, although what he remembers is only what she's just told him.

I gather Gilbert's "prose is fueled by a mix of intelligence, wit and colloquial exuberance that is close to irresistible" (*New York Times Book Review*), and if intelligence, wit, and exuberance are what you're looking for, Julia Roberts is an excellent choice as the movie's star. You can see how it would be fun to spend a year traveling with Gilbert. A lot more fun than spending nearly two and a half hours watching a movie about it. I guess you have to belong to the narcissistic subculture of Woo-Woo.

Here is a movie about Liz Gilbert. About her quest, her ambition, her good luck in finding only nice men, including the ones she dumps. She funds her entire trip, including scenic accommodations, ashram, medicine man, guru, spa fees, and wardrobe, with her advance to write this book. Well, the publisher obviously made a wise investment. It's all about her, and a lot of readers can really identify with that. Her first marriage apparently broke down primarily because she tired of it, although Roberts at (a sexy and attractive) forty-three makes an actor's brave stab at explaining they were "young and immature." She walks out on the guy (Billy Crudup), and he still likes her and reads her on the Web.

In Italy, she eats such Pavarottian plates of pasta that I hope one of the things she prayed for in India was deliverance from the sin of gluttony. At one trattoria she apparently orders the entire menu, and I am not making this up. She meets a man played by James Franco, about whom, enough said. She shows moral fiber by leaving such a dreamboat for India, where her quest involves discipline in meditation, for which she allots three months rather than the recommended lifetime. There she meets a tall, bearded, bespectacled older Texan (Richard Jenkins) who is without question the most interesting and attractive man in the movie, and like all of the others seems innocent of lust.

In Bali she revisits her beloved adviser Ketut Liyer (Hadi Subiyanto), who is a master of truisms known to us all. Although he connects her with a healer who can mend a nasty cut with a leaf applied for a few hours, his own skills seem limited to the divinations anyone could make after looking at her, and telling her things about herself after she has already told him.

Now she has found Balance and begins to dance on the high-wire of her life. She meets Felipe (Javier Bardem), another divorced exile, who is handsome, charming, tactful, forgiving, and a good kisser. He explains that he lives in Bali because his business is import-export, "which you can do anywhere"—although later, he explains, "I live in Bali because my business is here." They've both forgotten what he said earlier. Unless perhaps you can do import-export anywhere, but you can only import and export from Bali when you live there. That would certainly be my alibi.

The audience I joined was perhaps 80 percent female. I heard some sniffles and glimpsed some tears, and no wonder. *Eat Pray Love* is shameless wish fulfillment, a Harlequin novel crossed with a mystic travelogue, and it mercifully reverses the life chronology of many people, which is Love Pray Eat.

## The Eclipse ★ ★ ★

R, 88 m., 2010

Ciaran Hinds (Michael Farr), Aidan Quinn (Nicholas Holden), Iben Hjejle (Lena Morelle), Jim Norton (Malachy McNeill), Eanna Hardwicke (Thomas), Hannah Lynch (Sarah).

Directed by Conor McPherson and produced by Robert Walpole. Screenplay by McPherson and Billy Roche, based on Roche's *Tales from Rainwater Pond.*

The supernatural never seems far out of sight in Ireland, and it creeps in here and there during *The Eclipse,* a dark romance set at a literary festival in the County Cork cathedral town of Cobh. I'm not sure it's required, but it does little harm. The story centers on a quiet, enduring man named Michael Farr (Ciaran Hinds), who has lost his wife to cancer and is raising their two children. He volunteers to drive two visiting authors around town.

The authors have a history that is fondly recalled by only one of them. Nicholas Holden (Aidan Quinn) is a best-selling American novelist not a million miles removed from Nicholas Sparks. Lena Morelle (Iben Hjejle) is a British writer of upscale ghost stories. Once, at another festival, they had a brief fling, which only Nicholas thinks was a wise idea. Lena is warm and curious, a good person, and Nicholas, who after all is married, considers himself entitled to her comforts on the basis of her earlier mistake. Nicholas, when he drinks, can become quite unpleasant.

Of the other two key characters, one is dead and the other nearly so. Michael's late wife, Sarah (Hannah Lynch), is alive in his memory, and also occasionally turns up to offer advice or share his problems. She's simply there, seemingly in the flesh. Her father, Thomas (Eanna Hardwicke), his father-in-law, is still alive, but begins manifesting to Michael as a ghostly figure in the still of the night. Michael doesn't deserve this. His steadfast quality throughout the movie is goodness. Is he seeing a ghost, or is the old man prowling around?

Daytimes, Michael dutifully ferries Nicholas or Lena to their festival events, and shows them something of the town and its idyllic setting. He quickly picks up on the tension between them. If he were not so recently widowed, he might warm to Lena himself, but he isn't operating on that frequency. They slowly begin to bond in mutual sympathy.

Nicholas is a bit of an ass. Full of himself, fond of attention, lacking in insight, imperious. Michael, on the other hand, is almost too humble. He sees himself as an attendant, not a celebrant. And Lena? Smart, nice, increasingly worried about Nicholas's urgency, grateful for Michael as a port in the storm. All of this arrives at what I suppose is an inevitable crescendo involving lust, drinking, threats, and confusion, complicated by the increasingly dire supernatural manifestations Michael has experienced.

*The Eclipse* is needlessly confusing. Is it a ghost story or not? Perhaps this is my problem. Perhaps people who think they perceive the supernatural must simply incorporate that into their ordinary lives. Michael is a steady soul, and essentially does that. On another level, Aidan Quinn is superb at creating a man with the potential to behave as a monster, but with a certain buried decency. What of Lena and Michael? They deserve each other and will probably someday work that out.

## Edge of Darkness ★ ★ ½

R, 117 m., 2010

Mel Gibson (Thomas Craven), Ray Winstone (Darius Jedburgh), Danny Huston (Jack Bennett), Bojana Novakovic (Emma Craven), Shawn Roberts (Burnham). Directed by Martin Campbell and produced by Tim Headington, Graham King, and Michael Wearing. Screenplay by William Monahan and Andrew Bovell.

Can we think of Mel Gibson simply as an action hero? A star whose personal baggage doesn't upstage his performances? I find that I can. He has made deplorable statements in recent years, which may be attributed to a kind of fanatic lunacy that can perhaps be diagnosed as a disease. The fact remains that in *Edge of Darkness* he remains a likable man with a natural screen presence.

Here he plays a Boston cop named Craven (always a dependable movie name). The great love of his life is his daughter, Emma (Bojana Novakovic). She works for a giant secretive corporation named Northmoor. Few corporations with *moor* in their titles are wholly trustworthy; we think too much about bodies being buried there.

Emma comes home for a visit rather unexpectedly. She is having nosebleeds. A bleeding nose can be a symptom of numerous disorders, but in a thriller, as we all know, there's only one possible diagnosis. Emma has hardly arrived when there's a knock on the door, they answer it together, and a man in a hood screams "Craven!" and shoots her dead.

It is assumed that the detective Thomas Craven was the intended target. Craven's not so sure. His investigation leads him to Northmoor and its silky, sinister chairman, Jack Bennett (Danny Huston, ominously courteous just as his father was in *Chinatown*). Bennett tears himself away from planning Northmoor's campaign contributions long enough to greet Craven in his office, atop a towering aerie overlooking his feudal lands.

Because much of the movie is a cranked-up thriller with chases, fights, conspiracies, and all that stuff, permit me a digression on secretive, shadowy corporations. What kinds of headquarters buildings do they inhabit? I Googled. Blackwater, which supplies our mercenaries in Iraq, has a drab two-story building outside Cleveland with eight cars parked out in front. Halliburton, Dick Cheney's old company, recently moved from Houston to an anonymous skyscraper in Dubai, closer to its place of business.

I mention this because Northmoor, which you will not be surprised to learn traffics in illegal, traitorous, and dangerous activities, occupies a spectacular structure atop a tall riverside hill, visible from miles around: its tower, its modernistic design, and its curious enormous gleaming globe suggesting a planetarium. It is a building worthy of magazine covers, not least *Architectural Digest.*

One purpose of corporate architecture is to impress. Northmoor's desire is to impress us, the moviegoer. Its structure looks left over from a James Bond movie, and indeed, the *Edge of Darkness* director, Martin Campbell, made *Casino Royale* (2006). It's the kind of edifice that inspires such questions as, "What do they *do* in there?" Much of what they do takes place in enormous buried spaces within the hill. This low-profile corporation undertook a construction project on a par with a subway line.

I explain this not merely to avoid discussing the off-the-shelf thriller plot, but to illustrate that *Edge of Darkness,* like so many recent thrillers, has no ambition to be taken seriously. If the corporation were more realistic, the movie would be, too. And then the fate of the world wouldn't depend yet once again on One Cop . . . With Nothing to Lose . . . On a Personal Mission.

Gibson inhabits this gazebo with as much conviction as is probably possible. He's joined in this by the superb British actor Ray Winstone, as an intriguing free agent who turns up in Craven's garden one night with a cigar and an enigmatic line of patter. Whom does he work for? Why does he know so much? Why does he work alone? He reminds me of a man I know, Jean-Jacques de Mesterton, who told me: "If you have a problem, you go to the cops. If they can't help you, you go to the FBI. If they can't help you, you go to the CIA. If they can't help you, you come to me."

Winstone's interaction with Gibson provides the movie with much of its interest. For the rest, it's a skillful exercise in CGI and standard-order thriller supplies. Gibson is a credible, attractive hero, as he has always been, so if you want fast-food action, here's your movie.

It does have a useful subtext. It serves as a reminder that the purpose of a corporation is not to be patriotic, but to maximize profits for its officers and shareholders. This is required by its bylaws. I suppose if we, as shareholders, don't agree with its profit-making strategies, we can always sell our stock, assuming we can find out what those strategies are.

## Elite Squad: The Enemy Within ★ ★ ★

NO MPAA RATING, 115 m., 2011

Wagner Moura (Nascimento), Irandhir Santos (Diogo Fraga), Andre Ramiro (Captain Andre Matias), Pedro Van-Held (Rafael), Maria Ribeiro (Rosane), Sandro Rocha (Russo). Directed by Jose Padilha and produced by Padilha and Marcos Prado. Screenplay by Padilha and Braulio Mantovani.

Here is a Brazilian thriller that's so angry and specifically political it's hard to believe they got away with making it. "Based on real events," we're told, and it's one of the biggest hits in the history of Brazil and South America. If this is accurate, Costa Rica is about as far south as you can go and find an honest cop.

The movie is a sequel to *Elite Squad* (2007), by Jose Padilha, the same writer and director. I haven't seen that, but I don't believe you need to. It ended, I learn, with the retirement of Colonel Nascimento (Wagner Moura) from the state police militia. This one opens as he's recruited back into the force. After a prison hostage situation goes wrong and lots of bad guys are killed (against his wishes), he gets the credit, becomes a hero, and is placed in command of the entire militia.

Apparently the state governor and other bureaucrats don't know who they're dealing with. The last man they should want in the job is a man who knows about the corruption and is opposed to it. As the story unfolds, he discovers that earlier deadly raids against organized criminal gangs in the slums of Rio merely eliminated the competition for the police to take over and run the same rackets, only now under the protection of the law.

One honest man who already knows this is state senator Diogo Fraga (Irandhir Santos), who speaks out in the legislature and the press. As the first film closed, Nascimento was looking forward to the joy of fatherhood with his pregnant wife, Rosane (Maria Ribeiro). Now about seven years have passed (although the films are only three years apart), and Rosane is married to Senator Fraga. The two men are barely on speaking terms, although by the film's end they'll realize they're on the same side.

Watching *Elite Squad: The Enemy Within*, no one will complain about a shortage of two elements: (1) bloody, gruesome, pitiless violence, and (2) Nascimento's narration, which explains everything in such detail it sometimes sounds like an op-ed piece. He's in the process of discovering that drug dealing and other illegal businesses are a cartel run by Brazil's ruling elite. You see why I'm surprised the film got made? My notion is that this top group may be so embedded and powerful that there's no use opposing them, even though most people know what's going on—or will after they see this film.

Toward the end of the movie, there's a leisurely helicopter shot drifting over the enormous capital city of Brasilia, the boondoggle in the jungle, while Nascimento informs us this extravagance is a monument to money that came from the poor to provide a throne for the rich. After that, he spills *all* the beans in a speech at a legislative hearing targeted at the most corrupt cops and lawmakers. I was amazed that Nascimento was still alive at this point (although not because of any shortage of assassination attempts). (Spoiler!) I was even more amazed that a shot didn't ring out and kill him in the middle of his speech.

Who was this Nascimento, and why hasn't he won the Nobel? He's a fictional character, that's why. One of the small ironies in the film is that a real Nascimento was the robber who undertook the famous Bus 174 hostage crisis in 2000. You may have seen the 2002 documentary about that event. Jose Padilha certainly has because he directed it. Jose's little in-joke.

The slums of Rio have been the setting for many great films, including the great *City of God* (2002). Tiny tenement dwellings are piled one atop another as they jam together and mount the heights above the city. To be a cop there must be like being the monster in a video game. Guns are everywhere. Anarchy is the political system. Lots of money is made. And the characters of Fraga and Nascimento imply that lawlessness in the slums, or *favelas*, is almost deliberately encouraged because it's such a reliable source of corrupt income. The implication is that laws against drugs are a convenient form of price supports.

This is a good film, not a great one. Too little attention is paid to the complexities and personalities of the characters. We're always aware they stand for something. Wagner Moura, repeating in the role of Nascimento, is a big star, but doesn't seem especially charismatic; with his graying pompadour, he looks like a prosperous team owner or manufacturer. It's always a little startling when guys like this (and his archenemy, who is downright portly) can run up steep hills, leap gaps, and sock one antoher like ultimate fighters. Underneath its outrage, this is essentially a talky cop thriller.

## Elles ★ ★ ½

NC-17, 96 m., 2011

Juliette Binoche (Anne), Anais Demoustier (Charlotte), Joanna Kulig (Alicja), Louis-Do de Lencquesaing (Patrick), Francois Civil (Florent),

Pablo Beugnet (Stephane). Directed by Malgoska Szumowska and produced by Marianne Slot. Screenplay by Tine Byrckel and Szumowska.

*Elles* has a surprisingly deep performance in a disappointingly shallow movie. The performance, acute and brave, is by Juliette Binoche, who plays a Parisian writer researching a magazine article about young prostitutes in the city. What's disappointing is the way it attempts to equate her life as a married woman with prostitution. Yes, her husband is an unemotional louse and her two sons are a trial, but isn't it insulting to imply that her bright and independent character is simply selling out? Nobody said marriage was easy.

Binoche plays Anne, who has placed ads to contact young part-time call girls. The movie backs into this with her interviews with Charlotte (Anais Demoustier) and Alicja (Joanna Kulig). Both girls are frank about their motivation: Charlotte wants a nicer apartment, and Alicja, from Poland, likes the more-expensive clothes she can now afford. Neither seems traumatized by her experience; indeed, to Anne, they seem happier than she is.

Anne's sessions with them eventually lead to confidences and friendship; one ends with a hug. The director and cowriter, Malgoska Szumowska, intercuts these interviews with scenes of the two women servicing clients, which can look ever so much more pleasant than Anne, masturbating on her bathroom floor and then breaking into tears. The sex scenes are explicit enough to earn an NC-17 rating from the MPAA, a rating so rare I can't recall the last time I encountered one; films like these are usually released these days as "unrated."

Prostitution is an occupation both young women went into willingly, and their upper-scale clients and prices are in a different world from more desperate hookers. Still, *Elles* includes a particularly unpleasant scene involving one sadistic client; it is after Anne hears this described that she masturbates, suggesting—what? That's she's a masochist and was turned on? I don't think so, but the film doesn't provide a better explanation.

Anne's home life centers around her distant and demanding husband, Patrick (Louis-Do de Lencquesaing), and their sons, Florent (Francois Civil) and Stephane (Pablo Beugnet). The film begins on a day when Anne is racing to meet her magazine deadline, and is expected to prepare and serve a gourmet meal to her husband's boss and some business associates. Florent, an older teenager who is openly contemptuous of his parents and their marriage, drifts in a cloud of marijuana. Stephane, around twelve, is addicted to his generation's drug of choice, video games.

Anne can't seem to speak to any of the men in her family. Indeed, her only good relationships in the film are with the prostitutes. Binoche brings to these scenes an intimacy and ability to confide that transforms them from what could have been a more exploitative tone. There are moments of truth here, including a bleak closing scene with her husband. Binoche makes a strong impression, but the film seems inadequate to her character, and forces simplistic conclusions when more complex ones are needed.

## Even the Rain ★ ★ ★

NO MPAA RATING, 104 m., 2010

Luis Tosar (Costa), Gael Garcia Bernal (Sebastian), Juan Carlos Aduviri (Daniel), Karra Elejalde (Anton), Carlos Santos (Alberto), Raul Arevalo (Juan). Directed by Iciar Bollain and produced by Juan Gordon. Screenplay by Paul Laverty.

The genre of movies about movies coils back on itself in *Even the Rain.* The film involves the making of a film about Columbus and his discovery of America. That story shows how his arrival began centuries of exploitation of the native Americans he found. *Even the Rain* is about how the filming of this story begins yet another cycle of exploitation.

As the film opens, a cast and crew have arrived on location in the mountains of Bolivia, far from the Caribbean shores first found by Columbus. Here, as the producer Costa (Luis Tosar) boasts, the local Indians can be hired as extras for two dollars a day and count themselves lucky. They can also be used for manual labor, and Costa is happy to use them to haul a giant crucifix into position, saving the cost of tractor rental.

You may begin to glimpse some symbolism coming into view. The film will exploit the Indians just as Columbus did. The difference is that Columbus evoked Christianity as his excuse, while the modern film thinks it is denouncing him while committing the same sins. This is more clear to us than the characters, including Gael Garcia Bernal as Sebastian, the director, who has vague sympathies for his low-paid workers, but places his film above everything.

An opening scene establishes the poverty in the district. A casting call for extras draws a line of hopefuls that reaches out of sight. One of these is Daniel (Juan Carlos Aduviri), a worker who protests when the auditions are cut short. Sebastian ends up casting him in an important role, and then discovers that in real life Daniel is a leader in a local revolt against the privatization of the local water resources. A California company has bought land rights and plans to charge the Indians for water from their own wells.

A memory stirred uneasily within me. The James Bond movie *Quantum of Solace* (2008) involved a scheme to corner the Bolivian water supply, and this seemed ridiculous to me ("Ohooo! Nooo!" I wrote). A reader informed me that there was indeed such a scheme, and that in Cochabamba the Bechtel Corp. lost its fight to charge the locals for the water. *Even the Rain* has been filmed in Cochabamba, is based on that real event, and instead of James Bond, has Daniel as a Christ figure.

The personal dynamics of a movie location can be tricky. Here Sebastian faces not only a crusading local actor but an alcoholic leading man and a penny-pinching producer. Costa is obsessed with saving money, Sebastian thinks of himself as more humanitarian, but it is Costa who is eventually humanized by the plight of the workers. He grows fond of Daniel's sweet little daughter, and when local forces are brought in to subdue the demonstrations, the girl is injured and Costa suddenly sees things in a different light. This is not absolutely convincing, and depends too heavily on a race through riot-torn streets, but it provides a plot device to explain Costa's rediscovery of conscience.

The performance by Luis Tosar as the producer is confident and sturdy. Gael Garcia Bernal, as the director, is wimpy and not clearly defined, but that's in the nature of the character. The movie is brave to raise the questions it does, although at the end I looked in vain for a credit saying, "No extras were underpaid in the making of this film."

## Everything Must Go ★ ★ ★

R, 97 m., 2011

Will Ferrell (Nick Halsey), Rebecca Hall (Samantha), Laura Dern (Delilah), Christopher Jordan Wallace (Kenny Loftus), Michael Peña (Frank Garcia). Directed by Dan Rush and produced by Marty Bowen and Wyck Godfrey, based on the short story "Why Don't You Dance?" by Raymond Carver.

I found myself thinking during *Everything Must Go* that Will Ferrell is a gifted dramatic actor. That's sometimes the case with actors who specialize in comedy. Consider Robin Williams, Jack Lemmon, Jackie Gleason, Jim Carrey. Remember Adam Sandler in *Punch-Drunk Love.* To be good in comedy you need to be very skilled indeed, but talent doesn't always transfer to the heavy stuff. It's partly the matter of the physical presence. Ferrell has a presence. He reminds me sometimes of Fred MacMurray in his noir films.

*Everything Must Go* is not all the film it could have been, but is more worth seeing than a lot of other recent releases. It held my attention through Ferrell's performance as Nick Halsey, a man who drinks his way out of a job and a marriage. He isn't one of those flamboyant drunks, just a contained, dutiful man whose drinking has become the priority in his life. These are the kinds of alcoholics who break your heart: They mean to do well, they're not mean or violent, but over the years the need for booze has moved into the foreground.

They say you need to find your bottom before you're likely to stop. Every bottom is different. Nick finds his on the front lawn of his house, along with his furniture, his clothing, his keepsakes, and his life as a man whose wife has left him. He's locked out. His credit cards don't work. He deals with this by buying some beer and settling into his La-Z-Boy recliner. Fortunately, the nights can be mild in Arizona.

The idea for the movie, written and directed by Dan Rush, is based on the Raymond

Carver short story "Why Don't You Dance?" Carver was an alcoholic who lost most of the things in his life and then found them again through recovery and the love of his wife, the poet Tess Gallagher. In his story, the hero simply has a sale to sell everything he owns, which as we all know is better than dealing with the movers. In the film, the (never seen) wife is the deciding factor, but as the days and nights slide past, Nick Halsey gradually clears out not only his valued possessions but his excess inventory.

Of course neighbors complain. When a cop comes, it's Frank Garcia (Michael Peña), who was Nick's sponsor during an unsuccessful whirl through AA. Nick argues that he has a perfect right to use his lawn as he chooses, and I suppose if the law permits pink flamingos, anything goes. There is also the matter of the young woman named Samantha (Rebecca Hall), who has just moved in across the street, is pregnant, and is awaiting her husband. "What kind of a man lets his pregnant wife move halfway across the country by herself?" protests Nick, whose own wife may have been left on her own a time or two.

Into this situation comes an African-American teenager named Kenny (Christopher Jordan Wallace), a nice kid who rides up on his bike, asks the obvious questions, and enters into a tacit understanding to become Nick's business partner in the yard sale. This character is very well handled. He is not tiny and cute. He is not a cutup. He is not what Spike Lee calls a Magic Negro, one of those black people who enter into the lives of whites with wise advice. No, he is a normal kid, self-possessed, even thoughtful, who keeps his opinions to himself and has an instinctive tact. (Wallace is the son of late Notorious B.I.G., and played his dad as a kid in a movie about the rapper's life.)

The movie doesn't trick up this story much more than it needs. The spartan solemnity of the Carver story seems buried within it. Ferrell plays Nick straight from the shoulder, without spin, respectfully. What it amounts to is for you to decide. At the end I was expecting more of an emotional payoff; making a movie calm is one thing, and making it matter-of-fact is another. But make a note about Will Ferrell. There is depth there.

## Exit Through the Gift Shop ★ ★ ★ ½

R, 86 m., 2010

A documentary narrated by Rhys Ifans. Featuring Thierry Guetta, Banksy, Space Invader, Shepard Fairey, Neckface, and Swoon. Directed by Banksy and produced by Holly Cushing, Jaimie D'Cruz, and James Gay-Rees.

The widespread speculation that *Exit Through the Gift Shop* is a hoax only adds to its fascination. An anonymous London graffiti artist named Banksy arrives to paint walls in Los Angeles. He encounters an obscure Frenchman named Thierry Guetta, who has dedicated his life to videotaping graffiti artists.

The Frenchman's hundreds of tapes have been dumped unorganized into boxes. Banksy thinks they might make a film. Guetta makes a very bad one. Banksy takes over the film and advises Guetta to create some art himself. Guetta does, names himself Mr. Brainwash, and organizes an exhibition of his work, through which he makes a fortune in sales.

Surely Thierry Guetta cannot be real? With his dashing mustache and Inspector Clouseau accent, his long-suffering wife and his zealous risk taking to film illegal artists by stealth? Surely he didn't rent a former CBS television studio and transform it into an exhibition space? Surely people didn't line up at dawn to get in—and pay tens of thousands of dollars for the works of an artist who had never held a show, sold a work, or received a review? Surely not if his work looked like art school rip-offs of the familiar styles of famous artists?

Even while I sat spellbound during this film, that's what I was asking myself. But Thierry Guetta surely did. His art exhibition was written up in a cover story in *L.A. Weekly* on June 12, 2008. It mentions this film, which Banksy was "threatening to do." Common sense dictates that no one would rent a CBS studio and fill it with hundreds of artworks in order to produce a hoax indie documentary. Nor would they cast Guetta, indubitably a real person, as himself. Right? Right?

The film depends entirely on Guetta, a cross between a TV pitchman, a cartoon Frenchman, and a chatty con man. Its footage really has been edited from a decade of tapes made clandestinely while L.A. graffiti artists risked arrest and death to create their paintings in spectacular places. Guetta fearlessly followed them right out onto ledges and helped them carry supplies to places a human fly might balk at. And all the time he's talking, talking, telling his life story and his hero worship for these artists.

There are all kinds of graffiti. Much of it is ugly defacement, the kind of territorial marking a dog does so much more elegantly. Chicago mayor Richard Daley's Graffiti Busters have my support and admiration. Some graffiti, however, is certainly art, as Norman Mailer was one of the first to argue in his book *The Faith of Graffiti* (1974). Banksy and others at his level, such as Guetta's hero Shepard Fairey, find ways to visually reinvent public spaces and make striking artistic statements.

But what does Guetta do? One of his artworks, inspired by Andy Warhol's Campbell's soup can, shows a can of tomato paint spray. OK, that's witty enough for a nice editorial cartoon. How many thousands would you spend to have it in your house? Or a morph of Joan Crawford and Warhol's Marilyn? Then again, at the time, people said Andy Warhol wasn't creating art either. Surely Warhol's message was that Thierry Guetta has an absolute right to call his work art and sell it for as much as he can.

There are currently more than 3,600 comments on my recent blog headlined "Video Games Can Never Be Art." At least 95 percent of them inform me I am a fool and that "art is in the eye of the beholder." I believe video games are not an art *form*, for reasons I am certainly not going to bring up again. I am quite willing to agree that graffiti is Art, but I don't believe the act of painting them is an art form, if you see what I mean. Or maybe you don't. You may be too old to understand my argument.

Anyway, comment No. 3,307 on my blog was from Kristian, and it said: "The wafting smell of dried mung beans pervades my nostrils." That's kind of . . . poetic, don't you think? But I stray from my thoughts, which are (1) *Exit Through the Gift Shop* is an admirable and entertaining documentary; (2) I believe it is not a hoax; (3) I would not much want a Thierry Guetta original; (4) I like Thierry Guetta; and (5) Banksy, the creator of this film, is a gifted filmmaker whose thoughts, as he regards Guetta, must resemble those of Victor Frankenstein when he regarded his monster: It works, but is it Art?

## Extraordinary Measures ★ ★

PG, 105 m., 2010

Brendan Fraser (John Crowley), Harrison Ford (Robert Stonehill), Keri Russell (Aileen), Meredith Droeger (Megan), Diego Velazquez (Patrick), Sam Hill (John Jr.). Directed by Tom Vaughn and produced by Carla Santos Shamberg, Michael Shamberg, and Stacey Sher. Screenplay by Robert Nelson Jacobs, based on *The Cure* by Geeta Anand.

*Extraordinary Measures* is an ordinary film with ordinary characters in a story too big for it. Life has been reduced to a Lifetime movie. The story, based on fact, is compelling: Two sick children have no more than a year to live when their father determines to seek out a maverick scientist who may have a cure. This is *Lorenzo's Oil* with a different disease, Pompe disease, although it fudges the facts to create a better story. The film centers on two dying children, nine and seven. In life, most children with Pompe die before age two, and those in the real story were fifteen months and seven days old when they got sick, and five and three when they were treated.

With children that young, the drama would have focused on the parents. By making Megan Crowley (Meredith Droeger) a wise and cheerful nine-year-old, *Extraordinary Measures* improves her as a story element. Her father is John Crowley (Brendan Fraser), an executive at Bristol-Myers. Her mother is Aileen (Keri Russell). Neither is developed any more deeply than the story requires. Their personal relationship is defined by their desperation as the deadlines for their children grow nearer.

Crowley discovers on the Internet a professor at the University of Nebraska named Dr. Robert Stonehill (Harrison Ford). He's working on a controversial cure for Pompe that the medical establishment rejects, and when he won't return messages, Crowley impulsively flies to Nebraska to confront him.

Dr. Robert Stonehill doesn't exist in life. The Pompe cure was developed by Dr. Yuan-Tsong Chen and his colleagues while he was at Duke University. He is now director of the Institute of Biomedical Science in Taiwan. Harrison Ford, as this film's executive producer, perhaps saw Stonehill as a plum role for himself; a rewrite was necessary because he couldn't very well play Dr. Chen. The real Chen, a Taiwan University graduate, worked his way up at Duke from a residency to professor and chief of medical genetics at the Duke University Medical Center. He has been mentioned as a Nobel candidate.

I suspect Dr. Chen might have inspired a more interesting character than "Dr. Stonehill." The Nebraskan seems inspired more by Harrison Ford's image and range. He plays the doctor using only a few spare parts off the shelf. (1) He likes to crank up rock music while he works. (2) He doesn't return messages. (3) He's so feckless he accidentally hangs up on Crowley by pulling the phone off his desk. (4) He likes to drink beer from longneck bottles in a honky-tonk bar and flirt with the waitress. (5) "I'm a scientist, not a doctor." He's not interested in Pompe patients, only the chemistry of the disease.

This becomes tiresome. Later he becomes invested in the Crowleys, but of course he does. They hope to fund a high-tech startup and deal with venture capitalists whose scenes are more interesting than many of the medical ones. Contrast this with the character of Augusto Odone, played by Nick Nolte in *Lorenzo's Oil*—a self-taught parent who discovers his own cure for a rare nerve disease. Ford is given no lines that suggest depth of character, only gruffness that gradually mellows.

The film also fails to explain that the cost of the medication is $300,000 a year for life, which limits its impact in the United States because many American insurance companies refuse to pay for it. According to Wikipedia: "The vast majority of developed countries are providing access to therapy for all diagnosed Pompe patients."

Make no mistake. The Crowleys were brave and resourceful, and their proactive measures saved the lives of their children—and many more with Pompe. This is a remarkable story. I think the film lets them down. It finds the shortest possible route between beginning and end. And it sidesteps the point that the U.S. health care system makes it unavailable to many dying children; they are being saved in nations with universal health coverage.

## Extremely Loud and Incredibly Close ★ ★ ½

PG-13, 129 m., 2012

Tom Hanks (Thomas Schell), Sandra Bullock (Linda Schell), Thomas Horn (Oskar Schell), Max von Sydow (The Renter), Viola Davis (Abby Black), John Goodman (Stan the Doorman), Jeffrey Wright (William Black), Zoe Caldwell (Grandmother). Directed by Stephen Daldry and produced by Scott Rudin. Screenplay by Eric Roth, based on the novel by Jonathan Safran Foer.

No movie has ever been able to provide a catharsis for the Holocaust, and I suspect none will ever be able to provide one for 9/11. Such subjects overwhelm art. The artist's usual tactic is to center on individuals whose lives are a rebuke to the tragedy. They sidestep the actual event and focus on a parallel event that ends happily, giving us a sentimental reason to find consolation. That is small comfort to the dead.

*Extremely Loud and Incredibly Close* tells the story of an eleven-year-old boy named Oskar Schell, who is played by the gifted and very well cast Thomas Horn. His father, Thomas, was killed in 9/11. Indeed, intensely scrutinizing videos of bodies falling from one of the towers, Oskar fancies he can actually identify him. We see a lot of Thomas in flashbacks, and he is played by Tom Hanks, who has come to embody an American Everyman. As a father, Thomas was a paragon, spending countless quality hours with Oskar and involving the bright kid in ingenious mind games. Perhaps he suspected what Oskar now tells us about himself: He may have Asperger's syndrome, a condition affecting those who are very intelligent but lack ordinary social skills. For a kid like that, driven to complete tasks he has set himself, his dad's challenges are compelling.

The film opens with the father's funeral (the casket is empty). We meet Oskar's mother, Linda (Sandra Bullock), whom Oskar feels distant from and resents for being the parent who is still alive. He has no idea how much he hurts her. He is close with his grandmother (Zoe Caldwell) and learns that his paternal grandparents were Holocaust victims.

In a vase on the upper shelf of a closet, Oskar finds an envelope with the word "Black" in it. It contains a key. Oskar decides that the key might unlock a secret of his father's past—perhaps a message. Because the word is capitalized, he decides it is a name, and he sets out to visit everyone named Black in New York City. There are 472 of them. Oskar sets out on foot because one of his peculiarities is that he won't use public transportation. To boost his confidence, he takes along his tambourine. That he is able to undertake this task while apparently keeping it a secret from his mother is a tribute to his intelligence. That he thinks it's safe for an eleven-year-old to walk alone all over New York is not.

We don't follow him on every visit, but the first one makes a big impression. He knocks on the door of Abby Black (Viola Davis), who invites him in, hears his story, and tries to help him. Oskar's social skills don't extend to noticing that Abby is in the middle of a marital crisis with her husband (Jeffrey Wright). Davis and Wright are so good here, in roles that work mostly by implication, that Oskar's quest starts off on the right foot emotionally.

What do we learn during this quest? That more than four thousand may have died in the 9/11 terrorism, but millions more still live? That those named Black form a cross-section of the metropolis? That life goes on? Oskar is not entirely alone. He is seen off by his building's doorman (John Goodman), and soon he makes a new friend. This very old man, known only as The Renter (Max von Sydow), has moved in with Oskar's grandmother. He cannot or will not speak, communicating only with written notes, but he is a tall and reassuring companion. (Some will observe that Sydow played chess with Death in *The Seventh Seal*, a connection that might appeal to Oskar's analytical mind.) You will discover if the key unlocks anything, or if the search for its lock is itself the purpose.

The screenplay is by Eric Roth, whose *Forrest Gump* and *The Curious Case of Benjamin Button* were also about strange journeys in life. The director is Stephen Daldry, whose film *The Reader* also approached the Holocaust obliquely. There may be some significance in the name "Oskar," from Jonathan Safran Foer's original novel; that was the name of the hero of Gunter Grass's *Tin Drum*, about a little boy who travels around Europe during World War II and carries not a tambourine, but a drum.

You will not discover, however, why it was thought this story needed to be told. There must be a more plausible narrative about a boy who lost his father on 9/11. This plot is contrivance and folderol. The mysterious key, the silent old man, and the magical tambourine are the stuff of fairy tales, and the notion of a small boy walking all over New York is so preposterous we're constantly aware of it as a storytelling device. The events of 9/11 have left indelible scars. They cannot be healed in such a soothing way.

# F

## Fair Game ★ ★ ★

PG-13, 105 m., 2010

Naomi Watts (Valerie Plame), Sean Penn (Joseph Wilson), Sam Shepard (Sam Plame), Noah Emmerich (Bill), Michael Kelly (Jack), Bruce McGill (Jim Pavitt). Directed by Doug Liman and produced by Liman, Jez Butterworth, Akiva Goldsman, Bill Pohlad, Janet Zucker, and Jerry Zucker. Screenplay by Jez Butterworth and John-Henry Butterworth, based on the memoirs *The Politics of Truth* by Joseph Wilson and *Fair Game* by Valerie Plame Wilson.

It seems to come down to this: The Bush administration had decided to go to war in Iraq. Scrambling to find reasons to justify the war, it seized on reports that the African nation of Niger had sold uranium to Iraq. Joseph Wilson, a former ambassador to Niger, was sent to seek evidence. He found none. In fact, he found such sales would have been physically impossible.

His report was ignored. We went to war. The nonexistent uranium sales were cited. He wrote an article in the *New York Times* reporting on what he found, or didn't find, in Niger. In an attempt to discredit him, someone in the administration leaked the information to *Chicago Sun-Times* columnist Robert Novak that Wilson's wife, Valerie Plame, was a CIA agent.

Cheney's aide, Scooter Libby, was tried and convicted of obstruction of justice and perjury, sentenced to prison, and had his sentence quickly commuted by Bush. Cheney was angry he wasn't pardoned outright. In the film, we see that Plame, under a variety of aliases, ran secret networks of informants in Baghdad and other Middle Eastern cities. When the administration blew her cover, several of her informants were killed; some reports say seventy. Then the Bush spin doctors leaked the story that she was only a CIA "secretary."

The spinning is still going on. Doug Liman's *Fair Game*, based on memoirs by Valerie Plame and Joseph Wilson and starring Sean Penn and Naomi Watts, is unusually bold for a fictionalization based on real events. Using real names and a good many facts, it argues: (1) Saddam had no WMD; (2) the CIA knew it; (3) the White House knew it; (4) the agenda of Cheney and his White House neocons required an invasion of Iraq no matter what; and (5) therefore, the evidence was ignored and we went to war because of phony claims.

Well. That's what the film says. There will no doubt be dissent. Few people are happy to be portrayed as liars and betrayers. What amazes me is that *Fair Game* doesn't play the game of using fictional names. They're all right there, including Cheney personally ordering the intelligence to be falsified.

Naomi Watts looks uncannily like the real-life Plame, but that's beside the point; what I related to was the serious, workmanlike tone of her Plame, who doesn't see herself as a heroine but as a skilled operative. She has scenes where she devastates other characters with what she knows about them, and how she can use that information. Sean Penn plays Ambassador Wilson, more combative than his wife, outraged by the way administration leakers try to destroy them. The film is realistic about the ways the Plame-Wilson marriage almost failed.

What's effective is how matter-of-fact *Fair Game* is. This isn't a lathering, angry attack picture. Wilson and Plame are both seen as loyal government employees, not particularly political until they discover the wrong information. The implication is that if the Bush administration hadn't suppressed their information and smeared them, there might have been no Iraq war, and untold thousands of lives would have been saved.

This topic has been so poisoned by misinformation that a rational discussion seems impossible. I suppose the question becomes, How well does *Fair Game* work as a movie? I suspect it will work better the more you walk in agreeing with it. The portrait it paints of the Wilson-Plame marriage is a very personal one, based on conflicting personalities under pressure. Penn plays Wilson as a hotheaded idealist, fueled by outrage. Watts makes Plame an ideal spy: secretive, concealing, under the radar. Perhaps she would rather her husband had bitten the bullet like a good soldier.

They're surrounded by press attention, and she finds her CIA work belittled by the administration spin doctors and her contacts overseas trashed. Joe obviously didn't prevent the war. If he'd kept quiet, her own CIA work would not have been destroyed.

One interesting element in the movie's version is the cluelessness of George W. Bush. In this version, it's possible he didn't fully realize how flawed his information on Niger was. The Svengali is Cheney. That's the collective narrative that emerges from a group of such films, such as Rod Lurie's *Nothing but the Truth* and Oliver Stone's *W.* The implication was that Cheney wanted Scooter pardoned because Scooter was acting on his orders. It's unlikely Scooter would have been acting on his own.

## Fake It So Real ★ ★ ★ ½

NO MPAA RATING, 95 m., 2012

A documentary featuring Chris Baldwin, Alex Boyles, Gabriel Croft, David Hayes, Tyler Hayes, Howard Hill, Chris Isenberg, Van Jordan, Richie Owenby, Pitt, Zane Riley, Jeff Roberts, Brandon Weese. Directed by Robert Greene.

*Fake It So Real* filled me with affection for its down-and-out heroes, a group of semipro wrestlers in Lincolnton, North Carolina. On Saturday nights they rent a hall, construct their own ring, set out the folding chairs, stage a wrestling show, take the ring apart, truck it away, and start talking about next week. For this labor, one of them jokes, they get "twenty bucks, a hot dog, and a pat on the ass."

There are twelve or fourteen wrestlers in the film, and together they compose the entire Millennium Wrestling Federation, which seems to feature a title bout for its World Championship every few weeks. They have physical and relationship problems, most of them seem unemployed or in low-paying jobs, but for one shining night of the week they are stars. They have onstage personas, design their own flashy costumes, and play out scenarios of grudges, ferocity, and bad-ass moves. One says he knew he'd made it when three little girls asked him for his autograph.

This is show business. Is that why I liked them so much? In some circles they might be seen as losers, but they have taken admirable steps to bring about their dreams. During the week they post flyers for the Saturday match in gas stations and convenience stores, they meet daily to rehearse and collaborate on scenarios, and in the honorable tradition of Mickey Rooney and Judy Garland, what they're essentially doing is renting an old barn and putting on a show.

Darren Aronofsky's film *The Wrestler* (2008), the Mickey Rourke masterpiece, was about wrestlers performing in marginal, low-rent matches. Compared to these guys, they were flying first class. Their stardom in the ring is compensation for bad luck in other areas, trouble with wives and girlfriends, economic hardship, and a great deal of physical pain. Of that there's no doubt. Yes, it's true the fights are "fixed and faked," in the sense that the script and the winner are decided in advance. But let's say the script calls for an opponent to lift you over his head and slam you down on the mat, climb onto the ropes, and body slam you. What part of that, exactly, is not real?

The members of the federation all seem to be nice guys. Robert Greene's camera follows them through seven days before a big match and we get to know them. Many felt like outsiders until they found this family. One has a disproportionately big butt and was bullied about it in school. "I said, 'God, you gave me this big ass, now show me how to use it,'" he says, and on the back of his shorts he wears bright red lips inviting his opponent to kiss his ass.

One has asthma. One has an infection and is about to miss his first match in several years. One, Chris Solar, was born prematurely with his intestines and internal organs outside his body; that's why he lacks a navel. All are muscular enough for the considerable demands of wrestling, but many are overweight. One explains, "I'm in training. I smoke Marlboro Lights."

The best body belongs to the rookie, Gabriel Croft, a clean-cut kid who looks like Matt Damon. He gets a lot of instruction and encouragement from the veterans, who wonder if he has the right stuff. He plays a character named the Angel Gabriel, and gets some homophobic kidding, but homophobia is the water in which they all swim. There is a tenderness in the way they punish one another.

As showbiz, this is bottom rung. They play music from their own collections. They use Radio Shack strobe lights. One "villain" wears a dime-store Halloween mask. Admission is $5 (kids are free), and at the Saturday night show the crowd may be loyal and loud, but it's small. The rent for their venue, which looks like a school auditorium, is $240, and that would take forty-eight tickets. There must not be a lot left over. The possibility exists that they're wrestling at a net loss to themselves.

Greene, the documentarian, is a cousin of Chris Solar. He likes these guys and doesn't take cheap shots. The Rourke film contained a lot of painkiller use and illegal steroids. There are no drugs seen or referred to in this film, and my guess is they can't afford them. There is a rough nobility in the way they strive for fame and success. The film is alive at every moment. I'd like to attend one of their matches, but having seen this film I might find it too painful—and I'm not talking about physical pain.

## Faster ★ ★ ½

R, 98 m., 2010

Dwayne Johnson (Driver), Billy Bob Thornton (Cop), Oliver Jackson-Cohen (Killer), Maggie Grace (Lily), Moon Bloodgood (Marina), Carla Gugino (Cicero). Directed by George Tillman Jr. and produced by Tony Gayton, Liz Glotzer, Martin Shafer, and Robert Teitel. Screenplay by Tony Gayton and Joe Gayton.

*Faster* is a pure thriller, all blood, no frills, in which a lot of people get shot, mostly in the head. Rotate the plot, change the period, spruce up the dialogue, and this could have been a hard-boiled 1940s noir. But it doesn't pause for fine touches, and efficiently delivers action for an audience that likes one-course meals.

Dwayne Johnson stars, in the kind of role he's possibly been avoiding up until now. Once known as The Rock, he has developed a kinder, gentler screen persona that more closely fits him in real life. It's a melancholy fact of Hollywood today that *Faster* could be a good career move for him, moving him onto the trail blazed by Schwarzenegger and Bruce Willis. He has very broad shoulders, wicked tattoos, and a gun that seems to grow from his hand.

As the film opens, he's being released from prison after a ten-year term. He walks out the gate into a desert wilderness and begins to run—run—to a nearby city, where a circa 1970 Chevelle is waiting for him in a junkyard. This is because modern cars all look boring and most action heroes drive classics. He whips off the tarp and peels outta there. A private eye gives him a list of names, and he sets out to murder everyone on the list.

His character is named Driver. A clue to this, and the title, is that he invariably drives at the top possible speed, and obviously never took driver's ed in high school because he doesn't know how to turn around and drive in the other direction except by slamming on the brakes, twisting the wheel, and whipping through 180 degrees.

Driver is soon wanted for one, then two, then three murders. The cops know who he is. His photo is on the TV news. This all takes place in Bakersfield. What are the odds a tattooed killer with a shaved head could elude the Bakersfield police for long while piloting a classic Chevelle at 80 mph and laying rubber all over town? Excellent.

The cop on the case is Cicero (Carla Gugino). She finds herself saddled with a partner known as Cop (Billy Bob Thornton). He's two weeks from retirement. As we all know, anyone two weeks from retirement, be he cop, fireman, stuntman, prison guard, or kindly old dad, will never make it. Cop is also mainlining heroin, for no better reason than to show him doing it. One fix lasts him for the rest of the film.

Cicero and Cop try to track down Driver, who seeks vengeance on those who squealed about a bank heist and killed his brother. These people have moved into other lines of work, most notably Preacher (Buzz Belmondo), who runs revival tent meetings. We find out more about them. And we meet the fatuous Killer (Oliver Jackson-Cohen), a British addict of extreme sports, who is a professional hit man for fun. This is some guy. He informs his girlfriend, Lily (Maggie Grace), that he has "beaten" yoga, having mastered the most difficult three positions, and is ready to move on.

As Driver tracks his victims, Killer tracks Driver, and Cop and Cicero track them all.

Director George Tillman does a lean, efficient job of creating stark action scenes. Driver shows vestiges of a personality, reluctantly. Billy Bob creates a cop who looks like it's been all downhill for him since *Bad Santa.* Gugino, a good actress, gamely pretends to be in a more nuanced movie. And the hits keep coming.

## Fast Five ★ ★ ★

PG-13, 130 m., 2011

Vin Diesel (Dominic Toretto), Paul Walker (Brian O'Conner), Dwayne Johnson (Luke Hobbs), Jordana Brewster (Mia Toretto), Tyrese Gibson (Roman Pierce), Chris "Ludacris" Bridges (Tej), Matt Schulze (Vincent), Sung Kang (Han), Gal Gadot (Gisele), Joaquim de Almeida (Reyes), Elsa Pataky (Elena). Directed by Justin Lin and produced by Vin Diesel, Michael Fottrell, and Neal H. Moritz. Screenplay by Chris Morgan.

I don't think you can do this. I don't think you can take two midsize sedans, chain them to a bank vault, and haul it behind you on a high-speed chase through the streets of Rio de Janeiro while being chased by the cops. I think the traffic would be too bad.

I also don't think you can steal cars from a speeding train by driving a truck beside the tracks, cutting the side out of a freight car with an acetylene torch, flipping the cars onto the truck bed, tilting the bed, letting them roll to the ground, and then driving them away. I think there are more practical ways to steal cars.

I also think that while Houdini might have been able to make a bank vault disappear from the stage of the New York Hippodrome (and escape from it in the process), bank vaults in general tend to be hard to mess around with, as may occur to you during *Fast Five.* But you know what? It sort of doesn't matter. The movie is made of sheer preposterous nonstop impossible action, muscular macho guys, hot chicks, and platoons of bad guys who are eliminated by the dozens while the leading characters escape certain death so easily it gets to be a habit.

This is the third of the *Fast and the Furious* series, starring Vin Diesel, Paul Walker, and Jordana Brewster, and here they're joined by Dwayne Johnson, making it a sort of convention of reckless drivers. Apparently some of these characters have had, in the past, long conversations about their goals, dreams, abilities, and values, saving time at the present for terse verbal shorthand. When you hear as many as six words in a row, you suspect it's a tagline for a trailer ("We need to assemble a team.").

Justin Lin is emerging as a first-rate director in this second-rate genre, having shelved, temporarily I trust, the ambition suggested in his remarkable *Better Luck Tomorrow* (2002). Unlike a certain other maker of crash-crash-bang-bangs, whose name I trust you to summon effortlessly, Lin devotes attention to a story line that devises ingenious new things to do instead of obsessively blowing up things. He storyboards his impossible action sequences, instead of editing them with incomprehensible speed. And he hauls in fresh faces (played by such as Tyrese Gibson, Chris "Ludacris" Bridges, Matt Schulze, Sung Kang, Gal Gadot, Elsa Pataky, and Joaquim de Almeida) and gives them a specialty and a chance to demonstrate it. You couldn't say the supporting characters are developed beyond their defining labels, but at least they're in the mix.

The villain (de Almeida), a Rio drug kingpin, makes the usual error of ordering his flunkies into hot pursuit and then following them into danger. There's a reason generals don't fight in the trenches. His character, Reyes, is set up as a criminal tycoon, but $100 million is not, after all, very much drug money to have in a bank, not when Wachovia Bank (now absorbed by Wells Fargo) was recently revealed to have laundered drug money equal to a third of the Mexican GDP. One thing you know is that the United States will spend less time trying to put those bankers behind bars than the Brazilians do here, and lose many fewer squad cars in the process.

But facts will get me nowhere in reviewing a movie of this sort. What you want is advice about your genre expectations. The 2001 movie was sorta fun with its energy and ambition, placing Diesel and Walker in a Los Angeles street-racing story. The 2009 film, which made an impenetrable leap from the plot of the first one, was much more routine. Both made plenty of money. The *F&F* titles got confusing with the unrelated *The Fast and the Furious:*

*Tokyo Drift* and John Singleton's *2 Fast 2 Furious*, which is why, I suppose *Fast Five* drops the *furious*. But it isn't technically the fifth *F&F* unless you count the outliers. So I don't know what *Five* refers to. That doesn't bother me.

What it all comes down to is a skillfully assembled 130 minutes at the movies, with actors capable of doing absurd things with straight faces, and action sequences that toy idly with the laws of physics. That can be amusing for some people, not so much for me. What I missed were laughs, although I got a good one right at the end, when we were warned that the driving in the movie was done in a controlled environment by professionals, and we shouldn't try those stunts ourselves. Someday I would like to meet a driver who was planning to race his Hummer into a reinforced concrete wall before being persuaded otherwise by the closing credits.

## The Father of My Children ★ ★ ★ ½

NO MPAA RATING, 110 m., 2010

Louis-Do de Lencquesaing (Gregoire), Chiara Caselli (Sylvia), Alice de Lencquesaing (Clemence), Alice Gautier (Valentine), Manelle Driss (Billie), Eric Elmosnino (Serge). Directed by Mia Hansen-Love and produced by Oliver Damian, Philippe Martin, and David Thion. Screenplay by Hansen-Love.

"How much do I owe you?" the producer asks someone on his cell phone. He chuckles. "That much?" He is amused, busy, filled with energy. He handles two phones at a time while threading through Paris traffic and heading for a country weekend with his family. He smokes. He drives. He tells his wife, "I'm almost on the highway." He's stopped by the cops, who ask if he knows why they stopped him. "I have a vague idea," he says.

In the opening sequence, we meet a plausible human being. A French film producer, an honest hustler, a loving father and husband, confident of his powers, enjoying his work. *The Father of My Children* will watch this man come to pieces. It will not be dark melodrama or turgid psychology. It will simply be the story of a good man, well loved, who runs into a dead end.

The man is named Gregoire (Louis-Do de Lencquesaing). The actor, like many French actors, is good-looking without being improbable. He runs his business in his head. He explains, "I don't work with the kinds of directors who do television." He commits to a filmmaker and goes to the limit for the film not because he has lofty ideas about Art, but because that's the kind of man he is.

In the movie, he is plunging into debt while producing an obscure project of a temperamental auteur not a million miles distant from Lars von Trier. He gets phone reports from the set from his trusted assistant, hears of troublesome actors and bad weather, deals with money and debt, and loves his wife, Sylvia (Chiara Caselli), and three daughters, Clemence (Alice de Lencquesaing), Valentine (Alice Gautier), and Billie (Manelle Driss). Their country house evokes quiet family togetherness, which is the idea, but Gregoire's mind is often elsewhere, trying to find a way out of his troubles.

When very busy men are also essentially good men and working at something worthwhile, they tend to find themselves surrounded by supporters and enablers. Gregoire's office is also a family, in a way, and his employees share his vision. When calamity strikes, even his wife pitches in to help salvage his dream. The second half of the film is the most touching, because it shows that our lives are not merely our own, but also belong to the events we set in motion.

Louis-Do de Lencquesaing is effective here at *not* going into a manic mode. He runs his business while improvising from moment to moment, he has some plans for getting through, he tries some scenarios, and he doesn't need anyone to tell him when they're not working. I appreciate the ability of the director, Mia Hansen-Love, to allow the situation to develop through observation of her hero, not dialogue explaining everything.

Chiara Caselli, as Gregoire's wife, is, like many wives of workaholic men, better informed on his business than he can imagine. She believes in him, therefore in his hopes, and touchingly relates with the members of his office family as they all try to move things along. And the film gives due attention to the children, particularly Clemence (played by de Lencquesaing's own daughter), who negotiate unfamiliar emotional territory with their mother. The title (in French, *Le pere de mes enfants*) is appropriate.

SPOILER WARNING: The story is said to be inspired by the life of the real-life producer Humbert Balsan, who made Lars von Trier's *Manderlay* (2005). Balsan had considerable success, making nearly seventy films, including three by James Ivory, and even acting for Bresson. He committed suicide when his business imploded.

*Note: The film won the special jury prize in the Un Certain Regard section of Cannes 2009.*

## 50/50 ★ ★ ★ ½

R, 99 m., 2011

Joseph Gordon-Levitt (Adam), Seth Rogen (Kyle), Anna Kendrick (Katherine), Bryce Dallas Howard (Rachael), Philip Baker Hall (Alan), Anjelica Huston (Diane). Directed by Jonathan Levine and produced by Evan Goldberg, Ben Karlin, and Seth Rogen. Screenplay by Will Reiser.

Young people should not get sick and die. Most of us do eventually, but how sad it is to learn in your twenties that you have a dangerous cancer and your chances of survival are 50/50. How crueler still if the news is delivered by a doctor who seems almost deliberately sadistic. Start with those odds. They may indeed be accurate, but would it kill the son of a bitch to make them 60/40?

Adam (Joseph Gordon-Levitt) is a writer for public radio in Seattle, which makes him almost a poster boy for someone who should grow old and wise. He has a nagging back pain. The oncologist says it is a rare form of cancer of the spine. *50/50* was written by Will Reiser, who himself was diagnosed with a spinal tumor. Seth Rogen, who plays Adam's best friend, Kyle, is a close friend of Reiser in real life, and the movie is based on what happened in their friendship after the diagnosis.

After surgery and treatment, Reiser is currently in the sixth year of remission, and cheerfully observes, "Remission apparently lasts forever . . . or until you die." In an interview by Jen Chaney with the two of them in the *Washington Post*, they joke endlessly, which is perhaps inevitable between a comedy writer and a comic actor, and although *50/50* is structured with the efficiency of a sitcom, there's an undercurrent of truth and real feeling.

Adam turns to his best buddy for support and encouragement. Kyle rises to the occasion, unlike Rachael (Bryce Dallas Howard), his girlfriend, who (as he learns) wasn't all that committed even before the awful diagnosis. Rachael, of course, vows to stand by him and help him, as society says we must do, but in fact, cancer is a messy and depressing business, and she signed on to be a girlfriend, not a nurse. She doesn't have the right stuff. And believe me, the challenges Adam presents for her in *50/50* are nothing compared to real life. If you've been involved in the case of a loved one with cancer, you'll observe that the girl gets off easy.

Adam is also supported, maybe too much, by his mother, Diane (Anjelica Huston), who actually moves into the house. Her husband has Alzheimer's, and she's stuck by him, so she has the right stuff, but when you're sick you need quiet time, and the constant presence of a determined mother is not always what's called for.

The movie places Adam in a cancer patients' support group, where his fellow patient Alan (Philip Baker Hall) provides dry, realistic input. Alan is a model of acceptance, the fifth stage in Elisabeth Kubler-Ross's Five Stages of Grief. His work here is a reminder of what an effective actor Hall always is. Anna Kendrick plays Katherine, Adam's therapist, who gets just as involved as his oncologist is aloof. I know therapists are supposed to observe a certain distance, but in a case like this I don't see how one can. I would make a terrible therapist.

The screenplay perhaps benefits from Reiser's experience on television, and proceeds in an orderly way through a basic sitcom structure. Some of the comedy aspects may seem unlikely, but Seth Rogen has a winning way about him and reveals genuine affection. If a movie like this were as relentlessly realistic as a masterpiece like Mike Nichols's *Wit*, it would probably not be commercial and end up, as *Wit* did, on HBO. A spoonful of sugar helps the medicine go down.

What I appreciated was the third act. Sitcoms and film comedies in general have a way of going haywire with comic desperation toward the end. This one doesn't. Director Jonathan Levine (*The Wackness*) has established the characters with enough care that the audience is prepared when they reveal greater depth toward the end. Anjelica Huston is especially good at breaking free of what seem to be the boundaries of her role.

*50/50* isn't completely true to life, but the more you know about cancer the less you want it to be. Like another recent feel-good film about the disease, Gus Van Sant's *Restless*, it creates a comforting myth. That's one of the things movies are good for.

## The Fighter ★ ★ ½

R, 115 m., 2010

Mark Wahlberg (Micky Ward), Christian Bale (Dicky Eklund), Amy Adams (Charlene Fleming), Melissa Leo (Alice Ward). Directed by David O. Russell and produced by Dorothy Aufiero, David Hoberman, Ryan Kavanaugh, Todd Lieberman, Paul Tamasy, and Mark Wahlberg. Screenplay by Tamasy, Scott Silver, and Eric Johnson.

Micky Ward has less personality than the hero of any other boxing movie I can remember. Maybe that's because he can't get a word in edgeways. He has a motormouth crackhead for a half-brother, a mom who acts as his manager, and seven blond sisters who seem to be on a break from a musical being filmed on the next soundstage. It's easy to imagine Micky growing up in this family and sitting ignored in the corner.

David O. Russell's *The Fighter* is based on Ward's true story, and perhaps Micky (Mark Wahlberg) is flat and withdrawn here because he is in life. His family is spectacularly dysfunctional. Dicky Eklund (Christian Bale), his half-brother, is the failed version of what Micky hopes to become: a poor kid from Lowell, Massachusetts, who wins because of his ability to outlast savage punishment and finally land a winning blow.

Micky grew up hero worshipping Dicky, who lost a lot of fights but allegedly knocked over Sugar Ray Leonard once upon a time. Then Dicky got hooked on crack, and now we see him as a goofy, scrawny guy with a Skeezix haircut, a cigarette behind his ear, and an arm around his brother's shoulders. They're being filmed for an HBO documentary, which Dicky thinks is about his own unlikely comeback, and everybody else knows is about his decline and fall. Crackheads sometimes get the two confused.

As the movie opens, Micky doggedly begins a series of defeats in bad matchups. Then his life changes when he meets a sweet-faced, tough-talking barmaid named Charlene (Amy Adams). She knows the neighborhood, knows the story, and knows that Micky's problem is his family. His mother, Alice (Melissa Leo in a teeth-gratingly brilliant performance), sees both boys as performers in a long-running tribute to herself. She presides in a living room filled with her seven daughters, who smoke so much and use so much hair spray they must be considered fire hazards.

When Micky gets a chance to train seriously in Vegas, Charlene more or less forces him to take it. When Dicky and Alice follow him out there, it's showdown time and Charlene threatens to leave. But the movie is imprecise about how this plays out, and they're all at ringside at the end.

The weakness of the film is the weakness of the leading role. That's not a criticism of Mark Wahlberg, who has a quite capable range, but of how he and Russell see the character. Micky comes across as a proud, not very bright, very determined man who has apparently never given his family much constructive thought. To say of your family "They're my family!" is true enough, but may not be sufficiently analytical. His love for Charlene is real, but he never quite realizes he really must choose between her vision and his mother's. His character remains strangely unfocused.

That's not the case with Dicky, Alice, and Charlene, and those characters are where the life is. Christian Bale, who has played Batman *and* John Connor in *Terminator Salvation*, and for Werner Herzog played a man who survived in the jungles of Laos, so successfully transforms himself that you foresee a career as a cutup in the *Jackass* movies. Melissa Leo (*Frozen River*) is merciless in her depiction of Alice; steering her son to failure is more rewarding than having him succeed on his own.

She's one of those women, you know the type, who likes the way she looks posing with a freshly lit cigarette. And look at Amy Adams, our beloved *Junebug* and the nun in *Doubt*, who is clear-headed and has a strong will and tries to lend those qualities to the man she loves.

There are a lot of fight scenes, not as visceral as those in *Raging Bull*, *Rocky*, or *The Wrestler*, but designed more to represent the POV of a sportswriter or fan. Because we aren't deeply invested in Micky, we don't care as much as we should, and the film ends on a note that should be triumph but feels more like simple conclusion.

## Film Socialisme ★

NO MPAA RATING, 101 m., 2011

---

Most of the characters are not named. They are played by Catherine Tanvier, Christian Sinniger, Jean-Marc Stehle, Agatha Couture, Eye Haidara, Marie-Christine Bergier, Nadege Beausson-Diagne, Mathias Domahidy, Quentin Grosset, Olga Riazanova, Maurice Sarfati, Dominique Devals, Louma Sanbar, Gulliver Hecq, Marine Battaggia, Elizabeth Vitali, Patti Smith, Lenny Kaye, Alain Badiou, Bernard Maris, Elias Sanbar, Robert Maloubier, and Dominique Reynie. Directed by Jean-Luc Godard and produced by Ruth Waldburger. Screenplay by Godard.

---

One sunny day at Cannes, I sat at lunch with the British director Ken Russell, who had been well served and was feeling relaxed. As far as he was concerned, he said, he was pleased home video had been invented because now films could be watched on fast-forward, saving everyone's time. There was a quiet smile on Russell's face as he dozed off. "You're kidding!" I said. He awoke with a start. "Certainly not!" he said, and pushed back from the table.

I suppose it was only a matter of time until Russell's insight reached Jean-Luc Godard. The great director began with films that we would all agree fit the definition of "movie," and has relentlessly been putting more and more distance between himself and that form. With *Film Socialisme*, made in his seventy-ninth year, the pioneer of the French New Wave has been swept out to sea.

This film is an affront. It is incoherent, maddening, deliberately opaque, and heedless of the ways in which people watch movies. All of that is part of the Godardian method, I am aware, but I feel a bargain of some sort must be struck. We enter the cinema with open minds and good will, expecting Godard to engage us in at least a vaguely penetrable way. But in *Film Socialisme* he expects us to do all the heavy lifting.

When the film premiered at Cannes 2010, it was received with the usual bouquet of cheers, hoots, and catcalls. Defenders of Godard wrote at length about his content and purpose, while many others frankly felt insulted. In the spirit of Ken Russell, Godard actually posted an online video that used fast-forward to show his entire film in about four minutes. That, I concede, showed wit. You can see it here: http://bit.ly/lznp1u.

In the film, he shows us fragmented scenes on a cruise ship traveling the Mediterranean, and also shots which travel through human history, which for the film's purposes involve Egypt, Greece, Palestine, Odessa (notably its steps), Naples, Barcelona, Tunisia, and other ports. Then we see fragments of a story involving two women (one a TV camerawoman) and a family living at a roadside garage. A mule and a llama also live at the garage. There are shots of kittens, obscurely linked to the Egyptians, as well as parrots. The cruise ship is perhaps a metaphor for our human voyage through time. The garage is anybody's guess.

There is also much topical footage, both moving and still. Words are spoken, some of them bits of language from eminent authors. These words appear in uppercase subtitles, and are mostly nouns. These subtitles, Godard explained, are what he calls Navajo English. I guess he learned it from old Westerns.

His Navajo speakers touch on socialism, gambling, nationalism, Hitler, Stalin, art, Islam, women, Jews, Hollywood, Palestine, war, and other large topics. It all seems terrifically political, but there is nothing in the film to offend the most devout Tea Party communicant, and I can't say what, if anything, the film has to say about socialism.

Godard has sent my mind scurrying between ancient history and modern television, via Marxism and Nazism, to ponder—well, what? In addition to standard digital video, Godard uses a state-of-the-art iteration of high-def video; some shots, especially aboard the cruise ship, are so beautiful and glossy they could be an advertisement for something, perhaps a cruise ship. Other shots seem taken with cell phones, and there are bits and pieces from old movies.

The film closes with large block letters: NO COMMENT. I would have looked forward to attending Godard's press conference, but of course he didn't attend it. Once, at Montreal, I sat next to him at a little dinner for film critics, at which he arranged his garden peas into geometric forms on his plate and told us, "Cinema is the train. It is not the station." Or perhaps my memory has tricked me, and he said, "Cinema is the station. It is not the train." Both are equally true. Or not.

## Final Destination 5 ★ ★

R, 92 m., 2011

Nicholas D'Agosto (Sam), Emma Bell (Molly), Miles Fisher (Peter), Courtney B. Vance (Agent Block), Arlen Escarpeta (Nathan), David Koechner (Dennis), Tony Todd (Bludworth), P. J. Byrne (Isaac), Jacqueline MacInnes Wood (Olivia), Ellen Wroe (Candice). Directed by Steven Quale and produced by Craig Perry and Warren Zide. Screenplay by Eric Heisserer, based on characters created by Jeffrey Reddick.

*Final Destination 5* is one of those rare movies where the title itself is a spoiler. Yes, everyone in the movie dies, except for Coroner Bludworth. But you knew that because of the previous four films. The increasingly challenging task of the filmmakers is to devise ever more horrible and gruesome methods for them to be slaughtered.

*FD5* shows a lot of ingenuity. The recurring theme this time will be skewering and lots of it. The characters have names, but they might as well be called after items for a shish kebab: lamb, chicken, mushrooms, onions, tomatoes, some nice peppers (I like to use green, red, and yellow).

We get a tip-off in the opening credits, which use 3-D to thrust things at the audience. Before we have seen so much as a human face on the screen, we have been assaulted by skewers, knives, rods, stakes, and shards of glass. This is the "Ping-Pong effect" elevated to aggressive excess, a reminder that if we haven't already put on our annoying dark glasses, this is the time to bid farewell to bright colors. We have already bid farewell to the 3-D "premium" charge.

The actors in a movie like this are essentially doing product placement. By getting their names and faces out there in a splatter movie, they can perhaps catch the eye of a casting agent and get a shot at a decent film. They have studied their craft. They have struggled and dreamed. They have attended countless auditions. Now at last they have a role in a major Hollywood release and can call home: "Mom! I get impaled by the mast of a sailboat after I fall off a bridge!"

The fact is, the performances here are all effective. The actors bring more to the film than it brings to them. The caliber of performance in gruesome death movies has considerably improved since Herschell Gordon Lewis made *The Gore Gore Girls*. The direction by Steven Quale is efficient, and the special effects do an excellent job of beheading, incinerating, vivisecting, squishing, and so on.

I am amused by this credit: "Screenplay by Eric Heisserer, based on characters created by Jeffrey Reddick." Reddick, of course, was the writer of the original *Final Destination* (2000). Since all of the characters in that film were dead at the end of the film, his credit might more reasonably have read, "based on characters killed by Jeffrey Reddick."

I speak too soon. Bludworth (Tony Todd) always survives, his task to find ever more ominous ways of saying "I told you so." Reddick should also be given full credit for devising the ingenious logic of the first film, which consisted of many proofs that we can't cheat death. This truth struck the original characters with a force that has now been much diluted; you don't appear in a *Final Destination* movie and expect to get out alive.

I expect this movie to make a lot of money at the box office, spent by fans eager to see still more cool ways for hot young characters to be slaughtered. My review will not be read by any of these people. They know what they enjoy. They don't want no damn movies with damn surprises. I am always pleased when moviegoers have a good time; perhaps they will return to a theater and someday see a good movie by accident, and it will start them thinking.

## Fireflies in the Garden ★ ★

R, 89 m., 2011

Ryan Reynolds (Michael Taylor), Willem Dafoe (Charles Taylor), Emily Watson (Jane Lawrence), Carrie-Anne Moss (Kelly Hanson), Julia Roberts (Lisa Taylor), Ioan Gruffudd (Addison Wesley), Hayden Panettiere (Young Jane), Shannon Lucio (Ryne Taylor), Cayden Boyd (Young Michael), George Newbern (Jimmy Lawrence). Directed by Dennis Lee and produced by Sukee Chew, Vanessa Coifman, and Marco Weber. Screenplay by Lee. Inspired by a poem by Robert Frost.

Although *Citizen Kane* is one of my favorite films and it shuttles relentlessly between past and present, I'm often uneasy with movies where different actors play the same characters at different times. It helps when the character past and present has obvious distinctions. I lost too much time during *Fireflies in the Garden* reminding myself, "This must be young Jane," and suchlike. It doesn't help when some of the same locations persist over time. Directors have an obligation to include road directions. I followed *The Tree of Life* easily, for example, but am still getting queries from readers not sure whom Sean Penn was portraying as an older man.

*Fireflies in the Garden* is a fraught family drama that shows us the same family in past and present, twenty-two years separated. It might have been more effective if it had followed chronological order. It opens around the day when the family mother, Lisa Taylor (Julia Roberts), will graduate from college. The celebration is interrupted by a tragedy, and flashbacks lead us into the earlier lives of these people.

The Taylors live in a university town, where Charles (Willem Dafoe) is the cold, demanding father. There's a crucial event when his son Michael (Ryan Reynolds, and Cayden Boyd when younger) recites an "original poem" before his father's colleagues and the poem turns out to be plagiarized from Robert Frost. Charles is red-faced with rage. Yes, his son has committed an academic mortal sin, but when the response is as extreme as Charles's, it's an indicator he may feel a great deal of insecurity. His personality will make his family dysfunctional on down through the years. Feelings will grow more complicated because Charles the father is a would-be novelist in the past, and Michael the son has just published a successful novel in the present.

Other important characters: Lisa's teenage sister, Jane (Hayden Panetierre), Jane as a married adult (Emily Watson), her husband, Jimmy Lawrence (George Newbern), Michael's sister Ryne (Shannon Lucio), and Jane and Jimmy's two children, who unhelpfully live in the Taylor family home, so that time past and present seem to cross in the same space.

The screenplay shows signs of being inspired by personal memories that still hurt and are still piling up in Michael's mind. Fair enough, but the film doesn't sort this out clearly, and we experience vignettes in search of a story arc. The actors are all capable (Dafoe is fearsome), but they seem to drop in and out of the timeline as required.

We see literal fireflies in the garden in the movie, and the Frost poem supplies not only the occasion for plagiarism but also the title of Michael's novel—suggesting it settled old scores. Yes, but although fireflies are exemplary embodiments of transitory life and are often evoked by writers, I am never sure what they represent. The poem seems to suggest fireflies emulate real stars. The movie possibly suggests Charles fails in emulating his son. Or whatever.

## Fish Tank ★ ★ ★ ★

NO MPAA RATING, 123 m., 2010

Katie Jarvis (Mia), Michael Fassbender (Connor), Kierston Wareing (Joanne), Rebecca Griffiths (Tyler), Harry Treadaway (Billy). Directed by Andrea Arnold and produced by Kees Kasander. Screenplay by Arnold.

Andrea Arnold's piercing *Fish Tank* is the portrait of an angry, isolated fifteen-year-old girl who is hurtling toward a lifetime of misery. She is so hurt and lonely we pity her. Her mother barely even sees her. The film takes place in a bleak British public housing estate and in the streets and fields around it. There is no suggestion of a place this girl can go to find help, care, or encouragement.

The girl is Mia, played by Katie Jarvis in a harrowing display of hostility. She's been thrown out of school, is taunted as a weirdo by boys her age, converses with her mother and sister in screams, and retreats to an empty room to play her music and dance alone. She drinks what little booze she can get her hands on.

And where is her mother? Right there at home, all the time. Joanne (Kierston Wareing) looks so young she may have had Mia at Mia's age. Joanne is shorter, busty, dyed blond, a chain-smoker, a party girl. The party is usually in her living room. One day she brings home Connor (Michael Fassbender), a good-looking guy who seems nice enough. Mia screams at him, too, but it's a way of getting attention.

Joanne seems happiest when Mia isn't at home. The girl wanders the streets and gets in a fight when she tries to free a horse chained in a barren lot near some shabby mobile homes. She has no friends. She surfs in an Internet café, goes to an audition for sexy dancers, breaks into a house at random.

One day differs from the routine. Connor takes Mia, her mom, and her little sister, Tyler (Rebecca Griffiths), on a drive to the country. This isn't an idyllic picnic; they simply park in a field and hike to a river, Joanne staying with the car. Connor takes Mia in wading ("I can't swim"). Walking back barefoot she gets a ride on his back and rests her chin on his shoulder and what was in the air from the first is now manifest.

Some reviews call Connor a pedophile. I think he's more of an immoral opportunist. *Fish Tank* in any event isn't so much about sex as about the helpless spiral Mia is going through. The film has two fraught but ambiguous scenes—one when she goes to Connor's home, another involving a young girl—that we can make fairly obvious assumptions about. But the movie doesn't spell them out; Arnold sees everything through Mia's eyes and never steps outside to explain things from any other point of view. She knows who the young girl is, and we are left to assume. Whatever she thinks after the visit to Connor's house we are not specifically told. The film so firmly identifies with Mia that there may even be a possibility Joanne is better than the slutty monster we see. A slim possibility, to be sure.

In a film so tightly focused, all depends on Katie Jarvis's performance. There is truth in it. She lives on an Essex housing estate like the one in the movie, and she was discovered by Arnold while in a shouting match with her boyfriend at the Tilbury train station, which is seen in the movie. Now eighteen, she gave birth to a daughter conceived when she was sixteen.

We can fear, but we can't say, that she was heading for a life similar to the one Mia seems doomed to. Her casting in this film, however, led to Cannes, the Jury Prize, and contracts with British and American agents. She is a powerful acting presence, flawlessly convincing here. And Arnold, who won an Oscar for her shattering short film *Wasp* (2003), also about a neglectful alcoholic mother, deserves comparison with British director Ken Loach.

## Five Days of War ★ ½

R, 120 m., 2011

Rupert Friend (Thomas Anders), Emmanuelle Chriqui (Tatia Medoevi), Richard Coyle (Sebastian Ganz), Val Kilmer (Dutchman), Heather Graham (Miriam Eisner), Andy Garcia (Mikheil Saakashvili), Johnathon Schaech (Captain Rezo Avaliani), Mikko Nousiainen (Daniil), Rade Serbedzija (Colonel Alexandr Demidov). Directed by Renny Harlin and produced by Harlin, Mirza Davitaia, George Lascu, and Koba Nakopia . Screenplay by Mikko Alanne and David Battle.

At the end of this film there is a montage of sad people holding photographs of their grandparents, parents, husbands, wives, or children who were killed during the *Five Days of War* between Russia and Georgia. It is unforgivable to borrow human grief and evoke it to lend weight to an action movie scarcely deeper than a Michael Bay extravaganza. Here you will hear a great deal about the war but learn not so very much, and all from the Georgian point of view. Mind you, I'm not saying its POV is wrong—only that a cheesy war thriller financed with Georgian funds seems an odd way to publicize it.

The heroes of the film are war correspondents. The film opens with the fact that five hundred reporters have been killed in war in the last decade. That is a tragedy, but one must reflect that countless more soldiers and civilians have been killed during the same period, and so the focus seems a little misguided—especially since some of these reporters are less than noble. Consider Dutchman (Val Kilmer), an enigmatic journalist apparently in search of a good time.

The hero is Thomas Anders (Rupert Friend), a reporter who freelances for cable. His cameraman is Sebastian Ganz (Richard Coyle). In a prologue set in Iraq, they're teamed with Miriam (Heather Graham), his girlfriend, who is killed—sending him back to Los Angeles (so informs the subtitle) until Dutchman Skypes him from the bathtub with the joyous news: "This place is about to blow!" He's right, and Anders will go through most of the movie with an open wound on his nose, perhaps fearing that a Band-Aid would remind moviegoers of Jack Nicholson in *Chinatown.*

How, you may wonder, do actual Georgians figure in this film, except in the coda? Well, the reporters get invited to a wedding, which is attacked by Russian helicopters. Anders has become friendly with Tatia (Emmanuelle Chriqui), who is to be his translator, and after many deaths at the wedding, Anders and Sebastian end up fleeing with Tatia and family members. This consists of them running hunched over and ducking behind fences while accounting for the points of view of many unrelated action scenes.

None of the action is coherent; shots and shells are fired, people are killed or not, explosions rend the air, SUVs spin aloft (the same one more than once, I think), and there is no sense of strategy. Occasionally we cut to the state offices of Mikheil Saakashvili, the Georgian president, who is played by Andy Garcia, it being his misfortune to resemble Saakashvili. There are also vignettes involving a sadistic mercenary (Mikko Nousiainen) and a ruthless Russian (Rade Serbedzija), both of whom commit the Fallacy of the Talking Killer.

Renny Harlin is known for his action pictures (*Die Hard 2*, *Cliffhanger*) and not for his geopolitical insights. If the purpose of this film is to whip up sympathy for the Georgians, I doubt if few moviegoers not from that area will care. It's a lot of tough guys running around blowing up stuff real good, and getting so many good peeks at crucial action that we wonder why neither the Georgians nor the Russians can see people hiding behind a fence where even we can see them.

## Flipped ★ ★ ★ ½

PG, 90 m., 2010

Madeline Carroll (Juli Baker), Callan McAuliffe (Bryce Loski), Rebecca De Mornay (Patsy Loski), Anthony Edwards (Steven Loski), John Mahoney (Chet Duncan), Penelope Ann Miller (Trina Baker), Aidan Quinn (Richard Baker). Directed by Rob Reiner and produced by Reiner and Alan Greisman. Screenplay by Reiner and Andrew Scheinman, based on the novel by Wendelin Van Draanen.

There are moments in adolescence when your feelings about romance turn on a dime. Maybe it's hormonal. The girl you thought was a pest becomes the object of your dreams. The boy you've had a crush on for years begins to seem like a jerk. The timing is off. Sometimes you can look back half a lifetime and see how things might have happened differently if you hadn't been so stupid. Rob Reiner's *Flipped* does the looking.

Here is a lovely movie about a girl who has adored a boy ever since he moved into the neighborhood in the second grade. She even likes his smell, and it is true we cannot love someone who isn't aromatic to our hearts. All through grade school and into high school she pursues him; they're like the runners in Keats's "Ode on a Grecian Urn" who pursue each other for eternity without ever drawing closer. In Reiner's film they flip and start running in the other direction.

Madeline Carroll is Juli Baker, who was determined to get Bryce Loski (Callan McAuliffe) to like her when they were kids, but in eighth grade has turned her attention to more urgent matters, like sparing the life of the beautiful sycamore tree in her front yard. It is threatened with being chopped down by the forces of evil, and she climbs it and won't come down. That shows some character, muses Bryce's grandfather Chet (John Mahoney). If he were Bryce he'd notice a girl like that. Bryce begins to catch on.

There are difficulties and the possibility of heartbreak. There always are in high school. You wear your sleeve on your heart. There are parents. Not everybody has parents like Juno did. If Juno had ordinary parents, her story would be a grim morality play. But *Flipped* doesn't haul in standard Parents of Teenagers, either. Reiner wisely casts gifted actors (Aidan Quinn and Penelope Ann Miller as the Bakers, Anthony Edwards and Rebecca De Mornay as the Loskis). He knows that Mahoney can save a wise grandfather from cornball with sheer brute force of niceness.

There's a screenplay device used by Reiner and Andrew Scheinman, based on the novel by Wendelin Van Draanen, that could be arduous but works here because it has been thought through. The key events in the film are seen from both points of view: Bryce's and Juli's. Teenagers often lose the beat emotionally, and these two need John Philip Sousa. There isn't trickery: The scenes happen as they seem to, and not in alternate universes. But they *seem* so different depending on who is seeing them. There's one of those events so beloved by teenage girls in which they can exact excruciating embarrassment on boys while seeming to be blithely unaware. The boys are auctioned off to the girls as lunchroom partners to raise money for charity. Yeah, that's what a guy wants, to stand on the stage while the most patronizing teacher in the school handles the bidding. Of course, it all goes tragically wrong for Juli and Bryce, but for what seems like different reasons.

Reiner begins the movie in 1959, the same year as his classic *Stand by Me*, and I don't think it's just for nostalgia. In a way, that's the last year of American teenage innocence, before the '60s took hold. Madeline Carroll and Callan McAuliffe, who both look teeth-achingly vulnerable, who are sincere and pure and wholesome, are characters we believe can be hurt. Some of today's teenagers are more wounded and cynical than their parents ever were. And for some of them sex is not an undiscovered country.

Maybe what makes *Flipped* such a warm entertainment is how it re-creates a life we wish we'd had when we were fourteen. That's true for adults, and also I suspect true for some fourteen-year-olds. In a way the audience flips, too.

## The Flowers of War ★ ★

R, 142 m., 2012

Christian Bale (John Miller), Ni Ni (Yu Mo), Tianyuan Huang (George), Xinyi Zhang (Shu), Dawei Tong (Major Li), Atsuro Watabe (Colonel Hasegawa), Shigeo Kobayashi (Lieutenant Kato), Kefan Cao (Mr. Meng). Directed by Zhang Yimou and produced by Zhang Weiping. Screenplay by Heng Liu, based on the novel by Yan Geling.

One of the ancient ploys of the film industry is to make a film about nonwhite people and find a way, however convoluted, to tell it from the point of view of a white character. *The Help* (2011) is a recent example: The film is essentially about how poor, hardworking black maids in Mississippi empowered a young white woman to write a best-seller about them. *Glory* (1989) is about a Civil War regiment of black soldiers; the story is seen through the eyes of their white commander.

One of the last places you'd expect to see this practice is in a Chinese film. But what else can we make of Zhang Yimou's *Flowers of War*? It takes place during the Rape of Nanking (1937–38), one of the most horrifying atrocities in history, during which the Japanese Imperial Army invaded the Chinese capital city and slaughtered an estimated three hundred thousand civilians, usually raping the women first. It is one thing for civilians to die in the course of a war, and another for them to be hunted down and wiped out on a personal basis for the crime of their race. This chapter in history came to wide attention in the United States after the publication of *The Rape of Nanking* (1997), a best-seller by Iris Chang, a young Chinese-American whose depression over the facts she uncovered possibly led to her suicide.

Now we have the first fiction film about this event by one of the leading Chinese directors, who contrives to tell it through the experiences of a drunken American mortician named John Miller (Christian Bale). This man finds himself in Nanking at the time, misses a chance to escape the city, and ends up hiding out in a huge Catholic cathedral that is theoretically neutral ground.

Also sheltering in the cathedral are about twenty-five young Chinese women, divided between schoolgirls and prostitutes. Miller is a mess in the early scenes of the film, but slowly he pulls himself together, sobers up, dresses in a priest's vestments, and takes on the responsibility of protecting the women. He's assisted by a young man named George (Tianyuan Huang), whose owlish spectacles and little cap make him look ineffectual and set him up for heroism.

The cathedral is surrounded by Japanese troops, who occupy the whole city and are now routinely shooting all civilians on sight. For the time being those inside the walls of the cathedral grounds are safe, but to leave means the certainty of death. Miller's improvisations and quick thinking, and the partial cooperation of a Japanese officer who loves music and is therefore not all evil, you see, keeps the women alive despite some close calls. This episodic cliff-hanging sustains the narrative; a third of a million may be dead, but for our purposes all depends on the survival of these young women, and the redemption of the alcoholic American. Do you get my drift?

Spoiler warning. The Japanese outside the cathedral know about the schoolchildren but not about the hookers in the wine cellar. The music-loving Japanese officer invites the girls to come and sing at a party for his staff. It is virtually certain this will lead to their rape and murder. The prostitutes have also undergone a process of redemption and now, no longer crass and self-serving, they nobly volunteer to switch clothing with the girls and take their places. Then it will be up to "Father John" to somehow save the students.

*The Flowers of War* is in many ways a good film, as we expect from Zhang Yimou (*Ju Dou, Raise the Red Lantern, To Live*). It is handsomely photographed. Its exteriors were apparently shot on sets, including an impressive one of the cathedral and its surrounding grounds. Christian Bale grows tiresome as a drunk, but then straightens up and is an adequate hero, although lacking in depth and background. Yu Mo, the leader of the prostitutes, is played in an effective heart-of-gold way by Ni Ni. Tianyuan Huang is good as George, but there is never a danger of him stealing a scene.

Now let me ask you: Can you think of any reason why the character John Miller is needed to tell this story? Was any consideration given to the possibility of a Chinese priest? Would that be asking for too much?

## Footloose ★ ½

PG-13, 113 m., 2011

Kenny Wormald (Ren MacCormack), Julianne Hough (Ariel Moore), Dennis Quaid (Reverend Shaw Moore), Andie MacDowell (Vi Moore), Miles Teller (Willard), Ziah Colon (Rusty), Patrick John Flueger (Chuck Cranston). Directed by Craig Brewer and produced by Gary Barber, Roger Birnbaum, Neil Meron, Dylan Sellers, Brad Weston, and Craig Zadan. Screenplay by Brewer and Dean Pitchford.

There's one thing to be said for a remake of a 1984 movie that uses the original screenplay. This 2011 version is so similar—sometimes song for song and line for line—that I was wickedly tempted to reprint my 1984 review, word for word. But That Would Be Wrong. I think I could have gotten away with it, though. The movies differ in such tiny details (the hero now moves to Tennessee from Boston, not Chicago) that few would have noticed.

Was there then, or is there now, a town in Tennessee or any other state in which the city council has passed a law against "dancing in public"? There may have been a brief period, soon after Elvis first began grinding his pelvis and preachers denounced rock 'n' roll as "the devil's music." But for most young moviegoers this plot point is going to seem so unlikely as to be bizarre.

We again get a plot in which a high school beer party leads to a fatal crash, taking the lives of five teenagers. The city council bans the music, under the influence of Rev. Shaw Moore (Dennis Quaid). Rev. Moore, who seems to be the only preacher in town, acts as the de facto civic moral leader. He is paranoid about his daughter, Ariel (Julianne Hough), a free spirit who attracts the attention of a local bad kid, Chuck Cranston (Patrick John Flueger).

Ren MacCormack (Kenny Wormald) arrives in the hamlet of Bomont from Boston. He's got the Kevin Bacon role, but not the Kevin Bacon charisma; the Reverend Shaw Moore should be able to take one look at Ren and figure he's harmless. But Ren gets arrested for playing his car radio too loud, and soon is leading a movement of the town's kids to petition the council to allow dancing—in public, anyway. This is the setup for several dance scenes where those kids seem suspiciously well-choreographed for a town where they have allegedly never danced.

Meanwhile, the loutish Chuck Cranston, who considers Ariel his girl, resents Ren because he's attracting Ariel's smiles. This Chuck is a knuckle-dragging bully who patrols in his pickup truck with a posse of sidekicks. Attention, Posse Members of Bullies: When the local bully tools around in his pickup, but makes you guys all ride back there in the truck bed, you are being disrespected. What, aren't you good enough to ride up front with Chuck?

The bad boys and girls in high school movies always have a posse, usually two or three members, who follow close behind their leader and look ominous and slack-jawed. Are they issued instructions? Are they told, "Walk a few steps behind me and look worshipful"?

This new *Footloose* is a film without wit, humor, or purpose. It sets up the town elders as old farts who hate rock 'n' roll. Does it have a clue that the Reverend Shaw Moore and all the other city council members are young enough that they grew up on rock 'n' roll? The film's message is this: A bad movie, if faithfully remade, will produce another bad movie.

## Footnote ★ ★ ★ ★

PG, 106 m., 2012

Shlomo Bar-Aba (Eliezer Shkolnik), Lior Ashkenazi (Uriel Shkolnik), Alisa Rosen (Yehudit Shkolnik), Alma Zak (Dikla Shkolnik), Daniel Markovich (Josh Shkolnik), Micah Lewesohn (Yehuda Grossman). Directed by Joseph Cedar and produced by Cedar, Leon Edery, Moshe Edery, and David Mandil. Screenplay by Cedar.

When I describe *Footnote*, you may conclude that it offers little for you. In fact, it's one of the smartest and most merciless comedies to come along in a while. It centers on an area of fairly narrow interest, but in its study of human nature, it is deep and takes no prisoners. There are two main characters: The father has devoted his life to scratching out minute inconsistencies in various versions of the Talmud. His son is a great popularizer of Judaic lore, whose books are best-sellers and whose face is often on television.

Eliezer (Shlomo Bar Aba), the father, has labored for years without much recognition. He takes great pride in once having been mentioned in a footnote of a book by a legendary scholar. Uriel (Lior Ashkenazi), the son, is one of those facile popularizers to whom everything comes easily. The film opens in a teeth-grating ceremony where the son is receiving a prestigious prize, and his father is seated stony-faced in the audience. Uriel goes out of his way to praise the old man, but this serves only to reflect on the old man's obscurity and Eliezer knows it.

The film could be about a father-son rivalry in any field. I once had a professor who was a Great Man, the editor of a much-honored edition of Shakespeare. Among his other feats was the variorum edition of *Romeo and Juliet.* That involved the meticulous comparison of all the editions of Shakespeare's tragedy, noting every variance and allowing the reader to approach as closely as possible to Shakespeare's original words. I remember sitting in a campus coffee shop, buzzing with caffeine and underlining passages so that I, too, could determine the correct reading.

That may sound boring as hell to you, but I'd been to this man's book-jammed office in the English building, and his quest seemed to me grand and romantic. Imagine how he would have felt to know that in a few decades, all his heavy lifting would be done by a computer. Ah, but it was his *judgment* that mattered, not his years of footnotes. In that sense, Uriel has moved directly to the end stage and made his father's labor seem like busywork.

*Footnote*, a 2012 Oscar nominee for best foreign film, benefits from uncanny casting. Much of its success comes from the presence of the actors themselves. The story pendulum swings back and forth between father and son, who are both sympathetic and both tiresome and mean-spirited. We are expected to know nothing about the Talmud except that they believe it justifies their lifework. As we meet their wives, we sense that what benefit it has done them hasn't been reflected in their marriages. Nor has it inspired a good father and good son.

All of this leads up to a masterful series of ethical dilemmas in the last half of the film. The Talmud provides guidance to Jews about how to lead their lives, but these two Jews have learned nothing that helps them when they find themselves in an impossible situation. Please be aware that a plot point is about to be revealed.

The greatest honor available to either man is the Israel Prize. Eliezer receives a phone call congratulating him on having won it. Vindication at last for a lifetime of labor! Then Uriel is told a stunning piece of information. The father was mistakenly called. The prize was actually voted to the son. This cannot be. For the old man to be announced as the winner and then have the prize snatched away is a species of humiliation almost unimaginable.

So much for the spoiler. The film's richest scenes are still to come, and I will not spoil them. They involve an emergency meeting of the Israel Prize committee, and the involvement of the old curmudgeon Grossman (Micah Lewesohn), who is the chairman. There is a deadly serious meeting of six or seven scholars in an office large enough for two, and the choreography is hilarious. An apparent solution is arrived at. Grossman, who has been a lifelong saboteur of Eliezer's work, has demands that must be met. And then, in a brilliant montage, we see Eliezer at work. The most crucial textual reading of his life takes place, ironically, in connection with this personal crisis.

There's more comedy in the film, some of it involving Eliezer's ignorance of modern publicity and public relations, some of it indicating that in his ivory tower he doesn't know what security guards are. It's a rich irony that when Eliezer is interviewed by a reporter, he shoots himself in his own foot. What happens is a series of events involving academic scholarship, familial jealousy and pride, stubbornness, and poetic justice. All of these things come together wonderfully, and are so subtle that only the father and the son will completely understand them. Perfect.

## For Colored Girls ★ ★ ½

R, 134 m., 2010

Janet Jackson (Jo), Loretta Devine (Juanita), Michael Ealy (Beau Willie), Kimberly Elise (Crystal), Omari Hardwick (Carl), Hill Harper (Donald), Thandie Newton (Tangie), Phylicia Rashad (Gilda), Anika Noni Rose (Yasmine), Tessa Thompson (Nyla), Kerry Washington (Kelly), Whoopi Goldberg (Alice). Directed by Tyler Perry and produced by Perry, Roger M. Bobb, and Paul Hall. Screenplay by Perry, based on the stage play *For Colored Girls Who Have Considered Suicide When the Rainbow Is Enuf* by Ntozake Shange.

Some plays resist filming. They exist as stage fantasies that can't survive the greater realism of the cinema. When a stage character performs a soliloquy, we understand exactly what's happening. When a film character does it, it can feel strange. A monologue on film, sure—but not a poetic construction unlike the ordinary speech in the same film.

Tyler Perry's ambitious *For Colored Girls* is based on the famous play *For Colored Girls Who Have Considered Suicide When the Rainbow Is Enuf* by Ntozake Shange. Many in the audience will have seen it onstage, and that will be an advantage; they'll understand what Perry is attempting. Ordinary moviegoers, accustomed to Perry's mainline films, are likely to be thrown off by the unconventional approach here. Perry tries to be faithful to the stage play and also to his own boldly and simply told stories, and the two styles don't fit together.

He also paints a cluttered canvas. The play featured seven characters in seven places with seven kinds of problems. He adds three other significant roles in order to flesh out actions that the play described in prose. This is too literal. His actors do an effective job with their soliloquies, but the audience is tugged back and forth between the stylized speech and the straight dramatic material.

Too bad. What a cast he has assembled: Kimberly Elise (Crystal), Janet Jackson (Jo),

Loretta Devine (Juanita), Thandie Newton (Tangie), Anika Noni Rose (Yasmine), Kerry Washington (Kelly), Tessa Thompson (Nyla), and Whoopi Goldberg (Alice). Then there's Phylicia Rashad as a wise woman who lives in the same apartment house with six of the others, sees all, and provides a running commentary.

The Rashad character is new. So are Beau Willie (Michael Ealy), a war veteran and victim of posttraumatic stress syndrome who obsesses about Crystal; and Carl (Omari Hardwick), a rich, closeted gay conducting a doomed marriage with Jo. Crystal works for Jo, an imperious magazine editor, establishing some class conflict. The movie, like the play, distributes other problems among the women, so that we seem to be moving among episodes of a soap opera.

The award-winning Ntozake Shange play is justly respected, but I'm not sure it's filmmable, and I'm pretty sure it wasn't a wise choice for Perry. He seems more at home with everyday, human-comedy types of people, and here I think he is, if anything, too wary of his material. If he'd gone all the way in rewriting it into more conventional drama, he might have been criticized by lovers of the play, but he might have made a more entertaining and accessible film.

That's not to say *For Colored Girls* doesn't have its virtues. Seeing these actresses together is a poignant reminder of their gifts, and of the absence of interesting roles for actresses in general and African-American ones in particular. A generation has been often shut out of fruitful roles. I saw the movie twice, and although it never worked for me as a whole, the second time I found myself appreciating many of its parts more. The soliloquies don't fit, but taken as freestanding dramatic entries, they're strongly done. So there are elements here, but not a fully rounded film.

## Forget Me Not ★ ★ ½

NO MPAA RATING, 92 m., 2011

Tobias Menzies (Will), Genevieve O'Reilly (Eve), Gemma Jones (Eve's grandmother). Directed by Alexander Holt and Lance Roehrig and produced by Rebecca Long. Screenplay by Mark Underwood.

*Forget Me Not* seemed for an hour as if I had walked this way before, and then it took me in a new direction. The film is about a thirtyish couple who Meet Sorta Cute and end up sharing an all-night meander through London. They banter, they share, they separate and join up again, they even take a ride on the London Eye; and all the while I was wondering why *Before Sunrise* needed to be remade. Then the sun rose and the buried nature of the story became transformed.

The movie begins in a pub, where Will (Tobias Menzies) is the singer and Eve (Genevieve O'Reilly) is tending bar. He leaves, he walks to his nearby flat, and a very private moment is interrupted by a call from Eve: He forgot his guitar. Then he sees out the window that she's in a tussle with a drunk, hurries downstairs to rescue her, and they begin their all-night walk.

They are friendly. They exchange some personal information, not much. They're both taciturn, although she conceals that with cheerfulness. We know he is sad—more than she realizes. They have a small encounter with a bachelorette party, split, and later find themselves at the same club. The opening of the club scene is intriguing, showing dancers seemingly dancing to the sounds of their own shoes, until we figure it out.

They walk some more. They pretty much wander from above St. Paul's down the embankment, the streets mostly deserted, the Houses of Parliament making a background appearance. Like many Londoners, they seem impervious to the wonders they walk past. I'm glad I never lived in London after all. I would hate to ever get used to it.

On the next day, he goes along with her to the care home where her grandmother (Gemma Jones) will be taking one of those tests that ominously open by asking you what year it is, and how old you are. And now I will take a big step back from the plot and let it unfold on its own.

A couple of points: (1) If your hero is going to sing in the movie, give him better songs. (2) Although the cinematography is handsome, a couple of shots fall to the temptation of being about themselves and not the story—the foreground chess game in the coffee shop, for example, which has nothing to do with anything.

This is a civilized and empathetic film, but Will and Eve are so reserved and cautious, and as it moves along too deliberately you realize what a brilliant job Richard Linklater, Ethan Hawke, and Julie Delpy did with *Before Sunrise*. The ending conceals an emotional impact, sad and carefully orchestrated, but the film isn't very compelling.

## The Forgiveness of Blood ★ ★ ½

NO MPAA RATING, 109 m., 2012

Tristan Halilaj (Nik), Sindi Lacej (Rudina), Refet Abazi (Mark), Ilire Vinca Celaj (Drita), Cun Lajci (Ded), Zana Hasaj (Nik's girlfriend), Luan Jaha (Mark's Brother), Veton Osmani (Sokol). Directed by Joshua Marston and produced by Paul S. Mezey. Screenplay by Marston and Andamion Murataj.

Here is a film in which modern-day Albania, with cell phones, superhighways, and texting teenagers, comes into conflict with an ancient code of honor that threatens to place an entire family under indefinite house arrest. *The Forgiveness of Blood* could be a metaphor for many things, but it's most obviously about young people filled with life and old ones mired in a past of blood feuds and hatred.

We meet a family supported by Mark (Refet Abazi), who sells bread from a creaking one-horse cart. The cart looks overwhelmed by giant trailer trucks and speeding traffic. One day he takes the same shortcut his family has used for generations, but is stopped by a hot-headed neighbor, Sokol (Veton Osmani), who demands Mark stop crossing his land. To take the long way around would cost Mark's family its livelihood.

Sokol may have legal control of the right-of-way (which used to be in Mark's family), but how does a cart harm a road? He's looking for a fight, and he gets one. Mark and his brother return, and Sokol is killed. The death is not seen on-screen. Instead, we see the aftermath.

An Albanian code named the Kanun dictates that a member of the family guilty of murder must himself be killed or jailed. Mark's brother is jailed, but Mark goes into hiding, which means his entire family can be killed by members of Sokol's family if they venture outside their house. This is especially hard on Nik (Tristan Halilaj), a teenage son, and his slightly younger sister Rudina (Sindi Lacej). Cut off from his girlfriend, Nik goes stir-crazy and tells his father he should give himself up to the police and release the family from house arrest. Mark seems to think his family owes it to him to lock themselves up because he was defending their honor.

One is reminded of other societies ruled by foolish subservience to books written for other times and places. In this district men grow old, brandish fierce beards, and brood over the wrongs of the past. Women seem more sensible, and Rudina is the heroine of the film, a mediator in her family, a resourceful income earner.

Under a dispensation, Rudina can continue to sell bread and quickly upgrades to more profitable cigarettes. It is hard to see how a modern family could support itself from goods sold from the little cart, but never mind; they do.

The film was directed by Joshua Marston, an American whose previous work was the much-loved *Maria Full of Grace* (2004), about a pregnant young Colombian woman who in desperation works as a drug mule. Catalina Sandino Moreno was an Oscar nominee as best actress for that film. Both films show women as breadwinners in a male-ruled society.

What seems missing is a good notion of how this Albanian society functions on a daily basis. Surely a family cannot live under house arrest forever? Surely a modern police and court system can deal with matters leading to blood feuds? Apparently not. Although the villain here is the man who forbids passage to the cart, anyone could have been killed in the fight—the unseen fight, which makes the point. Apparently the right-of-way was only the occasion for bloodshed in a feud that had long been simmering.

Watching the film, I felt impatience with these bullheaded men and the women who endured them. That's what Marston intended, I'm sure, but the stupidity of the characters doesn't provide much of an emotional payoff here. And consider how the film ends, with shots of the brother and sister. What are their futures? Is a film obliged to provide us with a satisfactory ending? No, but this one seems especially passive and futile.

## For Greater Glory ★ ★ ½

R, 143 m., 2012

Andy Garcia (General Enrique Gorostieta Velarde), Oscar Isaac ("El Catorce" Ramirez), Catalina Sandino Moreno (Adriana), Santiago Cabrera (Father Vega), Ruben Blades (President Calles), Eva Longoria (Tulita Gorostieta), Peter O'Toole (Father Christopher). Directed by Dean Wright and produced by Pablo Jose Barroso. Screenplay by Michael Love.

In the years 1926 through 1929, Mexico fought a war over the freedom of Roman Catholics to worship. After the Mexican Revolution, the constitution of 1917 stripped great power from the Church, along with half of its enormous land holdings. But it was not until President Plutarco Elias Calles began to strictly enforce the constitution that he provoked an uprising. Supporters of the church, who called themselves Cristeros, began a campaign against federal troops, and had surprising success after they hired General Gorostieta Velarde to lead their forces.

An atheist and a hero of the revolution, Gorostieta signed on both for the cash and because he supported the principle of religious freedom. In the context of a new English-language epic called *For Greater Glory*, that principle apparently applies only to Catholics. No other religion is ever mentioned. The war took heavy casualties on both sides, and the United States played a behind-the-scenes role in protecting the interests of U.S. oil companies whose concessions controlled much of Mexico's oil.

This war has all the elements to make it well-known, but I confess I'd never heard of it. A close Mexican-American friend of mine, well informed on Mexico, told me yesterday she never has either. Is it in the usual history books? You'll learn a lot about it in *For Greater Glory*, the most expensive film ever made in Mexico; it is an ambitious production with a cast filled with stars.

It is well made, yes, but has such pro-Catholic tunnel vision that I began to question its view of events. One particularly important subplot involves a twelve-year-old boy choosing to die for his faith. Of course the federal troops who shot him were monsters, but the film seems to approve of his decision and includes him approvingly in a long list of Cristeros who have achieved sainthood or beatification after their deaths in the war.

The film's central figure is General Gorostieta, played by Andy Garcia with impressive strength and presence. He values his own leadership expertise, defends the fact that he is serving because of the money, and indeed is a brilliant general. There's an effective sequence where he warns a jealous Cristero leader he is probably leading his men into an ambush. The man won't listen. Gorostieta lets him go, and then leads his own troops up behind the ambushing *federales*, who are exactly where he predicted they would be.

President Calles (Ruben Blades), who at first can't believe the Cristeros can possibly be successful, pursues the war beyond what seems to be all common sense. It is one thing to enforce legal restraints on the church, and another—a riskier one—to order such extremes as sending all the bishops and foreign-born clergy out of the country and authorizing the murder of some priests in their own churches. Peter O'Toole stars in an early sequence as a seventy-seven-year-old priest who is killed by the *federales*, and it is young Jose (Mauricio Kuri), the altar boy who sees him die, who later becomes the martyr.

So dedicated are Jose and a young friend to the Cristero cause that they ride out on horseback and find the secret camp of General Gorostieta. He rejects them as soldiers and puts them to work caring for horses. But his love for the boy grows so much that he regards him as a son, and indeed the boy dies only because he is on a mission for Gorostieta. The general surely deserves some of the blame for putting a child in a hazardous position.

*For Greater Glory* is the kind of long, expensive epic not much made anymore. It bears the hallmarks of a labor of love. I suspect it's too long for some audiences. It is also very heavy on battle scenes, in which the Cristeros seem to have uncannily good aim. But in its use of locations and sets, it's an impressive achievement by director Dean Wright, whose credits include some of the effects on the *Lord of the Rings* films. If it had not hewed so single-mindedly to the Catholic view and included all religions under the banner of religious liberty, I believe it would have been more effective. If your religion doesn't respect the rights of other religions, it is lacking something.

## Forks Over Knives ★ ★ ★

PG, 90 m., 2011

Dr. T. Colin Campbell, Dr. Caldwell Esselstyn Jr., Dr. Neil Barnard, Dr. John McDougall, and others. A documentary directed by Lee Fulkerson and produced by John Corry. Screenplay by Fulkerson.

Here is a film that could save your life. So you'd better stop reading now, because you don't want to go to the trouble. You are addicted to fat, salt, sugar, and corn syrup. Your body has established a narcoticlike dependence on them, and you're comfortable with that, just like smokers know why they keep on smoking. If you have to die ten or twenty-five years sooner than necessary, if you need Viagra because your vascular system is compromised, if you're overweight, you can live with that.

Hey, I'm not going all holier-than-thou on you. Think how fat I was for years. I knew the solution; I was weak and lazy. Over twelve years I was eventually able to lose about seventy pounds with a proper diet, but my current weight and superb physical condition can be attributed to my illness. I am unable to eat or drink anything, and my (therefore) perfect diet of canned nutrition has given me an ideal weight and incredibly good blood numbers. I don't recommend that you get sick to get well, however.

What every human being should do is eat a vegetarian diet based on whole foods. Period. That's it. Animal protein is bad for you. Dairy is bad for you. Forget the ads: Milk and eggs are bad for you. Skim milk is no better because it contains proportionately more animal protein. What you're trying to avoid is dietary cholesterol. You also need to cut way down on salt and sugar, and run like hell from high fructose corn syrup.

*Forks Over Knives* is a documentary in which Lee Fulkerson enacts a mirror image of the journey taken by Morgan Spurlock in *Super Size Me.* Instead of eating only at McDonald's for a month and nearly killing himself, he eats a plant-based whole-food diet for six months, gets off all of his cholesterol and blood pressure medications, drops a lot of weight, sleeps better, and has more energy.

His film follows three other sick people, one with breast cancer, one given less than a year to live because of heart problems, one with murderously high cholesterol. All are well again after following the vegetarian diet. The movie opens with a warning that no one should take such steps without consulting a physician, and I quite agree; I would not have depended on nutrition to cure my cancer, but I'm convinced that I would always have been healthier if I'd eaten correctly.

The film hammers us with information. It centers on the work of the famed nutritionists Dr. T. Colin Campbell of Cornell and Dr. Caldwell Esselstyn Jr. of the Cleveland Clinic. Campbell conducted the awesome China-Oxford-Cornell study, which followed millions of Chinese over decades and found that increases in their incidence of cancer and heart disease directly paralleled their adoption of a Western diet. Short-term studies show the same thing: When Nazis commandeered all the food animals in Norway, and rationing forced Brits away from meat, disease rates plummeted. After the war, they moved up again. On the traditional Japanese diet, breast and prostate cancers are all but unknown.

These facts have long been established, not only by Campbell and Esselstyn but by such as Dean Ornish, John McDougall, and the researchers at Pritikin. There is a catch-22. The federal government subsidizes such crops as corn, which is used for lethal corn syrup and to feed animals that we then eat. It puts bad foods in school lunches. The lobbyists of agribusiness control national farm policy. The government spends millions to subsidize an unhealthy diet. We are raising the first generation of children who will not live as long as their parents.

Over the years I tried vegan and low-protein vegetarian diets, benefitted from them and enjoyed them. I found by experience that all one needed was a rice cooker, a knife, a chopping block, whole grains, and fresh fruits and vegetables. I got all the protein and calcium I needed. I enjoyed it. But I was tempted. I strayed into the elysian fields of pizza, steaks, hamburgers, and soft drinks. I once was blind and now I see.

*Forks Over Knives* is not a subtle film. It plays as if it had been made for doctors to see in medical school. Few doctors seem prepared to suggest proper nutrition as an alternative to pills, stents, and bypasses. Although regular exercise, especially walking, is invaluable, the film shows only a little exercise and focuses single-mindedly on nutrition.

The bottom line: I am convinced this message is true. A plant-based whole-foods diet is healthy. Animal protein is not necessary, or should be used sparingly as Asians did, as a flavoring and not a main course. This adds the advantage of allowing us to avoid the chemicals and carcinogens pumped into livestock and poultry. Fast food is lethal. Parents who feed it to their children are helping them get hooked on fat, salt, and sugar. The facts are in. Didn't I warn you to stop reading?

P.S. I have recently decided to ditch my canned nutrition and switch to a liquid diet based on fresh fruits and vegetables. Yes, I consulted my physician.

## Formosa Betrayed ★ ★ ½

R, 100 m., 2010

James Van Der Beek (Jake Kelly), Will Tiao (Ming), Kenneth Tsang (General Tse), Tzi Ma (Kuo), Wendy Crewson (Susan Kane), John Heard (Tom Braxton), Leslie Hope (Lisa Gilbert). Directed by Adam Kane and produced by Kane, David Allen Cluck, and Will Tiao. Screenplay by Tiao, Charlie Stratton, Yann Samuell, Brian Askew, Nathaniel Goodman, and Katie Swain.

*Formosa Betrayed* is a political thriller with an agenda. It argues that Formosa, now known as Taiwan, has been the pawn of great powers for centuries. Occupied by Japan in the prewar years, it was claimed by the Nationalists of Chiang Kai-shek after the war, and his army retreated there after its defeat by Red China. Although Americans have long been schooled that Chiang flew the banner of freedom, the film says he seized property, killed thousands of native Formosans, wiped out the leadership class, and established a dictatorship.

This history is related to an FBI agent named Kelly (James Van Der Beek), who has been sent to Taiwan to act as "liaison" in the search for the murderer of a prominent Taiwanese professor in Lake Forest, Illinois. Why Kelly—who speaks no Chinese and scarcely knows that Taiwan was once named Formosa? Perhaps precisely because of his ignorance. In the Cold War years, neither Washington nor Taipei want a scandal. The story takes place in 1983, but that hasn't changed.

Kelly flies in, is greeted by an American official named Susan Kane (Wendy Crewson), and is whisked off to a lavish welcome party while his key witness is being murdered. Secretly contacted by friends of the dead Lake Forest professor, he realizes their lives, and his, are in danger from the police state. At this point, the movie takes hold. Earlier, it seemed to linger overmuch on past history, including even newsreel footage from World War II and Chiang meeting Roosevelt and Churchill.

We realize, somewhat to our surprise, that *Formosa Betrayed* is a thriller that's actually *about* something. Most thrillers are about the good guy trying to outshoot and outrun the bad guys, and their settings are incidental. This one has a bone to chew. One of the screenplay writers is Will Tiao, who also plays Ming, the film's Taiwanese hero, an underground activist committed to regaining control of the island for its original Formosans.

I sense that his desire to make a point about history was equally or more important for the filmmakers than making a taut thriller. That explains the title *Formosa Betrayed*, which is completely accurate in terms of the story, but uses a name for the island that hasn't been current for fifty years. That it works fairly well as a thriller is a tribute to the actors, particularly Tiao, whose emotion can be felt as he relates his homeland's history.

James Van Der Beek's FBI agent might be skilled enough at domestic crime, but Kelly is out of his element in Taiwan. It's when he realizes this that the movie engages. One detail struck me: Van Der Beek insists on the official three-day beard required by all action heroes to signal their pumping testosterone. But in 1983, the FBI required its agents to be clean-shaven. And the action is set in the year before the first season of *Miami Vice,* which popularized the obligatory stubble.

Wendy Crewson's role seems thankless at first: She's limited to advising Kelly to cool it and asking him to keep his nose out of Taiwan's business. Turns out that she and Kelly's boss (John Heard) know many things the agent doesn't. As a result, *Formosa Betrayed* begins as rather clunky, but ends by making a statement that explains a great many things. One question left unasked: Why did we promise to defend Taiwan with nuclear weapons, but refuse to recognize it as a sovereign nation?

## 45365 ★ ★ ★ ★

NO MPAA RATING, 91 m., 2010

Featuring the townspeople of Sidney, Ohio. A documentary directed by Bill Ross IV and Turner Ross. Produced by Bill Ross IV.

The first shot tells us "45365 is the zip code of this city." In this achingly beautiful film, that zip code belongs to Sidney, Ohio, a handsome town of about twenty thousand residents. The brothers Bill and Turner Ross were born there perhaps thirty years ago. Of course they knew everybody in town, and when they spent seven months of 2007 filming its daily life, their presence must have eventually become commonplace. Their film evokes what *Winesburg, Ohio,* might have looked like as a documentary.

Take me for an example. I knew everyone in the film. I grew up there. Well, actually in zip code 61802, which is Urbana, Illinois. My hometown was close to Sidney, Illinois, just as 45365 is not far from Urbana, Ohio. There are also towns named Homer and Philo near both towns named Urbana. East central Illinois was settled by people from Ohio.

In my midwestern town, I knew these people, their homes, their friendliness, the trouble some of them got into, and I knew why after the high school football game some of the kids hung out under the arc lamps and others were in the shade of the bleachers with the hoods pulled up on their sweatshirts. I even recognized, because I once covered the police beat, exactly the tone of voice a policeman will use after stopping a drunk driver he's known for ten years.

The film is privileged. No one is filmed with a hidden camera. The camera must have been right there, in the living room, the riverbank, the barbershop, the backseat, the football practice, the front lawn when a man agrees to put up a sign supporting a judge running for re-election. The Rosses must have filmed so much they became both trusted and invisible. They know this town without even thinking about it.

There is a beautiful shot during a church service that pans slowly to the right over the congregation and pauses looking into a door to a stairwell. A woman and small girl come up the stairs. The camera follows them back to the left until the girl is deposited back in her pew, having obviously just been taken to the potty. Were those two people cued? Obviously not. I suggest the cameraman, Bill or Turner, observed them getting up, intuited where they were going and why, and composed the camera movement instinctively. A brief shot you may not even consciously notice, but a perfect shot, reading the room as our minds do. All human life is in it.

I've never seen a barbershop like the one in the film. All three barbers are surprisingly young; one seems to be a teenager. Yet there is the order and routine of a small-town barbershop with barbers as old as Moses. Do these kids own the shop? Well, why not? It would cost less than a Supercuts franchise. What do they talk about? What all barbers talk about: the Friday night football game.

Sidney has what can only be described as a great radio station. Local human beings sit before the mics and run the boards. This station isn't a robot from Los Angeles. They play hits of the '80s and '90s, they make announcements, they have a sports talk show about the Sidney Yellowjackets. The team has a chicken-dinner benefit coming up. Adults seven dollars, kids three dollars.

It looks like rain on the day of the parade, but the station's reporter is on the spot. He's hooked up via his cell phone, and interviews a woman on the street with a tiny mic he holds up to his mouth and then to hers. He tells everyone to come on downtown, the skies are clearing. At the carnival, Elvis Junior is onstage. It's pouring rain. A guy uses a broom to push up the canvas roof of the tent and spill out the rainwater. A mobile home has been painted up as an exhibit for "LIVE! The World's Smallest Woman!"

Trains rumble through Sidney on business of their own. The radio station is used for the judicial candidate to record ". . . and I approve of this message." A man goes to court for sentencing. Drunk. We've seen two of his former wives agreeing that he needs to get his act together. They argue over whether he left the one *for* the other, or left the one and *then* married the other. They don't exactly seem to be fighting over him.

Spring, summer, autumn, winter. Summer showers. The first snow falling out at the abandoned drive-in theater. Music on Radio 105.5. Lawns. Good-looking old buildings. Sidney still looks like a town, not a squatter's camp of fast-food outlets. One extraordinarily stupid review of the film complains "all of these situations are filmed as if we already know the story of who these people are. We don't even learn anyone's names." This isn't that kind of a documentary. If you need to know everybody's name, you'll never, ever understand this film. Hell, I could go to Sidney, Ohio, tomorrow and feel right at home.

*Note: 45365 won the $25,000 Roger and Chaz Ebert Truer Than Fiction Award at the 2010 Independent Spirits. The contest was independently judged.*

## Four Lions ★ ★ ★

R, 101 m., 2010

Riz Ahmed (Omar), Arsher Ali (Hassan), Nigel Lindsay (Barry), Kayvan Novak (Waj), Adeel Akhtar (Faisal), Preeya Kalidas (Sofia). Directed by Chris Morris and produced by Mark Herbert and Derrin Schlesinger. Screenplay by Morris, Jesse Armstrong, and Sam Bain.

There's a difference between blowing up people and blowing up things. When the African National Congress in South Africa was bombing power pylons, that made strategic sense. When terrorists blow up people (and themselves), it strikes me as self-defeating idiocy. Believing in heaven is commonplace. But surely only a stupid person would blow himself up to get there sooner.

*Four Lions* is a transgressive comedy about five such people. They live in an anonymous British suburb and dream of jihad. They speak such a fluent mixture of working-class Brit slang and argot, in such fluent accents, that it's odd to hear their radical beliefs in such commonplace slang.

All are Muslims. Four have Pakistani roots. One is a red-bearded Brit whose ideas are the most aggressive. They conduct a scheme to strap bombs to their bodies and strike against society. In this scheme they are so amateurish they fly below the radar of British intelligence. Nor do they have a very clear plan; Barry, the convert, believes they should blow up a mosque to radicalize Muslim moderates. The catch-22 here is that therefore the bomber should be a white Westerner. Hello, Barry.

*Four Lions* is impossible to categorize. It's an exceedingly dark comedy, a wicked satire, a thriller where the thrills center on the incompetence of the villains. It's fueled by both merriment and anger. It shows characters so dazzled by the prospect of the next life that they have no care for their present lives—or ours. It is about Muslims but also about the fundamentalist mind-set in general, which admits no doubt.

Consider Omar (Riz Ahmed), who I suppose is the film's closest thing to a hero. He has a loving wife, named Sofia (Preeya Kalidas), and a sweet child. He works as a security guard. He has a comfortable flat, where he studies terrorist videos on his laptop. He despairs of the ignorance of some of his comrades (one has "special needs"), but perhaps thinks even the stupid are useful as suicide bombers. Omar and his wife openly discuss his plans without a shred of doubt.

The others seem to be average blokes, apart from their fanaticism. They all seem serene about the prospect of blowing themselves up; they attach much importance to entering heaven with smiles on their faces. They have either not received or were unable to benefit from an education preparing themselves for reality. This is sad, and all the more so because the "four lions" (and a young recruit they pick up) are so satisfied with themselves.

There are elements of slapstick, particularly involving an unfortunate sheep (who was "harmed during the making of this film" the end titles tell us). And the climactic sequence involves the four men dressing up in bizarre clown costumes to run in the London Marathon. Why? To blow up other marathoners?

In the course of this plan, one lion locks himself inside a kebab shop, taking the owner and three customers hostage. When he's reached by a police negotiator and asked for his demands, he . . . doesn't have any. He seems, indeed, to have little idea why he has a bomb strapped to himself. The importance of blowing himself up and arriving in heaven with a smile has overshadowed any mundane considerations.

*Four Lions* was directed by Chris Morris, a British TV and radio satirist, and cowritten by Morris, Sam Bain, and Jesse Armstrong (who wrote the political satire *In the Loop*). They have made the film with heedless abandon. Its strategy is to regard imbecility with a poker face, and permit horrifying acts to occur absentmindedly. Sometimes this is funny and sometimes not at all, but you can't call it boring.

## Four Lovers ★ ½

NO MPAA RATING, 103 m., 2012

Marina Fois (Rachel), Elodie Bouchez (Teri), Roschdy Zem (Franck), Nicolas Duvauchelle (Vincent), Jean-Francois Stevenin (Rachel's Father), Alexia Stresi (Diane), Blanche Gardin (Rachel's Sister), Genevieve Mnich (Franck's Mother), Philippe Paimblanc (Franck's Father). Directed by Antony Cordier and produced by Pascal Caucheteux and Sebastien Lemercier. Screenplay by Cordier and Julie Peyr.

At one point in *Four Lovers*, the four lovers go into the pantry of an old French country house, pour bags full of white flour on the cobblestone floor, strip, and roll around on the flour while having sex. They begin languorously, in voluptuous caresses, but you can't fool me. Cobblestones have a decided detumescent effect. If you ever find yourself in such a situation, insist on being the missionary.

This is a movie about two married couples who decide to share each other's mates. There is little fascinating about them before they decide this, and still less after, because when it comes right down to it, looking at a lot of sex is not nearly as much fun as having it. The rolling around in the flour sequence is so tedious I had to fast-forward through part of it. You know there's something wrong with a sex movie when the good parts are the dialogue.

In Paris, we meet Rachel (Marina Fois), a designer of jewelry, and her husband, Franck (Roschdy Zem), who gives expert shiatsu massages and is writing a book titled *Feng Shui for Couples*. The book will explain why the bed has to face south and the cash register north, unless I have them mixed up. Their jewelry line needs help with its website, and they call in Vincent (Nicolas Duvauchelle), a software expert. As Vincent leans above Rachel at her keyboard, they feel unexpectedly strong erotic currents. Haven't we all sometimes felt that grateful for computer advice?

Not long after, the two couples, also including Vincent's wife, Teri (Elodie Bouchez), meet for dinner. Teri was an Olympic gymnast for France, and now sits on the floor because her back has been giving her some trouble. Franck offers her a back massage, which begins with his fingers pressing and counting off each vertebra while he names them, and when they reach the femur Teri is feeling a lot better all over. They kiss. Now both couples are in play, and they decide to begin trading partners.

Why? Why is not a word you should bring with you to this movie. *Pourquoi pas?* Is it possible for two couples to swap mates without jealousy? I doubt it. The men are the problem. When a husband is assured by his wife that he satisfies her just as much as the other man, I submit to you there's not a husband on earth capable of believing that. Women are more trusting, because sex is not the dominant theme in their lives from thirteen to decrepitude.

All four people are attractive, although Vincent has too many tattoos for my taste. He has a word in large letters running from one shoulder blade to the other, in an unreadable typeface he must have found on the Web. My advice: stick to Helvetica. The four lovers become best friends, while effortlessly raising three children. Can this idyll last forever? No. One afternoon while they're making love, Franck gets Teri to help him shift her bed closer to the window for feng shui reasons. They forget the time, and when Vincent returns home unexpectedly he is annoyed, not to find them in bed together, but to find the bed has been moved. That's going too far.

When Franck presses his wife to describe any of Vincent's problems, the best she can do is report that sometimes he has "trouble." What say? Trouble getting an erection? No, getting over it, if you see what I mean. I can understand why this might be a problem for Rachel, but Rachel, honey, it's not what Franck wants to hear.

The best parts of the film, for me, came toward the end, when the lives of the four lovers become bittersweet and melancholy. They were so happy for a time. They were inseparable. Now it is all over. There's a flashback where they walk together down to the farm pond to wash off the flour. As they dry contentedly in the sun, Teri still has a little flour behind her ear. You can't do better than that.

## Friends with Benefits ★ ★ ★

R, 109 m., 2011

Justin Timberlake (Dylan), Mila Kunis (Jamie), Patricia Clarkson (Lorna), Jenna Elfman (Annie), Bryan Greenberg (Parker), Richard Jenkins (Mr. Harper), Woody Harrelson (Tommy). Directed by Will Gluck and produced by Gluck, Liz Glotzer, Martin Shafer, Janet Zucker, and Jerry Zucker. Screenplay by Gluck, Keith Merryman, and David A. Newman.

*Friends with Benefits* follows romcom formulas as if directed on autopilot, but that's not to say it isn't fun. This is the second movie this year to ask whether it's possible to have sex with someone without falling in love, and the second to arrive at a mistaken conclusion—because of course it is. It's just not possible if you're Mila Kunis and Justin Timberlake, and the audience likes you and demands a romantic fadeout. I propose this as a rule: No movie with big stars and a big budget can allow them to enjoy big-time sex and then split them up at the end.

The news about this movie is that it makes it clear that both Timberlake and Kunis are the real thing when it comes to light comedy. Since they earlier proved themselves in dramas (*The Social Network* and *Black Swan*), that must indicate they're the real thing in general. Now all they have left are comic book superheroes.

She plays Jamie, an executive headhunter in New York City. He plays Dylan, a hotshot art director whose website gets six million hits a month. That allows him to hire an office full of employees. My website gets more hits and only has one employee, but obviously Dylan has a better head for business. Jamie persuades Dylan to fly to New York and interview for a dream job: being an art director for *GQ* magazine. He's cool to the idea, but she persuades him in one evening during which she is about as charming as it's possible for one person to be, even if she's Meg Ryan.

One dinner date leads to another. You know what's coming. They share that they've had bad luck with relationships, they swear they're not looking for a new one, and they agree to have pure physical sex with no emotional strings attached. This leads to activity under a blanket in which it's not difficult to figure out (from the way things move around under there out of sight) what's happening. This scene is well-written, well-directed, and well-acted—and such scenes involve a good deal of comic ability.

The formula now requires them to fall in love, to run into obstacles, to fight, to break up forever, and yadda yadda yadda. *Friends with Benefits* makes this process more entertaining because the cast is populated with good supporting actors. Patricia Clarkson is Jamie's mother, an unreformed product of the sexual revolution. Richard Jenkins plays Dylan's father, who suffers from Movie Alzheimer's. That's the form of the disease where the victim has perfectly timed lucid moments to deliver crucial speeches and then relapses.

At the *GQ* office, Dylan makes friends with the sports editor, Tommy (Woody Harrelson), who is loudly and enthusiastically gay and commutes to work in a speedboat. That leads me to idle thoughts about Dylan's work on the magazine's website, where he features such stories as "How to Wear White Pants at a Cookout." I consider *GQ* a little too cool for that feature, but not entirely: In addition to an excellent feature on Mila Kunis, its current website offers an update on plaid pocket squares ("How I wear my square really depends on my mood: Typically I'm a standard, straight-across-fold kind of guy").

But I stray. One of the movie's running

jokes is that Dylan and Jamie know all the clichés from movie love stories and are too hip to fall for them in their own lives. This indirection doesn't quite distract us from realizing their own lives are the embodiment of a movie love story. I guess that comes with the territory. What not every romcom has, however, is good dialogue, well-delivered at a fast clip. Mila Kunis fast-talks her way through the opening scenes as if she's channeling Juno, and Timberlake easily keeps up. At some fundamental level, I simply enjoyed watching them. That was sort of enough.

## Friends with Kids ★ ★ ½

R, 100 m., 2012

Adam Scott (Jason Fryman), Jennifer Westfeldt (Julie Keller), Jon Hamm (Ben), Kristen Wiig (Missy), Maya Rudolph (Leslie), Chris O'Dowd (Alex), Megan Fox (Mary Jane), Edward Burns (Kurt). Directed by Jennifer Westfeldt and produced by Westfeldt, Joshua Astrachan, Riza Aziz, Lucy Barzun Donnelly, Jon Hamm, Jake Kasdan, and Joey McFarland. Screenplay by Westfeldt.

There must be a better reason to have a baby than to provide a plot point in a romcom. Don't you think? *Friends with Kids* is altogether too casual about parenthood, and that supplies a shaky foundation to a plot that's less about human nature and more about clever dialogue. As a light entertainment it has its pleasures, but at the end I was left feeling sorry for the poor kid who emerges as such a great convenience.

We meet three couples who live comfortably in New York City and Brooklyn. They apparently chart their progress through life by comparing themselves to one another. That's possible in the sealed universe of a movie, although in life most couples have more than four friends, and there's a certain turnover rate.

Not here. Jason and Julie (Adam Scott and Jennifer Westfeldt) are very best friends who live in the same apartment building. They date around and don't have romantic feelings for each other—something they keep repeating lest we forget. They form what their friends treat as a virtual couple: They're not married, they're not sleeping together, and yet at a dinner party, you routinely invite them together.

Ben and Missy (Jon Hamm and Kristen Wiig) are married, and were once in such deep lust it was a standing joke in their circle. As passion has worn off, they are gradually suspecting there was never much else, and friends who once basked in the glow of their love now shiver in the chill of their sniping.

Leslie and Alex (Maya Rudolph and Chris O'Dowd), the Brooklynites, are closer to normal, comfortable with each other, and announce "We're pregnant!" That's one of the final straws for Jason and Julie, who are both increasingly fretful that they're childless. They're aware their clocks are ticking, and they decide to have a baby with each other and sidestep the whole marriage and divorce routine. They'll date other people, split the babysitting and child care fifty-fifty, and everybody will be happy, right?

Rather soon after they have this ideal child, they do indeed start dating other people: Jason meets Mary Jane (Megan Fox), and Julie is literally pushed into the arms of Kurt (Edward Burns), who is such an improbably nice man he borders on parody. I always wonder exactly what "dating other people" means. Is it assumed it won't affect the ideal platonic friendship Jason and Julie began with? If they fall in love with those "other people," how do those ideal people handle the notion of each contributing 25 percent of the baby-sitting and child care (and presumably costs) of the kid in the middle of all of this? How is this explained? How would you feel if you started seeing someone and he/she explained, "I love you enough to marry you and share with you a child I had with my best friend, who is still very much in my life and who we will be seeing every day and always have to live near"?

My guess is, it wouldn't go over. The old-fashioned marriage and divorce routine has a lot to be said for it. *Friends with Kids* isn't constructed as simply a comedy, and intends to have a measure of sincerity and even truth at its heart. But it smells off. It feels like an artificial screenplay concoction that's perhaps pitched at moviegoers fifteen or twenty years younger than the stars—audiences who don't have the experience to understand that the whole child-sharing scheme is cockamamie.

Yes, and we all know where the plot is headed anyway, because if there's one thing we know about a romcom, it's that conventional values invariably must win in the end. It's almost painful to watch characters jump through the obligatory story hoops in the third act. Even presumably real people don't behave like this.

## Fright Night ★ ★ ★

R, 106 m., 2011

Anton Yelchin (Charley Brewster), Colin Farrell (Jerry), Toni Collette (Jane Brewster), David Tennant (Peter Vincent), Imogen Poots (Amy), Christopher Mintz-Plasse (Ed), Dave Franco (Mark), Reid Ewing (Ben), Will Denton (Adam). Directed by Craig Gillespie and produced by Michael De Luca and Alison R. Rosenzweig. Screenplay by Marti Noxon.

*Fright Night* makes use of an ideal location: Las Vegas, a city of the night. It takes place in a suburban housing development of eerie isolation. Seen from the air, it is several square blocks of homes and streets entirely surrounded by barren desert. Whoever bought the first house here was an optimist.

Perhaps it was Jerry (Colin Farrell). He is a single man, handsome and charming, who lives next door to the Brewsters. Charley Brewster (Anton Yelchin) is a teen-something with the usual expertise about vampires, which is why he's sensitive to certain vibes from the neighbor. His divorced mother, Jane (Toni Collette), picks up more on the testosterone vibe. They both wonder why Jerry has an unsightly Dumpster in his front yard, and where all those chunks of debris come from. The exterior of his house remains unchanged.

To be sure, all of Jerry's windows are blacked out, but we're told that's not uncommon in Vegas, where so many people work the night shift and sleep all day. Sounds reasonable. The two houses are close together (especially considering the empty miles of desert surrounding the development), and Charley finds it easy to monitor Jerry's suspicious movements from his second-floor bedroom window. Charley's friend Ed (Christopher Mintz-Plasse) notices that students are going missing from their classroom and begins to suspect Jerry may be a vampire.

*Fright Night* was inspired by a somewhat similar 1985 vampire movie of the same name, which was actually pretty good and contained a rich performance by Roddy McDowall as an unemployed TV horror movie host named Peter Vincent, who was recruited by a teenager to advise on vampire killing. (The name is obviously a play on Peter Cushing and Vincent Price, although a diminishing number of movie fans may pick up on that.) This time Peter Vincent (David Tennant) is a Brit magician who headlines at a Vegas casino and claims to be a vampire expert.

Setting plot details aside, I can reveal that Charley has a hot girlfriend named Amy (Imogen Poots), that his mom, Jane, is a sturdy and grown-up character, and that no one will listen to Charley's suspicions about Jerry—especially not the cops, who, judging by the apparent size of the housing development, must have to commute from downtown Vegas.

David Tennant is droll and dissolute as Peter Vincent, occupying a penthouse filled with vampire artifacts and guzzling booze as if fighting chronic thirst. He is egotistical, rude, and aggressive, and not charmed by Charley's pleas for help. But . . . well, he does know a lot about vampires.

*Fright Night*, directed by Craig Gillespie and written by Marti Noxon, is several degrees superior to *Final Destination* 5, which opened a week earlier. I say this despite my dread certainty that it will be followed by *Fright Night*s 2, 3, 4, and 5, in which a series of increasingly suspicious neighbors will be introduced in increasingly exotic locations. My own needs are modest. Two movies based on this premise in twenty-six years are sufficient.

The movie has competent acting by the principals, who make an effort to surpass the generic requirements of their characters. It has decent CGI (including quite possibly most of the subdivision). The technical credits are first rate: production design (Richard Bridgland), art direction (Randy Moore), prosthetic makeup (Aurora Bergere), and cinematography (Javier Aguirresarobe).

As in the earlier film, this one dances always at the edge of comedy. It especially has fun with the Rules of Vampire Behavior, which Jerry even teases Charley about. Without spoiling a single thing, I can tell you that one of the inevitable stakes through the heart in this movie is an inspired use of product placement. As vampire movies go, *Fright Night* is a pretty good one.

## From Paris with Love ★ ★

R, 92 m., 2010

John Travolta (Charlie Wax), Jonathan Rhys Meyers (James Reece), Kasia Smutniak (Carolina), Richard Durden (Ambassador Bennington). Directed by Pierre Morel and produced by Luc Besson and India Osborne. Screenplay by Adi Hasak, based on a story by Besson.

Pauline Kael has already reviewed this movie in her book *Kiss Kiss Bang Bang,* and it only took her the title. I could go through my usual vaudeville act about chase scenes and queasy-cams and Idiot Plots, but instead I'd like you to join me in the analysis of something that increasingly annoys me.

Imagine we are watching *From Paris with Love* on a DVD with a stop-action button. We look at an action scene all the way through. John Travolta stars as Charlie Wax, an American Mr. Fix-It with a shaved head and goatee, who has been sent to Paris on a mysterious assignment. Not mysterious to him, mysterious to us. It involves Asian drug dealers and/or terrorists from the Middle East. Doesn't matter who they are or what they do, because their only function here is to try to kill Charlie and his fall-guy partner James Reece (Jonathan Rhys Meyers).

OK. We're on the sofa. We look at the scene. We take a second look. We focus on Travolta. This is an athlete. His reflexes are on a hair-trigger. He can deal with several enemies at a time. He can duck, jump, hurdle, spin, and leap. One slight miscalculation, and he's dead. He doesn't miss a beat. He's in superb condition, especially for a guy whose favorite food is Cheese Royales. That's a little joke reminding us of *Pulp Fiction,* and the *last* thing you should do is remind the audience of a movie they'd rather be watching.

Now we go through the scene a frame at a time. We don't miss much in the way of continuity because it's pretty much glued together a frame at a time. We see a dizzying cascade of images, but here's a funny thing: We don't see Travolta completing many extended physical movements, and none involving any danger. The shots of him involve movement, but in bursts of a few frames, intercut with similar bursts of action by his attackers. There is no sense of continuous physical movement taking place within a defined space. No overall sense of the choreography.

I hasten to say this is not criticism of John Travolta. He succeeds in this movie by essentially acting in a movie of his own. The fight construction is the same with most modern action movies. In past decades studios went so far as to run fencing classes for swordfights. Stars like Buster Keaton, Douglas Fairbanks Sr., and Errol Flynn did their own stunts and made sure you could see them doing them. Most of the stunts in classic kung fu movies, starring such as Bruce Lee and Jackie Chan, were really happening. Sure, they used camera angles, trampolines, and wires, but you try it and see how easy it is.

CGI makes that unnecessary. The stunt work is done by computers and the editing process. I fear that classic action sequences would be too slow for today's impatient action fans, who have been schooled on impossibilities. The actual stunt driving done in such chase landmarks as *The French Connection* and *Bullitt,* where you could observe real cars in real space and time, has been replaced by what is essentially animation.

I mention this because last week I saw a good South Korean thriller named *The Chaser,* and its best scene involved a foot chase through the narrow streets of Seoul by two actors who, you could see, were actually running down streets. In modern actioners, the only people who work up a sweat are the editors.

Anyway, that's what I had on my mind. As for *From Paris with Love,* it's mostly bang bang and not kiss kiss, and as an actress once asked Russ Meyer, what's love got to do with it?

## The Future ★ ★ ★ ½

NO MPAA RATING, 91 m., 2011

Miranda July (Sophie), Hamish Linklater (Jason), David Warshofsky (Marshall), Isabella Acres (Gabriella), Joe Putterlik (Joe). Directed by Miranda July and produced by Gina Kwon, Gerhard Meixner, and Roman Paul. Screenplay by July.

I suppose to some degree Miranda July's characters are autobiographical. Not literally; a woman like the heroine of *The Future* could never have written and directed *The Future.* Perhaps they're autobiographical more in the Woody Allen mode: characters created as avatars of fanciful whimsy. Christine, July's character in *Me and You and Everyone We Know,* was a thirtyish woman with life still ahead of her. Sophie, her character in *The Future,* is a thirtyish woman with life behind her—or, at very best, on hold.

Both women draw men into their vortex. These men tend to be male versions of herself, nice, sensitive, feckless, uncertain, tentative. In *The Future,* Sophie and Jason (Hamish Linklater) have been together about four years. They live in a sort of indefinitely attenuated present tense. They occupy a small apartment furnished by the accumulation of playful and ironic possessions. They have low-maintenance jobs adequate to support their undemanding lifestyle. He works on a help line for a tech company. She teaches dance to children, and when she dances, her style seems to have been learned from her students.

Children seem to be out of the picture. They are held together by habit, by familiarity with each other's peculiarities, by fond inertia. They're both easy to get along with. If she obsessively clings to a yellow "security T-shirt," perhaps an affection borrowed from old *Peanuts* strips, Jason accepts it. There are a lot of obsessions that are harder to live with. My friend Severn Darden used to gnaw on table napkins.

Change comes. They decide to adopt a sick cat. Caring for this cat will be a full-time task. Its illness is almost a requirement; seeking something to commit to, they prefer a sick cat to a well one. The cat cannot come home with them for thirty days. In that month, they budge from their inertia; Jason gets a job selling trees, and Sophie starts an affair with Marshall (David Warshofsky), a man who has no greater purpose in the story than that she can have the affair. Jason becomes friends with an old guy named Joe (Joe Putterlik), whose purpose is to be an old guy Jason becomes friends with.

In the world of Miranda July, magic is possible. Did I mention that some of *The Future* is narrated by the sick cat? In her films, the passage of time is not allowed to become routine. In an extraordinary scene in *Me and You and Everyone We Know,* the Christine character walks down a long block with a man she has just met, and she makes their passage down the block into a metaphor for their passage through life. In *The Future,* Jason is able to arrest the aimless meandering of his life by stopping time himself. He moves sideways from the time stream. The moon begins to speak to him.

This fantastical whimsy is delicate and fragile, and much depends on the personalities of Sophie and Jason, who despite all their self-conscious drifting are collaborating on a rather elaborate and defined idea of how to live. We are all on a voyage through life, but sometimes we even forget we're on a ship. Not these two. I see them standing side by side, leaning on a rail at the stern, focusing on the departure of the waves.

I suggested that Miranda July's characters are avatars, projections she invites us to focus on. I've met her, don't know her, but can guess something from her films. It takes a great deal of will to get an independent film made, particularly one that inhabits no known genre. If you direct it and star in it, it takes much more. If you make two of them, you are a focused and driven person. You are not a twee sprite like Sophie or Christine. You do not require a sick cat to provide meaning in your life. If you cling to a T-shirt (and July apparently sometimes really does), you must do it not out of weakness but from fierce determination. On the surface, this film is an enchanting meditation. At its core is the hard steel of individuality.

# G

## Gainsbourg: A Heroic Life ★ ★ ★

NO MPAA RATING, 130 m., 2011

Eric Elmosnino (Serge Gainsbourg), Lucy Gordon (Jane Birkin), Laetitia Casta (Brigitte Bardot), Doug Jones (La Gueule), Anna Mouglalis (Juliette Greco), Mylene Jampanoi (Bambou), Sara Forestier (France Gall), Kacey Mottet Klein (Lucien Ginsburg). Directed by Joann Sfar and produced by Marc Du Pontavice and Didier Lupfer. Screenplay by Sfar, based on his own graphic novel.

Serge Gainsbourg was one of the great performing artists of France from the 1960s until his death in 1991, but despite the title of *Gainsbourg: A Heroic Life*, I am not sure he was heroic, and I don't believe this film does, either. He was a star more because of his insouciant, defiant personality than for the quality of his voice, and a genius in getting himself into scrapes. His most notable controversy involved his reggae version of "La Marseillaise," the French national anthem. For Americans who loved Jimi Hendrix's guitar solo of "The Star-Spangled Banner," that doesn't seem like much of a transgression, but the French right wing didn't get the joke.

His music was consistently popular, he had international hits, and he had celebrated affairs with Brigitte Bardot and Jane Birkin, with whom he fathered the fearless actress Charlotte Gainsbourg (*Antichrist*). With Birkin he recorded the notorious *Je T'Aime . . . Moi Non Plus*, which apparently included the sound of a woman's orgasm and was denounced by no less than the Vatican. But he never seemed fully respectful of his talent, and in later years enjoyed notoriety on talk shows as a cut-up who sometimes went on drunk and lashed out at other guests.

Yes, he drank. But his overarching vice was smoking. Starting in this film as a child, he continues apparently nonstop, even in bed and the bath, until his probably inevitable heart attack at sixty-two. His brand of choice was Gitanes, the French cigarettes that scented all of Paris until the success of Marlboros. Someone, it may have been Art Buchwald, said Gitanes were made out of old socks and belly button lint. I point to his smoking not to be censorious, but to suggest that when someone endlessly does something harmful, there may be an aura of self-hate involved.

With Gainsbourg, it may have been connected with anti-Semitism—not because he objected to being Jewish, but out of defiance. That helped shape his personality at an early age. This eccentric biopic, directed by Joann Sfar from his own graphic novel, shows his attitude in an early scene: After the Nazis require all French Jews to wear yellow stars, the little Serge butts into the head of the line because, he explains, he wants his first. In a visual device that may have worked better on the page than on the screen, Sfar has him imagining an anti-Semitic face with a huge hatchet nose, atop a small body in the form of a caricature. This fantasy often follows him on the street and goads him into rebellious behavior.

The movie unreels his musical biography with an unending series of tastes of songs and performances. You may be surprised by how many you recognize. Along the way he was often outrageous not because he wanted to offend people, but because in a twisted way he simply didn't care.

The actors resemble those originals I know; Eric Elmosnino is the Gainsbourg I see in videos; Lucy Gordon resembles Jane Birkin's waifish look; and Laetitia Casta needs no dialogue to identify herself as Bardot. The affair with BB has an amusing payoff: Gainsbourg's father was a piano player who was a strict taskmaster in teaching his son the instrument, and disapproved when his boy began to hammer away in dives and bistros. What did Serge finally do to win his father's admiration? He brought home Bardot, which turned the old man into a fanboy.

Why was Gainsbourg a hero? The film leaves the question hanging. I am afraid it was only because, like Sinatra, he did it his way. Which no one can deny.

## Game Change ★ ★ ★ ½

NO MPAA RATING, 118 m., 2012

Julianne Moore (Sarah Palin), Woody Harrelson (Steve Schmidt), Ed Harris (John McCain), Ron

Livingston (Mark Wallace), Peter MacNicol (Rick Davis), Sarah Paulson (Nicolle Wallace), Jamey Sheridan (Mark Salter), Bruce Altman (Fred Davis), Colby French (Tucker Eskew), Spencer Garrett (Steve Biegun), David Barry Gray (Todd Palin), Brian Howe (Randy Scheunemann), Austin Pendleton (Joe Lieberman), John Rothman (A. B. Culvahouse). Directed by Jay Roach and produced by Gary Goetzman, Tom Hanks, and Amy Sayres. Screenplay by Danny Strong, adapted from the book by John Heilemann and Mark Halperin.

Sarah Palin lacked the preparation or temperament to be one heartbeat away from the presidency, but what she possessed in abundance was the ability to inflame political passions and energize the John McCain campaign with star quality. That much we already knew. What I didn't expect to discover after viewing *Game Change*, a new HBO film about the 2008 McCain campaign, was how much sympathy I would feel for Palin, and even more for John McCain.

The movie is largely told from the point of view of two McCain advisers, Steve Schmidt (Woody Harrelson) and Nicolle Wallace (Sarah Paulson). Schmidt was instrumental in the selection of Palin (Julianne Moore) as McCain's running mate, and Wallace was another senior adviser. During the campaign they share their concern as Palin reveals a comprehensive lack of knowledge about current events.

In the days before Palin's selection, it seemed so much simpler. McCain's inner circle shared a fear of Barack Obama as a formidable opponent. They had little enthusiasm for McCain's preference for running mate, Senator Joe Lieberman, a centrist independent from Connecticut. As they saw Obama drawing record-breaking crowds, Lieberman's appeal seemed tepid. What McCain (Ed Harris) needed, they became convinced, was a "game changer," a vice presidential candidate who would change the landscape.

On paper, the governor of Alaska was ideal. In person, she had delightful charisma. It's clear in the film that Schmidt and his team did only a superficial background check on her, and later Schmidt would berate himself for not asking her a single policy question. McCain, persuaded that she might be the game changer he needed, went along. Doubts began to form before the GOP convention, but they were swept away by her triumphant speech accepting the nomination. Backstage, the McCain troops hugged themselves with delight.

Watching that speech at home, I thought, "Obama's in real trouble." Some GOP pundits confessed they had crushes on her. Palin's crowd appeal was enormous. She went overnight from being an obscure governor to being a superstar. And then reality began to sink in: Palin knew virtually nothing about current events, world politics, history, geography. Wallace and Schmidt share their astonishment: She didn't know what the Fed was. She thought Korea was one country. She believed the queen was the British head of state.

In preparation for her first debate with Democratic vice presidential candidate Joe Biden, she hopelessly shuffled file cards and retained little. In an interview with Katie Couric of CBS, she came across as a deer caught in headlights. She had such an indifference to facts that she repeated the same errors (about the "bridge to nowhere," for example) no matter how often the staff corrected her. She knew an applause line that would please audiences, and that was enough for her.

But hold on a moment. Aren't I simply repeating a slanted, partisan view? Decide for yourself, if you see the film. Adapted from a best-selling book with the same title by John Heilemann and Mark Halperin, it draws on hundreds of interviews with McCain camp insiders, and although Palin's supporters are protesting its negative portrait, the facts and dialogue seem to be accurate. When *Newsweek*'s David Frum asked Schmidt what he thought about the film, he said it was "an out-of-body experience." Neither he nor Wallace (who confessed that after working with Palin she was unable to vote for McCain) has questioned its accuracy.

Palin was transformed by discovering her ability to mesmerize crowds. She grew intoxicated by her power and rejected guidance from advisers. Nothing like this had ever happened to her before. Exhilarated by the adulation she drew everywhere she went, she was wounded by questions from Couric and others, which she considered hostile "Gotcha!" attacks. Tina Fey's celebrated skits on *Saturday*

*Night Live* hurt her deeply. She found herself loved and ridiculed at the same time.

In her performance, Julianne Moore doesn't do an impersonation of Palin here, in the sense that Meryl Streep was uncanny in her resemblance to Margaret Thatcher. She looks about as much like Palin as she can, but that's not the point. She conveys the essence. In a way, she's unprotected. Not a hardened, cynical politician, but a woman who has gone through life expecting good things and usually found them. There is a moment here when she's alone and we see the hurt and sadness in her eyes because people are finding her lacking. She's like a student who studied hard for the exam and failed anyway. The people love her. Alaska still loves her; that's why she's so urgent about the results of an Alaska poll on her popularity. Why are these media creatures being so cruel? Why is everyone picking on her expensive wardrobe? She didn't want the damn fancy clothes anyway. Moore conveys these feelings with tenderness and subtlety. Her performance is not a barbed parody, but based on an actress's instinctive empathy with a character.

As John McCain, Ed Harris has more of a supporting role. He comes across in *Game Change* as a decent man of principle, who has honorable ideas about how a campaign should be conducted and sticks to them. There is a suggestion that he blames himself along with his staff for failing to properly vet Palin; they were too blinded by her appeal to take the time for a cool evaluation.

The film avoids scenes involving the personal lives of the Palins and McCains. Spouses are seen but rarely heard. Palin is depicted as an affectionate mother. This is proper because the sources for the book and film were expert on the campaign itself, but it wouldn't be appropriate for them to supply information about private lives.

Woody Harrelson makes Steve Schmidt a pillar at the center of the story, a man driven by frustration as he tries to manage a campaign that Palin is trying to manage herself. As late as election night, they had a shouting match because she wanted to join McCain onstage, where her own concession speech would join his. Schmidt roars at her: "It's never been done that way in American history! The candidate concedes!" As she walks onstage with McCain, his eyes are still shooting daggers at her as a warning not to grab the microphone for a few words of her own.

Sarah Palin was, Schmidt decided, the greatest actress in the history of American politics. Abandoning any attempt to brief her before the debates, he hit on the idea of assigning her twenty-five statements that she would memorize and then circle around to no matter what the question was. This she did brilliantly. She may have been a bad candidate, but she was a brilliant campaigner, astonishing the staff by her ability to save situations that looked perilous to them.

Seeing *Game Change* is like living again through the campaign of 2008. Much of the dialogue is words we've already heard. We're left with the conviction that Sarah Palin would have made a dangerously incompetent president of the United States, and that those closest to her in the campaign, including John McCain, came to realize that.

## Garbo the Spy ★ ★ ★

NO MPAA RATING, 87 m., 2011

A documentary featuring Nigel West, Mark Seaman, Xavier Vinader, Stan Vranckx, Aline Griffith, and Juan Pujol Garcia. Directed and produced by Edmon Roch. Screenplay by Roch, Maria Hervera, and Isaki Lacuestra.

It's widely known that the Nazis believed the Allied landing at Normandy to be a decoy strategy, and that the real invasion of Europe would come on the beaches of Calais and be led by George Patton. We know that Patton was moved to England to reinforce this view, while the Normandy operation was headed by Eisenhower. Even weeks after the landing at Normandy, the Nazis were still reinforcing Calais, waiting for an attack that never came.

What has hardly been known at all is how the Nazis were deluded. It was largely the work of a single man, Juan Pujol Garcia, a Spaniard who based himself in Lisbon and fed the Nazis a stream of misleading information from a spy network that existed entirely in his imagination.

Edmon Roch's *Garbo the Spy* is an engrossing documentary that is itself largely a work of the director's imagination. Garcia was codenamed "Garbo" because one of his handlers considered him "the greatest actor in the world." Impersonating a man who controlled sources that never existed, he sold the Nazis so convincingly that when he decided one of his spies had to die, the Nazis paid his "widow" a pension.

Based partly on Nigel West's book *Operation Garbo: The Personal Story of the Most Successful Spy of World War II*, the doc tells the story of an elusive young man from Barcelona who wanted to have an effect on the war and volunteered his services not once but four times to the British. They eventually accepted him after he had already set up as a freelancer, feeding his own Nazi contacts information from his fictional network.

Moving to Lisbon, a hotbed of intrigue in Nazi-occupied Europe, he made up most of the information passed on by his "network," and enough of it was true that the Nazis believed him. Over one period of nine months he even convinced them he was in London. His masterwork was to inform them that the Allies would fake a landing at Normandy to lure the German army there, and then unleash Patton's surprise attack at Calais. They believed him. The fiction worked so well that the Nazis never were up to strength at Normandy, and the fabled Panzer division, while en route there, was diverted to Calais instead.

By this point the Allies were working closely with Garcia. Three hours before the D-Day attack was timed to begin, Eisenhower personally authorized Garcia to tip off the Nazis, reckoning they wouldn't have time for troop movements. In a stroke of luck, when Garcia's message arrived, the Nazi communications center was unstaffed, and so when they discovered his timely warning hours later, he looked even more reliable.

Incredibly, weeks after the invasion, he continued to convince them the real target was elsewhere. When they asked why the attack at Calais never came, he explained: "They had such unexpected success at Normandy they decided to cancel it." The Nazis continued to believe Garcia to the end, and he became the only man decorated by both sides in World War II.

Only two early photographs of Garcia exist. *Garbo the Spy*, perhaps inspired by its subject, is made up partly of smoke and mirrors. Director Edmon Roch uses vintage newsreel footage and scenes from old spy movies to illustrate his story, which is narrated by a series of talking heads including Nigel West himself. Some of the footage shows Alec Guinness in *Our Man in Havana* (1959), a movie based on a Graham Greene novel inspired by Garcia.

Nigel West was able to trace Garcia's postwar movements to the Portuguese colony of Angola, where he reportedly died in 1949. Not so. He slipped away to Venezuela, operated a movie theater, married, and had children. The film concludes with an enormously affecting series of scenes in which the now elderly Garcia revisits the beaches of Normandy and an Allied cemetery. Perhaps fittingly, he never speaks.

## George Harrison: Living in the Material World ★ ★ ★

NO MPAA RATING, 208 m., 2011

A documentary featuring George Harrison, Paul McCartney, Terry Gilliam, Eric Idle, Ringo Starr, Jane Birkin, Eric Clapton, Yoko Ono, Tom Petty, Phil Spector, Dhani Harrison, Pattie Boyd, and others. Directed by Martin Scorsese and produced by Scorsese, Olivia Harrison, and Nigel Sinclair.

"Got up went to Twickenham rehearsed until lunchtime—left the Beatles—went home, and in the evening did King of Fuh at Trident studio, had chips later."

So George wrote in his diary on January 10, 1969. He returned a few weeks later, and then the band broke up for good after January 1970.

George Harrison always seemed to me the unhappiest of the Beatles. Of course, such an opinion is worthless. The Beatles are a screen upon which we project our own ideas, and George seemed the least willing to be projected upon. To be a member of that group, to have a hand in creating the pop music of our time most likely to be heard in later centuries, was to run the risk of losing yourself. George (we call them all by their first names) was the most defiantly individual.

In Martin Scorsese's new documentary *George Harrison: Living in the Material World*,

Harrison's journey is traced as a search for himself in the tumult of incoming distractions. It is clear, as Paul Theroux points out in a recent article, that in Harrison's life Scorsese saw much of his own reflected. They began as lonely, alienated children. They found escape and joy in music and film. They focused their lives on those arts. They resisted the possibility of being entirely consumed.

This is a long film, for which the expansiveness of cable television is appropriate. Over two nights on HBO, at 208 minutes, Scorsese has accomplished the best documentary that is probably possible. With George's faithful second wife, Olivia, as his coproducer, he has assembled all the archival material, all the photos, all the film and video, transient and lasting. With his own prestige, and because they loved George, Scorsese has been able to call on those who knew Harrison in all weathers: his son Dhani, Ringo and Paul, Yoko Ono, Eric Idle and Terry Gilliam, Eric Clapton, Jackie Stewart, and many others.

"In my beginning is my end," T. S. Eliot wrote. For George Harrison, raised in the working class in postwar Liverpool, one of those beginnings must have been his father's vegetable garden—victory gardens, they were called during and after the war, and my own father had one, too. All through his life, as money and fame came to him, he found pleasure seeking houses with gardens.

English country houses are known for their gardens, but many of their owners never get their hands dirty. George was obsessed by the physical act of gardening, working with his land every day that he could. When you garden, you imagine its effect for those who will see your garden—for future generations and strangers. It is a gift you give to the land and to others, and it shows love of beauty in a pure form.

George's professional life was caught up in a maelstrom almost from the day he first auditioned for John and Paul, playing "Raunchy" for them on the top deck of a bus. Scorsese's film deals fully with the rise of the Beatles, when pop stardom was transformed into a great deal more because it quickly became obvious that the Beatles were extraordinary.

Paul and John were the composers of most of the great Beatles hits. George wrote hundreds of songs, but somehow they kept being squeezed out of albums and not included on show lists. There is an invaluable scene here showing him in an argument with Paul. His songs were not valued as he thought they should be, and after he struck out on his own, we heard much more of his work.

Searching for inner quiet in the chaos of stardom, he found himself drawn to Eastern religion, and was instrumental in bringing the Beatles under the influence of Maharishi Mahesh Yogi and A. C. Bhaktivedanta Swami Prabhupada. He joined the Hare Krishna tradition and was a vegetarian from 1968 until he died.

George believed that a great purpose of life was to prepare oneself for death. With chanting and meditation, he turned inward. His serenity received a severe challenge when he and his wife were attacked by an invader in his home, and he was stabbed as they fought off the mentally disturbed man. Thoughts of the murder of John Lennon must have struck him with great force. In 1997 he was diagnosed with throat cancer, which later spread to his lungs and his brain. He died in 2001.

All of this, and a great deal more, is covered in this respectful film. This is a more objective, less personal documentary than Scorsese usually makes. Considering its length, there isn't much concert footage, and it focuses on archival interviews with George, news footage, and an impressive selection of talking heads.

Those who knew George loved and respected him. His use of LSD and other drugs is discussed, but he seems to have been seeking truth, not a high, and soon enough he was drug free and found his highs in spiritual practices. He left his music. Even now, there is something a little hidden and private about him. I suspect if we want to sense his presence, we should visit his gardens.

## Get Him to the Greek ★ ★ ★

R, 108 m., 2010

Jonah Hill (Aaron Green), Russell Brand (Aldous Snow), Elisabeth Moss (Daphne Binks), Rose Byrne (Jackie Q), Colm Meaney (Jonathan Snow), Sean Combs (Sergio Roma). Directed by Nicholas Stoller and produced by Judd Apatow,

David L. Bushell, and Rodney Rothman. Screenplay by Stoller.

Aldous Snow is the sort of rock star who can seriously propose himself for the role of White African Jesus. What would his duties be? He has no idea. It's just the sort of thing he throws out to keep people on their toes. Aldous was first seen as a rock star, clean and sober, in *Forgetting Sarah Marshall* (2008), and he returns in *Get Him to the Greek* as a wild man deep into a relapse.

It is the task of an earnest and square young man, Aaron Green, to fly to London and in exactly three days get him to New York for a *Today* show appearance and then to Los Angeles for a comeback concert at the Greek Theater. *Get Him to the Greek* is the story of those three days, and nights, which pass in a blur for the innocent Green. They are a blur for Aldous as well, but then, that's his lifestyle.

The movie is funny in the way of *The Hangover* about what trouble lads can get into when their senses are whirling. Unlike some depictions of binges, it doesn't shortchange vomit. The adventures of Aldous and Aaron remind me of a friend I used to meet on Saturday mornings for what we called Drunch. "Sometimes," she said, "it can be really exhausting having a good time." Aaron (Jonah Hill), who has been threatened with flaying if he doesn't deliver Aldous (Russell Brand) on time, panics when he can't get him to Heathrow airport for the right flight, can't get him to the *Today* show on time, can't get him to the sound check at the Greek, and very nearly can't get him to the Greek. Aldous, for the most part, floats benevolently above these small misunderstandings. When it comes to himself, he's a very understanding man.

There are really two movies here. One is a gross-out comedy that grows lyrical in its exuberant offensive language, its drug excesses, its partying, its animal behavior. The other movie, which comes into focus, so to speak, in the last half, is surprisingly sweet, and shows that Aldous and Aaron arrive at a friendship that has been tempered in the forge of their misbehavior. Both movies were produced by Judd Apatow, who does a nice line in gross-out comedies.

The lads share loneliness and a feeling of failure with women. Aaron is in love with Daphne Binks (Elisabeth Moss of *Mad Men*), a hospital intern who works endless shifts and gets a great job offer in Seattle, far from the music biz. Aldous has split from Jackie Q (Rose Byrne) as a consequence of his spectacular fall from sobriety. We learn they earlier collaborated on an album voted the worst of all time, but while Aldous has plunged, Jackie Q has soared. In a movie jammed with celebrity cameos (Paul Krugman?), we see bits of her music videos, which, incredible as they may be, aren't entirely improbable. We are so deep into post-irony that it's hard to be sure if a video is *intended* to be bad.

The reason the friendship works is that Russell Brand and Jonah Hill are good actors. Hill's character is required to be blotto half of the time, but there's the sense that he's desperately trying to do the right thing. Russell Brand is convincing as a rock star, imperious, self-destructive, smarter than he seems, calculating, measuring out wretched excess in survivable portions. When it comes time for him to sing, he does it convincingly, with songs that sound like real rock songs. I was reminded a little of Rod Stewart.

The urgency of Aaron's mission depends entirely on his fear of Sergio Roma (Sean Combs), the owner of Aldous's record label. Combs is convincing in an early scene as an egotistical, hard-driving music executive. Then his character has a comic flowering in later scenes, as he reveals his true rock 'n' roll roots. He can party at top speed *and* send Aldous onstage at the Greek despite a bleeding wound from a jump from a rooftop. That Aldous may collapse onstage doesn't occur to him. And indeed Aldous rises to the occasion, as from many reports a lot of rock stars are able to do. They may not remember their performances, but they were great.

What I'm backing into here is that under the cover of slapstick, cheap laughs, raunchy humor, gross-out physical comedy, and sheer exploitation, *Get Him to the Greek* is also fundamentally a sound movie. The writer-director, Nicholas Stoller, who also directed *Forgetting Sarah Marshall*, carefully places the foundations of the story and restrains himself from making Aldous and Aaron into *completely* unbelievable caricatures. The fundamentals are in place.

## Get Low ★ ★ ★

PG-13, 102 m., 2010

Robert Duvall (Felix Bush), Bill Murray (Frank Quinn), Sissy Spacek (Mattie Darrow), Lucas Black (Buddy Robinson), Gerald McRaney (Revered Gus Horton), Bill Cobbs (Reverend Charlie Jackson). Directed by Aaron Schneider and produced by David Gundlach and Dean Zanuck. Screenplay by Chris Provenzano and C. Gaby Mitchell.

We're asked to take Felix Bush on faith, and since he's played in *Get Low* by Robert Duvall, we must. Duvall is authentic right down to the bone, and lends his credibility to almost every character he plays. Felix requires a lot of credibility. He's a backwoods hermit with the kind of beard that suggests he took a box of Smith Brothers Cough Drops into the barber and said, "Give me one of those." He lives with a mule, a shotgun, and his secrets.

The film opens with a murky scene of a farmhouse on fire and a man running away through the night. Who could this man be? Given the Law of Economy of Characters, it must be Felix, and therefore at the end, the movie must account for this scene. Since Felix is an ornery rascal, it follows as the night the day that by the end he will be downright amenable to folks. We don't require him to shave off his beard, but he obliges.

In the present (the 1930s), Felix learns of the death of an old friend, and this inspires him to make his own plans. He makes a rare visit to town to meet with Frank Quinn, the undertaker (Bill Murray), and explains how he wants to "get low." He plans his burial plot, his stone, his farewell send-off, and even the designated speaker. He intends this all to happen now, while he's still alive and can enjoy getting the value for his money.

Frank, who is oleaginous even for a movie undertaker, has a fresh-faced young assistant, Buddy (Lucas Black), who has a wife and baby and ends up as Felix's unofficial minder. Frank dreams up a real corker of a getting low party, many of the townsfolk will come, and Felix gets a new spring in his step. He meets for the first time in years Mattie Darrow (Sissy Spacek), whom he used to be sweet on, and Frank even pulls Reverend Charlie Jackson (Bill Cobbs) out of his hat—or at least out of southern Illinois. The reverend may be the only man alive who knows what happened on that dark night.

All leads up to the big day, during which hearts are healed, truths told, secrets revealed, misunderstandings set straight, and Felix delivers a speech he must have been rehearsing for years. The movie, which opened in an unexpected and intriguing way, has by now long since been on autopilot. That's where Duvall comes in—and Murray.

After you get to a certain point with an actor, you don't much care what he does; you just want to watch him doing it. So it is with Duvall and Murray. They've played versions of these characters not a million miles distant. Duvall is a sly old twinkler, and Murray would take the bills out of your billfold before screwing you in, explaining he doesn't want you to spend eternity with a bump under your butt.

All of this is just plain enjoyable. I liked it, but please don't make me say it's deeply moving or redemptive and uplifting. It's a genre piece for character actors, is what it is, and that's an honorable thing for it to be. Perhaps Robert Duvall is the only man alive who could make his big speech here sound like the truth, and sincere. But he does.

## The Ghost Writer ★ ★ ★ ★

PG-13, 124 m., 2010

Ewan McGregor (The Ghost), Pierce Brosnan (Adam Lang), Kim Cattrall (Amelia Bly), Olivia Williams (Ruth Lang), Tom Wilkinson (Paul Emmett), Timothy Hutton (Sidney Kroll), Robert Pugh (Richard Rycart), James Belushi (John Maddox), Eli Wallach (Old Man). Directed by Roman Polanski and produced by Polanski, Robert Benmussa, and Alain Sarde. Screenplay by Polanski and Robert Harris, based on a novel by Harris.

In Roman Polanski's movie *The Ghost Writer,* a man without a past rattles around in the life of a man with too much of one. He begins by reading the work of an earlier ghost who mysteriously drowned, and finds it boring and conventional. Hired to pep it up to justify a $10 million advance, he discovers material to make it exciting, all right, and possibly deadly.

This movie is the work of a man who knows how to direct a thriller. Smooth, calm, confident, it builds suspense instead of depending on shock and action. The actors create characters who suggest intriguing secrets. The atmosphere—a rain-swept Martha's Vineyard in winter—has an ominous, gray chill, and the main interior looks just as cold.

This is the beach house being used by Adam Lang (Pierce Brosnan), a former British prime minister so inspired by Tony Blair that he might as well be wearing a name tag. Lang has one of those households much beloved by British authors of country house mysteries, in which everyone is a potential suspect—of something, anyway. His wife, Ruth (Olivia Williams), smart and bitter, met Lang at Cambridge. His assistant, Amelia (Kim Cattrall), smart and devious, is having an affair with him. The wife knows and isn't above referring to it before the Ghost (Ewan McGregor). Security men lurk about, and a serving couple look rather sinister.

Just as his ghost writer starts work, Lang is accused by his former foreign minister of sanctioning the kidnapping and torture of suspects. The World Court prepares an indictment. It would be unwise for him to return to Britain, and he flees to Washington for a photo op with the U.S. administration, unnamed, although the secretary of state looks a whole lot like Condi Rice.

The story is based on a best-seller by Robert Harris, who cowrote the screenplay with Polanski. He implies parallels between his story and the Blair and (both) Bush administrations, but uses a light touch and sly footwork so that not every viewer will necessarily connect the dots. There is also a loud, clanging alarm inviting comparison between Lang, an exile sought by a court, and Polanski himself. This is also the fourth thriller in recent months to make a villain of a corporation obviously modeled on Halliburton.

The Ghost is left to his own devices in a house haunted by the unsaid, and Polanski slips into a pure filmmaking mode. I won't describe what the Ghost searches for, but I will tell you that Polanski evokes Hitchcock in a conversation with an elderly local (Eli Wallach) and some forbidding beach scenes. And that he is masterful in the way he shows the dead former ghost providing the new one with directions, so to speak, leading to a possible source.

There is also a Hitchcock touch in visuals where an incriminating note is passed from hand to hand; the scene is so well done that it distracts from the fact that the Ghost didn't need the information in the note to arrive at the same inference.

There are a few other loose ends. The film seems to have a high incidence of black cars designed to be used as murder weapons. It's far from clear what Ruth Lang's emotional state is on one rainy night. The Ghost himself seems too much a lightweight to explain his daring sleuthing. But the performances are so convincing in detail that they distract us from our questions. McGregor's character has no family, little pride, and much insouciance, but is very smart and doesn't enjoy his intelligence being insulted. And Olivia Williams projects the air of a wife who is committed to her husband in more than expected ways.

*The Ghost Writer* is handsome, smooth, and persuasive. It is a Well Made Film. Polanski at seventy-six provides a reminder of directors of the past who were raised on craft, not gimmicks, and depended on a deliberate rhythm of editing rather than mindless quick cutting. The film immerses you in its experience. It's a reminder that you can lose yourself in a story because all a film really wants to do is tell it.

## Gigante ★ ★ ★

NO MPAA RATING, 88 m., 2010

Horacio Camandule (Jara), Leonor Svarcas (Julia). Directed by Adrian Biniez and produced by Fernando Epstein. Screenplay by Biniez.

We are all voyeurs, although some people fondly describe themselves as "people watchers." Going to the movies is at some level pure voyeurism—if they involve people, that is. Transformers don't count. I admire films that consist only or in large part of watching. *Vertigo* is the classic example, and *The Lives of Others* was voyeurism by eavesdropping.

*Gigante* is a film that has little meaningful dialogue; just incidental comments along the stream of a boring life. Jara (Horacio Camandule), is a big, strong, lonely man, who works the night shift in a huge supermarket in Montevideo, watching security monitors. He lives alone, and his social life is restricted to messing around with his young nephew. In the company lunchroom, he doesn't chat. Nor does he drink, smoke, watch TV, or much of anything else. He sometimes works as a nightclub bouncer.

One night on his video monitors, Jara notices Julia (Leonor Svarcas). She's a member of the corps of cleaning women, mopping the aisles. He observes her shoplifting something. He doesn't care. Clicking on his cameras, he's able to follow her around the store. Almost immediately, he starts following her around her life.

Since Julia is heard to say nothing until the very end of the film, all depends on the performance of Camandule. Since he says so little, it depends in turn on his presence, his aura. He is tall, broad, overweight, taciturn. He isn't the "gentle giant" type. On the other hand, because he can (as we see) efficiently wallop anyone, he has no need to act intimidating. He just sits or walks around, absorbed in his thoughts.

Of course he wants to ask Julia out. Of course he lacks the nerve. He follows her everywhere—shopping, home, to the movies, to an Internet café, even on a date with a pudgy nerd. Jara is innovative. Later he manages to strike up a conversation with the nerd and discovers the nerd doesn't think Julia liked him. It was their first date. Their tastes didn't match. For one thing, she likes heavy metal, and the nerd can't stand it.

This news is Tabasco for Jara. He has Metallica posters on his wall, listens to metal on his iPod, keeps rhythm with his hands. Does this give him courage? Not exactly. Is it creepy that he follows her? Technically, yes, but we sense he's no threat; his presence reads more as protective, and sad. We have no idea if they have a future together, but we hope he'll work up the courage to at least speak to her.

Because of the limitations imposed by the nature of *Gigante,* and because of Jara's simple, almost childish shyness, the film doesn't transcend its characters. Like Jara, it waits and watches. I kept watching. I was curious. We were both wondering if he would ever ask her out. I think I wanted him to more than he did.

## The Girl from the Naked Eye ★ ★

R, 84 m., 2012

Jason Yee (Jake), Samantha Streets (Sandy), Gary Stretch (Frank), Dominique Swain (Alissa), Ron Yuan (Simon), Sasha Grey (Lena). Directed by David Ren and produced by Henry Mu, Jason Yee, and Ron Yuan. Screenplay by Ren, Yee, and Larry Madill.

*The Girl from the Naked Eye* opens with a lurid cover from an old pulp detective magazine, and that's the look it achieves. This is a film noir crossed with a martial arts movie, taking place in the dark shadows of mean streets. And that's about all you need to know about the plot, which serves simply as a device to keep us moving right along from one bloody action sequence to the next.

It isn't a great movie, but it looks terrific, and makes me look forward to the next film by director David Ren. He has a good eye. I like his vertiginous high-angle shots, looking down into the gray, forbidding caverns between skyscrapers. I like the way he uses the reds and greens on neon signs, isolated in dark settings. I like the offices of nightclubs and mob bosses, where cigars are smoked and threats are made. I like the smoking in general: Some of the characters seem to be smoking at each other as an act of aggression. And the way the dialogue sometimes seems to be deliberately trying for satire, as when two guys go nose to nose and seem to be seeing which can shout the f-word the most.

It sounds, in fact, as if I like the movie. It was a pleasure to watch, but it never deserved its visuals. The story (which actually could come from one of those old pulps) is narrated in a hard-boiled voice-over by the hero, Jake (Jason Yee), who drives call girls for an escort agency and vows vengeance when his favorite girl, Sandy (Samantha Streets), is gruesomely murdered. His search for the killer leads him into one dangerous situation after another, especially since he seems to have stumbled into a situation where powerful men are not especially thrilled about finding the killer.

The movie is populated with don't-blink

cameos, including one by Dominique Swain, Adrian Lyne's Lolita, and another by porn star Sasha Grey. The rest of the cast is filled with hard-looking tough guys, more than half of them Asian-American, although no reference to ethnicity is ever made in the film. The movie seems destined for DVD, but would benefit by being seen on a big screen.

## Girl in Progress ★ ½

PG-13, 90 m., 2012

Eva Mendes (Grace), Cierra Ramirez (Ansiedad), Patricia Arquette (Ms. Armstrong), Matthew Modine (Dr. Harford), Raini Rodriguez (Tavita), Landon Liboiron (Trevor), Eugenio Derbez (Mission Impossible), Richard Harmon (Bad Boy), Russell Peters (Emile), Brenna O'Brien (Valerie). Directed by Patricia Riggen and produced by John Fiedler and Ben Odell. Screenplay by Hiram Martinez.

The high school lesson plan calls for a study of coming-of-age. The teacher approaches this topic as if it's uncharted territory for her teenage students. Maybe she's right. A student named Ansiedad (Cierra Ramirez) does some extra study outside class and begins a project to deliberately and consciously come of age.

Was it only a couple of weeks ago that the couples in *Think Like a Man* led their lives after studying Steve Harvey's self-help book? The only movie I've enjoyed based on a self-help book was *Everything You Always Wanted to Know About Sex (But Were Afraid to Ask).* Come to think of it, there have also been some good films based on the Bible. What Ansiedad discovers is that she has to go on full alert for epiphanies, become aware of tensions between adults and children, lose her virginity, and dump her best friend. The first three will likely occur by themselves, and the process of dumping her best friend is so mean-spirited it casts a pall over several scenes.

Ansiedad's mom is Grace (Eva Mendes), a woman with problems of her own. During the day, she cleans house for the married Dr. Harford (Matthew Modine), and in the evenings she's a popular waitress at a clam shack in Vancouver (which, of course, is not identified; Canada is playing America again). Grace and the doctor are having an affair, and Grace should read a few more books before believing him when he says he'll leave his wife and child and marry her.

Ansiedad's best friend is the appealing Tavita (Raini Rodriguez), who is loyal, true, and overweight. She's one of those pals you should keep around instead of dumping because of some goofy theory about rites of passage. When and how Ansiedad dumps her is so stupidly cruel that the subplot undermines the film and does serious damage to the character.

Ansiedad has chosen who she wants to lose her virginity to. This is a character actually identified in the credits as Bad Boy (Richard Harmon). Attention, women! You should never sleep with a man whose only attribute is that you want to sleep with him. I should write a book of my own. Because Ansiedad is a smart charmer, and well played by Cierra Ramirez, she should really be above this sort of thing—above the whole movie, really. It's rather hard to accept her as a heroine when she's treacherous to Tavita and shamelessly looking for stud service.

The movie, written by Hiram Martinez and directed by Patricia Riggen, finds parallels between the unwise relationships of Ansiedad and her mom, who both have unwise taste in men. The mom is not super-attentive to her daughter, which is why the kid is driven to grow up by studying books. Eva Mendes is another actress too good for this movie. I should add that the clam shack is also too good. It's another one of those movie restaurants where the regulars know everybody; it supplies the stage on which their lives are led.

I wonder if I've been coming across as a moralist recently. In reviewing Bobcat Goldthwaite's *God Bless America,* I felt it was necessary to point out that, gee, it's not right to go around killing people, even if they do offend you on reality TV. Now I wonder what teenage girls the makers of *Girl in Progress* had in mind, and whether they actually consider it progress.

## The Girl on the Train ★ ★ ★

NO MPAA RATING, 101 m., 2010

Emilie Dequenne (Jeanne), Catherine Deneuve (Louise), Michel Blanc (Samuel Bleistein), Ronit Elkabetz (Judith Bleistein), Mathieu Demy

(Alex Bleistein), Nicolas Duvauchelle (Franck), Jeremy Quaegebeur (Nathan). Directed by Andre Techine and produced by Said Ben Said. Screenplay by Techine, Odile Barski, and Jean-Marie Besset, based on the play *RER* by Besset.

The girl in Andre Techine's *The Girl on the Train* is Jeanne, who has never fully engaged in the society she occupies. She Rollerblades through French suburbs with her iPod blocking out other sounds, as the world glides past unobserved. Was it the job interview with the lawyer Bleistein that put Jews into her mind? One doubts she had given them, or anything else, much thought.

Jeanne (Emilie Dequenne) is sent to Samuel Bleistein by her mother, Louise (Catherine Deneuve). He was once in love with her. One of the nation's most powerful lawyers, he makes time to see the girl because of old memories. His secretary pages through her résumé and observes there isn't much there. Nor does the interview itself go well. Jeanne doesn't know much, hasn't done much, doesn't even realize how little she's done or what there is to be known. She lives in a cocoon of electronic distraction.

She doesn't care. She's having a romance with a young athlete, a wrestler, tattooed and a little strange. They break up. Now she's jobless, alone, and with her mother on her case—Louise, who provides home care for toddlers, works in the garden, and is gentle enough with her—but anything that interrupts Jeanne's reverie is annoying.

For no particular reason, perhaps hoping to win Bleistein's sympathy, perhaps not, perhaps she doesn't know, she makes up a false story of being assaulted on a train by North Africans who taunted her as a Jew, beat her, and carved a swastika on her stomach. She isn't Jewish, not that it's a point. The case becomes a national scandal. The French president can't get on the phone fast enough to express his sympathy and solidarity.

The police are not as sympathetic because there is absolutely no evidence to back up her claims. No witnesses, no evidence on security cameras—and why is the swastika drawn backward? Well, it can be difficult for the inexperienced. I don't know if I could draw one correctly.

These events occupy the first movement of the film, titled "Circumstances." The second is titled "Consequences," and is really the reason for the first. It deals more fully with Bleistein (the shortish, quite bald Michel Blanc) and his family: his son, Alex (Mathieu Demy), and son's wife, Judith (Ronit Elkabetz), and their child, Nathan (Jeremy Quaegebeur), who is preparing for his bar mitzvah.

The movie seems likely to be about anti-Semitism, but that's more the occasion than the subject. Bleistein gets involved in the case, sees there is nothing to do, doesn't consider Jeanne's lie a case of anti-Semitism so much as a case of utter cluelessness. Within his family, tensions uncoil that are typical of all families. What the film is really about is social embarrassment, and Bleistein's clear-headed, calm understanding that his old friend has a stupid daughter who has caused fraudulent trouble for a great many people.

The story, I understand, is based on a real French case not long ago. I can think of two similar cases—Tawana Brawley, the black girl who said she was attacked by whites, and Ashley Todd, who scratched a B on her face and made up a story that a black man robbed her and was angered by her McCain sticker.

Do these stories inspire others? Do dim TV viewers see them and come away with the impression that such stories inspire sympathy? Don't they hear about the later disgrace? Are they hungry for attention? Who knows? The perpetrators don't inspire much interest, but the effects do: How the media handles them, how politicians jump aboard, how false incidents reveal real racism.

Techine is a French master about the same age as Scorsese. His credits include such splendid films as *My Favorite Season* and *Les Voleurs.* He's worked before with Deneuve, who here strikes a nice balance of sweetness and vagueness. Perhaps she simply forgot to raise a girl with an idea in her head.

## The Girl Who Kicked the Hornet's Nest ★ ★ ★

R, 148 m., 2010

Noomi Rapace (Lisbeth Salander), Michael Nyqvist (Mikael Blomkvist), Lena Endre (Erika

Berger), Annika Hallin (Annika Giannini), Anders Ahlbom Rosendahl (Dr. Peter Teleborian), Mikael Spreitz (Ronald Niedermann). Directed by Daniel Alfredson and produced by Soren Staermose. Screenplay by Ulf Rydberg, based on the novel by Stieg Larsson.

Lisbeth Salander makes a transfixing heroine precisely because she has nothing but scorn for such a role. Embodied here for the third time by Noomi Rapace, she's battered, angry, and hostile, even toward those who would be her friends. Some of the suspense in the final courtroom showdown of *The Girl Who Kicked the Hornet's Nest* comes from the excellent question of whether she would rather be found guilty than provide anyone with the satisfaction of hearing her testify in her own defense.

By the time she comes to what is essentially a sanity hearing, she has returned to the ranks of punk fashionistas, with the black leather pants and jacket, the boots, the studs and buckles, the spikes, the body piercings, the eyeliner that looks like protective armor, and the stark black crest of her hair. She sits sullen and silent in the courtroom, as if saying, "I care nothing for you, although I have spent hours working on my look in front of the mirror."

She is formidably smart and deeply wounded from childhood, as we know from the earlier two films in the Stieg Larsson trilogy. Worse, she can't leave her pain behind in childhood. Again in her life are her freakish, gigantic half-brother Niedermann (Mikael Spreitz) and the psychologist who fabricated her incarceration in an asylum. And the murderous members of "the Section," a rogue killing unit within the Swedish national police, are determined to eliminate her once and for all.

The outlines of her dilemma will be clear to those who've seen *The Girl with the Dragon Tattoo* and *The Girl Who Played with Fire,* but this film has enough quick flashbacks to orient the first-timer. It begins literally when the second one ended, after the bloody confrontation in the barn with her father and half-brother. She's taken to the hospital with a bullet in her brain, and spends much of the film's first half in intensive care and refusing to speak.

That frees the director, Daniel Alfredson, to focus more time on Mikael Blomkvist (Michael Nyqvist), the investigative journalist who collaborated with her in the first film and has become her fierce defender—and perhaps more, a man who loves her. Their mutual affection was an intriguing subtext in the first film, but has been on hold ever since, while Mikael continues his relaxed intimacy with his editor, Erika Berger (Lena Endre). There are said to be two more Larsson novels in various stages of completion, but even if they're not publishable, Lisbeth Salander is too good a character to suspend after three films, and my guess is there must be sequels.

The sequels need not fret overmuch about plot. These films are really about personality, dialogue, and the possibility that the state has placed itself outside the law. That leads to an oppressive, doomy atmosphere that the characters move through with apprehension. We understand the basics of the Section conspiracy, we recognize most of the faces, but few of us could pass a test on exactly who is who. No problem; neither could Lisbeth nor Mikael.

The tension—and there is a lot of it—grows from the danger that Lisbeth brings upon herself by refusing to act sensibly for her own welfare. She has such a burned-in distrust of authority that even a friend like Mikael gets closed out, and Rapace takes a simple friendly "see you" and invests it with the effort it costs Lisbeth to utter. Her battle with herself is more suspenseful than her battle against her enemies, because enemies can be fought with and that provides release, but we spend much of *The Girl Who Kicked the Hornet's Nest* straining against Lisbeth's fear and sending her urgent telepathic messages about what she should do.

These are all very well made films. Like most European films, they have adults who are grown-ups, not arrested adolescents. Mikael and Erika, his boss and lover, have earned the lines in their faces and don't act like reckless action heroes. They make their danger feel so real to us that we realize the heroes of many action movies don't really believe they're in any danger at all. Lisbeth is in grave danger, but in great part because of her damaged obstinacy, and that scares us more than any number of six-foot-four Nordic blond homicidal half-brothers.

So what has happened is this uptight, ferocious little gamin Lisbeth has won our hearts, and we care about these stories and think there had better be more. The funny thing is I've seen the "real" Noomi Rapace on TV, and she has a warm smile and a sweet face. What a disappointment.

## The Girl Who Played with Fire ★ ★ ★ ½

R, 129 m., 2010

Noomi Rapace (Lisbeth Salander), Michael Nyqvist (Mikael Blomkvist), Lena Endre (Erika Berger), Annika Hallin (Annika Giannini), Per Oscarsson (Holger Palmgren), Malin Erikson (Sofia Ledarp), Peter Andersson (Nils Bjurman), Yasmine Garbi (Miriam Wu), Johan Kylen (Jan Bublanski), Tanja Lorentzon (Sonja Modig), Paolo Roberto (Himself), Georgi Staykov (Zalachenko). Directed by Daniel Alfredson and produced by Soren Staermose and Jon Mankell. Screenplay by Jonas Frykberg, based on the novel by Stieg Larsson.

The girl is an enigma. She has a dragon tattoo, she plays with fire, she kicks a hornet's nest. These are not personality traits. We learn in the second movie based on a Stieg Larsson thriller a little more about her childhood, and her fiery relationship with her father. What we don't learn is why she is content to live the life of a hermit, requiring very little human company. Even when she lends a woman her apartment for a year and makes love with her the night she moves in, it seems more like a social gesture.

Noomi Rapace returns as Lisbeth Salander in *The Girl Who Played with Fire.* She was electrifying in last year's *The Girl with the Dragon Tattoo.* She didn't look like your average young heroine. She was lean but not skinny, taut but not muscular, a solemnity rather than a gamin. Her mastery of computers allowed her to hack into almost any information, and the hatred of men's violence against women gave her a motive.

If you saw the earlier film, or have read the novels, you'll recognize some of the key players here. But you can walk in as a first-timer and understand. Mikael Blomkvist (Michael Nyqvist) is back as an investigative journalist. His *Millennium* magazine is negotiating with a researcher and her boyfriend to learn the names and details of trafficking in women between Russia and Sweden, and famous men are implicated as clients. Larsson paints a portrait of a corrupt Swedish climate in politics, the law, and business.

Although Mikael and Lisbeth are the leads, they don't meet until even later in this film than the last one. As before, they sense each other by tracks in cyberspace. Lisbeth has returned to Stockholm after learning of a case she has a personal interest in and finds herself on the trail of a killer. This trail grows complex as it leads back into her own past, and to the introduction of a onetime Soviet bad man and a hulking freak. In a Bond picture these would be stereotypes, but the Larsson stories aim closer to human dimensions and locate them firmly in a well-seen Sweden of cities and isolated country homes.

I suppose at its base this is a police procedural (although the police are on the wrong track all along). But Lisbeth and Mikael are quirky individuals and make up their detective work as they go, so it's hard to predict the story arc. It's also an advantage that the actors are *not* conventional star types. That will be the tricky part in the Hollywood versions. Carey Mulligan and Daniel Craig are cast for David Fincher's 2012 remake of *Dragon,* and they're very good, but are they too mainstream? How about, oh, say, Ed Norton and the non-*Twilight* Kristen Stewart?

The film is filled with strong supporting roles. Peter Andersson plays a twisted attorney. Georgi Staykov is the malevolent Russian, incredibly verbally cruel in one scene. I noted how good Lisbeth's old legal protector, Palmgren, was in an old people's home, as she allowed a little tenderness to show through. I discovered later he was played by Per Oscarsson, a great Swedish actor since 1944, star of *Hunger* and *Here's Your Life* (both 1966), who, incredibly, never worked with Bergman. Someone like that adds texture to a thriller, and with an actress like Rapace, creates an audience sympathy that pays off long after the scene is over.

*The Girl Who Played with Fire* is very good, but a step down from *The Girl with the Dragon Tattoo,* if only because that film and its casting were so fresh and unexpected. A thriller is incomparably more arresting when it involves plausible people doing plausible things, rather than archetypes costarring with animation.

## The Girl with the Dragon Tattoo ★ ★ ★ ★

NO MPAA RATING, 152 m., 2010

Michael Nyqvist (Mikael Blomkvist), Noomi Rapace (Lisbeth Salander), Lena Endre (Erika Berger), Sven-Bertil Taube (Henrik Vanger), Peter Haber (Martin Vanger), Peter Andersson (Nils Bjurman), Marika Lagercrantz (Cecilia Vanger), Ingvar Hirdwall (Dirch Frode). Directed by Niels Arden Oplev and produced by Soren Staermose. Screenplay by Nikolaj Arcel and Rasmus Heisterberg, based on the novel by Stieg Larsson.

*The Girl with the Dragon Tattoo* is a compelling thriller to begin with, but it adds the rare quality of having a heroine more fascinating than the story. She's a twenty-four-year-old Goth girl named Lisbeth Salander, with body piercings and tattoos: thin, small, fierce, damaged, a genius computer hacker. She smokes to quiet her racing heart.

Lisbeth is as compelling as any movie character in recent memory. Played by Noomi Rapace with an unwavering intensity, she finds her own emotional needs nurtured by the nature of the case she investigates, the disappearance of a young girl forty years earlier. As this case is revealed as part of a long-hidden pattern of bizarre violence against women, her own abused past returns with a vengeance.

Rapace makes the character compulsively interesting. She plays against a passive forty-something hero, Mikael Blomkvist (Michael Nyqvist), an investigative journalist who has six months of freedom before beginning a prison sentence for libel against a Swedish tycoon. Mikael, resourceful and intelligent, is hired by an elderly billionaire named Henrik Vanger (Sven-Bertil Taube), who inhabits a gloomy mansion on a remote island and broods about the loss of his beloved niece, Harriet. She vanished one day when the island was cut off from the mainland. Her body was never found. Because the access bridge was blocked, the killer must have been a member of Vanger's large and greedy family, which he hates. Three brothers were Nazi sympathizers during the war.

The notion of a murder with a limited list of suspects was conventional even before Agatha Christie. Niels Arden Oplev's *The Girl with the Dragon Tattoo* pays it lip service, with Mikael covering a wall with photos of the suspects. But this is a new age, and in addition to his search of newspaper and legal archives, he uses the Internet. That's how he comes across Lisbeth, who has been investigating *him.* She's described as Sweden's best hacker, a claim we have no reason to doubt, and the intensity of her focus, contrasted to her walled-off emotional life, suggests Asperger's.

They team up on the case, and might become lovers if not for Mikael's diffidence and her secretive hostility. They become efficient partners. Scenes involving newspaper photographs and Internet searches create sequences like a *Blow Up* for the digital age. The film is unique in my memory for displaying screen shots of an actual computer operating system, Mac OS X, and familiar programs like Google, e-mail, and iPhoto. Ever notice how most movie computers work like magic?

The forbidding island setting, the winter chill, the frosty inhabitants, all combine with dread suspicions to create an uncommonly effective thriller. It's longer than average, but not slow, not after we become invested in the depravity of the case. There are scenes involving rape, bondage, and assault that are stronger than most of what serves in the movies for sexual violence, but these scenes are not exploitation. They have a ferocious feminist orientation, and although *The Girl with the Dragon Tattoo* seems a splendid title, the original Swedish title was the stark *Men Who Hate Women.*

The novel, one of a trilogy that Stieg Larsson completed before his untimely death at forty-four, was an international best-seller. It is destined to be remade by Hollywood. That may be a good film, but if I were you, I'd be sure to watch this version. The Hollywood version will almost certainly tone down the sexual violence. I can't think of an American actress who could play Lisbeth. Kristen Stewart, whom I respect, has been mentioned. Dakota Fanning. I dunno. A younger Jodie Foster, maybe. Someone able to play hard as nails and emotionally unavailable. Make her a Swede, and simply cast Noomi Rapace.

This is not a deep, psychological study. But it's a sober, grown-up film. It has action, but not the hyperkinetic activity that passes for action in too many American movies. It has sex, but not eroticism. Its male lead is brave and capable, but not macho. Its female lead is sexy in the abstract, perhaps, but not seductive or alluring. This is a movie about characters who have more important things to do than be characters in an action thriller.

## The Girl with the Dragon Tattoo ★ ★ ★ ½

R, 158 m., 2011

Daniel Craig (Mikael Blomkvist), Rooney Mara (Lisbeth Salander), Christopher Plummer (Henrik Vanger), Stellan Skarsgard (Martin Vanger), Steven Berkoff (Frode), Robin Wright (Erika Berger), Yorick van Wageningen (Bjurman), Joely Richardson (Anita Vanger). Directed by David Fincher and produced by Cean Chaffin, Scott Rudin, Soren Staemose, and Ole Sondberg. Screenplay by Steven Zaillian, based on the book by Stieg Larsson.

The success of the heroine Lisbeth Salander suggests a hunger in audiences for an action picture hero who is not a white thirty-fiveish male with black stubble on his chin. Such characters are often effective, but they sometimes seem on loan from other pictures. There are few characters anywhere like Salander, played here by Rooney Mara and by Noomi Rapace in the original 2009 Swedish picture. Thin, stark, haunted, with a look that crosses goth with S&M, she is fearsomely intelligent and emotionally stranded.

It has been a fascination of the lean, fierce Salander that draws me into the *Girl* movies. We know horrible things happened to her earlier in life that explain her anger and proud isolation. Her apartment in Stockholm is like an eagle's aerie. She has an isolated life online, distant relationships with a few other technology geeks, and a bleak loneliness. One of the undercurrents of these movies is the very gradual rapport that grows between Lisbeth and Mikael Blomkvist (Daniel Craig), the radical investigative journalist. This is never the kind of movie where they're going to fall in love. That she even smiles is a breakthrough.

The stories churn in my mind. I've read two of the Stieg Larsson novels, seen all three of the Swedish films, and now am back for my third tour through the first story. It's an odd feeling to be seeing a movie that resembles its Swedish counterpart in so many ways, yet is subtly different under the direction of David Fincher and with a screenplay by Steven Zaillian. I don't know if it's better or worse. It has a different air about it.

Fincher is certainly a more assured director than Niels Arden Oplev, who did the 2009 Swedish film. Yet his assurance isn't always a plus. The earlier film had a certain earnest directness about it that seemed to raise the stakes. Emotions were closer to the surface. Rooney Mara and the earlier actress, Noomi Rapace, both create convincing Salanders, but Rapace seems more uneasy in her skin, more threatened. And as the male lead, Mikael Blomkvist, the earlier actor (Michael Nyqvist) seemed less confident, more threatened. In this film, Daniel Craig brings along the confidence of James Bond. How could he not? He looks too comfortable in danger.

The labyrinth of the story remains murky. The elderly millionaire Henrik Vanger (Christopher Plummer), cut off from the mainland on the family island, yearns to know how his beloved niece Harriet died forty years ago. Because apparently neither she nor her body left the island on the day she disappeared, and no trace has ever been found, suspicion rests on those who were there that day, in particular, other Vanger relatives whose houses overlook Henrik's from their own isolation.

They provide a snaky group of suspects. Many seem involved in corruption. Some have pasts with Nazi connections. Mikael arranges their photos and newspaper clippings and file cards in a collage pinned to a wall and connected with red lines of speculation, but his threads of suspicion seem to lead to . . . everyone.

In this film more than the other one, the stories of Mikael and Lisbeth are kept separate for an extended period. We learn about the girl's state-appointed guardian (Yorick van Wageningen), who abused her, stole from her, and embedded terror. Her attempts to avenge herself would make a movie of their own.

Zaillian's screenplay comes down to a series of fraught scenes between his leads and a distinctive gallery of supporting characters, given weight by such as Stellan Skarsgard, Robin Wright, and the iconic London actor Steven Berkoff. These people inhabit a world with no boring people. By providing Mikael with his own small cottage on the island, Henrik Vanger isolates him in a vulnerable situation, which sinks in as he realizes he's probably sharing the island with a murderer.

There's also the problem of why Henrik continues to receive watercolors of wildflowers on his birthday, a tradition his niece began but that inexplicably has continued after her death. If you subtract computers, geeks, goth girls, nose piercing, motorcycles, and dragon tattoos, what we have at the bottom here is a classic Agatha Christie plot. The island works as a sealed room.

I realize most people will be seeing the story for the first time in this version. Because it worked for me, I suspect it will work better for them because everything will be new. I'm happy to have seen both. If I had a choice of seeing one or the other for the first time, I'd choose the 2009 version. It seems closer to the bone, with a less-confident surface. Even the spoken Swedish adds to the effect; in English, the characters are concealing secrets but not so uncannily concealing themselves.

## God Bless America ★ ★

R, 100 m., 2012

Joel Murray (Frank), Tara Lynne Barr (Roxy), Melinda Page Hamilton (Alison), Mackenzie Brooke Smith (Ava), Rich McDonald (Brad), Maddie Hasson (Chloe). Directed by Bobcat Goldthwait and produced by Jeff Culotta, Sarah de Sa Rego, Richard Kelly, and Sean McKittrick. Screenplay by Goldthwait.

The first half hour or so of Bobcat Goldthwait's *God Bless America* promises so much more than the film is finally able to deliver. Here is a film that begins with merciless comic savagery and descends into merely merciless savagery. But wow, what an opening.

It consists of a man watching television, and the television he watches. The man is Frank (Joel Murray, Bill's brother). His head rests uneasily on his sofa as the screams of the wailing baby next door drill through the paper-thin walls. He suffers from migraines. On TV, he sees stupidity and cruelty. The news channels portray an America in decay. Such idiotic plagues as the Westboro Baptist Church are seen picketing veterans' funerals, TV rants are delivered by unhinged commentators, reality TV reduces civilization to the consumption of worthless consumer trash, and Frank stares in pain at the screen.

Of course the Westboro Church isn't mentioned by name, but there's no mistaking its "God Hates Fags" posters. Later in the film, daringly, Goldthwait's script does name names—even Diablo Cody, whom Frank despises for having created, in *Juno*, a heroine who is actually very much like the one in this movie. But I'm getting ahead of myself.

First Frank learns from his foul-mouthed doctor that he's dying of an incurable brain tumor. Then, at his hateful job (in an office filled with coworkers obsessed with celebrity gossip), he makes a thoughtful gesture and is fired for moronic reasons of political correctness. Then, on reality TV he sees a famous teenage brat throw a tantrum because her parents gave her a car, but it isn't the one she asked for, an Escalade.

All of this is especially effective because of Joel Murray's performance. He makes Frank a decent, levelheaded, respectable man, not an obvious comedy type. He is also smart and articulate in explaining his revulsion with aspects of current American civilization—so articulate, indeed, that sometimes he sounds like a combination of Al Franken, Rachel Maddow, and the "I'm as mad as hell!" speech in *Network*.

After getting the one-two punch of being fired and diagnosed with a brain tumor, something cracks. He sticks a gun in his mouth, and then decides, as a symbolic gesture, to first shoot the spoiled brat on reality TV.

That's when the film goes astray. His shooting is witnessed by Roxy (Tara Lynne Barr), a girl about the same age as his victim, who tells him it was awesome. She urges him not to stop when there are still so many worthy targets, and insists on coming along with him on what turns out to be a cross-country murder spree. While we understood why Frank might have been pushed over the edge with his first murder, you can't just go around killing people, y'know. And Roxy comes across as a deranged teenage psychopath.

Much of their relationship involves Frank trying to behave decently with her, despite her obliviousness to the idea that a forty-five-year-old man has no business in bed with an underage girl. Roxy is a disturbed creature. Yet they pal up and enjoy a strange immunity to being captured, despite how easy it should be to spot them. Everything finally leads to the live broadcast of an *American Idol*–type TV show, where Frank wants to vent his disgust at the way America has mocked a fat kid who sang off-key and was driven to attempt suicide.

In that subplot Goldthwait exhibits some of the sharp and perceptive intelligence that often informs the film. Turns out the fat kid didn't want to kill himself because people laughed at him, but because he might be taken off TV. Nice. It does seem true that a lot of people will do anything, however humiliating, for fame.

But by that point in the film, the air has gone out of Goldthwait's balloon. What he has created, in the name of comic social commentary, is an amoral movie about two psychopaths killing people they believe deserve to die. As a general rule, that's an evil reason for taking someone's life. If we agree with Frank and Roxy, we also agree with people who shoot at abortion clinics, kids who open fire at their schools, and road rage killings. I see what Goldthwait is trying to do and agree with many of his complaints about our society, but it finally became impossible to laugh.

## Goodbye First Love ★ ★ ★

NO MPAA RATING, 108 m., 2012

Lola Creton (Camille), Sebastian Urzendowsky (Sullivan), Magne-Havard Brekke (Lorenz), Valerie Bonneton (Camille's Mother), Serge Renko (Camille's Father), Ozay Fecht (Sullivan's Mother). Directed by Mia Hansen-Love and produced by Philippe Martin and David Thion. Screenplay by Hansen-Love.

It is Camille's first love, but it may not be Sullivan's. She is awash in it, consumed by it, made joyful. It is the center of her being. She is fifteen. Sullivan is nineteen, and yes, he loves her very much, but there is another part to him, elusive even to himself. It is far too simple to say he has trouble committing to her. His trouble is fully understanding his own desires.

Their parents know of their love and respect it. It is accepted as a natural part of growing up. Camille's parents are benign, only cautioning her against obsession. But obsession is very much where she is. She has never felt love before and is sure she never will again.

They go away alone for an idyllic holiday in her family's country cottage, near a little river in a pastoral setting. The sun dapples the water, the trees, the flowers, and their faces. I'm reminded of *Elvira Madigan*. And then, incredibly, it emerges that Sullivan (Sebastian Urzendowsky) has no plans to go back to school. He will leave with some friends for ten months to backpack through South America. Then he will return, and they will resume.

This is never deeply discussed. It is a given. His planning must have started some time ago, while his romance with Camille (Lola Creton) was still forming. She is shattered. Of course she is. I believe the movie is too easy on him, the egotistical pig, who thinks the world revolves around him. Yes, by all means, backpack through the Andes. But don't do it while talking with this young flower about how you will spend your lifetimes together.

*Goodbye First Love* is the third feature by Mia Hansen-Love, herself barely thirty, whose previous film was the perceptive *The Father of My Children* (2009), about a film producer whose sudden death exposes the fragile nature of his business dealings. There, too, we see the pattern of a man excluding a loved one (in this case, his wife) from his personal planning.

This film spans about eight years and focuses on Camille; Sullivan's travels in South America are represented by stickpins on a map, and the day comes when his letters stop, and Camille pulls the pins out of the map and puts them back in their box. She goes to architecture school and takes her professor as her mentor and then lover. This is Lorenz (Magne-Havard Brekke), a Dane whose lanky hair falls in disdain over his face, but who is older, more stable, responsible. They are in love in terms of their relationship, but there is no fire in her heart.

What has happened to Sullivan? When we find out, we couldn't be more astonished. Camille's reaction should be livid rage. This stupid man has not valued her love. He is irresponsible and careless. And, of course, then he expects to be understood and forgiven.

This is a fascinating film. I've withheld a lot of information from you. I wonder exactly what Hansen-Love means by it. It seems to me that a great deal more anger and contempt would be appropriate toward Sullivan—if not from Camille, then from the film. At the same time, Camille herself is a suitable case for study. Love is one thing. Even first love. But her love is so extreme and durable it qualifies as a psychiatric condition. If Sullivan were afraid of her intensity, we might understand the trip to Peru. But the suspicion remains that he never fully comprehends its depth.

We think of first love as sweet and valuable, a blessed if hazardous condition. This film, deeper than it seems, dares to suggest that beyond a certain point it can represent a tragedy.

## The Good Guy ★ ★ ★

R, 90 m., 2010

Scott Porter (Tommy), Alexis Bledel (Beth), Bryan Greenberg (Daniel), Anna Chlumsky (Lisa), Aaron Yoo (Steve-O), Andrew McCarthy (Cash), Andrew Stewart-Jones (Shakespeare). Directed by Julio DePietro and produced by DePietro, Rene Bastian, and Linda Moran. Screenplay by DePietro.

*The Good Guy* creates the interesting notion that Wall Street trading involves a gang of hard-partying goofs who pass their days playing video games with our money. They trade too fast to know much about the stocks they're selling—and besides, they mostly trade funds and may only vaguely know how the portfolios are weighted.

That at least is the impression given by *The Good Guy,* which contains not a moment in which any trader knows much about the fundamentals of a stock, but much about the dance of the numbers on a screen and the mind games he's playing with other traders. At the end of the day, all that matters is the score. Well, I guess that's the way it works.

At Morgan & Morgan, no relation to JPMorgan or Morgan Stanley, we meet a team of traders bossed by the legendary Cash (Andrew McCarthy). His team leader is Tommy (Scott Porter), who's making money hand over fist while leading the pack on sorties into bars that have a high babe count. These guys get drunk and play adolescent games and plow through conquests and keep laughing so it doesn't get quiet. There is charm in being seventeen, and pathos in being twenty-seven and acting as if you're seventeen.

The crew includes Shakespeare (Andrew Stewart-Jones), a black guy with a British accent who may realize, but doesn't care, that any babe impressed by a British accent belongs on Jaywalking. There's Steve-O (Aaron Yoo), master trader. And there's the new guy, Daniel (Bryan Greenberg), who, odd as it may seem, prefers not to horse around but stay home, fix himself some dinner, and read a good novel. You know, maybe by Dickens, whom many people don't know is about as much fun as any novelist who ever lived.

The section's top hotshot bails out to join another firm, and Cash orders Tommy to fill his chair. On a hunch, Tommy promotes Daniel. Everyone including Daniel is disbelieving. Under the delusion that a star trader must party hard and conquer the dollies, Tommy takes Daniel into the field for training; the Forty-Year-Old Virgin becomes a Twenty-Seven-Year-Old Reader.

During this process Daniel meets Beth (Alexis Bledel), Tommy's girlfriend. Beth isn't precisely Tommy's type; she belongs to a book club. Tommy is like one of those guys who might read if the library weren't always closed. Beth is a serious Green and believes Tommy's line that he is, too, but he has a line for every girl and is a serious liar. Daniel observes this dynamic.

Young men, let your old dad here impart some advice. If a woman has a choice of a man who makes sacks of money on the trading floor and a man who likes to stay home at night reading *Lolita,* and she's more attracted to the reader, choose that woman. She needs to pass one more test: Does she believe (a) *Lolita* is a sex novel, or (b) it's one of the greatest works of modern literature? Find that out on the second date. If she answers (b), there's your girl.

*The Good Guy* could have been just a dumb comedy, but actually it has a nice feel to it. It looks carefully at a lifestyle many people might thoughtlessly envy. The writer-director, Julio DePietro, is a former trader from Chicago, and he convinces us he knows that world. I hasten to add that I know some traders who are nice guys. I also add that I would trade the same way the guys in the movie do, because their clients care less about how much money they'll retire with than how rich they'll be tomorrow. Investing myself, I've trusted value guys over performance. That and buying Apple, just because I loved Macs, has turned out all right.

Readers may pick up on the clue that the title and some of the story are inspired by Ford Madox Ford's novel *The Good Soldier.* It opens with a famous line that makes it impossible to stop reading: "This is the saddest story I have ever heard." Tommy's story is another one.

I keep drifting off course. Will you like *The Good Guy*? I think you might. It has smart characters and is wise about the ones who try to tame their intelligence by acting out. And Beth and her friends are the women all these guys should be so lucky as to deserve.

## The Good Heart ★ ½

R, 98 m., 2010

Brian Cox (Jacques), Paul Dano (Lucas), Isild Le Besco (April). Directed by Dagur Kari and produced by Skuli Fr. Malmquist and Thor Sigurjonsson. Screenplay by Kari.

Every once in a while a movie comes along and you watch it and the credits come up and you sit there feeling a certain sadness. The actors are good ones and they work hard and the look and feel of the film are evocative—but good gravy! Where did that plot come from? The actors cast themselves adrift on the sinking vessel of this story and go down with the ship.

Few people know the name of Horatio Alger anymore. He was long outdated when I heard of him, but in those ancient times people still referred to "a Horatio Alger story." That would be a story sopping wet with cornball sentimentalism, wrapped up in absurd melodrama, and telling some version of the rags-to-riches story. Poor farm boy stops runaway carriage carrying banker's daughter, they fall in love, he inherits bank. I believe Alger used that actual plot.

*The Good Heart* isn't that obvious, but it's that corny. Poor homeless lad named Lucas (Paul Dano) lives in cardboard shack under the freeway, befriends forlorn kitten. Kitten is found hanged, lad attempts suicide, wakes up in intensive care next to nasty old banker. Sorry! Nasty old tavern owner. This barkeep, named Jacques (Brian Cox), has just had his fifth heart attack and is so foul-tempered even the nurses hate him. Jacques finds out the lad is homeless, brings him home, gives him a garret room above the bar, and tells him he can have the bar after he dies.

In my extensive research into the world of bars, I have observed that they survive by selling drinks at retail. The House of Oysters doesn't follow this time-tested model. Jacques has three business policies he drums into Lucas: (1) No walk-ins from the street. (2) No women allowed—and BTW it's not a gay bar. (3) No being nice to the customers.

Rule No. 1 seems paradoxical. If no walk-in customers are allowed, how does anybody ever get to be a regular? Presumably the regulars have all been there since Jacques got the place from a man who sold oysters. One of the oysters killed someone, the guy sold out, Jacques took over, discontinued food, and inherited the regulars.

They are a group who need fumigating. The bar itself is a skanky dump. Jacques throws customers out regularly, but they come back, maybe because they're barred everywhere else. One day the beautiful April (Isild Le Besco) walks in and orders champagne. She has a sad story. No, she's not a fallen woman with a heart of gold. She's a flight attendant from France, who can't go home again or find a job because, I kid you not, she's afraid to fly.

Lucas and April fall in love, Jacques hates her for violating all the rules, and now I am biting my hand hard enough to make it bleed in order to prevent myself from blurting out more plot details. No, I will not—I must not—tell you what happens at the end of this movie, except to say I was stupefied that anyone in modern times (i.e., since 1910) would have the gall to sell such cornball at retail.

So now my review must end. But wait. I haven't even mentioned the bar's pet goose. This goose is kept in a sturdy cage, but escapes from time to time and must be chased down by Lucas. The ending of *The Good Heart* is supposed to be sad, but for me the saddest thing in this movie is that Lucas didn't chop off the head of that goose when he had the chance. No animals are harmed during the filming of a picture, and look where it gets you.

## A Good Old Fashioned Orgy ★

R, 91 m., 2011

Jason Sudeikis (Eric), Leslie Bibb (Kelly), Lake Bell (Alison), Michelle Borth (Sue), Nick Kroll (Adam), Tyler Labine (McCrudden), Angela Sarafyan (Willow), Lindsay Sloane (Laura), Martin Starr (Duquez), Lucy Punch (Kate), Will Forte (Glenn). Directed by Alex Gregory and Peter Huyck and produced by James D. Stern. Screenplay by Gregory and Huyck.

An orgy provides an opportunity to perform in public what you cannot perform in private with sufficient satisfaction. To have an orgy with strangers is dangerous, and to have one with your best friends is unspeakably sad. My reactionary ideas make me unsuited as a grateful audience member for *A Good Old Fashioned Orgy*, which completes our long, hot summer of vulgar comedies.

This is a comedy without wit and soul. It strands fairly likable actors in a morass of the kind of dialogue only stupid characters ever say—and then only when reading stupid screenplays. No one in the movie has a morsel of intelligence. They all seem to be channeling more successful characters in better comedies. This would be touching if it were not so desperate.

To take off your clothing and engage randomly in sex with nine or ten other people reveals an appalling lack of self-respect. Is that all sex means to you, rummaging about in strange genitals? Masturbation seems healthier. It is performed with someone you admire. If a sexual orgy is as exciting as the people here pretend, why do they need to spice it up with costumes from fraternity toga parties, and sex toys from the remainder bins of adult stores across from truck stops on lonely interstate highways?

If the people in this movie had a plausible association with humanity, it would be painful and embarrassing. You don't want to witness the humiliation of people you believe in. I believed in none of these. They were a small step up from a porn movie starring Barbie and Ken, and, of course, their best friends Midge and Allan and Tanner the pooping dog. If Barbie had arrived in her pink Corvette convertible, I'd rather play with that.

There are actors here you have heard of and may like, such as Jason Sudeikis, Lucy Punch, Don Johnson, and David Koechner. The only one who will make an impression in this movie is Tyler Labine, who looks and behaves so much like Jack Black as makes no difference. The effect of a leopard-skin thong is wasted on him; it gets lost in the folds. He'd need a digital camera set on auto timer to admire the effect.

Lucy Punch plays Kate, who gets engaged to her one true love, Glenn (Will Forte). Of course they aren't invited to the orgy. There should be a sacred instant early in a romance when a couple's needs are fulfilled by each other, don't you agree? Yet Glenn and Kate turn up for it anyway, and are mad because they weren't invited: "We thought you were our friends!" If we don't all agree that newlyweds should be virgins on their wedding nights, we might compromise by suggesting they haven't attended any orgies with Jack Black types. I'll bet even Jack himself would go along with that.

The orgy is planned on Labor Day for a summer home in the Hamptons owned by Eric (Jason Sudeikis). This will be a farewell wallow: Eric's dad (Johnson) is selling the house. Dad's real estate agent, Kelly, played by Leslie Bibb, is an attractive woman who appeals to Eric. He tries to keep the orgy a secret from her. You know you're in a limited crowd when the designated adult is a real estate agent.

## Goon ★ ★ ★

R, 92 m., 2012

Seann William Scott (Doug Glatt), Jay Baruchel (Pat Houlihan), Liev Schreiber (Ross Rhea), Alison Pill (Eva), Eugene Levy (Dr. Glatt), Marc-Andre Grondin (Xavier Laflamme), Kim Coates (Ronnie Hortense), Nicholas Campbell (Rollie Hortense). Directed by Michael Dowse and produced by Jay Baruchel, Don Carmody, David Gross, and Andre Rouleau. Screenplay by Baruchel and Evan Goldberg, based on the book *Goon: The True Story of an Unlikely Journey into Minor League Hockey* by Adam Frattasio and Doug Smith.

Here's how much I know about hockey: Mike Royko and I were in a tiny bar one winter night and the radio kept reporting goals by the Blackhawks. I mentioned how frequently the team was scoring. "You're listening to the highlights," Royko observed.

If that's how much you know about hockey, you're nevertheless likely to enjoy *Goon*, which stars Seann William Scott as an enforcer for a minor league team in Massachusetts. An enforcer, I know by this time, is a brute who is put on the ice not to play hockey but to beat up opponents who are playing it too well. The charm of *Goon* is that Doug Glatt (Scott) is a genial guy from a nice family. Just because he hands around concussions doesn't mean he dislikes anybody. He's just happy to be wearing a uniform.

Having recently disliked a movie named *The Raid: Redemption* that was wall-to-wall violence, I now feel fondness for another movie that's also mostly mayhem. It's not violence itself I object to, but the absence of engaging characters and human interest. The best thing about *Goon* is not the hockey action, or who wins and who loses. It's Doug's rags-to-riches story.

One night he goes to a game with a friend named Pat (Jay Baruchel), who's one of those fans with a gift for getting under the skins of the players he heckles. One player grows so inflamed that he climbs into the stands. Pat is pitifully unable to defend himself, so Doug stands up and coldcocks the guy, actually splitting open his helmet. That draws the attention of talent scouts, and soon Doug is playing professional hockey. To be sure, he can't ice skate, but skating can be learned. Not everybody is a born enforcer.

The movie is enriched by a lot of material not specifically about hockey. Part of Doug's character is that he's modest about his achievements—and there's a lot to be modest about. His father (Eugene Levy) and brother (David Paetkau) are both doctors, and his parents have big ambitions for him. But Doug is a realist and accepts that he's not the reddest nose of the Rudolphs. To be offered a paying job in hockey is beyond his dreams.

Liev Schreiber would not be my first guess for a supporting role in *Goon*, despite what a good Hamlet he made. Here he plays Ross Rhea, a Canadian star who has always been Doug's hero. Now is he actually expected to butt heads with him? Yes. There is a *lot* of head butting in this movie. I'm aware of the depressing stories lately about an epidemic of brain injuries in football, hockey, boxing, and so on, but in *Goon* we have to accept that it's about a different era in hockey, or the world. If you start thinking too much about concussions, it will spoil the movie for you.

Doug becomes good pals with Xavier Laflamme (Marc-Andre Grondi), the star of his team, who has a name that sounds like one of Pepe Le Pew's romantic rivals. Laflamme is growing older, and Doug is assigned to be his protector, which means he shields Laflamme from assaults from opposing enforcers. What's clear pretty quickly is that this organized violence is sanctioned and expected in hockey, where a player like Doug might spend much of a game in the penalty box. The punishment these players take is unimaginable.

There's a sweet little subplot involving Doug and Eva (Alison Pill), who confesses she finds something irresistible about sweaty hockey players whose bruises are sexier than tattoos. Pill's performance has a comic quirkiness that responds to Doug's inner niceness, which isn't exactly her thing.

I've known only one hockey player myself. That was the legendary Eric Nesterenko of the

Chicago Blackhawks, who was a regular at O'Rourke's Pub (not precisely a sports bar). He was a big, genial guy, who attended university while he was playing, and was later a professor. He liked to talk literature. He was smarter than this movie's Doug, but arguably as tough, and that's another reason I liked *Goon*. The character is actually possible.

*Note: The movie is based on* Goon: The True Story of an Unlikely Journey into Minor League Hockey *by Adam Frattasio and Doug Smith. The real Doug Smith, also an enforcer, is seen in the credit cookies.*

## The Greatest ★ ★

R, 100 m., 2010

Pierce Brosnan (Allen Brewer), Susan Sarandon (Grace Brewer), Carey Mulligan (Rose), Johnny Simmons (Ryan), Aaron Johnson (Bennett), Zoe Kravitz (Ashley), Michael Shannon (Jordan Walker). Directed by Shana Feste and produced by Lynette Howell and Beau St. Clair. Screenplay by Feste.

*The Greatest* includes a great performance and a very good one at the center of vagueness and confusion. The film's people and situation are perfectly clear, and with this cast might have made a powerful film, but the screenplay contains baffling omissions, needless confusions, and questions we should not be thinking of.

The film opens with two teenagers deeply, joyously in love. It's the kind of love where they've flirted with their eyes and their hearts since they started school, and now, on the last day of their senior year, he finally finds the courage to speak to her, and her face lights up, and this is all they dreamed of, and they make love, and then he's killed when their car is hit by a truck.

Not a spoiler. It's the setup for the whole film. The girl is Rose (Carey Mulligan, the Oscar nominee from *An Education*). The boy is Bennett (Aaron Johnson, on screen briefly but with all the presence necessary to make their love significant). We cut to the funeral, and then to an extraordinary shot of three people in the backseat of a funeral limousine: Bennett's father, Allen (Pierce Brosnan), his mother, Grace (Susan Sarandon), and his kid brother, Ryan (Johnny Simmons).

They do not speak. They do not look at one another. They do not offer comfort. The shot lasts maybe a minute. It establishes that these people are grieving in their own private ways. Bennett was a wonderful boy, known as "the Greatest" since grade school because . . . well, he was. Grace is inconsolable. They all are, but she's the most intense, and Allen tries to hold the family together while Ryan disappears into his room and drugs and who knows.

Three months pass in this way. Rose appears at their door and tells Allen she is pregnant. It was the first time for both Rose and Bennett. She didn't even know you could get pregnant the first time. She moves in with them because—well, I don't know exactly. Apart from one enigmatic phone call late in the film, perhaps involving a mother, she seems to have no one. She attended high school in an affluent neighborhood for three years, she was a gifted pianist, she's in a fatal crash, and now she has no one? No family, no friends, not one single person, and this is never explained?

Maybe she comes from a troubled background? Hard to see. Carey Mulligan plays Rose as upbeat, cheerful, able to cope. Grace is cold and distant; Sarandon plays her as unforgiving. Rose overhears her saying she wishes it was Rose, and not Bennett, who had been killed. She doesn't give a damn about Bennett's child. She wants her own child back.

Allen tries to be friendly. There are a couple of scenes, indeed, that are oddly handled because there's no question of Allen and Rose growing intimate, but the film's staging allows such a question to occur. Meanwhile, Ryan starts attending a grief support group where the leader does what no support group leader should ever do, and offers a diagnosis and recommendation to members after one comment.

In this group, a young woman named Ashley (Zoe Kravitz) reaches out to Ryan, and he responds and improves emotionally, and they like each other, and a romance seems to be in the works, and then he knocks on her door and her sister (I guess) answers and says something (I'm not sure what) and he runs off, and Ashley runs after him but that's the end of that subplot. What's that about?

And what about the scene where Ryan consumes what may be Ecstasy and then smokes pot. OK . . . and then? Nothing. He gets high and comes down, I guess. Meanwhile, Grace sits at the bedside of Jordan (Michael Shannon), the truck driver who hit her son's car. She knows her son lived for seventeen minutes after the crash and that Jordan spoke to him, and she's obsessed to know what he said. But after the conversation Jordan went into coma. Some months later, we see her at his bedside, hearing the story of the seventeen minutes.

I will omit certain additional details involving Allen and Rose (separately), and I suppose I shouldn't describe the melodrama of the closing scenes, except to say they're an anthology of clichés. And there's a car ride in which way too much communication takes place, at long last, in a much too facile fashion.

So the screenplay is a soap operatic mess, involving distractions, loose ends, and sheer carelessness. Yet Sarandon creates a wrenching performance of a woman torn apart by grief, and Brosnan is convincing as a man holding it together as long as he can. As for Mulligan and Simmons, what can I say? There is nothing they do wrong, but this film written and directed by Shana Feste leaves both characters deprived of explanation, development, and revelation. And you can't get me to believe that after you have sex one time and get pregnant, and your lover is killed, and you have absolutely *nobody* to turn to except his parents, and his mother hates you, a teenage girl can have this much self-confidence. Even Juno would have disintegrated under the pressure.

## The Greatest Movie Ever Sold ★ ★ ½

PG-13, 86 m., 2011

A documentary directed by Morgan Spurlock and produced by Spurlock, Jeremy Chilnick, Abbie Hurewitz, and Jessica Wu. Screenplay by Chilnick and Spurlock.

Once, long ago, movie stars were trained to hold a can of beer or a pack of cigarettes in such a way that the brand could not be seen. Now when we notice a brand name in a movie we think "product placement!" and get on with it. Names like United Center and Staples Center may be so ingrained that we don't even think of airlines or office supplies stores anymore. Wrigley Field wasn't named for a chewing gum but for a family. I wonder if Chicagoans will allow it to be branded? Nothing is sacred. Just look at the new name on Marshall Field's.

Morgan Spurlock's new documentary, *The Greatest Movie Ever Sold,* finances itself by its own bootstraps. It is a movie about making a movie paid for by product placements. In fact, its official title is *Pom Wonderful Presents The Greatest Movie Ever Sold,* named in honor of the pomegranate juice that is, I now know, 100 percent pomegranate juice—unlike Minute Maid, which is mostly apple and grape juice, with pomegranate finishing under 2 percent.

The film also makes mention of Hyatt Hotels, Mini Coopers, OK Go, Old Navy, and JetBlue. (No promotional consideration was received by me for mentioning these products.) Spurlock is the star, just as he was when he ate only at McDonald's for a month in *Super Size Me.* He talks to agents, lawyers, product reps, movie directors, musicians, and placement specialists, and then makes calls on a series of would-be sponsors, some of whom are extremely wary of his scheme.

He strikes pay dirt with Pom Wonderful, which agrees to be a major sponsor, and then some of the other pieces fall into place. He raised $1.5 million and spent it on this film, he says, although this would be a perfect opportunity for a con of the sort exploited in *The Producers.*

Along the way he consults various learned experts, including Ralph Nader, Noam Chomsky, and Donald Trump (of the Trump Towers franchise), who appear as talking heads in so many docs these days they might almost be product placements for themselves. He finds directors such as Brett Ratner willing to talk on the record—and Quentin Tarantino, who complains he wanted to shoot scenes for *Reservoir Dogs* and *Pulp Fiction* in Denny's, but they wouldn't let him. Spurlock begins as almost serious about his subject, but about the time one of his authorities advises him to take the money and run, we realize that's what he's doing.

The movie is quick and cheerful, and Spurlock is engaging onscreen. I already knew what he was telling us, and I think many people do. I'm not sure Spurlock himself ever defined a purpose greater than raising the money on camera, but then he never claimed to. I can't exactly recommend the movie, but I do recommend drinking Pom Wonderful. Did you know it's a powerful antioxidant, and can provide some of the benefits of Viagra? Maybe if Minute Maid used more pomegranates it would be Ten Minute Maid.

## Greenberg ★ ★ ★ ½

R, 107 m., 2010

Ben Stiller (Roger Greenberg), Greta Gerwig (Florence Marr), Rhys Ifans (Ivan Schrank), Jennifer Jason Leigh (Beth), Brie Larson (Sara), Juno Temple (Muriel), Chris Messina (Phillip Greenberg), Susan Traylor (Carol Greenberg), Mark Duplass (Eric Beller). Directed by Noah Baumbach and produced by Jennifer Jason Leigh and Scott Rudin. Screenplay by Baumbach.

When you're angry with the world and yourself to the same degree, you're running in place. It takes a great deal of energy. It can be exhausting. You lash out at people. You're hard on yourself. It all takes place in your head. After a time people give up on you. They think you don't give a damn and don't care about yourself. If they only knew.

That's Roger Greenberg. I never knew who Ben Stiller was born to play, but now I do. I don't mean he *is* Greenberg, but that he makes him a convincing person and not a caricature. The hero of Noah Baumbach's new film was once, years ago, part of a rock band on the brink of a breakthrough. He walked away from it, stranding his bandmates, and never explained why. He fled Los Angeles and became a carpenter in New York.

He's been struggling. There has been some sort of vague period in an institution. Now he's returned to L.A. to house-sit his brother's big home and look after the dog. He glares out of the windows like old man Fredricksen in *Up*. He can live alone no more successfully than with others. He calls Florence Marr (Greta Gerwig), his brother's family assistant, who knows where everything is and how everything works. And the dog knows her.

Florence is someone we know. A bright, pleasant recent college graduate for whom the job market, as they say, has no use. We see her interacting with the family of Greenberg's brother; she does all the planning for them that she should be doing for herself. In a more conventional movie, Florence would be the love interest, and Greenberg would be fated to marry her. But Florence isn't looking for a man. She just broke up. "I don't want to go from just having sex to sex to sex," she says. "Who's the third 'sex'?" asks Greenberg. "You."

I have a weakness for actresses like Greta Gerwig. She looks reasonable and approachable. Some actresses are all edges and polish. This one, you could look up and see her walking dreamily through a bookstore, possibly with a Penguin Classic already in her hand. Greenberg treats her badly. He has no notion of his effect on people. When they end up having sex, and they do, it's like their right hands don't know what their left hands are doing.

Noah Baumbach made the inspired film *The Squid and the Whale* (2005), about a formidably articulate family torn apart by a divorce. Both parents were at fault to various degrees, and both sons could have done more in their own way to help the situation. Everyone obsessed on their grievances. Greenberg takes this a step further: He obsesses on the grievances against him.

He has a reunion with a former bandmate, Ivan (Rhys Ifans), a calm Brit, troubled by a trial separation, happy enough to see Greenberg and help him if he can. But Ivan is troubled that Greenberg *still* doesn't get it, doesn't understand how he crushed the dreams of his bandmates. Then there's Beth (Jennifer Jason Leigh), whom Greenberg once loved and was loved by. Life has moved on. She has a family. Does he recognize the look a woman gets in her eyes when she's thinking how that just would have never, ever worked out? Does he have enough self-knowledge to see how impossible he is?

The important relationship is the one between Greenberg and Florence. We look upon her and see wholesome health and abundant energy. She's happy when she has a purpose. She wishes she had a direction in life, but can be happy enough in the moment. It's as if when Greenberg moves a little in the direction of happiness, he gets jealous because that draws attention away from his miserable uniqueness. People driven to be constantly unique can be a real pain in the ass.

This is an intriguing film, shifting directions, considering Greenberg's impossibility in one light and then another. If he's stuck like this at forty, is he stuck for good? What Ben Stiller does with the role is fascinating. We can't stand Greenberg. But we begin to care about him. Without ever overtly evoking sympathy, Stiller inspires identification. You don't have to like the hero of a movie. But you have to understand him—better than he does himself, in some cases.

## The Green Hornet ★

PG-13, 108 m., 2011

Seth Rogen (Britt Reid/Green Hornet), Jay Chou (Kato), Christoph Waltz (Chudnofsky), Cameron Diaz (Lenore Case), Edward James Olmos (Michael Axford), Tom Wilkinson (James Reid), David Harbour (Scanlon). Directed by Michel Gondry and produced by Neal H. Moritz. Screenplay by Seth Rogen and Evan Goldberg.

*The Green Hornet* is an almost unendurable demonstration of a movie with nothing to be about. Although it follows the rough story line of previous versions of the title, it neglects the construction of a plot engine to pull us through. There are pointless dialogue scenes going nowhere much too slowly, and then pointless action scenes going everywhere much too quickly.

Seth Rogen deserves much of the blame. He cowrote the screenplay giving himself way too many words, and then hurls them tirelessly at us at a modified shout. He plays Britt Reid, a spoiled little rich brat who grows up the same way, as the son of a millionaire newspaper publisher (Tom Wilkinson, who apparently remains the same age as his son ages from about ten to maybe thirty). After his father's death, he shows little interest in running a newspaper but bonds with Kato (Jay Chou), his father's auto mechanic and coffee maker. Yes.

Kato is the role Bruce Lee played on TV. Jay Chou is no Bruce Lee, but it's hard to judge him as an actor with Rogen hyperventilating through scene after scene. Together, they devise a damn fool plan to fight crime by impersonating criminals. This they do while wearing masks that serve no purpose as far as I could determine except to make them look suspicious. I mean, like, who wears a mask much these days?

The crime lord in the city is Chudnofsky (Christoph Waltz, the Oscar winner from *Inglourious Basterds*). That provides the movie with a villain but hardly with a character. The war between Chudnofsky and the Hornet is played out in a great many vehicle stunts and explosions, which go on and on and on, maddeningly, as if screenwriter Rogen tired of his own dialogue (not as quickly as we, alas) and scribbled in: "Here second unit supplies nine minutes of CGI action."

There is a role in the film for Cameron Diaz as Lenore Case, would-be secretary for young Reid, but nothing for her to *do*. She functions primarily to allow us to cut to her from time to time, which is pleasant but unsatisfying. Diaz has a famously wonderful smile, and curiously in her first shot in the film she smiles for no reason all, maybe just to enter the smile in the record.

The director of this half-cooked mess is Michel Gondry, whose *Eternal Sunshine of the Spotless Mind* is as good as this one is bad. Casting about for something to praise, I recalled that I heard a strange and unique sound for the first time, a high-pitched whooshing scream, but I don't think Gondry can claim it because it came from the hand dryers in the men's room.

## Green Lantern ★ ★ ½

PG-13, 105 m., 2011

Ryan Reynolds (Hal Jordan/Green Lantern), Blake Lively (Carol Ferris), Peter Sarsgaard (Hector Hammond), Mark Strong (Sinestro), Angela Bassett (Dr. Amanda Waller), Tim Robbins (Senator Hammond), Temuera Morrison (Abin Sur), Jay O. Sanders (Carl Ferris). Directed by Martin Campbell and produced by Greg Berlanti and Donald De Line. Screenplay by Berlanti, Michael Green, Marc Guggenheim, and Michael Goldenberg.

*Green Lantern* presents yet another case of a human being given the responsibility of leading the battle of good versus evil, or, in this case, of the will versus fear. We learn that an ancient race of aliens has divided the universe into segments to enforce peace, but is being resisted by an alien named Parallax, who went off on his own, committed the sin of pride, and became a prince of darkness. If he reminds you of Satan, that can't be helped. Every superhero requires a malevolent egomaniac to battle.

The movie stars Ryan Reynolds as Hal Jordan, a test pilot who proves that humans are better at flying fighter planes than computers are. His fellow pilot is Carol Ferris (Blake Lively), the daughter of the tycoon Carl Ferris (Jay O. Sanders), who manufactures the fighters. Does Carl worry about his daughter flying in catfights at supersonic speeds? To answer that question would require him to reveal emotion, and he is locked immobile in superhero tycoon mode.

Far away in the universe, the benign aliens have created the Green Lantern Corps to spread out and combat the evil Parallax. One of these corpsmen is sent on a mission to find a worthy man on Earth to become a member of the Corps. His spaceship, which has survived a journey across the cosmos, crash-lands, and he lives long enough to hand over a green ring and a lantern to, of course, Hal Jordan. Hal learns that the ring gives him great power, but he must believe in the triumph of his will and conquer the weakness of fear.

If this sounds childish, of course it is. One of the absurdities of many modern superhero movies is how they adorn silly plots with great solemnity and millions of dollars in special effects. Nor does *Green Lantern* shortchange us on dialogue; indeed, it spends a great deal of time at the impossible task of explaining the logic and rules of its plot. I am amazed at how calmly humans absorb and accept the incredulities of these stories ("Waitaminit! I wear this magic green ring and I'm a superhero? Gee, that's every kid's dream!").

*Green Lantern* does not intend to be plausible. It intends to be a sound and light show, assaulting the audience with sensational special effects. If that's what you want, that's what you get. Among these are numerous split-second journeys across galaxies by speeding green spheres that shuttle between Earth and the domain of the aliens, while dismissing all technicalities of the speed of light. I nostalgically recalled *Thor*, in which Thor commutes to Earth to do battle with the avatars of his own satanic malevolent egomaniac.

The problem with many of these special effects is that they don't take on the gravity and substance of real events; they are an obvious extrusion of animation into the physical world. Often they take forms created by Hal Jordan's imagination, because whatever he wills becomes real. I suppose that goes with the territory.

Parallax, it must be said, is a well-imagined malevolence. Although he manifests a diabolical face, he seems otherwise to consist mostly of roiling tendrils of foul, polluted matter. There is a scene where the foreground is filled with terrified humans who are fleeing toward the camera, while behind them Parallax causes skyscrapers to tumble. Was it less than ten years ago that we wondered if movies could ever use such images again after 9/11?

The movie has a character I found interesting, if inconsistent. This is Hector Hammond (Peter Sarsgaard), a brilliant scientist nerd with a wispy mustache and a servile superiority. What becomes of Hector I will not say, but Sarsgaard gives him a dimension lacking in the cookie-cutter heroics of Hal Jordan. A subplot about Hector's mind-reading abilities is not developed very well. I also liked the fierce determination of Dr. Amanda Waller (Angela Bassett) and the composure with which Senator Hammond (Tim Robbins) deals with a haywire helicopter.

The bottom line: This is a comic book movie. Fans of the Green Lantern (in his intergalactic story mode and not his earthbound TV series) will no doubt enjoy its visualizations and its references to details of the backstory that escaped me. There's a whole lot going on. We don't really expect subtle acting or nuanced dialogue. We appreciate an effective villain. We demand one chaste kiss between hero and heroine, but no funny stuff. We enjoy spectacular visuals like the Green elders, who are immortal and apparently spend eternity balancing on top of towering pillars. *Green Lantern* delivers all of those things, and for what it's worth, I liked it more than *Thor.*

Perhaps there was a reason for that. The movie, as you know, was filmed in 3-D. But a screening was made available in 2-D, and I chose to attend the 2-D screening. The colors were bright, the images were crisp and clear, the impact was undeniable, the greens were . . . real green. I didn't see the 3-D version, so can't compare the two. I will be looking forward with interest to how other critics around the country describe it.

## Green Zone ★ ★ ★ ★

R, 114 m., 2010

Matt Damon (Roy Miller), Jason Isaacs (Briggs), Brendan Gleeson (Martin Brown), Greg Kinnear (Clark Poundstone), Amy Ryan (Lawrie Dayne), Khalid Abdalla (Freddy), Igal Naor (General Al Rawi). Directed by Paul Greengrass and produced by Tim Bevan, Eric Fellner, and Lloyd Levin. Screenplay by Brian Helgeland, inspired by the book *Imperial Life in the Emerald City* by Rajiv Chandrasekaran.

*Green Zone* looks at an American war in a way almost no Hollywood movie ever has: We're not the heroes, but the dupes. Its message is that Iraq's fabled "weapons of mass destruction" did not exist, and that neocons within the administration fabricated them, lied about them, and were ready to kill to cover up their deception.

Is this true? I'm not here to say. It's certainly one more element in the new narrative that has gradually emerged about Iraq, the dawning realization that we went to war under false premises. It's a thriller that makes no claim to be based on fact, but provides characters and situations that have uncanny real-life parallels. Its director made two of the Bourne films, and imports his approach to Baghdad, starring Matt Damon as an unstoppable action hero.

But this isn't merely a thriller. It has a point to argue: Critical blunders at the outset made a quick and easy victory impossible, and turned Bush's "Mission Accomplished" photo-op into a historic miscalculation. *Green Zone* argues, as many observers have, that the fatal error of the United States was to fire the officers and men of the Iraqi army and leave them at large with their weapons. The army had no great love of Saddam, and might have been a helpful stabilizing force. Instead, it was left unemployed, armed, and alienated.

Damon, playing Chief Warrant Officer Roy Miller, is seen at the outset leading a raid on a suspected storage site for WMDs. Nothing there. Another raid, intended to find weapons of chemical warfare, turns up years-old pigeon droppings. Because some of the raids produce casualties, he begins to question the intelligence reports the raids are based on. He speaks out at a briefing, and rather improbably finds himself face-to-face with a U.S. intelligence agent named Poundstone (Greg Kinnear). He's fed the usual line and told to perform his duty, but is overheard by Brown, a hulking, grizzled CIA man who's an old Middle East hand. Soon he's meeting with Brown to pass on his doubts. *Green Zone* indicates that the CIA, which lacked (as in real life) any evidence to back up the WMD claims, has been cut out of the loop, and that Poundstone is not only the architect of the neocon fictions, but their enforcer; he even has a military group answering directly to him.

Chief Miller also meets a New York newspaperwoman named Lawrie Dayne (Amy Ryan), whose reports about a secret Iraqi informer have given credence to the WMD claims. From her he discovers that General Al Rawi (Igal Naor) of the Iraqi army met with Poundstone in Jordan, but unlike the source Poundstone cited, flatly told him Saddam had no WMDs. So the bad intel was cooked up to justify the war the neocons desired.

Have I made the plot sound complex? Greengrass works with the screenwriter, Brian Helgeland, to tell it with considerable clarity. By limiting the characters and using typecasting, he makes a web of deceit easy to understand. Also a great help to Chief Miller is a local named Freddy (Khalid Abdalla), who risks his life to help him, acts as a translator, and is given the film's key line of dialogue.

The action in *Green Zone* is followed by Greengrass in the queasycam style I've found distracting in the past: lots of quick cuts between handheld shots. It didn't bother me here. That may be because I became so involved in the story. Perhaps also because unlike the Bourne films, this one contains no action sequences that are logically impossible. When we see a car chase that couldn't take place in the real world, we naturally think about the visual effects. When they could take place, and it's a good movie, we're thinking about the story.

*Green Zone* will no doubt be under fire from those who are still defending the fabricated intelligence we used as an excuse to invade Iraq. Yes, the film is fiction, employs far-fetched coincidences, and improbably places one man at the center of all the action. It is a thriller, not a documentary. It's my belief that the nature of the neocon evildoing has by now become pretty clear. Others will disagree. The bottom line is: This is one hell of a thriller.

## The Grey ★ ★ ★

R, 117 m., 2012

Liam Neeson (John Ottway), Frank Grillo (Diaz), Dermot Mulroney (Talget), Dallas Roberts (Hendrick), Joe Anderson (Flannery), Nonso Anozie (Burke), Ben Bray (Hernandez), James Badge Dale (Lewenden), Anne Openshaw (Ottway's Wife). Directed by Joe Carnahan and produced by Carnahan, Jules Daly, Mickey Liddell, Ridley Scott, and Tony Scott. Screenplay by Carnahan and Ian Mackenzie Jeffers, based on the story "Ghost Walker" by Jeffers.

*The Grey* is an unrelenting demonstration that wolves have no opinion. When they attack, it's not personal. They've spent untold millennia learning how to survive, naked and without weapons, in fearsome places such as the Arctic Circle in the dead of winter. They aren't precisely unarmed; they have their teeth and claws, but how far would that get us, even if we had rifles?

In the movie, a group of oil company workers gets the opportunity to find the answer to that question. They're workers at a pumping station in the Far North, described in the opening narration by Ottway (Liam Neeson) as a sort of prototype for hell, occupied by "men unfit for mankind." They have the kinds of jobs you might take if you were desperate for the good pay, or perhaps driven to seek a place far from society where it is assumed that when you are not working you are sleeping or drinking. The bar no doubt has cheap prices, and it's crowded during an early scene that establishes Ottway and some other characters.

He is a marksman for the oil company. His job is to shoot wolves. When I learned of Sarah Palin hunting wolves from a helicopter, my sensibilities were tested, but after this film, I was prepared to call in more helicopters. I was also stunned with despair. It so happened that there were two movies scheduled that day in the Lake Street Screening Room. After *The Grey* was over, I watched the second film for thirty minutes and then got up and walked out of the theater. It was the first time I've ever walked out of a film because of the *previous* film. The way I was feeling in my gut, it just wouldn't have been fair to the next film.

Ottway and a small planeload of other workers fly out on leave, on board a small airplane that crashes and strands them they know not where. Most are killed or die quickly. Seven are left alive. They hope they'll be found by rescuers, but Alaska is a big place, and their plane is small and rapidly being covered with snow. And then one of them walks a few steps away to take a pee and is struck by ravenous wolves.

Ottway is more experienced than the others and takes charge. He says their only chance is to walk below the tree line. It seems to me that wolves would be perfectly happy to hunt you among the trees, but I think I'd listen to Ottway.

They set off in bitter cold, slogging through snow, eating a little food from the plane, starting fires at night, intensely aware that they have attracted a large following of wolves. They use torches and a ring of smaller outlying fires to keep the wolves at bay. In the darkness, the eyes of the animals reflect the firelight in unblinking, hungry stares.

There's time for some conversation among the men, and this film, directed by Joe Carnahan and written by Carnahan and Ian Mackenzie Jeffers, treats them as individuals. They're not simply a group of victims. We learn the most about Ottway, who was on the brink of suicide on the day before the flight. Now that his life has become precarious, he fiercely clings to it.

The film advances with pitiless logic. There are more wolves than men. The men have weapons, the wolves have patience, the weather is punishing. I sat regarding the screen with mounting dread. The movie had to have a happy ending, didn't it? If not "happy," then at least a relief in some sense? Sit through the entire credits. There's one more shot still to come. Not that you wouldn't be content without it.

## Grown Ups ★ ★

PG-13, 102 m., 2010

Adam Sandler (Lenny Feder), Kevin James (Eric Lamonsoff), Chris Rock (Kurt McKenzie), David Spade (Marcus Higgins), Rob Schneider (Rob Hilliard), Maria Bello (Sally Lamonsoff), Salma Hayek (Roxanne Chase-Feder), Maya Rudolph (Deanne McKenzie), Joyce Van Patten (Gloria), Ebony Jo-Ann (Mama Ronzoni), Di Quon (Nanny Rita), Steve Buscemi (Wiley). Directed by Dennis Dugan and produced by Jack Giarraputo and Adam Sandler. Screenplay by Sandler and Fred Wolf.

*Grown Ups* is a pleasant, genial, good-hearted, sometimes icky comedy that's like spending a weekend with well-meaning people you don't want to see again any time real soon. They're the kind of people where, in the car driving home, you ask, "What was that all about?" Try to imagine the Three Stooges slapping one another's faces with dehydrated reconstituted bananas. No, really.

The pretense for the story: Five kids were on a basketball team in middle school. Their beloved old coach has died. To mourn him they return to the lakeside cabin where they celebrated their victory all those years ago. Wouldn't you know, the five kids on the team they beat are at the same lake for the same weekend.

The five buddies are played by Adam Sandler, Rob Schneider, Kevin James, Chris Rock, and David Spade. Sandler's wife is a famous designer (Salma Hayek). Schneider's much older wife is Joyce Van Patten. Rock's pregnant wife is Maya Rudolph. His Madea-style mother is Ebony Jo-Ann. James's wife is Maria Bello, who is still breast-feeding their four-year-old at every opportunity. Spade is unmarried, which, given the size of the cast, is just as well, since the characters have five children (I think), and there are also roles for Steve Buscemi as a guy who ends up in a body cast, Di Quon as Sandler's Asian nanny, and, of course, Schneider's three daughters from two previous marriages, two of them towering models, the third short and stout. There are so many characters in the movie that some scenes look like everyone lined up for a group shot.

The physical humor is not sophisticated. One character ends up with her face in a cake, and another has his face pushed twice into doggy-doo. The nursing mother squirts milk here and there, and her son is warned that if he doesn't wean himself soon he'll have a "got milk?" mustache with real hair. The gang all goes to a water park. There's a basketball game to settle old scores. And so on.

What's strange is how laid-back it all is. The five old pals at times sound positively like they're idly remembering old times. Lots of stuff seems intended only to be pleasant. When it looks like Sandler and his wife will be given the bedroom with the water mattress, for example, he says, naw, let the kids all share it. Does that sound like the set-up for a joke? There isn't one.

Joyce Van Patten (who is seventy-five) and Rob Schneider (who is forty-six) play a married couple, which generates some laughs, mostly on the nice side, and no vulgarities. See, they really like each other. And during the obligatory scene where every character makes a confession or relates one of life's lessons, she makes a warm and genuine speech that is well delivered, but hardly seems to belong in this movie.

The comedy talent here is seen but not much heard, given the human traffic jam of the cast. Chris Rock and Kevin James are underutilized. Maria Bello is reduced to breast-feeding and milk-pumping scenes. The character of Ebony Jo-Ann, with her farts, bunions, and pratfalls, comes perilously close to an insulting caricature. Maya Rudolph spends much of her time reacting to others and caressing her pregnancy. Adam Sandler plays a good guy who never does much more than be a good guy.

The direction by Dennis Dugan never overcomes the ungainly size of the cast. It's such a challenge to keep all the characters alive that he sometimes does round-robins of reaction shots—a fatal strategy when it comes to timing. Some of the dialogue is broken down into one-shots; some of the characters spend stretches of merely responding. It's all, as I said, pleasant and good-natured, but it feels too much as if all these nice people are trying to keep the conversation going. A comedy it is, but *The Hangover* or *Death at a Funeral* it isn't.

## The Guard ★ ★ ★ ½

R, 95 m., 2011

Brendan Gleeson (Sergeant Gerry Boyle), Don Cheadle (Agent Wendell Everett), Liam Cunningham (Francis Sheehy), David Wilmot (Liam O'Leary), Rory Keenan (Garda Aidan McBride), Mark Strong (Clive Cornell), Fionnula Flanagan (Eileen Boyle). Directed by John Michael McDonagh and produced by Chris Clark, Flora Fernadez-Marengo, Ed Guiney, and Andrew Lowe. Screenplay by McDonagh.

As an actor, Brendan Gleeson is a fact of life. Tall, shaggy, not thin, he demonstrates that it takes a heap o' living to make a body a character. Cast him in a role, and the plot and dialogue become adornments. In *The Guard*, he is paired with the equally effective actor Don Cheadle, who could not be more different, and that is the point.

To begin we should observe that *guarda* is the Gaelic word for policeman, and in that sense this Irish movie is titled *The Cop*. Gleeson plays Sergeant Gerry Boyle, who tells us what we need to know when he witnesses a high-speed crash on a coastal road and quickly searches the clothes of a victim for drugs that he can transfer to his own pockets.

Gleeson is not an evil cop, just a bad one. He loves his mother. That's a good sign. Eileen Boyle (Fionnula Flanagan) is dying in a retirement home, but perks up during Gerry's visits. He settles his great bulk next to her frail frame and they cheerfully share the f-word as if it's a punctuation mark. On the job, Boyle drinks, has warm friendships with hookers, and takes it easy. His life takes an inconvenient turn when McBride (Rory Keenan), a straight-arrow *guarda* from Dublin, is transferred to Galway and becomes Boyle's partner. The last thing Boyle wants is a partner. The last place he wants him to come from is Dublin, which is regarded in Galway with all the affection some downstaters reserve for Chicago.

A big drug deal is coming down. It may involve half a million dollars, or pounds, or something—everyone seems vague. After a killing associated with the deal, the FBI sends Agent Everett (Don Cheadle) to Ireland. He is the *very* last thing Boyle desires in a partner. Boyle is not a racist, but he is naive about black people and singularly lacking in tact. He seems to regard Everett almost as an expert on the ghetto lives he's seen portrayed on TV cop shows.

Gleeson has a way in this movie of making outrageous statements with such openness that we can't be sure if he means them—or what he means by them. He makes a lot of comments about blacks that exist in a twilight zone between ignorance and guile. Is he trying to offend Everett, or simply clueless? Is there a method to his cluelessness? It isn't limited to race-related subjects; one of the pleasures of this film is the way Gleeson's dialogue obliquely suggests a great deal of intelligence and wit. The agent tells him: "I can't tell if you're really [bleeping] dumb or really [bleeping] smart."

The movie has been written and directed by John Michael McDonagh, whose brother Martin McDonagh made such good use of Gleeson in *In Bruges* (2008). His fundamentals are formulas: good cop bad cop, fish out of water, odd couple. He leavens these familiar forms with an enchanting Irishness in which visitors at times suspect they are the butt of an unexpressed joke. As my friend McHugh explained to me as I entered my first pub in Sligo: "When they're not looking at you, they're studying you out of the corners of their eyes. And when they're not listening to you, they're not missing a word."

McDonagh makes little mystery of the identities of the big-time drug dealers. His dialogue, sly and delightful, allows the *guarda* and the FBI agent to begin to trust each other while evading cloying clichés. The local color is flawless; I especially liked the curious small boy on the bicycle who seems to be ubiquitous, and who is treated by Gleeson not as a lost child but as a useful informer.

All builds up to a shoot-out on a boat docked at an obscure pier. The framing and cinematography here are unobtrusive but efficient. The drama builds remorselessly. Much is at stake. I am exhausted by shoot-outs in which countless rounds are exchanged in displays of special effects. But a scene like this, which depends on topography, characters, and logistics, can be a gift of the cinema. This movie is a pleasure. I can't tell if it's really [bleeping] dumb or really [bleeping] smart, but it's pretty [bleeping] good.

## Gulliver's Travels ★ ★ ★

PG, 85 m., 2010

Jack Black (Lemuel Gulliver), Jason Segel (Horatio), Emily Blunt (Princess Mary), Amanda Peet (Darcy Silverman), Billy Connolly (King Theodore), Chris O'Dowd (General Edward). Directed by Rob Letterman and produced by Jack Black, Ben Cooley, John Davis, and Gregory Goodman. Screenplay by Joe Stillman and Nicholas Stoller, not based very much on the novel by Jonathan Swift.

I want to tread carefully here, and not because I might step on a Lilliputian and squish him. I want to explain who *Gulliver's Travels* is for, and who it might not be for. One person it is definitely for is Gloria DeMent, the eighty-four-year-old grandmother who wrote Associated Press film critic Christy Lemire in horror after spending $96 to take four generations of her family to see *The Nutcracker in 3-D.* She wrote: "It broke my heart when we left the theatre that my little great-granddaughters (5-13) had sad little, confused faces." Believe me, Auntie Glo, there would have been smiles on those faces after this movie.

On the other hand, this is not really a movie for Jack Black fans—not of the Jack Black of *School of Rock*, for sure. They're used to seeing Jack with his shirt off, but to see their bad boy getting tiny cannonballs embedded in his belly may not be what they have in mind, not even when he sticks out his gut and the cannonballs pop out again and demolish an enemy armada.

He is standing up to his waist in the ocean at the time. No, not near the shore. Way out where a big enemy navy has massed its warships. Not only is Gulliver a giant in the land of Lilliput, but the sea surrounding their land is apparently Lilliputian as well—about three feet deep, I'd guess, judging by Jack Black's not towering stature.

As the film opens, Black is celebrating his tenth year in the mail room of a New York newspaper. He has a crush on Darcy the travel editor (Amanda Peet), who is a good sport and gives him an assignment to write a piece from Bermuda. Jack falls asleep on board his speedboat and enters the Bermuda Triangle, which, come to think of it, of course is where Lilliput must be. In the land of these six-inch people, he awakens to find himself tied down with ropes staked to the ground, which is also what happened in Jonathan Swift's classic, but boy, would Swift ever not recognize the rest of this story.

Jack, or Lemuel Gulliver, soon finds himself not a captive but more like a hero, god, adviser, and warrior for the Lilliputians, whose society resembles an Arthurian, not a Swiftian, fantasy. On an island centered on a seaside castle, they wear the costumes and play the roles of medieval romantic swashbucklery. And they talk the talk. To paraphrase one Lilliputian, "Whyeth musteth we always speaketh with all these ETHS?"

The kingdom centers on the beloved and beautiful Princess Mary (Emily Blunt), and the rivals for her affection: King Theodore (Billy Connolly) and General Edward (Chris O'Dowd). Lemuel is able to participate in these intrigues by peering over ramparts or taking a seat on battlements. He is about twelve times as tall as they are. I wonder how he can so easily hear their little voices; if he said, "Speak up!" they'd be blown away. No matter. Darcy, of course, turns up in search of Lemuel, battles are waged, tables are turned, romances blossom, and so on.

It just occurred to me that you may be imagining this is an animated film, and that Jack Black is voicing Lemuel Gulliver. Not at all. This is live action, and despite the 3-D, it's sorta old-fashioned, not that that's a bad thing. The problem is to contain Lemuel and the Lilliputians in the same frame when he towers over them. Makes for (1) long shots, or (2) shots of Black's enormous face peering at the little folks from over the edge of something. As he stood on the beach with the little fellas, I was immediately reminded of the genie in Michael Powell's masterpiece *The Thief of Bagdad* (1940).

I wouldn't describe the special effects as

seamless. Far from it. But that brings us back around to our grandmother, Gloria DeMent. Do you think her great-grandchildren are going to be sitting there saying, "You can see that's done with green screen"? I don't think so. They're gonna be saying, "Thanks, Grandma Glo! This is ever so much better than that scary Nutcracker movie! There isn't a single Holocaust anywhere in it!"

(Well, in all fairness, the entire Earth is ripped to pieces in a brilliant cartoon that plays before the feature. *Scrat's Continental Crack-Up* stars the manic creature from the first *Ice Age*, who would destroy the globe to save a nut.)

# H

## Hall Pass ★ ★ ½

R, 105 m., 2011

Owen Wilson (Rick), Jason Sudeikis (Fred), Jenna Fischer (Maggie), Christina Applegate (Grace), Richard Jenkins (Coakley). Directed by Bobby Farrelly and Peter Farrelly and produced by Mark Charpentier, Bobby Farrelly, Peter Farrelly, J. B. Rogers, Bradley Thomas, and Charles B. Wessler. Screenplay by Pete Jones, Kevin Barnett, Peter Farrelly, and Bobby Farrelly.

I was just reading an article about the oddly prolonged adolescence of American males, especially those in the movies. There's a common fantasy where the guys get away from their wives and girlfriends and escape to where they're free to guzzle beer, eat sloppy, belch, fart, leave pizza boxes on the floor, scratch their butts, watch sports on TV, and in many other ways become irresistible to hot chicks. When was the last time you saw a man under thirty in the movies who had a stable marriage, a job, children, and a life where he valued his wife above his buddies?

*Hall Pass* extends the twenties and thirties into the forties, and imagines a world in which there are no grown-up men at all. We meet two pals named Rick and Fred (Owen Wilson and Jason Sudeikis) who are well married to Maggie and Grace (Jenna Fischer and Christina Applegate) and yet lust improbably after every nubile woman who strays into their target zone. Rick in particular is always being caught by his wife while checking out the passing parade.

It is perhaps hardwired into men that their eyes are constantly on the prowl. Maybe it's an evolutionary trait, and our species has developed it to encourage the sowing of human seed in many fields. Women, by contrast, have evolved to be sure their mates gaze in admiration at them alone and nobody else. There's a famous story by Irwin Shaw, "The Girls in Their Summer Dresses," about an estranged couple who decide to make up. They go for a stroll down Fifth Avenue, but break up all over again because the man can't prevent his eyes from straying. He loves her, yes he really does, but you see, the girls are so pretty in their summer dresses.

Maggie and Grace eventually get fed up with the vagrant eyeballs of their husbands and decide to call the bluff. They issue week-long "hall passes," which are permission slips to allow both men seven days of unsupervised and guiltless sexual freedom. Maybe then they'll get desire out of their systems? Rick and Fred rejoice, and so do the members of their posse, because of course, men when set free seek the protection of the pack. Any real man would hunt alone, the better to sneak up on his prey. A woman does not respond eagerly to flattery emanating from a booth jammed with guys at Fuddrucker's.

*Hall Pass* is the new comedy by the Farrelly brothers, Bobby and Peter, who are in the unfortunate position of forever being judged against the impossible standard of their movie *There's Something About Mary* (1998). That remains the only movie where I literally, cross my heart, saw a man laugh so hard he fell out of his chair. One of the essential qualities of *Mary* was the performance by Ben Stiller as a man with much dignity, easily offended. Stiller can evoke a kind of vulpine cunning that is funny when thwarted.

A problem with *Hall Pass*, I think, is that both Owen Wilson and Jason Sudeikis are affable, and the movie wants us to like them. It is often more useful for a comedy to have characters whose embarrassment we enjoy. I suspect we're expected to empathize with the lads here, in their inept attempts to plunder the netherlands of steamy chicks. The truest words in the film are spoken by Joy Behar, as a more experienced older woman who tells the two wives that their husbands, like all men, believe only marriage is preventing them from being irresistible to women. It is probably a good thing for the species that so many men believe they're irresistible because so few are.

The plot of the movie is meh. It involves the lads and their posse being cycled through several unsuccessful and quasi-slapstick situations showing their cluelessness, their immaturity, and how women easily see straight through them. Meanwhile, the wives and their posses have a great time on a getaway retreat.

Women seem to get along perfectly well when set free without men, but men seem uncomfortable without women. It probably all involves which sex has the greater need to be reassured.

## The Hangover Part II ★ ★

R, 101 m., 2011

Bradley Cooper (Phil), Ed Helms (Stu), Zach Galifianakis (Alan), Justin Bartha (Doug), Ken Jeong (Mr. Chow), Paul Giamatti (Kingsley), Jamie Chung (Lauren), Mason Lee (Teddy), Mike Tyson (Himself). Directed by Todd Phillips and produced by Phillips and Daniel Goldberg. Screenplay by Phillips, Craig Mazin, and Scot Armstrong.

Is this some kind of a test? *The Hangover Part II* plays like a challenge to the audience's capacity for raunchiness. It gets laughs, but some of them are in disbelief. As if making sure no one was not offended, it has a montage of still photos in the closing titles that includes one cruel shot that director Todd Phillips should never, ever have used. The MPAA's elaboration of the R rating says the movie has "pervasive language, strong sexual content including graphic nudity, drug use, and brief violent images." Also other stuff. Maybe their space was limited.

It's not that I was shocked. This is a raunchfest, yes, but not an offense against humanity (except for that final photo, which is a desecration of one of the two most famous photos to come out of Vietnam). The movie has its share of laughs. There's a wedding toast that deserves some sort of award for deliberate social embarrassment. And Alan (Zach Galifianakis), the character who stole much of the original 2009 film, walks off with a lot of this one, too.

If you saw that earlier film (which grossed $485 million, so you may have), there's not much need for me to describe the plot this time. It's the same story. Phillips seems to have taken the *Hangover* screenplay and moved it laterally from Las Vegas to Bangkok while retaining the same sequence of scenes: call to bewildered bride-to-be, flashback to wedding plans, ill-advised bachelor party, four friends waking up with terminal hangovers in unfamiliar hotel room, ominous signs of debauchery, desperate quest to discover what happened, etc.

As the picture opens, a few years have passed. The dentist, Stu (Ed Helms), is now the prospective groom. He's engaged to a beautiful Thai woman named Lauren (Jamie Chung). Her father (Nirut Sirichanya) is not happy. His son Teddy (Mason Lee) is a brilliant sixteen-year-old pre-med student at Stanford, and the father tells Stu: "In this country, we do not consider dentist a doctor." At a pre-wedding feast, he calmly and implacably offers a toast comparing Stu to a flavorless rice pudding.

Then the lads go down to the beach for one (1) beer, and the next thing they know, they're regaining consciousness in a sleazy Bangkok fleabag, Stu has a facial tattoo, and young Teddy is missing, except for a severed finger wearing a Stanford class ring. That sets off their search through the city's underbelly for people who might be able to help them reconstruct the missing hours? days? Let me just observe that no search of the Bangkok underbelly that involves Ping-Pong balls is going to be altogether reassuring.

Their adventures are punctuated by a series of behavioral eruptions by Alan (Galifianakis), who links passive aggression with clueless troublemaking. These interventions have a certain charm, but Alan's funniest scene takes place in his own bedroom before he ever gets to Thailand. Describing himself as a "stay-at-home son," he issues commands to his mother through a speaker system and seems determined to remain a fanboy for life. This character, as seen in this scene, could inspire a movie of its own that I would pay good money to see. (Galifianakis should regrow his hair, however; I like him looking like a shaggy bear more than like the bouncer in a biker bar.)

I'm no expert, but I've been to Bangkok, and while the city no doubt has a seamy side, let it be said that much of *The Hangover Part II* plays like an anti-travelogue paid for by a rival tourist destination—Singapore, maybe. Some of its surprises would shock only those who know little about the city's sex workers, but others are truly unexpected, including the appearance of Paul Giamatti as a crime boss, and Nick Cassavetes as a tattoo artist. The gangster Mr. Chow (Ken Jeong) is back for the second film, still in need of serious tranquilizing.

While many weekend comedies these days seem too timidly in search of the PG-13, *The Hangover* embraced its R, and *Part II* seems to be testing the MPAA's patience. I wonder if there will be an unrated director's cut. The sequel repeats the medical miracle of the first film, in that the characters are able to regain consciousness after horrifying debauches and quickly return to the land of the living. In real life, they'd check themselves into an emergency room.

## Hanna ★ ★ ★ ½

PG-13, 111 m., 2011

Saoirse Ronan (Hanna), Eric Bana (Erik Heller), Cate Blanchett (Marissa Wiegler), Tom Hollander (Isaacs), Olivia Williams (Rachel), Jason Flemyng (Sebastian), Jessica Barden (Sophie). Directed by Joe Wright and produced by Marty Adelstein, Leslie Holleran, and Scott Nemes. Screenplay by Seth Lochhead and David Farr.

*Hanna* is a first-rate thriller about the drawbacks of homeschooling. As it opens, a teenage girl is in the act of killing a deer with her bow and arrow, and then, as she's gutting the carcass, a man sneaks up behind her and says, "You're dead!" She engages in a fierce hand-to-hand battle with this man, who turns out to be her father. He has raised her, as they lived alone deep in the forest in a house that looks like it was inspired by lots of gingerbread.

Gradually most—not all—of the details come clear. Hanna (Saoirse Ronan) has been taught advanced and ruthless killing skills as a means of self-defense against her enemies, who are legion. Her father, Erik (Eric Bana), fears for her safety and his own. He is apparently an agent whose skills and knowledge are so formidable that a CIA officer named Marissa (Cate Blanchett) is obsessed with capturing him—and the child.

Hanna decides she is ready for the real world, and the two of them plunge back into a confrontation with the CIA. And then we get an odd cross between a fairy tale and a high-tech action movie. It could have been a fairly strained attempt at either, but director Joe Wright (*Atonement*) combines his two genres into a stylish exercise that perversely includes some sentiment and insight.

Consider how hard it is to be Hanna. You have never known anyone your own age. You have apparently never met a woman. You speak several languages fluently. You are the master of martial arts and adept at many weapons. Your dad has drilled you to memorize every word in a one-volume encyclopedia that looks like it came as a free gift for opening a new account at the savings and loan. So you are all topped up on facts, but have no knowledge at all of the real world.

Of course, the movie reminded me of *Kick-Ass*, the 2010 action fantasy about a deadly young girl. I like *Hanna* a good deal more, because in its quirky way it has something to say, a certain wit, and a command of the visual poetry of action. There is nevertheless something disturbing about the conversion of little girls into ruthlessly efficient fighters who can kill dozens of people and not give it a second thought. If Hanna were a sixteen-year-old boy, how would that feel?

Marissa, the CIA boss, is essentially a wicked step-mother figure. Why she hates and fears Hanna and Erik is hinted at in many ways, and they all amount to this: The father and daughter represent a threat to American security so great that millions of dollars are gladly spent in the effort to capture and neutralize them. Is there a more personal motivation? Is Hanna by any chance the daughter of Marissa and Erik? The thought occurs because Saoirse Ronan and Cate Blanchett resemble each other in their facial bone structures, and also because—well, there are vibes.

Joe Wright has been known until now for civilized literary adaptations, including the wonderful Keira Knightley version of *Pride and Prejudice*. He's not a vulgarian. He has a purpose here, and I think it's to stir some of the same fundamental emotional parts that are reached by fairy tales, especially of the Grimm variety. He demonstrates that action movies need not be mindless. There is a role for creative choreography in them, even in largely CGI scenes like a chase sequence involving shipping containers on a dock. Even when human bodies are not really there, their apparent movements must be choreographed, and that sequence is a beauty.

Wright and his writers, Seth Lochhead and David Farr, do something else that's effective. They introduce an element of reality. Too many action films exist always at the same unremitting level of violent fantasy. Here, he arranges for Hanna to come across an ordinary British family on vacation. There is a daughter named Sophie (Jessica Barden), who I believe must be the first girl her age Hanna has met. Indeed, this is her first encounter with a family, and it's all strange and unfamiliar. The touch of reality brings into focus how peculiar her life has been.

Cate Blanchett seems strange. She allows little humanity into her Marissa; she's as personable as Ilsa, She Wolf of the SS. Perhaps that's wise. A more human Marissa would introduce tones that might not fit. Her job is to command her minions and focus on the capture of the father and daughter. A chamber in which Hanna is held for a while amusingly reminds us of the James Bond convention that an extraordinary captive demands an extraordinary cell, apparently constructed at great expense for the occasion.

*Hanna* is good, sound filmmaking. It depends on stylistic order and discipline, a clear story map, and ingenious action sequences. It is not all banging and flashing. Saoirse Ronan takes on a difficult role and aces it with as much confidence as she did playing a much different character in *Atonement.* To see a movie like this is to gain a new understanding of the mindless confusion of something like *Battle: Los Angeles.*

## Happy Feet Two ★ ★ ½

PG, 99 m., 2011

Elijah Wood (Mumble), Ava Acres (Erik), Robin Williams (Lovelace/Ramon), Hank Azaria (Mighty Sven), Pink (Gloria), Sofia Vergara (Carmen), Brad Pitt (Will the Krill), Matt Damon (Bill the Krill). Directed by George Miller and produced by Bill Miller, George Miller, and Doug Mitchell. Screenplay by George Miller, Gary Eck, Warren Coleman, and Paul Livingston.

The opening musical number in *Happy Feet Two* reminded me of Zhang Yimou's choreography for the 2008 Olympics. There are thousands and thousands of penguins, all perfectly coordinated, singing and dancing. One wonders if, like the Chinese performers, they were getting their cues from tiny earpieces. On the other hand, where are a penguin's ears?

The fact is, penguins offer relatively little for an animator to work with. They can't smile or wink. They can't furrow their brows. They have flippers instead of hands. As for dancing, we look at two big feet extending a few inches from a spheroid body, and know we won't be reminded of Fred Astaire. By and large, penguins look much alike. I'm sure they can tell themselves apart, but I was thankful for the one wearing the rainbow knit sweater, and wish they'd all had baseball caps or tattoos—anything.

The youngish audiences for this movie may not agree with me. George Miller's original *Happy Feet* (2006) grossed $385 million and won an Oscar for best animated feature, and here again is the hero, Mumble (Elijah Wood), now with a young son, Erik (Ava Acres). The two of them and perhaps a dozen other penguins, krills, seals, and puffins are developed as characters; the thousands of others are as alike as members of a marching band. Some whole species are denied individual status; the birds are merely birds, and although we share the suffering of the krills as they risk being eaten, there is no sympathy for lots of fish that are gobbled alive.

Antarctica is still melting, as the first film warned. In *Happy Feet Two*, an enormous chunk of a glacier breaks off, stranding the so-called Penguin Nation in an isolated bowl from which there seems to be no escape. Luckily, Erik and a couple of his pals, who were bad penguins and ran away from home, are outside the bowl, and much of the action involves how the Nation can escape. Starvation is the alternative.

This is handled as a musical with a startling range of tastes; we get numbers all the way from Queen's "We Are the Champions" to a solo aria, "E Lucevan Le Stelle," from Puccini's *Tosca.* You wonder how these penguins found out about Puccini. Then you realize it's just as inexplicable how they found out about Queen.

No matter. Younger viewers, who have no idea what an aria is, may simply enjoy the music.

The lives of all the surface creatures are intercut with a parallel plot involving two new characters, bright orange krills voiced by Matt Damon and Brad Pitt. What would you give to see a behind-the-scenes documentary of the two of them doing a voicing session? A krill, in case an instant of doubt crossed your mind, looks something like a shrimp, with countless spindly legs. As the krills themselves discuss bitterly, they occupy the bottom of the food chain in Antarctica, and are scooped up in the millions by humpbacked whales and suchlike. These two survive only because they're individuals and have the pluck to leave their swarm. The very word "swarm" tends to reduce a krill's self-esteem, don't you imagine? It's one thing to be a member of a pack, a school, a herd, a team, a flock, or a pride, but—a swarm?

Because all the action must take place near the deep ice bowl where the penguins are trapped, there are two possibilities: climbing out or sliding down. Penguins are especially adept at sliding on their plump, sleek bellies, and some of their stunts resemble extreme sports. Along the way, the film teaches many wholesome lessons about family, self-confidence, and hope, as well as the importance of being as high in the food chain as possible.

For me, *Happy Feet Two* was pretty thin soup. The animation was bright and attractive, the music gave the characters something to do, but the movie had too much dialogue in the areas of philosophy and analysis. It occurred to me, not for the first time, that it is a hard life being a penguin.

## Happy Happy ★ ★ ★

R, 88 m., 2011

Agnes Kittelsen (Kaja), Joachim Rafaelsen (Eirik), Maibritt Saerens (Elisabeth), Henrik Rafaelsen (Sigve), Oskar Hernaes Brandso (Theodor), Ram Shihab Ebedy (Noa), Heine Totland (Choral Director). Directed by Anne Sewitsky and produced by Synnove Horsdal. Screenplay by Ragnhild Tronvoll.

Women sometimes have a way of bursting into shrieks of delight on seeing one another, as if calmer behavior could not contain their ecstasy. Kaja, the heroine of *Happy Happy*, lives in such a state of permanent exhilaration. She lives with her husband, Eirik, and son, Theodor, in a snowbound Norwegian landscape, and when they rent the house next door to a couple with a boy, she acts like she's won the lottery. Kaja (Agnes Kittelsen) explains to Elisabeth, her new neighbor, how they can flash the lights in their windows to signal each other, like a couple of giddy schoolgirls.

Eirik (Joachim Rafaelsen) is in a perpetual funk, a practitioner of passive aggression. Elisabeth (Maibritt Saerens) and her husband, Sigve (Henrik Rafaelsen), seem to be an ideal couple, although they don't seem to have much interaction with their adopted Ethiopian son, Noa (Ram Shihab Ebedy). The two families quickly have dinner, which leads to an unwise session of the Newlywed Game in which both sides make unwise revelations. We learn that Elisabeth and Sigve have moved to this remote district on a rebound from Elisabeth's affair. And that Kaja and Eirik have no sex life; he blames her yeast infection, she says it was cleared up a year ago, and the degree of her unhappiness can be gauged the same night when she unexpectedly performs oral sex on Sigve when they've stepped away from the table.

Sigve is ready for sex, perhaps to avenge his wife's affair, and there's one of those rollicking scenes in which Scandinavians seem immune to the cold. When Eirik is away on a "hunting trip," they romp naked in the snow, much to the disgust of Kaja's son, Theodor (Oskar Hernaes Brandso), who sides with his father and has withdrawn from his happy happy mother.

There is oddness all about. Eirik has constructed a free-standing wooden teepee in a field, to which he retreats for chilly solitude. After he makes a pass at Sigve and is rebuffed, we suspect his hunting trips may seek two-legged game. Meanwhile, Theodor shares with Noa his children's book about slavery, and explains to the silent African boy that he is his slave, and must carry baskets on his head and submit to whipping. Noa is a good sport and goes along. The parents never seem aware of this game.

The key performance is by Kittelsen, as

Kaja. She is so desperately needy. Her happiness is so sadly forced, it borders on hysteria. Her husband is so remote we understand why she was excited to get new neighbors. It's a fascinating performance.

The other cast members are all solid, in a plot that puts them through a below-zero soap opera. The slave play between Noa and Theodor makes us uncomfortable because it leads nowhere and seems to lack a purpose. Noa, such a small boy, simply goes along with it to be agreeable. He's passive and sometimes his adoptive parents seem almost to forget him.

Then there is a peculiar device by Anne Sewitsky, the director, who cuts at regular intervals to an American a capella singing quartet, which performs folk songs in English. Why? To what purpose? I think perhaps to provide ironic counterpoint in a misplaced attempt at cleverness. Kaja later finds the nerve to sing in the church choir, which is a breakthrough, I guess.

So this is a very strange film. Yet I was happy to be watching it. It is short and intense enough that it always seems on track, even if the train goes nowhere. The film won the grand jury prize in the Sundance World Cinema category.

## Happy Tears ★ ★ ★

R, 95 m., 2010

---

Parker Posey (Jayne), Demi Moore (Laura), Rip Torn (Joe), Ellen Barkin (Shelly), Christian Camargo (Jackson). Directed by Mitchell Lichtenstein and produced by Joyce M. Pierpoline. Screenplay by Lichtenstein.

---

In *Happy Tears,* two sisters—one poor, one rich, one steady, one obsessed with possessions—deal with their old dad's approach to senility and his girlfriend's approach to his money. This story takes on an eerie resonance with the performance by Rip Torn as the aging father. He was recently in the news for being arrested, at the age of seventy-eight, for breaking into a bank while intoxicated and carrying a firearm.

To be sure, it was late at night, he had apparently forgotten he had the firearm, and after all, the bank looked a lot like a house. Nor is senility his problem. He is now in alcohol rehab, and I wish him good fortune because he is a fine actor. Ann Landers wrote about the danger signals of alcoholism. His arrest in the bank is surely one of them. Still, to stir up such a scandal at seventy-eight is perhaps even a tiny accomplishment, when so many his age are no longer physically able to break into banks.

Even more worthy is Torn's work here as Joe, cantankerous, stubborn as a mule, and oblivious to the fact that his "nurse," Shelly (Ellen Barkin), does not practice medicine but a far older profession. This is evident to his daughter Laura (Demi Moore), who has flown in from San Francisco to decide what should be done with him. Of course he insists he's perfectly fine and will stay right at home, thank you.

As the film opens, Laura is on the phone with her sister, Jayne (Parker Posey), telling her it's her duty to fly east and help with Joe. Jayne is a shopaholic, and we see her buying a pair of boots so expensive that if it were my money I'd just buy a car. Posey is an actress with a nice line in flightiness, and here she blends it interestingly with selfishness and irresponsibility. Soon after her arrival, the need to tidy up after Joe's problems with number two becomes the first of several life lessons she'll learn.

*Happy Tears* centers on these two women, who have been opposites all their lives and yet like each other, and share a fondness for pot. Jayne can be infuriating, but Laura deals with it. Demi Moore is interesting here. In the role of a dialed-down, capable woman, she suggests dramatic possibilities for future roles. She projects a kind of calm, and it's attractive.

I was also intrigued by Ellen Barkin's work as the "nurse" Shelly, who optimistically believes that by wearing a stethoscope around her neck she can pass herself off. It's abundantly clear to Jayne and Laura that she learned her nursing on TV, but Joe is sold on her and cannot comprehend the possibility that he won't get his way. Instead of keeping Shelly at Level One of character complexity, writer-director Mitchell Lichtenstein wisely makes her a little more than she might seem. Barkin, a force of nature in such films as *Sea of Love,* here wades into a character role with zeal.

We assume the movie will mostly concern what the daughters should do with Joe. These scenarios are common enough, when estranged siblings are brought back together for the one reason it's hard to deny: the shared responsibility of family.

It's as well, too, that Joe is seen as a fairly clear-cut case. You want my opinion? He belongs in a home. In many films considering this question, the parents don't actually *need* such care, but it's such a convenience, you see, for their children. Joe presents not so much a problem for Jayne and Laura as an opportunity. It's time to grow up and be daughters and sisters. They've waited long enough. All of this, I must add, is done with a nice, screwy, sometimes stoned humor.

## Harry Brown ★ ★ ★

R, 103 m., 2010

Michael Caine (Harry Brown), Emily Mortimer (D. I. Frampton), Charlie Creed-Miles (D. S. Hicock), Ben Drew (Noel Winters), Liam Cunningham (Sid Rourke), Iain Glen (S. I. Andrew Childs), David Bradley (Leonard Attwell), Jack O'Connell (Marky Hathaway). Directed by Daniel Barber and produced by Keith Bell, Matthew Brown, Kris Thykier, and Matthew Vaughn. Screenplay by Gary Young.

*Harry Brown* is a revenge thriller poised somewhere between *Death Wish* and *Gran Torino*. All three depend on the ability of an older actor to convince us he's still capable of violence, and all three spend a great deal of time alone with their characters, whose faces must reflect their inner feelings. Charles Bronson, Clint Eastwood, Michael Caine. Those are faces sculpted by time.

Caine plays an old man with a dying wife. He lives in a London housing estate used by a drug gang as its own turf. Pedestrians are terrorized and beaten, drugs are openly sold, there are some areas understood as no-go. From his high window, Harry hears a car alarm and looks down to see the car's owner come out and be beaten by thugs. This is the daily reality.

Caine is a subtle actor who builds characters from the inside out. His voice has become so familiar over the years that it's an old friend. In this film he begins as a lonely, sad geezer, and gradually an earlier persona emerges, that of a British marine who served in Northern Ireland. All of that has been put in a box and locked away, he says, and thinks.

There's a pub on the estate, quiet in the daytime, where he and his old friend Leonard (David Bradley) meet for studious games of chess. The thugs have been shoving dog mess through Leonard's mail slot. His life is miserable. He shows Harry a gun. One day when the gang pushes burning newspapers through the slot, he goes to confront them in an underpass they control. Later Frampton, a young police inspector (Emily Mortimer), comes to tell Harry that Leonard has been killed.

The inspector is human, and sympathetic. Harry tells her the police have no control over the area, and she cannot disagree. Her superior officer has his own notions. And then the film takes the turn that we expect, and in the process takes on aspects of a more conventional police procedural.

What Caine is successful at, however, is always remaining in character. Like Eastwood, and unlike Bronson, he is always his age, always in the same capable but aged body. The best scene in the movie involves his visit to the flat of a drug dealer, where Harry plans to buy a gun. There's a semi-comatose girl on the sofa. The situation is fraught. How Harry handles it depends not on strength but on experience and insight. He carefully conceals his cards.

The police investigation is misdirected for political motives. Frampton has an excellent notion of who may be responsible for the killings of neighborhood hoods, but cannot get a hearing. It would not do for a geezer to outdo the police. Vigilante activity is, of course, not the answer to urban crime, but what is? In Chicago, Mayor Richard Daley floods one area with cops, and shootings continue nearby. It's all fueled by drugs and drug money, of course. You know, one of the areas where I think Libertarians may be right is about the legalization of drugs. There would be less of them with no profit motive for their sale. Less money for guns. Fewer innocent bystanders would die. Who knows?

This movie plays better than perhaps it

should. Directed as a debut by Daniel Barber, it places story and character above manufactured "thrills," and works better. We are all so desperately weary of CGI that replaces drama. With movies like this, humans creep back into crime films. There is a clear thread connecting this Michael Caine and the Caine of *The Ipcress File*. You may not be able to see it, but it's there.

## Harry Potter and the Deathly Hallows: Part 1 ★ ★ ★

PG-13, 146 m., 2010

Daniel Radcliffe (Harry Potter), Rupert Grint (Ron Weasley), Emma Watson (Hermione Granger), Helena Bonham Carter (Bellatrix Lestrange), Robbie Coltrane (Rubeus Hagrid), Ralph Fiennes (Lord Voldemort), Brendan Gleeson (Alastor "Mad Eye" Moody), Rhys Ifans (Xenophilius Lovegood), Jason Isaacs (Lucius Malfoy), Bill Nighy (Rufus Scrimgeour), Alan Rickman (Severus Snape), Imelda Staunton (Dolores Umbridge), Julie Walters (Mrs. Weasley), Mark Williams (Arthur Weasley), Michael Gambon (Albus Dumbledore), Richard Griffiths (Vernon Dursley), John Hurt (Ollivander), Fiona Shaw (Petunia Dursley), Timothy Spall (Wormtail), David Thewlis (Remus Lupin). Directed by David Yates and produced by David Barron, David Heyman, and J. K. Rowling. Screenplay by Steve Kloves, based on the novel by Rowling.

Harry, Hermione, and Ron have grown up. The horrors they met at Hogwarts are but nostalgic memories. They are cast out now into the vastness of the world, on their own, and Voldemort and his Death Eaters draw ever closer. Also drawing near is an equally unsettling phenomenon, sexual maturity. Both are barely kept at bay in this first installment of the last installment of the saga Harry Potter.

David Yates's *Harry Potter and the Deathly Hallows* is a handsome and sometimes harrowing film, and will be completely unintelligible for anyone coming to the series for the first time. At 146 minutes, it confronts us with a roll call of the many, many characters in the series, and requires a nearly encyclopedic recall of the previous chapters of the epic. I've seen all the films, and there were times when I had no idea what they were talking about here. Indeed, there are times when Hermione has to explain to Harry.

My cluelessness didn't bother me because the film depends more on mood and character than many of the others, and key actions seem to be alarmingly taking place off-screen. Our three heroes have left Hogwarts behind, Quidditch games are a thing of the past, and things have come to such a pass that Harry keeps his white owl in a cramped parrot cage.

The film opens with a frightening meeting of the Death Eaters, plotting the destruction of all three characters. Presiding is Lord Voldemort (Ralph Fiennes), his noseless face disturbingly like a snake's. Harry must be destroyed. That our hero survives after the myriad attacks on his life in the earlier installments does not speak well for Voldemort's minions, but this time they mean business.

Harry (Daniel Radcliffe) moves his family to a safe haven. He joins Hermione (Emma Watson) and Ron (Rupert Grint) in flight, sometimes literally. They seek counsel from old friends, and spend a great deal of time in wilderness isolation. They have the ability to materialize anywhere, and we find them in forbidding forests, beside mirrorlike lakes ringed by mountains, and in a harsh landscape where the rocks have been riven by deep cracks. That some of these locations are actual and others are CGI is usually not noticeable, although I doubt that Harry would have skipped so casually over these cracked stones if they were real.

This isolation serves two purposes. It helps conceal them from Voldemort. And, especially after Ron Weasley seems to live up to his name and weasel out, it allows Harry and Hermione to become closer friends than ever, confidants, and even, yes, in love. They share a kiss so chaste that passion seems a stranger to them; they might as well be observing a formal ritual. And they are nude, or almost nude, as they stand close to each other and ghostly CGI mists obscure all the naughty bits as efficiently as fig leaves.

Much has to do with tracking down missing pieces of Voldemort's soul. The late beloved Dumbledore (Michael Gambon) has left obscure clues to their whereabouts, leading to two observations: (1) Beyond a certain level of obscurity, a clue lacks usefulness, and (2) how extraordinarily careless of Voldemort to leave missing pieces of his soul lying about.

This installment ends in midstream, which we all knew it would, because Part 2 opens in July. That final installment must at last tie up all the loose ends, dispatch villains, celebrate heroes, and return some stability to the world of magicians. To hope a breeze blows through it and clears away the mists is too much to hope for. Hermione here has grown into an attractive young woman, Harry and Ron are both alert to that, and Harry now even needs to shave (although he has mercifully not graduated to the three-day stubble of the routine action hero).

The final film will be in 3-D. This installment was once planned for retro 3-D, but Warner Bros., a studio that enforces traditional standards, decided against that after observing the disastrous results of other 2-D films converted to 3-D. Presumably the next film will have 3-D done well. It will suffer in brightness and clarity, and that is a shame. Look closely at the 2-D opening Warner Bros. logo here and you will swear it's 3-D.

As we approach the end of a decade of Harry Potter, it's clear how wisely (and luckily) the studio cast the series. Radcliffe, Grint, and Watson have grown from children to young adults, still retain the qualities they had when younger, are practiced professionals, and carry the series. And they are surrounded by a supporting cast that's like an honor roll of great recent British actors.

Setting aside actors from earlier films who have passed away (Richard Harris) or are no longer needed (Emma Thompson), let me just make a list for those who know their actors: Helena Bonham Carter, Robbie Coltrane, Ralph Fiennes, Michael Gambon, Brendan Gleeson, Richard Griffiths, John Hurt, Rhys Ifans, Jason Isaacs, Bill Nighy, Alan Rickman, Fiona Shaw, Timothy Spall, Imelda Staunton, David Thewlis, Warwick Davis, Tom Felton, Toby Jones, Simon McBurney, Peter Mullan, and Julie Walters. Rather awesome.

I make it a custom to avoid becoming expert on the endless characters and plot strands of series movies. Life is too short to become an authority on all of the movies about James Bond, *The Lord of the Rings*, and so on. I'm sure students of Harry Potter will comprehend *Harry Potter and the Deathly Hallows* better than I was able to. They'll see a character and recall scenes from a movie made seven years ago. For me, it's more about the immediate experience. The important thing is that the characters know what's happening. At least by the end, anyway.

## Harry Potter and the Deathly Hallows: Part 2 ★ ★ ★ ½

PG-13, 131 m., 2011

Daniel Radcliffe (Harry Potter), Rupert Grint (Ron Weasley), Emma Watson (Hermione Granger), Helena Bonham Carter (Bellatrix Lestrange), Robbie Coltrane (Rubeus Hagrid), Ralph Fiennes (Lord Voldemort), Michael Gambon (Albus Dumbledore), John Hurt (Ollivander), Jason Isaacs (Lucius Malfoy), Kelly Macdonald (Helena Ravenclaw), Gary Oldman (Sirius Black), Alan Rickman (Severus Snape), Maggie Smith (Minerva McGonagall), David Thewlis (Remus Lupin). Directed by David Yates and produced by David Barron, David Heyman, and J. K. Rowling. Screenplay by Steve Kloves, based on the novel by Rowling.

After seven earlier films reaching back a decade, the Harry Potter saga comes to a solid and satisfying conclusion in *Harry Potter and the Deathly Hallows: Part 2*. The finale conjures up enough awe and solemnity to serve as an appropriate finale and a dramatic contrast to the (relatively) lighthearted innocence of *Harry Potter and the Sorcerer's Stone* all those magical years ago.

Harry, Hermione, and Ron are grown up now, and Harry has even grown the facial stubble required of all epic heroes. The time has come for him to face Lord Voldemort in their final showdown, and their conflict is staged in a series of special effects sequences containing power and conviction. I am still not sure what the bolts discharged by magic wands actually consist of, but never mind: They look wicked and lethal.

I dare not reveal a single crucial detail about the story itself, lest I offend the Spoiler Police, who have been on my case lately. Besides, you never know: Maybe they've completely rewritten J. K. Rowling's final book in the series. Maybe Harry dies, Voldemort is triumphant, and evil reigns.

What I can observe is that this final film is a reunion of sorts for a great many characters we've come to know over the years. So many distinguished British actors have played roles in the Potter films that those who haven't may be fitfully resentful. Here we see once again characters whose names were once new and now resonate with associations: Bellatrix Lestrange, Rubeus Hagrid, Albus Dumbledore, Ollivander, Lucius Malfoy, Sirius Black, Severus Snape, Remus Lupin, and even Minerva McGonagall, who is called upon to summon her powers and shield Hogwarts School from the powers of Voldemort.

You don't want to know what happens to Hogwarts here. Many of its shining spires and noble Gothic arches are reduced to ruin and ashes, providing an apocalyptic battleground. The school also seems to have mysteriously relocated adjacent to towering heights that permit vertiginous falls to the earth far below. There is no place in Britain that fits this geography, but then is Hogwarts quite in the real Britain?

What it does occupy is a Britain of the imagination. The series has remained faithful to J. K. Rowling's original conception, and resisted temptations to cheapen its action or simplify its complexity. She created a fictional world with its own logic and consistency, and here at the end there is some satisfaction in seeing loose ends tied up, lingering mysteries explained, and suspicions confirmed.

In a dreamy sequence close to the end, we are allowed to see the characters as they were in the beginning. They were so young. By spanning something like real time, the story has grown older along with them. Daniel Radcliffe, born in 1989, was eleven when he first played Harry Potter, and is twenty-one now. He and Ron Weasley (Rupert Grint) and Hermione Granger (Emma Watson) have luckily remained recognizable and soldiered on through what involved a great deal of hard labor. Not many young actors have been worked so relentlessly for a decade.

That said, it's apparent again in this film that the three leads are upstaged by the supporting characters. Their role is to be plucky, clean-cut, and stalwart. They sneak around and observe things. They eavesdrop. They speculate. They are lectured to. They endure a little low-key puberty. Harry struggles to master his magic. Meanwhile, such British legends as Maggie Smith, Helena Bonham Carter, Michael Gambon, Alan Rickman, and Ralph Fiennes steal scenes just by standing there. What chance does Harry or anybody have against Voldemort's smashed face with its nostril slits? Late in the film, leaving nothing to chance, Voldemort even appears as his own fetus, looking like it's been simmered in red sauce.

It is Fiennes's Voldemort who dominates this last installment, illustrating the old actors' axiom that it is better to play the villain than the hero. It takes a considerable villain to hold his own in the crumbled ruins of Hogwarts and force the remaining students to choose between the friends of Harry or joining him on the dark side. Considering what has happened to Hogwarts, it's a little surprising that the students haven't been sent home, but then, Dumbledore has had other things on his mind.

This movie is impressively staged, the dialogue is given proper weight and not hurried through, there are surprises that, in hindsight, seem fair enough, and *Harry Potter* now possesses an end that befits the most profitable series in movie history. These films will be around for a long time. And without spoiling a single thing, let me just observe that the final scene clearly leaves an opening for a sequel. I know, Rowling says there won't be one. Just sayin'.

## Hatchet II ★ ½

NO MPAA RATING, 85 m., 2010

Danielle Harris (Marybeth), Tony Todd (Reverend Zombie), Kane Hodder (Victor Crowley), Parry Shen (Justin), Tom Holland (Bob). Directed by Adam Green and produced by Derek Curl, Sarah Elbert, and Cory Neal. Screenplay by Green.

You want gore, you get gore. *Hatchet II* plays less like a slasher movie than like the highlights reel from a slasher movie. It comes billed as, I dunno, satire or homage. Homage it certainly is, to the tradition of movies where everyone starts out alive at the beginning and ends up pretty much dead at the end. If satire means doing what your target does but doing it twice as much, then it's satire, too.

This is the continuation of *Hatchet* (2006), by the same director, Adam Green. Having missed that film, incredibly enough, I learn it ended at the same moment this one begins, with a monstrous swamp creature savaging the heroine, Marybeth (Danielle Harris). Since Marybeth was played by Tamara Feldman in the earlier film, this may cause some confusion if the movies play as a double feature, but hey, if Luis Bunuel could make one movie with two women playing the lead, why can't Adam Green do it with two movies?

As an exercise, let's see how quickly I can summarize the plot. Marybeth escapes from the swamp into the shack of a swamp fisherman (John Carl Beuchler), who offers her a drink from a plastic hospital urinal. He finds out who she is, and throws her out. She appeals to the Reverend Zombie (Tony Todd), who runs Zombie Shop in the French Quarter. He musters a posse of armed men to venture into the swamp, retrieve any leftover body parts of Marybeth's father and brother, and shotgun the Swamp Thing, named Crowley (Kane Hodder). The nonswamp dialogue scenes are dispatched as swiftly as possible, and then Crowley sets about slicing, dicing, slashing, disemboweling, chainsawing, and otherwise inconveniencing the men in the boat.

Man, Adam Green must have run up a bill at the local butcher. Hundreds of dollars' worth of sweetmeats, livers, gizzards, hearts, lungs, and other organs of animals (none of them human, I trust) are seemingly ripped out of Crowley's victims, while blood helpfully obscures our view of the details of these eviscerations.

There is an explanation for Crowley's behavior, a revelation about who he is, an occult connection with Reverend Zombie, and some business involving the bounty hunters, and this information is used by Adam Green as sort of an *amuse-bouche*—you know, the little serving of sorbet that French chefs offer to cleanse your palate between main courses.

There are a number of good movies opening this weekend. *Hatchet II* is not one of them. Tickets are not cheap and time is fleeting. Why would you choose this one? That's a good topic for a long, thoughtful talk with yourself in the mirror.

## Haywire ★ ★ ★

R, 92 m., 2012

Gina Carano (Mallory Kane), Michael Fassbender (Paul), Ewan McGregor (Kenneth), Bill Paxton (John Kane), Channing Tatum (Aaron), Antonio Banderas (Rodrigo), Michael Douglas (Coblenz). Directed by Steven Soderbergh and produced by Gregory Jacobs. Screenplay by Lem Dobbs.

There must be Freudian insights explaining why so many young males respond positively to superwomen as heroines. At science fiction and comics conventions, a woman wearing a fetishistic superhero costume will almost certainly be the focus of a circle of intent fanboys. Maybe there's the prospect of an all-protecting mom. Or the promise of a cool female buddy. The possibility of sex seems to be secondary.

Mallory Kane, the heroine of *Haywire*, is a splendid example of the character type. Her first name springs from a Latin root for evil, and her last name inspires associations with British pornography ("Strict instruction for naughty schoolboys. Call Miss Kane"). Steven Soderbergh's new film is a thriller that has next to nothing to do with sex, except as an implement of distraction, but under the surface there's an appeal coiling to that part of many men that feels kinda needy about Lara Croft.

Mallory is played by Gina Carano, a retired mixed martial arts fighter. Her range is suggested by having placed number five on a Most Influential Women list on Yahoo! and number sixteen on *Maxim*'s Hot 100. On the basis of *Haywire*, I expect her to become a considerable box office success because the fact is, within a limited range, she's good. In the movie's first scene she walks into a little café in upstate New York, sits down, sips a little tea, and had me hooked. She has the no-nonsense beauty of a Noomi Rapace, Linda Fiorentino, or Michelle Monaghan.

She plays an employee of a murky special

contractor of the U.S. government, which specializes in performing dirty work on assignment. Its own agents and enemy agents, who sometimes seem interchangeable, spend a great deal of time deceiving and double-crossing one another, and Mallory discovers during the course of the film that (spoiler, I guess) she can't trust anyone. Why so many people want to kill her is a mystery, because she is so gifted at her job.

Carano is wonderfully athletic, which is just as well because she spends most of the film being wonderfully athletic. Although you never know in this age of special effects exactly what is real in a martial arts scene, let it be said she really does seem to be personally performing some impressive fight moves; there are the same elegant moments we remember from Bruce Lee and Jackie Chan, who were blindingly fast and ingenious in the way they improvised using walls, angles, furniture, and the bodies of others.

Soderbergh is a master craftsman whose work moves almost eagerly between genres. This is his first martial arts film, and he correctly assumes that the audience isn't interested in hearing a lot of dialogue. Lesser directors would use that as an excuse to rely entirely on action and lowball the words. Not Soderbergh and his screenwriter, Lem Dobbs, who wrote *Dark City*, is the son of the famous painter R. B. Kitaj, and lifted his pen name from the Bogart character in *The Treasure of the Sierra Madre.*

What they do is craft very precise words for a large group of supporting characters, and fill those roles with surprisingly big names. The result is that the film (although its plot is preposterous nonsense) has weight and heft and places Mallory at the center of a diabolical labyrinth. Consider that a relatively little-known actress costars with Michael Fassbender, Ewan McGregor, Bill Paxton, Channing Tatum, Antonio Banderas, and Michael Douglas, and you realize that (1) Carano can hold her own, and (2) like Woody Allen, Soderbergh is one of those directors who can get just about anybody he wants to act in his movies.

I call the plot nonsense. Ask yourself this: How could any organization or "contractor" survive for long with the death rate we see here? At the end of a year no one would be left alive except a few mail room clerks. Soderbergh seems to be amusing himself with the variety of his locations; we visit Barcelona, Dublin, New Mexico, New York state, and executive offices in unnamed cities. A film like *Haywire* has no lasting significance, but it's a pleasure to see an A-list director taking the care to make a first-rate genre thriller.

## Headhunters ★ ★ ★ ½

R, 100 m., 2012

Aksel Hennie (Roger Brown), Nikolaj Coster-Waldau (Clas Greve), Synnove Macody Lund (Diana Brown), Eivind Sander (Ove), Julie Olgaard (Lotte). Directed by Morten Tyldum and produced by Marianne Gray and Asle Vatn. Screenplay by Ulf Ryberg and Lars Gudmestad, based on the novel by Jo Nesbo.

It's not often a thriller keeps me wound up as well as *Headhunters* did. I knew I was being manipulated and didn't care. It was a pleasure to see how well it was being done. Unlike too many thrillers that depend on stunts, special effects, and a queasy-cam, this one devises a plot where it matters what happens. It's not all kinetic energy.

It's from Norway. Why has Scandinavia been producing such good thrillers? Maybe because their films can't afford millions for CGI and must rely on cheaper elements like, you know, stories and characters. *Headhunters* deserves comparison with *The Girl with a Dragon Tattoo*, *Insomnia*, and *Let the Right One In.*

At its center is an everyman, Roger Brown, who is an executive headhunter. While interviewing job candidates, he learns information that's invaluable in his second job, as an art thief. He needs the money and tells us why: He's keenly aware that he stands five-foot-six and is married to Diana, a statuesque blonde. On her he lavishes expensive gifts and a luxurious lifestyle, and he even sets her up with her own art gallery. He doesn't believe she could love him for himself.

Brown is played by Aksel Hennie, a smooth-talking type with the cool nerve necessary to enter homes and replace valuable paintings with deceptive reproductions. At a gallery opening, Diana (Synnove Macody Lund) introduces him to a new client: Clas Greve (Nikolaj Coster-Waldau). This man looks like trouble. Tall, chiseled, confident, he has just resigned as CEO of a multinational, and Brown would like to recruit him for a rival firm. He's persuasive. He won't stop until the man agrees to lunch.

Greve, as it turns out, inherited a Rubens from his grandmother. Perfect. Brown can place him with the firm and steal his painting. But when he learns the devastating news that Diana and Greve have been having an affair, he sabotages the job offer. Claus Greve is not a man you want to cross. Trained as a military commando, survivor of Bolivian torture, fiercely proud, he wants revenge. He's the sort of villain that a thriller needs: intelligent and remorseless. Not a gimmick character, but an implacable enemy.

Enough about the plot. What *Headhunters* has done, skillfully, is enlist our sympathy with Roger Brown and our interest in Claus Greve. They're not simply plot markers. And Diana is not simply a trophy blonde, but warm and nice, and if she had an affair, well, so did Brown—with Lotte (Julie Olgaard), whom he treats with disturbing callousness. We've seen Greve in a dressing room, his muscular back crisscrossed with whip marks. We know, and Brown knows, he means business.

*Headhunters* then opens up into a long, punishing chase, as Greve tracks Brown across Norway in a series of increasingly perilous situations. The short man proves courageous and resilient, and can think quickly. His method for hiding in an outhouse from Greve and his dog is admirably practical. It's incredible he hangs onto his life. Yes, this follows thriller formulas. What is important is that it has the unfaked weight of reality. No fancy effects, but flesh and blood and real locations.

Even though the film helpfully explains a few things in its closing scenes, it's unlikely you'll be able to follow the plot step by step. It's a labyrinth of double-crosses and deceptions. Brown doesn't know whom he can trust, and neither do we. The director, Morten Tyldum, has a gift for visual shocks and reveals. Everything can change in a single edit.

*Headhunters* is like an argument for the kinds of thriller I miss. It entertains with story elements, in which the scares evolve from human behavior. Pure action is boring. Chase scenes are boring, unless you devise one as *Headhunters* does, with a shaky farm tractor. Sex scenes can even be boring, unless there is the illusion that the partners care. *Headhunters* plays fair.

## The Hedgehog ★ ★ ★

NO MPAA RATING, 100 m., 2011

Josiane Balasko (Renee Michel), Garance Le Guillermic (Paloma Josse), Togo Igawa (Kakuro Ozu), Anne Brochet (Solange Josse), Wladimir Yordanoff (Paul), Sarah Le Picard (Colombe). Directed by Mona Achache and produced by Mark Lombardo and Anne-Dominique Toussaint. Screenplay by Achache, based on the novel *The Elegance of the Hedgehog* by Muriel Barbery.

*The Hedgehog* is a feel-good movie that masquerades at first as a feel-bad. It's narrated by Paloma, a precocious and almost infuriatingly self-assured eleven-year-old, who plans to kill herself on her twelfth birthday. This seems like a permanent solution to a trivial set of problems. Her complaints are common enough: Her mother talks to plants, her father is distracted by work, her sister is a snooty little snot-nose, and her sister's goldfish serves for Paloma as a metaphor for her own life lived in a bowl.

Paloma was the heroine of *The Elegance of the Hedgehog*, a French best-seller by Muriel Barbery. The hedgehog, as we know, is a creature that's all bristles on the outside and all cuddly on the inside. It is not Paloma who is the hedgehog in the film, but Madame Renee Michel (Josiane Balasko), the fifty-four-year-old concierge of the Parisian apartment building where Paloma lives with her family. Madame Michel refers to herself as old and ugly, dresses in an almost aggressively dowdy fashion, and "doesn't do anything with herself."

At first we fear the film will focus entirely on Paloma's tiresome narcissism. Then a deus ex machina arrives in the form of Kakuro Ozu (Togo Igawa), who moves into an empty apartment. Mr. Ozu is an elegant Japanese man of around sixty, and it should catch our attention that he happens to have the same surname as Yasujiro Ozu, that most civilized of Japanese directors.

We never learn very much about Mr. Ozu's history. He arrives fully formed in the building, well dressed, quiet, his gray hair cut youthfully short. He overhears Madame Michel saying impatiently, "Happy families are all alike." These are perhaps the most famous opening words of any novel, and Ozu supplies Tolstoy's next line: "Every unhappy family is unhappy in its own way."

This is the beginning of a beautiful friendship. Mr. Ozu is apparently the first person in some years to regard Madame Michel's bristly exterior and realize she is warm and good beneath the surface; feeling rejected by society, she has retreated to a small room in her apartment with her cat and her beloved books, and lives a life of the imagination.

There's little that happens in the building that Paloma doesn't observe, and often she records it on a video camera. This will presumably produce a document to explain her complaints about her family, and in particular her feelings about the goldfish, and why she has departed this life. But now a strange thing happens. She begins to see Madame Michel transformed by the quiet courtesy of Mr. Ozu, and she learns, by inference, that she must have more respect for her own warm insides and not be so fond of her pouty exterior.

*The Hedgehog* isn't one of those movies where the heroine is transformed by a beauty makeover. The actress Josiane Balasko is not a beautiful woman, although of course she would be attractive if she permitted her face to advertise a sunny personality. We get a hint of this in a single smile, so small, so astonishing. I won't go into the details of the polite relationship between the concierge and her new gentleman, nor will I mention a crucial event later in the film. All of that has to be experienced in context.

*The Hedgehog* is just a little too neat for me. Paloma is affected, Mr. Ozu is perfect to an unlikely degree, Paloma's family exists as comic types, and Madame Michel comes closest in the film to simple plausibility. Still, this is a movie with such a light, stylish touch, it makes no claims to profundity, and is a sweetly hopeful experience.

## The Heir Apparent: Largo Winch ★ ★

NO MPAA RATING, 108 m., 2011

Tomer Sisley (Largo Winch), Kristin Scott Thomas (Ann Ferguson), Miki Manojlovic (Nerio Winch), Melanie Thierry (Lea/Naomi), Gilbert Melki (Freddy), Karel Roden (Mikhail Korsky), Steven Waddington (Stephan Marcus), Benedict Wong (William Kwan). Directed by Jerome Salle and produced by Nathalie Gastaldo and Philippe Godeau. Screenplay by Julien Rappeneau and Jerome Salle.

Who could resist a movie with a title like *The Heir Apparent: Largo Winch*? Apparently not many fans of the comic books in Europe, where Largo Winch is a celebrity. Having first inspired a TV series, Largo starred in this film in 2008. If you can call a movie *Key Largo*, then why not *Largo Winch*?

The hero, played by the hardworking German actor Tomer Sisley, is the secretly adopted son of a billionaire named Nerio Winch (Miki Manojlovic). The old man, who is drowned in an opening scene, controls the Winch International Group. What does Winch International make? Mostly money, I think. It's one of those corporations where all you need to know about it is contained in a helicopter shot of a Hong Kong skyscraper.

Flashbacks reveal how a young lad was adopted by Nerio Winch from a Croatian orphanage and raised in hiding by a kindly couple against that day when Nerio might require an heir. Why Croatia? Because this is one of those movies that's always helping you with subtitles saying "Croatia," "Hong Kong," and "Brazil." The death of Nerio, explained as an accident, sets off a boardroom struggle for control of Winch International.

The acting head of Winch International is Ann Ferguson (Kristin Scott Thomas), who is one of the most visible actresses in the movies right now; she's made eight movies since this one, with five more in production. Her perfect French and crisp composure allow her to fit in Gallic romantic intrigues, historical roles, and even a thriller like this, in which she stares down a boardroom of tough executives.

She knows of the existence of young Largo, whom she produces from thin air with the aplomb of a magician holding up a wriggling rabbit. Not everyone is delighted that Largo exists, including Winch International's security officer (Steven Waddington) and vice president (Benedict Wong). It's also a good question whether Ann Ferguson herself is delighted. The plot thickens with the appearance of a second heir apparent, whom I dare not describe, because that would spoil a very tiny secret.

Much interest is added by the beautiful Lea (Melanie Thierry, reminding me of Maud Adams). She is either Largo's lover or his enemy, or both. Their contest involves complex financial instruments, and indeed I began to fear the whole movie would play out right there in the boardroom until the day was saved by a fight to the death high atop, yes, the Hong Kong skyscraper.

Do you sometimes get the feeling that you haven't seen a film before, but you might as well have? All of the ingredients are basic. You need a male lead with a permanent short stubble. A sensual woman who seems pretty young to be playing with grizzled veterans. Flashbacks to inexplicable locations that may have something do with production deals and tax shelters. An older, ruthless figure (gender optional) who is a puppet master. A giant, sinister corporation that plays the role formerly assigned in thrillers to Russia or China. And, of course, the rooftop struggle.

Gene Siskel was fond of a movie cliché he called the Climbing Killer Syndrome. This described the mysterious compulsion that forces killers to flee upward instead of sideways. If you climb to the top of a building, scaffold, tower, mountain, etc., your escape options relentlessly narrow. In movies like this, you should avoid the roof at all costs, because the plot will inevitably have you clinging by your fingertips above a vertiginous fall to the street far below.

Did I care if Largo Winch won his struggle for control of Winch International? Not at all. Did I care about him? No, because all of his action and dialogue were shunted into narrow corridors of movie formulas. Was I impressed by Kristin Scott Thomas's icy boardroom manner? No, because I've seen a great deal of her recently in such better movies as *Love Crime*, which opened here only two months ago, and *Sarah's Key*, which opened here only four months ago, and *I've Loved You So Long*, which opened three years ago, but will linger in my memory long, long after I will be able to remember if the name was Largo Winch or Winch Largo.

## Hell and Back Again ★ ★ ★ ½

NO MPAA RATING, 88 m., 2012

A documentary featuring Nathan Harris and Ashley Harris. Directed by Danfung Dennis and produced by Dennis, Martin Herring, and Mike Lerner.

Marine sergeant Nathan Harris is a natural leader of men. We sense that during the extraordinary combat footage in *Hell and Back Again*, not because he behaves heroically or makes eloquent speeches, but because he knows his job and believes in it. He's in his midtwenties and sometimes looks and sounds younger, and yet his sense of mission carries him forward, and we understand why men would follow him into danger. He seems to be a good man, brave, uncomplicated.

Near the end of a six-month tour in Afghanistan, a sniper's bullet "blows half his ass off," as he puts it. He is not shy about describing his wound. More than once during this film he pulls down his belt to allow people to see the crater left on his right hip by a bullet, and then he explains how it penetrated to his hip socket, "messed that up," and bounced off to shatter his leg lower down. The first time he explains this, he is sitting in a battery-powered cart in a Wal-Mart, talking to an elderly woman shopper in a matching cart. "Can I give you a hug?" she says, and his smile suggests how much backed-up tension that released.

Harris was lucky not to be paralyzed. He is disappointed to learn that it will take him a year of rehab before he can think about going into combat again. We privately understand his combat days are in the past. Hasn't he paid his dues? He doesn't think so. We don't know him well enough. Even when he was a kid, he says, he wanted a job where he could kill people. That's why he enlisted in the marines at eighteen. Now he's done a little growing up, he reflects, and things no longer seem that simple.

In Afghanistan, he clearly believes in the U.S. mission from deep in his heart. There are three scenes where he talks with village elders through a translator, explaining how he and fellow Americans are there to bring them freedom. The elders are not convinced. The Americans and the Taliban are all the same to them, destroying crops, disrupting rural life, causing many to flee from areas altogether. They seem to have no love for the Taliban, but foreigners come and go, and the Taliban is always there.

Director Danfung Dennis, a photojournalist, carried one of the new compact Canon cameras into the field with Harris's Echo Company, following them on foot as they run across fields and proceed gingerly into villages. Some are point-of-view shots of a man crawling on his stomach under fire—as Dennis was doing. We never actually see a Taliban fighter, but they're out there. On Echo Company's first day they lose a marine. Later comes the wound that changes Harris's life.

He returns home to North Carolina and his wife, Ashley, his high school sweetheart. She is lovely, sweet, patient. After surgery and rehab, her husband is released to her care, and we see her at a Walgreen's prescription counter, buying enough pills so that the orange plastic bottles fill a Ziploc bag. One contains Vicodin. Some wounded soldiers who miss dying in combat are struck down by prescribed medication.

Harris uses a wheelchair and then an aluminum walker to get around. He talks about trying again and again to take three steps on his own, falling and trying again. He and Ashley have a quiet home life that seems sad to me, because if he cannot go into battle, an essential part of him has been lost. There are times, she says, when it's like he's become different man.

*Hell and Back Again* presents his new reality with a stunningly good use of video and sound editing. His life at home, its sights and sounds, are intercut with his life in Afghanistan. His war memories are always with him, and in some respects seem more real than his home life. He was never a full-time husband, we sense; he was a soldier home on leave.

In its closing scenes, *Hell and Back Again* builds to an emotional and stylistic power that we didn't see coming. In the darkness of night, in pillow talk, Nathan tells Ashley of the thoughts and memories that haunt his dreams. We realize she has her own kind of heroism in standing by this man. He was most fully alive when he was leading his men into combat; he believed in his usefulness and the worth of his mission. Now that he cannot serve and can barely walk, he is beginning to understand how much he has lost. He hasn't lost only the full use of a leg. He has lost the full use of himself.

## The Help ★ ★ ★

PG-13, 146 m., 2011

Emma Stone (Skeeter Phelan), Viola Davis (Aibileen Clark), Octavia Spencer (Minny Jackson), Bryce Dallas Howard (Hilly Holbrook), Jessica Chastain (Celia Foote), Allison Janney (Charlotte Phelan), Cicely Tyson (Constantine Jefferson), Sissy Spacek (Missus Walters), Mary Steenburgen (Elaine Stein). Directed by Tate Taylor and produced by Michael Barnathan, Chris Columbus, and Brunson Green. Screenplay by Taylor, based on the novel by Kathryn Stockett.

*The Help* is a safe film about a volatile subject. Presenting itself as the story of how African-American maids in the South viewed their employers during Jim Crow days, it is equally the story of how they empowered a young white woman to write a best-seller about them, and how that book transformed the author's mother. We are happy for the two white women, and a third, but as the film ends it is still Jackson, Mississippi, and Ross Barnett is still governor.

Still, this is a good film, involving and wonderfully acted. I was drawn into the characters and quite moved, even though all the while I was aware it was a feel-good fable, a story that deals with pain but doesn't care to be that painful. We don't always go to the movies for searing truth, but more often for reassurance: Yes, racism is vile and cruel, but hey, not all white people are bad.

The story, based on Kathryn Stockett's best-seller, focuses on Skeeter Phelan (Emma Stone), a recent college graduate who comes home and finds she doesn't fit in so easily.

Stone has top billing, but her character seems a familiar type, and the movie is stolen, one scene at a time, by two other characters: Aibileen Clark (Viola Davis) and Minny Jackson (Octavia Spencer).

Both are maids. Aibileen has spent her life as a nanny, raising little white girls. She is very good at it, and genuinely gives them her love, although when they grow up they have an inexorable tendency to turn into their mothers. Minny is a maid who is fired by a local social leader, then hired by a white-trash blonde. Davis and Spencer have such luminous qualities that this becomes their stories, perhaps not entirely by design.

The society lady, Hilly Holbrook (Bryce Dallas Howard), is a relentless social climber who fires Minny after long years of service. The blonde is Celia Foote (Jessica Chastain, from *The Tree of Life*), who is married to a well-off businessman, is desperate to please him, and never learned anything about being a housewife.

Minny needs a job and is happy to work for her. Celia wants her only during the days, when her husband is away, so that he'll think he's eating her cooking and enjoying her housekeeping. Minny helps her with these tasks and many more, some heartbreaking, and fills her with realistic advice. Chastain is unaffected and infectious in her performance.

Celia doesn't listen to Minny's counsel, however, when she attends a big local charity event (for, yes, Hungry African Children), and the event provides the movie's comic centerpiece. Hilly Holbrook's comeuppance doesn't have much to do with the main story, but it gets a lot of big laughs. Some details about a pie seem to belong in a different kind of movie.

Skeeter convinces Aibileen and then Minny to speak frankly with her, sharing their stories, and as the book develops so does her insight and anger. A somber subplot involves the mystery of why Skeeter's beloved nanny, who worked for the family for twenty-nine years, disappeared while Skeeter was away at school. Her mother (Allison Janney) harbors the secret of the nanny's disappearance, and after revealing it she undergoes a change of heart in a big late scene of redemption.

Two observations, for what they're worth. All the white people in the movie smoke. None of the black people do. There are several white men with important speaking roles, but only two black men, including a preacher, who have much to say.

There was a 1991 movie named *The Long Walk Home* that starred Whoopi Goldberg and Sissy Spacek as a maid and her employer at the time of the Montgomery bus boycott. It had sharper edges than *The Help*. But I suppose the Stockett novel has many loyal readers, and that this is the movie they imagined while reading it. It's very entertaining. Viola Davis is a force of nature, and Octavia Spencer has a wonderfully expressive face and flawless comic timing. Praise, too, for Emma Stone, Bryce Dallas Howard, and Allison Janney. They would have benefited from a more fearless screenplay.

## Henning Mankell's Wallander ★ ★ ★ ½

NO MPAA RATING, 91 m., 2012

Krister Henriksson (Kurt Wallander), Lena Endre (Katarina Ahlsell), Sverrir Gudnason (Pontus), Nina Zanjani (Isabelle), Fredrik Gunnarsson (Svartman), Mats Bergman (Nyberg), Anna Ulrika Ericsson (Minister). Directed by Charlotte Brandstrom and produced by Malte Forssell. Screenplay by Hans Rosenfeldt, based on the books of Henning Mankell.

Here is one of the best and most provocative thrillers of the year, and maybe it says something that it's a ninety-one-minute installment of a Swedish TV series. Why see it at the movies? Because it's so very well done, and looks better on the big screen. *Wallander* played to great acclaim in Sweden, and a British remake starring Kenneth Branagh was on PBS's *Masterpiece Theater.* It's another in a series of first-rate crime dramas from Scandinavia.

This self-contained episode, titled *Revenge,* begins when a smallish Swedish city has a total power blackout. That happens as Kurt Wallander (Krister Henriksson), the police inspector, is just celebrating his new lakeside home. He takes charge, finds a power substation was destroyed by a perfectly timed blast, and later learns that a town councillor was shot dead in his home during the blackout.

Thus begins a taut police procedural in which Wallander and his men (and one new woman trainee, not entirely welcome) find a murder wave under way. The other victims are a woman who ran a local youth job placement agency and a nurse in a hospital. All are shot seventeen times with a similar handgun. What possible link could there be among them? That's the puzzle.

Wallander is the popular sixty-two-year-old hero of a group of novels by Henning Mankell, the best-selling Swedish crime novelist. The inspector lives alone except for his beloved dog, tends to be morose, and is a good cop and a liberal idealist.

His ideals are challenged when the townspeople become convinced the explosion and murders are linked to Islamist terrorism. The dead councillor approved the use of the town hall for a traveling international art exhibit on the Prophet Muhammad, and Muslim demonstrators have been holding daily protests. Should Wallander close down the exhibit? Absolutely not: "We must stand up for democracy."

The film becomes a display for various issues in modern Sweden, including the role of non-Swedish minority groups, the role of the army, and the roles of women in the workplace. Wallander is disturbed when the army sends in troops; he thinks his police are equal to the challenge, indeed having already found an obscure link joining the three murder victims. He isn't so advanced on women's roles; when two new trainees turn up, he assigns the man to work on the case and the woman to go out to his house and bring in his dog.

Then another woman gets in his hair. This is Katarina Ahlsell (Lena Endre), a public prosecutor who is just moving to town. In one of the best performances in a well-acted film, Endre, a tall, confident woman, treats him with quiet bemusement and also, we sense, with growing affection.

Things come to a crisis when another woman decides to come to town. The national defense minister (Anna Ulrika Ericsson) decides, probably unwisely, that this is a good time for her to visit with her husband and two small children and give a speech in the town square, urging citizens not to be intimidated by terrorism. This leads to a sequence of spellbinding tension, in which everything depends on Henriksson's calm, focused performance.

*Wallander* doesn't depend on overt action sequences but on mystery, suspense, and personality. It seems to know a lot about police procedures, and plays as an object lesson about scapegoating. There are also subtle human interactions, some romantic, some resentful, that are all the more effective for not being foregrounded. If Kurt Wallander is made into a hero of an American film (and you can probably bet on that), it's likely the actor playing him won't project Henriksson's reserve and intelligence. And you can just about bet the theme won't be freedom of speech.

Many thrillers follow such reliable formulas that you can look at what's happening and guess how much longer a film has to run. Not this one. I could never be sure what would happen next, and when it did, I never felt manipulated.

## Henry's Crime ★ ★

R, 108 m., 2011

Keanu Reeves (Henry Torne), Vera Farmiga (Julie Ivanova), James Caan (Max Saltzman), Peter Stormare (Darek Millodragovic), Judy Greer (Debbie Torne), Fisher Stevens (Eddie Vibes), Bill Duke (Frank), Danny Hoch (Joe). Directed by Malcolm Venville and produced by Stephen Hamel, David Mimran, Keanu Reeves, Jordan Schur, and Lemore Syvan. Screenplay by Sacha Gervasi and David White.

Keanu Reeves seems on mild sedation during most of *Henry's Crime.* I think that's intentional. He plays the feckless Henry Torne, an overnight toll booth attendant in Buffalo, who agrees to play in a softball game, drives a car filled with other players, and discovers that what they're actually planning is a bank robbery. Henry gets caught and thrown in the slammer, and takes it philosophically.

Our problem is finding a way to care about these events more than Henry apparently does. He seems to hover above his own life, detached, an observer. Into this life enter people who become more involved in it than he does. There's his conniving friend Eddie Vibes (Fisher Stevens), who tricked him into the bank robbery. His prison cell mate is Max Saltzman (James Caan), a wiseguy from way back who knows all the angles, except how to stay out of prison. Henry's wife, Debbie (Judy Greer), ends their marriage while he's behind bars, becoming preggers in a way that he should find particularly ironic, yet Henry remains calm.

Finally a woman discovers how to really get his attention. This is Julie Ivanova (Vera Farmiga), who hits him with her car. That'll do it. She's an actress rehearsing a production of Chekhov's *Cherry Orchard*, which is being directed by Darek Millodragovic (Peter Stormare—yes, who fed his friend into a wood chipper in *Fargo*). Henry begins to like Julie. Then he discovers that one of the dressing rooms in the theater is connected to an old tunnel that leads to the bank the softball team was trying to rob.

This is perhaps beginning to sound to you like a screwball comedy. Imagine such a comedy if it has gone forty-eight hours without sleep. All the elements are present: Henry needs to be cast in the play to gain access to the tunnel, Max and Eddie get involved, Julie is remarkably accepting, any romance between Julie and Henry hangs in the balance, split-second exits and entrances are called for, and so on. Now imagine everyone sprinting through quicksand.

Keanu Reeves has many strings in his bow, but screwball comedy isn't one of them. Vera Farmiga, James Caan, and Fisher Stevens can do it, but they often seem to be looking back, waiting for Reeves to pass the baton. What you need, I think, is someone nervous to play Henry. A Steve Buscemi, for example. Reeves maintains a sort of Zen detachment. Whatever happens is all right with him.

The film was directed by Malcolm Venville, who seems to muse when he should be fretting. How uninvolved is his direction? A friend of mine in Buffalo went to see the movie, at a premiere, I guess. He wrote me complaining a city block that supplies one of the locations "was shot from a boring angle." When a comedy inspires observations like that, you know you're in trouble.

## Hereafter ★ ★ ★ ★

PG-13, 129 m., 2010

Matt Damon (George Lonegan), Cecile de France (Marie LeLay), Jay Mohr (Billy), Bryce Dallas Howard (Melanie), George and Frankie McLaren (Marcus/Jason), Thierry Neuvic (Didier), Marthe Keller (Dr. Rousseau), Derek Jacobi (Himself), Richard Kind (Christos). Directed by Clint Eastwood and produced by Eastwood, Kathleen Kennedy, and Robert Lorenz. Screenplay by Peter Morgan.

Clint Eastwood's *Hereafter* considers the idea of an afterlife with tenderness, beauty, and a gentle tact. I was surprised to find it enthralling. I don't believe in woo-woo, but then neither, I suspect, does Eastwood. This is a film about the afterlife that carefully avoids committing itself on such a possibility. The closest it comes is the idea of consciousness after apparent death. This is plausible. Many near-death survivors report the same memories, of the white light, the waiting figures, and a feeling of peace.

One of the characters seems to have a genuine psychic gift. But is he, in fact, communicating with people beyond the grave? Some form of telepathy might be possible, and he may simply be receiving what his subjects desire or need to be told by their dead loved ones. He brings nothing from beyond the grave that his clients could not have formed in their living minds.

This is a subject that lends itself to sensation and psychic baloney. It's astonishing how many people believe New Age notions, which have the attraction of allowing believers to confer supernormal abilities on themselves and others without the bother of plausibility. Eastwood's film will leave such people vaguely uneasy. It believes most psychics are frauds. It introduced one who seems to be the real thing, but what, exactly, is he real about?

This is a film for intelligent people who are naturally curious about what happens when the shutters close. Eastwood tells three primary stories. The stories meet at the end, in one of those coincidences so beloved by multiple-strand movies. Is this possible? Yes. Is it likely? No. A coincidence never is. That's why we notice them. Throughout the film, the characters behave in ways that seem reasonable enough, and possibilities are left open, which is as it should be. We must live the lives we know and not count on anything beyond the horizon.

*Hereafter* stars Matt Damon as George, a man who sincerely believes he's able to have communication with the dead, but has fled that ability and taken a low-profile job; Cecile de France as Marie, a newsreader on French television; Bryce Dallas Howard as Melanie, a young cooking student with a fearful dark place inside; Richard Kind as a man mourning his wife; and George and Frankie McLaren as twin brothers, one of whom is struck by a truck and killed.

I won't describe here the traumatic surprises some of them experience. In the surprises as in everything else, *Hereafter* is believable. There are terrifying events, but Eastwood handles them not for sensation but to show how close we all are, at any moment, to oblivion. In the case of Marie, she undergoes the near-death experience we often hear reported, with the white light and the figures. Are people in such a state already dead, or are they experiencing visions generated by the human mind in its final shutdown mode?

The powers of the Damon character seem to be authentic, although what they prove is hard to say. There is a moment handled with love and delicacy in which he says something that is either true or isn't, but is a kindness either way. When he holds a stranger's hands, he experiences a flash of telepathic insight, but the movie never declares that his insights literally come from dead spirits.

Eastwood and his actors achieve a tone that doesn't force the material but embraces it: not dreamlike, but evoking a reverie state. These characters are not hurtling toward the resolution of a plot. There is no "solution" to their stories. There are various degrees of solace, or not. They don't punch the dialogue. They lack the certainty to impose themselves. George in particular is reserved and sad because his power has become a burden to him.

There's a sweet subplot involving Melanie (Howard), whom he meets as a partner in a cooking class. She has experienced loss. George doesn't want to enter her mind. He yearns for a normal life. The ability to read minds would be an unbearable curse. The way his gift affects their relationship is stark and poignant. Marie, the newsreader, is played by Cecile de France in such a fresh and likable way that our sympathy is engaged and we understand that whatever happened to her in the first terrifying scene has fundamentally changed her. George and Frankie McLaren, as the solemn and earnest little boy seeking his dead twin, take a character that could have been pathetic and make him simple and transparent. And notice Richard Kind, so affecting as a man who has lost his wife.

The movie is an original screenplay by Peter Morgan (*The Queen*). Eastwood told me Morgan doesn't believe in an afterlife. I don't know if Eastwood does, either. His film embodies how love makes us *need* for there to be an afterlife. It is the film of a man at peace. He has nothing to prove except his care for the living.

## Hesher ★ ★ ½

R, 105 m., 2011

Joseph Gordon-Levitt (Hesher), Devin Brochu (T.J.), Rainn Wilson (Paul), Natalie Portman (Nicole), Piper Laurie (Madeleine). Directed by Spencer Susser and produced by Susser, Lucy Cooper, Johnny Lin, Natalie Portman, Scott Prisand, Win Sheridan, and Matt Weaver. Screenplay by Susser and David Michod.

*Hesher* assembles a group of characters who aren't sure why they're in the same movie together. One by one they have an attraction, but brought together they're all elbows and angles. The title character (Joseph Gordon-Levitt) is hauled into the movie as a classic deus ex machina, as if he's been lowered by rope into the middle of a situation he has no connection with. He's a fearsome heavy metal creature with charming tattoos: on his back, an upraised middle finger, and on his chest, a man shooting his brains out.

He materializes in the life of young T.J. (Devin Brochu) and moves into T.J.'s house. The film makes no attempt to explain much about who he is, where he came from, or precisely what he thinks about T.J.'s family. At first he seems possibly an imaginary friend for the kid, but then we realize he's quite real, all right. Just inexplicable.

T.J.'s family is desolate. His mother was killed not long ago in an automobile accident. His father, Paul (Rainn Wilson), sits stunned by depression on the sofa, staring at the TV by default, not even really seeing it. His grandmother Madeleine (Piper Laurie) drifts on a cloud of vagueness through their lives, feeding them out of lifelong habit, not asserting herself, asking no questions even when T.J. brings Hesher home for dinner. Well, Hesher essentially brings himself along, but is explained as T.J.'s "friend." How has a ten-year-old acquired a friend who resembles a wasted rocker? Well you might ask, but Paul and Madeleine accept him in their sloughs of passivity.

It's not as if Hesher is really a sweet guy. He's willful, obscene, offensive, and easily angered; the tattoo covering his back must have been chosen after careful consideration. He sets up a camp in the family garage and parks his van in front, from which often pounds heavy metal at full volume. Hesher is not someone you want in your garage.

At the supermarket, T.J. meets the cashier Nicole (Natalie Portman), who has no more reason for being in the film than anybody else. In the store parking lot, she rescues T.J. from a school bully, and he develops a preadolescent crush on her, possibly seeing her as a protective mother substitute. Hesher attempts to subvert this friendship. He's just plain mean.

Portman's character is the most straightforward in the film; she is who she seems to be. Rainn Wilson and Piper Laurie are good actors, and so is, for that matter, Joseph Gordon-Levitt; and here we can see what good actors do with inexplicable situations and undefined characters. In a way, this is pure acting, generated from within, not supported by a narrative framework. Consider Wilson. He has that rare quality in an actor: Uncanny Presence. There are a few like him (Jack Nicholson, Christopher Walken, Bill Murray) who need only to look at something to establish an attitude toward it. Yes, they can get worked up, they can operate on high, but their passive *essence* is the point: dubious, wise, sadly knowledgeable, at an angle to the through-line. Other actors could sit on a sofa and watch TV, but Rainn Wilson makes it a statement. A statement of . . . nothing, which is the point.

In the long history of movies containing encounter groups or twelve-step meetings, few have given us a group inspiring less hope than the one here, where father and son attend a grief counseling session. When did grief counseling become an occupation, anyway? Whenever a demented loner opens fire at a school, grief counselors are platooned in. Just what a kid needs when his schoolmates have been murdered: a session with a stranger who wants to talk about how he feels. Perhaps grief is better dealt with among people one knows and trusts.

But I stray. Wilson brings a sad haplessness to this particular scene, and Devin Brochu's T.J. is throughout a steady, relatively uncomplicated presence. How T.J. will grow up is food for thought. Meanwhile, Hesher acts out in aggressive and offensive ways, directed only by fugitive instincts to help the kid. The film's eventual resolution of the Hesher character perhaps looked promising on the page, but doesn't bring much closure here.

Essentially, Spencer Susser's film is not strong or large enough to contain Hesher. I'm wondering how to evoke him for you. Have you ever seen *Withnail and I*? Hesher is the kind of man about whom Withnail would say: "Jaysus, and I thought I had problems."

## Hick ★ ½

R, 95 m., 2012

Chloe Grace Moretz (Luli), Blake Lively (Glenda), Eddie Redmayne (Eddie), Juliette Lewis (Tammy), Rory Culkin (Clement), Anson Mount (Nick), Alec Baldwin (Beau). Directed by Derick Martini and produced by Jonathan Cornick, Charles De Portes, Steven Siebert, and Christian Taylor. Screenplay by Andrea Portes, based on her novel.

*Hick* is a film about a damaged thirteen-year-old girl who runs away from an alcohol-soaked home and encounters only hateful, cruel, or moronic people. I cringed. It contains some effective performances, it does a good job of evoking bereft and empty landscapes, but what is it for? Has she learned anything? Have we?

The film stars Chloe Grace Moretz, the star of *Hugo* and *Let Me In*, who at fifteen looks all too convincing as a young adolescent. She plays Luli, who never goes anywhere without her drawing pad, and records her life in pictures much brighter than it is. Here's an idea of the kind of family she comes from. Her thirteenth birthday is celebrated in a tavern, with her drunken father (Anson Mount) half-conscious and sprawled in a booth. Her mother (Juliette Lewis) helps her unwrap presents, which include a .45. Everyone thinks it's a great present except perhaps the bartender, who later has to forcibly prevent her father from driving her home.

We see enough of her slovenly home life before she gets the idea from a TV show that she wants to seek happiness in Las Vegas. Wearing Daisy Dukes and a halter top, carrying a jean jacket and a handbag with the gun inside, she skips away from home to hitchhike.

Her first ride comes from Eddie (Eddie Redmayne), wearing a cowboy hat, driving a pickup truck, superficially charming, who knows only bad people. Then she's picked up by Glenda (Blake Lively), possibly a hooker, who takes her to the home of a sinister man, where she meets Eddie again. Their paths seem destined to cross. Later, he parks outside a pool hall, tells her to stay in the truck, goes inside, and plays pool for money. She defies him and comes inside. When he doubles down and loses, he seems to imply the winner can settle the bet with sex with Luli, but maybe that's not what he meant, because soon enough he interrupts a rape in the ladies' room by bashing in the man's head with a sink he rips from the wall.

Several other people die in *Hick*, one possibly of natural causes. I won't go into detail. Luli has a way of wandering off and not following Eddie's instructions, but he solves that by tying her to a bed. Then Glenda turns up again. All of Luli's travel seems to have been limited to a small area with an unsavory population.

*Hick* was directed by Derick Martini, who made the very good *Lymelife* (2009), and had a hand in writing the wonderful *Smiling Fish and Goat on Fire* (1999) and *Louis* (2010), a silent film about young Louis Armstrong. So you see we're dealing with a gifted filmmaker. No matter how I've made it sound, *Hick* does not play as an exploitation film, but shows every evidence of being a serious undertaking. I believe Martini has good films in his future. *Hick* was written by Andrea Portes, based on her own novel. They obviously hoped they were up to something.

But what? I'm at a loss. The character Luli comes from such an unhealthy family that it's a wonder she's as functional and outgoing as she is. But the screenplay lies in wait for her with one ugly encounter after another, and even after she calls home and is actually returning on a bus, she foolishly repeats her original mistakes on what promises to be an even more unhappy scale.

Is the movie intended as an object lesson? What's the lesson? Don't have a tragic life? Is it about pedophilia? Certainly it's filled with characters who have an unwholesome interest in an attractive, very young girl. Thinking of another film with a young heroine who has a similarly fraught life on the road, I recalled Agnes Varda's great *Vagabond* (1985). It was about a young woman who chose life on the road and eventually found it fatal. But it was an attentive and moving character study. After *Hick* I don't know much about Luli, and certainly nothing useful.

## Hidden Love ★ ★

NO MPAA RATING, 95 m., 2010

Isabelle Huppert (Danielle), Greta Scacchi (Dr. Nielsen), Melanie Laurent (Sophie), Olivier Gourmet (Nielsen's husband). Directed by Alessandro Capone and produced by Massimo Cristaldi and Mark Hammond. Screenplay by Capone and Luca D'Alisera, based on the novel *Madre e Ossa* by Danielle Girard.

*Hidden Love* is a movie that knows exactly who it is about but doesn't know what it thinks of them. That leaves us four clearly seen characters and a story wandering in the murk of despair. Its principal casualty is Isabelle Huppert, who creates a flawless performance to no particular effect. She gives director Alessandro Capone what few actresses would be capable of, and he leaves her hanging.

Huppert plays Danielle, a woman who has been institutionalized after three suicide attempts. We meet her in therapy sessions with Dr. Nielsen (Greta Scacchi, focusing her attention with growing empathy). As Danielle speaks, it begins to appear she's in the twenty-third year of postpartum depression. All she wants to talk about is the indifference she felt toward her daughter, Sophie (Melanie Laurent), at the moment of giving birth and ever since.

Danielle looks ragged and depressed, makes obsessive hand movements, goes long periods without speaking, stares into space, and assures the psychiatrist that Sophie cannot be believed. Sophie, on the other hand, says her mother is playacting and is a selfish narcissist. What we see of Sophie suggests she is a loving mother to her own little girl. There's a scene where Sophie seems grateful to her mother while being taken to an abortion clinic but angry afterward. So eventually having her daughter was a form of revenge for Sophie, or what?

That and other events in the film go unexplained, or are seen in more than one version, and at the end all we can be sure of is that Danielle is depressed for reasons we can choose from cafeteria-style. The relationship between Dr. Nielsen and her husband (Olivier Gourmet) is, in contrast, briefly but well portrayed, especially during a scene where she confesses her despair over the case.

Isabelle Huppert makes one good film after another, most recently *Home* and *White Material.* She is fearless. Directors often depend on her gift for conveying depression, compulsion, egotism, and despair. She can be funny and charming, but then so can a lot of actors. She is in complete command of a face that regards the void with blankness. She gives her director a valuable asset. He doesn't know how to spend it.

So remorseless is this film that the ending comes like a slap in the face. Presumably it's the original ending, but it feels like nothing so much as one of those upbeat emergency rewrites slapped onto a Hollywood drama a mogul thought was too depressing. The happy nature of this ending is one of the most depressing elements of the film.

## Hideaway ★ ★ ★

NO MPAA RATING, 105 m., 2010

Isabelle Carre (Mousse), Louis-Ronan Choisy (Paul), Pierre Louis-Calixte (Serge), Melvil Poupaud (Louis). Directed by Francois Ozon and produced by Chris Bolzli and Claudie Ossard. Screenplay by Ozon and Mathieu Hippeau.

The actress Isabelle Carre was pregnant during the filming of *Hideaway*, and the pregnancy of her character supplies the center of the film. It figures in the plot, but also in the yearning emotions that take uncertain form. Two men are fascinated by her swelling womb, and so is she. It is this promise of new life that overwhelms all of the other elements, and there are a lot of them.

Carre plays Mousse, an enigmatic thirtyish woman, girlish and yet sometimes with tired eyes, who as the film opens is in a room with her lover, Louis (Melvil Poupaud). Their drug dealer arrives and asks, "Is she all right?" Louis: "Now that you're here, she will be." Louis injects them both with heroin, and the next morning, rising early, he gives himself another shot, which is fatal. Mousse discovers he left her pregnant.

There are extraordinary scenes on the day of the funeral, involving Louis's pragmatic mother and his gay brother, Paul (Louis-Ronan Choisy). The family would prefer she not keep the baby. She agrees, then disappears to her "refuge," a lovely chateau overlooking a pastoral sweep of French countryside. There Paul arrives to visit, finding her off drugs and very pregnant. He stays for a time, and indeed connects quickly with Serge (Pierre Louis-Calixte), the young caretaker of the estate.

We have only fragmented information about Mousse's earlier life. Much can be guessed when she tells Paul that the chateau has been loaned to her by a man she slept with when she was sixteen: "He thinks he's my father." Whatever the real story is, that information helps explain her dispassionate approach to life. She's not cold, she's not hostile, but she has been wounded and is emotionally guarded. The camera spends a lot of time on her face, which is pleasant but not forthcoming.

She understands that Paul is gay. No big deal. Romantic formulas suggest Paul and Mousse stay together anyway, but this movie signals that it follows no formulas. Its romanticism is carefully buried, although there are two dream sequences suggesting the ability of a character to imagine ideal outcomes. Meanwhile, life goes on in a casual summertime way, with tea and coffee on the veranda, a trip to a disco in town, desultory conversation, landscape vistas, an idyll financed by the absent man who thinks he's her dad.

The film is by Francois Ozon, who is drawn to parents in awkward forms of love. His suspenseful *See the Sea* (1997) was about a mother staying at the seaside with a baby daughter, and how a woman traveler enters their lives; his strange *Ricky* (2009) was about a couple coping when their baby grows wings. *Hideaway* is deliberately more mundane, settled: It is about a situation that Mousse apparently accepts calmly.

There's an isolated scene. A man in a café boldly asks her to sleep with him. "You like pregnant women?" she asks. "Yes. Except for my wife. I couldn't sleep with her for nine months." There's another movie there. How this scene plays out has something to do with the rest of the film, and of that particular quiet urgency that many men feel about pregnant women. It's a heightened attention, and may be the product of evolution. For a time in her life, a woman's pregnancy is the most important thing about her. That is the subject of *Hideaway.*

## Higher Ground ★ ★ ★ ½

R, 109 m., 2011

Vera Farmiga (Corinne), Joshua Leonard (Ethan), Norbert Leo Butz (Pastor Bill), Dagmara Dominczyk (Annika), John Hawkes (CW), Bill Irwin (Pastor Bud), Ebon Moss-Bachrach (Mark), Donna Murphy (Kathleen), Taissa Farmiga (Teenager Corinne), McKenzie Turner (Child Corinne). Directed by Vera Farmiga and produced by Claude Dal Farra, Renn Hawkey, Carly Hugo, Matthew Parker, and Jon Rubinstein. Screenplay by Carolyn S. Briggs and Tim Metcalfe, based on Briggs's memoir *This Dark World.*

Vera Farmiga's *Higher Ground* is the life story of a woman who grows into, and out of, Christianity. It values her at every stage of that process. It never says she is making the right or wrong decision, only that what she does seems necessary at the time she does it. In a world where believers and agnostics are polarized and hold simplified ideas about each other, the film takes a step back and sees faith as a series of choices that should be freely made.

The woman's name is Corinne. We see her as a child, a young woman around twenty, and an adult around forty. As a child she invites Jesus into her life in a conventional, mainstream Protestant sort of way. Later she is born again, with full immersion and all the rest of it, after she and her husband credit God for saving them and their child from tragedy. Later still, she finds her evangelical congregation enforcing uncomfortable conformity upon her.

I would like to say *Higher Ground* never steps wrong in following this process, but it does. Sometimes it slips too easily into satire, but at least it's nuanced satire based on true believers who are basically nice and good people. There are no heavy-handed portraits of holy rollers here, just people whose view of the world is narrow. There are also no outsize sinners in the film; just some gentle singer-songwriters who are too fond of pot and whose lyrics are parades of clichés.

Corinne is played as a girl by McKenzie Turner, as an adult by Vera Farmiga, and as a teenager by Farmiga's sister, Taissa. At all of these stages in life, the character's face reflects awareness and intelligence, an inbred independence that is a little reluctant to go along with the crowd. At the discussions held by her prayer group, we can see her drawing a line between those who are thoughtful and those who are passive conformists. Corinne reads widely. She thinks about Scripture. She has opinions. She doesn't respond well when an older woman advises her that when she speaks out, it sounds too much like preaching. God forbid a woman should have an opinion.

Yet the preachers she comes into contact with are not bad men. The film carefully avoids stereotyping them. It's just that as she grows older, her congregation becomes a group where the others feel more included than she can. They accept. Even the men consider male dominance a duty, not a pleasure.

Corinne has a best friend, Annika (Dagmara Dominczyk), she confides in. They share thoughts about sex and other things. Farmiga might have been wise, however, to avoid the easy laugh when each woman draws her husband's penis. There is a point to be made, but there must be a more subtle way to make it.

Unhappiness strikes in the group. I will not supply details. I observe, however, that a person who suffers great misfortune is unlikely to be comforted by the assurance that God's will has been done. In the case of my own misfortune, I prefer to think that God's will had nothing to do with it. People who tell me it did are singularly tactless.

Ask yourself during the film where you think it takes place—which American state? I looked up the locations on IMDb and was surprised. Its location doesn't fit regional stereotypes. Nor do its characters. These are decent people, trying to do the right thing, and Corinne is a decent person who believes she must decide on the right thing for herself. When others inform her what that is, why are they rarely eager to have her input about them?

Vera Farmiga is such a warm actress. I don't know if she could play cruel. John Hawkes, who plays her alcoholic father, can play cruel—but not in a physically violent way. His is the kind of cruelty that shows a child her father is weak and pitiful, and doesn't deserve her respect. Perhaps that's how she began to doubt at an early age the paternalism of her social group.

We see the seeds of imagination growing through her reading. People in books sometimes do things we can understand because we have come to know those people. Nonreaders are likely to think they know what people should do because—well, they just should, that's all. You can read this in a book: "The unexamined life is not worth living."

## High School ★ ★

R, 99 m., 2012

Adrien Brody (Psycho Ed), Sean Marquette (Travis Breaux), Matthew Bush (Henry Burke), Colin Hanks (Brandon Ellis), Adhir Kalyan (Sebastian Saleem), Mykelti Williamson (Paranoid), Michael Chiklis (Dr. Leslie Gordon). Directed by John Stalberg Jr. and produced by Arcadiy Golubovich, Raymond J. Markovich, and Warren Zide. Screenplay by Stalberg, Erik Linthorst, and Stephen Susco.

*High School* is a pun. Get it? This is one of those stoner comedies that may be funny if you're high—but if not, not. The film premiered two years ago in the midnight movies section at Sundance, a wise decision. Midnight movies are often attended by audiences who walk in already giggling. I wouldn't advise seeing this during the daylight or early evening hours, unless you already have a running start. As a comedy expected to be funny without chemical reinforcement, it's labored and lame.

The plot: Henry, the school valedictorian, gets high on weed for the first time in his life. This happens on the very day a fellow student turns up stoned at the State Spelling Bee and blows her championship. The school principal is aghast and requires the entire student body to pee in little cups for compulsory drug testing.

Henry (Matthew Bush) envisions his scholarship to MIT going up in smoke (ho, ho). His best pal, Travis (Sean Marquette), a career pothead, is sympathetic. They dream up a plot to get the entire school high by switching the brownies at the school bake sale with their own recipe, spiked with powerful resin stolen from Travis's drug dealer.

Is this intrinsically funny? I suspect the filmmakers think so. But *nothing* is intrinsically funny. It depends on the characters and situation. The downfall of *High School* happens because the characters are carbon copies from countless earlier movies including, I am afraid, yet another school principal who is a pompous ass, and yet another drug dealer who is a grotesque sideshow act.

The dealer is Psycho Ed (Adrien Brody), who long ago was a brilliant student before he fried his brains. He seems to have spent the years since then in a project to make himself look as repulsive as possible. Or maybe it's just me. Maybe you like bodies densely covered with confusing tattooed doodles. Maybe you like one of those beards twisted into a scrawny, thin braid. Maybe you like eyes that, if they were drawn in, would be pinwheels.

Adrien Brody won an Academy Award and has spent years trying to live it down. Maybe times are hard. Maybe this was a role he needed. To give him credit, he throws himself into it with manic, violent acting-out. He tries to make Psycho Ed funny. Matthew Bush and Sean Marquette, as Henry and Travis, play their students as one-dimensional creatures of the plot requirements.

And spare me Michael Chiklis as Dr. Leslie

Gordon, the high school principal, who didn't get the memo that modern principals are usually pretty bright and in touch. His arch mannerisms and elaborate speech patterns remind me of nothing so much as a failed dinner theater actor auditioning for a public service announcement.

Anyway, the entire school gets stoned, even the teachers, and that's the joke. It's played in various permutations, all obvious. There is no suggestion that drugs might possibly be unwise for high school students, which, of course, they are. But the film offers proof that they are unwise as a subject for comedy unless the movie in question does something *funny* with them. It isn't funny to simply act high, except possibly for the person who is. Which leads us full circle to the subject of midnight movies.

## Holy Rollers ★ ★

R, 80 m., 2010

Jesse Eisenberg (Sam Gold), Justin Bartha (Yosef), Ari Graynor (Rachel), Danny A. Abeckaser (Jackie), Q-Tip (Ephraim), Mark Ivanir (Mendel Gold), Elizabeth Marvel (Elka Gold). Directed by Kevin Asch and produced by Danny A. Abeckaser, Jen Gatien, Per Melita, and Tory Tunnell. Screenplay by Antonio Macia.

One function of any traditional religious costume is to enforce the wearer's separation from the greater community. Those male Hasidic Jews who choose to dress in black and wear distinctive hats never seem to be anything else than Hasidic Jews. When they dress in the morning, they're making a decision to set themselves apart. This is not required in Jewish law, but is a sign of their devotion.

Apart from the hats, the side curls, and their religious beliefs, Hasidim are, well, a lot like everybody else. Sam Gold (Jesse Eisenberg) is a kid about twenty who is devout, naive, shy around women, loves his mom, respects his dad, and plans to go into the family business. Then his best friend's brother takes advantage of those qualities—and very specifically his dress style—to trick him into being a drug courier.

*Holy Rollers* is said to be based on a true story, circa 1990, of how Hasidic Jews from Brooklyn Heights were used to smuggle millions of Ecstasy pills from Amsterdam to New York. They weren't stopped by customs because they were so far from the profile of drug runners. In the movie, Sam is frustrated in his plans to build his father's business and accepts $1,000 from the brother to fly to Amsterdam and return with some "medicine."

Come on, you're thinking: How innocent can this kid possibly be? You should see him tongue-tied, sitting at the other end of a sofa from the girl he hopes to marry. Or even in Amsterdam, trying to avoid any body contact with women in a disco. Yes, the first trip he really does think the pills are medicine, and doesn't ask himself how what he's doing could possibly be legal.

He's a sweet kid as played by Eisenberg, who specializes in that line of work. The brother, Yosef (Justin Bartha), is persuasive, smooth, and hard to refuse. In Amsterdam, Sam meets a man named Jackie (Danny A. Abeckaser) and his girlfriend, Rachel (Ari Graynor), and is brought into their world of late-night clubs and loose living. On his second trip, things click into place, and he begins to put his good business sense to work.

It's that click that throws the movie off. Sam is moral and law-abiding, then changes seemingly overnight into a canny player in the drug trade. Before long he's instructing new Hasidim recruits on how to get past customs: "Act normal and look Jewish." It becomes apparent to his father and indeed his community what he's up to, but he's making good money and it seems so easy. For a long time he never even experiences Ecstasy.

The story may sound sensational, and you're possibly picturing traditional crime scenes: shoot-outs, chases, that sort of thing. But *Holy Rollers* is surprisingly matter-of-fact. Nobody gets shot, nobody gets chased, and Sam's anguish is internal.

The film's failure is to get from A to B. We buy both good Sam and bad Sam, but we don't see him making the transition. The film expects us to assume too much. Eisenberg is convincing as an essentially nice person who sounds confident but turns into a kid again when things start going wrong. But Kevin Asch, the director, keeps his distance from too many scenes; there's no particular suspense involved in getting past customs, for example. The movie relates to its story as Sam relates to women: look, talk, but don't get too close.

## Home ★ ★ ★ ½

NO MPAA RATING, 98 m., 2010

Isabelle Huppert (Marthe), Olivier Gourmet (Michel), Adelaide Leroux (Judith), Madeleine Budd (Marion), Kacey Mottet Klein (Julien). Directed by Ursula Meier and produced by Denis Delcammpe, Denis Freyd, Thierry Spicher, and Elena Tatti. Screenplay by Meier, Antoine Jaccoud, Raphaelle Valbrune, Gilles Taurand, and Olivier Lorelle.

There are two questions never answered in *Home.* How did this family come to live here? And why does the mother fiercely refuse to leave, even after a four-lane freeway opens in her front yard? Both are more satisfactory remaining as questions. In any event, as the film opens, they live in a comfortable small home in the middle of vast fields and next to the highway, which hasn't been used for ten years. So much is the road their turf that the story begins with them playing a family game of street hockey on its pavement.

Then big trucks arrive to lay down a fresh coating of asphalt, and steel guardrails are installed on each side and down the middle. Workmen wordlessly clear the highway of their hockey sticks, inflatable swimming pool, satellite dish, charcoal grill, and so on. On the radio, they hear breathless coverage of the road's grand opening, and eventually the first car speeds past their house.

The family seems ordinary enough, if not quite conventional. The parents snuggle, the small boy plays, the sister in her early twenties sunbathes and smokes in the front yard, the teenage daughter wears mostly black and sulks. Michel, the father (Olivier Gourmet), goes off to work every morning in the green Volvo station wagon. Marthe, the mother (Isabelle Huppert), does the laundry ("today is whites day"). There's horseplay in the bathtub, which the family seems to share rather freely.

The opening of the highway wasn't a surprise for them. Maybe they got the house cheap because it was coming. The heavy, unceasing traffic is a big problem. The two younger kids always ran across the bare pavement to cut through a field for school. Dad parked on the other side. Now even getting to the house is a problem. Marion, the smart younger sister (Madeleine Budd) is concerned about $CO_2$ poisoning. Young Julien (Kacey Mottet Klein) can't safely get to his pals. Judith (Adelaide Leroux) continues to sunbathe in the front yard and gives the finger to honking truck drivers.

Something will have to give, and it does, as the movie grows more and more dark. It's the skill of Ursula Meier, the director and cowriter, to bring us to those fraught passages by rational stages. What happens would not make sense in many households, but in this one it represents a certain continuity, and confirms deep currents we sensed almost from the first.

Do you remember Olivier Gourmet from his performance in the Dardenne brothers' movie *The Son* (2003)? Balding, middle-aged, nimble, and quick. Many secrets. Troubled. Isabelle Huppert you know since forever, usually looking fundamentally the same, always assuming a new character from the inside out. Intriguing us. There's thought in that face, but it's inscrutable. They work with the young actors here to face what it means when a home is not a house.

## Horrible Bosses ★ ★ ★ ½

R, 100 m., 2011

Jason Bateman (Nick Hendricks), Charlie Day (Dale Arbus), Jason Sudeikis (Kurt Buckman), Jennifer Aniston (Dr. Julia Harris), Colin Farrell (Bobby Pellit), Kevin Spacey (Dave Harken), Donald Sutherland (Jack Pellit), Jamie Foxx (MF Jones). Directed by Seth Gordon and produced by Brett Ratner and Jay Stern. Screenplay by Michael Markowitz, John Francis Daley, and Jonathan Goldstein.

*Horrible Bosses* is funny and dirty, in about that order. Of George Carlin's famous "seven words you can never say on television," it omits only the usual one, I think, makes free with the others, and adds several that didn't make Carlin's cut. It also contains what the MPAA describes as "crude and sexual content," which I guess means both kinds at once.

The story involves three horrible bosses and the three employees who vow to murder them. What makes the movie work is how truly horrible the bosses are, what pathetic victims the employees are, and how bad the employees are at killing; they'd be fired in a second by Murder Inc. The movie causes particularly painful twinges at this moment, when employees are in a weak position and their bosses know it.

The bosses display an impressive array of vile behavior. In a well-cast movie, each one plays to the strengths of the actor portraying him. Consider Dave Harken (Kevin Spacey), a supercilious sadist who toys with his middle manager Nick (Jason Bateman). Few are better than Spacey at regarding others with contempt and humiliating them with pleasure. Many other actors, given his dialogue in this film, would seem unconvincing and over the top. Spacey demonstrates why he is getting praise right now in London for his work as Shakespeare's *Richard III.* You remember him: the king who murdered Henry VI and his son Edward, and later during the funeral boasted of his plans to marry Edward's widow, Lady Anne.

The second boss we meet is Dr. Julia Harris (Jennifer Aniston), an erotomaniac dentist. Her target is Dale (Charlie Day), her dental assistant, who is engaged to be married, but so what? She wants him and she will have him, indulging in blatant and aggressive sexual harassment. You know those little Water Picks dentists have? You don't want to know what she does with one after aiming it at Dale's netherlands.

The third boss is Bobby Pellit (Colin Farrell, almost unrecognizable). Bobby has taken control of the company from his beloved father, Jack (Donald Sutherland), and uses it to fund a lifestyle of wretched excess. His employee Kurt (Jason Sudeikis) was a protégé of the old man and now watches with horror as Bobby runs roughshod over environmental restrictions in order to increase short-term profits.

Nick, Dale, and Kurt meet after work on too many days to bitch and moan about their bosses, and one night become inspired to murder them. This leads them to an unsavory bar in search of a hit man, and they meet a man named Jones (Jamie Foxx). Even the initials of his nickname don't belong in a family newspaper, qualifying as they do as a familiar adaptation of one of Carlin's seven words.

The movie, directed with cheerful and wicked energy by Seth Gordon, is situation slapstick, much of it set (as many desperate lad pictures are) outside the houses of the targets, as the plotters peep and spy. There's a particularly ingenious series of scenes involving Kevin Spacey, one of them finding a legitimate excuse to recycle perhaps the single most famous shot of *Pulp Fiction.*

Spacey is superb, but the surprise for many viewers may be Jennifer Aniston. Her career has drifted into such shallows that it's possible to forget how good she was in a movie like *The Good Girl* (1999). Here she has acute comic timing and hilariously enacts alarming sexual hungers.

The default rating for comedies these days is PG-13. A plain PG warns teenagers a movie is too tame, and an R (allegedly) means they can't get in. Every season brings a couple of R-rated comic raunch-a-ramas, however, and on the heels of the *Hangover* franchise here perhaps comes another one. In strict logic it's hard to see how a sequel would be possible, but they'll find a way. You wait and see.

## Hot Tub Time Machine ★ ★ ★

R, 100 m., 2010

John Cusack (Adam), Rob Corddry (Lou), Craig Robinson (Nick), Clark Duke (Jacob), Crispin Glover (Phil), Lizzy Caplan (April), Chevy Chase (Repairman). Directed by Steve Pink and produced by John Cusack, Grace Loh, Matt Moore, and John Morris. Screenplay by Morris, Josh Heald, and Sean Anders.

*Hot Tub Time Machine* may sound almost by definition like a bad comedy. I mean, how good can a movie named *Hot Tub Time Machine* possibly be? Yes? That's not what I thought. I saw the stand-up display in a movie lobby and perked up. With a title like that, the filmmakers aren't lacking in confidence. There was also the item of John Cusack in the lead. As a general rule, he isn't found in bad films.

I wasn't disappointed. This is a step or two below *The Hangover,* but occupying similar turf. It's another guy picture, which is like a buddy picture except usually without cops. The guys bond, they seek to relive their misspent youth, there are women and even wives around but they're strictly in supporting roles.

A forty-something party animal named Lou (Rob Corddry) gets drunk and passes out after he unwisely guns his car engine in time to the music while parked in his garage and listening to Mötley Crüe. This is interpreted as a suicide attempt by his best friends Adam (John Cusack) and Nick (Craig Robinson), and although he tells him they're mistaken, they're not so sure. They're worried about their friend. He's a full-bore, full-time alcoholic without a shred of maturity or caution. What this boy obviously requires is a return to the ski lodge where they all got blasted together in the 1980s. Over Lou's protests, they drag along Jacob (Clark Duke), Adam's nephew. Adam wants to keep him out of trouble (hollow laugh).

Today, this lodge is so shabby it looks not only like a poor excuse for a ski resort but even like a poor excuse for a movie set. That's part of the movie's charm. Did the Marx Brothers ever lavish money on sets? (Well, yes, but never mind.) The check-in routine is from Motel Hell, and the surly one-armed bellboy (Crispin Glover) kicks their luggage around, dumps it on the floor, and sticks out his remaining hand for a tip.

They get the same big room they had before. It's gone downhill. The hot tub seems to harbor growth from the Planet of Mold. But there's a cheerful repairman (Chevy Chase), who plays the role that George Burns used to play when you needed a guy who just looked like he knew the secrets of the universe. Chevy fixes the tub and it starts to bubble with an inner glow, like beer on the simmer. The guys jump in and are magically transported back in time to their youth in the 1980s. Jacob hadn't been born then, but never mind; it's their present selves who are transported.

This then becomes the premise for a comedy contriving more or less every possible problem and paradox, of which the high point is possibly Nick's boozy phone call to his wife, who at the time is still in grade school. A pretty girl named April (Lizzy Caplan) catches Adam's eye, although strict logic suggests they have little future together. And Corddry essentially steals the movie as Lou.

Remember how Corddry was always so earnest and sincere when assuring Jon Stewart of outrageous facts on *The Daily Show*? He brings the same focus to getting drunk. Comedy is a delicate art, with nothing so important as the performer never seeming to believe anything he does is funny. Corddry here achieves a level of comic confidence that seems almost uncanny; Cusack, as coproducer, and Steve Pink, the director (who wrote Cusack's *High Fidelity* and *Grosse Point Blank*), must have intuited this gift and been willing to give him free rein.

I can't be sure, but I think the density of the f-word reaches the saturation point in *Hot Tub Time Machine.* I may have heard it employed as three different parts of speech in the same sentence. One wonders if American spoken English could survive without it. What did we say in the old days? It must have been a quiet land.

The bottom line is, gross-out guy comedies open twice a month, and many of them are wretched excesses. *Hot Tub Time Machine,* which wants nothing more than to be a screwball farce, succeeds beyond any expectations suggested by the title, and extends John Cusack's remarkable run: Since 1983, in fifty-five films, he's never made a bad one. Well, I never saw *Grandview, USA.*

## The Housemaid ★ ★ ★

NO MPAA RATING, 106 m., 2010

Jeon Do-yeon (Eun-yi, the maid), Lee Jung-jae (Hoon, the husband), Ahn Seo-hyeon (Nami, the daughter), Seo Woo (Hae-ra, the wife), Park Ji-young (Mother-in-law), Yun Yeo-jong (Miss Cho). Directed and written by Im Sang-soo, based on the 1960 film directed by Kim Ki-young.

*The Housemaid* takes place almost entirely within the enormous modern house of a very rich man, and centers on the young woman he has hired as a maid. It involves primarily the man, his wife, his daughter, the older woman who runs his household, and his mother-in-law. Within this closed system the husband exercises his will, buying his power because of money and the enabling of the women, who are all subservient.

That something disturbing will happen is a given. Hoon (Lee Jung-jae) is a man who expects all of his wishes to be met without question, and in his hermetic household the introduction of the maid Eun-yi (Jeon Do-yeon) creates an imbalance. His wife, Hae-ra (Seo Woo), is content to live in expensive idleness, paging through magazines describing the world of consumer goods she inhabits. She is pregnant with twins, and her focus is on these two latest acquisitions of her marriage. The older servant, Miss Cho (Yun Yeo-jong), hates the family, but is mercilessly efficient in her service. The wife's mother (Park Ji-young) is pleased her daughter married well and wants her to continue to be well married.

Eun-yi is efficient, submissive, and very attractive. We learn little about her except that she needs the job. She is in awe of the man, who comes home from his job as a Master of the Universe and plays flawless classical piano while drinking rare vintages. His wife drifts through in couture designs. The daughter (Ahn Seo-hyeon) is a mystery, much loved and cared for, but not much needed. The maid and the daughter instinctively bond, because in this home they are the only two with affection to spend.

We know it's inevitable that the husband will attempt to seduce the maid. And it surely is a seduction and a coercion, even though the maid agrees and even seems to appreciate it. Sex is a bad bargain if only one party is free to set the terms. Miss Cho sees what is happening because she sees everything that happens. The mother-in-law also sees. Eventually, the housemaid's pregnancy is obvious.

It is not a problem for the others so long as it doesn't upset the financial equilibrium, in which the husband gets everything he pays for. His wife and her mother are like favored suppliers. The housemaid has opened up a new trading market with unfamiliar producers and negotiable prices. If you sell all the sugar, you don't want to hear about Sweet'n Low.

This story is told by the writer-director Im Sang-soo with cool, elegant cinematography and sinuous visual movements. The dominant mood is gothic, with the persistent sadomasochistic undertones that seem inescapable in so much Korean cinema. Why is that? The situation is obviously explosive, but we have no idea what will set it off.

The central questions are: Who has the most to lose? Who has the most to gain? Whose private agenda is not clearly perceived in the household? Will everyone put up with everything, as the husband expects? The film withholds even hints of the answers to these questions until the final grotesque series of shots, and then all of them are answered in one character's reaction in particular.

## House of Pleasures ★ ★ ★ ½

NO MPAA RATING, 125 m., 2012

Hafsia Herzi (Samira), Celine Sallette (Clotilde), Jasmine Trinca (Julie), Adele Haenel (Lea), Alice Barnole (Madeleine), Iliana Zabeth (Pauline), Noemie Lvovsky (Marie-France). Directed by Bertrand Bonello and produced by Bonello and Kristina Larsen. Screenplay by Bonello.

Bertrand Bonello's *House of Pleasures* is a morose elegy to the decline of a luxurious Parisian bordello, circa 1900, a closed world in which prostitutes and their clients glide like sleepwalkers through the motions of sex. Elegant and detailed production design creates L'Apollonide, a high-priced whorehouse on a respectable boulevard, where a madam and her women of commerce lead a life as cloistered as in a convent or a prison.

In only one scene, a swimming party on a riverbank, are the girls allowed outside. The house supplies all their needs. There is a stately entrance hall with marble statuary and a staircase leading up to a drawing room that is a cocoon of overstuffed furniture and sofas, plush cushions, Oriental rugs, ancient brass lamps, candles, sometimes music on a piano. Here rich men languish with champagne and tobacco while beautiful young women, expensively dressed or undressed, cuddle and caress them, and the madam's sleek black panther dozes on a velvet settee. Occasionally they go upstairs.

The house rules specify that the prostitutes remain on duty until the last client has gone home, but they can sleep as late as they wish. This is in a lazy dormitory, a separate, private area. The women sleep three to a bed like sisters, eat together around the same jolly table on which they submit to medical examinations, bathe together, dress and groom one another, gossip and console. They lead comfortable lives and always look fashionable, not for their comfort but for the clients.

Why do they come here to work? None has been forced. All are almost immediately in a state of servitude. L'Apollonide charges them for room, board, clothing, everything. From the first they are in arrears to Marie-France (Noemie Lvovsky), the madam, and they dream of a client who will free them by paying off their debts. Some have been there ten years and tell the young ones with resignation that they will never escape. Yet the house has a good name, and a provincial girl not yet sixteen comes with a letter of application at the urging of her parents.

Champagne is a constant presence in every scene. Clients and prostitutes all seem quietly drunk. One girl is addicted to opium, and offers another a puff on the pipe: "It makes the sex easier." Sex alone is not enough for jaded clients. One girl pretends to be a geisha, another an automaton. Madeleine (Alice Barnole) has the illusion that she and her favorite client love each other. "I want to tie you up," he says. She agrees. He tickles her neck and face with a knife. She doesn't like this game and asks him to stop. "I pay, I say," he says, and slices both her cheeks open from the lips.

She now becomes "The Woman Who Laughs," her face horribly disfigured behind a veil. The client continues to come to the house. A prostitute has no rights. Eventually, however, this man meets a gruesome fate. As the overhead and rent increase at L'Apollonide, Marie-France is forced out. She was not a cruel dictator, but remote and stately, gliding through rooms, softly issuing instructions. An epilogue suggests that all prostitution is a deadly form of bondage, and L'Apollonide was a comparatively more comfortable form of it.

Time and space are unclear. We never have a sense of where the rooms are in relation to one another. Some moments repeat. Others never happened. Modern music is heard when it should not exist. The girls like to move their wetted fingers on the rims of their champagne glasses to produce mournful music. No one, male or female, has any fun, but the men behave as if they do. They are all half-stupefied by the languor in which they drown.

## How Do You Know ★ ★

PG-13, 116 m., 2010

Reese Witherspoon (Lisa), Owen Wilson (Matty), Paul Rudd (George), Jack Nicholson (Charles). Directed by James L. Brooks and produced by Brooks, Julie Ansell, Laurence Mark, and Paula Weinstein. Screenplay by Brooks.

The one thing we don't see Reese Witherspoon doing in *How Do You Know* is playing softball. Considering that she portrays a softball player, this seems strange. To be sure, she's dropped from the team roster early in *How Do You Know*, so that's a reason. But there's something so deeply Witherspoonish about the idea of Reese stealing second that I am unconsoled.

It's established that she's a very good softball player indeed. Her teammates love her, her play is superb, she's a great role model, and her only problem is she's almost thirty. This is apparently past retirement age for women softball players. It's time for her to round third and collect a gold watch.

No sooner does she get some free time on her hands than two would-be lovers complicate her life. Matty (Owen Wilson) is a pro baseball pitcher with a multimillion-dollar contract, and George (Paul Rudd) is a big-time financial wheeler-dealer who works for the firm controlled by his father, Charles (Jack Nicholson). George is the nicer man. Matty is a two-timing, womanizing narcissist. But it looks as if George will be indicted and spend time in prison, and Lisa (Witherspoon) moves into Matty's penthouse, which is large enough for batting practice.

Lisa has sex with Matty and presumably with George, but it's that romcom kind of sex that remains, for an outsider, largely conceptual. Intimate personal behavior doesn't much enter in because all of the characters are limited to sitcom problems. Matty's troubles are shallowness and sex addiction. George is a nice man, ethical, who faces indictment on a technicality. In theory, he should have known every detail about the financial malfeasance of his father's company. It doesn't always work out that way.

I expected this movie to be better. The

writer-director is James L. Brooks, and this is the fourth time he's worked with Jack Nicholson (including *Terms of Endearment* and *As Good as It Gets*, for both of which he won acting Oscars). So let's start with Nicholson. Brooks hasn't given him much to work with. He plays a conniving tycoon who doesn't deserve his son's loyalty. It's a heavy role, and there's little to lighten it. In his best roles Jack always seems to be getting away with something. He is here, too, but it's not funny. We like to identify with his onscreen sins, and this is a rare time when Nicholson is simply a creep.

The best-written and funniest role in the film is for Owen Wilson, as the pro pitcher. You know how his characters can have that ingratiating niceness, that solicitude for you while they're serving themselves? Here he plays a man tone-deaf to the feelings of women and clueless about his own behavior. But he's so nice about it that Lisa agrees to move in, and that provides an opening for what every actress should master, the scene where she repacks her bags and marches out.

Rudd's George is very likable. This is the wrong time for him to fall in love. His world is collapsing, and he finds himself in a cheap rented apartment surrounded by packing boxes. He has nothing to offer Lisa, and not enough trust in himself or her to realize she loves him, the big dummy.

All of this whizzes along a few feet off the ground, like most romcoms. Reese Witherspoon is always immensely cuddly, but it's not Lisa's heart that's involved here; it's her story line. Nothing heats up. The movie doesn't lead us; it simply stays in step. Jack Nicholson is one of the few actors who always inspires a quiet chuckle of anticipation when he first appears in a movie. This is a rare movie that doesn't give him a chance to deserve it.

## Howl ★ ★ ★

NO MPAA RATING, 84 m., 2010

James Franco (Allen Ginsberg), David Strathairn (Ralph McIntosh), Jon Hamm (Jake Ehrlich), Bob Balaban (Judge Clayton Horn), Alessandro Nivola (Luther Nichols), Treat Williams (Mark Schorer), Mary-Louise Parker (Gail Potter), Jeff Daniels (Professor David Kirk), Todd Rotondi (Jack Kerouac), Jon Prescott (Neal Cassady), Aaron Tveit (Peter Orlovsky). Directed by Rob Epstein and Jeffrey Friedman and produced by Epstein, Friedman, Elizabeth Redleaf, and Christine K. Walker. Screenplay by Epstein and Friedman.

A few days after Allen Ginsberg died in 1997 there was a candlelight memorial service in a coffeehouse in Boulder, Colorado, just down Pearl Street from the Beat Bookshop. Ginsberg was familiar in Boulder as founder of the wonderfully named Jack Kerouac School of Disembodied Poetics at Naropa University. Poets read their work and his, listeners sat on chairs or on the floor, and for that time the beatnik era lived again.

The Beats created poetry, fiction, art, and music, but most of all they created the legend of themselves—"angelheaded hipsters burning for the ancient heavenly connection to the starry dynamo in the machinery of night." After rock 'n' roll they were the first decisive break with the orderly postwar years, and following them were the hippies, Woodstock, flower power, the Me Generation, and adults wearing Levis to the office. For anyone young in the late 1950s—a kid at Urbana High School, for example—to read the opening words of Ginsberg's "Howl" was to know, YES! that they described you: "I saw the best minds of my generation destroyed by madness, starving hysterical naked, dragging themselves through the negro streets at dawn."

Yes. Not that one was, but that one wanted to think of oneself in such terms. You wanted to steal the family car and drive all night and into the burning sun, driven by caffeine, and drive without stopping directly to City Lights bookstore in San Francisco, and have Lawrence Ferlinghetti publish *your* poems, which you would have scribbled on legal pads on the seat next to you as you drove.

The new film *Howl* evokes the first tender birth of that new age. Its Beats still wear jackets and ties. Allen Ginsberg has horn-rim glasses and seems touchingly young, and not at all an angelheaded hipster destroyed by madness. The secret was: He wanted to be one, too. And as the film gently reveals, he was reluctant to have his great early poem published because he wasn't eager to have his daddy find out things about him, such as that he was homosexual.

In years to come Allen Ginsberg would play the role of public poet as Robert Frost had for an earlier and much different generation. He was out when other brave souls were still only opening the closet door and waving. At a National Student Congress I saw him sit cross-legged on a rug and use finger cymbals and chant whatever it was he was chanting, because the act and not perhaps the words seemed to be the point.

What feels right about *Howl* is that it is set before those days, before the beard and the mysticism and Tibet, the public persona and the levitating of the Pentagon. The bold, outspoken man of later days is seen here as still a middle-class youth, uncertain of his gayness, filled with the heady joy of early poetic success, learning how to be himself.

The film is above all about "Howl" the poem. Ginsberg, played by James Franco with restraint and care, reads it as smoke fills a 1955 coffeehouse. There is a re-creation of an early Ginsberg documentary interview. We see scenes from the poem's trial for obscenity, with David Strathairn for the prosecution and Jon Hamm for the defense. (As ludicrous as some of the testimony is, it must be noted it's word for word from the transcript.) There is an uncertain attempt to animate some passages from "Howl," based on the miscalculation that the poem's striking imagery needs visuals, not words, to be realized.

And then there are straightforward biographical scenes involving Ginsberg's friendships with such Beats as Jack Kerouac and Neal Cassady, the charismatic legend who was the inspiration for the Dean Moriarty character in *On the Road*. It is during this time Ginsberg meets the man with whom he would spend the rest of his life, Peter Orlovsky. All of the biographical material is wisely done without the benefit of hindsight: It's possible to forget that "Howl," now a standard, was illegal to sell for a time, and that Ginsberg's own sexuality was against the law in many states. It took some courage to be Allen Ginsberg.

One of the qualities I like about this film is that the writer-directors, Rob Epstein and Jeffrey Friedman, are aware of the time when Beat was new. The coffeehouse reading could be archival footage. The re-created obscenity trial preserves the prim academic standards of the day (even in the 1960s, someone like Auden was not quite acknowledged as gay). The animation could be from an overheated student film. And the Orlovsky scenes focus more on idealized romance. Ginsberg also had a crush on Kerouac, who is seen here in much the same macho way as the early Brando and Newman: a hunk—but perfectly straight, of course.

## How to Live Forever ★ ★ ★

NO MPAA RATING, 94 m., 2011

Ray Bradbury, Phyllis Diller, Aubrey de Grey, Pico Iyer, Ray Kurzweil, Jack LaLanne, Buster Martin, John Robbins, Suzanne Somers, and Marianne Williamson. A documentary directed and produced by Mark Wexler. Screenplay by Wexler and Robert DeMaio.

If someone could give you a pill that allowed you to live for five hundred years, would you take it? Not me. Although I'm not keen on dying this minute or this year, I consider death to be the completion of the journey I embarked on at my birth, and do not expect the circle to be unbroken. For one thing, what would I do with all my memories? For another, where would the planet put everybody?

*How to Live Forever* is a documentary by Mark Wexler about scientific, nutritional, lifestyle, and philosophical approaches to a long life. Humans could once expect to live until about 23, we learn, and there are now 100,000 Americans over the age of 100. The oldest person in this film was 127, and there is a 101-year-old British woman who is quicker and smarter than most of the talking heads on TV.

How do they do it? Good genes, to begin with. Then diet: The key is a satisfying volume of low-calorie foods. Then staying active and taking an interest in things. We meet the Disney animator Tyrus Wong, 98, who flies kites of amazing complexity and beauty on the beach at Santa Monica. And a 101-year-old auto maintenance man in London who runs marathons (he took five rest stops, he explains, for a pint of beer and a smoke). There is a Brit punk rock group whose members, all over 90, put on a good show of destroying their guitars. And a 91-year-old heart surgeon.

Wexler journeys to Okinawa, where heart disease, cancer, and high blood pressure are all but unknown, apparently because of a diet with no meat, limited fish, and large quantities of seaweed and other vegetables. The Okinawans also seem to walk everywhere and keep working; a fisherman in his eighties dives into the sea to place and check his nets.

Back home, Wexler makes the obligatory visit to a cryonics center that promises to thaw you out at some point in the future. I can't think of anything more horrifying. He also learns about laughter yoga, Jack LaLanne's personal regime (he lived until ninety-six), Suzanne Somers's daily intake of hormones, and how Phyllis Diller keeps right on working ("Old age is when your feet are mistaken for alligator shoes"). There is even a Japanese actor in his seventies who stars in "elder porn," a field that seems to contradict Diller's theory that the best contraceptive among the aged is nudity.

Wexler meets a Cambridge biochemist named Aubrey de Grey who believes, with other antiaging experts, that we are approaching a medical "treatment" for aging. Given the undisputed fact that millions of humans live in conditions of starvation, drought, and disease, this strikes me as a mixed blessing. However, I know Wexler's father, the great cinematographer Haskell, and he is ferociously alive at eighty-seven. What keeps him going seems to be diet, exercise, work, and radical outrage. It's worth a try.

## How to Train Your Dragon ★ ★ ★

PG, 98 m., 2010

Jay Baruchel (Hiccup), Gerard Butler (Stoick), Craig Ferguson (Gobber), America Ferrara (Astrid), Jonah Hill (Snotlout), Christopher Mintz-Plasse (Fishlegs), Kristen Wiig (Ruffnut), T. J. Miller (Tuffnut). Directed by Chris Sanders and Dean DeBlois and produced by Bonnie Arnold. Screenplay by Sanders and DeBlois, based on the book by Cressida Cowell.

Some movies seem born to inspire video games. All they lack is controllers and a scoring system. *How to Train Your Dragon* plays more like a game born to inspire a movie. It devotes a great deal of time to aerial battles between tamed dragons and evil ones, and not much to character or story development. But it's bright, good-looking, and has high energy. Kids above the easily scared age will probably like the movie the younger they are.

This is another action animation with an improbable young hero. Remember when the heroes in this genre were teenagers? Now it's usually some kid who is ten at the most, revealing himself as stronger, wiser, and braver than older people, and a quick learner when it comes to discovering or mastering a new form of warfare. We are born knowing how to command dragons and spaceships, and we forget as up we grow.

Our hero is Hiccup Horrendous Haddock III (voice by Jay Baruchel), a young Viking who lives in Berk, a mountainside village surrounded by the crags and aeries of hostile dragons. Hiccup tells us that his village is very old, but all of the houses are new. An alarming omen. Led by his father, Stoick (Gerard Butler), and the dragon master, Gobber (Craig Ferguson), the villagers have been in combat with the dragons since time immemorial. It would seem to be an unequal struggle; the dragons are enormous and breathe fire, and the Vikings, while muscular, have only clubs, swords, and spears. They may, however, be smarter than the dragons, although you wouldn't know that just by listening to them.

Butler seems to be channeling his character from *300*, beefed up by many a hearty Viking feast. He joins Ferguson and others in muscular Scottish accents, since as we all know, that dialect of English was widely used among the Vikings. In appearance, the Vikings seem victims of a testosterone outbreak causing enormous sprouty growths of hair. Even the hair from their nostrils might knit up into a nice little sock. Oh, how I tried not to, but as I watched these brawlers saddled up on great flying lizards, I kept thinking, "*Asterix* meets *Avatar*."

The plot: Little Hiccup is ordered to stay inside during a dragon attack. But the plucky lad seizes a cannon, blasts away at the enemy, and apparently wings one. Venturing into the forest to track his prey, he finds a wounded little dragon about his age, already chained up. He releases it, they bond, and he discovers that dragons can be perfectly nice. With his new friend, Toothless, he returns to the village, and an alliance is formed with good dragons against the bad dragons, who are snarly holdouts and grotesquely ugly.

One evil beast is covered all over with giant warlike knobs, and has six eyes, three on either side, like a classic Buick. In one scene, a Viking hammers on an eyeball with his club. Not very appetizing. The battle ends as all battles must, with the bad guys routed and the youngest hero saving the day. The aerial battle scenes are storyboarded like a World War I dogfight, with swoops, climbs, and narrowly missed collisions with craggy peaks and other dragons. For my taste, these continued way too long, but then I must teach myself that I do not have a six-year-old's taste.

*Note: The movie is in both 3-D and 2-D. The 3-D adds nothing but the opportunity to pay more in order to see a distracting and unnecessary additional dimension. Paramount has threatened theaters that if they don't clear screens for* Dragon *despite the current glut of 3-D films, the studio won't let them show it in 2-D. This displays real confidence in 3-D.*

## Hugh Hefner: Playboy, Activist, and Rebel ★ ★ ★

R, 124 m., 2010

Hugh M. Hefner, Joan Baez, Tony Bennett, Pat Boone, Jim Brown, Susan Brownmiller, James Caan, Dick Cavett, Robert Culp, Tony Curtis, Dick Gregory, Jesse Jackson, Bill Maher, Jenny McCarthy, Mary O'Connor, Pete Seeger, Gene Simmons, David Steinberg, Shannon Tweed, Mike Wallace, and Ruth Westheimer. A documentary directed by Brigitte Berman and produced by Berman, Peter Raymont, and Victor Solnicki.

From the moment that Hal Homes and I slipped quietly into his basement and he showed me his father's hidden collection of *Playboy* magazines, the map of my emotional geography shifted toward Chicago. In that magical city lived a man named Hugh Hefner who had Playmates possessing wondrous bits and pieces I had never seen before. I wanted to be invited to his house.

I was trembling on the brim of puberty, and aroused not so much by the rather sedate color "centerfold" of an undressed woman, as by the black-and-white photos that accompanied them. These showed an ordinary woman (I believe it was Janet Pilgrim) entering an office building in Chicago, and being made up for her "pictorial." Made up! Two makeup artists were shown applying powders and creams to her flesh. This electrified me. It made Pilgrim a real person. In an interview she spoke of her life and ambitions.

The photographs that burned into my mind did not reveal any of Miss Pilgrim's wondrous bits. I sensed even then that bits were not what it was about. All depended on context. Miss Pilgrim would disrobe and have her body made up by two other women for her pictorial, and then . . . turning the page . . . and then she would put on a dressing gown and enter a photo studio and meet a serious and respectable-looking photographer . . . and then . . . she would drop the gown to the floor and then . . . I turned the page . . . she would pose for the centerfold.

It was the process that entranced me. I'd seen cheesecake pinups before; my own basement, across the street from Hal's, also contained certain hidden magazines we had studied. That our fathers concealed these magazines from our mothers and that we studied them secretly was surely a rite of passage into manhood. The women we found in those other magazines had no existence apart from their pages. They came into the world full-blown as we saw them, wearing polka-dot bikinis or holding Japanese umbrellas, and after the photo was taken they ceased to exist. They didn't come to work, go home from work, eat, sleep, sneeze, or have any corporeal existence. They were pinups. The women in *Playboy* were real, and lived only 135 miles from Urbana, Illinois, and in some unlikely but thinkable universe, I might meet them. My preteen hormones cried out: Yes! This is what we're hormones for!

In the years to come, Hugh Hefner was often in the news, and rarely in a story I didn't read. He lived in a Mansion. He drove a Mercedes two-seater. He smoked a pipe. In his Mansion, Tony Bennett, Julie London, and Bill Cosby hung out, and there were parties every night, and something was happening that was halfway between a bachelor's pad and a bacchanal.

I promised to myself that if I ever got a job in Chicago, I would get myself invited to the Mansion within six months. It didn't take that long. I was hired by the *Chicago Sun-Times* in the autumn of 1966, and two months later I was assigned to write a feature story about a party at the Mansion. It was a party for the top Chevrolet dealers of America. Julie London was nowhere to be seen. But there was a big buffet, and Hef was in the living room with his dressing gown, his slippers, his pipe, his Pepsi, and his date. I slipped into an alcove and found my way down to the Grotto with its plate-glass window opening onto the aquatic underwater vista of the pool.

And there I met not Miss December, but a young woman named Royal Kennedy. She worked in broadcasting and was also covering the party. She was amused by the Grotto. We later went out on one or two perfectly respectable dates. She had never met a Playmate. We had that in common. It gradually became clear to me that Bill Cosby might meet Miss December, but I never would.

I went back to the Mansion several more times, for parties and movie nights. When Russ Meyer came through Chicago with his new bride, Edy Williams, Hef had us over for dinner and gave us the tour. Russ shot some of the first Playmates. I covered the opening of the West Coast Mansion in Holmby Hills, and stood at the bar with Tony Curtis. Later, Chaz and I went to some of Hef's New Year's Eve parties out there. In *Playboy,* I'd read about parties at Hef's pad with people like Ray Anthony, Mel Torme, and Miss October of 1967. And now it was 1988, and OMG, there they still were! Ray Anthony, Mel Torme, and Miss October of 1967! And I went to one of Hef's "movie nights" at the Mansion, with Hef using notes on a yellow legal pad to introduce *Treasure Island.*

Many of you will find my comments deplorable. You may believe *Playboy* was the enemy of women. It objectified their bodies. It schooled men to regard them as sex objects. It stood for all that feminists fought to correct. There is some truth to that, but it doesn't impact upon my experience, and the best I can do here is be truthful.

Nobody taught me to regard women as sex objects. I always did. Most men do. And truth to tell, most women regard men as sex objects. We regard many other aspects of another person, but sex is the elephant in the room. Evolution has hardwired us that way. When we meet a new person, in some small recess of our minds we evaluate that person as a sex partner. We don't act on it, we don't dwell on it, but we do it. You know we do. And this process continues bravely until we are old and feeble.

Yes, *Playboy* presented women's bodies for our regard. Yes, they were airbrushed and Photoshopped to perfection. Not a blemish, not a zit, not one single chewed fingernail. This process of perfection doesn't deny nature; it reflects it. When we meditate on the partner of our dreams, the mental image we summon is without flaw. We don't dwell upon a pimple or a bad tooth or a little underarm fat. We meditate on the gestalt. We meditate on being accepted and loved by that wonderful person. Photographers like Diane Arbus photographed people realistically, and were called cruel.

Nor is it only women's bodies that have been objectified and turned into sex objects. Men have undergone the same process. If few women feel they can live up to a Playmate, few men believe they belong in a Ralph Lauren or Calvin Klein ad. *Vogue* doesn't publish seven-hundred-page holiday issues filled with models with zits. I'm not saying this is ideal. I'm saying it's the truth.

So now I move on to a larger view of Hugh Hefner. Yes, he has possibly experienced more orgasms with more different women than any other man who has ever lived. But his relationships have been consensual, and no woman has ever said, "Why, Mr. Hefner! I had no idea you were that kind of man!" It is also notable that in an age where sexual-harassment lawsuits are as common as bankruptcies, Hefner has never been charged with misbehavior. We must conclude that Hefner's behavior is that of a generous gentleman who likes to get laid. That is not the worst thing in the world.

I've just finished watching a new documentary named *Hugh Hefner: Playboy, Activist, and Rebel* by Brigitte Berman, who won an Oscar for *Artie Shaw: Time Is All You've Got*

(1985), and also directed *Bix: Ain't None of Them Play Like Him Yet* (1983). My guess is that Hefner and Berman met through their interest in jazz. The film is pro-Hefner, although it supplies Susan Brownmiller and Pat Boone to make the obligatory arguments for the prosecution. It presents Hefner as he would probably want to be seen, as a supporter of civil rights, civil liberties, freedom of speech, and freedom of choice.

His credentials in these areas have cost him some money and trouble. His syndicated TV program *Playboy After Dark*, which he owned and controlled, showcased mixed-race singing groups and blacklisted performers such as Pete Seeger at a time when networks enforced a ban on both. It also showed blacks and whites dancing together on a set supposed to be "Hef's Penthouse." Some stations in the South refused to carry it. The show went on the air not long after Nat King Cole's show left NBC after failing to find advertisers that would buy into a "black" show.

In New Orleans, Hefner franchised one of the first Playboy Clubs, later to learn it was forbidden by law to mix black and white patrons. He bought back the franchise, and reopened it to club members of all races. It was in that club that a black comedian performed before whites for the first time in Louisiana (although black musicians were "legal"). He was a young man from Chicago named Dick Gregory. Gregory appears in the film, recalling that he was a replacement for a white comic, Dr. Irwin Corey, and the *Playboy* event turned out to be a private party for three hundred white businessmen. "Three hours later, I was still talking," Gregory says. "Everything turned around on that day." For his career, it certainly did.

It became an old joke that people said they read *Playboy* because of the articles. But Hefner tried much harder than necessary to maintain a high editorial standard. His issues No. 2 through No. 4 serialized Ray Bradbury's *Fahrenheit 451*. He championed Vladimir Nabokov, Margaret Atwood, James Baldwin, and Jorge Luis Borges. His *Playboy* interviews were newsworthy, and his editors must have smiled when they sent Alex Haley to interview the American Nazi George Lincoln Rockwell. (Haley recalls, "I told him I'd been called 'nigger' many times, but this time I was being well paid to hear it.") *The Hurt Locker* was based on *Playboy* reporting.

Hefner and *Playboy* have been around so long that not everyone remembers what America used to be like. It was sexually repressed and socially restrictive. College students were expelled for having sex out of wedlock. Homosexuality and miscegenation were illegal. Freedom of choice was denied. McCarthyism still cast a pall over the freedom of speech. Many people joined in the fight against that unhealthy society. Hefner was one of them, and a case can be made that *Playboy* had a greater influence on our society in its first half-century than any other magazine.

No doubt *Playboy* objectified women and all the rest of it. But it also celebrated them, and freed their bodies from the stigma of shame. It calmly explained that women were sexual beings, and experienced orgasms, and that photographs of their bodies were not by definition "dirty pictures." Not many of today's feminists (of either gender) would be able to endure America's attitudes about women in the 1950s.

As Hefner speaks, you realize that he believes in civil rights and liberties so deeply that it's instinctive. Many people shared his politics in the 1950s and early 1960s, but not many of them ran corporations that (a) depended on mass audiences, and (b) stood to lose business because of political beliefs. When it came to African-Americans in his clubs or on his TV show (or as his centerfolds), Hefner did the right thing without calculation, and paid a financial penalty. When the (endless) *Playboy* philosophy argued for change, it is unlikely he gained a single reader. But he outlined and defended a progressive philosophy. And when magazine interviews were often revolting puffery about celebrities, he went long and in detail with people such as Malcolm X, Bertrand Russell, Ayn Rand, Jean-Paul Sartre, Elisabeth Kubler-Ross, and Marshall McLuhan. The fact is that sex made money for Hefner, and he used it to produce one of the best magazines in America.

He also spent money to free a man who faced a fifty-year prison term for fellatio. And helped overturn laws that made fellatio and cunnilingus a crime in all fifty states (for which many of us must be grateful). He fought against laws punishing homosexuality and interracial marriage. He supported Lenny Bruce's fight against an obscenity arrest in Chicago. He fought obscenity prosecutions brought by such as Charles Keating, founder of the Citizens for Decent Literature. He won. Berman's doc cannot resist juxtaposing shots of Keating lecturing on morality and Keating in handcuffs being led to prison for bank fraud. Hefner's Playboy Foundation fought for civil liberties in general. The cost for these activities came out of his profits, and that didn't give him a moment's pause.

Some argue, like Brownmiller, that *Playboy* was bad for women—that it made them objects for masturbation. I would suggest *Playboy* was several thousand years behind the curve in doing so. And not only women are used as subjects for meditation during masturbation. Masturbation is an equal opportunity employer. Others argue, like Boone, that *Playboy* promoted immoral behavior. I believe sex in our society, in general, is more moral today than it was when *Playboy* began. I think young people in particular have healthier attitudes toward it than they did when I was in high school. I agree that teen pregnancy and STDs are tragic, but it was Hefner who fought for birth control and protection when they were illegal in some states. I was taught that a woman's body was a possible Occasion for Sin. What kind of morality is that?

Hefner is returning to Chicago this week with his brother, Keith, to revisit their childhood home and their old high school, Steinmetz. I went along with them on their previous return home in 1994. I'd love for him to see the Audience Award winner in this year's Chicago Film Festival, *Louder Than a Bomb.* It's a documentary about the citywide High School Poetry Slam Contest, codirected by Jon Siskel, nephew of Hef's old poker buddy Gene. In its first year of competition, Steinmetz, now a troubled school in a black neighborhood, came out of nowhere and won the event with a gifted group of poet-performers. In the film, it's one of the finalists again. The students of Steinmetz may not much care that Hugh Hefner graduated from their school, but without the social changes he fought for and helped to influence, all of the members of their Poetry Slam team might be in jail today along with the ghost of Lenny Bruce.

## Hugo ★ ★ ★ ★

PG, 130 m., 2011

Ben Kingsley (Georges Melies), Sacha Baron Cohen (Station Inspector), Asa Butterfield (Hugo Cabret), Chloe Grace Moretz (Isabelle), Ray Winstone (Uncle Claude), Emily Mortimer (Lisette), Helen McCrory (Mama Jeanne), Christopher Lee (Monsieur Labisse), Jude Law (Hugo's Father). Directed by Martin Scorsese and produced by Scorsese, Johnny Depp, Tim Headington, and Graham King. Screenplay by John Logan, based on the novel *The Invention of Hugo Cabret* by Brian Selznick.

*Hugo* is unlike any other film Martin Scorsese has ever made, and yet possibly the closest to his heart: a big-budget 3-D family epic, and in some ways a mirror of his own life. We feel a great artist has been given command of the tools and resources he needs to make a movie about—movies. That he also makes it a fable that will be fascinating for (some, not all) children is a measure of what feeling went into it.

In broad terms, the story of his hero, Hugo Cabret, is Scorsese's own story. A bright young boy spends his childhood looking out at the world from a well-placed window, and schooling himself in the workings of artistic mechanisms. That runs in the family. Hugo's uncle is in charge of the clocks at a cavernous Parisian train station. And his father's dream is to complete an automaton, an automated man he found in a museum. He dies with it left unperfected. Rather than be treated as an orphan, the boy hides himself in the maze of ladders, catwalks, passages, and gears of the clockworks themselves, keeping them running right on time. He feeds himself with croissants snatched from station shops, and begins to sneak off to the movies.

His life in the station is made complicated by a toy shop owner named Georges Melies. Yes, this grumpy old man, played by Ben Kingsley, is none other than the immortal French film pioneer, who was also the original inventor of the automaton. Hugo has no idea of this. The real Melies was a magician who made his first movies to play tricks on his audiences. Leave it to Scorsese to make his first 3-D movie about the man who invented special effects. There is a parallel with the asthmatic Scorsese, living in Little Italy but not of it, observing life from the windows of his apartment, soaking up the cinema from television and local theaters, adopting great directors as his mentors and in such cases as Michael Powell rescuing their careers after years of neglect.

The way *Hugo* deals with Melies is enchanting in itself, but the first half of the film is devoted to the escapades of its young hero. In the way the film uses CGI and other techniques to create the train station and the city, the movie is breathtaking. The opening shot swoops above the vast cityscape of Paris and ends with Hugo (Asa Butterfield) peering out of an opening in a clock face far above the station floor. We follow his Dickensian adventures as he stays one step ahead of the choleric Station Inspector (Sacha Baron Cohen), in chase sequences through crowds of travelers. He always escapes back to his refuge behind the walls and above the ceiling of the station.

His father (Jude Law), seen in flashbacks, has left behind notebooks, including his plans to finish the automaton. Hugo seems somewhat a genius with gears, screws, springs, and levers, and the mechanical man is himself a Steampunk masterwork of shining steel and brass. One day Hugo is able to share his secret with a young girl named Isabelle (Chloe Grace Moretz), who also lives in the station and was raised by old Melies and his wife. She is introduced to Hugo's secret world, and he to hers—the books in the cavernous libraries she explores. These two bright kids are miles apart from the cute little pint-sized goofballs in most family pictures.

For a lover of cinema, the best scenes will come in the second half, as flashbacks trace the history and career of Georges Melies. You may have seen his most famous short film, *A Trip to the Moon* (1898), in which space voyagers enter a ship that is shot from a cannon toward the moon; the vessel pokes the man in the moon in the eye.

Scorsese has made documentaries about great films and directors, and here he brings those skills to storytelling. We see Melies (who built the first movie studio) using fantastical sets and bizarre costumes to make films with magical effects—all of them hand-tinted, frame by frame. And as the plot makes unlikely connections, the old man is able to discover that he is not forgotten, but indeed is honored as worthy of the Pantheon.

Not long ago I saw a 3-D children's film about penguins. I thought it was a simpleminded use of the medium. Scorsese used 3-D here as it should be used, not as a gimmick but as an enhancement of the total effect. Notice in particular his re-creation of the famous little film *Arrival of a Train at La Ciotat* (1897), by the Lumiere brothers. You've probably heard its legend: As a train rushes toward the camera, the audience panics and struggles to get out of its way. That is a shot that demonstrates the proper use of 3-D, which the Lumieres might have used had it been available.

*Hugo* celebrates the birth of the cinema and dramatizes Scorsese's personal pet cause, the preservation of old films. In one heartbreaking scene, we learn that Melies, convinced his time had passed and his work forgotten, melted down countless films so that their celluloid could be used to manufacture the heels of women's shoes. But they weren't all melted, and at the end of *Hugo* we see that thanks to this young boy, they never will be. Now there's a happy ending for you.

## The Human Centipede (no stars)

NO MPAA RATING, 90 m., 2010

Dieter Laser (Dr. Heiter), Ashley C. Williams (Lindsay), Ashlynn Yennie (Jenny), Akihiro Kitamura (Katsuro). Directed by Tom Six and produced by Tom Six and Ilona Six. Screenplay by Tom Six.

It's not death itself that's so bad. It's what you might have to go through to get there. No horror film I've seen inflicts more terrible things on its victims than *The Human Centipede*. You would have to be very brave to choose this ordeal over simply being murdered. Maybe you'd need to also be insane.

I'm about to describe what happens to the film's victims. This will be a spoiler. I don't care, because (1) the details are common knowledge in horror film circles, and (2) if you don't know, you may be grateful to be warned. This is a movie I don't think I should be coy about.

OK. Dr. Heiter is a mad scientist. He was

once a respected surgeon, but has now retreated to his luxurious home in the forest, which contains an operating room in the basement. His skin has a sickly pallor, his hair is dyed black, his speech reminds us of a standard Nazi, and he gnashes his teeth. He is filled with hatred and vile perversion.

He drugs his victims and dumps them into his Mercedes. When they regain consciousness, they find themselves tied to hospital beds. He provides them with a little slide show to brief them on his plans. He will demonstrate his skills as a surgeon by—hey, listen, now you'd really better stop reading. What's coming next isn't so much a review as a public service announcement.

Heiter plans to surgically join his three victims by sewing together their mouths and anuses, all in a row, so the food goes in at the front and comes out at the rear, you see. They will move on their hands and knees like an insect with twelve limbs. You don't want to be part of the human centipede at all, but you most certainly don't want to be in the middle. Why does Dr. Heiter want to commit such an atrocity? He is insane, as I've already explained.

He also wants to do it because he is in a movie by Tom Six, a Dutch director whose previous two films average 4 out of 10 on the IMDb scale, which is a score so low very few directors attain it. Six has now made a film deliberately intended to inspire incredulity, nausea, and hopefully outrage. It's being booked as a midnight movie, and is it ever. Boozy fanboys will treat it like a thrill ride.

And yet within Six there stirs the soul of a dark artist. He treats his material with utter seriousness; there's none of the jokey undertone of a classic Hammer horror film like *Scream and Scream Again* (1970), in which every time the victim awoke, another limb had been amputated. That one starred the all-star trio of Vincent Price, Christopher Lee, and Peter Cushing, and you could see they were having fun. Dieter Laser, who plays Dr. Heiter, takes the role with relentless sincerity. This is his sixty-third acting role, but, poor guy, this is seemingly the one he was born to play.

Tom Six is apparently the director's real name. I learn his favorite actor is Klaus Kinski, he is an AK-47 enthusiast, and wears RAF sunglasses and Panama hats. Not the kind of guy you want to share your seat on a Ferris wheel. He has said, "I get a rash from too much political correctness." I promise you that after this movie his skin was smooth as a Gerber baby's.

I have long attempted to take a generic approach. In other words, is a film true to its genre and does it deliver what its audiences presumably expect? *The Human Centipede* scores high on this scale. It is depraved and disgusting enough to satisfy the most demanding midnight movie fan. And it's not *simply* an exploitation film.

The director makes, for example, an effective use of the antiseptic interior of Heiter's labyrinthine home. Doors and corridors lead nowhere and anywhere. In a scene where the police come calling, he wisely has Heiter almost encourage their suspicions. And there is a scene toward the end, as the human centipede attempts escape, that's so piteous it transcends horror and approaches tragedy.

The members of the centipede are Ashley C. Williams, Ashlynn Yennie, and Akihiro Kitamura. The Japanese actor screams in subtitled Japanese, perhaps because he will broaden the film's appeal among Asian horror fans. In the last half of the film, the two American actresses don't scream at all, if you follow me.

I am required to award stars to movies I review. This time, I refuse to do it. The star rating system is unsuited to this film. Is the movie good? Is it bad? Does it matter? It is what it is, and occupies a world where the stars don't shine.

## The Human Centipede 2 (Full Sequence) (no stars)

NO MPAA RATING, 88 m., 2011

Laurence R. Harvey (Martin), Dominic Borrelli (Paul), Vivien Bridson (Martin's Mother), Bill Hutchens (Dr. Sebring), Ashlynn Yennie (Herself). Directed by Tom Six and produced by Tom Six and Ilona Six. Screenplay by Tom Six.

In the first *Human Centipede* movie, a young woman found herself sewn mouth-to-anus by a sadistic surgeon with two other victims. Every cloud has a silver lining. In *The Human Centipede 2 (Full Sequence)* we meet the same actress (Ashlynn Yennie), and from what we can judge she survived that ordeal with little permanent facial damage.

Despite what must have been an unhappy professional experience, Miss Yennie is a trouper, and soon after the beginning of *Human Centipede 2*, she optimistically looks forward to what she thinks will be a meeting with Quentin Tarantino. I can imagine her letter home: "Hi Mom and Dad! Thanks for not seeing my first movie! I've got great news! Tarantino wants to consider me!"

Alas, this is not to be. She is met by the singularly disquieting Martin (Laurence R. Harvey), a pudgy, nearsighted, pear-headed, clammy-skinned, mentally disabled momma's boy who works as a security guard in a mostly deserted subterranean parking garage. Since Martin very rarely ever says anything in this movie, how, you may ask, have I made my diagnosis of his mental condition? I submit to you that if this man spends his waking moments looking at the first *Human Centipede* movie over and over and over again, and wants to make his own version by connecting as many as twelve people, he is four tires short of a car.

Laurence R. Harvey is described as "a British performance artist." I raced off to the always helpful Google and discovered that his artistic career to date hasn't generated a single link. It may be that his performance art consists entirely of walking down the street as himself. Gene Siskel liked to amuse himself by people-watching and thinking, "When that person looked in the mirror before leaving the house, he thought he looked great."

Martin kills a lot of people in this movie, in addition to sewing others together. Perhaps the message is that the first movie influenced its viewers to do sadistic and cruel acts. Since both films were made by the same man, Tom Six, it is inarguable that the first film inspired him to make the second.

The film is reprehensible, dismaying, ugly, artless, and an affront to any notion, however remote, of human decency. It makes a point of Martin's lack of all surgical skills. He seems to have sewn his victims together with summer camp skills where you stitch the parts of a billfold together with leather thread. I am left with this question: After Ashlynn Yennie's first movie role was in the first *Human Centipede* movie, and now her second is in *Human Centipede 2*, do you think she'll leave show business?

## The Hunger Games ★ ★ ★

PG-13, 142 m., 2012

Jennifer Lawrence (Katniss Everdeen), Josh Hutcherson (Peeta Mellark), Liam Hemsworth (Gale Hawthorne), Woody Harrelson (Haymitch Abernathy), Elizabeth Banks (Effie Trinket), Lenny Kravitz (Cinna), Stanley Tucci (Caesar Flickerman), Donald Sutherland (President Snow), Wes Bentley (Seneca Crane), Willow Shields (Prim). Directed by Gary Ross and produced by Nina Jacobson and Jon Kilik. Screenplay by Ross, Suzanne Collins, and Billy Ray, based on the novel by Suzanne Collins.

Like many science fiction stories, *The Hunger Games* portrays a future that we're invited to read as a parable for the present. After the existing nations of North America are destroyed by catastrophe, a civilization named Panem rises from the ruins. It's ruled by a vast and wealthy Capitol inspired by the covers of countless sci-fi magazines and surrounded by twelve "districts," which are powerless satellites. As the story opens, the annual ritual of the Hunger Games is beginning; each district must supply a "tribute" of a young woman and man, and these twenty-four finalists must fight to the death in a forested "arena" where hidden cameras capture every move.

This results in a television production that apparently holds the nation spellbound and keeps the citizens content. Mrs. Link, my high school Latin teacher, will be proud that I recall one of her Daily Phrases, *panem et circenses,* which summarized the Roman formula for creating a docile population: Give them bread and circuses. A vision of present-day America is summoned up, its citizenry glutted with fast food and distracted by reality TV. How is the population expected to accept the violent sacrifice of twenty-four young lives a year? How many have died in our recent wars?

The story centers on the two tributes from the dirt-poor District 12: Katniss Everdeen (Jennifer Lawrence) and Peeta Mellark (Josh Hutcherson). The sixteen-year-old girl hunts deer with bow and arrow to feed her family; he may be hunkier, but seems no match in survival skills. They're both clean-cut all-Panem types, and although one or both are eventually required to be dead, romance is a possibility.

In contrast with these healthy young people, the ruling class in the Capitol are effete decadents. Effie Trinket (Elizabeth Banks), bedecked in gaudy costumery and laden with garish cosmetics, emcees the annual drawing for tributes, and the nation gets to know the finalists on a talk show hosted by Caesar Flickerman (Stanley Tucci), who suggests what Donald Trump might do with his hair if he had enough of it.

The executive in charge is the gamemaker, Seneca Crane (Wes Bentley), who has a beard so bizarrely designed that Satan would be envious. At the top of the society is the president (Donald Sutherland), a sagacious graybeard who harbors deep thoughts. In interviews, Sutherland has equated the younger generation with leftists and Occupiers. The old folks in the Capitol are no doubt a right-wing oligarchy. My conservative friends, on the other hand, equate the young with the tea party and the old with decadent elitists. *The Hunger Games*, like many parables, will show you exactly what you seek in it.

The scenes set in the Capitol and dealing with its peculiar characters have a completely different tone than the scenes of conflict in the arena. The ruling class is painted in broad satire and bright colors. Katniss and the other tributes are seen in earth-toned realism; this character could be another manifestation, indeed, of Jennifer Lawrence's Oscar-nominated character Ree in *Winter's Bone*. The plot even explains why she's adept at bow and arrow.

One thing I missed, however, was more self-awareness on the part of the tributes. As their names are being drawn from a fish bowl (!) at the Reaping, the reactions of the chosen seem rather subdued, considering the odds are twenty-three to one that they'll end up dead. Katniss volunteers to take the place of her twelve-year-old kid sister, Prim (Willow Shields), but no one explicitly discusses the fairness of deadly combat between girl children and eighteen-year-old men. Apparently, the jaded TV audiences of Panem have developed an appetite for barbarity. Nor do Katniss and Peeta reveal much thoughtfulness about their own peculiar position.

*The Hunger Games* is an effective entertainment, and Jennifer Lawrence is strong and convincing in the central role. But the film leapfrogs obvious questions in its path and avoids the opportunities sci-fi provides for social criticism; compare its world with the dystopias in *Gattaca* or *The Truman Show*. Director Gary Ross and his writers (including Suzanne Collins) obviously think their audience wants to see lots of hunting and survival scenes, and has no interest in people talking about how a cruel class system is using them. Well, maybe they're right. But I found the movie too long and deliberate as it negotiated the outskirts of its moral issues.

## The Hunter ★ ★ ★ ½

NO MPAA RATING, 90 m., 2012

Rafi Pitts (Ali Alavi), Mitra Hajjar (Sara), Saba Yaghoobi (Saba), Malak Jahan Khazai (Ali's Mother), Hassan Ghalenoi (Younger Cop), Ali Nicksaulat (Older Cop). Directed by Rafi Pitts and produced by Thanassis Karathanos. Screenplay by Pitts.

The hunter is also the hunted in *The Hunter*, a stark film from Iran about a man who is fed up and not going to take it anymore. This is a parable about modern Iran, and like many recent Iranian films it leaves its meaning to the viewer. One of the wise decisions by Rafi Pitts, its writer, director, and star, is to include no dialogue that ever actually states the politics of its hero, a security guard named Ali Alavi. Only in passing do we learn he has been in prison, and only by deduction do we conclude he may have been a political prisoner.

Pitts had no plans to play the lead in his own film, and I learn from *Variety* that he "was forced to take on the main role when his leading actor proved unreliable." He hardly feels like a replacement. He has uncanny presence. With his severe, tense face beneath a dark brow, he suggests Daniel Day-Lewis. In early scenes he shares the happiness of his wife and little daughter (Mitra Hajjar and Saba Yaghoobi), but then he comes home to an empty apartment and learns only after a long and frustrating wait that they have been identified as victims caught in a crossfire between insurgents and police.

They were not participants in whatever was happening. They were in the wrong place. When Ali learns the news, there's no emotional outburst. He remains contained and almost ominously silent as he identifies his wife's body and fails to identify a little girl in the morgue. He visits the scene of their deaths, with chalk body outlines still on the pavement, one smaller than the other. He parks for days outside his daughter's school, as if she would come smiling down the stairs.

Before this happened, sometimes he would take a hunting rifle into a forest outside Tehran. Now he returns to a vantage point overlooking an expressway, and fires at a police car. How he was identified as the shooter is unclear, but he was, and the second half of the film involves a police manhunt that comes down to him being led in handcuffs through the trees by an unhappy rookie cop and his bullying superior.

You are left free to determine what their long time in the woods represents. Or the personality conflict between the two cops. When they become lost while trying to bring their prisoner in, their three fates become linked. This dilemma won't develop as you may expect, and the more you consider what happens, the more labyrinthine and suggestive are the political undertones. As I followed step by step the unfolding of the ending, I could see how the plot makes perfect sense in a sinister way that adds one brilliant additional twist.

Ali, the hunter, has only a handful of words in the last half of the movie, and not many more before his family disappears. His existence supplies his dialogue. He is a man whose family's fate is not of much significance to the police bureaucracy, and whose life itself has no meaning except in his anguished actions. There is a deep irony in the scenes involving the police. And many long silences in which we're free to imagine his thoughts.

*A Separation*, another recent film from Iran, also centers on a married couple and their daughter. They have many thoughts and many words to express them. The solitary hunter here has been pushed outside his society's courts of appeal. His action itself, when he fires at the highway, takes lives of people unknown to him. By the same token, no one targeted his wife and daughter. They died as a result of the nature of their society. Nothing can be said.

## Hysteria ★ ★ ★

R, 100 m., 2012

Hugh Dancy (Mortimer Granville), Maggie Gyllenhaal (Charlotte Dalrymple), Jonathan Pryce (Dr. Robert Dalrymple), Felicity Jones (Emily Dalrymple), Rupert Everett (Edmund St. John-Smythe). Directed by Tanya Wexler and produced by Tracey Becker, Judy Cairo, and Sarah Curtis. Screenplay by Stephen Dyer and Jonah Lisa Dyer.

"First, do no harm," the Hippocratic Oath admonishes doctors. By this standard, Dr. Robert Dalrymple must have been one of the few practitioners of the Victorian era with a stainless record. He knew no more than most other doctors of his time, and was treating a condition that didn't exist, female hysteria. But give the doctor his due. His treatments consisted of inducing orgasms in his patients, and he didn't lose a one. In fact, his waiting room was usually jammed.

Tanya Wexler's quietly saucy *Hysteria* takes place in London at a time when medical authorities didn't know the word or the concept for "orgasm," and apparently many women never experienced one in practice. Dalrymple's treatments consisted of modestly covering a patient's private regions with a little tent, reaching delicately beneath it, and using digital stimulation to effect a cure. How he hit upon this method must be attributed to sheer genius.

We meet an ambitious young doctor named Mortimer Granville (Hugh Dancy), who has become nearly unemployable because of his habit of questioning the orthodoxy of the time. Desperate for work, he applies at the household of Dalrymple (Jonathan Pryce), who has more patients than he can handle. This also introduces him to the Dalrymple daughters, Charlotte (Maggie Gyllenhaal), a social activist, and the dutiful Emily (Felicity Jones), a student of phrenology who is also searching for a husband. Charlotte flatly rejects her father's theories as crackpot and his treatments as suspect, but uses family money to support her work among the London poor. Mortimer is intended to marry one, and falls in love with the other.

Curing hysteria is not a practice without its drawbacks, and Mortimer treats his patients with such dedication that he comes down with what was not then known as carpal tunnel syndrome. In despair, he consults his droll and dubious friend Edmund St. John-Smythe (Rupert Everett), who happens to be toying with an electrically powered duster. They try it on Mortimer's afflicted area, a light bulb illuminates over Mortimer's head, and the vibrator is invented.

This milestone in human progress has never received the respect it deserves, and yet vibrators have been selling widely and well ever since, even in the early Sears catalogs. They were advertised with such euphemisms as "personal massagers" for aches and pains, although why most of them had phallic shapes was wisely left unexplained.

One of the pleasures of Wexler's third feature is how elegantly it sets its story in the period. The costumes, the sets, the locations, and the behavior are all flawless, and the British characters in the screenplay by Stephen Dyer and Jonah Lisa Dyer are all masters of never quite saying what they mean. Of course, the Dalrymple practice is quite ethical because there is no such thing as a female having pleasure from sex; the exact nature of the complaint being treated is sometimes described as "wandering uterus," which for some reason makes me think of an albatross around its neck.

The film is based on fact. ("Really," an opening title assures us.) The performances are spot-on, and I especially liked the spunky Gyllenhaal, who with this film and the underrated *Secretary* (2002) has built up a nice sideline in sexual exploration. The subject of vibrators has been under discussion since the publication of *The Technology of Orgasm* by Rachel Maines, and it was Wexler's inspiration to see that the invention was all the more remarkable since it came at a time when it treated a condition that officially didn't exist. That was in contrast with many of its contemporary medical treatments, which didn't treat conditions that officially did exist.

# I

## I Am ★ ★

NO MPAA RATING, 78 m., 2011

Desmond Tutu, Howard Zinn, Noam Chomsky, Lynne McTaggart, Coleman Barks, and Thom Hartmann. A documentary directed by Tom Shadyac and produced by Dagan Handy.

There is a scene in *I Am* where a laboratory technician embeds sensors in a puddle of yogurt and attaches them to a Bio-Response Meter. When Tom Shadyac directs his thoughts at the yogurt, the needle on the meter bounces back and forth. It is important for you to know that Shadyac is not physically attached to the meter—or to the yogurt, for that matter. When he thinks about his lawyer, the needle redlines.

It's obvious that the yogurt is reading his mind, right? Right? Hello? For Shadyac and the technician, this experiment demonstrates that our minds are wired to the organic world. For me, it raises the following questions: (1) Was the yogurt pasteurized? (2) How did the yogurt know to read Shadyac's mind and not the mind of the technician who was just as close? (3) How did it occur to anyone to devise an experiment testing whether yogurt can respond to human thoughts? (4) Did anyone check to see if the technician was connected to the meter? (5) Is this a case for the Amazing Randi?

You see I am a rationalist. That means I'm not an ideal viewer for a documentary like *I Am*, which involves the ingestion of woo-woo in industrial bulk. When I see a man whose mind is being read by yogurt, I expect to find that man in a comedy starring, oh, someone like Jim Carrey. Since we all understand There Are No Coincidences, it won't surprise you to learn that *I Am* was directed by Tom Shadyac, who earned untold millions by directing Jim Carrey in such films as *Ace Ventura: Pet Detective.*

This documentary is often absurd and never less than giddy with uplift, but that's not to say it's bad. I watched with an incredulous delight, and at the end I liked Tom Shadyac quite a lot. He's a goofball, yet his heart is in the right place. But don't get me started on hearts. Did you know that Shadyac's friend Rollin McCraty, Ph.D., the director of research for HeartMath, has proven that the human heart controls the human brain via various types of biofeedback?

That's not all the heart can do. Try this on for size: When you are shown pleasant or frightening images on a computer screen, your brain (and heart) respond either positively or negatively. That makes sense. But wait. When the images are chosen at random from a big database, the heart sends positive or negative signals to the brain *two to three seconds in advance* of the image being chosen. In other words, the heart knows what the random image is going to be. Yes. Shadyac is grateful for this information. He doesn't ask any questions, like, for example, does the heart tell the brain what signal *would* have been displayed unless the power to the monitor went out in the milliseconds between when it was chosen and was to be displayed?

Dr. McCraty shares another piece of information that's interesting. There are random number generators distributed all over the world. Most of the time the numbers are truly random. But when a global catastrophe like 9/11 or the Japan calamity occurs, our collective minds send out such strong signals that the computers temporarily stop selecting random numbers. Yes. And the screen fills with lots of ones and zeroes to illustrate that.

So I'm thinking, not everybody found out about the Japan earthquake at once. Does McCraty have data showing if the globe's random number calculators failed simultaneously, or were timed to the spread of the news? (I can guess the answer: They all failed at once, because at a Gaia level we all sensed it simultaneously.)

What set Tom Shadyac to gather this information and make a film about it? In 2007 he was a multimillionaire living in a seventeen-thousand-square-foot mansion in Pasadena and flying in a private jet. Then he had a terrible bike accident, breaking bones and suffering a concussion. He became a victim of post-concussion syndrome, which meant the symptoms didn't clear up. He had blinding headaches and debilitating depressions, and contemplated suicide. Mercifully, the symptoms faded, leaving him sadder, wiser, and in search of truth.

He began with two questions: What's wrong with the world? What can we do about it? He traveled the world to pose these questions to many distinguished people, such as the linguist Noam Chomsky; Archbishop Desmond Tutu; Howard Zinn; Lynne McTaggart, an authority on consciousness and the new physics; people at the Institute of Noetic Sciences; his late father, Richard Shadyac, who was CEO of fundraising for St. Jude Hospital; and so on. None of these people necessarily agree with anything the others say. As for Shadyac, hey, he's just listening.

The thing is, he doesn't ask enough. He is not a skeptic. He asks his two questions and mashes together the answers with a lot of fancy editing of butterflies, sunsets, flocks of birds, schools of fish, herds of wild animals, and petri dishes filled with yogurt. From his tour emerges one conclusion: Everything is connected. Our minds, our bodies, our planet, our universe. This happens (you can see this coming) at the quantum level.

Another thing he learns is that money is the root of all evil. Like the fish, birds, animals, and untouched tribes, we have evolved to cooperate and arrive at consensus. By competing to enrich ourselves, we create bad vibes. Give Shadyac credit: He sells his Pasadena mansion, starts teaching college, and moves into a mobile home (in Malibu, it's true). Now he offers us this hopeful if somewhat undigested cut of his findings, in a film as watchable as a really good TV commercial, and as deep.

I leave you with a parting possibility raised by the film: What if your thoughts continue to affect the DNA you leave behind everywhere you go, all through life? At a quantum level, of course.

## I Am Love ★ ★ ★ ★

R, 120 m., 2010

Tilda Swinton (Emma), Flavio Parenti (Edoardo Jr.), Edoardo Gabbriellini (Antonio), Alba Rohrwacher (Elisabetta), Pippo Delbono (Tancredi), Maria Paiato (Ida), Gabriele Ferzetti (Edoardo Recchi Sr.), Marisa Berenson (Allegra). Directed by Luca Guadagnino and produced by Guadagnino, Francesco Melzi d'Eril, Marco Morabito, Tilda Swinton, Alessandro Usai, and Massimiliano Violante. Screenplay by Barbara Alberti, Ivan Cotroneo, Walter Fasano, and Guadagnino.

Did she understand when she married her husband what sort of family she was joining? She knew they were rich Italian aristocrats, operators of textile mills in Milan. But did she understand that as a wife from Russia she would serve and provide and even be loved, but would never truly be a member?

When we see Emma (Tilda Swinton), she is preparing the Recchi house for the birthday party of the patriarch. She seems to relate more as a caterer than as a hostess. At the head of the table is the grand old Edoardo (Gabriele Ferzetti). Among those gathered are his son, Emma's husband, Tancredi (Pippo Delbono). The old man makes an unexpected announcement: He is retiring and putting Tancredi in charge. But not Tancredi alone. His grandson, their son, Edo (Flavio Parenti), will also share the responsibility.

Is Emma filled with joy? Her husband and son will inherit the dynasty? She is so calm and expert, it's hard to say. Tilda Swinton is a daring actress who doesn't project emotions so much as embody them. *I Am Love* provides an ideal role for her, in that her actions speak instead of words. We learn she has her own private space, that after launching a family event she likes to leave it running smoothly and retire to her room upstairs.

The opening act of Luca Guadagnino's film establishes the stature of the Recchi family as surely as the Corleones are established in *The Godfather,* or the Salinas in Visconti's *The Leopard.* It may be impossible to write about this film without evoking *The Leopard,* not simply because they both involve Italian aristocrats, but because they involve matters of succession, and the way that love and lust can breach the walls aristocrats live behind. Guadagnino makes the connection inescapable by naming Tancredi; in *The Leopard,* Alain Delon pays the Salina nephew of that name.

The Recchi family has been living in a particular way for a long time. Cushioned by great wealth, working in an industry associated with style, never challenged, well educated, its hungers cloaked in tradition, it occupies its place of privilege effortlessly. Emma speaks Italian fluently, but with a Russian accent, a reminder that she is not . . . quite one of them.

Few actresses can embody urgent sexual desire so well as Swinton. She is realistic about such feelings. When she learns her daughter, Elisabetta (Alba Rohrwacher), is a lesbian, she reacts not as a mother, possibly with shock, but as a woman, in surprise and curiosity. She has heard of such things. The heart has its reasons.

The feast opening the film was prepared by Antonio (Edoardo Gabbriellini), a friend of her Edo's. She consults with this young chef, and a feeling passes into her. Later, on a visit to her daughter in San Remo, she happens to see Antonio, and with decision follows him through the streets. This is all done without dialogue. The camera is pursuer and pursued. The longer she follows him, the more certain they must meet.

Of course they make love. Actresses are often called upon to enact sex in the movies. Swinton does it differently with each character, understanding that sexuality is as distinctive as speech or taste. Emma is urgent as if a dam has burst, releasing not passion but happiness. Of course this affair threatens her relationship with her husband, her son, and her family. But most long-established families have overcome the inconveniences of adultery. Continuity is more important than commitment. The film now observes the ways, not predictable, in which this new sexual fact affects Emma's role.

All this time, Guadagnino has been paying due attention to other important members of the family. There is Allegra (Marisa Berenson), gatekeeper of her husband. There is the long-serving housekeeper, Ida (Maria Paiato), who sees and understands everything and in many ways is Emma's refuge in the household. There is the personality of her son, Edo, as yet untouched by the ordeals of business life, more open in his personal feelings. And there is the overarching sense in which the Recchi family embodies a tradition that, like a church, requires devotion if not belief.

*I Am Love* is an amazing film. It is deep, rich, human. It is not about rich and poor but about old and new. It is about the ancient war between tradition and feeling. For this role Tilda Swinton learned to speak Italian with a Russian accent, as Tilda Swinton would, but her performance is nothing as trivial as a feat of learning. She evokes Emma as a woman who for years has accepted the needs of the Recchis, and discovers in a few days to accept her own needs. She must have been waiting a long time for Antonio, whoever he would be.

## I Am Number Four ★ ½

PG-13, 110 m., 2011

Alex Pettyfer (John), Dianna Agron (Sarah), Callan McAuliffe (Sam), Jake Abel (Mark James), Timothy Olyphant (Henri), Teresa Palmer (Number Six). Directed by D. J. Caruso and produced by Michael Bay. Screenplay by Alfred Gough, Miles Millar, and Marti Noxon.

*I Am Number Four* is shameless and unnecessary. That's sad, when a movie casts aside all shame, demonstrates itself willing to rip off anything that might attract audiences, and nevertheless fails. What we have here is a witless attempt to merge the *Twilight* formula with the Michael Bay formula. It ends with sexy human teenagers involved in an endless special effects battle with sexy alien teenagers who look like humans, in a high school and on its football field.

Let's pause for a moment to consider this apocalyptic battle. It is all special effects. None of it is physically possible. It might as well be a cartoon; it's essentially CGI animation intercut with brief bursts of inane dialogue. Brief, because the global action market doesn't much care about dialogue, and besides, when people start talking about something, you could run into the hazard of having actual characters in a plot. Minute after relentless minute, creatures both human and alien, whom we care nothing about, wage war and occasionally disintegrate into clouds of tiny pixels for no particular reason.

I like science fiction. The opening shot of *I Am Number Four* holds promise, as John (Alex Pettyfer), the narrator, explains that he is a Mogadorian, no doubt from a planet named

Mogador. Specifically, he is Mogadorian Number Four. Don't expect me to explain the Mogadorian numbering system. He is hiding out on planet Earth, and doing everything possible to disguise himself as a box office attraction like Edward Cullen. They have already killed Numbers One, Two, and Three.

Consider. The *Twilight* movies were about a handsome and sexy teenager who exerted a powerful attraction upon a virginal young girl, and yet held himself aloof because he was a vampire. Here John is a handsome and sexy teenager who is technically unavailable because he is an alien, although it appears that Mogador may luckily have evolved teenage boys indistinguishable from humans to such as Sarah (Dianna Agron). John has been on the lam around America to remain in hiding from those who would kill him, and is accompanied by his fellow Mogadorian Henri (Timothy Olyphant), who poses as his father and cautions him that his real father didn't die only to see John marry an Earth girl. Whether John has the option of returning to Mogador and settling down with a nice Mogadoress to raise Mogadorlings, I am not certain.

The high school elements in the plot revolve around John's popularity in some areas (he's an ace on a Jet Ski) and nonconformity in others (his palms function like high-powered searchlights). He is also free of the ordinary constraints of gravity, and can leap for dozens of yards and even fly. What this means is that the climactic battle scene can take place largely in the air, and Harry Potter's Quidditch games join the honor roll of the plundered.

There is, no doubt, a degree of identification available for the primary audience of *I Am Number Four.* Many teenage girls have perhaps imagined themselves in love with a handsome hunk with tousled blond hair, a three-day stubble, incredible athletic abilities, and hands that glow in the dark. That he is Not From Around Here makes him all the more attractive.

In the film we see native Mogadorians, whose faces are deeply scarred with gill-like extrusions. I am not completely sure if this is how John really looks and he has somehow morphed into teenager form, or if he was forced to flee Mogador because he looked like an alien Edward Cullen. I'm sure this is all spelled out in the movie. Sometimes I find it so very, very hard to care.

Now imagine *I Am Number Four* as a "novelization." There would be the setup, a little dialogue, and then pages and pages of violent action: "John leaped one hundred yards into the air and struck him with a deadly ray! An enemy fighter disintegrated into an ashy gray cloud of pixels! Number Six, her hair flowing in slow motion, whirled around and kicked the Mogadorian commander! 'Look out!' John shouted. 'Behind you!' cried Sarah."

This would quickly grow old. Why audiences enjoy watching protracted sequences of senseless action mystifies me, but they do. There is no strategic or spatial way in which the battle in *I Am Number Four* makes any sense. It is movement and conflict edited together in incomprehensible chaos.

Where is Mogador? Why did nine of its citizens flee to Earth? How did they do so? How is it they breathe our air, eat our food, and make such expert use of our grooming products? Why didn't the other Mogadorians say to hell with it and leave them on Earth? What is a Mogadorian life span? Given what we know about the time and distance involved in space travel, are these the same nine individuals who fled Mogador or their descendants after many generations in an interstellar ark? What's the story on those spotlights in their hands? In all modesty, I think my questions are more entertaining than this movie.

## The Ides of March ★ ★ ★

R, 100 m., 2011

Ryan Gosling (Stephen Meyers), George Clooney (Governor Mike Morris), Philip Seymour Hoffman (Paul Zara), Paul Giamatti (Tom Duffy), Marisa Tomei (Ida Horowicz), Jeffrey Wright (Senator Thompson), Evan Rachel Wood (Molly Stearns), Michael Mantell (Senator Pullman). Directed by George Clooney and produced by Clooney, Grant Heslov, and Bran Oliver. Screenplay by Clooney, Heslov, and Beau Willimon, based on the play *Farragut North* by Willimon.

*The Ides of March* tells me something I already knew: that the experience of running an American political campaign is crushing for body and soul. By the time a winning candidate survives more than a year of primaries and the general election, it is a wonder he has the remaining strength to govern. The film also raises the question of whether it is possible for any candidate to win and yet remain true to his original values.

Although the movie stars George Clooney, well known as a Democrat, it doesn't target or even really consider Republicans. It takes place entirely within a Democratic primary campaign, and although our feelings about who is good and bad may evolve, they're all Democrats.

The central character is Stephen Meyers (Ryan Gosling), who as a press secretary is required to more or less lie as an occupation. He works for Governor Mike Morris (Clooney), an idealistic liberal contesting the Ohio primary. Philip Seymour Hoffman plays Paul Zara, his seasoned campaign manager; Michael Mantell plays Senator Pullman, his opponent; and Paul Giamatti plays Tom Duffy, Pullman's campaign manager. A strong cast. Perhaps because the screenplay is based on a play (*Farragut North* by Beau Willimon), it contains some front-of-the-stage monologues that Hoffman and Giamatti make plausible under the closer scrutiny of a camera.

All of these men, except young Stephen Meyers, are realists. They're cynical, compromised, and sometimes underhanded, but all in the cause of something they believe in. The Gosling character believes mostly in himself. Like many staff members of powerful men, he confuses reflected glory for the thing itself, and dreams not so much of Governor Morris winning as of being able to rise in the staff ranks and take over Zara's job.

This all happens in the pressure-cooker atmosphere of a primary, where the big picture is painted in tiny vignettes: campaign stops, hand shaking, speech writing, sleep loss, and bone-deep exhaustion that drives the characters almost to the breaking point. Imprudent sex under these circumstances is explicable, and Stephen puts the moves on a young intern named Molly (Evan Rachel Wood). This allows him to use her naïveté to learn information she doesn't realize she should never, ever share. He also develops a cagey relationship with a journalist (Marisa Tomei), as they work each other for information.

The screenplay, written by Clooney, Grant Heslov, and Willimon, is ingenious in the way it meshes personal and political ambitions, especially when Duffy (Giamatti), the manager of the rival campaign, reaches out and tries to recruit Stephen over to his side. His motives are suspicious: Does he really want the guy, or does he know that a job offer is a useful ploy? Certainly Stephen is on the make and looking for openings to his advantage.

Clooney as director seems attracted to stories about smart men under pressure (*Good Night, and Good Luck*, *Confessions of a Dangerous Mind*). He draws back from action and plunges into intrigue. Here he conceals certain of Stephen's inner workings (some planned, some improvised) to great effect, as the young man reveals an amorality that surprises even the hardened pros he works under. The last shot of the film, a close-up of Ryan Gosling, held for a long time, is chilling.

The movie really reveals no new information. Now that campaign managers shuffle between cable news shows and write their own books, few secrets stay in smoke-filled rooms (and besides, nobody smokes). There isn't the feeling, as there was with *Primary Colors* or *Nixon*, that we might be getting the inside story on actual candidates. *The Ides of March* is more about the nature of modern media politics, and younger players who are strangers to idealism.

The movie's strength is in the acting, with Gosling once again playing a character with an insistent presence. In roles as different as this one and *Drive*, he has a focus that sees through others and zeroes in on his character's goals. That intense conviction works in many ways; remember him in *Lars and the Real Girl*, where he played a secretive loner who fell in love with a love doll and found this companion a help in reentering society.

Hoffman has a great scene here with Gosling, in which he discovers the true nature of his situation. Jeffrey Wright has a small but important role as Senator Thompson, whose influential endorsement cannot be bought but may be available for rental. Clooney the director brings his actor's experience to the job and attends closely to performance. The impression remains, however, that he believes this movie to be more of an exposé than it is. The next election is more than a year away and many people seem already worn down by it.

## The Illusionist ★ ★ ★ ★

PG, 90 m., 2010

With the voices of: Jean-Claude Donda (Illusionist), Eilidh Rankin (Alice). Directed by Sylvain Chomet and produced by Chomet and Bob Last. Screenplay by Chomet and Jacques Tati.

*The Illusionist* represents the magically melancholy final act of Jacques Tati's career. Tati, of course, was the tall Frenchman, bowing from the waist, pipe in mouth, often wearing a trench coat, pants too short, always the center of befuddlements. If you've seen *Mr. Hulot's Holiday*, you know who he was, and if you haven't, it belongs in your holding pattern.

Tati, who died in 1982, wrote the screenplay for this film but never made it. He intended it for live action. As the story goes, his daughter Sophie Tatischeff still had the script and handed it to Sylvain Chomet, who made the miraculously funny animated film *The Triplets of Belleville* (2003). Chomet has drawn it with a lightness and beauty worthy of an older, sadder Miyazaki story. Animation suits it. Live action would overwhelm its delicate fancy with realism.

The story involves a magician named Tatischeff who fails in one music hall after another, and ends up in Scotland, where at last he finds one fan: a young woman who idealizes him, moves in with him, tends to him, cooks and cleans, and would probably offer sex if he didn't abstemiously sleep on the couch. He's a good magician on a small scale, flawless at every trick except producing a rabbit from a hat. His problem there involves his frisky rabbit, which likes to sleep on Tatischeff's stomach at night. The rabbit makes it a practice during the act to pop up and peep around at inopportune moments.

Tatischeff finally ends up in Edinburgh, a city that has never looked more bleak and beautiful in a film. Time has passed him by. Audiences prefer pop groups to aging magicians. He reaches the lowest stage in his career, performing in a shop window. He remains quiet, reflective, almost indifferent to the girl (although he buys her a pretty frock).

If you recall the opening scenes of *Up*, you know that animation is sometimes more effective than live action for conveying the arc of a life. This magician does what he does very well, but there's no longer a purpose for him. Did Tati feel the same when he wrote this in the 1950s, before *Hulot* was a worldwide success?

Important to the charm of *The Illusionist* is the grace with which the character of Tatischeff has been drawn. He looks like Tati, but much more important, he has the inimitable body language. The polite formality, the deliberate movement, the hesitation, the diffidence. His world is an illusion, which he produces nightly from a hat.

Tati became a legendary man of the cinema, a perfectionist producing a small body of enormously ambitious films that can be described as meticulous silent comedies with sound. The major works are *Jour de Fete* (1949), the worldwide hit *Mr. Hulot's Holiday* (1953), *Mon Oncle* (1958), *Play Time* (1967), *Trafic* (1971), and *Parade* (1974). He was admired and beloved.

He was also flawed, and one area of concern involves his family. After *The Illusionist* played at Cannes 2010, I received a letter from his middle grandson, Richard Tatischeff Schiel McDonald, telling me that the Chomet version "greatly undermines both the artistry of my grandfather's original script whilst shamefully ignoring the deeply troubled personal story that lies at its heart."

Briefly, he writes of Tati, "in the script he wrestles with the notion of publicly acknowledging his eldest daughter, my mother, who he had under duress from his elder sister heartlessly abandoned during the Second World War." It is a fraught family story, and the full and fascinating letter is here: http://bit.ly/dkigRT.

Becoming aware of these facts, and how they were apparently sublimated in Tati's more fanciful tale, only adds interest to *The Illusionist.* However the film stands on its own, and however much it conceals the real life events that inspired it, it lives and breathes on its own, and as an extension of the mysterious whimsy of Tati.

## I Love You Phillip Morris ★ ★ ★ ½

R, 98 m., 2010

Jim Carrey (Steven Russell), Ewan McGregor (Phillip Morris), Leslie Mann (Debbie), Rodrigo Santoro (Jimmy), Michael Mandel (Cleavon). Directed by Glenn Ficarra and John Requa and produced by Andrew Lazar and Far Shariat. Screenplay by Ficarra and Requa, based on the book by Steve McVicker.

If you wanted to make a movie about the life of Steven Russell, you might start with this question: Can we get Jim Carrey? You would need an actor who can seem both instantly lovable and always up to no good. That *I Love You Phillip Morris* is based on a true story is relevant only because it is too preposterous to be fiction. Russell is a con man, and his lifelong con is selling himself to himself.

That process begins when he discovers he isn't who he thought he was. His parents tell him he is adopted. My notion is that if you love your parents and they tell you you're adopted, you'd love them even more. It doesn't work that way for Steven Russell. Once that rug has been pulled from beneath his feet, he sets about creating a new reality for himself. He becomes a police officer. He marries Debbie (Leslie Mann), as wholesome as a toothpaste model. They have two children. He plays the church organ. He is a poster boy for truth, justice, and the American Way.

Continuing to seek truth, he discovers the identity of his birth mother. Shall we say she is a disappointment. After a traumatic accident, he has time in the hospital to reflect that his entire life has been constructed out of other people's spare parts. Who is he *really*? He decides he is gay. Not only gay but flamboyantly, stereotypically gay, and soon living with a Latin lover (Rodrigo Santoro) on Miami's South Beach. He begins to pass checks and defraud credit cards to finance their heady lifestyle.

Now when I wrote "he decides he is gay," did some of you think you don't "decide" to be gay—you simply are, or are not? I believe that's the case almost all the time. I'm not completely sure about Steven Russell. The movie reveals him as an invention, an improvisation, constantly in rehearsal to mislead the world because he has a *need* to deceive. Who could be less like a churchgoing cop and family man than a South Beach playboy? Does he like gay sex? Yes, and very energetically indeed. Does he like straight sex? You bet he does. He can sell himself on anything. I think gay sex is the easier sell.

The method of *I Love You Phillip Morris* provides great quantities of plot and then holds them at arm's length. It isn't really about plot. Plots are scenarios that characters are involved in. Steven Russell improvises his own scenario, so that most of what happens is his own handiwork in one way or another. Carrey makes the role seem effortless; he deceives as spontaneously as others breathe.

The authorities have a supporting role. He keeps breaking the law, and they keep arresting him. After he's imprisoned for theft and fraud, life changes when he's assigned a new cell mate: Phillip Morris (a blond Ewan McGregor as we've never seen him before). Steven falls in love. Or perhaps, as the song has it, he falls in love with love. After he's released, he creates a new persona, a lawyer, and floats this deception with a single shred of proof to pull off a stunt that gets Phillip out of prison. McGregor rises to this occasion like a dazzled ingénue.

Phillip is in love with Steven; that's not in doubt. But he is slow to understand the depth and complexity of Steven's fabrications. He's a sweet kid with a naive Southern accent, and not the brightest bulb on the tree. He's a bystander as Steven steals a fortune from a health care organization that has possibly never even employed him. Steven is soon back behind bars, and the movie unfolds into a series of increasingly audacious and labyrinthine confidence schemes.

All of this, as I said, is based on Russell's own story, as written by Steve McVicker of the *Houston Press*. Russell impersonated doctors, lawyers, FBI agents, and the CFO of a health care company. He convinced prison officials he had died of AIDS and later successfully faked a heart attack. He escaped from jail four times (hint: always on Friday the 13th). He is now serving 144 years in Texas in maximum security and solitary confinement, which seems a bit much for a man who never killed anyone and stole a lot less money than the officers of Enron.

## The Imaginarium of Doctor Parnassus ★ ★ ★

PG-13, 122 m., 2010

Heath Ledger (Tony), Johnny Depp (Imaginarium Tony 1), Jude Law (Imaginarium Tony 2), Colin Farrell (Imaginarium Tony 3), Christopher Plummer (Dr. Parnassus), Andrew Garfield (Anton), Verne Troyer (Percy), Lily Cole (Valentina), Tom Waits (Mr. Nick). Directed by Terry Gilliam and produced by Amy Gilliam, Terry Gilliam, Samuel Hadida, and William Vince. Screenplay by Terry Gilliam and Charles McKeown.

The traditional motto at Second City is Something Wonderful Right Away, and maybe Terry Gilliam has the words displayed on his mirror when he shaves every morning. He has never faltered. *The Imaginarium of Doctor Parnassus* could be seen as a sideshow version of his own life, with him playing the role of the pitchman who lures you into his fantasies. That they may seem extravagant and overheated, all smoke and mirrors, is, after all, in the nature of a pitchman's fantasies.

The story in Gilliam's fevered new film is all over the map as usual, but this time there's a reason for it. His wild inventions in character, costumes, and CGI effects are accounted for by a plot that requires revolving worlds. Elements of this plot were made necessary by the tragic death of Heath Ledger halfway into the shooting, but the plot itself, I think, was in place from the first.

It involves a bizarre, threadbare traveling show that unfolds out of a rickety old wagon in rundown pockets of London occupied mostly by drunks and grotesques. The show consists of the (very, very) old Dr. Parnassus (Christopher Plummer) perching ominously on a stool while his barker, Anton (Andrew Garfield), his daughter, Valentina (Lily Cole), and his angry dwarf, Percy (Verne Troyer), try to perform for an unruly handful of lager louts.

Percy and Anton save the life of a man hanging from a bridge. Why only they can perform this task is wisely not explained. The man on the rope is Tony (Heath Ledger). I know. He joins the show, is appalled by its archaic form, and suggests updates. The reason it's creaky is that Dr. Parnassus is many centuries old, having made a pact with Satan (Tom Waits, as usual) to live forever on condition that Satan can possess his daughter when she turns sixteen. You have to admit, Dr. Parnassus didn't rush into reproduction. Of course, he wants out of the deal. Satan frequently runs into credit payment risks.

Tony, it develops, can enter/evoke/control/create strange worlds on the other side of a looking glass on the shabby stage. In these worlds anything goes, which is always to Gilliam's liking. CGI allows the director and his designers to run riot, which they do at a gallop, and some wondrous visions materialize.

I believe Ledger was intended to be the guide through all of these. But Gilliam apparently completed filming all the outer-world London scenes, Ledger returned to New York for R&R, and the rest is sad history. Gilliam replaced him by casting Johnny Depp, Jude Law, and Colin Farrell as the Tonys of Imaginariums 1 through 3 and offering no other explanation, as indeed with Imaginariums he isn't required to do. Depp looks the most like Ledger, but it's a melancholy fact that Farrell steals the role.

My problem with Terry Gilliam's pictures is that they lack a discernible story line. I don't require A-B-C, Act 1–2–3, but I do rather appreciate having some notion of a film's own rules. Gilliam indeed practices Something Wonderful Right Away, and you get the notion that if a bright idea pops into his head, he feels free to write it into his screenplay under the Cole Porter Rule (Anything Goes). Knowing my history with Gilliam, whom I always want to like more than I do, I attended the Cannes screening of *Dr. Parnassus* in order to be baffled, which I was, and then the Chicago press screening, where I had an idea what was coming and tried to reopen my mind. Gilliam is, you understand, a nice man, and has never committed the sin of failing to amaze.

Now what I see are a group of experienced actors gamely trying to keep their heads while all about are losing theirs. Can it be easy to play one-third of a guide to one-third of an arbitrary world? You just have to plunge in. Ledger himself, who makes Tony relatively grounded in the "real" world, must have been prepared to do the same, and would have lent the story more continuity. Still, this movie is an Imaginarium indeed. The best approach is to sit there and let it happen to you: See it in the moment and not with long-term memory, which seems to be what Dr. Parnassus does. It keeps his mind off Satan's plans for his daughter.

## IMAX: Hubble 3-D ★ ★ ★

G, 45 m., 2010

Leonardo DiCaprio (Narrator). Featuring the astronauts Scott D. Altman, Andrew J. Feustel, Michael T. Good, John M. Grunsfeld, Gregory C. Johnson, Michael J. Massimino, and K. Megan McArthur. Directed, written, and produced by Toni Myers.

When I think of space travel, I get a sort of mental tingle. It intrigues and frightens me. I have nightmares, possibly illustrated by *2001*, in which the astronaut Poole has his tether clipped by HAL 9000 and goes tumbling away into the immensity. Mercifully, his oxygen tube has been cut, so he will quickly be dead. I remember, too, a science fiction story that curdled my blood about an astronaut who is lost in space *with* a full tank of oxygen, and drifts into the void, his vision field filled with the universe.

Then you would know how small you were, how powerless and insignificant. When the end comes, it would be good to be set adrift into space, I think, with time for reflection, or perhaps madness. Fatal, yes, but so much less boring than the ceiling of a hospital room. I have always been intensely interested in thoughts of space.

*IMAX: Hubble 3-D* offers two categories of images, both awesome. One involves footage filmed on board the space shuttle Atlantis on a mission to repair the Hubble Space Telescope one last time. The other involves a 3-D rendering of some of Hubble's photographs of the cosmos. It's remarkable how casual the astronauts are, joking and performing for the camera. Then we see space walks in which they drift weightless to replace, adjust, and tune up Hubble. There is nothing there but the shuttle, Hubble, Earth, and the abyss. If they lose a tool, it is lost . . . forever, or until it is found millions and millions of years from now in a galaxy far away.

The fact that this footage exists at all is enough to justify it. Someone like me would need to see it. I would be happier if the astronauts had been less confident and casual. I suppose that's the astronaut culture. Could they have acted? Pretended to be tense, scared, deadly serious? They're like the crew on the *Star Trek* command deck, which most of the time might as well be controlling the traffic grid of a subway system.

The important thing to understand about the 3-D photography of stars is that they are too far away to give any true idea of their distance. Almost all of the objects in the universe are very, very far apart. What they did was take Hubble photographs of small and old (therefore young) slices of the sky and use spectrum analysis and a computer to separate the stars according to their distance. Although the narration by Leonardo DiCaprio doesn't mention this, the third dimension we're regarding is really time, not space. As the viewpoint moves forward toward galaxies, we are hurtling at unimaginable speed toward light that originated longer and longer ago.

Beyond the most distant stars, at the end of our ability to see, there is black nothingness. If you stood there and looked outward, what would you see? A logical question. The answer is: more universe. Not another universe, but this one, because space is curved, you see, and therefore has no edge. This answer satisfies me, although I do not understand it and cannot picture how space can be curved. I understand how a circle has no beginning and no end, and that helps.

So these are thoughts I had while watching *IMAX: Hubble 3-D*. A movie like this can get you thinking.

## Immortals ★ ½

R, 110 m., 2011

Henry Cavill (Theseus), Mickey Rourke (King Hyperion), Stephen Dorff (Stavros), Luke Evans (Zeus), Isabel Lucas (Athena), Freida Pinto (Phaedra), John Hurt (Old Man), Kellan Lutz (Poseidon). Directed by Tarsem Singh and produced by Mark Canton and Gianni Nunnari. Screenplay by Charley Parlapanides and Vlas Parlapanides.

*Immortals* is without doubt the best-looking awful movie you will ever see. Eiko Ishioka's costume designs alone deserve an Oscar nomination. "They weren't at all historically accurate," grumbled a woman in the elevator after the sneak preview, as if lots of documentation exists about the wardrobes of the gods. She added: "I guess that's what we deserve for using free tickets we got at a Blackhawks game."

One image after another is gob-smacking, including the early one in which a prison cell of thick granite, buried inside a mountain, holds the imprisoned Titans. We see them from above, chained standing upright, their teeth clamped onto iron rods. They've been this way for *eons.* Other images include Greek villages carved from the sides of precipitous cliffs, spectacular temples and thrones, and a startling shot of the Oracles dressed in towering red costumes against a slate background. You look at these visuals and drink them in.

Alas, the movie makes next to no sense. It involves, in a very broad sense, the attempt by King Hyperion (Mickey Rourke) to conquer Greece and the battle to stop him led by a plucky peasant named Theseus (Henry Cavill). Much depends on the possession of the hidden Epirus Bow, which can fire arrows that materialize from thin air and guide themselves to a target. This sounds great, but when you're shooting arrows at tens of thousands of enemies, your fingers could get bloody pulling that bowstring.

The movie is sometimes completely CGI, and there must not be many scenes with no computer work at all. That allows for lots and lots of towering cliffs. In fact, all of Greece seems to be on the edge of a drop of hundreds or thousands of feet, although sometimes in the far distance we see flatlands, which are no doubt where the peasants live. No one is on the cliffs but gods, heroes, Oracles, warriors, and suchlike. These characters all seem compelled to live as close to the edge as possible, where they run nimbly, survey the horizon, push one another, and never look down to check their footing. You know how nervous that makes me get. One legendary character does dive into the sea, turning into a kind of missile and impacting like a bomb, creating a giant tsunami. You'd think the waves would wipe out civilization, but the payoff seems mostly when everybody finds themselves covered with mud.

There are no end of battle scenes, interminable and incomprehensible, in which beheading and skewering are routine. Theseus is so strong he actually stabs one enemy with the end of his pike and tosses him with great force against a rock wall. Try that sometime. I was encouraged by this because the actor, Henry Cavill, will soon be playing Superman, and here we see he can do that stuff for real.

There is a brief love scene involving Phaedra (Freida Pinto) and Theseus, of which I can say, as I have before, that Freida Pinto really has a lovely face. Also many scenes starring John Hurt, who plays, as he seems to in half the movies these days, an old man who's been there, done that, and knows it all. I also enjoyed Mickey Rourke doing his smash-everyone routine.

But a lot of the time I had no idea what was going on. Characters would turn up for the first time, seem terrifically important, and disappear. If at many moments I had stopped the film and asked anybody around me, "Who is that, and what are they doing and why?" I think they'd have been stuck for an answer. There are such puzzles as why an army stretches the width of the horizon and has to funnel four abreast through a narrow opening in a wall. And call me an idiot, but when they found the three people trapped inside the giant (golden? brass?) bull while being slow-roasted, I had no idea how they got there or who they were.

The movie was directed by Tarsem Singh, of whose wonderful *The Fall* (2006) I wrote: "It is a mad folly, an extravagant visual orgy, a free-fall from reality into uncharted realms. . . . [Tarsem] has made a movie that you might want to see for no other reason than because it exists. There will never be another like it." Now there is.

## I'm Still Here ★ ★ ★

NO MPAA RATING, 108 m., 2010

Joaquin Phoenix, Antony Langdon, Sean Combs, David Letterman, and many others. A documentary directed by Casey Affleck and produced by Affleck, Joaquin Phoenix, and Amanda White.

A mind is a terrible thing to waste. The tragedy of Joaquin Phoenix's self-destruction has been made into *I'm Still Here*, a sad and painful documentary that serves little useful purpose other than to pound another nail into the coffin. Here is a gifted actor who apparently by his own decision has brought desolation upon his head. He was serious when he said he would never act again. He was serious when he announced a career as a hip-hop artist. He wasn't goofing when he was on the Letterman show. He was flying into pieces.

For reasons that are unclear and sidestepped, this process was documented on video by the actor Casey Affleck, who is married to Joaquin's sister Summer. It's not well done technically—the image and sound are bad—but it has the advantage of access to private and tormented moments. After Phoenix imploded during a famous appearance on Letterman, we see him leaving a limousine in Central Park, crawling up an embankment into some shrubbery, and screaming that he has destroyed his life, his music sucks, he will never be able to act again, and "I'm totally f—ked!"

All of this is true. At least we must assume it is. If this film turns out to *still* be part of an elaborate hoax, I'm going to be seriously pissed. Actually, there are subtle signs it might be. The scene in Central Park: Is it a little too perfect dramatically? The scenes of cocaine sniffing, the nude parties including Joaquin's assistant Antony Langdon and two hookers: Were they really possible with a director, cinematographer, and sound man in the room? Would Casey Affleck release this devastating film with the acquiescence of his wife?

Apparently so. It exists, it was released, I've seen it, and Joaquin Phoenix, as the title assures us, is still here. One doubts he will be walking the red carpet if the film has a premiere. It documents a train wreck. A luxury train—one carrying Phoenix, his several personal assistants, his agent, his publicist, and apparently not one single friend who isn't on salary. A train that flies off the tracks and tumbles into the abyss.

Phoenix comes across as a narcissist interested only in himself. He is bored with acting. He was only a puppet. He can no longer stand where he's told, wear what he's given, say what is written. It's not him. He has lost contact with his inner self. He allows that true self to emerge here as a fearsomely bearded, deliberately shabby, chain-smoking egotist who screams at his patient assistants, blames himself on everyone else, and has deluded himself into thinking that there is a future in his dreadful hip-hop lyrics.

He thinks fame and fortune are due him. He earned them in his acting career, yes, but he will no longer act. He expects Sean Combs to *want* to produce his CD, although Combs has worked hard to earn the respect that Phoenix manifestly doesn't deserve. He's a little surprised that Combs remains sensible during their negotiations, expecting to be *paid* for his services and oh, you know, studios, musicians, sound engineers, those kinds of things. He stands in the middle of an airport, puzzled that no limousine awaits. He flies to Obama's inauguration, not invited, and doesn't make it outside of his hotel room. He is mystified that he may no longer be able to afford his Los Angeles home.

Phoenix's hip-hop performances are incomprehensible. The lyrics that we hear are lead-footed and stupid. During one performance he races from the stage and vomits copiously. He is enabled by his saintly staff, including Langdon, who has been with him for years and appears to be paid as a twenty-four-hour companion, since it's doubtful anyone would want to be with this man for free. Antony, we learn, has recently become a recovering alcoholic.

Which leads us to Phoenix's substance abuse problems. He doesn't drink much in the film. He smokes a great deal of what looks like pot. He says he scored cocaine in New York, and hardly seems to be using it for the first time. He has no onscreen moment when he appears clean or sober. Whether drugs alone could account for his condition, or whether mental illness is also involved, is not for me to say.

But I will say this: Joaquin Phoenix is a good actor. I was astonished by his performance as Johnny Cash in *Walk the Line* (2005). He was so good in other films, including the superb *Reservation Road* (2007), *Two Lovers* (2008), and *Gladiator* (2000), although I was unenthusiastic about the film. Whether he wants to be an actor is his business. Many great and worthy people have been, and in this film we see or hear about Paul Newman, Sean Penn, Jack Nicholson, and for that matter Danny DeVito (whom Phoenix dismisses).

I have hope that if Phoenix ever cleans up his body and mind, he can be restored and can be happy again. See how Robert Downey Jr. and Dennis Hopper came back from the edge of the grave. We do not desperately need another actor, but Joaquin is imprisoned within his illness, and he desperately needs to get well. If he wants a career as a singer—well, why not country music? In *Walk the Line* he proved he has a talent for it. In *I'm Still Here* all he proves is that he is hurtling toward the same pointless oblivion that killed his brother River. It is a waste of the privilege of life.

*Note: Regarding the film's three-star rating: It could be one, it could be four. What do stars have to do with it?*

## In a Better World ★ ★ ½

R, 113 m., 2011

Mikael Persbrandt (Anton), Trine Dyrholm (Marianne), Ulrich Thomsen (Claus), Markus Rygaard (Elias), William Johnk Nielsen (Christian), Kim Bodnia (Lars), Evans Muthini (Big Man). Directed by Susanne Bier and produced by Peter Aalbaek Jensen. Screenplay by Anders Thomas Jensen.

A new book by a Cambridge University scholar suggests that a lack of empathy is at the root of all cruelty. People are not intrinsically evil, argues Simon Baron-Cohen, but some lack the ability to identify with what others are feeling: "People who lack empathy see others as mere objects."

Although I doubt Susanne Bier knew of this book when she made *In a Better World*, it plays like a demonstration of the same insight. In parallel stories set in Denmark and Africa, it considers characters who act with cruelty and those who deliberately seek to act with empathy, and poses some moral choices for those who fall somewhere in the middle of the spectrum.

*In a Better World*, which won this year's Academy Award for best foreign film, centers on two boys and their fathers. Elias (Markus Rygaard) and Christian (William Johnk Nielsen) meet at the school where Christian has just transferred. Elias is a cute kid with braces, and when he's picked on by the school bully, Christian defends him in a sudden and bloody way. "Nobody will pick on me again," he explains.

Now pull back a step to their fathers. Elias's dad is Anton (Mikael Persbrandt), who commutes between Denmark and an unnamed African country, where he operates a free medical clinic. To his care come victims of all sorts, including women savagely sliced by the powerful local Big Man (Evans Muthini). Christian's dad is Claus (Ulrich Thomsen), whose wife has died of cancer and left Christian resenting his father.

Anton is often in Africa, and Claus is often in London. The two boys bond. One day when Anton is home, he and Elias see a foul-tempered local man named Lars (Kim Bodnia) pushing around people who innocently offended him. Anton steps in, and Lars slaps him. Thinking this over, Anton decides to set an example to his son, and takes him to Lars's auto shop for what is intended as a nonviolent confrontation. Lars is incapable of such a thing.

Christian, very inward, very intense, earlier defended Elias against the schoolyard bully, and now devises a plan for them to gain revenge against Lars. Meanwhile, back in Africa, Anton's clinic receives an emergency patient: Big Man, with an ugly, festering leg wound.

No more about the plot. What Susanne Bier does is cut between all of these stories to contrast the kinds of people who are instinctively cruel and those who are instinctively kind. The outcomes of the parallel stories are unpredictable, although they follow a certain logic.

I admired her *Things We Lost in the Fire* and her Danish and American versions of *Brothers*, but here her method is too foregrounded. The African events in particular don't fit organically into the rest of the film, playing more like a contrived contrast. The story of the boys works well (they're both good actors), and their fathers are well drawn and seen with sympathy. There's also an estranged mother who is drawn into the unhappiness.

There are two strong stories here, in Africa and Denmark. Either could have made a film. Intercut in this way, they seem too much like self-conscious parables. No doubt the film's noble intentions appealed to the Academy voters, but this seems to me the weakest of the five nominees. What does the title suggest? That in a better world there would not be such cruelty? True, no doubt.

## Incendies ★ ★ ★ ½

R, 130 m., 2011

Lubna Azabal (Nawal Marwan), Melissa Desormeaux-Poulin (Jeanne Marwan), Maxim Gaudette (Simon Marwan), Remy Girard (Notary Jean Lebel). Directed by Denis Villeneuve and produced by Luc Dery and Kim McCraw. Screenplay by Villeneuve, based on the play by Wajdi Mouawad.

After the death of their mother, twins in Montreal are called to the office of her employer. She had gone to work for him some twenty years ago in Canada after escaping sectarian violence and rage in a nation not unlike Lebanon. She left for her children, they learn, two letters. Jeanne (Melissa Desormeaux-Poulin) is asked to give hers to the father they never knew. Simon (Maxim Gaudette) is told to give his to a brother they didn't know they had.

This is a plot for a thriller, really, and Denis Villeneuve's Oscar-nominated *Incendies* doesn't shy away from that truth. But it wants to be much more than a thriller, and succeeds in demonstrating how senseless and futile it is to hate others because of their religion. Most people do not choose their religions but have them forced upon themselves by birth, and the lesson of *Incendies* is that an accident of birth is not a reason for hatred.

The heroine who comes to this conclusion is the author of the two letters, Nawal (Lubna Azabal), the twins' mother. Jeanne travels to the Middle East to carry out her mother's wishes. Simon stays resentfully in Canada until later in the story. In flashbacks spurred by Jeanne's meetings and conversations, we learn of Nawal's early life. Born a Christian, she fell in love with a Muslim. This was impossible for both of them in that time and place. It led her on a romantic, religious, and political odyssey, and inspired her to do unthinkable things.

All about her, others were also doing the unthinkable. People who were not murderers in their nature killed others and justified it, on both sides, in the names of their gods. And when enough people had died, they no longer needed their gods because they sought personal or tribal revenge. A season of murder by fanatics broadened into years of retribution by bystanders who took up their guns. Villeneuve is especially chilling when he shows young adolescents with rifles, killing others their own age when neither shooter nor target is old enough to understand the gift of life.

The plot of *Incendies* is based on a play by Wajdi Mouawad, described as consisting of poetic monologues. The screenplay by Villeneuve refashions the action in a way more suited to a film, where it is often better to show something than to evoke its mental image. The underlying story here could, with a few adjustments, be a noir set in any country, taking its choice of all the sad justifications men find for murder.

In its Middle Eastern setting, the film takes on a contemporary feel, and the scenes of battle, rape, and torture are concise and pitiless. The performance of Lubna Azabal, who plays Nawal over a range of years, is never less than compelling; she helps us understand in a visceral way why she acts as she does—as she must—under the circumstances she is unlucky enough to inherit. And Villeneuve's writing and direction do an effective job of making clear events that might have become cloudy. The specific way, in cryptic dialogue, that he reveals his film's shocking secret is flawless.

The film's ending, which you will not learn from me, is stunning in its impact. I am not sure it quite works out in terms of strict logic, but logic can be forgotten when the purpose is revelation. And that revelation, when it comes, lays bare the pathos of "justified" murder and the pathology of cruelty.

I am left with a question you might want to ask yourself after seeing the film: What was the mother's purpose in leaving the letters for her children? Yes, we can see, they deserve to know the truth about their father and their brother. She could have told them—either in life or, for that matter, in the letters. By sealing the letters she assigns them a mission that could easily have failed. If they had not found the recipients, they would not have learned the truth. Then what purpose did the letters serve?

Well, of course they provided the motive for Jeanne's journey, and later for Simon's. They're essentially MacGuffins. That's why I'm not so bothered by the device. A MacGuffin is a way of setting a story into motion, and *Incendies* tells a shocking one.

## Inception ★ ★ ★ ★

PG-13, 148 m., 2010

Leonardo DiCaprio (Dom Cobb), Ken Watanabe (Saito), Joseph Gordon-Levitt (Arthur), Marion Cotillard (Mal), Ellen Page (Ariadne), Tom Hardy (Eames), Cillian Murphy (Robert Fischer), Tom Berenger (Browning), Michael Caine (Miles), Dileep Rao (Yusuf). Directed by Christopher Nolan and produced by Nolan and Emma Thomas. Screenplay by Nolan.

It's said that Christopher Nolan spent ten years writing his screenplay for *Inception*. That must have involved prodigious concentration, like playing blindfold chess while walking a tightwire. The film's hero tests a young architect by challenging her to create a maze, and Nolan tests us with his own dazzling maze. We have to trust him that he can lead us through because much of the time we're lost and disoriented. Nolan must have rewritten this story time and again, finding that every change had a ripple effect down through the whole fabric.

The story can either be told in a few sentences, or not told at all. Here is a movie immune to spoilers: If you knew how it ended, that would tell you nothing unless you knew how it got there. And telling you how it got there would produce bafflement. The movie is all about process, about fighting our way through enveloping sheets of reality and dream, reality within dreams, dreams without reality. It's a breathtaking juggling act, and Nolan may have considered his *Memento* (2000) a warm-up; he apparently started this screenplay while filming that one. It was the story of a man with short-term memory loss, and the story was told backward.

Like the hero of that film, the viewer of *Inception* is adrift in time and experience. We can never even be quite sure what the relationship between dream time and real time is. The hero explains that you can never remember the beginning of a dream, and that dreams that seem to cover hours may last only a short time. Yes, but you don't know that when you're dreaming. And what if you're inside another man's dream? How does your dream time synch with his? What do you really know?

Cobb (Leonardo DiCaprio) is a corporate raider of the highest order. He infiltrates the minds of other men to steal their ideas. Now he is hired by a powerful billionaire to do the opposite: to *introduce* an idea into a rival's mind, and do it so well he believes it is his own. This has never been done before; our minds are as alert to foreign ideas as our immune system is to pathogens. The rich man, named Saito (Ken Watanabe), makes him an offer he can't refuse, an offer that would end Cobb's forced exile from home and family.

Cobb assembles a team, and here the movie relies on the well-established procedures of all heist movies. We meet the people he will need to work with: Arthur (Joseph Gordon-Levitt), his longtime associate; Eames (Tom Hardy), a master at deception; Yusuf (Dileep Rao), a master chemist. And there is a new recruit, Ariadne (Ellen Page), a brilliant young architect who is a prodigy at creating spaces. Cobb also goes to touch base with his father-in-law, Miles (Michael Caine), who knows what he does and how he does it. These days Michael Caine need only appear on a screen and we assume he's wiser than any of the other characters. It's a gift.

But wait. Why does Cobb need an architect to create spaces in dreams? He explains to her. Dreams have a shifting architecture, as we all know; where we seem to be has a way of shifting. Cobb's assignment is the *inception* (or birth, or wellspring) of a new idea in the mind of another young billionaire, Robert Fischer Jr. (Cillian Murphy), heir to his father's empire. Saito wants him to initiate ideas that will lead to the surrender of his rival's corporation. Cobb needs Ariadne to create a deceptive maze space in Fischer's dreams so that (I think) new thoughts can slip in unperceived. Is it a coincidence that Ariadne is named for the woman in Greek mythology who helped Theseus escape from the Minotaur's labyrinth?

Cobb tutors Ariadne on the world of dream infiltration, the art of controlling dreams and navigating them. Nolan uses this as a device for tutoring us as well. And also as the occasion for some of the movie's astonishing special effects, which seemed senseless in the trailer but now fit right in. The most impressive to me takes place (or seems to) in Paris, where the city literally rolls back on itself like a roll of linoleum tile.

Protecting Fischer are any number of gun-wielding bodyguards, who may be working like the mental equivalent of antibodies; they seem alternatively real and figurative, but whichever they are, they lead to a great many gunfights, chase scenes, and explosions, which is the way movies depict conflict these days. So skilled is Nolan that he actually got me involved in one of his chases, when I thought I was relatively immune to scenes that have become so standard. That was because I cared about who was chasing and being chased.

If you've seen any advertising at all for the film, you know that its architecture has a way of disregarding gravity. Buildings tilt. Streets coil. Characters float. This is all explained in the narrative. The movie is a perplexing labyrinth without a simple through-line and is sure to inspire truly endless analysis on the Web.

Nolan helps us with an emotional thread. The reason Cobb is motivated to risk the dangers of inception is because of grief and guilt involving his wife, Mal (Marion Cotillard), and their two children. More I will not (in a way, cannot) say. Cotillard beautifully embodies the wife in an idealized way. Whether we are seeing Cobb's memories or his dreams is difficult to say—even, literally, in the last shot. But she makes Mal function as an emotional magnet, and the love between the two provides an emotional constant in Cobb's world, which is otherwise ceaselessly shifting.

*Inception* works for the viewer like the world itself worked for Leonard, the hero of *Memento.* We are always in the Now. We have made some notes while getting Here, but we are not quite sure where Here is. Yet matters of life, death, and the heart are involved—oh, and those multinational corporations, of course. And Nolan doesn't pause before using well-crafted scenes from spycraft or espionage, including a clever scheme on board a 747 (even explaining why it must be a 747).

The movies often seem to come from the recycling bin these days: sequels, remakes, franchises. *Inception* does a difficult thing. It is wholly original, cut from new cloth, and yet structured with action movie basics so it feels like it makes more sense than (quite possibly) it does. I thought there was a hole in *Memento*: How does a man with short-term memory loss remember he has short-term memory loss? Maybe there's a hole in *Inception*, too, but I can't find it. Christopher Nolan reinvented *Batman.* This time he isn't reinventing anything. Yet few directors will attempt to recycle *Inception.* I think when Nolan left the labyrinth, he threw away the map.

## In Darkness ★ ★ ½

R, 143 m., 2012

Robert Wieckiewicz (Leopold Socha), Benno Furmann (Mundek Margulies), Agnieszka Grochowska (Klara Keller), Maria Schrader (Paulina Chiger), Herbert Knaup (Ignacy Chiger), Marcin Bosak (Yanek Grossmann), Kinga Preis (Wanda Socha). Directed by Agnieszka Holland and produced by Wojciech Danowski, Marc-Daniel Dichant, Eric Jordan, Patrick Knippel, Juliusz Machulski, Steffen Reuter, and Paul Stephens. Screenplay by David F. Shamoon, based on the book *In the Sewers of Lvov* by Robert Marshall.

*In Darkness* is yet another movie in which Jews escape death in the Holocaust through the actions of a gentile with a conscience. They survive because he helps them hide in the sewers of Lvov; that's bad luck for the audience, which has to peer for too long into dim, rat-infested shadows and endure standard melodramatic typecasting. Is there anyone who still requires this lesson in the evil of the Nazis and the resilience of human nature? *Schindler's List* (1993) said everything this film has to say, and much more. It was better directed, better written, better acted, and for that matter, more entertaining.

Is that a sacrilege, that I praise a Holocaust movie for being entertaining? The word doesn't imply that a movie need be cheerful. In my mind, entertainment in this genre springs from characters who are brought to full life, whom we care about, and who are set in a powerful story. My motto: "No good movie is depressing. All bad movies are depressing."

*In Darkness* is based on an extraordinary true story, told in the book *In the Sewers of Lvov* by Robert Marshall. It tells of a small group of Jews who were found hiding beneath the city streets by a man named Leopold Socha, a sewer worker. This Socha was no saint. An anti-Semite who before the war was exploiting and cheating Jews, he used the sewers to stash his loot, and realized he could make money by selling food and supplies to these survivors. He used his occupation as an excuse to come and go in the Nazi-controlled city, and even had a plausible reason to go down into the sewers.

The film doesn't inquire too closely into how Socha found adequate food, blankets, and medicine for so many people, at a time when such things were strictly rationed. The black market was his workplace, and he knew where to look. But the time came when this arrangement was no longer convenient or profitable for Socha. By then he had witnessed unspeakable atrocities carried out by the Nazis, and had come to know the Jews as individuals. He had a change of heart and became determined that they must survive no matter what. This involved many risks and much danger, and he was responsible for saving their lives.

So Socha was a flawed man rising to the occasion. The Jews were also not all saints, and one character in particular is such a rat that he leaves his wife behind to take his mistress into the sewers, and then abandons her after she becomes pregnant. Others are flawed in assorted very human ways, but together they and Socha boldly deceive the Nazis. This should be a more absorbing story than Agnieszka Holland, the director, is able to make of it. It must be said that Nazis in the movies seem strangely easy to deceive; how many movies have we seen in which heroic people escape them in tunnels, in disguise, in counterfeit ships, with bogus documents, or by concealing themselves in planes, trains, and automobiles?

It is not enough for a movie to be righteous. It must also be watchable. Recall, if you will, the opening of Quentin Tarantino's *Inglourious Basterds*, in which his Jewish heroine hides beneath floorboards while a Nazi sadist toys with his knowledge that she is there. The movie had no particular gravitas, but it was spine-tingling. *In Darkness* has the best of intentions, but is a boring dirge, lingering far too long in sewers and wringing as much righteousness as possible out of scenes so dimly lit they border on obscurity. It is curious that these desperate characters are made to engage in so much sex that we become distracted by how uncomfortable it must be.

The movie was nominated for an Oscar in the category of best foreign language film. It was a completely safe nomination for a film that is very long, very dark, against Nazis, and, of course, "based on a true story." Why Holland or anyone else would feel the need to make it after seeing *Schindler's List* I cannot say.

## In Memoriam ★ ★ ★

NO MPAA RATING, 101 m., 2011

Ian Forester (Jonathan), Kelly O'Sullivan (Kelly), Sadie Rogers (Sadie), Chris Carr (Ernest), Annabel Armour (Deborah), H. B. Ward (Tom), Hanna Dworkin (Nancy), Gerrit O'Neill (Jay Sr.). Directed by Stephen Cone and produced by Cone, Kathleen Cardoza, Keith Cardoza, and Gina LoPiccolo. Screenplay by Cone.

Someone sends Jonathan a snarky e-mail. Two naked students, apparently making love at the time, fell off the roof of a campus building in Chicago and were killed. Jonathan is appalled that anyone could find this funny. In the painfully true opening scenes of *In Memoriam*, he cannot get the deaths out of his mind. He's driven to begin what he calls an "investigation" into who the students were and what led them to the rooftop.

Stephen Cone's film *In Memoriam* never steps wrong in its first half hour, which I watched in fascination. Jonathan (Ian Forester) talks to the friends of the dead students and even to their parents (one set more willing than the other). It seems to him *wrong* that two people would die like that, in the midst of happiness. Forester is particularly effective in finding the right notes for his sorrow, which is not personal but existential.

I thought I vaguely recalled a real news item about deaths like that, but I couldn't find it online. What I did find were stories about four other students dying after falls from various campus buildings—one while doing a class project on "filming from high places." Those stories permitting comments included equally heartless snark. On the Internet, trolls can indulge the rotten festering of their shallow minds.

Jonathan eventually decides to reenact the last hours of the dead couple in the film. And that's where Cone's own film goes—not wrong, exactly, but in a less compelling direction. Jonathan recruits helpers, he finds a cameraman, he auditions actors, they all pitch in together on a tiny budget. They seem to be reasonable people engaged in a plausible undertaking. These elements are possibly not a million miles distant from what Cone himself did.

He's a sure-minded director, and *In Memoriam* is a touching film. Its final hour has convincing performances and avoids any horrors along the lines of "Hey, gang! Let's make a movie!" The scenes with the two sets of parents are acutely seen. There are some subplots, one involving a possible romance and the other a sublimated one, which are handled with admirable subtlety. A couple of moments with music seem somewhat obtrusive. The reality level is otherwise convincing.

And yet Cone never quite regains the force of his opening scene. I was thinking about that. How could he? I think perhaps Jonathan's initial obsession is so absorbing that we almost don't want it to find a release. If the opening Jonathan sequences were combined with one particular later moment, you would have an incredibly effective short film. Here is a paradox: Cone opens so well that he sets the bar too high for the rest of the film. "People die," one of his characters says. Yes, and mankind has spent a long time trying to deal with that fact, which has such an irrefutable finality.

## The Innkeepers ★ ★ ★

R, 100 m., 2012

Sara Paxton (Claire), Pat Healy (Luke), Kelly McGillis (Leanne Rease-Jones), Alison Bartlett (Gayle [Angry Mom]), Jake Schlueter (Young Boy), Lena Dunham (Barista), George Riddle (Old Man). Directed by Ti West and produced by West, Derek Curl, Larry Fessenden, and Peter Phok. Screenplay by West.

Truffaut said it's not possible to enjoy a film shot in the house where you were raised because you're always thinking about how they replaced the wallpaper. I had a little of that feeling during the new ghost movie *The Innkeepers*, which reminded me of the much-loved Boulderado in Boulder, Colorado. The movie is shot almost entirely within the (real) Yankee Pedlar Inn in Torrington, Connecticut. Both hotels are said to be haunted. I know someone who knew nothing about the Boulderado and saw a ghost standing in the closet of Room 506—and when we told the desk clerk, she said the ghost my friend saw matched the descriptions of earlier guests.

Cue the *Twilight Zone* theme. *The Innkeepers*, written, directed, and edited by Ti West, is set on the last weekend of the hotel, which is scheduled to close. The third floor is already shut down, and only four rooms are in use on the second floor, two of them occupied by twentyish Claire (Sara Paxton) and thirtyish Luke (Pat Healy). They're sorta friendly part-timers who've brought along a video camera and are determined to find evidence of haunting. It could go on Luke's Yankee Pedlar website, which he hopes to do some more work on one of these days.

One of the last guests is Leanne Rease-Jones (Kelly McGillis), an actress who has left her TV work to specialize in the supernatural. She's odd, standoffish, and a little hostile, until she takes pity on the kids and shares what she knows about the hotel, which is pretty much everything.

Ti West knows how to build suspense with quiet and timing. I admired his film *The House of the Devil* (2009), a POV story about a young college student who is hired as a companion for an old lady whose son (the spectral Tom Noonan) and his wife live way down at the end of a long, long road in the middle of a dark, dark forest. The architecture in both of these West films is like a character; the part-time innkeepers patrol long and lonely corridors, poke around in the basement, and stage-manage scenarios designed to coax any resident spirits to show themselves on video.

If this enterprise were treated in a high-voltage way, this would be another low-rent horror movie. West is more patient. He evokes the feeling of a long evening in a boring job, during which Claire and Luke speculate about ghosts as a way of amusing themselves. Their relationship, based on humor and enigmatic affection, would be entertaining enough that if no ghosts ever turned up, we would understand. *The Innkeepers* astonishingly creates characters who are not *only* specter-prey.

Supporting characters drift through. A mother angry with her husband; she brings along an obnoxious little boy. A waitress from a nearby coffee shop (Lena Dunham, director and star of *Tiny Furniture*). And then . . . someone . . . else turns up. Ghost movies like this, depending on imagination and craft, are much more entertaining than movies that scare you by throwing a cat at the camera.

## Inside Job ★ ★ ★ ★

PG-13, 108 m., 2010

A documentary narrated by Matt Damon. Directed by Charles Ferguson and produced by Ferguson and Audrey Marrs. Screenplay by Chad Beck and Adam Bolt.

I don't fully understand the workings of the derivatives and credit swaps we've heard so much about. But I'm learning. These are ingenious computer-driven schemes in which good money can be earned from bad debt, and Wall Street's Masters of the Universe pocket untold millions at the same time they bankrupt their investors and their own companies.

This process is explained in Charles Ferguson's *Inside Job*, an angry, well-argued documentary about how the American financial industry set out deliberately to defraud the ordinary American investor. The crucial error (in administrations of both parties) was to allow financial institutions to trade on their own behalf. Today many large trading banks are betting against their own customers.

In the real estate market, banks aggressively promoted mortgages to people who couldn't afford them. These were assembled in packages. They were carried on the books as tangible assets when they were worthless. The institutions assembling them hedged their loans by betting against them. When the mortgages failed, profits were made despite and because of their failure. This process has been targeted by financial reform measures, which many in both parties oppose because—well, lobbyists have persuaded them. There is no moral justification for how Wall Street functions today.

A Chicago group named Magnetar was particularly successful in creating such poisoned instruments for the sole purpose of hedging against them. Most of the big Wall Street players knew exactly what the "Magnetar Trade" was and welcomed it. The more mortgages failed, the more money they made. They actually continued to sell the bad mortgages to their clients as good investments. There was a famous exchange on C-SPAN as Senator Carl Levin grilled Daniel Sparks, head of the Goldman Sachs Mortgages Department, on why the company aggressively sold investments its own traders described to one another as "shitty." It was entertaining to watch Sparks maintain a facade of studious probity as Levin socked him with the word "shitty" again and again.

This Wall Street climate helps to explain one session of Senate testimony I have been fascinated by for almost two years: How Richard Fuld, CEO of Lehman Brothers, was able to defend the $484 million bonus he received after leading his firm into bankruptcy. Yes, the firm failed. But it failed because of poisoned investments it hedged against, and paid its executives bonuses on the profits from those hedges.

Lawrence McDonald, who wrote a book on Lehman's collapse, said on the *PBS NewsHour*: "Richard Fuld's driver would call Lehman Brothers, and one of the elevators in the southeast corner of the building would become frozen. A security guard would come over and hold it until Mr. Fuld arrived in the back door. . . . There's only fifteen feet where King Richard Fuld is exposed to the rabble, I guess you'd call us."

Some may say, well, he was the boss. I say, who the hell did he think he was? I've waited for elevators with my bosses, including Marshall Field and Rupert Murdoch. They seemed content enough that there *was* an elevator.

One of the most fascinating aspects of *Inside Job* involves the chatty on-camera insights of Kristin Davis, a Wall Street madam, who says the Street operated in a climate of abundant sex and cocaine for valued clients and the traders themselves. She's not talking about a few naughty boys. She says it was an accepted part of the corporate culture that hookers at $1,000 an hour and up were kept on retainer, that cocaine was the fuel, and that she and her girls didn't understand how some traders could even function on the trading floor after most nights.

That leads me to the matter of financial reform. We need it. We need to return to an era of transparency. We need to restore a market of investments that are what they seem to be. We need to deprive investment banks of the right to trade on behalf of their own accounts. We need to require them to work on behalf of their customers. In the days before deregulation, it was hard to get a mortgage from a bank that didn't believe you could make the payments. In recent years it was hard not to get one.

The bad mortgages were sliced and diced into so many derivatives that the banks themselves had no idea what paper they were holding. In one of the more refreshing moments during the housing meltdown, Representative Marcy Kaptur of Ohio advised her constituents: "If a bank forecloses on you, don't move, and demand they produce a copy of your mortgage. In many cases, they can't." She was prophetic; banks are now halting foreclosures all over the country.

Gene Siskel, who was a wise man, gave me the best investment advice I've ever received. "You can never outsmart the market, if that's what you're trying to do," he said. "Find something you love, for reasons you understand, that not everyone agrees with you about, and put your money in it." The stocks I thought of were Apple, Google, and Steak 'n Shake. I bought some shares. That was a long time ago. Reader, if I had invested every penny I had on Gene's advice, today I would be a Master of the Universe.

## Insidious ★ ★ ½

PG-13, 101 m., 2011

Patrick Wilson (Josh Lambert), Rose Byrne (Renai Lambert), Barbara Hershey (Lorraine Lambert), Lin Shaye (Elise Rainier), Ty Simpkins (Dalton Lambert), Angus Sampson (Tucker), Leigh Whannell (Specs). Directed by James Wan and produced by Jason Blum, Oren Peli, and Steven Schneider. Screenplay by Leigh Whannell.

*Insidious* is an affectionate visit to the Haunted House Movie, a genre that seems classic in contrast to queasy-cam gorefests. It depends on characters, atmosphere, sneaky happenings, and mounting dread. It's not terrifically good, but moviegoers will get what they're expecting. This is a new collaboration between director James Wan and writer Leigh Whannell, who launched the *Saw* franchise.

As the movie opens, an unsuspecting family is moving into a big old house they must have found through the Amityville Multiple Listing Service. It's the kind of house you require for a haunting movie, with lots of rooms, nooks, crannies, corridors, staircases, closets, and shadows—and an attic, of course. Although more modern houses were used in the *Paranormal Activity* movies, you really require all the creaky old bells and whistles.

The Lambert family seems to have been happy before this real estate transaction. Josh (Patrick Wilson) is a teacher, Renai (Rose Byrne) writes songs, and young Dalton (Ty Simpkins) is the most curious of the kids. That's why he sneaks into the attic, falls off a treacherous ladder, and immediately goes into a coma. Brain scans reveal no head injury. Could it be . . . something else?

Renai is positive something snaky is happening. Her boxes get moved around by unseen hands. Doors and windows open by themselves. We are even more sure than Renai is because we begin to see the stark apparition of a fearsome specter. Imagine a beast from Hades.

Dad begins to stay at work late. The movie probably wants us to blame him for not caring and trying to avoid the problems at home. We know better. We identify an example of the Absent Father Syndrome, that screenwriter's convenience for getting Dad out of the way so Mom can be home alone and told she's imagining things.

This is a family that needs help. They hire a psychic named Elise Rainier (Lin Shaye), who sends over two ghostbusters (Angus Sampson and the writer Leigh Whannell). These two seem singularly incompetent and provide some nice chuckles. Since the whole film teeters on the edge of being a comedy, it's probably a good idea that when Lin Shaye turns up, she brings in some cause for serious alarm. She's seen these cases before.

What is the malevolent presence? Why is it there? What does it want? What can it gain from the hapless Lamberts? The answers to such questions must necessarily remain theoretical at a metaphysical level, but at a practical level, the purpose of the presence is to generate startling bangs at frequent intervals, materialize unexpectedly, look horrifying, and be a nuisance. Its purpose, in short, is to go BOO!

## Inspector Bellamy ★ ★ ★ ½

NO MPAA RATING, 110 m., 2011

Gerard Depardieu (Paul Bellamy), Clovis Cornillac (Jacques Lebas), Marie Bunel (Francoise), Jacques Gamblin (Gentil/Leullet/Leprince). Directed by Claude Chabrol and produced by Patrick Godeau. Screenplay by Chabrol and Odile Barski.

Paul Bellamy is large, unkempt, sweet, blissfully married, and very calm for a police inspector. He doesn't solve a case so much as observe it with interest as it solves itself by the working of human nature. If you, like me, are a lover of Georges Simenon's Inspector Maigret, you will find his nature embodied here in the performance of Gerard Depardieu. If you are not, get your hands on a Maigret novel and thank me for the rest of your life.

As Claude Chabrol's *Inspector Bellamy* opens, Paul is on holiday with Francoise Bellamy (Marie Bunel), who, like Madame Maigret, understands her husband profoundly and is his sounding board as a case first baffles him and then unfolds under the gentle pressure of his low-key snooping. A man has been following them for days, and even now is creeping about in the garden. This man is named Gentil, and later will turn out to be Leullet, whom Gentil killed, *sort of,* while actually killing Leprince, who was in a sense only technically a victim. All three men are played by Jacques Gamblin. This is not at all confusing because of the ordered precision of Bellamy's approach, and Chabrol's.

Besides, it doesn't matter so much who did what and to whom. As in a Simenon novel, the solution is less interesting than the people encountered along the way and the sometimes sad lessons learned. *Inspector Bellamy* is only technically a murder mystery, and the critic Armond White is correct in observing, "Genre is Chabrol's MacGuffin." After hooking the audience with the mystery, Chabrol uses it as his avenue into the relationships between Bellamy and his wife, his loutish half-brother, Jacques (Clovis Cornillac), and two spritely local women who are mistresses, but not always the mistresses of those who claim them.

Chabrol, as always, shows a tenderness toward the lives of people who are exceptional only because crime touches them. He pays great attention to domestic details, and to the tone of the pillow talk between the Bellamys. He suggests that in their marriage, and perhaps in every marriage, things are not as simple as they seem. (Here he departs from Simenon; in Maigret's marriage, I believe things *are* as simple as they seem.) He introduces an extra character in Jacques—who is unnecessary in terms of the murder—really, not merely "seemingly" unnecessary. And Chabrol explores the unhappy history of Paul and Jacques, involving Francoise. In their relationship he uses the detective genre just as White says he does, as a device to involve us in another story thread.

Chabrol began making films at the dawn of the New Wave, in 1958. Depardieu began in 1970. Both worked prolifically. Hard to believe this was the first time they worked together. Chabrol and Odile Barski wrote the screenplay especially for Depardieu, and deliberately as homage to Simenon and Maigret; now that I see Depardieu as the famous inspector, I agree, yes, he makes a convincing Maigret, although at least two dozen other actors have played him. He is bulkier than I picture Maigret, and I've assumed the inspector's nose was less exceptional, but there is the inner quiet, the tranquillity in the face of violence, the curiosity and acceptance of human nature.

Here is a movie about a cop and a crime in which not one shot is fired. The only person who gets slapped is Bellamy. The movie ends with wisdom and resignation, not an orgasm of hyperactive computer effects. People talk about considerable things. They speculate about motives, even their own. They are articulate. Chabrol made many such films. He died on September 12, 2010, a survivor from the idealism of the New Wave, which he outlived. Which we have all outlived.

## The Interrupters ★ ★ ★ ★

NO MPAA RATING, 164 m., 2011

A documentary featuring Eddie Bocanegra, Ameena Matthews, Ricardo "Cobe" Williams, Tio Hardiman. Directed by Steve James and produced by James and Alex Kotlowitz.

Patiently, brilliantly, Steve James looks closely at our society. He begins documentaries with no easy end in sight and persists. How could he have guessed his masterpiece *Hoop Dreams* would develop into a story of such incredible power? Now, in *The Interrupters*, he has made his most important film, telling the story of ex-convicts who go daily into the streets of Chicago to try to talk gang members out of shooting at one another.

The interrupters are good people, and brave. All of them have done prison time. Some of them have murdered. They were young when they were seduced by the lure of street gangs, guns, easy money, and quick violence. Now they are older, wiser, and sad. They regard the death toll in Chicago and see young people throwing their lives away and often killing bystanders by accident.

On the news last night there was the story of a child killed by gunfire not intended for him. He was in the middle of a basketball game in a city park. One of his teammates told the camera: "It's a shame he never had the experience of life." There are fuzzy shots of a surveillance camera showing a white car with a sunroof speeding from the site. Inside were probably young black men empowered by firearms and an automobile to shoot stupidly into a park and make a pathetic gang gesture. The interrupters were once such young men—and women. They once were blind, but now they see.

James's film, mighty and heart-wrenching, follows members of CeaseFire, tough negotiators who monitor gang activity in their neighborhoods and try to anticipate developing warfare. They make it their business to know the gang leaders and members. They build trust. In some shots in this film they are physically in the possible line of fire—and so are Steve James and his small crew. They might as well be in a war zone. And indeed, the movie opens with the information that during early 2009 as many people died of street violence in Chicago as in Iraq and Afghanistan; twenty died in one night. Do not think only of Chicago. This is a national epidemic, its toll much larger than our deaths in war.

CeaseFire leaders hold harrowing roundtables to report on events in their districts and share their plans. James follows them on their rounds, watching as a knife fight is broken up by an interrupter. They're up against an embedded mind-set: Violence inspires retribution, and retribution inspires violence. It is no different on the South Side of Chicago than it has been in Ireland, Bosnia, or the Middle East. There is an obvious difference between those places and Chicago. In Europe and the Middle East, killings are usually driven by ethnic and religious differences. In an American inner city, where religious differences are irrelevant and everyone is of the same ethnicity, gangs take the place of race or belief. They provide an identity, no matter how paltry.

Are gangs protecting their turfs for drug sales? Not primarily. They are protecting it because it is theirs. If you walk on the wrong side of the street, you may be inviting death. This is pathetic, but enforcing gang turf provides some of these children and teenagers with the only source of self-esteem they find available. Sometimes they join gangs out of a fearful instinct for self-protection.

This is a universal human characteristic. When I was a grade-school child, I rode my bike home from school down a daily network of neighborhood streets. On one street some kids were sitting on a porch. They pulled me off my bike, punched me, and told me it was *their* street. They were white like me. They had no idea what school I went to. By protecting *their* street they were gaining esteem. I have no doubt they felt good afterward.

*The Interrupters* is based on a much-acclaimed article in the *New York Times Magazine* by Alex Kotlowitz, who followed a period of intense violence in Chicago. He joined with James to coproduce the film. It is difficult to imagine the effort, day after day for a year, of following this laborious, heroic, and so often fruitless volunteer work. Today when I read yet another story of a senseless gang killing, I find some small consolation in the thought that it could be worse.

## In the Family ★ ★ ★ ★

NO MPAA RATING, 169 m., 2012

Patrick Wang (Joey Williams), Trevor St. John (Cody Hines), Sebastian Banes (Chip Hines), Brian Murray (Paul Hawks), Park Overall (Sally Hines), Peter Hermann (Dave Robey), Susan Kellermann (Marge Hawks), Kelly McAndrew (Eileen Robey). Directed by Patrick Wang and produced by Wang, Robert Tonino, and Andrew van den Houten. Screenplay by Wang.

*In the Family* centers on one of the notable performances I've seen—if, indeed, it is a performance. Perhaps Patrick Wang is exactly like that. Then he must be a very good man. He wrote, directed, and stars in the film, but it's not a one-man show. It is about the meaning of "family." This is his first feature and may signal the opening of an important career.

Wang plays Joey Williams, a Chinese-American man who has been living happily for about five years with Cody Hines (Trevor St. John) and Cody's six-year-old son, Chip (Sebastian Banes). Chip's mother died in childbirth. Some months after that, to his own surprise, Cody fell in love with Joey, and they're raising Chip. This household is given enough screen time to establish it as a happy, healthy place.

Then Cody is killed in an accident. Chip stays with Joey, whose treatment of him is a study in wisdom and love. The little boy is so irrepressibly joyous that we sense what a happy life he has led. But Cody's sister, Eileen (Kelly McAndrew), reveals that he left a will years ago, granting her all of his property and custody of the child. This will, apparently written after the death of Cody's wife and before he met Joey, has never been updated.

On Thanksgiving Day, Joey drops the boy off at the sister's house and never sees him again. A lawyer in his small Tennessee town tells him flatly he doesn't have a child custody case, and no judge in the state will rule in his favor. Neither this lawyer nor anyone else in the film ever uses the words "homosexual" or "gay." It isn't in any sense a "gay rights" film, nor is it an "Asian-American" film. It is about a father and son who have been separated against their wishes.

Its objectivity in these terms is possible because of Wang's extraordinary performance. I've been unable to discover any details about him, but he speaks in a relaxed, natural Tennessee accent and creates Joey as a particularly convincing character, a contractor who drives a red pickup truck. (Cody was a schoolteacher.) His own parents died when he was very young. He was adopted by foster parents, who gave him their name, and who died when he was a teenager. As a man of Asian birth who has been raised apart from other Asians, as an orphan and a foster child who for years had no family, we sense how important stability and continuity are to him.

And there is something else. Without ever making a point of it, he has been treated as an outsider. Wang, as director, indicates this by several scenes with the back of the character's head to the camera, so that we see the other characters from his POV, instead of seeing Joey mixed in visually. He is not a hothead, not neurotic, not psychologically damaged, but in this crisis the entire basis of his being has been challenged. Having seen Cody, we can feel certain he would have granted child custody to Joey if he had ever made another will. Cody's sister doesn't see it that way. What does she think about homosexuality? She never says.

Joey's case looks hopeless. Friends try to console him, but helplessly. He's working on a house for a local attorney who has an ornate law library, and he reveals his skills in bookbinding—an art learned from his foster father. This attorney, Paul Hawks (the authoritative and wise Brian Murray), offers his help, and observes there may be no help within the court system but there may be a more human path around it.

Then follows a scene of depositions, during which Patrick Wang's performance, in long takes that feel entirely spontaneous, recounts his life story. Joey's treatment of the offensively hostile attorney for the other side is masterful:

He humiliates the other man simply by being a good person and telling the truth.

*In the Family* is a long film, and truth to tell could have been made shorter. (One dimly lit confrontation between Joey and a key participant seems unnecessary.) That said, I was completely absorbed from beginning to end. What a courageous first feature this is, a film that sidesteps shopworn stereotypes and tells a quiet, firm, deeply humanist story about doing the right thing. It is a film that avoids any message or statement, and simply shows us, with infinite sympathy, how the life of a completely original character can help us lead our own.

## In the Land of Blood and Honey ★ ★ ½

R, 126 m., 2012

Zana Marjanovic (Ajla), Goran Kostic (Danijel), Vanessa Glodjo (Lejla), Rade Serbedzija (Nebojsa), Boris Ler (Tarik), Alma Terzic (Hana). Directed by Angelina Jolie and produced by Jolie, Tim Headington, Graham King, and Tim Moore. Screenplay by Jolie.

Although the United States and the United Nations had troops involved, I have a feeling a good many Americans never worked up much interest in the Bosnian War. There were too many complexities for a sound bite. Was it Serbs against Croatians? Christians against Muslims? A free-for-all? Wasn't it all once Yugoslavia? Which side were we on? Or did we simply want all of them to stop fighting?

I hope I don't sound snarky. The indifference of many moviegoers to world events has an effect on the box office for any movie about such conflicts. It took a long struggle to get audiences worked up over *The Hurt Locker*, and even then the key words were "bomb disposal" and not "Iraq." Although we've spent a fortune in blood and resources in the Middle East, Hollywood has found audiences indifferent to events there. Even more so in the former Yugoslavia. When I say Bosnia, Serbia, and Croatia, how many nations have I named? Are they, in fact, nations? Here's a curveball: Where are the Balkans?

Given this reality, Angelina Jolie deserves admiration for making *In the Land of Blood and Honey* as her first filmmaking undertaking. She wrote it, directed it, and cared deeply about its issues, having spent a lot of time on the ground there, unlike so many movie stars who only turn up for the photo op. She has courage and convictions.

Her film is about a Serbian policeman named Danijel (Goran Kostic) and a Muslim artist named Ajla (Zana Marjanovic). Presumably Ajla is Serbian too, but as a Muslim, she is hated by her Christian fellow Serbs. As part of the old Yugoslavia, the movie explains, all races and religions lived together in peace; a convenience of Communism was that it dismissed such matters as bourgeois distractions from the class war. Now Marxism has fallen and humanity has returned to its familiar habit of hating thy neighbor.

If I understand Jolie correctly, she believes the Christian Serbs have blood on their hands, having carried out heartless genocidal massacres against Muslims. One of their pastimes is raping Muslim women. We see this in dismaying detail. On the other hand, Danijel's father, the veteran Serbian general Nebojsa (Rade Serbedzija), has a chilling monologue recounting Muslim atrocities against Serbs. It's the same as it always is in sectarian warfare: The side you're on contains the victims, and the other side is the spawn of Satan.

The film settles down into a more limited melodrama. Danijel and Ajla feel a spark of love at a carefree dance on the last night of peace. The bomb that rips through a nightclub defines them as enemies, and not long after that Danijel saves Ajla from certain rape and arranges for her special treatment in a prison. She gets her own sunny room, and in this privacy they luxuriate in love in the afternoon. This prompts the question of whether it is love, or whether Danijel wants to have sex with her and she feels it prudent to play along and buy her immunity with sex.

Danijel's brainstorm is to appoint Ajla the "official artist" of the Serbian army, and set her to work painting the portraits of Serbian generals. As a pretext this is fairly shabby, but it's a wonder how many powerful males would agree they should be the subject of an official portrait. Eventually the bitter General Nebojsa sees through his son's subterfuge, and then, well, you will see.

The film does what all war films must, which is to reduce the incomprehensible suffering of countless people into the ultimate triumph of a few. *Schindler's List* is a great film that employed this tactic, and indeed almost all fiction films about Jewish prisoners during World War II are about those who survived. This has nothing to do with race, religion, or nationality. It's all about the deeply embedded requirement of audiences to have an ending that provides happiness or at least catharsis.

One theme Angelina Jolie foregrounds with particular emphasis is the way women on both sides are singled out for suffering simply on the basis of their sex. For some men, wearing a uniform provides them with a license to rape, and this is true I fear in every war. The 2011 film *The Whistleblower* starred Rachel Weisz as a U.N. peacekeeping officer in Bosnia who discovered that an American private security firm was kidnapping underage girls and using them to staff profitable brothels.

I found *In the Land of Blood and Honey* to be moving and involving, but somehow reduced by its melodrama to a minor key. The scale of the ages-old evil and religious hatred in the region seemed to make the fates of these particular characters a matter of dramatic convenience. So what if Danijel shielded Ajla and his father found him out? It doesn't take much to see that the problems of three little people don't amount to a hill of beans in this crazy world.

## In Time ★ ★ ★

PG-13, 109 m., 2011

Justin Timberlake (Will Salas), Amanda Seyfried (Sylvia Weis), Vincent Kartheiser (Philippe Weis), Alex Pettyfer (Fortis), Cillian Murphy (Timekeeper Leon), Matt Bomer (Henry Hamilton), Olivia Wilde (Rachel Salas). Directed by Andrew Niccol and produced by Niccol, Marc Abraham, and Eric Newman. Screenplay by Nichol.

We are all of us engaged in the trade of buying and selling time. When we stop smoking, we hope we are buying years. When we drink and drive, we are willing to sell a few years. But those are gambles with the odds. *In Time* is a science-fiction movie in which time is a fungible commodity. Are you willing to pay for ten minutes of sex with an hour of your life?

The premise is damnably intriguing. Written and directed by Andrew Niccol, maker of such original sci-fi movies as *Gattaca* and *S1mOne*, it involves once again people whose lives depend on an overarching technology. In this case, they can buy, sell, and gamble with the remaining years they have to live.

The market in time is everywhere. On this imaginary Earth, humans have a DayGlo digital clock on their forearms, clicking off the years, months, days, and hours. It's like a population clock, except that it always grows smaller. By grasping hands and interfacing, I can upload and download time with you.

Justin Timberlake stars as Will Salas, a citizen of some unexplained future or parallel world (the settings and costumes are relatively contemporary), who finds himself on the run from the law. In this world, genetic engineering has been used to switch off everyone's body clock at twenty-five. At that point, they have one more year to live, but can work or make deals for more—or commit crimes. The twenty-five-year limit has the curious effect of making everyone more or less the same age, which explains the sexy Olivia Wilde as Will's mother.

One day, Will has a conversation with a morose man named Henry (Matt Bomer), who explains he is one hundred years old and has another century in the bank. He's tired of living. Their conversation drags on into philosophical depths, until both fall asleep. Will awakens with an extra century on his clock, and looks out the window to see Henry preparing to jump from a bridge. He runs out to stop him, is too late, and is caught by a security camera, making him a suspect in the death.

The plot now interweaves Sylvia Weis (Amanda Seyfried), daughter of the richest man alive, Philippe (Vincent Kartheiser), who has untold centuries on his clock and is essentially immortal. But enough about the plot.

The movie I suppose is an allegory in which time is money in a brutally direct way. For some of these people, time burns a hole in their pockets. For me, the most suspenseful scene involved a high-stakes poker game. Think about it. An opponent bets his whole pot: his life. Do you see him, or do you fold? If you lose, you're not broke; you're dead.

That said, a great deal of this film has been assembled from standard elements. Narrow your eyes to focus on them: Will Salas has the Identikit look of modern young action heroes: shaved head, stubble on his face. For contrived reasons, he is paired with a beautiful young woman and must drag her along with him as they're pursued by gunfire. The rich man moves nobly through a setting of opulence. The villain (Cillian Murphy) is androgynous and elegant, mannered in his cruelty. There are chases and so on. The only original element is the idea of timekeeping as a framework for these off-the-shelf parts. The only character of personal interest is Henry Hamilton.

Unanswered questions abound. The cars look like customized luxury boats from the 1970s; there's a Lincoln Continental with the slab sides but no nameplate. The time is said by the website to be "the near future," yet Henry has already lived a century. Don't even think to ask about the mechanism of the timekeeping, or how human life is stored up in what looks curiously like VHS cassette cases. And what of etiquette? Is allowing people to see your forearm as vulgar as flashing a big roll of cash?

Justin Timberlake continues to demonstrate that he is a real actor, with screen presence. But after the precise timing and intelligence he brought to *The Social Network*, it's a little disappointing to find him in a role that requires less. He has a future in the movies.

### Into the Abyss: A Tale of Death, a Tale of Life ★ ★ ★ ★

PG-13, 107 m., 2011

A documentary featuring Richard Lopez, Michael James Perry, Damon Hall, Lisa Stotler-Balloun, Charles Richardson, Jason Burkett, Jared Talbert, Amanda West, Delbert Burkett, Melyssa Thompson-Burkett, and Fred Allen. Directed, written, and produced by Werner Herzog.

*Into the Abyss: A Tale of Death, a Tale of Life* may be the saddest film Werner Herzog has ever made. It regards a group of miserable lives, and in finding a few faint glimmers of hope only underlines the sadness. The documentary centers on two young men in prison. Michael Perry is on death row in Huntsville, Texas, America's most productive assembly line for executions, and on the day Herzog spoke with him had eight days to live. Jason Burkett, his accomplice in the stupid murders of three people, is serving a forty-year sentence. They killed because they wanted to drive a friend's red Camaro.

Herzog opposes the death penalty, which America is the only developed nation still imposing. But the film isn't a polemic. Herzog became curious about the case, took a small crew to Huntsville and Conroe, Texas, where the murders took place, and spoke to the killers, and to members of their families and those of their victims. He obtains interviews of startling honesty and impact. I've learned that he met his subjects only once, on the day of the interviews, and the film presents their first conversations. I've long felt something about Herzog's personality is compelling and penetrating, and in evidence I could offer this film about Texans who are so different from the West German director.

Herzog keeps a much lower profile than in many of his documentaries. He is not seen, and his off-camera voice quietly asks questions that are factual, understated, and simply curious. His subjects talk willingly. He asks difficult follow-up questions. He is not very interested in the facts (there is no doubt about guilt here), but in looking into the eyes and souls of people who were directly involved.

Why did Perry die and not Burkett, when both were convicted for the same crimes? We meet Burkett's father, Delbert, who is also in prison serving a life sentence. In his testimony at his son's trial, he blamed himself for the boy's worthless upbringing. This apparently influenced two women jurors to pity the boy—or perhaps identify with the father. Delbert seems today a decent and reflective man. He bitterly regrets that he failed to take advantage of a college scholarship, dropped out of high school not long before graduation, and went wrong. He sees his mistake clearly now—too late for himself, too late for his son.

Perry and Burkett are uneducated, rootless,

callow, lacking in personal resources. Delbert perhaps has benefited from life in prison, as his son may. We meet Melyssa Burkett, who married Jason Burkett in prison and is now pregnant with his child—although, as Herzog observes, conjugal visits were not allowed. How did she become pregnant? She did, that's all. Herzog never sensationalizes, never underlines, expresses no opinions. He listens.

We also meet Captain Fred Allen, who was for many years in charge of the guard detail on Huntsville's death row, including the years in which George W. Bush turned down one appeal after another. He starts talking with Herzog and is swept up by memory and emotion, explaining why one day he simply walked away from his job and decided, after overseeing more than one hundred executions, that he was opposed to the death penalty. What he has to say about one crucial event in his life is one of the most profound statements I can imagine about the death penalty.

The people in this film, without exception, cite God as a force in their lives. The killers, their relatives, the relatives of their victims, the police, everyone. God has a plan. It is all God's will. God will forgive. Their lives are in His hands. They must accept the will of the Lord. Condemned or bereft, guilty or heartbroken, they all apparently find comfort in God's plan. What Herzog concludes about their faith he does not say.

Opposition to the death penalty, in part, comes down to this: No one deserves to be assigned the task of executing another person. I think that's what Captain Allen is saying. Herzog may agree, although he doesn't say so. In some of his films he freely shares his philosophy and insights. In this film, he simply looks. He always seems to know where to look.

## Intouchables ★ ★ ½

R, 112 m., 2011

Francois Cluzet (Philippe), Omar Sy (Driss), Anne Le Ny (Yvonne), Audrey Fleurot (Magalie), Clotilde Mollet (Marcelle). Directed by Olivier Nakache and Eric Toledano and produced by Nicolas Duval-Adassovsky, Laurent Zeitoun, and Yann Zenou. Screenplay by Nakache and Toledano.

It might help to think of *The Intouchables* as a French spinoff of *Driving Miss Daisy*, retitled *Pushing Monsieur Philippe.* A stuffy, rich employer finds his life enriched by a wise black man from the Paris ghettos, and takes lessons in funky music and the joys of marijuana. This is a story that has been told time and again in the movies, and sometimes the performances overcome the condescension of the formula.

The film was an enormous box-office hit in France, and indeed it is easy to enjoy. Philippe (Francois Cluzet) is a millionaire who was paralyzed from the neck down in a paragliding accident. Driss (Omar Sy) is a man out on parole for robbery, who applies for the job of Philippe's caregiver only so he can be rejected and get a signature on his application for unemployment benefits. As Philippe interviews one boring job applicant after another, we begin to understand that he needs not only physical help but someone to cheer him up. Driss's cheeky irreverence is refreshing, and Philippe astonishes him and his own household staff by offering him the job.

The movie tells the story of a growing relationship between these two likable men, based on Driss's confidence that Philippe will improve if he escapes his stuck-up lifestyle and samples the greater freedoms of a French immigrant from Africa. There may be a certain truth in this, but the education of Philippe proceeds in a series of essentially insulting clichés. Driss, you see, has rhythm and soul, and if only Philippe can absorb some of that he'll be a happier man. He'll still be a French millionaire surrounded by a protective staff, he'll still be paralyzed, but he'll be happier. How many times have we seen the scene where an uptight square inhales pot for the first time and a smile slowly spreads across his face?

The film has an element of truth that it never quite recognizes. The role of a good caregiver is hardly limited to lifting, bathing, grooming, dressing, pushing, and supplying medicines. The patient is faced with a reality he finds it difficult to accept: He has been deprived of all he once took for granted, such as the simple ability to walk across a room. A caregiver can't provide that, but he can provide something more valuable: companionship. Philippe's wife is dead, his teenage daughter is a snotty brat, and his staff is preoccupied by their salaries and status. Driss comes from a different world.

The success of the picture, in spite of its problems, grows directly from its casting. Francois Cluzet, who acts only with his face and voice, communicates great feeling. Omar Sy is enormously friendly and upbeat. He reminded me of the African immigrant played by Souleymane Sy Savane in Ramin Bahrani's *Goodbye Solo*—a film that avoided the traps that *The Intouchables* falls into.

The appeal of a film like this, and it is perfectly legitimate, is that when we begin to feel affection for the characters, what makes them happy makes us happy. Caught up in the flow of events, we allow many assumptions to pass unchallenged. The writer-directors, Olivier Nakache and Eric Toledano, are cheerfully willing to go for broad gags, and their style is ingratiating. But at the end, by looking through the foreground details, what we're being given is a simplistic reduction of racial stereotypes.

That was also true of *Driving Miss Daisy*, but it was a period picture set in the South in the late 1940s, with older characters who had been shaped by their times. There was a plausibility there. *The Intouchables* is more of a soothing fantasy.

## The Invisible War ★ ★ ★

NO MPAA RATING, 97 m., 2012

A documentary featuring Helen Benedict, Anu Bhagwati, Susan Burke, Kori Cioca, Susan Davis, Elle Helmer, Amy Herdy, Mary Kay Hertog, Jessica Hinves, Anthony Kurta, Rob McDonald, Stace Nelson, Loretta Sanchez, Hannah Sewell, Jackie Speier, Russell Strand, Loree Sutton, Niki Tsongas, Wilma Vaught, and Kaye Whitley. Directed by Kirby Dick and produced by Tanner Barklow and Amy Ziering.

If you're a young person thinking of enlisting in the U.S. military, you might want to give this some thought: A recent court decision ruled that rape was an "occupational hazard" of the job. Department of Defense official figures indicate 22,800 rapes took place last year. Most of the victims were women, but perhaps 10 percent were men.

Although the department itself provided the figure of 22,800, last year only 3,000 rapes were officially reported, and fewer than 200 of the accused were convicted. I was vaguely aware of the epidemic of military rape, but until watching this film, which follows the stories of a group of victims, I had no idea how widespread and urgent it was.

At about that time, the conviction of Jerry Sandusky was reported. He was found guilty of 45 of 48 charges. In every conversation I had, people asked how many additional assaults he committed—and why all of those at Penn State who knew about him remained silent.

*The Invisible War* suggests one reason. Both sports and the military are macho cultures that lay great emphasis on authority and teamwork. You follow the leader. You go along with the program. Your complaint not only casts your commanding officer in a bad light, but may involve him; the film says "25 percent of women didn't report an incident—because their commander was their rapist."

Until a few months ago, there was no way to go above your commander to report a rape. Then Defense Secretary Leon Panetta saw this film, and two days later issued an order changing that practice. But the overall problem remains. Rape is twice as common in the military as in civilian life, and "an estimated 15 percent of recruits attempted or committed rape before entering service."

The documentary focuses on the stories and experiences of a few women who joined in the lawsuit that led to the verdict that their experiences were an "occupational hazard." Their accusations were ignored or often not investigated, rarely led to prosecution, and almost never led to conviction. Those few who were convicted were usually sentenced to less than a year. Some of the accusers were themselves court-martialed. One wonders if military training and discipline itself help create such a culture. Complaining is a weakness. Even some military anti-rape campaigns send a mixed message; incredibly, one poster advises men: "Don't risk it—wait until she sobers up."

The film consists mostly of talking heads, congressional testimony, and a few glimpses of the home lives and sympathetic spouses of the victims. Although documentarian Kirby Dick is known for visually imaginative films (*This Film Is Not Rated, Outrage*), he wisely chooses to depend on the powerful stories told here. One of those stories in the film involves Kori Cioca, who served in the Coast Guard and was hit in the face by her rapist so hard that her jaw was broken. She will require some bone replacement, but has been refused treatment by the VA hospital system because her term of duty was not long enough to qualify her. Five years after the event, she is still on a diet of liquids and soft foods.

The film's implication, quite starkly, is that a strong military doesn't favor crybabies, that a certain degree of rape is unavoidable—and, inevitably, that some women may have been asking for it. One hearing noted that the victim was dressed provocatively. In her official uniform.

## Ip Man 2 ★ ★ ★

R, 108 m., 2011

Donnie Yen (Ip Man), Sammo Hung (Hung Chun-nam), Huang Xiao-ming (Wong Leung), Xiong Dai-lin (Cheung Wing-sing), Simon Yam (Chow Ching-chuen), Darren Shahlavi (The Twister). Directed by Wilson Yip and produced by Wong Bak-Ming. Screenplay by Edmond Wong.

*Ip Man 2* is a reminder of the pleasure of classic martial arts films in which skilled athletes performed many of their own stunts. In its direct and sincere approach, it's a rebuke to the frenzied editing that reduces so many recent action movies into incomprehensible confusion. I'm not saying deceiving camera angles and crafty stunt work isn't involved in the fight scenes here, but basically we see fighters in real time and space. That enormously increases the impact.

The movie is a sequel to an international 2008 hit that told the story of the legendary grandmaster who was Bruce Lee's teacher. In the first film, he fought against the Japanese occupiers of China, and this time his big showdown is with the Twister, a boxing champion of the British forces occupying Hong Kong. In both cases, his philosophy and strategy involve Wing Chun, the martial arts school adopted by Bruce Lee, which is now dominant in the West.

Ip Man (Donnie Yen) is a serious young family man with a second child on the way when he decides to open his own martial arts academy in Hong Kong. This is opposed by the syndicate that controls the sport, and that sets up an extended sequence where he must fight a series of their best fighters. The setup for these fights is daunting: A round table is balanced in the center of dozens of wooden stools turned upside down. The first fighter who is forced off the table loses the match, and lands on the waiting wooden legs. "I've seen this done with knives instead of stools," the head man sniffs.

I'm not naive. I don't believe Donnie Yen and his opponents were actually balanced on a teetering table while filming all of these scenes. You can work miracles with close-ups and camera angles. What I do appreciate is that the logic of time and space is respected, and there is a convincing illusion of realism. It's also obvious that you must be very skilled and experienced to act in such scenes, unlike the Hollywood stars who do all of their fighting with CGI.

Movies in this genre depend on an outsize villain for the climactic fight, and in the Twister (Darren Shahlavi) we get a character so over the top that he would have to dial down to become a pro wrestler. He's the champion of the British forces—symbolically defending British imperialism—and Ip Man is fighting for Chinese home rule.

The fight seems odd. The Twister is a boxer, wearing gloves. Ip Man, dressed in his usual quasi-clerical floor-length black costume, is a martial artist using his feet, elbows, fists, and so on. Midway in the match, the referee abruptly announces that kicking will no longer be allowed. That seems a fairly casual way to approach a championship.

I learn from online experts on this art form that Sammo Hung, who portrays the master of the Hong Kong martial arts syndicate, is himself a famous choreographer of these films, and that in fact he filmed his big scene here not long after having heart surgery. Sometimes the story behind a movie is the best one.

Donnie Yen makes an interesting martial arts star. He comes across as pleasant, sincere, never angry. His discipline involves control of mind and body. (He loves his wife, but isn't an ideal family man; she goes into labor and his duty is to his next fight.) He doesn't scream or make threats or seem to hate anyone, even The Twister. At the end of the film a five-year-old boy is brought to him as a possible student. He asks the kid for his name. "Bruce Lee," the kid says. He is destined to carry the Ip Man's message to the world.

## The Iron Lady ★ ★

PG-13, 105 m., 2012

Meryl Streep (Margaret Thatcher), Jim Broadbent (Denis Thatcher), Olivia Colman (Carol Thatcher), Anthony Head (Geoffrey Howe), Richard E. Grant (Michael Heseltine), Roger Allam (Gordon Reece), Nicholas Farrell (Airey Neave), Alexandra Roach (Young Margaret Thatcher), Harry Lloyd (Young Denis Thatcher). Directed by Phyllida Lloyd and produced by Damian Jones. Screenplay by Abi Morgan.

You have to be very talented to work with Meryl Streep. It also helps to know how to use her. *The Iron Lady* fails in both of these categories. Streep creates an uncanny impersonation of British prime minister Margaret Thatcher, but in this film she's all dressed up with nowhere to go. Director Phyllida Lloyd and writer Abi Morgan seem to have little clear idea of what they think about her, or what they want to say.

If there has ever been a biopic that required an opinion of its subject, that biopic would seem to be *The Iron Lady.* Thatcher held office for an unprecedented three terms, bitterly divided Great Britain, and led her nation during a Falklands War that seemed to be largely an exercise in hubris on both sides. Before the war (and now) no one frankly gave a damn about the Falkland Islands, and Thatcher's foreign policy amounted to: "They're ours and you bloody well can't have them." For this, brave troops on both sides were killed, and those who cared to could deceive themselves that there was one small spot of foreign soil that, as far as Thatcher was concerned, would be forever British. (Footnote: The British didn't consider it foreign.)

Of course the Argentines started the war by invading the Falklands, over which they had disputed Britain's claim since 1833. You can't say they didn't wait long enough before taking action. And if Argentina mounted a military invasion, what could Thatcher do? She was compelled to defend the islands. The loved ones on either side who lost someone in that war must have been hard-pressed to understand why the death was useful or necessary.

That wasn't Thatcher's concern. In a striking scene that takes place in her increasingly senile old age, she declares that ideas are more important to her than feelings. That seems to have been a governing principle in her life, allowing her to look with apparently limited concern at unemployment, hunger, and homelessness on the domestic front. In *Shanghai Express*, Marlene Dietrich utters the immortal words: "It took more than one man to change my name to Shanghai Lily." In a similar way the Iron Lady seems to have been well nicknamed.

Few people were neutral in their feelings about her, except the makers of this picture. They approach Thatcher as a figure in a time-honored biographical template in which a convenient fictional mechanism allows the heroine to revisit key chapters in her life so that we can understand that it was quite a life, indeed. From her humble beginnings as the proverbial "grocer's daughter from Grantham," she began on the lowest rungs of the Conservative Party and never paused in her climb. Her ambition was unlimited, her strategy ruthless, her victims many of the male generation the Conservatives thought they were grooming for power. Was hers a feminist triumph? She herself seems hardly to have thought of it that way, and there are scenes suggesting an emotional distance from her children and a marriage based on the self-effacement of her remarkably recessive husband (Jim Broadbent).

Was she a monster? A heroine? The movie has no opinion. She was a fact. You leave the movie having witnessed it. Whatever your feelings about Thatcher were before you saw it, you now have some images to accompany it. Part of its failure may be attributed to the director, Phyllida Lloyd, whose first feature also starred Streep. That was *Mamma Mia!* (2008), not a high point in Ms. Streep's career.

I witnessed Margaret Thatcher's extraordinary personal authority once. When Conrad Black numbered the *Sun-Times* among his holdings, he convened the International Advisory Panel of his Hollinger corporation in Chicago. Seated around a massive table were Lady Thatcher and assorted government officials, officeholders, pundits, and academics from around the world. To give you a notion, one of them was Henry Kissinger. (I was back along the wall with other underlings.)

Lady Thatcher was in command. Invisible psychic threads of respect and yearning extended toward her from the men. When she spoke, they fell silent. No one interrupted. No one disagreed. Her pronouncements were issued as recitals of fact. It was the most remarkable display of personal authority I have ever seen.

*The Iron Lady* suggests that only indirectly. It could have used a few behind-the-scenes moments showing what her rivals, particularly in the Conservative power struggles, really thought and said about her. Consider the invigorating new French film, *The Conquest*, about Nicolas Sarkozy's rise to power among the French Conservatives. Not here. Using flashbacks, period footage, montage, and dialogue bites, the film follows her rise. Streep is flawless, but the film, like a great many people at the time, is uncertain how to approach her.

## Iron Man 2 ★ ★ ★

PG-13, 124 m., 2010

Robert Downey Jr. (Tony Stark), Gwyneth Paltrow (Pepper Potts), Don Cheadle (Lieutenant Colonel "Rhodey" Rhodes), Scarlett Johansson (Natasha Romanoff), Sam Rockwell (Justin Hammer), Mickey Rourke (Ivan Vanko), Samuel L. Jackson (Nick Fury), Clark Gregg (Paul Coulson), Garry Shandling (Senator Stern). Directed by Jon Favreau and produced by Kevin Feige. Screenplay by Justin Theroux, based on the Marvel comic by Stan Lee, Don Heck, Larry Lieber, and Jack Kirby.

*Iron Man 2* is a polished, high-octane sequel, not as good as the original but building once again on a quirky performance by Robert Downey Jr. The superhero genre doesn't necessarily require good acting, but when it's there (as in *Iron Man* and *The Dark Knight*), that takes it up a level. Downey here gives us a Tony Stark who is cockier and more egotistical than ever. Or, and here's the key, he seems to be.

All heroes have a fatal flaw. That's one of the rules of the road in fiction. Tony Stark's flaw is that he is dying. The megalomaniac act comes naturally, but now it's useful as a cover-up. His chest-mounted battery pack, or life source, or whatever it is, is running low and poisoning his blood. It works by using the rarest element in the periodic table, and to renew it would require discovering or inventing a new element. Not easy.

So Tony stands aside at big events and uses a little blood monitor—helpfully named the "Stark Blood Monitor," in case anybody sees it—that tells him his blood toxicity is relentlessly climbing toward death. This is his private fear, not even shared with the loyal Pepper Potts (Gwyneth Paltrow), who is running his company.

Stark is sponsoring a Stark Expo at the site of the New York World's Fair, and he flies in for an appearance in the Iron Man suit and promises world peace. The arena is thronged with adoring fans. Imagine Steve Jobs announcing iPad 3. But trouble is brewing. His archrival Justin Hammer (Sam Rockwell) plans an army of rival iron suits. A congressional committee headed by the fatuous Senator Stern (Garry Shandling) wants Stark to make Iron Man the exclusive property of the Defense Department. And in Russia, the bitter Ivan Vanko (Mickey Rourke) believes Stark's father stole the Iron Man secrets from his own father.

Hammer hires Vanko to design a better suit than Stark's, the two suit designs go to war, we get half an hour of sensational special effects, and Bob's your uncle. But you also have a niece, a sexy martial arts expert played by Scarlett Johansson, who may be more than she seems. The character was named Black Widow in the comic books, never a good sign. Fighting at Stark's side is his comrade Lieutenant Colonel "Rhodey" Rhodes (Don Cheadle); while rocketing through a blizzard of enemy missiles, the two find time to talk. How slow must a missile be moving if your buddy has time to warn you to dodge it?

The best CGI sequence in the movie comes at midpoint, when Tony Stark decides to drive his own car in the Monaco Grand Prix, and Ivan Vanko stands fearlessly in the middle of the race, dressed like a kinky gladiator and wielding electric whips that can slice a car in two. He nearly destroys Stark, which is so exciting that we forget to wonder how he knew that Tony was driving his own car. It's after this race that Hammer signs him up.

Mickey Rourke gives us all the Ivan Vanko we could possibly wish for, unless he had a third arm to provide space for more tattoos. His performance features flashing his gold teeth in mirthless laughter, and lots of growling. Sam Rockwell gives a wry comic performance as Hammer, a querulous whiner who seems in over his head in the super weapons business.

You want a sequel, you got a sequel. *Iron Man 2*, directed like the first one by Jon Favreau, gets the job done. Since both movies have essentially the same story arc, there aren't a lot of surprises, however, which started me to wondering how the guys survive inside those suits. Sure, the suits are armored, but their bodies aren't. How many dizzying falls and brutal blows and sneaky explosions can you survive without breaking every bone in your body? Just askin'. At the end of a long day, those suits should be filled with bloody pulp.

## I Spit on Your Grave (no stars)

NO MPAA RATING, 108 m., 2010

Sarah Butler (Jennifer Hill), Jeff Branson (Johnny), Daniel Franzese (Stanley), Rodney Eastman (Andy), Chad Lindberg (Matthew), Andrew Howard (Sheriff Storch), Tracey Walter (Earl Woodason). Directed by Steven R. Monroe and produced by Lisa M. Hansen and Paul Hertzberg. Screenplay by Stuart Morse, based on a 1978 screenplay by Meir Zarchi.

This despicable remake of the despicable 1978 film *I Spit on Your Grave* adds yet another offense: a phony moral equivalency. In the original, a woman foolishly thought to go on holiday by herself in a secluded cabin. She attracted the attention of depraved local men, who raped her, one after the other. Then the film ended with her fatal revenge. In this film, less time is devoted to the revenge and more time to verbal, psychological, and physical violence against her. Thus it works even better as vicarious cruelty against women.

First let's dispatch with the fiction that the film is about "getting even." If I rape you, I have committed a crime. If you kill me, you have committed another one. The ideal outcome would be two people unharmed in the first place. The necessity of revenge is embedded in the darker places of our minds, and most hate speech is driven by "wrongs" invented in unbalanced minds. No one who commits a hate crime ever thinks his victim is innocent.

That set aside, let's see what this movie does. The woman, Jennifer (Sarah Butler), is a writer who rents a cabin in the woods where she plans to stay by herself. Once we know this, we start waiting for the gas station occupied by demented rednecks. There's always one. Of course that's where Jennifer stupidly asks directions and reveals where she's going to ignorant, leering phallus carriers.

There are four. One is their "ringleader." One is his sidekick. One compulsively makes video recordings. The fourth is mentally handicapped and they treat him as their pet "retard." After many scenes involving alarming noises in the night and the usual Woman in Fear sequences, the men enter her cabin and terrorize her.

They use words and guns. They insinuate. They toy with her answers. They enjoy her terror. This is rape foreplay, and they stretch it out as long as they can. There is a reason for this. Rape is a crime of violence, not sex, and the male rapist typically savors the fear he causes more than the sex. Indeed, if he enjoyed sex more, he might not be a rapist. The true pornography in this film involves the dialogue and situation in the cabin *before* the physical assault. It is well done. This is a professionally made film. The audience is very, very quiet. Some share Jennifer's terror. Some, I am afraid, may be aroused or entertained by it.

When the rape inevitably arrives, it is the hapless mental deficient, Matthew (Chad Lindberg), who is forced by the others to go first. Otherwise he crouches whimpering in a corner. The movie's exploitation of his handicap is on a par with the cruel sadism of the film. Eventually Jennifer is thoroughly raped and runs away into the woods barefoot and almost naked and, when they approach with a shotgun to eliminate her as a witness, jumps from a high bridge and disappears.

We will slip past the movie's nonexplanation for her survival and reappearance to consider her revenge. I choose not to describe her methods. Let me suggest that if you recall any of the torture scenes described in the novels of Cormac McCarthy or Larry McMurtry, I suspect the director and writer of this film remember them as well. Jennifer's methods are elaborate, bizarre, and cruel.

Oh, sure, they have it coming to them—except for the pathetic Matthew, who has been a victim all his life and is now punished by Jennifer even though she witnessed his grief and innocence. He is a man and must die. A couple of tortures here inspired groans from the audience, but this stuff isn't a novelty for connoisseurs of horror movies. Consider *Saw* and anything with *chainsaw* in its title.

No, it's the first half of the movie that's offensive. It implicitly assigns us the POV of the men as they taunt and terrorize Jennifer in plausible ways—which are different from her killing methods, which are implausible, probably impossible, and offered and received as entertainment.

Now here's an interesting thing: There were walkouts from the packed screening I attended. Not many, maybe eight or nine. Nobody walked out in the second half; they all left in the first half. And . . . they were all men. Most of the audience looked like they were on dates. For conversation afterward, if you see this loathsome film, here are some suggestions:

Men, ask your dates: What bothered you more, the first or second half? Would you recommend this movie to your girlfriends? Did you enjoy it? (It's OK; you can be honest.)

Women, ask your dates: What part did you like the most, the first or second half? Would you recommend this movie to your sister? Why did we go to this particular film? Did you know there were two new four-star films playing in the same multiplex?

Both men and women may find some food for thought in the answers. Certain answers may cause you to ask yourself if you have any future with this other person.

## I Will Follow ★ ★ ★ ½

NO MPAA RATING, 83 m., 2011

Salli Richardson-Whitfield (Maye), Michole White (Fran), Omari Hardwick (Troy), Dijon Talton (Raven), Tracie Thoms (Tiffany), Damone Roberts (Himself), Blair Underwood (Evan), Beverly Todd (Amanda). Directed by Ava DuVernay and produced by DuVernay and Molly M. Mayeux. Screenplay by DuVernay.

*I Will Follow* doesn't tell a story so much as try to understand a woman. Through her, we can find insights into the ways we deal with death. In one way or another, every emotion in this wonderful independent film is one I've experienced myself. Grief, of course. But also anger, loneliness, confusion, and a sense of lost direction. Above all, urgent conversations you have in your own mind with someone who is no longer alive to have them with you. How many people, now dead, have you wanted to ask questions you should have asked when they were alive?

The film takes place during one day in a home in Topanga Canyon, just a short drive above Los Angeles but with a sort of woodsy feeling. This is where a woman named Amanda (Beverly Todd) spent the last year of her life. She had breast cancer, she refused chemo, she wanted to die on her own terms in her own house, and died not long ago. We spend the day with her favorite niece, Maye (Salli Richardson-Whitfield), who lived with her for that last year.

Maye feels as if she's taking her next step into thin air. Amanda was a powerful and charismatic woman, a recording session drummer for rock 'n' roll and jazz groups. Maye has had success as a makeup artist in Hollywood, but it was her aunt who seemed glamorous and enchanting above everyone else. Now Maye is left behind.

The film opens with an argument with the movers. There's that tension you feel when someone touches anything left behind by the dead person, and it's like they're killing them just a little more. To help her pack up things, Maye has her nephew Raven (Dijon Talton), who is distracted, annoyed, unhelpful. People come by the house all day: two guys from the Goodwill, a woman repairman from the satellite company, a neighbor. All of these small roles are cast and written to create characters who are small but very human.

The key visitor is Amanda's daughter and Raven's mother, Fran (Michole White). Through her, we get an insight into Raven's attitude toward his grandmother. Fran always believed Maye was her mother's favorite. At the end, it was Maye whom Amanda chose to live with, Maye who nursed her, Maye who supported Amanda's desire to die at home without chemo. Fran blames Maye for Amanda's death—or at least for it coming so soon.

We're familiar with the five stages of grief: denial, anger, bargaining, depression, and acceptance. Are there also stages of mourning? One of them might be blame. We feel it's wrong for a person to die, and we want someone or something to blame. It must be someone's fault. By living with Amanda and sharing her feelings, Maye has accepted her death. But as her daughter, Fran feels closed out and blames the "favorite niece." A lifetime of resentment wells up in a powerful scene between the two women.

What is particularly human about *I Will Follow*, which was written and directed by Ava DuVernay, is that she understands why Fran feels that way. There's no attempt to make Maye the good character and Fran the bad one. They both have valid reasons for their emotions. And all the people who pass through the house that day (there are about twelve) come with feelings we understand and perhaps have shared. One who particularly struck me was the neighbor, maybe contemplating his own mortality, who didn't know Amanda that well. They apparently talked only over the fence. It's clear to me that as they talked about their gardens and the pleasant weather, they shared unspoken feelings that they were comrades in the process of leaving life. Another important visitor is Troy (Omari Hardwick), as Maye's sorta boyfriend. As they speak, we understand instinctively their fondness and also a certain reserve; these two don't easily give away their hearts.

Beverly Todd, a beautiful woman who has been in countless movies and TV shows since the late 1960s, has an important presence here in many flashbacks, some of them dreamy or fragmented, as Amanda. She easily evokes the magic Maye must have felt, and that gives weight to the present-day scenes. For Salli Richardson-Whitfield, the role of Maye is a great performance, as she embodies emotions the script wisely doesn't spell out. *I Will Follow* is an invitation to empathy. It can't have a traditional three-act structure, because every life closes in death, and only supporting characters are left onstage at the end. What goes unsaid, but not thought, is that we will all pass this way eventually.

Amanda's family is African-American. The neighbor and some of the visitors are white. Why do I mention race? I wasn't going to. This is a universal story about universal emotions. Maybe I mention it because this is the kind of film black filmmakers are rarely able to get made these days, offering roles for actors who remind us here of their gifts. Ava DuVernay, a documentarian making her first feature, has made *I Will Follow* as the first of a group of new indie African-American films.

## I Wish ★ ★ ★ ½

PG, 128 m., 2012

Koki Maeda (Koichi), Ohshiro Maeda (Ryunosuke), Ryoga Hayashi (Tasuku), Nene Ohtsuka (Nozomi), Joe Odagiri (Kenji). Directed by Hirokazu Kore-eda. Screenplay by Kore-eda.

The two brothers were inseparable, but now their parents have separated and they live, one with each, in distant towns. This is the problem that must be solved in *I Wish*, the new film by the Japanese master Hirokazu Kore-eda, who is as gentle and wise as any director now working. His film is built around performances by two real-life brothers who are as unaffected, spirited, and lovable as I can imagine, and one of the pleasures of *I Wish* is simply spending time with them.

During his entire career, Kore-eda, forty-nine, has been invested in sympathetic stories about people we warmly identify with. His frequent theme is parents and children. You may remember his well-received *After Life* (1998), about people asked after death to film one chosen event in their lives. Or the more painful *Nobody Knows* (2004), about a family of children left in an apartment to fend for themselves in their mother's absence. I was much moved by *Maborosi* (1995), about a young widow and her son who move to a coastal village where they know no one.

In *I Wish*, he enters easily into the lives of Koichi (Koki Maeda), a fourth-grader, and Ryunosuke (Ohshiro Maeda), a few years younger. These are blessed children. You can't just tell actors, especially young ones, to "act happy" and expect them to do it. They must in some essential way be happy. Here they're filled with the energy and hopes of childhood, their smiles are quick and open, laughter comes easily, and they seem to run everywhere, as if they never learned to walk.

Koichi lives with his mother. Ryunosuke decided to live with his father, although the reasons of neither boy are discussed. They talk all the time on their cell phones. Koichi's town lies downwind from an always-rumbling volcano, which covers everything with a daily layer of ash that he meticulously sweeps up. It strikes him that no one seems particularly concerned about the volcano, although an eruption would be a disaster. "I don't get it," he says. There are a lot of things he doesn't get, which may be his way of expressing misgivings.

He and his mother live with her parents, and the grandfather spends much time every day smoking and playing cards with cronies. They are all much absorbed in the fact that a high-speed bullet train will soon come to the town, one that Koichi knows will link it with the city Ryunosuke lives in. The old men discuss the possibility of opening a stand at the new train station to sell a traditional bean cake much loved in their childhoods; recipes are tried and tasted.

The boys become electrified when Koichi hears that at the moment when two 160 mph trains pass each other, some kind of magical field is generated to make wishes come true. He and a few friends decide to skip school and take a slow train to a point where the two fast trains currently pass; there the brothers will meet. This seems risky for kids their age, but the grandfather joins in the conspiracy and helps them deceive their teacher, and there's a moment when all the children shout out their wishes.

If this were a lesser film, that would be a sentimental moment, and maybe a successful one. Kore-eda is a realist. The journey becomes a coming-of-age experience for the kids, who are all changed, not in the ways they expected. Kore-eda's focus is not on the moving gears of a plot, but in the evolving emotions of these lives, and the movie's most intense pleasure comes because it allows us to share them.

All of the performances find the right tone, even that of Kenji, the father (Joe Odagiri), who has never been able to support his family with his dreams of becoming a rock musician. The brothers Maeda are pure gold; the film captures what feels like effortless joy in their lives, and it is never something they seem to be reaching for. They may be separated, they may have worries, the volcano may erupt, but for now, nothing can defeat their hopes.

# J

## Jack Goes Boating ★ ★ ★

R, 91 m., 2010

Philip Seymour Hoffman (Jack), Amy Ryan (Connie), John Ortiz (Clyde), Daphne Rubin-Vega (Lucy). Directed by Philip Seymour Hoffman and produced by Beth O'Neil, Peter Saraf, Marc Turtletaub, and Emily Ziff. Screenplay by Bob Glaudini, based on his play.

Philip Seymour Hoffman has a gift for playing quickly embarrassed men who fear rejection. He can convey such vulnerability in some roles that we're on his side without the screenplay needing to persuade us. We want to finish his sentences, clap him on the back, cheer him up. In other roles, such as *Synecdoche, New York*, he projects enough ego to enforce his will for years on end. There's an actor for you.

In *Jack Goes Boating*, Hoffman is not only the star but also the director. He is merciless in using himself as an actor. His face is often seen in close-up, sweaty, splotchy, red as if he suffers from rosacea. He seems perpetually blushing. In life Hoffman's skin is perfectly normal; not every actor would stand for this, but vanity is not one of Hoffman's sins.

In the movie he plays a limousine driver for a company owned by his uncle, which gives us an idea of his stature in the family. At dawn he meets for coffee with his best friend, Clyde (John Ortiz), and they sit in a parked limo and regard the unattainable towers of Manhattan. Jack is clueless. Clyde is effortless. Even in their forties, they have a student-teacher relationship. Clyde is going to teach Jack how to chat up a girl, make himself likable, swim, row a boat, even eventually cook a meal for her—which may be asking for too much.

Clyde is married to Lucy (Daphne Rubin-Vega). She works in a funeral home with Connie (Amy Ryan). Connie is the kind of person who you'd describe as sweet but terribly shy. Clyde and Lucy decide these two people belong with each other, perhaps by default because they appear to belong with nobody else.

This leads into a dinner that reminds me a little of Mike Leigh's *Abigail's Party*, in the sense that the wrong people are in the wrong room at the wrong time, and social embarrassment is the main course. The movie is based on an off-Broadway play by Bob Glaudini that Hoffman and Ortiz produced and acted in with Rubin-Vega. It has a touch of Leigh and more than a touch of kitchen sink drama; its stage origins are suggested by the way Jack lives in a flat where the kitchen, dining area, and living area are essentially one space—that works beautifully when his dinner for Connie goes wrong, as it must.

It's expected in a four-character play that all four characters will come into play, and they do, in an unexpected way. The interplay between Jack and Connie is awkward and initially promising, but it's clear they have a lot of shyness to overcome in catching up to Clyde and Lucy. Still, even happy marriages have secrets.

You can sense the familiarity the actors have with their roles, but there's not the sense they've been this way before. What has traveled this path is the screenplay, which follows a familiar pattern and is essentially redeemed by the meticulous performances. The actors make it new and poignant, and avoid going over the top in the story's limited psychic and physical space. Even at their highest pitch, the emotions of these characters come from hearts long worn down by the troubles we see.

## Jamie and Jessie Are Not Together ★★★

NO MPAA RATING, 95 m., 2011

Jacqui Jackson (Jamie), Jessica London-Shields (Jessie), Fawzia Mirza (Rhonda), Marika Engelhardt (Elizabeth), Sienna Harris (Dawn), Jen LaForte (Monica), Chris Meister (George). Directed by Wendy Jo Carlton and produced by Carlton and Anne T. Hanson. Screenplay by Carlton.

*Jamie and Jessie Are Not Together* is a sweet, appealing musical comedy about two lesbian roommates who, as they keep telling everyone, are "not together." Just friends. In fact, Jamie is two weeks away from leaving Chicago and moving to New York, where she plans a career on the stage.

The way Jessie takes that news ("Two . . .

weeks?") tells us what we need to know. She has a secret crush on Jamie. She walks out, goes to her job in an East Rogers Park coffee shop, confides in her understanding boss, and then, standing behind the espresso machine, begins singing a lament. Everyone in the shop joins in singing and dancing, including two men with Smith Brothers beards who pop up all during the movie and are never explained.

This scene is so charming I wish there were more like it. The movie is technically a musical, but doesn't have much music. Still, it's lighthearted as we meet the social circle of the two girls. Jamie is dating Rhonda (Fawzia Mirza), and the first time we see her, Jamie walks in the door and they begin a torrid love scene. At this point, I was still under the impression that Jamie (Jacqui Jackson) and Jessie (Jessica London-Shields) *were* together, and was a little disappointed in Jamie's promiscuity. But no, she and Rhonda are an item, and Jessie knows about them but keeps her feelings to herself.

"Come into my office," says Dawn, the coffee shop manager, and sits her down at a window table for a talking-to. She senses Jessie's feelings for Jamie, tells her there's no future there, and advises her to try some blind dates. We see bits of these, not successful, and then someone steals a wheel from her bike, and Elizabeth (Marika Engelhardt) happens along and offers to help her walk it home. In front of Jessie's house they kiss, they plan a date, and now it's Jamie who is none too pleased.

And that's about it, although this simple plot is charmingly written and acted, and as a low-budget indie, it makes splendid use of the Lake Michigan beach and lakefront. Admirably avoiding postcard shots, Wendy Jo Carlton and cinematographer Gretchen Warthen make practical use of these locations. The setting is always waiting, the lighting is always natural, and there are so few extras wandering around that there can be a little skinny-dipping. It's an alternative to conversations in apartments and the coffee shop, and it makes sense that if the roommates live in walking distance of the lake they'd have an agreed-upon beach rendezvous place.

The movie, let it be said, has a number of sex scenes, and although you can never be entirely certain who is doing what to whom, something is certainly being done. This is in no sense a sex film, but I suppose it will be marketed as soft eroticism for the appropriate audience, and where's the harm there?

## Jane Eyre ★ ★ ★ ½

PG-13, 118 m., 2011

Mia Wasikowska (Jane Eyre), Michael Fassbender (Rochester), Jamie Bell (Saint John Rivers), Sally Hawkins (Mrs. Reed), Judi Dench (Mrs. Fairfax). Directed by Cary Joji Fukunaga and produced by Alison Owen and Paul Trijbits. Screenplay by Moira Buffini, based on the novel by Charlotte Bronte.

Gothic romance attracts us with a deep, tidal force. Part of its appeal is the sense of ungovernable eroticism squirming to escape from just beneath the surface. Its chaste heroines and dark, brooding heroes prowl the gloomy shadows of crepuscular castles, and doomy secrets stir in the corners. Charlotte Bronte's *Jane Eyre* is among the greatest of Gothic novels, a page-turner of such startling power it leaves its pale, latter-day imitators like *Twilight* flopping for air like a stranded fish.

To be sure, the dark hero of the story, Rochester, is not a vampire, but that's only a technicality. The tension in the genre is often generated by a virginal girl's attraction to a dangerous man. The more pitiful and helpless the heroine the better, but she must also be proud and virtuous, brave and idealistic. And her attraction to the ominous hero must be based on pity, not fear; he must deserve her idealism.

This atmospheric new *Jane Eyre*, the latest of many adaptations, understands those qualities, and also that the very architecture and landscape embodies the Gothic notion. The film opens with Jane Eyre fearfully fleeing across the bleak moors, where even nature conspires against her. This is not the opening we expect, with Jane already fully grown, but later in flashbacks we'll be reminded of her Dickensian girlhood, her cruel aunt, her sadistic boarding school, and her need as a girl without means to earn her own way as a governess.

Jane is described in the novel as a plain girl; is that where the phrase "plain Jane" comes from? Here she's played by Mia Wasikowska (of Tim Burton's *Alice in Wonderland*), who is far from plain, but transforms herself into a pale, severe creature who needs to be watered with love. She is employed by the intimidating Rochester (Michael Fassbender) to supervise the care of his "ward," Adele Varens (Romy Settbon Moore), who is being raised in his isolated manor, Thornfield. How he came into the possession of a young girl as his "ward" is an excellent question, one among many that could probably be answered by Thornfield's dedicated housekeeper, Mrs. Fairfax (Judi Dench).

The classic *Jane Eyre* is the 1944 version with Joan Fontaine and Orson Welles. Fontaine was twenty-seven; Welles was twenty-nine. Mia Wasikowska is twenty-two and Michael Fassbender is thirty-four. In the novel, Jane is scarcely twenty and Rochester is . . . older. Whether in any version he is old enough to accomplish what he has done in life is a good question, but this film is correct in making their age difference obvious; Jane in every sense must be intimidated by her fierce employer. No version I know of has ever made Rochester as unattractive as he is described in the book.

Rochester is absent a good deal of the time, although represented by the foreboding atmosphere of Thornfield, the enigmatic loyalty of Mrs. Fairfax, and the sense that something is amiss in the enormous manor. Here Judi Dench's contribution is significant; the tone of her voice conveys so much more about Rochester than her words.

Either you know the plot or not. Its secret is a red herring with all the significance of "Rosebud." It functions only to provide Rochester with an honorable reason to propose a dishonorable thing, and thus preserve the moral standards of the time. The novel is actually about forbidden sexual attraction on both sides, and its interest is in the tension of Jane and Rochester as they desire sex but deny themselves. Much of the power comes from repressed emotions, and perhaps Charlotte Bronte was writing in code about the feelings nice women of her time were not supposed to feel.

The director here is Cary Joji Fukunaga, whose *Sin Nombre* was one of the best films of 2009. Its story, based on fearsome Mexican gangs, scarcely resembles *Jane Eyre*, but it showed an emotional intensity between characters who live mostly locked within themselves. He's a director with a sure visual sense, here expressed in voluptuous visuals and ambitious art direction.

Michael Fassbender is an Irish actor who can have a threatening charm; did you see him in *Fish Tank* (2009), a quite different film about a seductive man who takes advantage of a teenage girl? Mia Wasikowska, from Australia, is a relative newcomer who must essentially carry *Jane Eyre* and succeeds with restraint, expressing a strong moral compass. Judi Dench is firm, as a housekeeper must be firm, and observes everything, as a housekeeper must. All of the rest is decoration. Without the costumes, sets, locations, sound design, and the wind and rain, gothic cannot exist.

## J. Edgar ★ ★ ★ ½

R, 136 m., 2011

Leonardo DiCaprio (J. Edgar Hoover), Naomi Watts (Helen Gandy), Armie Hammer (Clyde Tolson), Josh Lucas (Charles Lindbergh), Judi Dench (Annie Hoover). Directed by Clint Eastwood and produced by Eastwood, Brian Grazer, Ron Howard, and Robert Lorenz. Screenplay by Dustin Lance Black.

J. Edgar Hoover was the head of the Bureau of Investigation from 1924 until he died in 1972; he added the word "Federal" to its title in 1935. Under the administrations of Coolidge, Hoover, Roosevelt, Truman, Eisenhower, Kennedy, Johnson, and Nixon he was, many believed, the second most powerful man in government. Now he has been dead for thirty-nine years, and what most people probably think they know about him is that he liked to dress up like a woman. This snippet of gossip, which has never been verified, is joined by the details that he never married, lived with his mother until she died, and had a close lifelong friendship with Clyde Tolson, the tall and handsome bachelor who inherited his estate.

It is therefore flatly stated that Hoover was gay, which would have been ironic since he gathered secret files on the sex lives of everyone prominent in public life and used that leverage to hold on to his job for forty-eight years and increase the FBI's power during every one of them. He was outspoken against homosexuality, and refused to allow gays (or many blacks, or any women) to become FBI agents. He was sure enough of his power that he sometimes held hands with Tolson in restaurants and shared rooms with him on vacations. There wasn't a president who could touch him.

Given these matters, and the additional fact that the screenplay for Clint Eastwood's *J. Edgar* was written by Dustin Lance Black, who wrote *Milk*, you would assume the film was the portrait of a gay man. It is not. That makes it more fascinating. It is the portrait of the public image that J. Edgar Hoover maintained all his life, even in private. The chilling possibility is that with Hoover what you saw was what you got. He was an unbending moralist who surrounded himself with FBI straight arrows. Those assigned closest to him tended to be good-looking. Agents wore suits and ties at all times. He inspected their shoe shines. . . . He liked to look but not touch.

In such famous cases as the capture of John Dillinger and the manhunt for the kidnapper of the Lindbergh baby, Hoover's publicity machine depicted him as acting virtually alone. He was not present when Dillinger was shot down outside the Biograph Theater, but America got the impression that he was, and he never forgave the star agent Melvin Purvis for actually cornering the Most Wanted poster boy. Doubt persisted that Bruno Hauptmann was guilty in the Lindbergh case—but not in Hoover's mind. The fight against domestic Communism in the years after World War II provided an ideal occasion for him to fan the Red Scare and work with the unsavory Joe McCarthy. Two of the reasons Hoover hated beatniks and hippies were their haircuts and shoe shines.

This man was closed down, his face a slab of petulance. He was so uncharismatic that it's possible to miss the brilliance of Leonardo DiCaprio's performance in *J. Edgar.* It is a fully realized, subtle, persuasive performance, not least in his scenes with Armie Hammer as Clyde Tolson. In my reading of the film, they were both repressed homosexuals, Hoover more than Tolson, but after love at first sight and a short but heady early courtship, they veered away from sex and began their lives as Longtime Companions. The rewards for arguably not being gay were too tempting for both men, who were wined and dined by Hollywood, Broadway, Washington, and Wall Street. It was Hoover's militant anti-gay position that served as their beard.

Two women figured importantly in Hoover's life. One was his domineering mother Annie Hoover (Judi Dench), who makes clear her scorn for men who are "daffodils." The other was a young woman named Helen Gandy (Naomi Watts). In an extraordinary moment of self-image control, Hoover concludes that it would be beneficial for him to have a wife. He asks Helen, an FBI secretary, out on one of the more unusual first dates in movie history; he demonstrates the workings of a card file system with great pride. It must have been clear to her that nothing was stirring in his netherlands. Their budding relationship segued smoothly into her becoming his confidential secretary for the rest of his life—the woman entrusted with the secret files.

Eastwood's film is firm in its refusal to cheapen and tarnish by inventing salacious scenes. I don't get the impression from *J. Edgar* that Eastwood particularly respected Hoover, but I do believe he respected his unyielding public facade. It is possibly Hoover's lifelong performance that fascinated him. There's a theme running through most of his films since *Bird* (1988): The man unshakably committed to his own idea of himself.

As a period biopic, *J. Edgar* is masterful. Few films span seven decades this comfortably. The sets, the props, the clothes and details look effortlessly right, and note how Eastwood handles the many supporting roles (some of them depicting famous people). These minor characters are all to some degree relating to Hoover's formidable public image. As a person or as a character, he was a star of stage, screen, radio, and print; he was said to have the goods on everyone. People tiptoed around him as they might have with Stalin. It's a nice touch, the way Eastwood and DiCaprio create a character who seems to be a dead zone and make him electrifying in other actors' reaction shots.

## Jeff, Who Lives at Home ★ ★ ★

R, 83 m., 2012

Jason Segel (Jeff), Ed Helms (Pat), Susan Sarandon (Sharon), Judy Greer (Linda), Rae Dawn Chong (Carol), Steve Zissis (Steve), Evan Ross (Kevin). Directed by Jay Duplass and Mark Duplass, and produced by Lianne Halfon, Jason Reitman, and Russell Smith. Screenplay by Jay Duplass and Mark Duplass.

Jeff is thirty, unmarried, unemployed, and lives in his mother's basement, wreathed in pot fumes. So large and unkempt his brother calls him Sasquatch, he watches the M. Night Shyamalan movie *Signs* over and over again, convinced it contains the key to the universe. That key, Jeff thinks, is that the universe is filled with meaningful coincidences, and all you must do is remain alert to them and your destiny will take care of itself. This is probably iron-clad logic if you smoke pot in the basement for long enough.

If Jeff (Jason Segel) is aimless, his brother, Pat (Ed Helms), is stuck in a lifeless marriage and doesn't realize it. His relationship with his wife, Linda (Judy Greer), is limited to registering her presence. While she focuses on saving money for a house, he reveals he's purchased a Porsche because . . . well, he got a good price. He takes her out to the deck of their condo to admire it in the driveway, and she startles him by dumping her breakfast on it. The nice breakfast (toasted waffles and Reddi-wip) he has just prepared for her! Women! What do they want?

Jeff and Pat share a widowed mother, Sharon (Susan Sarandon), who is approaching a birthday and demands that Jeff blast loose from the basement and perform one (1) simple task for her: replacing a kitchen shutter. Nothing can be simple when the universe is filled with signs and coincidences. Thus commences an eventful day for the family.

*Jeff, Who Lives at Home* is the new film by the brothers Duplass, Jay and Mark, who began in mumblecore with *The Puffy Chair* (2005), and created a comic gem in *Cyrus* (2010). The first involved two brothers and a shaky relationship. The second involved a mother and a demanding son who lives at home. In this film, the name "Kevin" seems to be a signpost from the universe. Jay's next film will be titled *Kevin*, a doc about an early hero of the brothers. Their basement must be a hotbed.

This film is a whimsical comedy, very whimsical, depending on the warmth of Segel and Sarandon, the discontent of Helms and Greer, and still more warmth that enters at midpoint with Carol (Rae Dawn Chong), Sarandon's coworker at the office. We get the impression they're all waiting around for the universe to whack them over the head with a two-by-four sign, and in the last act, it does.

All the major characters are stuck in a traffic jam on a bridge when an accident occurs. Now there's a coincidence that comes with a sign attached. What happens next can best be described as a melodramatic event that isn't terribly likely, but is terrifically effective in lowering a one-size-fits-all deus ex machina into the plot. It's all cute and self-aware, a pleasant joke on the audience, a happy ending for characters we like. It's not a feel-good movie, more of a feel-sorta-good movie.

One stylistic note: In nearly every scene, the Duplass brothers use quick little zooms in and out. Given the usual meaning of a sudden zoom in the grammar of the cinema (they translate as "Whoa!"), these have no meaning at all. They're simply devices to remind us that the story isn't really happening, but is being directed. Instead of "Whoa!" they translate as "Duplass!" They're good directors; they'll outgrow this.

## Jiro Dreams of Sushi ★ ★ ★

PG, 81 m., 2012

A documentary featuring Jiro Ono and Yoshikazu Ono. Directed by David Gelb and produced by Kevin Iwashina and Tom Pelligrini.

Jiro Ono is eighty-five years old. He ran away from home as a boy to become an apprentice in a restaurant, and has been making sushi for more than seventy years. He is apparently not happy doing anything else, and prefers to work all day, seven days a week, every day in the year. If an enforced holiday comes along, he considers that lost time.

His restaurant serves only sushi. It has ten

seats at a counter. It is in the basement of a Tokyo high-rise, not far from a subway stop. It has been awarded three stars, the highest possible rating, by the Michelin Guide. David Gelb's *Jiro Dreams of Sushi* is a documentary about a man whose relationship with sushi wavers between love and madness. He is a perfectionist, never satisfied, and if you go to work for him as an apprentice you will have to spend weeks learning how to properly squeeze out a towel before moving on to learn how to slice a hard-boiled egg.

He agonizes about the placement of mats on his counter. Great attention is paid to where along the counter the ten customers are seated in relationship to one another. Jiro's fifty-year-old son, Yoshikazu, works with him in the restaurant, and will inherit it someday. A younger son runs an associated sushi bar elsewhere in Tokyo. There is a three-month wait for a reservation. A typical meal will cost you more than $300. It will not take very long to eat.

This is a portrait of tunnel vision. Jiro exists to make sushi. Sushi exists to be made by Jiro. Do the math. Even at the high prices of his premium fresh ingredients, you realize he must be a rich man. But to what end? The existence of his sons is an indication that he has a wife, although we never see her. He must have a home, although we never visit it. There must be hours when he cannot be at work, but the film indicates no amusements, hobbies, or pastimes. The idea of his courtship of his wife fascinates me: Forgive me, but I imagine that even while making love he must be fretting about the loss of valuable sushi-making time.

As a documentary about world-class sushi, this film is definitive. It runs only eighty-one minutes, but the subject is finite. While watching it, I found myself drawn into the mystery of this man. Are there any unrealized wishes in his life? Secret diversions? Regrets? If you find an occupation you love and spend your entire life working at it, is that enough?

Standing behind his counter, Jiro notices things. Some customers are left-handed, some right-handed. That helps determine where they are seated. As he serves a perfect piece of sushi, he observes it being eaten. He knows the history of that piece of seafood. He knows his staff has recently started massaging an octopus for forty-five minutes and not half an hour, for example. Does he search a customer's eyes for a signal that this change has been an improvement? Half an hour of massage was good enough to win three Michelin stars. You realize the tragedy of Jiro Ono's life is that there are not, and will never be, four stars.

## Joan Rivers: A Piece of Work ★ ★ ★ ½

R, 84 m., 2010

Featuring Joan Rivers. A documentary directed by Ricki Stern and Annie Sundberg and produced by Seth Keal and Sundberg.

No one is ever too old. You may have that idea about Joan Rivers, who is seventy-five in this film and never tires of reminding us of that fact. Is that too old? It's older than she would prefer, but what are you gonna do? She remains one of the funniest, dirtiest, most daring and transgressive of stand-up comics, and she hasn't missed a beat.

*Joan Rivers: A Piece of Work* covers the events in about a year of her life. If the filmmakers didn't have total access, I don't want to see what they missed. In one stretch in this film she closes a show in Toronto, flies overnight to Palm Springs, does a gig, flies overnight to Minneapolis and performs another one. Try that sometime.

She has the energy, stamina, and aggression that a great stand-up needs. She assaults the audience. She pounds laughter out of us. If you've seen her only on television, you have no idea. I saw her in Vegas, and she had people weeping with laughter. I saw her at a memorial service in Toronto for a friend of hers, and she brought down the house. Was that wrong at a memorial service? Brian Linehan, her friend, wouldn't have expected anything less, and she knew it. If you need devout solemnity, Joan Rivers is not your girl.

The way she is funny is, she tells the truth according to herself. She hates some people. She has political opinions. Her observations are so merciless and her timing so precise that even if you like that person, you laugh. She is a sadist of comedy, unafraid to be cruel—even too cruel. She doesn't know fear. She seems to be curious about how far she can go and still get a laugh. That must feel dangerous on a stage with a live audience. Maybe she feeds on that danger.

This documentary began filming before she had her latest fifteen minutes of fame on Donald Trump's *Celebrity Apprentice.* God help Rod Blagojevich if he'd been on the show that season. Rivers has had hours of those fifteen minutes of fame. Her life is like a comeback tour. She is frank about her setbacks. She was Johnny Carson's resident cohost (and gave young Siskel & Ebert their first spot on *The Tonight Show*). She left Carson to begin her own nightly show on Fox. Carson never spoke to her again. NBC banned her from all of its shows until two years ago. The Fox show eventually failed, and it was discovered that her husband, Edgar, the show's manager, had been stealing from her. He killed himself. She never forgave him—for the suicide, not the other stuff.

She was down. She was up. Her daughter, Melissa, says, "Her career was like me having a sister." I wonder if Melissa appears with her on red carpet shows because it's a chance for some quiet time with Mom. She hardly mentions the red carpets for which she is now widely known. For her, it all comes down to this week: Does she have bookings? She looks at blank pages in her engagement calendar and says they're so white she needs sunglasses to read them.

What makes Joannie run? They say if a shark stops swimming, it dies. She's not a shark. She's a woman who for various reasons depends on making audiences laugh. They walk in knowing all of her problems, knowing her age, eagle eyed for the plastic surgery, ready to complain, and she *forces* them to laugh because she's so damned funny. I admire that. Bernard Shaw called it the Life Force. We see her in the film's first shot, without makeup. A minute later, *Joan Rivers* is before us. Her life is a performance of herself.

Yes, she's had plastic surgery. Well, why not? I think it's wrong for most people. But show business is cruel and eats its old, and you do what you have to do. She talks about it. She talks about everything. A portrait emerges of a bright little girl who walked onto a stage and never wanted to get off. If she can't have a network show, she'll work a dinner club.

There's that need in a lot of comics. Once in the Merchandise Mart, I was riding down in an elevator with Henny Youngman. The doors opened at the private club on the second floor, and there was a big placard there pointing to the room for a wedding. Henny didn't miss a beat. He walked off, asked to be introduced to the father of the bride, and told him, "My name is Henny Youngman. I'll do ten minutes for two hundred dollars."

I think *Joan Rivers: A Piece of Work* is fascinating and has a lot of laughs in it. It's more than that. It's the portrait of a woman who will not accept defeat, who will not slow down, who must prove herself over and again. A brave and stubborn woman, smart as a whip, superbly skilled. You want to see what it looks like to rage, rage against the dying of the light? Joan Rivers will not go gentle into that good night.

## John Carter ★ ★ ½

PG-13, 132 m., 2012

Taylor Kitsch (John Carter), Lynn Collins (Dejah Thoris), Samantha Morton (Sola), Mark Strong (Matai Shang), Ciaran Hinds (Tardos Mors), Dominic West (Sab Than), Willem Dafoe (Tars Tarkas), Thomas Haden Church (Tal Hajus). Directed by Andrew Stanton and produced by Lindsey Collins, Jim Morris, and Colin Wilson. Screenplay by Stanton, Mark Andrews, and Michael Chabon, based on *A Princess of Mars* by Edgar Rice Burroughs.

I don't see any way to begin a review of *John Carter* without referring to Through Time and Space with Ferdinand Feghoot. That was a series of little stories that appeared in the magazine *Fantasy and Science Fiction* from 1956 to 1973, and was to have a great influence on my development as a critic. In one of the Feghoot adventures, the hero found himself on Mars and engaged in bloody swordplay. He was sliced in the leg. Then in the other leg. Then an arm was hacked off. "To hell with this," Feghoot exclaimed, unholstering his ray gun and vaporizing his enemies.

I may have one or two details wrong, but you understand the point: When superior technology is at hand, it seems absurd for heroes to limit themselves to swords. When airships the size of a city block can float above a battle, why handicap yourself with cavalry charges involving lumbering alien rhinos? When it is possible to teleport yourself from Earth to Mars, why are you considered extraordinary because you can jump really high?

Such questions are never asked in the world of *John Carter*, and as a result the movie is more Western than science fiction. Even if we completely suspend our disbelief and accept the entire story at face value, isn't it underwhelming to spend so much time looking at hand-to-hand combat when there are so many neat toys and gadgets to play with?

But I must not review a movie that wasn't made. What we have here is a rousing boy's adventure story, adapted from stories that Edgar Rice Burroughs cranked out for early pulp magazines. They lacked the visceral appeal of his Tarzan stories, which inspired an estimated eighty-nine movies; amazingly, this is the first John Carter movie, but it is intended to foster a franchise, and will probably succeed.

Burroughs's hero is a Civil War veteran who finds himself in Monument Valley, where he has an encounter that transports him to the red planet Mars. This is not the Mars that NASA's rovers are poking into, but the Mars envisioned at the time Burroughs was writing, which the astronomer Percival Lowell claimed was crisscrossed by a system of canals. Luckily for Carter, it has an atmosphere he can breathe and surface temperatures allowing him to go without a shirt. In a delightful early scene, he finds that his Earth muscles allow him great leaps and bounds in the lower Martian gravity.

This attracts the attention of the inhabitants of Mars, represented by two apparently human cities at war with each other, and a native race called the Tharks, who look like a vague humanoid blend of weird green aliens from old covers of Thrilling Wonder Stories. They have four arms, and it was a great disappointment to me that we never saw a Thark putting on a shirt. John Carter feels an immediate affinity for the Tharks, and also gets recruited into the war of the cities—choosing the side with a fiery beauty named Dejah Thoris (Lynn Collins, who is the movie's best character).

John Carter is played by Taylor Kitsch, who costarred with Collins in *X-Men Origins: Wolverine*. Yes, I agree Kitsch is a curious name for a star in action movies. Still, it is his real name, and one can wonder how many fans of *Wolverine*, for example, are familiar with the word or its meaning. As an actor, he is perfectly serviceable as a sword-wielding, rhino-riding savior of planets.

The film was directed by Andrew Stanton, whose credits include *A Bug's Life*, *Finding Nemo*, and *WALL-E*. All three have tight, well-structured plots, and that's what *John Carter* could use more of. The action sequences are generally well executed, but they're too much of a muchness. CGI makes them seem too facile and not tactile enough. And although I liked the scene where Carter was getting his Mars legs with his first low-gravity steps, the sight of him springing into the air like a jumping jack could inspire bad laughs.

Does *John Carter* get the job done for the weekend action audience? Yes, I suppose it does. The massive city on legs that stomps across the landscape is well done. The Tharks are ingenious, although I'm not sure why they need tusks. Lynn Collins makes a terrific heroine. And I enjoyed the story outside the story, about how Burroughs wrote a journal about what he saw, and appears briefly as a character. He may even turn up in sequels. After all, he wrote some.

## Jonah Hex ★ ★

PG-13, 80 m., 2010

Josh Brolin (Jonah Hex), John Malkovich (Quentin Turnbull), Megan Fox (Lilah), Michael Fassbender (Burke), Will Arnett (Lieutenant Grass), Michael Shannon (Doc Cross Williams). Directed by Jimmy Hayward and produced by Akiva Goldsman and Andrew Lazar. Screenplay by Mark Neveldine and Brian Taylor, based on the DC Comics characters by John Albano and Tony Dezuniga.

*Jonah Hex* is a Western set around the town of Stunk Crick, although that doesn't entirely explain why the climactic scene involves an attack on the U.S. Capitol building in Washington. Using my powers of logic, I deduce that the characters traveled there from Stunk

Crick. The movie is not precise in its geography. Most of the location filming was in Louisiana, which is not named, perhaps because that might make it hard to explain its vast deserts and dusty frontier town.

The thriller involves a man named Jonah Hex (Josh Brolin), who is bent on vengeance. During the Civil War, the evil Quentin Turnbull (John Malkovich) strapped him to a cross and made him watch as a house containing his family was set afire. Then Turnbull branded Jonah's face with a hot iron, causing difficulties with leaks when he tries to throw back a shot of whiskey. You can see why Jonah would want his revenge. To be sure, Turnbull mutters something about Jonah having previously murdered HIS family, meaning he isn't entirely without motive.

Stunk Crick is your standard frontier town with a wide Main Street, a saloon, and a room over the saloon occupied by Lilah, a sexy hooker. The presence of Lilah in the film is easily explained: She is played by Megan Fox. If you want a woman in an old western town, there are only three occupations open to her, hooking, schoolmarming, and anyone called Ma.

Lilah and Jonah are in love, for reasons unexplained. It certainly isn't because of the quality of their conversation. The only hooker in a Western I've ever believed in was in *Lonesome Dove*, but I've seen *Lonesome Dove*, and *Jonah Hex* is no *Lonesome Dove*.

It's based on some DC Comics characters, which may explain the way the plot jumps around. We hear a lot about graphic novels, but this is more of a graphic anthology of strange occult ideas. Consider, for example, that Jonah was once so close to death that he wandered around on the Other Side and made valuable contacts there. He can even talk to the dead, and one corpse revives long enough to tell him precisely where Quentin Turnbull can be found.

In what is possibly a confused stab at allegory, Jonah finds himself trying to prevent Turnbull from blowing up the Capitol building with a terrorist super weapon. In scenes set in the Oval Office, the U.S. president is concerned about this threat by Turnbull, who is an embittered Confederate general, and decides that the wanted outlaw Hex is the only man who can prevent the plot from being carried out.

A climactic battle scene takes place in the Potomac River between two ironclad ships. In U.S. history, you will recall, there was such a battle between the USS *Monitor* and the Confederate ship *Virginia*. One of these ships looks like the *Monitor*, but I'm unclear. Anyway, Turnbull is onboard, directing the Weapon, which is a big cannon. He's previously tested it by blowing up a Western town. Now he trains it on the Capitol, depicted in special effects that suggest the Capitol and the Washington Monument were the only two structures in Washington at that time, at least for purposes of being fired on.

After Hex saves the day, he's invited into the Oval Office, thanked, and then presented with a big badge. What is this badge? The president tells Hex: "America needs a sheriff." This provided the audience with a big laugh, which sounded like it might have been bottled up for a while.

## The Joneses ★ ★

R, 96 m., 2010

Demi Moore (Kate Jones), David Duchovny (Steve Jones), Amber Heard (Jennifer Jones), Ben Hollingsworth (Mick Jones), Gary Cole (Larry), Glenne Headly (Summer), Lauren Hutton (KC). Directed by Derrick Borte and produced by Borte, Doug Mankoff, Andrew Spaulding, and Kristi Zea. Screenplay by Borte.

Everyone wants to keep up with the Joneses. They're good-looking, friendly, popular, affluent, and they always seem ahead of the curve when it comes to what they drive, wear, play, and consume. They never boast. They never have to. People just plain want to be just like them. And you had better stop reading now, because it's impossible to say more without a spoiler.

OK, for those still in the room, I wonder how many will really be surprised by the big plot "reveal." From the first moments of dialogue, there seems to be something off about the Joneses. Nothing is made explicit for a time, but they don't seem to relate to one another as family members. There's something they understand and we don't.

The fact is, they aren't a family; they're a marketing unit. Marketing people talk about "early adopters": People who influence a peer group by being the first to know about, use, wear, or attend something. At a conference I attended in Boulder, Colorado, total strangers followed Andy Ihnatko and his iPad around like a man with a T-bone at a dog pound. The Joneses are professional early adopters, paid to impersonate a family unit and consume the sponsor's products.

Among other advantages to this story idea, it makes product placement necessary, not merely venal. If you don't leave this movie more aware of the new Audi models, you slept through it. The Joneses never make a point of anything. It's just that Steve Jones (David Duchovny) makes great shots with his new golf clubs. Kate Jones (Demi Moore) entertains so brilliantly. Their teenagers, Jennifer (Amber Heard) and Mick (Ben Hollingsworth), wear such cool stuff. If the Joneses don't have a dog, maybe that's because there's not enough money in dog retailing.

It would seem to be a comfortable existence, consuming the best products ahead of the market and never having to pay for them. It's not that easy. It means denying your own impulses to be honest and confiding. Suppressing your own tastes. Not feeling genuine. Ask yourself who in your crowd insisted you had to see *How to Train Your Dragon* in 3-D, when you wanted to see it in 2-D, and what you *really* wanted to see was *My Son, My Son, What Have Ye Done*. That person is a Jones.

You, on the other hand, are a Larry or Summer (Gary Cole and Glenne Headly), the next-door neighbors who are always playing catch-up. You have ceded control of your taste to someone you admire for superficial reasons. This is a doomed enterprise, for you will never, ever catch up, and by definition you can never take the lead because the Joneses define the race.

*The Joneses* not surprisingly finds troubling flaws in the lives of this professional family. Try as they will to be disciplined and on message, they have emotions of their own. Some of them involve sex. Others involve a feeling of inner worthlessness. The strongest is Kate, played by the great-looking Demi Moore as a capable team leader aiming for a promotion. Steve is a former golf pro, so no stranger to the challenge of playing a role model, but his decency runs deeper than Kate's.

As for the kids, Jennifer and Mick, well, even their names are popular; Jennifer is the sixty-seventh most popular name in the nation and Michael is the third. But they're teenagers, and you know how that goes. So many raging hormones, either to follow or suppress. That Jennifer and Mick are so attractive, and so . . . advanced . . . for their age complicates their inner lives. At that age, you haven't been completely tamed by the corporate mind-set.

*The Joneses* was directed and cowritten by Derrick Borte, an advertising man, and contains a good deal of dark cynicism. It also hopes to entertain, and those two goals don't fit together easily. Either this is a tragic family or a satirical one, and the film seems uncertain which way to jump. In a perfect film, the noose of their inauthentic lives would draw more tightly, more swiftly, around the Joneses, and the movie might be angrier.

Still, Demi Moore is good as a corporate team player with no conscience (she could have played the George Clooney role in *Up in the Air*), and the others adequately act around the problems of the screenplay. It's just that somehow this movie should acknowledge how very close to life it is, and how in our society you don't have to pay the Joneses. They learn their roles from television and work for free.

## Journey 2: The Mysterious Island ★ ★ ½

PG, 94 m., 2012

Dwayne Johnson (Hank), Michael Caine (Alexander), Josh Hutcherson (Sean), Vanessa Hudgens (Kailani), Luis Guzman (Gabato), Kristin Davis (Liz). Directed by Brad Peyton and produced by Beau Flynn, Charlotte Huggins, and Tripp Vinson. Screenplay by Brian Gunn and Mark Gunn.

*Journey 2: The Mysterious Island* looks like nothing so much as one of those live-action adventures Disney used to grind out in the 1950s—and hey, here's Captain Nemo's Nautilus to prove it. Also a tree house to humble *Swiss Family Robinson*, which contains a shortwave radio that has been assembled from old spoons, I think I heard.

The movie is very, very loosely a sequel to *Journey to the Center of the Earth,* with only two connections: It's inspired by a Jules Verne novel, and it costars young Josh Hutcherson as the hero Sean. The picture opens with him on a motorcycle, being chased by cops, but not to worry; all he did was break into a satellite tracking station to boost the power on a message for help sent by his grandfather from a lost island in the Pacific.

Sean, whose father in the first film (Brendan Fraser) has disappeared (from the cast, anyway), now has to deal with Hank (Dwayne Johnson, aka The Rock). Hank is his new stepdad. Sean and Hank make friends by decrypting the grandfather's message; Hank glances at it and intuits that the two-syllable words stand for dots and the one-syllable words stand for dashes, which means Grandpa has had enough free time on his remote island to figure out a way to make Morse code several times longer than previously. Unanswered is why Grandfather would encrypt a call for help.

This Hank, what a swell guy. He proposes that the two of them fly off to the Pacific and find Grandpa. On arrival somewhere, they hire a tourist helicopter pilot named Gabato, played by Luis Guzman as another one of those low-comedy guys who get all worked up and are scared of stuff. (I enjoyed a reprise of this classic shot: Gabato runs toward camera, falls on stomach, looks up . . . and up . . . and up.)

Gabato has a daughter named Kailani (Vanessa Hudgens), a Polynesian beauty who wears a tank top and Daisy Dukes throughout the film. These four fly off in the helicopter, are trapped in a Category 5 hurricane, which rips it to pieces, and are lucky enough to find themselves alive on the beach of the Mysterious Island.

This is your complete island. It has an active volcano, waterfalls with no apparent water sources streaming down cliffs, elephants as small as dogs, and giant lizards that are nowhere big enough to account for the size of their eggs (Sean falls through the shell of one, splashes in a pool of yolk, and is attacked by an unborn lizard chick). Also on the island is the lost city of Atlantis, even though it's in the wrong ocean, and bees so big Sean and Kailani can both ride on the back of one. And Alexander Anderson, Sean's grandfather, who is played by Michael Caine, who will not be editing this role into his videos about how to act in movies.

I hope you understand I enjoyed most of this stuff. The director, Brad Peyton, apparently intended it as a genial parody of countless other movies in this spirit. There is, for example, a scene where Sean, Grandpa, Kailani, and Gabato all sit around the old campfire and listen while Hank strums a ukulele and sings "What a Wonderful World." And I mean he *sings* it: every word of three verses. It's not every day you see The Rock channeling Gene Autry.

Sean deduces that Verne's novel contains everything they need to know, and this comes in handy when the volcano explodes and the island begins to sink into the sea. Sure enough, Captain Nemo's submarine is still hidden underwater. Hank and Sean, trusting Verne, dive off a high cliff, and while holding their breaths and swimming underwater are able to (1) find the sub, (2) open the hatch by tugging and twisting it, (3) swim inside, (4) push a lever to fill it with air, and (5) get the power generator working by jump-starting it with an electric eel.

This is transcendently goofy. It isn't a "good" movie in the usual sense (or most senses), but it is jolly and good-natured, and Michael Caine and Dwayne Johnson are among the most likable of actors. Johnson is such a good sport he even shows young Sean how to impress girls by flexing your pecs so quickly that nuts will ricochet off of them. I can't think of any reason to pay extra for the 3-D.

## Joyful Noise ★ ½

PG-13, 117 m., 2012

Queen Latifah (Vi Rose Hill), Dolly Parton (G. G. Sparrow), Keke Palmer (Olivia Hill), Jeremy Jordan (Randy Garrity), Courtney B. Vance (Pastor Dale), Dexter Darden (Walter Hill), Jesse L. Martin (Marcus Hill). Directed by Todd Graff and produced by Joseph Farrell, Broderick Johnson, Andrew A. Kosove, Michael G. Nathanson, and Catherine Paura. Screenplay by Graff.

*Joyful Noise* is an ungainly assembly of parts that don't fit, and the strange thing is that it makes no particular effort to please its target audience, which would seem to be lovers of gospel choirs. There's a scene toward the end at a national gospel music competition that features a real gospel choir, and compared to them our team seems like a hasty gathering of unmatched character types. These are people we don't believe, with dialogue that sounds contrived and unconvincing.

The place: a small Georgia town, deep in poverty. The characters: the Pacashau Sacred Divinity Choir. The occasion: Just as the choir leader dies of a heart attack, the annual gospel choir competition is approaching. Two strong women are in competition for the job of choir director. Vi Rose Hill (Queen Latifah) and G. G. Sparrow (Dolly Parton). Pastor Dale (Courtney B. Vance) gives Vi Rose the position, although G. G. is the widow of the former director and believes she should have inherited the honor.

Now pause a moment. Imagine a choir. Not a large choir, but smallish, with most of its members looking typecast. It's a small church, but has plenty of empty seats during services (cutting corners on extras?). It is completely racially integrated, which I believe is not that common even in modern Georgia. The film has almost no specifically spiritual content; the purpose of the choir is not to praise God but to win contests. The choir members date a lot, leading to a scene in which a black woman and a small Asian man fall in love and sleep together. This is without the benefit of matrimony, although it must be admitted that the man seems to be quickly punished by the Almighty. (Later in the film, the woman meets another Asian man and they exchange warm smiles as part of the clunky happy ending.)

Dolly Parton and Queen Latifah seem, let it be said, too much for one choir. They provide an excess of subplots. The Parton character has a grandson named Randy (Jeremy Jordan) who has been sent to stay with her after "getting in trouble" in New York. The Latifah character has a daughter, Olivia (Keke Palmer). These two fall instantly in love. Olivia is sixteen. Randy is a "teenager" who looks every bit as old as the actor, who is twenty-six and poised to play Clyde in a Broadway production of *Bonnie and Clyde.* He and others were perhaps chosen by a casting director without a single thought about whether they seemed to belong in the same movie.

It's unclear why G. G. and Vi Rose hate each other or what their small-town history has been, but man, they have a grudge. The appointment of Vi Rose as choir director eventually leads to an epic confrontation between the two women in the local restaurant where Vi has a second job as a waitress. This has to be seen to be believed. While the customers look on in disbelief and the owner takes an amazingly long time to intervene, they scream insults at each other and Vi Rose throws baking powder biscuits at G. G., who blocks them with a tray.

A great many of the insults involve G. G.'s plastic surgery, which Vi Rose implies is mostly responsible for the G. G. standing before us today. G. G. shouts back, "Plastic surgeons have to make a living!" We all know that Dolly Parton has had some work and that she often jokes about it. Still, Vi Rose's dialogue seems over the top: too cruel, because it contains much truth. There is another problem. One look at G. G. and you suspect no one in a poverty-stricken small town could afford work like that.

The two "kids," Olivia and Randy, have a relationship that ticks off the time-honored clichés of all such movie romances, including the breakup and the reconciliation. The movie loads on another subplot involving Vi Rose's son Walter (Dexter Darden), who has Asperger's syndrome and is articulate about it, complaining to his mom that he wishes he knew how to behave better socially and know what people mean when they say things. Happily, he finds an appropriate way to express himself during the national finals, and fits snugly into the collective happy ending.

True gospel music can indeed be a joyful noise. The writers of this film, turning to the 95th Psalm, seem to have read it this way: "O come, let us sing unto the Lord: let us make a joyful noise to the rock and roll of our salvation." The climactic scene at the national finals is so inappropriate, so unexpected in terms of what's gone before, that its purpose is not so much to win the competition as to supply the audience with a big production number starring Dolly and the Queen. The only thing miraculous about it is that a big orchestra materializes on the sound track. In trying so awkwardly to include a little something for everyone, *Joyful Noise* succeeds in finding a little something to disappoint everyone, no matter what they were expecting.

## The Joy of Singing ★ ★ ★

NO MPAA RATING, 96 m., 2010

Marina Fois (Muriel), Lorant Deutsch (Philippe), Jeanne Balibar (Constance), Julien Baumgartner (Julien), Nathalie Richard (Noemie), Caroline Ducey (Anna), Guillaume Quatravaux (Joseph), Evelyne Kirschenbaum (Eve). Directed by Ilan Duran Cohen and produced by Anne-Cecile Berthomeau and Edouard Mauriat. Screenplay by Cohen and Philippe Lasry.

Don't get the wrong idea. *The Joy of Singing* could also be titled *The Joy of Singing Rather Than Being Murdered.* One of the meetings of Madame Eve's voice class begins with her tearful announcement that two of the group have been found dead. Her students eye one another uneasily. Who will be killed next? We wonder, too.

This is the goofiest thrill-sex-music-spy movie in many a moon, with a surprising amount of nudity and an even more surprising amount of singing, ranging from opera to "Amazing Grace" to "I'll Stand by You." Its MacGuffin is a missing USB memory stick containing unspecified uranium secrets.

I fully believe no one in the movie has any idea what these secrets could consist of, where they came from, and how they went missing, but never mind. The information belonged to the late husband of Constance (Jeanne Balibar), a student in the class. Therefore, French undercover agents *and* terrorists *and* possible Israeli and Russian agents enroll in the class to keep an eye on her. I'm trying to remember if anyone in the class has enrolled to improve their voice.

This is all done with a straight face. The students with their nefarious secrets all have to sing. Some aren't half bad. A couple are damn fine. Maybe there's something about singing in a small group of fellow spies that elevates the libido. Soon many, if not all, of these people (except for Madame Eve) are screwing like rabbits. Even the young hustler Julien (Julien Baumgartner), who doesn't give freebies for ethical reasons, is astonished to find himself growing tender about Noemie (Nathalie Richard). If there's one thing fatal to spying, it's sincerity.

At a different velocity this could be a screwball comedy, especially with those big apartments where people are always coming into and going out of rooms, but then it would be less fun. Death and sex are sort of serious, you see, and these people don't treat them lightly. They also have underlying concerns about growing old and never having children. The French agents, Muriel (Marina Fois) and Philippe (Lorant Deutsch), have a problem: She wants him to sleep with her, and he wants to be respected for more than his body. If Inspector Clouseau wandered in, he'd be out of his league,and soon out of his pants.

I'll award a shiny new dime to anyone who watches the film once and can tell me who is doing what and to whom and for what reason. It just doesn't matter. We get the basic idea, and realize we know more about what's happening than anyone on the screen. I doubt if anyone in the movie, in the audience, or among the filmmakers can offer a plausible explanation for why all these people have to attend music class, especially considering its fatality rate.

## Judy Moody and the NOT Bummer Summer ★ ★

PG, 91 m., 2011

Jordana Beatty (Judy Moody), Heather Graham (Aunt Opal), Parris Mosteller (Stink), Jaleel White (Mr. Todd), Garrett Ryan (Rocky), Preston Bailey (Frank), Janet Varney (Mom), Kristoffer Winters (Dad). Directed by John Schultz and produced by Gary Magness and Sarah Siegel-Magness. Screenplay by Kathy Waugh and Megan McDonald, based on the books by McDonald.

*Judy Moody and the NOT Bummer Summer* is a film that little kids might find perfectly acceptable. Little, little, little kids. My best guess is above fourth-grade level you'd be pushing it.

The kids, on the other hand, might enjoy its zany adaptation of Megan McDonald's best-seller. That makes this a good candidate for watching on video. I doubt many parents would enjoy it much, and I can't see grown-ups attending unless they're on duty.

The movie tells the story of red-headed Judy Moody (Jordana Beatty), who learns in disbelief that while all her friends will be spending the summer doing neat things, her own parents will be away from home on an important trip. They plan to abandon Judy and her kid brother, Stink (Parris Mosteller), to the care of her dreaded Aunt Opal (Heather Graham). That information immediately reminded me that one of my mother's best friends was named Opal Hollingsworth. I heard the name "Opal Hollingsworth" so often that it's difficult for me to think of an Opal not named Hollingsworth.

What, you may ask, does that possibly have to do with *Judy Moody and the NOT Bummer Summer*? I must be honest. Both while watching the movie and again while writing this review, when I got to the name "Aunt Opal," my mind veered off on a tangent. There was little in the film to draw it back on course. It may seem unfair of me to change the subject so arbitrarily, but I am trying to signal my grown-up readers that they may find themselves looking for stuff to think about while watching this film.

Anyway, Aunt Opal turns up and is not nearly so bad as Judy Moody fears. She draws up a Thrill Chart, a weirdly unconnected checklist of things to keep Judy and Stink occupied during the summer, and the film works its way through some of these topics with lots of bright colors and jolly music. There are also some jokes about those basic bodily functions that little kids seem to find hilarious.

Jordana Beatty is capable here, sweet and spirited, and my wish for her is that life brings her screenplays that I will find more interesting. She might excel in *The Life of Opal Hollingsworth*, who was quite a character.

## Jumping the Broom ★ ★ ★

PG-13, 107 m., 2011

Angela Bassett (Mrs. Watson), Paula Patton (Sabrina Watson), Laz Alonso (Jason Taylor), Loretta Devine (Mrs. Taylor), Meagan Good (Blythe), Tasha Smith (Shonda), Romeo Miller (Sebastian), DeRay Davis (Malcolm), Valarie Pettiford (Aunt Geneva), Mike Epps (Willie Earl). Directed by Salim Akil and produced by Tracey E. Edmonds, Elizabeth Hunter, T. D. Jakes, Michael Mahoney, Glendon Palmer, and Curtis Wallace. Screenplay by Hunter and Arlene Gibbs.

The groom's mother is a postal worker in Brooklyn. The bride's family lives in a seaside compound on Martha's Vineyard so spacious no neighbors are visible. The bride and groom are in love, but their families are not. That was good enough for *Romeo and Juliet*, and it still sorta works with *Jumping the Broom*.

This is one of those films during which I notice things I simply decide to disregard. It's a good time at the movies, and an excellent demonstration of why I dislike the word "flawed," which critics use as if they were gazing through jewelers' eyepieces. It's not a perfect movie. The mothers are exaggerated to the point of easy sitcommery. So OK: We're not going for the sociology. We're going for fun, and if characters are too broad, that, too, can be fun. There's such a thing as being picky, picky, picky, and in this case Angela Bassett and Loretta Devine have such good timing with their performances that to hell with nuance.

The marriage takes place across the class divide between two old African-American families. The Taylors are working class. The Watsons are members of the ruling elite; Mr. Watson basically just stands around posing like a sleek master of the universe.

We meet the Watson girl, Sabrina (Paula Patton), after another of the one-night stands apparently not unknown to her. She's fed up with these hit-and-run guys and tells her best friend, Shonda (Tasha Smith), from now on she's going to save her cookies like a good Girl Scout until she meets Mr. Right. The film was coproduced by Bishop T. D. Jakes, who possibly finds even retroactive abstinence to be commendable. It was Oscar Levant who said, "I go back so far, I knew Doris Day before she was a virgin."

Mr. Right is Jason Taylor (Laz Alonso), who may come from a blue-collar home but is a hot shot on Wall Street, and the kind of chap any mother should be proud to have her daughter marry. Not Angela Bassett's Mrs. Watson. As for Loretta Devine's Mrs. Taylor, she is affronted that the bride's mother contacts her by e-mail. E-mail! How insulting is that?

The mothers meet for the first time on the wedding day. Their meeting is not a masterpiece of subtle dialogue, but let it be said that Devine and Bassett slug it out boldly, as everyone present (and in the audience) winces. What saves this from being a bloodbath of social mayhem is the leavening presence of some amusing supporting characters.

It is written that couples who meet at weddings are under a special star, and young Sebastian (Romeo Miller) easily believes that when he lays eyes (and would like to lay so much else) on Sabrina's best friend, Shonda. She isn't quite old enough to be his mother, but easily old enough to be his mother's younger sister. He's love-struck, sincere, inexhaustible. She flees him and lectures him and is touched by his devotion and might secretly like to be touched by more than that.

There's an even broader romance between the bridesmaid Blythe (Meagan Good) and the chef (Gary Dourdan), which results in one of the most original explanations I can imagine for keeping flour off the knees of your pants.

The title *Jumping the Broom* comes from an ancient custom of slavery days, passed down in the Taylor family. When Mrs. Watson hears of this, she declares, "Our family weren't slaves. We owned slaves." While I have no doubt that was sometimes the case, I submit that neither Mrs. Watson nor any other African-American in the past century or more would choose to make that announcement in public.

The movie is elegantly photographed. There is something about a wedding that bestows a pleasing structure upon a film. We anticipate that inevitable moment when all happiness seems doomed. The cast is large, well chosen, and diverting. The ceremony is delightful. Sabrina and Jason make a lovely couple. Someday they will laugh in remembering their mothers. Not someday real soon.

## Just Go with It ★

PG-13, 116 m., 2011

Adam Sandler (Danny), Jennifer Aniston (Katherine), Brooklyn Decker (Palmer), Nick Swardson (Eddie), Nicole Kidman (Devlin Adams), Bailee Madison (Maggie), Griffin Gluck (Michael), Dave Matthews (Ian Maxtone Jones), Kevin Nealon (Adon). Directed by Dennis Dugan and produced by Jack Giarraputo, Heather Parry, and Adam Sandler. Screenplay by Allan Loeb and Timothy Dowling.

The people in this movie are dumber than a box of Tinkertoys. One fears they're so unfortunate it's not politically correct to laugh at them. That's not a problem because *Just Go with It* is so rarely funny. Here is a story that began as a French farce. Then it was adapted into a Broadway play named *Cactus Flower*. Then the play was made into a movie. Now it has been made into another movie. This process has diluted it like a homeopathic medicine, so that not an atom of the original formula can be found.

Consider. Danny (Adam Sandler) broke off his wedding at the last minute, but continues to wear the wedding ring. Women find the ring seductive and cannot resist having sex with a married man. Therefore, most (not all) of the women in his life are stupid. This works for him for approximately twenty-five years. In the meantime, he becomes a famous plastic surgeon in Beverly Hills. He is assisted by Nurse Katherine (Jennifer Aniston), who has two kids.

On the one day he isn't wearing his ring, he spends an idyllic night at the beach with the delicious twenty-three-year-old Palmer (Brooklyn Decker). Then she finds the ring in his pocket and thinks he is married, and he lies and says yes, but his divorce is almost final. She insists on meeting his wife. He makes Nurse Katherine pretend to be his wife. He buys her several thousand dollars' worth of clothes for her one (1) meeting with Palmer.

For reasons having to do with Palmer's love of children, they all fly to Hawaii together with Nurse Katherine's two kids and Danny's high school buddy Eddie (Nick Swardson), who pretends to be the nurse's fiancé. Eddie disguises himself with thick glasses and the worst German accent since the guy who worshipped Hitler in *The Producers*. He also brandishes a meerschaum pipe because everyone who has seen *Inglourious Basterds* knows all Germans smoke meerschaum pipes.

This might work as a farce. Maybe it did, in France. It worked as a Broadway play by Abe Burrows. It worked as a 1969 movie with Walter Matthau, Ingrid Bergman as the nurse, and Goldie Hawn as the young girl. It doesn't work now. The problem is the almost paralytic sweetness of the characters. Nobody is really trying to get away with anything. They're just trying to do the right thing in an underhanded way. Walter Matthau was crafty in the cradle. Goldie Hawn was the definitive ditz. Ingrid Bergman was *sigh.* The 1969 screenplay was by I. A. L. Diamond, who knew a thing or two about farce when he wrote *Some Like It Hot.* They made a good movie.

So nice is everyone here that even the completely surplus character played by Nicole Kidman is undermined. She plays the old standby, the popular girl who was mean to Nurse Katherine in high school. We know the cliché. Kidman could have done something with it, but the screenplay gives her nowhere to go. It's painful to endure the cloying scene where they kiss and make up.

*Just Go with It* is like a performance of the old material by actors who don't get the joke. The movie doesn't even have the nerve to caricature the Kidman character, who is presented as a true-blue, sincere Bo Derek clone. Adam Sandler stays well within the range of polite, ingratiating small-talk artists he unnecessarily limits himself to. Jennifer Aniston is alert and amused, but by giving her the fake boyfriend with the meerschaum the film indicates that she, too, is one tinker short of a toy.

There is one funny scene in the movie. It involves a plastic surgery victim with a roaming right eyebrow. You know the movie is in trouble when you find yourself missing the eyebrow.

## Just Wright ★ ★ ★

PG, 99 m., 2010

Queen Latifah (Leslie Wright), Common (Scott McKnight), Paula Patton (Morgan Alexander), James Pickens Jr. (Lloyd Wright), Phylicia Rashad (Ella McKnight), Pam Grier (Janice Wright). Directed by Sanaa Hamri and produced by Debra Martin Chase, Shakim Compere, and Queen Latifah. Screenplay by Michael Elliot.

One reason people like Queen Latifah is that she likes herself. In most of her roles, she radiates cheer. She can play grim, as in *Bringing Out the Dead,* but she has a natural sunniness that makes me, at least, feel good. And she is a real woman, not a skinny woman with too many sharp angles. Jennifer Aniston, who looks perfectly great, makes me worry about her mental health when she publicizes her new baby food diet.

Latifah has never been fat. She has always been plus size. There is a difference. She is healthy, fit, carries herself with confidence, and looks terrific in *Just Wright* in the kind of clothing a physical therapist might feel comfortable wearing. If you're dragging around feeling low about yourself, you want to know her secret.

This is not a discussion of the Queen's body, however; it's about the whole gestalt. One of the reasons she's the star of *Just Wright* is that few people, and certainly no one in this film, can hold the screen against her. In common with many other stars, when she's in a shot, it's about her.

Sure, we go along with the fiction that Scott (Common), the handsome pro basketball player in the movie, is going to marry Morgan (Paula Patton), Queen Latifah's BFF. Sure, we think Patton looks terrific and is a beauty. But, come on. Once Scott injures his knee and hires Miss Wright (Latifah) as his live-in physical therapist, we know he's going to fall in love with her. It's so much easier to fall in love with someone who is necessary to you than someone you are necessary to.

The plot involves Leslie Wright and Morgan as obsessed fans of the New Jersey Nets—Leslie because she loves basketball, and Morgan because she wants to be a player's wife. After Leslie has a Meet Cute with the handsome Nets star Scott McKnight at a gas station, she gets invited to his birthday party, and, of course, takes Morgan along. Scott zooms in on Morgan. Leslie, as loyal best friend, is accustomed to this.

After Scott gets a knee injury and Leslie becomes his special duty therapist, the trick is to not rush in the direction the movie is obviously moving. Director Sanaa Hamri accomplishes this. She and writer Michael Elliot add enough detail and actual dialogue (you know, people talking about things in more than one syllable) that we enjoy the growing-closer process. Paula Patton's Morgan is a self-centered egotist and no good at caregiving, but hey, that's built into the role.

Sanaa Hamri is herself an actor-director, with an interesting background; she directed two of Prince's TV specials and the very good *Something New* (2006), starring Sanaa Lathan (no relation). That was another film about a woman and man gradually discovering they're in love, which is always more fun than the first-sight deal. Here Common isn't called upon to do much heavy lifting in the acting department, but he plays well with Queen Latifah. Sure, the movie is a formula. A formula that works reminds us of why it became a formula.

# K

## Kaboom ★ ★ ½

NO MPAA RATING, 86 m., 2011

Thomas Dekker (Smith), Haley Bennett (Stella), Chris Zylka (Thor), Roxane Mesquida (Lorelei), Juno Temple (London), Andy Fischer-Price (Rex), Nicole LaLiberte (Red-Haired Girl). Directed by Gregg Araki and produced by Araki, Sebastien Lemercier, and Andrea Sperling.

*Kaboom* exists entirely in and for the moment. It brings some intriguing college students on-screen, watches them have sex with one another, and involves them in a plot in which there is not much difference between hallucination and everyday life. It raises only one question: Since the characters devote so much time to it, why don't they seem to care much about sex? It seems more like a pastime for idle hands and genitals.

The movie has been cast, designed, clothed, scored, and edited to the bleeding edge of hip, but it hasn't exactly been written. There's some nice dialogue, but sometimes it sounds like lines left over from other screenplays that were too good to throw away. The director, Gregg Araki, enjoys material of this sort; his characters draw the line only at heterosexual monogamy. What's curious is that his central character, Smith (Thomas Dekker), is filled with sexual yearnings despite the abundance of opportunities at hand.

Smith describes his sexuality as "undecided." As the film opens, he lusts for his hunky roommate Thor (Chris Zylka), who reminds me that the generation of kids named after Marvel superheroes must be approaching thirty. Thor isn't gay, he just plays gay in his life. His best friend, Stella (Haley Bennett), is a lesbian. Into her life comes Lorelei (Roxane Mesquida), who is a practicing witch—and I don't mean a Wiccan Earth goddess, but the kind of witch Aleister Crowley would approve of, with actual wicked powers. Lorelei and the character named the Red-Haired Girl (Nicole LaLiberte) appear in his dreams, even before he meets them. (Note: Nicole LaLiberte might have made a good wife for Rockets Redglare, had they overlapped in life.)

There are many other characters, including a pothead resident adviser and three hostile male figures wearing animal masks. Some of these figures are real, some dreams, some imposters, and then the line blurs and this microcosm of campus sex hobbyists turns out to be linked to the sort of secret global conspiracy that could inspire lots of Dan Brown novels.

None of this matters. If the events in *Kaboom* are anything, they're arbitrary. That helps justify the film's ending, which nobody can claim doesn't tie up all the loose threads. But this movie isn't about beginnings and endings—or middles, for that matter. If anything can happen, does it much matter? You could watch it like you listen to an album, not paying much attention to which cut you're on.

There's one thing that confuses me. *Kaboom* is as indulgent as a film school exercise. I thought Gregg Araki had outgrown messing about like this. His *Mysterious Skin* (2004) was lovingly controlled and mysteriously spellbinding. Now he engages his shallow and narcissistic characters on their level, not his.

## The Karate Kid ★ ★ ★ ½

PG, 131 m., 2010

Jaden Smith (Dre Parker), Jackie Chan (Mr. Han), Taraji P. Henson (Sherry Parker), Han Wenwen (Mei Ying), Wang Zhenwei (Cheng), Rongguang Yu (Master Li). Directed by Harald Zwart and produced by James Lassiter, Jada Pinkett Smith, Will Smith, Ken Stovitz, and Jerry Weintraub. Screenplay by Christopher Murphey.

If you've seen *The Karate Kid* (1984), the memories will come back during this 2010 remake of the original. That's a compliment. The original story was durable enough to inspire three sequels, and now we have an entertaining version filmed mostly on location in China, with fifty-six-year-old Jackie Chan in the role of Mr. Miyagi.

The original film was one of its year's best movies. The new one lacks the perfect freshness of that one; there aren't many surprises as it follows the 1984 almost point by point. But here is a lovely and well-made film that stands well on its own feet. The Chinese locations add visual interest, there are scenes of splendor in mountains and on the Great Wall, and the characters are once again engaging.

The original film's greatest asset was the Oscar-nominated performance by Pat Morita as Mr. Miyagi. Jackie Chan is so famous that it can come as no surprise here when Mr. Han, a reclusive janitor, reveals a hidden talent for the martial arts. But Chan has never been a strutting, macho fighter onscreen; his charm comes from a self-kidding quality. Here he does a good job of cooling down his usual cheerfulness and keeping his cards hidden.

In the role of his young pupil, Jaden Smith, son of Will and Jada Pinkett Smith, has a natural screen presence that glows. Dre Parker is calmer than the skitterish kid played by Ralph Macchio, but so much smaller than his opponents that we can well believe his fear of a bully at school. And when that happens, we can forget obsessing about the 1984 film and enjoy this one. That was then; this is now.

The story once again involves a kid being packed up by his divorced mom and forced to leave his hometown and friends and move far away—from Detroit to Beijing, this time. He hates it. Then a cute young violinist named Mei Ying (Han Wenwen) smiles at him, and life looks more promising—if it weren't for the school bully, Cheng (Wang Zhenwei). This creature is so hateful and sadistic it's hard to explain, until we meet his brutal kung fu coach, Master Li (Rongguang Yu). The monstrous Li teaches a new form of child abuse: kids beating up on each other.

The story proceeds, as it must, with Dre slowly softening the heart of Mr. Han, who saves him from a beating by Cheng and agrees to teach him the secrets of kung fu. Training goes well, and Dre and Mei Ying make a pact to attend each other's big days: his kung fu tournament, her recital. There's the usual nonsense about her parents disapproving of him. Gee, why in the world would the parents of a world-class classical musician disapprove of a kung fu student from Detroit who doesn't speak Chinese?

Luckily for Dre and the movie, everyone in China who needs to speak English can do so, even the little monster Cheng. Many Americans not only have small interest in learning another language, they have small interest in reading subtitles of their own. We believe, as Mark Twain put it in *The Innocents Abroad*, that any foreigner can speak English if only it is spoken slowly enough and loudly enough.

It goes without saying that the whole film leads up to a climactic kung fu tournament, and that Dre is pitted against Cheng for the championship. The lineage of the film is distinguished; the '84 version was directed by John Avildsen, director of *Rocky*. This film's climax is unusually well handled; the tension is constructed in a careful way, the characters are developed, and use of a scoreboard makes it seem orderly, not rushed. It's one of the better Obligatory Fight climaxes I've seen.

The director, Harald Zwart, has not been one of my favorites; he made last year's *Pink Panther 2*. But here, with a robust script by Christopher Murphey and cinematography by Roger Pratt (who filmed two Harry Potters), he makes a handsome, absorbing movie. It runs a little long, but during the championship, that's the last thing you're thinking of.

## Keyhole ★ ★ ★

R, 94 m., 2012

Jason Patric (Ulysses Pick), Isabella Rossellini (Hyacinth), Udo Kier (Dr. Lemke), Brooke Palsson (Denny), David Wontner (Manners), Louis Negin (Calypso/Camille), Kevin McDonald (Ogilbe). Directed by Guy Maddin and produced by Maddin, Jean Du Toit, Lindsay Hamel, and Jody Shapiro. Screenplay by Maddin and George Toles.

Surrounded by police on a dark and rainy night, a desperate armed gang is holed up inside a vast haunted house surrounding a courtyard holding a bog into which they will soon push two bodies. They hold a hostage. Their story is narrated by a naked old man chained in an attic room. Their leader, his hat dripping with rain, finds his way through the night with the body of a drowned woman slung over his shoulder.

Guy Maddin is creating another of his doomy nightmares. Although the Canadian director describes this film as his first exercise in pure narrative filmmaking, those aren't the first words that would leap into my mind. Narratives have a beginning, a middle, and an end, and a Maddin film has a disturbing way of always seeming to exist in the present, like a dream. You know what happened and you even know what will happen, but you also see it all shifting and changing. The drowned woman, for example. Once she is in the parlor with the others and has been dried off and dressed in clothes taken from an old woman, she appears to be alive.

In another sense, all the characters are dead. The man in the attic room tells us they are ghosts—I assume ghosts of the family that lived here long ago, which I think is the family living here now, with members of the gang, their gagged hostage and a large stuffed predator. The old man wanders chained in his daughter's bedroom. He is Calypso (Louis Negin). That is the name of a sea nymph in Greek mythology. His daughter's name is Hyacinth (Isabella Rossellini), another hero in Greek mythology. All right, I looked them up on Wikipedia. That's fair enough, because the gang leader's name is Ulysses Pick (Jason Patric), and at the film's premiere, Maddin cheerfully explained that the character was "based on *Ulysses*'s Wikipedia page."

Ulysses has come through the night with the drowned woman like an allusion from *The Waste Land.* His mission is to find his lost wife, who is upstairs with her father, Calypso, chained to her bed. Or perhaps not; "nobody knows where the other end of the chain is," Calypso tells us. This must be quite a large mansion, since Ulysses must search it for her room. How large can a mansion be, when the gang and its hostage made a crowd in the cluttered parlor, but an upstairs bedroom cannot be found? Ah, now he's found it, and appeals to his wife through the keyhole, not neglecting to thoughtfully finger a long wire that could be used to blind a person on either side of the door—or both of them at once, in the case of a most unfortunate occurrence.

Questions come up. The police dragnet is drawn tight around the house, and the lights on their squad cars flash incessantly through every window. Desperate gang members stand on alert behind curtains and doors with tommy guns and pistols. Yet the police issue no commands, and there is time for Ulysses Pick to talk with his wife and supervise the dumping of bodies into the bog. And he must deal with the squirming young man who is bound and gagged. Does he recognize him as his son?

This is one way to describe a Maddin film, and for *Keyhole* it may be the best way. He is the only avant-garde independent filmmaker I know who deals in the elements of the memory of cinema. It's said he makes film noir, and if by that you mean he uses black-and-white, melodramatic images, overwrought characters, and music driven by panic, you'd be right. But for me a movie like *Keyhole* plays like a fever dream, using the elements of film noir but restlessly rearranging them in an attempt to force sense out of them. You have the elements lined up against the wall, and in some mercurial way they slip free and attack you from behind.

## Kick-Ass ★

R, 117 m., 2010

Aaron Johnson (Dave/Kick-Ass), Christopher Mintz-Plasse (Chris/Red Mist), Mark Strong (Frank D'Amico), Chloe Grace Moretz (Mindy/Hit Girl), Nicolas Cage (Damon/Big Daddy). Directed by Matthew Vaughn and produced by Vaughn, Adam Bohling, Tarquin Pack, Brad Pitt, David Reid, and Kris Thykier. Screenplay by Vaughn and Jane Goldman, based on the comic book by Mark Millar and John S. Romita Jr.

Shall I have feelings, or should I pretend to be cool? Will I seem hopelessly square if I find *Kick-Ass* morally reprehensible, and will I appear to have missed the point? Let's say you're a big fan of the original comic book, and you think the movie does it justice. You know what? You inhabit a world I am so very not interested in. A motion picture camera makes a record of whatever is placed in front of it, and in this case it shows deadly carnage dished out by an eleven-year-old girl, after which an adult man brutally hammers her to within an inch of her life. Blood everywhere. Now tell me all about the context.

The movie's premise is that ordinary people, including a high school kid, the eleven-year-old, and her father, try to become superheroes in order to punish evil men. The flaw in this premise is that the little girl *does* become a superhero. In one scene, she faces a hallway jammed with heavily armed gangsters and shoots, stabs, and kicks them all to death, while flying through the air with such power it's enough to make Jackie Chan take out an AARP membership.

This isn't comic violence. These men, and many others in the film, are really stone-cold dead. And the eleven-year-old apparently experiences no emotions about this. Many children that age would be, I dunno, *affected* somehow, don't you think, after killing eight or twelve men who were trying to kill them?

I know, I know. This is a satire. But a satire of what? The movie's rated R, which means in this case that it's doubly attractive to anyone under seventeen. I'm not too worried about sixteen-year-olds here. I'm thinking of six-year-olds. There are characters here with walls covered in carefully mounted firearms, ranging from handguns through automatic weapons to bazookas. At the end, when the villain deliciously anticipates blowing a bullet hole in the child's head, he is prevented only because her friend, in the nick of time, shoots him with a bazooka shell at ten-foot range and blows him through a skyscraper window and across several city blocks of sky in a projectile of blood, flame, and smoke. As I often read on the Internet: Hahahahaha.

The little girl is named Mindy (Chloe Grace Moretz). She adopts the persona of Hit Girl. She has been trained by her father, Big Daddy (Nicolas Cage), to join him in the battle against a crime boss (Mark Strong). Her training includes being shot at point-blank range while wearing a bulletproof vest. She also masters the martial arts—more, I would say, than any other movie martial artist of any age I can recall. And she's gifted with deadly knife-throwing skill; a foot-long knife was presented to her by her dad as, I guess, a graduation present.

Big Daddy and Mindy never have a chat about, you know, stuff like how when you kill people they are really dead. This movie regards human beings like video game targets. Kill one, and you score. They're dead, you win. When kids in the age range of this movie's home video audience are shooting each other every day in America, that kind of stops being funny.

Hit Girl teams up with Kick-Ass (Aaron Johnson), the narrator of the film, a lackluster high school kid who lives vicariously through comic books. For reasons tedious to explain, he orders a masked costume by mail order and sets about trying to behave as a superhero, which doesn't work out well. He lacks the training of a Big Daddy. But as he and Hit Girl find themselves fighting side by side, he turns into a quick learner. Also, you don't need to be great at hand-to-hand combat if you can just shoot people dead.

The early scenes give promise of an entirely different comedy. Aaron Johnson has a certain anti-charm, his problems in high school are engaging, and so on. A little later, I reflected that possibly only Nic Cage could seem to shoot a small girl point-blank and make it, well, funny. Say what you will about her character, but Chloe Grace Moretz has presence and appeal. Then the movie moved into dark, dark territory, and I grew sad.

## The Kids Are All Right ★ ★ ★ ½

R, 104 m., 2010

Julianne Moore (Jules), Annette Bening (Nic), Mark Ruffalo (Paul), Mia Wasikowska (Joni), Josh Hutcherson (Laser). Directed by Lisa Cholodenko and produced by Gary Gilbert, Philippe Hellmann, Jordan Horowitz, Jeffrey Levy-Hinte, Celine Rattray, and Daniela Taplin Lundberg. Screenplay by Cholodenko and Stuart Blumberg.

*The Kids Are All Right* centers on a lesbian marriage, but is not about one. It's a film about marriage itself, an institution with challenges that are universal. Just imagine: You're expected to live much, if not all, of your married life with another adult. We're not raised for this.

The married couple involves Jules (Julianne Moore) and Nic (Annette Bening). They're raising a boy named Laser (Josh Hutcherson) and a girl named Joni (Mia Wasikowska). Each mother has one of the children, and because the same anonymous sperm donor was used, they're half-siblings. Home life is casual and happy, upper middle class. Nic is a doctor, Jules is unfocused and lately thinking she might go into landscape gardening. Like many couples, they're going through a little midlife crisis.

That's nothing compared with what awaits them, in a smart comedy by Lisa Cholodenko, whose *High Art* and *Laurel Canyon* showed those particular slices of Los Angeles we think we might find ourselves in for a period, before we got our acts together. The imperfect but stable home life of their family is disturbed by the decision of the children to seek out their birth father. Jules and Nic are staunchly liberal and approve of this in theory. In practice they find it disturbing.

The father turns out to be Paul (Mark Ruffalo), the kind of onetime hippie who says things like, "Sure, I mean . . . sure, yes, of course . . . I mean, why not? Sure . . ." He's with the program. He runs a cozy little organic restaurant with food from his own organic garden, has never married, has no other children, and is way cool in a way that involves no conscious effort. He thinks it's cool to meet his kids, it's cool their moms are married, it's cool they invite him for dinner. I mean . . . sure, yes, of course . . . I mean, why not? Sure.

Learning that Jules is taking up landscape design, he hires her to design the garden area sloping down behind his house in what looks like the Hollywood Hills. And what with bringing in bags of soil and standing in the rain with him discussing plans, Jules and Paul like, have sex. I mean, why not?

This causes a great deal of unhappiness when it's discovered, but not operatic grief and passion. More feelings of betrayal on Nic's part, and confusion from Jules and Paul, who didn't expect their secret to be discovered and, like, were not thinking of getting *married* or anything, and are really, truly sorry. So are the kids, because they love their moms, and they like Paul a lot, too.

Cholodenko, writing with Stuart Blumberg, is wise to keep her tone light. *The Kids Are All Right* isn't a laffaminit comedy, but it is a comedy, and fondly satirical of Nic's tendency to be quite serious. I refuse to call it a "gay film." I toyed with the idea of not even using the word "lesbian" and leaving it to you to figure out that the couple was female. This is a romantic triangle happening to involve these three people.

What interests Cholodenko is who they are. Moore and Bening are superb actors here, evoking a marriage of more than twenty years and all of its shadings and secrets, idealism and compromise. Nic is more of the mind, Jules is more of the heart. The film gives them convincing, intelligent dialogue, mannerisms that fit, and children who, having been raised outside homophobic hysteria, are nice and well adjusted. And with Mark Ruffalo's Paul, the film creates a slightly exaggerated version of characters like many we may have met: casually progressive, a little unfocused, pleasant, and agreeable. I mean, why not?

## The Kid with a Bike ★ ★ ★ ½

PG-13, 87 m., 2012

Thomas Doret (Cyril Catoul), Cecile de France (Samantha), Jeremie Renier (Guy Catoul), Egon di Mateo (Wes), Fabrizio Rongione (Le Libraire), Olivier Gourmet (Le Patron du Bar). Directed by Jean-Pierre Dardenne and Luc Dardenne and produced by Jean-Pierre Dardenne, Luc Dardenne, and Denis Freyd. Screenplay by Jean-Pierre Dardenne and Luc Dardenne.

The fierce young boy is always in motion, his face screwed up in determination, pedaling his bike, running through the streets, pounding on doors and windows, demanding, demanding. He demands the love of his father, but lacking that he wants his bike, and the acceptance of the woman who has become his foster mother on weekends, and recognition from Wes, the teenaged neighborhood hoodlum.

He is named Cyril, and as played here by Thomas Doret he becomes an indelible portrait of need. We meet him first in an official boys home, where he was dumped by a father who promised to return but never has. Like a young detective, he methodically tracks him down—visiting the bar and pastry shop his dad took him to, calling a number that is always disconnected, talking his way into his dad's former apartment, where he is sure he will find his bicycle and perhaps Guy (Jeremie Renier), his father.

*The Kid with a Bike* is another empathetic film by Jean-Pierre and Luc Dardenne, the brothers from Belgium who have strong sympathy for alienated children and young people, and who avoid melodrama and sensation in telling their stories so movingly. There are two things that could go seriously wrong in young Cyril's life, but they don't quite happen. The Dardennes don't wring us out like that. They prefer the drama of ordinary life, in which for a boy like Cyril things don't easily go right. In straightforward, realistic scenes, they show a boy who fears he has been thrown away, but persists in feeling that his father only lost him and will be happy to find him again.

He can't stand restraint. He doesn't accept instruction. When he sees another boy ride past on his bike, he chases him. Samantha (Cecile de France), who owns a local beauty shop, tracks down the boy and buys the bike from his father. What anguish Cyril must feel when he learns the other kid didn't steal his bike—Guy sold it. He sees a notice in a shop window, in his father's own handwriting. Cyril is about eleven, and will remind some viewers of the hero of Truffaut's film *The 400 Blows*. But that boy had a hero, Balzac, and Cyril has only his father, who cannot accept the role.

Cyril boldly asks Samantha if he can live at her house. She agrees to take him on weekends. It works out badly. Fearing rejection, he has a way of testing people beyond their endurance. "Why did you let me come here?" he asks. "I don't know," she says honestly. He keeps running away, and eventually is led into big trouble by Wes, a few years older, who slicks back his black hair, smokes, drinks, and leads a "gang." The Dardennes are masterful in showing how easily Wes is able to manipulate Cyril to do his will.

The film is only 87 minutes long, lean and efficient, intent on Cyril. It doesn't *explain* him, because he is all there to be seen: his need, his abandonment, his reckless determination, his unprotected youth. Young Thomas Doret fills the role with natural sincerity and focus, and not a second that seems contrived. The cast is small, but the Dardennes use some regulars: Cyril's dad, Guy, is played by Jeremie Renier, star of their *L'enfant* (2005), where he played a very young father who tries to raise money by selling his new baby. The man in the bar is Olivier Gourmet, who starred in their masterpiece *Le Fils* (2002), as a man who meets the boy responsible for his own son's death.

*The Child* and *The Son*. Over and over, their subjects are parents, children, alienation, rebellion. But the Dardennes love these characters and do not blame them. They attend to their pain. They find goodness and share happiness. The most mysterious character in *The Kid with a Bike* is not the kid, who after all has a story that's fairly easy to understand. It is the hairdresser, played by Cecile de France with her sad beauty. This actress carries lifetimes in her eyes. There is a moment here when she is forced to make a choice, and as she makes it, she reveals so much about how she got to this place in life. "Why did you let me come here?" Cyril asked her. She says she doesn't know. As she makes her choice, we sense that she knows very well.

*Note: Winner of the Grand Prize of the Jury at Cannes 2011.*

## Killer Elite ★ ★ ★

R, 105 m., 2011

Jason Statham (Danny), Clive Owen (Spike), Robert De Niro (Hunter), Dominic Purcell (Davies), Aden Young (Meier), Yvonne Strahovski (Anne), Ben Mendelsohn (Martin). Directed by Gary McKendry and produced by Michael Boughen, Steve Chasman, Sigurjon Sighvatsson, and Tony Winley. Screenplay by McKendry and Matt Sherring, based on *The Feather Men*, a novel by Ranulph Fiennes.

*Killer Elite* is inspired by a story that ingeniously finds a way to explain why two teams of ex–Special Air Service men would want to kill one another. That doubles the possibilities for casting, and here Jason Statham and Clive Owen, who in fact have no reason to dislike each other, are engaged in a deadly game of international murder. Robert De Niro plays a hostage taken by a sheik of Oman, who uses him to settle a score neither team has any reason to care about, so basically what's at stake is their professionalism.

Incredibly, this story is claimed to be based on fact. Author Ranulph Fiennes's novel is allegedly based on experiences he really had, and indeed the author of just such a book makes an appearance in the plot. I suspect the factual basis may be at a few degrees of separation from the pure action plot, but you never know, and recent movies like *The Debt* suggest spy organizations can get involved in events that seem lifted from fiction.

The story: De Niro plays Hunter, the mentor of Danny (Jason Statham). Both were skilled professionals. Danny has had one of those epiphanies where a man of action decides the killing must stop, and has retreated into hiding and seclusion in a remote quarter of the Australian outback. There he lives with the beautiful Anne (Yvonne Strahovski), who strictly speaking is not particularly essential to the plot. Danny's past life follows him to the outback after Hunter is kidnapped by the oil sheik. The sheik wants revenge against the killers of his sons, he knows Danny is the best in the world, and he correctly calculates that only the need to save his beloved teacher would lure him back into action.

The sons, it turns out, were murdered by four SAS men. Danny's assignment is tricky: He is to kill them—but make it look like each death is accidental, so no one will suspect the sheik. Diabolically clever. On his team are Davies (Dominic Purcell) and Meier (Aden Young). Meanwhile, Spike (Clive Owen) leads a shadowy group known as the Feather Men, whose mission is to protect ex-SAS men from retaliation. Their task is to shield the four targets from Danny and his boys. Got that?

This is actually a pretty good thriller, based more on character and plot than on action for its own sake. The need to construct killings that look like accidents adds to the interest. I find myself asking, really, how likely is it that one, let alone all, of these events could be stage-managed so precisely? Yet we learn that spy organizations are often behind "accidents."

Jason Statham is once again a hard-boiled man carved from solid macho. Clive Owen, who by disposition and facial expression seems more like a good guy, is also sufficiently cold-blooded. Do you ever find yourself looking at a movie involving steel-eyed killers with Brillo stubble on their chins and wondering if they would possibly seem as menacing if they were clean-shaven?

De Niro is good here, in a role that perhaps offered some small inspiration. My impression is that he feels he's paid his dues and his attention is now involved in his Tribeca activities. He still has his power when he chooses to use it.

The movie is a first feature by Gary McKendry, born in Northern Ireland, who previously directed many commercials and the twenty-minute short *Everything in This Country Must*, which was nominated for an Academy Award in the live-action short category. This is an impressive debut. He has the instincts of a storyteller, and understands that action is better when it's structured around character and plot and doesn't rely on simple sensation. *Killer Elite* is rather pure in its storytelling, because at the end we might be hard-pressed to divide the characters into good and bad guys.

## The Killer Inside Me ★ ★ ½

R, 109 m., 2010

Casey Affleck (Lou Ford), Kate Hudson (Amy Stanton), Jessica Alba (Joyce Lakeland), Ned Beatty (Chester Conway), Elias Koteas (Joe Rothman), Tom Bower (Sheriff Bob Maples), Simon Baker (Howard Hendricks), Bill Pullman (Billy Boy Walker). Directed by Michael Winterbottom and produced by Andrew Eaton, Chris Hanley, and Bradford L. Schlei. Screenplay by John Curran, based on the novel by Jim Thompson.

What we desire is not a happy ending, so much as closure. That often means simply that a film knows what it thinks about itself. *The Killer Inside Me* is expert filmmaking based on a frightening performance, but it presents us with a character who remains a vast, empty, lonely, cold space. The film finds resolution there somewhere, perhaps, but not on a frequency I can receive.

Michael Winterbottom's film is inspired by a 1952 pulp novel by Jim Thompson, perhaps the bleakest and most unrelenting of American crime novelists. The book is considered by some his finest work; other Thompson novels were filmed as *The Grifters, The Getaway, After Dark, My Sweet,* and *Coup de Torchon.* Stephen King wrote: "Big Jim didn't know the meaning of the word stop. There are three brave *lets* inherent in the forgoing: He let himself see everything, he let himself write it down, then he let himself publish it."

What Thompson saw in his character Lou Ford (Casey Affleck) was a mild-spoken, intellectual psychopath with no understanding of good and evil. He murders people he loves, *while* loving them, and has no idea why. The story's insights into this seem limited to the title. There is a killer inside him. The killer is not him. He doesn't understand that killer. He has no control over him and no doubt sincerely regrets the killer's crimes.

The story is set in West Texas in the early 1950s. Lou Ford, narrating his own story, is a deputy sheriff in a small town. He still lives in the home where he was raised. In the evenings he plays classical piano, reads books from his father's library, plays opera recordings. His voice, high-pitched but rough, bespeaks innocence. He has a girlfriend named Amy (Kate Hudson). He has the respect and affection of his alcoholic boss, Sheriff Bob Maples (Tom Bower). He is unfailingly calm and pleasant.

One day Maples gives him a job: Drive a few miles outside town and have a word with a prostitute, Joyce (Jessica Alba). A powerful local developer, Chester Conway (Ned Beatty), is concerned about her influence on his son, Elmer (Jay R. Ferguson). Ford pays the visit, has some words, and soon the two of them are urgently having rough sex. Why? Because this is the pulp universe, where a woman may be a prostitute with other men but she finds *you* irresistible. Female psychology is not the strong point with many pulp writers. Psychology in general is sketchy, based on simplified and half-understood Freudian notions. With Lou Ford, for example, we're given fragmented glimpses of childhood sexual abuse. Not the sort of abuse we've seen before: His mother liked Lou to slap her.

Indeed, Lou seems to attract women who like to be beaten. One apparently even likes to be nearly killed. The film attempts to account for this no more than it explains Lou's own nature. The best explanation probably is: When you buy a cheap paperback with a lurid cover, these are the sorts of events that will be described inside. In prose, the focus is through the point of view. In the film, we see the violence happening, and the first time it comes as a gut punch because we're not remotely expecting it.

Not from Lou Ford, anyway. Casey Affleck, an effective actor, is so convincing with his innocent, almost sweet facade that the movie sets us up to expect he'll be solving a crime, not causing one. He maintains that facade in the face of the most compelling challenges, not only from his own violence, but from two people with excellent reasons to suspect him: a labor leader (Elias Koteas) and the county attorney (Simon Baker). When Lou actually confesses to a kid who admires him (Liam Aiken), even what happens then doesn't faze him.

There is a point beyond which his implacability brings diminishing returns. While I admire Affleck's performance, I believe Winterbottom and his writer, John Curran, may have miscalculated. The reader of a pulp crime thriller might be satisfied simply with the prurient descriptions, and certainly this film visualizes those and has as its victims Jessica Alba and Kate Hudson, who embody paperback covers, but the dominant presence in the film is Lou Ford, and there just doesn't seem to be anybody at home.

## Kill List ★ ★ ★

NO MPAA RATING, 94 m., 2012

Neil Maskell (Jay), Michael Smiley (Gal), MyAnna Buring (Shel), Emma Fryer (Fiona). Directed by Ben Wheatley and produced by Claire Jones and Andrew Starke. Screenplay by Amy Jump and Ben Wheatley.

*Kill List* begins with verbal violence at a dinner table, continues with actual violence in a hit man scenario, and concludes with metaphysical violence that threatens to decapitate the movie itself. It's baffling and goofy, blood-soaked and not boring. The fact that it's well made adds to the confusion; it feels like a better film than it turns out to be.

We open with a dinner party for two rather ordinary couples, the men middle-aged, the women younger. The men have worked together before, and Jay (Neil Maskell) is desperate to find work again to support his Ukrainian wife (MyAnna Buring) and their young son. His friend Gal (Michael Smiley) has an offer that will bring in big money: a murder contract. It's casually established that they've worked before as hit men.

Now comes a sequence with Jay and Gal on

a business trip. They check into a businessman's hotel. A credit card is declined. The screen, at about this point, is filled from side to side with the words "THE PRIEST." Later we will meet "THE LIBRARIAN," "THE MP," and so on. These portentous titles, as large as the frame can contain, seem to announce a quasi-ritualistic murder agenda, but even later, after we see some decidedly bizarre events, the film conceals precisely what's going on.

The victims are apparently responsible for various manifestations of evil. It's not explained what the Priest did, but he himself thinks it bad enough that just before he's shot, he tells his killers, "Thank you." The Librarian seems to maintain a massive computer database, and a glimpse of some of its contents fills the lads with such disgust that Jay pounds his head with a hammer as if tenderizing a tough steak. Gal is appalled by his partner's behavior: A whack job is business, but enough's enough.

The movie is sneaking up on us. The director and cowriter, Ben Wheatley, plays the cards of his plot very close to his vest. There is an uneasy intimation of something growling beneath the surface, but the actors and their actions seem explicable on the level of ordinary reality. None of the incredible third act has been foretold in earlier scenes, and then there's a coda that isn't even hinted in the third act.

It's all done with command of camera, music, and lifelike dialogue. That's one of the fascinations. Many violent movies begin with a certain discipline and restraint, but then lose control and unleash a frenzy of action. *Kill List* proceeds in an ordered, mannered way as extraordinary events are introduced. It's tempting to find parallels with major films by famous directors, but to name one might be giving away too much.

Does it matter that nothing in the payoff makes sense? Does it need to? Has the movie jumped the rails and thrown itself into the hands of wild invention? It seems that way. But so careful was the setup, so convincing the characters, that we don't quite feel we're being toyed with. Somehow the eventual revelations seem to be in a direction the movie was headed.

The two lead performances are keys to the film's success. For one thing, they aren't the Identikit teenagers usually employed in horror films, but adults who look plausibly serious. Neil Maskell as Jay reminded me a little of Matt Malloy in *In the Company of Men*, and in Michael Smiley as Gal there are aspects of Peter Stormare. It makes sense that Smiley superficially looks like he might be more violent, but that turns out to be Maskell. MyAnna Buring, a Swede playing a Ukrainian, was apparently picked up during an assignment in Kiev. Emma Fryer as Fiona is apparently Gal's date, with no long-standing relationship. None of these things, or anything else, is entirely true.

The movie may leave you scratching your head way too much when it's over. Yet it proves Ben Wheatley not only knows how to make a movie, but he knows how to make three at the same time. I suppose one of the characteristics of horror is that it wears shifting faces.

## King of Devil's Island ★ ★ ★

NO MPAA RATING, 120 m., 2012

Stellan Skarsgard (Bestyreren), Benjamin Helstad (Erling/C-19), Kristoffer Joner (Brathen), Trond Nilssen (Olav/C-1), Morten Lovstad (Oystein), Daniel Berg (Johan), Odin Gineson Broderud (Axel), Magnar Botten (Lillegutt), Magnus Langlete (Ivar/C-5). Directed by Marius Holst and produced by Karin Julsrud. Screenplay by Dennis Magnusson and Eric Schmid.

I can't recall a juvenile home in a movie that wasn't hell on Earth. Both boarding schools and detention centers seem to attract sadists among the inmates and the administrators, and there's always at least one sex offender on the staff. *King of Devil's Island* is an effective drama set in Norway in 1915, where the mostly harmless boys are subjected to regimented punishment. Why are physical and mental cruelty considered to be rehabilitating?

A big-budget film that set box office records in its homeland, the movie tells a story more or less predictable, even though it's said to be based on the real story of one of the two times in history that the Norwegian Army fired on civilians. Set on Bastoy Island in a fjord near Oslo, it's said to be escape-proof. To this prison camp comes the teenager Erling (Benjamin Helstad), rumored among the boys to have committed murder while employed as a harpooner on a whaling ship. Like the other boys, he's dehumanized by being given a number in place of his name.

He becomes C-19 in the C Barracks. The dorm leader is C-1 (Trond Nilssen), who is scheduled to be released. C-19 is told by Bestyreren (Stellan Skarsgard), the school governor, that he has a good chance of becoming C-1 himself. But C-19 is not made for following rules. He doesn't misbehave for pleasure, but out of a sense of injustice. It becomes clear to him that the dorm master, Brathen (Kristoffer Joner), is sexually using the small and weak C-5 (Magnus Langlete) every night in the laundry room.

Does Bestyreren, the governor, suspect what is happening? C-19 bravely tells him what he knows, and the information is not welcomed by Bestyreren. Nevertheless, he calls in Brathen and pointedly asks him why he is still working at the institution after nine years. A young man with his abilities and prospects should set his sights higher, the governor says; there's no future in being a dorm master and living alone on an isolated island.

Brathen evades replying, and seems to sense that the governor is reluctant to know the true answer to his question because he doesn't want a scandal to threaten the school's sources of funding (mostly from the church). Here is an incident from history that seems to reflect Joe Paterno's reluctance to look too deeply into stories he heard about Jerry Sandusky.

Stellan Skarsgard is quite effective as Bestyreren, a man who mouths platitudes about how the school will help restore its boys to full and productive lives. He has an unreasonable optimism, given the reality of the school experience, which places emphasis on forced manual labor and punishment. Skarsgard evokes a studied detachment; he seems distracted from the reality at hand by his vague optimism.

C-19 eventually becomes the catalyst for an inmate uprising, dramatically staged by director Marius Holst with a balance between the latent wildness of the boys and their sometimes small stature. In one touchy scene, they allow the governor and his wife to safely leave a dangerous situation because they seem to have some grudging gratitude for his faith in them. There is a harrowing scene as two of the boys try to escape across thin ice. The film plays well, and is involving, but in one form or another this is a story often told.

## The King's Speech ★ ★ ★ ★

R, 118 m., 2010

Colin Firth (Bertie), Geoffrey Rush (Lionel Logue), Helena Bonham Carter (Elizabeth), Guy Pearce (Edward VIII), Jennifer Ehle (Myrtle Logue), Derek Jacobi (Archbishop Cosmo Lang), Michael Gambon (George V), Timothy Spall (Winston Churchill), Anthony Andrews (Stanley Baldwin). Directed by Tom Hooper and produced by Iain Canning, Emile Sherman, and Gareth Unwin. Screenplay by David Seidler.

*The King's Speech* tells the story of a man compelled to speak to the world with a stammer. It must be painful enough for one who stammers to speak to one other person. To face a radio microphone and know the British Empire is listening must be terrifying. At the time of the speech mentioned in the title, a quarter of the earth's population was in the empire, and of course much of North America, Europe, Africa, and Asia would be listening—and with particular attention, Germany.

The king was George VI. The year was 1939. Britain was entering into war with Germany. His listeners required firmness, clarity, and resolve, not stammers punctuated with tortured silences. This was a man who never wanted to be king. After the death of his father, the throne was to pass to his brother Edward. But Edward renounced the throne "in order to marry the woman I love," and the duty fell to Prince Albert, who had struggled with his speech from an early age.

In *The King's Speech*, director Tom Hooper opens on Albert (Colin Firth) attempting to open the British Empire Exhibition in 1925. Before a crowded arena and a radio audience, he seizes up in agony in efforts to make the words come right. His father, George V (Michael Gambon), has always considered

"Bertie" superior to Edward (Guy Pearce), but mourns the introduction of radio and newsreels, which require a monarch to be seen and heard on public occasions.

At that 1925 speech, we see Albert's wife, Elizabeth (Helena Bonham Carter), her face filled with sympathy. As it becomes clear that Edward's obsession with Wallis Simpson (Eve Best) is incurable, she realizes her Bertie may face more public humiliation. He sees various speech therapists, one of whom tries the old marbles-in-the-mouth routine first recommended by Demosthenes. Nothing works, and then she seeks out a failed Australian actor named Lionel Logue (Geoffrey Rush), who has set up a speech therapy practice.

Logue doesn't realize at first who is consulting him. And one of the subjects of the film is Logue's attitude toward royalty, which I suspect is not untypical of Australians; he suggests to Albert that they get on a first-name basis. Albert has been raised within the bell jar of the monarchy and objects to such treatment, not because he has an elevated opinion of himself, but because, well, it just isn't done. But Logue realizes that if he is to become the king's therapist, he must first become his friend.

If the British monarchy is good for nothing else, it's superb at producing the subjects of films. *The King's Speech*, rich in period detail and meticulous class distinctions, largely sidesteps the story that loomed over this whole period: Edward's startling decision to give up the crown in order to marry a woman who was already divorced three times. Indeed the Duke and Duchess of Windsor (as they became) would occupy an inexplicable volume of attention for years, considering they had no significance after the duke's abdication. The unsavory thing is that Wallis Simpson considered herself worthy of such a sacrifice from the man she allegedly loved. This film finds a more interesting story about better people; Americans, who aren't always expert on British royalty, may not necessarily realize that Albert and his wife, Elizabeth, were the parents of Queen Elizabeth II. God knows what Edward might have fathered.

Hooper makes an interesting decision with his sets and visuals. The movie is largely shot in interiors, and most of those spaces are long and narrow. That's unusual in historical dramas, which emphasize sweep and majesty and so on. Here we have long corridors, a deep and narrow master control room for the BBC, rooms that seem peculiarly oblong. I suspect he may be evoking the narrow, constricting walls of Albert's throat as he struggles to get words out.

The film largely involves the actors Colin Firth, formal and decent, and Geoffrey Rush, large and expansive, in psychological struggle. Helena Bonham Carter, who can be merciless (as in the Potter films), is here filled with mercy, tact, and love for her husband; this is the woman who became the much-loved Queen Mother of our lifetimes, dying in 2002 at 101. As the men have a struggle of wills, she tries to smooth things (and raise her girls, Elizabeth and Margaret). And in the wider sphere, Hitler takes power, war comes closer, Mrs. Simpson wreaks havoc, and the dreaded day approaches when Bertie, as George VI, will have to speak to the world and declare war.

Hooper's handling of that fraught scene is masterful. Firth internalizes his tension and keeps the required stiff upper lip, but his staff and household are terrified on his behalf as he marches toward a microphone as if it is a guillotine. It is the one scene in the film that *must* work, and it does, and its emotional impact is surprisingly strong. At the end, what we have here is a superior historical drama and a powerful personal one. And two opposites who remain friends for the rest of their lives.

*Note: The R rating refers to Logue's use of vulgarity. It is utterly inexplicable. This is an excellent film for teenagers.*

## Kinyarwanda ★ ★ ★ ★

NO MPAA RATING, 96 m., 2011

Cassandra Freeman (Lieutenant Rose), Edouard Bamporiki (Emmanuel), Cleophas Kabasiita (Francine), Marc Gwamaka (Patrique), Hadidja Zaninka (Jeanne), Jean Mutsari (The Mufti), Hassan Kabera (Ishmael), Kennedy Mpazimpaka (Father Pierre). Directed by Alrick Brown and produced by Brown, Dean, and Tommy Oliver. Screenplay by Brown and Charles Plath.

I thought I knew something about Rwanda, but I didn't really know very much. I was moved by

*Hotel Rwanda,* but not really shaken this deeply. Not like this. After seeing *Kinyarwanda* I have a different kind of feeling about the genocide that took place in Rwanda in 1994. The film approaches it not as a story line but as a series of intense personal moments.

The characters speak both English and the nation's own language. That language is called Kinyarwanda. The film's cowriter and director, a Jamaican named Alrick Brown, says he was surprised the first time he learned that all Rwandans speak the same tongue. Here was a nation in which the members of one tribe, the Hutu, set about to massacre the members of another tribe, the Tutsi. Yet were they really even members of different tribes?

There is a scene in the film in which this is discussed. Since time immemorial, people in Rwanda more or less got along. When Belgium colonized the nation, "ethnic scientists" came in with their calipers and found that the skulls and rib cages of two groups were somewhat different. Although they were already recognized as tribal groups before the Europeans arrived, it was convenient for the Belgians to name one of these groups, the Tutsi, the ruling class, and the Hutu as subservient. That led to a perhaps inevitable Hutu revolt, and some five hundred thousand to one million members of both tribes died.

This dreadful massacre was ignored by the world, apart from the ineffectual UN "peacekeeping mission" we saw in *Hotel Rwanda.* What Brown does in *Kinyarwanda,* working with research by his executive producer, Ishmael Ntihabose, is to weave together several compact interlocking stories to connect events before, during, and after the genocide. The United Nations is hardly to be seen. Rwandans commit the murders, suffer from the murders, recover, and repent. Here, over an unspecific period of several months, we see South Africa's Truth and Reconciliation process at work.

The vignettes establish a vivid group of characters. Jeanne and Patrique (Hadidja Zaninka and Marc Gwamaka), a young couple from different tribes who are in love. Lieutenant Rose (Cassandra Freeman), the head of a military unit trained in Uganda, who hopes to bring peace. Emmanuel (Edouard Bamporiki), the head of a Tutsi killing unit. Father Pierre (Kennedy Mpazimpaka), a Catholic priest. The mufti of Rwanda (Jean Mutsari), head of the nation's Muslims. Perhaps most memorable, a small boy named Ishmael (Hassan Kabera).

Each vignette adds to the mosaic. Characters from one turn up in another. Gradually a powerful outcome is arrived at. The mufti issues an edict declaring that the nation's Muslims must not participate in killing and must open the mosques as places of shelter for all, regardless of tribe or religion. The priest tries to operate his church in the same way, but lacks the courage. Yet finally, Muslims and Catholics link hands to face the bloodthirsty killers.

I mentioned Ishmael. This is a beautiful little boy who is sent out to buy cigarettes for his father, and overhears some soldiers searching for guns and cockroaches. "Cockroach" is the Hutu name for Tutsi. His father is hiding some Tutsi. He helpfully tells the soldiers where they can find cockroaches and leads them home. How this is resolved I will not say, but ask yourself this: Has Ishmael made a childish error, or does he do some agile last-minute thinking?

For all its greatness, *Hotel Rwanda* nevertheless used the conventional Hollywood technique of a movie star as a protagonist to serve as the audience's entry point. None of the actors in *Kinyarwanda* are stars, and their characters all live in the same world. By the equal weighting and linking of their stories in rotation, Brown prevents us from anticipating who will prevail. The criticism of this approach by the *Variety* critic is unfortunate. Here is a powerful film.

## Knight and Day ★ ★ ★

PG-13, 109 m., 2010

Tom Cruise (Roy Miller), Cameron Diaz (June Havens), Peter Sarsgaard (Fitzgerald), Viola Davis (Director George), Jordi Molla (Antonio), Paul Dano (Simon Feck), Maggie Grace (April Havens), Marc Blucas (Rodney), Celia Weston (Molly). Directed by James Mangold and produced by Todd Garner, Cathy Konrad, Steve Pink, and Joe Roth. Screenplay by Patrick O'Neill.

*Knight and Day* aspires to the light charm of a romantic action comedy like *Charade* or *Romancing the Stone,* but would come closer if it dialed down the relentless action. The romance part goes without saying after a Meet Cute contrived in an airport, and the comedy seems to generate naturally between Tom Cruise and Cameron Diaz. But why do so many summer movies find it obligatory to inflict us with CGI overkill? I'd sorta rather see Diaz and Cruise in action scenes on a human scale, rather than have it rubbed in that for long stretches they're essentially replaced by animation.

Have summer audiences been so hammered down by special effects that they require noise and fragmented visuals to hold their interest? Is it still possible to delight in a story unfolding with charm and wit? How many machine guns do you need in a romantic comedy? If you have charismatic stars like Cruise and Diaz and an A-list director, do you have to hedge your bet?

The movie is entertaining but could have been better. The director is James Mangold, whose previous two films were *Walk the Line* and *3:10 to Yuma.* I have a hunch there was an early draft of Patrick O'Neill's screenplay that was more in the Cary Grant romcom tradition, and then somebody decided the effects had to be jacked up. From the ads, you could get the notion this was a Michael Bay film.

The wonder is that Cruise and Diaz are effective enough in their roles that they're not overwhelmed by all the commotion surrounding them. They make the movie work because they cheerfully project that they know it's utter nonsense and pitch in to enjoy the fun. I've been reading that movie stars can no longer "sell" a blockbuster movie. Audiences buy the concept, brand name, packaging, whatever. If that's true, which I doubt, it would mean a victory of technology over humans. If it comes true, it will be because movies have lost interest in creating and shaping characters we care about—because they're using actors as insert shots in special effects.

The plot makes splendid use of a MacGuffin, the device that explains everything by explaining nothing. Roy Miller, the Cruise character, has something and there are bad guys who want it. I could tell you what it is, but what difference does it make? That's the whole point of a MacGuffin. Anyway, Roy *happens* to run into June Havens, the Diaz character, at an airport, for reasons you will discover. That's the manipulated Meet Cute. Now this next part you will want to follow closely.

They both end up on the same airplane, which has no other passengers except some men scattered here and there. She goes to the rest room. He kills all the men and both pilots, and sits the dead passengers upright, *Weekend at Bernie's* style. She comes out of the rest room, not having heard the gunshots. He crash-lands the plane in a field, and urges her to follow him in escaping FBI agents who are after them.

But . . . but . . . was there no other way for the bad guys to get the MacGuffin than by taking over a scheduled flight? Maybe, I dunno, snatch him on the ground? How did the FBI know the plane would crash—and where? Also, if you track who has possession of the MacGuffin during various times at the airport, you'll go crazy. Mind you, I'm not complaining. The movie knows this sequence is monumentally silly, and so do Cruise and Diaz, and Cruise keeps up a reassuring line of patter all during it, even while trying to crash-land safely.

That stuff is entertaining. There's also a running joke about how much ground they cover in an international chase. The movie was shot on location in Massachusetts, Spain (where they are chased by bulls), California, Jamaica, Austria, and Kankakee, Illinois, which has an excellent Steak 'n Shake out on I-57. Whether the actors were actually there on all those locations is a good question. Maybe only the green screen stuff was shot on location.

Such matters are irrelevant in a movie that makes not the slightest pretense of realism. Cruise and Diaz are fully scripted throughout with nonstop bantering and one-liners. They never seriously discuss their situation. They spend half the movie in dire danger. Thousands of bullets miss them. By motorcycle, car, train, airplane, and parachute, they survive anything.

That girl June, she's a trouper. She follows Roy everywhere and believes everything he says. But . . . but . . . why does she need to come along? Roy has the MacGuffin. She was a witness, you say? To what? I'll tell you why she has to be along. It's because this is a romantic action comedy starring Tom Cruise and Cameron Diaz, that's why.

So all of that I accept and even applaud, and I observe that Diaz has one of the most winning grins in the movies. Basically, what I wanted was more of it. Some of that Cary Grant dialogue. More flirtation. More of a feeling the characters, not the production, were the foreground. More of the stars. Because movie stars really do make a difference. I insist on it.

## Kung Fu Panda 2 ★ ★ ★ ½

PG, 90 m., 2011

Jack Black (Po), Angelina Jolie (Tigress), Dustin Hoffman (Shifu), Jackie Chan (Monkey), Seth Rogen (Mantis), Lucy Liu (Viper), David Cross (Crane), James Hong (Mr. Ping), Gary Oldman (Lord Shen), Michelle Yeoh (Soothsayer). Directed by Jennifer Yuh Nelson and produced by Melissa Cobb. Screenplay by Jonathan Aibel and Glenn Berger.

*Kung Fu Panda 2* is exactly as you'd expect, and more. The animation is elegant, the story is much more involving than the original, and there's boundless energy. I enjoyed it as fully as I possibly could, given the horror of its 3-D. The original film, in 2-D widescreen, was just fine. But never mind. Hollywood has brainwashed us (or itself) that 3-D is an improvement and not an annoyance.

What's best about this sequel is that it's not a dutiful retread of the original, but an ambitious extension. Of the many new elements, not least is the solution of the mystery of how Mr. Ping, a goose, could be the biological father of Po, a panda. In the original film, as nearly as I can recall, every character represented a different species, so I thought perhaps inscrutable reproductive processes were being employed. But no, Po's parenthood is explained here, and it has a great deal to do with new developments in the kingdom.

As we rejoin events in this mythical Chinese kingdom, Po (Jack Black), having attained the status of Dragon Warrior in the first film, still leads the Furious Five: Tigress (Angelina Jolie), Mantis (Seth Rogen), Monkey (Jackie Chan), Viper (Lucy Liu), and Crane (David Cross). Of these Tigress is clearly the most formidable, and Mantis remains the enigma; even though he sounds like Seth Rogen, how does he get past the weigh-in?

The kingdom now faces the prospect that it will be conquered and ruled by the evil peacock Lord Shen (Gary Oldman), whose minions have designed a new weapon that causes him to scour the land of scrap iron. This Shen is a wicked foe, hurling sharp, pointed feathers from his tail like a circus knife-thrower. It turns out that the mystery of Po's parentage is explained by Lord Shen's paranoia after a soothsayer (Michelle Yeoh) tells him to beware of pandas, so their destinies are linked more deeply than Po can imagine.

This is a film from Dreamworks, which is locked in competition with Pixar, and is swinging for the fences. The animation is much superior to your average 3-D feature about cute little animals, although the distortion caused by 3-D effects does it no favors. The story gets a lot of humor out of Po; Jack Black's voicing invests him with more personality than you'd expect from a character who resembles a balloon in the Macy's Thanksgiving Day Parade. (*Kung Fu Panda 3* could possibly open with Po working out with a personal trainer, maybe Tigress.) The director, Jennifer Yuh Nelson, broadens the scope of the animation to include more styles than your basic cartoon animals, and the imaginary sequences involving Po's history are rather beautiful.

Doing voice-over work must now count as an important part of every actor's repertory, and that has created a demand for actors who have distinctive voices. Dustin Hoffman is especially successful as a guru named Shifu. As he grows older, Hoffman is more and more mastering the timing and inflection of a smart stand-up comic. It's a gift.

Speaking of *Panda 3*, I wonder if the relationship between Po and Tigress will advance from its current status as what might be called a warm friendship. Tigress seems to occupy a favored position in Po's heart, reopening the possibility of cross-species pollination.

# L

## The Lady ★ ★ ½

R, 132 m., 2012

Michelle Yeoh (Aung San Suu Kyi), David Thewlis (Michael Aris), Jonathan Raggett (Kim Aris), Jonathan Woodhouse (Alexander Aris), Susan Wooldridge (Lucinda Philips), Benedict Wong (Karma Phuntsho). Directed by Luc Besson and produced by Besson, Andy Harries, Virginie Silla, and Jean Todt. Screenplay by Rebecca Frayn.

It was impossible to watch *The Lady* without thinking of *They Call It Myanmar*, a documentary I saw a few weeks ago. Both are set in the once-enchanted land of Burma, which, like its neighbor India, was ruled by British colonialism, and also like India suddenly received its independence in a disorderly fashion. In India that led to the troublesome partition of Pakistan. In Burma, it led to democratic elections whose outcome was overthrown by assassination. As it was said at the time, "The British stayed too long and left too quickly."

The central figure in both films is the Nobel Peace Prize winner Aung San Suu Kyi, whose father, Aung San, was elected to head the country and then assassinated, leaving the nation to a long period of repressive dictatorship under a military junta. The daughter, always called Suu Kyi (Michelle Yeoh), fled after her father's death to England, where in Oxford she married the professor Michael Aris (David Thewlis), had two children, and settled down as a housewife. Burma during those years disappeared behind a curtain of secrecy and paranoia. Many Burmese remained in exile because being "Westernized" might mean their imprisonment on return.

Only the illness of her mother drew Suu Kyi back to Burma, for a personal visit that the uneasy generals were told was nonpolitical. Once there, however, she was swept up in protests by the National League for Democracy, and implored by students to join their cause. She agreed to address a gathering. It was not publicized, but the news passed from ear to ear and a huge crowd overwhelmed police efforts to contain it. Her fate was clear: She was destined to be a leader of the struggle.

She was then kept under house arrest for most of the next fifteen years, even while winning the Nobel, and allowed to see her husband and children only a few times before he died of cancer back home in Oxford. This was a strong and stubborn woman—perhaps too stubborn, she confesses to Michael—but it required an iron will to play her role. Only in recent weeks have open elections been permitted; her movement swept into power, and Suu Kyi is now a member of Parliament.

This story is told in *The Lady*, directed by the prolific French director Luc Besson, who has great success in making action, sci-fi, and martial arts movies (*The Fifth Element*, *Subway*, *Leon: The Professional*). He has enormous resources at his command, including impressive crowd scenes staged in Thailand. The other film I mentioned, *They Call It Myanmar*, is in some ways an amateur film, however skillful and polished. It was shot secretly with a consumer HD camera by Robert H. Lieberman, a professor at Cornell, who covers a great deal of Burmese history and crucially has interviews with Suu Kyi herself. In person she seems much the same as the character played by Michelle Yeoh: composed, calm, resolute, with a firm British accent.

*The Lady* is more professional, but for me, *They Call It Myanmar* was more useful. Lieberman answers questions Besson does not think to ask. The Besson film, written by Rebecca Frayn, does indeed deal with a real life, but follows so faithfully the traditional shape of film biography that it feels less convincing. One of its distractions is the emphasis on Suu Kyi's marriage. There are too many domestic conversations, too many shots of Michael at home looking concerned while watching the news on TV. He is in Burma at the time of her first speech at the rally, and the film covers this momentous event mostly with reaction shots of his face in the huge crowd: proud, concerned, smiling, apprehensive, relieved.

This is not a criticism of David Thewlis's performance. He usually plays querulous or alarming characters, and this time he's a tousle-headed bookworm, kind to the core, who places his wife's politics above everything else. He was a good man. But this should not be his story or the story of their marriage. In a sense, he should be offscreen, as he was during the house arrest.

Michelle Yeoh is also strong in the film, embodying the qualities Suu Kyi seems to possess. Yeoh was the original force behind this film. What was needed, I think, was a different point of entry for the screenplay, so that it isn't such a conventional biopic. Luc Besson's busy career has centered on writing (44 credits) and producing (103). He usually matches talent to each project, and has directed only 17 times. Perhaps, given his strengths in genre films, he should have chosen not to direct this one, and selected a director such as Mira Nair or Deepa Mehta.

## La Mission ★ ★ ½

R, 117 m., 2010

Benjamin Bratt (Che Rivera), Erika Alexander (Lena), Jeremy Ray Valdez (Jes), Jesse Borrego (Rene), Talisa Soto Bratt (Ana), Max Rosenak (Jordan), Kevin Michael Richardson (Dee). Directed by Peter Bratt and produced by Peter Bratt, Benjamin Bratt, and Alpita Patel.

He is an admirable man, well liked in the Mission District of San Francisco. A single father whose son is headed for UCLA. A bus driver whose love is working on customized low-riders. A longtime recovering alcoholic. He got in trouble as a young man, did prison time, but now in his forties, he's put all that behind him.

This is the Che Rivera we meet at the beginning of *La Mission*, played by Benjamin Bratt as in a tattooed macho role—a man who isn't afraid to face down unruly passengers on his bus. He loves his son Jes (Jeremy Ray Valdez). After some disagreements with his upstairs neighbor Lena (Erika Alexander), he's beginning to see her in a new light. He's the anchor of a group of friends who work together on their lovingly customized cars.

Then he discovers his son is gay. That isn't part of his world, his culture, his comprehension. There is always violence coiled inside him, and he throws his son out of the house, fights with him on the sidewalk, and as a result assures that everyone in the neighborhood and at Jes's school knows the secret. They both sense a lot of stares and giggles and negative feelings from the Latino community.

Lena, as it turns out, works at a shelter for abused women. She is firm and unyielding in her distaste for violence. She'd started to like Che—there's a lot to like about him—but now she fears he's a type she's seen too often. He doesn't have a way to process anger. He explodes. He loves his son but hates homosexuality more.

This story is told earnestly and with some force in *La Mission*, written and directed by Benjamin's brother Peter. They worked together earlier on Peter's *Follow Me Home* (1996), an in-your-face film about a car full of minority graffiti artists on a cross-country odyssey. Here their hearts are in the right place, but the film tries to say too many things for its running time.

I believe Che's outrage at his son's personality. I do not believe his son would challenge him by suggesting Che found out something about gay sex in prison. At that moment I felt a screenplay talking, not a character. The film's treatment of Che's alcoholism is perfunctory—used for plot points, not character revelation. I believe an African-American woman and a Mexican-American man could certainly come together in the way the movie shows, but I was puzzled that the movie scarcely seemed to get deeper into that than the casting.

And Jes's lover is not simply too good to be true; he's too good to be interesting. This is Jordan (Max Rosenak), who is clean-cut, wholesome, and supportive, and of course has loving parents. I would have liked him a little more complex. I don't even know how they met; he's simply there because the story requires him.

Some crucial scenes take place in a hospital. These scenes, I think, overplay Che's feelings. I don't require acceptance and reconciliation, and the film is forthright in avoiding easy answers. But does the screenplay shortchange Che by painting him more broadly at the end than he seemed at the beginning? If experience does anything, it leaves us wiser.

## Larry Crowne ★ ★
PG-13, 99 m., 2011

Tom Hanks (Larry Crowne), Julia Roberts (Mercedes Tainot), Brian Cranston (Dean Tainot), Cedric the Entertainer (Lamar), Taraji P. Henson (B'Ella), Gugu Mbatha-Raw (Talia), Wilmer Valderrama (Dell Gordo), Pam Grier (Frances). Directed by Tom Hanks and produced by Hanks and Gary Goetzman. Screenplay by Hanks and Nia Vardalos.

*Larry Crowne* has Tom Hanks and Julia Roberts and a good premise and a colorful supporting cast, but what it doesn't have is a reason for existing. The screenplay carries blandness to a point beyond tedium. At some point the sinking realization sets in that Larry Crowne was born a nice guy, will always be a nice guy, will find few bumps in his road, and is destined for a happy ending. We watch not in suspense but in envy.

Hanks produced and directed the film, and cowrote the screenplay with Nia Vardalos, his pal since the days when Hanks's wife, Rita Wilson, produced Vardalos's *My Big Fat Greek Wedding* (2002). That was a good movie. Since then Vardalos wrote and starred in the awful *Connie and Carla* (2004), starred in the dismal *My Life in Ruins* (2009), and wrote and directed the train wreck *I Hate Valentine's Day* (2009). As a writer she seems drawn toward banality.

In *Larry Crowne*, Hanks plays a nice guy who gets fired from his retail job because he lacks the education to qualify him for a management position. This happens despite his countless awards for employee of the month. Larry cashes in his possessions, trades his car for a scooter, and decides to enroll in a local community college. As his economics teacher, he draws Dr. Matsutani (George Takei), the only character in the film interesting enough to have a movie made about him. As his public speaking teacher, he gets Mercedes Tainot (Julia Roberts), a character who seems to have drifted over from the auditions for *Bad Teacher.*

The story arc is simplicity itself: Larry Crowne is a nice man who becomes nicer with the encouragement of other nice people. He eventually inspires the bad teacher to become a good teacher, abandon her porn-surfing loser of a husband, cure herself of alcoholism, and fall in love with him. More than this a nice guy cannot be expected to do.

I watched the movie with all the pleasure I bring to watching bread rise. Don't get me wrong. I enjoy watching bread rise, but it lacks a certain degree of interest. You look forward to it being finished.

Larry is assisted in his lifestyle transition by the fetching Talia (Gugu Mbatha-Raw), who supervises a makeover; he ditches the regular-guy duds for basic black and gets a cool haircut. There is also character interest from his neighbors, Lamar (Cedric the Entertainer) and B'Ella (Taraji P. Henson), but that's what they're in the movie for: character interest. They don't seem essential. At the neighbor's garage sale, Larry buys a motor scooter and ends up as a member of a scooter club, which is like a motorcycle gang of environmentalists. How many scooter clubs are there in Los Angeles? Don't tell me. I don't want to know.

What we have here is a screenplay lacking in conflict. I often complain about screenwriters who slavishly follow the story arcs taught in screenwriting classes. Nia Vardalos might benefit from one of those classes. In place of conflict, the story substitutes cutesy whims. Tom Hanks on a motor scooter! Neat!

Julia Roberts is fine here, to the degree that the film permits it. She's pretty and has that warm smile and is transformed under the gentle pressure of Larry's sunny influence. Surely her marriage must be more deeply troubled than we ever see, but the movie's still waters don't run deep.

## The Last Airbender ½ ★
PG, 103 m., 2010

Noah Ringer (Aang), Nicola Peltz (Katara), Jackson Rathbone (Sokka), Dev Patel (Prince Zuko), Shaun Toub (Uncle Iroh), Aasif Mandvi (Commander Zhao), Cliff Curtis (Fire Lord Ozai), Seychelle Gabriel (Princess Yue). Directed by M. Night Shyamalan and produced by Shyamalan, Scott Aversano, Frank Marshall, and Sam Mercer.

*The Last Airbender* is an agonizing experience in every category I can think of and others still waiting to be invented. The laws of chance suggest that *something* should have gone right. Not here. It puts a nail in the coffin of low-rent 3-D, but it will need a lot more coffins than that.

Let's start with the 3-D, which was added as an afterthought to a 2-D movie. Not only is it unexploited and unnecessary, but it's a disaster even if you like 3-D. M. Night Shyamalan's retrofit produces the drabbest, darkest, dingiest movie of any sort I've seen in years. You know something is wrong when the screen is filled with flames that have the vibrancy of faded Polaroids. It's a known fact that 3-D causes a measurable decrease in perceived brightness, but *Airbender* looks like it was filmed with a dirty sheet over the lens.

Now for the movie itself. The first fatal decision was to make a live-action film out of material that was born to be anime. The animation of the Nickelodeon TV series drew on the bright colors and clear-line style of such masters as Miyazaki, and was a visual pleasure to observe. It's in the very nature of animation to make absurd visual sights more plausible.

Since *Airbender* involves the human manipulation of the forces of air, earth, water, and fire, there is hardly an event that can be rendered plausibly in live action. That said, its special effects are atrocious. The first time the Waterbender Katara summons a globe of water, which then splashes (offscreen) on her brother Sokka, he doesn't even get wet. The Firebenders' flames don't seem to really burn, and so on.

The story takes place in the future, after man has devastated the planet and survives in the form of beings with magical powers allowing them to influence earth, water, and fire. These warring factions are held in uneasy harmony by the Avatar, but the Avatar has disappeared, and Earth lives in a state of constant turmoil caused by the warlike Firebenders.

Our teenage heroes Katara and Sokka discover a child frozen in the ice. This is Aang (Noah Ringer), and they come to suspect he may be the Avatar, or last Airbender. Perhaps he can bring harmony and quell the violent Firebenders. This plot is incomprehensible, apart from the helpful orientation that we like Katara, Sokka, and Aang, and are therefore against their enemies.

The dialogue is couched in unspeakable quasi-medieval formalities; the characters are so portentous they seem to have been trained for grade-school historical pageants. Their dialogue is functional and action driven. There is little conviction that any of this might be real even in their minds. All of the benders in the movie appear only in terms of their attributes and functions, and contain no personality.

Potentially interesting details are botched. Consider the great iron ships of the Firebenders. These show potential as steampunk, but are never caressed for their intricacies. Consider the detail Miyazaki lavished on *Howl's Moving Castle.* Try sampling a Nickelodeon clip from the original show to glimpse the look that might have been.

After the miscalculation of making the movie as live action, there remained the challenge of casting it. Shyamalan has failed. His first inexplicable mistake was to change the races of the leading characters; on television Aang was clearly Asian, and so were Katara and Sokka, with perhaps Mongolian and Inuit genes. Here they're all whites. This casting makes no sense because (1) it's a distraction for fans of the hugely popular TV series, and (2) all three actors are pretty bad. I don't say they're untalented; I say they've been poorly served by Shyamalan and the script. They are bland, stiff, awkward, and unconvincing. Little Aang reminds me of Wallace Shawn as a child. This is not a bad thing (he should only grow into Shawn's shoes), but doesn't the role require little Andre, not little Wally?

As the villain, Shyamalan has cast Cliff Curtis as Fire Lord Ozai and Dev Patel (the hero of *Slumdog Millionaire*) as his son, Prince Zuko. This is all wrong. In material at this melodramatic level, you need teeth-gnashers, not leading men. Indeed, all of the acting seems inexplicably muted. I've been an admirer of many of Shyamalan's films, but action and liveliness are not his strong points. I fear he takes the theology of the bending universe seriously.

As *The Last Airbender* bores and alienates its audiences, consider the opportunities missed here. (1) This material should have become an A-list animated film. (2) It was a blunder jumping aboard the 3-D bandwagon with phony 3-D retrofitted to a 2-D film. (3) If it had to be live action, better special-effects artists should have been found. It's not as if films like *2012* and *Knowing* didn't contain "real-life" illusions as spectacular as anything called for in *The Last Airbender.*

I close with the hope that the title proves prophetic.

## The Last Mountain ★ ★ ★

PG, 95 m., 2011

William Sadler (Narrator), Maria Gunnoe, Bo Webb, Robert F. Kennedy Jr., Jennifer Hall-Massey, Joe Lovett, Bill Raney, Don Blankenship, Ed Wiley, Lorelei Scarbro, David Aaron Smith, and Susan Bird. A documentary directed by Bill Haney and produced by Haney, Clara Bingham, and Eric Grunebaum. Screenplay by Haney and Peter Rhodes.

Is there another state in the union more cruelly defaced than West Virginia? Its mountains have been blown up, its forests ripped out and thrown away, and the green new land that the settlers discovered now includes a wasteland of a million dead and toxic acres. Nationally, one in one hundred thousand people get brain tumors. In a small West Virginia town surrounded by strip mining, six neighbors have developed brain tumors. What are the odds of that?

*The Last Mountain* is a blunt and enraged documentary about how such things came to be. It is about Coal River Mountain, the site of a last stand against Massey Energy, a company it says disregarded environmental concerns, compromised the political process, and poisoned great stretches of the state in the name of corporate profits. Now lakes of sludge loom above towns, rivers are dead and dying, and heavy metals invade the bloodstreams and brains of the inhabitants.

Yes, we need coal. Yes, West Virginia has a lot of it and once had a lot more. Coal is a major contributor to global warming, but those very words, "global warming," are anathema to those whose minds have been bought and paid for by Big Energy. I would like to see a comparison of the dollars spent on (1) greener energy and (2) political lobbying by a company like Massey, the villain in *The Last Mountain.* Corporations by their nature exist to maximize profits. Their executives are compelled to enact draconian measures to further them. It's how they work.

The bad guy in *The Last Mountain* is Don Blankenship, who was chairman and CEO of Massey from 2000 until 2010. He doesn't believe in climate change and once equated energy conservation with communism. It was on his watch that twenty-nine miners were killed in the explosion at Massey's Upper Big Branch mine on April 5, 2010. Wikipedia: "In 2005, Blankenship wrote a memo to employees telling them that maximizing coal production was more important than spending time constructing things like support beams or ventilation shafts." Also Wikipedia: "When groundwater pollution from coal slurry injection by Massey Energy began contaminating wells around Blankenship's home, Massey paid to build a water line to his home from a neighboring town. Blankenship did not offer to provide uncontaminated water to any of his neighbors."

He fits my notion of a bad man. My notion of a heroine is Maria Gunnoe, a West Virginia woman who is one of the leaders of a campaign to defend Coal River Mountain. Articulate, plain-spoken, she has been transformed by the campaign.

A film like *The Last Mountain* fills me with restless anger. I have seen many documentaries like this, all telling versions of the same story: When there is money to be made at the cost of the environment, it is the environment that will suffer. And the suffering will be justified by denying global warming and "defending free enterprise." I understand that corporations exist to make profits, but I believe government exists to regulate them. Another hero in this film is Robert F. Kennedy Jr., who visits West Virginia frequently on behalf of the environmental activists, and lobbied Obama to reverse some (not all) of the Bush administration's moves to weaken green laws.

Still, it all comes back to the fact that we need energy. As I watched the film's aerial shots flying over the harsh and ugly landscapes left behind by Massey, it occurred to me that something was missing. No, not simply trees and other living things. I would have liked to see some wind turbines.

## Last Ride ★ ★ ★ ★

NO MPAA RATING, 100 m., 2012

Hugo Weaving (Kev), Tom Russell (Chook), Anita Hegh (Maryanne), John Brumpton (Max), Sonya Suares (Dr. Khan), Kelton Pell (Ranger). Directed by Glendyn Ivin and produced by Antonia Barnard and Nicholas Cole. Screenplay by Mac Gudgeon, based on the novel by Denise Young.

A father and his young son flee from the law across the limitless outback of Australia, and their doomed journey achieves a sad magnificence in *Last Ride.* Only gradually do we learn the reason for their flight. The father has a deep love for his boy, but he is a damaged man with a violent nature, and in the course of this great film, the son becomes capable of reaching hard conclusions and acting on them.

Before I tell you anything else, I want to describe one heartbreaking scene. There is a vast, flat salt lake in Australia, Lake Gairdner. When it is dry, they hold speed trials there. At some seasons it lies beneath a thin sheen of water. Kev and his son, Chook, driving a stolen SUV, set out across it and the visual effect is bewildering: There has been no explanation, and the car seems to be driving on water. The lake is miles across, and the SUV is the only moving thing to the horizon.

Chook (Tom Russell) has been along on this trip for days now, sometimes on foot, sometimes in stolen vehicles, sometimes eating canned beans, sometimes rabbits that they shoot. Most nights they sleep by a campfire under the stars. Kev (Hugo Weaving) steals money where he can, and when he ties up a woman who has been kind to Chook, the boy's eyes appeal to her for forgiveness.

His father won't tell him what happened to cause them to flee, but in flashbacks we see the boy's fragmented memories as he tries to piece it together. Sometimes his father strikes and frightens him. As they drive on the lake, Chook tells Kev, "You ain't a proper dad!" Kev stops the car and they fight. He throws his son out of the car and drives away. Soon the boy is alone, a moving speck on a shimmering mirror. He walks on defiantly, but finally halts and hunches down and begins to sob.

If *Last Ride* were made of scenes like this, it would be a bleak experience. It is not. A scene like this is balanced by a night when he rests in his father's arms and is told how to find the stars of the Seven Sisters, the Pleiades. "Black fellas reckon one of them came down to Earth," his dad says. The day before, while staying in a national park, they'd been warned by an Aboriginal ranger that camping was forbidden there. But Kev told the ranger he was trying to give his boy some experience in the bush, and that was good enough for the ranger.

Their odyssey has taken them through towns and down back roads and off-road. They have visited Maryanne (Anita Hegh), an old girlfriend of his dad's, who warned them they couldn't stay, but let them rest for one night. Chook and her dog made close friends. Then they had to move on. Walking in a dusty, empty town, they came across the Afghan Heritage Museum, a small house with a porch holding Afghan costumes and carvings. Here Chook was able to sleep secretly for a night. On another night, the boy shoplifted some sparklers from a gas station, and the father and son played with them on a small skateboard deck.

The film is astonishing in its visual beauty; cinematographer Greig Fraser (*Snow White and the Huntsman*) finds nobility in this arduous journey. As Kev, the veteran actor Hugo Weaving gives the performance of a lifetime. You may recall him as Elrond in the *Lord of the Rings* films. Here he plays a man who never tries to be nice, never tries to be cruel, only responds to his nature. He is down to his desperate final resources, and clings to the conviction that somehow he and the boy will find a place where he can be a father.

Tom Russell was a ten-year-old Adelaide schoolboy when he made this feature film debut. I have run out of words to account for young actors. Untrained, they seem able to reach an instinctive core of natural truth. Russell is in almost every scene, as authoritative as the adult actors. They say in a film or a story you must focus on the characters who change, and in *Last Ride* all of Kev's changes are behind him, but Chook is arriving at his young life's turning point.

For director Glendyn Ivin, this is also a

debut feature, although he won the Palme d'Or at Cannes for a short subject. Remarkable, how he begins with materials that could have given themselves so easily to a road movie formula, and finds such truth and beauty. He knows so surely where he's going that he arrives at a perfect final shot that tells us what we need to know about Chook.

## The Last Rites of Joe May ★ ★ ★ ½

NO MPAA RATING, 102 m., 2011

Dennis Farina (Joe May), Jamie Anne Allman (Jenny Rapp), Ian Barford (Stanley Buczkowski), Meredith Droeger (Angelina Rapp), Chelcie Ross (Billy), Gary Cole (Lenny). Directed by Joe Maggio and produced by Bill Straus and Stephanie Striegel. Screenplay by Maggio.

You meet guys like Joe May. They can get you a price on some merchandise that fell off the back of some truck. Dennis Farina depicts the type flawlessly in *The Last Rites of Joe May* in the performance of his career. He looks into the type and sees the man inside: proud, weary, fearful.

This movie takes place on the West Side of Chicago without a single "beauty shot." Not a skyscraper in sight. Only gray, cold streets, shabby bars, and forlorn bus stops. Joe May has just been released from Cook County hospital after a siege with pneumonia that nearly killed him. Before he goes home he goes to a bar. "Jeez, I thought you was dead," the bartender says. Nothing about how he's glad to see Joe is alive.

When he gets to his apartment Joe moves cautiously. Farina is a former Chicago cop and knows how to enter an apartment you're not sure about. It's been entered, yes—by Jenny Rapp (Jamie Anne Allman) and her daughter, Angelina (Meredith Droeger). They live there now. Joe lived there for years, but the landlord thought he was dead and rented it out.

Now begins the final act of Joe's life. He hunches his shoulders inside his coat, which is too thin against the chill wind. He goes to visit his old pal Billy (Chelcie Ross) in a retirement home, tapping on the ground floor window to announce his arrival. He goes to visit a man named Lenny (Gary Cole), whose office is a back table in a bar and who knows about stuff that falls off trucks. He sleeps one night outdoors, and then Jenny tells him he can sleep in his old apartment. This isn't romance. It's a rent-sharing arrangement.

Joe and Angelina, the daughter, get along right away. They feel natural together. You hardly ever see a bad performance by a child actor, but young Meredith Droeger is especially good in this role. Joe also encounters Stanley Buczkowski (Ian Barford), Jenny's boyfriend, who is a cop and who sometimes hits her. That goes down wrong with Joe May.

The film, written and directed by Joe Maggio, has only this handful of characters and looks at them carefully. The dialogue is right, the conflicts are simple and sincere, the hopes are touching. Joe talks Lenny into letting him move some stolen lamb chops, and has dreams even at his age of somehow becoming a big-time hustler. He carries himself as if he'd once been a bigger man in the neighborhood.

Hustling the hot merchandise doesn't work out so well. Without it being planned that way, Jenny and Angelina become the most important thing in Joe's life—not in terms of romance, but in terms of the responsibilities of a stand-up guy.

Joe Maggio is a sure-handed director with a good eye. I didn't see his straight-to-DVD horror film *Bitter Feast* (2010), but it got respectful reviews. Here he must have started writing with two elements in his mind: the winter streets of Chicago, and Dennis Farina, who has been so good for so long in supporting roles. *Joe May* evokes winters in Chicago neighborhoods far from the skyscrapers. The days grow short. Men with their fists punched into their pockets wish they had gloves. Some of them keep their coats on inside the bar. And Joe May, making the rounds of what's left of his life, gathers his will to make a last stand.

## The Last Song ★ ★ ½

PG, 107 m., 2010

Miley Cyrus (Ronnie Miller), Greg Kinnear (Steve Miller), Liam Hemsworth (Will Blakelee), Bobby Coleman (Jonah Miller), Kelly Preston (Kim Miller). Directed by Julie Anne Robinson and produced by Jennifer Gibgot and Adam

Shankman. Screenplay by Nicholas Sparks and Jeff Van Wie, based on a novel by Sparks.

Now that Miley Cyrus is seventeen, it's about time she played a sixteen-year-old. That she does fetchingly in *The Last Song*, and wins the heart of a beach volleyball champion a foot taller than she is. Well, actually 12.5 inches. She also learns to love her dad, played by Greg Kinnear, whose aura suggests a man easier to love than, say, Steve Buscemi. She does this on an idyllic island paradise offshore from Savannah, Georgia, where her dad is a classical composer whose pastime is restoring stained glass windows.

I was trying to remember the last time I felt the way about a girl that Miley Cyrus's fans feel about her. That would have been in 1959, when I saw Hayley Mills in *Tiger Bay*. Oh, she was something. A brave tomboy. She was twelve, but I could wait. It's a bit much to ask for the same innocence from Miley, who has already had her first world tour, but the fact is, she does a good job of making her character, Ronnie, engaging and lovable. That's despite her early Alienated Teen scenes. You know it's an Alienated Teen when it's a lovely day on an island paradise, but she has her hands pulled up inside the sleeves of her sweater and huddles against the chill of the cold, cruel world.

I like Miley Cyrus. I like her in spite of the fact that she's been packaged within an inch of her life. I look forward to the day when she squirms loose from her handlers and records an album of classic songs, performed with the same sincerity as her godmother, Dolly Parton. I think it'll be a long, long time until she plays a movie character like the freestanding, engaging heroines of Ashley Judd, but I can wait.

*The Last Song* is about how Ronnie (Miley) and her little brother, Jonah (Bobby Coleman), are taken by their mother (Kelly Preston) to spend the summer with their dad, Steve (Kinnear). She blames her dad for the divorce, is sullen and withdrawn. Ten minutes after she hits the beach (dressed in Gothic black), her milk shake is spilled by a flying volleyball player named Will (Liam Hemsworth). Talk about your Meet Cutes. Gradually she overcomes her hostility to men and realizes Will is a nice and honorable kid, even though he lives in a vast Southern mansion with insufferable rich parents.

Ronnie and Will make an attractive couple, possibly because Miley is standing on a box below camera range. I suspect Hemsworth may have been cast for his appeal to fangirls, rather like Robert Pattinson in *Twilight*. He's a little too tall, blond, blue-eyed, and hunky to be super plausible. He can definitely become a star, but it may be in the Peter O'Toole tradition; I can more easily imagine him in a remake of *Lawrence of Arabia* than as a settled spouse in a domestic drama.

Miley Cyrus, on the other hand, is attractive in the way of a girl you might actually meet. Her acting is unaffected, she can play serious, and she works easily with a pro like Kinnear, whose light comedy skills are considerable and undervalued. She even seems sincere in the face of a plot so blatantly contrived it seems like an after-school special. Would you believe that she and Will bond over sea turtle eggs?

Yes, she scares off a raccoon trying to raid a nest of eggs buried in the sand and mounts an all-night vigil over them. Then she calls the aquarium, and who do you think is the handsome volunteer who responds to the call? Standing watch together the second night, Ronnie and Will start talking, and it's only a matter of time until they regard together the itty bitty turtles hurrying toward the sea.

The other big crisis of her summer is that she's a trained classical pianist, but has just turned down a scholarship to Juilliard because her dad, you see, is such a snake. In a world containing divorce, what's the use of Mozart? The film's title relates to this situation, I believe, in some obscure way. Miley does, however, sing in the movie. She's mad at her dad, but not her fans.

*The Last Song* is based on the novel by Nicholas Sparks, who also wrote the screenplay. Sparks recently went on record as saying he is a greater novelist than Cormac McCarthy. This is true in the same sense that I am a better novelist than William Shakespeare. Sparks also said his novels are like Greek tragedies. This may actually be true. I can't check it out because, tragically, no really bad Greek tragedies have survived. His story here amounts to soft porn for teenage girls, which the acting and the abilities of director Julie Anne Robinson have promoted over its pay scale.

The movie is intended, of course, for Miley Cyrus admirers, and truth compels me to report that on that basis alone, it would get four stars. But we cannot all be Miley Cyrus fans, and these days you rarely hear Hayley Mills mentioned. Yet I award the film two and a half stars.

To be sure, I resent the sacrilege Nicholas Sparks commits by even mentioning himself in the same sentence as Cormac McCarthy. I would not even allow him to say, "Hello, bookstore? This is Nicholas Sparks. Could you send over the new Cormac McCarthy novel?" He should show respect by ordering anonymously. But it seems unfair to penalize Miley Cyrus fans, Miley, and the next Peter O'Toole for the transgressions of a lesser artist.

## The Last Station ★ ★ ★

R, 110 m., 2010

Helen Mirren (Sofya), Christopher Plummer (Tolstoy), Paul Giamatti (Chertkov), Anne Marie Duff (Sasha), Kerry Condon (Masha), James McAvoy (Valentin). Directed by Michael Hoffman and produced by Bonnie Arnold, Chris Curling, and Jens Meurer. Screenplay by Hoffman, based on the novel by Jay Parini.

Watching *The Last Station,* I was reminded of the publisher Bennett Cerf's story about how he went to Europe to secure the rights to James Joyce's *Ulysses.*

"Nora, you have a brilliant husband," he told Joyce's wife.

"You don't have to live with the bloody fool."

If Joyce was a drunk and a roisterer, how different was the Russian novelist Leo Tolstoy, who was a vegetarian and pacifist, and recommended (although did not practice) celibacy? *The Last Station* focuses also on *his* wife, Sofya, who after bearing his thirteen children thought him a late arrival to celibacy and accused him of confusing himself with Christ. Yet it's because of the writing of Joyce and Tolstoy that we know about their wives at all. Well, the same is true of George Eliot's husband.

*The Last Station* focuses on the last year of Count Tolstoy (Christopher Plummer), a full-bearded Shakespearian figure presiding over a household of intrigues. The chief schemer is Chertkov (Paul Giamatti), his intense follower, who idealistically believes Tolstoy should leave his literary fortune to the Russian people. It's just the sort of idea that Tolstoy might seize upon in his utopian zeal. Sofya (Helen Mirren), on behalf of herself and her children, is livid.

Chertkov, who as the quasi-leader of Tolstoy's quasi-cult, hires a young man named Valentin (James McAvoy) to become the count's private secretary. In this capacity, he is to act as a double agent, observing moments between Leo and Sofya when Chertkov would not be welcome.

It may be hard for us to understand how seriously Tolstoy was taken at the time. To call him comparable in stature to Gandhi would not be an exaggeration, and indeed, Gandhi adopted many of his ideas. Tolstoy in his eighty-second year remained active and robust, but everyone knew his end might be approaching, and the Russian equivalent of paparazzi and gossips lurked in the neighborhood. Imagine Perez Hilton staking out J. D. Salinger.

Tolstoy was thought a great man and still is, but in a way his greatness distracts from how good he was as a writer. When I was young the expression "reading *War and Peace*" was used as a synonym for idly wasting an immense chunk of time. Foolishly believing this, I read Dostoyevsky and Chekhov but not Tolstoy, and it was only when I came late to *Anna Karenina* that I realized he wrote page-turners. In *Time* magazine's compilation of 125 lists of the ten greatest novels of all time, *War and Peace* and *Anna Karenina* placed first and third. (You didn't ask, but *Madame Bovary* was second, *Lolita* fourth, and *Huckleberry Finn* fifth.)

*The Last Station* has the look of a Merchant-Ivory film, with the pastoral setting, the dashing costumery, the roomy old country house, the meals taken on lawns. But did Merchant and Ivory ever deal with such a demonstrative family? If the British are known for suppressing their emotions, the Russians seem to bellow their whims. If a British woman in Merchant-Ivory land desires sex, she bestows a significant glance in the candlelight. Sofya clucks like a chicken to arouse old Leo's rooster.

The dramatic movement in the film takes place mostly within Valentin (James McAvoy), who joins the household already an acolyte of Tolstoy. Young and handsome, he says he is celibate. Sofya has him pegged as gay, but Masha (Kerry Condon), a nubile Tolstoyian, pegs him otherwise. Valentin also takes note that Tolstoy, like many charismatic leaders, exempts himself from his own teachings. The thirteen children provide a hint, and his private secretary cannot have avoided observing that although the count and countess fight over his will, a truce is observed at bedtime, and the enemies meet between the lines.

As the formidable patriarch, Christopher Plummer avoids any temptation (if he felt one) to play Tolstoy as a Great Man. He does what is more amusing; he plays him as a Man Who Knows He Is Considered Great. Helen Mirren plays a wife who knows his flaws, but has loved him since the day they met. To be fair, no man who wrote that fiction could be other than wise and warm about human nature.

Some women are simply sexy forever. Helen Mirren is a woman like that. She's sixty-four. As she enters her seventies, we'll begin to develop a fondness for sexy septuagenarians.

Mirren and Plummer make Leo and Sofya Tolstoy more vital than you might expect in a historical picture. Giamatti has a specialty in seeming to be up to something, and McAvoy and Condon take on a glow from feeling noble while sinning. In real life, I learn, Tolstoy provided Sofya with more unpleasant sunset years, but could we stand to see Helen Mirren treated like that?

## Last Train Home ★ ★ ★ ★

NO MPAA RATING, 87 m., 2010

---

Chen Suqin, Zhang Changhua, Zhang Qin, and Zhang Yang. A documentary directed by Lixin Fan and produced by Mila Aung-Thwin and Daniel Cross.

---

This is inevitable: Painful social conflict will arise between those Chinese citizens who produce consumer goods for the world, and those Chinese who want to consume them. *Last Train Home*, an extraordinary documentary, watches that conflict play out over a period of three years in one family. It's one of those extraordinary films, like *Hoop Dreams*, that tells a story the makers could not possibly have anticipated in advance. It works like stunning, grieving fiction.

The film opens like a big-picture documentary, showing us a huge crowd being directed by police as it grinds its way forward. We are informed that these are some of the 130 million Chinese citizens who make an annual train journey from urban centers to their provincial villages—"the largest human migration in the world." Umbrellas of every description protect them. They carry enormous bundles—gifts, perhaps, or food for the journey. They're headed home for Chinese New Year.

We gradually center on Zhang Changhua and Chen Suqin, a married couple. Years ago they left their home in the Szechuan province to take low-paying jobs in a textile factory in Guangzhou, which is the huge industrial city on the mainland next to Hong Kong. Here, in row after row, they work bent over sewing machines, assembling perhaps the jeans I'm wearing right now. They live in dormitories—married adults, with next to no privacy.

They save every yuan they can to send home. They left their children behind to be raised by a grandmother. Their dream is that by fifteen years of this toil, they will pay for the children to finish school and live better lives. For that dream they have sacrificed the life of parenthood, and are like strangers at home to children who know them as voices on the telephone, seen on the annual visit.

This is a reality Dickens could hardly have imagined. The fruit of their toil has contributed to China's emergence as a global economic power. But their lives are a grim contrast to the glittering Beijing of the Olympics, the towers of Shanghai, the affluent new business class. And here is the part you may sense coming: Are their children grateful for what amounts to the sacrifice of two lifetimes?

The filmmaker, Lixin Fan, follows this family for three years, in the city and in the village. We hear much about how Chinese parents pressure their children to study hard and excel. Overseas, they frequently do succeed. But China is a huge nation, so large that a generation may not be long enough to rise from poverty.

Their daughter, Zhang Qin, is in high school, and comes to regard her parents as distant strangers—and nags. She's had enough of it. But what she does is beyond heartbreaking. She moves to Guangzhou and gets a factory job. She does the math. If she keeps her wages instead of sending them home, she'll have them to spend on herself. Does it occur to her to suggest her parents move back home with her brother, while she helps support and repay them? Not a chance.

There is so much to say about this great film. You sense the dedication of Lixin Fan and his team (he did much of the cinematography and editing himself). You see once again the alchemy by which a constantly present camera eventually becomes almost unnoticed, as people live their lives before it. You know the generations almost better than they know themselves because the camera can be in two places and they are usually in one or the other.

There is a quiet moment in a mall. On their day off, Zhang Qin and her friends go shopping. They like a pair of jeans: "Are these made in our factory?" No, in another. Of course they want them. Of course their generation wants them. But their generation doesn't want to work years leaning over a sewing machine and sleeping in a dorm.

We read about the suicides in Apple's plants in China. Seeing this film, you suspect there are many suicides among workers in factories whose brands are less famous than Apple. Chinese peasants no longer live without television and a vision of another world. They no longer live in a country without consumer luxuries. *Last Train Home* suggests that the times they are a-changin'. The rulers of China may someday regret that they distributed the works of Marx so generously.

## Late Bloomers ★ ★ ½

NO MPAA RATING, 95 m., 2012

William Hurt (Adam), Isabella Rossellini (Mary), Doreen Mantle (Nora), Kate Ashfield (Giulia), Aidan McArdle (James), Arta Dobroshi (Maya), Luke Treadaway (Benjamin), Leslie Phillips (Leo), Hugo Speer (Peter), Joanna Lumley (Charlotte), Simon Callow (Richard). Directed by Julie Gavras and produced by Bertrand Faivre and Sylvie Pialat. Screenplay by Gavras and Olivier Dazat.

"I'm getting old. And you're getting old, too." Mary looks her husband in the eyes and says out loud something they both know, but which only she is willing to deal with. Isabella Rossellini and William Hurt star in *Late Bloomers,* an uneven but touching comedy with a cheery score that sounds too much like whistling on the way past the graveyard. Without even trying to be profound, the film communicates a great deal of truth. Perhaps it seems particularly true to me because Rossellini and I both have our birthdays coming up on the eighteenth of this month. If she's old, I'm ten years older.

Hurt plays Adam, an architect working in London. Rossellini plays his wife, born in Italy. They've been married for thirty years. The film opens with her undergoing a medical examination, which returns good news, but something like that can help you imagine the bells tolling. We see Mary taking exercise classes in a local swimming pool and looking for more to do with her time; her friend Charlotte suggests the old standby, volunteer work. Adam has just received the sort of award that comes near the end of a career and is incapable of thinking of his career in such a way.

They seem happy enough, although the actors are useful in suggesting their differences: Rossellini glows and has a warm smile as usual, and Hurt is detached and has his angular look as usual. Their three grown children sense something is shifting in the marriage.

Adam's firm was founded to take unpopular assignments and find exciting solutions for them. Now he's asked to design a senior retirement home, the last thing he could have wished for. Charlotte (Joanna Lumley) lines Mary up for volunteer work at a foundation. The woman in charge there is unbearably condescending to a room full of her older volunteers. Although Mary was an advanced teacher of Italian, this horrible woman asks her to bake cakes.

Mary begins to improve their home with a

telephone with enlarged numbers, grab bars above the bathtub, and lift-off bars on either side of the toilet. You never know when you might need such things. Adam is offended. At work, he skulks over the old-age home until some young colleagues express their admiration for him, and then he makes them a secret task force to work on the project with him. Part of his renewed interest may involve a warm-eyed young woman (Arta Dobroshi) who considers him a hero. Communication between Mary and Adam begins to shut down.

*Late Bloomers*, directed by Julie Gavras, doesn't use fraught scenes and heated dialogue to reflect their troubles. They aren't those kind of people, and this isn't that kind of film. It offers shallow pleasures and the satisfaction of seeing two actors in performances better than the film deserves. They're surrounded by easy supporting turns: Simon Callow plays Adam's boss, Doreen Mantle plays Mary's mother, and their three children are the dry and stuffy James (Aidan McArdle), the sweet Giulia (Kate Ashfield), and the feckless Benjamin (Luke Treadaway). Not much communication here among the generations.

If *Late Bloomers* contains good acting and useful truths, it also contains some condescension of its own. There's one of those familiar but unbelievable movie scenes where a man opens his door and about fifteen complete strangers sweep past him without a word, followed by his wife with a smug smile. They're all old people, and should have better manners.

## Leap Year ★ ★ ★

PG, 97 m., 2010

Amy Adams (Anna), Matthew Goode (Declan), Adam Scott (Jeremy), John Lithgow (Jack). Directed by Anand Tucker and produced by Gary Barber, Chris Bender, Roger Birnbaum, and Jake Weiner. Screenplay by Deborah Kaplan and Harry Elfont.

Amy Adams and Matthew Goode have the charm necessary to float a romantic comedy like *Leap Year*, and this is a story that needs their buoyancy. A sort of conspiracy forms between the audience and the screen: We know what has to happen, and the movie knows what has to happen, and the point is to keep us amused. *Leap Year* did better than that: It made me care. It did that by not being too obvious about what it was obviously trying to do.

Let's start off on the same page. A sweet but over-organized young woman named Anna (Amy Adams) has been dating a high-powered heart surgeon named Jeremy (Adam Scott) for four years. He's pleasant, attentive, presentable, and shares her goal of buying a condo in the best building in Boston. He does nothing, absolutely nothing wrong. For veteran filmgoers, he has one fatal flaw: He has a healthy head of hair, and every strand is perfectly in place. No modern movie hero can have his hair combed.

When, oh when, will Jeremy ask Anna to marry him? After dashing her hopes once again, he hurries off to Dublin for a cardiologists' convention because as we all know it's a professional necessity for cardiologists to meet in faraway places. Anna is told that in Ireland on Leap Day, every four years, a woman can ask a man to marry her. Anna double-checks on the Web, somehow not discovering that this is believed nearly everywhere, and if a man in Denmark turned her down, he would have to buy her a pair of gloves.

Anna flies off to Ireland. The flight lasts only long enough for her to survive severe turbulence. The plane is diverted to Cardiff. Is there *anyone* in the theater surprised that she didn't arrive in Dublin on schedule? Despite canceled ferry boats, she makes her way to Ireland by hiring a tugboat. The skipper says they can't land at Cork but must head for Dingle. Dingle in Ireland is more or less as far as you can get from Wales (or Dublin), but never mind.

We know what's coming. Anna must meet her costar, Declan, played by Matthew Goode as the owner of the local pub. I suspect business has fallen off there ever since Robert Mitchum left after filming *Ryan's Daughter* in 1969. Anna is now wet and tired, but still plucky. In the pub, she asks Declan how she can get to Dublin. Turns out Declan is not only the publican but the taxi driver and runs the local hotel. They get a good smile out of this, but wouldn't you be asking yourself why neither one mentions "Local Hero"?

OK, enough fooling with the plot. Let's agree it stays firmly on course, and that Anna and Declan argue all the way to Dublin through adventures that, by law, must include getting all muddy and being forced to share a bedroom together. Therefore, the success of the film depends on the acting and direction.

Amy Adams and Matthew Goode sell it with great negative chemistry and appeal. Adams has an ability to make things seem fresh and new; everything seems to be happening to her for the first time, and she has a particularly innocent sincerity that's convincing. (Who was it that said if you can fake sincerity, you can fake anything?) Goode is wisely not made too handsome. Oh, you could shoot him as handsome; he's good-looking, let's face it. But the director, Anand Tucker, shoots him as annoyed, rude, and scruffy. Hair not too well combed.

Then take another look at Jeremy (Adam Scott). I'm not going to say he's too handsome. All I have to say is that in a silent movie he could simply walk on the screen and you'd know he's not going to get the girl. The movie carefully avoids making him a heavy. It's rather clever: He smoothly does more or less exactly what she's trained him to do, and what he doesn't understand is that she no longer believes in that version of him.

Bottom line: This is a full-bore, PG-rated, sweet romantic comedy. It sticks to the track, makes all the scheduled stops, and bears us triumphantly to the station. And it is populated by colorful characters, but then, when was the last time you saw a boring Irishman in a movie?

## Leaves of Grass ★ ★ ★ ★

R, 105 m., 2010

Edward Norton (Bill Kincaid, Brady Kincaid), Tim Blake Nelson (Bolger Tim), Susan Sarandon (Daisy Kincaid), Keri Russell (Janet), Richard Dreyfuss (Pug Rothbaum), Steve Earle (Buddy Fuller). Directed by Tim Blake Nelson and produced by Nelson, Elie Cohn, Kristina Dubin, John Langley, William Migliore, and Edward Norton.

Tim Blake Nelson's *Leaves of Grass* is some kind of sweet, wacky masterpiece. It takes all sorts of risks, including a dual role with Edward Norton playing twin brothers, and it pulls them off. It is certainly the most intelligent, philosophical, and poetic film I can imagine that involves five murders in the marijuana-dealing community of Oklahoma and includes John Prine singing "Illegal Smile."

Sometimes you can't believe your luck as a movie unfolds. There is a mind behind it, joyful invention, obvious ambition. As is often the case, I had studiously avoided reading anything at all about *Leaves of Grass* before going to see the movie, although I rather doubted it would be about Walt Whitman. What I did know is that the actor Tim Blake Nelson has written and directed three films I enormously admired: *Eye of God* (1997), *O* (2001), and *The Grey Zone* (2001), all three dealing in a concrete dramatic way with important questions: religion, redemption, race, the Holocaust; and that the actor Edward Norton has never agreed to appear in a film he didn't believe he had reason to respect.

The film opens with Norton as a philosopher named Bill Kincaid giving a lecture on Socrates to a packed classroom of starstruck students at Brown. It's a measure of Nelson's writing and Norton's acting that this lecture isn't a sound bite but is allowed to continue until the professor develops his point, and it's an interesting one. Only as I think back do I realize what an audacious way that is to open a movie about the drug culture of rural Oklahoma.

SPOILER WARNING: Kincaid is on the fast track. He's published books, is a crossover intellectual superstar, is offered a chance to open his own department at Harvard. Then he gets a telephone call telling him his twin brother, Brady, is dead. He has long since severed his old family ties, but he flies home for the funeral to Little Dixie, Oklahoma, and is met at the airport by his twin's best friend (Nelson). As it turns out, Brady is not dead, and the story was a lie designed to lure him back home for two purposes. One is to force him to see his mother, a 1960s pothead played by Susan Sarandon. The other is to act as his double to establish an alibi while Brady goes up to Tulsa for a meeting with the region's dominant marijuana dealer, Pug Rothbaum (Richard Dreyfuss).

Now I will abandon synopsis and consider

the pleasures of the film. First there's the dual performance by Norton, who is flawless as both an elite intellectual and a good ol' boy. In appearance, movement, and dialect he's for all intents two different people, one who has reinvented himself and shed his down-home roots, the other who is growing the best marijuana around. I like the way the film makes the twins equally brilliant; Brady has designed and built a hydroponic farm that is producing its seventh generation of top-quality weed. He is also something of a philosopher himself. In writing his dialogue, Nelson doesn't condescend. He is a Tulsa native who dismisses the widespread notion that a man's "hick" accent (the movie's word) provides a measure of his intelligence. Brady sounds like a semiliterate redneck, but he's very smart.

Faithful readers will know I am much occupied with the various definitions of God. Here is Brady's theory, as explained to his best buddy: There is a God, but man can never conceive of him or know him, because God is perfect and we cannot know perfection. Take for an example parallel lines extending to infinity. There can never be indefinitely parallel lines demonstrating themselves in the real, physical world, because it does not admit of parallelism. That is widely understood. Ah, but man can conceive of parallel lines, and prove them absolutely by mathematics. Just so with Brady's God. We can form an idea of perfection reaching into infinity, but we live in a universe that will never—can never—intersect with his. Rather elegant thinking, wouldn't you say, as expressed in Brady's own pothead barroom vernacular in the cab of a pickup truck with a shotgun rack.

I suspect there's a lot of Tim Blake Nelson in this film that is buried out of sight. Some elements are visible. That would include the Jewish community of Tulsa, which Nelson affectionately describes as "wildly eccentric, unlikely, and exotic." The plot includes not only Rothbaum, the drug lord and well-known charitable benefactor, but Ken Feinman (Josh Pais), the financially desperate orthodontist who finds himself bizarrely drawn into the plot. As is Rabbi Zimmerman (Maggie Siff), who explains to Billy Kincaid her belief that the world is broken and our duty is to try to fix it.

Another valuable character is Janet (Keri Russell), a local English teacher and poet, who quotes Whitman to Billy and entrances him in a way he has never before allowed. I suspect Janet has personal meaning to Nelson. In a press conference he said he is grateful to have been raised around books and rhetoric, and much of his dialogue here may be payback. Yes, but also always perfectly appropriate and in tune.

The plot involves as many dead and severely wounded bodies lying around as in *Blood Simple*, and Nelson weaves it expertly without a lot of visible "plotting." The story is the terrain the characters move through, and they are always the foreground. What stands out is the ability of both Billy and Brady (perhaps even more Brady) to understand the world philosophically and deal with it intellectually.

Here's a quote for the video box: "One of the year's best!" No, Tim Blake Nelson . . . thank *you*.

## Leaving ★ ★

NO MPAA RATING, 85 m., 2010

Kristin Scott Thomas (Suzanne), Sergi Lopez (Ivan), Yvan Attal (Samuel). Directed by Catherine Corsini and produced by Michel Seydoux and Fabienne Vonier. Screenplay by Corsini and Gaelle Mace.

The French are considered, especially by themselves, to be expert in the arts of romance. Their films about love are often adult, thoughtful, perceptive, and observant. In order to preserve that reputation, they should have refused an export license to *Leaving*. Here we have characters who couldn't figure their way out of a Dr. Phil show.

We begin with the premise that sexual passion is sufficient to compel a French woman in her forties to abandon her husband and two children, her home, her profession, her reputation, and her credit cards in order to recline in the arms of a Spanish handyman who is an ex-con with no funds. He must be very handy indeed. She experiences love at first sight, a *coup de foudre*.

Suzanne (Kristin Scott Thomas) is in a loveless marriage with Samuel (Yvan Attal), a doctor. He is proper and polite, expects his meals on time, takes pride in his possessions, and agrees to remodel a room in one of their outbuildings so she can resume her practice of reflexology. Ivan (Sergi Lopez) turns up to perform this task, and soon they are reflexing to the same drummer.

Oh, it is love. Mad, heedless love. She can hardly wait to confess to her husband, because she cannot lie. Perhaps this compulsion can be understood because Suzanne is British. It explains something about the two nations that in the United Kingdom people sometimes have tea between five and seven, and in France they sometimes have *cinq à sept,* which you're going to have to look up for yourself. Suzanne could have avoided much unhappiness if she had only been able to keep a secret.

Suzanne is not only impetuous, but doesn't seem to know her husband very well. Samuel isn't a good sport. He demands his wife back. She should get out in that kitchen and rattle those pots and pans. He cuts off her allowance, freezes the bank account, cancels the credit cards, pulls strings to make both Ivan and Suzanne unemployable, and otherwise inconveniences them.

This makes no difference. In Ivan's arms she's like a teenager with her first boyfriend. He takes her to visit a ruined stone cottage on a remote hillside, and she dreams that they'll build a little love nest. Ivan keeps a cool head. He usually has good advice. He's in love, but he's not nuts. Now with Suzanne: I knew you could get galloping pneumonia, but I hadn't heard about galloping erotomania.

Still, I want to say a word in praise of Kristin Scott Thomas. She is a splendid actress. Because she's perfectly bilingual, she finds challenging roles in France while Hollywood would reduce her to playing Magical Women. (These are like Spike Lee's Magical Negroes—wise and kind characters who have nothing to do in the plot but stand around being wise and kind.) Sometimes in the past Thomas has seemed to be, well, a little brittle. Here she is warm, soft, and lovable. When she cuddles Ivan he purrs. Thomas walks around in jeans and a T-shirt and has that Isabelle Huppert lifelong little girl look. She's good. Pity about the movie.

## Le Havre ★ ★ ★ ★

NO MPAA RATING, 103 m., 2011

Andre Wilms (Marcel Marx), Kati Outinen (Arletty), Jean-Pierre Darroussin (Monet), Blondin Miguel (Idrissa), Elina Salo (Claire), Evelyne Didi (Yvette), Jean-Pierre Leaud (Denouncer), Pierre Etaix (Dr. Becker), Roberto Piazza (Little Bob), Quoc-Dung Nguyen (Chang), Francois Monnie (Grocer), Laika (Dog). Directed, written, and produced by Aki Kaurismaki.

Here is the sunniest film I've seen by Aki Kaurismaki, and he reveals a lot of sunshine inside for a director whose world is usually filled with deadpan losers. His dour films are comedies, too, and baffle some viewers while others grow unreasonably fond of them. Apprehensive loners fail at unpromising enterprises and their hopes are crushed by an uncaring society, but it's piled on so deep you're pretty sure Kaurismaki is grinning. Who else could run, along with his brother Maki, a summer film festival so far north in Finland that the sun never sets?

Le Havre is much farther south, a French port where many of the cargoes are human—illegal immigrants arriving from Africa. The police find a container filled with them, and a young boy slips under their arms and runs away. This is Idrissa (Blondin Miguel), from Gabon, solemn, shy, appealing. The cops announce a manhunt. The film's hero, Marcel Marx (Andre Wilms), is fishing near a pier and sees the boy standing waist-deep in hiding, mutely appealing to him. He returns, leaves out some food, and finds the food gone the next day. And so, with no plan in mind, Marcel becomes in charge of protecting the boy from arrest.

The movie's other characters are all proletarians from a working-class neighborhood, and in Kaurismaki's somewhat sentimental view, therefore in sympathy with the little underdog and not with the police. We meet Marcel's wife, Arletty (Kati Outinen, long the director's favorite actress), who joins her husband in his scheme. Their dog, Laika, is also a great help. Marcel, probably in his fifties, is a hardworking shoe-shine man who knows everyone, including such as a snoop, a woman grocer (Francois Monnie), a fellow Vietnamese shoe shiner, Inspector Monet (Jean-Pierre Darroussin), and a local rock singer named Little Bob (Roberto Piazza), whose act is unlike any you have ever seen.

Marcel and Arletty are long and happily in love. They cherish each other. Childless, they care for the boy and enlist others in the neighborhood to hide him from the inspector, who perhaps is not looking all that hard. The snoop is a throwback to informers during the Resistance. Idrissa is resourceful and clever, and moves in and out of hiding places like a figure in a French farce. The dog fully deserves its listing by name in the credits.

Early in the conspiracy, Arletty falls ill and is rushed to the hospital, concerned only that her sickness will make Marcel worry. In a priceless scene, she meets Idrissa for the first time when Marcel dispatches him to the hospital on a mission. Note her perfect acceptance of any emissary from her husband, even an inexplicable young African boy. Note, too, the precise sequence of events during which Marcel believes his wife has died and discovers otherwise. Even Kaurismaki's miracles are deadpan.

This movie is as lovable as a silent comedy, which it could have been. It takes place in a world that seems cruel and heartless, but look at the lengths Marcel goes to find Idrissa's father in a refugee camp and raise money to send the boy to join his mother in England. *Le Havre* has won many festivals, including Chicago 2011, and comes from a Finnish auteur, yet let me suggest that smart children would especially like it. There is nothing cynical or cheap about it, it tells a good story with clear eyes and a level gaze, and it just plain makes you feel good.

## Le Quattro Volte ★ ★ ★ ½

NO MPAA RATING, 88 m., 2011

Giuseppe Fuda (Shepherd), Bruno Timpano and Nazareno Timpano (Charcoal Workers). Directed by Michelangelo Frammartino and produced by Philippe Bober, Marta Donzelli, Elda Guidinetti, Gabriella Manfre, Susanne Marian, Gregorio Paonessa, Andres Pfaffli. Screenplay by Frammartino.

Here is a film that invites philosophical musing. Made without dialogue and often in long shots, it regards the four stages of existence in a remote Italian village. Those stages, as set down 2,500 years ago by Pythagoras, are animal, vegetable, mineral, and intellectual. It's not necessary to know that or anything else to watch *Le Quattro Volte*, which doesn't require active interpretation but invites meditation and musing. I drifted pleasantly in its depths.

The camera usually keeps a certain distance, so it isn't telling a story but observing daily life. A very old shepherd climbs with effort after his goats on a hillside, while his dog barks and is a busybody. The shepherd returns to the village and waits as an old woman sweeps the dust from the church floor. Some of this dust he mixes with water and drinks as a remedy.

Events unfold slowly. In one unbroken shot of some duration, we see the dog somehow sets into motion a truck, which rolls down an incline and breaks open an enclosure holding the goats. The goats wander into the village. In another shot, the dog hurries down a road, encounters some walkers, and hurries back. Usually trained animals don't perform at such a distance from their masters. That's not the point of the shots, but of course you think of things like that.

Other shots. A smoldering coal-black heap, tamped down by workers. A tall tree felled. The erection of the tree in the town. Processions. A funeral. The sudden and unceremonious birth of a goat. The adventures of this kid. Human affairs seen at such a distance they seem isolated by the objectivity of history. Goat affairs seen closely as the mother licks her newborn.

The director, Michelangelo Frammartino, has made a serene and beautiful film. Its visuals cover the animal, vegetable, and mineral stages in our infinitesimal bit of the universe. Our thoughts, and his, supply the fourth stage. The title can be translated as *The Four Realms*. The four realms . . . of what? It doesn't say. Perhaps the four realms of everything that is.

Often I felt no need to bring the images up to the level of verbal thought. I observed the old shepherd's difficult passage through life, I noticed how quiet and empty the village seems to be, I actually thought about what it would be like to live there, who one would talk with, how one could find books or movies, and whether all the citizens are as ritual-bound as those we see.

I also thought about charcoal. I had no idea how it was created. Then I thought about goats. I like to visit them in their enclosure in the farm at the Lincoln Park Zoo. Their step is so nimble, their behavior so alert. They are tactful animals, ever so much more graceful than pigs or sheep. I started thinking, forgive me, about goat curry. Then I started thinking about what I was thinking. You might be surprised how absorbed you become during this film.

## Let Me In ★ ★ ★ ½

R, 115 m., 2010

Chloe Grace Moretz (Abby), Kodi Smit-McPhee (Owen), Richard Jenkins (The Father), Elias Koteas (The Policeman), Cara Buono (Owen's Mother), Sasha Barrese (Virginia). Directed by Matt Reeves and produced by Alexander Yves Brunner, Guy East, Donna Gigliotti, Carl Molinder, John Nordling, Simon Oakes, and Nigel Sinclair. Screenplay by Reeves, based on the screenplay and novel *Let the Right One In* by John Ajvide Lindqvist.

"I've been twelve for a very long time."

*Let Me In*, like the Swedish film that inspired it, deals brutally with the tragic life of the vampire. It's not all fun, games, and Team Edward. No lifestyle depending on fresh human blood can be anything but desperate. A vampire, like a drug addict, is driven by need. After a certain point, all else is irrelevant and the focus is on the craving.

The film is remarkably similar in tone and approach to *Let the Right One In*, and it is clear the American writer-director, Matt Reeves, has admiration for the Swedish writer-director, John Ajvide Lindqvist. He understands what made the first film so eerie and effective, and here the same things work again. Most U.S. audiences will be experiencing the story for the first time. Those who know the 2008 version will notice some differences, but may appreciate them.

The core story remains similar. Owen, a boy on the brink of adolescence, lives a lonely life in a snowbound apartment complex with an alcoholic mother, hardly seen. He is bullied at school by a sadistic boy, much larger. A girl named Abby and her father move into the next apartment. She announces, "I can never be your friend," but some latent kindness causes her to feel protective toward the lonely and abused child. Abby is a vampire, but vampires have their reality forced upon them and, having lived for a long time, may have seen much to make them pity the living.

The story focuses tightly on Owen (Kodi Smit-McPhee) and Abby (Chloe Grace Moretz, of *Kick-Ass*). Two other adults are of consequence: Her "father" (Richard Jenkins), who can hardly be her father and was probably, long ago, in Owen's shoes. In vampire lore he is her Familiar. The other adult is a local policeman, played by Elias Koteas as a saturnine and solemn man. He's investigating a serial killer in the region. Where there are vampires, there must always be serial killers.

The night and the cold are also characters. The film is shot in chill tones of blue and gray, Owen and Abby have uncanny pale skin, there is frost on his breath, but not on hers. She doesn't feel the cold, we gather. Or the warmth. Many of the events are the same in both films, although the U.S. version adds one surprise that comes at a useful time to introduce frightening possibilities: This is not a safe world, and bad things can happen.

Both films end with scenes set in a swimming pool at night. The windows, high up under the ceiling to admit sunlight, are dark and cold. We can imagine the clammy tiles, the chill in the locker room where Owen is so often picked on. The bullies call him a "girl," and seem obsessed with seeing his genitals—homophobic cruelty that casts a sad light on the first film's revelation about Abby's body. Both these characters feel sexually threatened or inadequate. It may only be me, but as I recall indoor swimming pools at night in winter (at high school, or the YMCA), they always had a whiff of mournful dread.

In the *Twilight* films, sexuality is treated as a tease. The handsome Edward is cast as a sexy but dangerous threat, who manfully holds back from sex with Bella Swan. She's tempted, but the films are cautionary fables about the danger of teenage sex. In *Let Me In*, sex is seen more as a troubling encroachment on privacy. Owen and Abby for their own reasons quail from intimacy and contact, and their only sensuous moments involve the comfort of close, tender hugs.

Where this will lead is easy to guess. Owen will move into Abby's life as her next Familiar. She will protect him. Among the things she will save him from is the necessity of growing up and functioning as a normal male. She will control everything. Thus Bella's sweet masochism will become Owen's hunger to give over control. To be a servant is the price for not being a victim. Those hoping to see a "vampire movie" will be surprised by a good film.

## Letters from the Big Man ★ ★ ★

NO MPAA RATING, 104 m., 2011

Lily Rabe (Sarah Smith), Jason Butler Harner (Sean), Isaac C. Singleton Jr. (The Big Man), Jim Cody Williams (Barney Baxter), Fiona Dourif (Penny), Don McManus (Forest Superintendent), Karen Black (Sean's Colleague). Directed, written, and produced by Christopher Munch.

*Letters from the Big Man* makes no secret that it involves the mysterious forest creature known as Sasquatch, or more popularly as Bigfoot. No wonder. Legends about Bigfoot have inspired more than twenty previous films, from exploitation pictures to the big-budget *Harry and the Hendersons.* Two things are different about this film. It is serious, and it isn't shy about showing us the creature. Instead of blurred shots of something vaguely seen through trees, we see the Sasquatch clearly and even in contemplative close-ups.

The story involves a U.S. Forest Service employee named Sarah Smith (Lily Rabe), who is on the rebound from a failed relationship and accepts a commission to study the rainwater runoff in a remote area devastated by forest fires. She packs camping gear, heads into the wilderness, measures the depths of streams, and enjoys her solitude so much that she actively repels a young Green activist named Sean (Jason Butler Harner) when she meets him on a trail. Lily Rabe's performance exudes self-confidence and determination. (She's the daughter of Jill Clayburgh and playwright David Rabe.)

Sarah is aware she's being followed. She thinks Sean is the stalker. In a gradual way, without a dramatic turning point, she absorbs the fact that her shadow is Sasquatch. She isn't electrified with curiosity, nor is she frightened. She accepts his presence, and he accepts hers. Often she is aware of him without seeing him. A few shots show him transparent, hinting at metaphysical powers or invisibility.

Sarah keeps a journal and makes a great many sketches and watercolors. She also treats herself in the evening to red wine—a great deal of wine, actually, considering how hard supplies must be to come by in these remote Oregon woods. The activist, Sean, encounters her again and this time they do a little necking on the deck of a Forest Service cabin while Sasquatch watches them from behind a tree with—what? Curiosity? Disappointment? His eyes seem very sad.

The creation of the Bigfoot costume, by Lee Romaire, is so much better here than in previous movie appearances. He looks like a very tall cross between a gorilla and a bear, and inside is the actor Isaac C. Singleton Jr. At night, Sasquatch begins leaving little arrangements of twigs, sticks, and stones where Sarah will find them. These are his "letters." There is also an indistinct voice heard on the sound track, suggesting men and Sasquatch must find acceptance and peace.

Left unestablished is what Sasquatch thinks, how "human" he is, or indeed, any details of his life. Does he mate? Have children? Live in groups? What do his thumpings of logs on trees mean? His mournful night cries? ("That's no coyote," Sarah says.) In the film he seems to be as much a manifestation of the forest as an inhabitant.

This film is unlike anything else the indie writer-director, Christopher Munch, has done, such as *The Hours and Times*, a biopic about John Lennon and Brian Epstein. Asked if he believes in Bigfoot, he says yes. He also apparently believes there is, or was, a CIA plan to investigate if the Sasquatch has extrasensory powers. Well, the CIA has investigated more cockamamie schemes.

*Letters from the Big Man* will mystify some,

please others with its serenity, and be unlike any Bigfoot movie you have ever imagined.

## Letters to Juliet ★ ★ ★

PG, 101 m., 2010

Amanda Seyfried (Sophie), Vanessa Redgrave (Claire), Christopher Egan (Charlie), Gael Garcia Bernal (Victor), Franco Nero (Lorenzo Bartolini). Directed by Gary Winick and produced by Ellen Barkin, Mark Canton, Eric Feig, Caroline Kaplan, and Patrick Wachsberger. Screenplay by Jose Rivera and Tim Sullivan.

I know *Letters to Juliet* is soppy melodrama, and I don't mind in the least. I know the ending is preordained from the setup. I know the characters are broad and comforting stereotypes. In this case, I simply don't care. Sometimes we have personal reasons for responding to a film.

*Letters to Juliet* is about Sophie (Amanda Seyfried), an American girl who visits Verona with the man she's engaged to marry (Gael Garcia Bernal). He's always leaving her behind to investigate wine and truffles for his New York restaurant. She visits the house allegedly inhabited by Shakespeare's Juliet. Below the balcony there, lovelorn women for years have posted "letters to Juliet" asking for advice.

Sophie finds a letter fifty years old, written by a young British girl about a Tuscan boy she met, fell in love with, and allowed to fall out of her life. Sophie writes to the girl, the letter amazingly finds its way, and soon Claire (Vanessa Redgrave) and her grandson, Charlie (Christopher Egan), arrive in Verona. So now, if we're experienced moviegoers, we know what must happen by the end of the story.

All of this is wrapped up in unimaginably beautiful shots of the Italian countryside, the warmth of the friendship between Sophie and Claire, and visits to many men named Lorenzo Bartolini, which was the name of the boy Claire loved so long ago. A hard-hearted realist would suggest that Sophie help Claire check out the possible Lorenzo Bartolinis on the phone, but no. *Letters to Juliet* requires the three of them to visit the candidates in person, leading to a series of false leads and at last, of course, to the real Lorenzo Bartolini (Franco Nero).

As it happens, this story stirred romantic memories in my own life. Once in a small hill town outside Rome, under a full moon, I stood before the balcony being used by Franco Zeffirelli for his great film *Romeo and Juliet* (1968), and heard Nino Rota hum his theme music to Zeffirelli. Some years later, I stood beneath Juliet's balcony in Verona itself with a woman dear to my heart, and saw the notes pinned to the wall.

And the very first movie set I ever visited, before I was yet a movie critic, was *Camelot* (1967). On that set I met and interviewed Vanessa Redgrave, who was not yet thirty, and Franco Nero, who was twenty-six. They played Guenevere and Lancelot. They fell in love on the set and had a child. They took separate paths for years, but on New Year's Eve 2006, they married. Even earlier, Franco walked Vanessa's daughter Natasha Richardson down the aisle when she married Liam Neeson.

So you see, when Vanessa marries Franco forty years after falling in love with him, and they are playing characters who meet after fifty years, and this all has to do with Juliet's balcony—reader, what am I to do? I am helpless before such forces.

Vanessa Redgrave recently lost her sister, Lynn. I met Lynn once in London. I went to her house for tea. This was not long after the success of *Georgy Girl.* My interview has been lost in the past, but I remember the feeling of the day, Lynn sitting cross-legged on the carpet beside her coffee table, smoking and jolly, a famous actress friendly to an unknown kid her own age.

I have strayed far from the film. But I've told you what you need to know about it. I also want to observe that our response to every film depends on the person we bring to it. Pauline Kael said she went to a movie, and the movie happened, and she wrote about what changed within her after she saw it. This is quite valid. Sometimes, however, we go to a movie, and our lives have happened, and we write about what hasn't changed.

## The Lie ★ ★ ★

R, 80 m., 2011

Joshua Leonard (Lonnie), Jess Weixler (Clover), Mark Webber (Tank), Kelli Garner (Brianne),

Alia Shawkat (Seven), Jane Adams (Dr. Bentel), Gerry Bednob (Radko). Directed by Joshua Leonard and produced by Mary Pat Bentel. Screenplay by Jeff Feuerzeig, Mark Webber, Jess Weixler, and Leonard, based on a short story by T. Coraghessan Boyle.

The hero of *The Lie* tells a lie that no one should ever tell. It cannot be forgiven. It can be explained, but not understood. Many of us may have felt like telling such a lie in the extremities of desperation. No reasonable person, no matter how lacking a conscience, ever actually would—because the inevitable consequences are so predictable and sad.

I'm not going to tell you the lie, but let me set the stage. This is a well-written and -acted movie about Lonnie and Clover, a thirtyish married couple with a baby daughter. He works in a Los Angeles video production house. She is about to move into a good corporate job. When Lonnie consults a therapist, he describes his depression and says one of the reasons for it is that "my wife works a lot." This is before she has even gone to work, so obviously he's feeling threatened by her new job. From her point of view, it comes with good health benefits, and is an ideal move for a new mom.

Lonnie (Joshua Leonard) is a pothead, although this isn't a movie about addiction. He's also a good liar; listen to him manipulate the therapist (Jane Adams) into a prescription for medical marijuana by explaining his preference for Eastern and organic medicines over man-made chemicals. Uh-huh. He also tells people he's in a band, although the band hasn't played in a long time and exists only in a technical sense. What he really does is time video shots of ketchup drops, over and over again. This is driving him crazy. One day he calls the boss from the company parking lot and says he's not coming in to work. When the boss explodes, he tells a lie.

He takes the day off. He drives out to the beach and meets his friend Tank (Mark Webber). They smoke a lot of pot. He goes home and has an especially nice evening with Clover (Jess Weixler). The next day, again, he can't force himself to go to work. He tells The Lie.

Lonnie's problem is that he fears he's at that point in life where your dreams stop being ahead of you and start being behind. His wife's newfound job stability is too conventional for a guy who still sees himself as cool, a rebel, a "musician." He doesn't resent fatherhood—he's crazy in love with baby Xana—but he resents the sense that life is tightening his chains. His terrible job is like a life sentence of failure.

Joshua Leonard directed this movie, and cowrote it with Jeff Feuerzeig, Jess Weixler, and Mark Webber—Clover and Tank. It's based on a short story by T. Coraghessan Boyle, which I gather is darker. *The Lie* is dark enough, but it has affection for its characters and doesn't destroy them. It paints them in three fallible human dimensions, and the actors are warm and plausible, even Tank the druggie dropout, who lives in an RV, so home is where he parks. The day that Lonnie drives out to see him, he suggests it would have been nice if he'd phoned ahead. "But you don't have a phone," says Lonnie. "Then I'll call you," Tank says.

It's easy to imagine this movie going wrong: pumping up the drama, punching the big developments, using the wrong music. It keeps its cool. One test of a new director is how he handles a scene that has cliché written all over it. In *The Lie*, Lonnie, Clover, and Baby Xana go on a weekend camping trip, and we see they truly do make up a family, and Leonard does this in a convincing and affectionate way.

This scene is crucial for setting up the agonizing scene in which The Lie is revealed. Without it, we wouldn't believe how that scene eventually pays off. I can't explain why, but you'll see. Observe then at the same time how flawless Jess Weixler's timing and acting are—how she holds a moment long enough for us to read her mind.

Here's a film in which the actors create plausible people we would probably like. They're loose inside the skins of their characters. Even Mark Webber's Tank, who must be intimate with more drugs than pot, has a level of wisdom and insight. His self-knowledge is so much better than poor Lonnie's.

I didn't even remotely see the film's conclusion coming. I consider it unlikely. I also consider it unwise. But I don't consider it impossible, because in a way, *The Lie* has been preparing us all along for such a decision. This movie isn't dry goods, measured by the yard.

It has a pulse. At the end, I think Baby Xana will still have two happily married parents when she grows up. At the end of a lot of movies, you never ever give a thought to the characters again.

## Life, Above All ★ ★ ★ ★

PG-13,102 m., 2011

Khomotso Manyaka (Chanda), Keaobaka Makanyane (Esther), Harriet Manamela (Mrs. Tafa), Lerato Mvelase (Lillian), Aubrey Poolo (Jonah). Directed by Oliver Schmitz and produced by Oliver Stoltz. Screenplay by Dennis Foon and Schmitz, based on the novel *Chanda's Secrets* by Allan Stratton.

Oliver Schmitz's *Life, Above All* earns the tears it inspires. The film is about deep human emotions, evoked with sympathy and love. It takes place entirely within a South African township near Johannesburg, one with modest prosperity and well-tended homes. It centers on the twelve-year-old Chanda, who takes on the responsibility of holding her family together after her baby sister dies.

As the film opens, Chanda (Khomotso Manyaka) visits an undertaker to examine the inexpensive coffins on display. This is a task no twelve-year-old should ever have to bear. But her mother, Lillian (Lerato Mvelase), is immobilized by grief and illness and her father by drink. The next-door neighbor woman, Mrs. Tafa (Harriet Manamela), helps her care for two younger siblings.

Suspicion spreads in the neighborhood that the real cause of the family's problems is AIDS, although the word itself isn't said aloud until well into the film. Its absence forms a fearful echo chamber—reflecting South Africans' own insistence, until recent years, of denying the reality of AIDS. A family linked to the disease by rumor or gossip is ostracized, which is why Mrs. Tafa facilitates Lillian's "visit" to distant relatives.

Chanda does what she can to care for her siblings, attend school, and keep up appearances. Her own good heart is demonstrated by her friendship with a schoolmate named Esther (Keaobaka Makanyane), who is forced into prostitution to earn the funds for survival. It goes unspoken between them that this could lead to AIDS for Esther herself. The South African tragedy was that former president Thabo Mbeki persisted in his puzzling denial about the causes and treatment of AIDS, so many who suffered and died of AIDS need not have. This contributed to a climate of ignorance and mystery surrounding the disease, which only increased its spread.

By directly dealing with the poisonous climate of rumor and gossip, the film takes a stand. But in nations where AIDS has been demystified, *Life, Above All* will play strongly as pure human drama, about two women, one promptly and one belatedly, rising courageously to a challenge.

The performances by the two young girls are remarkable here. They have seen and internalized unspeakable experiences. Their faces are young, but their eyes are wise. Whenever I see such early performances by inexperienced actors, I wonder where they come from. No doubt director Oliver Schmitz had much to do with these. The casting process must have been crucial. But Manyaka and Makanyane have grave self-possession; they never even slightly overact. I met Khomotso Manyaka at Ebertfest 2011 and found her a cheerful, friendly teenager. Where did she find these resources? Where does any actor?

As for Harriet Manamela as Mrs. Tafa, she has a central role. This township is far from the poorest in South Africa. In the terms of that neighborhood, many households are middle-class. Mrs. Tafa embodies authority. She is fiercely proud of her son, a star athlete. She shares the general taboos about AIDS, but she is a good person, kind, sympathetic, which she sometimes keeps concealed.

There is a scene here where fearful neighbors gather outside Chanda's house, inflamed by their suspicions about her mother. Mrs. Tafa confronts them, surprising even herself, perhaps, by how she rises to the occasion. Schmitz's camera placements here are confident and underline the drama.

The film's ending is improbably upbeat: magic realism, in a sense. It works as a deliverance. Dennis Foon's screenplay is based on the novel *Chanda's Secrets,* by the Canadian writer Allan Stratton. It is a parable with biblical undertones, calling back to *Cry, the Beloved Country.*

## Life As We Know It ★ ★

PG-13, 113 m., 2010

Katherine Heigl (Holly Berenson); Josh Duhamel (Eric Messer); Josh Lucas (Sam); Alexis, Brynn, and Brooke Clagett (Sophie); Hayes MacArthur (Peter Novack); Christina Hendricks (Alison Novack). Directed by Greg Berlanti and produced by Paul Brooks and Barry Josephson. Screenplay by Ian Deitchman and Kristin Rusk Robinson.

Awww. Their best friends are killed in an auto accident, leaving behind their cute little one-year-old daughter, Sophie. Holly and Messer are appointed in the will as Sophie's joint custodians. Alas, Holly and Messer (Katherine Heigl and Josh Duhamel) can't stand each other. But the will specifies they should move into their friends' home, so Sophie won't miss her own room.

Awww. Sophie is just as cute as most one-year-old babies. She's always ready to roll, maybe because she's got backup; the character is played by triplets (Alexis, Brynn, and Brooke Clagett). Holly and Messer know nothing 'bout raisin' no babies. The first emergency comes when Sophie does do-do in her diaper.

Awww. This is really sad. Holly and Messer have to share the same enormous Atlanta mansion. I think it has room for an indoor one-hundred-yard dash. Although their friends Peter and Alison (Hayes MacArthur and Christina Hendricks) were young, they must have been loaded. "The mortgage is prepaid for a year," the lawyer tells Holly and Messer. How many people can say that?

Awww, this is never gonna work out. Messer is a tomcat on the prowl. Hell, that first night he met Holly on a blind date set up by Peter and Alison, he had another date lined up for later. And Holly—well, she's one of your organized types, spic and span, not a mess like Messer. Plus, she maybe has a crush on Sam (Josh Lucas), the handsome pediatrician.

Awww, I gotta admit, I liked the actors. Katherine Heigl and Josh Duhamel do what they can with this off-season TV material, and Josh Lucas is awfully nice, which of course a kindly young pediatrician would have to be to almost win the heart of Katherine Heigl. But the film is so clunky. It's not every rom-com that starts out with the tragic deaths of the parents of a one-year-old and moves right on to the poop jokes.

So anyway, what happens in the movie? You'll never guess in a million years. Never. You might just as well give up. I don't like spoilers, so just let me say Holly and Sam adopt Sophie and live happily in the mansion forever after. Awww.

## Life During Wartime ★ ★ ½

NO MPAA RATING, 98 m., 2010

Shirley Henderson (Joy Jordan), Ciaran Hinds (Bill Maplewood), Gaby Hoffman (Wanda), Allison Janney (Trish Maplewood), Michael Lerner (Harvey Weiner), Chris Marquette (Billy Maplewood), Rich Pecci (Mark Weiner), Charlotte Rampling (Jacqueline), Paul Reubens (Andy), Ally Sheedy (Helen Jordan), Dylan Riley Snyder (Timmy Maplewood), Renee Taylor (Mona Jordan), Michael Kenneth Williams (Allen). Directed by Todd Solondz and produced by Derrick Tseng and Christine K. Walker. Screenplay by Solondz.

There's always rationing in wartime. What's rationed in Todd Solondz's *Life During Wartime* are feelings of hope, kindness, and optimism. His people are disturbed, pleading, and often perverse, and indeed some of them are so badly off they're dead and must appear as ghosts to make their complaints. Always the kvetching, from beyond the grave yet.

Solondz describes the film as "a quasi-sequel" to his great *Happiness* (1998). If ever there was a film where the characters' lives were over at the end, it's that one. Solondz brought closure. Now, twelve years later, wondering what happened to his people after that film ended, he approaches entropic collapse.

Well, they aged at different rates. They turned into different people, played by different actors, while keeping the same names. Allen, played by Philip Seymour Hoffman in the first film, morphed into a black man (Michael Kenneth Williams), although Hoffman and Williams are still two of the three actors in either film with three names. The genders of the various characters are the same, although the gender behavior is far from conventional. These people are stuck in their minds and can't bring happiness to themselves or others. Only the children can be happy, and in the Solondz world their innocence is a time bomb.

I could supply here a listing of the major characters in the 1998 film and the actors who played them. Can you remember the names of movie characters for twelve years? I can't, not unless they're named Marge Gunderson or Anton Chigurh, but in this film, Joy (Shirley Henderson) talks like a middle-age little girl, and once again finds herself stuck in restaurants in mutual misery with a man. This time it's Allen (Williams), who has moved on from dirty phone calls and wankery to gangbanging and despair.

The man Joy had her agonizing date with in the first film has now become the dead Andy (Paul Reubens), whose ghost torments her (again in a restaurant booth) with piteous pleas. Later, Williams also appears to her as a ghost, urging her to kill herself. Her men have a way of not getting everything done in one lifetime.

Trish (Alison Janney) has moved to Florida to help her children escape the reputation of their pedophile father. They think he's dead. But Bill (Ciaran Hinds) is on parole and unwisely wants to meet his older boy at college. Trish is dating Harvey (Michael Lerner), so devastated by a divorce he fears he's forgotten how to perform sex. To the degree that he remembers, he's sure that he can't. Trish's younger son, Timmy (Dylan Riley Snyder, in a performance that evokes great sympathy), is preparing for his bar mitzvah when he discovers his father was a pedophile—not good news on the day he becomes a man.

Trish has tried to break with her past and start anew in Florida. Her sister Helen (Ally Sheedy) is a thriving Hollywood screenwriter, driven and unfulfilled. Joy is the third sibling. For these three sisters, Chekhov would be the Marx Brothers. One of the best performances in the film is by Charlotte Rampling as the last woman in the world who Bill, the reforming pedophile, should choose as his partner in grown-up sex. These people live in interiors as barren as demonstration homes. They don't have much stuff around. Ed Lachman, the cinematographer, almost sees them as on a stage set, "suggesting" the rooms where they live.

This is the Solondz world. I think he's a brilliant filmmaker. He evokes so effectively his own point of view, which is appalling and compulsive. You can imagine his screenplays being read aloud in his distinctive voice, which seems to embed in every word a querulous complaint against—well, everything. When he's good (*Palindromes*, *Storytelling*, *Welcome to the Dollhouse*), few can touch him. Here he's made a film that is sad without energy, dead without life. As a sequel to *Happiness*, it regards the same lives, then as tragedy, now as farce.

## Like Crazy ★ ★ ★

PG-13, 90 m., 2011

Anton Yelchin (Jacob), Felicity Jones (Anna), Jennifer Lawrence (Sam), Charlie Bewley (Simon), Alex Kingston (Jackie). Directed by Drake Doremus and produced by Jonathan Schwartz and Andrea Sperling. Screenplay by Doremus and Ben York Jones.

From the very start, Anna is more in love than Jacob. They meet in a college class in Los Angeles, she leaves a note on his windshield, they start to date, it goes very well, and because she can't bear the thought of separating, she overstays her student visa and doesn't return home to London on schedule. Later, when she tries to return to California, she's nabbed by the airport immigration officials and put in one of those bare white rooms with one table and two chairs.

They will have to be apart—not forever, but for who knows how long? This makes her feel terrible, and we do, too, because they're young and beautiful and *Like Crazy* shows them in an intelligent, graceful indie style, not a clunky romcom, but sweeter and more intimate. The question in my mind is, how deeply does he care?

I ask this as a male who brought some cynicism to my viewing. It may be love at first sight, and Anna (Felicity Jones) may not have spent a lot of time with Jacob (Anton Yelchin), but she is deep and true and trusts her heart, and she wants to build a nest with this man. Jacob, on the other hand, feels sincerely for her, but what's required is loony love, not sincerity. If you're in love like crazy, you do what the situation requires.

Anna can't get into the United States. Jacob can get into London, but he can't move there because, you see, he designs and builds chairs, and his business is in Santa Monica. Say what? You can't design chairs in London? You wouldn't rather live in London with the girl you love than build chairs in Santa Monica? His chairs look ordinary to me. The one we see is a straight chair made of wood. We see him lovingly perfecting a sketch of it. Assemble a dozen second graders, assign them to draw a chair, merge their drawings into one, and they would look like a Jacob Chair. This guy is no Eames.

I discuss these things because I think they expose a problem. It's easy to identify with Anna, because the character is wonderfully well drawn and acted; Felicity Jones, a rising star, has a face that glows when she smiles, and radiates her love and sense of loss. She reminds me of Helena Bonham Carter. You may recall her as Miranda in Julie Taymor's *The Tempest.* She may have only a case of first love, but what love is more urgent and presents a more desperate challenge?

Anton Yelchin has all the tools he needs to play Jacob, but the screenplay doesn't serve him. He doesn't seem to be as involved as Anna. And for a man so involved in the design and crafting of chairs, isn't he on the young side? (He is twenty-two, three years younger than Jones.) There should be a time in your youth when you're free to act impulsively on signals from your heart.

That said, this is a well-made film. The scenes showing Jacob and Anna falling in love have a freshness, and I learn Doremus handed his actors an outline and together they improvised every scene. Some of the whispered endearments under the sheets are delightful.

It is probably impossible to film a love story in Los Angeles without the lovers running on the beach, usually within sight of Santa Monica pier. I also understand why young lovers in movies inevitably end up on bumper cars and share ice cream cones. There's an impulse in first love to reenact childish pastimes, as if to start anew and grow up together.

It should be noted that both Jacob and Anna, while separated, have transient affairs. Well, they're not married or even engaged, and the song says when you're not with the one you love, you love the one you're with. Jacob's affair is more interesting because it involves his work partner, Sam (Jennifer Lawrence, from *Winter's Bone*). She is too good an actress to ever fit neatly into the slot of the Other Woman; she emerges full-blown and convincing, even in a small role, and if the actors improvised their dialogue, she created some that's very good. Anna hooks up with Simon (Charlie Bewley), her neighbor in London, but their dalliance doesn't have the same weight because she's not really available.

What am I arguing? That the movie requires a happy ending? It's not that it doesn't have one. It's more that the complications over the visa feel like a contrivance to separate them so we can share their loss. Since one of them, Jacob, is free to do something about that, we have two choices here: (1) they mourn sadly on two sides of the ocean, or (2) he bites the bullet, shuts up shop, and moves to London. That would open the way for authentic grown-up challenges, in which they find it can be harder to make sacrifices and live together than it is to suffer narcissistically while apart. As convincing as it is when it begins, *Like Crazy* tilts too much in the direction of a weepie and not enough in the direction of the facts of life.

P.S. Both of these actors are destined to become genuine stars.

## Limitless ★ ★ ½

PG-13, 105 m., 2011

Bradley Cooper (Eddie Morra), Abbie Cornish (Lindy), Robert De Niro (Carl Van Loon), Anna Friel (Melissa), Andrew Howard (Gennady). Directed by Neil Burger and produced by Leslie Dixon, Ryan Kavanaugh, and Scott Kroopf. Screenplay by Dixon, based on a novel by Alan Glynn.

I know how Eddie Morra feels. Like him, I know almost everything but have forgotten most of it. We are told time and again that we use only a small portion of our brains and have enough left over to run nations in our down time. *Limitless* is about Eddie's adventures after his ex-brother-in-law gives him a pill that suddenly puts his entire brain online.

He finishes his novel at typing speed. He wins at poker, invests in the market, and runs it up to millions. He fascinates a woman who had rejected him as a loser. He knows intuitively how to handle situations that used to baffle him. He is hailed as the Wall Street guru of the age.

Eddie is played by Bradley Cooper as a schlub who becomes a king. This sort of mental rags-to-riches progression has inspired a lot of movies; ever see Cliff Robertson in *Charly* (1968)? The difference here is that Eddie Morra remains himself before and after, and all that changes is his ability to recall everything he ever saw or heard. *Limitless* assumes that would be a benefit and make him rich, but what if most of what he ever saw or heard about Wall Street was wrong (as it usually is)?

The movie sidesteps the problem that what we need is more intelligence and a better ability to reason, not a better memory. For memory, modern man has Google. There's no need to stumble over such technicalities, however. Given its premise, *Limitless* is passably entertaining. Abbie Cornish plays Lindy, the successful young professional woman who dumps Eddie as a loser and falls for him all over again when he becomes a winner. This is not sneaky on her part; there is every reason to dump the original Eddie and many good ones to return.

Eddie grows entangled in three problems. One has to do with the source of the magic pills; the ex-brother-in-law is no longer in a position to reveal it. The second has to do with a mob loan shark who liked being smart and wants to get that way again.

The third involves Carl Van Loon, played by Robert De Niro as one of the richest men in America. He hires Eddie as an investment magician, Eddie loses his touch when he runs out of pills, he regains it, and so on. De Niro is not well used in the role because he plays Van Loon straight and in one dimension. Don't you suppose he could have been supplied with a quirk of his own? The twist at the end comes too late.

Bradley Cooper fits well into the two versions of Eddie Morra, and director Neil Burger does inventive visual effects in showing how time telescopes for Eddie and the answers to problems seem to materialize before his eyes. A subplot about a murder, however, raises questions it doesn't answer, and all the quasi-criminal stuff seems a little perfunctory. The movie is not terrifically good, but the premise is intriguing; it doesn't really set out to explore what such a pill might really do to a person. *Limitless* uses only 15, maybe 20 percent of its brain. Still, that's more than a lot of movies.

## The Lincoln Lawyer ★ ★ ★

R, 118 m., 2011

Matthew McConaughey (Mick Haller), Marisa Tomei (Maggie McPherson), Ryan Phillippe (Louis Roulet), Josh Lucas (Ted Minton), John Leguizamo (Val Valenzuela), Michael Peña (Jesus Martinez), Frances Fisher (Mary Windsor), Bryan Cranston (Detective Lankford), William H. Macy (Frank Levin). Directed by Brad Furman and produced by Sidney Kimmel, Gary Lucchesi, Tom Rosenberg, Scott Steindorff, and Richard S. Wright. Screenplay by John Romano, based on the novel by Michael Connelly.

I like movies about smart guys who are wiseasses and think their way out of tangles with criminals. I like courtroom scenes. I like big old cars. I like *The Lincoln Lawyer* because it involves all three, and because it matches Matthew McConaughey with a first-rate supporting cast while so many thrillers these days are about a lone hero surrounded by special effects. People have words they actually say in this movie. After *Battle: Los Angeles*, that is a great relief.

Let's start with the big old car. It's a Lincoln, and a lawyer named Mick Haller (McConaughey) does most of his work out of the backseat. Apparently he drove it himself until he was socked with a DUI; given how much he drinks in the film, it's amazing he remembered where he parked it. Now he has a chauffeur (Laurence Mason) who ferries him around to the Los Angeles dealers, hookers, bagmen, and lowlifes who are his clientele. Mick's specialty is getting people off, sometimes in a perfectly legal way.

There were decades in the movies when heroes drove new cars, unless it was a period picture. Carmakers used to pay for product placement. We saw Mustangs, GTOs, Chargers. But in recent years, action and thriller heroes have driven mostly classic cars, or oddballs like Hummers. The reason for this is obvious: Modern cars all look mostly the same, and none of them look heroic. Can you imagine James Bond in a Camry? My Ford Fusion gets good mileage, but Mick Haller would just look silly doing business out of the backseat. The only new cars still popular in movies are big black SUVs with tinted windows, which usually prowl in packs.

Anyway, Haller is a streetwise defense attorney with connections who knows how to collect and invest prudent envelopes full of cash. So connected is this guy that a motorcycle gang materializes more or less when he needs one. One day a bondsman (John Leguizamo) comes to him with a higher-class client than usual. Louis Roulet (Ryan Phillippe) is a rich kid from Beverly Hills accused of beating up a woman. He's clean-cut, looks Mick in the eyes, seriously insists he is innocent, and wants to go to trial to prove it.

Mick senses there is something fishy. So do I. If Roulet has unlimited funds and really is innocent, why is he hiring a guy who works out of the backseat of a car? I've seen a lot of crime movies and read my Raymond Chandler and Ross Macdonald. I know, even if Mick doesn't, that he's being used in some way.

Let's not get into the details. Details are interchangeable in movies like this. What you want is a laconic wise guy in the lead, and McConaughey does a nice line in those. You need a good dame in the picture. Marisa Tomei plays his ex-wife, courtroom opponent, and (still) friend. When Tomei walks into a movie, it's like the queen came into the room. I want to stand up. I know why Lady Gaga wants Marisa to play her in a biopic. It's not because they look like sisters. It's because every woman, and many men, would love to have a smile like Marisa Tomei's.

We also meet Mick's opposing attorney (Josh Lucas); a former client he plea-bargained into prison (Michael Peña); a cop who considers him a shyster (Bryan Cranston), and, most valuable, Mick's private investigator (William H. Macy). The PI role isn't very big, but Macy makes it distinctive; he brings it a quirky familiarity that creates a history between the two men without a lot of setup. You care for the hardworking sap.

All of this comes together in a satisfactory way. It isn't brilliant, it's far from foolproof, and the second appearance of the motorcycle gang technically qualifies, I think, as a miracle. The Law of Seemingly Unnecessary Characters comes nicely into play as events from the present turn out to be connected to the past. I did feel undercut by the movie's final revelation—which is, let's face it, completely arbitrary. The plotting seems like half-realized stabs in various directions made familiar by other crime stories. But for what it is, *The Lincoln Lawyer* is workmanlike, engagingly acted, and entertaining.

## A Little Help ★ ★ ★ ½

R, 108 m., 2011

Jenna Fischer (Laura Pehlke), Chris O'Donnell (Bob Pehlke), Rob Benedict (Paul Helms), Daniel Yelsky (Dennis Pehlke), Kim Coates (Mel Kaminsky), Brooke Smith (Kathy Helms), Lesley Ann Warren (Joan), Ron Leibman (Warren), Zach Page (Kyle Helms). Directed by Michael J. Weithorn and produced by Joe Gressis and Dena Hysell. Screenplay by Weithorn.

*A Little Help* is about a woman who is very far from perfect, and that's why it's appealing. Laura limps through her days using Budweisers as a crutch. She never gets falling-over drunk, just buzzed enough to screw up when things go wrong, which they do relentlessly. I liked her. I've had days like hers. Every once in a while I appreciate a change of pace from mothers who are brave heroines.

Laura is a New Jersey dental hygienist, played by Jenna Fischer (*The Office*) in such a way that although the plot is loaded against her, she's so real she wins our sympathy. She's not a bad person. Life piles up on her. She has a husband (Chris O'Donnell) who cheats, a son (Daniel Yelsky) who is a lying little brat, a mother (Lesley Ann Warren) who has been criticizing her from birth, a father (Ron Liebman) who won't shut up about his greatness as a sportswriter, and a sister (Brooke Smith) who isn't as pretty but is, oh, so much better organized. There are two men in her family she can stand: her brother-in-law (Rob Benedict), and her nephew (Zach Page), whose garage band may be an excuse to get out of the house.

These people almost seem to coordinate their picking on Laura. Someone is always on her case. The screenplay by Michael J. Weithorn, who also directed, is ingenious in setting the stage for one calamity after another—one that should remain a surprise, and the others all developing inexorably out of Laura's tendency to fib her way out of a corner. This is a talent shared by her son, who in order to fit in at his new school shares that his father was a fireman who died while saving people in 9/11. Since the movie is set only a year after that tragedy, the kid is rewarded with instant popularity; Laura keeps quiet about his lie and actually participates in a patriotic memorial service at the school.

If you're in for a dime, you're in for a dollar. Laura gets in for about five bucks. Money she doesn't have—because she learns her husband was far from provident. This leads to painful sessions with a salivating litigator (Kim Coates), who thinks she could win a big-time lawsuit. She only agreed to meet the guy in the first place because her controlling sister insisted on it. Laura doesn't like lawsuits. I agree. You may win, you may lose, but the lawyers on both sides always get paid.

I haven't given a good enough notion of why *A Little Help* worked so well for me. It's manipulative, yes, but clever and persuasive in its manipulations. It has a bittersweet revelation when the brother-in-law confides he only married Laura's hateful sister so he could be her brother-in-law. There is a day of crisis at her son's school that Laura tries desperately to head off, and I was with her all the way.

And mostly I just plain liked Jenna Fischer. She plays a woman who is smart, plucky, trying to do the right thing, and going through a period when every damn thing goes wrong. She deserves better. We believe that, and it's why the movie succeeds. Yes, she could be a better mother for little Dennis, her brat. But he's going through one of those phases when a kid idolizes one parent and pretends to hate the other. Something like that gets on your nerves.

## Littlerock ★ ★ ★

NO MPAA RATING, 83 m., 2011

Atsuko Okatsuka (Atsuko), Cory Zacharia (Cory), Rintaro Sawamoto (Rintaro), Brett L. Tinnes (Jordan). Directed by Mike Ott and produced by Sierra Leoni, Laura Ragsdale, and Frederick Fulton Henry Thornton. Screenplay by Ott, Atsuko Okatsuka, and Carl McLaughlin.

Not often have I been more certain of the direction a movie is heading, or more wrong. *Littlerock*, a sensitive indie feature by Mike Ott, plays fair. I was misled only by my own cynicism. I arrived at quick assumptions about the characters, and didn't credit them for being young and aimless but not evil or violent. Within the terms of their relationships, they all come out fairly well—not happy, but not tragic, and they had some good times.

Littlerock is a small town in the remote drylands of Los Angeles County. From the looks of its Fourth of July parade, it may be a nice place to live, but the characters we meet are all unemployed, living in poverty, spending their days drinking and smoking pot. When they offer to take a visitor biking around town, it's not on motorbikes but child-sized bicycles that look like they've had them since they were eight or nine.

There are two visitors, Atsuko and Rintaro, a brother and sister from Japan. Their rental car has broken down. They were driving toward San Francisco. The brother (Rintaro Sawamoto) speaks a little English, the sister (Atsuko Okatsuka) none. They check in to a motel, and fall into the orbit of some kids about their age when they go to complain about the noise in the next room. They are friendly enough, offer them beers, share smokes, and let them hang out.

One of the local boys is Cory (Cory Zacharia), who is pleasant to the attractive girl, but sort of slow, as if he's smoked too much pot. Her brother looks on coolly. Where is this going? Atsuko is headed for trouble, right? Not at all. She doesn't drink too much, she isn't assaulted, and these layabouts don't belong to a local chainsaw gang.

Atsuko regards them with curiosity and, in the case of the attractive musician Jordan (Brett L. Tinnes), guarded lust. She likes it here. Her brother, who seems older and certainly wiser, thinks they should stick to their original plans once the car is repaired. She wants to stay for a while. He argues there is nothing here for her: "They just sit around all day drinking." He is correct. The actress Atsuko Okatsuka, who cowrote, has a cautious face where curiosity and emotions are at play.

Her brother leaves her in Littlerock for a few days. She has no idea what anybody is saying, which Jordan understands, but Cory persists in protesting: "You don't know a word I'm saying!" What happens with her and these two boys you will discover. You will also get a vivid portrait of the clueless Cory, his dreams of artistic success, and his difficulties with reading body language.

Much is still to happen, which I will not disclose. Let me say we learn a great deal more about all of the characters, and we understand as Atsuko learns that only a chance of history has prevented her from growing up in America very much like this. We also note that the locals are not racist toward the Japanese, although the pot dealer is vicious toward a Mexican. Later we can consider that there are shifting fashions in racism.

*Littlerock* tells a confident story that knows precisely where it's going. Its characters all learn a little and grow a little and one of them cries a little. And this is how Atsuko and Rintaro spent their summer vacation.

## Lockout ★ ★ ½

PG-13, 95 m., 2012

Guy Pearce (Snow), Maggie Grace (Emilie Warnock), Peter Stormare (Scott Langral), Lennie James (Harry Shaw), Joseph Gilgun (Hydell), Vincent Regan (Alex). Directed by Stephen St. Leger and James Mather and produced by Marc Libert and Leila Smith. Screenplay by St. Leger, Mather, and Luc Besson.

It's a mission so impossible that not even the U.S. Marines can do the job. No, this one will take—don't hold your breath—yes, One Man. The invention of the One Man Movie has been one of the handiest story devices to come along since the fruit cart. All I need do is quote two sentences from the trailer and in your mind you know exactly how the Deep-Voiced Trailer Guy sounds when he says them: "My daughter . . . is on a goodwill mission on that station. There's only One Man who can get her out. . . . Snow!

OK, now, hold onto your seat. The worried father who is speaking is—why, the president of the United States, of course. And where is the station where his daughter, Emilie (Maggie Grace), is on a goodwill mission? I'll bet you can guess this one. It's a maximum-security prison in orbit around the Earth, naturally. And what about One Man Snow? He is a brilliant and versatile man of action, capable of all things, and yet the Secret Service is pursuing him because he has his hands on a briefcase and is suspected of spying. And what is in the briefcase? My best guess is: a MacGuffin.

I probably mention MacGuffins half a dozen times a year. I wonder if there's anyone left who doesn't know what one is. First defined by Alfred Hitchcock, the MacGuffin is whatever everyone in the movie is in a lather about. All we need to know is that Snow has it and the Secret Service wants it. It doesn't matter in the slightest what's in the briefcase; Snow doesn't know, so why should we?

Snow, played by Guy Pearce, is an overwritten hero who talks like a character on a sitcom. Every line is a wisecrack, a gag, or what he fondly thinks of as a witticism. If you were on a mission to rescue the president's daughter, who was being held hostage on a space station in Earth orbit by a tattooed psychotic with glowing eyeballs (Vincent Regan), would you have time to think up one-liners? Of course you wouldn't. That's why this job can only be undertaken by . . . One Man Snow!

They say no one has ever escaped from Alcatraz by swimming. A prison in orbit is even more escape proof. And there's another detail. Many of the prisoners have been cryogenically frozen and are being held in suspended animation. A prisoner like that, he isn't going anywhere.

Why, you might ask, would the president's daughter take it into her head to go on a goodwill mission to an orbiting prison? She wants to be sure the deep-frozen prisoners aren't being mistreated. This woman is all heart. Unluckily, some of the most violent prisoners have taken over the prison, and with Emilie as their hostage, they're in a powerful position.

The generator of this story is the inexhaustible French producer Luc Besson (*The Fifth Element, Leon: The Professional, La Femme Nikita, Ong-Bak*, and dozens of others). He has skillfully assembled the story elements and left them in the hands of directors Stephen St. Leger and James Mather, who reason that with breakneck action and shiny special effects, we will have no complaints. It just about works. The idea of the president's daughter being held captive isn't blindingly original (it's an alarmingly dangerous occupation), but placing the story on a space station is a masterstroke, since we're about filled up to here with prison movies set on Earth.

I imagine the movie's intended audience will enjoy itself. I enjoyed myself in my own peculiar way. I like to ask myself how real people would feel in a situation like this. If I were sent on Snow's mission, I would be paralyzed by fright most of the time. But then I'm not One Man. I would be dead several times over by the ending of this film. But not to worry. I'm not gonna tell you they parachute to Earth and land in New York City. Nothing like that.

## Lola Versus ★ ★

R, 87 m., 2012

Greta Gerwig (Lola), Joel Kinnaman (Luke), Zoe Lister-Jones (Alice), Hamish Linklater (Henry), Bill Pullman (Lenny), Debra Winger (Robin), Cheyenne Jackson (Roger). Directed by Daryl Wein and produced by Jocelyn Hayes, Michael London, and Janice Williams. Screenplay by Wein and Zoe Lister-Jones.

Greta Gerwig plays Lola, the woman we're expected to feel sorry for in *Lola Versus*, and that would be easier if she had more to complain about. She's twenty-nine, approaching her Ph.D., engaged to be married, and apparently the heir to a fortune. How do I guess that? Her only job is waiting on tables in her mother's restaurant, and yet she and her b.f. live in one of those Manhattan lofts that you don't even want to know how much it costs.

As the movie opens, Lola is radiant at a fitting for her wedding dress. Brimming with joy, she hurries home to her fiancé, Luke (Joel Kinnaman), takes one look at him, and intuits something is wrong. "Have a stroke?" she asks. He's calling off the wedding. He can't go through with it.

I think I'd feel worse about that if I knew Luke, and had maybe lived through some of Lola's history with him. When I'm given only one piece of information—he's abandoning her virtually at the altar—all I can conclude is that Luke is a jerk, and Lola's better off without him.

Lola seems to be a nice enough person, which goes without saying, because Greta Gerwig is an actress you like just by looking at her. Unfortunately, Lola lives in a sitcom that deprives her of any intrinsic interest. Her entire life consists of being jilted, being consoled and advised by her best friend, Alice (Zoe Lister-Jones), and then rather carelessly sleeping around in an attempt to accumulate makeup sex.

One of her partners is a nice guy, Henry (Hamish Linklater), who is her best friend—and Alice's. In fact, Alice and Henry seem to be in the early stages of their own romance, but sweet Lola plows right through that and keeps on smiling. Among her other partners is a guy whose penis is apparently somehow strangely shaped. "I was a preemie," he explains, having stripped and faced her. (We're looking from behind, thank God.) "I was in an incubator." How the incubator caused his problem is left unexplained, but never mind: The entire purpose of this scene is to show us Gerwig's face as she regards the penile carnage. She looks . . . thoughtful. That's the punch line, see? And later she'll have a story to share with Alice.

The movie is basically constructed like that all the way through. It sets up a situation, pays it off with a gag, and hurries on its way. The setups are usually clever enough to deserve better. Let's circle back to her waitress job. A rude customer demands sangria, even though it's an Italian restaurant. She tries to explain this, fails, and tells the bartender to just dump a can of fruit cocktail in a pitcher of red wine. Wouldn't you agree that's a solution that could support more than the customer's reaction shot?

Alice has many of the film's best lines, and indeed the screenplay was cowritten by Zoe Lister-Jones and the director, Daryl Wein. Her girlfriend role is nevertheless handled in a standard way: She consoles, she advises, and she empathizes, while Lola eats lots of junk food and bathes in self-pity. A sitcom, as I said. There's not enough here to support eight-seven minutes. The best reason to see this is that Gerwig is lovable and she's on the screen a lot.

## London River ★ ★ ★

NO MPAA RATING, 87 m., 2012

Brenda Blethyn (Elisabeth), Sotigui Kouyate (Ousmane), Francis Magee (Inspector), Sami Bouajila (Imam), Roschdy Zem (Butcher), Marc Baylis (Edward). Directed by Rachid Bouchareb and produced by Bouchareb and Jean Brehat. Screenplay by Bouchareb, Zoe Galeron, and Olivier Lorelle.

A tall old African man makes his way through an olive grove. A sturdy market gardener on the island of Guernsey takes the ferry to the British mainland. They have both been set in motion by the same events in 2005: Terrorists have exploded bombs on London underground trains and a bus. They are seeking news of their children.

*London River* tells the story of how these parents meet in the course of their journeys. It also shows a London set ajar by the cruel and senseless attacks. The searches of these parents have one thing in common: Neither one knows very much about their children, who have left home and started unknown lives in the city.

Elisabeth (Brenda Blethyn) learns about the bombs on the telly and calls her daughter Jane just to be reassured. We gather they don't talk often; at first she isn't alarmed when there's no reply. She calls again and again, and eventually unease grows within and she travels to London. Peering out the window of a London taxi, she asks anxiously, "Is this it?" The door of Jane's flat is in a mews next to an Arabic butcher shop. The butcher (Roschdy Zem) tells her he's the landlord.

Ousmane (Sotigui Kouyate) begins his search with the imam of a London local mosque, who knows his son from an Arabic class. The man sees a photo of his son with Jane, and connects it with "Missing" posters Elisabeth has stuck up. He calls the number on the poster, but after meeting him, she's hostile: What would her daughter have to do with a French-speaking old Muslim with dreadlocks halfway down his back?

The development of *London River* is somewhat predictable from that moment forward, but no less useful. As the parents make their separate ways through a bewildering and discouraging series of encounters with the police and people who knew their children, it becomes clear that the two young people were a couple living together. Ousmane knows even less about his child than Elisabeth knows about hers: "I do not know my son. I did not have the raising of him." He'd left French Africa many years ago for France, to become a forester working with elm trees. Elisabeth, a widow, raised Jane on Guernsey through working her farm.

The film is a matter of Brenda Blethyn's performance versus Sotigui Kouyate's presence. Thin to the point of gauntness, leaning on a worn wooden cane, his clothes too large, his eyes dark and deep-set, he embodies a figure of solitude. She speaks French, but their conversations begin very slowly; their guards are up because they both, we eventually learn, suspect the other's child of having misled their own. There is no evidence that either was involved in the terrorism—and indeed nobody knows if either was on the doomed bus—but as they follow a dreary route of hospitals and morgues, a dread sinks upon them.

Blethyn's character resembles in some ways the woman she played in Mike Leigh's *Secrets and Lies* (1996), for which she won an Oscar nomination. In that film, she is discovered by the black daughter she gave up for adoption as a baby. In this one, she doesn't know why her daughter would be dating an African or studying Arabic. She lives in insular befuddlement. "Who speaks Arabic?" she asks the woman who was Jane's teacher. "Well," the woman smiles, "we do."

The film has been directed by Rachid Bouchareb, the French-Algerian filmmaker whose two previous films, *Days of Glory* or *Indigenes* (2006) and *Outside the Law* (2010), were both Oscar nominees for best foreign film. Both were deeply involved politically. *London River* is more concerned with these two searching parents.

There is good news and bad along the way of Elisabeth and Ousmane's quest. Unexpected information. Gradual insights. Self-discovery. The film has been criticized by some as too politically correct. Perhaps so. But the reality of these two characters rises above its ideas and makes it human. People never think of themselves as choosing to be politically correct. They simply think in the way that they do.

## Looking for Eric ★ ★

NO MPAA RATING, 116 m., 2010

Steve Evets (Eric Bishop), Eric Cantona (Himself), Stephanie Bishop (Lily), Gerard Kearns (Ryan), John Henshaw (Meatballs), Lucy-Jo Hudson (Sam), Stefan Gumbs (Jess). Directed by Ken Loach and produced by Rebecca O'Brien. Screenplay by Paul Laverty.

*Looking for Eric* is the last film I would have expected from Ken Loach, the great British director of films about working-class lives. His strength is social realism and a critique of the limited options within a class system. He works close to the earth and to his characters.

Here now is a most unexpected comedy, appealing to world soccer fans and based on a common enough daydream: A man's sports hero appears in his life and carries on friendly conversations with him. I call it a fantasy, but Loach approaches it as if it were quite real. He uses Eric Cantona, a famed star of Manchester United, and places him right there in the room with Eric Bishop (Steve Evets), a Manchester postal worker badly in need of encouragement.

The outlines of Eric's life are grim. The film begins after he survives a car crash and involves his two worthless grown sons, Ryan and Jess, and his lingering feelings for his estranged wife, Lily (Stephanie Bishop), who has refused to speak to him in seven years.

Into this sad man's life steps Cantona, a superstar in all the soccer-playing world, who becomes his confidant and confessor. Cantona, it must be said, is quite successful in his role: warm, persuasive, a source of common sense. He diagnoses Eric's problem: He should get back together with Lily. This is also the plan of Sam (Lucy-Jo Hudson), Eric and Lily's grown daughter.

This counsel provides a reason for flashbacks showing Eric and Lily's romance in earlier years, very touching, causing us to hope they'll fall in love all over again. But, excuse me, why does this require brokering by an imaginary sports star? Cantona himself produced the film and may have been involved in the financing, which could explain how it came to be made. What I can't explain is why Loach chose to make it. Maybe after so many great films he simply wanted to relax with a genre comedy. It has charm and Loach's fine eye and an expected generic payoff. But it doesn't make any sense.

I had another problem I'm almost ashamed to admit. Loach has always made it a point to use actors employing working-class accents, reflecting the fact that accent is a class marker. I've usually been able to understand the characters in his movies; it's the music as much as the words to begin with, and then I start to hear the words. This time his star, Steve Evets, uses a Manchester accent so thick many of the English themselves might not be able to understand it. Ironically Eric Cantona, who is French, is easier to understand.

*Looking for Eric* is inexplicable. It has elements of a Loach social drama, which might have been better used as the entire story. Cantona is nice enough, but so what? If there seem to be any comic possibilities in the story, Loach doesn't find them. If your world doesn't revolve around Eric Cantona, he'll come over as just a nice enough guy, no big deal. And can the great Ken Loach actually have fallen prey to the Obligatory Action in the Third Act virus?

## The Losers ★ ★ ★ ½

PG-13, 98 m., 2010

Zoe Saldana (Aisha), Jeffrey Dean Morgan (Clay), Chris Evans (Jensen), Idris Elba (Roque), Columbus Short (Pooch), Oscar Jaenada (Cougar), Jason Patric (Max). Directed by Sylvain White and produced by Kerry Foster, Akiva Goldsman, and Joel Silver. Screenplay by Peter Berg and James Vanderbilt.

*The Losers* is a classical action movie based on a comic strip. It does just enough nodding toward the graphics of drawn superheroes, and then gets that out of the way and settles down into a clean, efficient, and entertaining thriller. It's a reminder of how exhausting this kind of material can be when it's brought to a manic level by overwrought directors. It looks, feels, and plays like a real movie. There is another reason to be grateful: It's not in 3-D. You have to treasure movies like this before they're entirely eaten away by the marketing gimmicks.

Story, straightforward, no gargoyles. Five tough guys on a mission against a drug lord in Bolivia. They abort the mission when they see a bus full of little kids arrive at the target. No luck. A voice named "Max" orders a plane to carry out a bombing run. The tough guys break in and rescue the kids just in time. A helicopter is sent for them. No room on the copter except for the kids. The copter is shot down, the kids die.

"That was supposed to be us," they say, regarding the smoldering wreckage. Close-up of flames still licking at a toy bear that was established earlier as belonging to a cute kid. Note: Whenever a kid gets on a copter in an action film and is told to take good care of his bear, the kid and the bear will go down in flames.

The tough guys rip off their dog tags and throw them on the flames. Now they're The Losers, dedicated to bringing the mysterious Max to justice. Who is he? They guess maybe CIA–Special Forces–Black Ops . . . nobody knows. Meanwhile, they're officially dead and stranded in Bolivia with no passports and no money.

Think I'm giving away too much? That's only the pre-title sequence. Then we meet them one by one: Clay (Jeffrey Dean Morgan), Jensen (Chris Evans), Roque (Idris Elba), Pooch (Columbus Short), and Cougar (Oscar Jaenada). Each has a specialty: command, ordnance, rockets, sniper, etc. They're rugged, macho, wisecracking. Clay is the highest-ranking officer, but he keeps saying, "We're not in the military now." Later, of course, he pulls rank.

Then we meet Aisha (Zoe Saldana). Saldana is a seriously beautiful woman. You didn't notice that so much in *Avatar*. She poses as a bar girl to seduce her way into Clay's room, and then they have a deadly fight, destroy the room, and burn down the hotel, and after that they're friends on the same side and Clay is convincing the others to trust her. I didn't quite follow this every step of the way.

Aisha knows who Max really is, where he is, and how to get him. And she has the resources to get The Losers into the United States, arm them, rent them helicopters, and so on. They want to avenge those kids. Can Aisha be trusted? It's not always clear. Nor is it clear at first exactly what Max is up to, although here's a first: He demonstrates the first green weapon of mass destruction. It totally destroys a target, yet adds no pollution to the atmosphere. How's that for progress? How he plans to use the weapon and what his super-secret computer files are for provide the movie's MacGuffin.

Max is played by Jason Patric, who can make a very snaky snark. The director, Sylvain White, contrives a nice little scene on the beach where Max's curvaceous servant shades him with an umbrella. The wind blows the umbrella aside for a second, and the shot becomes a perfect steal of that butler on the beach in the Jack Vettriano painting that became the largest-selling poster in British history. Then Max shoots her. That's not in the Vettriano.

*The Losers* knows what it's doing and how to do it. Sylvain White doesn't have a lot of credits, but he knows how to direct and not trip over his own feet. The movie gets the job done, and the actors show a lot of confidence in occupying that tricky middle ground between controlled satire and comic overkill. It's fun.

I noted that Zoe Saldana is beautiful. I noted something else. In keeping with the current popularity of cafe au lait complexions, the movie uses lighting and filters to bathe the romantic scenes in a kind of golden glow, so that Saldana and Morgan come out looking about the same. We're no longer making people of color look whiter in the movies; we're tinting people of whiteness. Time marches on.

## The Loss of a Teardrop Diamond ★ ★ ★

PG-13, 102 m., 2010

Bryce Dallas Howard (Fisher Willow), Chris Evans (Jimmy Dobyne), Ellen Burstyn (Miss Addie), Mamie Gummer (Julie), Ann-Margret (Aunt Cornelia), Will Patton (Old Man Dobyne),

Jessica Collins (Vinnie). Directed by Jodie Markell and produced by Brad Michael Gilbert. Screenplay by Tennessee Williams.

Soft summer nights, the moon low above the river, "Alice Blue Gown" drifting on the breeze, a rich Southern girl who tasted freedom in Paris and now pretends to desire Memphis society, a poor but honest boy, bitchy debutantes in pastel gowns, wary old ladies in wide-brimmed hats, an opium addict in agony, a good but drunken father, and down by the levee the ghosts of sharecroppers drowned by a rich man's dynamite.

The voice of Tennessee Williams calls to us across the twenty-six years since his death. It is not strong and fierce, but it is his. *The Loss of a Teardrop Diamond* is an original screenplay he wrote in the 1950s, never produced, long forgotten. It has been filmed in a respectful manner that feels like a touring production of an only moderately successful Broadway play. Understand that, accept it, and the film has its rewards and one performance of great passion.

That would be by Ellen Burstyn, Miss Addie, who plays it all in bed in her sickroom in a Tennessee country mansion with a debutante party going on downstairs. She has snared Fisher Willow (Bryce Dallas Howard) away from the party and ordered her to lock the doors. Addie lived for many years in Hong Kong, consoled by opium for her lost dreams. She remembers Fisher from a brief visit home. The girl struck her as hard and brave. Now she asks her to do something for her. Give her the pills that will allow her to die.

Fisher is very agitated, a word Tennessee might have liked. She has hired Jimmy Dobyne (Chris Evans), the good-looking poor boy whose alcoholic father manages her father's commissary, to be her escort to the party. She even measured him for his evening wear. Jimmy's grandfather was governor, but the family has fallen back to its knees. Addie senses all has not gone well on their date, discovers Jimmy didn't want to kiss Fisher when she parked on the riverbank, advises her to escape and go back to Europe.

These are all Williams tropes. The paralyzing stupidity of genteel society. The lure of Europe and the "arts," and escape itself. The drink, the drugs, the decay. The not-as-young woman hiring a gentleman caller and hoping for the kindness of strangers. Bryce Dallas Howard is affecting as Fisher, but not electrifying because the material doesn't have it in it. Chris Evans, as Jimmy, is reserved to the point of oddness: a straight arrow without the arrowhead. He may think he's channeling Paul Newman, but he evokes instead the new male lead on a soap opera.

There are extended scenes involving the party downstairs, everyone perfectly dressed. No one talks unless they have dialogue provided. They stand around murmuring like extras. Remember the party scene in Visconti's *The Leopard*, all told in one shot, establishing characters and relationships? This party is as lifeless as the "pageant" staged earlier in a garden by drilled girls for bored old ladies.

And yet I relax and take it for what it is. I feel Tennessee's yearnings. I saw something of his life indirectly, at a remove. His brother Dakin lived in Chicago and was a frequent player on the newspaper drinking circuit; he announced his candidacy for governor at a press conference at Riccardo's. He wore a white pinstripe suit and a Panama hat. He had a platform, but the only plank you ever heard about was that he was the brother of Tennessee—and of Rose, you remember, the sister. He was a friendly man, courteous, sharing I suspect the joke of his several runs for office. He was the comedy, Rose was the tragedy, and Tennessee was the recording angel.

You will want to see this film if Tennessee means anything to you. Does he, to most people, anymore? And do Albee and Miller? A nonmusical play can hardly open on Broadway these days, and the twentieth century's playwriting history flourishes elsewhere in places like Chicago. But this *is* a Tennessee Williams screenplay. And in it one of the great Williams women, Miss Addie, and one of the great Williams actresses, Ellen Burstyn. That ought to mean something. Well, shouldn't it?

## Louder Than a Bomb ★ ★ ★ ½

NO MPAA RATING, 100 m., 2011

Kevin Coval, Adam Gottlieb, Elizabeth Graf, Kevin Harris, John Hood, Lamar Jorden, Peter Kahn, Jesus Lark, Nate Marshall, She'Kira McKnight, Preye Porri, James Sloan, Charles

Smith, Robbie Q. Telfer, and Nova Venerable. A documentary directed and produced by Greg Jacobs and Jon Siskel.

Poetry slams began in Chicago in 1984 and have become an international phenomenon without most people probably having heard of them. They're poetry readings as a spectator sport. Individuals and teams are scored by judges on the Olympic ten-point scale, but while Olympic diving judges claim to be looking at specific elements in a dive, slam judges are responding to emotion, charisma, and—well, poetry. Some slammers are also rap artists, but slam and rap are different art forms, and slammers rely only on their voices.

*Louder Than a Bomb* is about the 2008 Chicago-area slam of the same name, the nation's largest. Teams and soloists from sixty high schools compete, and the finalists face off in a citywide slam that fills a theater usually used for rock concerts. The suspense that year initially centered on Steinmetz, a troubled inner city school that had never entered before it won the 2007 Bomb in a thrilling upset. Can Steinmetz and its coach, James Sloan, repeat?

The film was directed by Greg Jacobs and Jon Siskel (Gene's nephew), who followed several competitors for months and guessed well in choosing those they focused on. The 2008 Steinmetz team had some gifted repeaters, and we also meet three outstanding solo talents:

—Nova Venerable from Oak Park/River Forest High School, who helps her mom with the complex needs of a disabled kid brother and then writes about that and her absent father.

—Nate Marshall from Whitney Young Magnet High School, whose parents were addicts but who, when asked to choose between basketball and poetry, chooses words, and masters them with almost bewildering fluency.

—Adam Gottlieb, from Northside College Prep, whose poems are so joyous and whose performances so charismatic that he makes it possible to think of a slammer as a rock star.

—The Steinmetz team, calling themselves the Steinmenauts, are Lamar Jorden, Kevin Harris, Jesus Lark, Charles Smith, and She'Kira McKnight. They develop artistic and personal differences, which Coach Sloan helps them work out during tense scenes. When they triumphantly appear onstage, their very presence is a tribute to their poetry.

Siskel and Jacobs focus on the performances, which are inspiring and electrifying. Their film left me wondering why American television must be so gutless and shallow. If these kids and others like them were programmed against *American Idol* or *Dancing with the Stars*, the shabbiness of those shows would be placed in dramatic contrast. Here are real performers with real feelings and important things to say.

I hesitate to hint about the outcome of the contest, nor to steal some of the thunder and surprises from the performers. I'll end on this: After *Louder Than a Bomb* plays theatrically, it will air on the Oprah Winfrey Network. Why doesn't Oprah consider it a pilot for a series? America's got talent, all right, but maybe we've been looking for it in the wrong places.

## A Love Affair of Sorts ★ ½

NO MPAA RATING, 91 m., 2011

Lili Bordan (Enci), David Guy Levy (David Guy), Ivan Kamaras (Boris), Jonathan Beckerman (Himself). Directed and produced by David Guy Levy. Screenplay by Levy and Lili Bordan.

*A Love Affair of Sorts* answers the question of whether you can make a feature film with a Flip camera, and leaves open the question of whether you can make a good one. It's a "shakycam" meander through an unconvincing relationship, with detours considering the process of making the film. At ninety-one minutes it seems very long.

The stars are David Guy Levy, the director, and Lili Bordan. They share writing credits, although much of the film seems unwritten. He plays "David Guy" and she plays "Enci," so it's not a documentary, but I imagine these characters are not a million miles apart from the actors in real life. He is a pudgy geek, likable and low-key, with an almost hostile taste in T-shirts. She is an attractive Hungarian-American. They live in places their characters don't seem able to afford.

They meet when he Flipcams her shoplifting. He persuades her to take another Flip so they can collaborate on a film. It's a good question whether he intends this as a project or a pickup technique. She agrees, and the film is edited from their separate footage. There is much talk about where the camera is, who is on cam, what they film when apart, and so on.

There is also the snaky "love affair of sorts." She kinda likes David, but we meet Boris (Ivan Kamaras), the testosterone engine she's sleeping with. A woman like her should have better taste than to date a man who wears a gigantic watch on one arm and a studded wristband on the other. The movie's dramatic highlight is when she discovers he left the camera pointed at the bed while they were preparing to make love. Yes, but after all, it's her camera.

David takes her to lunch and dinner; he has excellent taste in Formica diners. They go for walks. They talk a lot. They grow fond. He entertains either illusions or delusions of romance. She smokes all the time, with a certain style, and decides to stop smoking. That is the other dramatic high point. If Boris is the "wham, bam, thank you ma'am" type, David is more like wh . . . wh . . . wh . . .

And that's it. The movie lacks a purpose other than its own existence. It is largely about filming itself. David's friend named Jonathan Beckerman appears and apparently doesn't know he is in a movie. So what difference does that make? There could possibly be an interesting story here about David and Enci, but that would involve imposing narrative and stylistic discipline. It could be filmed with a Flip, but why? Better cameras are also cheap. The movie's lasting contribution is to serve as an illustration of sub-mumblecore.

## Love and Other Drugs ★ ★ ½

R, 112 m., 2010

Jake Gyllenhaal (Jamie Randall), Anne Hathaway (Maggie Murdock), Oliver Platt (Bruce Winston), Hank Azaria (Dr. Stan Knight), Josh Gad (Josh Randall), Gabriel Macht (Trey Hannigan). Directed by Edward Zwick and produced by Pieter Jan Brugge, Marshall Herskovitz, Charles Randolph, Scott Stuber, and Zwick. Screenplay by Randolph, Zwick, and Herskovitz, based on the book *Hard Sell: The Evolution of a Viagra Salesman* by Jamie Reidy.

*Love and Other Drugs* stars Jake Gyllenhaal as Jamie Randall, a pharmaceutical salesman who sells love, Zoloft, Viagra, and other products with equal sincerity. He's a charmer, determined to sell his way out of Ohio and into the big Chicago market, and if that involves flirting with the receptionists in doctors' offices, it's a tough job but somebody's got to do it.

The movie takes place at that point in the 1990s when Viagra was tumescing in the marketplace, and Jamie is riding the success of his employer, Pfizer. He infiltrates hospitals, befriends doctors, pushes drugs, and sabotages the best efforts of his aggressive rival, Trey Hannigan (Gabriel Macht), whose product Prozac is outselling Zoloft. Whether these products, or any of their products, work very well is not a concern of the salesmen. They sell.

Jamie is egged on by his supervisor, Bruce Winston (Oliver Platt), and it seems quite possible he'll make it to Chicago when his life makes an unexpected course correction. He's buddies with Dr. Stan Knight (Hank Azaria), who introduces him as his intern and allows him to observe as he palpates the breast of his lovely patient Maggie Murdock (Anne Hathaway). Strictly speaking, doctors aren't supposed to do that. Maggie discovers the fraud, and in the course of an argument with Jamie about it they both grow so passionate that, well, they rip off each other's clothes and fall upon the bed in a confusion of sheets and moans.

Maggie and Jamie discover that they really, really like each other. She has something she wants to tell him. She is in the early stages of Parkinson's disease. This introduces an unexpected note into what seemed to be a screwball comedy. Hathaway brings such tenderness and solemnity to her role that she moves the film away from comedy and toward *Love Story*, and from then on we never quite know where we're headed.

The emotional tug-of-war intensifies because of the presence of Jamie's brother, Josh (Josh Gad), who seems to have been imported directly from an Odd Buddy Movie. Josh is helpless in the area of appropriate behavior, seems to have selected his wardrobe in high school for the rest of his life, has made millions of dollars in the markets, and has a disastrous personal life. Although he could buy a hotel, he lacks the skill or the courage to check into one, and seems intent on living for the rest of his life on the sofa in Jamie's small apartment.

That would be permissible in another kind of movie. Not in this one, where matters grow serious between the two lovers—so serious, indeed, that they begin to discuss how their love will prevail through the difficult road ahead. The movie gives full weight and attention to the subject of Parkinson's and doesn't trivialize it or find jokes in it (how could it?).

But the more weight the story of Maggie and Jamie takes on, the more distracting is the screenplay's need to intercut updates on the pharmaceutical wars. Nor do we continue to care much about Bruce and Trey. The most effective single scene in the movie takes place at a meeting of people with Parkinson's and their loved ones. The husband of a victim describes to Jamie in stark, realistic detail the possible course of the disease, and how it may affect the woman he loves. After this scene, the movie has definitively introduced a note that makes the rest seem trivial.

The director is Edward Zwick, a considerable filmmaker. He's essentially working with a screenplay (by Charles Randolph, Marshall Herskovitz, and himself) that doesn't work. Given that problem, you have to observe that he is a capable filmmaker even in bad weather. He obtains a warm, lovable performance from Anne Hathaway, and dimensions from Gyllenhaal that grow from comedy to the serious. The scene with the husband of the Parkinson's survivor has a simple grandeur. As a filmmaker by nature, Zwick gives that scene its full weight, no matter that it's not a good fit in his movie. That counts for something.

## Love Crime ★ ★ ★

NO MPAA RATING, 104 m., 2011

Ludivine Sagnier (Isabelle), Kristin Scott Thomas (Christine), Patrick Mille (Philippe), Guillaume Marquet (Daniel), Gerald Laroche (Gerard), Julien Rochefort (Lawyer), Olivier Rabourdin (Judge). Directed by Alain Corneau and produced by Said Ben Said. Screenplay by Corneau and Nathalie Carter.

Alain Corneau's *Love Crime* is a diabolical mystery movie with one of those plots where we suppose we understand everything that's happening, and then get the rug pulled out from under us. It's a contest of will between two women executives in the French headquarters of an American multinational, and involves bloodthirsty office skullduggery and intrigue. The two lead performances make it work, even if the plot eventually seems devious for its own sake.

Kristin Scott Thomas, once again fluently bilingual, plays Christine, the boss, who is one step away from being promoted to the American office. When we first see her with Isabelle (Ludivine Sagnier), they're in Christine's home working on business when Christine's affection for her protégé shows hints of being more personal. Is she really attracted to the younger woman, or simply trying to seduce her loyalty? She speaks tenderly, touches her gently, gives her a scarf.

When Isabelle discovers Christine has also taken credit for her work, she's stunned. Christine smoothly explains that it's the way corporations work; it's known as teamwork. Isabelle seems to be a naive and vulnerable underling compared to Christine's cold-eyed calculation. Intrigue deepens as Christine sends her lover Philippe (Patrick Mille) with Isabelle on a business trip to Cairo, they sleep together, and that triggers Christine's fury against them both.

The screw tightens. Philippe is trapped. Now Isabelle feels betrayed by both. Daniel (Guillaume Marquet), a friendly colleague, opens her eyes to office secrets, setting in motion a labyrinthine plot in which the seemingly naive young woman turns out to be more than the equal of her boss.

Spoiler: I must reveal that Christine is murdered. I won't say who does it. Isabelle is arrested and brought before a fair, conscientious magistrate (Olivier Rabourdin), and the police assemble a damning case against her, all based on circumstantial evidence. Demoralized by pills, deeply depressed, Isabelle confesses. But then the whole plot turns on itself.

One of the pleasures is watching the gears mesh. The screenplay has been written by Corneau and Nathalie Carter with meticulous attention to detail. Like classic mystery authors, they play fair, so that the surprises at the end are consistent with what we've seen—although we didn't realize it at the time.

Kristin Scott Thomas is good at roles like these, with the combination of sensuality and ruthlessness. Her fluency in the language has given her a new career as a French star, at a time when French filmmakers are more interested than Americans in middle-aged women. The movie depends, however, on Ludivine Sagnier, who is convincing both in early scenes when she's helpless and clueless, and later when she holds the cards and pulls the strings.

This was the final film by Alain Corneau, who died last year at sixty-seven. His best film was *Tous les Matins du Monde* (1991), which starred Gerard Depardieu in one of his best performances as a regretful old musician. Corneau directed a favorite of mine, *Fear and Trembling* (2003), which also involved two women in competition. It starred Sylvie Testud as a Belgian woman who returns to Japan, where she was raised as a child, to work under an executive she idolizes (Kaori Tsuji). *Love Crime* is equally involving.

## Loveless ★ ★ ★

NO MPAA RATING, 104 m., 2010

Andrew von Urtz (Andrew), Cindy Chastain (Joanna), Genevieve Hudson-Price (Ava), Gary Wilmes (Tad), Kendra Hurley (Kendra), Sabin Streeter (Sabin), Scott Cohen (Ricky), Ramin Serry (Ramin), Shauna Lyon (Shauna). Directed by Ramin Serry and produced by Shauna Lyon. Screenplay by Serry.

We all know someone like Andrew, with his intense vagueness. It's important for him to convey to you that he has something important to tell you. The precise nature of that always seems to reside in his next unspoken sentence. He's like a fortune-teller, trying to get you to reveal what you want to hear him say.

Andrew, the hero of Ramin Serry's *Loveless*, is a midthirties office worker in Manhattan, who tirelessly drinks and tries to pick up women and has a low-key cluelessness that some women find attractive. Besides, anyone this unskilled at claiming he's looking for an actress for his new movie might possibly be telling the truth. Andrew is played by Andrew von Urtz in his movie debut, and played so easily and convincingly that you not only believe such a person might exist, but that you are probably looking at him.

Half-drunk, he tries out the actress routine on Ava (Genevieve Hudson-Price), whom he meets in a bar. She stalks out to go to a party, he follows her, and finds himself at her brother's birthday. Her brother, Ricky (Scott Cohen), has many other brothers (I counted three), and they all worship the memory of their dead father. Indeed, Ava and Ricky believe they talk to him and receive daily guidance.

Andrew finds himself at another party, this one given by friends, where he meets his ex-girlfriend Joanna (Cindy Chastain). That isn't surprising because Andrew is the kind of man whose friends would possibly rather stay in touch with his ex-girlfriend than with him. Not that he's obnoxious. It's more that he's perfectly nice, but wearying. He and Joanna start up again, sort of, and, meanwhile, Ava's brothers decide to finance Andrew's movie, Ava smothers him in lust, Joanna meets her, and Andrew, who would possibly like to be left in peace to drink, finds himself loveless but not loverless.

*Loveless* is a movie about behavior, not plot. It doesn't much matter which woman, if either, Andrew ends up with, or whether his movie (or Ricky's movie) ever gets made. Andrew is a character whose life is about process, not plot. He doesn't get from A to C but spends his best years circling B. He wanders. He wanders in his drinking, in his sex life, in his plans. He's indulged by his boss, who is a friend, and probably has a gift for inspiring indulgence. Certainly the women in his life accept a lot.

Although Andrew von Urtz and Cindy Chastain are in their first film and Genevieve Hudson-Price has only two previous credits, all three have a natural ease on camera. In genre, *Loveless* is a romantic comedy, and their comfort level in the form is a contrast to the tense energy you often sense in romcoms. Nobody is obsessed with an imaginary finish line, least of all Andrew, who ends as he begins, circling B.

## The Lovely Bones ★ ½

PG-13, 136 m., 2010

Mark Wahlberg (Jack Salmon), Rachel Weisz (Abigail Salmon), Susan Sarandon (Grandma

**Lynn), Stanley Tucci (George Harvey), Michael Imperioli (Len Fenerman), Saoirse Ronan (Susie Salmon), Rose McIver (Lindsey Salmon). Directed by Peter Jackson and produced by Jackson, Carolynne Cunningham, and Fran Walsh. Screenplay by Jackson, Walsh, and Philippa Boyens, based on the novel by Alice Sebold.**

*The Lovely Bones* is a deplorable film with this message: If you're a fourteen-year-old girl who has been brutally raped and murdered by a serial killer, you have a lot to look forward to. You can get together in heaven with the other teenage victims of the same killer and gaze down in benevolence upon your family members as they mourn you and realize what a wonderful person you were. Sure, you miss your friends, but your fellow fatalities come dancing to greet you in a meadow of wildflowers, and how cool is that?

The makers of this film seem to have given slight thought to the psychology of teenage girls, less to the possibility that there is no heaven, and none at all to the likelihood that if there is one, it will not resemble a happy gathering of new Facebook friends. In its version of the events, the serial killer can almost be seen as a hero for liberating these girls from the tiresome ordeal of growing up and dispatching them directly to the Elysian Fields. The film's primary effect was to make me squirmy.

It's based on the best-seller by Alice Sebold that everybody seemed to be reading a couple of years ago. I hope it's not faithful to the book; if it is, millions of Americans are scary. The murder of a young person is a tragedy, the murderer is a monster, and making the victim a sweet, poetic narrator is creepy. This movie sells the philosophy that even evil things are God's will and their victims are happier now. Isn't it nice to think so. I think it's best if they don't happen at all. But if they do, why pretend they don't hurt? Those girls are dead.

I'm assured, however, that Sebold's novel is well written and sensitive. I presume the director, Peter Jackson, has distorted elements to fit his own vision, which involves nearly as many special effects in some sequences as his *Lord of the Rings* trilogy. A more useful way to deal with this material would be with observant, subtle performances in a thoughtful screenplay. It's not a feel-good story. Perhaps Jackson's team made the mistake of fearing the novel was too dark. But its millions of readers must know it's not like this. The target audience may be doom-besotted teenage girls—the *Twilight* crowd.

The owner of the lovely bones is named Susie Salmon (Saoirse Ronan, a very good young actress, who cannot be faulted here). The heaven Susie occupies looks a little like a Flower Power world in the kind of fantasy that, murdered in 1973, she might have imagined. Seems to me that heaven, by definition outside time and space, would have neither colors nor a lack of colors—would be a state with no sensations. Nor would there be thinking there, let alone narration. In an eternity spent in the presence of infinite goodness, you don't go around thinking, "Man! Is this great!" You simply *are*. I have a lot of theologians on my side here.

But no. From her movie-set Valhalla, Susie gazes down as her mother (Rachel Weisz) grieves and her father (Mark Wahlberg) tries to solve the case himself. There's not much of a case to solve; we know who the killer is almost from the get-go, and, under the Law of Economy of Characters, that's who he has to be because (a) he's played by an otherwise unnecessary movie star, and (b) there's no one else in the movie he *could* be.

Here's something bittersweet. Weisz and Wahlberg are effective as the parents. Because the pyrotechnics are mostly upstairs with the special effects, all they need to be are convincing parents who have lost their daughter. This they do with touching subtlety. We also meet one of Susie's grandmothers (Susan Sarandon), an unwise drinker who comes on to provide hard-boiled comic relief, in the Shakespearean tradition that every tragedy needs its clown. Well, she's good, too. This whole film is Jackson's fault.

It doesn't fail simply because I suspect its message. It fails on its own terms. It isn't emotionally convincing that this girl, having had these experiences and destined apparently to be fourteen forever (although cleaned up and with a new wardrobe), would produce this heavenly creature. What's left for us to pity?

We should all end up like her, and the sooner the better; preferably not after being raped and murdered.

## The Lucky One ★ ★ ½

PG-13, 101 m., 2012

Zac Efron (Logan Thibault), Taylor Schilling (Beth Green), Blythe Danner (Ellie Green), Riley Thomas Stewart (Ben), Jay R. Ferguson (Keith Clayton). Directed by Scott Hicks and produced by Denise di Novi and Kevin McCormick. Screenplay by Will Fetters, based on the novel by Nicholas Sparks.

A marine sees a photograph almost buried in rubble in the middle of a combat scene. He steps over to pick it up, and with that small movement he saves his life. A nearby explosion would have wiped him out. The photo stays with him through his third tour of duty, and when he comes home he determines to find the girl in the photograph. He doesn't know her name or where she lives, but wouldn't you know, through happy chance he happens to be passing through Louisiana—and there she is!

I'm not going to say anything at all about the odds of that happening. The odds are overwhelmingly against anything in any movie happening, so I should just shut up and pay attention. This is yet another love story adapted from a Nicholas Sparks novel, and it has been cast with appealing romantic leads, a snaky villain with a drinking problem, a grandmother with infallible instincts, and a lot of adorable dogs. It also has leaves bursting into bright autumn colors, and a lake just right for a couple to steal away for a quiet chat on a rowboat.

Nicholas Sparks has a good line in stories like this. They usually involve the triumph of love over adversity, they are usually set in beautiful natural settings, they usually involve such coincidences as finding a message in a bottle, and they usually make me stir restlessly, because such escapism is shameless. Still, credit must be given to a film that delivers the goods, and if you've ever liked a Nicholas Sparks movie, you're likely to enjoy this one. I've seen him in interviews, where he's better looking than some of his leading men and comes across as sincere. I think he really does believe in his stories, and I think readers sense that.

The marine is Logan (Zac Efron), an engaging actor who is natural onscreen without the insufferable self-confidence of a lot of leading men. If he wins the love of a woman, he has the grace to seem a little surprised. The girl in Louisiana is Beth (Taylor Schilling), who looks plausible as the owner and operator of a first-rate dog kennel in a picturesque rural setting, and no character who loves dogs is going to have a problem with me. Beth is pretty much perfect, but she made a big mistake when she married Keith Clayton (Jay R. Ferguson), a local deputy sheriff who is an insufferable bully with an inferiority complex. Keith did, however, serve as the father of Beth's cute, spunky son, Ben (Riley Thomas Stewart). The moment he sees Logan hanging around Beth, of course, he begins to threaten her custody of the child.

The journey that brings Logan to the dog kennel in the Louisiana woods is one happy chance after another, but is Beth going to wonder if he's a stalker? Not every guy tracks down one person out of the total population without being a little obsessive. Also, who was the marine who was carrying her photo, and why?

Luckily, Logan doesn't have to answer such questions because Beth assumes he has turned up in response to a help-wanted poster. He never gets around to explaining her mistake. That sort of mistaken identity is commonplace in the movies and rare in life, and for that matter wasn't Lucille Ball incessantly being mistaken for whoever she needed to be—or not to be?

Beth's nana is Ellie, played by Blythe Danner as a reminder of what a cheery, commonsense presence she can be. Just sitting there in the same room, she intuits in a few seconds that this strange man, who has drifted in from nowhere, is husband material. Too bad she wasn't around to shoo Keith off the property.

*The Lucky One* is at its heart a romance novel, elevated by Nicholas Sparks's persuasive storytelling. Readers don't read them because they're true, but because they ought to be true. You can easily imagine how many ways this story would probably go wrong in real life, but who wants to see a movie where a marine leans over to pick up a photo and is blown up? And a mom trying to raise her son and feed lots of hungry dogs while her abusive ex-husband gets drunk and hangs around? That kind of stuff is too close to life.

## Machine Gun Preacher ★ ★

R, 127 m., 2011

Gerard Butler (Sam Childers), Michelle Monaghan (Lynn Childers), Michael Shannon (Donnie), Kathy Baker (Daisy), Souleymane Sy Savane (Deng), Madeline Carroll (Paige). Directed by Marc Forster and produced by Forster, Robbie Brenner, Craig Chapman, Deborah Giarratana, and Gary Safady. Screenplay by Jason Keller.

If the Lord moves in mysterious ways his wonders to unfold, rarely can he have worked more mysteriously than in the case of Sam Childers, a Pennsylvania ex-con, drug addict, and thief who was born again and since 1998 has been leading a crusade on behalf of the wretched orphans of South Sudan. *Machine Gun Preacher* is a combination of uplift and gritty violence, and the parts don't fit.

We hear about Sudan all the time. There is little ambiguity there. A warlord named Joseph Kony runs something called the Lord's Resistance Army that has murdered hundreds of thousands, burned villages, and kidnapped some fifty thousand children, forcing the boys to become soldiers and making the girls sex slaves. He is an evil man, and while we're occupied in trying to bomb Gadhafi we might profitably drop a few on him.

In Pennsylvania, we meet Childers (Gerard Butler), who with his buddy Donnie (the always effective Michael Shannon), drinks, drugs, raises hell, and makes things hard on his wife, Lynn (Michelle Monaghan), and daughter. While Sam was in the pen, Lynn found God. One Sunday morning, after a bloody night of violence, Sam allows himself to be dragged along to a church service, where he confesses himself a sinner and undergoes a baptism of full immersion.

It takes. One day he hears a sermon from a missionary from Sudan, describing the plight of the orphans. Sam knows the construction business and informs his astonished wife that he feels called to go to Africa and see what he can do to help. There is a lot. Faced by the specter of overwhelming suffering, he builds an orphanage, raises money from home to help out, and becomes a driven man.

Eventually, so dire is the situation, Sam Childers returns to the instincts of his violent past and finds himself fighting against the Lord's Resistance Army as a commander in the Sudan People's Liberation Army. Thus the movie's title. Well, Childers isn't the first to go to war in the name of the Lord.

The enigma at the heart of the film is the quality of his actual spirituality. He's born again, yes, but he seems otherwise relatively unchanged. He still gives full vent to his drives and instincts, and still, if you get down to it, gives himself license to break the laws, such as they are, in Sudan. I learn from an article by Brett Keller in *Foreign Policy* magazine that as Childers was fund-raising in the United States, the Sudan People's Liberation Army issued a statement saying, "The SPLA does not know Sam Childers. . . . We are appealing to those concerned to take legal measures against him for . . . misusing the name of an organization which is not associated with him."

There's more, about "his narcissistic model of armed humanitarianism." That's what bothered me. He seems fueled more by anger and ego than spirituality, and essentially abandons his family to play with his guns. It's intriguing, however, how well Gerard Butler enlists our sympathy for the character. The film has been directed by Marc Forster (*Monster's Ball*), from a screenplay by Jason Keller that's efficient scene by scene, but seems uncertain where it's going or what it's saying. Since much of the killing in Northern Uganda and Southern Sudan is driven by sectarian and tribal prejudice, I'm not sure that shooting back is a solution—particularly when it's done by a self-anointed white savior from the West.

The sight of Sam Childers with his machine gun and his ammo belt reminds me of the night at O'Rourke's when a guy flashed a handgun for my friend McHugh. "Why are you sportin' that pistol?" he asked. "John," the guy said, "I live in a dangerous neighborhood." McHugh replied: "It would be safer if you moved."

## Made in Dagenham ★ ★ ★ ½

R, 113 m., 2010

Sally Hawkins (Rita O'Grady), Bob Hoskins (Albert Passingham), Miranda Richardson (Barbara Castle), Geraldine James (Connie), Rosamund Pike (Lisa Hopkins), Rupert Graves (Peter Hopkins), Andrea Riseborough (Brenda), Daniel Mays (Eddie O'Grady), Kenneth Cranham (Monty). Directed by Nigel Cole and produced by Elizabeth Karlsen and Stephen Woolley. Screenplay by William Ivory.

Ford is having a great year, and I just bought one of their new Fusions. How would I feel if I discovered the women building it had been paid less than the men simply because they were . . . well, women? If a woman does the same job as a man, should she receive the same pay? Yes, says common sense. No, say corporations that will disregard anything in the search for profits.

Ford, let me hasten to add, has a policy of equal pay for equal work. It was not always that way, with Ford and, to be fair, most corporations. *Made in Dagenham* takes place so recently as 1968, when the British Ford plant in Dagenham paid women significantly lower wages than men—with the agreement of their own unions and the Labour government of Harold Wilson.

Why was this so? Did they do less work? No. In fact, they were highly productive. It was so because the unions, the company, and the government were run by men and, I dunno, I guess they just weren't used to thinking about women in that way. *Made in Dagenham* is a delightfully entertaining movie based on fact. The women went on strike, annoyed their unions and their husbands, and embarrassed Wilson, who was caught with his principles down.

Sally Hawkins, that emerging dynamo of British acting, stars as Rita O'Grady, who sews automobile seat covers in what is literally a sweatshop; she and her coworkers have to strip down to bra and panties because of the unbearable heat. Her union organizer, Albert Passingham (Bob Hoskins), is a left-winger whose principles run deeper than his union's. He was raised by a brave mother, instinctively admires women, and sees with his own eyes that unequal pay is wrong.

Rita is a quiet woman who almost by accident becomes the shop steward. Albert spots the way her spontaneous humanity cuts through politics. Using her first as a surrogate, he encourages the idea of a strike. The head of the union at Ford (Kenneth Cranham) "works closely with management," as they say, and the government is also not eager to alienate a big corporate employer. All Rita O'Grady knows is that she works hard and believes that what's fair is fair.

A brief strike escalates into a much larger one. Her own husband, Eddie (Daniel Mays), is against her. The usual alarms circulate about left-wing influences. But when Rita is seen on the telly (and she is), she makes it all seem so simple (because it is). The strike at Dagenham changed history, in England and America, at Ford and many other manufacturers, and elsewhere in the developed world. It's one reason so many jobs are outsourced to places where labor unions and equal pay do not find favor.

The struggle is far from over. Only last week, a Republican filibuster in the U.S. Senate prevented passage of the Paycheck Fairness Act, which would have added teeth to measures for equal pay. You don't see many GOP ads saying it's against equal pay, but it is. So are corporations, and there may be a connection, but it's harder to say now that corporate political contributions can be secret.

But back to Dagenham. Although Albert set the ball rolling, Rita quickly found tons of support, some of it in unlikely places. One backer of the strike was the government's minister for labor, Barbara Castle (Miranda Richardson). A "fiery redhead" (Why are all redheads "fiery"?), she defied the pipe-puffing Wilson, who didn't want to alienate Ford. She explained her reason: "Harold, you are wrong." Probably the movie's best scene is when Castle receives O'Grady and her coworkers in her office and astonishes them by giving her support. Her decision put the Labour party on the spot.

Another ally is much more unlikely. She is Lisa Hopkins (Rosamund Pike), who is married to a top executive at Ford. She received a first-class education, could have had a career, but now finds herself playing the role of a well-trained and tamed corporate wife. Her husband, Peter (Rupert Graves), assumes that of course she opposes the striking women. Not so fast there, Pete.

Niki Caro's 2005 film *North Country* starred Charlize Theron in a similar story about a woman who won the first American sexual-harassment lawsuit. That was in 1984. Some men are slow to figure these things out. The unexpected thing about *Made in Dagenham* is how entertaining it is. That's largely due to director Nigel Cole's choice of Sally Hawkins for his lead. In Mike Leigh's *Happy Go Lucky* (2009) and again here, she shows an effortless lightness of being. If she has a limitation it may be that she's constitutionally ill adapted for playing a bad person.

## Magic Mike ★ ★ ★

R, 110 m., 2012

Channing Tatum (Magic Mike), Alex Pettyfer (Adam), Matt Bomer (Ken), Matthew McConaughey (Dallas), Joe Manganiello (Big Dick Richie), Cody Horn (Brooke), Olivia Munn (Joanna), Adam Rodriguez (Tito), Kevin Nash (Tarzan). Directed by Steven Soderbergh and produced by Reid Carolin, Gregory Jacobs, Channing Tatum, and Nick Wechsler. Screenplay by Carolin.

Whether you're a man or a woman, making money by allowing people to push cash inside your G-string is, I think we can agree, demeaning. It's probably worse for women because the big spenders with two dollars probably harbor some vague dream of sleeping with them. In the case of male strippers, I suspect their female fans are looking more for fun and some laughs on their girls' night out.

I could be wrong about this. I'm right about the job, however. Selling anyone the right to touch near your genitals for a couple of bucks is not a good way to build self-esteem. Steven Soderbergh's *Magic Mike* makes this argument with a crafty mixture of comedy, romance, melodrama, and some remarkably well-staged strip routines involving hunky, good-looking guys. I have a feeling women will enjoy it more than men.

Or maybe not. The sculpted bodies on display in the film are a monument to narcissism; a guy who spends hours a day improving his pecs and abs may offer limited conversation skills. Kelly Oxford, the famous Canadian housewife who won a Hollywood contract for her Tweets, just the other week tweeted: "FWIW, I'd rather f—— a 260-pound guy than a body builder."

*Magic Mike* has the fascination of most backstage movies: It shows a naive kid being drawn into the world of show business. He is Adam (Alex Pettyfer), a good-looking nineteen-year-old, who meets Magic Mike (Channing Tatum) while they're working on a roofing job. Mike dances three nights a week at Xquisite, a marginally successful Tampa strip club. Mike brings Adam along to the club, where he's fast-talked by the boss, Dallas (Matthew McConaughey). The kid has no desire to strip, but is pushed onstage wearing his street clothes and told to take them off down to his jockey shorts. He is awkward and embarrassed—and not surprisingly an enormous hit because the ladies think his shyness is an act, and they love it.

The film seems to know a lot about male strip clubs; Channing Tatum worked as a dancer when he was nineteen; he coproduced this film, which was written by his producing partner Reid Carolin. We learn what the rules are, how the money is shared, and how there's extra income when the guys guest-star at private parties. There's backstage humor as these muscle men powder their noses and make themselves up like burlesque queens, and a dark side, as the kid Adam begins to be pulled toward drugs.

Matthew McConaughey plays Dallas, the charismatic impresario of the business, which essentially involves him renting a club, paying for costumes and productions, and allowing his dancers to keep their own tips. He's the first one we see onstage, using his hands to point to his naughty bits, asking the ladies if they'd like to touch them, and then wagging his finger at them and saying, "No-no-*no*-no!" That may not sound like much of a scene, but think how easily it could go wrong. This is actually one of McConaughey's best performances, as a hardheaded businessman who understands his product and his audience.

Channing Tatum's Magic Mike has a long-range plan to own a custom furniture business, but is having trouble raising capital (there's a timely scene with a bank loan officer). Having recruited Adam for the club, he now meets the kid's protective sister Brooke (Cody Horn), and promises her no harm will come to her brother. They begin to fall in love, and this subplot feeds off the gradual revelation of the more dismaying aspects of male stripping. Tatum is a likable actor and we believe Mike's good intentions, but like all the dancers, he has become the captive of the nightly paydays.

The choreography, costumes, and production values of the shows look slick and professional, considering the fly-by-night nature of Dallas's business. We see the strippers as soldiers, construction workers, and other Village People archetypes, and the stage flows with smoke from dry ice. The movie sidesteps such details as stagehands, lighting directors, and so on, and there is no suggestion that any of the dancers may be gay.

Adam's descent into drug-fueled depravity is portrayed with merciless detail; when you sleep with a girl who has a pet piglet and wake up with the little fella eating your vomit, surely you've hit bottom. *Magic Mike* starts as fun and grows steadily darker, and Soderbergh and Tatum tell a realistic and vivid story. You get a feeling of realism and research, for example, when a chubby fan throws herself into the arms of a muscular dancer and the poor guy throws his back out.

## Make Believe ★ ★ ★

G, 90 m., 2011

Siphiwe Fangase, Hiroki Hara, Bill Koch, Krystyn Lambert, Derek McKee, Nkumbuzo Nkonyana, Jeff McBride, and Lance Burton. A documentary directed by J. Clay Tweel and produced by Steven Klein. Screenplay by Cleven S. Loham.

Oh, I wanted to be a magician. I memorized a biography of Houdini and mailed off to Johnson Smith Co. for boxes that made coins disappear, trick card decks, and wands that contained weights to make tassels rise and fall. I ordered the neighborhood kids into the basement and staged a laborious performance by The Great Ebertini. Tassels rose and coins disappeared, but the cards needed more work.

A lot more work, I learn in *Make Believe.* This is a charming documentary about the finalists in the Teenage Magician Contest at the annual World Magic Seminar in Las Vegas. From Malibu, Chicago, Colorado, Japan, and South Africa they come, dreaming of being presented with first place by the great Lance Burton. The documentary visits their homes, gets their stories, talks to their friends and parents, and follows them backstage in Vegas.

But mostly it watches them practice, over and over and over. Hiroki Hara, who lives in Kitayama, Japan, uses the village hall and rehearses relentlessly all day, every day, mentioning that he grows lonely there all by himself, but his goal makes it worthwhile. The others practice, too, and one sheds a few tears when two coaches tell him he's not ready for the finals. He rehearses some more, and on the big day, he is ready and then some.

Not a single rabbit is pulled from a hat. Most of the tricks are small-scale—locking rings, disappearing scarves, card production. A deck of cards in their hands seems to have a life of its own. One kid turns cards into iPods while they're fanned between his fingers. We see him in his basement, building the props.

Hara is the most inventive. He appears as a ghost monster with flashing green eyes, and presents an elegantly choreographed act. Siphiwe Fangase and Nkumbuzo Nkonyana, from a township in Cape Town, are the most entertaining, with their act based on music, dance, and magic soccer balls in honor of the World Cup held in South Africa.

For one contestant, everything goes wrong. A ball drops during a ball-production trick, and a trap in a hat doesn't work. It's not the magician's fault; both tricks *always* work. It's one of those days. The other contestants, backstage, discuss this with a kind of dread, knowing that no matter how often they practice, the same thing could happen to them.

One question not really addressed by the movie is whether these kids are wise to skip classes and put social life and college on hold in order to focus single-mindedly on magic. Apparently they all think they'll find professional careers, maybe not in Vegas, but at conventions and so forth. I hope so.

One thing we don't find out is how any of the tricks are done. The secrets in some cases (the steel rings, the vanishing scarves) are pretty widely known. In card manipulation, most of the people in the audience know in theory exactly how it's done, but are connoisseurs judging how well they are performed. Magicians have a saying: "The trick is told when the trick is sold." These kids are sold on tricks.

## Man on a Ledge ★ ★

PG-13, 102 m., 2012

Sam Worthington (Nick Cassidy), Elizabeth Banks (Lydia Mercer), Jamie Bell (Joey Cassidy), Anthony Mackie (Mike Ackerman), Genesis Rodriguez (Angie), Ed Harris (David Englander), Edward Burns (Jack Dougherty), Kyra Sedgwick (Suzie Morales). Directed by Asger Leth and produced by Lorenzo di Bonaventura and Mark Vahradian. Screenplay by Pablo F. Fenjves.

Faithful readers know I'm not fond of heights. That doesn't mean I object to them in movies. I responded strongly to Tom Cruise clinging to the walls of the world's tallest building in *Mission Impossible: Ghost Protocol.* With a movie such as *Man on a Ledge*, however, I feel toyed with. The movie cuts back and forth between two preposterous plots, and uses the man on the ledge as a device to pump up the tension.

Fair enough. I've played along with more than one absurd plot in my life. But how should we react when the man on the ledge doesn't take it seriously? I believe if you are standing on a twenty-first-floor ledge in a fair wind, you take it very seriously indeed. To be sure, the man is threatening to commit suicide, so if he fell, that would fit into his plan. But since we know he's not serious, what is this goofball *thinking*?

His name is Nick Cassidy (Sam Worthington). He's an ex-cop, serving a prison term. Let outside for a day under armed escort to attend his father's funeral, he escapes from his guards, ditches his prisoner's uniform, makes it into Manhattan, checks into a hotel, tucks into a big breakfast, and climbs out on the ledge.

At this point, if we're experienced moviegoers, we have a good idea he isn't going to jump anytime real soon, because then the movie would be over, get it? No, we're going to get a lot of point-of-view shots looking straight down past the toes of his shoes. Man, is he high up. He collects a big crowd, which brings traffic to a halt.

At the same time, the movie cuts away to David Englander (Ed Harris), a wealthy Master of the Universe whose offices are in a high-rise across the street. He's preparing to unveil his grandiose scheme to erect a skyscraper. I've forgotten its name, so let's call it the Englander Tower, in honor of the Donald.

Now we cut between Nick Cassidy, David Englander, and Joey (Jamie Bell) and Angie (Genesis Rodriguez). Why do I always think people named Joey and Angie are New Yorkers? I'm sure there are lots of them elsewhere. Anyway, Angie emulates the new breed of female action heroes by squeezing herself into a skin-tight latex costume that incorporates a push-up bra designed along the same lines that made the Sydney Opera House possible. Then she begins crawling through air shafts.

Across the street, a cop named Jack Dougherty (Edward Burns) arrives in the hotel room to talk down the jumper. Soon he's replaced by an NYPD psychologist named Lydia Mercer (Elizabeth Banks). Down below, on cue, the crowd chants "Jump! Jump!" while hoping to film the death on their iPhones and pick up some change from Eyewitness News. TV news reporter Suzie Morales (Kyra Sedgwick) breathlessly covers the story. Her station's NewsChopper helpfully flies so close to the ledge that its downdraft threatens to blow Nick into a thousand YouTube postings.

How much should I reveal? I could explain the connection, if any, between the events on both sides of the street. Let me just say it's all part of a tricky scheme to steal the world's largest diamond. Therefore, Nick's role is to attract attention and tie up traffic, right? Yes, and pretend to almost fall at just the right moment so an explosion will be overlooked, and so on.

But hold on. What we have here is a master plan that absolutely depends on Nick (1) being released for the funeral, (2) escaping two armed guards, (3) getting safely into Manhattan, (4) checking into a room on the correct floor and side of the hotel, and (5) not falling off the ledge prematurely, which would not only kill him but spoil the whole plan. And meanwhile, Joey and Angie have to *find* the world's largest diamond, which is not where it's supposed to be. Maybe it has been disguised as a diamond-plated Ferrari? No, that was *Tower Heist.* And also there has to be time for the TV reporter to sum up the meaning of everything and bring about the happy ending.

You say that all sounds plausible to you? OK. But here's what I doubt: You know those big mattresses that firemen inflate to break falls from high places? Do you believe that when it becomes urgent for Nick to be at street level right now, he would take a deep breath, get a running start on the ledge, jump into thin air, and land safely after his fall of twenty-one floors? That's where I draw the line.

## The Man Who Fell to Earth ★ ★ ★

R, 158 m., 1976 (rereleased in 2011)

David Bowie (Thomas Jerome Newton), Rip Torn (Nathan Bryce), Candy Clark (Mary-Lou), Buck Henry (Oliver Farnsworth), Bernie Casey (Peters), Rick Riccardo (Trevor). Directed by Nicolas Roeg and produced by Michael Deeley and Barry Spikings. Screenplay by Paul Mayersberg, based on the novel by Walter Tevis.

In the thirty-five years since its first release, Nicolas Roeg's *The Man Who Fell to Earth* has attained such cult status that it was remade in 1987 for television, and its poster can be glimpsed in the recent *Green Lantern.* It centers on an eerie performance by David Bowie, as an alien from a drought-stricken planet who journeys to Earth in search of water. Bowie, slender, elegant, remote, evokes this alien so successfully that one could say, without irony, this was a role he was born to play.

His character, named Thomas Jerome Newton, splashes to Earth in a remote western lake, walks into a town, sells some gold rings to raise cash, and searches out a patent attorney named Farnsworth (Buck Henry). He offers plans for a group of advanced electronics products (one of them, not so amazing, is a disposable camera that develops its own film). Farnsworth establishes the World Enterprises Corp. to market these inventions, and Newton grows wealthy. His plan, we learn, is to build a spaceship and transport water to his home planet.

This is seen as a desolate desert world whose only visible inhabitants are his family. They wear plastic suits to conserve precious bodily fluids. They apparently live or travel in something that looks like a hunting lodge with wings and runs on a monorail. There is no dialogue on this planet, only sad, spectral gestures.

On Earth, Newton (a name with a lot of gravity) isolates himself and communicates with Farnsworth only by telephone. In a motel he meets a chirpy young woman named Mary-Lou (Candy Clark). They begin an affair, and she introduces him to gin and tonic and television. He becomes addicted to both, eventually watching several channels at the same time.

The plot thickens. The CIA becomes involved. He is taken captive, and so on. You will discover the story for yourself. The movie is intriguing primarily because of Bowie's performance as Newton, and Clark's as the girl (Buck Henry, and Rip Torn as a scientist, could be playing their characters in any movie).

Bowie has an enviable urbane charm. I met him once, and rarely have I been so impressed by someone's poise. If he hadn't been a rock star he could have had success as an actor, playing roles such as those given to James Fox or William Hurt. He demonstrated that in such films as *Merry Christmas, Mr. Lawrence*; *Absolute Beginners*; *The Hunger*; and *Labyrinth.* Apart from a few moments involving special effects, he and Roeg make no overt attempt to show Newton as particularly alien. They simply use his presence. He is . . . other. Apart. Defined within himself.

And lonely. From his body language on his home planet as he takes leave of his family, we assume he misses them. His plans to return with water get mislaid as he loses focus with too much gin and television, as has happened to many humans. It's hard to say what actual connection he feels with Mary-Lou. His personal style, reflected in his wardrobe, seems to be reality rotated through conscious design. He's curiously passive—not one of those aliens hell-bent on a mission, but a man almost dreamy at times.

As science fiction films go, this is a unique one. It focuses on character and implied ideas, not on plot and special effects. It's very much a product of the 1970s, when idiosyncratic directors deliberately tried to make great films. A production of this style is almost unthinkable today; it's too challenging and abstract for the Friday night mobs, and requires too much thought.

Nicolas Roeg was on a roll when he made this film in 1976. In 1970, his first film, *Performance*, also centered on a nontraditional role for a rock star, Mick Jagger. In 1971 he made the visionary *Walkabout*. In 1973 there was *Don't Look Now*, recently voted the best British film of all time. Then this.

It's slow going at times, and the plot isn't worthy of the performances. Too many shots of limousines and an unexplained big truck. Too many unfocused conversations in offices. I gave it 2 1/2 stars in 1976. That was about right. But I'm nudging it up to three stars for the 2011 rerelease. Star ratings are meaningless anyway, so consider this just a quiet protest vote against the way projects this ambitious are no longer possible in the mainstream movie industry.

## Margin Call ★ ★ ★ ½

R, 109 m., 2011

Kevin Spacey (Sam Rogers), Paul Bettany (Will Emerson), Jeremy Irons (John Tuld), Zachary Quinto (Peter Sullivan), Penn Badgley (Seth Bregman), Simon Baker (Jared Cohen), Mary McDonnell (Mary Rogers), Demi Moore (Sarah Robertson), Stanley Tucci (Eric Dale). Directed by J. C. Chandor and produced by Robert Ogden Barnum, Michael Benaroya, Neal Dodson, Joe Jenckes, Corey Moosa, and Zachary Quinto. Screenplay by Chandor.

It may have happened something like this. *Margin Call* depicts the last night of good times on Wall Street, as a deadly certainty travels up the executive ladder at an investment firm: Disastrous speculation in the mortgage markets is leading to the firm's collapse. We can still recall those days in the summer of 2008, during the Obama-McCain campaign, when America seemed awash in prosperity and the stock market was setting records. Then one firm after another was forced to declare bankruptcy, the nation's economic structure was threatened, and Congress ponied up its huge bailout.

*Margin Call* begins on a day at an unnamed investment firm that must certainly have an inkling of what's coming, since 80 percent of the workforce is laid off. One of the victims is Eric (Stanley Tucci), a senior risk analyst who, like many of his colleagues, was incapable of seeing that the real estate market was built as a house of cards. Although writer-director J. C. Chandor's film has sympathy for most of its characters, it is important to remember that they all felt they had to play along with the deals that were bringing their firms such huge profits and bonuses.

On his way out the door, Eric slips a USB drive to Peter (Zachary Quinto), a younger analyst who wasn't fired. There's information on it that disturbs Peter. So it should. While the office is empty and the survivors are out partying to celebrate not being fired, Peter realizes the firm and the market are clearly trembling on the brink. He contacts his supervisor Will (Paul Bettany), who takes one look and calls his boss Sam (Kevin Spacey). Others are called in for an all-night emergency meeting until at dawn a helicopter brings in the CEO, John (Jeremy Irons).

You don't need to understand a lot about the markets to follow the film. John is a cool, polished Brit who likes to say things like, "Speak to me in plain terms," because his job requires him to manage the corporation, but not necessarily understand its business. Indeed, as we now know, a fresh young college graduate could have looked at the balance sheets and clearly seen Wall Street was doomed.

It is up to John to make the margin call. In other words, to order his company to start dumping worthless holdings before the word spreads that they are worthless—essentially, betraying their customers. It has now been established that some firms created hedge funds *intended* to fail, so they could make money betting against them. These they sold to their customers knowing they were worthless.

I think the movie is about how its characters are concerned only with the welfare of their corporations. There is no larger sense of the public good. Corporations are amoral and exist to survive and succeed, at whatever human cost. It is this the Wall Street protesters are angry about: They are not against capitalism, but against Wall Street dishonesty and greed.

*Margin Call* employs an excellent cast who can turn financial talk into compelling dialogue. They can also reflect the enormity of what is happening: Their company and their lives are being rendered meaningless. This scenario was enacted at many Wall Street institutions in the autumn of 2008, and fundamental financial reform is still being opposed. No particular firm is named, but doesn't it seem to you that the name of the Jeremy Irons character, "John Tuld," has an echo of Richard Fuld, CEO of Lehman Brothers, who collected enormous bonuses for leading his company into bankruptcy?

Irons is sly in the role, a man who knows his own financial stability is unassailable, who considers his job as an amoral exercise, who has made it to the top by not particularly caring about people. A great corporate executive must have a strain of ruthlessness. I also admired Kevin Spacey, who projects incisive intelligence in his very manner, and Demi Moore, as a senior executive who has risen to just below the glass ceiling and knows she will stay there.

The physical world of the film itself is effective. It's all glass, steel, and protocol, long black cars and executive perks, luxurious lifestyles paid for with what was inescapably fraud. One of the characters has a sick dog. The dog is the only creature in the entire film that anyone likes.

## Marley ★ ★ ★ ½

PG-13, 144 m., 2012

A documentary featuring Bob Marley, Ziggy Marley, Cedella Marley, Rita Marley, Neville "Bunny Wailer" Livingston, Chris Blackwell. Directed by Kevin Macdonald and produced by Charles Steel.

At the time of Bob Marley's death in 1981, I was struck by how different the obituaries were from those of most musical stars. Due credit was given to such classic albums as *Burnin'* and many of his great hits were listed, but even then his memoirists were drawn to a wider frame. Marley was the most important Jamaican, a figure who stood above race and politics, who sang for the globe and at a time of racial upheaval and surging African independence sang the anthem "One Love" ("Let's get together and feel all right"). People of color and young people everywhere felt his passion.

*Marley*, an ambitious and comprehensive film, does what is probably the best possible job of documenting an important life. Authorized by all the members of his scattered family and with rights to all of his music and a wealth of previously unseen film and video footage, it shows the growth of a legend. What is interesting is that Marley seems not to have had a concrete goal for his career other than to use music to bring people together. His instincts were good and he followed them, and to an unusual degree he found independence in a white-ruled music industry.

Marley was born in 1945 in the hamlet of Nine Mile in Saint Ann Parish, Jamaica. Footage shows rude shacks, no electricity, staring barefoot children, and a sense of community. His mother, Cedella, was eighteen. His father, Norval Sinclair Marley, was sixty, a white captain in the Royal Marines. Norval married Cedella and provided cash support, but was all but unknown to the boy, who was bullied because of his mixed ancestry. It was his Rastafarian religion that helped him think above racial categories.

Using interviews from survivors of those years, *Marley* recalls how Bob began performing in grade school and recorded his first singles in 1962, with friends who were later to be part of his group, the Wailers. His mother got work as a hotel maid in Wilmington, Delaware, and musical history might have been different if he'd stayed in America, but after two visits he returned home, formed the Wailers with Bunny Wailer and Peter Tosh, and began to create the kind of music that attracted local and then world audiences. Underlying it was the reggae beat that was the foundation stone of modern Caribbean music.

With his longtime wife and frequent singing partner, Rita, he had three children and adopted two of hers. The film says he had eleven children in all. What is rather miraculous is that they all agreed to this film by Kevin Macdonald, and granted rights to his music. Contemporary footage shows his crowds swelling so rapidly that he was soon doing stadium concerts and traveling with a rock star entourage. Yet he remained concerned with Jamaica. He turned down offers to run for office, but returned to Jamaica at the height of a hard-fought election, bringing about the film's most powerful moment, when he brings two opposing politicians on stage to shake hands.

In 1977, Marley seems to have developed symptoms of malignant melanoma. He chose to overlook them, and a cancer that could have been treated in its early stages claimed him when he was only thirty-six.

The passages in the film showing his final years are tremendously touching. He began to seek treatment when it was already probably too late, and continued to tour even though his fans noted with concern his weight loss and increasingly frail appearance. Finally he went to a clinic in Switzerland, where the snow-covered mountains provided an alien landscape against which his death approached. The documentary talks to some of those who treated him and developed great affection for him; he had now become in a sense a secular saint. He flew to warmer weather in Miami, where he died on May 11, 1981.

This film has no great revelations and will start no scandals—if indeed there are any. It's a careful and respectful record of an important life, lived by a free spirit, whose "One Love" seems to be known in every land.

## Marmaduke ★ ★

PG, 87 m., 2010

Lee Pace (Phil Winslow), Judy Greer (Debbie Winslow), William H. Macy (Don Twombly). With the voices of: Owen Wilson (Marmaduke), Emma Stone (Mazie), George Lopez (Carlos), Christopher Mintz-Plasse (Giuseppe), Steve Coogan (Raisin), Stacy Ferguson (Jezebel), Kiefer Sutherland (Bosco). Directed by Tom Dey and produced by Dey and John Davis. Screenplay by Tim Rasmussen and Vince di Meglio, based on the comic strip by Brad Anderson and Phil Leeming.

Dogs cannot talk. This we know. Dogs can talk in the movies. This we also know. But when we see them lip-synching with their dialogue, it's just plain grotesque. The best approach is the one used by *Garfield* in which we saw the cat and heard Bill Murray, but there was no nonsense about Garfield's mouth moving.

The moment I saw Marmaduke's big drooling lips moving, I knew I was in trouble. There is nothing discreet about a Great Dane with a lot on his mind, especially when he's the narrator of the film and never shuts up. And when his master, Phil, moves the Winslow family from Kansas to Orange County and he joins the crowd at the dog park of a vegetarian pet food company, well, what can I say about a movie that has more speaking parts for dogs (and a cat) than for humans?

This is a congenial PG-rated animal comedy. If you like the comic strip, now in its fifty-sixth year, maybe you'll like it, maybe not. Marmaduke's personality isn't nearly as engaging as Garfield's. Then again, if personality is what you're in the market for, maybe you shouldn't be considering a lip-synched talking-animal comedy in the first place.

The plot. In California, Marmaduke likes his new backyard, but gets in hot water with his family for a dumb reason and runs away. Mazie, the collie he's been romancing at the park, goes searching for him, and it rains, and Marmaduke gets lost, and his family piles in the station wagon and searches, and—long story made short—they all end up where a burst sewer has caused a big sink hole (although not as big as the one in Guatemala). Mazie falls in, Marmaduke leaps in after her, they're swept into a sewer, they come out in an aqueduct, Phil Winslow (Lee Pace) leaps in, and so on and so forth.

Great Danes can be your best friends, but they are not gifted comedians. Mazie is typecast as a sexy collie; just once couldn't a pug play the female lead, in a little nontraditional casting? And speaking of that, what's with William H. Macy as the owner of the pet food company? If you admire Macy as I do, you can imagine dozens of ways he could be funny as a pet food tycoon. The movie sidesteps all of them and has him play the role right down the middle as a businessman. Then why hire Macy in the first place?

And then . . . but enough. Why am I writing, and why are you reading, a review of a talking-animal movie? Little kids may like it. It's not offensive. I don't find Marmaduke particularly photogenic, but that's just me. Great Danes look like they have extra elbows. The movie gets two stars. It could have done a little better if Marmaduke had kept his mouth shut.

## Martha Marcy May Marlene ★ ★ ★ ½

R, 101 m., 2011

Elizabeth Olsen (Martha), John Hawkes (Patrick), Sarah Paulson (Lucy), Hugh Dancy (Ted), Brady Corbet (Watts). Directed by Sean Durkin and produced by Antonio Campos, Patrick Cunningham, Chris Maybach, and Josh Mond. Screenplay by Durkin.

"Martha" is her name. "Marcy May" is the name given to her by the leader of a cult group. "Marlene" is the name all the women in the group use to answer the telephone. The cult occupies a white frame farmhouse in rural New York state, where there are many more women than men, and all of them are under the control of the leader, Patrick. That this man is compelling and charismatic helps explain his power; softly, gently, maintaining tight eye contact, he coaxes agreement from his followers, who are all damaged or vulnerable in some way.

Martha (Elizabeth Olsen) has had things go wrong earlier in her life. Their nature is left murky in this persuasive film. When she escapes the cult and picks up a phone to call her older married sister, Lucy (Sarah Paulson), we sense no joy when she hears Lucy's voice. Home is the place where, when you have to go there, they have to take you in. Lucy lives with her husband, Ted (Hugh Dancy), in a lakeside "cottage" large enough to be a bed-and-breakfast. Ted is a British architect, stuffed with pretension. Lucy is sensible and cares for Martha, but doesn't seem to pick up on how damaged the younger girl really is. Maybe there was not much closeness when they were all growing up.

The movie's timeline moves freely, sometimes with deliberate confusion, between the two years Martha spent on the farm and the present, on the lake with Lucy and Ted. We get the feeling that these two times are intermingled in her mind. She knows she has left the cult, she knows she is with her sister, but so deeply did Patrick indoctrinate and seduce her that he lives on, a presence in her mind. As small as the cult is and as large as the world is, it may be a long time before Martha feels safe anywhere.

Clearly she was unformed when she entered the cult. Her early life gave her an insecure self-image. First she was taught the sunny good things (working on the farm, preparing meals, caring for babies, meditating) and then, slowly, introduced to the bad ones (all the women are expected to sleep with Patrick). This is rape in the sense that they have no choice, but Patrick is so effective that they are mind-controlled into the illusion that it is their desire. Later, Martha even helps prepare another girl for the initiation. Group unanimity is the overarching reality; there is enormous pressure to fit in and go along. And it is very hard, Martha discovers, to leave.

She needs skilled help. Certainly she needs more insight than Ted and Lucy are prepared to provide. They treat her as if she's been "away" for her own loony reasons, and have little idea of her psychological earthquake. Ted in particular wants nothing to upset his narcissistic, affluent lifestyle. He didn't go to all the cost and trouble of building his dream house only to hear some girl observe it is way too big for two people.

Performances make a great contribution to the film's effectiveness. Elizabeth Olsen, a sister of the Olsen twins, is a genuine discovery here: childlike and yet deep, vulnerable but with a developing will, beautiful in a natural and unforced way. Her appeal reminds of Michelle Williams. She has a wide range of emotions to deal with here, and in her first major role she seems instinctively to know how to do that.

The other essential performance is by John Hawkes, as the cult leader. All of these types seem to have something. Charles Manson's followers became the puppets of his mind. Hawkes's performance is carefully modulated to convincingly suggest how a man might enlist your trust, then your love, and finally your will. He is so warmly seductive in early scenes with Martha that they could work as well if this were an actual love story. Add to the equation that Martha desperately needs a "home" and "parenting," and you see how he walks right into her mind.

I think it's a flaw that the film tries to draw parallels between the farm and the lake home. We gather Martha has been sold on the cult's lifestyle of subsistence (all the women sleep in the same room) and values (they have no shyness about nudity and sex), and that the crass materialism of her sister's life offends her. One wonders what she took with her to the farm, that only two years later she has changed enough she can casually crawl into bed with Lucy and Ted at the very moment when they seem to be sharing an orgasm. Martha, it's just not done. If she objects to the wealth around her, some of Patrick is still doing her thinking for her. Now that she's free she can find resources from her sister to relocate and rebuild.

In cutting back and forth in time, the first-time writer-director Sean Durkin is a shade too clever. In a serious film, there is no payoff for trickery. If the audience is momentarily confused about when and where they are, there should be a point. I suppose he's showing Martha's confusion about the nature of reality, and at the end there's an unsettling development. But a linear story, or one that was fragmented more clearly, could have been more effective.

Still, a good film, ambitious and effective, introducing a gifted young actress and a director whose work I'll anticipate. And Elizabeth Olsen can know that no one will ever ask, "Which one is she?"

## The Mechanic ★ ★

R, 92 m., 2011

Jason Statham (Arthur), Ben Foster (Steve), Donald Sutherland (Harry), Tony Goldwyn (Dean), Mini Anden (Sarah). Directed by Simon West and produced by Rene Besson, Robert Chartoff, John Thompson, David Winkler, Irwin Winkler, William Chartoff, Rob Cowan, Marcy Drogin, and Avi Lerner. Screenplay by Richard Wenk and Lewis John Carlino.

*The Mechanic* tells a story as old as *Hamlet* in a style as new as unbaked bread. What's the point? An intriguing plot is established, a new character is brought on with a complex set of problems, and then all the groundwork disintegrates into the usual hash of preposterous action sequences. Is there an action director left who knows it isn't all about the sound and the fury?

The movie is a remake of sorts of the 1972 Charles Bronson film, which seemed fairly good at the time and might only seem better today. It follows a cool professional killer, "The Mechanic" (Jason Statham), who works for a sinister killing corporation and specializes in murders that don't seem like murders or are deliberately misleading in other ways.

My guess is that in real life such operators are lonely, brutal, and tending toward paranoia. Statham's character, Arthur Bishop, on the other hand, is a hedonist and esthete who lives alone in elegance, prizes his classic car, and apparently believes a hooker isn't a hooker if you overpay her. For twenty bucks, you're buying sex, but for thousands you are identifying yourself as a consumer of the highest degree.

Bishop is, then, a worthless creature who prizes himself highly. It is assumed we make no moral judgment on his murders because nothing in this film has human meaning and few of its viewers will expect any. It's all an exercise in technique. George Clooney played a similar character in *The American*, an infinitely superior film that was also about an untraceable solo killer working for a murder corporation. But that film was fascinated by the Clooney character, whose attempts to deal with sex without feeling got him into trouble.

There are two human elements in *The Mechanic*. Donald Sutherland plays another killer under contract to the same company—a veteran in this line of work, who is wise and bearded and was Bishop's mentor. This would be touching if their field was science or the law, but less so since their field is killing people for money. That we are expected to be moved by what are presented as Sutherland's ethical instincts is a peculiarity best not meditated upon. The fact is that Sutherland pulls it off on the surface level, and brings more humanity than the character deserves.

The other character is Steve (Ben Foster), the son of a character I will not name. Bishop has killed this man, the son doesn't know that, and Bishop takes the kid under his arm and teaches him the theory and practice of the trade. Steve has problems with immaturity, substance abuse, and other issues that the suave, shaven Bishop is a stranger to, but Bishop works with him and has faith that the young man will grow up into a killer to make his father proud.

The film is well made by Simon West (*Tomb Raiders*), a technician in the tradition of Michael Winner, who made the Bronson film. Directors like this must be very good, regardless of whether their films are worth making in the first place. Audiences have been drilled to accept noise and movement as entertainment. It is done so well one almost forgets to ask why it has been done at all.

## Meek's Cutoff ★ ★ ★ ½

PG, 104 m., 2011

Michelle Williams (Emily Tetherow), Bruce Greenwood (Stephen Meek), Paul Dano (Thomas Gately), Zoe Kazan (Millie Gately), Will Patton (Solomon Tetherow), Shirley Henderson (Glory White), Neal Huff (William White), Tommy Nelson (Jimmy White), Rod Rondeaux (The Indian). Directed by Kelly Reichardt and produced by Elizabeth Cuthrell, Neil Kopp, Anish Savjani, and David Urrutia. Screenplay by Jon Raymond.

To set aside its many other accomplishments, *Meek's Cutoff* is the first film I've seen that evokes what must have been the reality of wagon trains to the West. They were grueling, dirty, thirsty, burning, and freezing ordeals. Attacks by Indians were not the greatest danger; accidents and disease were. Over the years from movie Westerns I've developed a composite image of wagon trains as Conestoga parades led by John Wayne, including lots of women wearing calico dresses, and someone singing "Red River Valley" beside the campfire.

Not here. Director Kelly Reichardt's strategy is to isolate her story in the vastness of the Oregon Trail, where personalities seem to weaken in the force of the wilderness. She shows three families who bring reality to Robert Frost's phrase "vaguely realizing westward." They are gradually understanding that they are hopelessly lost. Their guide, Stephen Meek (Bruce Greenwood), boasts of his accomplishments, but members of the group sense that he is pushing ahead blindly in the hope that somehow the way through the Cascade Mountains will reveal itself.

The group includes Emily Tetherow (Michelle Williams), her husband, Solomon (Will Patton), the young couple Millie and Thomas Gately (Zoe Kazan and Paul Dano), and the Whites: Glory, William, and Jimmy (Shirley Henderson, Neal Huff, and Tommy Nelson). In their wagons they bring a few household furnishings, some clothes, and a forlorn bird in a cage, whose pathetic smallness echoes their own in this landscape. The men withdraw to discuss their mistrust of Meek, and it is significant that Reichardt identifies with the women as they attempt to overhear what's said.

Her focus in general is on the "womenfolk," as Westerns liked to call them. She centers on Michelle Williams as Emily, and of course Reichardt and Williams worked together on *Wendy and Lucy*, the evocative 2008 film about a drifter and her dog. Both films were written by Jonathan Raymond. Michelle Williams appears at first to be a slight, unprepossessing person, but in *Meek's Cutoff* she then reveals inner certainty. She is sure their guide is lost, she is certain they face death by thirst, and it is she who determines how they must use an Indian (Rod Rondeaux) they capture: He will find water.

The Indian, first seen alone on a high ledge watching them, is portrayed in a particular way. Unlike the fierce close-ups of Indian warriors we've been trained on in many Westerns, he is an enigmatic man, self-contained, observing, mostly held in the film's usual long and medium shots. We don't know what he's thinking. Why should we? In circa 1845, the two races were alien to each other.

At a time when many directors fall contentedly into the rhythm of a standard visual language, Reichardt devises a strategy that suggests the distance and isolation of these travelers. This is the first new feature film I've seen in a long time that has been photographed in the 1:1.33 screen ratio (as all movies were before the early 1950s). That's the ratio of many, maybe most, classic Westerns, but we expect widescreen these days, and her frame encloses her characters—not in the landscape (it appears limitless) but in their dilemma. They are such a small, helpless group, bound up with their hopes and fears. Imagine what it involved 165 years ago to set out in an ox-drawn covered wagon and trek across a continent in search of rumors.

I'm sure the women of the period wore hooded sunbonnets. They're always seen that way in Westerns. But Hollywood costume departments made sure the bonnets didn't obscure the famous faces of their stars (Joanne Dru, for example). The bonnets in *Meek's Cutoff* bury faces deep in shadow, are hard to see into, and must create tunnel vision. They not only protect women, but limit them. The men are also hidden; Meek's biblical beard and the deep shadow of his hat make him concealed and enigmatic.

The distinctive thing here is the subservience of the characters to the landscape. These pioneers do not stand astride the land; they wander it in misery and exhaustion. The wheels of their wagons are little match for the terrain. There is a heartbreaking accident. The peeps of the caged bird become a mocking reminder of the domesticity they've left behind.

*Meek's Cutoff* is more an experience than a story. It has personality conflicts, but isn't about them. The suspicions and angers of the group are essentially irrelevant to their overwhelming reality. Reichardt has the courage to establish that. She doesn't make it easy for us with simplistic character conflict. She's genuinely curious about the hardly educated pioneers who were brave, curious, or hopeful enough to set out on such a dangerous journey. It goes without saying that they had nothing to keep them home where they started from. Many started from hopelessness and died on the journey toward hope. Or wandered in the mountains. I learn that *Meek's Cutoff* was based on a true story. I didn't need to be told that.

*Note: Although you'll see the movie in 1:1.33, Steve Kraus of the Lake Street Projection Room in Chicago writes me: "It was true 1.37:1 Academy Ratio. By 'true' I mean similar on-screen results could be had by pillar boxing 1.33 within the conventional cropped widescreen 1.85:1 aperture, which would make it easier for mainstream theaters to show such films correctly, but* Meeks *was the real deal, in the format of films from before the widescreen era. Correct lenses and aperture plates are required to show."*

*Of course, Steve has the lenses and plates. If you see this movie projected in widescreen, it is being projected wrongly.*

## Megamind ★ ★ ★

PG, 95 m., 2010

With the voices of Will Ferrell (Megamind), Tina Fey (Roxanne Ritchi), Jonah Hill (Hal/Tighten), David Cross (Minion), Brad Pitt (Metro Man). Directed by Tom McGrath and produced by Lara Breay and Denise Nolan Cascino. Screenplay by Alan Schoolcraft and Brent Simons.

*Megamind* was the third 3-D movie I'd seen in a row, and as I struggled to free my glasses from their industrial-strength plastic envelope, I wasn't precisely looking forward to it. Why do 3-D glasses and DVDs come so securely wrapped they seem like acts of hostility against the consumer? Once I freed my glasses and settled down, however, I was pleased to see a 3-D image that was quite acceptable. Too dim, as always, but the process was well used and proves again that animation is incomparably more suited for 3-D than live action is.

I'd just been rewatching *Superman* (1978), and felt right at home with the opening, narrated by a bright blue alien over flashbacks to his infancy. Born on a distant planet, he's packed into a rocket ship and blasted off to Earth, just like the Man of Steel. En route he meets his lifetime nemesis, a golden child who also lands on Earth in the lap of wealth. The blue child, alas, lands in a prison and is raised by hardened convicts.

As they grow up, these two super beings are destined to play crucial roles in nearby Metro City, where they're named Megamind (voice by Will Ferrell) and Metro Man (Brad Pitt). We may remember that Superman was given his name by Lois Lane, and here the story of the two super beings is covered by a TV reporter named Roxanne Ritchi (Tina Fey). Roxanne's cameraman Hal (Jonah Hill, looking rather Jonah Hill-like) later morphs into yet a third super being named Tighten.

This setup is bright and amusing, even if it does feel recycled from bits and pieces of such recent animated landmarks as *The Incredibles* with its superpowers and *Despicable Me* with its villain. *Megamind* even goes so far as naming Megamind's fishy sidekick Minion (David Cross), a nod to the Minions who serve the despicable Gru. I enjoyed Megamind's conclusion, after being bullied as a child, that if he can't get credit for doing anything good he might as well become a villain.

It is a truth universally acknowledged that a hero requires a villain, and *Megamind* has some fun by depriving Megamind of Metro Man. Left without an opponent, he loses his zeal for evildoing, and actually clones Tighten to cure his loneliness. All of this of course is accomplished with much slapstick and sensational action, in a population that consists entirely of super beings, plus Roxanne, the prison warden, and cheering thousands of anonymous humans.

Tina Fey does a spirited job with Roxanne, and again I was reminded of *Superman* and Margot Kidder's high-spirited, unafraid Lois Lane. This time Roxanne isn't smitten by anyone, which is just as well because these guys are aliens, after all.

*Megamind* is an amusing family entertainment and gains some energy from clever dialogue and the fun Will Ferrell has with his character. I like the way he pronounced Metro City like "metricity," for example. The 3-D is well done, if unnecessary. Nothing in the movie really benefits from it, and if you can find it in 2-D that's the best choice. Save the surcharge and see those colors nice and bright.

## Melancholia ★ ★ ★ ½

R, 135 m., 2011

Kirsten Dunst (Justine), Charlotte Gainsbourg (Claire), Kiefer Sutherland (John), Alexander Skarsgaard (Michael), Stellan Skarsgaard (Jack), Jesper Christensen (Little Father), Charlotte Rampling (Gaby), John Hurt (Dexter), Udo Kier (Wedding Planner), Cameron Spurr (Leo), Brady Corbet (Tim). Directed by Lars von Trier and produced by Meta Louise Foldager and Louise Vesth. Screenplay by von Trier.

Lars von Trier's *Melancholia* opens with music from Wagner's *Tristan und Isolde*, mourning and apocalyptic, and disturbing images of a world not right. A woman dressed as a bride runs through a forest whose branches seem to grab at her in a Disney nightmare. She floats in a pond, holding flowers, like Ophelia. Another woman makes her way with a child over marshy grass that sucks at her. Looming in the sky is another planet, vast in size. The earth is about to end.

These scenes are isolated prologue. As time begins to run, we meet a newlywed couple being driven to their wedding party at a grand estate. It is a small gathering, only large enough to establish that few in this family can abide one another, and some may be mad. The bride is Justine (Kirsten Dunst). Her husband is Michael (Alexander Skarsgaard). Her sister is Claire (Charlotte Gainsbourg). Their estranged parents are Gaby (Charlotte Rampling) and Dexter (John Hurt). The mansion is owned by the brother-in-law John (Keifer Sutherland). Joining the party is Jack (Stellan Skarsgaard), Justine's boss, who owns an ad agency and is attending primarily to wrest an advertising tagline from her. The wedding planner is played by the ominous Udo Kier, who you will agree is correctly cast to run a wedding at the end of the world.

Not much of an attempt is made to fashion these people into a plot anything like a wedding party you've seen in a movie before. Even when the bride steals out of her husband's bed to have rough sex in the sand trap of a golf course, there is no sense of intrigue, just a desperate acting out. Every moment is saturated with the common knowledge that Earth is about to collide with an enormous planet named Melancholia. I'm not sure if the planet has been officially named, or if the name simply attached itself. One thinks of Robert Burton's book *The Anatomy of Melancholy*, published in 1621, which marshaled all the arts and sciences known to him into a study of what we could call clinical depression.

The new planet is first seen by Justine as they pause on their way to the party. It is the brightest of the evening stars. During an undefined period of days it will grow larger and larger, until it fills the sky. Curiously, the characters do not spend all of their time talking about it, and we pick up little information about when it was first seen. Von Trier limits himself entirely to the meandering conversations at the house party. He avoids all the usual sci-fi clichés; there are no TV news updates, no Cabinet meetings, no nuclear rockets fired at it, no surging mobs in the streets. It looms larger. It "appeared from behind the sun."

If I were choosing a director to make a film about the end of the world, von Trier the gloomy Dane might be my first choice. The only other name that comes to mind is Werner Herzog's. Both understand that at such a time silly little romantic subplots take on a vast irrelevance. Doctor Johnson told Boswell: "Depend upon it, sir, when a man knows he is to be hanged in a fortnight, it concentrates his mind wonderfully." In the cast of von Trier's characters, impending doom seems to have created a mental state of dazed detachment. They continue to act as if their personal concerns have the slightest relevance. Von Trier has never made a more realistic domestic drama, depicting a family that is dysfunctional not in crazy ways but in ways showing a defiant streak of intelligent individualism.

The film is divided into two halves, titled "Justine" and "Claire." It appears that the two sisters exchange personalities, but to no great effect. Maybe the approach of an overwhelming event has dissolved the membranes of personalities. Notice how Jack, the ad man, continues to place importance on his ad slogan. And how Gaby lashes out at the very notion of a wedding or a party. There is displacement here that is frightening.

In any film involving the destruction of the globe, we know that, if it is not to be saved, there must be a "money shot" depicting the actual cataclysm. I doubt any could do better than von Trier does here. There are no tidal waves. No animals fleeing through burning forests. No skyscrapers falling. None of that easy stuff. No, there is simply a character standing on a hill and staring straight at the impending doom, as von Trier shows it happening in what logically must be slow motion, with a fearsome preliminary merging of planetary atmospheres.

Violent death is often a shabby business in the movies. It happens in depressing bedrooms, bloody bathtubs, shattered cars, bleak alleys. Its victims are cast down empty of life. Here is a character who says, "I see it coming, I will face it, I will not turn away, I will observe it as long as my eyes and my mind still function." Is it fair of me to speculate that von Trier himself regards death in that way? He tends to be grandiose, but if one cannot be grandiose in imagining one's own death, then when is grandiosity justified?

## Men in Black 3 ★ ★ ★

PG-13, 103 m., 2012

Will Smith (Agent J), Tommy Lee Jones (Agent K), Josh Brolin (Young Agent K), Jemaine Clement (Boris the Animal), Michael Stuhlbarg (Griffin), Emma Thompson (Agent O). Directed by Barry Sonnenfeld and produced by Laurie MacDonald and Walter F. Parkes. Screenplay by Etan Cohen, inspired by the comic book by Lowell Cunningham.

*Men in Black 3* comes fifteen years after the entertaining original and ten years after the sequel laid an egg, and the surprise is it's better than the first one. Given the passage of time, the entire concept may be new to some audience members, but it still does service: There is a secret agency assigned to keeping track of all aliens on Earth, and there are as many of them as makeup expert Rick Baker can possibly devise. I am not sure how undercover an MiB agent can be when he dresses exactly like the Blues Brothers, but never mind, they get the job done.

The story until now: Veteran Agent K (Tommy Lee Jones) and his younger recruit Agent J (Will Smith) are under the supervision of Agent O (Emma Thompson) when there's an emergency. The hideously ugly alien Boris the Animal (Jemaine Clement) has escaped from a maximum security prison on the moon. He is the last surviving member of his race and still angry because Agent K shot off one of his arms. His plan: Travel back in time and kill Agent K before that can happen.

An arm like his, you don't want to lose. Its palm apparently serves as a condo for a nasty little insectoid creature that will leap over and take chunks out of you. Indeed, Boris is one of those aliens whose entire body seems to contain openings from which unappetizing things can forage on his victims.

Time travel can become very complicated. To make it simple: Agent J (Will Smith, you remember) tries to travel back in time to prevent Boris the Animal from killing K. This results in a young K existing in the same time period as J, who is the same age he started as, so the old man and the rookie are now contemporaries.

How this is achieved is the movie's most impressive achievement. Young Agent K is played, not by Tommy Lee Jones in prosthetic makeup, but by Josh Brolin. The casting is spot-on. He looks like a young Tommy Lee Jones, and he sounds so uncannily like him that director Barry Sonnenfeld, hearing him, allegedly shed tears of relief. While watching the movie, I was convinced Jones dubbed his own voice. But remember, Brolin was also a good soundalike for George W. Bush in *W.*

Anyway, Agent J travels back to save Agent K, and not content to populate the film with countless gob-smacking aliens from Rick Baker's fertile imagination, Sonnenfeld and his writers also show a Hitchcockian flair for using iconic locations. For reasons I don't understand, in order to return to the "present," it's necessary to fall from a very great height and push a button on a gizmo at the last second. This involves Agent J crawling out on one of those medieval-looking eagles atop the Chrysler building, something you can imagine Hitch assigning Cary Grant to do.

A virtuoso final sequence takes place at the (then named) Cape Kennedy on the day of the first moon-landing attempt. Another gizmo must be placed on the moon to save humanity, and this involves a last-minute attempt to crawl out to the Apollo 11 pilot capsule, slap on the gizmo, and escape using one of those chutes provided for the astronauts in case of an emergency. Since the first moon launch was telecast with many TV cameras and scrutinized by countless binoculars, it seems unlikely this would have gone unnoticed. Maybe there's a loophole—like if the attempt succeeds, it changes the future and turns out to be unnecessary.

Whatever. The movie gets comic relief from a sidekick character named Griffin (Michael Stuhlbarg), who wears a knitted Elmer Fudd hat and has the ability to see all the possible variations resulting from various events during time travel. "Uh-oh," he's always saying, "this is the one where . . ."

Let me say that although I liked the first MiB movie, I wasn't particularly looking forward to this belated sequel. But I had fun. It has an ingenious plot, bizarre monsters, audacious cliff-hanging, and you know what? A closing scene that adds a new and sort of touching dimension to the characters of J and K.

## Mercy ★ ★

NO MPAA RATING, 87 m., 2010

Scott Caan (John Ryan), Wendy Glenn (Mercy Bennett), Troy Garity (Dane), John Boyd (Erik), James Caan (Gerry Ryan), Dylan McDermott (Jake). Directed by Patrick Hoelck and produced by Scott Caan, Vince Palomino, and Phil Parmet. Screenplay by Caan.

I have a problem with movies about men whom women cannot resist. If a man knows that, how did he find it out? By succeeding with one woman after another? If he's thirty-five, never been married, and doesn't like to date the same woman twice, he probably has a problem, and he probably *is* a problem. Even in a town as big as Los Angeles, word would get around. You wouldn't want to be the woman watched by everyone in the room to see if you fall for the Irresistible Man.

John Ryan is apparently such a man. Played by Scott Caan as a man who is surgical in his focus, he sees, decides, and moves in. He seems to succeed. If the woman is gone when he wakes up in the morning, that was a successful date. If they go to his place, they can't even feel a kindly urge to help him clean up a messy bachelor pad. Unless there is a toothbrush in the bathroom, there seems to be nothing in his apartment that didn't come with the demonstration unit.

One night at a party his moves don't work. It must be said he uses hopelessly outdated lines. When a man says, "You are the most beautiful woman I have ever seen," a woman should reply: "I know. But why would that make me want to sleep with you?" At the party, where he has already lined up a date with a waitress, he zeroes in on Mercy Bennett

(Wendy Glenn), a classy woman with a British accent. "Mercy?" he asks. "Is that a joke?" He explains that (*cough*) the party is in his honor.

He thought it might be a joke because his new novel is named *Mercy*. He chats her up, gets nowhere, and the next day is horrified to read Mercy Bennett's review of the novel. She hated, hated, hated it. He's intrigued. He calls her up and asks her to meet, not for a date, but for a talk about the book. (It doesn't occur to him, then or ever, that if she reviewed his book and was invited to the party she probably knew who he was.)

These scenes are in the half of the film titled "Before." It also establishes his married best friend (Troy Garity) and his agent (Dylan McDermott). There is his lovelorn pal Erik (John Boyd), whose own girl is manifestly trying to dump him. John tutors Erik on the theory and practice of picking up women and dumping them.

In the film's second half, titled "After," we meet a changed John Ryan. He hasn't been shaving, he's deeply depressed, for the first time in years he goes to visit his father (James Caan), an English professor. His dad says he hasn't read his books, which is probably as well; he writes "romance novels" and, as we have seen, knows nothing about romance. Father and son share the same jaundiced view of women. The apple has not fallen far from the tree.

The time shifting (in a screenplay written by Scott Caan) may leave you adrift at times. There are flash-forwards, flashbacks, and possibly imagined scenes. The point is the same. They add up to a playboy getting his comeuppance. This story arc is predictable and not very satisfying, and the film's strengths are in the performances. Scott Caan is effective as a heartless creep, Wendy Glenn is devastating as a woman so assured she can perform verbal emasculation, and James Caan relates with his (own) son in scenes that inspire speculation the screenplay might be a little autobiographical.

What's lacking is a little more depth. This is a movie that covers a lot of distance in only eighty-seven minutes. We know the basics: The pickup artist gets hurt and becomes sadder but wiser. What we'd like to know is more about the people, especially Mercy Bennett. She never has a scene without Ryan. The women in the film don't seem to talk to one another about him, or themselves. And how does a bad novelist become a good one at the age of thirty-five after one life-changing experience?

## Mesrine: Killer Instinct ★ ★ ★ ½

R, 113 m., 2010

Vincent Cassel (Jacques Mesrine), Cecile de France (Jeanne Schneider), Gerard Depardieu (Guido), Roy Dupuis (Jean-Paul Mercier), Gilles Lellouche (Paul), Elena Anaya (Sofia). Directed by Jean-Francois Richet and produced by Thomas Langmann. Screenplay by Abdel Raouf Dafri.

Jacques Mesrine was a brutal man who shot dead thirty-nine victims during his twenty-year run as a bank robber and kidnapper. That total doesn't include the prisoners, possibly dozens, he executed point-blank after they'd been tortured during France's war against Algeria. He escaped from two high-security prisons, kidnapped a millionaire, broke back into one of the prisons in an attempt to free his friends, and went on the lam in Quebec, Arizona, and Florida.

Yes, but he was a particularly French criminal who claimed he was an anarchist, protested prison conditions, described all his killings as acts of revolution against the state, and wrote two best-sellers that were compared by some to Camus. When he was France's Public Enemy Number One and every police officer in the nation was participating in a manhunt, he granted exclusive interviews and wrote tender love poems to his lawyer.

This is too much man for one movie, and so he has gotten two, *Mesrine: Killer Instinct* and *Mesrine: Public Enemy No. 1*. They're rolling out one after the other in North America, which usually doesn't work at the box office, but *Killer Instinct* ends with his car trapped behind a truck when its back canvas goes up and French cops open fire, killing his girlfriend, Jeanne Schneider (Cecile de France), and his dog, and wounding him fourteen times in the chest and head. Only wounding him? Yes, and then the screen promises *Mesrine: Public Enemy No. 1.* (I'm assuming he wasn't murdered; if he was, the second movie would have to be in reverse chronology or extremely slow motion.)

Mesrine, played with rough intensity by Vincent Cassel, was the most famous criminal in French history, and he came to that role only late in his career, after he was already famous in Canada and the United States. The Montreal papers called him and Jeanne "the French Bonnie and Clyde," he outdid Dillinger by robbing two banks across the street from each other within ten minutes, and like Dillinger he was an expert in self-publicity. Was the police ambush an assassination attempt? The police denied it, but he predicted it, and he promised he would never be taken without gunfire. He was known as a master of disguise, moved boldly in public when his face was on every TV screen, and in a touch too good for fiction, he took Jeanne to Cape Kennedy to watch the Apollo moon launch.

Jean-Francois Richet's *Mesrine: Killer Instinct* has parallels with Michael Mann's *Public Enemies*, particularly in the suggestion that both men began to feed on their publicity. They walk into banks almost as celebrities making guest appearances. But Dillinger tried to stay out of shooting situations, and Mesrine seemed addicted to danger. He wrote a newspaper explaining that after he committed his first robbery he felt free because he had crossed a line separating him from control of the state. He declared war, and when authorities raided his apartment they found an arsenal, including automatic weapons and grenades.

Vincent Cassel in his forties is France's leading hard-boiled actor. Have you seen *The Crimson Rivers, Read My Lips, Irreversible*, or *Eastern Promises*? As Mesrine he affects the sideburns and mustache of a bad guy who studies himself in the mirror and doesn't know his look isn't working. He makes Mesrine self-absorbed, arrogant, and detached from the meaning of his murders. He depends on the charisma of his evil to attract women, and it does—although it didn't work for his first wife, the mother of his two children. Well, he wasn't very famous then. Unlike some American stars, Cassel makes no attempt to protect his image. Gaspar Noe's *Irreversible*, in particular, would be unthinkable for most of them. In it Cassel stars in a story I described as "so violent and cruel that most people will find it unwatchable."

Don't get the wrong idea. Cassel isn't his characters. He also plays nice guys and did the voice of the French hoodlum in *Shrek*. Here he even seems a sympathetic underdog until you reflect he has chosen the role for himself and murdered innocent people along his road to romance. He had an ordinary enough start in life, but then was attracted to the petty criminals who infest the Paris district called Clignancourt—that's where the tourists go to shop in *les puces*, the flea market. By then, his father believed, he had already been morally destroyed by his experiences in Algeria.

Yes, but some people become addicted to being bad. If you're trained as a paratrooper, you don't routinely seek work as a torturer and executioner. Mesrine seems to have had little concept of other people; life for him perhaps contained no more emotion than a point-and-shoot video game. The director Richet, who made the Ethan Hawke–Laurence Fishburne *Assault on Precinct 13* (2005), treats him as an insect more than a psychological case study.

The acting is macho understatement. Mesrine is a character who might have been played years ago by Gerard Depardieu, who appears here as Guido, a bullet-headed impresario of larceny. The two are business partners, not friends, and there's the suggestion none of his underworld pals understand the depth of Mesrine's pathology. They know they're bad guys, but Jacques takes it to another level.

*Note: I obtained information on Mesrine from an article by John Lichfield in the* Independent.

## Mesrine: Public Enemy No. 1 ★ ★ ★ ½

R, 133 m., 2010

Vincent Cassel (Jacques Mesrine), Ludivine Sagnier (Sylvie Jeanjacquot), Mathieu Amalric (Francois Besse), Samuel Le Bihan (Michel Ardouin), Gerard Lanvin (Charlie Bauer), Olivier Gourmet (Commissaire Broussard), Anne Consigny (L'avocate de Mesrine). Directed by Jean-Francois Richet and produced by Thomas Langmann, Maxime

Remillard, and Andre Rouleau. Screenplay by Abdel Raouf Dafri.

Because *Mesrine: Public Enemy No. 1* covers essentially the same material in the same style as *Mesrine: Killer Instinct*, there's not much to add in reviewing the second film of the pair. There are some personnel changes; Ludivine Sagnier replaces Cecile de France as the woman in Mesrine's life, Mathieu Amalric appears as a jumpy accomplice, the stout-hearted Olivier Gourmet is the prosecutor, and Anne Consigny is the attorney he has much need of. She was the one he wrote love poetry to.

The central enigma remains the same: Jacques Mesrine was born in a stable middle-class home, well educated, then sent to Algeria as a paratrooper who soon became a torturer and executioner and found he liked the work. He escaped from four prisons, killed perhaps forty people, kidnapped in France and Quebec, and stuck up banks the way other people use ATM machines.

Women were inexplicably willing to commit themselves to him. *Killer Instinct* ended with Mesrine and Sylvie being sprayed with a hail of police bullets, and *Public Enemy No. 1* opens with the same ambush. Since Mesrine was always heavily armed and had promised he would not be taken alive, Sylvie must, or should, have known that being attached to him placed her in the fire zone. Why did she do it? Was it love? After the gunfire, she doesn't even look to see what happened to Jacques, but starts screaming at the cops because they killed her dog.

Both of these films are directly and forcibly made, and indeed won Cesars for best director (Jean-Francois Richet) and best actor (Vincent Cassel). They have an impact recalling the days when gangster movies and action pictures in general had a meaty realism and weren't weakened by absurd CGI. No cars, guns, or people do anything here that cars, guns, and people cannot do in real life. If there's ever a film titled *Bourne vs. Mesrine*, the bout will end in the first round and the crown will return to Paris.

Vincent Cassel is the overwhelming fact of both films. He doesn't give Mesrine great depth, because how can he? The man was a psychopath, immune to movie psychology. But he gives him great presence. He is brutal, ugly, powerful, and inscrutable. In other roles Cassel is none of those things; he looks nice when he smiles. But he finds such cold ferocity in Mesrine that he's like a wild animal who kills for survival. I don't think Mesrine likes killing. He just frequently has to.

A great many bullets are fired by Mesrine, who stands up from behind parked cars and starts shooting at the cops in full view. In most movies we know the police bullets will never find their target. With Mesrine (1) sometimes they do, and (2) in real life, he survived an incredible twenty years with the police firing at him at least annually.

Cassel speaks excellent English and appears in many English-language films. Hollywood seems in need of a credible new action star, one who isn't worn out by trekking down red carpets. Here's the man.

## Micmacs ★ ★ ½

R, 104 m., 2010

Dany Boon (Bazil), Andre Dussollier (De Fenouillet), Omar Sy (Remington), Dominique Pinon (Buster), Julie Ferrier (Elastic Girl), Nicolas Marie (Francois Marconi), Marie-Julie Baup (Calculator), Michel Cremades (Tiny Pete), Yolande Moreau (Mama Chow), Jean-Pierre Marielle (Slammer). Directed by Jean-Pierre Jeunet and produced by Jeunet, Frederic Brillion, and Giles Legrand. Screenplay by Jeunet and Guillaume Laurant.

Here's a movie with visual invention and imagination up the wazoo. *Micmacs* is a whimsical fantasy about how a weapons manufacturer is set upon by a man with a bullet in his head and a motley crew of weirdos who live in a cave inside a junkyard. It may be a little too much for one meal.

I say this with reluctance, because this kind of visual energy is rarely found in the movies. I should be grateful for the change after several recent films in which the camera freezes in its tracks and stares stupefied at the action. I suppose I am. But the invention upstages the story without seeming necessary to it.

The director is Jean-Pierre Jeunet. Recall his magical *Amelie* (2001) and *A Very Long Engagement* (2004) and you'll understand its fancies. Recall his *The City of Lost Children* (1995) and you'll understand its problems. In an age when special effects can show us almost anything, there can come a tipping point when a movie is essentially only showing off. I'm not flatly against that, but in general I like to delude myself that the story is in the foreground. It's a judgment call. You may enjoy *Micmacs* more than I did.

The story is about a sad-sack clerk in a video store, named Bazil (Dany Boon). His father was killed with a land mine. As a child, opening a box of his father's effects, he finds the trademark of the manufacturer. He grows up into a feckless young man who passes his time in the video store by reciting the dialogue of movies in synch. One day, after a series of, shall we say, improbable events, he's shot in the middle of the forehead. The bullet lodges. The doc flips a coin and decides to leave it in, even though he could die at any moment.

Naturally, he's replaced at work. He's taken under the wing of a band of scavengers who live in a sort of Aladdin's Cave inside a mound of junk. This may sound sordid, but it's not. Imagine steampunk heaven. These people have the resources of a troupe of itinerant troubadours. They could start their own circus.

There's the contortionist named Elastic Girl (Julie Ferrier). The Guinness book–obsessed type named Buster (Dominique Pinon). A master thief named Slammer (Jean-Pierre Marielle), perhaps because of where he's spent a lot of time. A woman Calculator (Marie-Julie Baup), whose mind does mathematical wonders. A sage from the Congo (Omar Sy), who speaks Fortune Cookie. And Mama Chow (Yolande Moreau), who feeds and mothers them. Oh, and a human cannonball.

These oddballs enlist in Bazil's cause so quickly he hardly realizes he has a cause, and conspire with him to destroy the enterprises of the munitions experts. They zero in on the chief malefactor, Nicolas Thibault de Fenouillet (Andre Dussollier), and conspire against him with schemes so improbably labyrinthine that Rube Goldberg would have advised them to dial down.

The production values of the film are splendid. Jeunet's camera is so liberated that *Micmacs* might as well be animated. But there's a lack of urgency. The characters seem defined by the requirements of the plot. Dany Boon, in the lead, seems to be mostly along for the ride. The villain de Fenouillet is the most compelling character, particularly because of his fondness for collecting spare parts from the cadavers of evil men.

I look at a film like this and must respect it for its ingenuity and love of detail. Then I remember *Amelie* and its heroine played by Audrey Tautou, and I understand what's wrong: There's nobody in the story who much makes us care.

## Midnight in Paris ★ ★ ★ ½

PG-13, 94 m., 2011

Owen Wilson (Gil), Rachel McAdams (Inez), Kathy Bates (Gert), Adrien Brody (Salvador), Carla Bruni (Museum Guide), Marion Cotillard (Adriana), Michael Sheen (Paul). Directed by Woody Allen and produced by Letty Aronson, Jaume Roures, and Stephen Tenenbaum. Screenplay by Allen.

This review contains spoilers.

Oh, yes it does, because I can't imagine a way to review *Midnight in Paris* without discussing the delightful fantasy at the heart of Woody Allen's new comedy. The trailers didn't give it away, but now the reviews from Cannes have appeared and the cat is pretty much out of the bag. If you're still reading, give yourself a fair chance to guess the secret by reading through the list of character names in the credits. "Gert." Which resident of Paris does that make you think of?

This film is sort of a daydream for American lit majors. It opens with a couple on holiday in Paris with her parents. Gil (Owen Wilson) and Inez (Rachel McAdams) are officially in love, but maybe what Gil really loves is Paris in the springtime. He's a hack screenwriter from Hollywood who still harbors the dream of someday writing a good novel and joining the pantheon of American writers whose ghosts seem to linger in the very air he breathes: Fitzgerald, Hemingway, and the other legends of Paris in the 1920s.

He'd like to live in Paris. Inez would like to live in an upper-class American suburb, like her parents. He evokes poetic associations with every café where Hemingway might once have had a Pernod, and she likes to go shopping.

One night he wanders off by himself, gets lost, sits on some church steps, and as a bell rings midnight, a big old Peugeot pulls up filled with revelers. They invite him to join their party. They include Scott and Zelda Fitzgerald.

Allen makes no attempt to explain this magic. None is needed. Nor do we have to decide if what happens is real or imaginary. It doesn't matter. Gil is swept along in their wake, and finds himself plunged into the Jazz Age and all its legends. His novel was going to be about a man who ran a nostalgia shop, and here he is in the time and place he's most nostalgic for.

Some audience members might be especially charmed by *Midnight in Paris.* They would be those familiar with Fitzgerald, Hemingway, Gertrude Stein, and Alice B. Toklas, and the artists who frequented Stein's famous salon: Picasso, Dali, Cole Porter, Man Ray, Luis Buñuel, and, yes, "Tom Eliot." Allen assumes some familiarity with their generation, and some moviegoers will be mystified because cultural literacy is not often required at the movies anymore. Others will be as charmed as I was. Zelda is playfully daffy, Scott is in love with her and doomed by his love, and Hemingway speaks always in formal sentences of great masculine portent.

Woody Allen must have had a great time writing this screenplay. Gil is, of course, the Woody character (there's almost always one in an Allen film), and his fantasy is an enchanted wish fulfillment. My favorite of all the movie's time-lapse conversations may be the one Gil has with Buñuel. He gives Buñuel an idea for a film: A group of guests sit down to dinner and after the meal is over they mysteriously find themselves unable to leave the house. "But why not?" Buñuel asks. "They just can't," Gil explains. Buñuel says it doesn't make any sense to him. If the story idea and perhaps the name Buñuel don't ring a bell, that's a scene that won't connect with you, but Allen seems aware that he's flirting with Inside Baseball, and tries to make the movie charming even for someone who was texting all during high school.

Owen Wilson is a key to the movie's appeal. He makes Gil so sincere, so enthusiastic about his hero worship of the giants of the 1920s. He can't believe he's meeting these people and they are so nice to him—although at the time, of course, they didn't yet think of themselves as legends; they ran into ambitious young writers like Gil night after night in Miss Stein's salon. Another treasure in the film is Kathy Bates's performance. She is much as I imagine Gertrude Stein: an American, practical, no-nonsense, possessed with a nose for talent, kind, patient. She's something like the Stein evoked by Hemingway in *A Movable Feast*, his memoir of this period. She embodies the authority that made her an icon.

Then there's Adriana (Marion Cotillard), who has already been the mistress of Braque and Modigliani, is now Picasso's lover, and may soon—be still, my heart!—fall in love with Gil. Compared with her previous lovers, he embodies a winsome humility, as well he might. Meanwhile, life in the present continues, with Gil's bride-to-be and future in-laws increasingly annoyed by his disappearances every night. And there's another story involving a journey even further into the past, indicating that nostalgia can change its ingredients at a movable feast.

This is Woody Allen's forty-first film. He writes his films himself, and directs them with wit and grace. I consider him a treasure of the cinema. Some people take him for granted, although *Midnight in Paris* reportedly charmed even the jaded veterans of the Cannes press screenings. There is nothing to dislike about it. Either you connect with it, or not. I'm wearying of movies that are for "everybody"—which means, nobody in particular. *Midnight in Paris* is for me, in particular, and that's just fine with moi.

## The Mighty Macs ★ ★

G, 95 m., 2011

Carla Gugino (Cathy Rush), David Boreanaz (Ed Rush), Marley Shelton (Sister Sunday), Ellen Burstyn (Mother St. John), Lauren Bittner (Mary Margaret O'Malley), Malachy McCourt (Monsignor). Directed by Tim Chambers and produced by Whitney Springer. Screenplay by Chambers and Anthony L. Gargano.

*Mighty Macs* is a sweet, innocuous family movie about a young feminist who defies her husband, becomes a basketball coach, and leads the team of a nearly bankrupt Catholic women's college to the sport's first national championship. There is nothing to complain about except the film's deadening predictability and the bland, shallow characters. Kids up to a certain age may like it just fine.

Carla Gugino stars in a lovable performance as the real-life Cathy Rush. Herself a college basketball star, she's recently married to Ed Rush (David Boreanaz), an NBA referee, who expects her to be a dutiful little wait-at-home housewife. That's not her nature. She's the only applicant for the coaching position at tiny Immaculata College in Pennsylvania. The school owns one basketball. Its gym has just burned down. The salary is $450 a season. Her mission is explained by the school president, Mother St. John (Ellen Burstyn): The point isn't winning; it's keeping the girls' hormones under control.

From this point, we know from countless other movies that Immaculata will win the national championship. In case there's a shred of doubt, the ads reassure us. You don't get a movie made about you by starting without a gym and going on to build a good second-place team. We also know with certainty that the film will end with the Big Game. That is right and proper. What we hope for, however, are memorable characters, colorful dialogue, and a few surprises along the way.

The biggest surprise for me was the character of Ed Rush, Cathy's husband. In a film populated by nice people, he comes across as a louse. Remember, the movie is set in 1971, when "male chauvinist pig" was a term in everyday use. Ed is a gold-plated MCP. He complains that Cathy's coaching duties mean she's late getting home and doesn't tend to her wifely duties. He takes no interest in her team. Nor, although they are recently married, does he seem to feel any stirrings of affection or lust. The basketball team is certainly working to keep *his* hormones under control.

You know the movie, written and directed by Tim Chambers, is going to have to move the louse's character from A to B. The turning point is a solid brass cliché. On an away trip, he phones home, says he's delayed, and then says, "How was your game?" "We won," she says. "And . . . thanks for asking." Because he never had before. He takes a beat. "I love you," he says.

What changed? I dunno. Maybe he heard the team was winning. In movies like this there's always a climactic scene where the absent parent/teacher/authority is found sitting in the stands. Sure enough, for the final game, cut to Ed in the bleachers, who gives his wife a proud, if not effusive, nod.

Men are not prized in *Mighty Macs*. The other male of consequence is the monsignor, played by the legendary Malachy McCourt. He is only seen chairing board meetings at which the trustees agree the school is broke and must be closed. He's always talking about the "best offers." Mother St. John is a realist and agrees. Cathy Rush doesn't get the drift. She's forever bursting through a closed door with pleas for money for uniforms or transportation to out-of-town games. The monsignor also turns up at the national championship game and smiles. So you see what men care about.

The other major character is a young nun, Sister Sunday (Marley Shelton). She confesses to Mother St. John that she's not sure she should be a nun. She's having a crisis of faith. Then she signs on as Cathy's assistant coach, and now she has a mission. Spiritual matters don't seem to enter into this. In fact, this movie has about as little religion in it as it's probably possible for a movie set at a Catholic school. The team doesn't even pray before games. Sister Sunday does walk into chapel and demand, in a clear, ringing voice, a message from God. Apparently the assistant coaching position is God's answer. He moves in mysterious ways.

I'm not unhappy with this movie. It's good-hearted and pleasant, and tells an uplifting story. Younger viewers may love it. It has an innocence that today's movies have almost lost. Consider. Even 3-D animated movies about animated animals are now usually rated PG. How long has it been since you've seen a G-rated sports film?

## The Mill and the Cross ★ ★ ★

NO MPAA RATING, 92 m., 2011

Rutger Hauer (Pieter Bruegel), Michael York (Nicholas Jonghelinck), Charlotte Rampling (Mary). Directed by Lech Majewski and produced by Majewski and Dorota

Roszkowska. Screenplay by Majewski and Michael Francis Gibson.

Here is a film before which words fall silent. It contains little dialogue, and that simple enough. It enters into the world of a painting and the man who painted it. If you see no more than the opening shots, you will never forget them. It opens on a famous painting, and within the painting a few figures move and walk. We will meet some of those people in more detail.

The painting is *The Road to Calvary* (1564) by the Flemish master Pieter Bruegel the Elder. We might easily miss the figure of Christ among the five hundred figures in the vast landscape. Others are going about their everyday lives. That's a reminder of Bruegel's famous painting *Fall of Icarus*, about which Auden wrote of a passing ship "that must have seen something amazing, a boy falling out of the sky, had somewhere to get to and sailed calmly on." Extraordinary events take place surrounded by ordinary ones.

There is a bitter subtext for Bruegel's great painting. The soldiers on horseback are not Romans persecuting Jews, but Spanish Catholics persecuting the Protestants of Flanders. Not that the film explains that. In the Middle Ages painted allegory spoke in terms its audience would understand. Here Christ is carrying his cross through another land subjugated by outsiders for sectarian reasons.

The film is an extraordinary mixture of live action, special effects, green screen work, and even an actual copy of the painting itself (painted by Lech Majewski, the Polish director of the film). The compositions are painterly, the colors Bruegelian. Only three "characters" are named: Bruegel (Rutger Hauer), his patron Nicholas Jonghelinck (Michael York), and his mother, Mary (Charlotte Rampling), who was Bruegel's model for the Virgin at two different ages.

But other characters are more memorable. In a rustic home, we meet the most piteous: a man and his wife who live in close quarters with their lovable calf. They set off with it to market. They are young and carefree. Spanish troops seize the man, whip him, and bind him to a cart wheel. This they hoist into the sky atop a tree trunk we have earlier seen them cutting down in the forest. As his young wife weeps below, carrion birds feast on the delicacies of his face.

We never learn what transgression the man was being punished for. Not long after, a young woman (I was not sure if it was his wife) is buried alive. It is the fate of these peasants to be treated so by the Spanish. These events take place on a vast plain, and elsewhere children play, people are on journeys, dogs conduct their doggy affairs.

Towering above is an extraordinary sight: a craggy pinnacle, topped by a huge grain mill, its sails revolving. Inside live the miller and his wife, at the bottom of a helter-skelter stairway that zigzags into the far shadows above. Its massive wheels grind.

From time to time we observe Bruegel outlining sketches for his painting and discussing it with his patron. Certain diagonals are important to his proportions. The mill in the left background stands above the weeping Virgin in the right foreground. Sometimes Majewski, the director, freezes part of the painting while other parts of it move and live. Thus life is transformed into the greater permanence of art.

We regard most of the events from one angle: the front, as looking at the painting. But the camera sometimes enters into the action. There are many closer shots of the peasants, solemnly, sadly regarding the pain they witness. They are as passive as beasts. Others in the same frame may be engaged in indifferent occupations. At the center is the death of Christ, but it, too, is only a detail.

Here is a film of great beauty and attention, and watching it is a form of meditation. Sometimes films take a great stride outside the narrow space of narrative tradition and show us things to think about. Here mostly what I thought was, why must man sometimes be so cruel?

## Mirror Mirror ★ ★ ½

PG, 106 m., 2012

Julia Roberts (The Queen), Lily Collins (Snow White), Armie Hammer (Prince Alcott), Nathan Lane (Brighton), Mare Winningham (Baker Margaret), Michael Lerner (The Baron), Robert Emms (Charles Renbock), Sean Bean (The King),

Jordan Prentice (Napoleon), Mark Povinelli (Half-Pint), Joe Gnoffo (Grub), Danny Woodburn (Grimm), Sebastian Saraceno (Wolf), Martin Klebba (Butcher), Ronald Lee Clark (Chuckles). Directed by Tarsem Singh and produced by Bernie Goldman and Brett Ratner. Screenplay by Marc Klein and Jason Keller, based on stories by the Brothers Grimm.

*Mirror Mirror* is a sumptuous fantasy for the eyes and a pinball game for the mind, as story elements collide and roll around bumping into one another. This is not a faithful retelling of the versions by the Brothers Grimm or Walt Disney, but neither is it a satire, nor much of a story in its own right. But it's great to look at. If there's a major difference in the earlier versions, it's the beefed-up roles for the Seven Dwarfs, who here seem to be a merry band in search of Robin Hood. Nor do I recall earlier battles with a giant winged griffin.

The look of the film owes everything to the director, Tarsem Singh, an India-born former TV commercial maker, famous for two of the best-looking movies I've ever seen, *The Cell* (2000) and *The Fall* (2006). He's in love with spectacular landscapes and architecture, and in all of his films (including the underwhelming *Immortals* in 2011) the costumes of the late Japanese designer Eiko Ishioka dominate every scene they're in and every character they're worn by.

Julia Roberts seems particularly well-suited to wear them, and when first seen is wearing a magnificent orange gown and seated on a seashell throne that acts as a frame and a continuation of the costume. Roberts plays the queen in a kingdom we're introduced to by her opening narration—which uses animated doll figures to fill us in on her early life, during which she was married to a king (Sean Bean) who promptly set off into the forest and was not seen again. That left her as the autocratic ruler of a kingdom with painfully high taxes, and the stepmother of Snow White (Lily Collins), who is a captive in the castle until she's eighteen.

There is a financial crisis. Brighton (Nathan Lane), her aide and accountant, tells her she's broke. That comes at an inconvenient time, because Prince Alcott (Armie Hammer) has wandered into the kingdom, and the queen knows if she marries him, he can solve her finances. Problem is, she can't even afford the royal ball at which she plans for them to fall in love.

The prince has already met Snow White; they were both wandering in the woods when they encountered the Seven Dwarfs, jolly bandits with good hearts. It is Snow White and not the prince in this version who bestows a life-changing kiss. It's almost uncanny in some scenes here, how Lily Collins (daughter of Phil Collins) looks like Audrey Hepburn.

She's all sweet, all innocent, but Julia Roberts steals the show with her imperious and autocratic queen. She consults her own image in a mirror, located as only Tarsem would place it in a weird structure in the middle of a lake. She never asks who is the fairest of them all, and thus never has to hear the inevitable answer, but the queen's vanity and fear of aging give Roberts some plum scenes. Consider the one where she's having a spa-style beauty makeover before the ball. Her lips become bee-stung with the help of real bees, she gets a manicure from disgusting wormy creatures, and her skin is refreshed with a preparation made up from parrot droppings. Yes, parrot droppings, and we see the parrots dropping them.

All of this is in place and looks great, but the dialogue is rather flat, the movie sort of boring, and there's not much energy in the two places it should really be felt: between the queen and Snow White, and between Snow and the prince. The story is a listless tale that moves at a stately pace through settings that could have supported fireworks. Indeed, the characters who seem to care the most about each other are the dwarfs.

## Mission Impossible: Ghost Protocol ★ ★ ★ ½

PG-13, 132 m., 2011

Tom Cruise (Ethan Hunt), Jeremy Renner (William Brandt), Simon Pegg (Benji Dunn), Paula Patton (Jane Carter), Michael Nyqvist (Kurt Hendricks), Vladimir Mashkov (Anatoly Sidorov), Josh Holloway (Trevor Hanaway), Anil Kapoor (Brji Nath), Lea Seydoux (Sabine Moreau), Tom Wilkinson (IMF Secretary).

Directed by Brad Bird and produced by J. J. Abrams, Bryan Burk, and Tom Cruise. Screenplay by Josh Appelbaum and Andre Nemec, based on the television series created by Bruce Geller.

*Mission Impossible: Ghost Protocol* is a terrific thriller with action sequences that function as a kind of action poetry. The best one has Tom Cruise hanging more than one hundred stories up on the glass windows of the Burj Khalifa in Dubai, the world's tallest building. He has been equipped with gloves that cling when you slam them against the surface and release when you kinda curl them back.

Tricky enough in concept alone. But it has been claimed that Cruise "insisted on doing his stunts himself." Say what? The character Ethan Hunt is seen like a human fly clinging to glass thousands of feet in the air, and you're telling me we aren't looking at CGI? If that's really Tom Cruise, he seems like a suitable case for treatment.

If it is or isn't, the sequence is one of the most spellbinding stretches of film I've seen. In the way it's set up, photographed, and edited, it provided me and my vertigo with scary fascination. The movie has other accomplished set pieces as well. It opens with Hunt's breakout from a Russian prison. There is a staggering fight scene inside a space-age parking garage where moving steel platforms raise and lower cars, and the fighters jump from one level to another. There's a clever scene in the vaults of the Kremlin archives in which a virtual reality illusion is used to fool a guard. And a scene at a fancy Mumbai party in which Indian star Anil Kapoor thinks he's seducing the team member Jane (Paula Patton) in an elaborately choreographed diversionary technique.

Ethan and Jane are joined by Mission mates Brandt (Jeremy Renner) and Benji (Simon Pegg) in an attempt to foil a madman named Hendricks (Michael Nyqvist), who has gained control of a satellite and possession of Russian nuclear codes, and wants to start a nuclear war. His reason, as much as I understand it, is that life on Earth needs to be annihilated once in a while so it can get a fresh start, and Hendricks is impatient waiting for a big asteroid to come along in his lifetime.

The movie benefits greatly from the well-defined performances of the Mission team. Cruise, hurting from the death of his wife (remember her in the third *MI* picture?), plays a likable man of, shall we say, infinite courage. Simon Pegg, with his owl face and petulance, is funny as Benji the computer genius—one of those guys who can walk into the Burj Khalifa with a laptop and instantly grab control of its elevators and security cameras. Paula Patton is an appealing Jane, combining sweet sexiness with vicious hand-to-hand fighting techniques. And Jeremy Renner's Brandt, entering the plot late as an "analyst" for the IMF secretary (Tom Wilkinson), is revealed to have a great many extra-analytical skills.

Brandt and Benji have a scene that reaches a new level of action goofiness even for a *Mission Impossible* movie. Brandt's mission, and Ethan makes it clear he has to accept it, is to wear steel mesh underwear and jump into a ventilating shaft with wicked spinning fan blades at the bottom. Benji will halt his fall with a little mobile magnet at the bottom, so Brandt can break into massive computers. Renner does an especially nice job of seeming very scared when he does this.

The movie has an unexpected director: Brad Bird, the maker of such great animated films as *The Iron Giant*, *The Incredibles*, and *Ratatouille.* Well, why not? Animation specializes in action, and his films are known for strong characterization. You'd think he'd been doing thrillers for years.

Now I want to get back to Tom Cruise, whom we left clinging to the side of the Burj Khalifa, allegedly doing his own stunts. I'm not saying he didn't. No doubt various unseen nets and wires were also used, and at least some CGI. Whatever.

I remember a story Clint Eastwood told me years ago, after he made *The Eiger Sanction* (1975). There's a scene in the movie where Clint's character dangles in midair at the end of a cable hanging from a mountain. He's thousands of feet up. Clint did the scene himself.

"I didn't want to use a stunt man," he said, "because I wanted to use a telephoto lens and zoom in slowly all the way to my face—so you could see it was really me. I put on a little disguise and slipped into a sneak preview of the film to see how people liked it. When I was hanging up there in the air, the woman in front of me said to her friend, 'Gee, I wonder how they did that?' and her friend said, 'Special effects.'"

(I should add that I saw the film on an IMAX screen. Wow. The skyscraper scene had incredible impact.)

## Miss Minoes ★ ★

PG, 86 m., 2011

Carice van Houten (Minoes), Theo Maassen (Tibbe), Sarah Bannier (Bibi), Pierre Bokma (Meneer Ellemeet), Hans Kesting (Harrie de Haringman), Kees Hulst (Meneer van Dam), Olga Zuiderhoek (Mevrouw van Dam). Directed by Vincent Bal and produced by Burny Bos. Screenplay by Tamara Bos, Burny Bos, and Bal, based on the novel by Annie M. G. Schmidt.

*Miss Minoes* is a film I suspect would be adored by young girls who love cats. I am not that young woman. It's nominally a children's film, based on a children's book, but in its native Holland it won awards for both best film and best actress. Best film I don't understand. Best actress—well, the role is certainly challenging.

The Miss Minoes of the title begins life as a Siamese cat. After exposure to a barrel filled with chemicals that falls off a passing truck, Minoes turns into a woman (Carice van Houten) who speaks, dresses, and moves like a human but also climbs into trees when chased by dogs, and eats sardines without using her fingers. The movie doesn't look into her response to a litter box.

Tibbe (Theo Maassen), a local newspaper reporter, meets Miss Minoes one night when she is crawling on the roof outside his window. The movie sidesteps any romantic implications in their encounter, and uses Minoes as a news source for the young reporter, who is shy and not very good at his job.

If anyone knows everything that's going on in town, it is a cat, and Minoes is wired into the local feline hotline. She begins to produce a series of scoops that moves Tibbe into the top ranks of his paper, and eventually leads to an exposé about the nefarious schemes of a local villain who runs an animal welfare organization as his cover.

The cats all speak. If their lips were synched in the original Dutch, we'll never know, because the movie has been dubbed into English—just as well for younger audiences. It is also kid-friendly in its simplicity, and a bit too simpleminded for me. I was frustrated that it avoids countless logical questions. For example, after Miss Minoes changes into a human, she is fully clothed. Shouldn't she be nude?

Still, the movie is probably ideal for those proverbial young girls who adore cats, and young boys, too. I can't recommend it for adults attending on their own, unless they really, really love cats.

## Modus Operandi ★ ★ ½

NO MPAA RATING, 78 m., 2010

Randy Russell (Stanley Cashay), Danny Trejo (Director Holiday), Mark Borchardt (Dallas Deacon), Michael Sottile (Squire Parks), Barry Poltermann (Casey Thunderbird), Nikki Johnson (Black Licorice). Directed by Frankie Latina and produced by Shalyse Dominique, Laurie Foote, Mark Foote, Sasha Grey, Jon Krill, Zebedee LeTendre, Barry Poltermann, Andrew Swant, Gilbert Trejo, and Sean Williamson. Screenplay by Latina.

You need to have paid your dues to appreciate *Modus Operandi.* Have you marinated in exploitation films? The cheap kind from the '60s and '70s, made by fly-by-night filmmakers on starvation budgets? Where you can almost sense them gasping as they try to accumulate enough footage to qualify as a feature? And where the female characters are wearing bikinis even in business offices?

It's not enough to like such films because they're "so bad they're good." You need to specialize and like the films because they're so good about being so bad, they're good. *Modus Operandi*, a film by Frankie Latina that has won praise on the midnight movie festival circuit, is such a film.

Yes, it has babes in bikinis. Yes, it has a "plot" about spies and assassins. Yes, it's filmed in Cheapo-Color, which is used interchangeably with black and white. Yes, it has scenes set in "Siberia," "Russia," and "Tokyo, Japan." But what makes it special is that it was mostly filmed in Milwaukee, and one of its stars is

Mark Borchardt, whom you may recall as the subject of the great documentary *American Movie.* That was about the making of his own bargain-basement horror film, *Coven,* which a British actor informed him he was mispronouncing.

If you have paid those dues, there is a special pleasure to be had in *Modus Operandi* sequences like this one: The evil Dallas Deacon (Borchardt), apparently wearing the same glasses he wore in the doc ten years ago, is being chased in black and white across an open field by a helicopter, in homage to *North by Northwest.* He runs and runs and runs, and then disappears into some trees that didn't exist in the previous shots. The (unseen) pilot shouts, "We lost him down by the river!" Cut to high-quality new color footage of some ducks floating past, but no Borchardt. Cut to unmatched Cheapo-Color footage of three babes in bikinis, feet astride, standing menacingly on the prow of a speedboat on a lake, not a river. One babe means business. A second babe unties the top of the first babe's bikini and she dives in the water—because, of course, she is unable to swim while wearing the top. Cut to Borchardt wading into the (river? lake?) fully clothed.

Do you understand why I enjoyed *Modus Oprandi*? You don't. Millions agree with you. The film is touring the nation in search of those like Quentin Tarantino and John Waters who would stay planted in their seats and watch it a second time.

Often the (satire?) is embedded in the very arrangement of the characters. Know the crime movie cliché in which an evil boss sits enthroned in a restaurant, flanked by hit men and babes? Here they are obviously in the seating area of a Chinese restaurant's waiting room. Know how the bad guy shouts commands in a phone while his babes make out with each other? Here his headquarters is obviously a bench on the balcony of a hotel. His phone is a pastel 1970s desk model. Know how bad guys give orders to those around them? In one shot here, they're lined up parallel, so they have to look sideways to talk.

The plot involves two briefcases, I guess. Who cares? They were stolen from a U.S. presidential candidate. The briefcases are brought up by a scuba diver through a hole in the ice of a frozen lake in "Siberia, Russia" after unmatched footage pretty obviously of Wisconsin ice fishermen. Only CIA agent Stanley Cashay (Randy Russell) can find the briefcases. When we meet him, he's passed out with his head resting in a tavern urinal, with unfortunate results. At one point the search for them involves a mission to fly to "Tokyo, Japan" to shove a letter under the door of the mysterious Black Licorice (Nikki Johnson), who invariably wears huge 1970s sunglasses, even at night or while receiving a massage. Pay close attention to the footage incorporating Black Licorice in shots of crowds crossing a street in Tokyo.

I dunno who's still reading. You know who you are. If the film doesn't sound unique enough, reflect that it's one of the few in its genre to incorporate (1) a full-screen quote by Alexandre Dumas, and (2) a walking-down-the-street shot in homage to *Berlin Alexanderplatz,* and (3) a tavern still using a Blatz Beer sign. The Dumas quote doesn't make clear if it was said by père or fils, but you can't have everything.

## Moneyball ★ ★ ★ ★

PG-13, 133 m., 2011

Brad Pitt (Billy Beane), Jonah Hill (Peter Brand), Philip Seymour Hoffman (Art Howe), Robin Wright (Sharon), Chris Pratt (Scott Hatteberg), Stephen Bishop (David Justice), Kerris Dorsey (Casey Beane). Directed by Bennett Miller and produced by Michael De Luca, Rachael Horovitz, and Brad Pitt. Screenplay by Steven Zaillian and Aaron Sorkin, based on the book *Moneyball: The Art of Winning an Unfair Game* by Michael Lewis.

In the 2002 season, the nation's lowest-paid Major League Baseball team put together a twenty-game winning streak, setting a new American League record. The team began that same season with eleven losses in row. What happened between is the stuff of *Moneyball,* a smart, intense, and moving new film that isn't so much about sports as about the war between intuition and statistics.

I walked in knowing what the movie was about, but unprepared for its intelligence and depth. It centers on the character of the Oakland Athletics' general manager Billy Beane (Brad Pitt), who after a bad start as a major league player, moved over to management and was driven by his hatred of losing. In his previous season, he'd taken the A's to the World Series, only to have them lose and their best three players hired away by richer teams offering bigger salaries.

Faced with rebuilding the team at bargain basement prices, Beane became persuaded by the theories of Peter Brand (Jonah Hill), a nerdy recent Yale graduate who crunched numbers to arrive at a strict cost-benefit analysis of baseball players. He persuaded Beane that he should hire based on key performance statistics that pointed to undervalued players. Together, they assembled a team that seemed foolhardy at first, but during the course of an agonizing season proved itself the biggest bargain in baseball.

"Peter Brand" is based on people described in the 2003 book *Moneyball: The Art of Winning an Unfair Game* by Michael Lewis. Jonah Hill's performance is understated and fascinating in the film; a pudgy kid who has never played a baseball game in his life, Peter has analyzed decades of baseball stats to prove that game-winning qualities are not always the ones veteran scouts look for. He's shy and quiet, advancing his theories tentatively but with firm certainty; he's an amusing contrast with the team's grizzled, tobacco-chawing scouts—who are looking for all the wrong things, he argues.

Brad Pitt's Billy Beane, based on the team's real general manager, is an inward and lonely man, recovering from a failed marriage and doting on his daughter Casey (Kerris Dorsey). He's so driven he can't bear to watch a game in the stadium, and sometimes drives aimlessly while listening to it on the radio. He's fully aware that if he follows his theories for the full season and they fail, he will be unemployable. He faces fierce opposition from his bullet-headed team manager, Art Howe (Philip Seymour Hoffman), who feels his experience is being insulted by a GM mesmerized by some half-baked Ivy League theorist. The director is Bennett Miller, who also directed Hoffman in the title role of the radically different *Capote*.

*Moneyball* is not a traditional sports movie, and indeed should be just as gripping for non–sports fans. It's not a series of Big Games. When it goes to the field, it's for well-chosen, crucial moments. Its essence is in terse, brainy dialogue by the two accomplished screenwriters Aaron Sorkin (*The Social Network*) and Steven Zaillian (*Gangs of New York*). As in *The Social Network*, abstract discussions reflect deep emotional conflicts. There are a lot of laughs in this film, but only one or two are inspired by lines intended to be funny. Instead, our laughter comes from recognition, an awareness of irony, an appreciation of perfect zingers—and, best of all, insights into human nature.

This is really a movie about business. None of the individual players have major roles. The drama all happens in the minds of a manager and his numbers guy. They bet against tradition and in favor of numerical analysis. That goes against a century of baseball history, although for all of those years fans have thumbed through their baseball almanacs and issued mind-numbing statistical theories on talk shows. What the number crunchers demonstrated is that a computer can assemble a team better than human instinct.

That's melancholy, but then this is a melancholy movie. Pitt has some soul-bearing scenes with Jonah Hill in which he wonders what it all means, anyway. It doesn't matter if you have a twenty-game winning streak. All that matters is that you win the last game of the season. Even the players are merely inventory, and there are dramatic moments here of players being traded or moved down to the minors. Baseball is a business. Only we fans love it as a game.

## Monsieur Lazhar ★ ★ ★ ½

PG-13, 94 m., 2012

Mohamed Fellag (Bachir Lazhar), Sophie Nelisse (Alice L'Ecuyer), Emilien Neron (Simon), Danielle Proulx (Madame Vaillancourt), Brigitte Poupart (Claire Lajoie), Louis Champagne (Concierge), Jules Philip (Gaston). Directed by Philippe Falardeau and produced by Luc Dery and Kim McCraw. Screenplay by Falardeau, based on the play by Evelyne de la Cheneliere.

In an opening scene of *Monsieur Lazhar*, it's Simon's day to pick up cartons of milk and deliver them to his Montreal fourth-grade classroom before the school day begins. Looking in through the door, he realizes that his teacher has hanged herself from a ceiling pipe. Only one other student sees this before the teachers usher all the students back onto the playground.

This incident, reported in a Quebec newspaper, is the inspiration for Bachir Lazhar (Fellag) to present himself at the office of the school principal and volunteer to teach the class. He is a legal immigrant from Algeria, he explains, where he taught primary school for nineteen years. The principal is Madame Vaillancourt (Danielle Proulx), who, like most school administrators these days, is rigid in conforming to the rules. Hiring Monsieur Lazhar is a bit of an excursion for her, but he is a well-spoken, presentable man and makes a good impression.

*Monsieur Lazhar*, which begins in the dead of winter, follows his work in the classroom all the way through until summer. During that time he, and we, get to know the students, who are generally cheerful and well behaved, and get on well with their new teacher. They are assumed to be traumatized by their teacher's suicide, and a psychologist is assigned to spend closed-door sessions with the class. We, and Monsieur Lazhar, are closed out of these sessions, but Lazhar on his own tells the students some gentle truths and assures them it wasn't their fault.

For this and other transgressions he is criticized by the principal; to follow the rules, a teacher seems hardly allowed to be human. A student throws a paper ball at a classmate, and Lazhar, standing right there, taps him sharply on the head. This, too, is wrong; teachers are forbidden to touch students in any way. God forbid they would hug one, or pat one on the shoulder. I now realize that when Sister Ambrosina in the first grade at St. Mary's in Champaign snapped us with a strict fingernail it was brutality, although I always knew why I had it coming.

Lazhar has some challenges. French is spoken differently in Algeria and Quebec—and in France, too, perhaps. He dictates some Balzac for the students to write down, and is informed by them it is *prehistoric*. He finds a sympathetic fellow teacher to confide in, and perhaps she also rather likes him.

There is a great deal more to be known about Monsieur Lazhar's personal life, which I won't reveal. It adds an additional dimension to the trauma of the students. Simon in particular blames himself for the suicide; the dead teacher must have known he would bring the milk to class that day, he reasons, and must have known he would find her hanging body. Why else would a teacher choose to hang herself in her schoolroom?

This is a question without an answer. One of the qualities of *Monsieur Lazhar* is that it has no simple questions and simple answers. Its purpose is to present us with a situation, explore the people involved, and show us a man who is dealing with his own deep hurts.

## Monsters ★ ★ ★ ½

R, 93 m., 2010

Scoot McNairy (Andrew Kaulder), Whitney Able (Samantha Wynden). Directed by Gareth Edwards and produced by Allan Niblo and James Richardson. Screenplay by Edwards.

A movie named *Monsters* must contain monsters. But in its breathtaking final scene, we realize they should not be called monsters but perhaps simply beings. They're aliens from Europa, a moon of Jupiter that has a thin oxygen atmosphere and possibly an ocean of water under its surface. It's one of the prime candidates for life elsewhere in the solar system, and if it's hard to understand how that life might be fifty-foot-high spiders that float and have a pulsing inner glow, well, that's an alien for you. The bastards are always up to something.

I've read some complaints from fanboys that the monsters aren't monstrous enough. You don't hear any complaints about Godzilla, Mothra, or the clicking grasshoppers in *District 9*, but let a filmmaker dare to imagine a truly alien life-form, and it's whine, whine, whine. So let me say that *Monsters* is a rather special achievement. Think of it as a movie that M. Night Shyamalan (and we) would be happy he made. It's based on characters, relationships, fear, and mostly unseen menace, and although its special effects are important, it's not *about* special effects.

I recently came across a collection of covers from a 1950s comic book named *Tales to Astonish!* Each issue featured a different low-rent monster ("Mummex," "Droom," "Titano," "Vandoom," "Rommbu"). The most intriguing was "X," described as "THE THING THAT LIVED!!" The monsters invariably towered high above puny humans who were running for their lives in the foreground. The beings in *Monsters* tower above humans, but that's not because they're giant versions of B-movie clichés. It's because they are different in structure and nature from the life-forms on Earth.

The story, set some years in the future, explains that a probe was sent to Europa to search for life. On its return it crash-landed in Mexico. Whatever was on board found the conditions here suitable. The beings have occupied a wide swath of northern Mexico, known as the Infected Zone, and travel through it is forbidden. The two nations are connected only by boats and airplanes. A massive wall has been constructed to keep the creatures out of the United States, and air force planes fire missiles at them.

Whoops. I just hopped over one allegory and tripped on another one. There's an obvious parallel with our current border situation and the controversy over illegal aliens. And another one with our recent wars, where expensive and advanced aircraft are used to fire missiles at enemies who are mostly invisible. A process of demonization is also going on: Are these beings actually a threat?

Oh, sure, the journey in the film takes us through wastelands of devastation (my guess is they filmed in the aftermath of hurricanes). Boats are in trees, planes are in rivers, and so on. A brief comment, almost a throwaway line, suggests the creatures grow agitated when attacked. Many a creature does. There isn't a single shot on camera of a being actually assaulting anything without provocation.

The story involves Andrew Kaulder (Scoot McNairy) and Samantha Wynden (Whitney Able). He's a freelance photographer. She's the daughter of Kaulder's boss. Her father calls Kaulder and orders him to be sure Sam gets out of Mexico unharmed. He reluctantly agrees. They begin a journey north that, after many setbacks, leaves them trying to navigate a river through the Zone on a boat crewed by hired gunmen.

We see evidence of the aliens. We hear their mournful sounds. We see them unclearly in night-vision images on television news. Apparently they don't come out in daytime. The river journey, like the one in *Apocalypse Now*, often goes smoothly enough, but there's always the invisible threat in the jungle. Andrew and Samantha, like many a movie couple before them, start out antagonistic and gradually lower their guard as they share the journey. But theirs is not a conventional romance. It's more about learning to see another person.

*Monsters* was written and directed by Gareth Edwards. He also created all the special effects. He shot on location. All of the characters except the leads are played by locals. They're untrained, which means they're all the more convincing. Edwards had a minuscule budget, but he knew how to spend it.

The film holds our attention ever more deeply as we realize it's not a casual exploitation picture. We expect that sooner or later we'll get a good look at the aliens close up. When we do, let's say it's not a disappointment. They're ugly and uncannily beautiful. We've never seen anything like them. And their motives are made clear in a sequence combining uncommon suspense and uncanny poetry. Edwards is brilliant at evoking the awe and beauty he has been building toward, and at last we fully realize the film's ambitious arc. I think the lesson may be: Life has its reasons. Motives are pretty universal. Monsters are in the eye of the beholder.

## Monte Carlo ★ ★

PG, 109 m., 2011

Selena Gomez (Grace/Cordelia), Katie Cassidy (Emma), Leighton Meester (Meg), Cory Monteith (Owen), Andie MacDowell (Pam), Brett Cullen (Robert). Directed by Thomas Bezucha and produced by Denise Di Novi, Alison Greenspan, Nicole Kidman, Per Saari, and Rick Schwartz. Screenplay by Bezucha, April Blair, and Maria Maggenti.

*Monte Carlo* is a harmless, innocuous tweener fantasy that seems constructed out of bits and pieces of movies we must surely have seen before, but can't quite place because there's nothing much to remember. It's chirpy, it's bright, there are pretty locations, and lots happens. This is the kind of picture that can briefly hold the attention of a cat.

It stars Selena Gomez, a Disney discovery who is eighteen but looks fourteen and, let it be said, is cute as a button. I liked her in the movie, with her round-eyed astonishment and unaffected energy. She plays Grace, a new high school graduate who has been saving up for four years to pay for her dream, a graduation trip to Paris.

In another movie, in another universe, this would be a movie about Grace's trip to Paris. *Monte Carlo* is a movie about Grace's trip to a wheezy plot involving mistaken identities, a handsome guy who falls in love with her, and her whirlwind trip through a lifestyle of the rich and famous.

Grace has acquired a stepsister, Meg (Leighton Meester, of *Gossip Girl*), and is devastated when she finds that her mom and stepdad have arranged for Meg to join her on the trip. And Grace will bring along her BFF, Emma (Katie Cassidy, also of *Gossip Girl*). This actually may be prudent because Meg is in her twenties and will perhaps provide a chaperone for Grace and Emma.

Such a possibility is not considered by the movie, which treats the trio more as a unit, bopping through a heady series of adventures after Grace is mistaken for Cordelia Winthrop Scott, a rich little British girl who is heir to a vast fortune and is perhaps not six degrees separated from Paris Hilton. Grace is a dead ringer for Cordelia, and in playing both characters Gomez essentially has only to look like herself.

That sets up the girls for a PG-rated version of *Sex and the City*, except with no sex, one fewer girl, and different cities. Otherwise, the escapism is the same: Through the miraculous intervention of outside forces (a Middle Eastern sheik, or in this case, the mistaken identity), they are whisked off in a private jet and find themselves pampered in a luxurious hotel suite, gowned in haute couture, served thirty-pound lobsters and courted by handsome young guys. And, hey, Owen (Cory Monteith of *Glee*) likes Grace . . . for herself!

There is a puzzlement about the selection of Monte Carlo. Given any role in the decision, what girl in her right mind would want to leave Paris and go to Monte Carlo? Venice, maybe. Monte Carlo is an overbuilt condo tax shelter with bargain-basement royalty. Its sights, in this film anyway, seem to consist mostly of hotel rooms. The adventures of the girls have less to do with traveling in Europe than with conspicuous consumption. The movie gives its tweener target audience credit for little intelligence or curiosity about Europe, and dishes out the same old love-at-first-sight formulas.

I enjoyed two details. One was the budget fleabag hotel they check into. If they had only stayed there, some promising comedy might have been generated. The second was the whirlwind tour by sightseeing bus they take after arriving in Paris. As they trot through the Louvre, their guide seems to be trying to set a speed record. Then again, nothing about these characters suggests they would have ever found the Louvre on their own.

## Moonrise Kingdom ★ ★ ★ ½

PG-13, 94 m., 2012

Jared Gilman (Sam Shakusky), Kara Hayward (Suzy Bishop), Bruce Willis (Captain Sharp), Edward Norton (Scout Master Ward), Bill Murray (Walt Bishop), Frances McDormand (Laura Bishop), Tilda Swinton (Social Services), Jason Schwartzman (Cousin Ben), Bob Balaban (The Narrator). Directed by Wes Anderson and produced by Anderson, Jeremy Dawson, Steven M. Rales, and Scott Rudin. Screenplay by Anderson and Roman Coppola.

Wes Anderson's mind must be an exciting place for a story idea to be born. It immediately becomes more than a series of events, and is transformed into a world with its own rules, in which everything is driven by emotions and desires as convincing as they are magical. *Moonrise Kingdom* creates such a world and takes place on an island that might as well be ruled by Prospero. It's set in 1965, and might as well be set anytime.

On this island no one seems to live except for those involved in the story. There is a lighthouse in which the heroine, Suzy, lives with her family, and a scout camp where the hero, Sam, stirs restlessly under what seem to him childish restrictions. Sam and Suzy met the previous summer and have been pen pals ever since, plotting a sort of jailbreak from their lives during which they could have an adventure out from under the thumbs of adults, if only for a week.

Sam (Jared Gilman) is an orphan, solemn behind oversized eyeglasses, an expert in scout craft. Suzy (Kara Hayward) is bookish, a dreamer. When they have their long-planned secret rendezvous in a meadow on the island, Sam is burdened with all the camping and survival gear they will possibly need, and Suzy has provided for herself some books to read, her kitten, and a portable 45 rpm record player with extra batteries.

Because this is a Wes Anderson film, you know Bill Murray will appear in it. He has worked in six of Anderson's seven films, beginning with *Rushmore* (1998). In *Moonrise Kingdom* he plays Walt Bishop, Suzy's father, and Frances McDormand is the mother. Murray is always right for a role in an Anderson picture, and I wonder if it's because they share a bemused sadness. You can't easily imagine Murray playing a manic or a cutup; his eyes, which have always been old eyes, look upon the world and waver between concern and disappointment. In Anderson's films, there is a sort of resignation to the underlying melancholy of the world; he is the only American director I can think of whose work reflects the Japanese phrase *mono no aware*, which describes a wistfulness about the transience of things. Even Sam and Suzy, sharing the experience of a lifetime, seem aware that this will be their last summer for such an adventure. Next year they will be too old for such irresponsibility.

It is not a large island, but they think it must have a place where they can hide out. Sam has come prepared with maps for their trek, and they follow an old Indian trail to a secluded cove they name Moonrise Kingdom. Here they make their camp, which a scout leader is later to tell Sam is "the best-pitched camp I have ever seen." And here, as they sit side by side and look out over the water, in a sense, they regard the passage of innocence and the disturbing possibility of maturity.

Meanwhile, the adult world has launched a worried search for them. Suzy's parents call in the police, led by Captain Sharp (Bruce Willis). Scout Master Ward (Edward Norton) leads Sam's fellow scouts, who were not terrifically fond of the way he seemed to take the troop with less than utter dedication. A character known only as Social Services (Tilda Swinton) gets involved, because as an orphan Sam is of special interest.

Anderson always fills his films with colors, never garish but usually definite and active. In *Moonrise Kingdom* the palette tends toward the green of new grass, and the scouts' khaki brown. Also the right amount of red. It is a comfortable canvas to look at, so pretty that it helps establish the feeling of magical realism.

The approaching turmoil of adolescence is foretold, however, by a threatening hurricane that places the lives of the young explorers in danger. Their trek, their camp, and the search for them under the mounting danger reminds me of the sort of serials I used to follow in *Boy's Life* magazine, although those regrettably were not co-ed.

I think the success of *Moonrise Kingdom* depends on its understated gravity. None of the actors ever play for laughs or put sardonic spins on their material. We don't feel they're kidding. Yes, we know these events are less than likely, and the film's entire world is fantastical. But what happens in a fantasy can be more involving than what happens in life, and thank goodness for that.

## Morning Glory ★ ★ ★ ½

PG-13, 110 m., 2010

Rachel McAdams (Becky Fuller), Harrison Ford (Mike Pomeroy), Diane Keaton (Colleen Peck), Patrick Wilson (Adam Bennett), Jeff Goldblum (Jerry Barnes). Directed by Roger Michell and produced by J. J. Abrams and Bryan Burk. Screenplay by Aline Brosh McKenna.

*Morning Glory* is a funny entertainment to begin with, and then Rachel McAdams transforms it. And Harrison Ford transforms himself. She plays as lovable a lead as anyone since

Amy Adams in *Junebug*, and he bestirs himself from his frequent morosity and creates with gusto a TV newsman who is described as a great man, *but* the third worst person of all time. Diane Keaton is pitch-perfect as a morning TV host who can, and must, smile through everything.

Comedies open every week. This is the kind I like best. It grows from human nature, and is about how people do their jobs and live their lives. It is wisely not about a May-October romance between McAdams and Ford. It's more about their love for their work. It isn't deep, and it doesn't approach *Broadcast News* in its examination of the TV producer mentality, but it's the kind of sitcom you can get happily carried along with.

McAdams plays Becky Fuller, a little Energizer bunny of a morning TV producer, who gets fired from her thankless job in New Jersey and then has the good, or bad, luck to be hired to produce a last-place network morning show. Her boss is the dubious Jerry Barnes (Jeff Goldblum), who possibly views himself as the hiring agent for the *Titanic*. Becky plunges with zeal into a show that is not merely stuck in its tracks, but congealed. At the first staff meeting she comes across as a featherbrained lightweight until, in a nice burst of dialogue, she reveals she has heard everything, had strong opinions about it, and fires Keaton's current coanchor.

Her assignment: Turn the show around. The network has one of her heroes hanging around, working off the end of his contract. This is Mike Pomeroy (Ford), who detests what has happened to network news. Becky discovers how much time he has left on his contract and forces him into taking her show's coanchor gig. This involves precisely the kind of news he hates, and he'll have to do some of it, even though Diane Keaton's game enough to kiss a frog.

I suppose the outcome of the story is preordained. And we can hardly stir ourselves to care about the story within the story, about Becky's affair with Paul Newmanish fellow producer Adam Bennett (Patrick Wilson), which forces her to choose between love and her Blackberry. If you think teenagers are tethered to texting, you've never seen a TV producer.

What the movie has is charm and a light-footed smartness. In its version of story meetings and problems with talent, it's not a million miles away from what I've seen taking place. Morning news has a certain caffeinated jollity that's comforting. I sit in grumpy sleepiness and allow myself to be kidded out of it with the on-air "family" and the goofy weathermen. I don't expect hard news and investigative reporting. Pomeroy does. He expects it all the time, which is perhaps why he's sitting out the rest of his contract.

*Morning Glory* could have been routine. It's Rachel McAdams's life force that illuminates it. She positions herself barely on the right side of manic. She's always on, always optimistic, always hoping. She loves her work. There's a scene where she runs from NBC at Rockefeller Center across town to her network, "IBS," and she does it like a hungry colt. She makes Becky impulsive, determined, frisky, and, yes, cute. She grinds away at Harrison Ford's stone face and carves a smile out of it.

The film was directed by Roger Michell (*Notting Hill*) and written by Aline Brosh McKenna, whose *The Devil Wears Prada* is also about a spunky young woman up against a living legend. They know how to handle this material. They're also fortunate in the casting.

Ford is not a demonstrative actor. Sometimes he can barely rouse himself to growl. Here he's kind of inspired. When he's anchoring with Keaton, his double takes are flawless. When they get into a duel of who says "bye" last, they do it with impeccable timing. Ford doesn't venture beyond his usual acting range, but within it he creates a character with a reluctantly human inside.

I mentioned goofy weathermen. Matt Malloy plays a funny one here. He lives for the weather. He collects weather vanes. He also loves being in TV. Becky is ruthless in how she uses him on outside locations, and those scenes remind us of all the hapless TV people doing absurd things at some risk to their bodies or souls, simply to produce a few minutes of anything to perk us up at home. Back in the studio, the producers like Becky aren't heartless, exactly. It's just that they'll gladly toss human beings on the bonfire of "good TV."

## The Most Dangerous Man in America ★ ★ ★

NO MPAA RATING, 94 m., 2010

Featuring Daniel Ellsberg (Narrator), Patricia Ellsberg, Anthony Russo, Howard Zinn, Janaki Natajaran, Randy Koehler, Tom Oliphant, Egil Krogh, Max Frankel, John Dean, Leonard Weinglass, Hendrick Smith, and Mike Gravel. A documentary directed and produced by Judith Ehrlich and Rick Goldsmith. Screenplay by Goldsmith, Ehrlich, Lawrence Lerew, and Michael Chandler, partly based on Daniel Ellsberg's *Secrets: A Memoir of Vietnam and the Pentagon Papers.*

I thought I was pretty much familiar with the story about how the Pentagon Papers were leaked to the press in 1971. I knew that Daniel Ellsberg, a high-level analyst at the Pentagon and the Rand Corporation, had Xeroxed the Pentagon's secret history of the war in Vietnam and leaked it to the press, notably the *New York Times.* I recalled his arrest and trial. Ironically, his case was dismissed because White House plumbers broke into his psychiatrist's office and Nixon offered to make Ellsberg's judge head of the FBI. Said Judge William Matthew Byrne Jr.: "The bizarre events have incurably infected the prosecution of this case."

I knew all that. What I never realized was what a high-ranking employee Ellsberg really was, and how secret the Pentagon Papers really were. Locked in safes, their existence was a secret even from President Lyndon B. Johnson, who, it was believed, would have been infuriated by such a history. Ellsberg didn't merely leak the papers; he played a key role in contributing to them.

His first day on the job, cables came in from the celebrated Gulf of Tonkin incident, used by LBJ to justify escalating the war in Vietnam. Later the same day, cables from the commodore in command over the "attacked" ships said there was a "problem" with the reports—which turned out to be false. Johnson didn't want to hear it. He was ready to escalate the war, and he escalated.

His was the latest in a series of presidential decisions beginning with Truman, and continuing through Kennedy, Johnson, and Nixon, who financed France in its Indochinese war, propped up corrupt regimes in South Vietnam, prevented free elections, and eventually wreaked destruction in an unwinnable war.

Ellsberg, a marine company commander in the 1950s, wanted firsthand information. He went to Vietnam personally, shouldered a weapon, and led a patrol. What he learned convinced him that a false portrait of U.S. success was being painted. On a flight back to Washington with Robert McNamara, the defense secretary agreed the war could not be won, and we see the two men leaving the aircraft together before McNamara lied to the press that America was winning it. Later McNamara resigned, for reasons he didn't make clear at the time, nor even later in his confessional Errol Morris documentary, *The Fog of War.*

Ellsberg, in short, could not be dismissed as merely a sneak and a snitch, but a man who had direct knowledge of how the American public had been misled. He saw himself not as a peacenik war protester, but as a government servant exercising a higher moral duty. The documentary *The Most Dangerous Man in America,* by Judith Ehrlich and Rick Goldsmith, traces his doubts about authority back to a childhood tragedy and forward to the influence of young men who went to prison for their convictions.

It is a skillful, well-made film, although, since Ellsberg is the narrator, it doesn't probe him very deeply. We see his version of himself. A great deal of relevant footage has been assembled, and is intercut with stage recreations, animations, and the White House tapes of Richard Nixon, who fully advocated the nuclear bombing of Hanoi. Kissinger was apparently a voice of restraint. If you can think of another war justified by fabricated evidence, and another cabinet secretary who resigned without being very clear about his reasons, you're free to, but the film draws no parallels.

## Mother ★ ★ ★ ½

R, 128 m., 2010

Kim Hye-ja (Mother), Won Bin (Do-joon), Jin Goo (Jin-tae). Directed by Bong Joon-ho and produced by Choi Jae-won, Park Tae-joon, and Seo Woo-sik. Screenplay by Park Eun-gyo and Bong Joon-ho.

The strange, fascinating film *Mother* begins with what seems like a straightforward premise. A young man of marginal intelligence is accused of murder. A clue with his name on it and eyewitness testimony tie him to the crime. His mother, a dynamo, plunges into action to prove her son innocent. So there we have it, right? He's either guilty or not, and his mom will get to the bottom of things. Or not.

Is it that I've seen so many movies? Is that why I grow impatient with formulas, and am grateful for films that upset my expectations? If you faithfully remade *Mother* for a mass American audience (let's say with Helen Mirren and Ed Norton), mainstream moviegoers would likely be furious because: (a) "You can't do that!" and (b) "Uh, what is it that you did, exactly?"

This is a new South Korean film by Bong Joon-ho, his first after *The Host* (2006). That was a popular thriller about a giant squid created by toxic waste who dragged away a victim. Her family members learn she's still alive, but can't get the authorities to listen. Once again, in *Mother,* blood ties go up against the state.

The mother of the title, played by a respected South Korean actress named Kim Hye-ja, is a force of nature. In a village, she runs a little shop selling herbs, roots, and spices. Her sideline is prescribing herbal cures. Her son, Do-joon (Won Bin), in his late twenties, lives at home and they sleep in the same bed. He's a few slices short of a pie. Early in the film, he's saved from death in traffic when his mother races to the rescue.

Do-joon has a best friend named Jin-tae (Jin Goo). Jin-tae can easily manipulate him, persuade him to his will. Do-joon's mental fogginess may be his most attractive quality. In the town, a shocking murder takes place. A young girl's body is left where all can see. A golf ball with Do-joon's name on it is found near the death site.

Did he do it? We can't be sure. Did Jin-tae do it and plant the evidence? Or persuade Do-joon to do it when he was drunk? Again, we can't be sure. Under the Law of Economy of Characters, Jin-tae must have been involved because there are no other eligible characters. You can't simply produce a killer out of your hat. Of course, Do-joon could be guilty and Jin-tae had no involvement. Or, at least technically, the mother could have done it.

Mother (she's given no other name) marches tirelessly around the village, doing her own detective work. She questions people, badgers them, harasses the police, comforts her son, hires a worthless lawyer. We learn everything she learns. It seems she's getting nowhere. And it's at this point that the movie might become upsetting for a mass audience, because *Mother* creates not new suspects from off the map, but new levels in the previously established story.

The film is labyrinthine and deceptive, and not in a way we anticipate. It becomes a pleasure for the mind. Long after a conventional thriller would have its destination in plain sight, *Mother* is still penetrating our assumptions. So much depends on Kim Hye-ja's performance as a remorseless parent defending her fledgling. Likely she has spent years helping her clueless son escape one dilemma after another, and now she rises to the great occasion of her life. Her struggle is made more difficult because the police found it child's play to extract a confession from him.

*Mother,* and South Korean films in general, provide a case study of the situation of alternative films in this country. Many Americans have never seen a South Korean film and never will. I once spoke to a class for would-be foreign correspondents at the University of Illinois, and only two of them had ever seen a subtitled film from anywhere.

A film like *Mother,* and the recent *Chaser,* are adult films, not in the sense that they contain X-rated material, but in the sense that they appeal to intelligent grown-ups. A bright ten-year-old can understand most of today's Hollywood films. Disney recently announced it will make only 3-D "event" movies, comic hero stories, and extensions of franchises like *Pirates of the Caribbean.* It has essentially abandoned movies about plausible human beings. It isn't a luxury to see indie and alternative films. It's a necessity.

*Mother* will have you discussing the plot, not entirely to your satisfaction. I would argue: The stories in movies are complete fictions and can be resolved in any way the director chooses. If he actually cheats or lies, we have a case against him. If not, no matter what strange conclusions he arrives at, we can be grateful that we remained involved and even fascinated. Why do we buy a ticket? To confirm that a movie ends just the way we expect it to?

## Mother and Child ★ ★ ★ ½

R, 126 m., 2010

Naomi Watts (Elizabeth), Annette Bening (Karen), Kerry Washington (Lucy), Jimmy Smits (Paco), Samuel L. Jackson (Paul), S. Epatha Merkerson (Ada), Cherry Jones (Sister Joanne), Elpidia Carrillo (Sofia), Shareeka Epps (Ray). Directed by Rodrigo Garcia and produced by Lisa Maria Falcone and Julie Lynn. Screenplay by Garcia.

Three mothers in need of a child. Three children, one not yet born. Three lives that are obscurely linked. Rodrigo Garcia has made his career of films sympathetic to the feelings of women, and *Mother and Child* is so emotionally affecting because it is concerned only with their feelings. The story lines coil and eventually join, but that's just a narrative device. If these characters had no connection, their lives would be equally evocative.

The film is founded on three performances by Annette Bening, Kerry Washington, and Naomi Watts. All have rarely been better. Bening plays Karen, a caregiver at work, where she's a physical therapist, and at home, where she cares for her mother (Eileen Ryan). There will be no one to care for her: When she was fourteen, she gave up a child for adoption, and now she yearns to have that child back. This is not a film about the wisdom of adoption, however, but about Karen's desire for her child.

Kerry Washington plays Lucy, happily married, childless, trying to adopt a child. She finds one she loves, but the baby's birth mother, Ray (Shareeka Epps), is a piece of work. She considers it a seller's market, and is fiercely determined that her unborn baby will find a good home with worthy parents. She's more exacting than an adoption agency. Epps is very good, very focused here.

Naomi Watts plays Elizabeth, a lawyer who is focused not so much on her career but on her power, and how her sexuality can be a part of that. She goes to work for a Los Angeles law firm and makes it her business to have an affair with one of the partners (Samuel L. Jackson). She calls the shots, perhaps because she never knew her own parents, and fears a feeling of abandonment.

A quiet, nurturing person at the intersection of these lives is Sister Joanne (Cherry Jones), a nun at a church adoption bureau. She is childless, of course, but content; she accepts her state as part of her service to God, and is devoted to her clients. The nun is one of several important supporting characters who give *Mother and Child* richness. There is a large cast here, but the actors are gifted and well cast, down to the smaller roles, and each one is important to the development of the story—not just added for diversion or variety.

These include Sofia (Elpidia Carrillo), Karen's maid, who has a daughter who sometimes comes to work with her and embodies some of Karen's regrets. Paul, the Samuel Jackson character, has daughters of his own, as does Paco (Jimmy Smits), Karen's friend at work. They have what she doesn't. Lucy's mother (S. Epatha Merkerson) is a nurturing example of motherhood; not so her mother-in-law, who is cruel about the absence of a grandchild.

Garcia, whose credits include *Things You Can Tell Just by Looking at Her* (2000) and *Nine Lives* (2005), has created an interwoven plot here, not just for the purpose of being clever. Each facet revolves to illuminate the others. The characters reflect aspects of the central dilemma of mothers without children. It doesn't argue that all mothers require children, and indeed the nun may be the happiest woman here. It simply argues that these mothers believe that they do.

Of all the performances, Samuel L. Jackson's is the most surprising. It sometimes appears that the busy Jackson will take almost any role to stay working (remember *Black Snake Moan*?). This film provides a reminder of his subtlety. He is a powerful, successful man, relatively helpless with a demanding and sexually skilled woman. They like the sex, there is no love, she doesn't want to be involved in his personal life, and there is something there that disturbs him.

Bening, Watts, and Washington create three distinct beings with three distinct lives. They don't all "share the same problem," but they believe they share the same solution. Garcia embeds their needs in the details of their lives, so we don't emerge with ideas about them, but feelings.

## Mozart's Sister ★ ★ ★ ½

NO MPAA RATING, 120 m., 2011

Marc Barbe (Leopold Mozart), Marie Feret (Nannerl), Delphine Chuillot (Frau Mozart), David Moreau (Wolfgang), Clovis Fouin (Dauphin), Lisa Feret (Louise de France). Directed by Rene Feret and produced by Rene Feret and Fabienne Feret. Screenplay by Rene Feret.

The image that springs to mind is of the young Mozart touring the royal courts of Europe and being feted by crowned heads. He was a prodigy, a celebrity, a star. The reality was not so splendid, and even less so for his sister, Nannerl, who was older by four and a half years and also highly gifted.

The family Mozart, headed by the ambitious impresario Leopold and cared for by his wife, traveled the frozen roads of the continent in carriages that jounced and rattled through long nights of broken sleep. Some royalty were happy to keep the Mozarts waiting impatiently for small payments. There was competition from other traveling prodigies—none remotely as gifted as Mozart, but how much did some audiences know about music? Toilet facilities were found in the shrubbery along the roads.

Still, theirs was largely a happy life, as shown in Rene Feret's *Mozart's Sister*, a lavishly photographed period biopic that contrasts the family's struggle with the luxuries of its patrons. Papa Mozart (Marc Barbe) was a taskmaster but a doting father. Frau Mozart (Delphine Chuillot) was warm and stable. And this is crucial: Nannerl (Marie Feret) and Wolfgang (David Moreau) loved music. They lived and breathed it. They performed with delight. The great mystery of Mozart's life (and now we must add his sister) is how such great music apparently came so easily. For them, music was not labor but play.

One understandably hesitates to say Nannerl was as gifted as her brother. We will never know. She played the violin beautifully, but was discouraged by her father because it was not "a woman's instrument." She composed, but was discouraged because that was not "woman's work." She found her family role at the harpsichord, as Wolfgang's accompanist. The feminist point is clear to see, but Leopold was not punishing his daughter so much as adapting his family business to the solidly entrenched gender ideas of the time.

There's a trenchant conversation late in the film between Nannerl and Princess Louise de France (Lisa Feret), the youngest child of Louis XV. From such different walks of life, they formed almost at first meeting a lifelong friendship, and shared a keen awareness of the way their choices were limited by being female.

A royal princess who was not close in line to the throne (she was the tenth child), Louise had two career choices: She could marry into royalty, or give herself to the church. She entered a cloistered order, and it's her good fortune to accept its restrictions joyfully. "But think if we had been males!" she says to Nannerl. Each could have ruled in their different spheres of life.

Nannerl also has a close relationship with Louise's brother, the Dauphin prince (Clovis Fouin), a young widower. It seems to have been chaste but caring. Nannerl was always required in the wings of her brother's career, and after his death at only thirty-five she became the guardian of the music and the keeper of the flame. She found contentment in this role, but never self-realization.

The movie is an uncommonly knowledgeable portrait of the way musical gifts could lift people of ordinary backgrounds into high circles. We hear Papa in a letter complaining about the humiliations his family experienced from tight-fisted royals (they were kept waiting two weeks as one prince went out hunting). Leopold was a publicist, a promoter, a coach, a producer. It is possible that without him, Mozart's genius might never have become known.

The film focuses most closely on Nannerl, a

grave-eyed beauty whose face speaks volumes. She aspires, she dreams, she hopes, but for the most part she is obedient to the role society has assigned her. Marie Feret, the director's daughter, is luminous in the role. Another daughter, Lisa, plays the princess, and Rene Feret himself turns up as a music master; does his family have a Mozartian dynamic?

David Moreau supplies a different Wolfgang than the one we remember so clearly by Tom Hulce in *Amadeus* (1984). He is younger, rounder-faced, more angelic, more childish. As he and his sister have a pillow fight, all of the mystique evaporates from the notion of "a great composer." Through some happy chance, the child and man who created such bountiful music in so many styles and fashions was motivated by sheer enjoyment of the gift he had been given. It is one of those lives that make you wonder at the glory of men. Not so much at the opportunities of women.

## Mr. Popper's Penguins ★ ½

PG, 97 m., 2011

Jim Carrey (Mr. Popper), Carla Gugino (Amanda), Angela Lansbury (Mrs. Van Gundy), Ophelia Lovibond (Pippi), Madeline Carroll (Janie), Clark Gregg (Nat Jones), Jeffrey Tambor (Mr. Gremmins). Directed by Mark Waters and produced by John Davis. Screenplay by Sean Anders, John Morris, and Jared Stern, based on the novel by Richard Atwater and Florence Atwater.

*Mr. Popper's Penguins* is a stupefyingly dumb family movie proving that penguins have limited charisma as pets. I mean, what do they do? They sit on eggs, they waddle, they eat fish, and they squawk. Sometimes they might snap at you. The movie stars Jim Carrey, who is in his pleasant mode. It would have helped if he were in his manic mode, although it's hard to get a rise out of a penguin.

The movie is inspired by a 1938 children's book, apparently beloved by many. I haven't read it, so I'm trying to imagine why kids might like it. My best guess is that the idea of living in your home with penguins is more delightful than the experience. Penguins look cute in their little tuxedos, and kids can imagine being friends with them. The problem with a movie is that they take on an actual presence that gets old real fast.

This is, perhaps I should make clear, not an animated film. If the penguins were zooming into outer space in 3-D, that might change things. Weighted down by their apparent reality, they're more limited, although sometimes they slide down stuff on their bellies. One goes hang gliding, but not very convincingly. I assumed that all of the penguins in the movie were created with CGI, but no. I learn from IMDb: "Some are, some aren't." Since they all look and behave much the same, either the CGI is very good or the real penguins are well trained.

Jim Carrey plays Mr. Popper, a man involved in architecture and real estate, who must have great wealth because he lives in a Manhattan duplex with a spacious deck and travels in stretch limos. He is divorced from his wife, Amanda (Carla Gugino), although they seem on such good terms it is eerie. The unit of mother and two children is always available to turn up at his co-op at a moment's notice, smiling and cheerful. It's one of those cases, I guess, where the parents are apart only for the good of the children.

Mr. Popper inherits six penguins from his father. Never mind why. At first he doesn't want them in his apartment, which is modern and sleek and looks decorated by a designer with ice water in his or her veins. There is no sign of daily habitation in his living space. What with one thing and another, Mr. Popper comes to love the little creatures; guess how Stinky gets his name. You would think the spic-and-span apartment would soon be deep in penguin poop, but no, Mr. Popper squeezes them over the toilet.

There is a subplot involving Popper's employers, who also move in a unit of three like his family. Also a matter involving the sale of the historic Tavern on the Green by the rich Mrs. Van Gundy (Angela Lansbury). These need concern us no more than they will concern the kiddies in the audience. There is also some weirdly bland courtship by which Mr. Popper attempts to convince Mrs. Popper to return.

Of more interest may be the blessed event when the penguins produce three eggs, a tip-off (given penguin mating habits) that three of them are male and three female. You could have fooled me. Two eggs hatch. The third does not. That is the movie's tragic low point. Mr. Popper seems more distressed than the parents, or perhaps Carrey is the better actor.

## Mugabe and the White African ★ ★ ★

NO MPAA RATING, 90 m., 2010

Mike Campbell and Ben Freeth. A documentary directed by Lucy Bailey and Andrew Thompson and produced by David Pearson and Elizabeth Morgan Hemlock.

After the colonial invasions of Africa, all power was held in white hands. Of the colonial powers, the Portuguese were perhaps the best to live under, the Belgians the worst. The British in Southern Africa had a way of doing about as much mischief as everybody else but talking about it in idealistic terms. Cecil Rhodes, whom Northern and Southern Rhodesia were named for, saw himself as a force for civilization. When I visited those two lands in 1962, then not yet independent and renamed Zambia and Zimbabwe, I visited farms not unlike Mike Campbell's in this documentary.

When independence came, many white Rhodesians chose to leave for South Africa or "home," which meant the United Kingdom, even if they'd been born in Africa. Others decided to stay. Campbell bought his farm and regularly made his payments, under the existing law of the black government at the time. He wasn't bothered by the regime of Robert Gabriel Mugabe, which came to power in 1980. Mugabe began land reform, turning many farms over to black control. His government often paid far below market value. In Campbell's case, Mugabe waited until he had made his final payment before claiming the farm. He deemed it would become the possession of a member of his ruling party, and perhaps wanted to free that crony from the task of paying off the mortgage.

Campbell refused to leave. Supported by the five hundred Africans who worked on his farm, he resisted armed raids during which his workers and his family were beaten. This film tells the story of the complaint against Zimbabwe filed in a regional African court. He won, but not until he and his family were nearly beaten to death. After he won, his farm buildings were burned to the ground. Little happens in Zimbabwe without Mugabe's knowledge.

There is an excellent case to be made that whites were guilty of the theft of Africa from its native peoples. There is also a case, which South Africa has been making, that all races should be able to coexist peacefully there. The spirit of Nelson Mandela's Truth and Reconciliation Commission is far from the brutal vision of Mugabe. In a continent where despotic rule is not uncommon, there is little argument that Mugabe is the most monstrous of rulers. He has gladly proclaimed Hitler as his role model.

It seems to me that Campbell has a good case here—good enough, anyway, to convince the judges on the African court. One could understand the government buying his farm at a fair price under eminent domain and installing an African staff to manage it. Mugabe pays pitiful sums and his political cronies, not interested in farming, loot their new properties and deprive the resident laborers of their livelihood. Zimbabwe, which was one of the most prosperous lands in Africa, today has 80 percent unemployment and widespread disease and starvation.

That being said, *Mugabe and the White African* could certainly have looked more deeply. The filmmakers travel to Kent in England to speak with the family of Campbell's son-in-law, but never have any meaningful conversations with the African workers on Campbell's farm. They support him, fight for him, are beaten by Mugabe's thugs for their efforts. What do they think? Possibly their understanding of the situation is less theoretical than ours, and they don't see how they can feed their families without stable employment. Apart from skin color, the difference between Mike Campbell and Robert Mugabe is that Campbell wants to run a farm.

## Mulberry Child ★ ★ ★ ½

NO MPAA RATING, 85 m., 2012

Lisa Xia (Lisa Xia), Jody Choi (Little Jian), Bruce Akoni Yong (Father/Hou Kai), Christine Chiang (Mother/Gu Wenxiu), Yang Juan Xue (Nainai), Vanessa Chiu (Big Jian), Charlotte Kong (Ping),

Kayley Kong (Wen), Jacqueline Bisset (Narrator). Directed and produced by Susan Morgan Cooper. Screenplay by Cooper, based on the book by Jian Ping.

Lisa Xia was born in China but moved to Chicago at the age of three and has been thoroughly Americanized. This is not entirely pleasing to Jian Ping, her mother. Even though they live in the same city, she doubts if her daughter visits her every two months. Lisa thinks it's more like once a month. Whatever it is, it's unthinkable in her mother's culture. Lisa no doubt finds her mother boring and demanding. Her mother no doubt finds Lisa distant and lacking in filial affection. She'd like her daughter to come more often to, you know, have dinner, or talk, or even watch television. "TV isn't something I do," Lisa replies. We gather she goes out after work with friends, goes on dates, likes to travel—lots of things other than watching TV with her mom.

*Mulberry Child* is a documentary mixed with reenactments, based on a book Jian Ping wrote to tell her daughter what it was like for her, her husband, and their parents to grow up in China. The parents (Lisa's grandparents) lived through the ordeal of Mao's Cultural Revolution, were deprived of jobs and honor, were sent to live and labor in the countryside in poverty. For Lisa, a fortunate child, her life has been nothing like that. She wasn't much interested in reading the book. She isn't cruel or heartless—just not much interested in lives that were nothing like her own.

Finally Jian Ping decided to take her daughter on a trip to China so they could find out more about each other. As Jian Ping comes from a family that tried to mask its emotions, perhaps such a journey would release some truths. And it does, not just for the two women, but for us. There's a universal story here about immigrant parents and children, and how American culture can swamp family traditions and make parents and children culturally unrecognizable to one another.

This is a powerful and touching film, but I think it will help you to know at the beginning that many of the "documentary" scenes are recreated by actors. *Mulberry Child* makes no secret of that (the actors are profiled on the movie's website), but neither does it make it clear at the outset, and although it's logically necessary to use actors, you may have some uncertainty at the outset. This film is never boring, and it might have been slow going if the director, Susan Morgan Cooper, had been limited to the scant real material available. As it is, she artfully cuts in her new scenes and archival news footage from the Cultural Revolution.

What an upheaval that was! A society steeped in tradition was uprooted, families were separated, relatives were forced to testify against one another. Then Mao died, the chaos was over, people moved back home, and today China is a success story. That's not because of the Cultural Revolution. But to the end, we learn, Jian's father was loyal to Chairman Mao, and her mother, Gu Wenxiu, still alive, says in the film she believes in the Communist Party.

From Zhang Yimou's great film *To Live* (1994), I remember a scene that *Mulberry Child* says could happen in real life. Ordered to name a "counterrevolutionary" in their ranks, the members of a Communist Party committee would wait until someone left for a visit to the restroom, then name him. Living conditions were cruel; Jian Ping and her mother were not only exiled to the countryside but made to live in a rude shack with no heat, water, or plumbing. The father was in prison at the same time, yet still loyal to Mao.

If the film has a weakness, it's the lack of information about the lives of Lisa Xia and Jian Ping in Chicago today. We see them talking in the mother's apartment, we see them on the street, we see Lisa meeting with friends, but we don't learn about their jobs or life trajectories.

True, what happened in the past is more interesting than the present. (Ancient Chinese curse: "May you live in interesting times.") I have recently written my own memoir, and received no indication that our grandchildren have read it. On the other hand, I had a cousin who spent a lot of time writing the story of Great-Grandmother Gleeson, who set out from Ireland in a sailing ship and was blown back to shore many times. This book was carefully mimeographed and bound into bright blue covers, with real photographs stuck to some of the pages. That would have been in the 1940s. I'm afraid I haven't read it yet.

## Munger Road ★ ★ ★

PG-13, 90 m., 2011

Bruce Davison (Chief Kirkhoven), Randall Batinkoff (Deputy Hendricks), Trevor Morgan (Corey LaFayve), Brooke Peoples (Joe Risk), Hallock Beals (Scott Claussen), Lauren Storm (Rachael Donahue), Art Fox (Mayor Swanson), Maggie Henry (Nancy), Bill J. Stevens (Father McCroy). Directed by Nicholas Smith and produced by Kyle Heller. Screenplay by Smith.

It is the middle of the night in a small town on the eve of the annual Scarecrow Festival. A notorious local serial killer has escaped from a prison bus and apparently stolen a van. The mayor is alarmed because the town will fill up with visitors: "This town needs to leave him in the past." The police chief and his deputy go on the prowl.

This is a standard setup for a horror film. All depends on how well it is done. *Munger Road* does an efficient, skillful job of audience manipulation, using the techniques of darkness and vulnerability, and the truth that a horror not seen is almost always scarier than one you can see.

This is a low-budget film written and directed by Nicholas Smith, filmed where he lives in St. Charles, Illinois. It proves yet again that horror films don't require big stars because the genre itself is the star. All you need is a poster with a skeletal handprint on the back window of an SUV on a lonely road, and you've got an audience.

In the SUV are four teenagers who have made the unwise decision to drive out to Munger Road, scene of a legendary local tragedy when a school bus was hit by a train. Legend has it that one night a . . . well, you always need a legend in a movie like this. And teenagers foolish enough to challenge it.

Their SUV stalls, starts, and then stalls for good. Their phones can't pick up a signal. No traffic passes by. Meanwhile, back in town, the serial killer's stolen van has been found abandoned on Main Street. This calls for extended passages of the kids being scared in the car, and the cops penetrating dark and frightening places. There is also an ominous tunnel beneath the town, which looks like it must have taken a lot of work to construct, and I don't completely understand why it needs to extend as far as it does.

But never mind. Commonsense questions are rarely appropriate with horror films. The unbelievable is part of the game. *Munger Road* stars the fine actor Bruce Davison as the police chief, all these years after his debut in Frank Perry's *Last Summer* (1969) and his Oscar nomination for *Longtime Companion* (1991). He and the four kids (Trevor Morgan, Lauren Storm, Hallock Beals, and newcomer Brooke Peoples) are all smooth and accomplished, and *Munger Road* gets the job done.

I'd say the ending leaves it open for a sequel. What do you think?

## The Muppets ★ ★ ★

PG, 98 m., 2011

Jason Segel (Gary), Amy Adams (Mary), Chris Cooper (Tex Richman), Rashida Jones (Executive). And the Muppeteers: Steve Whitmire, Eric Jacobson, Dave Goelz, Bill Barretta, David Rudman, Matt Vogel, and Peter Linz. With cameos by Jack Black, Mickey Rooney, Zach Galifianakis, Selena Gomez, Whoopi Goldberg, Neil Patrick Harris, and Sarah Silverman. Directed by James Bobin and produced by David Hoberman and Todd Lieberman. Screenplay by Jason Segel and Nicholas Stoller, based on Jim Henson's Muppet characters.

The popularity of the Muppets is given new life in *The Muppets*, a funny, wickedly self-aware musical that opens by acknowledging they've outlived their shelf life. There's some truth in that; this is the first Muppet movie since *Muppets from Space* (1999), and there wasn't exactly a clamor for a revival. Yet for those who grew up with them, they had lovable personalities and (shall we say?) character defects.

What's rather canny about this revival is that it sidesteps the fact that some younger members of the family may not actually be very familiar with the Muppets. Their parents will be the fans. The movie opens with the Muppets disbanded; their movies and TV shows are all in the past. They've moved on. Miss Piggy, we discover, became the editor of a Paris fashion magazine.

It's a human fan that misses them most. Jason Segel plays Gary, who not only loves the Muppets but actually lives with Walter, who is his brother. This relationship is a problem, as well it might be, for Gary's girlfriend, Mary (Amy Adams). Walter likes Mary well enough, but feels like a displaced person. After all, he's a Muppet.

Gary, Mary, and Walter take a bus trip to Hollywood, only to discover the historic Muppet Studios are abandoned and derelict. Walter discovers that a millionaire (Chris Cooper) plans to buy the studios and drill for oil. This is not preposterous; didn't they strike oil under the Twentieth Century Fox ranch? The three tourists vow to raise money to save the studios, and the early appearance of Mickey Rooney in the movie should have been a tip-off of the old Rooney-Garland formula: "Hey, kids! Let's put on a show!"

Time is short. The search for the Muppet diaspora is difficult. The plan is to do a TV benefit. Since the Muppets aren't as big as they once were, human stars are also recruited to appear on the benefit. Famous bit parts are a tested element of the Muppet formula; I remember when I was all set up to interview Orson Welles on the day he was costarring with Miss Piggy. The interview never happened. There was some problem with Miss Piggy.

The remarkable thing about the Muppets, then and now, is what distinctive personalities and presences they have. When *The Muppet Movie*, the first in the series, came out in 1979, there was astonishment that—ohmigod!—Kermit was riding a bicycle! How could a Muppet do that? Today characters can do anything in the movies, but these Muppets are still played by Muppeteers, and they're still endearing.

## Musical Chairs ★ ★ ½

PG-13, 102 m., 2012

Leah Pipes (Mia), E. J. Bonilla (Armando), Priscilla Lopez (Isabel), Jaime Tirelli (Bernardo), Laverne Cox (Chantelle), Nelson Landrieu (Wilfredo), Angelic Zambrana (Rosa), Morgan Spector (Kenny), Auti Angel (Nicky). Directed by Susan Seidelman and produced by Janet Carrus, Joey Dedio, Brian Herskowitz, and Marty Madden. Screenplay by Madden.

Susan Seidelman's *Musical Chairs* is a feel-good romantic fantasy that is likely to inspire a hollow laugh among some people in wheelchairs. Either it knows little about the realities of disability, or it knows too much. Certainly people using wheelchairs can lead full and active lives, including the kind of ballroom dancing shown here. They also play basketball and do track and field, but first they must go through months or years of arduous rehabilitation.

My guess is that the filmmakers know more about disability than they reveal, because events might have grown way too complicated. The movie tells the story of Mia (Leah Pipes), a beautiful dance instructor, who is struck by a taxi and paralyzed from the waist down. She has earlier touched the heart of Armando (E. J. Bonilla), who works in his family's restaurant and is also a gifted dancer. Now follow this timeline. Mia had been dating the creepy owner of the dance studio. But it's Armando who visits her in the hospital, while the creep begs off over the phone; he's been "too busy" to come and see her. We get the impression that only two weeks have passed since the accident.

One night while taking out the restaurant garbage, Armando's attention is caught by a trash can on wheels, and something about the way they pivot together inspires him to perform a pas de deux right there in the alley. Inspiration hits. He shows Mia Internet videos of wheelchair ballroom dancers and starts a class to teach it in Mia's hospital. He recruits such fellow patients as a wounded soldier, a busty transgendered woman, and a hard-boiled Goth girl, and finally Mia also attends. It turns out that New York's first wheelchair ballroom dancing competition is in three months, and . . .

It's unlikely that anyone paralyzed from the waist down is going to be taking ballroom dancing classes a few weeks later. The physical and mental trauma would make it impossible. Why am I telling you this? You already assumed as much, didn't you? So let's back way up and bring the movie into focus in a different way. It isn't a docudrama. It's an escapist fantasy. It uses a group of Identikit stereotypes in a formula story.

One is Isabel, Armando's Puerto Rican

mother (Priscilla Lopez), who has a neighborhood beauty all lined up for him to marry and wants grandchildren and lots of 'em. Then there are Mia's rich WASP parents, eager to have her move back home with them; they'll have the house outfitted with ramps. Chantelle (Laverne Cox), the transgender woman, falls in love with one of Armando's older Puerto Rican relatives. This clicks in another set of stereotypes: The man allegedly has no idea Chantelle has a little something extra, although it is the worst-kept secret in the hospital. Chantelle never gets around to telling him, and oops! They truly fall in love, although she's not exactly his type, whether or not she was in a chair. Love conquers all.

These implausibilities are ignored by the movie. It knows that with characters we like, we want good things to happen to them. We know who we're cheering for in the dance competition. I saw the movie with a registered nurse who cared for me at the Rehabilitation Institute of Chicago, and she loved it. It was life affirming, she said. If anyone knew firsthand how inaccurate it was, she knew. But she didn't mind. And neither, to a degree, did I. That's what fantasies are for, to help us imagine that things are better than they are.

There are, however, two areas where the movie is guilty of misinforming audiences. Armando's mother believes that if her son marries Mia, they cannot have children. Nobody corrects her. Many disabled women can and do become mothers. The other area is wheelchair dancing. It is a beautiful and demanding performance art. Even assuming you've had a full course of rehabilitation, it's unlikely you'll be winning many trophies after three months of night classes taught by instructors with no experience in wheelchairs. I've seen wheelchair dancing. It can be transcendent. It is not easy.

All of these things having been said, *Musical Chairs* is a success at its intended level. Leah Pipes, a rising young actress, has a luminous screen presence (and let's hear no complaints that she isn't really disabled because key scenes in the movie require her to walk). Priscilla Lopez, as the mother, is high-spirited. Laverne Cox (who really is transgendered) brings a nice warmth and humor to her performance. And Nicky (Auti Angel) makes an original out of her disabled Goth girl. Sneaking a smoke outside a party, she finds some little kids staring at her. They want to know how she got that way. "Got drunk and fell out a window," she all but snarls, and they are properly impressed.

## My Afternoons with Margueritte ★ ★ ★

NO MPAA RATING, 86 m., 2011

Gerard Depardieu (Germain), Gisele Casadesus (Margueritte), Maurane (Francine), Patrick Bouchitey (Landremont), Jean-Francois Stevenin (Jojo), Francois-Xavier Demaison (Gardini), Claire Maurier (Mother), Sophie Guillemin (Annette). Directed by Jean Becker and produced by Louis Becker. Screenplay by Becker and Jean-Loup Dabadie, based on the novel by Marie-Sabine Roger.

Germain is a handyman/gardener in a sloppy flannel shirt and overalls, overweight and hulking. Margueritte is a little (eighty-five pounds) old (ninety-five years) lady. They meet on a park bench, where both know that exactly fourteen pigeons hang out, and both recognize them by sight.

Germain may be a hulk (he's played by Gerard Depardieu, who certainly is), but he is gentle and has a good heart, despite having been treated with cruelty by a mother who still survives to make his life miserable. He lives in a small trailer parked near his childhood home and lovingly tends his garden, where his mother displays sporadic violence against leeks.

Margueritte is played by Gisele Casadesus, who made her first film in 1934 as a member of La Comedie-Francaise. She is so slight and fragile she reminds Germain of a glass figure. She once worked for the World Health Organization, now lives in a retirement home with her beloved books.

Germain believes he cannot read. Actually, we discover later, he was taught to read but never taught to have a shred of self-confidence. She begins to read to him—*The Plague* by Camus—and he is an ideal listener. With her as his catalyst, he makes slow steps toward self-esteem.

This happens in an improbably sweet film

that will strike many as too upbeat. Germain is cuddled by his adorable bus-driver girlfriend, Annette (Sophie Guillemin), and pals around with his buddies at a local café. He suffers through flashbacks to his unhappy childhood, but seems on the whole serene. He loves Francine, but he declares himself *in love* with Margueritte.

So are we, a little. She is bright-eyed and high-spirited, and never overplays the heart tugging. The director, Jean Becker, is the son of the great French noir director Jacques Becker, who was eight when Gisele Casadesus was born. There's history here. The happy ending lays it on too thick, but what the hell: in for a dime, in for a dollar. Besides, the movie started me rereading *The Plague.*

## My Dog Tulip ★ ★ ★ ★

NO MPAA RATING, 83 m., 2011

Voices of: Christopher Plummer (J. R. Ackerley), Lynn Redgrave (Nancy/Grocer's Wife), Isabella Rossellini (Miss Canvenini). Directed by Paul and Sandra Fierlinger and produced by Howard Kaminsky, Frank Pellegrino, and Norman Twain. Written by Paul and Sandra Fierlinger, based on the memoir by J. R. Ackerley.

*My Dog Tulip* is the story of a man who finds love only once in his life, for fifteen perfect years. It is the love of a dog. It may be the only love he is capable of experiencing. As other men write books about a woman in their life, J. R. Ackerley wrote a book about a German shepherd bitch he rescued from a cruel home. *My Dog Tulip* has been a private discovery by many readers for years, and now it becomes an animated film combining elating visuals with a virtuoso voice performance by Christopher Plummer.

The film is animated but not intended for children. It is told from and by an adult sensibility that understands loneliness, gratitude, and the intense curiosity we feel for other lives, man and beast. The story is narrated by Plummer, in the voice of a man in his sixties who works for the BBC and lives in London near Putney Common. We know from the book that Ackerley was homosexual, and that is implied without the film making anything of it. For our purposes he is a soloist, cantankerous, crabby, lonely.

Tulip gives him unconditional love. Evolution, which produced humans who could think and were self-aware and knew loneliness, also in an act of serendipity produced dogs that could know us and love us. How strange that an animal could evolve as a wolf, self-select as a wolf that sought human company, and become an animal that values human company and considers its owners to be wonderful gods. People who do not like dogs do not know dogs. It is very difficult to dislike a being who worships you and would gladly die for you—especially when it is handsome and frisky and empathetic, and a good, good doggie, yes it is.

In a sense, *My Dog Tulip* is a natural history. Ackerley is educated by Tulip in the needs and ways of domesticated dogs. He attends to the feeding of Tulip, the training, the grooming, the walking, the territorial marking behavior, the sexual needs, the illnesses, the personality, the life and death. No parents of a child have ever been more observant or taken better care.

To this story, directed and animated by Paul and Sandra Fierlinger, *My Dog Tulip* brings Sandra's watercolors. Fierlinger is the sort of watercolorist one would collect. Her colors, her line, her ability to saturate or wash, are well suited to the story. She makes London with its black cabs and red buses come alive, and then turns pastoral on Putney Common. Her animated paintings have life and impact. She is an original, but if you know of an artist named David Gentleman you'll get the idea.

Given Ackerley's apparent celibacy, it becomes a source of some humor when he struggles to find Tulip a suitable mate. It isn't clear that Tulip much *wants* to become pregnant, but Ackerley is determined that she be impregnated. Perhaps she is a surrogate through which he achieves fertility. Lord knows they struggle together, J. R. and Tulip, through the travails of courtship.

*My Dog Tulip* has no stupid plot, no contrived suspense. Tulip grows old and dies, as must we all. J. R. Ackerley misses her and writes a book about his loss. Through this dog he knew love. And through J. R., so did Tulip.

## My Piece of the Pie ★ ★ ½

NO MPAA RATING, 109 m., 2012

Karin Viard (France), Gilles Lellouche (Steve Delarue), Audrey Lamy (Josy), Jean-Pierre Martins (JP), Zinedine Soualem (Ahmed), Raphaele Godin (Melody), Lunis Sakji (Alban), Flavie Bataille (Lucie). Directed by Cedric Klapisch and produced by Simona Ferraro and Caroline Levy. Screenplay by Klapisch.

You can forgive someone for wanting their piece of the pie. But what if they want your piece, too? The heroine of *My Piece of the Pie* has just lost her factory job of twenty years because a stock trader has manipulated the company's share price to force a failure. When these two people meet each other, the stage is set for—what? Drama? Satire? Comedy? Farce? Romance?

Writer-director Cedric Klapisch supplies a little of all five in *My Piece of the Pie*, a film about the everyday ways in which the markets deal in abstract numbers without the slightest interest in the lives that might be affected. In the French city of Dunkirk, a factory closes suddenly, families are uprooted, people lose their incomes and suddenly find themselves poor. In the most interesting element of the film, we see how a man seated before six computer screens in his Paris luxury apartment taps a key here and a key there, and behaves as what Tom Wolfe immortalized as a Master of the Universe.

This man is Steve Delarue (Gilles Lellouche)—thirty-five, rich, single, and a right proper bastard. There's a sequence here in which he boldly picks up a model named Tessa (Marine Vacth), flies her in his private plane to Venice, and is shocked that she won't have sex with him because she'd sort of prefer to, you know, like him first. WTF? Now he's heard everything.

The detailed savagery of his behavior indicates a man with no heart, no conscience, and not even much common sense; Tessa tells him he will never be happy because he will never be able to love anyone but himself. Into his wretched life comes a pretty fortyish woman named France (Karin Viard), a single mom who lost her job when he manipulated her factory out of existence. In Paris looking for work, she gets a job as Steve's house cleaner, a task that expands to include managing his clueless life. She doesn't know or care who he is. But she is practical and copes, for example, when Steve's ex-wife, Melody (Raphaele Godin), dumps off their son, Alban (Lunis Sakji), without warning and announces she'll be in Thailand for a month.

Steve needs a nanny. He doesn't like children, doesn't understand them, hardly knows his three-and-a-half-year-old son. France takes over, bedding down on a futon next to the boy in Steve's gym (formerly "Alban's room"), and they form a virtual family; she also doubles as his date at two social occasions, at which her brassy confidence stands out.

The movie is best when showing us the lives of France and the odious Steve. It loses its way with France's decision to pack up Alban and take him home with her to Dunkirk. She has well-meaning reasons for this trip, but to the world it looks like a kidnapping, and there's nothing in her character, up until that point, that suggests she's remotely capable of such lunacy. The third act turns into an unlikely and contrived confrontation between Steve and unemployed workers.

Movies make unwritten contracts with us. While it's permitted for characters to reveal enormous surprises about themselves, I believe that by the last act they should act more or less consistently in terms of the intelligence and judgment we've been led to expect of them. France unfortunately behaves entirely at the convenience of an unlikely plot turn. True, the movie sidesteps a couple of clichés it seems headed directly toward, but I might have preferred them to the preposterous melodrama it substitutes.

## My Son, My Son, What Have Ye Done ★ ★ ★

NO MPAA RATING, 87 m., 2010

Willem Dafoe (Detective Hank Havenhurst), Michael Shannon (Brad McCullum), Chloe Sevigny (Ingrid), Michael Peña (Detective Vargas), Udo Kier (Lee Meyers), Brad Dourif (Uncle Ted), Grace Zabriskie (Mrs. McCullum), Irma P. Hall (Mrs. Roberts), Loretta Devine (Miss Roberts), Verne Troyer (Midget).

**Directed by Werner Herzog and produced by Eric Bassett. Screenplay by Herzog and Herbert Golder.**

Werner Herzog's *My Son, My Son, What Have Ye Done* is a splendid example of a movie not on autopilot. I bore my readers by complaining about how bored I am by formula movies that recycle the same moronic elements. Now here is a film where Udo Kier has his eyeglasses snatched from his pocket by an ostrich, sees them yanked from the ostrich's throat by a farmhand, gets them back all covered with ostrich mucus, and tells the ostrich, "Don't you do that again!"

Meanwhile, there is talk about how the racist ostrich farmer once raised a chicken as big as, I think, forty ordinary birds. What did he do with it? "Ate it. Sooner pluck one than forty." Knowing as I do that Herzog hates chickens with a passion beyond all reason, I flashed back to an earlier scene in which the film's protagonist talks with his scrawny pet flamingoes. Is a theme emerging here? And the flamingo who regards the camera with a dubious look: Is it inspired by the staring iguana in Herzog's *Bad Lieutenant*?

For me it hardly matters if a Herzog film provides conventional movie pleasures. Many of them do. *Bad Lieutenant,* for example. *My Son, My Son, What Have Ye Done,* on the other hand, confounds all convention and denies the usual expected pleasures, providing instead the delight of watching Herzog feed the police hostage formula into the Mixmaster of his imagination. It's as if he began with the outline of a stunningly routine police procedural and said to hell with it, I'm going to hang my whimsy on this clothesline.

He casts Willem Dafoe as his hero, a homicide detective named Hank Havenhurst. Dafoe is known for his willingness to embrace projects by directors who work on the edge. He is an excellent actor, and splendid here at creating a cop who conducts his job with tunnel vision and few expected human emotions. It is difficult to conceive of a police officer showing a more measured response to a madman ostrich farmer.

His case involves a man named Brad McCullum, played by Michael Shannon as a man with an alarming stare beneath a lowering brow. He kills his mother with a wicked antique sword as she sits having coffee with two neighbors. He likes to repeat "razzle dazzle," which reminded me of "helter skelter," and yes, the movie is "inspired by a true story." His mother (Grace Zabriskie) is a woman who is so nice she could, possibly, inspire murder, especially in a son who has undergone life-altering experiences in the Peruvian rain forest, as this one has—and why, you ask? For the excellent reason, I suspect, that Herzog could with great difficulty revisit the Urubamba River in Peru, where he shot much of *Aguirre, the Wrath of God* (1972) and part of *Fitzcarraldo* (1982). Perhaps whenever he encounters an actor with alarming eyes, like Klaus Kinski or Shannon, he thinks, "I will put him to the test of the Urubamba River!"

Detective Havenhurst takes over a command center in front of the house where Brad is said to be holding two hostages (never seen), and interviews Brad's fiancée, Ingrid (Chloe Sevigny), and a theater director, Lee Meyers (Udo Kier). Both tell him stories that inspire flashbacks. Indeed, most of the film involves flashbacks leading up to the moment when Brad slashed his mother. Ingrid is played by Sevigny as a dim, sweet young woman lacking all insight and instinct for self-protection, and Meyers is played by Kier as a man who is incredibly patient with Brad during rehearsals for the Greek tragedy *Elektra.* That's the one where the son slays his mother.

The memories of Lee Meyers inspire the field trip to the ostrich farm run by Uncle Ted (Brad Dourif). If you've been keeping track, the film's cast includes almost *only* cult actors often involved with cult directors: Dafoe, Shannon, Sevigny, Kier, Dourif, Zabriskie, and I haven't even mentioned Oscar nominee Irma P. Hall and Verne Troyer. Havenhurst's partner is played by Michael Peña, who is not a cult actor but plays one in this movie. Little jest. For that matter, the film's producer is David Lynch, one of the few producers who might think it made perfect sense that a cop drama set in San Diego would require location filming on the Urubamba River.

There is a scene in this movie that involves men who appear to be yurt dwellers from Mongolia, one with spectacular eyebrow hairs. I confess I may have had a momentary attention lapse, but I can't remember what they had to do with the plot. Still, I'll not soon forget those eyebrows, which is more than I can say for most scenes at the 60 percent mark in most cop movies. I am also grateful for two very long shots, one involving Grace Zabriskie and the other Verne Troyer, in which they look at the camera for thirty or forty seconds while flanked with Shannon and another one of the actors. These look like freeze frames, but you can see the actors moving just a little. What do these shots represent? Why, the director's impatience with convention, that's what.

Herzog is endlessly fascinating and always surprising. I have now performed an excellent job of describing the movie. Can you sense why I enjoyed it? If you don't like it, you won't be able to claim I misled you. I rode on an ostrich once. Halfway between Oudtshoorn and the Cango Caves, it was.

## Mysteries of Lisbon ★ ★ ★ ½

NO MPAA RATING, 272 m., 2011

Adriano Luz (Father Dinis), Maria Joao Bastos (Angela de Lima), Ricardo Pereira (Alberto de Magalhaes), Jose Afonso Pimentel (Pedro da Silva), Joao Arrais (Young Pedro), Clotilde Hesme (Elisa de Montfort), Joao Baptista (D. Pedro da Silva), Lea Seydoux (Blanche de Montfort), Melvil Poupaud (Colonel Ernest Lacroze). Directed by Raul Ruiz and produced by Paulo Branco. Screenplay by Carlos Saboga, based on the novel by Camilo Castelo Branco.

I got a little lost while watching *Mysteries of Lisbon*, and enjoyed the experience. It's a lavish, elegant, operatic, preposterous nineteenth-century melodrama, with characters who change names and seemingly identities, and if you could pass a quiz on its stories within stories, you have my admiration.

I didn't feel it was necessary to understand it during every moment. It is hypnotically beautiful, playful, coiling between past and present. It tells its stories within narratives by several characters. As in *Citizen Kane*, it sometimes feels as if we've entered a flashback through the eyes of one character, and emerged from it through the eyes of another. All of the characters are memorable, even the little priest, Father Dinis (Adriano Luz), so small and quiet, so omniscient, so omnipresent, who relates some of the fates of the characters and seems to have shaped others. How was he present at so many key moments, early and late?

The film opens with the voice of young Pedro da Silva (Joao Luis Arrais), an orphan who boards at a school run by Father Dinis. The boy is teased because he has no family name; he must be a bastard, cruel boys say. But the padre begins to tell him a story of his mother, a great noblewoman, and then she appears in her carriage, beautiful and severe, and we are sinking into the labyrinth of the past.

The film by Raul Ruiz is based on a modern Portuguese novel of the same title, by Camilo Castelo Branco, unread by me. I admired Ruiz's 1999 film *Time Regained*, inspired by Proust, and now here is an even more complex film about memories, but with the richness of Dickens. We meet brigands, pirates, prelates, nobility, cuckolds, and soldiers in the Napoleonic wars, and an abundance of great beauties who swoon at their feet, and are swooned at. Many trenchant letters are written, and many thrown unread into the flames. Secrets of paternity are revealed. Betrayals are related.

All of this is told in narration illustrated by reconstructions of history, and sometimes illustrated by figures on a miniature stage given to Pedro by his mother. Ah, but the stage appears more than once. Indeed, all of the characters here seem to be on stage, and Ruiz consistently shows others observing from afar, or eavesdropping. Observe one magical scene in which an old monk begins to tell a story, and closes a window in his room. When he opens it again, three other monks are standing solemnly outside making no effort to conceal themselves. In other scenes, unexplained strangers frankly stare in through windows, and servants make no effort to hide that they are eavesdropping. Much seems to take place with random witnesses. A ballroom scene is attended by people who are keeping snaky eyes on one another.

The film painstakingly re-creates the world of nobility in Portugal, France, Spain, and

Italy. Everyone behaves in a formal manner. They are dressed with great attention to detail. There is an obsessive focus on the codes of gentlemen. Women are given that degree of exaggerated worship that is a form of possession or subjugation: By defining them as above humanity, men deny them simple humanity itself.

The movie is long—272 minutes. It played as a miniseries in sixty-minute installments in some countries. It doesn't hurtle through its plot, nor does it seem to dawdle. It immersed me, it wove a spell, it was very serious about its absurd coincidences, about characters who might almost be shape-shifters. If occasionally you are not certain who is at the center of a scene, do not be concerned; more likely than not, that person will turn out to be someone you remember from earlier in the film, under another name and with a different identity.

## My Week with Marilyn ★ ★ ★ ½

R, 101 m., 2011

Michelle Williams (Marilyn Monroe), Eddie Redmayne (Colin Clark), Kenneth Branagh (Laurence Olivier), Julia Ormond (Vivien Leigh), Dougray Scott (Arthur Miller), Judi Dench (Sybil Thorndike), Dominic Cooper (Milton Greene), Emma Watson (Lucy), Toby Jones (Arthur Jacobs), Derek Jacobi (Owen Morshead), Zoe Wanamaker (Paula Strasberg). Directed by Simon Curtis and produced by David Parfitt and Harvey Weinstein. Screenplay by Adrian Hodges, based on the diaries by Colin Clark.

By some tantalizing alchemy Marilyn Monroe imprinted an idea in the minds of a large percentage of the human race in around 1950, and for many that idea is still there. In the early 1950s, my friends and I required only one word to express it: "marilynmonroe." It wasn't a name. It was a summation of all we yearned and guessed about some kind of womanly ideal. Sex didn't seem to have much to do with it. It was more a form of devotion, a recognition of how she embodied vulnerability and sweetness and hope and fear.

The success of *My Week with Marilyn* centers on the success of Michelle Williams in embodying the role. With the blond hair, the red lipstick, and the camera angles, she looks something like Monroe, although she's more petite. What she has is the quality that was most appealing: She makes you want to hug her, not have sex with her. Monroe wasn't bold in her sexuality, not like her contemporaries Jane Russell or Brigitte Bardot. She held it tremulously in her grasp, as if not knowing how to set it down without damaging it.

*My Week with Marilyn* is based on the true story of a young man named Colin Clark, who talked his way into a job on *The Prince and the Showgirl*, a movie being directed in England by Sir Laurence Olivier, the nearest thing to royalty among British actors. For one troubled week, while her husband, the playwright Arthur Miller, was absent in Paris and production was on hiatus, she asked the worshipful twenty-three-year-old kid to join her at a getaway cottage. She was thirty. They were alone. One night they went skinny-dipping in the moonlight. That's about it. There's a suggestion they had sex, but the movie is coy. The way I read it, it was about a gift. Aware of what "marilynmonroe" meant to someone like Colin Clark, grateful for his sympathy and protectiveness, in need of company, she gave herself. Apparently she had a way of sometimes taking mercy like that.

For serious relationships, she preferred alpha males: Joe DiMaggio, Arthur Miller, by some accounts Robert Mitchum, and John and Bobby Kennedy. She admired their brains. She was smart, but had no confidence. She was in search of mentors and father figures. In her acting she fell into the orbit of Lee Strasberg's Method, and his second wife, Paula. She brought Paula to England with her and seemed incapable of making a move without her. This aroused the anger of Olivier, who despised the Method and considered acting a job to train for and work at without any bloody nonsense.

Gifted with this week, Colin Clark recorded it in a dairy, which later became a book. Diaries ran in the family. His older brother Alan Clark wrote one of the greatest of twentieth-century political diaries. For Colin Clark, the week with Marilyn wove a spell that never freed him.

This film is a fragile construction. There is no plot to speak of. The character of Colin Clark (Eddie Redmayne) is surrounded by many others who have more presence and charisma: Lord Olivier, played by Kenneth Branagh with barely concealed fury that his own crush on Monroe was impossible; Arthur Miller (Dougray Scott) with his deep American accent, disengaged from her world; Paula Strasberg (Zoe Wanamaker), fixated on Monroe, deaf and blind to others.

Julia Ormond plays Vivien Leigh, Olivier's wife, who sees through him, weighs the threat from Monroe, and sees he isn't the equal of a Miller or DiMaggio. Judi Dench is Dame Sybil Thorndike, also acting royalty, who patiently explains to Olivier that it doesn't matter if Monroe can't act because when she's onscreen nothing else matters. And Toby Jones is the press agent, who is crass, belligerent, and irrelevant. Eddie Redmayne is well cast as Colin Clark. He plays him as young, brash, but somehow unworldly, with a helplessness that may remind Monroe of herself.

The movie seems to be a fairly accurate re-creation of the making of a film at Pinewood Studios at the time. It hardly matters. What happens during the famous week hardly matters. What matters is the performance by Michelle Williams. She evokes so many Marilyns, public and private, real and make-believe. We didn't know Monroe, but we believe she must have been something like this. We're probably looking at one of this year's Oscar nominees.

# N

## The Names of Love ★ ★ ★

R, 84 m., 2011

Jacques Gamblin (Arthur Martin), Sara Forestier (Baya Benmahmoud), Zinedine Soualem (Mohamed), Carole Franck (Cecile), Jacques Boudet (Lucien), Michele Moretti (Annette). Directed by Michel Leclerc and produced by Caroline Adrian, Fabrice Goldstein, and Antoine Rein. Screenplay by Leclerc and Baya Kasmi.

If more fascists slept with Baya Benmahmoud, there would be fewer fascists. That is her theory anyway, and a good many fascists allow her to test it during *The Names of Love*, a wacky French satire about the supercharged political climate in France. Baya (Sara Forestier) is the child of a gentle Algerian father and a fervently political French mother. Sexual abuse by her childhood piano teacher has inspired her, somewhat obscurely, to use sex as a weapon of political persuasion.

The film swims in the waters of French politics, which are a good deal more diverse than our own, spanning communists on the left and neo-fascists on the right. The Socialist Party of Dominique Strauss-Kahn, in this company, is close to the center. Baya's evangelical recruitment is further eased by her freedom in defining "fascist," which for her seems to embrace anyone even slightly shy of the activist left.

The movie centers on her love affair with Arthur Martin (Jacques Gamblin), a studious specialist in the diseases of birds. She meets him after breaking into a talk show he's on. After a first sexual encounter leads nowhere, she breaks the news to him: She always sleeps with men on a first date. Furthermore, as a sincere socialist, he is not quite right-wing enough for her tastes.

Their star-crossed affair develops in an ingenious story structure by director Michel Leclerc and his cowriter, Baya Kasmi. We meet Baya and Arthur as children, as in (adult) voice-overs they explain their ancestral backgrounds. These children rematerialize from time to time to discuss developments with their adult selves.

Arthur's Jewish mother, Annette (Michele Moretti), escaped the Holocaust that claimed her family, by being hidden under a non-Jewish name in an orphanage. Neither she nor his Catholic father, Lucien (Jacques Boudet), ever, ever reveal her Jewish background—not even to Arthur, who has apparently been named after a popular brand of washing machines.

Baya's father, Mohamed (Zinedine Soualem), is a nonreligious Algerian immigrant who is a brilliant artist but too modest to admit it; he works as a paid and sometimes voluntary Mr. Fix-It who is forever setting things right again. Her mother, Cecile (Carole Franck), grew up as a French leftist and married Mohamed in part out of political conviction of a milder sort than that adopted by her daughter.

So we have a hero who doesn't *seem* half-Jewish, and a heroine who doesn't *seem* half-Arab, engaged in a love affair that brings them and their parents into contact with the past. Sometimes this leads to dark humor. Arthur, for example, is reluctant to introduce Baya to his parents because talking with his mother is like tiptoeing on eggshells. She's so sensitive that any reference to her past is likely to inspire anxiety and despair. When Arthur and Baya finally do have a meal with the Martins, Baya is warned to make no reference whatever to anything remotely suggesting the Holocaust, and of course her subconscious mercilessly generates such words as "oven" and "camp."

This scene is funny in concept, but not so much funny in execution. That's sort of the whole story of *The Names of Love*. We see it's a comedy, we appreciate the satire, but our laughter is easily contained. What I admired was the story of these characters themselves. What an odd couple. An intent scientist and a wild child half his age. A straight arrow and a sexual predator. A neatly buttoned-up man and a woman whose blouses and sweaters have a way of spontaneously revealing her breasts.

So free is Baya with her body, indeed, that after receiving an urgent phone call she pauses long enough to put on her shoes but neglects to put on anything else before rushing out into Paris and onto the Metro completely nude. This results in a predictable scene of a Muslim couple being offended; it might have been funnier if a couple her age had said, "Far out!" in calling her attention to her undress.

Sara Forestier is uninhibited in the role and has great comic energy. She won the Cesar for best actress for this performance. She makes a good contrast with Jacques Gamblin's dutiful, responsible Martin. What a fate, to be separated from his real name and given the name of a washing machine. Imagine an American named Facebook Martin. I enjoyed this film. I know I was intended to laugh more. It didn't bother me that I didn't.

## Nate and Margaret ★ ★ ★

NO MPAA RATING, 80 m., 2011

Natalie West (Margaret), Tyler Ross (Nate), Conor McCahill (James), Gaby Hoffmann (Darla). Directed by Nathan Adloff and produced by Adloff and Ash Christian. Screenplay by Adloff and Justin D. M. Palmer.

Here is a sweet, delicate story about friendship. Margaret is fifty-two. Nate is nineteen. They're neighbors in a Chicago building. They're best friends. The gorilla in the room is our memory of *Harold and Maude*, but *Nate and Margaret* has nothing in common with that film except the age difference, which is essentially irrelevant. This is a smart, observant movie about two very particular people, and its casting is pitch-perfect.

Nate and Margaret seem alone in the world. There is no mention of family. They like to do things together: shop at the Goodwill store, have brunch, hang out. Margaret has never been married. Nate, who is gay, has never had a boyfriend, or even been kissed.

Margaret (Natalie West) is a pleasant-looking woman without much of a style sense. She looks you straight in the eye and says what's on her mind. She has a day job as a waitress in a coffee shop, and spends her evenings at the open mike nights at obscure comedy clubs. Her plan is to become a stand-up comic.

Nate (Tyler Ross) is boyishly handsome, soft-spoken, private. He's a student of film at a school in the Loop. Sometimes he compares notes with a fellow student, Darla (Gaby Hoffmann). He's directing his thesis film and has enlisted Margaret as his sound person.

This situation would continue indefinitely, but Nate is startled one day to be kissed on the lips by James (Conor McCahill). At a party the next night, James steers him into a sudden romance and seems particularly turned on that it's Nate's first time. (Advisory to new lovers: When the other person wants you to keep repeating the same words as a turn-on during sex, they are having sex with an idea and not with you.)

Nate is swept away by young love, and one of the film's achievements is to make this feel realistic. There are no clichés in dialogue or visuals, no overacting, no straining for effect. Tyler Ross is a precise and quiet actor who's very effective portraying a young man having an experience for the first time. And Conor McCahill is a good choice as James; we can understand why Nate likes him. We can even understand why Nate stands up Margaret on their regular brunch date.

Margaret is not thrilled to learn about Nate's new friend, but bravely invites the two of them over for dinner. And the dynamics of this scene are carefully modulated to allow the morphing of James into the jerk he really is.

The story of *Nate and Margaret*, directed by Nathan Adloff, cowritten with Justin D. M. Palmer, is a minefield of things that could go wrong. It goes right because Adloff focuses on his characters and doesn't concern himself with big scenes and theatrical payoffs. He allows Margaret and Nate to be exactly who they are without any manipulation or hyped-up drama. Theirs isn't an earth-shaking relationship, but it's real and it's important to them, and worth preserving. That's what the movie is about: friendship. The film respects that, and doesn't get distracted by sex or age.

## Natural Selection ★ ★ ★ ½

R, 90 m., 2012

Rachael Harris (Linda), Matt O'Leary (Raymond), Jon Gries (Peter), John Diehl (Abe). Directed by Robbie Pickering and produced by Brian Hambel and Paul Jensen.

Linda and her husband, Abe, have every reason to believe she cannot conceive a child.

They share a fundamentalist faith, but only Abe carries it so far as to believe sex with his wife would be a sin because procreation is not a possibility. This is a terrible cross to bear for poor, sweet, lonely Linda, but as a loyal wife, she goes along with it. Then it comes as a blow when Abe (John Diehl) suffers a stroke at a sperm bank, where he has been spilling his seed for years.

Linda is a truly good woman, and Rachael Harris's performance illuminates *Natural Selection.* The film avoids most temptations to take easy shots at her religion, although some of those around her don't get off as easily. Linda sincerely believes. And when her husband, on what could be his deathbed, expresses a desire to meet one of the children of his years of sperm donation, she faithfully sets out cross-country from Houston to Tampa in order to track down the one she finds a record for.

Raymond (Matt O'Leary) is not a son you would wish for, although writer-director Robbie Pickering invents a rather brilliant way to bring him on-screen. Using his own knife, Raymond delivers himself by cesarean from inside the bag of grass clippings he has used to smuggle himself out of prison. When Linda finds him, he's living a feral existence in a foul shack that seems to have done duty as a crack house.

Raymond has no particular desire to meet his sperm father, nor does he have anything in common with kind, sympathetic Linda. But she does have a car and wants to drive them both back to Houston, and that comes as a godsend for a man who has just escaped from prison.

Thus begins a road trip that is not much different from any other road trip in the movies, except for the redeeming presence of Linda behind the wheel. Pickering's inspiration is to see her in a positive light, as a completely good and yet human character; if he'd mocked or satirized her beliefs, the movie might have left a sour taste, but in Rachael Harris's work we sense forgiveness and charity at work.

We also sense other things at work. Reflect that Linda has possibly never had sex. Reflect that Raymond cleans up pretty well. Consider that Abe is essentially out of the running. And that if you want to get technical, for Linda to have sex with Raymond would not be incest.

It's not that they do have sex. It's that the possibility hovers there in the air between them. Yes, Linda is old enough to be his mother, but Rachael Harris plays one of those women who, if she took off her glasses and did something with her makeup and hair, would easily qualify as beddable. And she knows it.

*Natural Selection* is not so much about sex as about communication across a vast divide. Linda and Raymond have nothing in common except the meaningless existence of Abe. But Linda lives her life, as a good Christian must, as an example to others. And Raymond is not a bad seed, but simply a young man brought down by drugs, as so many are. Linda provides a healing presence, reminding him that once, years ago, he might have been a nice boy.

Rachael Harris has one of those faces you think you've seen before—but where? She's done a ton of television, was a regular on *Fat Actress,* and played Ed Helms's potty-mouthed fiancée in *The Hangover.* Here she comes across as relaxed and comfortable, a good soul. That's probably harder than playing a horrible person; she engages our affection in the opening scenes and never lets go. She's the big reason *Natural Selection* is so engaging.

*Note: The film won the Grand Jury Prize, the Audience Award, and five other prizes at SXSW 2011.*

## Never Let Me Go ★ ★ ★ ★

R, 104 m., 2010

Carey Mulligan (Kathy), Andrew Garfield (Tommy), Keira Knightley (Ruth), Sally Hawkins (Miss Lucy), Isobel Meikle-Small (Young Kathy), Ella Purnell (Young Ruth), Charlie Rowe (Young Tommy), Charlotte Rampling (Miss Emily). Directed by Mark Romanek and produced by Alex Garland, Andrew Macdonald, and Allon Reich. Screenplay by Garland, based on the novel by Kazuo Ishiguro.

In my will I have left to the next generation such parts of my poor body as it can salvage. That is the Golden Rule. I suppose if you take it literally, you would accept life as a donor in *Never Let Me Go,* since after all, that is the purpose for which you were born. In the film there is a society within the larger one consisting of children who were created in a laboratory to be donors. They have no parents in the sense we use the term. I'm not even sure they can be parents. They exist to grow hearts, kidneys, livers, and other useful items, and then, sadly, to die after too much has been cut away.

When I read Kazuo Ishiguro's novel, the donors' purpose was left murky until midway in the book. In the film, it's clear to us but not, up to a certain point, to the children. They live within a closed world whose value system takes pride in how often and successfully they have donated. They accept this. It is all they have ever known. One of the most dangerous facts of human society is that children believe what they are told. Those who grow out of that become adults, a status not always achieved by their parents.

We meet three donor children, first when young and then later. They are Kathy, Tommy, and Ruth, played in their twenties by Carey Mulligan, Andrew Garfield, and Keira Knightley. They were raised at Hailsham, a progressive boarding school for donors—progressive in the sense that it's an experiment based on the possibility that these test-tube babies are real human beings. Well of course they are, we think. But it doesn't suit the convenience of the larger society to think of them in that way. If you are about to get someone's heart, don't you tend to objectify the source? You should. If you get my heart, I don't want you moping around about me. It's your heart. You pay the bills.

The teachers at Hailsham aren't precisely progressives in the John Dewey tradition, but the school is the last one that still encourages the children at all. The society wants these donors for one purpose and doesn't want to waste resources on them for any other. If you can walk through this plot without tripping over parallels to our own society and educational systems, you're more surefooted than I.

The director, Mark Romanek, wisely follows Ishiguro in burying any meanings well within a human story. The film is about Kathy, Tommy, and Ruth, and their world, and not some sort of parable like *1984*. Essentially it asks, How do you live with the knowledge that you are not considered a human being but simply a consumer resource? Many hourly workers at big box stores must sometimes ponder this question.

*Never Let Me Go* would have made a serious error in ramping up contrived melodrama toward some sort of science-fiction showdown. This is a movie about empathy. About how Ruth realizes Kathy and Tommy were naturally in love with each other as young adolescents, and how she selfishly upset that process. About how now, when it may be too late, she wants to make amends. About the old rumor at Hailsham that if two donors should fall deeply in love they might qualify for some sort of reprieve—short-term, to be sure. But if their masters can believe they can love, they would have to believe they are human. Two of the requirements for a being with a soul in Thomist philosophy are free will and the ability to love. Donors qualify for both.

This is such a meditative, delicate film. I heard some snuffling about me in the darkness. These poor people are innocent. They have the same hopes everyone has. It is so touching that they gladly give their organs to us. Greater love hath no man, than he who gives me his kidney, especially his second one.

This is a good movie, from a masterful novel. *Remains of the Day*, also inspired by an Ishiguro novel, was similar: What is happening is implied, not spelled out. We are required to observe. Even the events themselves are amenable to different interpretations. The characters may not know what they're revealing about themselves. They certainly don't know the whole truth of their existence. We do, because we are free humans. It is sometimes not easy to extend such stature to those we value because they support our comfort.

## Newlyweds ★ ★

NO MPAA RATING, 95 m., 2012

Edward Burns (Buzzy), Kerry Bishe (Linda), Marsha Dietlein (Marsha), Caitlin Fitzgerald (Katie), Johnny Solo (Miles), Dara Coleman (Dara), Max Baker (Max). Directed by Edward Burns and produced by Burns, Aaron Lubin, and William Rexer. Screenplay by Burns.

Edward Burns's *Newlyweds*, I learn from *Variety*, played at the Tribeca Film Festival and is a "$9,000-budgeted comic love letter to that

Gotham neighborhood, hastily assembled expressly for the fest." I don't ordinarily mention the budgets of low-priced films because that can unfairly diminish their worth, but if there was ever a $9,000 movie hastily assembled for a fest, this is it.

That means it has both the charms and the shortcomings of the indie fringe. Although a great deal happens in the lives of the characters, it often seems hasty and perfunctory, as if we are being urged ahead by an invisible production schedule. The performances rely on the considerable charm and presence of the actors, who are working with improvised dialogue that has been worked with but not polished.

It begins like some Woody Allen films, with two couples having a meal in a Manhattan eatery. Their dialogue is not up to Allen's standard, nor is their intrinsic interest, but here they are: Buzzy (Burns) and Katie (Caitlin Fitzgerald), near the beginning of their second marriages, and Marsha (Marsha Dietlein) and her husband, Max (Max Baker), who are in the eighteenth year of their marriage. Marsha is Katie's older sister.

Buzzy and Katie explain that they have the ideal "setup." He works days, she works nights, and they see each other only on weekends. Although this description is accompanied by a lot of affection and smiling, I dunno. The advantage of their setup, they reason, is that they don't get on each other's nerves, which sounds to me like an ominous hint that the possibility exists. Marsha and Max have not a setup but a long-running status quo, and a son now safely away in college.

Katie owns a successful restaurant. Buzzy is a personal trainer in a "gym" so small it looks suspiciously like someone's personal exercise room. She has the money. One day a bomb drops into the middle of their setup in the form of Buzzy's half-sister, Linda (Kerry Bishe), whom he hasn't seen since she ran away to Los Angeles at sixteen. As he observes, the prospects aren't favorable for sixteen-year-old runaways. She plans to move in.

Linda is a ditzy blonde with a shaky grasp on reality and personal property. She has arrived in New York in winter without a coat, borrows Katie's expensive designer coat, and "forgets" it somewhere. Her purpose for the visit is to ring up Miles (Johnny Solo), an old boyfriend whom she has now decided to marry. This despite the fact that he is a newlywed—although none too solidly, it appears.

The function of Linda is to put the marriage of Buzzy and Katie to a severe test, which she does with an array of bizarre behavior. In the meantime, the contentious regular dinners of the foursome in the opening scene drive a wedge into the stability of Marsha and Max's union. Events lead to Marsha's desire to move in with Buzzy and Katie, so that each might have a sister in residence. Adult siblings living under the same roof is a subject that has involved Burns since his well-regarded first film, *The Brothers McMullen* (1995).

All this develops in a series of conversations between various combinations of the characters, who after a scene may begin speaking directly to the camera in docudrama style. This feels like test footage from an earlier stage of the same film, although I have little doubt it was intended for this one. The insights of the direct speech aren't especially useful.

Edward Burns deserves credit for persisting in ambitious, low-budget indie projects. Issues involving siblings seem to tug at him, and *Newlyweds*, like *The Brothers McMullen*, also involves issues of morality. This is an honorable film, and Kerry Bishe's performance in particular is winning. But it plays more like a rehearsal than an opening night. As Gene Siskel once told a filmmaker who mentioned the low budget of his film, "I wish you'd had more."

## New Year's Eve ★

PG-13, 118 m., 2011

Halle Berry (Nurse Aimee), Jessica Biel (Tess Byrne), Jon Bon Jovi (Jensen), Abigail Breslin (Hailey), Chris "Ludacris" Bridges (Brendan), Robert De Niro (Stan Harris), Josh Duhamel (Sam), Zac Efron (Paul), Hector Elizondo (Kominsky), Katherine Heigl (Laura), Ashton Kutcher (Randy), Seth Meyers (Griffin Byrne), Lea Michele (Elise), Sarah Jessica Parker (Kim), Michelle Pfeiffer (Ingrid), Til Schweiger (James), Hilary Swank (Claire Morgan), Sofia Vergara (Ava). Directed by Garry Marshall and produced by Richard Brener, Toby Emmerich, Mike Karz, Wayne Allan Rice, and Josie Rosen. Screenplay by Katherine Fugate.

*New Year's Eve* is a dreary plod through the sands of time until finally the last grain has trickled through the hourglass of cinematic sludge. How is it possible to assemble more than two dozen stars in a movie and find nothing interesting for any of them to do? What sins did poor Hilary Swank commit, that after winning two Oscars she has to play the role of the woman in charge of the New Year's Eve ball in Times Square? And if you don't think there's dialogue about getting her ball to drop, you're barking up the wrong movie.

I'm not even going to begin to summarize the paltry series of subplots the all-star cast is trapped in. I like you too much. How many films have you seen where two pregnant moms are in a race to push out the first New Year's baby and win the cash prize? Where Robert De Niro plays a dying man whose last wish is to have his wheelchair pushed out into the cold so he can see the ball drop? Where two people fall in love while trapped in a freight elevator, and that gives the woman courage to sing "Auld Lang Syne" in Times Square at midnight, taking the place of Jon Bon Jovi, who has skipped the gig so he can propose to the pastry chef whose feelings he hurt a year ago tonight?

I never watch those New Year's Eve specials. The stories about Dick Clark's retirement were more interesting to me than any of the shows. So help me out on this. You know those tens of thousands of people in Times Square? Are more than half of them usually wearing foam hats given to them by some company? Because in *New Year's Eve* we look out over the surging throng of ecstatic celebrants and the sea of humanity is blue. They're all wearing freebie hats from Nivea Skin Creme. No hats for the Knicks, Budweiser, or I Heart New York. All Nivea Skin Creme. Countless hats of Nivea blue. I've heard of product placement, but this is carpet bombing.

The cinematographer was Charles Minsky. Did there ever come a moment when he peered into his view finder, turned to the director Garry Marshall, and asked, "Uh, Garry . . . do you think we have maybe a little too much blue here?" No, probably not, because most of the overhead crowd shots look like special effects. There are lots of close-ups of people wearing Nivea, however. It must have taken a supreme effort of will for the filmmakers to resist showing any of the characters actually using Nivea. Not even Robert De Niro, the dying man who is consoled in his final hour by nurse Halle Berry. He wants to see that ball drop and die. Despite his excellent nursing care, he has a five-day beard. Not a regular beard, an action-star five-day-stubble beard. Have mercy on this man. Give him a shave and a little Nivea Skin Creme.

## The Next Three Days ★ ★ ½

PG-13, 133 m., 2010

Russell Crowe (John Brennan), Elizabeth Banks (Lara Brennan), Brian Dennehy (George Brennan), Lennie James (Lieutenant Nabulsi), Olivia Wilde (Nicole), Ty Simpkins (Luke), Helen Carey (Grace Brennan), Liam Neeson (Damon Pennington). Directed by Paul Haggis and produced by Haggis, Olivier Delbosc, Marc Missonnier, and Michael Nozik. Screenplay by Haggis, based on the film *Anything for Her* (*Pour Elle*), directed by Fred Cavaye.

Russell Crowe slumps comfortably into the role of a junior college teacher in *The Next Three Days*, and then morphs into an unlikely man of action determined to spring his wife from jail. The film might have been more convincing if he'd remained the schleppy English teacher throughout. Once glimmers of *Gladiator* begin to reveal themselves, a certain credibility is lost. The movie is a competent thriller, but maybe could have been more.

That's because the filmmaker is Paul Haggis, director of such powerful films as *Crash* and *In the Valley of Elah* and writer of *Million Dollar Baby*. Here he's remaking a 2008 French film named *Anything for Her*, unseen by me. What he makes of it really doesn't seem worthy of his time, and the performances by Crowe and Elizabeth Banks could have been put to better use.

Crowe and Banks play John and Lara Brennan, a Pittsburgh couple with a young son, who find their world collapses in twenty-four hours. After a nice night out, their doors burst open the next morning, cops charge in, and Lara is hauled away on murder charges. John *knows* his wife did not—could not—commit the crime. But the evidence is compelling: She has the opportunity, it appears she had the motive, and the blood on her coat matches the victim's. Looks bad.

John tries to continue teaching and raising their son. He's conventional, intelligent, settled. The arrest has triggered a deep outrage. First he backs appeals to the sentence. When they all fail, he learns Lara will be transferred to the state penitentiary in three days. The deadline is dire because he plans to break his wife out of the jail she's being held in.

How do you, a bookish English teacher, go about doing that? The movie becomes a prison-break procedural, and the steps John takes and the plans he makes are interesting, as such matters often are in the movies. How he transforms into a man capable of fulfilling them is sort of slipped in. He does them, ergo he could do them. He does a lot of online research, solicits advice from a man who has broken out of a lot of prisons (Liam Neeson), and descends into the Pittsburgh underworld to obtain a weapon.

English teachers are ordinarily not terrifically good at buying guns from dope dealers, and the deal doesn't go smoothly, shall we say. But by now Russell Crowe the hero of *Master and Commander* has surfaced, almost on command. It's not his fault the role requires such a stretch. It's perfectly possible for ordinary people to cleverly break into and out of things, which they do all the time. But there's a requirement in the marketplace that there must be action scenes; Haggis supplies them, and Crowe rises to the occasion, as he must.

There are intriguing subcurrents. Did Lara Brennan perhaps actually commit the murder? There are indistinct black-and-white flashback scenes that are ambiguous. They raise the possibility. I consider them cheating: A movie knows whodunit. If it includes scenes that deliberately mislead us and then later clears up our confusion, that's a form of cheating, and the movie knows it. Better if you can use POV scenes in which another observer (John, say) misleads himself. Here, that's not possible.

Elizabeth Banks plays many of her scenes behind bars and begins to despair. Her son, picked on at school, refuses to talk nicely with her. The family's money is gone. She has little reason to think John can do anything at this point and sinks into depression. Then we get to the third act, and personalities take second place to action.

It's not a bad movie. It's sort of slow, because it spells out a lot of details, but it kept me involved. It's just that, after it was over, I felt it was a waste of the talent involved. I'd like to see Crowe and Banks in a smart Haggis original that wasn't about a jailbreak. I'm not sure, unfortunately, that the people financing the film would agree with me.

## Nick Nolte: No Exit ★ ★

NO MPAA RATING, 74 m., 2010

Featuring Nick Nolte, Jacqueline Bisset, Rosanna Arquette, Barbara Hershey, Ben Stiller, Paul Mazursky, Alan Rudolph, Powers Boothe, James Gammon, F. X. Feeney, Mike Medavoy. A documentary directed and produced by Thomas Thurman.

Nick Nolte is an interesting actor. Perhaps too interesting to appear in an independent documentary about himself. Perhaps too interesting to be interviewed by someone else. In *Nick Nolte: No Exit,* he interviews himself. The way he does this does what it can to assist a fairly pointless documentary.

Seated behind a silver laptop, well groomed and wearing a big white Stetson, Nolte asks questions. Seated behind a black desktop computer and looking disheveled and squinty-eyed (well, all right, hungover), Nolte replies to them. It would be going too far to say he "answers" them.

Here is a fine actor who has made many very good films. On the wall behind him is the poster for Paul Schrader's *Affliction* (1997), the one he and James Coburn both won Oscar nominations for (Coburn won). His credits include *Hotel Rwanda, The Thin Red Line, Who'll Stop the Rain, North Dallas Forty, Lorenzo's Oil, Q&A,* and many others.

He mentions several of these films, and others, but doesn't really discuss them. He's proud of them, and of his work, as he should be. He admires Marlon Brando, who encouraged him. He has nothing to say about his private life. He mentions "the most famous celebrity mug shot," which he posed for after a DUI arrest in 2006, but doesn't go into details.

Nolte is intercut with sound bites about him by Nick Nolte, Jacqueline Bisset, Rosanna Arquette, Barbara Hershey, Ben Stiller, Paul Mazursky, Alan Rudolph, Powers Boothe, James Gammon, F. X. Feeney, Mike Medavoy. He's worked with them all, but doesn't go into detail. Most of them he doesn't mention.

Yet despite everything, the film has a certain fascination because Nolte is such a charismatic enigma. I've interviewed him several times, including at Telluride, which he attended in a bathrobe, and at Cannes, where we did a Q&A that was light on the A's. I enjoyed his company. Can't say that he confided many secrets.

## Night Catches Us ★ ★ ★

R, 90 m., 2010

Anthony Mackie (Marcus), Kerry Washington (Patricia), Jamie Hector ("DoRight" Miller), Tariq Trotter (Bostic), Wendell Pierce (Detective Gordon), Jamara Griffin (Iris), Amari Cheatom (Jimmy). Directed by Tanya Hamilton and produced by Sean Costello, Jason Orans, and Ron Simons. Screenplay by Hamilton.

In the late 1960s revolution seemed to be in the air. Not a revolt powerful enough to topple the government, but one intense enough to threaten its expectations. Then the war was over, the draft ended, and the moment passed. *Night Catches Us* takes place in Philadelphia at a time when the Black Panthers are still alive in memory.

The film doesn't open with that large canvas, however, but with a small one. Marcus (Anthony Mackie) walks past a Cadillac in a driveway and into a house, and is told "your father is in the living room." The father's introduction is an example of one shot doing the work of much dialogue. Marcus has a brother, Bostic (Tariq Trotter), who harbors much anger against him, and slowly we learn that Marcus is believed in the neighborhood to have betrayed a Panther comrade and been responsible for his death.

So deep was this belief that Marcus left town for some years, and it's still not comfortable for him to walk in the neighborhood. One person who doesn't hold him accountable is the dead man's widow, Patricia (Kerry Washington). She's a lawyer, a widow with a daughter, and we sense immediately that there's unfinished passion between them. Perhaps people suspected that and tied it to the dead Panther's betrayal.

This is not an action movie. It is a movie about loss, sadness, and regret, and the feeling that history has moved on. Bostic, the brother, symbolizes that by having joined the Black Muslims, a group that by then represented a similar rejection of white society and even a somewhat similar iconography. Bostic is finished with the past. He can't wait to sell the family house.

*Night Catches Us* wisely avoids many of the situations this setup might suggest—situations that have been played out in countless other films. It doesn't turn into a street war or a whodunit. Its emotional center is the understanding that grows between Marcus and Patricia. They're good people, capable of useful lives, trying to free themselves from the chains of the past. She never believed he was a snitch. Perhaps they can find reconciliation and acceptance.

The film leads to no showy conclusion, no spectacular climax. It is about movement possible within the soul even in difficult times. The writer-director, Tanya Hamilton, faces the problem of all directors of period films, and solves them here by re-creating the Black Panther period in black-and-white news photos. That's about right. Even a few years later, that's somehow how it's remembered in the mind. The Panthers feeding kids breakfast. The Panthers in their black berets. The fiercely identical anger and resolve in their faces. All over with. Leaving Marcus and Patricia to get on with things.

## A Nightmare on Elm Street ★

R, 95 m., 2010

Jackie Earle Haley (Freddy Krueger), Kyle Gallner (Quentin Smith), Rooney Mara (Nancy Holbrook), Katie Cassidy (Kris Fowles), Thomas Dekker (Jesse Braun), Kellan Lutz (Dean Russell). Directed by Samuel Bayer and produced by Michael Bay, Andrew Form, and Bradley Fuller. Screenplay by Wesley Strick and Eric Heisserer.

Forget about the plot, the actors, and the director. What you require to make a new *Night-*

*mare on Elm Street* are these three off-the-shelf sound effects:

1. A sudden, loud clanging noise mixed with a musical chord.
2. Snicker-snack sounds, which Freddy Krueger's steel finger claws make every time they are seen.
3. A voice deepener, to drop Freddy's speaking voice to an ominous level.

On top of that, you need your sudden cuts, your lighting from below, your thump-thump-thumps, and, of course, a dog that barks at something unseen in the night, so that your teenage heroine can go out onto the lawn in bare feet and flimsy PJs and call, "Rufus! Rufus! Here, boy!" You know in your bones that Rufus is now checking into Doggie Heaven.

Oh, and actors. Lots of Dead Teenagers, seen in the last moments of their lives, when they enjoy a farewell Moment of Deceptive Safety just before there's a sudden, loud clanging noise and the snicker-snack claws disembowel them and Freddy rumbles, "You have nothing to worry about. This won't hurt one . . . little . . . bit."

The 2010 edition of *A Nightmare on Elm Street* is number 8½ in the series. I arrive at that number not out of a desperate desire to be seeing the Fellini film instead, but because *Freddy vs. Jason* (2003) should in all fairness count for half a film on this list, and half a film on the *Friday the 13th* list.

It is sad to think of all those Dead Teenagers. They were played by ambitious, talented young actors, some of them now in their forties, who survived grueling auditions for the honor of being slashed by Freddy. Some of them are now successful: Johnny Depp, for example. Robert Englund became famous playing Freddy, but where can that lead when you're always wearing a mask of makeup? Now Jackie Earle Haley plays the role. For what purpose? He might as well play Santa Claus.

It was twenty-six long years ago when Freddy first began to haunt the nightmares of the children of Elm Street in Springwood, Ohio. At least 137 victims have been claimed by Freddy in the years since then, but the shady little street is still lined with handsome homes and hasn't been leveled, covered with ashes and sprinkled with holy water. The franchise was founded by Wes Craven, the Ray Kroc of horror, who made the excellent *Wes Craven's New Nightmare* (1994), about Freddy haunting the dreams of the *makers* of the *Nightmare* movies.

Freddy is not a good argument for a supernatural existence. He can live inside wallpaper, appear anywhere, and has no need of physical existence except, arguably, when he inflicts actual physical damage. Yet he's such a bore, always growling away with his deep-voiced *hahahahaha.* If a man leads an interesting life he ought to be able to make good conversation, is what I say.

I stared at *A Nightmare on Elm Street* with weary resignation. The movie consists of a series of teenagers who are introduced, haunted by nightmares, and then slashed to death by Freddy. So what? Are we supposed to be scared? Is the sudden clanging chord supposed to evoke a fearful Pavlovian response? For Rufus, maybe, but not for me. Here, boy.

## 9500 Liberty ★ ★ ★ ½

NO MPAA RATING, 80 m., 2010

With Greg Letiecq, Corey A. Stewart, Charlie T. Deane, Guadencio Fernandez, Alanna Almeda, Elena Schlossberg, Frank J. Principi, Martin E. Nohe, and Annabel Park. A documentary directed by Annabel Park and Eric Byler and produced by Chris Rigopulos. Written by Park and Byler.

A few years before Arizona passed its new immigration law, a similar law was passed and then repealed in Virginia's Prince William County. The new documentary *9500 Liberty* tells the fascinating story of how that happened and possibly foretells what lies ahead for Arizona. In Virginia, the law was eventually overturned by a combination of middle-class whites, Republican officeholders, the police chief, Latinos, and economic reality.

When Prince William experienced a major building boom in the 1990s, a shortage of labor created a demand for workers, which led to an increase in the Latino population. Some of the newcomers were legal immigrants. Some were not. A blogger named Greg Letiecq began to write about his unhappiness with hearing Spanish spoken in public places. Finding an audience, he fomented about rising crime rates, rising taxes to pay for services for the newcomers, overcrowded dwellings, music played too loud, fast driving, and so on. He included Latino crime reports from the local police blotter. He even claimed armed members of the Zapatistas Mexican revolutionary group were moving to Prince William.

His organization, Help Save Manassas, issued saucer-sized red lapel stickers and soon they were seen around the town. He and board of supervisors president Corey A. Stewart created a law that would require local police to stop people for "probable cause" and ask them to show their proof of citizenship. This measure seemed to have popular support, and there was resentment against a Mexican-American citizen who erected a large sign on his property (at 9500 Liberty Street) to differ with it.

At about this time filmmakers Eric Byler and Annabel Park (a Filipino-American and a Korean-American) began to post videos on YouTube that weren't so much political as the raw material for a documentary. They showed discussions and arguments among local residents, testimony before the county board, Stewart, Letiecq and other pro-law figures, and ordinary citizens. As the videos went viral, they inspired another local blog to counter Letiecq, and a growing community discussion about the law.

Among its opponents was Charlie T. Deane, the long-serving, widely respected local police chief, who testified the law would cost about $14 million over five years to enforce, who said his officers had more important things to do, and who said (along with the county attorney) that without video cameras in every police car, the officers and the county would be open to lawsuits. Cameras would cost another $3.1 million.

Ironically, the law was partly to blame for a tax rate increase of 25 percent a year. There was another problem. Latinos began to move out of Prince William or take their business to nearby friendlier areas. There was a retail slump, badly timed to coincide with the collapse of the housing market. The county tax base dropped as taxpaying "legals" left. Restaurants and shops closed. Prince William County and Virginia have sales taxes, income taxes, and other taxes that even noncitizens pay.

Chief Deane met with a Mexican government official and was incredibly accused of treason by the right-wingers (for "negotiating with a foreign power"). This did not go over well. The Republican woman who had hosted a fundraiser for board president Stewart testified against him at a board meeting. There was a rising tide of opposition to the law and the negative image it gave the area. A motion to raise taxes to keep the law and pay for the cameras drew a tie 4–4 vote. Stewart recessed for a caucus and returned with a new "compromise" motion ending the "probable cause" mandate, which resulted in an 8–0 vote. On the board at that time were six Republicans and two Democrats.

The most rewarding element of this deeply involved documentary involves the board meetings. Local citizens stand up to speak their minds, and we hear a great many of them. Some board meetings lasted until well past midnight. They were in the great tradition of New England town meetings. Latinos were united in opposing the law. Many were longtime, well-known American citizens. But the balance was finally tipped by the voices of thoughtful Republicans and their distaste for the hate stirred up by Letiecq and his group. Calling Chief Deane a traitor was the last straw.

Annabel Park and Eric Byler began as objective documentarians who found this story being pressed upon them. They become advocates and are clear about that. They try to show both sides of the debate, but (inevitably, perhaps?) the anti-law faction comes across more positively.

The outcome was this: Passing the law led to higher taxes, not lower ones. The tax base decreased. And as for the crime rate? Chief Deane has charts showing that crime dropped every single year over the past decade.

## Norman ★ ★ ★

R, 97 m., 2011

Dan Byrd (Norman Long), Emily VanCamp (Emily Parrish), Richard Jenkins (Doug Long), Adam Goldberg (Mr. Angelo), Billy Lush (James), Camille Mana (Helen Black). Directed by Jonathan Segal and produced by Segal, Kim

Blackburn Bowen, Rich Cowan, Dan Keston, and Hawk Koch. Screenplay by Talton Wingate.

*Norman* tells the story of a high school senior who finds too great a burden of challenges piling up all at once. His mother has died in a car crash. His father is dying of stomach cancer. This is all made known to us at the outset. The film will not be about these tragedies happening to him, but about how he deals with them. That's a worthy change from a more ordinary teen movie.

Norman (Dan Byrd) is quiet and private, with a way of hesitating before speaking as if he can barely find the will. His father, Doug (Richard Jenkins), is a doctor who understands his own condition all too well, and has made a decision to refuse one more round of chemotherapy and essentially supervise his own hospice care at home. He and his son love each other; they argue only over his decision to end care, and he is painfully aware that he will be leaving behind an orphan. He treats Norman like an adult, inviting him to discuss with an attorney how he wants to live after Doug's death, but Norman is unable to even listen to such questions.

Norman is smart, and therefore a loner in school. In his English class, he makes an ironic comment at a moment when no one else in the class can supply a definition of irony, and is spotted for his intelligence by an English teacher (Adam Goldberg). At tryouts for a drama club, he applauds an offbeat audition by Emily Parrish (Emily VanCamp), after they've earlier had an ancient classic Meet Cute (they collide in the hall and he helps pick up her books, not awesomely original). She sweetly reveals that she likes him, and he confesses he's never been out on a date.

All of that could be in a conventional film. It is impending death that gives this one depth. In a foolish attempt to explain his behavior, he tells his best friend, James (Billy Lush), that he has cancer, and soon the whole school, and especially Emily and the English teacher, have the news. When Emily insists on meeting his father, that creates an obviously insoluble dilemma, not least because of the way his lie would make his father feel.

The film, directed by Jonathan Segal from an original screenplay by Talton Wingate, has the nerve to play this plot straight. The high school, in Washington state, seems relatively free of the cretins inhabiting most high school movies and avoids many opportunities for cheap laughs. Dan Byrd, whom you may have seen on *Cougar Town*, is a dead ringer for Bud Cort, but sidesteps the danger of excessive cuteness. Emily VanCamp (a longtime regular on TV's *Brothers and Sisters*) has a standard role, the friendly girl, but she handles it with delicacy and doesn't overplay; her performance depends above all on her ability to project empathy. When she learns Norman doesn't have cancer, that takes the need for empathy to another level, and the movie wisely finds a way to communicate that without the risks of dialogue. For me, Richard Jenkins was the heart of *Norman*. How often I've admired him, even in unworthy roles; he has such strength he needs never seem to try.

## North Face ★ ★ ★

NO MPAA RATING, 126 m., 2010

Benno Fuermann (Toni Kurz), Johanna Wokalek (Luise Fellner), Florian Lukas (Andi Hinterstoisser), Simon Schwarz (Willy Angerer), Georg Friedrich (Edi Rainer), Ulrich Tukur (Henry Arau). Directed by Philipp Stoelzl and produced by Benjamin Herrmann, Gerd Huber, Danny Krausz, Rudolf Santschi, Boris Schonfelder, Kurt Stocker, and Isabelle Welter. Screenplay by Stoelzl, Christoph Silber, Rupert Henning, and Johannes Naber.

The movies have long been convinced that any story can be improved by adding a romance. Not true. Any story can be improved by leaving out as much as you reasonably can. Consider *North Face*, the bone-chilling, superbly mounted record of an assault on the north face of the Eiger, which is known by the grim understatement as "the last remaining problem in the Alps."

Mountain climbing terrifies me because it has such a ruthless digital simplicity. It is either zero or one: (1) You are holding on. (Zero) You are falling. Time's arrow flies in one direction. Once you aren't holding on, there is nothing you can do. No skill, no courage, no training, nor any rope or piton.

These fears explain why in its scenes on the

Eiger itself *North Face* starts strongly and ends as unbearably riveting. They also explain why it was a strategic error to believe this story needed romantic and political subplots. You know something has gone wrong when a story about mountain climbers gives the sorta girlfriend of one of them second billing.

*North Face* is based on the true story of a May 1936 attempt on the Eiger by four climbers—two Germans and two Austrians who meet on the mountain in the movie but began together in real life. All four are experienced and confident. One is not very wise. Using the long-tested rope-and-piton method, they hope to reach the top after spending only one night in sleeping bags secured to the mountain. They have little petrol burners to heat tea or broth. They are very fit.

One of the Germans has doubts about making an attempt on a peak that has never been scaled and that froze two Germans to death the year before. The Eiger is known for its weather shifts and avalanches of snow and rocks. Meanwhile in Berlin, the Nazi editor (Ulrich Tukur) of a daily newspaper wants to produce German heroes for Hitler in the run-up to the Olympics. The two Germans, Toni Kurz and Andi Hinterstoisser (Benno Fuermann and Florian Lukas), both in the army, are such lackluster Nazis that they're assigned to cleaning latrines.

The editor's secretary, Luise Fellner (Johanna Wokalek), was sweet on Toni when they were young; Toni and Andi took her climbing with them. When her editor discovers she knows them, he orders her to go to the Eiger and convince them it's their patriotic duty to climb. Toni is convinced more by Luise than by Hitler. Setting off from the base, they eye two Austrians, Willy Angerer (Simon Schwarz) and Edi Rainer (Georg Friedrich). Higher up, their climbs will intersect.

The director, Philipp Stoelzl, is uncanny in his ability to convince us these four are actually climbing a mountain. Because the four actors could hardly be climbing themselves, he must use doubles for some shots. That is easier because of sunglasses, hoods, and blowing snow. Some of the shots must have been made on sets. None of that matters. I was on the side of that mountain all the way.

If the film had stayed there, it might have been devastatingly good. It's powerful enough as it is. But consider the 2004 film *Touching the Void*, about a climber who broke his leg, driving a bone through a knee socket, and later fell into an ice crevice, and agonizingly, unbelievably, made his way alone back down the mountain. That semi-documentary by Kevin Macdonald showed only the two climbers. That was more than enough.

In *North Face*, Stoelzl cuts to the luxury hotel at the base and even back to Berlin. There's a lot about the editor's ego and his desire to please Hitler. And much about Luise's fears for her friends and her determination to bring help to them after they disappear from view before the second night. We learn that railway tunnels through the mountain have occasional openings to the surface to admit air, and that the climbers might be approached by that means. Sounds reasonable, although some of her later decisions are dubious.

I believe audiences will enjoy this film. I did. But there's too much baggage along for the ride. It involves not only Luise but also the Nazis. A love story is not needed here, particularly when the reputed lovers got along perfectly well apart for ten years. And as for the Nazis, must every German film set in the '30s involve Nazism? Do you climb a mountain for Hitler and think about him all the way up? Not these climbers. They don't give a damn about Hitler.

*Note: Speaking of mountains and special effects, when Clint Eastwood made* The Eiger Sanction, *he personally performed in a scene showing him dangling at the end of a rope three thousand feet in the air. A telephoto lens zoomed in on him from a distance to prove it was really him. He told me he attended a sneak preview in disguise and overheard: "It really looked like it was Clint up there. I wonder how they did that."*

## Norwegian Wood ★ ★ ★

NO MPAA RATING, 133 m., 2012

Kenichi Matsuyama (Toru Watanabe), Rinko Kikuchi (Naoko), Kiko Mizuhara (Midori), Reika Kirishima (Reiko Ishida), Kengo Kora (Kizuki), Eriko Hatsune (Hatsumi), Tetsuji Tamayama (Nagasawa). Directed by Tran Anh Hung and produced by Shinji Ogawa. Screenplay by Hung, based on the novel by Haruki Murakami.

> "I once had a girl, or should I say, she once had me."
>
> —"Norwegian Wood" by Lennon and McCartney

There's something depressing about a young couple helplessly in love. Their state is so perfect it must be doomed. They project such qualities on their lovers that only disappointment can follow. Perhaps such truths help explain the success of Haruki Murakami's international best-seller *Norwegian Wood.* It's easier to identify with loss than love, because we have had so much more experience of it.

The novel has been filmed by Tran Anh Hung, born in Vietnam, long resident in Paris, whose *Scent of Green Papaya* (1993) was a gorgeous romance I thought was one of the best films of the year. He seems to fall in love with his actors, finding beautiful faces and then caressing them in close-up. Here he begins with two best friends and the girlfriend of one of them. I thought of *Jules and Jim.* Life is joyous and carefree. Then Kizuki (Kengo Kora) commits suicide. At the risk of sounding crass, may I suggest he wanted to quit while he was ahead? Do suicidal young lovers realize that romance is short but death is long?

Kizuki leaves behind his girlfriend, Naoko (Rinko Kikuchi), and his best friend, Toru Watanabe (Kenichi Matsuyama). It feels wrong to them that they are only two. On her twentieth birthday, Naoko loses her virginity to Toru, and explains why Kizuki, who was so close to her ever since sixth grade, never made love with her. The reason is not what you may be thinking.

Naoko disappears. Toru occupies himself with school, and then meets Midori (Kiko Mizuhara), a ribald girl who likes sex and flavors her speech with cheerful obscenities. Midori was the most popular character with the readers of Murakami's novel, probably because she wasn't as gloomy as the others. Here she is much toned down because Tran is more drawn to poignancy about the transience of happiness.

Word comes that Naoko is living in some sort of retreat in a beautiful distant area, a place that seems halfway between a spa and a sanatorium. Here she is inseparable from an equally beautiful woman who is a fellow patient who teaches music there. Toru comes to visit and what follows between Naoko and him are dreamy scenes of languorous caresses and whispering, poetic love talk. They are photographed in scenes of nature and snow, as if Tran seeks to create in his visuals the tenderness of their love. Let's hope Naoko doesn't learn about Midori. The naughty girl isn't all that important to Toru, really, but she represents a flaw in Naoko's idea of Toru, and she is too fragile to sustain such a blow.

I'm sure there are ages and personalities that would find the young love in *Norwegian Wood* irresistible. Maybe a loving young couple would find their own story in it, as so many have found themselves in *Romeo and Juliet.* There is something in the nature of director Tran Anh Hung, however, that seems to resist happy endings. In the emotional arc of his art, the high point seems to be bittersweet. It's sweet all the way up, wavers in dread, and slides down to doom.

The movie's cinematography, by Mark Lee Ping Bin, paints each frame in rapture. The actors are so attractive they could be models for *Vogue,* and perhaps they are; certainly they're effective in their roles, which require a lot of soft, intimate dialogue. There are a couple of points in the film when the Beatles song slips in; I wonder if Watanabe took note of this lyric: "When I awoke, I was alone, this bird had flown."

## No Strings Attached ★ ★

R, 106 m., 2011

Natalie Portman (Emma), Ashton Kutcher (Adam), Cary Elwes (Dr. Metzner), Kevin Kline (Alvin), Greta Gerwig (Patrice), Lake Bel (Lucy), Olivia Thirlby (Katie), Chris "Ludacris" Bridges (Wallace), Ophelia Lovibond (Vanessa). Directed by Ivan Reitman and produced by Reitman, Jeffrey Clifford, and Joe Medjuck. Screenplay by Elizabeth Meriwether.

*No Strings Attached* poses the question: Is it possible to regularly have sex with someone and not run a risk of falling in love? The answer is yes. Now that we have that settled, consider the case of Emma (Natalie Portman) and Adam (Ashton Kutcher), who met when they were six and now meet when they're maybe twenty-six. Busy people. He's a low-rent TV producer and she's a medical student. She doesn't have time for romance, and he's dating the sexy Vanessa (played by the well-named Ophelia Lovibond).

Still, one must do something about sex, lest the pipes run rusty, as my friend Henry Togna Sr., the London hotelier, instructed me when he was well into his seventies. Adam and Emma see each other at a party, remember each other after all those years, yet do not realize they're having a Meet Cute. Then Adam discovers Vanessa has dumped him and moved in with his father (Kevin Kline). In response, he begins to drink, which is what the Jack Lemmon character always does in these situations, and what with one thing and another he wakes up naked in Emma's apartment while she and three roommates reassure him they're all interns and it's deja vu when it comes to viewing the male netherlands on display.

Is there something a little, I dunno, *dated* about a comedy where a guy clutches a towel to his privates while girls giggle at him? And when he asks if he slept with anyone last night, why does that remind me of Doris Day in *Where Were You When the Lights Went Out?* Here is a titillating sex romp in 2011, when the very words "titillating" and "romp" have outlasted their shelf lives. The movie is rated R, but it's the most watery R I've seen. It's more of a PG-13 playing dress-up.

Anyway, finding out he hasn't slept with Emma, Adam engages in sitcom badinage that quickly leads to the old rumpy-pumpy, and they find the pipes running marvelously clear. What a discovery! They can have sex and remain just friends! This is a great convenience. They proceed to frolic like two bunnies in clover, using their cell phones and texting skills to arrange emergency trysts in roughly anything except a bed.

All of this is fun while it lasts. Then the wheels of Hollywood morality begin to grind. There was a time when the very premise of this film would have been banned, but times change, and now characters can do pretty much anything as long as they don't get away with it. Although *No Strings Attached* might have been more fun if Adam and Emma had investigated the long-term possibilities of casual sex, it is required that the specter of Romantic Love raise its ominous head. Are they . . . becoming too fond? Emma suggests they try sleeping with others so, you know, they won't get too hung up on each other. If you've ever seen a romantic comedy, you know how that works. Experience shows that *not* sleeping with others is the foolproof way of not getting too hung up, etc.

This is a strange film. Its premise is so much more transgressive than its execution. It's as if the 1970s never happened, let alone subsequent decades. Emma and Adam aren't modern characters. They're sitcom characters allowed to go all the way like grown-ups. As the wheels of the plot creak and groan, we're like kids in the backseat, asking, "Are we there yet?" Some diversion is supplied by the subplot involving Adam's dad, Alvin (Kline), an aging TV star trapped forever in his own misspent youth. Alvin is a dedicated hedonist, which Vanessa finds to her liking because hedonists are always happy to pay, one way or another, for their hedonism, and Vanessa is happy to be paid, one way or another.

Natalie Portman won an Academy Award for *Black Swan*. Why she helped produce this I cannot say. Ambitious actors usually do dreck like this in order to afford to produce a movie like *Black Swan*. All the same, she does what she can; she has an edge, aggressive timing, and impressive enthusiasm for sex romping. Of Ashton Kutcher I have less to say. He seems to be a very nice guy, a little too large for agile romping and still too young for a Brendan Fraser role. When I saw him in *The Butterfly Effect* (2004), I registered that he could act, but in this material he's essentially just the Male Unit. There is no character there.

## Nowhere Boy ★ ★ ★ ½

R, 97 m., 2010

Aaron Johnson (John), Kristin Scott Thomas (Mimi), Anne-Marie Duff (Julia), Thomas Sangster (Paul), David Morrissey (Bobby), Ophelia Lovibond (Marie), David Threlfall (Uncle George). Directed by Sam Taylor-Wood and produced by Robert Bernstein, Kevin Loader, and Douglas Rae. Screenplay by Matt Greenhalgh, based on a memoir by Julia Baird.

John Lennon wrote the song "Julia" about his mother, and it is a strangely objective love song, as if about a real girlfriend and not a mom. Perhaps that's how he thought of her. When he was very young, he came under the care of his Aunt Mimi, whom he regarded as his mother, and in the telling in *Nowhere Boy*, he didn't see Julia again until the day of his uncle's funeral. The film is based on a memoir written by Julia Baird, his half-sister, who must be presumed to have good information.

"Julia" is a song of longing and regret, written some years after Julia's sudden death. Their relationship was close and did not have the time to grow old. There's a video online of Sean Lennon singing it, in front of back-projected photographs of his father and Julia, and also of his mother, Yoko Ono. "This song is for my mother," he says, and as he sings it, he sounds eerily like his father, in intonation, arrangement, emotion. Perhaps it is for both his parents. He was young when he lost John, and John was young when he lost Julia. Both memories are of interrupted love.

The young man John Lennon (Aaron Johnson) in *Nowhere Boy* was cocky and vulnerable. He was raised in an ordinary lower-working-class home, not far from Strawberry Fields in Liverpool, by an aunt (Kristin Scott Thomas) who loved him, but was reserved and cool. She and her husband had taken the child in after her younger, prettier sister proved incapable of caring for him; John learns the details of his adoption late in the film. He knew Mimi was not his mother, but had no idea that all during his childhood Julia lived only a few blocks away.

She must have seen him often, if he had only known it. Did she stay away out of respect for Mimi? He glimpses her at the funeral of his uncle and instinctively knows who she is. When he discovers where she lives, he knocks on her door and she greets him with instant, embracing love; we get the sense that she was a woman quick to love, impulsive, more spontaneous than the responsible Mimi. Because John and Julia are essentially strangers, their relationship has elements of unrealized romance. There is the tension between joy and sadness we often feel in Lennon's songs, and perhaps we see some of the origin of his place in the flow of British Romanticism.

*Nowhere Boy* is deliberately *not* about the future John Lennon, Paul McCartney, and George Harrison, nor about the birth of the Beatles. The cataclysm of their future global fame is nowhere on the horizon. It is about a not remarkable childhood and youth in Liverpool, marred by the sudden death of his Uncle George (David Threlfall), also warm and playful, more spontaneous than Mimi. The two men must have formed a club of their own in the Mimi-ordered household.

There are times when I would have liked a little more detail about the gestation of the future musicians. The only actual Beatles note in the film is its opening chord, from the distinctive first sound of *A Hard Day's Night.* We see John meeting Paul, and through Paul, George, in the ways that teenage boys meet. No heartfelt conversations, no elaborate daydreams; music seems to have been a natural way of expression for them. The seminal Beatles moment in the film may be when John goes to the cinema and sees Elvis Presley singing in a newsreel. Later generations can hardly comprehend how, or perhaps even why, Elvis represented a moment of decisive social change.

What do we really learn from *Nowhere Boy*? We don't really learn much about the actual early days of the Beatles as a band. Of course there is no Ringo Starr, who may deserve his own film. What we do learn is that it could be said of the teenage John Lennon that he:

*Doesn't have a point of view,*
*Knows not where he's going to,*
*Isn't he a bit like you and me?*

I think we also learn something more important. We learn that the emotional roller coaster of his formative years probably contributed to the complexity of his lyrics. We learn why there's so often in his music the top level of what seems clear, and then, below, echoes of something else. We feel elation and sadness as simultaneous possibilities. We arrive at the possibility that if Julia had always been there for him, he might not have been there for us. We reflect that even if all you need is love, that isn't always all you get.

## Nuremberg: Its Lesson for Today ★ ★ ★

NO MPAA RATING, 78 m., 2011

Liev Schreiber (Narrator). A documentary directed by Pare Lorentz and produced by Lorentz, Budd Schulberg, and Stuart Schulberg.

Of all the many documentaries about the Holocaust, this was the first, made before the term was routinely linked to the event more properly called the Shoah. *Nuremberg: Its Lesson for Today* was edited from many hours of film taken at the eleven-month Nuremberg Trial, which, starting in 1945, placed twenty-two high-ranking Nazis on trial for crimes that together amounted to an outrage against decency. Assembled and edited by Stuart Schulberg with U.S. government funding, the film was exhibited throughout Germany in 1948 and 1949, and then taken from release and never seen in America.

It gave audiences the spectacle of seeing such iconic Nazis as Goring, Bormann, Hess, and Speer now humbled in an international courtroom, earphones clamped to their heads as they listen to the irrefutable evidence of their infamy. The film intercuts statements by the prosecution and defense and brief statements by some of the defendants.

As the record of crimes is read out, the film edits in horrifying footage from other documentaries made for the U.S. Army by such as John Ford. I hadn't seen all of these images before. Jews being marched naked through the streets, gloating mobs empowered by flimsy armbands, skeletal "subjects of medical experiments," the impossibly emaciated survivors of the death camps. An unspeakable sequence of corpses being piled into a mass grave, raising the question of why such film was shot, and why anyone agreed to be seen in it. The systematic extermination of six million Jews and nearly as many others was carried out boldly and openly, without apology, and when the unrepentant Goring is asked in the dock if he ever said human life was worthless, his answer rings out: *"Jawohl!"*

Most of the others seem repentant, and many in their final statements express resentment at what they see as Hitler's betrayal of their values, whatever they thought those were. It is revealing that even then, with the horrifying portrait of their evil deeds laid bare, they instinctively glorified Hitler so much that it was all his fault. Every single one of them was apparently only following orders, even those shown to have personally signed documents ordering the murder of children and those too weak to be useful slaves.

The film is not sophisticated; it is a bludgeon in words and images that cannot be presented otherwise. It was seen as a weapon of "denazification." Some of it feels anachronistic because at Nuremberg, for the first time, evidence was assembled and presented that has later become well known. Many Germans claimed at the time they didn't know what was being done in their names; for some of them it must have been true, and the purpose of this film was to show them their evil leaders, sitting in the dock—never, ever, in the footage here, even looking at one another.

The film, as I said, was never seen in America. This print has been assembled under the supervision of Sandra Schulberg, Stuart's daughter, and Josh Waletzky, who began with an archival print found in Berlin. They have made the decision to restore the original film. Good enough, but there could have been two modern additions. Subtitles would be invaluable to identify the defendants. And there could have been an explanation of why the film was suppressed.

At the time of the Nuremberg trial, it was a growing embarrassment that Stalin, an ally during the war, was as guilty of atrocities as anyone in the dock. And, as Robert McNamara much later said that General Jimmy Doolittle told him after the bombing of Tokyo, that, too, was a war crime.

This point is well made by Salon's film critic, Andrew O'Hehir, who writes: "Even amid all the contradiction and ambiguity of the Nuremberg process, the argument made there was clear: All the nations of the world had to be held to the same standard, and every nation that waged aggressive warfare and committed war crimes, no matter how large or rich or powerful, would be judged accordingly."

## The Nutcracker in 3-D ★

PG, 107 m., 2010

Elle Fanning (Mary), Nathan Lane (Uncle Albert), John Turturro (The Rat King), Frances de la Tour (The Rat Queen), Richard E. Grant (Father), Yulia Visotskaya (Mother/Snow Fairy), Shirley Henderson (The Nutcracker), Aaron Michael Drozin (Max), Charlie Rowe (The Prince). Directed by Andrei Konchalovsky. Produced by Konchalovsky and Paul Lowin. Screenplay by Konchalovsky and Chris Solimine.

From what dark night of the soul emerged the wretched idea for *The Nutcracker in 3-D*? Who considered it even remotely a plausible idea for a movie? It begins with an awkward approximation of the story behind the Tchaikovsky ballet, and then turns it into a war by the nutcracker prince against the Holocaust. Am I exaggerating? At one point, the evil Rat King (John Turturro) has his troopers snatch toys from the hands of children so they can be tossed into furnaces, and the smoke will emerge from high chimneys to blot out the sun.

Yes. And the Rats are dressed in fascistic uniforms. And against them stand our heroine, Mary (Elle Fanning), and her Christmas present, a nutcracker (voice of Shirley Henderson) that has imprisoned a handsome prince (Charlie Rowe). And two-legged helicopters swoop low over screaming children, and the city is laid waste, and the Rats dream of world domination.

You may be in disbelief. I was. This is one of those rare holiday movies that may send children screaming under their seats. Their parents, naively hoping to see a sweet version of *The Nutcracker Suite*, will be appalled or angry, take your choice. Yes, there are melodies that began with Tchaikovsky at one point, but now they have (are you sitting down?) lyrics by Tim Rice.

*The Nutcracker in 3-D* easily qualifies as one of the most preposterous ideas in the history of the movies. It isn't a story; it's a gag line for one of Letterman's "Top 10" lists (No. 9, *It's a Horrible Life;* No. 8, *A Christmas Carol in Hell* . . .).

Andrei Konchalovsky, who wrote and directed it, says this has been a dream project for twenty years. That is tragic. Konchalovsky made the great films *Shy People* and *Runaway Train*, and perhaps he became obsessed with this folly. But what did others think? What about Nathan Lane, who plays a character not previously associated with *The Nutcracker*, Albert Einstein? Yes, he gets to sing a song about the theory of relativity, but not since he played Jacqueline Susann's adoring husband in *Isn't She Great* has a role been more thankless.

Only one thing could have made this premise worse, and they haven't neglected it. That would be to present it in 3-D. They have. The movie was filmed in Hungary in 2007, and perhaps those screening it sensed a certain lack of enthusiasm. Maybe they thought that by retrospectively "adapting" it to 3-D, it would play better. No luck. I've seen bad retro 3-D. I have never seen 3-D as bad as this. The picture is so dim and dingy you almost wonder if the smoke from those burning toys is drifting between you and the screen.

# O

## October Baby ★ ★

PG-13, 105 m., 2012

---

Rachel Hendrix (Hannah), Jason Burkey (Jason), John Schneider (Jacob), Jennifer Price (Grace), Shari Rigby (Cindy), Jasmine Guy (Mary), Chris Sligh (B-Mac). Directed by Andrew Erwin and Jon Erwin and produced by Jon Erwin, Dan Atchsion, and Cecil Stokes. Screenplay by Jon Erwin and Theresa Preston.

---

*October Baby* tells the story of a nineteen-year-old college student named Hannah, who is introduced by collapsing onstage in the first act of a college play. In a fraught scene with her doctor and her parents, she learns that her collapse was likely associated with childhood epilepsy, and that it might be related to her birth. "We aren't your birth parents," says her father (John Schneider), adding somewhat hurriedly that they always meant to tell her, but . . .

Hannah (Rachel Hendrix) discovers that she was born as the result of a failed late-term abortion. Her father doesn't want her to know this, but her mother (Jennifer Price) silently hands over her birth certificate. After a long lakeside discussion with her lifelong friend Jason (Jason Burkey), she decides to join Jason and a group of friends in a trip to Mardi Gras; they can stop off on the way in Baton Rouge to meet Hannah's birth mother, which seems a rather casual way to treat that emotional event.

The trip is unhelpful to the plot, which surrounds a potentially strong story with distracting changes in mood and style. Low-rent comedy relief centers around Jason's cousin B-Mac (Chris Sligh), the bearded, roly-poly owner of an old Volkswagen van he treasures as a "classic." There are too many scenes along the way, as the old van (the vehicle of choice in countless 1960s road movies) rolls down highways while the soundtrack bursts with middle-of-the-road pop rock.

An undetermined number of friends share the van with them, including a young black woman who is placed prominently in several shots but is never mentioned, identified, or spoken to. Her purpose is to show that they have a black friend. Then there's an ungainly scene in a hotel where Hannah and Jason are so determined to not share the same bed that they end up camping out in the lobby. This comes after the night clerk offers them the deluxe luxury suite, but they request a regular room. Turning down the free suite doesn't sound typical of college students—hey, maybe it had two bedrooms?

This whole stretch feels like padding. I was painfully unconvinced when Hannah finds the hospital mentioned on the birth certificate, which looks like a boarded-up motel, and she and Jason break in—expecting, I guess, to find Hannah's files still waiting around. They're arrested for breaking and entering, and in a clunky coincidence, the cop on duty just so happens to know the nurse who signed the certificate.

Now, at last, comes a scene with the weight and dialogue the story deserves. Jasmine Guy plays nurse Mary, who is able to describe to Hannah the entire story of her birth and the trauma of her mother. (The mother feared her law career would be threatened by having the baby of a man she met only once, in a bar, while drunk.) So shaken was Mary that she never assisted in such a procedure again. In another convenient coincidence, she *happened* to run into the birth mother (Shari Rigby) a few weeks ago, luckily recognizing her after nineteen years, and is able to hand Hannah her business card. Not every birth mother is tracked down so efficiently. Jasmine Guy's monologue here is so well performed and effective that we almost forgive it for being such a contrivance and shoehorning in all the film's necessary background detail.

There is a scene with Hannah and the birth mother, but it's a disappointment. This woman is detached and uninterested, and stays in the movie only long enough for Hannah to stand on the sidewalk and see her and her husband with their own beautiful baby girl, who solemnly waves at Hannah (apparently sensing they are sisters?). Shari Rigby appears again in the end credits, where at last the movie finds more time to let her speak.

Now comes another monologue dropped from the sky. Hannah wanders into a Catholic church and a priest (Rodney Clark), luckily hanging around, asks if he can help. She's a Baptist, Hannah says, but fortunately a priest can help even a Baptist, and the priest quotes from one of Paul's epistles and follows it with brief advice about the importance of being able to forgive. Having discovered forgiveness, Hannah and the movie use it to resolve all the outstanding conflicts in the story involving the birth mother, her adoptive parents, and Jason.

*October Baby* is being promoted as a Christian film, and it could have been an effective one. Rachel Hendrix is surprisingly capable in her first feature role, and Jasmine Guy is superb in her scene. Unfortunately, the film as a whole is amateurish and ungainly, can't find a consistent tone, is too long, is overladen with music that tries to paraphrase the story, and is photographed with too many beauty shots that slow thc progress.

## October Country ★ ★ ★

NO MPAA RATING, 80 m., 2010

Featuring members of the Mosher family. A documentary directed by Michael Palmieri and Donal Mosher and produced by Palmieri. Screenplay by Palmieri and Mosher.

"We wouldn't know normal if it fell on us," Donald Mosher says. He sits and smokes on the front porch of one of two adjacent houses that are home to four generations of his family. The Moshers are a sad and dysfunctional family, which they are curiously willing to explain, as if they've spent years rehearsing their mistakes. "Bad taste in men runs in the family," observes Desiree, Donald's eleven-year-old granddaughter.

The Moshers live in the beautiful Mohawk Valley in upstate New York. "Here is where we were born, and here, I guess, is where we'll die," says Dottie Mosher, the matriarch. She and Donald are the enduring centers of a family of a daughter, Donna, who has a history of abusive men; a granddaughter, Daneal, who seems to be following the same pattern; her sister, Desiree, who explains, "I'm a lot smarter than the rest of them"; and Daneal's daughter, Ruby. There is also Don's sister, Denise, who dresses in a black cape, haunts cemeteries to videotape ghosts, and is a Wiccan.

None of the husbands are seen in the film. The only male apart from Donald is Chris, a foster child he and Dottie took in. He's been in jail, explains in one scene how he likes Walmart because it's "easy to steal from," warns the Moshers he'll be trouble for them, and proves it by stealing two computers. Dottie wipes aside a tear as Chris goes back behind bars.

What happened to this family? One of the two codirectors is Donal Mosher, another son, who is never mentioned in the film. His photographs of his family inspired the film, made with his partner, Michael Palmieri, a director of TV commercials. The film is often lovely to regard, and sees the Moshers surrounded by the beauty of the seasons between one Halloween and the next.

The legacy of sadness started when Donald went to serve in Vietnam. Dottie remembers him as a cheerful, upbeat kid when he went away. Something happened there to change him forever. He never talks about it—or about much of anything else. He watches old war movies on TV, makes doll house furniture in his attic workshop, and watches with dour passivity as the generations go awry.

He worked at first in the Remington Arms Factory, the chief employer in the valley, but found his job so boring "an ape could do it." He observes, "Remington executives get an eight-hundred-thousand-dollar Christmas bonus, and the workers get a damn belt buckle after thirty years." He quit, went to work as a police officer, and on his first day on the job covered a suicide that left brains all over a garage wall.

Donna and Daneal seem to move through a cloud of gloom. They know all about abusive men, but seem to feel that is their fate. The spark of hope is Desiree—"Desi"—who is spirited and sarcastic, and seems to have gotten the family's entire allotment of senses of humor. Even at her age, she sees the problems and refuses to enlist in them. I hope her school can set her on a good path in life; she seems ready for one.

One understands how Donal Mosher could obtain access to these moments of stark honesty and bleak truth. One wonders what the family thought of the film when they saw it. This is the face of dysfunction. Apparently alcohol and drugs are not involved, except perhaps with some of the missing men. The drug here is despair. They seem to treat it with cigarettes.

*Note: The photographs that inspired the film are here: http://donalmosher.com/.*

## Of Gods and Men ★ ★ ★

PG-13, 122 m., 2011

Lambert Wilson (Christian), Michael Lonsdale (Luc), Olivier Rabourdin (Christophe), Philippe Laudenbach (Celestin), Jacques Herlin (Amedee), Loic Pichon (Jean-Pierre), Xavier Maly (Michel), Jean-Marie Frin (Paul), Abdelhafid Metalsi (Nouredine), Sabrina Ouazani (Rabbia). Directed by Xavier Beauvois and produced by Pascal Caucheteux and Etienne Comar. Screenplay by Beauvois and Comar.

"Men never do evil so completely and cheerfully as when they do it from religious conviction." So wrote the French philosopher Pascal in the seventeenth century, and his words are quoted by one of the monks in this solemn and engrossing film. *Of Gods and Men* is based on an event in Algeria in 1996, when eight Trappist monks were taken hostage by terrorists. The film centers on the fact that the monks could easily have evaded this but chose not to.

Every scene in the film involves these monks, and most of the scenes are set in their monastery. Several times a day they put on white robes and pray and sing in a little chapel. The rest of the time they tend crops, keep bees, sell honey, treat the sick of the district, eat bread and soup while being read to, and hold community meetings around a table with a candle on it.

They make no attempt to convert anyone to Catholicism. They live peacefully in a Muslim community, attend a service for a child, employ some of the nearby people as workers. There is a deep serenity in their way of life. Although we learn to know the monks by face and name, the film makes no particular attempt to focus on their personalities, except for two: Brother Christian (Lambert Wilson), whom they have elected as leader, and Brother Luc, played by gentle old Michael Lonsdale, whom I first saw in 1962 in Orson Welles's *The Trial*—that time, too, playing a cleric.

Luc is the doctor, himself old, sick, and asthmatic, but seeing countless patients every day and sometimes imparting benevolent advice, as when a village girl questions him about love. Christian is clear-eyed and resolute in his idea of their mission in this place distant from their birthplace in France; they have been called by God to minister to the sick and hungry.

There is revolution in the land. A group of Serbian migrant workers have their throats cut by terrorists. The government urges the monks to leave, the army offers protection, but Christian refuses; there is no place for the army in a monastery. They will deal with what comes.

The most fraught scene comes when terrorists break in on Christmas Eve, demanding that old Luc come with them to care for a wounded comrade. Christian turns them away, after quoting what the Quran has to say in favor of Christians. Their leader, Rabbia (Sabrina Ouazani), is, somewhat unexpectedly, convinced. The next group of terrorists will not be so forgiving.

*Of Gods and Men* asks us to admire these monks, whose lives are wholly devoted to good works. There is an uplifting scene when they welcome an old friend with a dinner at which wine is served, the music of *Swan Lake* plays, and joy shines from their faces. After some discussion, they follow Christian in deciding to stay at the monastery, no matter what.

The movie has a narration making a sharp distinction between radical Islamic terrorists and the peaceful Muslims who share the district with the monks. But stay. There is another side to the Algerian question, the side of the forcible French occupation and its decades of repressive rule. This land is not France. Technically, which side could be called terrorist?

The film doesn't raise such political questions, except in one enigmatic sentence by a local official. It focuses entirely on the nobility of the monks in choosing to stay with their vocation and their duty in the face of quite probable death. Did they make the right choice? In their own idealistic terms, yes. In realistic terms, I say no. They have the ability to help many who need it for years to come. It is egotism to believe their help must take place in this specific monastery. Between the eight of them they have perhaps a century of life of usefulness remaining. Do they have a right to deprive those who need it of their service? In doing so, are they committing the sin of pride?

I found myself resisting the film's pull of easy emotion. There are fundamental questions here, and the film doesn't engage them. I believe Christian should have had the humility to lead his monks away from the path of self-sacrifice.

## Once Upon a Time in Anatolia ★ ★ ★ ½

NO MPAA RATING, 157 m., 2012

Muhammet Uzuner (Doctor Cemal), Yilmaz Erdogan (Commissar Naci), Taner Birsel (Prosecutor Nusret), Ahmet Mumtaz Taylan (Driver Arab Ali), Firat Tanis (Suspect Kenan), Ercan Kesal (Mukhtar). Directed by Nuri Bilge Ceylan and produced by Zeynep Ozbatur Atakan. Screenplay by Ercan Kesal, Ebru Ceylan, and Nuri Bilge Ceylan.

*Once Upon a Time in Anatolia* is 157 minutes long and its story unfolds slowly and obliquely. I tell you now so you won't complain later. It needs to be long, and it needs to be indirect because the film is about how sad truths can be revealed during the slow process of doing a job. The Turkish director Nuri Bilge Ceylan doesn't slap us with big, dramatic moments, but allows us to live along with his characters as things occur to them.

The first two hours of the film take place at night on a vast plain in Anatolia, undulating greenly beneath the moon. From a great height, we see three sets of headlights snaking down an empty road. Distant figures get out, meander in a field, return to the cars. In closer shots, we discover the caravan is in search of a corpse. The cars contain a police chief, a prosecutor, a doctor, a driver, two suspects, and a man with a laptop who will type out testimony.

This search will not end until just before dawn. Suspect One has already signed a confession, but is having trouble remembering where the body was buried because he was drunk at the time. Suspect Two seems incompetent to remember anything. All the men know the local countryside, but it looks much the same; one watering trough for livestock looks like another, and what does Suspect One mean by a "round tree"?

The men are tired. They know one another well. They get out of the cars many times and poke around. The night is filled with barking dogs. Rain clouds are drawing in front of the moon. There is distant thunder. The driver offers the prosecutor a cream biscuit, and he asks for another. A story is told about a woman who predicted the day of her death and keeled over on schedule. A local mayor is awakened and offers them tea and food.

The mayor has a beautiful daughter. The men grow morose as they reflect how in this district she will not find the life she deserves. They are also sad, as many men are when regarding a woman too beautiful for them to hope for. The mayor complains that he cannot get funds for a new morgue. The young people all leave. The old people die, and the young people want to come home for the first time in years to view them. But bodies do not keep well in the old morgue, and they start to smell.

How does this sound to you? I'm told we movie critics praise movies that are long and boring. I can imagine many people finding this movie an ordeal. That depends on how easily they can be drawn into the story that is taking place under the surface and within these minds. A life has been taken. A bureaucratic procedure is being followed. The body is dug up and returned for an autopsy to another morgue, where the coroner complains he needs a small power saw. The doctor looks out the window and sees something that inspires him to lie about the results of the autopsy.

We discover in these parting passages how the night has affected them all, especially the prosecutor and doctor, but also Suspect One, who begins to cry, and the son of the dead man. The little story about the woman who died on schedule takes on a great importance. This night has been of crucial importance to some of the characters, and we could not understand that in a different film. Nuri Bilge Ceylan, one of Turkey's best directors, has a deep understanding of human nature. He loves his characters and empathizes with them. They deserve better than to be shuttled around in a facile plot. They deserve empathy. So do we all.

*Note: The film won the Grand Jury Prize at Cannes 2011.*

## One Day ★ ★ ★

PG-13, 108 m., 2011

Anne Hathaway (Emma), Jim Sturgess (Dexter), Jodie Whittaker (Tilly), Patricia Clarkson (Alison), Romola Garai (Sylvie), Rafe Spall (Ian), Tom Mison (Callum). Directed by Lone Scherfig and produced by Nina Jacobson. Screenplay by David Nicholls, based on his novel.

With some people we are destined to become lifelong friends. It can't be planned that way. Chance plays a role. There is an underlying harmony that persists in spite of the whims of fate. When childhood sweethearts marry after not seeing one another for thirty or forty years, it makes perfect sense to me. The instinctive understanding is there.

*One Day* is a film based on the David Nicholls best-seller about a boy and girl who graduate from the University of Edinburgh on July 15, 1988, and spend the night together. The story follows them by dropping in on July 15 of their lives for year after year, which is a useful device, because it eliminates the need to show us the events of the other days of their years. Success, failure, marriages, divorce can take place off-screen if necessary. What matters is their accumulating effects.

Dexter (Jim Sturgess) is a twit. In the 1970s he might have been known as a Hooray Henry. Emma (Anne Hathaway) is an earnest, hardworking girl. Dexter is upper class. Emma is middle class. Dexter goes into television production. Emma gets a job as a waitress in a Tex-Mex restaurant in London I believe I have actually dined at. It wasn't bad. Dexter becomes famous quickly, and fades inexorably because there is really nothing there. Emma becomes obscure quickly, and only gradually becomes successful because she persists in believing in herself and her gift for writing.

Life has its way of bringing them together for periodic updates. Some of these meetings are intentional, some accidental. The thread is never broken, not even after Dexter marries and Emma takes up with Ian (Rafe Spall, son of Timothy). Since Emma and Dexter are both beautiful people, there is no imbalance there. It is all in character. Emma has it.

The film depends on a reliable fictional element, the redeeming power of the love of a good woman. Dexter is a superficial fool who descends through ever-lowering levels of humiliation on TV, cable, and the Internet, until he has been reduced to a punch line. Emma stays her course. Her persistence and success are like a rebuke to Dexter. But it is important for us, and Emma, to realize that he is fundamentally a good person at heart—potentially.

The movie tells their story in a palatable romcom manner, much enriched by its locations in Edinburgh, London, Paris, and elsewhere. Such characters never live in forlorn places. The film is carefully crafted to make even its sad moments seem not all that bad, and it modulates its progress toward happiness without unseemly haste. But it unfolds as it must: A film cannot begin with two such attractive people and follow them for years into unhappiness and misery. Every single joyous love story ends in death if you follow it long enough. The movies make life easier for us by usually stopping in the middle.

In a season of movies dumb and dumber, *One Day* has style, freshness, and witty bantering dialogue. Anne Hathaway is so attractive that she would be advised to sometimes play against type (the eyeglasses she wears at the beginning are a bit over the top). Jim Sturgess contributes the film's most versatile performance, one that depends on exact timing and control of the balance between pathos and buffoonery. It's a decent night at the movies, if however a letdown after *An Education*, the previous film by Lone Scherfig. Why July 15? That's St. Swithin's Day, although Dexter and Emma eventually find it has a more direct relevance.

## 127 Hours ★ ★ ★ ★

R, 93 m., 2010

James Franco (Aron Ralston), Amber Tamblyn (Megan), Kate Mara (Kristi), Clemence Poesy (Rana), Treat Williams (Aron's Dad), Kate Burton (Aron's Mom), Lizzy Caplan (Sonja). Directed by Danny Boyle and produced by Boyle, Christian Colson, and John Smithson. Screenplay by Boyle and Simon Beaufoy, based on the book *Between a Rock and a Hard Place* by Aron Ralston.

Sometimes a person will make an enormous mistake and get a lot of time to think about it.

There was a man who went over Niagara Falls sealed inside a big rubber ball. It never made it to the bottom. The ball lodged somewhere on the way down. He'd counted on his team to cut him out at the bottom. Oops! Aron Ralston, the hero of *127 Hours*, had an Oops! moment. That's even what he calls it. He went hiking in the wilderness without telling anyone where he was going, and then, in a deep, narrow crevice, got his forearm trapped between a boulder and the canyon wall. Oops.

We all heard about this. Ralston stumbled out to safety more than five days later, having cut off his own right arm to escape. He is an upbeat and resilient person and has returned to rock climbing, although now, I trust, after filing a plan, going with a companion, and not leaving his Swiss Army knife behind. The knife would have been ever so much more convenient than his multipurpose tool. I imagine that every time he considers his missing right forearm, he feels that, under the circumstances, he's better off without it.

What would you have done? What about me? I don't know if I could have done it. It involves a gruesome ordeal for Ralston, and for the film's audience, a few of whom have been said to faint. But from such harrowing beginnings, it's rather awesome what an entertaining film Danny Boyle has made here. Yes, entertaining.

For most of the film he deals with one location and one actor, James Franco. There's a carefree prologue in which Ralston and a couple of young women hikers have a swim in an underwater cavern. And during moments of hallucination other people from his life seem to visit. But the fundamental reality is expressed in the title of the book he wrote about his experience: *Between a Rock and a Hard Place.*

Franco does a good job of suggesting two aspects of Ralston's character: (1) He's a cocky, bold adventurer who trusts his skills and likes taking chances, and (2) he's logical and bloody-minded enough to cut through his own skin and bone to save his life. One aspect gets him into his problem, and the other gets him out.

Is the film watchable? Yes, compulsively. Films like this don't move quickly or slowly, they seem to take place all in the same moment. They prey on our own deep fear of being trapped somewhere and understanding that there doesn't seem to be any way to escape. Edgar Allan Poe mined this vein in several different ways. Ralston is at least fortunate to be standing on a secure foothold; one can imagine the boulder falling and leaving him dangling in midair from the trapped arm.

Suddenly his world has become very well defined. There is the crevice. There is the strip of sky above, crossed by an eagle on its regular flight path. There are the things he brought with him: a video camera, some water, a little food, his inadequate little tool. It doesn't take long to make an inventory. He shouts for help, but who can hear? The two women campers have long since gone their way and won't report him missing because they won't realize that he is. For anyone to happen to find him is unthinkable. He will die or do something.

*127 Hours* is like an exercise in conquering the unfilmable. Boyle uses magnificent cinematography by Anthony Dod Mantle and Enrique Chediak, establishing the vastness of the Utah wilderness and the very specific details of Ralston's small portion of it. His editor, Jon Harris, achieves the delicate task of showing an arm being cut through without ever *quite* showing it. For the audience the worst moment is not a sight but a sound. Most of us have never heard that sound before, but we know exactly what it is.

Pain and bloodshed are so common in the movies. They are rarely amped up to the level of reality because we want to be entertained, not sickened. We and the heroes feel immune. *127 Hours* removes the filters. It implicates us. By identification we are trapped in the canyon; we are cutting into our own flesh. One element that film can suggest but not evoke is the brutality of the pain involved. I can't even imagine what it felt like. Maybe that made it easier for Ralston, because in one way or another his decision limited the duration of his suffering.

He must be quite a man. The film deliberately doesn't make him a hero—more of a capable athlete trapped by a momentary decision. He cuts off his arm because he has to. He was lucky to succeed. One can imagine a news story of his body being discovered long afterward, with his arm only partly cut through. He did what he had to do, which doesn't make you a hero. We could do it, too. Oh, yes we could.

## One Lucky Elephant ★ ★ ★

NO MPAA RATING, 84 m., 2011

A documentary featuring David Balding, Laura Balding, Carol Buckley, Willie Theison, Raul Gomez, Scott Blais, and Flora. Directed by Lisa Leeman and produced by Christina Colissimo. Screenplay by Leeman and Colissimo.

"Animals and men regard each other across a gulf of mutual misunderstanding." So said W. G. Sebald, whom I have quoted more than once when confronted by a film like *One Lucky Elephant*, which is simple enough to delight a child and complex enough to baffle a philosopher.

Here are the stories of Flora, an African elephant, and David Balding, who runs a St. Louis circus. Flora witnessed her mother killed, and was shipped in a crate to the United States at a tender age, where after training and bonding with Balding, she became the star performer and namesake of Circus Flora. This is a one-ring circus that was created as a commissioned work for the 1986 Spoleto Festival in Charleston, South Carolina, and has performed annually in St. Louis since 1987.

Flora was its star from the first. We see her performing in close harmony with Balding, a portly bewhiskered man who is one of those few humans born to wear a ringmaster's uniform. Flora was gifted and obedient. But when she reached adolescence, she went through a puzzling period of sleepiness attributed to hormonal changes, and gradually began to exhibit impatience and a temper.

She didn't go on a rampage or anything, but Balding and his wife, Laura, decided she was reaching the end of her show business career and deserved a pleasant retirement. *One Lucky Elephant* follows their search for a home for Flora, which began in 2000 and became a great challenge. Her native Botswana was ruled out because of local problems. She later resided for short periods in zoos in Miami and Pittsburgh before finally finding what seems to be a permanent home at a large elephant sanctuary in Tennessee.

Balding loves Flora. He believes Flora loves him. That's where it gets complicated. The motives for the behavior of an elephant are not always easily comprehended across the gulf that Sebald described. Certainly Flora was accustomed to Balding, who treated her well and fed and cared for her generously. When they were separated, she sometimes exhibited aggression with other humans—not her fault, Balding believes, and it may have been provocative or ignorant behavior on the part of strangers.

A larger question coils beneath the surface of the film. What happens to an elephant that is "trained"? Are the chains, ropes, prods, and other training tools kind to the creature? Should any wild animal be trained in such a way? (Domestic animals have trained themselves to be our guests and dine at our tables.)

The owner of the Tennessee sanctuary believes it would be best for Flora to have a definite split with Balding, and learn to live in a natural habitat with other elephants. This is very hard on Balding. He and his wife consider Flora their daughter, and he even compares her departure with a child going away to school.

Along the way we get a good knowledge of the Baldings, who can only be described as good people. David's love for Flora is real. Circus Flora seems to be a wonderful institution, a one-ring tented circus that is still performing. I wish we saw more of it. But the question remains: Is it wise to take an elephant out of its home and train it as a circus performer? I have a sense Flora and David regard that question with mutual incomprehension.

## On the Ice ★ ★ ★

R, 96 m., 2012

Josiah Patkotak (Qalli), Frank Qutuq Irelan (Aivaaq), Teddy Kyle Smith (Egasak), Adamina Kerr (Michelle), John Miller (James), Rosabelle Kunnanna Rexford (Aaka), Sierra Jade Sampson (Uvlu). Directed by Andrew Okpeaha MacLean and produced by Lynette Howell, Marco Londoner, and Cara Marcous. Screenplay by MacLean.

There is a murder in *On the Ice*, but not really a crime. Two best friends try to escape the blame and then to take it. The story is set in the icebound town of Barrow, Alaska, among three generations of the Inupiat people. There's not an igloo or dog team in sight, snowmobiles are used more than cars, and the kids are into hip-hop and a couple of them are into meth.

If only because of the setting, this is an uncommonly involving thriller. I could call it a film noir except that the sun never sets in the film. That makes a perfect contrast with the only other feature filmed in Barrow, the vampire movie *30 Days of Night* (2007), in which it never rises.

In a film that lives comfortably among the local residents, we meet two pals: the round-faced Qalli (Josiah Patkotak), who will be going to college, and the long-faced Aivaaq (Frank Qutuq Irelan), who figures he might as well look for a job now that his girlfriend is pregnant. Egasak (Teddy Kyle Smith), Qalli's father, is the head of the local search and rescue team.

One night the teens party hearty, some drugs are consumed, and there's a fight. Bad feelings are carried over the next day when Qalli and Aivaaq join their friend James (John Miller) to go seal hunting. This trip ends with James dead. In the meticulous morality of the plot by writer-director Andrew Okpeaha MacLean, responsibility for his death is, in a way, shared by all three.

MacLean and all of his actors are Inupiat, although the politically incorrect word "Eskimo" is used in the lyrics of one of their hip-hop songs. Their town seems bereft of entertainment (apparently the bar in *30 Days of Night* has closed). Sometimes the kids climb the water tower to smoke pot. The homes are small and simple, the people decent, and Qalli's father and grandmother provide him with love and support. Aivaaq has it harder; his mom is an alcoholic who hardly stirs from a stupor.

What happens out on the ice I will leave for you to discover. Qalli and Aivaaq push James's body and his snowmobile into a hole in the ice, return to town, and say he went too fast toward a patch of fog and drove into the water. This leads to a helicopter search for a floating body and a demonstration of local expertise as the pilot uses the direction and speed of the current to calculate where it should come up.

It doesn't, and people notice how oddly the two boys are behaving. The search and rescue officer suspects something and begins to poke around on his own. There is also a nicely handled sequence in which the paranoid Aivaaq moves some bloody evidence from one Dumpster to another. It all comes down to an invitation the boys cannot refuse: to go on a "hunting trip" with Qalli's father. They're not too sure what he might be hunting for.

*On the Ice* has an unforced conviction permeating every scene. The local actors are persuasive (guilt almost paralyzes Qalli), and their lives seem limited by the opportunities in Barrow. Qalli's plans for college are the pride not only of his family, but probably of many other residents. This bleakness provides a backdrop for what is essentially a morality play, in which MacLean shows the characters trying to decide how to do the right thing. In one stunning moment, Qalli's father leaves them with a cold moral choice, and MacLean finds impressive suspense in it.

## Oranges and Sunshine ★ ★ ★

R, 103 m., 2011

Emily Watson (Margaret Humphreys), Hugo Weaving (Jack), David Wenham (Len), Richard Dillane (Merv), Lorraine Ashbourne (Nicky), Federay Holmes (Charlotte). Directed by Jim Loach and produced by Camilla Bray and Iain Canning. Screenplay by Rona Munro, based on the book *Empty Cradles* by Margaret Humphreys.

Starting in the 1930s and continuing until as recently as 1967, hundreds of thousands of British children, some as young as four, were separated from poor families and single mothers and shipped to Australia, where in church institutions they were used as child labor and sometimes abused and raped. Their parents were assured they had been sent to "a loving family" and given no other information. This treatment was licensed by the social work norms of the time.

The story was never made public. In 1986, in Nottingham, a social worker named Margaret Humphreys (Emily Watson) was told by an adult woman named Charlotte (Federay Holmes), "I want to know who I am." She had grown up being fed conflicting stories about her mother, many of them suggesting she was dead. She was, in fact, still alive, and Humphreys, in bringing them together, realized she had stumbled over an outrage of monstrous proportions.

Another woman, Nicky (Lorraine Ashbourne), is seeking her brother Jack (Hugo Weaving), who was deported. Together they go to Australia and find him. Jack introduces Humphreys to others who came out from the United Kingdom apparently orphans, and they visit the remote Christian Brothers school where he was raised and abused. There is an electric, painful scene in which Humphreys approaches the brothers at tea and asks if any of them care to discuss the past. They stare silently at their cups and plates of cake, none stirring or meeting her eyes. Some of them are young. The older ones must have known this day was coming.

This is all true. When Margaret Humphreys went on TV in Australia to tell the story, she drew crowds of adults who knew they came from the United Kingdom, but had never believed the stories they had been told. If their parents were dead, did they have brothers or sisters? Grandparents? Anyone who could tell them about themselves? As the scandal grows, Humphreys establishes an organization and raises a fund for it, and finally, in 2009, there were formal apologies by the British and Australian governments to the victims.

Emily Watson, a delicate English rose, has never seemed more sturdy than here. In the movie, directed by Jim Loach (son of Ken), she doesn't play a fiery, charismatic heroine, but a quietly stubborn force of nature, who persists in a cause no one else cared to fight. Often she and her helpers, especially Jack and another deportee, Len (David Wenham), are unfunded and seem to be drifting from one remote clue to another in the vast land. Sometimes she is made to feel in physical danger. She carries on.

One question is not addressed by the movie: Why were the children deported in the first place? Yes, we know the "reasons," but what were the motives? If hundreds of thousands of children without parents are arriving in Australia, why are there those eager to receive them? They must be fed, sheltered, and educated for years. Where's the money? Are they needed for something as dismaying as to provide a reason for church institutions and jobs for clergy? Are they a growth industry? Does the government pay a subsidy that is welcomed? Are the children simply a pretext for the flow of funds?

The movie doesn't say. A crime was committed, it has been exposed, and presumably many family members have been reunited. We move on.

## OSS 117: Lost in Rio ★ ★ ★

NO MPAA RATING, 101 m., 2010

Jean Dujardin (Hubert Bonisseur de la Bath), Louise Monot (Delores), Alex Lutz (Heinrich), Rudiger Vogler (Von Zimmel), Reem Kherici (Carlotta), Ken Samuels (Trumendous). Directed by Michel Hazanavicius and produced by Eric Altmeyer and Nicholas Altmeyer. Screenplay by Michel Hazanavicius and Jean-Francois Halin, inspired by the OSS 117 novels by Jean Bruce.

Hubert Bonisseur de la Bath, French Agent OSS 117, looks like a parody of James Bond, British Agent 007, but it may be the other way around. Pretty much unknown over here, he first appeared in print in 1949. I haven't read a single OSS 117 novel (there are more than 250!), but it appears Ian Fleming may have found some inspiration from Jean Bruce, the creator of 117.

The OSS man first appeared in a film in 1957, and was once played by John Gavin, of all people. The character was revived in *OSS 117: Cairo, Nest of Spies* (2006), but while the original stories were played straight, *Cairo* and now *OSS 117: Lost in Rio* are parodies—of the James Bond movies, appropriately enough.

The star is Jean Dujardin, who in some shots looks something like Sean Connery, and who has the same gift of understatement and drollery. He's also surrounded by babes, in particular a sexy Mossad agent named Delores Koulechov (Louise Monot). The movie is set in the early 1960s, and 117 is sent to Brazil to retrieve a secret list of French collaborators with the Nazis. This leads to an action climax atop the right arm of the immense statue of Christ that towers above Rio de Janeiro. Hitchcock set *Notorious* in Rio, but didn't quite have the nerve to use that location.

Imagine that the film looks exactly like a slightly faded thriller from 1967. The makers have gone to a great deal of trouble to get not only the costumes, the sets, the props, and the cars right, but even the film stock; some audience members may wonder if they wandered into a revival house. The stunts are as stagy as 007, the villains as absurd, and 117 as unflappable.

One thing that will strike North American audiences as odd is that 117 is cheerfully racist. Working with an Israeli agent gives him plenty of opportunities to voice his anti-Semitism, which is not intended to hurt, but grows directly out of his ignorance. I think (or hope) the filmmakers are making a commentary on the everyday anti-Semitism of the DeGaulle era.

But 117 is an equal-opportunity offender and makes unbelievably gross statements to women. He somehow gets away with it because Dujardin is a polite charmer with an eager smile and a quick laugh, and you see he doesn't mean to offend; he's only trying to make conversation. That he is clueless is the joke.

There's too much of that for my taste, but the movie depends mostly on wild exaggerations of 007, and here it does something right: It shows stunts and special effects that *look* like they might have been staged in 1967. The movie almost goes out of its way to reveal it's using rear projection on a studio set. The music is appropriate, too: that kind of cheesy pop that has a good time no matter what's happening on the screen. The sound track reminded me of nothing so much as a forced laugh.

I sort of liked the 2006 film, and I sort of like this one, too. I may like it a little more because Dujardin grows on you. The film opens with him singing "Everybody Loves Somebody" in a voice that sounds so much like Dean Martin that maybe it is. But the way he smiles and moves . . . well, surely you've heard of the Trololo Man?

If you haven't, Google him.

## Our Family Wedding ★ ★

PG-13, 101 m., 2010

Forest Whitaker (Brad Boyd), America Ferrera (Lucia Ramirez), Carlos Mencia (Miguel Ramirez), Regina King (Angela), Lance Gross (Marcus Boyd), Diana Maria Riva (Sonia Ramirez). Directed by Rick Famuyiwa and produced by Edward Saxon and Steven J. Wolfe. Screenplay by Famuyiwa, Wayne Conley, and Malcolm Spellman.

*Our Family Wedding* is a perfectly good idea for a comedy: A wedding between a Mexican-American woman and an African-American man leads to culture clash. The film, unfortunately, deals with the situation at the level of a middling sitcom. You almost miss the laugh track. Difficult problems are sidestepped, arguments are overacted, and there are three food fights involving wedding cakes. Well, two, actually, and the destruction of a third cake.

At the center of the wedding are Lucia Ramirez (America Ferrera), who was a law student at Columbia, and Marcus Boyd (Lance Gross), a Columbia med school graduate. The young couple plan to move to Laos, where he will work with Doctors Without Borders. They've been living together in New York, but keeping it a secret from her parents because her mom, Sonia (Diana Maria Riva), expects her to remain a virgin before marriage, and her father, Miguel (Carlos Mencia), would be crushed if he learned she had dropped out of law school. In a plot twist of startling originality, she is not pregnant.

A slimmed-down Forest Whitaker plays Marcus's father, Brad, a popular Los Angeles all-night DJ. He's doing all right and inhabits a huge house in the hills with a pool, stairs leading to a terrace, and a lawn big enough to hold a wedding party. Plus his ride is a Jaguar. Not bad for an all-night DJ.

Miguel is also well off, with the daughter at Columbia, the big luxurious house, and the passion for restoring classic cars. He owns a towing service, which is how he and Brad have a Meet Cute: All his drivers call in sick. Miguel fills in, and he and Brad meet when he tows the Jag.

The dads meet again at dinner when their

children pop the big news and are immediately screaming insults and shaking each other by the throat. This scene, like all the stagy arguments between the fathers, is completely unconvincing. Their fights are drummed up for the purposes of the screenplay, and the actors hardly seem to believe them. Their families flutter their hands and beg them to calm down. Their running feud feels phony to begin with, and painfully forced by the end.

All of the family difficulties seem trumped up. Although Lucia is terrified that her mother will discover she had sex before marriage, that revelation, when it comes, is almost a throwaway. Marcus is embarrassed that his dad dates much younger women, but when he turns up at the family dinner with a girl who was Lucia's softball teammate, there's barely a mild stir. Lucia's grandmother faints when she sees Lucia's fiancé is a black man, but when she comes to, this is forgotten. (Didn't anyone tell her?) Oh, and speaking of softball, the game played between the two family teams is so badly staged, I wasn't sure which side many of the players were on, nor who won the game.

The bright spots are America Ferrera, the kind of cuddly beauty who plunges right in and kisses a guy without worrying about her makeup, and Lance Gross as the guy, who has a thankless task as the Perfect Fiancé but doesn't overplay it. Regina King steals many scenes as Brad's longtime lawyer and secret admirer; her character is smart, focused, and sympathetic, and King's costumes showcase those Michelle Obama arms.

*Our Family Wedding* is a pleasant but inconsequential comedy, clunky, awkward for the actors, and contrived from beginning to end. Compare it with *Nothing Like the Holidays* (2008) to see how well a movie can handle similar material.

## Our Idiot Brother ★ ★ ★

R, 96 m., 2011

Paul Rudd (Ned), Elizabeth Banks (Miranda), Zooey Deschanel (Natalie), Emily Mortimer (Liz), Steve Coogan (Dylan), Rashida Jones (Cindy), Adam Scott (Jeremy), Shirley Knight (Ilene). Directed by Jesse Peretz and produced by Anthony Bregman, Peter Saraf, and Marc Turtletaub. Screenplay by Evgenia Peretz and David Schisgall.

This movie is so nice. Its hero is so sweet. His sisters consider him such an idiot. His sisters are so correct. He's an idiot in the sense that he doesn't lie or cheat. He doesn't calculate the odds on getting away with things. He trusts people. He always tells the truth. Wasn't there a study proving that human society would collapse if we didn't lie?

Ned is sort of a saint. He has a beatific smile, wishes you the best, and doesn't hold grudges. He also doesn't hold jobs very well. He reminds me a little of Harold Skimpole, the Dickens character who never grasped how money worked, or why it mattered if he didn't have any. When we meet Ned he's selling organic vegetables at a farmers' market, with a little sideline in under-the-counter weed. And when a uniformed cop says he's having a bad day and wonders if he might have something to sell him, he slips him a twenty-dollar bag with his rhubarb. A *uniformed* cop.

Ned (Paul Rudd) is released from prison early (he was Model Prisoner four months in a row). He returns to the farm he worked with his girlfriend (Kathryn Hahn), discovers she has a new boyfriend, and just about apologizes to the guy for turning up unexpectedly. Deprived of his home, he begins to depend on the hospitality of his three sisters, who in their three ways are three pieces of work.

This movie wouldn't work without Paul Rudd. He walks such a fine line. He has to be nice, but not a fool. Sweet, but not saccharine. Honest enough to cause trouble, but always innocently. Not only doesn't he lie, he never knows when he has been lied to. When the genes were being shaken up in his family tree, all of the kind ones must have fallen into his pool.

The movie circles with nimble wit through an A-list of supporting characters. Ned's sisters are Liz (Emily Mortimer), a doting mom married to a filmmaker (Steve Coogan); Miranda (Elizabeth Banks), who has ambitions to write for *Vanity Fair* magazine; and Natalie (Zooey Deschanel), who may be a lesbian and is certainly in love with Cindy (Rashida Jones). Their mother is Ilene, played by the legendary Shirley Knight, who is one of those rare all-day wine drinkers who can stay topped up and never get hammered. It goes without saying, I suppose, that the Steve Coogan character is a bit of a rat; his characters usually are. But Cindy the lesbian is free of all the tiresome clichés about lesbians in comedies, and daringly plots with Ned to regain ownership of Willie Nelson, his beloved dog.

I know someone just like Ned. She is a woman. She has an uncanny gift for making a statement, looking puzzled when a hush falls upon the room, and saying, "Uh-oh. I thought everyone knew that." In Ned's case, his startling honesties seem to be blessed. He appears to cause harm and dismay, but in the workings of the screenplay he usually ends up doing good, however accidentally.

It was refreshing, this late in the summer, to find a hot-weather comedy that doesn't hate its characters and embed them in scatology and sexual impossibilities. *Our Idiot Brother*, directed by Jesse Peretz and written by Evgenia Peretz and David Schisgall, is as good-hearted as its hero. I've seen Paul Rudd in a lot of movies, but never realized he could be as lovable as Amy Adams or Mary Steenburgen. Jesse and Evgenia Peretz are the children of Martin Peretz, the publisher of the *New Republic*, and the other day my friend Margo Howard was tweeting that she's known the Peretz kids since they were born, "and going back years, he always did used to sit on her!" Twitter doesn't encourage detailed elaboration.

The film ends with a series of unlikely happy endings, which I might ordinarily object to. But since one outcome produces an iron-clad reason why the dog must be named Willie Nelson, all is forgiven.

## Outrage ★ ★ ½

R, 109 m., 2012

Soichiro Kitamura (Mr. Chairman), Tomokazu Miura (Kato), Tetta Sugimoto (Ozawa), Jun Kunimura (Ikemoto), Beat Takeshi (Otomo), Kippei Shiina (Mizuno), Ryo Kase (Ishihara), Renji Ishibashi (Murase). Directed by Takeshi Kitano and produced by Masayuki Mori and Takio Yoshida. Screenplay by Kitano.

*Outrage* opens by bringing a large number of Japanese gangsters onscreen, a lot of them efficiently introduced at a banquet. Then it depicts the merciless, cruel, and sometimes bizarre murders of all of them, and as many more as the film has room for. Its director, a favorite of mine named Takeshi Kitano, went a decade without any particular violence in his films, and now gives us almost nothing else. It's like a version of *Cinema Paradiso* where all the murders were saved up by a censor and strung together for a bloodbath.

Kitano is one of the great originals of the Japanese cinema. He usually works alone, writing, directing, and acting. Perhaps to save confusion, or maybe to create it, he directs as Takeshi Kitano and acts as Beat Takeshi—a nod to the beatniks, which may explain his fondness for dark glasses. In 1994 he had a motorcycle accident that reportedly paralyzed half his body, and he lost some control of his facial muscles. Whether later treatment was able to repair any of the damage is a good question; at no time in this or his other post-1994 films does he seem to be particularly handicapped.

That may be because his personal acting style provides a cover. He is very quiet and still, the embodiment of cool. He reminds me of a snake, waiting to strike. In one of his films, he stands unwavering as an enemy approaches and taunts him, and then in a lighting movement too fast to see, skewers him in the brain through an eyeball.

If that's not your idea of a good time, stay far, far away from *Outrage*. The movie is wall-to-wall violence. I could spend thousands of words outlining the plot and its labyrinth of double-crosses, but I can do that just as well in a handful of words: Rival gangs of *yakuza* (Japanese gangsters) become involved in a blood feud that involves the death of everyone. (Everyone but Kitano, you're wondering? I'm not saying.)

Some of the deaths are horrible, such as a decapitation involving a rope and an automobile. Others involve messy slaughter, crazed gunplay, and the ironic turning of tables. This happens relentlessly. It would be more depressing, but Kitano takes mercy on us and provides no one in the film, including his own character, with a shred of personality. We know no one, we like or hate no one, we observe their murders as a form of kinetic action.

Because Kitano has dealt so long and well with violence, the film has been greeted by his admirers as a personal statement, perhaps "existential," that most convenient all-purpose word when you want to say nothing and sound meaningful. It is also a film of controlled visual style; Kitano's compositions are like arrangements of bodies in space and time.

That said, and with all due respect, I expected a better time. One of his *yakuza* movies involved as much percussion as a marching band, and many of them are often very funny. This one almost expresses impatience: "You wonder why I haven't given you violence? Very well; please have some violence."

## Outside the Law ★ ★ ★

NO MPAA RATING, 138 m., 2010

Jamel Debbouze (Said), Roschdy Zem (Messaoud), Sami Bouajila (Abdelkader), Bernard Blancan (Colonel Faivre), Chafia Boudraa (Said's Mother), Sabrina Seyvecou (Helene), Assaad Bouab (Ali), Thibault de Montalembert (Morvan). Directed by Rachid Bouchareb and produced by Jean Brehat. Screenplay by Bouchareb and Olivier Lorelle.

For France, the Algerian War was like our experience in Vietnam, but closer, more personal, and with bloodshed on domestic soil. France had already lost its war to retain French Indochina as a colony when we moved in. At about the same time, it was facing a revolt in French Algeria, which was much more important to it; indeed, many families had members living in either place and supporting either side.

*Outside the Law* is a big, expensive historical film that considers the war from an Algerian point of view. It assumes in a straightforward manner that the National Liberation Front's attempts to throw the French out of Algeria were directly comparable to the attempts of the French Resistance to throw the Nazis out of France. This is heresy in some circles, and indeed caused right-wing demonstrations against the film, but as attitudes about colonialism shift, this view is gradually becoming more accepted.

Much of the film involves FLN activities in Paris as well as Algeria. But it isn't an explanation of how or why the insurgent tactics were impossible to defeat; *The Battle of Algiers* (1966) has never been improved on for that. This is a more traditional personal melodrama, telling its story through a few characters seen against the backdrop of history. At a reported cost of $25 million, it's unusually expensive for a French film, and it's a sign of changing times that the financing was available.

Rachid Bouchareb, a French director of Algerian descent, tells his story through the lives of three brothers. We meet them first in 1925 when French authorities throw them off the land their family has farmed for generations in Algeria. Homeless and without a livelihood, they form a lifelong resentment, which will express itself in different ways.

They move with their family to Paris. Said (Jamel Debbouze) takes to the streets, works as a pimp, opens a club, and sponsors boxing matches. Messaoud (Roschdy Zem) fights for the French in Indochina, where he observes the Viet Cong firsthand and begins to see parallels between its resistance to colonialism and the struggle for Algeria. He returns to France a revolutionary and joins his brother Abdelkader (Sami Bouajila) in organizing for the FLN in Paris.

Their tactics involve violence. Abdelkader is inspired more by ideas and theory, and Messaoud's energy comes from more basic emotions of resentment and hatred for how the French dispossessed his family. Abdelkader the cerebral is able to kill dispassionately; Messaoud finds it more personal and agonizing. After a certain point it matters not what they think, because they've passed a point of no return and are desperate and wanted armed men, fighting in an invisible army.

We meet Colonel Faivre (Bernard Blancan), who organizes a secret branch of the French police named the Red Hand. He tells those under him that he works on direct orders from the top. They do not officially exist. Their activities will be denied. They will work outside any restraints of the law to do what is necessary to put down the insurgency.

Bouchareb takes these elements and essentially constructs a superior action picture. I'm sure it plays differently here than in France, where emotions on the subject are old and run deep. Imagine the feelings of Americans about a film where the Confederacy is viewed as heroic and the Union as murderous invaders. It all depends on which side you think is the right one. *Outside the Law* votes with the FLN.

The film is very well made. The actors create individual characters, within the limitations of what is essentially a formula. The flaw in the film is that, as Truffaut said, action in movies argues for itself. If we are assigned three protagonists and they're in gunfights with people trying to kill them, we identify with the protagonists. If the cops are the heroes, then we identify with them. So simple action is idea-neutral. If the point is to inspire sympathy for the Algerians, it may be effective, but lacks meaning.

There's a scene early in the film, during a boxing match Said stages for gambling purposes, when the cops raid what they perceive as a dangerous gathering of Algerians and open fire, causing a massacre. I understand this is a fictional version of a real event, about which there is much disagreement. We foreign viewers, not clued in, can only assume we know Said, and so the authorities are wrong.

Compare that with *The Battle of Algiers*, which is much more thoughtful about the methods of the resistance. Its sentiments are on the side of the FLN, but its focus is on the day-to-day reality of the struggle. There is a point in that film where the FLN seems crushed. It is not. The argument is that an indigenous movement cannot be crushed by force because its inexorable causes remain. In *Outside the Law*, the matter seems more simply about strategy and victory.

*Outside the Law* is at the very least a superior action film, in which the action sequences are plausible and grounded in reality. It is also a parable in support of anticolonialism. What it isn't, at the end of the day, is a film about the larger picture. It's about these characters and their stories. Well, most films are. It's just helpful to be clear that you're not finding out much about the larger issue.

# P

## Page One: Inside the *New York Times* ★ ★ ★

R, 88 m., 2011

David Carr, Brian Stelter, Bruce Headlam, Tim Arango, Bill Keller, Michael Hirschorn, Shane Smith, Gay Talese, David Remnick, Andrew Ross Sorkin, Larry Ingrassia, Markos Moulitsas, Seth Mnookin, Nick Lemann, Carla Baranauckas, Katherine Bouton, Katrina vanden Heuvel, Nick Denton, Jimmy Wales, Rick Lyman, Dean Baquet, Ken Auletta, Brian Lam, Charles Strum, Carl Bernstein, John Carr. A documentary directed by Andrew Rossi and produced by Alan Oxman and Adam Schlesinger. Screenplay by Rossi and Kate Novack.

When the *New York Times* started to charge for Web access to more than twenty articles a month, I signed up. I can't imagine a month when I wouldn't exceed that number. The paper remains, as it has long been, the most essential source of news in this country. *Page One: Inside the New York Times* sets out to examine its stature in these hard times for print journalism, but ends up with more of the hand-wringing that dominates all such discussions. People who are serious about the news venerate the past, hope for the future, and don't have a clue about the present.

Andrew Rossi's documentary had unlimited access to limited areas within the paper. There is extensive coverage of the staff of the *Times'* media desk, which covers other media, but the film lacks the skill of that staff in covering the *Times.* Nor does it eavesdrop on any strategic conversations among *Times* managers about the bottom line and the hopes for Web revenue.

Instead, what happens is what sometimes happens in many stories: A charismatic hero comes along and distracts from the big picture. That man here is David Carr, the paper's raspy-voiced, oracular star media reporter. I can think of no greater compliment than that he reminds me of the reporters I held in awe when I first went to work for newspapers. Like Mike Royko, he combines cynicism, idealism, and a canny understanding of how things *really* work. As we watch him meticulously report the story that exposed the lamentable "frat house" management of Sam Zell's *Chicago Tribune,* we see the reporter as a prosecutor, nailing down an air-tight case.

Carr is a survivor, an indicted crack addict and single parent who remade himself. We also meet Bruce Headlam, his boss on the media desk, and Brian Stelter, who won a job on the *Times* on the basis of his personal blog (How many bloggers share the dream of winning that lottery?). We follow them through a year in which they write about new media and old, Carr snorts at the idea of media "brands," and Headlam vets the devastating Carr coverage that would bring about regime change at the *Tribune* in a matter of weeks.

What he was essentially covering was the collapse of the print journalism culture. When Sam Zell entrusted the leadership of the *Tribune* to a slaphappy gang of callow radio executives, he revealed he had no idea what he had purchased, or why. There are certain ethical assumptions embedded in traditional journalism that are now being shredded not only by the Zells but by the heady, hit-and-run style of gossip Web sites.

In assuming that they must compete with celebrity gossip and scandal, newspapers abandon what they do well and devote their resources to what they do badly. They do this in pursuit of a "youth demographic" that doesn't read newspapers anyway, and shows symptoms of increasing illiteracy. I suspect that at the bottom of the crisis in print media is a crisis in American education, and that many of today's college graduates cannot read and write as well as grade school graduates did a few decades ago.

But back to the film. You would have to walk into it already knowing a great deal about the *Times.* Moving with no apparent plan, the doc touches on the Pentagon Papers, Judith Miller, Jayson Blair, and Gay Talese's *The Kingdom and the Power.* It doesn't have or find a theme. Attention is paid to Bill Keller, the executive editor, seen at a news meeting to determine the stories for the next day's paper. You won't discover here that he has been replaced by managing editor Jill Abramson (glimpsed a couple of times), whose mission is reportedly to focus on the Internet.

That said, I enjoyed the film very much. It was a visceral pleasure to see a hard-boiled guy like David Carr at its center. There's a scene in a bar, a farewell party for a correspondent going to the Middle East, and the other Timesmen sort of cluster around Carr to hear what he has to say. It was the same with Royko. Some people in this business just seem to *know.*

## Paradise Lost 3: Purgatory ★ ★ ★ ½

NO MPAA RATING, 121 m., 2012

A documentary featuring Jason Baldwin, Damien Wayne Echols, and Jessie Misskelley. Directed by Joe Berlinger and Bruce Sinofsky and produced by Berlinger, Sinofsky, and Jonathan Silberberg.

When a documentary named *Paradise Lost: The Child Murders at Robin Hood Hills* played on HBO in 1996, it left little doubt that the three young men convicted of the crimes were innocent. When *Paradise Lost 2: Revelations* played in 2000, it left less doubt. Now it is 2012 and a third film, *Paradise Lost 3: Purgatory,* shows them being set free in August 2011 after seventeen years in jail. One of them was on death row.

The case of the West Memphis Three became famous. The Dixie Chicks held a concert to help pay their defense fund. The original conviction was based on flawed, circumstantial evidence and a confession obtained from Jessie Misskelley, one of the defendants, who had an IQ of 72 and was questioned by police for twelve hours without a parent or attorney present, and then tape-recorded only long enough to recite a statement he later retracted. A police transcript shows Jessie shifting the time of the crimes from morning to noon to after school to evening (when they actually occurred) under leading suggestions by police.

This new film is the culmination of years of extraordinary persistence by the documentary filmmakers Joe Berlinger and Bruce Sinofsky, whose work freed the three men. So flawed was the evidence against them that at the end, the state decided to avoid a court hearing on their appeal by offering this unique deal: They could go free and could even state their innocence if they would sign an admission of guilt—a technicality shielding Arkansas from lawsuits for wrongful imprisonment.

*Lost 3* does a smooth job of retelling the entire story, so you needn't have seen the first two. The naked bodies of three Cub Scouts were found in a creek in a wooded area near an interstate exchange in West Memphis, Arkansas. Within a month police had charged three teenagers with the crime: Damien Echols, Jason Baldwin, and Jessie Misskelley. There was no physical evidence against them, and they all had alibis.

The area had been aflame with rumors of satanic cults and ritual sacrifices. The West Memphis Three fit a profile: They liked heavy metal music, they wore black, and Echols's notebooks contained sketches of demonic symbols. Many people in the area literally believed in Satan, and heard dark accounts in their churches of the spread of devil worship. The prevailing mood was perhaps not unlike that during the Salem witch trials.

At the end of the second film, an alternative suspect had drawn attention: John Mark Byers, the stepfather of Chris Byers, one of the victims. It was he, amazingly, who handed the filmmakers a hunting knife that held traces of blood, suggesting it could have been the murder weapon.

In *Paradise Lost 3,* the case grows far murkier with the emergence of another suspect, Terry Hobbs, the stepfather of another victim. DNA testing not available at the time of the murders links him with a hair found at the crime scene. There was new eyewitness testimony linking him with the three victims at a crucial time, and one of his alibi witnesses recanted. The DNA tests, supported by four expert witnesses, including the head of an FBI forensics lab, seemed to eliminate the three teens as suspects, which is why they were so suddenly released. Even the prosecutors seem less than enthusiastic about their own case.

This third film contains earlier footage not used in the first two, so there's reason to see it if you've seen them. There's a better reason. For most of the film, it seems headed for the same conclusion as the earlier ones: As evidence piles up that the WM3 are innocent, they will lose on appeal and go back behind bars. Indeed, the original version of this film had already been scheduled on HBO and for the Toronto Film Festival when the DNA bombshell burst. The defendants and their attorneys were summoned without warning to a courtroom and set free; you can sense the excitement even in how the camera moves. After their release, *Lost 3* was updated and expanded by twelve minutes.

I've been involved in an online discussion recently about the death penalty. Without reopening that subject, I will note that a great many people were convinced the West Memphis Three were guilty, and after seeing this film there seems no doubt they are innocent. This is one of the most fascinating of all true crime stories. By the end of this film, you'll never guess who believes Terry Hobbs is the real murderer: John Mark Byers.

## Paranormal Activity 2 ★ ½

R, 91 m., 2010

Micah Sloat (Micah Sloat), Katie Featherston (Katie Sloat), Sprague Grayden (Kristi), Brian Boland (Daniel), Molly Ephraim (Ali), Vivis (Martine). Directed by Tod Williams and produced by Jason Blum and Oren Peli. Screenplay by Peli and Michael R. Perry.

*Paranormal Activity 2* is an efficient delivery system for gotcha! moments, of which it has about nineteen. Audiences who want to be gotchaed will enjoy it. A gotcha! moment is a moment when something is sudden, loud, and scary. This can be as basic as the old "it's only a cat" cliché, or as abrupt as a character being hit by a bus. *PA2* starts slyly with pre-gotcha! teasers, such as a door or a child's toy moving on its own. Then there are obscure offscreen rumbles, like an uneasy stomach. Then loud bangs. Then loud bangs with visible causes. Then all the doors in a room banging open at once. And eventually, well, you can see for yourself, because all the activity is captured by twenty-four-hour security cameras.

The cameras, which function perfectly, never capture the Presence on the screen. For the house is indeed haunted by a ghostlike supernatural presence, I guess. I say "I guess" because there is a scene of a victim being dragged downstairs, and the entity doing the dragging is invisible. On the other hand, the movie ends with a strong suggestion that the malefactor was, in fact, a living human being. So would that be cheating? Hell yes.

But who cares? People go to *Paranormal Activity 2* with fond memories of the original film, which was low-tech and clever in the way it teased our eyes and expectations. It scared them. They want to be scared again. They will be. When there's a loud unexpected bang, it will scare you. The structural task of the gotcha! movie is to separate the bangs so they continue to be unexpected.

Any form of separation will do. The characters include the Sloats (Micah Sloat and Katie Featherston), who are back from the first movie. But this story begins earlier in time than that one and takes place in the home of her sister, Kristi (Sprague Grayden), her husband, Daniel (Brian Boland), teenage daughter, Ali (Molly Ephraim), brand-new baby, Hunter, and his nanny, Martine (Vivis). Martine is ethnic, and we know what that means: She has an instinctive knowledge of ghosts, breaks out the magic incense at a moment's notice, and can't get anyone to listen to her.

There are six speaking roles, not counting the nonspeaking baby and the dog. Good odds, you'd think, that at least one of them would have something interesting to say, but no. The movie isn't about them. They function primarily as gotcha! separators, going through vacuous social motions between gotchas! They are not real swift. The movie numbers the days as they tick away, and along about Day No. 12 I'm thinking, "Why are these people still here?" The screening I attended was treated to a surprise appearance by three stars of that cable show about Chicago's paranormal detectives. These are real Chicago detectives. If the Sloats lived in Chicago, they'd have a SWAT team out there by Day No. 7.

The movie is presented as a documentary with no setup, unless the first movie was the setup. It begins with little Hunter being brought home, and then we get titles like "Day No. 3." Of what? One peculiar title says, "Nine days before the death of Micah Sloat." I probably have the number of days wrong, but you get the idea. What are we supposed to do with this information? I guess we should think, "Sloat, you poor bastard, you only have nine days to go." This knowledge is about as useful as the farmer who tells you to make a left turn five miles before you get to the barn. There are also titles saying things like "1:41:15 a.m.," as if we care.

The character who suffers the most is poor little Hunter. Something is always bothering him in the middle of the night. When a security camera is on the staircase, we hear his plaintive little wail. When it's focused on his bedroom, he's standing up in his wee crib and bawling. The dog is always there barking at something, because dogs, like ethnic nannies, Know About These Things. Hunter screams and screams in the movie. If you were Hunter's parents and your house was haunted, wouldn't you move the poor kid's crib into the bedroom?

My audience jumped a lot and screamed a lot, and then laughed at themselves, even after one event that wasn't really funny. Then they explained things to one another, and I could overhear useful lines like, "She got the $#!+ scared outta her!" I understand they attended in hopes of seeing gotchas! and explaining them to one another. I don't have a problem with *Paranormal Activity 2*. It delivers what it promises, and occupies its audiences. Win-win.

## Paranormal Activity 3 ★

R, 85 m., 2011

Katie Featherston (Katie), Sprague Grayden (Kristi Rey), Lauren Bittner (Julie), Chris Smith (Dennis), Chloe Csengery (Young Katie), Jessica Tyler Brown (Young Kristi Rey), Brian Boland (Daniel Rey), Dustin Ingram (Randy), Mark Fredrichs (Dr. Fredrichs). Directed by Henry Joost and Ariel Schulman and produced by Jason Blum, Oren Peli, and Steven Schneider. Screenplay by Peli and Christopher B. Landon.

*Paranormal Activity 3* is a prequel, revealing that the characters in *PA1* and *PA2* had already been through the all-night video surveillance ordeal. At least in this film they are undergoing it for the first time, which is less than can be said for us. The formula for the films involves pallid characters, perfunctory dialogue, and very long waits for something to happen.

When something does, it's often a sudden shock accompanied by a startling musical chord. Sometimes there are loud bangings and other noises. Sometimes the shocks are false alarms. The audience screams, and then laughs. At my screening, it also did a lot of talking. Usually I find that obnoxious, but this time I wish they'd spoken louder; the *Mystery Science Theater* approach might enrich this film.

What we have to accept in all three films is that a house is occupied by an entity intent on being a pain in the butt and zapping us with gotcha! moments. These are cruel limitations for a supernatural being; one rather hopes the Other Side would produce more interesting company. When the origin of the manifestations is revealed or hinted at, the film closes soon after, as if the terminal scene explained the slightest thing.

This film involves the two sisters who were seen in earlier episodes as adults. Katie (Katie Featherston) and Kristi Rey (Sprague Grayden) share a two-level home with their mother, Julie (Lauren Bittner), and her boyfriend, Dennis (Chris Smith). The girls are aware of a presence in the house, perhaps an imaginary friend, although perhaps not so imaginary.

In a series of shots destined to be repeated tediously, we cut between video cameras left to run all night in the bedrooms of the girls and the adults, and a camera on an oscillating fan platform that pans back and forth between the living room and the kitchen/dining area. Long periods pass without activity. Some activity is subtle. Occasionally it's sudden and startling. Sometimes (a "ghost" in a sheet) it's like Casper the Friendly Ghost playing a practical joke. The slow deliberation of the oscillations adds implacable delays while we wait to pan back again and see what has changed. In the best shot in the film, all the tables and chairs and pots and pans in the kitchen have disappeared, and then we find out with perfect logic where they are.

Inexplicably, there are people who still haven't had enough of these movies. The first was a nifty novelty. Now the appeal has worn. Since they already know more or less what will happen and it's lame-brained, why do audiences continue to turn out for new *Activities*? Yet you mark my words: *Part 3* will gross untold millions on opening weekend. If you like horror, dread, and a twisty plot, try to find the Michael Shannon film *Take Shelter.* Let's say you like popcorn during a movie. *Paranormal Activity 3* is like eating the cardboard box.

## Pariah ★ ★ ★ ½

R, 86 m., 2012

Adepero Oduye (Alike), Pernell Walker (Laura), Aasha Davis (Bina), Charles Parnell (Arthur), Sahra Mellesse (Sharonda), Kim Wayans (Audrey). Directed by Dee Rees and produced by Nekisa Cooper. Screenplay by Rees.

Alike is seventeen and never been kissed. She dreams of being kissed by a girl. The bright Brooklyn high school student has accepted her lesbianism for some years, it appears, but hasn't come out to her parents, her sister, or really anyone except her gay friend, Laura. Yet everybody sort of knows. She lives in a condition familiar to many families, where something has long been sensed but never acknowledged. Home life is a process of evasion. Words take on more than one shading.

Alike (pronounced a-LIE-kee) is played by Adepero Oduye, in a performance so natural and touching that she does what every director hopes for: She brings the character into being without the need of explanatory dialogue or obligatory setup scenes. She is an A student, being raised by Arthur (Charles Parnell), an affectionate policeman, and Audrey (Kim Wayans), a churchgoing mother. It's clear that both parents know their daughter is gay, but that's never acknowledged out loud and is consigned to that unspoken category of family realities that are either (1) behavior the girl will outgrow and correct, or (2) somehow the other parent's fault.

Situations like this are not uncommon in many families, and apply not only to homosexuality but to any area in which a teenager has entered a realm of her life that parents choose to remain blind to. Alike shares a room with her sister, Sharonda (Sahra Mellesse), who, like many siblings, knows the story, thinks it's no big deal, and goes along with the official family denial. Alike's best friend is the butch Laura (Pernell Walker). They go to a nearby lesbian club together, which Alike visits with sweet shyness, making wardrobe adjustments between home and destination so she can pass in two roles.

Her mother knows the story on Laura and wants Alike to stop seeing her. She encourages a friendship with Bina (Aasha Davis), the daughter of one of her church friends. Ironic: Laura has never made a pass at Alike, but Bina wants to cuddle and kiss, and Alike at last acts on her sexual feelings. But Bina is the solution to no problems.

*Pariah* is probably too loaded a word to be the title of this film. Alike lives in a world where homosexuality is far from unknown, and her problems will grow smaller in a few years as she moves away from home. This story, so tellingly written and acted, is about the painful awkwardness of that process. What makes it worse is that there's repressed hostility between her parents, and Alike's sexuality becomes the occasion for tension with deeper sources.

The film is an impressive debut for Dee Rees. It's said to be somewhat autobiographical. It began as a 2007 short subject, was brought to maturity at a Sundance laboratory, and one of its producers is Spike Lee, whose presence in Brooklyn must have been an inspiration for Rees. On a low budget, she takes advantage of the vibrant photography of Bradford Young, who also shot the short subject. So what we're seeing here is the emergence of a promising writer-director, actor, and cinematographer who are all exciting, and have cared to make a film that seeks helpful truths.

## Passione ★ ★ ★ ½

NO MPAA RATING, 91 m., 2011

A documentary hosted and narrated by John Turturro. Featuring Mina, Spakka-Neapolis 55 (Monica Pinto, Antonio Fraioli), Avion Travel, Misia, Pietra Montecorvino, Massimo Ranieri, Lina Sastri, M'Barka Ben Taleb, Gennaro Cosmo Parlato, Peppe Barra, Angela Luce, Max Casella, Raiz, James Senese, Fausto Cigliano, Fiorello, Fiorenza Calogero, Daniela Fiorentino, Lorena Tamaggio, Enzo Avitabile, and Pino Daniele. Directed by John Turturro and produced by Alessandra Acciai, Carlo Macchitella, and Giorgio Magliulo.

John Turturro's mother was Sicilian and his father was born in Italy, but he'd never been to Italy until he went there for location shoots about a decade ago. He fell in love, especially with the music. It tells you something that his actress cousin is named Aida. In his ideal world, music is as much a part of life as speech, and in his magical film *Romance and Cigarettes* (2005), the characters will walk out of a dramatic scene into the street and start to sing.

In the Naples we see in his new film, *Passione*, it feels as if everyone in Naples has that freedom. Here is a music documentary filmed in the streets of Naples and with the people of Naples. It doesn't have a single slick or cynical frame. It's a happy ramble through the storied streets with Turturro as our guide, not pretending to be an expert; it's more like having a good friend take you to this place he really loves.

Although the many singers and instrumentalists he features are no doubt well-known in Italy, they were new to me. What they shared was an immediacy. There was none of the fake pop glitter spawned by the *American Idol* virus. They were performing, yes, but they were also behaving—living their lives in song. Turturro sometimes devises small dramas for them in which he implies their histories and relationships.

There's a freedom in his structure. This isn't a formal documentary, but a meander. Some songs are built as music videos. Some are shot like scenes from neorealism. In some, musicians plant themselves in front of a microphone in a city square and perform for the camera. In others, they engage in freestyle dancing.

The city's music was formed from many sources. It is the city of Caruso, whose standing three old-timers discuss with the exactness of baseball fans. The music of Turkey and France steeped in North Africa was a major influence; remember Ethiopia was an Italian colony. Most recently and perhaps most audibly, the arrival of African-Americans in World War II left behind a heritage of gospel and rhythm and blues.

One of the musicians, James Senese, was fathered by a black American soldier who returned to the States, leaving him to grow up amid prejudice but also with an inherited musical tradition that has brought him great success. There is a lovely woman here named M'Barka Ben Taleb, who is Neapolitan by way of Tunisia. She's North African, but moves through the streets as if she rules. That's Turturro's theme: Once you visit Naples, you will never fall out of love with it.

## Patang ★ ★ ★ ★

NO MPAA RATING, 105 m., 2012

Seema Biswas (Sudha), Nawazuddin Siddiqui (Chakku), Sugandha Garg (Priya), Aakash Maheriya (Bobby), Mukkund Shukla (Jayesh), Hamid Shaikh (Hamid), Pannaben Soni (Ba). Directed by Prashant Bhargava and produced by Jaideep Punjabi. Screenplay by Bhargava.

*Patang* plunges headfirst into a family based in Ahmedabad, where India's largest annual kite festival is celebrated. It reflects the way Indians live in one another's pockets. Homes and businesses, temples and roadways, are all crowded close together, neighbors know one another, and it's all held together by a network of the most baffling traffic in the world.

This film is joyous, but more than that: It's lovely in its construction. The director, Prashant Bhargava, born and raised in Chicago, knows what his basic story line is, but reveals it subtly. The story in outline would be simple enough for a made-for-TV movie. There is nothing simple about *Patang*.

The bare bones of the story: An affluent uncle from Delhi named Jayesh (Mukkund Shukla) pays a much-delayed visit back home to his family in Ahmedabad, bringing along his daughter Priya (Sugandha Garg), who hasn't seen these relatives in years. He meets his sister-in-law (Seema Biswas), his mother, Ba (Pannaben Soni), and his nephew—the son of his brother, who died of a heart attack. The nephew, Chakku (Nawazuddin Siddiqui), resents the way this distant man descends grandly on the small-town relatives and feels he has the right to make suggestions and changes.

The story line becomes fully clear only toward the end. In form, *Patang* looks almost like a cinema verité documentary of this family, surrounded by the city and the kite festival. Many key shots were obtained during the festival itself, and we see the skies over the city filled with thousands of dancing, dueling kites, as every single rooftop is occupied by people. Below in the streets, bands, fireworks, and food vendors create a tumult.

There is a little romantic subplot, involving the daughter from Delhi and Bobby (Aakash Maheriya), who begin a flirtation on the rooftop and continue it during a motorbike ride. On a bridge, her eyes dance with merriness. They've been together a few hours. In a lesser film, this would be a love story with a happy ending. "But Bobby," she says, "we hardly know each other. Do you expect me to leave behind thousands of friends in Delhi?"

He does. Their flirtatious conversation is filmed in close-ups and closer-ups. The effect is intimate and sensual. In one shot only, cigarette smoke coils from her mouth. We never otherwise see her smoking. This establishes in a moment that she is more worldly than the boy. She kisses him, but that will be that: This is only a few days' visit.

The family house itself is a character, and there are a few extended shots of its graceful, playful architecture and happy colors. Many interiors involve a photograph of the dead brother, whose soul seems to inhabit it. Meals are prepared and shared on a table in the street. The food looks delicious; fingers are often used. People are teased to perform songs. Gossip and chatter run wild. We are immersed in the life and sort it out for ourselves. The effect is curiously like being invited into this home and learning while we stay.

Prashant Bhargava, the director, was born and raised on the South Side of Chicago, where he went to grade school and to high school at the Kenwood Academy. How did his background produce such a lovely and successful indie film in India? He explains: "The seeds for the movie were based on the memories of my uncles' dueling kites. In India kite flying transcends boundaries. Rich or poor, Hindu or Muslim, young or old—together they look toward the sky with wonder, thoughts and doubts forgotten. Kite flying is meditation in its simplest form.

"In 2005, I visited Ahmedabad to experience their annual kite festival, the largest in India. When I first witnessed the entire city on their rooftops, staring up at the sky, their kites dueling ferociously, dancing without inhibition, I knew I had to make this film in Ahmedabad."

And that's what happened. His film took three years of research, was six years in the making, had 90 percent nonactors, improvised its takes based on the script. And it flies as free and colorfully as a kite.

## Paul ★ ★ ½

R, 104 m., 2011

Seth Rogen (Paul), Simon Pegg (Graeme Willy), Nick Frost (Clive Gollings), Jason Bateman (Agent Zoil), Kristen Wiig (Ruth Buggs), Bill Hader (Haggard), Blythe Danner (Tara Walton), John Carroll Lynch (Moses Buggs), Joe Lo Truglio (O'Reilly), Jeffrey Tambor (Adam Shadowchild), Sigourney Weaver (The Big Guy). Directed by Greg Mottola and produced by Tim Bevan. Screenplay by Simon Pegg and Nick Frost.

Here's a movie that teeters on the edge of being really pretty good, and loses its way. I'm not quite sure what goes wrong, but you can see that it might have gone right. Maybe Paul, its alien hero, should have been sent back to the shop for a rewrite. He isn't merely voiced by Seth Rogen, he *is* Seth Rogen, if Seth Rogen looked like your usual bulb-headed, big-eyed being from outer space.

The premise is lovable. Graeme and Clive (Simon Pegg and Nick Frost) play two average fanboys from England who breathlessly embark on their dream trip to America. Their destination: Comic-Con in San Diego, and then they plan to rent an RV and tour such American landmarks as Roswell, New Mexico, where (as we all know) a flying saucer landed years ago and the event has been covered up ever since, becoming famous for allegedly being covered up.

The Comic-Con scenes are priceless, as our lads vibrate with excitement in the presence of the legendary sci-fi author Adam Shadowchild, whom Jeffrey Tambor invests with a dour impatience for the species of fanboys. I don't know where Tambor got the inspiration to wear that hat, but sometimes you see a prop and your heart leaps up because it is so right.

After San Diego, the boys drive to Area 51 in Nevada, the first leg of their odyssey. Pegg and Frost bring a wide-eyed innocence and sweetness to their characters, for whom just about everything in America is more or less alien. That includes Paul, whose van crashes in front of them on the highway. If you are an alien and a bad driver, Graeme and Clive are the first two humans you want to meet. They've been inflamed for so long by images of creatures that look exactly like you, that they aren't particularly surprised when you appear. So you join them in their RV and enlist them in your trip toward a rendezvous with your Mother Ship.

Along the way they all meet Ruth Buggs (Kristen Wiig), an intelligent-design advocate with a black lens in her glasses, who finds most of what they say shocking, but joins them in the RV for excellent reasons, even though the existence of an alien poses a considerable challenge to her creationism.

As you expect with a movie that begins at Comic-Con, *Paul* revels in its geekdom. The movie is wall-to-wall with references to other sci-fi movies, some overt, some subtle, as we gradually catch on that this one little creature, Paul, must have been single-handedly behind most of the close encounters of the last seventy years. The movie even supplies a new ending for one sci-fi classic, which brings it to a total of three.

But Paul himself may be a miscalculation. He is Seth Rogen in every aspect except physical appearance. His voice, his vocabulary, his thinking, even his wardrobe (such as it is). And he uses even more four- and ten-letter words than Seth Rogen characters usually do. I think that's a mistake in two ways: (1) If you're going to involve Seth Rogen in a live-action movie, put him on the screen. (2) Paul isn't alien enough. The joy in characters like *E.T.* and *Starman* is that they *are* aliens. Their thinking is strange. Their reactions are unexpected. Paul is somehow too . . . ordinary.

So the movie's a miss, but not without its pleasures. One of them is the appearance of Sigourney Weaver, who knows a thing or two when it comes to aliens who are not ordinary.

## Paul Goodman Changed My Life ★ ★ ★

NO MPAA RATING, 89 m., 2012

A documentary featuring Geoffrey Gardner, Taylor Stoehr, Susan Goodman, Sally Goodman, Judith Malina, Vera Williams, Grace Paley, Noam Chomsky, Ned Rorem, Jerl Surratt, and Michael Walzer. Directed by Jonathan Lee and produced by Lee and Kimberly Reed.

*Paul Goodman Changed My Life* is a documentary about a man who changed mine. Now largely forgotten, Paul Goodman (1911–72) was an omnipresent influence on young people in the 1960s. His book *Growing Up Absurd* (1960), a radical critique of how America raises its young men, was an improbable best-seller from the day it was published, predicting and influencing the '60s generation. "It was impossible to enter a college dorm without seeing it everywhere," remembers one of the people in this doc, and you didn't have to enter my room to see mine, which was often carried in my sports coat pocket or displayed for effect on my desk at the *Daily Illini.*

The readers of that paper were regaled by my weekly columns, which were often applications of Goodman's ideas, and when the great man came to lecture on campus, I devoted two pages to an interview with him, which I insisted our printers set in the American Typewriter type font. "Who is this guy?" moaned Orville Moore, the foreman of our press room. "Times Roman was good enough for Jesus Christ."

Who was this man? Articles about Goodman have a way of beginning with lists. He was a writer, poet, novelist, critic, anarchist, teacher, pacifist, activist, publicly bisexual father of three, city planner, anticommunist godfather of the New Left. He resisted definition. He also resisted authority and convention, as those who remember him here make clear. He would cheerfully go out of his way to state his views plainly. He said he was bisexual when people didn't often say things like that. On the very weekend of the March on the Pentagon, he had been invited to address an official government conference of defense contractors and military leaders, and he informed them they were the devil incarnate. He had such a winning way about him that they sat there and listened. After all, this was the show they had asked to see.

The Goodman books that had the greatest impact on me were *The Community of Scholars* (1962) and *Compulsory Mis-Education* (1964).

They followed logically after *Growing Up Absurd*, arguing that American higher education was largely to blame for the production of narrow-minded specialists and careerists. A university should be a place to gather a general education, Goodman argued. A graduate should know the way around history, literature, philosophy, art, music, politics, and science. Instead, he said, universities were organized for the convenience of their various departments, which focused narrowly in their specialties. Students shouldn't hasten to define themselves too quickly; he recommended a year between high school and college to roam free and discover what life paths beckoned.

Those books, published nearly fifty years ago, were uncannily prophetic. Today some kids are already on a career path in grade school. Before they really know themselves, it is determined what they will do in life. The idea of spending a couple of years in a college of liberal arts and sciences before choosing a specialty is, I fear, losing favor.

*Paul Goodman Changed My Life* is filled with abundant evidence of Goodman as a public intellectual, assembled by its director, Jonathan Lee, who believes the time is here for a rediscovery of his ideas. That seems inescapable. Time and again, we see him on television panels (William F. Buckley raising a dubious eyebrow), behind lecterns, attending conferences, teaching classes, haranguing demonstrations and rallies. He was a tireless campaigner for his ideas. How he found time to write all those books is a mystery. And he was a pipe smoker. In photo after photo, clip after clip, always the pipe.

His life was untidy. He never knew his father. He never married Sally, the mother of his children, although they were together for decades. His sexual promiscuity got him in trouble; he would reportedly give a try at seduction in the most inappropriate situations. An enemy of specialists, his own career defied definition. When I was accepted as a PhD candidate at the University of Chicago, I proposed a thesis on three "generalists," authors who wrote a little of everything: Edmund Wilson, Dwight Macdonald, and Goodman. The world was spared my thesis when the *Sun-Times* made me its film critic. By then his ideas had already changed my life.

## Peace, Love, and Misunderstanding ★ ★ ★

R, 96 m., 2012

Jane Fonda (Grace), Catherine Keener (Diane), Jeffrey Dean Morgan (Jude), Chace Crawford (Cole), Elizabeth Olsen (Zoe), Nat Wolff (Jake), Marissa O'Donnell (Tara), Rosanna Arquette (Darcy), Kyle MacLachlan (Mark). Directed by Bruce Beresford and produced by Jonathan Burkhart, Brice Dal Farra, Claude Dal Farra, and Lauren Munsch. Screenplay by Joseph Muszynski and Christina Mengert.

*Peace, Love, and Misunderstanding* is one of Jane Fonda's rare leading roles in recent years, and it provides a wink at what we probably imagine she's been up to in her spare time. She plays Grace, a hippie grandmother with untamed graying hair who is known as the freest spirit in town—and since she lives in Woodstock, that's saying something.

On her farm with its pond and purebred chickens roaming inside the house, she seems to throw a party every night for the local wild spirits. On the night of the full moon, she gathers a circle of women to worship the Goddess and smoke amazing quantities of pot. If there's a local music festival, it's taken for granted that Grace will be the emcee, and that she's probably slept with most of the musicians.

Into this hedonistic world, her daughter Diane (Catherine Keener) arrives unannounced one day with her children, Zoe (Elizabeth Olsen), twentyish, and Jake (Nat Wolff), around fifteen. Grace has not seen them in twenty years. Diane broke off relations in reaction to her mother's flamboyant lifestyle—but now, having decided to divorce her stolid husband, Mark (Kyle MacLachlan), she has piled her kids into the SUV and headed upstate. All she asks is that Grace somewhat curtail her wildness around the kids. It is not to be.

*Peace, Love, and Misunderstanding* is an undemanding formula picture that's a lot of superficial fun and not much more. Would it surprise you that within twenty-four hours Diane and both of her children have commenced romances with locals, and that many truths will be exchanged between Diane and

Grace? Woodstock is presented as a place where the 1969 festival still more or less continues, many of the flower children apparently having never left. It's very upscale in a laid-back way, like Aspen or Telluride, and Grace, for example, seems to have unlimited funds, although there's a reason for that.

Because Fonda was (very capably) playing a send-up of her image, the character I found most interesting was Catherine Keener's Diane. She's a Manhattan lawyer, nursing anger with her mother after all these years, and making it a point not to drink or smoke—as a rebuke, perhaps. She quickly falls into the aura of Jude (Jeffrey Dean Morgan), a local furniture maker and guitarist, age-appropriate, handsome, understanding. Meanwhile, her daughter, Zoe, locks hearts with Cole (Chace Crawford), even though she is a vegetarian and he is a butcher. Young Jake is smitten with Tara (Marissa O'Donnell), a waitress in a coffee shop who wins him with a shy smile and superb latte.

These three interlocking romances mesh with Grace's nonstop adventures and assorted heart-to-heart talks, and that's about the size of it. The director, Bruce Beresford, seems content to deliver a charming comedy and sidestep the deeper family issues he could have dealt with.

So, all right, on that level the film worked for me. It essentially focuses on the three women, and Fonda, Keener, and the fast-rising Elizabeth Olsen look plausibly like three generations from the same genes. Olsen, indeed, looks a great deal like Keener, and that is a sincere compliment. It's the cheekbones when they smile.

## People Like Us ★ ★ ½

PG-13, 115 m., 2012

Chris Pine (Sam), Elizabeth Banks (Frankie), Michael Hall D'Addario (Josh), Michelle Pfeiffer (Lillian), Olivia Wilde (Hannah), Mark Duplass (Ted), Sara Mornell (Dr. Amanda), Jon Favreau (Richards), Philip Baker Hall (Ike Rafferty). Directed by Alex Kurtzman and produced by Bobby Cohen, Roberto Orci, and Clayton Townsend. Screenplay by Kurtzman, Orci, and Jody Lambert.

*People Like Us* is a good-hearted and well-intentioned film that depends on a movie device we could name the Ninety-Minute Delay. That describes the technique of waiting through most of a movie for one simple line to be spoken that would clear up all of the confusion. In this case, that line would be, "We are brother and sister." There might be a good reason for not wanting to tell someone that, but not in this story, where it serves mostly to string us along.

The siblings in question are the children of a famous Los Angeles record producer, who spent his career masterminding the albums of rock legends and found time to start a second family on the side. Now we meet his son Sam (Chris Pine), a slick-talking New York salesman, who gets the news that his father has died. He sets off for the airport with his girlfriend, Hannah (Olivia Wilde), but is so reluctant to attend the funeral he tries to manage for them to miss their flight.

No luck. Apparently the old man was a distant father, wrapped up in his own legend. When he arrives belatedly at home, his mother, Lillian (Michelle Pfeiffer), gives him a good slap and then says she's happy to have him home. He enters at last a room in their house that was his father's man cave, a repository of his tapes, albums, souvenirs, archives, and privacy. It's unclear how much money the old man left, but Sam's legacy seems to be a shaving kit with $150,000 inside—and information on who to deliver it to.

That would be Frankie (Elizabeth Banks), his half sister. In a reasonable world he might implore his father's trusted attorney, Ike Rafferty (Philip Baker Hall), to perform this mission, or at least accompany him on it. Sam prefers a stealth approach, "happens" to meet her at an AA meeting, and learns she has a young son, Josh (Michael Hall D'Addario). He begins to befriend them, grows close to the son, and behaves in a way that, in another movie, might seem alarming. Not here. His help is welcomed, although Frankie grows curious.

As Hannah returns home and Sam settles in for an indefinite stay, he is tempted to keep the cash for himself; he's deeply in debt because of a boxcar-load of exploding juice boxes. But never mind. He and Frankie begin to share confidences, an unmistakable affection grows between them, and all this time Sam keeps the crucial secret.

A truth untold can interest me up to a certain point, and then it grows tiresome. Alex Kurtzman, who directed and cowrote this film, says it is loosely based on a true story, his own. I don't suppose it's a close parallel, but for the sake of discussion, at which point does Sam's keeping the secret qualify as a sadistic manipulation of his sister? If the old man was cool and distant, has the fruit fallen far from the tree?

*People Like Us* paints engaging portraits of its characters, who feel close enough to plausible people—so close that the delayed secret undermines them. Characters cannot linger in ignorance indefinitely without suffering. I like smart movies about smart people, and enjoy it when most of the facts are on the table and we can contemplate them together.

Sam and Frankie are certainly interesting enough that a movie about them coming to grips with this hidden truth would have been justified. It would also probably have been harder to write than this one, so *People Like Us* marches on with a coy little smile, toying with Frankie and the audience.

## Percy Jackson and the Olympians: The Lightning Thief ★ ★ ★

PG, 119 m., 2010

Logan Lerman (Percy), Alexandra Daddario (Annabeth), Brandon T. Jackson (Grover), Uma Thurman (Medusa), Sean Bean (Zeus), Pierce Brosnan (Chiron), Steve Coogan (Hades), Catherine Keener (Sally Jackson), Joe Pantoliano (Gabe Ugliano), Melina Kanakaredes (Athena), Rosario Dawson (Persephone), Kevin McKidd (Poseidon). Directed by Chris Columbus and produced by Michael Barnathan, Thomas M. Hammel, Guy Oseary, Mark Radcliffe, and Karen Rosenfelt. Screenplay by Craig Titley, based on the novel by Rick Riordan.

Every movie involving superheroes requires an origin story, and *Percy Jackson and the Olympians: The Lightning Thief* has a doozy. The Greek gods on Mount Olympus sometimes descend to Earth to have children, you see, and these half-god, half-humans are demigods. They live among us. One is Percy Jackson (Logan Lerman), who is the teenage son of Poseidon and Sally Jackson (Catherine Keener). He doesn't know this. I wonder if his mom noticed. Kind of a letdown to discover Greek gods are runaway dads.

Percy finds he can think best when underwater for ten minutes at a time. Poseidon was the god of the sea, you will recall. His best buddy is Grover (Brandon T. Jackson), who is revealed as a sort of assistant-demigod assigned to watch over him. His teacher is Mr. Brunner (Pierce Brosnan), who is actually Chiron, a centaur. Give Brosnan a lot credit for wearing the back half of a horse as if he'd been doing it for years.

The movie, based on a novel by Rick Riordan, has fun working out modern parallels for Greek mythology. Percy, for example, thinks he is dyslexic, but it's only that his eyes instinctively turn English into Greek letters. No help in class. After learning of his real identity, he goes off to Chiron's demigod training camp with Grover, and he becomes friends with Annabeth (Alexandra Daddario), a demigoddess if ever I've seen one.

The plot heats up. Zeus (Sean Bean) and Poseidon (Kevin McKidd) meet atop the Empire State Building to discuss Zeus's missing lightning bolt, which he believes Poseidon's son Percy has stolen. (The story requires a certain suspension of disbelief.) Why, when, or how he allegedly might have done so begins as a mystery to Percy, but eventually the situation leads to slam-bam special effects sequences, as the gods and demigods do battle.

Undoubtedly the biggest attraction among the gods is Medusa, and Uma Thurman demonstrates she can wear a snake-filled head as gracefully as Pierce Brosnan can trot around with a horse's netherlands. There is also the advent of Steve Coogan as Hades. Yes, Steve Coogan. Hades, you recall, is the brother of Zeus and Poseidon.

Or maybe you don't recall. It's one of my weaknesses that I was never able to work up much of an interest in the Greek gods, who made for discouraging fiction because they were entirely defined by their attributes. They had no personalities to speak of, but simply went about doing what they did. You can understand why Zeus is so upset about losing his lightning bolt. That's what he does, is hurl that lightning bolt. What is Zeus without his bolt?

Director Chris Columbus has fun with this goofy premise, but as always I am distracted by the practical aspects of the story. Does it bother the Greek gods that no one any longer knows or cares that they rule the world? What are the genetic implications of human-god interbreeding? And, forgive me, I'll have to double back to Sally Jackson, Percy's mother. How did she meet Poseidon? At the beach, I suppose. Did he reveal his true identity? If a guy picks you up at the beach and says he's Poseidon, do you say, fine, let's not date, let's just mate? And then when the bastard dumps you and disappears leaving you pregnant, what way is that for a god to behave?

My remaining question involves the title. Call me foolish, but I don't consider *Percy Jackson and the Olympians: The Lightning Thief* an ideal title. The movie's original title was *Percy Jackson and the Lightning Thief,* which at least has the advantage of sounding less like a singing group.

*Note: This is the first film I recall with end credits including the names of the actors who played Parthenon Janitors. I know, it's the Parthenon in Nashville, but even so.*

## The Perfect Game ★ ★ ★

PG, 118 m., 2010

Clifton Collins Jr. (Cesar Faz), Cheech Marin (Padre Estaban), Jake T. Austin (Angel Macias), Ryan Ochoa (Norberto), Emilie de Ravin (Frankie), Moises Arias (Mario), Patricia Manterola (Maria), Louis Gossett Jr. (Cool Papa Bell), Bruce McGill (Tanner). Directed by William Dear and produced by Daniel de Liege, Michael O. Gallant, Mark W. Koch, David Salzberg, Christian Tureaud, and W. William Winokur. Screenplay by Winokur.

Once upon a very long time, a film "based on a true story" was both true and almost too good to be a story. Perhaps anticipating any suspicion, William Dear intercuts newsreel footage from 1957 with *The Perfect Game,* frequently piping into the past for black-and-white and then segueing into the color of the present day. These players really lived, and this game was really played.

The film begins in Monterrey, Mexico, seen here as an impoverished town with many baseball fans, who follow the Brooklyn Dodgers on the radio with nearly religious intensity. We meet young Angel Macias (Jake T. Austin), who aims at a bucket fastened to a wall as a strike zone and dreams of greatness on the mound. His father is not so enthusiastic.

The setup is traditional. The town's boys have time on their hands and need an activity to keep them out of mischief. Enter wise, gentle Padre Estaban (Cheech Marin), who thinks a baseball team might help. Newly returned to town is Cesar Faz (Clifton Collins Jr.), who was a prospect for the St. Louis Cardinals but was devalued and shunted aside, possibly because he was Mexican. Unable to take more of the racism of management, he returned home and is recruited by Padre Estaban, not without difficulty, to coach the kids' team.

Because the film is titled *The Perfect Game,* you expect one to be pitched. You do not expect it to be pitched in Monterrey. You sort of know how these underdog sports movies turn out. Doesn't matter. *The Perfect Game* so expertly uses the charisma and personalities of the actors, especially the young ones, that it's thrilling anyway.

The scenes at the Little League World Series in Williamsport, Pennsylvania, make the contrast seem so dramatic between the teams in the final game—the Mexicans seemingly a foot shorter on average than their American counterparts. William Dear cannot, by the very nature of his story, avoid certain clichés, but the way he orchestrates the big game is sure and confident, and there's that life we often feel at the end of an underdog story.

In the years since, the Little League World Series has become blown out of proportion, verging on the exploitation of the players. They're trained within an inch of their lives, placed under enormous pressure, and subjected to punishing media scrutiny. It's not a game anymore. In 1957, these kids were *playing.* And it was a perfect game.

## Phunny Business: A Black Comedy ★ ★ ★

NO MPAA RATING, 84 m., 2011

A documentary narrated by John Ridley and featuring Doug Banks, Bill Bellamy, Cedric the Entertainer, Mike Epps, Jamie Foxx, Chris

Gardner, Adele Givens, Steve Harvey, D. L. Hughley, Honest John, Raymond C. Lambert, Ali LeRoi, Bernie Mac, Carlos Mencia, J. B. Smoove, Aries Spears, Sheryl Underwood, George Willborn, and Damon Williams. Directed by John Davies and produced by Davies, Reid Brody, and Raymond C. Lambert. Screenplay by Davies and Lambert.

What Second City was for *Saturday Night Live*, a comedy club in Chicago was for virtually every black comedian who emerged in the 1990s. All Jokes Aside was a black-owned enterprise that seemed to have infallible taste in talent, perhaps because it was the only club in the country that didn't relegate blacks to "special nights" or "Chocolate Sundays." Its opening-night act was Jamie Foxx, then unknown. It introduced or showcased such as Bernie Mac, Cedric the Entertainer, Steve Harvey, D. L. Hughley, Carlos Mencia, A. J. Jamal, Sheryl Underwood, George Wallace, Bill Bellamy, Dave Chappelle, Adele Givens, and on and on, including the personnel of the touring Kings of Comedy and Queens of Comedy.

*Phunny Business: A Black Comedy* is a most unexpected documentary about the rise of a club that often sold out three houses a night for ten years, wasn't on the radar of many Chicagoans, and closed, in a way, as the victim of its own success: When the young comics it launched made it big, they found more money doing concerts on big stages than gigs in a small room.

This is a film not so much about black comedians, although we see and hear a lot of them, but about black entrepreneurs. Raymond C. Lambert, who cofounded the club, began as a stock trader for the firm of the black Chicago millionaire Chris Gardner (who himself inspired the character played by Will Smith in *The Pursuit of Happyness*). After a visit to Budd Friedman's Improv in Los Angeles, he wondered why a club like that wouldn't work in Chicago.

Turned out, it would. He opened on Wabash Avenue in the South Loop, booked the best of a new generation, insisted on impeccable manners, dress, and training for his staff, made headliners wear suits and ties, and drew affluent crowds. He was also providing almost the only venue in the nation for black female comedians, the threatened subspecies of a threatened species, and booked black gay comics at a time when that was unheard of. He even booked one white comic, Honest John, who backstage one night advised Deon Cole, "Try some of this real California weed instead of that Chicago &#!+," after which Cole went onstage and found himself suddenly gifted with telescopic tunnel vision.

The film goes in depth about business details, including the peculiarity that All Laughs Aside paid its performers their full fees, promptly, with checks that didn't bounce, no matter how many tickets had been sold—an achievement few comedy clubs of any description could boast, then and now. One of Lambert's partners was a woman named Mary Lindsey, herself a trader at the Chicago Board Options Exchange, who supervised talent with a firm hand, a ready tongue, and dress code inspections.

The film, directed by John Davies, has access to a lot of archival footage, going back to the earliest days when the "stage" was a curtain on a back wall. We get bites from many of the comics, but no extended stretches; the narration and editing often seem to be upstaging the comedians. I would have preferred more comics and fewer montages about Chicago's weather, women, and food. It is also safe to say that we see enough of Raymond Lambert in the film, from the opening titles onward. He's heard not as a doc-style talking head, but in scripted material that sells itself a little too hard. The comedians come across as more relaxed and natural. Former *Sun-Times* reporter Ernie Tucker shares warm memories, as do Second City's John Kapelos and Tim Kazurinsky.

The club on Wabash was the victim of larger paychecks paid by big stages (like the Chicago Theater, not far away), a rent that doubled, and gentrification as the South Loop underwent a boom. Lambert invested $1 million in a move a mile north to the "entertainment district," only to face ruinous delays in getting a liquor license (despite a record of ten years with no incidents). White and Asian owners of nearby galleries and restaurants signed a petition protesting a change in the "ambience" of the area—meaning, "more blacks." So it goes.

Still, it was a grand run, and it is good to have it memorialized. Today Lambert says he looks back with satisfaction. He created All Laughs Aside at a time when it was needed, and it achieved what it set out to achieve, and on its stage many of today's most successful black actors and comedians got their start. Consider his opening-night act. Jamie Foxx went on to win an Academy Award. And he still gives back: He was the headliner at this year's benefit for Chicago's Gene Siskel Film Center.

## Pina ★ ★ ★ ½

PG, 103 m., 2012

A documentary featuring Malou Airaudo, Andrey Berezin, Damiano Ottavio Bigi, Clementine Deluy, Josephine Ann Endicott, Lutz Foerster, Silvia Farias Heredia, Barbara Kaufmann, Nayoung Kim, Dominique Mercy, Ditta Miranda Jasjfi, Cristiana Morganti, Nazareth Panadero, Jean-Laurent Sasportes, Julie Shanahan, and Yu Tsai-chin. Directed by Wim Wenders and produced by Wenders and Gian-Piero Ringel.

Pina Bausch was a much-loved German choreographer whose work was unlike anybody else's, incorporating earth, water, stones, and city streets into music and movement. She was greatly admired by the German director Wim Wenders, who delayed the notion of filming her work until the recent developments in 3-D. It is an irony that as he was preparing *Pina*, the choreographer discovered she had cancer and died a few days before filming began.

Ideally, Pina and her voice would have stood at the center of this film. Hauntingly, it seems to circle the empty space she left behind. There are only a few obviously dated shots of her. And there are the memories of her dancers. Admission to the close ranks of her troupe was an arduous and demanding process, and we sense her dancers are as closely associated as the nuns or monks in a cloister. As they speak of her, their voices are reverential. We do not need to be told she very recently died; we hear the sorrow and shock in their voices.

We do not, indeed, even see them speaking. Wenders uses techniques to set their voices aside from their physical presence. Instead of talking heads, he uses carefully composed close-ups, and we hear their thoughts in voice-over. Some look at the camera, some into space. They are young, middle-aged, older, coming from all races, representing (perhaps she thought) the human race.

How can words describe dance? All I can tell you is what I saw. There are four dance pieces here, mixed together, none seen straight from start to finish. One of them, titled "Cafe Mueller," I remembered seeing in Pedro Almodovar's *Talk to Her* (2002), in which dancers wander blindly in a room where other dancers rearrange chairs and tables so that in their wanderings they might fall over them. The parallel with life is there to be seen.

Another uses Stravinsky's *Rite of Spring*, which takes place on a stage covered with earth and sand. Dancers leave traces on this surface as they walk, slide and even crawl on it, and perhaps they represent living things making their way from the soil to the sun. And there is "Vollmond," with its onstage waterfall. The dancers soak themselves and one another, hurling sprays of water into the air like extensions of their movements.

Wenders has spoken a lot about his use of 3-D here. Like other thoughtful directors (Scorsese, Herzog, Spielberg), he uses it only when he knows why and how it should be employed. Here he visually dramatizes the spaces between the actors by moving his camera on a crane so that the POV places us on the stage and moves among the dancers.

Although Pina Bausch knew Wenders planned to use 3-D, I wonder what she would have thought of the result. Most dance is choreographed to be seen from one point of view, the audience's. I imagine a choreographer creates it, however, from an omniscient point of view positioned above and among the dancers. That would be necessary to anticipate how the dancers would relate to one another in space; they aren't cut-out silhouettes, but figures in a landscape. Imagine the difference between ordinary chess and 3-D chess. There are different lines of force.

I watched the film in a sort of reverie. The dancers seemed particularly absorbed. They had performed these dances many times before, but always with Pina Bausch present. Now they were on their own, in homage.

## Pirates of the Caribbean: On Stranger Tides ★ ★

PG-13, 136 m., 2011

Johnny Depp (Jack Sparrow), Penelope Cruz (Angelica), Geoffrey Rush (Barbossa), Ian McShane (Blackbeard), Kevin R. McNally (Gibbs), Sam Claflin (Philip), Astrid Berges-Frisbey (Syrena), Stephen Graham (Scrum), Keith Richards (Captain Teague). Directed by Rob Marshall and produced by Jerry Bruckheimer. Screenplay by Ted Elliott and Terry Rossio.

Before seeing *Pirates of the Caribbean: On Stranger Tides*, I had already reached my capacity for Pirates of the Caribbean movies, and with this fourth installment, my cup runneth over. Indeed, so doth Captain Jack Sparrow's, as he obtains two chalices to use while drinking from the Fountain of Youth, and seeks a mermaid's tears to invest them with magic. There's always a catch-22. You fight Spanish conquistadors and the British Navy to find the bloody fountain, and now you need a weepy mermaid.

I had fleeting hopes for this episode of the Disney franchise. An opening sequence is fun, as Captain Jack impersonates a British judge, is chased through London, and discovers his old amour Angelica (Penelope Cruz) attempting to impersonate him while raising the crew for a ship. That anyone would still want to sail under Jack's command is a tribute to the daring of British seamen. The movie is fun until they set sail.

Johnny Depp, who confesses he's rather tired of playing his relentless hero, nevertheless does a plucky job here. He plays Jack Sparrow as an insouciant wise guy, rarely ruffled, always ready with a quip. Whether he is a competent swashbuckler is hard to say because the fight sequences here are composed in the editing room and do not seem to exist in an actual space-time continuum. We no longer see truly great sword fighting, the kind performed by Liam Neeson and Tim Roth in *Rob Roy* (1995). It's all impossible leaping and incomprehensible cutting, giving us all of the movement of action and none of the excitement.

The best way to describe the plot is by explaining that the Fountain of Youth is the MacGuffin. Angelica and Jack set sail for the New World aboard a ship commanded by Blackbeard (Ian McShane), who is said to be her father. The ship's crew includes zombies, which is a step up from previous crew members in the series, skeletons. Blackbeard is in a race to find the fountain before Captain Barbossa (Geoffrey Rush), who is being financed by King George, who needs to drink from the fountain none too soon. Rush is as always a dependable actor, but his sandpapery skin complexion is rather alarming here. Get this sailor some Lubriderm.

Also in the race is a boatload of Spanish sailors sent by their king. All three boats pitch up on the same beach and fight one another to the fountain. But wait. The mermaids. Yes, a special reflector used in an old lighthouse casts light on one of the longboats, and light attracts mermaids, and it's a nasty sight. We get to meet only one of the mermaids, the well-named Syrena (Astrid Berges-Frisbey), who is comely and doe-eyed, and has one of those official hairdos that cleverly conceals the delightful bits.

Syrena and Philip (Sam Claflin), a cleric, lock eyes and hearts, but Syrena is needed for her tears, and is held captive and transported through the jungle in a large water tank, wherein she nearly drowns because she cannot breathe, establishing at last what I have always argued, that mermaids are amphibians.

One improvement this time is the dropping of the superfluous nonpirate characters played earlier by Orlando Bloom and Keira Knightley. I was never sure what essential function they fulfilled; Depp and Cruz are so over-the-top they function as their own supporting characters.

Even in his first Pirates movie, Depp seemed to be channeling large parts of the persona of Keith Richards, not to mention all of the eyeliner. Here the Rolling Stone himself turns up again, playing Jack Sparrow's father. The hairdressers for these two characters seem to have involved themselves in some sort of a grudge bet.

*Pirates of the Caribbean: On Stranger Tides*

is about what you'd expect. It is long, expensive, and bombastic, and the beautiful mermaid has a tantalizing way of not coming quite far enough out of the water. For me, it's too much of a muchness. The whole series was inspired by a ride at Disney World. There's a bright side to that. At least no movie has yet been inspired by "It's a Small World."

## Please Give ★ ★ ★ ½

R, 91 m., 2010

Catherine Keener (Kate), Amanda Peet (Mary), Oliver Platt (Alex), Rebecca Hall (Rebecca), Ann Morgan Guilbert (Andra), Sarah Steele (Abby). Directed by Nicole Holofcener and produced by Anthony Bregman. Screenplay by Holofcener.

There is an evil-tempered old woman in *Please Give* whose greatest accomplishment is having survived into her nineties without being pushed down a steep flight of stairs. She finds fault with everyone and everything, is ungrateful, is a whiner, and brings nothing to the party. How do people like this live with themselves?

Her next-door neighbors are waiting for her to die so that her apartment will become available and they can break down some walls. This is in New York, the city that drains a cruel price per square foot of living space from its inhabitants. I know New Yorkers happy to find an apartment that for a somewhat poor Chicagoan would be the bedroom. It is one of the pleasures of Nicole Holofcener's new film that everyone, including the old lady, knows this.

The couple next door are Kate and Alex (Catherine Keener and Oliver Platt). They run an antique-furniture store specializing in furniture from the 1950s—you know, the kind your family accumulated at great expense, which sat there in the house looking superior. They often obtain their stock from grandchildren who consider a 1952 coffee table to be the graceless blotch it surely is, but which metrosexuals consider an ironic statement on how cool they are.

The old lady, Andra, is played by Ann Morgan Guilbert with exact cunning: She makes Andra expert at seeming unaware of her monstrous selfishness. Andra is looked after by two granddaughters, Mary (Amanda Peet) and Rebecca (Rebecca Hall). Rebecca is constant and kind, Mary is a distracted heavy drinker, both are attractive, and they live together in one of those roommate arrangements that can be explained only by madness or the cost of apartments.

Kate is another of those Catherine Keener characters you feel like you've known somewhere before. She and her husband have a nice life as a couple who seem to be winning their own version of *Antiques Roadshow.* They have a daughter, Abby (Sarah Steele), who is pudgy, has skin problems, and is a little antisocial right now but is smart, has good timing, and will eventually get life sorted out. Abby is incredulous at the way her mom is a pushover for street beggars, as if she's making some kind of amends. Kate can hardly enjoy a meal without taking a doggie bag to a homeless man. She's an innocent; she's shocked to find that another dealer bought a table from her and marked it up in his own store.

Kate and Alex are reasonably happy. They run errands for old Andra to calm their consciences, and decide to have a dinner party for the old lady and her granddaughters. This scene shows Holofcener demonstrating that recognizable life is almost always more engrossing than fantasy; it's an exercise in social embarrassment, one of those Bunuelian scenes in which people unexpectedly tell the truth and say what should not be said.

Nicole Holofcener, who made the great *Lovely and Amazing,* pays close attention to women. She doesn't define them by their relationships with men. In a Holofcener movie, women actually have their *own* reasons for doing things—and these are even allowed to be bad reasons, and funny ones. The movie is about imperfect characters in a difficult world, who mostly do the best they can under the circumstances, but not always. Do you realize what a revolutionary approach that is for a movie these days?

## Poetry ★ ★ ★ ½

NO MPAA RATING, 139 m., 2011

Yun Jung-hee (Mija), Lee David (Wook), Kim Hira (M. Kang). Directed, produced, and written by Lee Chang-dong.

There is perhaps something in the river. It floats slowly closer on the current. It is the body of a young woman. *Poetry* opens with this extended shot, so that our realization can slowly grow. Then we meet an old woman named Mija. She learns from her doctor that she is in the early stages of Alzheimer's. It is difficult to be sure what effect this news has. She continues with her life.

Mija (Yun Jung-hee) lives in a South Korean city where she looks after her grandson, Wook (Lee David), and is a caregiver for an old man who is half-paralyzed by a stroke. She is a small, unremarkable woman, cheerfully dressed, quiet, getting things done. She signs up for an adult class in poetry writing at a local community center. The teacher is not a bad teacher, maybe even a good one, although he acts as if you can be taught to write poetry. All you can do is write it. Whether it is good or not isn't up to you.

The teacher encourages his students to look, *really* look, at things. He asks them if they have ever *really* looked at an apple. Mija goes home and really looks at an apple. It is such a perfect fruit. But then, every fruit is perfect. Mija's grandson is a sullen lout, a layabout with worthless friends. She is told one day that he has been implicated with five other boys in the rape of a young woman. That was the young woman in the river.

She carries on. She still attends class. It is very difficult to be sure what she is thinking, and this kind of film is more absorbing than those with characters who wear their emotions on their sleeves. We peer at her, we want to see into her. Yun Jung-hee's performance is delicately given, in that she seems to be concealing nothing and yet we remain outside. Aware of her diagnosis, we look for signs of memory loss, but she remembers, all right. It's just that she is more focused on poetry at the moment.

There is a scene here that is heartrending. The fathers of the other boys meet with Mija and explain they're getting up a fund to pay off the dead girl's mother. Mija is made to feel she must raise the money as a duty to her grandson. She deals with this in her own way, which I will not specify, except by saying that she begins to *really* look. And the poetry class, with its promise of transcendence, takes a place in her soul that we sense, rather than see.

This is the second of Lee's films I've seen after *Oasis* (2002). That film also approached extreme cruelty with outward composure. It deals with a disturbed and worthless ex-con who killed a man in a hit-and-run accident. After prison, he meets the severely disabled daughter of his victim, he assaults her, and this begins a relationship that seems somehow to meet their mutual needs. Believe me, I know how horrifying that sounds. But Lee doesn't make exploitation films and he doesn't find conventional answers. He is puzzled by the mysteries of inexplicable behavior.

In *Poetry*, we have a movie that is outwardly more calm. It is not seeking answers, either. It begins with events and sees how they develop. Mija, at the center, is perhaps determined not to fill her remaining memories with despair, and to avoid adding to the sum of the world's misery. Maybe it's as simple as that. And I must add that the film contains certainly the most poignant badminton match I can imagine.

*Note:* Poetry *won the prize for best screenplay at Cannes 2010.*

## Point Blank ★ ★ ★

R, 84 m., 2011

Gilles Lellouche (Samuel Pierret), Roschdy Zem (Hugo Sartet), Gerard Lanvin (Commandant Werner), Elena Anaya (Nadia Pierret), Mireille Perrier (Commandant Fabre), Claire Perot (Captain Susini). Directed by Fred Cavaye and produced by Cyril Colbeau-Justin and Jean-Baptiste Dupont. Screenplay by Cavaye and Guillaume Lemans.

*Point Blank* is an ingenious thriller that doesn't make much sense, but doesn't need to because it moves at breakneck speed through a story of a man's desperation to save his pregnant wife after she has been kidnapped. This is the kind of movie where you get involved first and ask questions later.

Samuel (Gilles Lellouche) is a male nurse in a Parisian hospital, deeply in love with the very pregnant Nadia (Elena Anaya). It goes without saying that her pregnancy is not uncomplicated; in other words, the last thing she needs is to be kidnapped.

Working on the night shift, Samuel happens upon a murder attempt directed against one of his patients, Sartet (Roschdy Zem). We met Sartet earlier in the pre-title sequence, when the film hit the ground running with a headlong chase through Paris. He was almost killed then. Now someone wants to finish the job. Samuel saves the man's life.

This makes him a hero, and he even boasts a little to his wife. His joy is short-lived. She is kidnapped, and Samuel gets a phone call: He must remove Sartet from the hospital or she will die.

Everything else in the film expands from his dilemma. The details of the removal. His relationship with Sartet. The identity of the kidnappers. The involvement of a police commandant named Werner (Gerard Lanvin, very effective). Nadia's health. Ethical dilemmas. Moral choices.

To go into any detail would be to rob the movie of its essence. It has to happen to you. It does, with a fearsome urgency. When the movie ended I looked with a little surprise at my watch. You know that instinct you have about where a movie is in its story? You get a feeling for the approach of the ending.

*Point Blank* didn't feel incomplete; indeed, it had a rare economy and unity. But it was only eighty-four minutes long. That was more or less exactly how long it needed to be. I learn there will be an American remake. You can count on it approaching the two-hour mark as Hollywood pumps in the helium.

*Note: This movie has no connection to the Lee Marvin/John Boorman classic.*

## Polisse ★ ★ ½

NO MPAA RATING, 127 m., 2012

Karin Viard (Nadine), Joey Starr (Fred), Marina Fois (Iris), Nicolas Duvauchelle (Mathieu), Maiwenn (Melissa), Karole Rocher (Chrys), Emmanuelle Bercot (Sue Ellen), Frederic Pierrot (Balloo). Directed by Maiwenn and produced by Alain Attal. Screenplay by Maiwenn and Emmanuelle Bercot.

I'm not sure I feel more at ease after seeing this prize-winning film about a child protection unit in Paris. No doubt a lot of children get protected, but the professional standards of the police sometimes seem inspired by TV cop shows, on which the plots center on the camaraderie of the cops.

Consider this scene. A female officer is questioning a teenage girl who was asked to provide oral sex for a group of boys. Why did she agree? Because they took her cell phone. The policewoman can barely suppress her laughter. She calls some colleagues into the interrogation room and tries to keep a straight face as she briefs them: "She gave a blow job to get her cell phone back." The girl doesn't think she was so stupid. "It was a smartphone!" she explains. Now all the cops are laughing at her.

The police in the film seem to move as a posse. They make raids together, sit in on one another's interrogations, have dinners at each other's houses, and carry on various sexual affairs. Their dynamics threaten to upstage the importance of their work. Yes, there are serious scenes, some heartbreaking, including the questioning of a great many adults who talk defensively about their behavior as if they don't see anything wrong with it.

The message is that the sexual abuse of children is more common in Paris than anyone would believe, and although some of it involves child prostitution, most of it involves family members. It's not that the cops chortle through one interrogation after another, but more that they seem to have a streak of voyeurism. Having seen so much evil, they're curious about what they haven't seen before. One cop asks for a case because he hadn't had "one like that."

The film opens with a flurry of activity, intercutting case details while only gradually orienting us to the characters. But it does a good job of setting apart their individual stories, and the dismay and disgust about what they have to see every day. Sometimes a case is too much for them, as when they meet a young African immigrant who has been living on the streets with her little boy. The cops try to find her a shelter and fail, and one cop wants to bring them home with him, which is against the rules. Mother and son end up separated, probably permanently.

Another searing story involves a cop named Iris (Marina Fois), who is present during a miscarriage. Told the infant must have a name in order to be logged and buried, she replies simply, "Iris." In her case, and probably some others, this job is more than they can withstand.

The director and cowriter is Maiwenn, an

actress and now third-time filmmaker, who is accomplished at following her several story lines and weaving them together. If her subject matter had been less fraught with despair, her approach would have been more appropriate. She has a central role in the film, as Melissa, a photographer who is assigned to document the unit by the justice ministry. Fair enough, but she actually gives herself one of those scenes where a cop she likes tells her she'd be really beautiful if she took off those glasses and let down her hair.

Maiwenn, who was earlier known as Maiwenn Le Besco, is said to have inspired the role played by Natalie Portman in Luc Besson's *Leon: The Professional* (1994). Born in 1976, pushed into acting by her actress mother, she met Besson when she was fifteen and had a child by him a year later. To know that is to ask yourself many questions about this film.

*Note:* Polisse *won the Jury Prize at Cannes 2011. The title is a child's misspelling of the word "police."*

## Potiche ★ ★ ½

R, 103 m., 2011

Catherine Deneuve (Suzanne Pujol), Gerard Depardieu (Maurice Babin), Fabrice Luchini (Robert Pujol), Karin Viard (Nadege), Judith Godreche (Joelle), Jeremie Renier (Laurent Pujol). Directed by Francois Ozon and produced by Eric Altmeyer and Nicolas Altmeyer. Screenplay by Ozon, adapted from a play by Pierre Barillet and Jean-Pierre Gredy.

It has been years since I sensed that Catherine Deneuve and Gerard Depardieu were acting. They are, of course, and as a wide variety of characters. But they give their directors what Billy Wilder once asked Jack Lemmon to do: "Nothing." There is never a note wrong, never the slightest strain, always such an unforced ease in the sight of the camera that they might have been born onscreen.

Here they are in Francois Ozon's comedy *Potiche*. The title is a French word that combines aspects of "trophy wife" and "status symbol." Here she comes now, the *potiche*, jogging down a forest path in a red running suit: Suzanne (Deneuve), the bourgeois wife of a provincial factory owner.

Her father created the factory, which manufactures umbrellas. Her husband, Robert (Fabrice Luchini), became the boss after the old man's death. It appears that she brought the factory into their marriage, but Robert behaves as if he built it from the ground up with his own hands, one *parapluie* at a time. He is an arrogant man, the ruler of his little kingdom, who cheats on his fragrant wife with his secretary—who herself seems not very pleased by him.

Suzanne lives a serene and comfortable life, loves her adult son and daughter, understands that her husband has a mistress and is perhaps happy to have the mistress relieve her of some of her duties. That Deneuve so convincingly inhabits this character is a demonstration of effortless skill.

It is 1977. France is shaken by strikes. I recall Cannes in those years, annually shut down for a day or two by striking workers who took their own strolls on the red carpet. The workers go on strike at the umbrella factory, Robert marches out to denounce them, and they make him a hostage. Suddenly all the labor problems have become the business of Suzanne.

She has been depicted as just slightly bubble-brained. She carries around a little pocket notebook in which she writes little poems that are more than a little banal. The method of Deneuve's approach to the role is not to pretend Suzanne becomes suddenly serious, but to show Suzanne as still exactly the same person, as only the circumstances change.

She needs help. She calls upon the town mayor, Maurice (Gerard Depardieu). He is a communist, as many French mayors were at that time. He is also a fond man in late middle age, running a little to seed, who remembers Suzanne warmly from his past. (Their unforced onscreen affection must owe something to the fact that they have appeared in eight films together, and have lived in each other's pockets for decades as glories of the French cinema.) They work together to find a way past the stupidity of her husband and the anger of the workers. Along the way Suzanne reengages in life; we sense her strategy for dealing with her unbearable husband was to partition him into a soundproof room in her mind.

The film is a whimsical comedy, based on a

popular Parisian stage success of some years ago. It plays like one, although Ozon uses more locations than a play would find possible. There's little effort at psychological depth, and the characters float along on the requirements of comedy. But it's sweet comedy, knowing about human nature, and Deneuve and Depardieu, who bring so much history to the screen, seem to create it by their very natures.

## Predators ★ ★

R, 106 m., 2010

Adrien Brody (Royce), Topher Grace (Edwin), Danny Trejo (Cuchillo), Alice Braga (Isabelle), Walton Goggins (Stans), Oleg Taktarov (Nikolai), Laurence Fishburne (Noland). Directed by Nimrod Antal and produced by Elizabeth Avellan and John Davis. Screenplay by Alex Litvak and Michael Finch.

*Predators* may be the first film in history to open with a deus ex machina. Yes, the entire plot and all the human characters drop into the movie from the heavens. The last thing they remember is a blinding flash of light. Now they're in free fall, tumbling toward the surface, screaming, grabbing for rip cords on the parachutes they didn't know they had.

The first to land, with a mighty thump, is Royce (Adrien Brody). The others start dropping all around him. These people are savage professional killers from all over: a mercenary, a Japanese samurai, an Israeli markswoman, a mass murderer, an African warlord, and so on. How did they get in this thick jungle, and why?

They discover they're on another world: a perfectly terraformed world, it would seem. The gravity allows them to walk normally, and they can breathe the air and drink the water. Royce notices something odd: The sun never moves. They arrive in a clear space and realize there are three or four moons in the sky, which are either very close or very huge, since their discs are many times that of our moon.

Now hold on here. As every science-fiction fan knows, if a planet always presents the same face to its sun, and is ringed by bodies apparently larger than it is, it will quickly become molten lava pulled hither and yon by vast tidal forces. But never mind. After the visitors are attacked by humongous beasts of prey, Royce figures it out: They're in a game preserve. He figures out a lot of things in the movie, which might have been more fun if he hadn't.

Who runs this game preserve, and why? If you recall the first *Predator* (1987), Arnold Schwarzenegger and other killers found themselves in the Amazon fighting an unseen predatory alien. Has that race of aliens imported humans to its solar system for a rematch? Is it a wise use of resources to transport several mammals untold light-years through space just so you can watch them getting their asses predatored?

No time to think about them. Here come some really vicious warthog-looking creatures. They weigh about half a ton apiece, move as fast as lions, and have so many horns and spikes sticking out of them that fornicating must have to be a sometime thing.

Look at an illustration of one of these fearsome beasts. Can you spot the design flaw? Its horns or fangs, whatever they are, extend too far in front of its mouth! After they kill their prey, how do they eat it? I thought, maybe they lie on their backs and shovel the food in with their feet. But no, how's that gonna work with all the spikes on their backs?

Never mind. The movie is mostly about our nasty heroes being attacked by terrifying antagonists in incomprehensible muddles of lightning-fast special effects. It lacks the quiet suspense of the first *Predator*, and please don't even mention the *Alien vs. Predator* pictures, which lacked the subtlety of *Mothra vs. Godzilla*. The resident aliens view everything in POV shots through what looks like a video monitor with a haywire color adjustment, and they appear in ways I will not go into.

There are always a few characters who get killed in attack movies like this. What confuses me is why they don't all get killed. Look at the illustration again. If that thing hit you at 20 mph and got you down on the ground and all you could do was stab it with your knife, would you expect to have dialogue later in the movie?

There is, of course, one woman in the film, Isabelle (Alice Braga). She and Royce slowly bond, and eventually at the end . . . but no, I can't tell you if they kiss. That would be a spoiler. One thing you know for sure: The alien warthogs don't spend a lot of time frenching.

## Prince of Persia: The Sands of Time ★ ★

PG-13, 116 m., 2010

Jake Gyllenhaal (Dastan), Gemma Arterton (Tamina), Ben Kingsley (Nizam), Alfred Molina (Sheikh Amar), Steve Toussaint (Seso), Toby Kebbell (Garsiv), Richard Coyle (Tus), Ronald Pickup (King Sharaman). Directed by Mike Newell and produced by Jerry Bruckheimer. Screenplay by Boaz Yakin, Doug Miro, and Carlo Bernard, based on the video game by Jordan Mechner.

*Prince of Persia: The Sands of Time* is a children's story beefed up to appeal to young teens. It's based on a video game, but don't make me play it, let me guess: The push-button magic dagger is used in the game to let you rewind and try something again, right? Since anything in the story (any death, for example) can be reversed, the stakes are several degrees below urgent. And there's a romance in which the boy and girl spend endless moments about to kiss for every nanosecond they actually do. If I were the Prince of Persia, I'd push the button, go back in time, and plant a wet one on Tamina's luscious lips.

The movie is set in ancient Persia, which is now named Iran. This is a land with truly astonishing landscapes: deserts, canyons, craggy monument valleys, and a mountain range that resembles the Himalayas. Fair enough, since Persia reaches "from the steppes of China to the shores of the Mediterranean," but even more impressive since it's all within a day's journey of the capital city.

That city, whose name escapes me, is ruled by the noble King Sharaman (Ronald Pickup). One day in the marketplace he sees a brave young urchin defend a boy being beaten and escape pursuit by running across rooftops. This is Dastan, who will grow up to be played by Jake Gyllenhaal. He's an orphan; his birth parents are two movies, the Douglas Fairbanks (1924) and Michael Powell (1940) versions of *The Thief of Bagdad*.

Dastan is adopted by the king and raised with two brothers, Garsiv (Toby Kebbell) and Tus (Richard Coyle). The names of the movie's characters seem to have been created by a random-word generator. The king has a brother named Nizam (Ben Kingsley), first seen in a sinister close-up that could be subtitled, "I will turn out to be the villain." He has a Vandyke beard and eyes that glower smolderingly.

Dastan is good at running on rooftops. He can also leap from back to back in a herd of horses, jump across mighty distances, climb like a monkey, and spin like a top. This is all achieved with special effects, ramped up just fast enough to make them totally unbelievable. Fairbanks has a 1924 scene where he hops from one giant pot to another. He did it in real time, with little trampolines hidden in the pots, and six pots in that movie are worth the whole kitchen in this one.

Anyway, the evil Nizam insists that the Persian army invade the peaceful city of Alamut. This is a beautiful city surrounding a towering castle. King Sharaman has ordered the city not be sacked, but nooo. Nizam has secret information that Alamut is manufacturing weapons of mass destruction for Persia's enemies. Poor Dick Cheney. He can't even go to a Disney swashbuckler without running into finger wagging.

Anyway, Dastan climbs the city walls, pours flaming oil on its guards, etc., and then encounters the beautiful Princess Tamina (Gemma Arterton). She possesses the Dagger of Time, which is an honest-to-God WMD, since if it's switched on too long, all the sands of time will run out, and it's back to the Big Bang.

The plot involves portentous dialogue ("The only way to stop this Armageddon is for us to take the Dagger to the Secret Guardian Temple"), which separates tiresome CGI sequences in which clashing warriors do battle in shots so brief we can see people getting whacked, but have no conception of actual physical space. Of course, this must all lead to Tamina and Dastan fleeing from the evil Nizam, who has framed the lad for regicide.

Their flight brings them under the sway of the film's obligatory Comic Supporting Character, Sheikh Amar (Alfred Molina), a con man who runs rigged ostrich races, and those who have tried to fix an ostrich race will know that the bloody ostriches are impossible to reason with. My interest perked up with the prospect that Dastan and Tamina might try to flee by ostrich-back, but no luck. Imagine the scene! Gemma in foreground, Jake right behind her, compressed by telephoto, jerking up and down at terrific speed while sand dunes whiz past on the green screen in the background.

The irritating thing about special effects is that *anything* can happen, and often you can't tell what the hell it is. Dastan, for example, seems to fall into a vast sinkhole as the sand is sucked from beneath him at dizzying speed. Exactly how he is saved of this predicament isn't exactly clear.

Other key events are obscure. It looked to me as if Garsiv was killed on two occasions, yet is around for the end of the movie, and I don't think the Dagger of Time was involved in either of them. The workings of the Dagger are in any event somewhat murky; when you push the button in its base, it makes you light up like Sylvester the Puddy Cat sticking a paw in an electric socket, and everyone fast-reverses into their starting positions. How do people in movies always know how to do this stuff without practice?

The two leads are not inspired. Jake Gyllenhaal could make the cover of a muscle mag, but he plays Dastan as if harboring Spider-Man's doubts and insecurities. I recall Gemma Arterton as resembling a gorgeous still photo in a cosmetics ad. If the two actors had found more energy and wit in their roles (if they'd ramped up to the Alfred Molina level, say), that would have been welcome. Oh, almost forgot: Molina's ostrich racer is outraged at government taxes. If big government can't leave a man alone to race his ostriches, they're all Alamutist sympathizers.

## Princess Kaiulani ★ ★ ½

PG, 97 m., 2010

Q'orianka Kilcher (Princess Ka'iulani), Barry Pepper (Thurston), Will Patton (Sanford Dole), Shaun Evans (Clive Davies), Jimmy Yuill (Archie), Julian Glover (Theo Davies). Directed by Marc Forby and produced by Forby, Lauri Apelian, Ricardo S. Galindez, Nigel Thomas, and Roy Tijoe. Screenplay by Forby.

In the late nineteenth century, American corporations backed by U.S. Marines overthrew the legitimate monarchy of Hawaii. One of the conspirators was Sanford B. Dole, of pineapple fame.

Princess Ka'iulani, niece of King David Kalakaua, was in England at the time, getting a thorough Victorian education. After Kalakaua's death, Queen Lydia Lili'uokalani became his successor to the throne and resisted the outsiders. Then Ka'iulani returned and took up the doomed struggle.

Princess Ka'iulani (Q'orianka Kilcher) is much remembered in Hawaii, much forgotten on the mainland, and the subject of this interesting but creaky biopic. She was the child of a Hawaiian mother who died when she was young, and a Scottish father, Archibald Cleghorn (Jimmy Yuill). It was he who feared his young daughter's life was in danger from the Americans, and returned her to Britain and to the household of his friend Theo Davies (Julian Glover). In the United Kingdom she attended a rigorous boarding school, where there was some rudeness but the children of foreign royalty were not unknown. And she fell in love with Davies's son, Clive (Shaun Evans).

News of the uprising was withheld from her, but when she learned, she blamed the Davies family for concealing telegrams, hurried home, and moved into the Iolani Palace. (The film opens with her throwing a switch to illuminate the place and bring electricity to Honolulu; it had electric lighting before the White House.)

The real Iolani Palace, usually closed to the public but handsomely maintained, was made available to the filmmakers, and is one of a wealth of Hawaiian locations that make the film effortlessly authentic. Indeed, in production values the film is flawless. But it plays too sedately, moves too slowly, and contemplates the occupation of a sovereign kingdom with a curious impassivity.

The presence of Q'orianka Kilcher in the lead is a suggestion of what might have been. You may recall her as the tall, grave fourteen-year-old playing the somewhat similar historical figure Pocahontas in Terrence Malick's *The New World* (2005). In both films a native princess sees her nation conquered by

Europeans and is removed to England, educated, and falls in love with a Brit. The difference is that Malick finds mystery, poetry, and beauty in his film, and *Princess Kaiulani* plays more like a history lesson.

When the film was premiered at the 2009 Hawaiian Film Festival, there was much complaint about its original title, *The Barbarian Princess.* For so she was called, just as Pocahontas was sometimes described as a savage. She seems to have been a woman of uncommon intelligence and strength of will, and so loyal to her land that in the film she breaks off with Clive Davies and chooses Hawaii over love.

*Princess Kaiulani* shows the European business community conspiring against King David's efforts to secure Hawaiians' title to their own land, and indeed the rights were stripped away and the Doles and other old white families converted much of Hawaii into their own private plantation. The film's treatment of these results seems somewhat muted; more drama would have been welcome.

Q'orianka Kilcher seems an intriguing Ka'iulani, as she was a Pocahontas. Of Peruvian and German descent, she was raised in Hawaii, was a hula dancer by five and a student of classical voice at the University of Hawaii by six. Unlike a standard young starlet, she evokes great depth and sympathy in her role, and seems to have created Ka'iulani from the inside out. That she has admired the character since childhood is a help. It's a shame more help didn't come from greater passion in the filmmaking.

## The Princess of Montpensier ★ ★ ★ ½

NO MPAA RATING, 139 m., 2011

Melanie Thierry (Princess Marie), Lambert Wilson (Comte de Chabannes), Gregoire Leprince-Ringuet (Prince de Montpensier), Gaspard Ulliel (Henri de Guise), Raphael Personnaz (Duc d'Anjou), Judith Chemla (Catherine de Guise), Philippe Magnan (Marquis de Mezieres), Michel Vuillermoz (Duke of Montpensier). Directed by Bertrand Tavernier and produced by Frederic Bourboulon, Laurent Brochand, and Eric Heumann. Screenplay by Tavernier, Jean Cosmos, and Francois-Olivier Rousseau.

*The Princess of Montpensier* enters the field of the swashbuckling romance so littered with our memories of other films, and conquers it with a startling freshness. So well does Bertrand Tavernier suggest the period that he evokes tangible physical qualities: the warmth of flesh, the coldness of steel, the green fields on which men fight and die. This world of France in 1562 might be idyllic, if it were not being torn by the need of Catholics and Protestants to kill one another.

We meet a fierce soldier, the Count of Chabannes (Lambert Wilson), who after unknowingly plunging his blade into the belly of a pregnant woman decides he is disgusted by war. That places him outside the pale, a traitor to one side, a deserter to the other. He's redeemed by an affectionate student and becomes the tutor to the beautiful Marie de Mezieres (Melanie Thierry), a rich and famous beauty who in short time is forced into an arranged marriage with the callow Philippe de Montpensier (Gregoire Leprince-Ringuet). The negotiations between the fathers of these two young people are a straightforward business contract involving the transfer of lands, with not the slightest thought of Marie's desires.

On her part, she's indifferent to Philippe, but drawn passionately to Henri de Guise (Gaspard Ulliel), a rugged and arrogant man who proudly displays his scarred face. The de Guise family is also powerful and also desires Marie; a cardinal in their family represents the only appearance of religion in this film, and he is a politician, not a man of prayer. Ironic that although France is in a civil war over religion, it comes down to tribes rather than theology.

Establishing the major players and some minor ones slightly impedes the early scenes, but soon the characters are vivid and the intrigue begins. It centers on Marie, and on Melanie Thierry, who looks a decade younger than her thirty years, a classic heroine with a fresh, proud beauty. She is duly handed over to the attentions of her husband for a humiliating wedding night attended by witnesses to testify that the sheet is bloody, and then her husband hurries off to a new war and she responds quickly to the tutoring of Chabannes.

He falls in love with her and admits it, although neither is moved to act on the fact.

Henri de Guise comes back into her life, and so does the powerful Duc d'Anjou (Raphael Personnaz). She makes it clear she's drawn to both. Her husband becomes a monster of jealousy, and one night during a masked ball she unwisely confides in the wrong masked figure. Of course, this is 1562, and Marie hasn't seen many movies demonstrating how hazardous it is to confide in anyone at a masked ball without being absolutely sure who is behind the mask.

Tavernier has an uncanny success in showing the life within a medieval castle, which provides staircases, nooks, crannies, closets, corners, and retreats for intrigues. One night there is a compelling set piece during which Chabannes the tutor tries to prevent a disastrous discovery. We realize that for all the massive size of a medieval castle, its inhabitants lived more or less in earshot of footfalls and passion.

Bertrand Tavernier's career has been a celebration of many kinds of films. He began in 1974 with *The Clockmaker of St. Paul*, one of the best films ever made from a Simenon novel, and has made films about war (*Coup de Torchon*), jazz (*'Round Midnight*), biography (*Daddy Nostalgia* with Dirk Bogarde), an old artist (*A Sunday in the Country*), young cops (*L.627*), and French filmmaking under the Nazis (*Safe Conduct*). He is one of the most prolific and generous of directors, and there is no word that summarizes a Tavernier film except, usually, masterful.

All the dramatic mechanism he sets in motion here hinges on the reality that the princess of Montpensier is, at the same time, a possession and an object of desire. The moment she is officially sold off into marriage, powerful men feel free to disregard that contract, and so does she. To our modern eyes her natural romantic partner should be her tutor, but neither Marie nor Chabannes, who buy into the norms of their world, thinks of acting on that. There are only three possible partners in her constrained world, and she prefers the two who are more desirable than her husband.

Princess Marie becomes quite a sympathetic figure in the story: smart, yearning for knowledge, resentful that she has no personal choice, not valued for her mind, with no sympathy even from her own mother. Tavernier takes leave of her in a beautiful shot where she is alone. All alone. As all rich women then were, unlike the lucky poor.

## Project Nim ★ ★ ★ ½

PG-13, 99 m., 2011

A documentary featuring Nim, Herbert Terrace, Stephanie LaFarge, Jenny Lee, Laura-Ann Petitto, Joyce Butler, Bill Tynan, Renee Falitz, Bob Ingersoll, and James Mahoney. Directed by James Marsh and produced by Simon Chinn.

Can a chimpanzee learn to speak by using sign language? Yes. But in what sense does it know what it is saying? *Project Nim*, a fascinating documentary, follows the life of a chimp named Nim Chimpsky as it's raised like a human baby and then shuttled from one set of "parents" and "homes" to another. The chimp emerges from this experience as a more admirable creature than many of its humans.

Nim was born in captivity in Oklahoma and taken from his mother after a few days by Herbert Terrace, a Columbia professor who recruited his student Stephanie LaFarge to be his foster mother. This was in the 1970s, a decade that helps explain why Stephanie breast-fed Nim and allowed him to smoke pot and have the occasional beer. In his early years, Nim was a bright and affectionate child, quickly learning what would eventually grow into a vocabulary of 125 signs. He even made progress at potty training, although I doubt he ever quite saw the point.

I call Nim "he" rather than "it" because that's how his humans see him. The movie is more about how we see them. *Project Nim* is a new film by James Marsh, who made the Oscar-winning *Man on Wire*. Like Errol Morris on occasion, Marsh weaves dramatic recreations into his film, so that sometimes we are seeing actual documentary footage and at other times we're seeing actors or even (although you won't notice it) animatronics. Stephanie, for example, is played by Reagan Leonard because original doc footage of Nim's early days might well be scarce. How this substitution fits with traditional documentary ethics I will set aside. It produces a very absorbing film.

The real people depicted here don't always come across very well, especially professor Terrace, who seems to be less hands-on with Nim than with two of his attractive research assistants, Stephanie and Laura-Ann Petitto. The foster parents, later including a hippie type, Bob Ingersoll, do love and worry about Nim, and forgive him a great deal, especially when in adolescence his natural aggression begins to grow.

There comes a point after which a chimp can no longer safely be kept as what we might call a house pet. This is not the fault of the chimp, which is programmed by evolution to develop anger and other self-protective mechanisms. Chimpanzees are five times as strong as humans of the same weight, and you don't want one to grow impatient with you. In the film various handlers show the scars on arms, legs, and cheeks of Nim's aggression.

After severely biting one researcher on the cheek, Nim signs "Sorry." But is Nim truly sorry, or is that merely the sign he learned to use after sensing human displeasure? His name is a play on "Noam Chomsky," the linguist who suggested some human language skills might be hardwired at birth. It's an excellent question whether chimps are in fact "speaking" in a human sense at all. Yes, Nim knows the sign for "banana." But when a dog wants a Milk Bone and begs on its hind legs, it's not precisely thinking, "Please, master, give me one of those excellent cereal-based treats from the Milk Bone box."

Nim's later life is melancholy. After first seeming destined for medical research, he is saved only to be consigned to a small cage. He then moves through what must have been a baffling series of homes, his early language skills no longer needed or praised. The movie suggests that humans benefitted little from Project Nim, and Nim himself not at all.

## Prometheus ★ ★ ★ ★

R, 124 m., 2012

Noomi Rapace (Elizabeth Shaw), Michael Fassbender (David), Guy Pearce (Peter Weyland), Idris Elba (Janek), Logan Marshall-Green (Charlie Holloway), Charlize Theron (Meredith Vickers). Directed by Ridley Scott and produced by Ridley Scott, David Giler, Walter Hill, and Tony Scott. Screenplay by Jon Spaihts and Damon Lindelof.

Ridley Scott's *Prometheus* is a magnificent science fiction film, all the more intriguing because it raises questions about the origin of human life and doesn't have the answers. It's in the classic tradition of golden age sci-fi, echoing Scott's *Alien*, but creating a world of its own. I'm a pushover for material like this; it's a seamless blend of story, special effects, and pitch-perfect casting, filmed in sane, effective 3-D that doesn't distract.

A scene at the outset shows a world with apparently only one animal being, a pale humanoid who stalks a high ridge surrounded by spectacular scenery. This person eats something that causes painful vomiting and quick body decay. The vomit is followed into flowing water, where it seems to morph into living cellular structures. Where is this place? Is it Earth? Who is the being, and why alone and naked? Is the scene a visualization of the theory that life first arrived on Earth from outer space?

Cut to a human spaceship in the year 2093, qualifying *Prometheus* for a flash-forward spanning more years than the opening of *2001*. The trillion-dollar ship *Prometheus* is en route to a distant world that seems pointed to in prehistoric cave paintings. There's reason to believe human life may have originated there. It's an Earth-sized moon orbiting a giant planet, and at first it seems a disappointment: no growing things, unbreathable atmosphere. But the crew notices straight lines on the surface, and as we all know, nature makes no straight lines.

The lines lead to a vast dome or pyramid, and the film will mostly take place inside the dome and the *Prometheus*. But let's put the plot on hold and introduce two of the crew members: Elizabeth Shaw (Noomi Rapace) wears a cross around her neck and believes life ultimately had a divine origin. Her boyfriend, Charlie Holloway (Logan Marshall-Green), accuses her, a scientist, of dismissing centuries of Darwinism. What they find in the pyramid leaves the question open. Alien humanoids, found in suspended animation, incredibly have DNA that is a perfect match for our own. So they could somehow have brought life to

Earth—but why? And from this moon where they slumber inside their pyramid, or from another planet around a distant star? Why did they stop here? What are they waiting for?

The film then develops horror scenes comparable to *Alien,* although it depends more on action and weaponry than on *Alien*'s use of shadows and silence. For me the most spellbinding scenes involved the crew members exploring the passages and caverns inside the pyramid, obviously unvisited in eons, and their experiences with some of the hibernating alien beings. One of the key members of the crew is David (Michael Fassbender), an android, who knows or can figure out more or less everything, even alien languages, and is sort of a walking, talking, utterly fearless HAL 9000.

The alien race in *Prometheus* shares a body characteristic that reminded me of *Alien* and countless films since: Elements can detach from them and enter into other bodies as hostile parasites. This leads to an astonishing sequence in which Elizabeth, alone on the ship, discovers she is pregnant with an alien Something, and somehow finds the will to control a robot surgery device that removes it. Her later showdown with a waning oxygen supply shows equal resourcefulness; Noomi Rapace (*The Girl with the Dragon Tattoo*) continues here the tradition of awesome feminine strength begun by Sigourney Weaver in *Alien.*

There is another strong woman on board, Meredith Vickers (Charlize Theron), who represents the corporation that privately financed the *Prometheus.* She treats the others like her employees, which they are, and believes she always speaks for the company's wishes. The ship's captain, Janek (Idris Elba), makes no pretensions of scientific expertise like the others but is a no-nonsense, working pilot. Janek has the most interesting evolution in the film, from an irreverent hipster in his first scenes into a man with the ability to intuit the truth about what he's seeing.

The most tantalizing element of the film is how it plays with the role of these DNA twins of ours. Did they create life on Earth? The possibility of two identical DNAs as a coincidence is unthinkable. Charlie digs at Elizabeth, suggesting their existence disproves her beliefs. Her obvious response: Where did they come from? This puzzle is embedded in an adventure film that has staggering visuals, expert horror, mind-challenging ideas, and enough unanswered questions to prime the inevitable sequel.

## A Prophet ★ ★ ★ ★

R, 154 m., 2010

Tahar Rahim (Malik el Djebena), Niels Arestrup (Cesar Luciani), Adel Bencherif (Ryad), Reda Kateb (Jordi le Gitan), Hichem Yacoubi (Reyeb), Jean-Philippe Ricci (Vettorri). Directed by Jacques Audiard and produced by Lauranne Bourrachot, Martine Cassinelli, and Marco Cherqui. Screenplay by Audiard and Thomas Bidegain.

There is a murder at the center of Jacques Audiard's *A Prophet* that is unlike most murders I've seen in films. It's clumsy, messy, and brutal, and leaves the killer shaking. Whether he shakes with grief, relief, or anger we cannot say. That's the key to this film. We look, we see, but we cannot say. It often must be that way when we witness violence. Those capable of murdering live in another country.

The movie follows the life of Malik, a young Frenchman of Arab descent, who enters prison as a naive outsider and is shaped into an evil adult criminal. He wasn't born evil; he was born a shy, passive loser. Prison made him all that he can be. He seems an unlikely protagonist for a prison movie. Played by Tahar Rahim, he's skinny, insecure, trying to raise a mustache. He's behind bars for unclear reasons; he says he's innocent, although it doesn't matter. Prison efficiently strips him of privacy and self-respect and serves him over to the Corsican gang that controls everything behind bars through violence and bribes.

This gang is run by Cesar Luciani (Niels Arestrup), a man who has the presence of Don Corleone but colder eyes. He walks everywhere followed by bodyguards. His spies see all that happens. He gives an order, and it is followed out. He makes it his business to intimidate the new man, who is useful because he provides entrée into the wing housing the Arabic prisoners.

There is a prisoner there (Hichem Yacoubi) whom Cesar wants killed. This man must not live to testify. Malik is instructed by Cesar's lieutenant how to conceal a razor blade in his mouth and slit the man's throat. It is very simple. If Malik doesn't do this, he will die. When Malik seeks help from the warden, he quickly sees that Cesar is right: Kill or die.

Well, it's an unforgiving Darwinian choice. Malik has never killed. He makes a botch of it. There is a horrible struggle. Everything is covered in blood. Malik escapes only because Cesar has had the wing cleared out. It is a baptism. Now that he has killed, he is not a "man," but he is a survivor who will do what is necessary.

In the years to come, Malik undergoes a transformation. He's a quick learner. Outside society never got a chance to fashion him. Now he learns how to observe, how to measure motives, how to devise strategy, how to rise. He also learns to read, although that's more important for his self-confidence than for anything he learns. It's not as if he becomes Jean Genet. He is an outsider to the Corsicans, a "dirty Arab," but there is no purpose in resenting that. He keeps his own counsel.

Eventually he becomes Cesar's most trusted confidant, perhaps because he is Arab, cannot band with the other Arabs, and has no other place to turn. Prisoners sometimes are given a few days' leave. He performs a task for Cesar on the outside, and it also allows him to better position himself. *A Prophet* becomes a young man's bleak, remorseless coming-of-age story.

The best performance in the film is by Niels Arestrup, as Cesar Luciani. You may remember Aerstrup from Audiard's *The Beat That My Heart Skipped* (2005), where he played a seedy but confident father who psychically overshadows his son. That one was very loosely inspired by James Toback's *Fingers*, with Harvey Keitel as the vulnerable son of a gangster.

Aerstrup sees but does not want to be perceived. He keeps his own deep counsel. He rules by passive aggression. He has held absolute power over life and death for so long that he acts as if it's innate. Most of his big moments involve silent reaction shots: decisions and realizations.

The newcomer Tahar Rahim is an enigma. What is he thinking? I believe that's the quality Jacques Audiard wants. He's a newly poured man, and when the mold sets, it happens inside. He learns from Cesar to reveal nothing. Many movies and actors are too ready to inform us what everyone is thinking, and why. It's more absorbing for us to read significance from mystery. An actor who reveals nothing, like Alain Delon in Melville's *Le Samourai*, is fascinating.

But what does go on inside Malik? That's the frightening part. We can only judge by what he does. Now he is prepared to kill. If we must be killed, don't we all rather hope it will be by someone for whom the act has meaning? For whom our life has importance? Malik was such a man once, but that ended in the bloody mess of the prison cell. Now prison has prepared him to return to the streets.

*Note:* A Prophet *swept all major categories in this year's Cesar Awards, the "French Oscars." It won the Grand Jury Prize at Cannes 2009.*

## Puncture ★ ★ ★

R, 100 m., 2011

Chris Evans (Mike Weiss), Vinessa Shaw (Vicky), Marshall Bell (Jeffrey Dancort), Brett Cullen (Nathaniel Price), Kate Burton (Senator O'Reilly), Michael Biehn (Red), Mark Kassen (Paul Danziger). Directed and produced by Adam Kassen and Mark Kassen. Screenplay by Chris Lopata, based on a story by Ela Thier and Paul Danziger.

One of the greatest health risks for medical professionals is an accidental needle puncture. If the needle has just been used on a patient with AIDS or another disease, the caregiver risks infection. As an opening ER scene depicts, such an accident is not uncommon if a patient is thrashing in a seizure.

*Puncture* dramatizes this dilemma with its based-on-life story about two low-rent Houston lawyers who take on the personal injury case of Vicky (Vinessa Shaw), a nurse who contracts AIDS after an accidental stick. They learn that her friend Jeffrey Danfort (Marshall Bell) has designed a retractable needle that could not stick a second person, but that the safety needle faces an unofficial national boycott by medical suppliers and hospitals that object to its slightly higher cost. Anyone who has ever looked at the itemized printout of what hospitals charge for everything will find that incredible, but the movie is based on fact.

The lawyers are Mike Weiss (Chris Evans) and Paul Danziger (Mark Kassen). Kassen and his brother Adam codirected; the real Danziger cowrote the story. He's seen as a serious family man, concerned about their joint practice. Weiss, his friend from college days, is his polar opposite: an out-of-control cokehead who often misses meetings and court dates and, in a few fascinating scenes, test-drives his court summations before audiences of pimps and druggies. His marriage breaks up near the start of the movie, and as he plunges more deeply into drugs, the amazing thing is that he manages to show up at all.

But he does. With a frenzied energy perhaps fueled by crack, he becomes obsessed with the case, risking the firm itself in the process. He's brilliant; that seems clear enough. Time and again, all seems lost and he pulls it out of the fire. The movie becomes a showdown between his brilliance and his addiction.

That's a problem, in a way. Weiss is played so well by Chris Evans that his character upstages the issues. It seems clear that the health care system is corrupt, and that health industries will spend unlimited funds to avoid a court defeat. One of the industry's high-priced lawyers is Nathaniel Price (Brett Cullen), who is all confidence and polish, surrounded by mahogany and brass, and tends to refute Weiss by his very presence. But he and the other supporting actors, good as they are, find themselves upstaged by Weiss and by Evans's performance.

It's unfair to complain that Weiss seems over the top. The portrayal seems to be accurate. He died at thirty-two of a drug overdose, and an online obituary says he achieved wonders "working only a couple of hours a day." Chris Evans is electrifying in the role, reminding me of other great out-of-control druggies played by Al Pacino and Nicolas Cage. A movie like this is a reminder that box office success can be unfair and limiting to gifted young actors. Evans is famous in great part because of *Captain America: The First Avenger* and *Fantastic Four.* They give little hint of his powers. Movies like this can be career changers.

Yet I read in one review that the "pic might prove too commercially downbeat for Evans's *Captain America* fans, while purists might prefer a straight-ahead docu approach." I suspect the film was made for neither *Captain America* fans nor purists, and though the movie's not a complete success, Evans is always riveting on screen and the story is yet another parable about our venal health care industry.

## Putty Hill ★ ★ ★ ★

NO MPAA RATING, 85 m., 2010

Sky Ferreira (Jenny), Zoe Vance (Cory's older sister), James Siebor Jr. (Cory's brother), Dustin Ray (Cory's best friend), Cody Ray (Dustin's brother), Charles Sauers (Tattooist), Cathy Evans (Cory's mom), India Streeter (Cory's girlfriend). Directed by Matthew Porterfield and produced by Eric Bannat, Steve Holmgren, Joyce Kim, and Jordan Mintzer. Screenplay by Mintzer and Porterfield.

In a way rarely seen, *Putty Hill* says all that can be said about a few days in the lives of its characters without seeming to say very much at all. It looks closely, burrows deep, considers the way in which lives have become pointless and death therefore less meaningful. It uses fairly radical filmmaking techniques to penetrate this truth and employs them so casually that they seem quite natural.

Matthew Porterfield's film, which takes place in a poor, wooded suburb of Baltimore, involves the death by overdose of a young man named Cory. We never meet him, although we see his portrait at a memorial service. The portrait tells us nothing: He projects no personality for the camera. His family and friends gather for his funeral, and we meet them in unstructured moments that tell us much about them but little about Cory.

The sad truth is, nobody knew Cory that well. There seems to have been little fierce love for him, even from his girlfriend (whose identity I only learned from the Web site), because little is made of her in the film as she sits quietly at a memorial gathering, impassive. Everyone knows he died from an overdose of heroin; no one is much surprised. One conversation is philosophical about how he "wasn't able to handle it."

Sometimes Porterfield's camera steps aside with some of the characters, and an off-screen voice (his?) is heard interviewing them. How old are you? Do you have brothers and sisters? Have you come back for the funeral? Have you attended many funerals? This voice seems to come from outside; it doesn't necessarily know who these characters are. The illusion is that the film is an ongoing narrative, and the interviewer is asking characters questions in order to clarify it for himself. Oddly, this seems perfectly natural.

So do all the actors. None of them, I learn, are professionals. Only the lead, Sky Ferreira, as Cory's sister Jenny, has any performing experience; she's a C&W singer. Few experienced actors could be this convincing, sound this authentic, seem to be there in the moment and not in any way acting. The dialogue isn't "written"; everything feels spontaneous, and it *just sounds right*, if you know what I mean.

Cory lived in a mostly lower-class white neighborhood, although at his memorial service there are a fair number of blacks, including his unidentified girlfriend, a woman possibly her mother, and others. His mourners mostly seem people without resources. The only occupation we see onscreen is held by a tattoo artist, who learned his trade while in prison for second-degree murder after revenging the rape of his wife ("and you can fill in the rest").

The film opens with contemplative shots inside a barren apartment we later learn was Cory's. It returns there at the end, as two of the mourners break in, sit in the dark and smoke, and are surprised he could live like that. Where is all his stuff? Probably sold to buy drugs, we suppose. Only a miserable life could have been lived in these rooms.

Casually, we meet Jenny as she arrives back in town. She hasn't seen Cory much in recent years. Doesn't miss home: "God, no." We follow four girlfriends as they hang out in an aboveground pool, go walking in a woods, meet two cops with rifles, watch TV, smoke, are bored. Later they go to a swimming hole but don't seem to have as much fun as they should. Notice the body language as a boy and girl lie on a rock, hands idly entwined; why do we feel eroticism is behind them and has been played out?

The most extraordinary scene is the memorial service. Everyone sits crowded together passing around pitchers of beer. A professional karaoke emcee has been employed along with his equipment. Family members sing standard songs—in Cory's memory, I guess. Some of the mourners say a few awkward words about the deceased. The karaoke man asks, "Does anyone else want to say something at this time?" His words "at this time," reflecting a dutiful solemnity, attempt to lend a sense of ceremony. Tributes are inarticulate and trail off into uncompleted thoughts.

No one seems to know exactly where Cory was or what he was doing. He made little impression. No one has learned anything from his death other than, perhaps, that it was to be expected. None of these people seem to have hopes and plans. A grandmother in "sheltered living" won't attend the funeral because "I simply can't take it. I want to remember things as they were."

Porterfield takes no cheap shots. He respects these people, their lives, their unspoken hopelessness. He doesn't go for dire colorful dialogue. He has no social commentary. *Putty Hill* makes no statement. It looks. It looks with as much perception and sympathy as it is possible for a film to look. It is surprisingly effective. I know what the budget was, but the figure is irrelevant. He had all the money he needed to make this film, his cinematography by Jeremy Saulnier always simply and evocatively visualizes; there is not one wrong shot. He has internalized his characters, knows them, understands them, shows them in just such a way that we can, too. If there had been a real Cory, this would be his memorial. Watching *Putty Hill*, we don't have to be told there are real Corys.

# Q

## Queen of the Sun: What Are the Bees Telling Us? ★ ★ ★

NO MPAA RATING, 82 m., 2011

A documentary directed by Taggart Siegel and produced by Siegel and Jon Betz.

In the Central Valley of California, there are five hundred thousand acres of almond trees. All almond trees. Nothing but almond trees. This is wrong. It is not natural. For these trees to bear almonds, they must be pollinated. But bees cannot live there, for there is nothing to sustain them when the trees are not in blossom. So hives containing millions of bees must be trucked more than a thousand miles, and then trucked back again.

Almonds are an agribusiness, run by corporations concerned only with their profits. In *Queen of the Sun*, you will learn that bees would prosper in the valley if there were year-round nectar for them. Would it kill a corporation to set aside some tracts of land for flowers and vegetables? Wouldn't that be easier and more pleasant than mile after mile and row after row of almond trees? Easier for the corporations and easier for the bees?

From time to time a bee truck will be involved in a highway accident. These aren't cute little yellow trucks, but long, flatbed trailer-trucks. The bees escape, motorists panic, the cops are called, TV helicopters circle, exterminators swarm in, and no one asks—why in the *hell* are we trucking bees across the country?

We need bees. If bees were to become extinct, animals would be threatened because so much plant life would cease to exist. On your table you would find limited choices and high prices. Yet when I mentioned this on my Facebook page, the first reader was prompt to comment: "I could care less they're creepy I'm allergic sooner they go the better."

There are other kinds of pollination, by the wind, by ladybugs, by the coats of animals, but bees do the heavy lifting. We have native bees, but our beloved honeybee was imported from Europe and thrived here until recently. Now they're suffering from colony collapse disorder, in which the beekeeper goes out in the morning and finds his bees are dead or have disappeared. One culprit seems to be the use of insecticides. Bees do a marvelously complex dance to communicate distance and direction to one another, and insecticides can apparently so confuse their navigation that they fly out one morning and forget the way home.

This I have learned from Taggart Siegel's *Queen of the Sun: What Are the Bees Telling Us?*, a remarkable documentary that's also one of the most beautiful nature films I've seen. In exquisite photography by Siegel, we go inside hives and follow bees as they sip on flowers. We also meet beekeepers in sylvan settings (Illinois, Germany, New Zealand, Italy) and even on rooftops in Manhattan. Yes, there's a movement supporting rooftop hives and gardens.

It's true that bees sting. A wasp sting is worse, but a bee sting is no fun. Since the bee dies, it's even less fun for the bee. The beekeepers in *Queen of the Sun* often wear masked hoods, gloves, and so forth, but just as often they seem unprotected. One guy with a luxuriant mustache even runs it across the backs of bees on a honeycomb and says, "They like it." He was a brave man who first found this out.

Honey and beeswax are valuable cash crops, but if bees didn't make honey or wax, they would still be essential to the environment. Bees moved around by truck pollinate $15 billion in crops every year, including your next honey almond. The value of the crops that are naturally pollinated by bees is incalculable.

Bees, the film argues, are part of an intricately choreographed ecosystem that we meddle with at our peril. The same almond trees that must be pollinated via interstate commerce have so depleted their soil that they must be fertilized by chemicals. Crops in rotation have worked for millions of years. Why do corporations poison the environment in order to produce inorganic produce?

Taggart Siegel is known to me as the director of an earlier documentary, *The Real Dirt on Farmer John*, about an eccentric but inspiring organic farmer in Illinois. I was looking for Farmer John and his Dr. Seuss hat in this film, but no luck. Siegel's message remains the same: We need to trust the earth to its own hands. The campaign to legalize beekeeping in Manhattan is an example. Are you putting out some flowers this summer, and maybe planting a garden? The bees are ready to pitch in for free.

## Queen to Play ★ ★ ★ ½

NO MPAA RATING, 96 m., 2011

Sandrine Bonnaire (Helene), Kevin Kline (Dr. Kroger), Francis Renaud (Ange), Valerie Lagrange (Maria), Alexandra Gentil (Lisa), Jennifer Beals (American Woman), Dominic Gould (American Man). Directed by Caroline Bottaro and produced by Dominique Besnehard and Michel Feller. Screenplay by Caroline Bottaro and Caroline Maly, based on the novel *The Chess Player* by Bertina Henrichs.

I'd like to be playing a game of chess right now. I'd like to be sinking down into its cool depths and staring infinity in the face. I'd like to be competing with the player across the board from me in terms of implacable logic rather than motor skills and hand-eye coordination. When I play chess, I temporarily leave time.

I wonder if someone who doesn't love chess as much as I do would like *Queen to Play* as much as I did. Such a person could enjoy the transformation of a Corsican chambermaid into a strong chess player. It might be read as a story of female empowerment, of a woman asserting herself in her marriage and in her job. That would be fair enough.

But what I enjoyed was the way the film summons up the pure obsessive passion that chess stirs in some people. I never got to be very good (although I could maybe beat you), but I spent 1965 partly sidetracked by chess. I bought books. I played through classic games. I joined a chess club. I became a fan of queenside strategies because I figured most of my opponents would know a lot more about kingside. These thoughts gave me much pleasure. Then I fell back into being what I really was, a mediocre patzer, because when you get to a certain point in chess you realize what a very long way you still have to go.

*Queen to Play* stars Sandrine Bonnaire as Helene, a hotel maid who cycles to work through the pastoral beauty of Corsica, where Napoleon no doubt played chess many years ago. She is married to Ange (Francis Renaud), who works at a boatyard. One morning at work she sees, through a filmy white curtain, two of the guests (Jennifer Beals and Dominic Gould) seated on the terrace and playing a game of chess that looks for all the world like foreplay. They seem so in love they're on their honeymoon—or cheating.

Something in the scene sends an arrow through her heart. Ange is an all-right guy—she thinks of him as handsome—but they no longer look at each other like that couple. For his birthday she buys him one of those computer chess game boards that will play against you if you can't find anyone else. "I don't play chess!" he says in astonishment. "Maybe you will learn," she says.

Awake in bed, her eyes still open, she knows he never will. In the middle of the night she takes out the game and reads the rules of chess. She finds it grand that the most powerful piece is the queen and holds it protectively.

Her other job is cleaning for an American, a widower named Dr. Kroger (Kevin Kline). She sees a fine wooden chess set on his shelf and asks him to play. Of course he checkmates her in a few moves. But they continue to play, he teaches her fundamentals, and it turns out that she's a natural. Some people are. Not people like me.

Where this all leads I will leave for you to enjoy. The film has some sly fun with the way chess consumes Helene's mind: Even bread crumbs begin to represent chess pieces for her. The floors in hotel lobbies are often black and white squares, and the tablecloths in Italian restaurants are red and white, and so on.

The most observant element of the movie is the way it handles the changing relationship between Helene and Dr. Kroger (with Kevin Kline speaking his own French). The story is based on the novel *The Chess Player* by Bertina Henrichs, and what it knows is the way the minds of two players can become engaged, not in a romantic way, but in the pure contact of their thinking. There are often no words in the mind during a chess game. Just rules of spatial relationships. It can get pretty intimate.

## Quill: Life of a Guide Dog ★ ★ ★

NO MPAA RATING, 100 m., 2012

Kaoru Kobayashi (Mitsuru Watanabe), Keiko Toda (Yoshiko Watanabe), Kippei Shiina (Satoru Tawada), Teruyuki Kagawa (Isamu Nii), Shinobu Terajima (Mistuko Nii), Tomoka Kurotani (Masumi Kubo), Yuko Natori (Ren Mito). Directed by Yoichi Sai and produced by Ichiro Yamamoto. Screenplay by Shoichi Maruyama and Yoshihiro Nakamura.

What sets this film above so many movies about animals is that it's about a dog who is realistic in every aspect. *Quill: Life of a Guide Dog* doesn't use fake close-ups to show the dog being cute or funny. It doesn't dub Quill's "dialogue" or, even worse, use CGI to move his jaw and show him "speaking." Quill is a dog, and that is quite enough.

The movie is a fictional story, based on fact, about the life span of a yellow Labrador retriever from his puppyhood to old age. Not for a moment did it lose my interest. It answers questions I've always had about guide dogs for the blind—and why blind people trust them without hesitation.

Quill's trainer, Satoru Tawada (Kippei Shiina), narrates parts of the story, and the rest is depicted in dramatic scenes. It shows that much of the training of a guide dog is based on common sense. For example, imagine a group of puppies. You call them to come to you. They all eagerly run forward, except for one. Is that the dunce of the litter? Not at all. His hesitation shows he is naturally thoughtful and cautious. He's the one with guide dog potential.

We follow Quill as he lives for a year with a trainer, learning to obey so well that when told to "stay," he will stay even in the face of temptations such as food. Obedience is combined with training in decision making. If an owner tells a dog to lead him into traffic, the dog will think it over and decide, maybe not.

Quill learns how to pause at curbs and steps. How to gently stand in front of an owner to cue him to pause, without tripping him. How to deal with corners and street crossings. How to ignore other dogs (and cats). When this training has been completed, Quill begins a training regime with the blind man who will become his owner. This is Mitsuru Watanabe (Kaoru Kobayashi), who is not some lovable little child, but a grouchy man who doesn't much like dogs. Quill has to be more accepting than his owner.

Labradors are now considered even better guide dogs than German shepherds, we learn, and Quill seems eager to be a good dog, even though his new human family makes him stay outside in a doghouse that isn't large enough. As John McPhee wrote in a memorable essay, dogs for some reason have evolved to consider humans their gods. They love us, listen to us, are happy when they help us. The only bad dogs are those with bad masters.

Recent studies have found that dogs follow the eye lines of humans in order to find out what they're looking at. Few other animals have a conception of the gaze of those not of their species. Dogs notice, they share, they draw conclusions, they like it when they're able to be of service, and are touchingly grateful when they're praised.

*Quill* is not a children's movie, but it would be excellent for children who can read the easy subtitles. Its storytelling is clear enough that the titles might not even be necessary. Kids may appreciate an honest film about a real dog after being regaled with the stupidities of animated pigs. Adult viewers may find lots of interest, too. For example, in Japan, guide dogs are trained to respond to commands in English. Why? Because everyone around them speaks Japanese, so there's a possibility of misunderstood commands from others. Makes sense to me.

# R

## Rabbit Hole ★ ★ ★ ½

PG-13, 91 m., 2010

Nicole Kidman (Becca), Aaron Eckhart (Howie), Dianne Wiest (Nat), Tammy Blanchard (Izzy), Miles Teller (Jason), Giancarlo Esposito (Auggie), Jon Tenney (Rick), Sandra Oh (Gaby). Directed by John Cameron Mitchell and produced by Nicole Kidman, Gigi Pritzker, Per Saari, Leslie Urdang, and Dean Vanech. Screenplay by David Lindsay-Abaire, based on his play.

In *Rabbit Hole,* Becca and Howie are trying their best to get on with things. This is the tricky and very observant story of how a married couple is getting along eight months after their four-year-old ran out into the street and was struck dead by a car. They were leveled with grief. Their sex life stopped. They lived for a time in a daze, still surrounded in the house by the possessions of the child who no longer lived there.

But their lives are no longer a daily agony. Life is beginning again. *Rabbit Hole,* based on an acclaimed play by David Lindsay-Abaire, occupies the drafty spaces between the clichés of this situation. Becca (Nicole Kidman) and Howie (Aaron Eckhart) are rattling unhappily in an emotional emptiness. As a couple they attend a group therapy session for mourners, and Becca finds it's a room full of self-righteous therapy addicts while Howie finds a sympathetic ear from Gaby (Sandra Oh). And that's just what he finds—an ear. He finds someone who can hear him, and he feels he must have been speaking past Becca.

She is also not hearing her mother (Dianne Wiest) or a younger sister (Tammy Blanchard). She's not even on good terms with the dog. Sadness for her has settled into discontent. As a couple, they've reached that point of touchiness where nothing ever seems to be the right thing to say. What makes John Cameron Mitchell's film so interesting is that it bravely investigates what you say then.

I know all this sounds like a mournful dirge, but in fact *Rabbit Hole* is entertaining and surprisingly amusing, under the circumstances. The film is in a better state of mind than its characters. Its humor comes, as the best humor does, from an acute observation of human nature. We have known people something like this. We smile in recognition.

I was interested in Nicole Kidman's performance. I've always believed her to be talented, since all those years ago when she and Thandie Newton starred in the wonderful *Flirting* (1991). She seems to be two people: the glamorous star of *Moulin Rouge* and *Nine,* and the risky, daring actress in *Birth, The Hours,* and *Eyes Wide Shut.* Celebrity has clouded her image; if she were less glamorous, she would be more praised. Age will be only an asset to her.

Here she plays the character who changes: the balance point of the story. Aaron Eckhart's Howie has things that happen in his life, but he essentially remains the same man. Becca is troubled and disturbed beyond the depths created eight months ago, and *Rabbit Hole* is about how she's pulled by inner tides.

The wonder is that Mitchell and his screenplay see her confusion fairly clearly. Apart from anything else, *Rabbit Hole* is a technical challenge. It is simple enough to cover the events in the story, not so simple to modulate them for humor and even warmth. I knew what the movie would be about, but I was impressed by how it was about it.

## The Raid: Redemption ★

R, 101 m., 2012

Iko Uwais (Rama), Joe Taslim (Jaka), Doni Alamsyah (Andi), Yayan Ruhian (Mad Dog), Pierre Gruno (Wahyu), Tegar Satrya (Bowo), Ray Sahetapy (Tama). Directed by Gareth Evans and produced by Evans and Ario Sagantoro. Screenplay by Evans.

This film is about violence. All violence. Wall-to-wall violence. Against many of those walls, heads are pounded again and again into a pulpy mass. If I estimated there are ten minutes of dialogue, that would be generous.

What am I to say? *The Raid: Redemption* has a rating of 93 percent on the Tomatometer. It is being hailed as a breakthrough in martial arts films. It is "hard-driving, butt-kicking, pulse-pounding, bone-crunching, skull-smashing, blood-curdling" (*Hollywood Reporter*) and "largely a hand-to-hand, fist-to-face, foot-to-groin battle, with a few machetes and guns tossed in for good measure" (*Variety*).

The trade papers are correct. I am dismayed. I have no prejudice against violence when I find it in a well-made film. But this film is almost brutally cynical in its approach. The Welsh director, Gareth Evans, knows there's a fanboy audience for his formula, in which special effects amp up the mayhem in senseless carnage.

There's obviously an audience for the film, probably a large one. They are content, even eager, to sit in a theater and watch one action figure after another pound and blast each other to death. They require no dialogue, no plot, no characters, no humanity. Have you noticed how cats and dogs will look at a TV screen on which there are things jumping around? It is to that level of the brain's reptilian complex that the film appeals.

*The Raid: Redemption* is essentially a visualized video game that spares the audience the inconvenience of playing it. There are two teams, the police SWAT team and the gangsters. The gangsters have their headquarters on the top floor of a fifteen-story building, where they can spy on every room and corridor with video surveillance. The SWAT team enters on the ground floor. Their assignment: Fight their way to the top, floor by floor.

Most of the residents of the building are living rent-free and are loyalists to the gang lord. Young kids are "spotters," who sound the alarm. Most fighters on both sides are armed with automatic weapons, swords, machetes, clubs, and knives, but they *prefer* hand-to-hand combat. One fighter explains: "Squeezing a trigger? That's like ordering takeout."

The film opens by introducing the rookie cop Rama (Iko Uwais), who recites his morning prayers on a prayer rug, undergoes a grueling physical workout, and then tenderly kisses his pregnant wife good-bye. He will be our avatar. The van carrying his team parks in front of the building and is met by a gray-haired man wearing a bulletproof vest over a bright sports shirt. He is the lieutenant who has set up the raid. Wearing clothes that make you stand out from all the others is a dimwitted move, but then again, how bright is Tama (Ray Sahetapy), the crime lord, by barricading himself on the *top* floor? Elementary strategy suggests he can be cornered there. He reminds me of my beloved movie cliché, the Climbing Killer.

What country are we in? The movie never tells us. (It was filmed in Indonesia.) Establishing Rama as a Muslim seems pointless, except as a cheap fake out in character development. No one in the film has a personality; they are all ruthless fighters without a brain in their heads. Is the lieutenant up to something? What? And why?

I neglected one plot point that is major by default, since there are so few. One of the gangsters is Rama's brother. Thus it is inevitable they eventually will hold each other's lives in their hands and resolve deep childhood feelings to their satisfaction, if not to ours. At the end we see a lone figure walking slowly away from the camera while the music supplies a paroxysm of significance. Can we hope to see Rama's baby?

Some of the hand-to-hand battles are shameless in how they mimic video games. A fighter stands in a corridor and demolishes an enemy. As the enemy falls, another springs into position from around the corner, ready to be demolished in turn. Then another. It's like they're being ejected by an automatic victim dispenser.

A detail. What does *Redemption* mean in the title? Who, or what, is redeemed, and how? If you kill lots of people and are still alive, have you been redeemed? If you and your brother don't kill each other after almost everyone else does, is that redemption? Or is "redemption" just one of those title words like "reloaded" or "destiny" to help people tell movies apart?

## Ramona and Beezus ★ ★ ★

G, 103 m., 2010

Joey King (Ramona), Selena Gomez (Beezus), John Corbett (Robert), Bridget Moynahan (Dorothy), Ginnifer Goodwin (Aunt Bea), Josh Duhamel (Hobart), Sandra Oh (Mrs. Meacham), Hutch Dano (Henry Huggins). Directed by Elizabeth Allen and produced by Denise

Di Novi and Alison Greenspan. Screenplay by Laurie Craig and Nick Pustay, based on the novels by Beverly Cleary.

Kids who started reading anytime between the 1950s and today may know the books of Beverly Cleary, and at ninety-four she's still writing. Her books are set on Klickitat Street in Portland, Oregon, which is a real street not far from her childhood home; she must have filed it away for future reference.

On that street, those readers will know, live a nine-year-old girl named Ramona, her fifteen-year-old sister, Beatrice, their parents, Robert and Dorothy, their Aunt Bea, and Ramona's friend Henry Huggins. Life has stayed lively for these characters for sixty years because of the inexhaustible Ramona (Joey King), who gets up to so much mischief that I think she must have indirectly inspired *Leave It to Beaver.*

It's not that Ramona is a bad girl. Winningly played by King, no one can look more innocent, and indeed even think herself more innocent. She's a virtuoso of the "But I was only standing here!" routine. Yet every day in an astonishing number of ways she disrupts her family more than that insurgent Labrador in *Marley and Me.* Considering that the story revolves around her father losing his job, I don't even want to think about the bills for property damage.

Without ever meaning to, of course, Ramona survives as chaos erupts around her, and in her daydreams she dangles by precarious handholds over a roaring gorge, for starters. She was causing mischief even when she was too young to know better: She saddled her sister Beatrice with the hated nickname Beezus.

This is a featherweight G-rated comedy of no consequence, except undoubtedly to kids about Ramona's age. Joey King and the Disney star Selena Gomez are both appealing, and the movie is wisely populated with grown-ups who are content to play straight men; Sandra Oh is a calming presence as Ramona's sensible teacher. The adults hint that normality exists in some form on Klickitat Street, and prevent the movie from going totally wacko and running off the rails.

It's surprising that these books by Beverly Cleary didn't inspire a TV series in the 1950s or 1960s like *Leave It to Beaver.* (Sarah Polley played Ramona in a 1980s PBS series.) Maybe they'd still work on Nickelodeon or the Disney Channel, but not these days on general TV. We no longer all watch the same TV shows, we are no longer as innocent, and the world of Klickitat is fading into timeless nostalgia. *Ramona and Beezus* is a sweet salute.

## Rampart ★ ★ ★ ★

R, 112 m., 2012

Woody Harrelson (Dave Brown), Ned Beatty (Hartshorn), Ben Foster (General Terry), Anne Heche (Catherine), Ice Cube (Kyle Timkins), Cynthia Nixon (Barbara), Sigourney Weaver (Joan Confrey), Robin Wright (Linda Fentress), Steve Buscemi (Bill Blago). Directed by Oren Moverman and produced by Ben Foster, Lawrence Inglee, Ken Kao, and Clark Peterson. Screenplay by Moverman and James Ellroy.

Woody Harrelson is leaner in *Rampart,* the skin tight over the skull, the jawline defiant. His eyes are busy. He is a cop in the Los Angeles police district that became notorious in 1999 as a cesspool of corruption, but this man takes corruption with him wherever he goes. The movie is cowritten by the unsurpassed crime writer James Ellroy, who no doubt knows enough stories about Rampart to write a dozen movies, but his inspiration here is to make this cop a stand-alone character study, isolated within himself. He doesn't require the reprehensible environment of Rampart. He's self-fueled.

Harrelson is an ideal actor for the role. Especially in tensely wound-up movies like this, he implies that he's looking at everything and then watching himself looking. His character, Dave Brown, has no moral center, but he has the survival instincts of a rat, and I say that with all due respect for rats. He always likes to know the way out of a tight corner. He knows an angle he can play or a squirm he can call on.

Why is he this way? That question helps explain why the movie is so absorbing, because there is no answer. *Rampart* lacks the usual plot engines behind crime films, in which motivation comes from money, lust, or revenge.

Brown behaves in this film primarily just to do bad things. He reminds me of one of the most evil characters in American fiction, Judge Holden in Cormac McCarthy's *Blood Meridian*, a man who likes to torture and kill for no other reason than simply to cause pain. The Harrelson of *Rampart* could play Judge Holden, and not many actors could.

He is an overt racist. He has such contempt for women he cannot always be bothered to use them sexually. He was married to two women (Anne Heche and Cynthia Nixon) who are sisters, and apparently this meant so little to all of them that they live in houses next to one another. There was no emotional commitment there for them to engage. He has a daughter by each, and is said to have once murdered a rapist because of his feelings for his daughters. Only with a man like Brown would you suspect that was an excuse; more likely, he got started killing the man and didn't feel like stopping.

It's that feeling that seems to empower Brown when he does the last thing the Rampart district needs in 1999. Eight years after the brutality against Rodney King, he is videotaped while beating a suspect. He seems to approach this task like a skilled workman performing a job he loves. Recently there's been a movement to make videotaping of police officers illegal. That would get Dave Brown's vote.

This time he doesn't seem to have an escape route ready. The district attorney's office sees him as an ideal target, and Sigourney Weaver is finely focused as an assistant DA who has him in her sights. He also makes the error of trying to pick up a defense attorney (Robin Wright) in just the wrong way at just the wrong time. And he casually insults a black investigator for Internal Affairs (Ice Cube).

*Rampart* is deeply embedded in Los Angeles in the summertime, every day a reminder of the desert that waits patiently to take back the land stolen from it by sprinkler systems. It is hot, the sun is blinding, Brown is sweating, he feels rotten. You cannot live forever with amorality and sadism eating away at you. Even other immoral people around you stand back, because they recognize themselves and fear to go that far.

*Rampart* was directed and cowritten with Ellroy by Oren Moverman, whose directorial debut was *The Messenger* (2009). He was nominated for an Oscar for that screenplay. It also starred Woody Harrelson, playing an army veteran whose job is to inform the next of kin that a soldier has been killed. He's training his new partner on the job, and advises him not to take it personally: Don't have physical contact with anyone, let alone hug them. Better for you, better for them. These are their lives. They need the news, not a new best friend.

In that film, Harrelson's character turns out to have feelings after all. He's such a versatile actor, able to point one way and act in another. We know he can do that, and maybe that's why he's so fascinating in *Rampart.* Is it really possible for a man to be as evil and indifferent as Dave Brown, and be empty inside? Apparently so. What made him that way? Maybe nothing did. Maybe it's just the way he is.

## Rango ★ ★ ★ ★

PG 107 m., 2011

With the voices of: Johnny Depp (Rango), Isla Fisher (Beans), Abigail Breslin (Priscilla), Alfred Molina (Roadkill), Bill Nighy (Rattlesnake Jake), Harry Dean Stanton (Balthazar), Ray Winstone (Bad Bill), Timothy Olyphant (Spirit of the West), Ned Beatty (Mayor). Directed by Gore Verbinski and produced by Verbinski, John B. Carls, Graham King, and Jacqueline M. Lopez. Screenplay by Verbinski, John Logan, and James Ward Byrkit.

*Rango* is some kind of a miracle: an animated comedy for smart moviegoers, wonderfully made, great to look at, wickedly satirical, and (gasp!) filmed in glorious 2-D. Its brilliant colors and startling characters spring from the screen and remind us how very, very tired we are of simpleminded little characters bouncing around dimly in 3-D.

This is an inspired comic Western, deserving comparison with *Blazing Saddles*, from which it borrows a lot of farts. The more movies you've seen, the more you may like it; it even enlists big bats to lampoon the helicopter attack in *Apocalypse Now.* But let's say you haven't seen lots of movies. Let's say you're a kid. *Rango* may surprise you because it's an animated film that plays like a real movie and really gets you involved.

The title character is a lizard, voiced by Johnny Depp. Just an ordinary lizard. You know, green and with scales and pop eyes. But to this humble reptile comes the responsibility of bringing civilization to Dirt, an untamed Western town tormented by villains and running desperately short on water.

The other characters are outsize versions of basic Western types. There is, for example, Rattlesnake Jake (Bill Nighy), the bad man whose gang holds the town in a grip of terror. After Rango accidentally kills the eagle that has been dining on Dirt's citizens, he is persuaded by the mayor (Ned Beatty) to wear the sheriff's badge and bring law to Dirt. This involves tough talk in saloons, face-downs on Main Street, and a chase sequence between high canyon walls that's a nod in the direction of *Star Wars*.

*Rango* loves Westerns. Beneath its comic level is a sound foundation based on innumerable classic Westerns, in which (1) the new man arrives in town, (2) he confronts the local villain, and (3) he faces a test of his heroism. Dirt has not only snakes but vultures to contend with, so Rango's hands are full. And then there's the matter of the water crisis. For some reason, reaching back to the ancient tradition of cartoons about people crawling through the desert, thirst is always a successful subject for animation.

The movie is wonderfully well drawn. The characters are wildly exaggerated, yes, but with an underlay of detail and loving care. The movie respects the tradition of painstakingly drawn animated classics, and does interesting things with space and perspective with its wild action sequences. The director is Gore Verbinski, who directed Johnny Depp in all three of the *Pirates of the Caribbean* movies. I think he benefits here from the clarity of animation drawings, as compared with the tendency of the *Pirates* to get lost in frenzies of CGI. Yes, animation is also computer-generated imagery these days, but it begins with artists and drawings and paintings and a clearly seen world.

The movie is rated PG. I hope it will be huge at the box office. Godard said that the way to criticize a movie is to make another movie. *Rango* is a splendid and great-looking entertainment with a strong story, limitless energy, and a first-rate voice cast, including Abigail Breslin, Ned Beatty as the disabled mayor, Alfred Molina, Bill Nighy, Stephen Root, Timothy Olyphant, Ray Winstone, and, yes, Harry Dean Stanton. No Sam Elliott, but you can't have everyone.

Here's what I hope: Lots of families will see this. They won't have a single thought about it being in 2-D. They will pay ordinary ticket prices. They will love the bright colors and magnificent use of space. In a few weeks, they'll go to a 3-D movie and wonder, why did we have to pay extra for this?

## Rapt ★ ★ ★

NO MPAA RATING, 125 m., 2011

Yvan Attal (Stanislas Graff), Anne Consigny (Françoise), Andre Marcon (Andre Peyrac), Françoise Fabian (Marjorie), Alex Descas (Attorney), Michel Voita (Le Commissaire Paoli), Gerard Meylan (Le Marseillais). Directed by Lucas Belvaux. Screenplay by Belvaux.

Here is a millionaire industrialist who has inherited control of the family company. He is well-married and well-respected. He maintains a secret life with a love nest populated with mistresses who are no doubt well-paid. We meet him in midstride at the dawn of another day of playing a master of the universe.

Then he's kidnapped. That wasn't in the plan. It's an efficient operation. Stanislas Graff (Yvan Attal) is pulled from his car, blindfolded, and held chained and captive in a cold, dark room of an abandoned factory, where he will never be found by accident. Enormous ransom demands are made.

Our sympathies are with him. Then the police start sniffing around rumors that he was a big loser in private poker games. The press finds out about the mistresses. Weeks pass. His wife (Anne Consigny) and daughters are humiliated by news of his infidelities. There isn't nearly as much money in his bank account as they would have expected. The kidnappers grow impatient.

*Rapt*, written and directed by Lucas Belvaux, is based on a real-life case, but the industrialist could probably have been inspired by many men. I thought first of Dominique Strauss-Kahn. To be sure, all charges have been dropped against him, but his alleged behavior seemed consistent with his reputation, and aren't many of us rather persuaded that something wrong happened in the hotel room? Berlusconi is another exhibit.

What lends *Rapt* its fascination is that it represents such a dramatic fall from grace for its hero. The kidnappers took from him his freedom, one of his fingers, the respect of his family, and the public facade that he required as the leader of a big corporation. He finds in the end that he doesn't require ten fingers, or even nine, to count his real friends. Indeed, the kidnapper named "Marseillais" (Gerard Meylan) seems to see him more clearly as a human being than anyone else. A master of the corporate universe requires the acquiescence of the universe or his power is built on sand.

What a harrowing performance this must have been for Yvan Attal. He begins the film as a powerful, sleek animal, becomes a haggard victim, and ends as a pitiful case study. His success and prosperity were not necessary for a single person. His experience has demonstrated that his status was an illusion of smoke and mirrors. In a sense, he made himself an attractive target for kidnapping by pretending to be much more than he was. We now know that DSK will not be the Socialist candidate for the French presidency. He may discover still other things he will never be.

## Rare Exports: A Christmas Tale ★ ★ ★ ½

R, 84 m., 2010

Onni Tommila (Pietari), Jorma Tommila (Rauno), Per Christian Ellefsen (Riley), Tommi Korpela (Aimo), Rauno Juvonen (Piiparinen), Ilmari Jarvenpaa (Juuso), Peeter Jakobi (Santa). Directed by Jalmari Helander and produced by Anna Bjork, Francois-Xavier Frantz, Petri Jokiranta, and Knut Skoglund. Screenplay by Helander.

*Rare Exports: A Christmas Tale* is a rather brilliant lump of coal for your stocking hung by the fireside with care. How else to explain an R-rated Santa Claus origin story crossed with *The Thing*? Apart from the inescapable fact that the movie has Santa and reindeer in it, this is a superior horror film, a spot-on parody of movies about dead beings brought back to life. Oh, and all the reindeer are dead.

I need to help you picture this. It is the day before Christmas in the far Arctic north. Young Pietari lives on a reindeer ranch with his dad and other men who would feel right at home shooting reindeer from a helicopter. Yes, they are hunting food. The Scandinavians eat reindeer. God knows they do. I once visited Finland, Norway, and Sweden on a tour for the Scandinavian Film Institute, and at every single meal some sort of reindeer appetizer was served as a "delightful surprise." Between meals or when lost in the snow, they gnaw on reindeer jerky.

I stray. Nearby, there is a huge mound that looks vaguely sinister. The Americans have been blasting away up there with dynamite. Very sinister. Pietari (Onni Tommila) and his friend Juuso have been sneaking through the fence to spy on the Yanks. Pietari is a dead ringer in every way for Ralphie in *A Christmas Story.*

There is a legend that centuries ago the citizens were threatened by fearsome monsters. They were able to trick them onto the lake, where they froze. One of them was cut out inside a giant block of ice and buried deep beneath the mound. And now . . .

It's an idea from *The Thing,* where an alien was found in Antarctica and brought frozen into a hut, where drip . . . drip . . . drip . . . it began to thaw. We approach this possibility on the Night Before Christmas. Pietari's mother is dead (lots of lumps of coal in this stocking), and his dad, Rauno (Jorma Tommila), keeps telling him to stay in the house, and Pietari, an earnest, stubborn Ralphie type, keeps sneaking out. He's the only one who figures out what's happening: Inside the mound, inside the ice, is Santa Claus.

Well, not Santa precisely. A savage, scrawny beast of a man with a beard, who eventually does admittedly end up wearing a Santa suit, but strictly for warmth. This creature is, however, arguably of the species *Santus clausium.* The director of *Rare Exports: A Christmas Tale,* the Finnish Jalmari Helander, has made two *Rare Export* short subjects about the capture and taming of wild Santas, who are then supplied to the worldwide market for Santas. Those Finns, what cutups.

Don't let it get lost in the confusion that this is a fine film. An original, daring, carefully crafted film that never for one instant winks at us that it's a parody. In its tone, acting, location work, music, and inexorably mounting suspense, this is an exemplary horror film, apart from the detail that they're not usually subtitled *A Christmas Tale* and tell about terrifying wild Santas.

*Note: The R rating was earned by the F word and a nekkid Santa. Did I mention the reindeer slaughter?*

## The Raven ★ ★

R, 111 m., 2012

John Cusack (Edgar Allan Poe), Luke Evans (Detective Fields), Alice Eve (Emily Hamilton), Brendan Gleeson (Colonel Charles Hamilton), Oliver Jackson Cohen (John Cantrell), Kevin McNally (Henry Maddox), Sam Hazeldine (Ivan), John Warnaby (Griswold). Directed by James McTeigue and produced by Marc D. Evans, Trevor Macy, and Aaron Ryder. Screenplay by Hannah Shakespeare and Ben Livingston.

It is widely known that on October 3, 1849, Edgar Allan Poe was found wandering the streets of Baltimore, raving and incoherent. He died on October 7. He was forty. His death was about as much of a surprise as the passing of such modern icons as Kurt Cobain and Amy Winehouse. Poe was an acute alcoholic, particularly fond of the notorious spirit absinthe. He also used opium and who knows what other substances, and as a man supported only by his writings, may have been badly nourished. This is a lifestyle known to lend itself to incoherent wanderings.

*The Raven*, a feverish costume thriller, attempts to explain Poe's death by cobbling together spare parts from thrillers about serial killers. It should not be mistaken for a movie about Edgar Allan Poe, although to be sure he buys a drink for a man in a tavern who is able to complete this line of poetry: "Quoth the Raven . . ."

When I heard that John Cusack had been cast for this film, it sounded like good news: I could imagine him as Poe, tortured and brilliant, lashing out at a cruel world. But that isn't the historical Poe the movie has in mind. It is a melodramatic Poe, calling for the gifts of Nicolas Cage.

The film opens with Poe on a Baltimore park bench, beneath a tree limb holding a large, malevolent raven. *Mad* magazine would know what to do with that image. Then it flashes back to Poe, broke and in serious need of a drink, bursting into a tavern and expecting to drink on credit. He boasts of his fame, issues the Raven-quoting challenge, and immediately establishes himself as a disappointment to those who find Poe a complex and fascinating man.

Poe wrote fiction that is read for pleasure to this day. He has possibly inspired more movies than anyone except Shakespeare. We quickly meet one of his editors, Henry Maddox (Kevin McNally), editor of a trashy Baltimore tabloid, who orders Poe to return to the lurid horror tales he's famous for, instead of his more introspective recent stuff. Poe soon finds the inspiration for macabre material.

Two women are discovered murdered in a locked room. Emmett Fields (Luke Evans), the detective on the case, discovers that the killer must have escaped in the same way used in Poe's "The Murders in the Rue Morgue." It has slipped from Fields's memory that the killer in that tale was an orangutan, but never mind: Poe becomes a suspect. Shortly after, a man is discovered sliced in two in the manner used in Poe's "The Pit and the Pendulum." It is a grievous death: The victim cries out that he is too insignificant to justify such a laborious means of death; after all, he screams, "I'm only a critic."

Now Poe and Fields find themselves working in tandem, since the killer is apparently a man willing to go to a lot of trouble to draw attention to the works of Poe. A rich young woman named Emily (Alice Eve) is kidnapped, and ransom notes demand that Poe write an account of their investigation for Henry Maddox's scandal sheet. *The Raven* now indulges in a plot that will remind you of any number of serial killer movies, in which we're expected to believe that a madman goes to astonishing trouble while killing a lot of people simply to devise an elegant puzzle for the hero to solve. This can work nicely, as in *Se7en*, but in *The Raven* it is all concoction, a device to link Edgar Allan Poe with modern serial killer formulas and shovel in a great deal of special effects violence.

The use of sensational effects may be a temptation for a director such as James McTeigue, whose first feature, *V for Vendetta* (2005), was actually pretty good. They create a problem of proportion for a period film like this, where personality and atmosphere should create suspense; extreme violence is unnecessary, although I realize that at least some Friday night moviegoers will be hoping for it and have only a vague notion of when 1849 might have been.

## Real Steel ★ ★ ★

PG-13, 126 m., 2011

Hugh Jackman (Charlie Kenton), Dakota Goyo (Max Kenton), Evangeline Lilly (Bailey Tallet), Anthony Mackie (Finn), Kevin Durand (Ricky), Hope Davis (Deborah Barnes), James Rebhorn (Marvin Barnes). Directed by Shawn Levy and produced by Levy, Susan Montford, Don Murphy, and Robert Zemeckis. Screenplay by John Gatins. Story by Dan Gilroy and Jeremy Leven, based in part on the short story "Steel" by Richard Matheson.

*Real Steel* imagines a near future when human boxers have been replaced by robots. Well, why not? Matches between small fighting robot machines are popular enough to be on television, but these robots are towering, computer-controlled machines with nimble footwork and instinctive balance. (In the real world, bots are threatened with being rendered helpless on their backs, like turtles.) It must also be said that in color and design, the robots of *Real Steel* are glamorous and futuristic-retro enough to pose for the cover of *Thrilling Wonder Stories.*

The movie's story is not from the future but from the past, cobbling together Rocky's rags-to-riches trajectory and countless movies in which estranged fathers and sons find themselves forced together and end up forging a deep bond. Hugh Jackman stars as Charlie Kenton, a former boxer who is now hanging onto the fringes of the fight game as the owner-operator of a ramshackle robot he tours with. It's no match for the competition, and when the desperate Charlie replaces it with another battered veteran, it can't even outfight a real bull.

Even during these early fight scenes, however, it's clear that the movements of the robots are superbly choreographed. My complaint about the battling Transformers was that they resembled incomprehensible piles of auto parts thrown at each other. Fast cutting was used to disguise the lack of spatial continuity. *Real Steel*, on the other hand, slows down the fight action enough so that we can actually perceive it, and the boxing makes sense.

OK, OK, it doesn't completely make sense, because when one of these behemoths slugs another with a right cross to the jaw, we're wondering (1) shouldn't one of those punches cause as much damage as a car wreck, and (2) why do robots have jaws? For that matter, why are they humanoid at all? *Real Steel* doesn't pause for logical explanations. In this world, robots do the work that human boxers used to do. (Sugar Ray Leonard was a consultant on the fight scenes.) The director is Shawn Levy, who didn't endear himself to me with the *Night at the Museum* movies, but gets on base with this one.

If the movie were all robot fights it might be as unbearable as—well, a Transformers title. Drama enters in the person of Charlie's son, Max Kenton (Dakota Goyo), a smart, resilient preteen who, like all kids, seems to have been genetically programmed to understand computers, video games, and all allied fields. Charlie is a very bad absent father, and as played by Hugh Jackman he is actually mean toward his boy. Charlie's sister (Hope Davis) and her husband (James Rebhorn) plan to adopt the boy, but in a complicated arrangement, Charlie first has to take care of Max for a summer.

This Max is some kid. He loves robots. During a scouting expedition in a bot junkyard he comes upon an ancient training robot named Atom literally covered in mud and convinces his dad this relic still has fighting potential. Amazingly, it hasn't entirely rusted away, and father and son rehab it and teach it some new tricks. One of its abilities is a "mirror mode," which allows it to mimic the motions of its controller. Since Charlie is a has-been boxer, Max has faith that Atom can win as his dad's avatar.

All, of course, leads up to a Big Match with a fearsome juggernaut named Zeus. To my amazement, this fight scene was as entertaining and involving as most human fights, and the off-screen story (involving Zeus's odious owners) adds interest. It's hard to hate a robot, but not its owners.

Curiously, however, it's easy to love Atom. With his blue eyes glowing behind a face of steel mesh, and his skinny, muscular body facing off against giants, he's a likable underdog. Steven Spielberg was one of the producers of this picture, and knowing of the research he put into making E.T. lovable, I wonder if screen-testing was used to help design Atom. You wouldn't say he looked cute, but there's something about him that's much more appealing than his shiny high-tech rivals.

*Real Steel* is a real movie. It has characters, it matters who they are, it makes sense of its action, it has a compelling plot. This is the sort of movie, I suspect, young viewers went to the Transformers movies looking for. Readers told me they loved and identified with their Transformers toys as children. Atom must come close to representing their fantasies. Sometimes you go into a movie with low expectations and are pleasantly surprised.

## RED ★★

PG-13, 110 m., 2010

Bruce Willis (Frank Moses), Morgan Freeman (Joe Matheson), John Malkovich (Marvin Boggs), Mary-Louise Parker (Sarah Ross), Helen Mirren (Victoria), Karl Urban (William Cooper), Brian Cox (Ivan Simanov), Rebecca Pidgeon (Cynthia Wilkes), Ernest Borgnine (Henry), James Remar (Gabriel Singer), Richard Dreyfuss (Alexander Dunning). Directed by Robert Schwentke and produced by Lorenzo di Bonaventura and Mark Vahradian. Screenplay by Jon Hoeber and Erich Hoeber, based on the graphic novel by Warren Ellis and Cully Hamner.

This would have been a hell of a cast when we were all younger. *RED* plays like a movie made for my Aunt Mary, who was always complaining, "Honey, I don't like the pictures anymore because I don't know who any of the actors are." If the name Ernest Borgnine sounds familiar, here's the movie for you.

Borgnine at ninety-three is still active and has a project "in development," I learn from IMDb, even if it's ominously titled *Death Keeps Coming.* Says here it's a supernatural Western being produced by Tarantino. Borgnine himself is a heck of a guy. I flew out of Cartagena with him one morning with a terrible hangover, and we got stranded in some forgotten Colombian airport where he fed me aspirin crushed in milk. An actor like that is a role model.

Bruce Willis stars in the title role of *RED,* which refers to his alert level ("retired: extremely dangerous") and not his hair. He's a former CIA agent who discovers bad guys want to kill him. So he summons the members of his old killing squad and they prepare a defense. The team includes Joe Matheson (Morgan Freeman), Marvin Boggs (John Malkovich), Victoria (Helen Mirren), and Ivan (Brian Cox).

(Notes: Victoria requires no second name because she is a woman in a thriller; Ivan is a Russian because the Russian in every thriller is named Ivan; Malkovich may have taken the role because he is never considered for characters named Boggs; and Freeman reveals early that he is dying of liver cancer. We know that as the black member of the team he must die first, because that's how he would have wanted it. So once again poor Morgan Freeman is hung out to dry. He'd rather play the villain. As he once explained to me: The villain is usually the most interesting character in the movie, and one thing you *know* is, he'll still be around for the last scene.)

In addition to his old comrades, Frank Moses takes along Sarah Ross (Mary-Louise Parker), a telephone operator, for his retirement plan. He's fallen in love with her voice. He explains she has to go on the run with him because her life is in danger. Like any federal employee, she finds this reasonable. Her life will be much safer with a man who is the target of thousands of rounds of automatic weapon fire. The villains in thrillers are such bad shots they'd suck at video games.

The bad guys are in the upper reaches of the CIA, and the conspiracy reaches all the way to a vice president with connections to a huge private defense contractor. This man is played by Richard Dreyfuss, who subtly signals to us, "You only *think* this is my Dick Cheney imitation, but if the studio let me loose, I could nail this role." Are sinister Dick Cheney roles growing uncommonly frequent? Hollywood is always fearful of running out of villains and, having run through Russians, Chinese, Nazis, and Mongols, seems to have fallen upon poor Cheney with relief.

*RED* is neither a good movie nor a bad one. It features actors we like doing things we wish were more interesting. I guess the movie's moral is, these old people are still tougher than the young ones. You want tough? I'll show you tough. In one scene, Helen Mirren is gut-shot and a blood stain spreads on her white dress. In a closing scene not a day later, she's perfectly chipper, and has had time to send the dress out to the cleaners.

## The Red Machine ★ ★ ★ ½

NO MPAA RATING, 84 m., 2010

Lee Perkins (F. Ellis Coburn), Donal Thoms-Cappello (Eddie Doyle), Meg Brogan (Aggie Driscoll), Maureen Byrnes (Stella Snyder), Eddie Lee (Ichiro Shimada), Madoka Kasahara (Naomi Shimada), David Ross Paterson (Admiral McAdams). Directed by Stephanie Argy and Alec Boehm and produced by Argy, Boehm, and Ken Cortland. Screenplay by Argy and Boehm.

*The Red Machine* is a lean, intense thriller about a disgraced spy for the U.S. Navy and a jailed safecracker who team up to steal the secret of the Japanese version of Enigma, the Nazi cryptography machine. It's set in Washington in the 1930s when Japan and the United States still had diplomatic relations, and the target is a red cipher machine.

Something happened to Lieutenant F. Ellis Coburn (Lee Perkins) in Tokyo seven years earlier to turn him into the man we see. He looks to be a flawlessly turned-out navy officer, but he's locked behind a stone face and a reputation all his superiors know about. In a climate of expanding promotions as the navy prepares for war, everyone notices he's stuck at lieutenant.

Eddie Doyle (Donal Thoms-Cappello) is a cocky young thief straight from a 1930s pulp crime magazine. He approaches his craft as a science, noiselessly breaking and entering, cracking combinations, slipping into the night. He can pick locks and pockets, and works within a tight criminal fraternity ruled by Stella Snyder (Maureen Byrnes), a wise-talking hard case.

Navy intelligence has broken all the Japanese codes but this one. The red machine baffles them. They assign Coburn to the task because of his undoubted skills, and get Eddie released from jail for his particular specialty. Eddie will get them into the guarded embassy, and when Coburn sees the machine he'll know what he's looking at. The machine itself can't be stolen; the Japanese must never suspect it has been compromised.

The drama also involves the Japanese ambassador Shimada (Eddie Lee) and his wife, Naomi (Madoka Kasahara), who, almost inevitably, have links to the mysterious events in Tokyo seven years ago. And that's about it. These people, this stage, the red machine.

The movie, written and directed by the married pair of Stephanie Argy and Alec Boehm, doesn't fall back on stunts, chases, or extended gun battles; it's in the honorable tradition of the heist movie. That involves blueprints, plans, and the need to be very, very quiet. There's a nice scene when a safe is opened just behind an open door in Shimada's office. The Coburn character becomes so desperate to stall that he plays every card in his hand, including personal secrets.

*The Red Machine* is deeper than it first seems. The plot has hidden levels, and so do the characters, particularly the unlikely team of Doyle and Coburn. They don't like each other and don't like working together, and any possible personal progress is shut down by Coburn's fearsome reserve. He is taciturn to the point of aggression.

Neither actor overplays. Perkins's role doesn't allow him. Donal Thoms-Cappello's thief is supposed to be brash and dubious, which he is, but within reason. There's some subtle shifting going on that the directors suggest with visuals, not dialogue; an unspoken agreement to conspire takes place below the surface.

Here's a film with an elegant simplicity. Not a shot doesn't do its work. It may remind you of a 1940s B crime movie, and I mean that as a compliment. When you don't have a lot of explosions and special effects to exploit, you have to turn to the imagination—yours and the audience's.

## Red Riding Hood ★

PG-13, 120 m., 2011

Amanda Seyfried (Valerie), Gary Oldman (Solomon), Billy Burke (Cesaire), Shiloh Fernandez (Peter), Max Irons (Henry), Virginia Madsen (Suzette), Lukas Haas (Father Auguste), Julie Christie (Grandmother). Directed by Catherine Hardwicke and produced by Leonardo DiCaprio, Jennifer Davisson Killoran, Alex Mace, and Julie Yorn. Screenplay by David Leslie Johnson.

Of the classics of world literature crying out to be adapted as a sexual fantasy for teenage girls, surely *Red Hiding Hood* is far down on the list. Here's a movie that cross-pollinates the *Twilight* formula with a werewolf, and adds a girl who always wears a hooded red cape, although I don't recall her doing any riding. It's easy to imagine a story conference in which they said: "Hey! Let's switch the vampires with a werewolf and recycle the theme of a virgin attracted to a handsome but dangerous hunk, only let's get two hunks!"

What this inspiration fails to consider is that while a young woman might toy with the notion of a vampire boyfriend, she might not want to mate with a wolf. And although she might think it was, like, cool to live in the woods in Oregon, she might not want to live in the Black Forest hundreds of years ago because, like, can you text from there?

*Red Riding Hood* has the added inconvenience of being dreadfully serious about a plot so preposterous it demands to be filmed by Monty Python. The only scene that amused me was a dream sequence where Grandma says, "The better to eat you with." I'm asking myself, "How can Red Riding Hood dream about dialogue in her own fairy tale when she hasn't even gone over the hill and through the dale to Grandmother's house yet?"

The movie was directed by Catherine Hardwicke, who made *Twilight.* It opens with aerial shots of hundreds of square miles of forests, dotted here and there by stubby, grim castles. Then we meet the narrator, Valerie, who always wears a red cape. She is but a lass when she steals away with her prepubescent boyfriend, Peter, so they can trap a bunny rabbit and possibly slit its throat, although the camera moves away from the bunny at the crucial moment to focus upon their faces as the young actors think, "OK, this is where they flash forward and we are replaced by Amanda Seyfried and Shiloh Fernandez."

They live in a village which is one of the most peculiar nonplaces in the history of production design. Because the original fairy tale was by the Brothers Grimm, I suppose there's a chance the village is in Germany, but it exists outside time and space and seems to have been inspired by little plastic souvenir villages in airport gift shops. You know, populated mit Hansel und Gretel.

Valerie (Seyfried) wants to marry Peter (Fernandez), who is a woodchopper, but her parents have promised her to a rich kid named Henry (Max Irons). The village since time immemorial has been terrorized by a werewolf, who turns up when the moon is full and must be pacified by a pathetic little piggie left chained to a stump, lest it develop an appetite for villagers. Alarmingly, Valerie's sister is found dead, amid distracting cone-shaped haystacks dotted with blue flowers, which is not the sort of detail you want to be noticing when a young girl has been killed but (spoiler) not eaten by a werewolf.

The villagers send off for Father Solomon (Gary Oldman), a famed werewolf fighter, and he arrives with his band of warriors and a very large metal elephant. Solomon, an expert, knows that werewolves are not werewolves all the time, and in between full moons take the form of men. Therefore, one of the villagers must be a werewolf. This has enormous implications for Valerie's possible future love life.

But I know you, my readers. Right now you aren't thinking about Valerie's romance. You're thinking, "Did I just read that Father Solomon arrived with a very large metal elephant?" Yes, he did. A very large metal elephant. I thought the same thing. That must have been a *hell* of a lot of trouble. Even harder than Herzog dragging the boat over the mountain. Showing Father Solomon's men dragging a metal elephant through the woods—there's your movie right there.

## Red Riding Trilogy ★ ★ ★ ★

NO MPAA RATING, 302 m., 2010

Andrew Garfield (Eddie Dunford), Paddy Considine (Peter Hunter), Mark Addy (John Piggott), David Morrissey (Maurice Jobson), Warren Clarke (Bill Molloy), Sean Bean (John Dawson), Peter Mullan (Martin Laws), Robert Sheehan (BJ), Rebecca Hall (Paula Garland), Sean Harris (Bob Craven). Directed by Julian Jarrold (*1974*), James Marsh (*1980*), and Anand Tucker (*1983*) and produced by Wendy Brazington, Andrew Eaton, and Anita Overland. Screenplay by Tony Grisoni, based on the novels by David Peace.

*Red Riding Trilogy* is an immersive experience like *Best of Youth, Brideshead Revisited,* or *Nicholas Nickleby.* Over the course of 302 minutes, we sink into a virtual world: the corrupt police and establishment figures of West Yorkshire in England, at the time of the real-life Yorkshire Ripper. Peter Sutcliffe, the Ripper, was convicted of killing thirteen women, and may have killed more. The fictional Ripper here enjoys the same inexplicable immunity to police investigation.

This is the sort of undertaking the UK's Channel 4 excels at and is approached in the United States only by ambitious cable TV series. The experience could give you the impression that the three parts were filmed at separate times. The visual style proceeds from 16 mm to 35 mm to high-def video, different actors play some of the characters at different times, and there are three directors, each with a distinctive style. But that was all part of the Channel 4 plan, and the completed trilogy aired in March 2009.

There's a large cast of characters involved in a complex series of events. Few viewers could be blamed for failing a test on what happens and who (in addition to the Ripper) is guilty. Strict continuity is sidestepped to such a degree that some characters do not quite seem to remain dead. This is a way to reflect the shifting nature of reality in which there are many concealed motives and the police version of events is fabricated entirely for their own convenience.

The police have their reasons, chillingly dramatized in a scene where conspirators drink a toast to "the North!" Yorkshire is in northern England, traditionally hostile to the South (London), but what does that have to do with a license for corruption? The toast is an example of the human willingness to excuse behavior by evoking meaningless abstractions (The South! The Young! Party Time! Der Fuhrer!). Where they are is irrelevant to what they do.

They are in a society that seems, to our North American eyes, clearly distinct from other parts of Britain. In some segments, the Yorkshire accents are so pronounced that Channel 4 wisely adds subtitles. We are inhabiting a subculture. In the early scenes, our attention is focused on an investigative reporter, new in town, Eddie Dunford (Andrew Garfield), who looks deeper into the murders, but is unlucky enough to get personally involved with a woman linked to a separate series of crimes. Their intimate scenes together are the closest the trilogy will come to human kindness.

Dunford is an unalloyed hero. Much of the rest of the story involves conspirators who plot among and against themselves. Any sense of objective morality is lacking. We get the sense that no one rises high in the police without knowing the rules and playing by them. They arrange for their own immunity.

There is a public outcry as the Ripper continues to kill and evade capture. It was the same in real life. Scotland Yard was brought in, represented indirectly here by a veteran cop named Peter Hunter (Paddy Considine). He makes little progress, in large part because the officers he's working with have guilt to conceal and much to cover up.

Without revealing anything crucial, the reality is that the Ripper murders are invisibly connected to a police cover-up of a deadly real estate conspiracy, and if you pull a string from the Ripper, the whole ball of yarn of the larger conspiracy may unravel. A central figure becomes a vile chief of police, played by David Morrissey, who is so alarming that one searches the Web to discover he looks a nice enough man in real life. The casting here and throughout is essential to the trilogy's effect.

All this time a mentally challenged suspect has been held as the alleged Ripper. He has even confessed, which after police interrogation in Yorkshire, is a foregone conclusion. His guilt is convincingly challenged, which leads to a reopening of the case, as well it might, because the murders didn't stop with his imprisonment.

One wants to believe no police department in North America has ever been as corrupt as this one from Yorkshire. That may not be true, but the chances of a television trilogy about it are slim. *Red Riding Trilogy* hammers at the dark souls of its villains until they crack open, and it is a fascinating sight. We're in so deep by the final third that there can hardly be a character whose hidden evil comes as a surprise: Can innocence exist in this environment?

The directors, who worked on their segments more or less simultaneously, have impressive credits that do not, however, suggest the different feels they bring to their segments. *Red Riding 1974* is by Julian Jarrold, whose *Brideshead Revisited, Becoming Jane,* and *Kinky Boots* are all some distance from the immediacy of his 16 mm. *Red Riding 1980* is by James Marsh, whose documentaries *Man on Wire* and *Wisconsin Death Trip* don't suggest the 35 mm feature feel of his segment. And *Red Riding 1983*'s Anand Tucker (*Shopgirl, Hilary and Jackie*) is a specialist in clearly delineated ambiguity, at odds with the moral anarchy of his segment. I gather they were not hired to reproduce their strengths, but to find the right approach for this material.

I have given only the sketchiest of plot outlines here. The trilogy isn't so much about what happens objectively (which can sometimes be hard to determine), but about the world in which it takes place, a miasma of greed and evil. I have no idea whether the real Yorkshire police were led by monsters such as these. Someone must have thought so. Channel 4 aired these segments as they stand.

## Red Tails ★ ★ ½

PG-13, 125 m., 2012

Terrence Howard (Colonel A. J. Bullard), Cuba Gooding Jr. (Major Emmanuel Stance), Nate Parker (Marty "Easy" Julian), David Oyelowo (Joe "Lightning" Little), Ne-Yo (Andrew "Smokey" Salem), Elijah Kelley (Samuel "Joker" George), Andre Royo (Antwan "Coffee" Coleman), Kevin Phillips (Leon "Neon" Edwards). Directed by Anthony Hemingway and produced by Rick McCallum. Screenplay by John Ridley and Aaron McGruder, based on a book by John B. Holway.

The Tuskegee Airmen were a group of African-American fighter pilots who were trained despite the racism entrenched in the U.S. armed services at the time, were deployed in action, and achieved fame and many decorations for their skills against German pilots, which included engaging and shooting down Messerschmitt Me 262s, the first jet fighters. So successful were they at providing escort for American bombers that the white bomber pilots requested them—contradicting a "study" at the time that claimed "Negroes lack the intelligence to operate heavy machinery."

The story of the Tuskegee Airmen has been told before, in a 1995 HBO movie that stuck close to the facts and included much material about the training of the airmen in the racist South of the 1940s. That film represented the first time the fliers became widely known to the American public.

Now George Lucas has personally financed a big-budget mainstream action movie about the airmen in the hope of reaching a larger audience. He has had *Red Wings*, directed by Anthony Hemingway, under development for twenty-three years, and credit is due for his perseverance. The emphasis here is on *action,* and this is not so much a social or historical document as a war thriller. A great deal of the film is devoted to aerial dogfights, with POV shots of the pursuit of enemy fighters. The combat dialogue comes down to many close-ups of pilots in flight masks, barking brief words of command. The dramatic scenes on the ground in Europe don't have much substance, although there are effective scenes showing bureaucratic infighting at the top of the Air Corps' chain of command.

George Lucas is known for his enthusiasm about combat dogfights, and is said to have studied William Wellman's early Oscar winner *Wings* (1927) and its footage of World War I aerial battles. He used it as a template for creating the dogfights in outer space in the *Star Wars* movies. Now substitute 1940s fighters for spaceships, move them closer to Earth, and you have the audience appeal of this movie.

The cast is large and distinguished, a roll call led by such actors as Terrence Howard and Cuba Gooding Jr. (who also starred in the earlier film). The film is entertaining. Audiences are likely to enjoy it. The scenes of aerial combat are skillfully done and exciting. It makes the point that the airmen were skilled and courageous, and played a historic role in the eventual integration of our armed services. *Red Tails* could have done more than that by more firmly establishing the atmosphere of the time in the Jim Crow South that surrounded most of the airmen in their childhoods. They had a higher mountain to climb than many white pilots, and reached higher on its slopes.

At a premiere of his film, and again on *The Daily Show*, Lucas has said he financed the movie himself because Hollywood doesn't want to finance expensive movies with all-black casts. "They don't believe there's any foreign market for it, and that's 60 percent of their profit," he told Jon Stewart. "I showed it to all of them and they said, 'No. We don't know how to market a movie like this.'" He also made an oblique reference to the aerial combat footage: "This is as close as you'll get to *Episode VII*."

True enough, no doubt. But Lucas's point prompts the question: Did this have to be an expensive movie? Was the purpose to make a blockbuster, or to make a statement? I imagined a film that contained more history and drama—and that was angrier. Years ago my father had a friend who flew bombers over Germany. He spoke of the immediate reality that each mission could very likely be the last. Here, I didn't feel fear as the pilots took off. They had pride, patriotism, and zeal, yes, but their hands must have been sweating and their guts must have been churning. I would have appreciated their thoughtful late-night conversations about the meaning of it all. In Spike Lee's *Miracle at St. Anna* there is a flashback to a scene of black American soldiers in the Deep South being refused service by a restaurant that does accept Nazis from a nearby POW camp.

I'm also not sure Lucas did his movie a favor by speaking so widely about the industry's reluctance to finance all-black casts. If I were a PR person, I'd advise him to talk up the selling points ("In a way, this is *Episode VII!*") and give the movie a chance to open.

## Rejoice and Shout ★ ★ ★

PG, 115 m., 2011

Smokey Robinson, Andrae Crouch, Mavis Staples, Ira Tucker, Marie Knight, Willa Ward, Ira Tucker Jr., Anthony Heilbut, Bill Carpenter, Jacquie Gayles Webb, the Selvey Family, and Darrel Petties. A documentary directed by Don McGlynn and produced by Joe Lauro.

Black gospel music in one way or another created a great deal of the blues, jazz, and rock and roll. Born on the plantations of the South, it merged the Christian hymns of the slave owners with rhythms from Africa and created a new musical form not heard before but reflected everywhere today, even in hip-hop. *Rejoice and Shout* is a consistently entertaining documentary bringing together a remarkable variety of surviving performances on films and records, going back to circa 1900.

Where some of these films came from and how they were preserved isn't a question the film answers, but without them we couldn't see rare 1902 footage of the Dinwiddie Colored Quartet, not the first gospel singers but the first to be filmed. We also see joyous work by the Dixie Hummingbirds, the Staple Singers, the Swan Silvertones, Sister Rosette Tharpe, Mahalia Jackson, and an onstage duel between the Blind Boys of Alabama and the Five Blind Boys of Mississippi.

Smokey Robinson, one of the sources interviewed by Don McGlynn for his film, links the music to his own religious beliefs, which of course is appropriate, but some of the singers, Rosetta Tharpe in particular, seem drawn toward more secular venues. There's even the suggestion that Mahalia Jackson might have liked to do more show tunes and pop music, but was kept in line by her churchgoing mother.

Mavis Staples, whose father links back to the earliest days of gospel, is a warm presence throughout the film, calling on personal memories of many of the artists. Other experts such as Anthony Heilbut, Bill Carpenter,

Ira Tucker Jr., and Darrel Petties have a wealth of information, connections, and memories. And *Rejoice and Shout* doesn't show snippets of old performances, but entire songs, so we get a more complete idea of the talents.

My own knowledge of gospel music is limited mostly to what I learned through the (much better) documentary *Say Amen, Somebody*, which told the stories of Thomas A. Dorsey, Willie May Ford Smith, and others. Dorsey wrote an astonishing number of gospel standards (*Precious Lord, Take My Hand* among them), but is only mentioned in passing here. I suppose the footage from *Say Amen, Somebody* wasn't available to McGlynn. Indeed his own footage here is limited to his talking head interviews; all the performance footage is archival. Still, this is an engaging film filled with love for the music.

*Note: My review of* Say Amen, Somebody *is here: http://bit.ly/iKCje3.*

## Remember Me ★ ★ ★

PG-13, 113 m., 2010

Robert Pattinson (Tyler Hawkins), Emilie de Ravin (Ally Craig), Chris Cooper (Sergeant Neil Craig), Pierce Brosnan (Charles Hawkins), Lena Olin (Diane Hirsch), Tate Ellington (Aidan Hall), Ruby Jerins (Caroline Hawkins). Directed by Allen Coulter and produced by Trevor Engelson and Nick Osborne. Screenplay by Will Fetters.

*Remember Me* tells a sweet enough love story, and tries to invest it with profound meaning by linking it to a coincidence. It doesn't work that way. People meet, maybe they fall in love, maybe they don't, maybe they're happy, maybe they're sad. That's life. If a refrigerator falls out of a window and squishes one of them, that's life, too, but it's not a story many people want to see. We stand there looking at the blood seeping out from under the Kelvinator and ask with Peggy Lee, "Is that all there is?"

You can't exactly say the movie cheats. It brings the refrigerator onscreen in the first scene. It ties the action to a key date in Kelvinator history, one everybody knows even if that's all they know about refrigerators. But, come on. This isn't the plot for a love story; it's the plot for a Greek tragedy. It may be true, as *King Lear* tells us, that "As flies to wanton boys are we to th' gods." But we don't want to think of ourselves as flies, or see fly love stories. Bring on the eagles.

The fact is, *Remember Me* is a well-made movie. I cared about the characters. I felt for them. Liberate them from the plot's destiny, which is an anvil around their necks, and you might have something.

The film opens on a New York subway platform. A young girl witnesses the senseless murder of her mother. We meet her again as a young woman. She is Ally Craig (Emilie de Ravin, from *Lost*), the daughter of a police sergeant (Chris Cooper). She's in college. Having lost his wife, he is intensely protective of her.

We meet a feckless young man named Tyler Hawkins (Robert Pattinson). He slouches about trying to look like a dissipated Robert Pattinson. Drinks too much, smokes too much, has the official four-day stubble on his face, hair carefully messed up, bad attitude. He lives in a pigpen of an apartment with a roommate named Aidan (Tate Ellington), who might have been played by Oscar Levant back in the days when roommates were obnoxious, OK, but bearable.

Tyler gets drunk one night, is thrown out of a club, gets in a fight, the cops are called, and when it's almost all over, he shoves one of the cops—Sergeant Craig, of course. Young drunks: It is *extremely unwise* to shove the cop who is about to let you off with a warning. Tyler is thrown in the slammer. Not long after in school, the snaky Aidan tells Tyler that their pretty classmate Ally is the daughter of that very cop. He dares Tyler to ask her out and then dump her in revenge.

Aidan is a jerk, but logically Tyler is too, because this is morally reprehensible. However, to the surprise of no one in the audience, Tyler falls for Ally and neglects to break up with her. Their courtship is a sensitive, well-acted progression through stages of mutual trust and Tyler's gradual rediscovery of his own real feelings.

There's an intriguing subplot. Tyler's parents are divorced. His father is the immensely wealthy Charles Hawkins (Pierce Brosnan), whose office looks larger than small airplane terminals. His mother, Diane (Lena Olin), has remarried. Tyler's beloved kid sister, Caroline (Ruby Jerins), lives with her. Only with Caroline can Tyler relax and drop the sullen facade, showing warmth and love. Until he meets Ally—and then there are two safe harbors, and his rebirth begins.

Pierce Brosnan plays a key role in the process. He has only a few significant scenes in the movie, but plays them so well that he convincingly takes a three-step character development and makes it into an emotional evolution. Meanwhile, Ally and Tyler encounter fierce opposition to their relationship from her dad, who can't be blamed because as a cop he saw Tyler at his drunken worst.

These people and their situation grow more involving as the movie moves along. Then there's a perfect storm of coincidences to supply the closing scenes. That's what I object to.

If we invest in a film's characters, what happens to them should be intrinsically important to us. We don't require emotional reinforcement to be brought in from outside. The movie tries to borrow profound meaning, but succeeds only in upstaging itself so overwhelmingly that its characters become irrelevant. I'm guessing the message is: Parents, when you have a rebel child who hates you, someday you will learn what a good person that child really was. It's the dream of every tormented adolescent. Many of them become parents themselves and get their turn at being resented. Such is life.

## Repo Men ★ ★

R, 111 m., 2010

Jude Law (Remy), Forest Whitaker (Jake), Liev Schreiber (Frank), Alice Braga (Beth), Carice van Houten (Carol). Directed by Miguel Sapochnik and produced by Mary Parent and Scott Stuber. Screenplay by Eric Garcia and Garrett Lerner, based on Garcia's novel *The Repossession Mambo.*

*Repo Men* makes sci-fi's strongest possible case for universal health care. In a world of the near future, where they still drive current cars, a giant corporation named the Union will provide you with a human heart, kidney, liver, or other organ. Let's say a pancreas costs you, oh, $312,000. No, it's not covered by insurance, but the sales guy says, "You owe it to yourself and your family." For a guy in need of a pancreas, this is an eloquent argument. Interest rates are around 19 percent.

Now let's say you can't make the payments. If you fall behind more than three months, they send around a repo man who shoots you with a stun gun, slices open your body, reaches in, and repossesses the organ. To be sure, he puts on latex gloves first. I don't believe the gun kills you, but after they leave you on the floor with an organ missing, your prognosis is poor.

Let's say you were conscious during such a procedure. Would it hurt? You bet it would. At one point in the film, our heroes Remy and Beth (Jude Law and Alice Braga) decide the only way to outwit the company's computer is to repossess themselves. He has a donor heart, and as for Beth, her heart is her own, but it is surrounded by guest organs. They don't actually carve themselves open and *remove* the organs. No, that would be fatal. But they have to reach inside each other with a bar-code scanner and scan them in. As Remy carves into his chest with a big old knife, you oughta see the way his fist clenches and he grits his teeth. He's thinking, I wish I had the public option.

I don't know if the makers of this film intended it as a comedy. A preview audience regarded it with polite silence, and left the theater in an orderly fashion. There are chases and shootouts, of course, and a standard overwrought thriller sound track, with the percussion guy hammering on cymbals and a big bass drum. Even then, you wonder.

Remy and Beth find themselves locked in a corridor with a dozen guys from the evil corporation who are well armed. They dodge the bullets and wham some guys with karate, and then Remy pauses, strips off his shirt, reveals his bare (pre-repo) chest, and is wearing kinky leather pants with buckles. From scabbards in the back, he withdraws two long knives that help explain why he wasn't seated earlier in the scene. He slices some other guys. Then he shouts "Hacksaw!" to Beth and she slides it to him on the floor, and he whirls around and *decapitates* three guys, it looked like, although it happened real fast.

What are people supposed to think? Is this an action scene, or satire? Does it make any difference? I dunno. I know the actors play everything with deep, earnest seriousness. The head of the Union corporation is Frank (Liev Schreiber), who demands complete dedication from his repo men and is humorously not humorous. Maybe he's not the head of the whole Union, but only their immediate boss. The Union's headquarters building is maybe one hundred stories high, and Remy stumbles into a room with guys in white suits working at tables that stretch farther than a football field. There are enough props in this movie to clean out the organ department at Moo & Oink's. When I say they're up to their elbows in blood, I mean it. This work takes its toll. Remy's friend at work is a repo man named Jake, played by Forest Whitaker. Like most Forest Whitaker characters and Whitaker himself, he is a warm, nice man. I noticed for the second time in a week (after *Our Family Wedding*) that Whitaker has lost a lot of weight and looks great. I hope the extra pounds weren't repo'ed.

## Restless ★ ★ ★

PG-13, 91 m., 2011

Mia Wasikowska (Annabel), Henry Hopper (Enoch), Ryo Kase (Hiroshi), Schuyler Fisk (Elizabeth), Jane Adams (Mabel), Lusia Strus (Rachel), Chin Han (Dr. Lee). Directed by Gus Van Sant and produced by Brian Glazer, Bryce Dallas Howard, and Ron Howard. Screenplay by Jason Lew.

Gus Van Sant's *Restless* is an uncommonly touching romance about a young man and woman who essentially worship at the shrines of their own deaths. The girl with infinite tact and sweetness is able to coax the boy back into the world of the living, even though we learn cancer will allow her only three more months of life.

They begin to notice each other among the mourners at funerals. They stand back a bit and don't speak to anyone, and by the time she turns and smiles at him it's probable she realizes they're both up to the same game: requiem watching. Well, lots of people crash weddings. Why should funerals be exempt?

Enoch (Henry Hopper, son of Dennis) is obsessed with death. When we first see him he is drawing a chalk outline on the floor around his body—a murder scene technique that works without words to tell us what we need to know. Annabel (Mia Wasikowska) has a brain tumor and has been given three months to live. Tenderly, shyly, they develop an affection for each other. As it grows it helps him renew his interest in living. She sets one condition: Her illness is not to be the subject of their relationship. Because her death is near in her future she wants to simply ignore it, and in the weeks she has remaining experience, as much as she can, the first real romance of her young life.

There is a third major character, an inexplicable one, a friend of Enoch's named Hiroshi Takahashi (Ryo Kase), who died in World War II as a kamikaze pilot. The nature of this character is unclear. Reincarnated? Van Sant wisely doesn't explain and simply uses him in a matter-of-fact way as someone who is there. I don't believe kamikaze pilots were in love with death, but simply willing to give up their lives for their country. Perhaps his presence indicates that Enoch can travel in some sense to that undiscovered country, from whose bourn no traveler returns.

Annabel has a confidante, too: her sister, Elizabeth (Schuyler Fisk), who is wary of this strange boy who has come tentatively stumbling into Annabel's complicated life. You can't always trust a man, Elizabeth counsels, but Annabel knows she can trust this one.

All of the performances are pitched correctly. Nobody pushes too hard. Nobody underlines anything. Perhaps calmed by Van Sant, the characters seem peaceful, not troubled (as they should be). Few people can be this composed in the face of death. The most problematic character is Hiroshi, who has literally been dropped in from nowhere. Because he speaks English and knows about Nagasaki (which would have happened after his death), perhaps he is entirely an imaginary friend? In any event, Hiroshi and Enoch speak in matter-of-fact terms, as ordinary best pals.

Where Van Sant and the screenwriter, Jason Lew, found the idea for this story, I have no idea. It is wholly fresh and beguiling. It's not a facile fantasy or a dreamy romantic comedy, but an attempt by these two characters to steal a little happiness from the inexorable march of time. Much of it could play as a gentle romance. It's illness and the shadow of death that lend it poignancy.

The story raises some practical problems. Annabel's cancer functions primarily as a plot device. For much of the movie, it is kept in the background. We deduce from her close-cropped hair that she has had chemotherapy, a treatment that probably made her feel very sick indeed. Details of her progress and continued treatment are postponed or avoided, and in general she seems in good health for a terminal cancer patient. They swim, they walk through nature, she extols Darwin, they kiss but are more ethereal than physical.

This is a film of escapism and consolation. Their time together, like the plot of *Love Story*, depends on illness to elevate an ordinary romance into transcendence. That creates an uplifting story as long as the hard reality of cancer is kept off-screen. The posters for Errol Morris's movie *Gates of Heaven* quote one of the characters: "Death is for the living and not for the dead so much." It could also be used on the posters for *Restless*.

## Restrepo ★ ★ ★ ½

R, 94 m., 2010

With Dan Kearney, Lamont Caldwell, Kevin Rice, Misha Pemble-Belkin, and Kyle Steiner. A documentary directed and produced by Tim Hetherington and Sebastian Junger.

"Afghanistan" is a word on the news, debated in terms of our foreign policy. Almost an abstraction. Nobody thinks about foreign policy in *Restrepo*, a documentary shot during the fifteen months an American company fought there under almost daily fire. They were in the Korengal Valley, described on CNN as the most dangerous place in the world.

It is also one of the most desolate, even in the arid land of Afghanistan. Sparse vegetation clings to the rocky, jagged terrain. There is dust everywhere. It is too hot in the summer and too cold in the winter, and in the movie, at least, the troops only actually see one Taliban fighter—and the man who saw him thought it was the last sight he would ever see.

The Taliban is an elusive presence, moving freely through the landscape and population, and there is one point when the company is ambushed and takes fire from 360 degrees. That all of them were not killed seems surprising. The film is named after the first one of their number to die, a twenty-year-old medic, Private First Class Juan S. Restrepo.

Battle Company is led by Captain Dan Kearney, whose plan is to establish an outpost at a key point on Taliban battle routes. The men occupy the position at night and start digging in, using the earth to build fortifications. They catch the enemy off guard. The successful maintenance of Outpost Restrepo, named for their dead comrade, turns the tide of war in the hostile valley and frightens the Taliban. But the hearts and minds of the locals remain an uncharted terrain.

Kearney holds a weekly council with the local elders, a group of men who could not look more aged, toothless, and decrepit if they tried. A portrait of one would be all you needed to suggest the poverty of the region. One elder complains he has lost a cow. It's explained that the cow became tangled in razor wire and had to be put out of its misery. He is offered compensation: the cow's weight in rice, beans, and sugar. He wants cash. His heart and mind are not won.

The location footage is intercut with debriefings of the survivors conducted soon after they've been flown out to Italy. They use understatement to express strong emotions. The deaths of men they fought with are almost impossible for them to speak of. The memory of Restrepo lived on in the guitar lessons he provided and his book of flamenco songs. He was a great favorite. After Outpost Restrepo grew from a dugout into a proper position with shelter and fortifications, they felt right having named it for him.

They all speak with special dread about an operation named Operation Rock Avalanche, through deadly country, where Kearney says the enemy was so close a Taliban fighter once took a man's weapons from him. They come under fire three, four, five times a day. There are many firefights in the film, but they all share one feature: We never see the enemy, and we never see the American targets.

This is hard, hard duty. A fifteen-month tour. Our admiration for these men grows. Their jobs seem beyond conceiving. I cannot imagine a civilian thinking he could perform them. It would take much training—and more important, much bonding. There is the sense they're fighting for each other more than for ideology. At a low point when a nearby company has taken heavy losses, Kearney talks to his men not in terms of patriotism, but in terms of finding the MFs who are shooting at them, and going out and killing them.

The film is nonpolitical. It was filmed at great personal risk by the war photographer Tim Hetherington and the author Sebastian Junger (*The Perfect Storm*). It raises for me an obvious question: How can this war possibly be won? At the end of the film, a title tells us U.S. troops have withdrawn from the Korengal Valley and therefore Outpost Restrepo. No reason is given.

## Resurrect Dead: The Mystery of the Toynbee Tiles ★ ★ ★

NO MPAA RATING, 85 m., 2011

A documentary featuring Justin Duerr, Steve Weinik, Colin Smith, and Jon Foy. Directed by Jon Foy and produced by Foy and Colin Smith. Screenplay by Foy and Smith.

It's possible you've stepped on a Toynbee Tile yourself. These are hundreds of crudely lettered tiles stuck with tar to pavements and sidewalks in cities up and down the Eastern Seaboard, as far west as Kansas City, and in three South American cities. They might have started appearing in 1983.

They all bear the same message, sometimes with additions:

TOYNBEE IDEA
IN MOVIE '2001'
RESURRECT DEAD
ON PLANET JUPITER

What does this possibly mean? That's the question. Who devises and places them? That's the mystery examined in a quirky and persistent documentary named *Resurrect Dead: The Mystery of the Toynbee Tiles.*

*Toynbee* is no doubt the distinguished scholar Arnold Toynbee. The movie *2001: A Space Odyssey* involves a journey "to Jupiter . . . and beyond." Its ending is enigmatic enough that it could support a case that Dave Bowman, the astronaut, had been resurrected, reborn, or something.

Excellent. Now what action or beliefs do the tiles suggest? They are apparently intended to speak for themselves. Is it unfair to suggest they seem to be a product of mental illness? This doc is interesting not because of the explanation, but because of the investigation.

Writer-director Jon Foy follows three tile sleuths: Justin Duerr, Steve Weinik, and Colin Smith. Starting with a small handful of meager clues, their detective work leads them to strange places: a paragraph in an old *Philadelphia Inquirer*, a play by David Mamet, addresses in South Philadelphia, a convention of ham radio operators. They find websites filled with tile photos and rumors.

Foy, a first-time director, shows a gift here for bringing together reenacted scenes, talking heads, graphics, and many shots of the tiles, and driving them with his own urgent score. The film is confoundingly watchable.

Sometimes a solution seems tantalizingly close. Duerr walks out of a Philadelphia deli at 3 a.m. and finds a new tile that has just been laid, the tar still soft. He runs around the block, shouting, "Toynbee Idea! I agree!" No luck. The person behind the tiles seems like a shadow. There is even one at the mouth of the Holland Tunnel—a place not easy to work, a tile not easy to see.

Do they solve their quest? Would it be a spoiler if I told you?

## Revenge of the Electric Car ★ ★ ★

PG-13, 90 m., 2011

A documentary featuring Tim Robbins (narrator), Bob Lutz, Elon Musk, Carlos Ghosn, and Greg Abbott. Directed by Chris Paine and produced by Jessie Deeter and P. G. Morgan. Screenplay by Paine and Morgan.

As recently as 2006, in his film *Who Killed the Electric Car?*, Chris Paine portrayed an auto industry guilty of all but conspiracy as General Motors introduced the EV1, an electric car that won fervent admirers and then abruptly and inexplicably was withdrawn from the market. Using the fine print in its contracts, GM repossessed all of the EV1s from their owners and (in a heartbreaking sequence) junked and crushed them.

Now it is 2011, proclaimed as the year of the

electric car in Paine's new doc, *Revenge of the Electric Car.* The Chevy Volt and the Nissan Leaf are the high-profile leaders, the legendary Tesla boasts 100 mph, and hybrid vehicles like my Ford Fusion are popular. But many people consider setting out on a trip in an all-electric like being in a boat without a paddle, and the Volt offers reassurance in a backup gas engine.

Never addressing what murky conspiracies doomed the EV1 in the first place, Paine returns to the villain of that film and makes him the unlikely hero of this one. That would be Bob Lutz, a GM veteran who has always been identified with high horsepower. With the auto industry threatened by the economic meltdown and its executives excoriated for flying to a congressional hearing in their corporate jets, Lutz led the charge for the development of the Volt. Somewhat daringly inviting Daniel into the lion's den, he gives Paine access to GM planning sessions, production lines, and even its top-secret testing grounds. What comes across is that, gasoline or electric, Lutz is a car man and knows the business.

The other hero is Carlos Ghosn, head of Renault/Nissan, who all but bets the store on the Nissan Leaf. Then there's Elon Musk, an entrepreneur who developed the Tesla and his own private spaceship ventures, seems constantly on the edge of financial disaster, somehow always pulls off rescues (including a successful IPO), and has undeniably developed a nice car at a risky price: $100,000.

At the low end of the spectrum, we meet Greg ("Gadget") Abbott, who buys existing cars and loads them with an electric motor and batteries. He works out of storefronts in Los Angeles, one of which is destroyed by arson, another discovered to have mercury poisoning, and yet his seat-of-the-pants operation is still standing at the end of the film.

So did electric cars get their revenge? Yes and no. They made a comeback, they proved workable and attractive to many buyers, and in their hybrid cousins they've impacted the marketplace. So Paine's 2006 doc has a happy sequel. His film is just as polished and good-looking as his first one, gives us a good look at automakers we like, and is entertaining. But the first film was charged with drama. *Revenge* is somewhat anticlimactically charged with a wall plug.

## Ricky ★ ★

NO MPAA RATING, 89 m., 2010

Alexandra Lamy (Katie), Sergi Lopez (Paco), Melusine Mayance (Lisa), Arthur Peyret (Ricky), Andre Wilms (Doctor), Jean-Claude Bolle-Reddat (Journalist). Directed by Francois Ozon and produced by Chris Bolzli, Claudie Ossard, and Vieri Razzini. Screenplay by Ozon, based on the short story "Moth" by Rose Tremain.

Parables are stories about other people that help us live our own lives. The problem with *Ricky* is that the lesson of the parable is far from clear, and nobody is likely to encounter this situation in their own life. That would be pretty much impossible. The story begins in gritty realism, ends in pure fantasy, and leaves out most of the alphabet as it makes its way from A to Z.

The story begins with Katie (Alexandra Lamy), a morose French factory worker who has been abandoned, she thinks, by the man she lives with. It's hard to pay the rent. We flash back to the beginning, see her living with her peppy seven-year-old daughter, Lisa (Melusine Mayance), and working in a French chemical factory. There she meets a Spanish worker named Paco (Sergi Lopez). He's warm and attracted, they smile, they live together and have a baby.

These events take place in a series of time jumps that are momentarily jolting, but easy enough to follow. Not so easy is what happens to their son, Ricky (Arthur Peyret), as he grows up. In appearance he seems at first like an outtake from *Babies,* but then when Paco cares for him at home alone, Katie discovers bruises on his shoulders. Paco is enraged to be accused of child beating and stalks out, explaining Katie's opening scene.

These scenes are absorbingly created and well acted, and we settle in for a French slice of life. I can hardly deal with any more of the film without revealing details. Here goes, after a spoiler warning.

Those aren't bruises, they're the beginning of wings. Yes. Little wings, which at first look so much like poultry parts that Katie tape-measures a turkey wing at the supermarket, just to get an idea. One night, in slow-mo, the wings begin to sprout tiny feathers, which in close-up look like one of those life forms you don't want to make friends with. Soon the little lad has flapped his way to the top of an armoire.

No, he isn't an angel. Maybe more likely the result of his parents working at the chemical factory, although the movie doesn't make that a point. It doesn't much make anything a point. Katie and Lisa are about as amazed as if the child had a lot of hair on its head. You'd think babies with wings were born every day. Later, after Paco rejoins the family, baby Ricky gets a little injury, and the family doctor seems, to me, insufficiently amazed. Surely this is an OMG case?

Because the film is directed by the esteemed Francois Ozun (*Swimming Pool, Under the Sand, See the Sea*), I waited to see where it would take me. At the end, I wasn't sure. The ending has the form of a statement, but not the content of one. Its last half seems to be building to a life lesson, and perhaps the lesson is: "Parents! If you have a baby with wings, don't be this calm about it!"

I couldn't help myself. All during the film I was distracted by questions of aeronautics. In early scenes, those wings are way too small to allow a healthy baby to fly. Even later, the ratio of wingspan to baby weight seems way off. A scene where Ricky breaks free and flies around a supermarket seems designed for comedy, but doesn't play that way. And what kind of a cockamamie idea is it to hold a press conference and let Ricky fly with only Katie holding a string around his ankle? This is worse than the hot air balloon kid, if there had been one.

The film is bewildering. I don't know what its terms are, and it doesn't match any of mine. I found myself regarding it more and more as an inexplicable curiosity. It's so curiously flat in tone that when a baby grows wings and flies (think about that!), people in the film and in the audience seem to watch with no more than mild interest. *Ricky* makes a good case for lurid melodrama.

## Rise of the Planet of the Apes ★ ★ ★

PG-13, 105 m., 2011

James Franco (Will Rodman), Freida Pinto (Caroline Aranha), John Lithgow (Charles Rodman), Brian Cox (John Landon), Tom Felton (Dodge Landon), Andy Serkis (Caesar). Directed by Rupert Wyatt and produced by Peter Chemin, Dylan Clark, Rick Jaffa, and Amanda Silver. Screenplay by Jaffa and Silver, based on the novel by Pierre Boulle.

*Rise of the Planet of the Apes* is a title suggesting need for a sequel, since in this film the chimpanzees only get as far as crossing the Golden Gate Bridge. Today San Francisco, tomorrow the world. The movie develops the notion that chimps, who as we know are only a few genes separated from humans anyway, require only a new wonder drug to become fairly good at chess.

The film opens at a big drug company, where Will Rodman (James Franco) is a scientist who has developed ALZ 112, a possible treatment for Alzheimer's. He tests it on chimpanzees, who unexpectedly zoom up the IQ charts and develop enormous sign language vocabularies.

Alas, a test animal goes berserk and attacks a board meeting, and the experiment is called off—odd, because scientists should have known what all the rest of us know, which is that chimps are charming until they sexually mature, after which they develop the characteristics of, well, wild animals. Assuming that ALZ 112 works, it might be safe to test on Grandpa without running much of a risk of him pounding on people with his walker.

Will is touched by the plight of a helpless baby chimp and privately takes him home "for a few days." Days turn to weeks and years, and Caesar exhibits incredible intelligence and the body language of a Marcel Marceau. During the same period, Will grows close with a primatologist named Caroline (Freida Pinto), who becomes Caesar's mother surrogate. Whether she becomes Will's wife surrogate is an excellent question; the movie displays the usual PG-13 shyness about intimate details, and when she kisses him some years into their relationship, it's as if she's finally making a statement. I expected her to be employed as a device for getting lots of info about chimps into the dialogue, but no, she doesn't know much more than anyone else.

By a benign coincidence, the fascinating documentary *Project Nim* has been playing around the country, and provides a sort of briefing for this film. It also has much more interesting relationships involving men and women and humans and apes. It teaches us that chimps may be very smart and friendly, but they are not humans, and when they grow large, they can turn nasty. The chimp experts in this movie can be seen running around the Golden Gate Bridge crying out "Caesar! Caesar!" long after they should have realized Caesar has played his last pawn to king four.

That said, the movie has its pleasures, although human intelligence is not one of them. Caesar, to begin with, is a wonderfully executed character, a product of special effects and a motion-capture performance by Andy Serkis, who earlier gave us Gollum. One never knows exactly where the human ends and the effects begin, but Serkis and/or Caesar gives the best performance in the movie.

James Franco struggles with an underwritten role that shies away from philosophical and ethical questions and limits itself to plot points in basic English. Freida Pinto's Caroline, the primatologist, is no Dian Fossey and indeed gives no hints that she has even heard of her, but man, is she gorgeous. Tom Felton plays a keeper in a primate facility who is deliberately cruel to his chimps, which is unlikely but serves a purpose. People who make faces at chimpanzees are telling us more about themselves than they should share. Oh, and John Lithgow is here as the hero's dad, once a beloved music teacher, now disappearing into Alzheimer's. He is in the film to do exactly what he does and, apparently, not one thing more.

There's a big climactic action scene that is more engaging than the countless similar scenes I've seen with zombies. And a conclusion that is uplifting and inspiring for the apes, I assume, and proves that Caesar is so smart that when he sees a place from another place he knows how to find his way back to the other place from the first one, which is what humans need GPS for.

Bottom line: This is the movie you may have been expecting. No less, no more.

## The Rite ★ ★ ★

PG-13, 112 m., 2011

Anthony Hopkins (Father Lucas Trevant), Colin O'Donoghue (Father Michael Kovak), Alice Braga (Angeline), Ciaran Hinds (Father Xavier), Toby Jones (Father Matthew), Rutger Hauer (Istvan Kovak). Directed by Mikael Hafstrom and produced by Beau Flynn and Tripp Vinson. Screenplay by Michael Petroni, based on the book by Matt Baglio.

*The Rite* takes exorcism more seriously than I expected it to. It begins with the supposition that Satan is "alive and active in the world" and assumes that satanic possession takes place and that the rite of exorcism works. Otherwise, we wouldn't have a movie, would we? In metaphysical terms I must immediately jump on the word "alive." In what sense can a being that exists outside of time and space be said to be alive? Active, yes.

The movie is based on the actual experiences of Father Gary Thomas, a California priest who was assigned by his bishop to study exorcism at the Vatican. In *The Rite* he becomes Father Michael Kovak (Colin O'Donoghue) from Chicago, and the closing credits tell us he's now working in a Western suburb. That's a fib. The director, Mikael Hafstrom, should say three Hail Marys and make a good act of contrition.

Father Michael is not a saint. He enters the seminary as a way to get a four-year college education before taking his vows, and then tries to leave the novitiate. Discovering the cost of his education would then roll over into a $100,000 student loan, he reconsiders and agrees to attend a monthlong course in Rome. This sort of detail is more refreshing than shots of him silhouetted against ancient desert structures while monks intone Gregorian chants.

In Rome, he attends classes, debates scripture, and then is advised to spend some time with an experienced exorcist, Father Lucas Trevant (Anthony Hopkins). This, too, is from the book by Matt Baglio, although in the book this priest is Italian. As Hopkins appears onscreen, *The Rite* slips into gear and grows solemn and effective. Hopkins finds a good note for Father Trevant: friendly, chatty, offhand, self-effacing, realistic about demonic possession but not a ranter. He takes the kid along while treating the apparent possession of a pregnant young woman.

That something happens to make people

seem possessed I have no doubt. Diagnosing whether Satan is involved is above my pay grade. What I must observe is that demonic possession seems very rare, and the church rejects the majority of such reports. Yet it approaches epidemic proportions in *The Rite*, almost as if it were a virus. The film is like one of those war movies where everybody gets wounded but John Wayne.

Still, I found myself drawn in. It is sincere. It is not exploitative; a certain amount of screaming, frothing, and thrashing comes with the territory. My own guess is that people get the demons they deserve. While true believers go into frenzies, the Masters of Wall Street more cruelly lose joy in their wives and homes.

In Rome, Father Lucas meets a journalist named Angeline (Alice Braga), who like most women in the movies, even journalists, lacks a second name. She follows them on assignment, but it is one of the virtues of the film that she does not get romantically involved. In a correct casting decision, Braga is attractive but not a sexpot. This movie was filmed largely in Hungary. In Hollywood, the role would have had Megan Fox written all over it.

Hafstrom uses what I assume are some Hungarian interiors to go with his exteriors in Rome. A centuries-old library is especially impressive. The ancient presence of the Vatican is evoked to great effect; a reminder that although Satan is in fashion in many denominations, when you want to exorcise, you call in the experienced professionals. The priests are not blind believers. Father Kovak argues at one point that a psychiatrist might be more appropriate. When they get into the trenches with the demons there is spiritual hand-to-hand fighting, but Father Trevant, Father Kovak, and Angeline are as realistic as probably possible.

This is, I suspect, a more realistic film than *The Exorcist*, although not its equal. The real Father Gary Thomas has cited *The Exorcism of Emily Rose* (2005) as more accurate. I admire *The Rite* because while it delivers what I suppose should be called horror, it is atmospheric, its cinematography is eerie and evocative, and the actors enrich it. It has given some thought to exorcism. Grant its assumptions, and it has something to say.

## Road to Nowhere ★ ★

R, 121 m., 2011

Shannyn Sossamon (Laurel Graham), Tygh Runyan (Mitchell Haven), Dominique Swain (Nathalie Post), Waylon Payne (Bruno Brotherton), Cliff De Young (Rafe Tachen). Directed by Monte Hellman and produced by Monte Hellman, Melissa Hellman, and Steven Gaydos. Screenplay by Gaydos.

*Road to Nowhere* plays like an exercise in frustrating audiences. Imagine a jigsaw puzzle where you assemble as many pieces as seem to fit, but have pieces left over and gaps left in the puzzle. One of the pleasures of puzzle films is that we understand, or at least sense, the underlying pattern of their solution. Here is a film that seems indifferent to that satisfaction.

It is the first film in twenty-one years by the cult legend Monte Hellman, whose *Two-Lane Blacktop* (1971) offers less determined frustrations. Clarity of narrative is unimportant in both films. They're more about their own making. It is one thing for a director to express his vision, and another thing for him to make a film about it, especially a fragmented film. *Two-Lane Blacktop* at least followed linear, if enigmatic and unexplained, characters. *Road to Nowhere* keeps pulling the rug out from under the characters' feet.

The film opens with a shot of a DVD being loaded. The DVD is titled *Road to Nowhere.* So therefore this film exists outside another film of the same name. We are seeing a film about the film. The *inner* film is being made by a director named Mitchell Haven (Tygh Runyan), who has the same initials as Monte Hellman. So is the outer film about the making of the inner one, or are the two films simply not synched in time and space? And for that matter, is there a third level, a "reality," that neither film completely reflects?

We see Haven working with an actress, Laurel Graham (Shannyn Sossamon), whom he has discovered and convinced to play her role. She doesn't think of herself as an actress. Perhaps Haven doesn't care. He spends a great deal of time in the sorts of earnest discussions with her that men use to impress their importance upon women. These often take the form of wise teacher and attentive student. God, women must sometimes grow weary of listening to us.

We see Laurel Graham acting in apparently fictional scenes involving a fraud case. This fraud was blogged about by Nathalie (Dominique Swain), who we learn is the person watching the DVD seen at the beginning of the movie. On her blog, a "real" crime was described, and Laurel apparently greatly resembles Velma Duran, one of the perps, who is now dead. We gather that because Laurel visits her grave. On the other hand, everyone notes that Laurel looks exactly like Velma. The possibility is left hanging that Velma faked her death and changed her name to Laurel, which would go a long way toward explaining Laurel's reluctance to accept the movie role. The film doesn't consider the question of who, therefore, is buried in the grave.

Velma and her partner in crime, Rafe (Cliff De Young), died in the crash of a small plane into a lake, we are told. Or possibly not. Rafe is also much seen in the movie, sometimes calling in from Rome. It is unclear to me, however, which movie Rafe is in—or if he's in both. Is he calling, then, into the inner movie or into the movie about it?

I submit that there is no answer. Further complicating matters is the existence of Bruno Brotherton (Waylon Payne), a detective Mitch hires. Is he hired in the inner story or the outer story? Actually he seems to suggest the existence of a third, still more encompassing story that involves Mitch's meta-role in both of the others.

Are you following this? I'm not. Some scenes are intended as fiction within a larger reality, and then of course all realities in the film may be part of a larger fiction. The levels seem to be leaking into each other. The screenplay is by Steven Gaydos, an editor at *Variety* I know and like, who has been a friend and confidant of Hellman for a long time. He also wrote Hellman's little-seen *Iguana* (1988), and reportedly this is the screenplay that persuaded Hellman to return to feature films.

I have no doubt *Road to Nowhere* is exactly the film they intended to make. It is not a failure in that it sets out to do exactly what it does, and does it. The question remains of why it should have been done. Hellman's skill is everywhere evident in precise framing and deliberate editing (he likes contemplative shots). Each scene works within itself on its own terms. But there is no whole here—at least none that I could piece together. I've rarely seen a narrative film that seemed so reluctant to flow. Nor perhaps one with a more accurate title.

## The Robber ★ ★ ½

NO MPAA RATING, 97 m., 2011

Andreas Lust (Johann Rettenberger), Franziska Weisz (Erika), Markus Schleinzer (Probation Officer). Directed by Benjamin Heisenberg and produced by Burkhard Althoff, Nikolaus Geyrhalter, Markus Glaser, Peter Heilrath, Michael Kitzberger, and Wolfgang Widerhofer. Screenplay by Heisenberg and Martin Prinz, based on the novel by Prinz.

*The Robber* might as well be called *The Loneliness of the Long-Distance Runner.* It tells the story of a man who runs so well he's a marathon contender, but is compelled to rob banks and then run away from the scene of the crime. That is what the movie is about: bank robberies and running, and a bleak life that seems to contain nothing else of much interest for him.

It is a good question whether Johann Rettenberger (Andreas Lust) actually feels joy when he pulls off a successful robbery and escapes. He seems to have sentenced himself to loop indefinitely through the same actions, punctuated by intervals of prison time. When we first see him, he's running around a prison track and then, back in his cell, pounding on a treadmill.

One assumes that champion endurance athletes must be monomaniacs, at least while training and performing. Lance Armstrong comes to mind. In the case of Rettenberger, there seems to be nothing else in life. He doesn't engage with people. His answers are curt and defiant. When he encounters a woman he was apparently involved with, he is cold and hostile. He makes no effort to ingratiate himself with his parole officer (Markus Schleinzer).

He trains. He plans. He runs. Is he exhilarated when he escapes after a bank job? Not apparently. His successful escape simply signals the beginning of the next job. He doesn't even show any interest in spending the loot.

*The Robber* is based on the story of a real man, Johann Kastenberger, who won a marathon and many other races in Austria in the 1980s. He also robbed several banks, wearing a Ronald Reagan mask and carrying a shotgun, gaining himself the nickname "Shotgun Ronnie." Once, when cornered by police in a stolen car on a motorway, he fled into the woods, ran cross-country, and stole another car.

Director Benjamin Heisenberg based his film on a novel by Martin Prinz, who cowrote the screenplay. They depict their hero as a psychological void; a man who deliberately tries to project no personality. One is reminded a little of the hero of Jean-Pierre Melville's *Le Samourai* (1967), a killer for hire played by Alain Delon. He also was a solitary man of few emotions, but that film surrounded his loneliness with characters and embedded him in a great maze of plot.

*The Robber* has not so much a plot as a series of events. The relationship with the woman is left open-ended. The attempts of the parole officer to care about him result in violence. He wants to rob banks and run. What brought him to this point remains an enigma.

The movie therefore offers meager pleasures of character. Where it excels is in staging and cinematography. The running sequences, in races, on city streets, and through forests, are very well handled. (The film inserts him in real races.) His expertise in stealing cars and dealing with their owners is direct and efficient. Curiously, we care so little about him that it doesn't much matter to us if he escapes or not; we watch with the same interest that we bring to a race with no runners we care about. Here is a well-made movie with insufficient interest in its hero.

## Robin Hood ★ ★

PG-13, 131 m., 2010

Russell Crowe (Robin Longstride), Cate Blanchett (Marion Loxley), Mark Strong (Godfrey), William Hurt (William Marshal), Mark Addy (Friar Tuck), Oscar Isaac (Prince John), Danny Huston (Richard the Lionheart), Eileen Atkins (Eleanor of Aquitaine), Kevin Durand (Little John), Scott Grimes (Will Scarlet), Alan Doyle (Allan A'Dayle), Max von Sydow (Sir Walter Loxley). Directed by Ridley Scott and produced by Scott, Russell Crowe, and Brian Grazer. Screenplay by Brian Helgeland.

Little by little, title by title, innocence and joy is being drained out of the movies. What do you think of when you hear the name of Robin Hood? I think of Errol Flynn, Sean Connery, and the Walt Disney character. I see Robin lurking in Sherwood Forest, in love with Maid Marian (Olivia de Havilland or Audrey Hepburn), and roistering with Friar Tuck and the Merry Men. I see a dashing swashbuckler.

That Robin Hood is nowhere to be found in Ridley Scott's new *Robin Hood*, starring Russell Crowe as a warrior just back from fighting in the Third Crusade. Now Richard is dead, and Robin is essentially an unemployed mercenary. This story is a prequel. It takes place entirely *before* Robin got to be a folk hero. The idea of taking from the rich and giving to the poor was still in storyboard form. Grieving Richard the Lionheart and now faced with the tyrant King John, he leads an uprising.

This war broadens until, in the words of the movie's synopsis, "it will forever alter the balance of world power." That's not all: "Robin will become an eternal symbol of freedom for his people." Not bad for a man who, by general agreement, did not exist. Although various obscure bandits and ne'er-do-wells inspired ancient ballads about such a figure, our image of him is largely a fiction from the nineteenth century.

But so what? In for a penny, in for a pound. After the death of Richard, Robin Hood raises, arms, and fields an army to repel a French army as it lands on an English beach in wooden craft that look uncannily like World War II troop carriers at Normandy. His men, wielding broadswords, backed by archers, protected from enemy arrows by their shields, engage the enemy in a last act devoted almost entirely to nonstop CGI and stunt carnage in which a welter of warriors clashes in confused alarms and excursions, and Russell Crowe frequently appears in the foreground to whack somebody.

Subsequently, apparently, Robin pensioned

his militia and retired to Sherwood Forest to play tag with Friar Tuck. That's my best guess; at the end the film informs us, "and so the legend begins," leaving us with the impression we walked in early.

Ah, you say, but what of Maid Marian? In this telling, Marion (Cate Blanchett) is not a maid but a widow, and not a merry one. At one point she threatens to unman Robin with her dagger, which is unlike the Maid Marians I've known and loved. Blanchett plays the role with great class and breeding, which is all wrong, I think. She's the kind of woman who would always be asking Robin, "Why do you let that smelly so-called friar hang around you like a fanboy?"

If you listen closely to the commercials, you may hear of a royal edict being issued against "Robin of the Hood." A hood, in medieval English, was, of course, a wood, or forest—a point that may be lost on many of the commercial's viewers.

*Robin Hood* is a high-tech and well-made violent action picture using the name of Robin Hood for no better reason than that it's an established brand not protected by copyright. I cannot discover any sincere interest on the part of Scott, Crowe, or the writer Brian Helgeland in any previous version of Robin Hood. Their Robin is another weary retread of the muscular macho slaughterers who with interchangeable names stand at the center of one overwrought bloodbath after another.

Have we grown weary of the delightful aspects of the Robin Hood legend? Is witty dialogue no longer permitted? Are Robin and Marion no longer allowed to engage in a spirited flirtation? Must their relationship seem like high-level sexual negotiations? How many people need to be covered in boiling oil for Robin Hood's story to be told these days? How many parents will be misled by the PG-13 rating? Must children go directly from animated dragons to skewering and decapitation, with no interval of cheerful storytelling?

The photography is, however, remarkable, and Crowe and the others are filled with fierce energy. Ridley Scott is a fine director for work like this, although in another world Hollywood would let him make smarter films. God, he must be tired of enormous battle scenes.

*Note: The film was the opening night attraction at the 2010 Cannes Film Festival. There must be a reason for that.*

## Rock of Ages ★ ★ ★

PG-13, 123 m., 2012

Julianne Hough (Sherrie Christian), Diego Boneta (Drew Boley), Russell Brand (Lonny), Paul Giamatti (Paul Gill), Catherine Zeta-Jones (Patricia Whitmore), Malin Akerman (Constance Sack), Mary J. Blige (Justice Charlier), Alec Baldwin (Dennis Dupree), Tom Cruise (Stacee Jaxx). Directed by Adam Shankman and produced by Shankman, Jennifer Gibgot, Garrett Grant, Carl Levin, Tobey Maguire, Scott Prisand, and Matt Weaver. Screenplay by Justin Theroux, Chris D'Arienzo, and Allan Loeb.

*Rock of Ages* is a rags-to-riches rock 'n' roll musical set mostly in a music club on the Sunset Strip, and winning no prizes for originality. A lot of it is zesty entertainment, there are some energetic musical numbers, and several big names (Tom Cruise, Russell Brand, Alec Baldwin) prove they can sing well enough to play the Strip if they lose their day jobs. The two leads are Diego Boneta, playing Drew, a bartender in the Strip's hottest club, and Julianne Hough, as Sherrie, a naive kid just off the bus from the Midwest. They're both gifted singers and join the others in doing covers of 1980s rock classics.

Of course they also fall in love. Of course they have heartfelt conversations while standing behind the Hollywood sign. Of course they break up because of a tragic misunderstanding. Of course their mistake is repaired and (spoiler!) they're back together at the end. Has ever a romance in a musical been otherwise?

They're sweet and likable, but for me the better story involves the fate of the club, the Bourbon Room. Dennis Dupree (Alec Baldwin), its owner, is desperate because he owes back taxes and will have to close the doors at any moment. His only confidante is a weathered rock-and-roller named Lonny (Russell Brand), whose primary function is to lean over him during phone calls and frantically tell him what to say. The person on the other end of the line is usually a venal music manager named Paul Gill (Paul Giamatti), who claims he will save the club by supplying his legendary client Stacee Jaxx (Tom Cruise) for a one-night farewell concert.

If you're tracking those names you're perhaps impressed. Adam Shankman's *Rock of Ages* not only has a high-profile cast, but they never seem to be slumming; they play their roles with great intensity and earnestness, which is really the only way to do satire.

A subplot is recycled directly out of old Beach Party musicals. If you are very old, you may remember them. Frankie, Annette, and the gang were always having a great time down at the beach when some stuffy local politician decided to run them out of town as a campaign tactic. In this case, the politician is Mayor Whitmore (Bryan Cranston), who gets all of his instructions from his domineering wife, Patricia (Catherine Zeta-Jones). She leads a group of protesters across the street from the Bourbon Room, while Baldwin and Brand look grimly out the window.

There isn't an original idea in sight in the screenplay by Justin Theroux, Chris D'Arienzo, and Allan Loeb, based on a Broadway hit. Even the songs are oldies. And that's OK, because the actors are having a lot of fun, and the production values of the musical numbers are slick and high-spirited. The only problem is that the plot meanders when nobody is singing. If you're making the kind of movie where everybody in the audience knows for sure what's going to happen, best not to linger on the recycled bits. If Drew misunderstands something he sees and thinks Sherrie was cheating on him with Stacee Jaxx, then let them clear that up without a lugubrious return visit to the Hollywood sign.

In a movie where all the stars except the leads are essentially satirizing themselves, Tom Cruise is the most merciless on himself. Stacee Jaxx, his muscular body a quilt work of tattoos, travels with a couple of grim bodyguards (Kevin Nash, of all people, and Jeff Chase, a giant six-foot-seven bodybuilder). Stacee has such a big ego that when he's interviewed by a *Rolling Stone* reporter (Malin Akerman), he's so narcissistically seductive he almost seduces himself. Meanwhile, Alec Baldwin and Russell Brand have a big scene I'll bet neither one saw in his future.

## The Rum Diary ★ ★ ½

R, 119 m., 2011

Johnny Depp (Paul Kemp), Aaron Eckhart (Sanderson), Michael Rispoli (Bob Sala), Amber Heard (Chenault), Richard Jenkins (Lotterman), Giovanni Ribisi (Moburg). Directed by Bruce Robinson and produced by Christi Dembrowski, Johnny Depp, Tim Headington, Graham King, Robert Kravis, and Anthony Rhulen. Screenplay by Robinson, based on the novel by Hunter S. Thompson.

In the early 1960s, after he had discovered booze but before he had stumbled across drugs, the young Hunter S. Thompson got an uncertain start in journalism. By the time he was twenty, he had already been fired as a copy boy for *Time* magazine for "insubordination," and from the *Middletown (N.Y.) Daily Record* for destroying the office candy machine. He moved to San Juan, Puerto Rico, seeking a job on the *San Juan Star*, where he was turned down.

This career path looks marginally sunnier in *The Rum Diary*, based on a novel he wrote in the early 1970s. The story goes that Johnny Depp found the manuscript among Thompson's papers in his cabin on Woody Creek, and was instrumental in getting it published and now produced as a film. The writer-director, Bruce Robinson, was a good choice, having already directed a landmark, *Withnail & I*, about an alcoholic who was Thompson's equal—or inferior, or superior, whichever fits.

The film opens as the ambitious young hero, Kemp (Depp), sporting a white suit, a straw hat, and the dark glasses Thompson would wear for a lifetime, applies for a reporting job at the *Star*. It doesn't appear to be the kind of paper that attracted the ambitious in those days. Lotterman (Richard Jenkins), the editor, spots him for trouble and immediately asks him how much he drinks. "The high end of social."

He is the only applicant for the job and gets it. He falls in with Sala (Michael Rispoli), the paper's veteran photographer, and Moburg (Giovanni Ribisi), a shambling wreck who has been fired but still hangs around the newspaper office. San Juan in those days appears to have been a lively little metropolis in which a reporter on an English-language newspaper was a stranger in a strange land. One of Kemp's stories concerns Sanderson (Aaron Eckhart), a property developer who has grown rich through shady deals, and occupies a palatial beach home where he entertains local investors.

The movie is cast as autobiographical, assuming that Thompson had been given the job in the first place. He was a writer with lifelong trouble with deadlines, not a good trait when you're one of the few reporters on a daily. For all the movie makes clear, Kemp may have been the only one. He is of great value to the snaky Sanderson, however, because what appears in a newspaper has the illusion of fact, and Sanderson hopes to bribe him to write favorable coverage of his property schemes. This he does with a shiny red Corvette to match the shiny red lipstick on his mistress, Chenault (Amber Heard), who is Kemp's for the taking. One suspects Kemp could have been bought for far less.

Depp has a deep attraction for Hunter Thompson, whom he played earlier in *Fear and Loathing in Las Vegas* (1998). Thompson was apparently good company; my friend Bill Nack, an otherwise sensible man, logged time with him covering prizefights and liked him. The mystery involved how Thompson possibly consumed so many intoxicants and hallucinatory drugs, lived until he was sixty-seven, and wrote a great deal of invaluable prose, most of it turned in late.

Thompson had a speaking style that Depp re-creates accurately in *The Rum Diary.* He mutters in a low voice, as if marginally short on breath, or as if fearful of jarring something loose inside his head. He never seems particularly drunk, but sometimes it's more like he went through drunk and came out the other side.

There is the dim purpose, in the film and I guess in the novel, that Kemp is fighting corruption in the form of American money being used to defraud Puerto Ricans. This is no doubt his purpose, but his mind is so muddled and his days so haphazard that he often seems to be drifting toward a vaguely seen destination.

The mistress, Chenault, is played by the sensuous Heard as a woman who is tired of Sanderson's wealth and ego and inexplicably drawn to Kemp's shabby life and disreputable friends. True, Sanderson is a rat and Kemp is a crusader, but a girl like Chenault doesn't find herself living with a millionaire on the beach if she has a taste for shaky drunks.

We have the feeling that Kemp/Thompson saw much of life through the bottom of a dirty glass, and did not experience it with any precision. The film duplicates this sensation, not with much success. The difference between Kemp and Withnail is that Withnail is seen from outside, partly through the eyes of his horrified friend. As Kemp loses focus, so does the story.

I can imagine a tightly written newspaper story set in San Juan and populated with colorful characters, but Kemp's view seems clouded by his uncertain perception. At the film's end we're informed that Kemp saw that the bastards got what was coming to them, but I suspect San Juan was much the same when Kemp (and Thompson) left.

## The Runaways ★ ★ ★

R, 100 m., 2010

Kristen Stewart (Joan Jett), Dakota Fanning (Cherie Currie), Michael Shannon (Kim Fowley), Stella Maeve (Sandy West), Scout Taylor-Compton (Lita Ford), Alia Shawkat (Robin), Riley Keough (Marie Currie). Directed by Floria Sigismondi and produced by Art Linson, John Linson, and William Pohlad. Screenplay by Sigismondi, based on the book *Neon Angel: The Cherie Currie Story* by Cherie Currie.

An all-girl rock band is named and trained by a rock manager of dubious sexuality, goes on the road, hits the charts, has a lesbian member and another who becomes a sex symbol but crashes from drugs. This is the plot of a 1970 film named *Beyond the Valley of the Dolls,* which inadvertently anticipated the saga of the Runaways five years later. Life follows art.

*The Runaways* tells the story of a hard-rock girl band that was created more or less out of thin air by a manager named Kim Fowley. His luck is that he started more or less accidentally with performers who were actually talented. Guitarists Joan Jett and Lita Ford are popular to this day, long after the expiration of their sell-by dates as jailbait. The lead singer, Cherie

Currie, costarred in the very good *Foxes* (1980) with Jodie Foster, had drug problems, rehabbed, and "today is a chainsaw artist living in the San Fernando Valley." The ideal art form for any retired hard rocker.

The movie centers on the characters of Jett (Kristen Stewart), Currie (Dakota Fanning), and the manager Fowley (Michael Shannon). Jett was the original driving force, a Bowie fan who dreamed of forming her own band. Fowley, known in the music clubs of Sunset Strip as a manager on the prowl for young, cheap talent, told her to give it a shot, and paired her with Currie, whose essential quality is apparently that she was fifteen. That fit Fowley's concept of a jailbait band who would appeal because they seemed so young and so tough. He rehearses them in a derelict trailer in the Valley, writing their early hit "Cherry Bomb" on the spot.

Shannon is an actor of uncanny power. Nominated for a role as an odd dinner guest in *Revolutionary Road* (2008), he was searing as he turned paranoid in William Friedkin's *Bug* (2006). Here he's an evil Svengali, who teaches rock 'n' roll as an assault on the audience; the girls must batter their fans into submission or admit they're losers. He's like a Marine drill sergeant: "Give me the girl. I'll give you back the man." He converts Cherie, who begins by singing passively, into a snarling tigress.

The performance abilities of the Runaways won respect. The rest was promotion and publicity. The film covers the process with visuals over a great deal of music, which helps cover an underwritten script and many questions about the characters. We learn next to nothing about anyone's home life except for Currie, who is provided with a runaway mother (Tatum O'Neal), a loyal but resentful sister (Riley Keough), and a dying alcoholic father. Although this man's health is important in the plot, I don't recall us ever seeing him standing up or getting a clear look at his face.

So this isn't an in-depth biopic, even though it's based on Currie's 1989 autobiography. It's more of a quick overview of the creation, rise, and fall of the Runaways, with slim character development, no extended dialogue scenes, and a whole lot of rock 'n' roll. Its interest comes from Shannon's fierce and sadistic training scenes as Kim Fowley, and from the intrinsic qualities of the performances by Stewart and Fanning, who bring more to their characters than the screenplay provides.

Another new movie this week, *The Girl with the Dragon Tattoo* from Sweden, has a role for a young, hostile computer hacker. Stewart has been mentioned for the inevitable Hollywood remake. Reviewing that movie, I doubted she could handle such a tough-as-nails character. Having seen her as Joan Jett, I think she possibly could.

*Note: Many years ago, while I was standing at a luggage carousel at Heathrow Airport, I was approached by a friendly young woman. I'm Joan Jett, she told me. I liked* Beyond the Valley of the Dolls.

*Just sayin'.*

# S

## Safety Not Guaranteed ★ ★ ★ ½

R, 94 m., 2012

Aubrey Plaza (Darius), Mark Duplass (Kenneth), Jake Johnson (Jeff), Karan Soni (Arnau), Jenica Bergere (Liz), Kristen Bell (Belinda), Jeff Garlin (Mr. Britt), Mary Lynn Rajskub (Bridget). Directed by Colin Trevorrow and produced by Trevorrow, Derek Connolly, Stephanie Langhoff, Peter Saraf, and Marc Turtletaub. Screenplay by Connolly.

Few descriptions of *Safety Not Guaranteed* will do it justice. It's a more ambitious and touching movie than seems possible given its starting point, which is this classified ad in an alternative newspaper:

"WANTED: Someone to go back in time with me. This is not a joke. You'll get paid after we get back. Must bring your own weapons. Safety not guaranteed. I have only done this once before."

That sounds like a setup for a comedy, maybe like *Hot Tub Time Machine*. It is a comedy in many ways, but there's a serious undertow, kindhearted attention to the characters, and a treatment of time travel that (a) takes it seriously, and (b) sidesteps all of the well-known paradoxes by which time travel is impossible.

That's not to say time travel takes place in the film. Or that it doesn't. A rather brilliant ending is completely satisfying while proving nothing. What it means is that the story takes place entirely at this time, and time travel provides the subject and not the gimmick.

The classified ad comes up at a story conference for *Seattle* magazine. A writer named Jeff (Jake Johnson) volunteers to try to track down whoever placed the ad. He demands two interns to help him, and is assigned Darius (Aubrey Plaza) and Arnau (Karan Soni). She's an intense, quirky loner. He's a virginal nerd with big glasses. Jeff is a slacker who actually wants to cover the story because it will help him hook up with a high school girlfriend.

The reporting team goes to Ocean View, Washington, and fairly easily finds the guy who placed the ad: a midthirties grocery store clerk named Kenneth (Mark Duplass). Jeff quickly alienates him, but Darius has a better approach: She's sarcastic, aggressive, and challenging. The more she discovers about Kenneth, the more intriguing he becomes. He lives in a shabby home in the woods, unchanged since his parents died, and focuses with tunnel vision on his method for time travel. His ad is completely realistic, as far as he's concerned.

Here's where the movie, directed by Colin Trevorrow and written by Derek Connolly, takes a decisive turn for the good. In reviewing a lot of movies I complain that the characters speak in short bursts of basic English, to make them easier to subtitle. They never really say anything. There's no reason for us to care about them. Their dialogue is used only as a function of the plot.

*Safety Not Guaranteed* not only has dialogue that's about something, but characters who have some depth and dimension. Kenneth is goofy and paranoid, but also smart, sincere, and vulnerable. Darius is more than a wiseass fresh college grad on her first job. When the two of them reveal their reasons for wanting to travel back through time, they're reasons we can understand. Jeff, the senior writer, essentially blows off the assignment while he goes searching for Liz (Jenica Bergere), who made an impression twenty years ago he hasn't been able to stop thinking about. When they meet, the movie avoids the many clichés we can easily imagine. Arnau does resemble the stereotypical Indian-American sidekick, but even he has life-changing experiences.

Mark Duplass has all of a sudden emerged as an engaging actor with real presence. This is really his movie; the role is borderline impossible, and he carries it. He and his brother Jay emerged from the mists of mumblecore (*The Puffy Chair*, 2005), and now he's a leading man in three other 2012 movies: *Your Sister's Sister*, *Darling Companion*, and *People Like Us*. His brother is emerging as a gifted director (*Cyrus*; *Jeff, Who Lives at Home*).

In this film, Mark walks a fine line between paranoia and caricature, and yet when he tells Darius he's being followed by government agents, it turns out he's telling the truth. There are a couple of Men in Black types who follow him around, but the movie wisely suggests they don't take this assignment entirely seriously. How wrapped up would you be in an investigation about some goofball in the woods who advertises for time-travel partners?

As I said, the movie doesn't make it absolutely clear whether time travel actually takes place. Or whether it doesn't. You'll see what I mean, and that the filmmakers have found an ingenious solution for their challenge.

## Saint John of Las Vegas ★ ★

R, 85 m., 2010

Steve Buscemi (John Alighieri), Romany Malco (Virgil), Sarah Silverman (Jill), Peter Dinklage (Mr. Townsend), Emmanuelle Chriqui (Tasty D Lite), Tim Blake Nelson (Ned). Directed by Hue Rhodes and produced by Mark Burton, Lawrence Mattis, Kelly McCormick, and Matt Wall. Screenplay by Rhodes, based on the story by Dante Alighieri.

If you were to view the trailer of *Saint John of Las Vegas*, it would probably look like a good time. It seems to have so much great stuff. Promise me a movie with Steve Buscemi, Sarah Silverman, Peter Dinklage, and Tim Blake Nelson, and I'm there. But this movie is all elbows. Nothing fits. It doesn't add up. It has some terrific free-standing scenes, but they need more to lean on.

Consider the burning man. This is a sideshow performer who wears a suit designed to burst into flames. Unfortunately, the suit has malfunctioned and he can't take it off until the fuel is exhausted. He waits it out on a folding chair behind the carnival midway, consumed in flames every thirty seconds. That's funny, especially when he's dying for a cigarette. But . . . what? He exists only to be existing.

Well, not quite. The flaming also seems to fit into the movie's overall symbolism. The screenplay, we learn, was written by the director Hue Rhodes, based on the story by Dante Alighieri. That name may not ring a bell with a lot of moviegoers and had better not be a question on the Tea Baggers' literacy test. We all recall that Dante's *Inferno* told the story of a journey into hell, with the poet Virgil as the tour guide.

In the movie, Steve Buscemi plays John Alighieri, an insurance claims adjuster who is assigned a partner named Virgil (Romany Malco) and sets off on a journey through the desert to Las Vegas (hell).

Let's have some fun. Dante's First Circle of Hell was Limbo. In the movie, that would be the main office of the insurance company. People in Limbo have trouble controlling their weaknesses. John's weakness is compulsive gambling. Second Circle is Lust. He lusts for Jill (Silverman), a chirpy coworker who labors in the next cubicle. Later, in a lap-dance bar, he undergoes but resists temptation from a stripper (Emmanuelle Chriqui), who sprained her neck in a car crash but tries to give him a lap dance from her wheelchair. It's her crash the insurance company doesn't want to pay the claim on.

Third Circle, Gluttony. In this circle are rain and hail, which the two drive through. Fourth Circle, Avarice. John dreams of winning the lottery and spends every dollar on scratch cards. Virgil also has greed, revealed later. Fifth Circle, Anger. They argue with a cop and arrive at a senseless flaming gateway in the desert, guarded by Tim Blake Nelson and other naked men with guns. Sixth Circle, Heresy. Virgil seems not to take the insurance company seriously.

Seventh Circle, Violence. In a used car lot, they are led into a trap and John, knocked senseless, barely escapes with his life. The lot is guarded by a savage dog, no doubt based on Cerberus, the watchdog of Hell. Eighth Circle, Fraud. John discovers the nature of a scheme to defraud the insurance company. Ninth and last Circle, Treason against God—or, in this case, Mr. Townsend (Dinklage), who is their boss at the insurance company.

If you recall Dante very well, or jot some reminders on your palm with a ballpoint, you can possibly follow the movie in this way. But if like most people your command of the *Inferno* is shaky, the film may seem disjointed and pointless. There is also this inescapable storytelling dilemma: Once you arrive in the Ninth Circle of Hell, what do you do for an encore?

The acting is first-rate. Buscemi is an

apologetic loser who fled Vegas after losing his net worth, and now unwisely returns. Malco's Virgil, now that we think of it, is a guide who seems to have been this way before. Silverman's Jill is part temptress, part saint. It must have taken all of Rhodes's willpower to avoid naming her character "Beatrice," although of course Beatrice was Dante's guide into heaven. That would be the sequel.

And who is Saint John of Las Vegas? That would be John the Baptist or "John of the desert," divine messenger, not to be confused with the brother of Jesus. Why is he "of Las Vegas"? I think the answer must relate to John's gambling history. When Anna Dudak, my landlady on Burling Street, would take a trip to Las Vegas, her husband, Paul, would tell me she had gone to Lost Wages.

## Salmon Fishing in the Yemen ★ ★ ½

PG-13, 111 m., 2012

Ewan McGregor (Dr. Alfred Jones), Emily Blunt (Harriet Chetwode-Talbot), Amr Waked (Sheikh Muhammed), Kristin Scott Thomas (Patricia Maxwell), Tom Mison (Robert Mayers), Rachael Stirling (Mary Jones). Directed by Lasse Hallstrom and produced by Paul Webster. Screenplay by Simon Beaufoy, based on the novel by Paul Torday.

Salmon fishing in the *what*? The title is no doubt intended to inspire incredulity. In a river in the deserts of western Yemen, that's where. *Salmon Fishing in the Yemen* is based on Paul Torday's novel, a political satire that was a best-seller in the United Kingdom, and allows an opening into the worlds of British and Yemeni politics, the devotion of salmon fishermen, and the possibilities of romance among humans and salmon, who in this story must both swim upstream.

There is a kind of character in British comedies I am fond of, the eccentric scientist with a narrow focus. Recall Alec Guinness as *The Man in the White Suit*. Here the role is played by Ewan McGregor, as Dr. Alfred Jones, a salmon expert in the British fisheries, who is known not only for his vast knowledge but also for some of the famous fishing flies he has designed. It seems a little callous to both study salmon and fish for them, but he is an affable young man who finds himself in over his head when a sheikh hatches a plan to transport his favorite pastime to his Middle East homeland.

Briefly, the sheikh intends to construct a dam to convert a previously undistinguished river into a home where salmon can sport and spawn. He counts on Jones to supply him with ten thousand salmon from waters farther north. Will the salmon like it in the desert waters? For them, it's sink or swim.

The sheikh (Amr Waked) is an incredibly wealthy man who seemingly has only a single interest in life, salmon fishing. He's clearly a member of the 1 percent. He seeks the cooperation of the British government for his project, and this involves the prime minister and, in particular, his supercharged personal assistant Patricia Maxwell (Kristin Scott Thomas). On the sheikh's team is Harriet Chetwode-Talbot (Emily Blunt), hired to handle the financial details from the Yemini side. It's her job to sign up Alfred.

If I were a poor citizen of Yemen, struggling to feed my family, I wouldn't find this project charming, and indeed terrorists are stalking the sheikh and even blow up a dam to drown him. The sheikh's response to the death attempts is disappointment: "They thought it was all about the fish!" Well, I did, too. Apparently his motives are pure and green.

Dr. Jones and Ms. Chetwode-Talbot are destined to fall in love almost from the moment they set eyes on each other. This is an inconvenience because she is engaged to Robert (Tom Mison), a soldier who is missing in action, and he is married to Mary (Rachael Stirling). They try to remain at respectful arm's length, which is not easy, while the inappropriately dressed Patricia Maxwell turns up on a fact-finding visit to possibly the biggest public works project in the region.

This perhaps sounds to you like a hilarious movie. So it could be, in the hands of the masters of classic British comedy. Unfortunately, the director is the Swedish Lasse Hallstrom (*Chocolat*), who sees it as a heartwarming romance and doesn't take advantage of the rich eccentricity in the story. The sheikh in particular is an enigma. Is he a public servant, a foolish hobbyist, a spoiled rich man, or a still water that runs deep? Middle East politics have become so touchy that Hallstrom and his writer, Simon Beaufoy, refrain from making him a comic figure at all.

What's left is the love story, which waltzes along with the schmaltzy score by Dario Marianelli. I'll be curious to see what kinds of audiences the movie attracts. Few people in this country have probably read the novel. The trailer promises a sweeping romantic comedy. The movie comes down to a missed opportunity. The happy ending is cornball. Only Kristin Scott Thomas, as the hypercharged operative for the prime minister, seems to understand she's in a comedy.

## Salt ★ ★ ★ ★

PG-13, 100 m., 2010

Angelina Jolie (Evelyn Salt), Liev Schreiber (Ted Winter), Chiwetel Ejiofor (Peabody), Daniel Olbrychski (Orlov), Andre Braugher (Secretary of Defense). Directed by Phillip Noyce and produced by Lorenzo di Bonaventura and Sunil Perkash. Screenplay by Kurt Wimmer.

*Salt* is a damn fine thriller. It does all the things I can't stand in bad movies, and does them in a good one. It's like a rebuke to all the lousy action movie directors who've been banging pots and pans together in our skulls. It winds your clock tight, and the alarm doesn't go off for one hundred minutes.

It's gloriously absurd. This movie has holes in it big enough to drive the whole movie through. The laws of physics seem to be suspended here the same way as in a Road Runner cartoon. Angelina Jolie runs full speed out into thin air and doesn't look down until she's in the helicopter at the end.

Jolie is one fine-looking woman. You don't need me to tell you that. It's why she gets the big bucks. The movies have celebrated her eyes, lips, profile, biceps, boobs, waist, butt, thighs. *Salt* pays tribute to her ankles. Anyone who can jump from the heights she does here, in the way she does it, may die from a lot of causes, but a sprained ankle won't be one of them.

You know *parkour*? Wikipedia defines it as "the physical discipline of training to overcome any obstacle within one's path by adapting one's movements to the environment." Jolie's character, Evelyn Salt, makes it look as if *Run, Lola, Run* was about walking. There's a scene when she descends eight stories in an elevator shaft by simply jumping across it to one wall support lower than the last. Each time she lands, she says, "Oof," but that's about it.

You're not going to hear much about the plot here. Nothing I could tell you would be necessary for you to know, and everything could be fatal to your enjoyment. Let's just make it simple: She plays a woman determined to single-handedly save the world from nuclear annihilation. Oh, it's not that the plot holds water or makes any sense, but it's a pleasure to be surprised here and there along the way, and it's not like the movie lingers over each twist and turn as if it's just pulled an elephant out of a hat.

No, each revelation is the occasion for another chase scene. Evelyn Salt escapes from, or breaks into, one inescapable and/or impenetrable stronghold after another. And she does it all by herself, and with her bare hands, plus a few guns, grenades, and a homemade rocket launcher. You know how Ginger Rogers did everything Astaire did, except backward and wearing heels? Evelyn does everything James Bond did, except backward and barefoot in the snow.

At one point in the movie, Evelyn is chained to a concrete floor in a North Korean dungeon while a rubber hose is charmingly stuck into her mouth and gasoline is poured in. That's at the *beginning* of the film. I'm not going to tell you what she survives later. She plays a spy for the CIA—but now I'm giving away too many details. Important supporting roles are played by Liev Schreiber and Chiwetel Ejiofor.

The movie has been directed by Phillip Noyce, an Australian whose work ranges from Tom Clancy thrillers to the great and angry drama *Rabbit-Proof Fence.* Here he performs as a master craftsman, aided by the cinematography of Robert Elswit and the editing of Stuart Baird and John Gilroy. The movie has a great many chase scenes, and faithful readers will know that these, in general, have lost their novelty for me. But a good chase scene is a good chase scene. It demands some sense of spatial coherence, no matter how impossible; some continuity of movement, no matter how devised by stunt work and effects; and genuine interest for the audience.

It's in that area that Angelina Jolie really delivers. She brings the conviction to her role that such a movie requires. She throws herself into it with animal energy. Somehow, improbably, she doesn't come off as a superhero (although her immunity suggests one), but as a brave and determined fighter. How does she look? She looks beautiful by default, and there's a scene in an office where she looks back over her shoulder to talk with Schreiber and you think, oh, my. But neither Jolie nor Noyce overplay her beauty, and she gets gritty and bloody and desperate, and we get involved.

Although the movie finds an ingenious way to overcome history and resurrect the Russians as movie villains, neither that nor any other element of the plot demands analysis. It's all a hook to hang a thriller on. It's exhilarating to see a genre picture done really well.

## The Salt of Life ★ ★ ★

NO MPAA RATING, 89 m., 2012

Gianni di Gregorio (Gianni), Valeria de Franciscis Bendoni (Gianni's Mother), Alfonso Santagata (Alfonso), Elisabetta Piccolomini (Gianni's Wife), Valeria Cavalli (Valeria), Aylin Prandi (Aylin), Kristina Cepraga (Kristina), Michelangelo Ciminale (Michelangelo), Teresa di Gregorio (Teresa). Directed by Gianni di Gregorio and produced by Angelo Barbagallo. Screenplay by Gregorio and Valerio Attanasio.

The three happiest men in Gianni's world are no doubt the three old-timers who sit all day every day on plastic chairs lined up in front of a café in Rome and chat endlessly. There's also the old dude who walks his toy poodle, "a beautiful dog." Certainly Gianni's best friend, Alfonso, is unhappy, despite his tireless quest for women a third his age. Least happy of all is Gianni, who lacks the will to stop looking, and the nerve to begin.

Gianni (Gianni di Gregorio, the film's director) is sixty. The most notable features on his careworn face are the bags under his eyes. He lives in a spacious apartment with his wife, his daughter, and his daughter's boyfriend, Michelangelo, who talks with him more than the other two combined. On the ground floor of his building lives the cheerful Aylin (Aylin Prandi), who pretends to be madly in love with him. He walks her Saint Bernard and his own inconspicuous family dog, whose breed he doesn't even know or care about.

The bane of his existence is his ninetyish mother (Valeria de Franciscis Bendoni), deeply tanned no doubt from the many poker games she plays with her peers in the garden of her luxurious house. She has all the money. Gianni lives on a pension and his wife's income, and grits his teeth as his mother serves champagne to her poker buddies and buys designer gowns for her caregiver. His marriage is peaceful and his wife affectionate, but seems focused elsewhere. It is probably an omen for the boyfriend that he spends so much time with his future father-in-law commiserating about the women in the family.

One look at Gianni's mother's caregiver and Alfonso can't believe Gianni isn't carrying on with her. Gianni's only response is the body language for "meh." His carrying-on days are over. But he begins to be persuaded by Alfonso that sixty is too young to retire completely from the chase. *The Salt of Life* tells his story in an affectionate, low-key way, not as a smutty sex-com, but as a gentle look at a harmless man who realizes he has become invisible, except to people who need something from him. His mother, for example, needs him to come over twice in the same day to adjust the TV set.

The movie is alert to his wounds. He thanks a bartender for his drink. Is ignored. Thanks her again. And again. "She can't hear me," he tells Alfonso. He passes a group of young women on the street. They can't see him. The busty middle-aged daughter of his mother's friend invites him to her house on Sunday afternoon. He buys a summer suit for himself and a bouquet for her. When he arrives, she is taking a music lesson, and he realizes she set up the visit to make her teacher feel possessive.

I know women are mistreated by men in countless ways every day. Men sometimes get their turn. In this movie, only two women are actually cruel to Gianni (the music student and his mother—who is polishing off ninety years of emasculation). On the other hand, at least they have uses for him. This is a movie about a man who is past his shelf life. Sooner or later he'll end up sitting in front of that café with the other guys. He knows it. He even tries it one day. The sexy Aylin comes past, throws her arms around his neck, and whispers, "What are *you* doing sitting here?" I can think of so many answers, none of which would much cheer him.

## The Samaritan ★ ★ ★

NO MPAA RATING, 90 m., 2012

Samuel L. Jackson (Foley), Luke Kirby (Ethan), Ruth Negga (Iris), Tom Wilkinson (Xavier). Directed by David Weaver and produced by Suzanne Cheriton, Andreas Hamori, and Tony Wosk. Screenplay by Elan Mastai and Weaver.

One difference between film noir and more straightforward crime pictures is that noir is more open to human flaws, and likes to embed them in twisty plot lines. *The Samaritan* isn't a great noir, but it's true to the tradition and gives Samuel L. Jackson one of his best recent roles.

He plays Foley, a con man who was forced to kill his best friend and fellow grifter. He did twenty-five years in prison for murder, and as we meet him, he's just getting out on parole. He makes a promise to himself that he will never go behind bars again, and that means having nothing to do with crime in any form. He gets a job working construction.

It's not that easy. A man named Ethan (Luke Kirby) approaches him with an offer: an easy "Samaritan" con, which means the con man poses as a friend doing the mark a favor. Foley says no. Ethan continues to follow him, turning up everywhere. Foley tells him to go to hell, using that anger beneath lowered brows that Jackson does so well.

The film takes place in Toronto, not a city often identified with noir, but then noir has no geographical requirements. Perhaps that accounts for the mid-Atlantic polish of a crime boss like Xavier (Tom Wilkinson), who has given Ethan a compelling reason to mastermind the con: He will kill him if he doesn't.

Here, as so often, Wilkinson has a compelling screen presence. He's a British actor I first remember particularly noticing in *In the Bedroom* (2001), but he was in many films before and since—more than one hundred credits in all. You may recall him from *Michael Clayton*, and he has the most touching role in *The Best Exotic Marigold Hotel.*

Anyway, Ethan has his reason to recruit Foley. And he eventually reveals another one, which I won't reveal. The strategy is to make it *necessary* for Foley to return to a life of crime, and Ethan has cards in his hand Foley doesn't even suspect.

The film does a good job of establishing Foley's lonely single life. He works, he lives in a little flat, he hangs out at a bar from the old days, he learns most of his onetime pals are dead or locked up. And now there must be a woman. All noirs have one, usually one with secrets. In the bar he befriends Iris (Ruth Negga), a slight, sweet-faced girl who needs defending. There's something about her vulnerability that appeals to him. She's like a wounded bird. Hers isn't an erotic appeal, at least not obviously, but who knows where it could lead?

I think we're at the point in the story now where I'd better make my excuses and leave. In a proper noir, nothing is as it seems, and I'll leave it at that. I will observe, however, that director David Weaver, who cowrote with Elan Mastai, does a precise job of springing his surprises and drawing all the plot threads together into a knot that he yanks in one of those delicious showdown scenes where personal urgencies and moral compulsions get all mixed up with death and blood.

Jackson was a coproducer on this film, probably because he liked the complexity of the role. *The Samaritan* has the patience to establish its setup, and that's important in a noir, in which action deferred is more important than action indulged. The final resolution is perhaps a little hasty. But there's something here.

## Sanctum ★ ½

R, 109 m., 2011

Richard Roxburgh (Frank), Rhys Wakefield (Josh), Ioan Gruffudd (Carl), Alice Parkinson (Victoria), Dan Wyllie (Crazy George). Directed by Alister Grierson and produced by Ben Browning, James Cameron, Ryan Kavanaugh,

Michael Maher, Peter Rawlinson, and Andrew Wight. Screenplay by Wight and John Garvin.

*Sanctum* tells the story of a terrifying adventure in an incompetent way. Some of it is exciting, the ending is involving, and all of it is a poster child for the horrors of 3-D used wrongly. The film is being heavily marketed as a "James Cameron Production," but if this were a "James Cameron Film," I suspect it would have fewer flaws and the use of 3-D would be much improved.

The movie, based on a true story, involves a scuba-diving expedition into the Esa-ala Caves of New Guinea, said to be the largest cave system in the world. The plan is to retrace an already explored route to reach a "base camp" somewhere far beneath the surface, and then to press on, perhaps to find how the surface water draining into the caves finds its way to the sea. There's no *need* to discover this, you understand, but after some loss of life, Frank (Richard Roxburgh), the leader of the expedition, tells his son, Josh (Rhys Wakefield), that only in a cave does he feel fully alive; the humdrum surface world is not for him and "human eyes have never seen this before."

After awkward opening scenes of almost startling inanity, we find ourselves deep inside the cave system, and our heroes deep in trouble. They are combining dangerous climbing with risky diving, and it's a good question why an inexperienced girlfriend was allowed to come along. Still, tactical errors are not what concerned me. I only wanted to figure out what was happening, and where, and why.

This movie should be studied in film classes as an example of inadequate film continuity. At no point are we oriented on our location in the cave as a whole or have a clear idea of what the current cave space looks like. If you recall Cameron's *Titanic*, its helpful early animation briefed us on the entire story of how the great ship sank. That was a great help in comprehending the events of its final hour. In *Sanctum*, there's a computer animation showing the known parts of the cave, but as the POV whizzes through caverns and tunnels, it achieves only a demonstration of computer animation itself. We learn damn little about the cave. The animated map even flips on its horizontal axis, apparently to show off. Hey, I can do stuff like that on my Mac, and then my hair is parted on the other side!

The movie is a case study of how not to use 3-D. *Sanctum* takes place in claustrophobic spaces with very low lighting, which are the last places you want to make look dimmer than they already are. The lighting apparently comes from battery-powered headlamps, and the characters are half in darkness and half in gloom. Now why put on a pair of glasses and turn down the lights?

One purpose of 3-D is to create the illusion of depth. One way to do this is to avoid violating the fourth wall by seeming to touch it. Let me give a famous example from *Jaws 3-D*. The problem with that movie is that when the shark attacked, it was so big its body touched the sides of the screen, and the 3-D illusion was lost. (The movie has a scene of an eel attack, and *that's* scary.)

Alas, the cinematographer of *Sanctum*, Jules O'Loughlin, consistently touches the side of the screen. He even has the curious practice of framing middle action with large, indistinct blocks of foreground stones and stuff. These are out of focus so that the midrange can look sharp, and 3-D only makes us wonder why the closer objects are less distinct. In close quarters he has to use many close-ups, and those, too, get old in a hurry in 3-D. The Brendan Fraser 3-D movie *Journey to the Center of the Earth* (2008) did a much better job of placing its actors in its spaces. Of course, the spaces were mostly f/x, but there you are.

In its editing continuity, *Sanctum* doesn't make clear how the actions of one character relate to another's. There is great spatial disorientation in the use of the close shots. There is a scene where a character gets in trouble underwater, and I invite anyone to explain exactly what happens. The movie has a tactic to distract from this visual confusion. Three team members follow many of the events from above on a large computer monitor. Alas, we don't see what they see. We only get reaction shots of them seeing it. Where does their screen image come from? Head-mounted webcams? A cam in that submersible lighting device? I dunno. How is the image transmitted? I doubt the cell phone service is great in a cave in the jungles of New Guinea. Maybe they set up a LAN? How is it powered? They even complain about the batteries on their headlamp.

There are a few closing scenes that involve the ruthless reality of who survives in a cave and who doesn't. One of these involves Frank and Josh. We've had a long wait, but the scene works. It has absolutely no need for 3-D. I wonder if people will go to *Sanctum* thinking the James Cameron name is a guarantee of high-quality 3-D. Here is a movie that can only harm the reputations of Cameron and 3-D itself.

## Sarah's Key ★ ★ ½

PG-13, 111 m., 2011

Kristin Scott Thomas (Julia Jarmond), Melusine Mayance (Sarah Starzynski), Niels Arestrup (Jules Dufaure), Frederic Pierrot (Bertrand Tezac), Michel Duchaussoy (Edouard Tezac), Dominique Frot (Genevieve Dufaure), Natasha Mashkevich (Madame Starzynski), Gisele Casadesus (Mame), Aidan Quinn (William Rainsferd). Directed by Gilles Paquet-Brenner and produced by Stephane Marsil. Screenplay by Paquet-Brenner and Serge Joncour, based on the novel by Tatiana De Rosnay.

*Sarah's Key* cuts back and forth between a tragic story involving the Holocaust and an essentially trivial, feel-good story about a modern-day reporter. It's an awkward fit, and diminishes the impact of the story set earlier.

In Paris in the early 1940s, we meet a Jewish family that is targeted by the Nazis for deportation to a death camp. Acting quickly, the family's young daughter, Sarah (Melusine Mayance) shoves her kid brother into a closet and tells him to keep quiet and stay there. The key mentioned in the movie's title is her key to that closet, and stays with her during a harrowing series of events.

In the present day, we meet a reporter named Julia Jarmond (Kristin Scott Thomas) whose research leads her into events of that period. The French have been none too forthcoming about their record under the Nazis (apart from a remarkable number of them claiming to be Resistance fighters), but Julia is focused on a more narrow subject, that first targeting of the Parisian Jews.

The link between the two stories is an improbable coincidence. The family of Julia's husband, Bertrand (Frederic Pierrot), came into possession of that apartment and its (by then empty) closet, and now he's remodeling it for them to live in. If his family had seized it from Sarah's family, that would be fraught with meaning, but no, it just happened to work out that way, and his family was not actively evil.

The center of interest in the story involves Sarah, whose life is spared because of extraordinary events and her own ingenuity and courage. She is taken in by a rural couple, survives the war, and emigrates to America. To lend urgency to Julia's story, we learn she is pregnant and must decide whether, at her age, to have the baby.

Doesn't this feel to you like an issue cobbled together for narrative purposes? Now that she has explored the horrors of the past and discovered she and Sarah have only a few degrees of separation, is it acceptable, in movie terms, for her to decide against the baby? And whatever she decides, what difference does that make to the members of Sarah's family, and millions of others, who died in the Holocaust?

Kristin Scott Thomas is excellent, as she so often is. Flawlessly bilingual, she has taken advantage, in films like this, *Tell No One* (2006), and *I've Loved You for So Long* (2008) of the greater openness in France to dramas about grown-ups. She does all that is probably possible to invest Julia's story with the emotional weight of Sarah's, but it is Sarah's key, and this is Sarah's story.

## Saving Face ★ ★ ★ ½

NO MPAA RATING, 40 m., 2012

A documentary directed by Sharmeen Obaid-Chinoy and Daniel Junge.

Every year in Pakistan, at least one hundred men feel entitled to throw acid into the faces of their wives, some of them still in early adolescence. Many of these attacks go unreported. In some cases, the women feel they must return to their husbands' homes after the hospital because they have no other way to pay for the care of their children.

One of the women in *Saving Face* looks as if

half her face has melted. Her lips are twisted and distorted, her left eye socket so damaged it cannot accept a glass eye, her throat a mass of scars. We follow her through a series of plastic surgeries performed by Dr. Mohammad Jawad, a Pakistani doctor from London who volunteers his time. He is able to make the lips seem more normal, and to cover some of the damaged facial area with a synthetic skin substitute. It no longer looks melted, but now seems rubbed flat of its features.

Another woman says her husband threw acid into her face, and then her sister-in-law threw gasoline on her and her mother-in-law set her afire. They locked her into a room, intending her to die. The husband was arrested, and looks straight into the camera while saying his wife set herself on fire. If you look in the burn unit of the Islamabad hospital, he claims, you'll find that most of the women there set themselves on fire, or threw acid at themselves.

Dr. Jawad, a large, affable man, enlists a colleague from Dubai to construct a prosthesis for the woman without an eye socket. He confides that he can barely endure listening to the stories he is forced to hear. When he learned about the acid attacks in London, he says, he felt obligated to return to his homeland and volunteer his surgical skills to mend the faces and the lives of women who in some cases feel unable to step outside the door.

This film, which won the 2012 Academy Award for best short documentary, is only forty minutes long. It has the impact of an epic. Instead of giving us outraged speeches, it takes a realistic, level-headed view of the people involved and of the surgical process. It follows the efforts of a woman member of the Pakistan Parliament to introduce a bill establishing life sentences for those guilty of acid attacks, and it passes unanimously.

That is progress. But the victims are still faced with the challenge of raising a family, and given local interpretations of Muslim law, they often feel they must remain in the house of their husband's family. One woman files for divorce—but her husband refuses her one because that would shame him. He feels no shame about attacking her with acid. I forgot: She attacked herself.

This heartbreaking film has relevance to the cruelties toward women that are sanctioned in many lands. There is no justification for such behavior in the laws of the Muslim religion, but in many societies the dominance of men over women is so interpreted as to almost sanction physical violence. Men own women, who have few rights. One woman shows us a brick wall that blocks a doorway in her home, preventing her from ever seeing her daughter again. In some lands, women accused of adultery are bricked inside sealed rooms for the rest of their lives.

I find it notable that the women victims in this film repeatedly evoke the name of God, even assuming that God has permitted such things. Words fail me.

The codirectors of *Saving Face,* Sharmeen Obaid-Chinoy and Daniel Junge, shared the Oscar, and Obaid-Chinoy is the first Pakistani to ever win one. A friend of mine noted that the subject of the film was never mentioned on the Academy Awards broadcast.

## Scrappers ★ ★ ★ ½

NO MPAA RATING, 90 m., 2010

A documentary directed by Brian Ashby, Ben Kolak, and Courtney Prokopas.

In the alley I see them at least once a week, the men with their grocery carts, collecting tin cans and other treasure. Some will have a heap as tall as themselves. I learn from the new film *Scrappers* that the same trade happens in Chicago on a larger scale, with men trolling the city for scrap metal and emptying their trucks at scrap-metal yards. For this valuable work they could make a living, until the economy collapsed.

An urban legend has grown up that such men steal copper gutters and the aluminum off the sides of garages. Such theft has been committed, but by desperate creatures of the night, not family men like Otis and Oscar who are the backbone of the scrapper trade. "I paint my name and my phone number on the side of my truck," Otis says. "They know this truck down to 157th Street."

These are happy men. Otis is almost poetic about his joy in cruising alleys and vacant lots for salable metals. He's on his own, alone in the truck, chatting with his wife every half hour or so. Housewives know him and flag him down to carry out an old refrigerator. For one lady he removes two old boilers from her basement, no charge, just for the resale value, and considers himself lucky.

They are strong. With dollies but no forklifts, they lever heavy loads into the backs of pickups with high plywood sides. Their trucks are weighed on the way into a scrapyard and on the way out—they're paid for the difference. They work in all weather, fourteen hours a day, collect cash money at the end, come home to their wives and kids. The film says there are thousands of scrappers in Chicago. I'm reminded of Agnes Varda's great *The Gleaners and I* (2000), about the French vocation of scavenging.

Otis is seventy-three, born in Chicago. Oscar looks to be in his forties and is from Honduras, and I have the impression he may be undocumented. They do useful work. "Mayor Daley is supposed to be a green mayor," says one housewife as she watches a heavy load hauled out of her basement, "but it doesn't seem like they pick up much."

Scrappers look for wire, pipes, aluminum, brass, copper, plain iron, and steel. The scrap yards heap it up, process it into particles about the size of Cheerios, and ship it mostly to China, where it comes back to us and ends up in the alley again. In 2007, we learn, a scrapper could earn $200 to $300 a ton. In 2008, when the market collapsed and new construction ended, the price dropped to $20. Scrappers became desperate.

Fortunate people sneer at them, write them off as bums or thieves. Few in the middle class work as hard all day as these men do—and, quite possibly, work as usefully. You cannot be a drunk and work this hard. You can't support a drug habit. But you can support a family, and *Scrappers* goes into the homes of Otis and Oscar to meet their wives—stable, stalwart women—and their kids. The loyalty in these homes is palpable.

Otis lives in senior housing, but moves out because of bedbugs and water leaking everywhere. He has worked as a scrapper for more than forty years, but it's in his own hallway that he slips on water and gets a concussion. He sits by a hospital window and tells his wife how much he wants to get back to work. I think it's Oscar who compares scrapping to fishing—you go out in the morning hoping for a good catch.

The film was made by Chicagoans Brian Ashby, Ben Kolak, and Courtney Prokopas. They put in the hours in the alleys and brought back a human document. It is necessary we have these films because our lives are so closed off we don't understand the function these men perform. You want green; there ain't nobody greener than Oscar and Otis.

## Scre4m ★ ★

R, 111 m., 2011

Neve Campbell (Sidney Prescott), Courteney Cox (Gale Weathers), David Arquette (Dewey Riley), Emma Roberts (Jill Roberts), Hayden Panettiere (Kirby Reed), Rory Culkin (Charlie Walker). Directed by Wes Craven and produced by Craven, Iya Labunka, and Kevin Williamson. Screenplay by Williamson.

The great pleasure in the *Scream* movies is that the characters have seen other horror films. At times they talk as if they're in the chat room of a horror site. Wes Craven's *Scre4m*, the typographically skewed fourth movie in the series, opens with a clever series of horror scenes that emerge one from another like nested Russian dolls, and Kevin Williamson's dialogue is smart and knowing. All through the movie, *Scre4m* lets us know that it knows exactly what it's up to—and then goes right ahead and gets up to it.

The premise is that a psychopath has returned to the town of Woodsboro, which has already seen so many fatal slashings you question why anyone still lives there, let alone watches horror movies. This killer seems at times to be supernormal, is able to appear simultaneously at the front and back doors of a house, and predict precisely where victims will be, and when. As a result, the body count in *Scre4m* mounts relentlessly until you wonder whether everyone in the cast is going to be killed, with the movie ending on an empty room (with the phone ringing—heh, heh).

There is a dark nihilism here that seems to appeal to *Scream* fans. No one deserves to die, but so many do, and horribly, with geysers of blood spurting from their wounds. Why must they die? Why is the killer, "Ghost Face," so driven? The motive is eventually revealed, but I wouldn't go so far as to say it's explained.

Neve Campbell returns as Sidney Prescott, a hometown girl who has written a best-seller and has returned to Woodsboro to promote it. My own inclination would be to stay the hell away from the location of the killings in the original *Scream*, but hey, that's just me. Also back are David Arquette as the local sheriff, and Courteney Cox, the newscaster who is now his wife.

Sidney's cousin Jill (Emma Roberts) has a posse of fellow teenagers who spend most of the time picking up the phone and answering the door when they absolutely shouldn't. They're sophisticated; they know that in a horror movie when you walk past a dark doorway, something is likely to jump out at you. But when they get a call from someone saying, "My face will be the last sight you see," and then the doorbell rings—do they answer it? Of course they do. Survival of the fittest needs another million years to take effect in Woodsboro.

Karl Malden once said the hardest thing he ever had to do as an actor was act as if he didn't know he was about to be hit in the head with a beer can. He could have taken lessons from these girls, who go through the whole movie acting as if they're not about to be stabbed to death.

Wes Craven is a good director, and the film is done with some wit and style. The actors do what they can in a film that doesn't care about human insights. The characters are almost preternatural in their detachment; if you were embedded in events like these, wouldn't you be paralyzed with panic? Let's say you were the sheriff. Would you act so competent when you were obviously powerless? What about the film's many ambulance drivers? In *Bringing Out the Dead,* Nicolas Cage was in a constant frenzy, and that was supposedly a realistic story. In *Scre4m,* the locals are almost catatonic in their ability to carry on dialogue. How can you dissect a plot when you know you're next on the dissection table?

Maybe that's the point. Perhaps Craven and Williamson are making an ironic and cynical comment on the bloody tradition of the genre. Are they counting on their knowing fans to pick up all their self-aware nods? Could be. Does anyone—*anyone*—watch a movie like this as if it's in any way depicting reality? I dunno. *Scre4m* provides exactly what its audience will expect: one victim after another being slashed, skewered, stabbed, gutted, and sliced, with everyone in on the joke. Maybe that's your idea of a good time.

## A Screaming Man ★ ★ ★ ½

NO MPAA RATING, 92 m., 2011

Youssouf Djaoro (Adam Ousmane), Dioucounda Koma (Abdel Ousmane), Emile Abossolo M'bo (District Chief), Hadje Fatime N'Goua (Mariam), Marius Yelolo (David), Djeneba Kone (Djeneba), Heling Li (Madame Wang). Directed by Mahamat-Saleh Haroun and produced by Florence Stern. Screenplay by Haroun.

Adam was the swimming champion of central Africa years ago and now rules over the swimming pool of a luxury hotel. Tall, stately, and middle-aged, he provides towels and services for the mostly white and Asian guests, and cleans up the area at day's end. He's assisted by his son, Abdel, and as *A Screaming Man* opens, the two of them have a contest to see who can hold his breath the longest underwater.

Somewhere offscreen, indirectly alluded to, a civil war is under way in this nation, Chad. Business at the hotel falls off. It has been purchased by a Chinese group, and now Madame Wang, the manager, makes staff cuts. She informs Adam (Youssouf Djaoro) that he will be replaced at the pool by his son, Abdel (Dioucounda Koma), and made a security guard in charge of the hotel gates. He's lucky to have a job. His best friend, David (Marius Yelolo), the hotel chef, loses his.

"But the pool is my life!" Adam says. His long-ago swimming medal validates his existence. Moving sadly to the front gate, he wears a hotel uniform and becomes, in a way, a mirror image of the hero of Murnau's famous *The Last Laugh* (1924). In that film, a hotel doorman measures his worth by his uniform and identity; a similar job is, for Adam, devastating. He regards his son, now holding "his" job, balefully.

The unique quality of the movie is to look

at Adam's life, the way he values his job more than his son, and the way status conferred by a Western hotel has bewitched him. He pours out his discontent with his wife, and shares it with the district police chief (Emile Abossolo M'bo), who has been charged with raising troops to fight in the war. These elements play out in an agonizing choice that Adam feels he must make between his son and his "life" as the pool man.

The film was directed by Mahamat-Saleh Haroun, and won the Jury Prize at Cannes 2010 (Haroun himself was a member of the 2011 jury). He is a clear and confident filmmaker. It's easy to imagine how the story, as I have simplified it, could have been a clunky melodrama, but *A Screaming Man* is about what happens within the characters, especially Adam. He never screams, but we feel him screaming.

Haroun was born in Chad, a former French colony, and moved to France at about the age of twenty-one. He has cited Ozu as one of his influences, and like the master he is attentive to the way compositions and body language create dramatic effects. His strategy here is not to have Adam act out his crisis, but to allow us time to empathize with him and understand the emotional choices he is making. One of the crucial events in the film takes place offscreen, and that is the best place for it because what happens isn't as important as its effects.

The movie makes no obvious statements about postcolonial Africa, but it is clear that colonialism in Adam's case requires not so much colonial rulers as those who were ruled. The hotel to begin with, and his job itself, and the Chinese who buy it, are all part of an economic process that dictates his life. He finds his whole value as a man in a job that essentially involves only a title.

*A Screaming Man* is being released by Film Movement, whose members received their DVDs in the mail quite some time ago. FM is a valuable enterprise that searches festivals and elsewhere for films worthy of being seen, which are perhaps not commercial in today's market. Members get the first (sometimes the only) look. The films are chosen well; I saw this film at Cannes 2010, admired it, and wondered at the time if it would find a release. As we find our way through a troubled time for foreign and art films, enterprises like Film Movement give hope.

*Note: Film Movement on the Web: http://www.filmmovement.com.*

## Season of the Witch ★ ★

PG-13, 95 m., 2011

Nicolas Cage (Behmen), Ron Perlman (Felson), Stephen Campbell Moore (Debelzaq), Claire Foy (The Girl), Stephen Graham (Hagamar), Ulrich Thomsen (Eckhart), Robert Sheehan (Kay), Christopher Lee (Cardinal D'Ambroise). Directed by Dominic Sena and produced by Alex Gartner and Charles Roven. Screenplay by Bragi Schut Jr.

I lost track of the sieges and battles. *Season of the Witch* opens with a series of helpfully labeled sequences in which desert battles are fought, cites are sacked, buttresses stormed, redoubts doubted, enclosures enclosed, and so on. I didn't take notes, but an example might be "The Siege of Synecdoche, April 1, AD 1239."

Anyway, there's a slew of them. Crusaders in armor do battle with fierce desert tribesmen under the blazing sun. Heads are lopped off and roll across the plain. Horses whinny, women scream, children flee, warriors are disemboweled, limbs are severed, dogs would bark if there were dogs. The horror!

After about a dozen years of this, we pause for a discussion between the two hero Crusaders, Behmen (Nicolas Cage) and Felson (Ron Perlman). Yes, Cage and Perlman, so you suspect *Season of the Witch* will not be an exercise in understatement. "The killing of the women and children must stop!" they agree. Having arrived at this conclusion after twelve years of rape and pillage, they do not qualify as quick studies. The comrades abandon the armies of the Crusades, hit the road, and happen across a town somewhere in the vastness.

They have an excellent reason for ending up here, of all places: Why, this is the very same town of the pretitle sequence! Where three women were forced to confess to witchcraft, thrown backward off a bridge with nooses around their necks, hanged dead, and then prudently drowned in the river below! We liberals are earnestly deploring the superstition that forced them to confess Salem-style, until they spring back up from the dark waters and, hey, they *were* witches. Sometimes Glenn Beck is right.

Time has passed since that day (whether the full twelve years, I cannot say), and Behmen and Felson are quickly assigned to convey a surviving (if technically dead) witch (Claire Foy) to a distant monastery where there is a crumbling ancient tome containing the only known incantation that can exorcise her and bring an end to the Black Plague—so hey, we're back in medieval Europe now, specifically Hungary. A possible clue to this film's mind-set as a guy flick is that the Claire Foy character has no name and is known only as The Girl. Not even The Witch.

I am about out of Astonishments for you, but buckle your seat belt for this one: The director, Dominic Sena, has been inspired by Ingmar Bergman's *The Seventh Seal* (1957), that classic tale of a knight who returns from the Crusades and encounters Death on the road. Audiences for *Season of the Witch* may not be thickly larded with students of *The Seventh Seal*, but those few will be rewarded by sundry parallels and allusions. Ever since Bergman's *The Virgin Spring* was remade as *The Last House on the Left*, his work has suggested a rich mine for homage.

You know I am a fan of Nic Cage and Ron Perlman (whose very existence made *Hellboy* possible). Here, like cows, they eat the scenery, regurgitate it to a second stomach found only in actors, and chew it as cud. It is a noble effort, but I prefer them in their straight-through *Human Centipede* mode.

## Secretariat ★ ★ ★ ★

PG, 122 m., 2010

Diane Lane (Penny Chenery), John Malkovich (Lucien Laurin), Dylan Walsh (Jack Tweedy), Dylan Baker ((Hollis Chenery), Margo Martindale (Miss Ham), Nelsan Ellis (Eddie Sweat), Otto Thorwarth (Ronnie Turcotte), Fred Dalton Thompson (Bull Hancock), James Cromwell (Ogden Phipps), Scott Glenn (Chris Chenery), Kevin Connolly (Bill Nack). Directed by Randall Wallace and produced by Mark Ciardi, Pete DeStefano, and Gordon Gray. Screenplay by Mike Rich, suggested by *Secretariat: The Making of a Champion* by William Nack.

When Secretariat died at nineteen, my friend Bill Nack told me, the autopsy revealed that his heart was two and a half times the size of an average horse's. Bill had followed the horse for its entire life and wrote the book *Secretariat*, which inspired this film. Bill and I became good friends at Illinois in 1962. I remember him telling me in the 1970s about a racehorse he admired with great passion. I thought it was curious that Nack, who could recite long passages from Fitzgerald and Eliot by heart, had been lured away from literature by a racehorse. Now I understand. He found literature in a racehorse.

Bill has been the close friend of a lifetime. I would call that not a conflict of interest in writing this review, but more of a declaration. I have no fear in suggesting that his twenty years as Secretariat's biographer and his daily presence on the set contributed materially to this film. *Secretariat* just *knows* all sorts of things, and many of them I knew from Bill telling me over the years. They also grow from his love of horses, which began when he was a stable boy. Let me tell a story: When Bill was a reporter at *Newsday*, he climbed on a desk at an office party and recited the names of every Derby winner, correctly, in order. When he climbed down, the editor quietly called him aside and said, "How do you know that?" Then he made Bill the paper's turf writer, in some way setting this movie in motion.

You don't need me to tell you Secretariat was the crowning glory of the Sport of Kings. It is thirty-seven years since he set records in the Kentucky Derby and the Belmont, and those records stand today. It was said by some he was better over shorter distances, and that at the Belmont he would fade against his great rival Sham, who would show more endurance. He won the Belmont by thirty-one lengths. I knew that. Everybody knows that. Bill has shown me video of that race, with the astonishing gap between Secretariat and the rest of the field. So why, when I saw the race in the film, did I have tears in my eyes?

It was because *Secretariat* is a movie that allows us to understand what it really meant.

This isn't some cornball formula film. It doesn't have a contrived romance. It's certainly not about an underdog: At the Belmont, Secretariat paid only $2.20 on a $2 bet, and 5,617 holders of winning tickets held them as souvenirs (a wise investment; those tickets go on eBay for as much as $1,000). *Secretariat* takes none of those mundane paths. It is a great film about greatness, the story of the horse and the no less brave woman who had faith in him.

Penny Chenery (Diane Lane) was the daughter of a Virginia horse farm owner. Her father (Scott Glenn) was ill, and his family thought they should sell the farm. But she could read lineages. She flipped a coin with a millionaire and "lost," but won the mare she wanted—and she was there in the stable when the mare gave birth. The groom said he'd never before seen a horse stand up on its legs that soon after birth.

There was something about Secretariat. Bill, who was a regular visitor at Meadow Farm throughout the horse's life, tried to get me to understand: The people around the horse felt it was blessed. Penny Chenery refused to sell the farm, turned down an offer of $7 million for the still-untested horse, and left her husband and family behind in Colorado to commute to Virginia. She had faith. So did the groom, Eddie Sweat (Nelsan Ellis), who was with Secretariat more than any other human being during the horse's life. And so did Lucien Laurin (John Malkovich), the trainer who had been trying to retire when Penny hauled him away from his golf clubs.

The movie focuses closely on the owner, the trainer, and the groom. It has no time for foolishness. When the time comes for the coin flip with millionaire Ogden Phipps (James Cromwell), we understand why Mrs. Chenery wants the mare she does, and director Randall Wallace underlines that with admirable economy, using a close-up of Malkovich studying a breeding chart that works better than five minutes of dialogue.

Gene Siskel used to say his favorite movies were about what people actually do all day. That's what *Secretariat* is. It pays us the compliment of really caring about thoroughbred racing. In a low-key way, it conveys an enormous amount of information. And it creates characters who, because of spot-on casting, are vivid, human, and complex. Consider how it deals with the relationship between Penny and her husband, Jack Tweedy (Dylan Walsh). They became estranged because of her decision, Nack says, but the movie only implies that rather than getting mired in a soap opera.

As a woman, Penny is closed out of racing's all-boys club. If a man neglected his family for a racehorse, that might be common. But a woman is committing some sin against nature. And when she refuses to sell, her whole family—husband, brother, everyone—put enormous pressure on her. They were sure her decision was taking money out of their pockets. How she raises money to keep the farm is ingenious lateral thinking, and best of all, it's accurate.

This whole movie feels authentic. Diane Lane, who is so good in so many kinds of roles, makes Penny as a smart woman with great faith in her own judgment and the courage to bet the farm on it. Every hair in place, always smartly turned out, she labors in the trenches with Lucien and Eddie, negotiates unflinchingly with the Old Boys, eats the stomach-churning meals at the diners where the track crowd hangs out. She looked at the greatest racehorse in the world and *knew* she was right, when all about her were losing their heads and blaming it on her.

Of the actors, I especially enjoyed John Malkovich. He has a way of conveying his reasoning by shorthand and implication. He creates a horse trainer slow to tip his hand, which is correct. No role in Mike Rich's screenplay is overwritten, or tries to explain too much. Like *The Social Network*, another contender for year-end awards, it has supreme confidence in its story and faith that we will find it fascinating. This is one of the year's best films.

To my shame, I used to kid Bill that he wrote stuff like, "Big Red knew it was an important day," as if he could read Secretariat's mind. He wrote nothing of the sort. We would speculate about what a horse does know. W. G. Sebald wrote: "Men and animals regard each other across a gulf of mutual incomprehension." Yes, I think so. But between Secretariat and his human family, something was comprehended. There's a scene here when Penny Chenery and her horse look each other in the eye for a long time on an important morning. You can't tell me they weren't both thinking the same thing.

## The Secret in Their Eyes ★ ★ ★ ★

R, 129 m., 2010

Ricardo Darin (Benjamin Esposito), Soledad Villamil (Irene Menendez Hastings), Guillermo Francella (Pablo Sandoval), Pablo Rago (Ricardo Morales), Javier Godino (Isidoro Gomez). Directed by Juan Jose Campanella and produced by Campanella, Mariela Besuievski, and Carolina Urbieta. Screenplay by Campanella, based on the novel by Eduardo Sacheri.

*The Secret in Their Eyes* opens with the meeting, after many years, of Benjamin (Ricardo Darin) and Irene (Soledad Villamil). She is a judge. He is a retired criminal investigator. They are just a little too happy to see each other. Twenty-five years ago, when she was assistant to a judge and he was an investigator under her, they were involved in a brutal case of rape and murder. Benjamin visited the crime scene, and the corpse of the dead woman spoke eloquently of the brutality of the crime. Two workmen were arrested and convicted. Benjamin was never convinced of their guilt. Now he tells Irene that on his own time he wants to write about the case.

This commences an absorbing back-and-forth journey through time, between Buenos Aires in 1974 and 2000, which reopens both the crime and the unacknowledged feeling that has remained all these years between Irene and Benjamin. That's where their personal appeal comes into play. The actress Soledad Villamil is, forgive me, my idea of a Woman. Grown-up, tallish, healthy, brunette, sane, and perhaps she was cast for her eyes because the film contains a lot of close-ups and they're required to conceal secrets. Think of Anne Archer. Playing Irene at ages twenty-five years apart, she is never too young or too old, but standing right there.

Ricardo Darin makes her a worthy partner as Benjamin. His rank was too low, his pay too small, her presence too assured for him to trust the signals he must have known she was sending. He's one of those men on whom a beard seems inevitable. There is a sadness about him. He has never stopped thinking about the murder case, and we understand—although the movie is indirect about this—that the investigation was mishandled at the time because of Argentina's diseased right-wing politics.

Without being too obvious about it, the film reassembles the strands of two stories, the murder case and the unfinished emotions between Benjamin and Irene. It is filled with vivid characters. Sandoval (Guillermo Francella) is Benjamin's alcoholic assistant in the investigation, one of those drunks who may be incompetent but is not useless. He and Benjamin, and all the legal side, engage in the droll formality of addressing one another by fanciful titles. Morales (Pablo Rago) is the husband of the dead woman, still obsessed with her death. Gomez (Javier Godino) has always been Benjamin's real suspect, and there is a scene involving him in a soccer stadium that I have no idea how it could have been filmed, special effects or no.

Juan Jose Campanella is the writer-director, and here is a man who creates a complete, engrossing, lovingly crafted film. He is filled with his stories. *The Secret in Their Eyes* is a rebuke to formula screenplays. We grow to know the characters, and the story pays due respect to their complexities and needs. There is always the sense that they exist in the *now*, and not at some point along a predetermined continuum. Sometimes I watch a film unspool like a tape measure, and I can sense how far we are from the end. Sometimes my imagination is led to live right along with it.

*The Secret in Their Eyes* surprised many by winning the 2010 Academy Award for best foreign-language film. Michael Haneke's *The White Ribbon,* another considerable film, was thought to be the front-runner. The Academy did a good thing when it reformed the foreign language voting, requiring all voters to see all five finalists. In 2009, with the Japanese winner *Departures,* and again in 2010, the voters had an advantage over the rest of us. Who is to say whether they were right? They voted as they felt, and in today's unhappy distribution scene, the Oscar means your chances of seeing this film are much increased. You won't regret it. This is a real movie, the kind they literally don't make very much anymore.

## The Secret of Kells ★ ★ ★

NO MPAA RATING, 75 m., 2010

With the voices of: Evan McGuire (Brendan), Christen Mooney (Aisling), Mick Lally (Brother Aidan), and Brendan Gleeson (Abbot Cellach). Directed by Tomm Moore, codirected by Nora Twomey, and produced by Moore, Didier Brunner, Viviane Vanfleteren, and Paul Young. Screenplay by Fabrice Ziolkowski.

When I went to Ireland to visit the set of *Ryan's Daughter,* the studio sent a car to ferry me and my cohort McHugh to the Dingle Peninsula. As we drove along we crossed an old bridge and the driver said, "Leprechauns made their home under this bridge." We stopped for petrol, and I quietly said to McHugh, "He doesn't know you're Irish and is giving us the tourist treatment." "Ebert," said McHugh, "he means it."

Did he mean it? Did McHugh believe that he meant it? With the Irish, the answer is yes and no. McHugh and his brothers told me how as lads they picked up change by discovering the Irish surnames of Yankee tourists and offering to show them where their ancestors lived. They always led them to the same shop in a little cottage, where the owner gave them a "consideration" for any purchases made.

What does this possibly have to do with *The Secret of Kells,* the new film that was one of this year's Oscar nominees for best animation? Quite a bit, I think. Here is a film about a young and very brave medieval monk named Brendan, a sacred book, a storied monastery, a fairy girl, and an alarming creature, a forest containing little nuts that make brilliant green inks. The fairy girl is quite real, as Brendan can see for himself. If there are any leprechauns, she no doubt knows them. If there are not, how does she know for sure?

The Irish are a verbal people, preserving legends in story and song, and although few Chicagoans may know there's a First Folio of Shakespeare in the Newberry Library, few Dubliners do NOT know that the Book of Kells reposes in Trinity College. I viewed it once. It is a painstakingly illuminated medieval manuscript preserving the four Gospels, and every page is a work of art. Many monks created it over many years.

Perhaps little Brendan was one of them. Perhaps some of that brilliant emerald green was his, extracted from nuts he gathered in the forest. Brendan (voice by Evan McGuire), the youngest and pluckiest monk in the walled monastery, befriends old Brother Aidan (Mick Lally), a traveler who has arrived bearing the precious book. Some pages remain to be created, and Aidan says Brendan must help. He can start by disobeying the Abbot (Brendan Gleeson), venturing outside the walls, and gathering the nuts.

This and his further adventures are related in Tomm Moore's film, which is a little like an illuminated manuscript itself. Just as every margin of the Book of Kells is crowded with minute and glorious decorations, so is every shot of the film filled with patterns and borders, arches and frames, doodads and scrimshaw images. The colors are bold and bright, the drawings are simplified and 2-D. That reflects the creation of the original book in the centuries before the discovery of perspective in the Renaissance.

Like the people in Nina Paley's *Sita Sings the Blues,* these move mostly back and forth within the same plane, which is only correct since perspective hasn't yet created spatial dimension. But there's no feeling of limitation. Indeed, in a season where animated images hurl themselves from the screen with alarming recklessness, I was grateful that these were content merely to be admired.

The movie has a wide appeal, with a gap in the middle. I think it will appeal to children young enough to be untutored in boredom, and to anyone old enough to be drawn in, or to appreciate the artistry. For those in between, the *Transformers*-damaged generation, it will seem to be composed in a quaint, unknown language.

## Seeking a Friend for the End of the World ★ ★ ★

R, 101 m., 2012

Steve Carell (Dodge), Keira Knightley (Penny), Connie Britton (Diane), Adam Brody (Owen), Rob Corddry (Warren), Gillian Jacobs (Waitress/Katie), Derek Luke (Speck), Melanie Lynskey (Karen), T. J. Miller (Chipper Host/Darcy), Mark Moses (Anchorman), Patton

Oswalt (Roache), William Petersen (Trucker). Directed by Lorene Scafaria and produced by Steve Golin, Joy Gorman, Steven M. Rales, and Mark Roybal. Screenplay by Scafaria.

If he were told the world were ending tomorrow, Martin Luther said, he would plant a tree. Werner Herzog would start a film. In *Seeking a Friend for the End of the World*, Steve Carell plays an insurance salesman, but finds little point in selling a life policy. An asteroid seventy miles wide is on a collision path with Earth, and governments have announced it will slam into its target in three weeks' time.

To me, even worse than this catastrophe would be foreknowledge of it. To die is one thing. How much worse to know that all the life that ever existed on this planet, and all it ever achieved, was to be obliterated. Dodge, the Carell character, looks a little gloomy at the best of times. Now life is really piling on. A space shuttle mission to destroy the asteroid has failed, and to make things worse, his wife has walked out on him and joined the man she really loves.

The end of the world is hardly a rare subject for movies; recently we've had *Melancholia* and *Another Earth*, and who could forget Don McKellar's bittersweet *Last Night* (1998). Lorene Scafaria, the writer-director of this film, approaches the subject as an opportunity for melancholy satire and some gentle romance. It amounts to sort of a romantic comedy, although it makes no promises of providing a happy ending.

Some people riot in the streets. There are looters, determined to have a new big-screen TV no matter how few days are left to watch it. There are orgies and mass baptisms. Cable news inevitably attaches a catchphrase and some theme music to the apocalypse. Radio stations have countdowns. Dodge, alone and lonely in his apartment, unexpectedly finds himself caring for a dog. That's when I realized what I would do if I knew the world was ending. I would find a homeless mother dog with puppies, and be calmed by her optimism.

Dodge meets Penny (Keira Knightley), a woman who lives in the next building. They begin to talk and become kindred spirits. She talks him into a road trip that would bring together two of their desires. He can look for the girl he's always thought he should have married, and she can seek her family.

The destination of this trip isn't really the point. Road trips are about who you meet along the way. They meet a man (William Petersen) who has hired a contract killer to shoot him, and a survivalist (Derek Luke) who unreasonably believes all of his preparations will help him, and they come across a chain restaurant named Chipper's. The shtick at this place is that the staff are all your best friends. The approaching Armageddon has cranked this routine into high gear, and everybody in the place is so desperately friendly it borders on madness.

How do you end a movie like this? I mean before the inevitable end, which logically must be a blank screen? How does Scafaria as a filmmaker create a third act? She produces a couple of unexpected characters who inspire some moments of truth, and there is a Hemingwayesque flight in a small aircraft that is supposed, I guess, to indicate that we face the worst with stoic endurance. These scenes are good enough in themselves, but aren't really adequate to bring a sense of closure.

The best parts of this sweet film involve the middle stretches, when time, however limited, reaches ahead, and the characters do what they can to prevail in the face of calamity. How can I complain that they don't entirely succeed? Isn't the dilemma of the plot the essential dilemma of life?

## Seeking Justice ★ ½

R, 105 m., 2012

Nicolas Cage (Will Gerard), January Jones (Laura Gerard), Guy Pearce (Simon), Jennifer Carpenter (Trudy), Harold Perrineau (Jimmy), Xander Berkeley (Lieutenant Durgan). Directed by Roger Donaldson and produced by Ram Bergman, Tobey Maguire, and James D. Stern. Screenplay by Robert Tannen.

Faithful readers are baffled by my loyal praise for Nicolas Cage. He seems to have been dismissed by the blogosphere as a lost cause, a bat$#!* overactor whose thrashing in some roles threatens to endanger bystanders. I continue to consider Cage a gifted (if uneven) actor, but a movie like *Seeking Justice* challenges my faith. Here is a story hammered together from discards at the Lunacy Factory. Attempting to find something to praise, I am reduced to this: Cage's performance is not boring.

He plays Will Gerard, a New Orleans high school English teacher, whose wife, Laura (January Jones), plays cello in an orchestra. One dark night on her way home she's assaulted and raped, and in the hospital waiting room, Will is approached by a creep named Simon (Guy Pearce), who offers to have Laura's attacker "taken care of." No money is involved; Will must simply promise to do Simon a small favor at some point in the future. Will resists at first, but becomes convinced that the Big Easy's leaky justice system will soon have the perp back on the street. If he decides he wants the bad guy whacked, Simon says, he should signal his decision by purchasing two chocolate bars from a vending machine outside the oncology department.

At which point, so early in the movie, I am asking myself: (1) Was Laura the victim of a random attack? (2) If so, how would Simon know all about the attacker only a few hours later the same evening? (3) If not, was the perp *assigned* to assault Laura as part of a larger plan? (4) Was the assault intended to provide a reason for Will to owe a favor to Simon? And my favorite: (5) Why the cockamamie signals with the chocolate bars? And (6) is either, or neither, of the men skulking about near the vending machines in on the scheme?

Because the movie has been directed with technical skill by Roger Donaldson, who has a lot of good movies to his name, we're inspired to care about such matters as the chocolate bars. Suspense is generated while Cage's fingers shake as he extracts dollar bills from his wallet. It builds as he steals sideways glances at the skulkers. (No one can glance sideways better than Nic Cage; remember how he stared down that shifty iguana in Werner Herzog's *Bad Lieutenant*?) One chocolate bar is dispensed by the machine. He pushes in more bills. A second chocolate bar! Why two? So he won't be mistaken by someone else who coincidentally was buying only one chocolate bar from that exact same vending machine in the middle of the night? Why not play it safe and have him buy three? Also, if he wants in on the revenge plan, why not bypass the chocolate bar routine and simply reply, "OK. I'm in."?

I ask because we never find out who was monitoring the chocolate sales, and my hopes were dashed when the chocolate bars were never required later in the movie—not even to be eaten! I was thinking maybe they'd have a message inside their wrappers.

Why do I carry on like this over such an early scene? Because all of *Seeking Justice* is constructed of such preposterous scenes. The only way to make sense of the movie is to conclude that an unlimited number of New Orleans citizens are in on the revenge scheme, are on call twenty-four hours a day, and have nothing better to do than shadow Will Gerard. These people include the police, an investigative journalist, and several people Will doesn't trust, or does trust but shouldn't. Despite the vast size of the conspiracy, which must require tens of thousands of dollars and unlimited man-hours, I still never found out the whole story behind the revenge operation, or Simon's precise role in it.

Nor did I understand how cars could be stationed one night outside *everywhere* Will might go. Nor how a highway chase was motivated, since its only obvious purpose was to have a chase scene in the movie. It did, however, supply the pleasure of seeing a middle-aged English teacher leap from his car, jump over the railing of a highway overpass, and crawl along beneath it before leaping to the lanes below and narrowly evading being hit by the usual honking and swerving trucks.

If you can imagine how worked up Nic Cage gets during all of that (and more! and more!), you may begin to comprehend why I admire the man. He may be the only actor in the world who could rise to this occasion and then keep right on rising even beyond it. I'd say he's earned the candy bars.

## Senna ★ ★ ½

PG-13, 104 m., 2011

A documentary featuring Ayrton Senna, Alain Prost, and Jean-Marie Balestre. Directed by Asif Kapadia and produced by Tim Bevan, Eric Fellner, and James Gay-Rees. Screenplay by Manish Pandey.

*Senna* is a documentary that focuses on the popular image of the great auto racer and leaves us to ponder the mystery. Ayrton Senna won the Formula One world championship three times, was cheated of it a fourth, was the beloved hero of his native Brazil, and died in a crash at thirty-four—when he was in the lead. All of that racing fans may already know. This film implies that he was consumed, inflamed, devoured by the need to win. Perhaps no one, least of all Senna, can say why.

He is a good-looking, nice boy when he has a surprise success in the Monaco Grand Prix. Earlier, he'd done well on the top-level go-kart circuit; his wealthy family could afford to send the boy to Europe for a world competition. In a few short years he leaped into the front ranks of Formula One drivers and exhibited an ability to come from far back in a pack and blaze past other cars.

At first he was happy to be a McLaren teammate of Alain Prost, the French champion. Then they became cool, and finally bitter rivals who did not speak. Between them was Jean-Marie Balestre, the French president of the Federation Internationale du Sport Automobile. When Senna and Prost collided during a 1989 Grand Prix in Japan, it looks to us as if Prost left a gap and moved too late to try to fill it again. The Federation ruled against Senna, gave him a suspended disqualification, and fined him. Much is said about Prost being better at the "politics" of Formula One than Senna; the implication is that Balestre was prejudiced in favor of his countryman.

The movie is edited entirely from Formula One archival video. There is no new footage in the film. The well-chosen voice-over narration is by Senna, his parents, his sister, Prost, and a great many television commentators. *Senna* lives entirely in the moment. The race footage is thrilling; much of it, including the seconds leading up to Senna's final crash, is from the camera mounted on his car.

That final one-car crash is an enigma. Senna, having joined the Williams-Renault team, has been complaining about his car. It failed him in two earlier races. He doesn't like the steering or the suspension. Experts later suggested the crash was due to mechanical failure. A man who believed deeply in his connection with God, he awakened on his final day, felt uneasy, and consulted his Bible, coming upon a passage in which God told him he would be united with Him on that day. Not precisely good news.

As I looked at Senna's face before the race, I felt I was looking at a man who expected to die. His doctor advised him to retire. "I can't," he said. What drove him? The film is enigmatic about his inner life. He "loved women," and is seen with many, but we learn nothing about his relationships. He drove faster than anyone else, in a sport where success is a hair's breadth from disaster. In a competition among risk takers, he took the most. But apparently that isn't why he crashed.

Earlier, Alain Prost, having finally won the world title, retired on the spot. Good for him. Senna won it three times, kept right on racing—and would have continued, I suspect, until he finally died on the track. That is not the portrait of a happy man, and although he pours magnums of champagne over his head on one podium after another, he doesn't look joyous so much as vindicated.

*Senna* is a documentary that does the job it sets out to do. I wish it had tried for more. It is a competent TV sports doc, the sort you'd expect to see on ESPN. Unless you are a big fan of Senna or Formula One, I don't know why you'd want to pay first-run prices to see it.

## A Separation ★ ★ ★ ★

PG-13, 123 m., 2012

Leila Hatami (Simin), Peyman Moadi (Nader), Shahab Hosseini (Hodjat), Sareh Bayat (Razieh), Sarina Farhadi (Termeh), Babak Karimi (Judge), Ali-Asghar Shahbazi (Nader's Father), Shirin Yazdanbakhsh (Simin's Mother), Kimia Hosseini (Somayeh), Merila Zarei (Miss Ghahraei). Directed, written, and produced by Asghar Farhadi.

*A Separation* is a film in which every important character tries to live a good life within the boundaries of the same religion. That this leads them into disharmony and brings them up before a judge is because no list of rules can account for human feelings. The film involves its audience in an unusually direct way because, although we can see the logic of everyone's position, our emotions often disagree.

The movie takes place in present-day Iran, a modern nation that attempts to live under Islamic law. Its story has no quarrel with Islam, but it demonstrates that the inflexible application of the letter of the law may frustrate the spirit of the law. This is true in all nations under all religions and all laws. Laws are an attempt to regulate hypothetical situations before they may arise. If laws were replaced by principles, they might be a better fit with human nature.

Imagine this situation. Nader and Simin (Peyman Moadi and Leila Hatami), a happily married middle-class couple in Tehran, have a sweet eleven-year-old daughter, Termeh (Sarina Farhadi), and Nader's senile father also lives with them. They have agreed in principle to move abroad, where they hope Termeh's prospects might be better. Simin is ready to leave now. Nader wants to stay for his father's sake.

"But he doesn't know you!" his wife says. "No, but I know him." Both are correct. Here we have the universal dilemma of Alzheimer's. At an impasse, Simin moves to her mother's apartment and as a necessity sues for divorce, although the two want to remain married. Nader hires a caregiver for his father. She is Razieh (Sareh Bayat). She keeps the nature of her job a secret from her husband, Hodjat (Shahab Hosseini), who as a strict Muslim would never allow her to work in a man's household without his wife present.

Nader returns one day to find his father tied to the bed and Razieh absent. She has a good reason for this, but Nader doesn't know it and neither do we. He fires her, and she accuses him of pushing her downstairs and causing a miscarriage. Hodjat sues Nader for manslaughter. One of the witnesses will be Miss Ghahraei (Merila Zarei), the daughter's tutor, who is sincere but may not be as reliable as she thinks herself.

That's what you must know about the plot. The case ends up in the office of an official interrogating judge (Babak Karimi), whose task is to hear evidence and evaluate it. He is a fair man, open-minded, and all the witnesses testify as truthfully as they can. But none of them has possession of all the facts, and the findings must be in accordance with religious law. Nader and Simin are moderate Muslims. Razieh is so religious that she questions whether she can change the underpants of a man, even though he is so old and sick. What drives her is the family's desperate poverty.

The writer-director, Asghar Farhadi, tells his story with a fair and even hand. His only agenda seems to be to express empathy. Although the judge may be tending against our own sympathies, we understand why he does so and may be correct to do so. That a director can make such a sympathetic film in such a troubled time is a tribute to his strength of character.

The actors, as sometimes happens, create those miracles that can endow a film with conviction. Moadi and Hatami, as husband and wife, succeed in convincing us their characters are acting from genuine motives; they love each other and want the best for their family, but are divided on how to act. That this leads them into a manslaughter case is by unhappy chance. Nor is the judge eager to punish.

*A Separation* provides a useful portrait of Iran today. Some inflamed American political rhetoric has portrayed it as a rogue nation eager to start nuclear war. All too many Americans, I fear, picture Iranians as camel-riding harem keepers. Certainly some of the punishments for adultery that we read about seem medieval. But this film portrays a more nuanced nation, and its decent characters are trying to do the right thing. To untangle right and wrong in this fascinating story is a moral challenge. I'd love to see the film with wise judges from American divorce courts and hear their decisions. Sometimes the law is not adequate to deal with human feelings.

## 7 Days in Slow Motion ★ ★ ★

NO MPAA RATING, 100 m., 2010

Teja (Ravi), Shiva Varma (Onka), Kunal Sharma (Hamid), Rajeshwari Sachdev-Badola (Ravi's Mom), Ayesha Jalil (Hamid's Mom), Vivek Mushran (Ravi's Dad). Directed and produced by Umakanth Thumrugoti. Screenplay by Thumrugoti.

Ravi, the young narrator of *7 Days in Slow Motion*, is obsessed with movies, and so are his friends Hamid and Onka. So when a professional-quality HD video camera falls into their hands, of course they are compelled to go immediately into production. There are two problems: They have to return the camera at the end of seven days, and on the seventh day they have to sit for final exams at their school.

That's the setup for an unexpected and entertaining look at upper-middle-class life in Hyderabad, a prosperous central Indian city that is the home of many digital industries and a large movie studio. These are privileged kids. Their parents chatter about the Ivy League schools they want them to attend. All depends on the all-important exams, however, and in an opening scene, Ravi (Teja) produces a pie chart picturing how his mother wants him to spend his time: 60 percent for studying, 2 percent for fun.

After the camera literally falls off the proverbial passing truck, they seize their opportunity to secretly produce a film while allegedly studying for exams. They need a story. One suggestion: "The plot from *Indecent Proposal,* the villain from *Terminator,* and the plot from *Titanic.*" They need expertise. Ravi buys *Directing for Dummies.*

And they need a cast. Here there is a problem. Ravi's seventeen-year-old cousin would seem to be ideal, but suddenly she's matched up with a forty-year-old man for an arranged marriage, and their plans (and her hopes of college) are upset.

The movie Ravi eventually edits out of his material turns out to have a much greater effect on his family than anyone could have anticipated. We are also not sure that he could have actually obtained all of those shots, but never mind.

The movie addresses two subjects much discussed in India: the pressure put on children to excel in school, and the unequal opportunities for boys and girls. It's a comedy, not a serious film, but those themes are there. American audiences, long taught to imagine India in terms of Mother Teresa's homeless, may be surprised by this portrait of go-getter, upward-bound Indians; India is said to have a larger middle class than the United States. Another element that goes without comment is that everyone in the movie speaks English fluently (as a great many Indians do).

The adventures of the boys in making the movie would be right at home in a Disney family comedy, and no wonder; Umakanth Thumrugoti, the writer and director, worked at Disney Animation for years, and did visual effects on *Chicken Little, Treasure Planet,* and *Pocahontas.*

The kids, around ten years old, are all good-looking and energetic on camera. Teja, who plays Ravi, and Shiva Varma, who plays Onka, are seasoned veterans of "Tollywood," the Telugu film industry that's sort of a popular, low-rent version of Bollywood. Varma is so good-looking, indeed, that when his cousin forcibly makes him up to step into the female lead, he's almost too comely.

The Indian love of riotous displays of bright colors is everywhere on display. And the film contains several songs and a dance number, which seem to be obligatory in films from India. *7 Days in Slow Motion* is a cheerful family entertainment, completely accessible to English-speaking audiences. Will it get much distribution? As nearly as I can tell, its current engagement at Chicago's Facets Cinematheque is the North American premiere.

## Seven Days in Utopia ★

G, 105 m., 2011

Lucas Black (Luke Chisholm), Robert Duvall (Johnny Crawford), Melissa Leo (Lily), Deborah Ann Woll (Sarah), Jerry Ferrara (Joe Buckner), Joseph Lyle Taylor (Martin Chisholm). Directed by Matt Russell and produced by Jason Berman and Mark G. Mathis. Screenplay by Russell, David L. Cook, Rob Levine, and Sandra Thrift, based on the novel *Golf's Sacred Journey: Seven Days at the Links of Utopia*, by Cook.

I would rather eat a golf ball than see this movie again. It tells the dreadful parable of a pro golfer who was abused by his dad, melts down in the Texas Open, and stumbles into the clutches of an insufferable geezer in the town of Utopia (population 375) who promises him that after seven days in Utopia he will be playing great golf. He will also find Jesus, but for that you don't have to play golf, although it might help.

The geezer is named Johnny Crawford. He is played by Robert Duvall. Only a great actor could give such a bad performance. Duvall takes the arts and skills he has perfected for decades and puts them at the service of a flim-flam man who embodies all the worst qualities of the personal motivation movement. That is the movement that teaches us that if we buy a book, view some DVDs, or sit for hours in the "Conference Center" of some crappy motel, we won't be losers anymore.

How do we know we were losers? Because we were suckers for the fraud. How will we know we are winners? When we rent our own motel rooms and fleece the innocent. The formula of the movement can be seen at work in this classified ad: "Send 25 cents for the secret of how to receive lots of quarters in your mail."

The movie stars Lucas Black as Luke Chisholm, whose father (Joseph Lyle Taylor) browbeat him sadistically since childhood to force him to become a pro golfer. When Luke's game blows up on the final hole of the Texas Open, the old man turns his back on him and stalks away in full view of the TV cameras. Devastated, Luke drives blindly into the night and stumbles across the town of Utopia, where he has a Meet Cute with Johnny Crawford. Johnny runs a nearby golf resort, and, wouldn't you know, it will take exactly seven days to repair Luke's truck, which is how long Johnny needs to work his spells on the young man.

Robert Duvall can play crafty con men as well as anyone. I was looking for a twinkle in his eye as he inflicts young Luke with his bull$#!t, but unfortunately I'm afraid the character is intended to be real. Only exposing him as a boring fraud could possibly redeem him. The three great secrets of golf, we learn, are to "See it. Feel it. Trust it."

Johnny Crawford's approach is a variation on the methods always used in the movies by wise old gurus to redeem clueless young men. To make Luke a better golfer, he makes him paint landscapes, go fly fishing, and attend church with him on Sunday. He forgets to train him to capture flying golf balls with a pair of chopsticks. Johnny has a wife (Melissa Leo) who nurtures the forlorn youth. There is a pretty waitress (Deborah Ann Woll) who has been kept on hold for a lifetime waiting for Luke's putt shot. The landscape is majestic, and Luke spends much time regarding its vistas from horseback from high plateaus while the sound track swells devoutly.

Utopia is another one of those movie towns where every single citizen, without exception, knows all the others and can always be found in the local restaurant. There is a TV on the wall where they all watch nothing but golf, and know exactly who poor Luke is. One of the local men has his eye on the comely waitress, but when the slicker turns up, does he get mean and possessive? Not a chance. The good people of Utopia have such charity that they give up their homes, families, horses, cows, waitresses, and dogs to the wayfaring stranger.

Let me give you an idea what good people these are. Many things go wrong during the week. Many, many things. All this in the land beyond San Antonio. Do we hear the f-word? Do we hear the s-word? Do we even hear the d-word or the h-word? No, dear reader. This is the first general audience movie in quite some time that is rated G. Robert Duvall must seldom have had a greater challenge to overcome.

## Sex and the City 2 ★

R, 146 m., 2010

Sarah Jessica Parker (Carrie Bradshaw), Kim Cattrall (Samantha Jones), Kristin Davis (Charlotte York), Cynthia Nixon (Miranda Hobbes), Chris Noth (Mr. Big), John Corbett (Aidan Shaw), David Eigenberg (Steve Brady), Evan Handler (Harry Goldenblatt), Jason Lewis (Smith Jerrod), Willie Garson (Stanford Blatch), Mario Cantone (Anthony Marantino). Directed by Michael Patrick King and produced by King, John P. Melfi, Sarah Jessica Parker, and Darren Star. Screenplay by Patrick King.

Some of these people make my skin crawl. The characters of *Sex and the City 2* are flyweight bubbleheads living in a world that rarely requires three sentences in a row. Their defining quality is consuming things. They gobble food, fashion, houses, husbands, children, vitamins, and freebies. They must plan their wardrobes on the phone, so often do they appear in different basic colors, like the plugs of a Playskool workbench.

As we return to the trivialities of their lives

for a sequel, marriage is the issue. The institution is affirmed in an opening sequence at a gay wedding in Connecticut that looks like a Fred Astaire production number gone horribly overbudget. There's a sixteen-man chorus in white formal wear, a pond with swans, and Liza Minnelli to perform the ceremony. Her religious or legal qualifications are unexplained; perhaps she is present merely as the patron saint of gay men. After the ceremony, she changes to a Vegas lounge outfit and is joined by two look-alike backups for a song-and-dance routine possibly frowned upon in some denominations.

Then it's back to the humdrum married life of our gal Carrie Bradshaw (Sarah Jessica Parker) and the loathsome Mr. Big (Chris Noth). Carrie, honey, how can you endure life with this purring, narcissistic, soft-velvet idiot? He speaks loudly enough to be heard mostly by himself, his most appreciative audience. And he never wants to leave the house at night, preferring to watch classic black-and-white movies on TV. This leads to a marital crisis. Carrie thinks they should talk more. But sweetheart, Mr. Big has nothing to say. At least he's provided you with a Manhattan apartment that looks like an *Architectural Digest* wet dream.

Brief updates. Miranda Hobbes (Cynthia Nixon) is a high-powered lawyer who is dissed by her male chauvinist pig boss. Samantha Jones (Kim Cattrall) is still a sexaholic. Charlotte York (Kristin Davis) has the two little girls she thought she wanted, but now discovers that they actually expect to be raised. Mothers, if you are reading this, run this through your head. One little girl dips her hands in strawberry topping and plants two big handprints on your butt. You are on the cell to a girlfriend. How do you report this? You moan and wail out: "My vintage Valentino!" Any mother who wears her vintage Valentino while making muffin topping with her kids should be hauled up before the Department of Children and Family Services.

All of this is pretty thin gruel. The movie shows enterprise and flies the entire cast away to the emirate of Abu Dhabi, where the girls are given a $22,000-a-night suite and matching Maybachs and butlers, courtesy of a sheikh who wants to have a meeting with Samantha and talk about publicity for his hotel.

This sequence is an exercise in obscenely conspicuous consumption, which the girls perform in so many different outfits they must have been followed to the Middle East by a luggage plane. I don't know a whole lot about fashion, but I know something about taste, and these women spend much of the movie dressed in tacky, vulgar clothing. Carrie and Samantha also display the maximum possible boobage, oblivious to Arab ideas about women's modesty. There's more cleavage in this film than at a pro wrestling wedding.

And crotches, have we got crotches for you. Big close-ups of the girls themselves and some of the bulgers they meet. And they meet some. They meet the Australian World Cup team, for example, which seems to have left its cups at home. And then there's the intriguing stranger Samantha meets at the hotel, whose zipper-straining arousal provokes the fury of an offended Arab guest and his wife. This prodigy's name is Rikard Spirt. Think about it.

Samantha is arrested for kissing on the beach, and there's an uncomfortable scene in which the girls are menaced by outraged men in a public market, where all they've done is dress in a way more appropriate for a sales reception at Victoria's Secret. They're rescued by Arab women so well covered only their eyes are visible, and in private these women reveal that underneath the burka they're wearing Dior gowns and so forth. Must get hot.

I wondered briefly whether Abu Dhabi had underwritten all this product placement, but I learn that *SATC2* was filmed in Morocco, which must be Morocco's little joke. That nation supplies magnificent desert scenes, achieved with CGI, I assume, during which two of the girls fall off a camel. I haven't seen such hilarity since *Abbott and Costello in the Foreign Legion.*

The movie's visual style is arthritic. Director Michael Patrick King covers the sitcom by dutifully cutting back and forth to whoever is speaking. A sample of Carrie's realistic dialogue in a marital argument: "You knew when I married you I was more Coco Chanel than coq au vin." Carrie also narrates the film, providing useful guidelines for those challenged by its intricacies. Sample: "Later that day, Big and I arrived home."

Truth in reviewing: I am obliged to report that this film will no doubt be deliriously enjoyed by its fans, for the reasons described above. Male couch potatoes dragged to the film against their will may find some consolation. Reader, I must confess that while attending the sneak preview with its overwhelmingly female audience, I was gob-smacked by the delightful cleavage on display. Do women wear their lowest-cut frocks for one another?

*Note: From my understanding of the guidelines of the MPAA Classification and Rating Administration, Samantha and Mr. Spirt have one scene that far, far surpasses the traditional MPAA limits for pumping and thrusting.*

## Shame ★ ★ ★ ★

NC-17, 99 m., 2011

Michael Fassbender (Brandon), Carey Mulligan (Sissy), James Badge Dale (David), Nicole Beharie (Dale Marianne). Directed by Steve McQueen and produced by Iain Canning and Emile Sherman. Screenplay by McQueen and Abi Morgan.

There is a close-up in *Shame* of Michael Fassbender's face showing pain, grief, and anger. His character, Brandon, is having an orgasm. For the director, Steve McQueen, that could be the film's master shot. There is no concern about the movement of Brandon's lower body. No concern about his partner. The close-up limits our view to his suffering. He is enduring a sexual function that has long since stopped giving him any pleasure and is self-abuse in the most profound way.

Brandon is a good-looking, fit man in his early thirties, who lives alone in a sterile condo in Manhattan. He works in a cubicle with a computer. Never mind what his company does. It makes no difference to him. Sometimes in the evening he and his boss David (James Badge Dale) go out to drink in singles bars. David is a little hyper with his pickup lines. Brandon just sits there, his face impassive, and has better luck. He doesn't hope to get lucky. He doesn't think of it as luck. Sex is his cross to bear.

I remember when the notion of sexual addiction was first being mentioned. People treated it as a joke. It was featured in late-night monologues. The American Psychiatric Association in 1987 defined it as a mental disorder involving "distress about a pattern of repeated sexual conquests . . . involving a succession of people who exist only as things to be used." The APA is no longer certain it is a disorder. Whatever it is, Brandon suffers from it. In *Shame*, however, he himself is the thing only to be used. One or two of his sexual partners in the film may be attracted to him in the sense that some men are attracted to nymphomaniacs. There is such a sadness involved.

*Shame* makes into a lie the universal assumption in movies that orgasms provide a pleasure to be pursued. Its opening shot shows Brandon awake in the morning, staring immobile into space. He could be a man prepared to commit suicide. He gets out of bed, goes into the shower, and masturbates. It will be the first of his many orgasms, solitary and with company, that day. He never reveals emotion. He lives like a man compelled to follow an inevitable course.

He is cold to people. To prostitutes, to coworkers, to strangers. On the subway, he trades eye contact with a woman who may be flirting. Is he flirting? To boldly maintain eye contact is a form of flirting, and an aggressive challenge. But he doesn't smile. His is a dreadful life.

One day he comes home to his apartment and someone is there. We think it may be an intruder. It is Sissy (Carey Mulligan), his sister, although for a time we don't know that. He flies at her in a rage, telling her to get out. She has nowhere to go. He doesn't care.

His shame is masked in privacy. He wants no witnesses to his hookers, his pornography, his masturbation. Does he think he is incapable of ordinary human contact? In time we will suspect that Brandon and Sissy shared childhood experiences that damaged them. Steve McQueen wisely is not specific about them.

Brandon lives in a cold, forlorn Manhattan. When he is in a group, he is alone. The sidewalks seem unusually empty. He knows where to go in order to have sex. In one sequence, that involves a gay bar. He isn't gay, in my opinion, but then how is he heterosexual? He loves no one, is attracted to no one, is driven to find occasions for orgasm—whether alone or in company hardly seems to matter.

The introduction of Sissy allows the film

some spontaneity and life. She is as passionate and uninhibited as he is the opposite. She needs him desperately. He fears need. They rage at each other. She works sometimes as a cabaret singer, and in one scene she performs a song in close-up. It is done heartbreakingly. This close-up also shows pain and grief, but no anger.

Not many actors would have the courage it took Michael Fassbender to play this role. He showed similar courage in Steve McQueen's *Hunger* (2009), about the IRA hunger striker Bobby Sands. The actor and director seem to have found a common resolve in these films to show the thing itself, unalloyed by audience-pleasing techniques. Brandon can't even be said to visibly suffer. He is compelled to repeat the same behavior over and over, and all he gets from it is self-loathing. *Shame* is the correct title.

*Shame* contains unblinking truth. I have no doubt it depicts behavior that can be accurately called "sex addiction." The film suggests no help for Brandon, although toward the end he moves somewhat in the direction of being able to care for another human being. For him that involves being able to care for himself, despite the truth that he feels unworthy to be known. This is a great act of filmmaking and acting. I don't believe I would be able to see it twice.

## Sherlock Holmes: A Game of Shadows ★ ★ ★ ½

PG-13, 129 m., 2011

Robert Downey Jr. (Sherlock Holmes), Jude Law (Dr. John Watson), Noomi Rapace (Madam Simza Heron), Rachel McAdams (Irene Adler), Jared Harris (Professor James Moriarty), Stephen Fry (Mycroft Holmes), Paul Anderson (Colonel Sebastian Moran), Kelly Reilly (Mary Watson), Geraldine James (Mrs. Hudson), Eddie Marsan (Inspector Lestrade). Directed by Guy Ritchie and produced by Susan Downey, Dan Lin, Joel Silver, and Lionel Wigram. Screenplay by Michele Mulroney and Kieran Mulroney, based on characters created by Sir Arthur Conan Doyle.

I suppose any hope of an authentic Sherlock Holmes movie is foolish at this epoch in movie history. No matter that a story is set in 1895 in Victorian London, it must be chock-ablock with explosions, gunfire, special effects, and fights that bear no comparison to the "fisticuffs" of the period. As an Anglophile, I've luxuriated in the genial atmosphere of the Conan Doyle stories, where a step is heard on the stair, a client tells his tale, and (Dr. Watson reports) Holmes withdraws to his rooms to consider his new case during a period of meditation (involving such study aids as opium).

We see a great deal of Victorian London (and Paris and Switzerland) in *Sherlock Holmes: A Game of Shadows*, but we must look quickly. The movie all but hurtles through episodes that would be leisurely set pieces in a traditional Holmes story. This is a modern action picture played in costume. I knew it would be. After Guy Ritchie's 2009 *Sherlock Holmes* with Robert Downey Jr. and Jude Law grossed something like half a billion dollars, this was no time to rethink the approach. What they have done, however, is add a degree of refinement and invention, and I enjoyed this one more than the earlier film.

*Sherlock Holmes: A Game of Shadows* opens with an emergency that threatens to rock Holmes's world: Watson (Law) is getting married. In the first film we learned of his engagement to Mary Watson (Kelly Reilly), and now a date has been set for the poor girl. Holmes (Downey), who considers himself every bit as much good company as the doctor could possibly require, deplores this development, and indeed even joins the blissful couple on their honeymoon train journey. At one point he throws Mary off the train, but to be fair it's to save her life.

Most of the film centers on a climax in the long-standing feud between Holmes and professor James Moriarty (Jared Harris), who beneath his cover as an Oxford don is the mastermind of an anarchist plot to use bombings and assassinations to push Europe into war. Moriarty would profit handsomely from that because he operates an enormous secret munitions factory, turning out everything from machine pistols to gigantic cannons. The lives of many European heads of state are threatened, and Holmes is the only hope to keep the peace.

Once this game is afoot, it seems too large

to be contained by the eccentric investigator of 221B Baker Street and Watson his intimate (I am using "intimate" as both a noun and an insinuation). It's more of a case for James Bond, and Moriarty's grandiosity seems on a scale with a Bond villain. Guy Ritchie and his writers, Michele Mulroney and Kieran Mulroney, however, wisely devote some of their best scenes to one-on-ones between Holmes and Moriarty.

Their struggle comes to a head in an elegant high-stakes chess game, held for some reason in Switzerland in the dead of a winter night on a snowy outdoor balcony. Moriarty is played by Jared Harris, who doesn't gnash or fulminate, but fences with Holmes in barbed language. This returns the story somewhat to the tradition that Holmes did most of his best work in his mind.

Watson has a more proactive role this time than previously. The movie opens with him recalling these events on a typewriter that is too modern for 1895 but maybe suggests he's writing years later. He's not just a confidant and a chronicler but a hero, too, involved in fights and shoot-outs. His wife must be thankful that Holmes abruptly eliminated her from most of the action.

Holmes's brother, Mycroft, turns out to be well placed at the center of European diplomacy; Stephen Fry has plummy good fun in the role, especially in nude moments where he shields his netherlands from view by employing artfully arranged foregrounds in the *Austin Powers* tradition. Two women characters are prominent. Back again is Irene Adler (Rachel McAdams), the enigmatic figure in much romantic speculation about Holmes. And we meet for the first time a gypsy fortune-teller named Madam Simza Heron, who is played by Noomi Rapace, the original Girl with the Dragon Tattoo. She capably discharges the duties required of her as Madam Heron, but demonstrates how really brilliantly conceived the Dragon Girl was. Heron is pale by comparison.

It's Downey's movie. With his cool, flippant manner, his Holmes stands apart from the danger, thinking it through visually before performing it, remaining insouciant in the face of calamity. He appears in many disguises, one with a markedly bad wig, and another as a remarkably convincing chair. The thing to do, I suppose, is to set aside your memories of the Conan Doyle stories, save them to savor on a night this winter, and enjoy this movie as a high-caliber entertainment.

## She's Out of My League ★ ★ ★

R, 106 m., 2010

Jay Baruchel (Kirk), Alice Eve (Molly), T. J. Miller (Stainer), Mike Vogel (Jack), Nate Torrence (Devon), Krysten Ritter (Patty), Geoff Stults (Cam), Lindsay Sloane (Marnie). Directed by Jim Field Smith and produced by Eric Gold, David B. Householter, and Jimmy Miller. Screenplay by Sean Anders and John Morris.

Molly is a perfect ten. Kirk is a five. This scoring is provided by his best friends, who sadly inform him, "You can't jump more than two." Because of reasoning like that, Aristotle Onassis remains a hero to fours and fives everywhere. *She's Out of My League,* which is sortofa good comedy, tells the story of a five who meets a ten who believes there is a ten inside of him fighting to get out.

Kirk (Jay Baruchel) works as a TSA security screener at the Pittsburgh airport. He's competent enough, but the behavior of his colleagues should all by itself raise the national security level to red. Apparently unsupervised, they brighten up their jobs by trying to pick up every cute girl who comes through security. This is made more possible because there never seem to be five hundred impatient passengers waiting in line.

Baruchel looks as if he could indeed be a five, but he has that essential quality of turning into a ten with his attitude alone. Here he will find what I have long observed, that everyone is beautiful when they're looking at you with love in their eyes. Kirk has recently become the victim of the sort of perfect storm that strikes the heroes of movies like this. His girlfriend, Marnie (Lindsay Sloane), has broken up with him. But having lacked a warm family relationship, she latched onto Kirk's family, and now hangs out at his house with her new boyfriend, whom Kirk's parents approve of. Think about that.

Molly is also fresh from romantic disaster. When she loses her iPhone and Kirk finds it and returns it, she asks him out to dinner. He's stunned because, yes, she's out of his league. But it turns out Molly is ready to play in a different league, one where being a ten on the outside is less important than being a ten on the inside. Kirk's innate decency melts her heart.

Jay Baruchel has that quality of seeming like someone we might actually have known outside of a movie. He plays Kirk as apologetic, easily embarrassed, with low self-esteem—plain and simple, a nice guy. Alice Eve, who is despite all evidence British, is pretty, yes, but not actually quite a ten. A 9.5, easy. Isn't that scoring system loathsome? Her best friend, Patty (Krysten Ritter), thinks Kirk is beneath her, possibly because Patty likes to bask in the reflected glow of Molly's tenhood. Kirk's own three best buddies include two party animals and one nice pudgy guy, whose combined wisdom on women is a perfect two.

There are some funny set pieces here, one involving guys rummaging through each other's netherlands, one involving a family trip to Branson, Missouri, in matching sweatshirts. Do you ever get the feeling you're the last American alive who hasn't been to Branson? That *Titanic* attraction sounds great to me. Anyway, much depends on whether Kirk will actually make this journey.

The movie is not a comedy classic. But in a genre where so many movies struggle to lift themselves from zero to one, it's about, oh, a 6.5.

## A Shine of Rainbows ★ ★ ½

PG, 101 m., 2010

Connie Nielsen (Maire O'Donnell), Aidan Quinn (Alec O'Donnell), John Bell (Tomas), Jack Gleason (Seamus), Niamh Shaw (Katie), Tara Alice Scully (Nancy). Directed by Vic Sarin and produced by James Flynn, Tina Pehme, and Chris Rudolph. Screenplay by Sarin, Catherine Spear, and Dennis Foon, from the novel by Lillian Beckwith.

As you can possibly guess from the title, *A Shine of Rainbows* is a feel-good movie. Hey, what's not to like about cute orphans, baby seals, sweet moms, and gruff dads with hearts of gold? And rainbows? If your heart is going thumpety-thump at such a prospect, here is the movie for you.

No, I'm serious. And kids may really love it. It's too much of an emotional heart tugger for me, but then I prefer my orphans by Dickens, where the little rascals pick pockets for a living. I'll admit one thing: I wish there were still an Ireland (or anywhere else) where a couple looking like Connie Nielsen and Aidan Quinn could live in an isolated and charming home on a high meadow overlooking the sea, operate a small family farm, and make a living.

The film is set on Corrie Island, off the western coast of Ireland, and I'll grant you one thing: You can find dozens of photos of it at http://j.mp/cnQWBU, and it looks just about the way it does in the film. It is a wonderful place for small Tomas (John Bell), who has become a punching bag for bullies at the orphanage, but is swept up by the heaven-sent Maire O'Donnell (Connie Nielsen), popped aboard a ferry, and carried across to this idyllic setting.

All is fine, except . . . why does his new dad, Alec (Aidan Quinn), glower at him so darkly? Alec confides to his wife that the boy doesn't look sturdy enough. Why didn't she pick a brawnier model? Alec is possibly in the Dickens tradition of a cruel stepfather who demands only a brisk twenty-hour day of hard labor in return for the lad's bowl of gruel. Good thing Tomas is Irish. If he'd been Russian, there'd be no telling.

Maire unfortunately contracts Ali MacGraw's Disease, defined in an ancient edition of the Glossary as that disease of young women whose only symptom is that after they take to a hospital bed they grow more and more beautiful. That leaves Tomas with Alec. Oh, but Tomas finds a new friend, a baby seal stranded down on the beach. He knows another orphan when he sees one.

As Tomas and Alec slowly bond over the seal, Alec's heart melts, as it must. It's the seal I'm worried about. Tomas brings him fish to wolf down, but I dunno . . . how long can a young seal lie helpless on a beach in full sun and remain happy? Couldn't he, like, you know, sort of crawl into the sea? Isn't that kind of programmed into seals? The movie offers some reason for his immobility, which didn't lock into my memory bank. Essentially he stays there day after day because the plot requires him.

I know, I know. I'm being unsentimental. I

should make this clear: *A Shine of Rainbows* is a sweet, good-looking film about nice people in a beautiful place, and young John Bell is an appealing performer in the tradition of the Culkins. Quinn and Nielsen are pros who take their roles seriously, and Vic Sarin's direction gets the job done. If I were six . . . but then I'm not, am I?

## Sholem Aleichem: Laughing in the Darkness ★ ★ ★

NO MPAA RATING, 93 m., 2011

A documentary directed, written, and produced by Joseph Dorman.

How could Solomon Rabinovich have guessed, while he was going bankrupt in the stock market, that fame would come to him from the fiction he wrote in a dying language for little newspapers? When two of his plays opened on the same night in New York and closed after the critics hated them, would he have thought that his work would inspire one of the greatest hits in the history of the musical theater?

Yes, my dear friends, I can hear you asking, who is this big shot Solomon Rabinovich, whom I have never heard a word about? That's not so important. Maybe you should call him by his other name, Sholem Aleichem. While he worked all day losing his father-in-law's money in the markets and bragging he was becoming successful, he was coming home to write his stories late at night, and writing more of them so early in the morning that God himself was not awake.

He was rich for a while, after marrying a rich girl and inheriting her father's money. He lost it all because he was maybe paying more attention to his writing than to these tipsters who told him sell when they should have told him buy. When things went bad in Russia, he immigrated to America, the land of opportunity, where a man could make something of himself, and grew so discouraged he returned to Europe and never owned his own home again.

But all the time he was writing the stories, filled with humor and irony, inspired by his childhood in a shtetl so small he had to leave town to change his coat. He created a world of characters who often seemed to be speaking in their own voices, and even writing him letters. He wrote a story a week, sometimes two, and every Friday night the readers of the Yiddish papers came home to read a new one.

He was a nice-looking man. He was a family man, and had six children, none of whom could speak or write Yiddish, so in his own household these children couldn't read the words of the greatest Yiddish writer who ever lived. He sold the rights to most of his work to raise cash, and at fifty he was so broke he had to go on lecture tours.

Don't think he was unsuccessful. He didn't manage his money well, but he was very popular. When he fell sick on one of his tours, his young admirers spread straw on the cobblestones outside the window of his inn so his sleep wouldn't be disturbed by the passing carriages. He returned to America, and when he died in 1916, only fifty-seven years old, two hundred thousand people participated in his funeral. To call him beloved would be putting it mildly.

This documentary by Joseph Dorman tells the story of Sholem Aleichem with many photographs and early films, most of them not showing him but re-creating the world that produced him. There are many scholars and critics here, most of them useful and pleasant, who obviously love him. Most remarkably, there is his granddaughter, Bel Kaufman, still looking terrific at one hundred, who had writing in her blood and wrote *Up the Down Staircase.*

Of all his many characters, his best known is without a doubt Tevye the milkman, who is the hero of the great musical *Fiddler on the Roof.* Although Sholem Aleichem's work is easily available in English, I'd never heard of him when I saw that musical. If I'd known more, it would have helped me to better understand "If I were a rich man, a ha deedle deedle, bubba bubba deedle deedle dum."

## Shutter Island ★ ★ ★ ½

R, 138 m., 2010

Leonardo DiCaprio (Teddy Daniels), Mark Ruffalo (Chuck Aule), Ben Kingsley (Dr. Cawley), Michelle Williams (Dolores), Emily Mortimer (Rachel 1), Patricia Clarkson (Rachel

**2), Max von Sydow (Dr. Naehring). Directed by Martin Scorsese and produced by Scorsese, Brad Fischer, Mike Medavoy, and Arnold Messer. Screenplay by Laeta Kalogridis, based on the novel by Dennis Lehane.**

*Shutter Island* starts working on us with the first musical notes under the Paramount mountain, even before the film starts. They're ominous and doomy. So is the film. This is Martin Scorsese's evocation of the delicious shuddering fear we feel when horror movies are *about* something and don't release all the tension with action scenes.

In its own way it's a haunted house movie, or make that a haunted castle or fortress. Shutter Island, we're told, is a remote and craggy island in Boston bay, where a Civil War fort has been adapted as a prison for the criminally insane. We approach it by boat through lowering skies, and the feeling is something like the approach to King Kong's island: Looming in gloom from the sea, it fills the visitor with dread.

To this island in rainy weather in 1954 travel U.S. Marshal Teddy Daniels (Leonardo DiCaprio) and his partner, Chuck Aule (Mark Ruffalo). They're assigned to investigate the disappearance of a child murderer (Emily Mortimer). There seems to be no way to leave the island alive. The disappearance of one prisoner might not require the presence of two marshals unfamiliar with the situation, but we never ask that question. Not after the ominous walls of the prison arise. Not after the visitors are shown into the office of the prison director, Dr. Cawley, played by Ben Kingsley with that forbidding charm he has mastered.

It's clear that Teddy has no idea what he's getting himself into. Teddy—such an innocuous name in such a Gothic setting. Scorsese, working from a novel by Dennis Lehane, seems to be telling a simple enough story here; the woman is missing, and Teddy and Chuck will look for her. But the cold gray walls clamp in on them, and the offices of Cawley and his colleagues, furnished for the Civil War commanding officers, seem borrowed from a tale by Edgar Allan Poe.

Scorsese the craftsman chips away at reality piece by piece. Flashbacks suggest Teddy's traumas in the decade since World War II. That war, its prologue and aftermath, supplied the dark undercurrent of classic film noir. The term "post-traumatic stress disorder" was not then in use, but its symptoms could be seen in men attempting to look confident in their facades of unstyled suits, subdued ties, heavy smoking, and fedoras pulled low against the rain. DiCaprio and Ruffalo both effect this look, but DiCaprio makes it seem more like a hopeful disguise.

The film's primary effect is on the senses. Everything is brought together into a disturbing foreshadow of dreadful secrets. How did this woman escape from a locked cell in a locked ward in the old Civil War fort, its walls thick enough to withstand cannon fire? Why do Cawley and his sinister colleague Dr. Naehring (Max von Sydow, ready to play chess with Death) seem to be concealing something? Why is even such a pleasant person as the deputy warden not quite convincingly friendly? Why do the methods in the prison trigger flashbacks to Teddy's memories of helping to liberate a Nazi death camp?

These kinds of questions are at the heart of film noir. The hero is always flawed. Scorsese showed his actors the great 1947 noir *Out of the Past,* whose very title is a noir theme: Characters never arrive at a story without baggage. They have unsettled issues, buried traumas. So, yes, perhaps Teddy isn't simply a clean-cut G-man. But why are the others so strange? Kingsley in particular exudes menace every time he smiles.

There are thrilling visuals in *Shutter Island.* Another film Scorsese showed his cast was Hitchcock's *Vertigo,* and we sense echoes of its hero's fear of heights. There's the possibility that the escaped woman might be lurking in a cave on a cliff or hiding in a lighthouse. Both involve hazardous terrain to negotiate, above vertiginous falls to waves pounding on the rocks below. A possible hurricane is approaching. Light leaks out of the sky. The wind sounds mournful. It is, as they say, a dark and stormy night. And that's what the movie is about: atmosphere, ominous portents, the erosion of Teddy's confidence and even his identity. It's all done with flawless directorial command. Scorsese has fear to evoke, and he does it with many notes.

You may read reviews of *Shutter Island* complaining that the ending blindsides you. The uncertainty it causes prevents the film from feeling perfect on first viewing. I have a feeling it might improve on second. Some may believe it doesn't make sense. Or that, if it does, then the movie leading up to it doesn't. I asked myself: OK, then, how *should* it end? What would be more satisfactory? Why can't I be one of those critics who informs the director what he should have done instead?

Oh, I've had moments like that. Every moviegoer does. But not with *Shutter Island.* This movie is all of a piece, even the parts that don't appear to fit. There is a human tendency to note carefully what goes before and draw logical conclusions. But—what if you can't nail down exactly what went before? What if there were things about Cawley and his peculiar staff that were hidden? What if the movie lacks a reliable narrator? What if its point of view isn't omniscient but fragmented? Where can it all lead? What does it mean? We ask, and Teddy asks, too.

## Silent House ★ ★

R, 85 m., 2012

Elizabeth Olsen (Sarah), Adam Trese (John), Eric Sheffer Stevens (Peter), Julia Taylor Ross (Sophia), Adam Barnett (Stalking Man), Haley Murphy (Little Girl). Directed by Chris Kentis and Laura Lau and produced by Lau and Agnes Mentre. Screenplay by Kentis and Lau, based on a film by Gustavo Hernandez.

*Silent House* is another one of those "scream at the screen" movies, in which you want to shout out advice to a character. In this case, a nubile young woman is trapped inside an apparently haunted house for most of the time, and what you want to shout is, "Get out of the damn house!" Finally, a little beyond the halfway mark, she does escape, running out the front door, and flees, weeping and stumbling, down a country road until her Uncle Peter drives along and they return to the house and *she goes back inside.*

Soon she's reduced to tiptoeing through the darkness calling out "Uncle Peter?" when not long before she was calling "Dad? Daddy?" This is an optimistic girl. Her name is Sarah, and she's played by Elizabeth Olsen, the younger sister of Mary-Kate and Ashley. We saw her not long ago in the challenging lead role of *Martha Marcy May Marlene.* In that film she demonstrated she's a gifted actress, and in *Silent House* she performs a rite of passage for many young actresses, as the endangered heroine of a horror film.

I said the house is "apparently" haunted because . . . well, you'll see. It's nothing as simple as that. The movie is a remake of a horror film from Uruguay, and both the original and the remake claim to have been shot in a single take. I doubt it. If it is, it's the most amazing single take since *Russian Ark*, beginning with an overhead crane shot on a lake shore and then traveling down a road and into a house and following the heroine upstairs and downstairs and into the basement. That would take one hell of a cameraman, and there are all kinds of shots where the screen goes dark and cuts could obviously be concealed.

Whatever. The camera remains always close to Sarah, sometimes almost resting on her shoulder, and what's impressive is Elizabeth Olsen's ability to sustain that kind of intense on-cam scrutiny and stay convincingly in character. She has a pretty face, expressive and delicate, and carefully modulates her performance: not overacting, not mugging, not trying to sell us on anything. Some of her best moments communicate silent terror.

The Silent House is her family's summer house, quite large, three floors, with a seemingly unlimited number of doors located at right angles to other doors, so that in another world this would be a good location for a slapstick farce. There's also an unreasonably high number of closet doors and doors opening onto staircases.

Sarah and her dad, John (Adam Trese), and Uncle Peter (Eric Sheffer Stevens) enter the house. It's daylight, but window boards make it pitch black inside. They carry bright lamps. Left alone, she begins to hear things. Tappings, squeakings, scuttlings, breathings, creakings, moanings, clickings. This house embodies a full rhythm section.

Creeping through the dark, she finds her dad again, and then Uncle Peter leaves for a while and things get really heavy. The secret of the plot is revealed to be unexpectedly fraught, and a surrealistic element enters with bodies in bathtubs and a toilet mounted vertically on a wall and dripping a stream of blood.

My attention was held for the first act or so. Then any attempt at realism was abandoned, and it became clear that the house, and the movie containing it, were devices to manufacture methodical thrills. The explanation, if that's what it was, seemed devised and unconvincing. To some degree, the ending of a film should seem vaguely necessary, don't you think?

Truth in reviewing: I saw the film with a sneak preview audience. Most of my fellow audience members sat quietly, but there was a cadre of girlfriends three rows down and on the right who shrieked on cue, and then laughed—which is proper, because that's why people go to these thrillers, to be amused that they were frightened. If that's the case with you, *Silent House* delivers, although you may be left suspecting there's more to the mold in the walls than they're telling us.

## Silent Souls ★ ★ ★ ★

NO MPAA RATING, 75 m., 2011

Igor Sergeyev (Aist), Yuri Tsurilo (Miron), Yuliya Aug (Tanya). Directed by Aleksei Fedorchenko and produced by Igor Mishin and Mary Nazari. Screenplay by Denis Osokin, based on the novel *The Buntings* by Aist Sergeyev.

Road movies take many forms, and *Silent Souls* is the road movie as metaphysical memory and meditation. This profound and immensely touching film in only seventy-five perfect minutes achieves the profundity of an epic. I read the description (two friends from the ancient Merjan tribe in Russia take a funeral trip involving the wife of one), and wasn't much interested; it sounded like ethnography without impact. Yet not often have I been more deeply touched.

The film is narrated by a mill worker, Aist (Igor Sergeyev). His friend and coworker Miron (Yuri Tsurilo) receives news that his much younger wife has died. There is a Merjan tradition, we learn, that when his wife dies a husband asks his closest friend to join him in rituals surrounding this event. They set out together in Miron's car to drive to the deathbed in the distant town of Neya.

Joining them on the trip are two fluttery little birds, buntings, that Aist has just purchased at a market stall and is afraid to leave behind untended. These birds in their cage may represent souls trapped in bodies. Together the two men undress Tanya (Yuliya Aug), the dead wife, bathe her, tenderly wrap her, and place her in the back of their car. Aist's narration explains that water is of supreme importance to the Merjans, who were originally from Finland but long ago were absorbed by Russia. Only such rituals survive of their history.

While the two friends take the body to a lake, they engage in a practice called "smoke." This means the husband is permitted, indeed expected, to share frankly about his love life and his wife's sexuality. This in no sense is offensive; it is fond and loving. Miron's wedding night included a Merjan practice in which the bride's friends tie bright threads to her pubic hair, and the husband later unties them and hangs them over a branch of a yew tree. This is much more loving than the way certain European countries display with triumph a bloody sheet.

The movie contains very little on-screen dialogue between the two men, permits itself long shots of them simply driving, listens to their "smoke," and we learn that, as it happens, Aist was also in love with Tanya, and Miron knew that. In flashback we see some of their memories.

At the end, on a beach, the men build a bonfire, cremate Tanya, and scatter her ashes on the water. This appeals to me much more than being screwed into a casket. The buntings all this time have been rather enervating with their (may I say) bird-brained chirps and incessant leaps around the perches in their little cage. Now they have their appointment with destiny.

*Silent Souls* is fearlessly simple. In part it is an act of mourning not simply for Tanya but for the traditions of the Merjan peoples and their lost villages. I was reminded of the books of W. G. Sebald, who undertakes journeys through the half-abandoned remainders of the past, through signs that men had once been here and are now forgotten.

## The Sitter ★

R, 81 m., 2011

Jonah Hill (Noah), Max Records (Slater), Ari Graynor (Marisa Lewis), J. B. Smoove (Julio),

Sam Rockwell (Karl), Landry Bender (Blithe), Kevin Hernandez (Rodrigo). Directed by David Gordon Green and produced by Michael De Luca. Screenplay by Brian Gatewood and Alessandro Tanaka.

A genial layabout gets talked into babysitting for three rambunctious children, and by the end of the evening they've gotten him into trouble all over town, involving cocaine, auto theft, cops, party crashing, and sex, in what the star, Jonah Hill, genially describes in his own trailer as "the filthiest R-rated babysitter movie ever made."

I am so very, very tired of movies like this. Does the story line strike you as original? It sounds to me like another slice off the cheesecake of dreck. The one cliché I neglected to mention earlier was the standard scene where a white dude walks into a situation involving a lot of mean black twelve-letter-ers and of course they all hate white people and loom over the camera exuding danger, until—hey, what do you know!—they end up liking this doofus and later materialize to save his butt in another tricky situation.

The three kids are blameless. They are smartass Slater (Max Records), cutie pie Blithe (Landry Bender), and explosives hobbyist Rodrigo (Kevin Hernandez), who has been adopted into the family because this movie will try anything to get a Latino into the cast. Rodrigo provides at least a spark of humor. He "has issues about running away," which he does several times, causing Noah (Jonah Hill) to pack up the other two kids and track him down. His issues are so chronic that he has a location beeper chip sewn into his clothing. His specialty is using giant-sized fireworks to blow up toilets. Of course, it is inevitable that this talent will eventually save the day.

*The Sitter* is another example of an emerging genre, the Potty Mouth Movie. Remember the words George Carlin said could not be said on TV? There's now a kind of movie that cannot be made without using all of them except one. Even the online trailer may startle you. It's one of those adults-only red-band trailers that you have to give your age in order to view. I lied about my age. Nobody under seventeen would ever do that.

It causes me a real pang to report that *The Sitter* was directed by David Gordon Green, who on the basis of his early work seemed destined to become one of the great American directors. Now he is lost and wandering in the wilderness of Friday night specials. I hope this is a temporary aberration. I know how hard it is to get financing for good and ambitious movies. I know how attractive sex, violence, cars, and cocaine are for producers. I don't blame Green for working in the genre. But I blame him for making a bad movie that isn't funny. And as for Jonah Hill: Here is one of the nicer and warmer actors in the movies. He's even warm and nice in *The Sitter.* Too bad it doesn't get him much of anywhere.

## The Skin I Live In ★ ★ ★

R, 117 m., 2011

Antonio Banderas (Robert Ledgard), Elena Anaya (Vera), Marisa Paredes (Marilia), Jan Cornet (Vicente), Roberto Alamo (Zeca), Eduard Fernandez (Fulgencio), Blanca Suarez (Norma). Directed by Pedro Almodovar and produced by Agustin Almodovar and Esther Garcia. Screenplay by Agustin Almodovar and Pedro Almodovar based on the novel *Mygale* by Thierry Jonquet.

With a Pedro Almodovar film we expect voluptuous sexual perversion, devious plot twists, and a snaky interweaving of past and present, all painted on a canvas of bright colors with bold art and clothing. His new film *The Skin I Live In* does not disappoint. Although I usually take pleasure in Almodovar's sexy darkness, this film is queasy-making.

What it provides is a glossy, smooth, luxurious version of the sorts of unspeakable things that occupied classic horror films involving mad scientists, body parts, twisted revenge, personal captives, and hidden revenge. Usually such films are stylistically elevated enough that there's an irony involved, a camp humor.

Although camp is not unknown to Almodovar, here he maintains an emotional intensity showing that his bizarre story must be taken seriously. Yes, there is a mad scientist: the driven, brilliant Dr. Robert Ledgard, played by Antonio Banderas with rare intensity. Robert is driven by his science to try to repair tears in his heart. To do this, he assumes he has the godlike right to use the bodies and minds of other people: Their sacrifices are necessary to heal his pain.

As the film opens, he holds the beautiful Vera (Elena Anaya) captive in his huge mansion in the Spanish city of Toledo. She has every luxury except freedom. She is dressed from toes to chin in a flesh-colored costume that looks like a compression suit. She has a stack of books, a routine of yoga, around-the-clock service, everything but her freedom. She is not his patient but his prisoner, and perhaps she believes there are only two ways to free herself: suicide, or forcing the doctor to fall in love with her. She is narcissistic enough to know how beautiful she is, and seduction is a challenge to her.

We learn pieces of the back story. Robert's young wife was horribly burned in a car accident. His specialty has become face transplants ("I have performed three of the nine in history, and nothing has given me more satisfaction"). I briefly thought Vera was his wife, but no, she's dead and Vera was kidnapped. He watches her on closed-circuit TV like an artwork, and seems intent on using plastic surgery to create an ideal woman who will be, to put it plainly, fireproof.

There's much clinical detail involving laboratory work, cloning, the blood of living pigs, and sheets of newly grown skin. Some sequences could come from a documentary. This program of surgery is embedded in a plot so devious that the audience knows more than Robert ever does—for example, the identity of his mother and his brother. That's Almodovar for you: It makes no difference who those people are, or whether Robert knows it. Pedro is just thickening the soup.

There is also a rape whose nature Robert misunderstands. And the faithful older housekeeper, Marilia (Marisa Paredes), whom all mad scientists are required to have on staff. And Zeca (Roberto Alamo), a man dressed as a tiger, who comes to the house and explains to Marilia that he is a wanted man and must be given sanctuary; only during Carnival can he move through the city disguised as a tiger. And Vicente (Jan Cornet), whom Robert kidnaps for mistaken reasons and holds captive in the basement. You see how this film could star Vincent Price.

It looks so silky. Few directors have used colors, especially red, as joyfully as Almodovar. Every scene vibrates. There is passion, but not chemistry; although we believe Vera actually does hope to seduce the doctor, his feelings for her seem psychopathic, not sexual. He wants to prove something. The full depth of his depravity is revealed in the unexpected final sequence, when we discover that Robert's emotional engine is fueled not by lust, jealousy, or anger, but by a need to treat others as his scientific playthings.

Robert is an unwholesome character. The feelings of others mean nothing to him. That he expresses them on the rich canvas of Almodovar lends them a superficial beauty, but he is rotten to the core. This film must be credited with expressing exactly what Almodovar wanted to say, but I am not sure I wanted to hear it. The three-star rating is a compromise between admiration for the craftsmanship and the acting, and disquiet about the story.

## Sleep Furiously ★ ★ ★

NO MPAA RATING, 94 m., 2011

A documentary directed by Gideon Koppel.

Here is a portrait of a farming community in Wales in which the people, animals, and crops live together in pastoral harmony. It's the sort of place you might fall in love with if you stayed there in a bed-and-breakfast and had a picnic under a tree on a hilltop. If you had to live there, however, I suspect you might start scheming to move to the bright lights of Cardiff.

*Sleep Furiously* is a lovely film, but maddeningly complacent. Let me begin with the loveliness. It was filmed in and near Trefeurig, where the director, Gideon Koppel, was born, and where his mother still walks her dog. Here the year rotates through the seasons, calves and piglets are born, the choir sings in church, there are bake sales and village meetings, and in music class the students bang away on rhythm instruments while their teacher plays the piano.

It is quiet here. If you didn't have a dog, you would need one. In one wonderful shot, a dog sees its master into his van, and as it drives away it trots behind. The road falls gently into a valley, and there is a gradual turn in the road. The dog keeps the van in view as long as it can, stops and looks after it after it has disappeared, and then rouses itself from reverie and resumes doggy business. All in one unbroken shot.

I know that the director's mother is in the film only because I read some of the press materials. She is not introduced. Individual people are not the point. They have little dialogue, and that not of much consequence ("Will you have leeks or cabbage for dinner?"). There are some events; the local school is closing, for example, but the reaction is more of regret than rebellion. We see a few TV sets, and the farms use modern machinery, but with such exceptions life here must be the same as it was fifty years ago.

The connecting thread is a man who drives a cheerful yellow van on a regular route. This is the bookmobile. He knows his customers and suggests books he thinks they'd like—we suspect he's checked them out from a central library in a larger town. People check out fresh books and return the ones they borrowed last month. Yes, the yellow van comes around only monthly.

The older people speak Welsh. Younger people are bilingual in English. Everyone must know all the others, if only by sight and habit. There must certainly be pubs and places where young people hang out, but we don't see them. There is no sign of a cinema. I daresay most of you, dear readers, will agree that this is a tranquil and bucolic district, but after a long winter you might want to consider moving.

## Small, Beautifully Moving Parts ★ ★ ★

NO MPAA RATING, 72 m., 2012

Anna Margaret Hollyman (Sarah Sparks), Richard Hoag (Henry), Andre Holland (Leon), Mary Beth Peil (Marjorie), Sarah Rafferty (Emily), Susan Kelechi Watson (Towie). Directed by Annie Howell and Lisa Robinson and produced by Howell, Jen Dougherty, and Robinson. Screenplay by Howell and Robinson.

Sarah Sparks is your friendly local technology guru. She can debug your computer, teach you how your cell phone works, and repair your toaster. She seems compelled to disassemble every device she comes across, and when she uses a drugstore pregnancy test, she's fascinated by the typeface used on the product.

The part she can't deal with is her pregnancy. She has no interest in babies and no desire to become a mother. The baby growing within her is like a computer bug that has invaded her drive. Her boyfriend, Leon (Andre Holland), is thrilled. So is her father, Henry (Richard Hoag). So is her sister, Emily (Sarah Rafferty), who throws her a shower in LA. And also Leon's sister, Towie (Susan Kelechi Watson), who joins her in Las Vegas for a few days to offer massages and pick up the vibes of her chi.

*Small, Beautifully Moving Parts*, written and directed by Annie Howell and Lisa Robinson, is effortlessly engaging in introducing us to these people. That's possibly because Anna Margaret Hollyman, who plays Sarah, has a lovable screen presence. In this early leading role of a brief career, she has the sort of charm we felt from the first films of Sandra Bullock or Greta Gerwig. She deals with a lot of emotions in the film's compact running time, and always feels natural and spontaneous.

After learning she's pregnant, she becomes obsessed with motherhood and her own mother, who disappeared from her life years ago. She learns vaguely that her mom is living "off the map" somewhere in the Nevada desert. Leon encourages Sarah to contact her, but her father and sister advise against it. Her father confesses he's baffled by the behavior of his former wife.

Sarah perhaps unwisely sets off alone to drive off the map and back into her mother's life. This takes her near the Grand Canyon, where she snaps a family photo of some tourists and quizzes them like she's Errol Morris doing a blog on photography: "Is taking family photos a way to run away from despair?"

The deeper Sarah penetrates into the wilderness, the more her technology fails her. The GPS gives up. Her phone battery runs out. When she finally arrives at the Dome, which her mother is said to inhabit, she's been reduced to just . . . herself.

The pleasure of everything up until this

point has been intrinsic. Hollyman and the other actors are good company, and an obsession with technology could inspire a complete film. (Indeed, it has: Aronofsky's *Pi* comes to mind.) But when Sarah finally encounters her mother (Mary Beth Peil), the movie itself goes off the map, in a good way. It offers no answers, no facile psychological observations, just the mystery of personality. So I must not discuss those scenes.

This is a small film, and knows exactly how to be a small film. Like many *New Yorker* short stories, its purpose is to strike a particular note and allow it to reverberate. Life is made up of challenges that cannot be solved but only accepted. And Sarah will discover that her child will need a lot more maintenance than a microwave oven.

## A Small Act ★ ★ ★ ½

NO MPAA RATING, 98 m., 2010

With Chris Mburu, Jane Wanjiru Muigai, and Hilde Back. A documentary directed and written by Jennifer Arnold.

The heartwarming documentary *A Small Act* centers on the life story of Chris Mburu, who as a small boy living in a mud house in a Kenyan village had his primary and secondary education paid for by a Swedish woman. This cost her fifteen dollars a month. They had never met. He went on to the University of Nairobi, graduated from Harvard Law School, and is today a United Nations human rights commissioner.

The film shows Mburu seeking the Swedish woman who "made my life possible." She is Hilde Back. Before even meeting her, in gratitude he started a foundation named the Hilde Back Education Fund to fund scholarships for poor village children. She is now eighty-five years old, a German Jew who was sent to Sweden as a child. Her family died in the Holocaust. She never married, has lived in the same apartment for thirty-five years, was a schoolteacher. She is a tiny woman, but robust and filled with energy. We see them meeting for the first time.

She is flown to Kenya, serenaded by the choir from Mburu's village, feasted, thanked, gowned in traditional robes. She says that her fifteen dollars was an insignificant sum to her, but she kept it up because she thought even a small act was worth performing.

In the film, we see the mud house Chris grew up in. Then we follow Kimani, Ruth, and Caroline—three Kenyan students who hope to win high scores and continue in school. This will depend on winning one of the scholarships. Their families pin all of their hopes on these kids.

One says she would miss her family at a boarding school, but would enjoy being able to study by electric light. In this village the students study by the light of a single oil flame. Most families in Kenya want their children to attend high school, seeing that as the key to success in life. They lack the money, but recently, Kenya has been able to make primary education free.

The schools we see are not physically impressive; the one focused on in the film is a very basic brick structure with no amenities and crowded classrooms with simple board benches and desks. A gym? Don't make me laugh.

Education focuses on reading (in English) and math, with some history and geography. The students are impressed by their ability to be in school at all. Their parents sacrifice to send them; child labor could add to the family income. At the end of primary school, they take tests to qualify for secondary education if they can afford it. The film shows some of the test questions. To me, they look difficult for kids that age. They pass or fail; too many American schools graduate students who are functionally illiterate.

Hilde Back is asked if, since she never had children, she thought of Chris as a son. We see in the film that they stay in close touch. "But I have had children," she replied. "I was a teacher. I had many, many children." And one lived in a mud house in Kenya.

## Snow Flower and the Secret Fan ★ ★

PG-13,103 m., 2011

Gianna Jun (Snow Flower/Sophia), Li Bingbing (Nina/Lily), Vivian Wu (Aunt), Jiang Wu (Butcher), Russell Wong (Bank CEO), Coco Chiang (Anna), Hu Jingyun (Mrs. Liao). Directed by Wayne Wang and produced by Wendi

Murdoch and Florence Sloan. Screenplay by Angela Workman, Ron Bass, and Michael K. Ray, based on the novel by Lisa See.

The Chinese, who have been innovators in so many areas, are now revealed to have formalized the BFF relationship as long ago as 1839. In Hunan, when two women were Best Friends Forever, they were *laotong*. This was a relationship that could begin with the agreement of their parents before birth and persist independent of marriage, children, or the changing fortunes of life. It is at the heart of Lisa See's period best-seller *Snow Flower and the Secret Fan,* and has inspired a film that carries it into the present day.

Whether *laotong* represents empowerment or weakness for women is a good question. In the film's period story, parents link their daughters so that both will have someone to depend on in a world run by men. In the modern story, Sophia (Gianna Jun) and Lily (Li Bingbing) use the concept to describe a bond that forms between them as children, becomes almost a fetish in adolescence, and then is threatened when their adult lives take different pathways. We wonder if lesbian feelings are involved; the film provokes that possibility but never addresses it.

As movies about female bonding go, *Snow Flower and the Secret Fan* is thin tea. Soppy and sentimental, it evokes *Divine Secrets of the Ya-Ya Sisterhood* without improving on it. More of *Fried Green Tomatoes* would have been preferable. The story opens in modern Shanghai, where we meet Lily, an upward-bound executive, and Sophia, who has abandoned her own career path. After a traffic accident, Sophia is comatose, and Lily abandons an important trip to New York to be at her bedside.

She discovers the manuscript of Sophia's novel, which involves a nineteenth-century *laotong* between Snow Flower (also played by Gianna Jun) and Nina (also Bingbing). Snow Flower was subjected to the cruel practice of foot binding, which in crippling her won her a desirable husband. Nina stood by her side. Despite a class difference and the fact that Nina was Korean, their families sealed the *laotong* pact because, apparently, their astrological signs were in such close harmony.

I haven't read the novel by See, but I find it takes place entirely in the past. Director Wayne Wang and his screenwriters have invented the parallel modern story, and cut back and forth between the two. This isn't persuasive, because in the nineteenth century *laotong* was apparently an embedded social custom and a survival tool, and in the twenty-first it seems—well, about as momentous as being someone's BFF. Oprah and Gayle, meet Sophia and Lily.

Wayne Wang made the best Western film I've seen about friendship between Asian women, *The Joy Luck Club.* Now he has made the most soporific. Both stories here suffer by focusing more on *laotong* than on the actual lives of the women, as if their bond transcended daily experience and was more like a vow taken by a nun or monk. Men are entirely secondary, and that conspicuously includes an inexplicable character played by Hugh Jackman, who becomes Sophia's mere BF.

The film has been scored with music too sweet and saccharine, insisting on how bittersweet everything is, when in fact the storytelling seems to find it all rather lovely. Tragic, perhaps, but lovely. Nor am I sure what parallels to draw between the two stories, other than that the earlier functions as a fiction created by Sophia to idealize her closeness to Lily. Apparently Lisa See considered it adequate on its own terms.

We in the West tend to view China through eyes much influenced by art. Today's China is no more comparable to Hunan Province in 1839 than today's Texas is comparable to the time of the Alamo. By running the stories in parallel, Wang's approach causes needless interruptions in both and makes it difficult to tell two stories that are, after all, separate. Presumably the connection is that Sophia sees her novel as representing her friendship with Lily. The need to tell the two stories in 103 minutes leads to some vagueness. I am no more sure than Lily is why Sophia acted to forfeit her education and professional future. She is the film's most intriguing character, and I wanted more.

I believe, however, that some audience members will admire this film specifically because of what I've referred to as soppy and sentimental. The actresses are evocative, and

Wang sees them with a sympathetic eye. The visuals are too pretty for me but not for everyone. The music, lushly arranged, will find fans. And there was one detail I found fascinating: During the Hunan period *laotong* pals could communicate in a written language only they understood. I suppose this is true, and if it is, why hasn't that become better known?

## The Snowtown Murders ★ ★ ★ ½

NO MPAA RATING, 114 m., 2012

Daniel Henshall (John Bunting), Lucas Pittaway (Jamie), Louise Harris (Elizabeth), Anthony Groves (Troy), David Walker (Mark), Aaron Viergever (Robert), Richard Green (Barry), Beau Gosling (David), Frank Cwertniak (Jeffrey), Aasta Brown (Verna). Directed by Justin Kurzel and produced by Anna McLeish and Sarah Shaw. Screenplay by Shaun Grant, inspired by the books *Killing for Pleasure* by Debi Marshall and *The Snowtown Murders* by Andrew McGarry.

In a dismal and defeated Australian suburb, we meet a family that seems put upon Earth to chain-smoke and stare blankly into space. The dog has the most self-esteem. One of the sons, Jamie, has been molested by his mother's worthless boyfriend and by Troy, one of his own brothers. It doesn't occur to him to seek help. He is so powerless he seems to regard victimhood as his fate.

In the world of this family a man appears who at first appears to a benefactor. John Bunting materializes at the kitchen table, seems to assign himself the role of father, starts preparing meals and beaming with reassurance at everyone. Learning of the molestation, he kills some kangaroos, chops off their heads, and enlists Jamie in helping him pound them into bloody mash and dumping them on the molester's front porch.

Bunting was to become Australia's most notorious serial killer, now serving consecutive life sentences for eleven murders. What instinct led him to this family whose actions he was able to completely control? Jamie is presented as weak and passive, and is sobbing as he helps strangle his own half brother almost as an act of mercy to end the torture.

The film is a chilling study of an evil, dominant personality and his victims. It works primarily through an astonishingly good performance by Daniel Henshall, as Bunting. Compact, stout, muscular, he has beady eyes that twinkle as he plays the provider and protector. He ladles food on everyone's plate and has a way of asking them if they're happy that's merciless and aggressive. Listen to him ask a seemingly friendly question and follow it too quickly with "Right?" or "Yes?" or "You do?" so that he is commanding an answer. Look at the sunny smile and encouraging expression that feel so sinister. With inexorable slowness, he tightens his grip on the family until he has complete mastery. He is presumably the lover of the mother, Elizabeth (Louise Harris), but uses her primarily for access to her three sons. She is a drab, unkempt woman, hardly even speaking, the light dead in her eyes.

The film is a directorial debut by Justin Kurzel, who has an impressive command of mood. His colors tend toward gray and lifeless. His characters sit exhausted in the house or on the porch and smoke, smoke, smoke. Bunting is the only one who doesn't smoke, and Kurzel frequently shows him eating. There is something disgusting about his manner of feeding himself; how is he able to suggest that he would be entitled to every bite even if he were in a room of starving people?

The movie isn't structured like most true crime stories. The plot and characters are slightly muddled. Not everything is explained. It's not a procedural. Kurzel's purpose is to bury the characters in a miasma of evil. Bunting enlists neighbors in kitchen table conversations about pedophiles and gays, and directs the talk about what should be done to them: "Right? Right?" I'm not sure if he actually cares about molestation and so on; it is simply a pretext to control the will of others and force them to murder through mind control.

Serial killers are often described as loners. Bunting is sociable, pleasant, friendly. He likes company. One wonders how his puppets feel as they realize he has charmed his way into ruling their lives. *The Snowtown Murders* is distressing and almost unbearably painful, the most frightening film about a psychopath I've seen. There is no way to understand John Bunting. He is quite bluntly an evil man.

## Snow White and the Huntsman ★ ★ ★ ½

PG-13, 127 m., 2012

Kristen Stewart (Snow White), Charlize Theron (Queen Ravenna), Chris Hemsworth (Eric the Huntsman), Sam Claflin (William), Sam Spruell (Finn), Ian McShane (Beith), Bob Hoskins (Muir), Ray Winstone (Gort), Nick Frost (Nion), Eddie Marsan (Duir), Toby Jones (Coll), Johnny Harris (Quert), Brian Gleeson (Gus). Directed by Rupert Sanders and produced by Sam Mercer, Palak Patel, and Joe Roth. Screenplay by Evan Daugherty, John Lee Hancock, and Hossein Amini.

*Snow White and the Huntsman* reinvents the legendary story in a film of astonishing beauty and imagination. It's the last thing you would expect from a picture with this title. It falters in its storytelling, because Snow White must be entirely good, the queen must be entirely bad, and there's no room for nuance. The end is therefore predetermined. But oh, what a ride.

This is an older Snow White than we usually think of. Played for most of the film by Kristen Stewart, capable and plucky, she spent long years locked in a room of her late father's castle, imprisoned by his cruel second wife (Charlize Theron). When she escapes and sets about righting wrongs, she is a mature young woman, of interest to the two young men who join in her mission. But the movie sidesteps scenes of romance, and in a way, I suppose that's wise.

The huntsman (Chris Hemsworth) is a heroic, mead-guzzling hunter who is assigned by the queen to track down Snow White and bring her back to the castle. After encountering her, however, he is so impressed he changes sides. There is also Prince William (Sam Claflin), smitten with her since childhood, and the two men join in an unstated alliance.

The queen lives in terror of losing the beauty of her youth, and constantly tops up with the blood of virgins to restore it. She tests her success with the proverbial mirror on the wall, which melts into molten metal and assumes a spectral form, not unlike Death in *The Seventh Seal*, although its metallic transformation process reminds us of *Terminator 2*.

The castle, which sits in eerie splendor on an island joined to the mainland only at low tide, is a Gothic fantasy that reminded me of *Gormenghast*. The queen is joined there by her brother, somewhat diminished by his blond pageboy haircut, who does her bidding but seems rather out to lunch. Extras appear when needed, then disappear. The queen commands extraordinary supernatural powers, including the ability to materialize countless black birds that can morph into fighting demons or shards of cutting metal.

All of this is rendered appropriately by the special effects, but the treasure of this film is in two of its locations: the harsh, forbidding Dark Forest, and an enchanted fairyland. Both of these realms exist near the castle, and the huntsman is enlisted in the first place because he knows the Dark Forest, where Snow White has taken refuge.

This is a forbidding realm where nothing lives, and is thick with the blackened bones of dead trees, as if a forest fire had burned only the green. There is no cheer here and not a living thing, except for a monstrous troll whom Snow White confronts in a dramatic staredown. After the huntsman frees her from the Dark Forest, they are delighted to find, or be found by, the Eight Dwarves.

Yes, eight, although one doesn't survive, reducing their number to the proverbial seven. These characters look strangely familiar, and no wonder: The magic of CGI has provided the faces of familiar British actors such as Ian McShane, Bob Hoskins, Ray Winstone, Nick Frost, Eddie Marsan, and Toby Jones. While this technique is effective enough, it nevertheless deprives eight working (real) dwarves of jobs, which isn't really fair.

The dwarves lead them to my favorite realm in the film, an enchanting fairyland, which is a triumph of art direction and CGI. Mushrooms open their eyes and regard the visitors. Cute forest animals scamper and gambol in tribute to a forest scene in Disney's 1937 film. The fairies themselves are naked pale-skinned sprites with old, wise faces. The spirit of this forest is embodied by a great white stag with expressive eyes and horns that spread in awesome complexity. This is a wonderful scene. The director, Rupert Sanders, who began in TV commercials, is clearly familiar with establishing memorable places.

As for the rest, there is a sufficiency of medieval battle scenes, too many for my taste, and a fairly exciting siege of the castle, aided by the intervention of the dwarves and featuring catapults that hurl globs of burning tar, always enjoyable.

There is a great film here somewhere, perhaps one that allowed greater complexity for the characters. But considering that I walked in expecting no complexity at all, let alone the visual wonderments of the film, *Snow White and the Huntsman* is a considerable experience.

## The Social Network ★ ★ ★ ★

PG-13, 120 m., 2010

Jesse Eisenberg (Mark Zuckerberg), Andrew Garfield (Eduardo Saverin), Justin Timberlake (Sean Parker), Armie Hammer (Cameron/Tyler Winklevoss), Max Minghella (Divya Narendra), Brenda Song (Christy Ling), Rooney Mara (Erica). Directed by David Fincher and produced by Dana Brunetti, Cean Chaffin, Michael De Luca, and Scott Rudin. Screenplay by Aaron Sorkin, based on the book *The Accidental Billionaires* by Ben Mezrich.

*The Social Network* is about a young man who possessed an uncanny ability to look into a system of unlimited possibilities and sense a winning move. His name is Mark Zuckerberg, he created Facebook, he became a billionaire in his early twenties, and he reminds me of the chess prodigy Bobby Fischer. There may be a touch of Asperger's syndrome in both: They possess genius but are tone-deaf in social situations. Example: It is inefficient to seek romance by using strict logic to demonstrate your intellectual arrogance.

David Fincher's film has the rare quality of being not only as smart as its brilliant hero, but in the same way. It is cocksure, impatient, cold, exciting, and instinctively perceptive. It hurtles through two hours of spellbinding dialogue. It makes an untellable story clear and fascinating. It is said to be impossible to make a movie about a writer, because how can you show him only writing? It must also be impossible to make a movie about a computer programmer, because what is programming but writing in a language few people in the audience know? Yet Fincher and his writer, Aaron Sorkin, are able to explain the Facebook phenomenon in terms we can immediately understand, which is the reason five hundred million of us have signed up.

To conceive of Facebook, Zuckerberg (Jesse Eisenberg) needed to know almost nothing about relationships or human nature (and apparently he didn't). What he needed was the ability to intuit a way to involve the human race in the Kevin Bacon game. Remember that Kevin Bacon himself need not know more than a fraction of the people linking through him. Same on Facebook. I probably know 40 of my Facebook friends well, 100 glancingly, 200 by reputation. All the others are friends of friends. I can't remember the last time I received a friend request from anyone I didn't share at least one "mutual friend" with.

For the presence of Facebook, we possibly have to thank a woman named Erica (Rooney Mara). *The Social Network* begins with Erica's date with Zuckerberg. He nervously sips a beer and speed talks through an aggressive interrogation. It's an exercise in sadistic conversational gamesmanship. Erica gets fed up, calls him an asshole, and walks out.

Erica (a fictional character) is right, but at that moment she puts Zuckerberg in business. He goes home, has more beers, and starts hacking into the "facebooks" of Harvard dorms to collect the head shots of campus women. He programs a page where they can be rated for their beauty. This is sexist and illegal, and proves so popular it crashes the campus servers. After it's fertilized by a mundane Web site called the Harvard Connection, Zuckerberg grows it into Facebook.

In theory there are more possible moves on a chessboard than molecules in the universe. Chess masters cannot possibly calculate all of them, but using intuition they can "see" a way through this near-infinity to a winning move. Nobody was ever better at chess than Bobby Fischer. Likewise, programming languages and techniques are widely known, but it was Zuckerberg who intuited how he could link them with a networking site. The genius of Facebook requires not psychological insight but its method of combining ego with interaction. Zuckerberg wanted to get revenge on all the women at Harvard. To do that he involved them in a matrix that is still growing.

It's said there are child prodigies in only three areas: math, music, and chess. These nonverbal areas require little maturity or knowledge of human nature, but a quick ability to perceive patterns, logical rules, and linkages. I suspect computer programming may be a fourth area.

Zuckerberg may have had the insight that created Facebook, but he didn't do it alone in a room, and the movie gets a narration by cutting between depositions for lawsuits. Along the way we get insights into the pecking order at Harvard, a campus where ability joins wealth and family as success factors. We meet the twins Cameron and Tyler Winklevoss (both played by Armie Hammer), rich kids who believe Zuckerberg stole their Harvard Connection in making Facebook. We meet Eduardo Saverin (Andrew Garfield), Zuckerberg's roommate and best (only) friend, who was made CFO of the company, loaned it the money it needed to get started, and was frozen out. And most memorably we meet Sean Parker (Justin Timberlake), the founder of two legendary Web start-ups, Napster and Plaxo.

It is the mercurial Parker, just out of work but basked in fame and past success, who grabbed Zuckerberg by the ears and pulled him into the big time. He explained why Facebook needed to move to Silicon Valley. Why more money would come from venture capitalists than Eduardo would ever raise with his hat-in-hand visits to wealthy New Yorkers. And he tried, not successfully, to introduce Zuckerberg into the fast lane: big offices, wild parties, women, the availability of booze and cocaine.

Zuckerberg was not seduced by this lifestyle. He was uninterested in money, stayed in modest houses, didn't fall to drugs. A subtext the movie never comments on is the omnipresence of attractive Asian women. Most of them are smart Harvard undergrads, two of them (allied with Sean) are Victoria's Secret models, one (Christy, played by Brenda Song) is Eduardo's girlfriend. Zuckerberg himself doesn't have much of a social life onscreen, misses parties, would rather work. He has such tunnel vision he doesn't even register when Sean redrafts the financial arrangements to write himself in and Eduardo out.

The testimony in the depositions makes it clear there is a case to be made against Zuckerberg, many of them sins of omission. It's left to the final crawl to explain how they turned out. The point is to show an interaction of undergraduate chaos, enormous amounts of money, and manic energy.

In an age when movie dialogue is dumbed and slowed down to suit slow-wits in the audience, the dialogue here has the velocity and snap of screwball comedy. Eisenberg, who has specialized in playing nice or clueless, is a heat-seeking missile in search of his own goals. Timberlake pulls off the tricky assignment of playing Sean Parker as both a hotshot and someone who engaged Zuckerberg as an intellectual equal. Andrew Garfield evokes an honest friend who is not the right man to be CFO of the company that took off without him, but deserves sympathy.

*The Social Network* is a great film not because of its dazzling style or visual cleverness, but because it is splendidly well made. Despite the baffling complications of computer programming, Web strategy, and big finance, Aaron Sorkin's screenplay makes it all clear, and we don't follow the story so much as get dragged along behind it. I saw it with an audience that seemed wrapped up in an unusual way: It was very, *very* interested.

## The Soft Skin ★ ★ ★

NO MPAA RATING, 113 m., 2011

Jean Desailly (Pierre Lachenay), Francoise Dorleac (Nicole Chomette), Nelly Benedetti (Franca Lachenay), Daniel Ceccaldi (Clement), Sabine Haudepin (Sabine). Directed by Francois Truffaut and produced by Truffaut and Antonio da Cunha Telles. Screenplay by Truffaut and Jean-Louis Richard.

Francois Truffaut's *The Soft Skin* is being revived at the very moment when it seems uncannily prophetic. It tells the story of a wealthy and famous French man who has an affair with an airline hostess and foolishly thinks he can keep it a secret from his wife. The difference between Pierre Lachenay and Dominique Strauss-Kahn is that Pierre is timid and guilty, although he would have saved himself a great deal of grief by being even more timid.

This 1964 melodrama was a change of direction for Truffaut, whose *The 400 Blows* (1959), *Shoot the Piano Player* (1960), and *Jules and Jim* (1962) helped define the French New Wave. Here is material more suited to bourgeoisie soap opera, although it is fairly scathing about France's intellectual elite. Pierre (Jean Desailly) is a Parisian literary editor and author, which means that in France he is a good deal more famous than he would be in many countries. So famous that the young air attendant Nicole (Francoise Dorleac) is quite willing to be seduced, and must be considered an accomplice in the process.

Pierre is perhaps forty, an impeccably groomed, well-spoken married man with a delightful wife and a lovable daughter. Truffaut must have cast Jean Desailly for his appearance of ordinary respectability. His hair is always neatly parted, his tie is always in place, he is polite almost to a fault. He isn't a caricature of a lustful, cheating husband; he seems almost abashed by his sexual feelings.

And Nicole? What does she see in him? She sees his fame. She knows who he is. She is staying in his hotel in Lisbon, where he has gone to give a speech about (Truffaut's hero) Balzac. She met his eyes on the airplane, they saw each other again at the airport, and they shared the same elevator at the hotel—he rather pointedly staying on past his floor. Her eyes in the elevator made her willingness clear. He calls her from his room, to, yes, apologize for not helping her with her packages. Although this polite meekness allows their affair to begin, it also contains the seeds of its destruction.

There seems no reason for Pierre to stray. His wife, Franca (Nelly Benedetti), seems an ideal spouse: smart, loving, competent, sexy. They get along in bed. He strays because . . . he can? He is flattered by the company of this younger woman? In the film, Truffaut gives Nicole no particular qualities other than beauty and availability; indeed, it is Pierre's panic and secretiveness that bring out her best qualities, of self-respect and pride.

This happens during the film's centerpiece, Pierre's trip to Reims to introduce a film. He goes only so that Nicole can accompany him. But the chairman of the event is a friend of Pierre's from Paris, so Nicole must be hidden. They check into a different hotel, there is no ticket for Nicole at the screening, and later he's trapped over drinks with the chairman while through the window he sees Nicole being hit on by a creep and does nothing. She will not allow herself to be treated in this way.

What it comes down to is: Pierre is a lousy adulterer. He lacks the desire, the reason, and the skill. Truffaut nicely portrays the crisis of social embarrassment that develops when he tries to keep Nicole out of sight. Part of his dilemma is that he tries so desperately to do the safe and prudent thing. This only leads, as you will see, to catastrophe, in an ending that is perhaps justified but is unconvincing. How could anyone care about mundane Pierre that much?

*Note: Francoise Dorleac was the older sister of Catherine Deneuve and costarred with her in Jacques Demy's* The Young Girls of Rochefort *(1967). On June 26 of that year, she died in a car crash near Nice.*

## Solitary Man ★ ★ ★ ½

R, 90 m., 2010

Michael Douglas (Ben Kalmen), Mary-Louise Parker (Jordan Karsch), Jenna Fischer (Susan Porter), Jesse Eisenberg (Cheston), Imogen Poots (Allyson Karsch), Susan Sarandon (Nancy Kalmen), Danny DeVito (Jimmy Merino). Directed by Brian Koppelman and David Levien and produced by Heidi Jo Markel, Paul Schiff, and Steven Soderbergh. Screenplay by Koppelman.

For an actor with so many films, Michael Douglas hasn't played many conventional heroes. Yes, he did those *Romancing the Stone* roles, and he's been more memorable as a villain (*Wall Street*), but his strongest roles are as sinners: not big or bad enough to be villains, more ordinary men, smart, glib, conniving, trying to get by on short dues. Here is where he best uses his considerable screen presence. And he gets better at it as he grows older because his characters keep on sinning when they just don't have the stamina for it anymore.

In *Solitary Man,* he plays Ben Kalmen, once a regional celebrity as "New York's Honest Car Dealer." Ben is good-looking, still has that great head of hair, and is as persuasive as—well, as a good car dealer. In business he can sense what car to put you in. In sex he can sense what mood to put you in. He closes a lot of deals.

He isn't solitary by choice but by default. He cheated on his good wife, Nancy (Susan Sarandon). He disappointed their daughter, Susan (Jenna Fischer), one time too many. He cheats on his current companion, Jordan (Mary-Louise Parker), in a particularly unforgivable way. He uses the offer of his experience in life to charm Cheston (Jesse Eisenberg), a college student, and then betrays him. He has lied to his customers so often that, as everyone knows, "Honest Ben Kalmen" spent time behind bars.

Yet he's charming and persuasive. He looks like a winner until you look too close. *Solitary Man* follows him for several days after he agrees to accompany Jordan's daughter, Allyson (Imogen Poots), as she goes to Boston to settle in for her freshman year at college. This is the same school he attended. He knows the dean, which may be a help.

You want to like Ben. He works on encouraging that. When he was younger and less of a sinner, he must have been good to know, and there's an effective character in *Solitary Man* who suggests that. This is his old school-years buddy (Danny DeVito) who still runs a greasy spoon diner. On campus, Ben befriends the sophomore Cheston with man-of-the-world advice about sex, success, and how to sell yourself. With women, his approach is solicitous: Do some men misunderstand you? Are your qualities recognized? What are you getting out of the transaction?

The film is all about Ben Kalmen, but one of the strengths of Michael Douglas's performance is that he isn't playing a character. He's playing a character who is playing a character. Ben's life has become performance art. You get the feeling he never goes offstage. He sees few women he doesn't try seducing. As a car dealer, he was also in the seduction trade. His business was selling himself. At a dealership, it's hard to move a lemon. What about in life when you need a recall?

What happens with Ben and the people in his life, especially the women, I should not hint at here. The movie depends on our fascination as we see what lengths this man will go to. Reading in the gossip sheets that Douglas in years past was led astray by lust, we suspect that some of his performance is based on experience. Why is a man a serial seducer? To prove to himself that he can, which to a woman is not a compelling reason to be seduced.

This is a smart, effective film, a comedy in many ways even though it's bookended with reasons for Ben to see it as a potential tragedy. It's a serious comedy, perceptive, nuanced, with every supporting performance well calibrated to demonstrate to Ben that he can run but he can no longer hide. One of the best is by DeVito, who has been standing behind his counter for years and is perfectly content. He doesn't have that hunger that gnaws at Ben.

Imogen Poots is good, too, as the girl going away to school. She could sell Honest Ben the Brooklyn Bridge, and he would think he was talking her into it. As the trip upstate begins to fall apart, so does Ben's shaky financial future, and he has a meeting with a banker (Richard Schiff) that plays out with relentless logic.

Here is one of Michael Douglas's finest performances. Because the other characters, no matter what they think, never truly engage Ben Kalmen, he's on that stage by himself. Everyone else is in the audience. Douglas plays Ben as charismatic, he plays him as shameless, he plays him as brave, and very gradually, he learns to play him as himself. That's the only role left.

## Something Better Somewhere Else ★ ★ ★

NO MPAA RATING, 76 m., 2010

With Christian Stolte, David Pasquesi, John G. Connolly, Stephanie Childers, Naomi Ashley, Tim Polk, and Megan Moore Burns. Directed by Ron Lazzeretti and produced by Ed Amaya. Screenplay by Lazzeretti.

*Something Better Somewhere Else* is a delightful film and in some stretches a flawless one. It tells four stories, each one immediately engaging, and gets in and out without overstaying its welcome. In a world of bloated and dumbed-down entertainment, here's a movie with the quickness and acute observation of a good short story.

So what is the flawless part? That would be the execution by director Ron Lazzeretti. Yes, he wrote and directed it, and we'll get back to that. But what I kept noticing was the excellence in details. The acting, the casting, the dialogue, editing, music, and meticulous camera placement. The feeling that not a shot was careless. The film knows what it's doing.

The four stories have one theme: moving on. We live much of our lives, I suspect, in a state of tension between the belief that there must be *Something Better Somewhere Else* and a fear of abandoning what we know and are familiar with. The four segments apply this truth to work, love, marriage, and home.

The first short, *Last Day,* involves a man leaving a job he hates at a place everyone else hates, too. He inspires admiration, envy, and (after farewell drinks) even some hatred. Notice how economically Lazzeretti directs his supporting actors to make each one stand out as an individual. And watch the scene in the bar when his hero uneasily watches one conversation while mired in another.

*Wedding Night,* the second, is like an O. Henry story, and the ending creates some of the same dissatisfaction he was sometimes guilty of. Still, there's a nice narrative bait and switch.

The third film, *Flowers,* is surprisingly evocative. Set the plot aside for a moment and see how observant the camera is in noticing there is something about a man sitting on a bench at a bus stop and holding a big bouquet of flowers that just makes some women need to smile. This stretch of the film would fail if a single shot seemed "acted," but none does.

The fourth, *Move,* takes place on a family's last day before moving to California. It was the wife who wanted this move, and now she's having second thoughts, and her husband doggedly tries to keep everyone on schedule. In the process we listen to a farewell conversation between the girl and her boyfriend that is written and acted so convincingly we realize we don't hear many authentic teenage voices in teenage movies.

Lazzeretti's perfectionism shows with a shot showing two extras. Observing emotion during the family's departure process, one kid looks at his pal (with the round wire-rim glasses) and that's all that happens, but look at how it's photographed and edited, and realize how much you think you know about those kids. Storytelling is as much a matter of technique as laborious plotting.

Lazzeretti is a Chicago-based commercial director, and that's a form that requires every frame to do heavy lifting. He wrote and produced Michael Keaton's memorable directing debut, *The Merry Gentlemen* (2009). *Something Better Somewhere Else* is only seventy-six minutes long, but three of the four films remain in my mind with as much psychic weight as features.

## Something Borrowed ★ ★

PG-13, 112 m., 2011

Kate Hudson (Darcy), Ginnifer Goodwin (Rachel), John Krasinski (Ethan), Colin Egglesfield (Dex), Steve Howey (Marcus), Ashley Williams (Claire). Directed by Luke Greenfield and produced by Broderick Johnson, Andrew A. Kosove, Aaron Lubin, Pamela Schein Murphy, Molly Smith, and Hilary Swank. Screenplay by Jennie Snyder Urman, based on the novel by Emily Giffin.

One of the curious problems with *Something Borrowed* is that Kate Hudson's performance is too effective. She plays Darcy, the lifelong best friend of the heroine, Rachel (Ginnifer Goodwin). Blond, rich, and headstrong, Darcy always gets her way in their relationship. And as the film opens she's about to be married to Dex (Colin Egglesfield), whom Rachel has had a crush on since law school. No good can come of this.

The plot mechanics are more or less inevitable. Thrown together again as the ceremony approaches, Rachel and Dex realize they have always been in love. But what to do? Rachel doesn't want to hurt her best friend. And Dex has a mother who struggles with depression; only the marriage seems capable of cheering her up.

To be married as an aid to someone else's mental health calls, I think, your own into question. This is especially true because the depressed mother (Jill Eikenberry) doesn't have a single line in the movie, and is seen only looking sad sometimes and happy sometimes. I believe, but cannot be sure, that a surprise decision made late in the film is triggered by her single ambivalent expression.

Now as to Kate Hudson. She plays an alcoholic. This is as clear as day, although I'll bet you won't see her described that way in many other reviews. Among the danger signals of alcoholism must certainly be playing badminton on the beach with a glass of wine in your hand, sitting down in a bar and ordering six shots of tequila, and drinking in every scene where she is not literally being fitted for a wedding dress. If you are marrying an alcoholic and are not one yourself, you shouldn't do it to cheer up your mom.

Kate Hudson plays Darcy so well that she almost forces the film apart at the seams; her character is too strong for it. Dex and Rachel, on the other hand, are sweet, inoffensive, beautiful people, who let others determine key decisions in their lives. As played by Ginnifer Goodwin and Colin Egglesfield, they are also extraordinarily attractive, and I almost held that against them until the story developed some of their depths. Goodwin has one of those faces of which you can think no bad things.

The movie supplies two other male characters, Ethan (John Krasinski) and party animal Marcus (Steve Howey). Ethan is Rachel's confidant during their lunch hours together. He figures out the whole story and pleads with Rachel to express her own feelings for once and not always let Darcy be the winner. It was even Rachel who introduced Darcy to Dex, for criminy sakes, and all but gave him away. Ethan avoids the clutches of their lustful friend Claire (Ashley Williams), a woman whose appearance can only be explained by the need for someone clutchy.

If Dex's mother says nothing, his father (Geoff Pierson) has a speech that is succinct and powerful, essentially ordering his son to go ahead with the wedding. The problem with that is that few fathers order their sons to marry ditzy drunks, but then again, maybe he doesn't know about Darcy's style at badminton.

*Something Borrowed* gathers an undeniable narrative momentum in its last half because all of the characters are treated sincerely and played in a straightforward style. It's just that we don't love them enough. Dex is too weak, Rachel is too sweet, Ethan has the same problem he accused Rachel of, and only Marcus finally seems to get what he deserves.

## Somewhere ★ ★ ★ ★

R, 96 m., 2010

Stephen Dorff (Johnny Marco), Elle Fanning (Cleo), Chris Pontius (Sammy). Directed by Sofia Coppola and produced by Sofia Coppola, Roman Coppola, and G. Mac Brown. Screenplay by Sofia Coppola.

Don't distinguish what he feels with the word "existential." It has nothing to do with philosophy. He believes he's nothing, and it appears he's correct. This is called depression, but it may simply be a realistic view of the situation. Johnny Marco sits in a suite of the Chateau Marmont, that little hotel for generations of Hollywood hideouts, and finds himself a hollow man.

He is a movie star. With that comes such options as money, fame, sex, drugs. Fame is a joke because he gets nothing from it. Sex involves mechanics of the genitals. He drinks and takes drugs and gets a little wound up, but pleasure doesn't seem to be involved. On two occasions he hires twin blond strippers to come to his room, set up their portable equipment, and do choreographed pole dances. No sex is involved. He is demonstrating the truth that if you stare long enough at a wall, it will break the monotony if blond twins do pole dances in front of it.

Sofia Coppola's new film *Somewhere* involves, as did her *Lost in Translation* (2003), a man separated from his family and sitting alone in a hotel room. Its opening resembles Vincent Gallo's *The Brown Bunny* (2003): a long shot of a vehicle tearing around a track. A man racing madly to nowhere. Bill Murray's Bob in *Lost in Translation* makes dutiful but cheerless phone calls home from Japan. Stephen Dorff's Johnny spends dutiful time with his eleven-year-old daughter, Cleo (Elle Fanning). Neither seems meaningfully connected.

Because so much of *Somewhere* is set at the Chateau Marmont, it might be useful to discuss it. It isn't cheap, but nobody goes there to indulge in conspicuous consumption. What it offers above all is a management that minds its own business. What happens at the Chateau Marmont stays at the Chateau Marmont. It's often linked with another semiresidential legend a few blocks away, the Sunset Marquis. The Chateau, I sense, is more useful for clients who want not so much privacy as retreat. There's a scene where Johnny nods to Benicio Del Toro in the elevator. I'll bet you Del Toro was staying there at the time. They are both simply waiting for their floors.

The notion of a star sinking into seclusion and depression isn't new. Gus Van Sant's *Last Days* (2005) starred Michael Pitt as a character unmistakably inspired by Kurt Cobain. What distinguishes Coppola's film is the detail in her portrait of celebrity life. Remember that she was a little girl and later a young actress on the sets of her father's movies. Now that we see how observant she is, we can only speculate about what she understood right from the start. She played Michael Corleone's baby.

The movie has, for example, an unusually accurate portrait of how publicists work from the client's point of view. Some become friends, some remain employees, but during work they function as parents and guardians. The star's contract requires him to do some press. The phone rings and the publicist tells the star where to go and what to do. He takes on a certain passivity. The car is there; he takes the car. The press is there; he talks to the press. Some stars are more interested and interesting. Not Johnny. He flies to Milan to accept an award, and the event plays like a bus ride with a Jacuzzi.

He seems to suffer from anhedonia, the inability to feel pleasure. Perhaps he hardly feels anything. The film only indirectly suggests some of the reasons he got this way. It is not a diagnosis, still less a prescription. Johnny stares at the wall and the film stares back. This is more interesting than it may sound. Coppola watches this world. The familiar strangers on the hotel staff are on a first-name basis because a star's world has become reduced to his support. Hookers and sex partners come and go. There are parties filled with strangers, most of them not excited to see a star because they see stars constantly.

Then his daughter. What led to the divorce Cleo probably knows better than he does. The child of an actor, she has learned to play a star. She observes his drinking, his detached attempts at fatherhood, the woman he makes no attempt to explain at breakfast. Why does a man like this inflict partial custody on a blameless child?

Coppola is a fascinating director. She sees, and we see exactly what she sees. There is little attempt here to observe a plot. All the attention is on the handful of characters, on Johnny. He has attained success in his chosen field, and lost track of the ability to experience it. Perhaps you can stimulate yourself so much for so long that your sensitivity wears out. If Johnny has no inner life and his outer life no longer matters, then he's right: He's nothing.

*Note:* Somewhere *won the Golden Lion at Venice 2010.*

## The Son of No One ★ ★

R, 90 m., 2011

Channing Tatum (Jonathan "Milk" White), Tracy Morgan (Adult Vinnie), Katie Holmes (Kerry White), Ray Liotta (Captain Marion Mathers), Juliette Binoche (Loren Bridges), Al Pacino (Detective Charles Stanford), Brian Gilbert (Young Vinnie), Jake Cherry (Young Jonathan). Directed by Dito Montiel and produced by Montiel and Avi Lerner. Screenplay by Montiel.

Here's a bad movie with hardly a bad scene. How can that be? The construction doesn't flow. The story doesn't engage. The insistent flashbacks are distracting. The plot has problems it sidesteps. Yet here is a gifted cast doing what it's asked to do. The failure is in the writing and editing.

The movie takes place in the same Queens police precinct in 1986 and 2002. The opening involves a reference to 9/11, but with no clear purpose. In 1986, Jonathan White (Jake Cherry) is a pre-adolescent who is chased into a housing project bathroom by two rampaging junkies, grabs a pistol, and shoots them. From what we see, they were asking for it, and Jonathan was saving his own life. His best friend, Vinnie (Brian Gilbert), witnesses it all.

Detective Charles Stanford (Al Pacino), Jonathan's godfather and the police partner of his late father, is early on the scene, covers up for the boy, and tampers with evidence. Now sixteen years pass, the adult Jonathan (Channing Tatum) is a cop in the same precinct, and anonymous letters are being sent to the editor of a neighborhood newspaper (Juliette Binoche) alleging that a top cop was involved in the cover-up of two homicides.

What he did when he was young gnaws at Jonathan. The letters gnaw at his commanding officer, Captain Marion Mathers (Ray Liotta). Jonathan's wife, Kerry (Katie Holmes), can see her husband coming apart at the seams. Like all cops in police movies, he won't confide in her. As the letters continue, Jonathan grows convinced they must come from the only witness, the adult Vinny (Tracy Morgan), and he is willing to consider murdering his estranged friend.

Fair enough. Were you clocking the names of that incredible cast? The ringer is Binoche, who seems oddly cast as the only employee of a storefront newspaper. Of course, a woman from France could end up with such a job, but no point is made of her origins, nor do we understand why her paper devotes front-page headlines to anonymous scrawled notes. Every paper receives many such messages, and has excellent reasons they never print them.

But here's another problem: Jonathan was a minor when the deaths occurred. They were in self-defense. A kid his age isn't likely to go looking for junkies to shoot. The Pacino character knows this, and the right thing to do would be to see that charges are dropped and the minor's name suppressed. The only chargeable crime committed is his own—suppressing evidence. Another small difficulty is that if Vinny is the source of the notes, why would he be concerned sixteen years later about actions protecting his blameless best friend?

These questions do not find answers. Instead, good actors circle them in a series of scenes that lead nowhere, and the final scenes end everything without concluding anything, if you see what I mean. Moment by moment, *Son of No One*, written and directed by Dito Montiel, seems to be adding up, but its drama and urgency are without purpose.

## The Sorcerer's Apprentice ★ ★ ½

PG, 108 m., 2010

Nicolas Cage (Balthazar), Jay Baruchel (Dave Stutler), Teresa Palmer (Becky Barnes), Alfred Molina (Maxim Horvath), Monica Bellucci (Veronica), Toby Kebbell (Drake Stone), Alice Krige (Morgana), Jake Cherry (Young Dave), James A. Stephens (Merlin). Directed by Jon Turteltaub and produced by Jerry Bruckheimer. Screenplay by Matt Lopez, Doug Miro, and Carlo Bernard.

Having seen *The Last Airbender* gross untold millions despite the worst reviews in many a year, I confess myself discouraged at the prospect of reviewing *The Sorcerer's Apprentice.* This is a much better film than *Airbender,* which is faint praise, but it's becoming clear that every weekend brings another heavily marketed action "comedy" that pounds tens of millions out of consumers before evaporating.

I use the word "consumer" deliberately. This genre doesn't require an audience in the traditional sense. It attracts children and young teenagers with the promise of cinematic fast food: It's all sugar and caffeine, no nutrition. In place of a plot there's a premise, in place of carefully crafted action there are stupefying exercises in computer-generated imagery, and in place of an ending there's a hook for the sequel and, if all goes well, a new franchise.

*The Sorcerer's Apprentice* is in small part inspired by the famous sequence in Walt Disney's *Fantasia* (1940) where Mickey Mouse does battle with bewitched brooms and buckets while Leopold Stokowski conducts the famous music by Paul Dukas. Here there's an amusing sequence involving enchanted mops and such, with music that shares most of the same notes as Dukas but none of Stokowski's conducting flair. No matter. Most consumers have likely never heard of the music—or of *Fantasia,* for that matter. Even this shadow of the original is more charming than anything else in the film.

Nicolas Cage is the star, playing Balthazar, a good magician who has long held captive the forces of magical evil. A prologue explains how, 1,300 years ago, the Arthurian magician Merlin (James A. Stephens) warred with the evil magicians Morgana (Alice Krige) and Horvath (Alfred Molina). Merlin sealed them and their despicable minions in the deepest interior of a nested doll. Mankind will be safe as long as they stay there. If Morgana and Horvath escape, the planet will be doomed. They're as bad as BP.

As the story opens, ten-year-old Dave (Jake Cherry) chases a stray love note as it blows through the mail slot of an ancient curiosity shop in New York. This shop is chockablock with weird gimcracks, and presided over by Balthazar, who instantly intuits that Young Dave may have the potential to become the long-awaited Prime Merlinian—the great magician who can vanquish Morgana's forces once and for all.

The purpose of this sequence is crystal clear: It's to establish the protagonist as a kid, before he grows for ten years and becomes the movie's hero (Jay Baruchel). That way grade-schoolers will identify with twenty-year-old Dave. Others can identify with Balthazar, who is played by Cage with his usual admirable energy. It gets a chuckle early in the movie when Young Dave asks Balthazar how he knows something, and Cage spins and snarls: "Because I can read minds!" Next question?

There's a needless subplot involving Dave's crush on the fragrant Becky Barnes (Teresa Palmer), who in grade school all those many years ago was the intended recipient of the love note. Balthazar informs Dave he is The One and commands mighty magical powers. Balthazar then has to leave his shop briefly and asks Dave to guard the Prison Doll with extreme care. Naturally, Dave manages to open it and release the evil magicians. Balthazar should know better than to ever tell the hero of a Jerry Bruckheimer movie about the one thing he should never, never, ever, ever do.

That's it for the story setup. The rest is all centered on special effects. The director, Jon Turteltaub (*National Treasure*) and his several writers devise some clever set pieces, such as a dragon in a Chinatown parade that starts breathing smoke and fire, and it's up to Balthazar and Dave to vanquish the villains. I also liked it when Balthazar brought to life a steel eagle on top of the Chrysler Building and flew around on its back.

Cute Becky Barnes, now a college student, takes it pretty well that this Dave guy who wants to date her is a sorcerer's apprentice. I kept waiting for her to tell Dave she would still be there waiting for him after he finished annihilating the fiends, so maybe he should focus on saving the planet instead of putting the moves on her.

*The Sorcerer's Apprentice* is a perfectly typical example of its type, professionally made and competently acted. Imagine a graph with one line indicating the consumer's age and the other line representing his degree of enjoyment. These lines would intersect at about the age of Young Dave.

## Soul Surfer ★ ★ ½

PG, 106 m., 2011

AnnaSophia Robb (Bethany Hamilton), Helen Hunt (Cheri Hamilton), Dennis Quaid (Tom Hamilton), Lorraine Nicholson (Alana Blanchard), Carrie Underwood (Sarah Hill), Kevin Sorbo (Holt Blanchard), Jeremy Sumpter (Byron), Ross Thomas (Noah Hamilton), Sonya Balmores (Malina Birch), Chris Brochu (Timmy Hamilton). Directed by Sean McNamara and produced by McNamara, David Brookwell, Dutch Hofstetter, Douglas Schwartz, and David Zelon. Screenplay by McNamara, Deborah Schwartz, Douglas Schwartz, and Michael Berk, from the book by Bethany Hamilton.

*Soul Surfer* is based on the true story of Bethany Hamilton, a champion surfer who in her early teens was attacked by a shark and lost almost all her left arm. One month later, she was back on a surfboard, has since won several championships, and is at age twenty-one a professional surfer. All of those are remarkable facts.

My problem with the movie is that it makes it look too simple. Bethany has a loving family of professional surfers and a big, friendly dog. She lives in walking distance of the beach. She was and is a committed churchgoer, she got great support from her spiritual leaders, and she was an indomitable optimist with a fierce competitive spirit.

But there had to be more to it than that. I applaud her faith and spirit. I give her full credit for her determination. I realize she is a great athlete. But I feel something missing. There had to be dark nights of the soul. Times of grief and rage. The temptation of nihilism. The lure of despair. Can a thirteen-year-old girl lose an arm and keep right on smiling?

The flaw in the storytelling strategy of *Soul Surfer* is that it doesn't make Bethany easy to identify with. She's almost eerie in her optimism. Her religious faith is so unshaken it feels taken for granted. The film feels more like an inspirational parable than a harrowing story of personal tragedy.

Even its portrait of her recovery and rehabilitation is perfunctory. There's a particularly unconvincing scene where she's fitted with a prosthetic arm and refuses to wear it. They're making remarkable progress in the field of prosthetics. The arm she's offered looks no more useful than the arm she rips off her Barbie doll the same night (in one of the movie's rare moments of depression). Although I can understand a good prosthetic might not help her balance on a surfboard, I believe one might be of use in other situations—and I don't mean cosmetically. Maybe I'm mistaken.

Because Bethany actually was in the water a month after the attack, there can be no quarrel with those scenes in the film. What I missed was more information about her medical condition. What did her doctors advise? What risks were there to the wound? Having totaled almost a year in three trips through the Rehabilitation Institute of Chicago, I've known people who lost limbs, and I know it's very difficult and complicated. Maybe Bethany was so young and resilient, and in such a happy situation with her family and her church, that it was this easy for her. But it feels too simple.

One of the best sequences in the film involves a trip her church group makes to Thailand to bring aid and supplies to the survivors of the tsunami. This episode looks so realistic it's uncanny. It has one detail that made me smile: Bethany packs cans of Spam for the victims. I don't know how you feel about Spam, but I know that in Hawaii it's considered one of the basic food groups. (I like it with Colman's English Mustard—but I'm drifting.)

*Soul Surfer* is a wholesome movie, intended as inspirational. Whether it will cheer viewers who are not as capable as Bethany is an excellent question. AnnaSophia Robb is a convincing, cheerful heroine. Dennis Quaid and Helen Hunt, as Bethany's parents, are stalwart and supportive, although the screenplay indeed leaves them with no other choice. One character I question is Malina Birch (Sonya Balmores), one of Bethany's competitors, who sneers and is mean and does cruel things and of course always wears black. Why? Does she know she has been cast as the villain?

## Sound of My Voice ★ ★ ★

R, 85 m., 2011

Christopher Denham (Peter), Nicole Vicius (Lorna), Brit Marling (Maggie), Davenia McFadden (Carol Briggs), Kandice Stroh (Joanne), Christy Meyers (Mel), Richard Wharton (Klaus). Directed by Zal Batmanglij and produced by Brit Marling, Hans C. Ritter, and Shelley Surpin. Screenplay by Batmanglij and Marling.

*Sound of My Voice* is a sci-fi thriller made with smoke and mirrors. No special effects, no other worlds, only the possibility of time travel, which you can't show but can only talk about. In fact, it's probably not science-fiction at all, but belongs in some related category, like a story from *Weird Tales* magazine.

We meet Peter and Lorna, a young couple who are members of that most common Los Angeles population group, would-be filmmakers. Peter (Christopher Denham) is interested in a San Fernando Valley cult group, and has enlisted Lorna (Nicole Vicius) in his plan to clandestinely make a documentary exposing it. His preparations include swallowing a radio transmitter to collect sound and dialogue, although one hopes it doesn't collect any intestinal gurglings.

It's a low-rent cult. After being told to strip and shower, the two are blindfolded and led into a drab, ordinary basement occupied by several cult members dressed in white garments. They learn the drill, including a complex handshake that includes so many secret grips and twists one could surely infiltrate any fraternity with it.

A hush falls, and Maggie (Brit Marling) enters in a white veil. She is tethered to an oxygen tank, sits cross-legged in the circle, and gradually shares her story. She is from the year

2054, where a civil war is raging. Her body is so vulnerable to present-day toxins that she can consume only organic food grown by her followers, and her source of protein is their blood. She is never dire or dramatic and sounds comforting, but she makes strange demands. For example, the cult members must vomit to purge themselves, something Peter claims he can't do ("not even as a child"). Under Maggie's spell, he successfully hurls, which tells you something.

The film is divided into parts, numbered in big, bold letters on the screen, and one part shows Maggie's arrival in the present day as she wanders dazed on a highway while wearing only a sheet. Of course, there could be more than one explanation for that condition, and *Sound of My Voice* never precisely declares whether her story is true. Without going into detail, I can say that the film never precisely declares anything to be true.

The key figure here is Brit Marling, who cowrote with the director, Zal Batmanglij. She also starred in and cowrote *Another Earth* (2011), a much better film. In that one, she played a young astrophysicist distracted by the appearance in the sky of a second Earth. I won't go into detail. Both films use their sci-fi premises as an avenue into human stories that might not be quite as compelling without them.

She is a talent. She has an understated presence that conveys in this film an insidious conviction: What is her motive, really? And she demonstrates with Batmanglij that you can conjure out of a very small budget a quietly compelling film. *Sound of My Voice* makes me very interested in what she'll come up with next.

## Source Code ★ ★ ★ ½

PG-13, 93 m., 2011

Jake Gyllenhaal (Colter Stevens), Michelle Monaghan (Christina Warren), Vera Farmiga (Colleen Goodwin), Jeffrey Wright (Dr. Rutledge). Directed by Duncan Jones and produced by Mark Gordon, Philippe Rousselet, and Jordan Wynn. Screenplay by Ben Ripley.

*Source Code* is an ingenious thriller that comes billed as science fiction, although its science is preposterous. Does that matter, as long as everyone treats it with the greatest urgency? After all, space travel beyond the solar system is preposterous, and we couldn't do without *Star Trek*. The "science" in this case is used to prop up an appealing story of a man who tries to change the past.

His name is Colter Stevens (Jake Gyllenhaal). That he is sure of. That's why it's strange when he finds himself on a Chicago commuter train talking to Christina Warren (Michelle Monaghan), a woman he's never met. It's even stranger when he goes into the toilet and sees a face in the mirror that doesn't belong to him.

How can this be? We are far from sure in the early scenes, which embed us in his confusion. Because some of the pleasure comes from unwinding the mystery, I'd advise you to stop reading now—unless the helpful TV ads have already hinted at the secret.

Spoilers ahead. Colter gains consciousness to find himself (as himself) in a secret army lab talking to a scientist named Goodwin (Vera Farmiga). He gradually understands that the commuter train was destroyed by a terrorist bomb, and that the brain of one of the victims was harvested for memories of the last eight minutes before the explosion. That's a first cousin to the old theory that a killer's image remains imprinted on his victim's retinas.

But listen. Goodwin and her army intelligence team believe that by rerunning those eight minutes, they can discover the identity of the terrorist and prevent a larger explosion that could destroy Chicago. This is because the terrorist unwisely detonated the small bomb as a warning, or something, I dunno. In the movies, evildoers love to pass out alarms and clues so they can be prevented from carrying out their schemes. This is a more sophisticated variation of the Talking Killer Syndrome.

Now comes the human touch. As he returns again and again to those fateful eight minutes, Colter finds that he can remember his previous visits, even though for Christina and others on the train, they are, of course, happening for the first time. This is the *Groundhog Day* paradox: You remember your previous passages through the same span of time. Colter begins to care for Christina, as well he might, as anyone who loved Michelle Monaghan in *Trucker* (2008) will understand. As the conscious occupant of this borrowed body, he apparently possesses free will and need not duplicate exactly what the original memory donor did.

This involves the possibility that he could relive the memories of a man's final eight minutes and act in such a way as to affect the outcome. If the man were to survive—whose memories would he have, his own or his visitor's? (Don't go there.) The army's no-doubt-brilliant Dr. Rutledge (Jeffrey Wright) starts out to account for the experiment, but abandons his explanation, which is our loss. If you had a speech in this movie actually saying in so many words how this was possible, it would rival the findings of such great thinkers as Dr. Moreau, Dr. Jekyll, and Dr. Frankenstein.

No matter. The director and writer, Duncan Jones and Ben Ripley, hurtle ahead with the speed of their commuter train, which, like the man on the Grecian urn, always speeds forward and never gets anywhere. Colter's challenge increases in complexity. The city grows ever closer to destruction. Christina becomes more poignant. The scientists grow more desperate.

What we have here, setting aside the fancy editing involving the time travel, is something that looks like hard science fiction. That's a threatened genre. Movies with plots are threatened in general; much modern "science fiction" involves blowing stuff up. The good classic sci-fi involved starting with an idea and exploring its implications.

Duncan Jones previously made *Moon* (2009), with Sam Rockwell as a character apparently nearing the end of a contract to man a station on the far side of the moon. Characters in Duncan Jones movies should learn not to be so sure of things. But Jones has the right spirit, Gyllenhaal and Monaghan are adept at playing their variations on the eight minutes, and here's a movie where you forgive the preposterous because it takes you to the perplexing.

## Special Treatment ★ ★ ★

NO MPAA RATING, 95 m., 2011

Isabelle Huppert (Alice), Bouli Lanners (Xavier), Richard Debuisne (Pierre), Sabila Moussadek (Juliette), Valerie Dreville (Helene), Mathieu Carriere (Robert). Directed by Jeanne Labrune and produced by Jani Thiltges. Screenplay by Richard Debuisne and Jeanne Labrune.

Although Isabelle Huppert often plays very private characters, she allows us to be private with them. She can embody self-possession and a detached intelligence, and part of the appeal of one of her performances is the intrigue about what she's thinking and how she's behaving. In *Special Treatment*, she plays a high-priced Parisian prostitute whose age, fiftyish, has perhaps only enhanced her appeal.

She plays Alice, a lover of antiques, a student of art when young, who now specializes in role-playing. She's good at what she does. Alice tells a psychiatrist she's "forty-three . . . well, a little more," but she can be any age her clients desire. Who else her age could portray a little French schoolgirl? She has aged very subtly. Huppert is now in real life fifty-seven years old and has had no apparent plastic surgery, but it's scary how much she looks the same as she did in 1977 when I met her at Cannes.

I would not usually be preoccupied with the age of an actress, but Alice, as a prostitute, has a professional motive for concern about her shelf life. She deals with affluent professional men, she meets only those recommended by other clients, she is as meticulous about her hourly rate as a lawyer, she makes no attempt to pretend pleasure, and her clients seem to prefer her that way. Both sides feel safer maintaining a certain distance.

We can see she is tired, very tired, of prostitution. She confides in a friend, Juliette (Sabila Moussadek), who is also in the profession, and when she's with Juliette we see another side of Alice, more relaxed, warmer, with her feelings closer to the surface. For her, life has come down to money. The film opens in an antiques store where she sees a beautiful piece of glassware she'd like, and tells Juliette how many times she'd have to perform fellatio to pay for it. She wants the bowl, but not the work.

A new client is recommended to her: Xavier (Bouli Lanners). We've already met him. He's a psychiatrist, as distant and uninterested in his profession as she is in hers. His wife, who is a colleague, says he's neglecting his patients. She leaves him. At his first session with Alice, Xavier is so inhibited he's unable to think of anything he wants them to do. She charges up-front for ten sessions, no refunds, but this is a challenge she rarely faces.

It occurs to her that perhaps she should also seek professional help—a psychiatrist, to help her leave prostitution. Xavier suggests Pierre (Richard Debuisne), a colleague he barely knows. Pierre helps run a mental hospital, and Alice is somewhat shaken when she meets some of his clients. Pierre is a good man. We sense it, and so does Alice.

The questions are: Will Pierre take her into therapy? Will Xavier be able to relax enough to use her services? Can Pierre help her? Can she help Xavier? At a certain level in society, prostitutes are more therapists than sex retailers. *Special Treatment* circles these questions as it circles the characters and their intersecting lives. A seventeenth-century wooden sculpture of an angel passes among them, reflecting their relationships—and progress. At the end, there is no great revelation, but Huppert has succeeded once again in making us wonder what's going on in there.

## Splice ★ ★ ★

R, 107 m., 2010

Adrien Brody (Clive Nicoli), Sarah Polley (Elsa Kast), Delphine Chaneac (Dren), Brandon McGibbon (Gavin Nicoli), Simona Maicanescu (Joan Chorot), David Hewlett (William Barlow), Abigail Chu (Child Dren). Directed by Vincenzo Natali and produced by Steven Hoban. Screenplay by Natali, Antoinette Terry Bryant, and Douglas Taylor.

Well timed to open soon after Craig Venter's announcement of a self-replicating cell, here's a halfway serious science fiction movie about two researchers who slip some human DNA into a cloning experiment and end up with an unexpected outcome, or a child, or a monster, take your pick. The screenplay blends human psychology with scientific speculation and has genuine interest until it goes on autopilot with one of the chase scenes Hollywood now permits few pictures to end without.

In the laboratory of a genetic science corporation, we meet Clive and Elsa (Adrien Brody and Sarah Polley), partners at work and in romance, who are trying to create a hybrid animal gene that would, I dunno, maybe provide protein while sidestepping the nuisance of having it be an animal first. Against all odds, their experiment works. They want to push ahead, but the corporation has funded quite enough research for the time being, and can't wait to bring the "product" to market.

Elsa rebels and slips some human DNA into their lab work. What results is a new form of life, part animal, part human, looking at first like a rounded SpongeBob and then later like a cute kid on Pandora, but shorter and not blue. This creature grows at an astonishing rate, gets smart in a hurry, and is soon spelling out words on a Scrabble board without apparently having paused at the intermediate steps of learning to read and write. Clive thinks they should terminate it. Elsa says no. As the blob grows more humanoid, they become its default parents, and she names it Dren, which is nerd spelled backward, so don't name your kid that.

Dren has a tail and wings of unspecific animal origin, and hands with three fingers, suggesting a few sloth genes, although Dren is hyperactive. She has the ability common to small monkeys and CGI effects of being able to leap at dizzying speeds around a room. She's sweet when she gets a dolly to play with, but don't get her frustrated.

The researchers keep Dren a secret, both because they ignored orders by creating her, and because, although Elsa wanted no children, they begin to feel like her parents. This feeling doesn't extend so far as to allow her to live with them in the house. They lock her into the barn, which seems harsh treatment for the most important achievement of modern biological science.

Dren is all special effects in early scenes, and then quickly grows into a form played by Abigail Chu when small and Delphine Chaneac when larger. She also evolves more attractive features, based on the Spielberg discovery in *E.T.* that wide-set eyes are attractive. She doesn't look quite human, but as she grows to teenage size, she could possibly be the offspring of Jake and Neytiri, although not blue.

Brody and Polley are smart actors, and the director, Vincenzo Natali, is smart, too; do you remember his *Cube* (1997), with subjects trapped in a nightmarish experimental maze? This film, written by Natali with Antoinette Terry Bryant and Douglas Taylor, has the beginnings of a lot of ideas, including the love that observably exists between humans and some animals. It questions what "human" means, and suggests it's defined more by mind than body. It opens the controversy over the claims of some corporations to patent the genes of life. It deals with the divide between hard science and marketable science.

I wish Dren had been more fully developed. What does she think? What does she feel? There has never been another life form like her. The movie stays resolutely outside, viewing her as a distant creature. Her "parents" relate mostly to her mimetic behavior. Does it reflect her true nature? How does she feel about being locked in the barn? Does she "misbehave" or is that her nature?

The film, alas, stays resolutely with human problems. The relationship. The corporation. The preordained climax. Another recent film, *Ricky*, was about the French parents of a child who could fly. It also provided few insights into the child, but then Ricky was mentally as young as his age, and the ending was gratifyingly ambiguous. Not so with Dren. Disappointing, then, that the movie introduces such an extraordinary living being and focuses mostly on those around her. All the same, it's well done and intriguing.

## Spoken Word ★ ★ ★

NO MPAA RATING, 116 m., 2010

Kuno Becker (Cruz), Ruben Blades (Senior), Miguel Sandoval (Emilio), Persia White (Shae), Antonio Elias (Ramon), Monique Gabriela Curnen (Gabrielle). Directed by Victor Nuñez and produced by William T. Conway and Karen Koch. Screenplay by Conway and Joe Ray Sandoval.

*Spoken Word* opens with the startling sound of a gunshot, but the gun appears only in a poem being performed by the hero, Cruz Montoya. He's a star on the San Francisco poetry slam scene and teaches a class for young students at what looks like might be Dave Eggers's 826 Valencia workshop for neighborhood kids. He lives with a warm and loving artist, and his life seems good.

He gets a call from home, in the country outside Santa Fe. His father is dying. He returns not only to his father but to his earlier life. Pops (Ruben Blades) is pleased to see him but reserved. Cruz (Kuno Becker) hasn't stayed in close touch. They're not estranged; it's more that, as Cruz observes, "The men in this family don't talk much." It's clear he has a history in the area; old friends welcome him, but he keeps his distance.

We pick up on his circumstances. His married brother Ramon (Antonio Elias) was given half the family land as a wedding present and sold it to Emilio (Miguel Sandoval), who runs a dance club and sells drugs through it. We've seen Cruz taking pills and being asked about that by his brother and father, in different tones of voice, and we assume they're illegal. We also see Cruz edging reluctantly back into the bar scene, and he begins getting drunk and sleeping all day.

But *Spoken Word* is not at all the expected story you might assume given this setup. Cruz Senior was a local teacher. He is also a painter. Unlike the clichéd patriarch of a Mexican-American family, Pops doesn't oppose his son being a poet, doesn't nag him about grandchildren, is proud of the kid. And Cruz himself is a lot more complex than we assume.

A small but useful supporting role is played by Persia White (of *Girlfriends*) as Shae, the girlfriend back in San Francisco. She worries. Cruz can be remote and fearfully private, but she has some ideas why that is. It would make sense for her to join him in New Mexico—for them, but not for the plot—so she's often on the phone. She doesn't nag. She waits.

Victor Nuñez is a leading American filmmaker who has always worked with stories deeply embedded in American regions. In Florida he made *Gal Young 'Un* (1979), based on the novel by Marjorie Kinnan Rawlings; *A Flash of Green* (1984), based on a John D. MacDonald story and with one of Ed Harris's best performances; *Ruby in Paradise* (1993), which with her first role established Ashley Judd as a great actress; *Ulee's Gold* (1997), which won Peter Fonda an Oscar nomination.

Now Nuñez moves to New Mexico and gets far from obvious performances by Kuno Becker and Ruben Blades. He knows his places and the people who live in them.

I met him in 1979, when he was beginning. You can see gaps between those films showing how hard it is to find backing for an independent vision. There was a 2002 film named *Coastlines* that never even got a decent release. Now this rich and textured film. I can easily see alterations that would move it into the mainstream (an abusive father, more addiction, a violent drug dealer instead of a mild businessman, elements of prejudice), but they're all lacking, and the film grows in their absence.

It also grows in the presence of a parallel narrative made of Cruz's poetry and drifting, fragmented images from his past. They're not "flashbacks" but more of meditations on memories. They help to deepen the way we understand his relationship with his father. After all, they don't talk much in their family.

## The Spy Next Door ★ ½

PG, 92 m., 2010

Jackie Chan (Bob Ho), Amber Valletta (Gillian), Madeline Carroll (Farren), Will Shadley (Ian), Alina Foley (Nora), Magnus Scheving (Poldark), Katherine Boecher (Creel), Lucas Till (Larry), Billy Ray Cyrus (Colton James), George Lopez (Glaze). Directed by Brian Levant and produced by Robert Simonds. Screenplay by Jonathan Bernstein, James Greer, and Gregory Poirier.

Let's see. Jackie Chan is a spy working for China and the CIA, who falls in love with a widow with three kids. He retires to be with them, but his job follows him home. Mom goes to be with her sick dad. Evil Russians have a plot to control the world's oil supply, and this requires them to chase Jackie and the kids through shopping malls, large empty factories, and so on. Jackie's character is named Bob Ho, which reminds me of someone.

Truth in reviewing requires me to report that *The Spy Next Door* is precisely what you would expect from a PG-rated Jackie Chan comedy with that plot. If that's what you're looking for, you won't be disappointed. It's not what I was looking for.

There are things you learn from movies like this. (1) All kids know how to use weapons better than Russian mobsters. (2) A villainess in a spy movie always dresses like a dominatrix. (3) Hummers are no help. (4) Kids always hate the guy their mom is dating until they survive in battle with him, and then they love him. (5) Whenever an adult turns away, a small child will instantly disappear. The smaller the child, the more agile. (6) Even in New Mexico, Russian gangsters wear heavy long black leather coats, which they just bought in customs at Heathrow. These, added to their six-foot-five-inch heights and goatees, help them blend in. (7) The mole in the CIA is always the white boss, never the Latino.

What else? Oh, (8) if you put a cell phone under a rock with iron in it, it cannot be traced. Only such a rock miles into the desert will work. No good putting it in the stove. (9) Little girls would rather dress in a pink princess outfit than wear a Hulk mask. (10) Spies always have fiery kitchen disasters the first time they cook for kids, and the second time produce perfect French toast with powdered sugar on it. Oh, and (11) no spy has the slightest idea of a reasonable ratio of oatmeal to water.

Such sights made a young Saturday morning audience happy. Nothing to a kid is quite as funny as a food fight. A cat trapped on a roof is a suspense builder. They don't like the guy dating their mom until they save him with their well-timed action moves. And all young audiences find it perfectly reasonable that when a kid runs away from a residential neighborhood on a bike, that kid will, of course, pedal into the large empty factory where Jackie Chan is facing the Russian mob giants.

Jackie Chan is fifty-five. Just sayin'. He no longer runs up walls by using the leverage of a perpendicular surface. Back in the days before CGI, he used to really do that. OK, maybe some wires were involved, but you try running up a two-story wall with wires. I wouldn't even want to be winched up.

Chan was famous for doing his own stunts. He had so many accidents it's a wonder he can walk. Everybody knew to wait for the outtakes during the closing credits because you'd see him miss a fire escape or land wrong in the truck going under the bridge. Now the outtakes involve his use of the English language. What's that? Your name *isn't* Bob Hope?

## The Square ★ ★ ★ ½

R, 116 m., 2010

David Roberts (Ray), Claire van der Boom (Carla), Joel Edgerton (Billy), Anthony Hayes (Smithy), Peter Phelps (Jake), Bill Hunter (Gil Hubbard). Directed by Nash Edgerton and produced by Louise Smith. Screenplay by Joel Edgerton and Matthew Dabner.

*The Square* moves with implacable logic toward catastrophe, as its desperate heroes try to squirm out of a tightening noose. Step by step, mistake by mistake, their delusion is trampled on by reality. More horrible things happen in this film than are probable in any scenario short of a large anvil falling from the sky and flattening the town, but it remains mostly plausible from scene to scene.

Crime doesn't pay. This we all know. Adultery has a way of making itself known. Adulterers who hope to steal cash and live happily ever after are really asking for trouble. Note to adulterers with such a plan: Never try to carry it out until you first join your partner in sin on a seventy-two-hour bus ride.

In a small Australian town, Ray (David Roberts) works as the harried supervisor of a housing development. Carla (Claire van der Boom) is married to Smithy (Anthony Hayes), a lowlife. Ray and Carla, both unhappily married, have been having an affair for quite some time. In each other's arms they console themselves with the dream that someday they will run away from their lives and live happily ever after—in hiding, I guess.

Carla dreams that this will happen. Ray plays along with it. Note to other women, if younger and without resources: A gray-haired married man with a good job is lying when he says he'll surrender everything for you. Lying. But Carla calls his bluff. She discovers that Smithy has a lot of cash hidden in the house. Enough to finance their flight. It's undoubtedly illegal cash. If they steal it, how can the theft be reported?

Well, sure, yeah, great, Ray says, possibly hoping for something to come up. You know, like maybe Smithy will move the money. Nothing comes up, and Ray finds himself involved in a plan that goes wrong and wronger and wrongest.

The delight of this film, directed by Nash Edgerton and written with his brother Joel Edgerton and Matthew Dabner, is that it never pushes too hard or moves too fast. It lovingly, almost sadistically, lays out the situation and deliberately demonstrates all the things that can go wrong. And I mean *all* the things.

At the center of these things is a very large hole filled with concrete, the "square" of the title. Note to people with dead bodies on their hands: If you cover a corpse with several feet of concrete, it is difficult to dig it up discreetly. It is also hard to keep all of your stories straight, to control what people may notice, to deal with the moment when the cash is found missing, and to say thanks but no thanks when the police try to be helpful.

One of the best elements of *The Square* is how well it establishes the rhythms and layout of its small town, which is in New South Wales, cane toad country. I was waiting for a cane toad to figure in the plot, but Edgerton is admirably disciplined. That's why the movie is so effective. The acting is convincing, the characters are realistic, nobody is looking for trouble, fate plays a role, and we clearly understand who everybody is. There is a shot from a high bluff down to a house on fire, and we already know whose that house is.

*The Square* has been compared to *Blood Simple* and *A Simple Plan*. High praise, but not undeserved. It's so good to find filmmakers with quiet, firm confidence in story and character. An unseemly number of people die here, but never in "thrilling" scenes, which are so rarely even interesting. They die because, despite their best efforts, something happens to them. Note to thieves and adulterers: Live so as to prevent things from happening to you.

## Stake Land ★ ★ ★

NO MPAA RATING, 96 m., 2011

Nick Damici (Mister), Connor Paolo (Martin), Danielle Harris (Belle), Kelly McGillis (Sister Anna), Sean Nelson (Willie), Michael Cerveris (Jebedia). Directed by Jim Mickle and produced by Derek Curl, Larry Fessenden, Adam Folk,

Brent Kunkle, and Peter Phok. Screenplay by Mickle and Nick Damici.

Zombies are a great convenience. They provide villains who are colorful and frightening, require no dialogue, motivation, or explanation, and yet function efficiently as a negation of all that is good. Just the very word "zombie" can persuade people to buy tickets for a movie, and "sex" hasn't done that in years. At the risk of using the word "MacGuffin" twice in the same week—well, that's what zombies are, aren't they?

Humans are survivors in an undead world that has gone horribly wrong, where all the good times are past and gone. That's what our modern world feels like to me sometimes; the morning news is filled with more ominous portents than the opening montage of a disaster movie. When Japan is torn by earthquakes and airports are attacked by tornadoes and the economy is melting and radiation is leaking and honeybees are dying, obviously the zombies are only waiting for the globe to warm a little more.

One advantage of zombie movies, and indeed all monster and horror movies, is that they provide a port of entry for new filmmakers. The genre itself is the star. I don't like to say this about David Arquette, who is a jolly nice guy, but I doubt many people went to *Scre4m* to see him; they wanted to see the slasher in the mask.

That said, there are substantial qualities in *Stake Land*, a movie that probably uses zombies as little as it can get away with. Considering that the dialogue calls them *vamps* for short, they're apparently some kind of zombie/vampire hybrid, previously unidentified by horror science. The dead have merged with the undead. You see what spraying with insecticides can lead to.

The movie mercifully focuses on a handful of characters as they journey toward a perhaps mythical New Eden. We begin with the voice of a young narrator, Martin (Connor Paolo), who explains how after his family was massacred he came under the protection of Mister (Nick Damici). How they are driving in a big boat of a classic car through a wasteland of threat and paranoia. How Mister instructs him in the skills of survival. There are echoes here, less eloquent, of *The Road*.

Mister has hard-earned expertise about vamps. A bullet will slow them down, but all that will kill them is the proverbial stake, driven into the base of the skull, where allegedly resides the Reptile Brain. He schools Martin in eternal vigilance, and they survive surprise attacks by zombies that sometimes seem suspiciously well coordinated with one another (given their presumed inability to communicate).

Mister is like a Western hero committed to doing the right thing. When he sees Sister Anna (Kelly McGillis) being attacked by zombies, he rescues her. Their little band grows to include Belle (Danielle Harris), a pregnant young girl, and Willie (Sean Nelson), who was a marine.

On the road they encounter rare safety zones, carefully guarded communities barricaded against strangers. Some of these are run, however, by religious cultists looking forward to the end of days. The scariest is a venomous loony named Jebedia (Michael Cerveris). This is not so unlikely. I just saw a report on CNN about Branch Davidian members looking for the resurrection of David Koresh.

Director Jim Mickle, who cowrote with his star, Nick Damici, has crafted a good-looking, well-played, and atmospheric apocalyptic vision. There are pauses for thoughtful character moments and some nicely written dialogue evoking the looming despair. The cinematography makes this new world look as bleak as—well, as a lot of empty strip malls and seldom-traveled badlands. What with one thing and another, *Stake Land* is, if not precisely entertaining to my taste, certainly attention-getting.

## Steve Jobs: The Lost Interview ★ ★ ★

NO MPAA RATING, 70 m., 2011

A documentary featuring Steve Jobs and Robert X. Cringely. Directed by Paul Sen. Screenplay by Robert X. Cringely.

If Steve Jobs was right in 1995 and the computer is the most important tool in the history of the human race, then he was the most important toolmaker. In that year he was in exile from Apple, fired by the company he cofounded, and running his own much smaller company named NeXT. Soon he would sell NeXT to Apple and become Apple's CEO. Ahead lay a new generation of Macs and iPhones, iPods, and lots of cool iStuff.

Jobs, who died on October 5, 2011, rarely sat down for interviews. He was highly conscious of message control as a part of marketing; note how tight Apple's security is on new product introductions. In 1995 he sat down for a seventy-minute interview with Robert X. Cringely, technology writer and blogger. Bites from it were used in *Triumph of the Nerds*, Cringely's PBS series. Most of it has never been seen and was thought to be lost en route from London to New York. Recently, Cringely says in his intro to this doc, a copy was found in London.

Jobs and Cringely (a former Apple employee) were on good terms, and Jobs was unusually open. One of his motives was that he believed Apple was on a slow slide into extinction. He's frank about John Sculley, the executive he hired and who pushed him out: Sculley knew little about computers, but a great deal about survival.

Jobs was forty when this interview took place. He recalls with savor the early days when he and Steve Wozniak built the Apple I in a garage, and unknowingly invented cell phones by rigging it to send a telephone call around the world to ring the pay phone next door a minute later.

"We realized we two could control billions of dollars in infrastructure!" he says with a smile. He also remembers them calling the pope and hanging up when they realized they'd actually gotten through.

He tells the story of how he saw a Graphical User Interface in Xerox's PARC lab in Palo Alto and realized in an instant it represented the future of computing. He tells other hardware and software stories, but seems more interested in the process of running a company in which diamonds in the rough can polish each other by constant friction. He discusses his management theories, which made him arguably the best chief executive of his time, and remembers his first visit, as a twelve-year-old nerd, to Hewlett-Packard.

"It was the only company I'd ever seen," he tells Cringely. "I thought it was great how they had free coffee and doughnuts."

Steve Jobs has held a special fascination for me since I bought one of the first Macs. And you? It's likely you already know if you want to see this documentary, which isn't really a film; it's raw material for a film, in the form of Jobs speaking in close-up. It's a tribute to the singular popularity of Steve Jobs that he's probably the only talking head people would pay to watch for more than an hour.

## Stone ★ ★ ★

R, 105 m., 2010

Robert De Niro (Jack Mabry), Edward Norton (Gerald Creeson), Milla Jovovich (Lucetta), Frances Conroy (Madylyn). Directed by John Curran and produced by David Mimran, Jordan Schur, and Holly Wiersma. Screenplay by Angus MacLachlan.

*Stone* has Robert De Niro and Edward Norton playing against type and at the top of their forms in a psychological duel between a parole officer and a tricky prisoner who has his number. Norton plays Gerald Creeson, imprisoned for his role in a crime that resulted in the murder of his grandparents and the burning of their house. De Niro is Jack Mabry, who plays everything by the book to protect himself from a dark inner nature.

De Niro is an old hand at playing inner demons. His classic weakness was jealousy in *Raging Bull*. Here it is anger, which perhaps leads to lust. The film opens with a younger Jack Mabry enacting a terrifying scene with his young wife and infant. Years later, they are still married, in a loveless gridlock based on passive aggression. He does nothing "wrong." It is his duty to stay married. His wife, Madylyn (Frances Conroy), seems to be hunched against blows that never come. He mechanically sips whiskey and stares at the TV, the wall, anything.

It's time for his retirement. He could pass his caseload on to his successor, but no: He will do his duty to the last detail. That includes handling a parole plea by Creeson, who is very smart, an emotional manipulator whose wife, Lucetta (Milla Jovovich), is such a woman that such a man might use and be used by. Creeson senses that De Niro, the duty-bound straight arrow, might be vulnerable to temptation.

Lucetta is smart enough to try, not a bold seduction, but a mental game in which Mabry essentially seduces himself.

This is a process which cannot be dispatched in a neat prison caper package. It involves plotting about personalities. Jovovich's Lucetta has a key role in finding and exploiting an avenue through Mabry's defenses. What does Creeson think about the possibility she will have sex with Mabry? What does he think about her sex life in general? Is her promiscuity useful to him? Does she know it? Apart from whatever she does, she loves her husband without reserve, which is peculiar because he doesn't seem to deserve it, but then you never know.

*Stone* could have been some sort of a procedural, a straightforward crime movie, but it's too complex for that. It is actually interested in the minds of these characters and how they react to a dangerous situation. De Niro is so good at playing a man who has essentially emasculated himself because of fear of his anger, so that sex and anger may be leashed in precisely the opposite way as in *Raging Bull.* And Norton, the puppet master—it may not even be freedom he requires, but simply the pleasure of controlling others to obtain it.

## Straw Dogs ★ ★ ★

R, 110 m., 2011

James Marsden (David Sumner), Kate Bosworth (Amy Sumner), Alexander Skarsgard (Charlie), James Woods (Tom Heddon), Dominic Purcell (Jeremy Niles), Rhys Coiro (Norman), Billy Lush (Chris), Laz Alonso (John Burke), Willa Holland (Janice Heddon), Walton Goggins (Daniel Niles), Anson Mount (Coach Milkens). Directed by Rod Lurie and produced by Marc Frydman. Screenplay by Lurie, based on an earlier screenplay by David Zelag Goodman and Sam Peckinpah, and *The Siege of Trencher's Farm*, a novel by Gordon Williams.

This new version of *Straw Dogs* is a reasonably close adaptation of the 1971 film by Sam Peckinpah. Change the location from England to Mississippi, change a mathematician into a screenwriter, keep the bear trap and the cat found strangled, and it tells the same story. It is every bit as violent. I found it visceral, disturbing, and well made.

James Marsden and Kate Bosworth star in the roles originally played by Dustin Hoffman and Susan George, as an intellectual and his wife who move to a rural area where he can work undisturbed. There is something about this man and his sexy wife that disturbs the locals down at the pub, and what begins as a subtle competition over territorial rights (in the Darwinian sense) escalates implacably into a full-blown lethal struggle. The lesson learned is that the egghead contains the possibility of using great violence when his home and wife are threatened. At the beginning he doesn't know that.

Something within me has shifted in the forty years since *Straw Dogs* was released and its original x rating in England got it banned from theaters. Four decades of screen violence must have tempered me, and I am no longer as vulnerable to images of barbarism and mayhem. Peckinpah at the time was notorious for his violence; his masterpiece, *The Wild Bunch* (1969), was considered in some quarters to be unreleasable. I praised it, and yet drew the line at *Straw Dogs*, which crossed some sort of line with me.

Since Rod Lurie, the director of the new version, cannot be accused of having softened the material, my own feelings must have changed. Perhaps I am more in touch with them now, and recognize how close to home the movie strikes. I fear the story's hero represents me, and finds me lacking machismo. Not since grade school have I ever willingly been in a fistfight. I have never fired a rifle except in ROTC classes and never touched a handgun. I avoid physical confrontation. When somebody tries to cut me off on an expressway, I let them.

I depend on society to protect me. I have always feared I couldn't do it myself. A man isn't supposed to admit that, but there's no purpose in denying it. Now here is Marsden playing David, a Hollywood screenwriter who has moved with his wife, Amy (Kate Bosworth), back to her old hometown on the Gulf Coast, where they will live in a handsome fieldstone house with a barn much damaged by a hurricane. Amy was a cheerleader here in high school, left for California, and has had a little success on a TV crime series.

Their first day they go into a bar and grill where any sensible person would know to make an immediate U-turn and walk out again. You've seen this place in dozens of movies. Everybody knows one another. They inhabit a macho bar culture where violence is always close to the surface. When the former beauty queen walks in with her new husband (who wears glasses and drives a classic Jaguar of about the vintage of the Peckinpah movie), she is the immediate focus of passively aggressive attention. Comments are made that are not quite intended to be heard.

Charlie (Alexander Skarsgard), Amy's high school boyfriend, comes over to their booth to say hello. He is tall, muscular, cold-eyed, superficially nice. David treats him with just a shade too much friendliness. You know what I mean. He smiles too readily, falls into pleasant cadences, and is subtly condescending. His attitude translates as: "I may not be a bar-bum redneck like you, but if it makes you feel better, I'll pretend to be."

Bad luck. Charlie and his posse have been hired to repair the barn. An unspoken aggression develops. They arrive for work too early. David stupidly climbs their ladder in *bedroom slippers* to complain they were awakened. One of the crew walks into the kitchen and helps himself to several beers, complaining they aren't cold enough. David complains to Charlie. "Don't you trust us?" Charlie asks. There is no way this situation is going to get better.

The local men are sexual predators capable of rape. Amy, who comes from their culture, resents the way their eyes drink in her nipples under a sweaty T-shirt. David suggests maybe she should have worn a bra. She is offended that she can't wear what she wants on her own property. Later, she commits an act of sexual provocation against the men that amounts to psychological violence, or maybe simple stupidity.

A subplot involves the way the town centers on high school football and local church services, which interlock sports and religion. One of the regulars in the bar is the former coach, Tom Heddon (James Woods). It's possible to wonder if being coached by this vicious man has influenced a whole local generation. James Woods is spellbinding in the role: hard, mean as hell, quick-triggered.

The situation all comes down to a siege at the farmhouse, with Charlie and the others trying to break in and cause harm. This involves a sustained passage of blood-curdling mayhem, more violent than we're used to, because so much movie violence these days is CGI and not very realistic, and this all looks like real bodies causing great pain to each other. In a logical world one might wonder if a guy with a prized pickup truck might be willing to damage it by using it as a battering ram, but anti-intellectualism on this coast apparently knows no limits.

After the first movie, I must have been disturbed by what kinds of acts the hero found himself capable of. After this one, perhaps I was relieved? Fantasy is one of the things we seek in the movies. Whatever. Rod Lurie has made a first-rate film of psychological warfare, and yes, I thought it was better than the Peckinpah. Marsden, Bosworth, and Skarsgard are all persuasive, and although James Woods has played a lot of evil men during his career, this one may be the scariest.

## Strongman ★ ★ ★

NO MPAA RATING, 113 m., 2011

Stanley and Michael Pleskun and Stan's girlfriend, Barbara. A documentary directed by Zachary Levy.

*Strongman* is a tantalizing example of the kind of documentary I find engrossing: a film about an unusual person who invites us into the mystery of a human life. Stanley Pleskun bills himself as "Stanless Steel, the Strongest Man Alive." Whether this is true is beside the point. Stanless, as I will call him, believes it absolutely. His girlfriend, Barbara, and his brother Michael agree, I gather, although they never actually say so.

How does the Strongest Man in the World support himself? He works as a freelancer in the scrap metal industry, collecting scrap and hauling it to a yard. We see him heaving heavy loads into the bed of his truck. Does this help him train? No, I learn from the film's notes, it tires him out and makes it harder to train. Although Zachary Levy, the filmmaker, followed him over a course of years and shot hundreds of hours of film, we see him actually training only twice: once squeezing a hand grip, and again staggering for several yards while carrying heavy concrete blocks.

He is a strict vegetarian who does not smoke or drink, and lives on fruit and vegetable juices. We see him demolish a dozen ears of corn in a single brief sitting. We also see him, perhaps during times of stress, smoking, having a beer, and sharing a pizza. Nobody's perfect. Stanless is convinced he doesn't smoke and advises Barbara to cut it out. He also bums smokes from her.

Barbara is a great mystery to me. She is a good-looking woman about the same age as Stanless. Old photos show her with the facial structure of a model. Her skin remains unlined. She wears her hair in a graying ponytail or braids. She has a presence. She has a beauty. Stanless moves in with her. She rehearses to introduce his act: "Ladies and gentlemen, boys and girls! Presenting Staaaaaanless Steeeel! The Strongest Man in the Woooorld!" He makes appearances at events in New Jersey and New York, bending steel bars, lifting trucks, and so on. He is paid $1,000 and expenses to appear on a British TV show.

He meets with an agent who has "represented all the top strong men." The agent tells him his act lacks a "hook." Indeed, it seems quickly over. Before an audience of maybe two hundred in a parking lot, he positions himself on his back below the rear end of a pickup truck and lifts it high enough with his feet for his brother to slip a sheet of paper under a real wheel. He can also bend pennies and quarters. He puts a bent penny on a chain and gives it to Barbara as a necklace.

What is it with those two? They hug, they kiss, but their relationship seems to center on his strong-man status and her acceptance and support of it. Eventually there's a complex scene in which they argue, although she remains calm and composed, and his complaints seem recycled out of New Age beliefs about the soul and the essence of goodness. He also has moments of offended anger, when he reminded me uncannily of Bruno S., the star of Herzog's *Stroszek*.

Stanless's family life is the stuff of Diane Arbus. Forced to move in with Michael, he shouts: "How can you expect the Strongest Man in the World to live in a space ten by twelve feet?" Michael's living room is an indoor-outdoor carport. Their mother and grandmother live in an ordinary house, where the grandmother, apparently a stroke victim, has to be carried about.

Zach Levy has the deadpan approach of a filmmaker like Errol Morris. You're not sure what he thinks about these people. They are very definitely *themselves*, and we've never seen anyone else like them. Levy's camera simply regards them. The film ends with a flashback to a historic moment: the first meeting between Stanless and Barbara. It solves nothing. I watched the film with quiet fascination.

## Submarine ★ ★ ★

R, 97 m., 2011

Craig Roberts (Oliver Tate), Yasmin Paige (Jordana Bevan), Noah Taylor (Lloyd Tate), Sally Hawkins (Jill Tate), Paddy Considine (Graham Purvis). Directed by Richard Ayoade and produced by Mary Burke, Mark Herbert, and Andy Stebbing. Screenplay by Ayoade, based on the novel by Joe Dunthorne.

Craig Roberts, who plays Oliver Tate, the hero of *Submarine*, looks a lot like the very young John Lennon: fresh and hopeful, with the soul of a poet and the self-importance of—well, of a teenage boy who struggles under the weight of his virginity. He also looks so much like young Bud Cort that if you gave him a pair of Harry Potter glasses he could remake *Harold and Maude*. The British tone of the film helps; it's set in Swansea, Wales.

Oliver seems to be the author of *Submarine*, his own biopic—sometimes literally, sometimes more in the way its tone evokes his preoccupations. Sex is much on his mind, but he sees himself as too serious and cultured to seek it in vulgar ways. True, he rather mistreats Jordana Bevan (Yasmin Paige), a girl in his school, but he immediately regrets that pushing incident, and besides, awkward boys sometimes mask tenderness with roughhouse.

Jordana understands this, and a great many other things about adolescent boys. For example, she knows some of them need leadership or they will stew forever in self-doubt. She isn't a tart, nor is she any more experienced than Oliver, but she's more confident. Their relationship begins with earnest exchanges of searching looks in the school corridor, and soon progresses to having dinner at Oliver's house when his parents aren't home.

His parents are much on his mind. His father (Noah Taylor) is an oddly quiet man, withdrawn, not quite there in the room. His mother (Sally Hawkins) is, like many Sally Hawkins characters, earnestly engaged in whatever occupies her. Right now she is entranced by a self-styled mystic named Graham Purvis (Paddy Considine), who has the gift of holding an audience spellbound with utter nonsense he seems to make up as he goes along.

Oliver is concerned that his mother may be growing too involved with Graham Purvis. He reports to us that his parents have stopped having sex, and explains the ingenious method he used to figure this out. Simultaneously, Oliver very much wants to start having sex—with Jordana Bevan, who for now occupies all the space available in his mind for possible partners.

*Submarine* isn't an insipid teen sex comedy. It flaunts some stylistic devices, such as titles and sections and self-aware narration, but it doesn't try too hard to be desperately clever. It's a self-confident work for the first-time director, Richard Ayoade, whose purpose I think is to capture that delicate moment in some adolescent lives when idealism and trust lead to tentative experiments. Because Craig Roberts and Yasmin Paige are enormously likable in their roles, they win our sympathy and make us realize that too many movies about younger teenagers are filtered through the sensibility of more weathered minds.

## Sundance 2012 Short Subjects

A pet alligator. A submarine crew going ballistic. A woman trapped in her girdle. Sometimes the idea itself is the film. These seven short films are part of the Sundance Institute Art House Project, which also includes local screenings of new features at about the same time they play in Park City.

Almost every filmmaker starts with a short subject. Some end there. Others become great directors. The rewarding thing about programs like this is that there are countless shorts submitted to Sundance every year, and those selected are the very best.

Here are brief reviews in the order they play:

*The Eagleman Stag*: All animated in shades of white, a summary of the life of a taxonomist from the day in childhood when he noticed a wondrous worm to the day in his eighties when his body seems to have copied a beetle's ability to generate lost parts of itself. Elegant in a macabre, white purity. You can read it any way you like; the program informs us, "If you repeat the word 'fly' for long enough, it sounds like 'life.'" (Mikey Please, UK, 9 min.)

*The Strange Ones*: The sound of a useless car ignition awakens a young boy. He's in a car at the roadside with an older youth, presumably his brother. They start walking down the highway and find a motel with a swimming pool. The kid jumps in. The older makes friends with the woman running the hotel, who offers them a ride to a towing service. Then she starts talking to the younger, and the reality goes through a shift. We no longer know what to believe. (Christopher Radcliff and Lauren Wolkstein, USA, 14 min.)

*Incident by a Bank*: Told entirely in long shot from a POV across the street, a bank robbery seen at a distance. We're told the film reconstructs an incident actually witnessed in Stockholm in 2006. As two young men drive up on a moped and stick up the bank, some passersby ignore them, and we hear the voice of whoever is holding the camera: "Are they really holding up that bank?" There's humor. A man comes out of a store, sees a security guard wrestling with one of the crooks on the sidewalk and asks, not very enthusiastically: "Is there anything I can do to help?" For some people in the area, it's as if the robbery is hardly taking place at all. (Ruben Ostlund, Sweden, 12 min.)

*Worst Enemy*: A woman has a negative self-image. She thinks she's too fat, but she's not. TV ads for weight-loss products do nothing to help. She takes her dog for a walk and is rudely propositioned by some construction workers, who are thrown off their game when she thanks them. Back home again, she tugs and struggles to get herself into a girdle, which fits so tightly she needs to go to a doctor to get it off. The doctor is more than helpful. This would make a scene in a comedy about the woman. (Lake Bell, USA, 13 min.)

*The High Level Bridge*: A short documentary about the enormous span linking the two halves of the city of Edmonton, the capital of Alberta. The narrator supplies a dry assembly of facts: It is often used for suicides, one of the men who was building it is entombed in one of its supports, the city fathers were going to paint it gold to commemorate Canada's centennial, but they never did. One anecdote involves a woman who slipped on a patch of ice, dropped her cell phone, and indirectly saved a life. (Trevor Anderson, Canada, 5 min.)

*We're Leaving*: Rusty and Veronica live with Chopper, their pet alligator, who seems a friendly reptile. They get a notice to move in thirty days from an unfriendly manager. Few rental units accept alligators. Rusty is fed up with Chopper's fondness for nicking wires and hiding them in crevices. One of the intriguing aspects of this film is that I assume it is a documentary but cannot be absolutely sure. It certainly gave me new ideas about alligators as pets. (Zachary Treitz, USA, 13 min.)

*Deeper Than Yesterday*: The weight of a feature in a twenty-minute film. Takes place on a submarine after ninety days at sea. Nerves are worn ragged. Some men are on the edge of violence ("Piss in the shower again and I'll kill you"). Through the periscope, a body is found floating in the ocean. They surface and bring it on board. It is an attractive young woman, whose glittery dress suggests she fell from a cruise ship. The hero, a big man with a shaved head, who has tried to be a peacemaker, is faced with a considerable challenge. The director of this film knows exactly what he's doing. (Ariel Kleiman, Australia, 20 min.)

And actually, all of the directors do. Moviegoers have a certain reluctance to attend programs of short subjects, although when one is shown before a feature (all too rarely), they're grateful. This program may be better, minute for minute, than most of the features at your friendly multiplex.

## Super ★ ★

NO MPAA RATING, 96 m., 2011

Rainn Wilson (Frank/Crimson Bolt), Ellen Page (Libby/Boltie), Liv Tyler (Sarah), Kevin Bacon (Jacques), Nathan Fillion (The Holy Avenger), Gregg Henry (Detective John Felkner), Michael Rooker (Abe), Andre Royo (Hamilton). Directed by James Gunn and produced by Miranda Bailey and Ted Hope. Screenplay by Gunn.

*Super* is being sold as a comedy, but I doubt it will play that way. It begins as the portrait of a lovable loser named Frank, and as it ends we're pretty sure he's an insane, ruthless killer. That's not a joke. Maybe the filmmaker, James Gunn, intended it as a joke, but after the camera lingers on the young heroine with a third of her face blown off, it's hard to laugh.

I quite understand that this could all be seen as an ironic commentary on audience expectations; when Ellen Page of *Juno* stars in a movie, we don't much expect to see her brains dripping. But let's face it: Most audiences have little appetite for irony about themselves. One possible way to like the movie might be to observe how unenjoyable it is for people expecting something funny and upbeat, but that would be unkind.

Rainn Wilson stars as Frank, a short-order cook who is married to the lithesome Sarah (Liv Tyler). He's a loser who is content to be a loser. He is also palpably stupid and clueless, a pawn in the hands of the slickster Jacques (Kevin Bacon). Sarah is a recovering addict, a paragon of sweetness until she falls in among low companions, including Jacques, a big-time drug dealer involved with a strip club.

When Jacques comes to Frank's house looking for Sarah, so clueless is Frank that he cooks eggs for his rival. It must be said that Kevin Bacon plays the scene (and praises the eggs) with such wicked comic timing that you can imagine the whole film centering on that scene and flowering in other directions.

It was not to be. Jacques steals Sarah, hooks her on drugs, and requires her for ominous obscure purposes. Frank dissolves into self-pity. While watching a Christian cable channel, he sees a half-witted drama about a superhero and is inspired to imitate it. He goes to a comic book store seeking instructional reading, and meets a clerk named Libby (Ellen Page), who claims she is twenty-two, but has the savvy of a credible eight-year-old.

Frank identifies Jacques with evil in general and reinvents himself as the Crimson Bolt, a masked superhero wearing a tight-fitting red suit he ran up himself on his wife's sewing machine. He then (this is kind of funny) hides behind Dumpsters, hoping to spot crimes being committed, and later, after getting beaten senseless, arms himself with a big wrench and starts pounding drug dealers. The Crimson Bolt becomes a big local news item; Libby figures out who he is and recruits herself as his junior sidekick, Boltie.

This isn't necessarily funny. It approaches humor, however, with the work by Rainn Wilson and Ellen Page, and with the cool, mocking detachment of the Kevin Bacon character, who visits as if an ambassador from another, better movie. There's something I like very much about Wilson, who plays an unaffected klutz with about as much grace and humor as possible. He never seems to be trying to be funny, and that's a strength. But what can he do with this screenplay?

Setting aside the details of the plot mechanics (Jacques, his gated mansion, his henchmen, his drugs, his evil), what we're left with are scenes of Frank the madman appointing himself as the wrath of God and smashing people senseless. When one of the Three Stooges gets beaned with a wrench, it's funny. When presumably actual characters are maimed and possibly killed, not so much.

The movie plunges into nihilistic despair in its third act. This isn't a black comedy because it isn't a comedy. It's a trick played on our expectations, I concede, but to what end? Is there any requirement that a film develop organically from beginning to end? No. There's no rule book. But audiences feel uneasy when they feel toyed with. I'm all for movies that create unease, but I prefer them to appear to know why they're doing that. *Super* is a film ending in narrative anarchy, exercising a destructive impulse to no greater purpose than to mess with us.

## Super 8 ★ ★ ★ ½

PG-13, 112 m., 2011

Joel Courtney (Joe Lamb), Kyle Chandler (Jack Lamb), Elle Fanning (Alice Dainard), Riley Griffiths (Charles), Noah Emmerich (Nelec), Ron Eldard (Louis Dainard), Ryan Lee (Cary), Gabriel Basso (Martin), Zach Mills (Preston). Directed by J. J. Abrams and produced by Abrams, Bryan Burk, and Steven Spielberg. Screenplay by Abrams.

With its night skies filled with mystery, its kids racing around town on bicycles, and its flashlights forming visible beams in the air, *Super 8* has the visual signatures of an early Spielberg movie. Its earnest young heroes stumble upon an awesome mystery and try to investigate it themselves. And as a small town in Ohio experiences frightening events, we feel poised between *The Goonies* and a 1950s sci-fi picture with the characters lined up side by side and looking in alarm at an awesome sight.

The associations are deliberate. Steven Spielberg produced the film, and its director, J. J. Abrams, worked in lowly roles on early Spielberg pictures before going on to make *Mission Impossible III* (2006) and *Star Trek* (2009). What they're trying here is to evoke the innocence of an *E.T.* while introducing a more recent level of special effects. There are really two movies here, one about the world of the kids and one about the expectations of the audience, and *Super 8* leads a charmed life until the second story takes command.

Set in the 1970s, it opens with its twelve-year-old hero, Joe Lamb (Joel Courtney), helping his intense friend Charles (Riley Griffiths) make an 8 mm zombie movie for a local film festival. This, of course, must be done in secret, not so much because parents would forbid it, but because it's fun to operate with stealth. Besotted by stories of other young directors (no doubt including Spielberg), they scout locations, improvise costumes, and energetically apply zombie makeup. In this they are greatly assisted by fourteen-year-old Alice (Elle Fanning), who not only plays the zombie mother but, just as importantly, sneaks out with her father's car to drive them all to a midnight shoot at the local train station.

A great opportunity develops when a train comes rumbling out of the night. "Action!" Charles shouts, and Martin and Alice try to perform their dialogue as the train rumbles past. Then a pickup truck appears, racing on the tracks toward the train. The train wreck goes on and on and on, tossing railroad cars around like dominoes. You would think a freight car loaded with heavy metals couldn't fly very high into the sky, but you'd be wrong. This is a sensationally good action sequence, up there with the airplane crash in *Knowing*.

Yes, something ominous is happening, but I'd better not say what. Part of the delicious fun of the film is the way it toys with portents. For example, Joe's dog disappears. He tacks up a card on a notice board. We see that countless dogs have disappeared. Later there's a map of where missing dogs have been found. The dots form a ring around the city. All the dogs ran out of town. This moment reminded me of the great shot in *The Thing* (1952), when the scientists stood on the outline of something in the Antarctic ice and when Howard Hawks's camera drew back, we saw they were in a circle.

Meanwhile, human elements come into play. Joe's mother was killed not long ago in an accident at the steel mill. He mourns her. His father, Deputy Sheriff Jack Lamb (Kyle Chandler), has grown distant and depressive. Joe begins to bond with Alice, who is two years older, but sympathetic and nice. There's an oddly touching scene where he helps her with her zombie makeup.

It is a requirement of these films that adults be largely absent. The kids get involved up to their necks, but the grown-ups seem slow to realize strange things are happening. Here, the mystery centers on the cargo of the cars in the train wreck, and on the sudden materialization of U.S. Air Force investigators and troops in town. If we don't instinctively know it from this movie, we know it from a dozen earlier ones: The authorities are trying to cover up something frightening, and the kids are on the case.

During the first hour of *Super 8*, I was elated by how good it was. It was like seeing a lost early Spielberg classic. Then something started to slip. The key relationship of Alice and her troubled father, Louis (Ron Eldard), went through an arbitrary U-turn. Joe's own father seemed to sway with the requirements of the plot. The presentation of the threat was done with obscure and unconvincing special effects. We want the human stories and the danger to mesh perfectly, and they seem to slip past one another.

All the same, *Super 8* is a wonderful film, nostalgic not for a time but for a style of filmmaking, when shell-shocked young audiences were told a story, not pounded over the head with aggressive action. Abrams treats early adolescence with tenderness and affection. He uses his camera to accumulate emotion. He has the small-town locations right.

And he does an especially good job with Joe, Alice, Charles, and their friends—especially Cary (Ryan Lee). You know how a lot of heist and action movies have an explosives expert? Cary is the kid who is always playing with matches and fireworks. There was always some kid like that in school. The grown-ups said if he kept on like that he'd blow off a finger. We were rather grateful for the suspense.

## Survival of the Dead ★ ★

R, 90 m., 2010

Alan Van Sprang (Sarge Crocket), Kenneth Welsh (Patrick O'Flynn), Kathleen Munroe (Jane O'Flynn), Richard Fitzpatrick (Seamus Muldoon), Devon Bostick (Boy). Directed by George A. Romero and produced by Paula Devonshire. Screenplay by Romero.

For the purposes of watching *Survival of the Dead*, I'm perfectly willing to believe in zombies. It's a stretch, however, to believe in an island off the coast of Delaware where life looks like outtakes from *Ryan's Daughter*, everyone speaks with an Irish accent, and there's a bitter feud between those who believe in capital punishment for zombies, and those who call for their rehabilitation and cure.

How can you kill *or* rehabilitate a zombie, since by definition it is dead? Here's my reasoning: If it can attack you and dine on your throbbing flesh, it isn't dead enough. George A. Romero is our leading researcher in this area, having reinvented zombies for modern times with *Night of the Living Dead* (1968), and returned to them from time to time, most successfully in the excellent *Dawn of the Dead* (1978).

Zombies, as I have noted before (and before, and before), make excellent movie creatures because they are smart enough to be dangerous, slow enough to kill, and dead enough we need not feel grief. Romero has not even begun to run out of ways to kill them. My favorite shot in this film shows a zombie having its head blown apart, with the skullcap bouncing into the air and falling down to fit neatly over the neck. If that doesn't appeal to you, nothing will.

I've seen a whole lot of zombies killed. I've been cordial over the years with Romero, who in addition to reinventing zombies demonstrated how horror movies were a low-cost point of entry for independent filmmakers. To him we possibly owe such directors as David Cronenberg and John Carpenter. *Dawn of the Dead* was a biting indictment of the culture of the shopping mall, with most of its action in a landscape of modern retailing and merchandising. It was also funny.

All true. But after you've seen, oh, I dunno, twenty or thirty zombie movies, you sort of stop caring very much, unless something new is going on, as in *Zombieland*. At this point, I find myself watching primarily to spot and appreciate entertaining new ways to slaughter zombies. That's why the skullcap moment appealed to me. It was new.

Not much else is new in *Survival of the Dead*. After a vaguely explained plague of zombies has broken out, America has descended into post-apocalyptic warfare. The zombie disease is spreading. If one bites you, you become a zombie. That ability to infect others was once the special gift of vampires, and I suspect it has now been bestowed on zombies by gene-splicing at the genetic level. All zombies share one characteristic: They take a lickin' and keep on tickin'.

On the island off Delaware, we meet the O'Flynns and Muldoons, who are in the dependable tradition of the Hatfields and McCoys. The O'Flynns believe zombies exist to be destroyed. The Muldoons, more humane, want to chain them up and keep them around until a cure is discovered. How do you vote? How would you feel if the Muldoon scheme worked, and you were a cured zombie? Would your flesh still look a little decomposed? Would you mention it in your entry on Match.com?

The leader of the O'Flynns is exiled to the mainland via rowboat, and in Philadelphia we encounter paramilitaries who are fighting off zombies and considering going to . . . the island off the Delaware coast. I was unable to stir up the slightest interest in the O'Flynns and Muldoons, the military types reminded me of the better *28 Days Later*, and finally, all that kept my attention were the ingenious ways Romero killed the zombies. The man is a fount of imagination. Scarcely a zombie dies in a boring way. So there's that.

## Surviving Progress ★ ★ ★ ½

NO MPAA RATING, 86 m., 2011

A documentary featuring Ronald Wright, Mark Levine, Robert Wright, Marina Silva, Kambale Musavuli, Vaclav Smil, Colin Beavan, Michael Hudson, Jane Goodall, Chen Ming, Chen Changnian, J. Craig Venter, Raquel Taitson-Queiroz, Gary Marcus, Daniel Povinelli, Margaret Atwood, Simon Johnson, Enio Beata, David Suzuki, Jim Thomas, and Stephen Hawking. Directed by Mathieu Roy and Harold Crooks, based on the book *A Short History of Progress* by Ronald Wright.

Before the rise of Rome, nations and city-states forgave all debt from time to time, and started again. I have somewhat simplified that fact from *Surviving Progress*, but bear with me. After Rome, debt began to be treated as more durable, and the result was a steady suctioning of wealth to the top. In modern times, that process has been speeded up by the rise of the idea of a corporation, which exists for one purpose: to maximize its own profits.

One of the most efficient means of making money is to create debt. In the buildup to the recent collapse, we saw that starkly demonstrated by Wall Street traders who knowingly sold worthless mortgages to their own customers, while at the same time creating that debt by encouraging consumers to sign mortgages they had no realistic means of repaying. The traditional banker who wanted to know how you would repay your mortgage was replaced by a new breed that gleefully sold you mortgages it knew you couldn't repay. They made profits on your interest, and then foreclosed on your principal.

*Surviving Progress*, a bone-chilling new documentary, argues that the world has financed an unsustainable growth rate by essentially encouraging whole nations to take out unpayable mortgages on their own futures. Brazil is given as an example. Enormous loans are given to the nation, which cannot meet the payments, and then it is encouraged to liquefy its own natural assets—the rain forests. When the assets are gone, the wealth will have been taken out in the same process, and corporations will leave behind a drained nation and move on to another loan customer.

I wince while realizing how I have oversimplified the movie's argument. I am really just trying to dramatize the point. All but a very few of us are in debt. We exist as entities who borrow money and spend the rest of our lives making interest payments on principal that never seems to budge. Whatever wealth we have, in labor, property, or cash, is suctioned to the top. That is the basic fact being referred to by the current term "the 1 percenters," and why we are "99 percenters." We exist to have our wealth moved up the economic chain out of our reach.

All of this is justified by "progress." More population, more consumers, more material goods, more cars, highways, housing, retail sales. More franchises, fewer small entrepreneurs. It is even possible to think of war as a way of speeding up the creation of debt. In anything short of total destruction by nuclear war, the top 1 percent on both sides—winners and losers—end up accumulating the wealth that the other 99 percent go into debt to create—and often their capital is represented by their own lives. If I die in a war, you have whatever I am worth.

*Surviving Progress* is a bright, entertaining (!), coherent argument in favor of these principles I have simplified so briefly. It seems to me that it is self-evident, and tells the truth. It is an irony that the actual victims of the process are often those most in support of it. Think of the opposition to "tree huggers." In Brazil, they are seen as a cause of unemployment in the lumber and logging industries. Actually, they are opposed to the nation essentially tearing its wealth out of the ground and shipping it overseas, resulting not only in unemployment but in devastation.

T

## Tabloid ★ ★ ★ ★

R, 87 m., 2011

A documentary featuring Joyce McKinney. Directed by Errol Morris and produced by Julie Ahlberg and Mark Lipson.

If *Tabloid* is a love story, it is one only Errol Morris could film. He says its subject, Joyce McKinney, is his favorite protagonist, which means she places ahead of Robert McNamara, Stephen Hawking, and the expert on naked mole rats. Certainly she is the most enigmatic.

In 1977, McKinney was involved in the infamous "Case of the Manacled Mormon," which was made to order for the British tabloids we've been reading about during the *News of the World* scandal. A former Miss Wyoming, she was alleged to have kidnapped an American Mormon missionary in the United Kingdom, handcuffed him to a bed, and made him a sex slave. All lies, she says in *Tabloid*, and says she was intervening to rescue him from a cult. British police said she fled the country with an accomplice, donning a red wig and flying into Canada, where they posed as a mute mime troupe.

McKinney's life seems ideal for sensational headlines. Years later she found herself in the news again after a Korean scientist allegedly cloned her beloved dog, producing five puppies. In 2008, McKinney faced burglary charges in Tennessee while trying to find funds to purchase a false leg for her three-legged horse.

Is McKinney speaking the truth when she gives her version of the story? Or are the other versions offered by Morris more accurate? I believe Morris doesn't think it matters. It is Joyce McKinney he cares about. How she presents herself, how she copes, who she is to herself, what she does to explain a bizarre and contradictory story. Watching the film is a tantalizing experience. Everything seems right here in our grasp, like Truth in a philosophy class. Yet there are so many questions that cast Truth into doubt. When you leave at the end you may feel you have the necessary materials, but don't know how to assemble them.

*Rashomon* will inevitably be evoked in discussions of this film. Many scenarios fit the facts. Morris presents officials with boundless reasons to think McKinney guilty of stalking, abduction, and possible rape. He also allows McKinney to offer a perky alternative perspective on the same events. Her alleged victim is portrayed in murky ambiguity (once unshackled, he has prudently refused all interviews). Morris surrounds his story with unexpected asides, blindsides us with surprise revelations, and weaves in an ominously insidious score by John Kusiak.

Morris has gained full access to McKinney, who in the early 1970s was a somewhat shady nude model and is now a poised and persuasive sixty-something who proclaims full innocence and has an explanation for everything. As is often the case with Morris, we can never be sure what he thinks, only that he wants to baffle us with the impenetrable strangeness of reality.

Morris makes intensely personal films, which are about neither his subjects nor himself, but about the intensity of his gaze. No wonder he invented the Interrotron, which allows Morris and the person he is speaking with to peer directly into each other's eyes. He, and we, are constantly asking what we think of this person—and what's really going on here.

Even in his first film, *Gates of Heaven* (1978), Morris was looking but not judging. Every audience I've seen that film with has been divided about whether he loves its subjects or is mocking them. Impossible to say. And Joyce McKinney? She is so likable and sounds so plausible, and yet what was the deal with the red wig and the mime troupe? She sounds wounded in explaining the early nude photos are Photoshopped. But they sure do look like her—and how did they get printed in real magazines before the invention of Photoshop, and why would anyone back then have wanted to substitute her face on somebody else's body?

What is amazing is that Morris gets McKinney to talk at all. And not only her, but others who were involved, all staring directly into the Interrotron and all sounding uncannily as if they're speaking the truth. I've seen *Tabloid* twice. It is a spellbinding enigma, and one of the damnedest films Morris has ever made.

## Take Me Home Tonight ★ ½

R, 114 m., 2011

Topher Grace (Matt Franklin), Anna Faris (Wendy Franklin), Dan Fogler (Barry Nathan), Teresa Palmer (Tori Frederking), Chris Pratt (Kyle Masterson), Michael Biehn (Bill Franklin). Directed by Michael Dowse and produced by Sarah Bowen, Topher Grace, Gordon Kaywin, James Whitaker, and Dany Wolf. Screenplay by Dowse, Jackie Filgo, and Jeff Filgo.

I follow the Darwin Awards carefully. Those are the mentions given out on the Internet every year of people whose deaths may have improved the species by removing them from the gene pool. Many of the characters in *Take Me Home Tonight* might make a contribution in that way.

Let me run this past you. Your name is Matt (Topher Grace). You are maybe ten years out of high school. You work at a Los Angeles video store. You want to impress a girl named Tori (Teresa Palmer) you lusted after in school. She walks into the video store. You lie and tell her you are a trader with Goldman Sachs. You end up at a party, and she's there. It turns out she's also in banking, and happens to know that Goldman Sachs doesn't have a Los Angeles office.

Everybody then gets drunk and exchanges inane dialogue during the longest scene set at a party since the forty-five-minute formal ball in Visconti's *The Leopard* (1963). Your most hated rival is throwing the party. Your high school class had some kind of cockamamie ritual test involving the Ball (I may have the name wrong, but I'm close). This is a large metal sphere, apparently hammered together out of old junkyard parts. It's in the bed of your rival's dump truck.

You decide one way to regain your self-respect and win esteem in Tori's eyes is to risk the challenge of the Ball. The idea is, you climb inside the Ball, he tilts the truck bed, and the Ball rolls out of control downhill on a canyon road above Los Angeles. To get into the Ball is to qualify yourself as a finalist for the Darwin Award. To aid and abet anyone involved in this process is to act as an accessory to murder.

Now let me get back to that party scene. It is unendurably long. There are endless camera setups to define various groupings of characters who perform badly written dialogue. Among these characters are Matt's twin sister, Wendy (Anna Faris), and her boyfriend, Kyle (Chris Pratt). Wendy got all the brains in the family. Matt got to be Topher Grace. In that family, a trade-off. Wendy is holding an envelope that will tell her if she has been accepted to "Oxford University." Kyle thinks they should get married. He doesn't know where Oxford is. This gives you a notion of the depth of his interest in her.

I put the words "Oxford University" in quotes to mislead you into thinking nobody calls Oxford by that name. Actually, that's its official name, but it is uncool to say "Oxford University." Most people say "Oxford" and people know what you're talking about. You know, like "Berkeley." Anybody tells you they're going to the "University of California at Berkeley," they must think you just got off the train.

*Take Me Home Tonight* must have been made with people who had a great deal of nostalgia for the 1980s, a relatively underprivileged decade. More power to them. The movie unfortunately gives them no dialogue expanding them into recognizable human beings. They speak entirely in plot points and punch lines, and seem to be motivated only by lust, greed, and ego. Well, we all are, but few bring to this motivation so little intelligence and wit.

Besides, I have news for Tori, who works in banking and thinks she's so smart. If she thinks Goldman Sachs doesn't have a Los Angeles office, she should pay a visit to Suite 2600 in Fox Plaza at 2121 Avenue of the Stars.

## Take Shelter ★ ★ ★ ★

R, 124 m., 2011

Michael Shannon (Curtis LaForche), Jessica Chastain (Samantha LaForche), Shea Whigham (Dewart), Katy Mixon (Nat), Kathy Baker (Sarah), Ray McKinnon (Kyle), Lisa Gay Hamilton (Kendra), Robert Longstreet (Jim), Tova Stewart (Hannah LaForche). Directed by Jeff Nichols and produced by Tyler Davidson and Sophia Lin. Screenplay by Nichols.

Here is a frightening thriller based not on special effects gimmicks but on a dread that seems quietly spreading in the land: that the good days are ending, and climate changes or other sinister forces will sweep away our safety. It takes place in a quiet Ohio countryside with big skies and flat horizons, and involves a happy family whose life seems contented.

It is the gift of the actor Michael Shannon, however, that while appearing to be a stable husband and father with a good job in construction, he can also evoke by his eyes and manner a deep unease. Curtis LaForche has what he needs to be happy. He fears he will lose it. His dreams begin to be visited by unusually vivid nightmares: The family dog attacks him, for example, or storms destroy his home.

To the puzzlement of his wife, Samantha (Jessica Chastain), and their hearing-impaired daughter, Hannah (Tova Stewart), he builds a pen in the backyard for the dog, which had been living peacefully indoors. The storm dreams are not so easily managed. Ominous black clouds gather, their heavy raindrops brown and oily, and so subtle is the direction of Jeff Nichols that some of this poisoned rain seems to be real, not imaginary. They live on the outskirts of town, in an area that is swept from time to time with tornados.

His behavior begins to concern his best friend and workmate Dewart (Shea Whigham), who helps him as much as he can. Their friendship dramatizes the thin ice beneath so many people these days, when employment is threatened by uncontrolled forces, and if you lose a job, there may not be another one. Stories about Curtis begin to spread in the community, and Curtis is not paranoid when he thinks people are talking about him. His explosion at a community benefit dinner is terrifying in its energy.

This is the second collaboration by the director and star, whose powerful *Shotgun Stories* (2007) established Nichols as a gifted new filmmaker, and further cemented Shannon's growing reputation as an actor of uncommon force: the young Christopher Walken, my wife says, and he does embody the same shifting air of disquiet. As his wife, Jessica Chastain is effective in her seventh major role this year; since *The Tree of Life*, has any young actress ever put together such a series of roles?

A few jolting shots early in the film establish the possibility that bad things could happen. But writer-director Nichols builds his suspense carefully. Curtis is tormented but intelligent; fearing the family's history of mental illness, he visits his schizophrenic mother (Kathy Baker) in a care facility to ask if she had ever been troubled by bad dreams. He checks books out of the library. He turns to the area's obviously inadequate public health facilities.

But he also acts as if his warnings should be taken seriously. He is driven to guard the family he loves. He borrows money from the bank and equipment from work to greatly expand an old tornado shelter in his backyard. His wife grows frightened by his behavior. His job and health insurance are threatened.

And then a storm comes. Its nature need not be discussed here. It leads to a scene of searing power in which Samantha tells Curtis that it is safe once again to return to the surface—that it is a step he must take personally. The story seems somewhat resolved. Then the film concludes not with a "surprise ending," but with a series of shots that brilliantly summarize all that has gone before. This is masterful filmmaking.

In films like *Shotgun Stories*, William Friedkin's *Bug*, Sam Mendes's *Revolutionary Road*, and Werner Herzog's *My Son, My Son, What Have Ye Done?* Shannon has attracted the best directors with his uncanny power. His virtually one-man performance in *Mistakes Were Made* was one of the most amazing performances I've ever seen. Thinking again over what he does in *Take Shelter*, I think an Oscar nomination for best actor is well-deserved.

## Tamara Drewe ★ ★ ★ ½

R, 110 m., 2010

Gemma Arterton (Tamara Drewe), Roger Allam (Nicholas Hardiment), Bill Camp (Glen McCreavy), Dominic Cooper (Ben Sergeant), Luke Evans (Andy Cobb), Tamsin Greig (Beth Hardiment), Jessica Barden (Jody Long), Charlotte Christie (Casey Shaw). Directed by Stephen Frears and produced by Alison Owen, Tracey Seaward, and Paul Trijbits. Screenplay by Moira Buffini, based on the graphic novel by Posy Simmonds.

*Tamara Drewe* is one of those British comedies in which, one way or another, we envy all of the characters—even, briefly, the one run over by stampeding cows. If one must be vain, lustful, egotistical, or long-suffering, let it be here, at a writers' retreat in the Dorset village of Ewedown, where everyone lives across the street from a field and there are no bank branches to deface the rustic charm.

The writers' colony is run by Nicholas Hardiment (Roger Allam) and his good wife, Beth (Tamsin Greig). He is a best-selling crime novelist and serial adulterer, and she is a saintly helpmate who runs the retreat, befriends the guests, bakes fresh pastries for tea, and is reconciled to his tomcatting because at the end of the day he always returns to her—for the pastries, possibly.

Into this pastoral idyll drops the fragrant Tamara Drewe (Gemma Arterton). Once, long ago, she was a village lass with a big nose. She went off to London to make her fortune and find a plastic surgeon, and has returned to sell the family home. She is now a famous newspaper columnist with a standard-issue nose, the kind of woman men describe as healthy, when they mean so very much more.

The Hardiments are assisted by a robust local lad named Andy Cobb (Luke Evans), who has fallen on bad fortune but cheerfully does odd jobs and harbors a resentment against Tamara, whose family purchased what he still considers *his* family home. Once, in their teen years, Andy and Tamara apparently rummaged a bit among each other's netherlands, notwithstanding her nose.

Nicholas the crime novelist is drawn to Tamara like a cat to tuna. He wears his fame like a backstage pass, and Tamara, after all, is not so very difficult to seduce. She is, in fact, a woman who calls her own shots, and about her lovers is less likely to feel gratitude than pity. Into the mix now comes a famous London rock 'n' roller, Ben Sergeant (Dominic Cooper). I believe it possible that his eyeliner is tattooed.

His presence in town inflames the adolescent girls Jody Long and Casey Shaw (Jessica Barden and Charlotte Christie), who spend their days moping about bored in bus shelters, and lurk behind hedgerows to spy on everyone. Tamara dumps Nicholas for Ben, flirts with Andy, and is one of the many victims of Jody and Casey's meddling with private lives.

The movie was adapted from a graphic novel by Posy Simmonds, and *it* was inspired by Thomas Hardy's *Far from the Madding Crowd*, although there seems to have been an uncredited infusion of French farce along the way. To the game of romantic musical chairs already under way, a new player is added: McCreavy (Bill Camp), a morose American academic who is laboring away at the poetry of Hardy and has come here to Ewedown to be inspired by a village that is indeed far from the madding crowd. He finds a sympathetic ear from Beth, and begins to entertain ambitions about other bits of her anatomy.

*Tamara Drewe* resembles another British village comedy, *Local Hero*, in which everyone lived in each other's pockets. Its director is Stephen Frears, a master of many genres (*High Fidelity*, *The Grifters*, *Dirty Pretty Things*, *The Queen*). Here he knows exactly what he's dealing with: foolish and flawed people who harbor desires that may not be good for them. Not all of them can be happy, and it must be said that Frears, with his writer Moira Buffini and Simmonds and Hardy lurking in the background, gives us a story in which everyone gets more or less what they deserve. If these people are silly, they are no sillier than most of us. There is admirable craftsmanship at work in the scene of the unfortunate cattle stampede, and although we regret the fate of its victim, we must admit that no one is really to blame, and a rough justice has been served.

There is another pleasure here. All of the characters, except for the two naughty girls, are adults with grown-up ideas and aspirations, however lamentable. I find myself growing weary of the overgrown adolescents who impersonate adult characters in too many recent American films. Even a jolly comedy like this has characters with more depth. For example, at no time in the film does anyone come right out and explain who Thomas Hardy was. The characters are all presumed to already know. Not that you need to know in order to enjoy the film, but it's nice to know stuff you don't need to know, don't you think?

## Ted ★ ★ ★ ½

R, 106 m., 2012

Mark Wahlberg (John Bennett), Mila Kunis (Lori Collins), Seth MacFarlane (Ted [voice]), Joel McHale (Rex), Giovanni Ribisi (Donny), Aedin Mincks (Robert), Patrick Stewart (Narrator). Directed by Seth MacFarlane and produced by MacFarlane, Jason Clark, John Jacobs, Scott Stuber, and Wellesley Wild. Screenplay by MacFarlane, Wild, and Alec Sulkin.

The funniest movie character so far this year is a stuffed teddy bear. And the best comedy screenplay so far is *Ted*, the saga of the bear's friendship with a thirty-five-year-old man-child. I know; this was also hard for me to believe. After memories of Mel Gibson's bond with a sock puppet, *Ted* was not high on the list of movies I was impatient to see.

The opening scenes find the right tone. A treacly narrator (Patrick Stewart) describes a Christmas that reminds us of *A Christmas Story*, except for the jolts of four-letter words and anti-PC one-liners. We meet young John Bennett, the most unpopular kid in the neighborhood, so disliked that while the Jewish kid is being beaten up, he feels envious.

All young John wants is a true friend for life. For Christmas his parents give him an enormous teddy bear the size of a first-grader, and that night under the sheets with a flashlight, John asks Teddy to be his real and true forever friend, and Teddy comes to life and agrees.

The miracle of a walking, talking teddy bear, of course, makes the little stuffed creature an overnight celebrity, and he appears on the Carson show. But his fame fades ("like Corey Feldman," the narrator explains), and he settles in as John's roommate for life. Years pass. Teddy is now a little frayed, and John (Mark Wahlberg), at thirty-five, has a counter job at a rental car agency. Against all odds he also has a fragrant girlfriend named Lori Collins (Mila Kunis), who has been waiting four years for a marriage proposal.

John and Ted lead an *Animal House*–like existence, inhaling wholesale quantities of weed and recalling their early years as Flash Gordon fans. American movies have recently featured a lot of male characters who are victims of arrested adolescence, but few who have resisted growing up more successfully than John.

The laughs in *Ted* come largely through the teddy bear's dialogue. With an edgy Beantown accent and a potty mouth, Ted insults and offends everyone he comes into contact with, and sees Lori as a threat to his friendship with John. This despite his own pastimes, which include drugs, hookers, and, as we later discover, a torrid early 1990s affair with absolutely the last female vocalist you could imagine having sex with a teddy bear—and I mean the *last.*

The movie was cowritten and directed by Seth MacFarlane (*The Family Guy*), who also does Ted's voice, and gives himself the same freedom he has in animation. The bear itself is a CGI creation, striking a reasonable balance between the agility of a sexual athlete and the clumsiness of Pooh. It appears that Ted is stuffed with cotton wool and feels no pain when an ear is ripped off, but he behaves as a living, breathing best buddy.

The plot is fairly standard, but greatly embellished by MacFarlane's ability to establish comic situations and keep them building. One crucial scene takes place when Ted convinces John to leave Lori at a party ("Just for five minutes") and come to Ted's own party, where their childhood hero has turned up. This is Sam J. Jones, the star of *Flash Gordon* the movie, who in middle age has become a party animal. How this situation ends up with an enraged duck attacking Ted you will have to discover for yourself.

There's also peril involving a creepy dad (Giovanni Ribisi) who as a child passionately wanted Ted to be his own teddy, and his pudgy spoiled son (Aedin Mincks), who wants Ted now. Their desire is pitched at such a perverse level that it approaches teddy bear predation.

The remarkable thing about *Ted* is that it doesn't run out of steam. MacFarlane seems unwilling to stop after the first payoff of a scene. He keeps embellishing. In Ted, he has an inexhaustible source of socially obnoxious behavior and language, and it's uncanny the way a teddy bear can get away with doing and saying things that we wouldn't necessarily accept from a human character. This is partly because Ted is a stand-up insult comedian trapped inside the body of a teddy bear.

I must end on a note of warning. *Ted* is not merely an R-rated movie, but a *very* R-rated movie—"for crude and sexual content, pervasive language, and some drug use," says the MPAA, and what it means by *some* is hard to figure, because it could hardly contain more. No matter how much kids want to see the teddy bear movie in the ads on TV, steer them to *Brave*. Trust me on this.

## The Tempest ★ ★ ½

PG-13, 110 m., 2010

Helen Mirren (Prospera), Russell Brand (Trinculo), Reeve Carney (Prince Ferdinand), Tom Conti (Gonzalo), Chris Cooper (Antonio), Alan Cumming (Sebastian), Djimon Hounsou (Caliban), Felicity Jones (Miranda), Alfred Molina (Stephano), David Strathairn (King Alonso), Ben Whishaw (Ariel). Directed by Julie Taymor and produced by Taymor, Robert Chartoff, Lynn Hendee, Jason K. Lau, and Julia Taylor-Stanley. Screenplay by Taymor, based on the play by William Shakespeare.

The only way to read Shakespeare's *The Tempest* is as a farewell: a play written, if you will, for his retirement banquet, to be performed before he's handed his gold watch and finally has more time to spend with his family. It is my favorite of all his plays, containing a line I embrace as my consolation: "We are such stuff as dreams are made on, and our little life is rounded with a sleep." The writer who saw more deeply into human nature than any other looked into himself and decided he had finished his work.

Julie Taymor's film *The Tempest* doesn't feel like a farewell. She does not abjure her rough magic. In a film filled with sound and fury, she rages against the dying of the light. There is no reconciliation or closure. What reads as a poetic acceptance of human mortality plays as the defiance of a magician clinging to familiar tricks.

She doesn't capture Shakespeare's tone (or his meaning, I believe), but she certainly has boldness in her reinvention. The best thing she does is change the sex of Prospero, the exiled Duke of Milan who has fled to a remote island with his daughter. Here Prospero becomes Prospera, and is magnificently played by Helen Mirren with more ferocity than resignation. Prospera's daughter, Miranda (Felicity Jones), now seems more suited at her side; Prospera empathizes with her as Prospero never did. Indeed, all the relationships on the island curiously seem more natural when the character becomes a woman.

Consider Ariel (Ben Whishaw), the androgynous sprite who follows Prospera's bidding and performs her magic. Ariel is neither male nor female, and while Prospero seemed to treat the spirit as an extremely skillful pet, Prospera relates more to Ariel's functions as a companion and helpmate. And there is Caliban, the original inhabitant of the island before the first boat arrived from Milan. He resents the usurpers and invokes one of the most terrible curses in literature: "All the infections that the sun sucks up from bogs, fens, flats, on Prosper fall, and make him by inch-meal a disease!" Here, played by Djimon Hounsou as an African, he evokes parallels with colonialism, and Prospera seems more ready to see him beneath her instinctive rejection.

Taymor has gathered a cast that, for the most part, would be ideal for a traditional stage version of the play, and embedded them in special effects that begin with the word "tempest" and build to a frenzy. The dialogue is pure Shakespeare (proving again that he is easier to understand when spoken than read), but these gifted actors sometimes seem to be saying the words as someone with a chainsaw cuts firewood in the next room.

Taymor's stagecraft is bold but not measured. If the top is in sight, she aims for it. This worked with her passionate film *Titus*, based on Shakespeare's *Titus Andronicus*. That's a bloody early play suited to extremes. *The Tempest* contains more resignation; it is a search for sunset. There's a gentle finality to it, despite some quite violent scenes. The best performance I've seen is Barbara Gaines's 2002 production for the Chicago Shakespeare Company, where she used daring rigging to float some actors like performers for Cirque du Soleil. With her you felt love; with Taymor this time, determination.

Many gifted actors join Mirren in finding their own moments within the melee. Felicity Jones as Miranda is hopeful and virginal. King Alonso is played with sad resignation by

David Strathairn. Djimon Hounsou plays an angry and almost politicized Caliban. Russell Brand and Alfred Molina are bawdy as two seafarers who wander off and enlist Caliban as a drinking buddy. Alan Cumming and Chris Cooper play Sebastian and Antonio as filled with ominous ill will. Tom Conti is the good king Gonzalo.

They inhabit locations (Hawaii) and remarkable soundstage sets for Prospera's Milan lab and island spaces. Interiors are sensational: her alchemist's workshop and a room with alarming stair steps climbing at an angle. There are all the cliffs you could possibly desire for Prospera to stand atop and howl at the sea.

All of these elements are in place. Taymor might have turned down the heat. You do not have to insist with *The Tempest* because it is a play that puts all assertion behind it and is content to cast its magic staff into the sea. It is the play with which Shakespeare shows that he knew how good he was.

## Terri ★ ★ ★ ★

R, 105 m., 2011

John C. Reilly (Mr. Fitzgerald), Jacob Wysocki (Terri), Creed Bratton (Uncle James), Bridger Zadina (Chad), Olivia Crocicchia (Heather). Directed by Azazel Jacobs and produced by Alison Dickey, Hunter Gray, Lynette Howell, and Alex Orlovsky. Screenplay by Patrick Dewitt.

I found a rare absorption while watching Azazel Jacobs's *Terri*, the story of a fat kid who is mocked at school. Movies about high school misfits are common; this is an uncommon one. Terri, so convincingly played by Jacob Wysocki, is smart, gentle, and instinctively wise. His decision to wear pajamas to school "because they fit" may be an indication that later in life he will amount to a great deal. He has character.

All of that lies ahead in this story, which observes him for two or three weeks as he survives some turning points. Terri's parents are not in the picture. He lives in a cluttered little house with his Uncle James (Creed Bratton), whose books and music indicate he was once a much different man. Now he is drifting into senility, and Terri cares for him with quiet affection.

The house is in a wooded semi-rural area, which Terri cuts through to reach the school. He has been missing a lot of school days and is called in by Fitzgerald (John C. Reilly), the assistant principal. This is a school administrator unlike those we usually see, containing kindness, anger, and hard-won lessons learned in his own difficult life. He and Terri slowly begin to communicate person-to-person, and this process is subtly constructed by Jacobs.

Indeed, the entire film moves at a human pace, not prodded by impatience or a desire to rush through the story. To view *Terri* after the manic thrashing of *Transformers 3* was soothing and healing: It demonstrates how films can engage us in human life, rather than mocking it.

There are two more important characters. Chad (Bridger Zadina) is another of Fitzgerald's problem children, a morose, slouching outsider driven to pluck hairs from his head. Heather (Olivia Crocicchia) is a pretty young student whom Terri observes, during a home economics class, as a boy takes liberties with her body. When this threatens to lead to her expulsion, Terri steps up and defends her to Fitzgerald, in a way that shows he respects her and empathizes.

Terri and Heather begin a friendship based on shy notes using mostly smiley faces. This leads to a strange and uneasy evening involving the two of them, Chad, a bottle of booze, and some of Uncle James's pills. This session, like the rest of the film, has a timing and sympathy that sets it apart from many similar scenes I've seen.

There's an element of Terri's life left for us to make of what we will. Told by his uncle to set some mousetraps in the attic, Terri captures some mice and lines up their bodies on a log in the woods. Later he sees a bird of prey gobbling one of them, and his face fills with wonderment. He catches more mice and keeps baiting the log. Does this make him an unwholesome sadist? Not at all. The movie invites no hasty conclusion. In honesty, I believe his reaction is normal.

Five characters. Terri, Fitzgerald, Uncle James, Chad, Heather. All original. None limited by story conventions. None seen by me in previous movies. Observed with attention and sympathy. Not oversimplified, although it would help to know more about Heather. And a fat kid who is fat, and weird, but much more than fat and weird.

The actor Jacob Wysocki is unknown to me, but he brings such quiet confidence to the role that he creates absolute conviction. A newcomer, he goes one-on-one with the masterful John C. Reilly in scenes of actual communication between two people rarely seen in any movie. He's more of a John Candy than a Chris Farley, if you see what I mean.

*Note: The* R *rating is absurd. This film is incomparably more relevant and wholesome for younger teenagers than the* PG-*13* Transformers 3.

## Terribly Happy ★ ★ ★

NO MPAA RATING, 100 m., 2010

Jakob Cedergren (Robert), Lene Maria Christensen (Ingelise Buhl), Kim Bodnia (Jorgen Buhl), Lars Brygmann (Dr. Zerlang), Anders Hove (Kobmand Moos), Mathilde Maack (Dorthe). Directed by Henrik Ruben Genz and produced by Tina Dalhoff and Thomas Gammeltoft. Screenplay by Genz and Gry Dunja Jensen, based on a novel by Erling Jepsen.

The cow gave birth to a calf with two heads, and they weren't just any two heads. Into the bog it went. All sorts of village problems sink in the bog. No telling what's rotting down there. This beginning may make *Terribly Happy* sound like a modern-day *Motel Hell*, where Farmer Vincent buried people to their necks and fattened them like geese. But no, this is a dour and deadpan film noir from Denmark, and a good one.

Robert (Jakob Cedergren), a young policeman from Copenhagen, has been exiled as punishment to a dismal village in South Jutland. He's about thirty, single, and made a "terrible mistake" he doesn't talk about. The town doesn't look like some cheery Danish hamlet, but more like a rundown grain elevator town in the Old West. When he steps into the bar, he's made to feel not only unwelcome, but in some subtle way threatened. The drinkers regard him with a level, cold gaze. They laugh at him behind his back. When he goes to get a bicycle repaired, he finds the repairman missing. He's told it's not uncommon for folks to go missing.

He asks a young woman for directions. This is Ingelise (Lene Maria Christensen). She has that Shirley MacLaine gamine look. She's not a raving beauty but has undeniable sex appeal. Robert senses it—he feels an attraction—but no, that would be wrong. But what happens when wrong starts to look right?

Something very wrong is happening in this town. The guys in the bar were unfriendly because they have every reason to believe Robert is kidding himself if he thinks he can get anything accomplished as the new town marshal. It gradually develops that Jorgen (Kim Bodnia), the husband of Ingelise, is feared by everyone, not least Ingelise, whom he beats. The film's most eerie detail involves their little daughter. When she parades alone down the abandoned main street with her baby buggy and its squeaky wheels, everyone knows domestic violence is taking place at Jorgen's house.

Bodnia, who plays Jorgen, is alarming in appearance and manner. He isn't one of those jumped-up ex-bouncers who stands six foot six and has big arms and a shaved head. He's alarming not for how he looks but for what he signals he's capable of. If Robert was a bad cop before, he's in way over his head now.

But there's another level. The townspeople seem to have little reason to fear if they'll just go along. They keep their heads low and their thoughts to themselves. Is this intended by the director, Henrik Ruben Genz, as some sort of a parable? I have no idea. It works well enough just at creating an intimidating atmosphere for Robert, who is disoriented when people don't just naturally accept him as, you know, the law.

Genz creates a distinctive look and feel in the film. The town is drab, the people wrung out, and the moments of passion are smoothed back down into the tired routine. You could almost get to feel comfortable in a town like this. Play ball and you won't be disturbed. Jakob Cedergren plays the marshal as a man born to be ordered around. He could only be a policeman in a town where people take cops seriously. Whatever happened to him in Copenhagen has him still in shock, and it's almost like he feels he deserves the way the town treats him. Even in his romantic transgression he seems to be going with the flow.

*Terribly Happy* at heart plays like a classic Western: the frontier town, the local bad man, the new marshal, the townspeople, cute and vulnerable Ingelise. I've only been to Denmark twice and have no idea if this is even remotely a Danish situation, but it could fit right fine in the Old West.

## Texas Killing Fields ★ ★

R, 105 m., 2011

Sam Worthington (Mike Souder), Jeffrey Dean Morgan (Brian Heigh), Jessica Chastain (Pam Stall), Chloe Grace Moretz (Little Anne Sliger), Jason Clarke (Rule), Annabeth Gish (Gwen Heigh), Sheryl Lee (Lucie Sliger), Stephen Graham (Rhino). Directed by Ami Canaan Mann and produced by Michael Jaffe and Michael Mann. Screenplay by Don Ferrarone.

You won't find the Texas Killing Fields on a map, but round about Texas City, Texas, that's where everybody knows a murder victim's body is likely to be found. It's said even the Native Americans feared to enter them. They're bayou country, soggy and forbidding, and two local detectives are looking here for clues to the murder of a young girl.

Mike Souder (Sam Worthington) and Brian Heigh (Jeffrey Dean Morgan) are on the case. Souder's former wife, Pam (Jessica Chastain), a detective in a nearby jurisdiction, is investigating the murder of another young woman, and of course suspects answers will be found not far from a killing field. Heigh agrees with Pam that there seems to be some pattern in the two almost simultaneous murders, but Mike doesn't want to get involved in a case with his ex. Bad memories.

*Texas Killing Fields* begins along the lines of a police procedural, and might have been perfectly absorbing if it had played by the rules: strict logic, attention to detail, reference to technical police work. Unfortunately, the movie often seems to stray from such discipline. Scenes do not always necessarily follow one another. I was sometimes unclear who some of the characters were. Developments were explored that seemed of great importance to the detectives, and then the film would seem to lose track of them.

The locations and cinematography distract from these problems because they have great intrinsic interest. If nothing riveting is happening, it seems to be taking place in a locale where it could happen; the fields and the worn little towns around them seem pregnant with possibilities.

One line of investigation involves a young local girl, Little Anne Sliger (Chloe Grace Moretz), who is being raised by a slatternly mother (Sheryl Lee), who works a step down from prostitution because she is a service provider who essentially wants not money but company. Little Anne was, for me, the most interesting character in the movie, and somehow if the story could have been rotated to focus on her, the other elements might have been lined up better.

Cop movies seem to require chase scenes and shoot-outs. This movie has both, and the chase is well done. But there seems no urgent reason to have made this movie; no character stands out, the plot seems absentminded, and what we're left with are the Killing Fields, which supply a great title but not much of a resolution. The movie was produced by Michael Mann, father of the director, Ami Canaan Mann, but it doesn't reflect his usual tight grip on structure.

## That Evening Sun ★ ★ ★ ½

PG-13, 110 m., 2010

Hal Holbrook (Abner Meecham), Ray McKinnon (Lonzo Choat), Walton Goggins (Paul Meecham), Mia Wasikowska (Pamela Choat), Carrie Preston (Ludie Choat), Barry Corbin (Thurl Chesser), Dixie Carter (Ellen Meecham). Directed by Scott Teems and produced by Terence Berry, Walton Goggins, Ray McHinnon, and Laura D. Smith. Screenplay by Teems, based on the story "I Hate to See That Evening Sun Go Down" by William Gay.

One of the reasons *That Evening Sun* works so well is that the good character isn't all good and the bad character isn't all bad, although they both come close. That leads to a drama set on a Tennessee farm that begins by looking like your standard old-codger story and turns out, as Clint Eastwood's *Gran Torino* did, to be a lot more.

Hal Holbrook, that rock-steady actor with a face off Mount Rushmore, stars as Abner Meecham, an eighty-something who up and walks out of a retirement home one day and takes a taxi to his farm outside of town. It is his farm as far as he's concerned, anyway, although his lawyer son has power of attorney and has rented it to the Choat family. This family is well known to Abner, who dislikes them. He and his neighbor Thurl (Barry Corbin) agree that Lonzo Choat (Ray McKinnon) doesn't amount to much.

While his son, Paul (Walton Goggins), busy with a court case, issues ineffectual commands into his cell phone, Abner sets up an outpost in the bare-boards sharecropper cabin and keeps a hostile eye on the house. Lonzo's sixteen-year-old daughter, Pamela (Mia Wasikowska), comes to visit, is instinctively nice, and sort of disregards Abner's hostility. When she confides that her father hates barking dogs, Abner adopts one of Thurl's barkingest dogs and moves him into the cabin.

Choat has been living on disability, can't make payments on the house, is in no shape to work the farm, and usually has a beer in his hand. If the inside of the farmhouse looks warm and inviting, that's because of two women: Choat's long-suffering wife, Ludie (Carrie Preston), and Abner's own dead wife, Ellen (Dixie Carter). There is poignancy in that role now that Carter, Holbrook's wife, has herself died.

Ellen fixed up the house, Ludie keeps it up, and the two men snarl at each other in the yard. Abner cheerfully calls Choat a white trash redneck, which seems true as we see him drunkenly whipping his wife and daughter with a garden hose. Abner brings this to a stop with a couple of pistol shots. But this situation isn't as simple as who has the gun.

We begin to sense that Choat acts mean but is scared and uncertain inside. By flashbacks and other means, we learn that Abner hasn't always been a sterling husband and father himself. Because both men are flawed, the story takes on an interest and complexity that the setup doesn't hint.

It's a story confined by time and space, adapted by the director, Scott Teems, from the story "I Hate to See That Evening Sun Go Down" by William Gay. Although the setting is a gentle Tennessee landscape and the houses look like illustrations for a calendar of farm life, the situation owes more to Eugene O'Neill or Tennessee Williams. The actors are more than successful at creating deeply plausible characters. There may have been temptations to go broad, but they're all subtle, even McKinnon, in a role that could have gone over the top.

Watching Hal Holbrook, I was reminded again of how steady and valuable this man has been throughout his career. I saw his famous *Mark Twain Tonight* three times in the 1960s, I remember him and Dixie one night at the Royal Court Theater in London where a lamp came crashing to the stage and they handled it with perfect grace and humor, and I remember him most recently as the old man who cares and worries about the doom-seeking hero of *Into the Wild.* Here he incorporates everything he knows about getting to the age of eighty (he's actually eighty-five) and conveys it without the slightest sign of effort. This isn't a performance; it's an embodiment. You know, I think he's about old enough to play Mark Twain.

*Note:* That Evening Sun *won the Audience Award and a jury prize for ensemble acting at the 2010 SXSW film festival.*

## That Girl in Yellow Boots ★ ★ ★ ½

NO MPAA RATING, 103 m., 2011

Kalki Koechlin (Ruth), Prashant Prakash (Prashant), Naseeruddin Shah (Divakar), Gulshan Devaiya (Chittiappa Gowda), Puja Sarup (Maya), Kumud Mishra (Lynn), Shivkumar Subramaniam (Himself), Divya Jagdale (Divya), Thani (Henchman), Mushtaq Khan (Visa Officer). Directed by and produced by Anurag Kashyap. Screenplay by Kashyap and Kalki Koechlin.

She is a figure of instant enigma. A young white woman in Mumbai, speaking Hindi, living alone, rarely smiling, consumed by an obsession. Judging by her accent, she was raised in England. We learn she is half Indian. She has received a letter from the father she has never seen. "If you ever come to India," he writes, "look me up." He unhelpfully provides no contact information.

In Anurag Kashyap's *That Girl in Yellow Boots*, we follow Ruth (Kalki Koechlin) through the labyrinth of Indian customs and visas, which apparently involves endless numbers of men shuffling obscure sheets of paper and sending her to another office. "Why are you here?" they ask. "Because I love India," she says, which doesn't allay their suspicions that she is a foreigner seeking employment.

She lives in a shabby little apartment and supports herself by working in a massage parlor, where she can charge one thousand rupees extra by providing a "handshake," if you follow me. Her free time is spent in the search for her father, who abandoned his family when she was too young to remember him. There is a snaky man named Prashant (Prashant Prakash) who considers himself her boyfriend, although she refuses him intercourse and sees him off with actual handshakes. Prashant is a cokehead, and provides a current of humor when he lugs a giant bottle of water into her flat and handcuffs himself to the radiator to force himself to get clean and sober.

Ruth is a slim, morose beauty with long hair, full lips, and a slight overbite; she's described as "Bugs Bunny crossed with Julia Roberts." We sense an inner rage. She isn't seeking her father for sentimental reasons, and still grieves over the suicide of her older sister. Her skill at massage is not really tested by most clients, who are happy enough to move directly to the happy ending. We meet several of her regulars, including one man who doesn't want her to look at any part of his body. "Where should I look?" she asks. "At the wall." She stares at the wall while her head bobs in time with her hand, and her face betrays nothing—not amusement, annoyance, or even boredom.

She makes little effort to be pleasant. There is one older man, Divakar (Naseeruddin Shah), who actually does want only a massage, and she is marginally happier to see him. Most of the time, she broods, often staring at the cityscape and smoking. The cokehead Prashant is obnoxious by constantly following her and cluelessly interrupting her life, and she tells him to get lost.

As the story finds its way to a conclusion, we realize it was all about character, not plot. What happens at the end doesn't please or especially surprise us—except that it sidesteps a cliché. The value of the film is in its portrait of Ruth, and her independence as a solo outsider in a vast uncaring city. Kalki Koechlin, who cowrote with her husband, the director, Anurag Kashyap, creates a memorable woman who is sad and old beyond her years.

This is Kashyap's third feature. He is said to be a leader of a growing independent film movement in India. I hope it prospers; a film like this provides a radically different view of India than you can find in the pleasures and excesses of Bollywood. Kalki Koechlin herself, who is twenty-eight but looks younger, was born in India of French hippie parents, studied theater in London, and has worked before with Kashyap. They were correct to sense that the very presence of a young foreign loner in Mumbai was a good place to begin with a film.

## They Call It Myanmar: Lifting the Curtain ★ ★ ★

NO MPAA RATING, 70 m., 2012

A documentary directed by Robert H. Lieberman.

I've never seen a documentary with more smiling faces. The people of Burma seem sunny and cheerful, kind and eager to accept visitors. No, not all of them. Not the unsmiling ruling military class with their comic-opera official hats, and not the little girl with untreated tuberculosis that has caused an ulcer to open a hole in her chest. But most of them. They have an inner glow. See for yourself.

*They Call It Myanmar: Lifting the Curtain* is the much-discussed new documentary about the sealed-off nation of Burma. The film could also have been titled, *The British Renamed It Burma.* Under any name, it is a beautiful nation, sharing borders with Thailand, Laos, China, Bangladesh, and India.

Here is a nation that has undergone much hardship after winning independence from Britain in 1948. It was controlled until 2011 by a military dictatorship. It is currently in the process of democratic elections, and on April 1, 2012, its famed Nobel Peace Prize winner, Daw Aung San Suu Kyi, apparently won a seat in parliament.

She is one of the subjects of *They Call It Myanmar*, a film that was shot secretly by Cornell professor Robert H. Lieberman during four visits there arranged by the U.S. Department of State. Held under house arrest for most of her adult life, Suu Kyi is the leader of the main opposition party. She is composed and serene, sounding not like an angry dissident but like a reasonable and balanced person. She embodies gentle intelligence. As it turns out, her fifteen years of house arrest ended not long after this interview was filmed.

It is reckless to make broad generalizations about any group of people. I don't want to imply that the Burmese under military rule are happy. What I do observe is a land where the precepts of Buddhism are so embedded that philosophical acceptance is widespread. It is not a successful nation. The national economy lags far behind its neighbors in Southeast Asia, its educational level is unusually low, and although its tourist business thrives, the nation (at least as seen here) has not yet been colonized by fast food and chain stores that make much of the world look like a Western shopping mall. Even Lieberman, an outspoken critic of its military regime, loves it.

His film, made unofficially and on a shoestring, is nevertheless a thing of beauty; its cinematography, music, and contemplative words make it not an angry documentary but more of a hymn to a land that has grown out of the oldest cultures in Asia.

The movie lacks a tight agenda. Lieberman and others poke around here and there, asking people questions; voice-overs are anonymous, and some of the on-camera interviews have the faces of the subjects blanked out. There is a devastating contrast between the rich and poor. At the wedding of a general's daughter, she boasts of a necklace of real diamonds, and we see luxury resorts and consumer goods. But few of the masses receive more than one year of schooling, there are no child labor laws, and although we learn that the girl with the ulcerous hole in her chest is "treatable and curable," that would cost five dollars. Medical care for most people is limited to "quacks"—that's the actual local word—who may have picked up a little knowledge by sweeping the floors at a clinic and watching doctors at work.

Lieberman's film is the only doc about Burma available. I gather he may not be an infallible source. He's informed by a fellow foreign passenger that the buses leading up a steep hillside to a temple often plunge off the road, killing everyone on board. Douglas Long, in the *Myanmar Times*, writes: "The drivers, the man further explains to the camera, are not bothered by the prospect of dying. On the contrary, they consider it an honor to sacrifice their own lives while performing the meritorious deed of carrying pilgrims to one of the most sacred Buddhist sites in Myanmar."

Long says in his nine years of working for the newspaper such an accident has never occurred, and "those who live in Myanmar . . . will immediately recognize the man for what he is: a charlatan unable to resist the compulsion to impress others with 'special knowledge' about the supposed dangers of visiting 'exotic' locales like Myanmar." I am reminded of the tall tales told by local guides in Mark Twain's *Innocents Abroad.*

Such footnotes aside, the importance of the film is simply to provide us images for the words "Myanmar" or "Burma." Here is the second-largest country in Southeast Asia, and most Americans know hardly anything about it. What I've come away with is a notion of a land that, despite its crushing problems, has produced a population that seems extraordinarily radiant.

## The Thing ★ ★ ½

R, 103 m., 2011

Mary Elizabeth Winstead (Kate Lloyd), Joel Edgerton (Sam Carter), Adewale Akinnuoye-Agbaje (Jameson), Ulrich Thomsen (Dr. Sander Halvorson), Eric Christian Olsen (Adam Finch), Trond Espen Seim (Edvard Wolner). Directed by Matthijs van Heijningen and produced by Marc Abraham and Eric Newman. Screenplay by Eric Heisserer, based on the short story "Who Goes There?" by John W. Campbell Jr.

Imagine a creature that can exactly imitate the body and behavior of another life form—so well it could fool you into thinking it was your best friend. This Thing journeys the cosmos and mimics the aliens it encounters. Then it reveals its true appearance, which is a hideous and leaky smorgasbord of palpitating organs, claws, teeth, crab legs, lobster tails, beaks, snaky appendages, and gooey dripping eyeballs. It doesn't say much for life in the universe that with whole galaxies to choose from, that's the best body it could come up with.

The source is one of the most durable science fiction stories of all time. Written as "Who Goes There?" by John W. Campbell Jr., it inspired a 1951 film by Howard Hawks and a 1982 remake by John Carpenter. Its idea for an alien also transmuted into two versions of *Invasion of the Body Snatchers* and all of the *Alien* movies. In the 1950s the movies were read as allegories of the Communist menace: Ordinary Americans were infested with Marxism, and although they continued to resemble your husband, cousin, or boss, secretly they were a manifestation of an alien ideology.

The movie's setup: Scientists have discovered a spacecraft buried in the ice of the South Pole. A body is dug out in a block of ice and . . . thaws. In the first film, scientists used instruments to determine the edges of the buried craft, and then chillingly realized they were standing in a saucer-shaped circle. It was the best shot in the film.

This new film once again finds useful the notion that the story takes place entirely within a closed system—a research station in Antarctica, or a spaceship traveling the void. Since the Thing prefers to inhabit its hosts secretly and remain in disguise, the plot comes down to a deadly puzzle: Of the people in the research station or on the spaceship, which are real and which are Things? Paranoia drives the plot.

There is a logical flaw here: Why would the Thing reveal itself before it had infected everyone? Why tip off the humans that there's a problem? Why, for that matter, wouldn't the Thing race travel the universe and simply become every race, so that all life was Things?

The answer, obviously, is that such a story would be impossible. All these people would be in the research station, they'd look and behave like themselves for the whole movie, nothing exciting would happen until the last scene—and then, wow, what happened? We're all Things!

You don't ask questions like that. You accept the genre. It consists of people being horribly sucked up and digested and having their teeth fillings spit out. The interest would seem to be in the special effects: What do the Things really look like? I saw the 1951 film with my mother in a movie theater in West Point, New York, where we were attending my cousin Tommy's graduation from the military academy. It was the most terrifying experience I have ever had in a movie theater.

What did the creature look like? I'm not quite sure. I know it was played by James Arness and was humanoid (a guy in a Thing suit, you could say). The point wasn't its appearance; it was the suspense. The long, cold corridors of the Antarctic structure, the dark and cluttered storerooms, could be concealing a Thing that would leap out at you. Characters persisted in wandering off recklessly by themselves. I kept ducking down behind my seat.

The contribution by John Carpenter was to take advantage of three decades of special effects to make his creatures Awful Gooey Things from space. That was done well in his film, and it is done with even more technical expertise here—but to what point? The more you see of a monster, the less you get. It is the unseen, the imagined, that scares you. This version of *The Thing*, directed by Matthijs van Heijningen, provides such graphic and detailed views of the creature that we are essentially reduced to looking at special effects, and being aware that we are. Think how little you ever really saw in the first *Alien* movie, and how frightening it was.

I expect this movie will do well at the box office. It has a lot of gory *gotcha!* moments, and many scenes in which an endless supply of Things are incinerated by flamethrowers. It seems like such an ignominious end for such a versatile species.

## Thin Ice ★ ★ ★

R, 93 m., 2012

Greg Kinnear (Mickey Prohaska), Billy Crudup (Randy), Alan Arkin (Gorvy Hauer), David Harbour (Bob Egan), Lea Thompson (Jo Ann Prohaska), Bob Balaban (Leonard Dahl), Michelle Arthur (Karla Gruenke). Directed by Jill Sprecher and produced by Mary Frances Budig, Elizabeth Redleaf, and Christine K.

Walker. Screenplay by Jill Sprecher and Karen Sprecher.

---

There's an explanation of the plot at the end of *Thin Ice*, including flashbacks to key moments and shots explaining otherwise inexplicable matters. This explanation essentially builds a different movie out of the one we thought we just saw, and rather makes us want to see it again knowing what we now know. That's not complete consolation. *Thin Ice* could have been more coherent in the first place.

An ordinary life supplies room for only so many twists and turns. The life of Mickey Prohaska (Greg Kinnear) is all too commodious. He's an insurance salesman in Kenosha, Wisconsin, who drives a flashy Cadillac, but is deep in debt and estranged from the wife (Lea Thompson) he expropriated money from. Since the insurance business requires much use of the telephone, he finds it dispiriting that most of his calls come from bill collectors.

We meet Mickey at an insurance convention where he lectures on how to strike up conversations. (Question to Mickey: How much do you charge for supplying audiences with such conversation openers as, "Do you have the correct time?") After his speech, trying out his own line in the hotel bar, he falls for a con so old that Nancy was pulling it on Sluggo.

Back in Kenosha, he calls on a possible client, a farmer named Gorvy Hauer, played by Alan Arkin as a man wandering in the fog of his own befuddlement. Gorvy needs insurance on his TV so he can call a guy to get it to work; Mickey observes that it's not plugged in, but signs him up anyway for a high-priced package. He assures Gorvy his house looks worth $400,000; it looked to me as if it had been stapled together from a house trailer and a couple of prefabricated sunrooms. While he's at the house, a violin appraiser (Bob Balaban) calls to offer Gordy $25,000 for an old family violin. Mickey, a heartless bastard, immediately decides to steal the violin and sell it himself.

Already we're seeing some good typecasting at work. Kinnear is a likable actor, who possibly would make a trustworthy insurance salesman. As his problems begin to pile up, however, he could have used a greater ability to vibrate in terror. William H. Macy, as the car salesman in *Fargo*, comes to mind. Indeed, a lot of *Fargo* comes to mind in *Thin Ice*'s snowbound Wisconsin locations.

Arkin has always had a good line in confused naïveté. His Gorvy is so hapless, and yet with such occasional streaks of insight, that we don't know if his stupidity or his intelligence is an act, but we suspect one or the other is. Balaban evokes a man who knows everything about violins, including a lot he isn't sharing. His violin shop looks remarkably authentic despite occupying an upper floor of an industrial building.

Now enters the engine of the movie's energy, an installer of security systems. This is Randy (Billy Crudup), a man with a police record who isn't above stealing the odd alarm clock. This would be the last man you'd want in charge of your security, but how is old Gorvy expected to know that? Mickey, who can resist anything but temptation, seems to have found a partner in crime.

More of the plot I must not describe. This is a devilishly ingenious screenplay by the sisters Jill and Karen Sprecher. Jill directed, and they shared the same credits on two wonderful films, *Clockwatchers* (1997) and *Thirteen Conversations About One Thing* (2001). The construction of the plot must have taken a great deal of effort, and I feel churlish in raising a couple of points: (1) As these things are happening to Mickey Prohaska, there comes a point—perhaps when the guy was being pounded on the head with a hammer—when they're rather over the top; (2) the explanation, when it comes, cannot be said to fall into place with a smoothly oiled click, but feels more like an alibi.

Never mind. As it was actually happening, *Thin Ice* kept me interested and entertained. There's nothing like the macabre to bring intrigue to an ordinary life, and nothing like the logistics of body disposal to challenge an insurance salesman. The acting helps to float the movie. These actors are quirky in complementary ways, and I've never seen Crudup anywhere near this weirded out. My objections are more like technical fouls.

*Note: This review was written before I received a letter from Jill Sprecher that may explain my problems with the film: "The producers and distributor of our film completely reedited it without me. Nearly twenty minutes were cut; the structure rearranged; outtakes used; voiceover and characters dropped; key plot points omitted; a new score added. Although our names contractually remain on the film, my sister and I do not consider* Thin Ice *to be our work."*

*I showed Jill and Karen's* Thirteen Conversations About One Thing *at Ebertfest 2003. I loved their* Clockwatchers. *They know film construction. This seems to account for the questions I raised.*

## Think Like a Man ★ ★

PG-13, 122 m., 2012

Michael Ealy (Dominic), Jerry Ferrara (Jeremy), Meagan Good (Mya), Regina Hall (Candace), Kevin Hart (Cedric), Taraji P. Henson (Lauren), Terrence J (Michael), Romany Malco (Zeke), Gabrielle Union (Kristen), Jenifer Lewis (Loretta), Gary Owen (Bennett), Chris Brown (Alex). Directed by Tim Story and produced by William Packer. Screenplay by Keith Merryman and David A. Newman, based on the book *Act Like a Lady, Think Like a Man* by Steve Harvey.

Anyone who reads advice books about romance has one problem to begin with: bad taste in literature. The idea that a book can advise a woman how to capture a man is touchingly naive. Books advising men how to capture women are far less common, perhaps because few men are willing to admit to such a difficulty. For both sexes I recommend a good novel, offering scenarios you might learn from, if only because they reflect a lot of doubt.

Nevertheless, in 2009 the comedian and radio host Steve Harvey wrote a best-seller titled *Act Like a Lady, Think Like a Man: What Men Really Think About Love, Relationships, Intimacy, and Commitment.* This was advice for women. It apparently left some questions, because in 2010 Harvey felt the demand for another book, *Straight Talk, No Chaser: How to Find, Keep, and Understand a Man.* A small industry had been set in motion, which inspired Maria Bustillos's *Act Like a Gentleman, Think Like a Woman: A Woman's Response to Steve Harvey's Act Like a Lady, Think Like a Man* (2009). What are Bustillos's qualifications? One month before that book, she published *Dorkismo: The Macho of the Dork.*

Among Harvey's qualifications are that he's been married three times and possibly gained some insights from his two ex-wives about how they failed to keep him. This is not a history to inspire confidence, but in the new movie *Think Like a Man,* we're expected to believe that every woman in the film bought the book and started living her life according to it. The twist comes when the men in their lives discover their secret reading and study the book themselves. Now the men know the women's game plan.

Starting with its title, this movie must be one of the greatest examples of product placement in history. We see Steve Harvey plugging the book on a daytime talk show, and then he appears again from time to time to deliver advice straight to the audience. It's a promising device for a sitcom, especially as the film assigns the characters to categories from the book, such as "The Dreamer vs. The Woman Who Is Her Own Man." This is somewhat limiting because each character is required to behave in a way consistent with his or her label.

But that isn't the real problem. The movie's mistake is to take the book seriously. This might have worked as a screwball comedy or a satire, but can you believe for a moment in characters naive enough to actually live their lives following Steve Harvey's advice? The result is a tiresome exercise that circles at great length through various prefabricated stories defined by the advice each couple needs (or doesn't need).

The cast is superb. It's depressing to find them locked inside this formula. My favorite is Mya (Meagan Good), discouraged by her own promiscuity, who tries to follow the book's advice in dealing with Zeke (Romany Malco). He's a fast-moving ladies' man. She decides he must wait ninety days for sex. This is contrary to both of their natures, and builds up such a head of steam we expect a gasket to blow.

Kevin Hart is funny, too, as a living rebuke to his pals who are studying the book: He spends most of his time in so-called gentlemen's clubs, having thirty-minute relationships that all have happy endings, and it's hard to argue he isn't happy.

Given that the book advises women about how to capture men, it's an irony that the actresses in the film are among the most beautiful in Hollywood. In addition to Good, I give you such as Gabrielle Union, Regina Hall, Taraji P. Henson, and Jenifer Lewis. Does it make me a chauvinist if I suggest that finding men must be the least of their problems? The movie is as appropriate for men seekers as a diet movie starring thin girls.

Let's pretend you're a studio executive. Having read this far, did you spot in this review the brilliant title (and premise) for a new comedy? Maybe you skipped right over it. It was: *Dorkismo: The Macho of the Dork.*

## 13 Assassins ★ ★ ★ ½

R, 126 m., 2011

Koji Yakusho (Shimada), Takayuki Yamada (Shinrokuro), Yusuke Iseya (Koyata), Goro Inagaki (Lord Naritsugu), Masachika Ichimura (Hanbei Kitou), Mikijiro Hira (Sir Doi), Hiroki Matsukata (Kuranaga), Ikki Sawamura (Mitsuhashi). Directed by Takashi Miike and produced by Minami Ichikawa, Toichiro Shiraishi, and Michihiko Yanagisawa. Screenplay by Daisuke Tengan.

*13 Assassins* has what many action pictures need, a villain who transcends evil and ascends to a realm of barbaric madness. Against this creature and his private army, a band of samurai is mustered to end his terror. Their heroism against impossible odds is a last hurrah for the samurai code; the film is set in 1844, toward the end of the medieval Edo period, when true samurai warriors were growing rare.

The film is terrifically entertaining, an ambitious big-budget epic, directed with great visuals and sound by Takashi Miike. The last forty-five minutes are devoted to an inventive and ingenious battle scene, but it's not the sort of incomprehensible mayhem we often find in recent action. It's a lesson to the queasy-cam auteurs, because Miike choreographs the action to make it comprehensible—and, more important, has spent his first two acts establishing the characters. We know who the thirteen samurai are, and we understand why many of them behave as they do under threat of death. The care taken with the screenplay and the shot composition deserves comparison to Kurosawa's (even better) *Seven Samurai.*

The film opens with stark, bloody simplicity. A man kneels in a courtyard and disembowels himself in protest against Lord Naritsugu (Goro Inagaki), the half-brother of the shogun. This seppuku was inspired by Naritsugu's cruelty, which we see demonstrated in appalling detail. He amputates some victims, kicks the severed heads of others across rooms, and exercises the right to rape anyone in his domain. He isn't a twisted caricature but a preening narcissist; the shogun inexplicably plans to promote him.

To correct this evil in the land, Sir Doi (Mikijiro Hira) seeks the samurai Shimada (Koji Yakusho), and finds him peacefully fishing atop a ladder in the sea—but with his sword, of course, nearby. Shimada then seeks another dozen warriors to join him, and this process is familiar to us from countless other movies. Each of the recruits has his own personality and backstory, some more elaborate than others, and of course there must be a little comic relief, although Koyata (Yusuke Iseya) grows more serious in the heat of battle.

The odds for these heroes seem impossible; they are only thirteen and Lord Naritsugu fields at least two hundred against them. Miike spares us the whimsy that thirteen good men can defeat two hundred evil ones, and has his samurai rig an entire village as a trap. It's clear this is planned, but the details remain vague, and when the surprises begin it would be logical, I think, to ask exactly how the assassins found the time and resources to marshal such an elaborate ambush. Logical, but not fair; you don't ask questions like that in movies that require your belief.

Samurai films have a rich history, and Miike evokes it elegantly with traditional costumes, idealistic dialogue, sharp characterizations, and a gloriously choreographed fight sequence that must extend in one form or another for forty minutes. I often find fight scenes in movies boring because they substitute movement for drama. But in *13 Assassins,* characters are involved who we know and understand, and the general melee is broken down into structured vignettes. Hollywood action directors could study this film, especially in the way it focuses on story in the midst of violence.

There is a subtext in the film. The thirteen assassins are essentially making a last stand for the traditional samurai code. Modern times are encroaching on Japan, and the shogunate is corrupt, decadent, and a hive of nepotism. I was reminded in a lateral way of Yamata's *Twilight Samurai* (2004), a very good film set in 1868, about a samurai who works for his clan as an accountant and is forced to recall the code of his tradition.

While watching *13 Assassins* I was sure CGI effects must have been used, but I was rarely able to notice them. That's the point, as it always was in traditional special effects: to deceive the eye, not insult it. Most of the movement here is at least somewhat plausible in terms of the real world. Too often CGI is an excuse for what amount to live-action cartoons. Here is a film that could be studied for its lessons by the manufacturers of Friday night action blockbusters.

## 30 Minutes or Less ★ ★

R, 83 m., 2011

Jesse Eisenberg (Nick), Danny McBride (Dwayne), Aziz Ansari (Chet), Nick Swardson (Travis), Dilshad Vadsaria (Kate), Michael Peña (Chango), Bianca Kajlich (Juicy), Fred Ward (The Major). Directed by Ruben Fleischer and produced by Stuart Cornfield and Ben Stiller. Screenplay by Michael Diliberti.

I should do a little more research, but I think *30 Minutes or Less* is the first R-rated slacker comedy based on a true recent story in which a man was blown up by a bomb strapped around his neck. You may recall the 2003 case of a pizza delivery man who dreamed up a scheme to rob a bank with the bomb strapped on. He thought it was a fake bomb, but his treacherous partners double-crossed him.

Now here is a movie about a guy who drives for a Grand Rapids pizzeria that promises your pizza in thirty minutes or less. That, of course, establishes him as a breakneck stunt driver, which will be useful in the inevitable chase scene. The driver, named Nick, is played by Jesse Eisenberg, in an unfortunate career move after *The Social Network*. He was so good in that film that it is impossible to believe him as a character as dumb as Nick. Try to imagine George Clooney, Ben Kingsley, and John Malkovich playing the Three Stooges.

His best buddy is Chet (Aziz Ansari), who goes ballistic when he discovers Nick has slept with his beautiful twin sister, Kate (Dilshad Vadsaria). That causes complications when Nick turns to Chet in desperation with a bomb strapped to his chest.

How did this happen? We meet two slacker layabouts, Dwayne (Danny McBride) and Travis (Nick Swardson). Hapless, luckless, and witless, they make ten bucks an hour cleaning the pool of Dwayne's father (Fred Ward). One night during a lap dance Dwayne mentions his dad is a lottery winner. Juicy (Bianca Kajlich), the dancer, promises that Dwayne's lap need never be untenanted again if he steals a million from his dad. She even suggests a hit man from Detroit: Chango (Michael Peña).

Their brainstorm: Order a pizza, strap a bomb to the guy, and have him rob a bank to get them the money to pay the hit man, who will then kill the lottery-winning dad. Need I explain that everyone involved in this plot is stupid enough to go along with it?

The time bomb deadline ramps up the urgency and leads to great desperation. The movie's strategic error is to set the deadline too far in the future. There is something annoying about a comedy where a guy is strapped to a bomb and nevertheless has time to spare for off-topic shouting matches with his best buddy. A buddy comedy loses some of its charm in a situation like that.

Certain moments in the film elicit mechanical laughs. The chase is well-staged, but then staging a good chase, in this era of CGI, is becoming routine. Eisenberg is a good actor, which may be why he's wrong for this. The tension over his buddy's sister feels contrived, and only one line is devoted to the intriguing implications that she's a twin sister.

Oh, and the only purpose of the sister, Kate, is to be beautiful. She is plugged into the plot, used to establish her existence, and dropped. If she had been more involved, that might have been an improvement—or might have shown up the plot's shaky contrivance. Better to devote more screen time to the lap dancer, right? If you occupy the demographic this film is aimed at, Hollywood doesn't have a very high opinion of you.

### 35 Shots of Rum ★ ★ ★ ★

NO MPAA RATING, 99 m., 2010

Alex Descas (Lionel), Mati Diop (Josephine), Gregoire Colin (Noe), Nicole Dogue (Gabrielle), Julieth Mars Toussaint (Rene), Ingrid Caven (Jo's Aunt). Directed by Claire Denis and produced by Karl Baurmgartner and Bruno Pesery. Screenplay by Denis and Jean-Pol Fargeau.

Here is a movie about four people who have known each other for a long time, and how their relationships shift in a way that was slow in the preparation. The film makes us care for them, and so our attention is held. I've seen films where superheroes shift alliances, and I only yawned. It's not the scope of a story; it's the depth.

Part of the pleasure in Claire Denis's *35 Shots of Rum* is working out how these people are involved with each other. Two couples live across a hallway from each other in the same Paris apartment building. Neither couple is "together." Gabrielle and Noe have the vibes of roommates, but the way Lionel and Josephine obviously love each other, it's a small shock when she calls him "papa."

Lionel (Alex Descas) is a French train engineer. Jo (Mati Diop) works in a music store. Gabrielle (Nicole Dogue) drives her own taxi. Noe (Gregoire Colin) is of uncertain plans. He claims only his much-loved cat is preventing him from moving to Brazil. The four people are in and out of both apartments, and we sense they're a virtual family. Small events take place. A guy flirts with Jo at her store. Gabrielle deals with a talkative customer. Lionel and Jo both bring home rice cookers, so Jo puts hers aside so as not to hurt his feelings.

At work, Lionel attends a retirement party for a longtime engineer, Rene. His fellow workers love him, but Rene is miserable. He has no desire to retire. Afterward on a bus, he confesses to Lionel he has no idea how he got into his life to begin with. He has no desire to be an engineer. Spending his life on trains and buses is no way to live.

Lionel seems content. All four of the neighbors seem content, yes, but not completed. One night they head out together in Gabrielle's taxi to attend a concert. The taxi breaks down, they get out of the rain in a Jamaican café, there's good music on the jukebox, they dance with one another, the woman who owns the café, and others.

And in that long scene with its familiar music, Clare Denis achieves the shift. She does it not with dialogue, not with plot points, but with the eyes. This is what movies are for. They begin happy enough, but . . . incomplete. During the dancing and kidding around, it becomes clear to them, and to us, what must happen for the parts to fall into place.

Denis has long been interested in the former French colonies of West Africa, and in those who came from there to France. Lionel did, and married a German woman; she has died, but they go to visit her sister, Jo's aunt (Ingrid Caven). It is part of Lionel taking care to raise his daughter well and launch her into life. Lionel is handsome, Jo is beautiful, neither one cares.

Nicole Dogue glows in a quiet way as Gabrielle, in her forties, once no doubt stunning, now beautiful in a comfortable way. It's clear she has long been in love with Lionel. No pressure. It's clear Lionel has put that side of his life on hold to be a good father. What does he think about his job? It is a job; he's good at it. The tragedy of the retired Rene will not be his.

You can live in a movie like this. It doesn't lecture you. These people are getting on with their lives, and Denis observes them with tact. She's not intruding; she's discovering. We sense there's not a conventional plot, and that frees us from our interior moviegoing clock. We flow with them. Two are blessed; two are problematic. Will all four be blessed at the end? This is a wise movie and knows that remains to be seen.

### This Is Not a Film ★ ★ ★ ½

NO MPAA RATING, 78 m., 2012

Directed by Jafar Panahi and Mojtaba Mirtahmasb and produced by Panahi. Screenplay by Panahi.

*This Is Not a Film* is not a film because its director is not a director. In December 2010, Jafar Panahi of Iran was sentenced to six years in prison and banned for twenty years from making movies. His crime was "propaganda against the Islamic Republic." He was a supporter of the enormous crowds that filled the streets of Tehran to protest the suspicious reelection of Iranian president Mahmoud Ahmadinejad.

Panahi, who is on camera almost constantly in *This Is Not a Film*, has a trustworthy face. He seems kind and philosophical—especially on this particular day, when he is awaiting a judge's ruling on his appeal. Alone in a spacious high-rise apartment, except for his daughter's pet iguana, Igi, he has some flatbread and jam for his breakfast, calls his lawyer, is told Iranian judges almost never overturn sentences, but he might hope for a "discount" off the twenty years.

What comes next is an extraordinary act of courage. He has been filming himself, and now calls his friend Mojtaba Mirtahmasb to come over and join him. He's not sure what to do. Forbidden to even say "action" or "cut," he wanders about the apartment, feeds the iguana, begins to describe the most recent screenplay he was forbidden permission to film, and comments on the DVDs of three of his films: *The White Balloon* (1995), *The Circle* (2000), and *Crimson Gold* (2003).

This man, who has been silenced, now finds things in the films he did not plan. In the first, the little girl who is playing his heroine gets fed up with the process, tears off the cast she's wearing for the scene, and stalks out of camera range. "I'm not acting anymore!" she announces. The second is a drama about the difficulties of a group of women who attempt to move about the city without male companions (chaperones?). The third is about a large, stolid man who loses patience with himself. The actor is, in fact, schizophrenic (which the film doesn't mention). He cannot take direction, but spontaneously he makes a gesture with his hands that expresses enormous frustration.

I've seen these films and they are very good. They've won awards at many major festivals—Cannes, Venice, Berlin, and so on. I realize my description doesn't begin to evoke the experience for you. That is precisely Panahi's point. He demonstrates it in an agonizing scene where he begins to tell his friend the story of his banned film, and uses tape on the carpet to mark out the floor plan of his heroine's room. (She has been accepted by a university but forbidden by her father to attend and locked in the room.) He grows frustrated and tears up the tape.

Things happen. Carry-out food arrives. A neighbor drops off her dog for Panahi to watch, but the dog freaks out at the sight of the iguana. He watches the news on TV. It is Fireworks Wednesday, the Persian New Year's, and in the evening the city by tradition will be crowned by fireworks. Ahmadinejad has banned fireworks, murmuring darkly that they are in violation of Islamic law. The film never says the Islamic Republic shows great insecurity in the face of anything it doesn't control. It doesn't have to. I would like to show *This Is Not a Film* to those in the United States who are in favor of a close union of church and state.

There is nothing remotely political in Panahi's films. But they can be read as parables. That is how Iranian directors must work these days. Even a domestic drama such as last year's Oscar-winning *A Separation* can be read in more than one way. And when religious fundamentalists are doing the interpretation, what chance does the human spirit have?

Little by little, detail by detail, *This Is Not a Film* leads to a final scene of overwhelming power. I don't think it was even planned—no more than Panahi expected the little actress to take the cast off her arm. It simply happens, and then the film is over, having nothing more to say. Because, after all, it is not a film.

## This Means War ★ ½

PG-13, 97 m., 2012

Reese Witherspoon (Lauren), Chris Pine (FDR Foster), Tom Hardy (Tuck), Til Schweiger (Heinrich), Chelsea Handler (Trish), Angela Bassett (Collins). Directed by McG and produced by Simon Kinberg, James Lassiter, Robert Simonds, and Will Smith. Screenplay by Kinberg and Timothy Dowling.

If there's anything I hate more than a stupid action comedy, it's an incompetent stupid action comedy. It's not so bad it's good; it's so bad it's nothing else but bad. At the center of *This Means War*, poor Reese Witherspoon is poised, playing Lauren, a perky single woman who meets two hunks through an online dating service. These two guys both work for the CIA, with their desks facing each other. What a hilarious coincidence, eh?

I could comprehend this story gimmick in a movie involving sixteen-year-olds. Witherspoon and her costars, Chris Pine and Tom Hardy, have an average age of 33.33, and that's how old they look, 33.33-ish. Their agents should be old enough to warn them against this movie. That they are all single is possible. That the two guys meet the same girl and fall instantly in love and engage in bitter romantic struggle is . . . not. Reese Witherspoon is as cute as a button on Raggedy Ann's overalls, but irresistible raw sex appeal is not one of her qualities.

Now consider her CIA buddies, FDR Foster (Chris Pine) and Tuck (Tom Hardy). Although Reese is not convincing as the woman they go to war over, she would be ideally cast as a straight roommate giving them advice about their romance. Because surely they're gay. They do everything together, ranging from deadly fights on top of a Hong Kong skyscraper to an office contest to see who can shoot the most baskets by tossing wadded-up paper into a wastebasket.

Here's how creepy it gets. They divert apparently millions of dollars' worth of high-tech electronic surveillance equipment in order to monitor Lauren's private life every moment of the day. This means they can watch each other trying to seduce her and eavesdrop as she gets advice from Trish (Chelsea Handler), her BFF. Often they review the surveillance videos *together*. Is there something about that that's not entirely consistent with a heterosexual competition? Lauren is obviously only the nexus for their plexus.

The two agents are assigned to the case of Heinrich (Til Schweiger), whose robbery they interrupted in Hong Kong. Their boss at the agency is Collins (Angela Bassett). Heavens, it must grow tiresome to be a big German movie star asked only to stand there and look tall, unshaven, and menacing. Goodness, Angela Bassett must feel underemployed asked only to look tall, shaven, and menacing. She can play no-nonsense strong women as well as anyone, but what can she do with a role that amounts to delivering zingers and stalking off on high heels?

I've often observed that characters in movies tend to live in nicer apartments than they ought to be able to afford. I don't know what the CIA pays, but FDR has a Los Angeles apartment where the ceiling of a hallway consists of the glass bottom of a swimming pool. Uh-huh. Are you asking yourself why his name is FDR? You can be excused for guessing it's short for Franklin Delano Roosevelt, but I have a better idea. *This Means War* was directed by a man whose entire and complete name is McG. He's probably always wanted a name he didn't have to explain nine times a day.

## Thor ★ ½

PG-13, 114 m., 2011

Chris Hemsworth (Thor), Natalie Portman (Jane Foster), Tom Hiddleston (Loki), Anthony Hopkins (Odin), Stellan Skarsgard (Erik Selvig), Kat Dennings (Darcy Lewis), Clark Gregg (Agent Coulson). Directed by Kenneth Branagh and produced by Kevin Feige. Screenplay by Ashley Miller, Zack Stentz, and Don Payne.

I didn't attend the critics' screening for *Thor* because it was at the same time Ebertfest was showing *A Small Act*, about an eighty-eight-year-old woman named Hilde Back. She'd flown from Sweden, and I wanted be onstage to present her with the Golden Thumb. Missing *Thor 3-D* was not an inconsolable loss, because I was able to see it in Chicago in nice, bright 2-D. The house was surprisingly well populated for an 8:50 p.m. screening on a Monday, suggesting that some people, at least, will make an effort to avoid 3-D.

*Thor* is a failure as a movie, but a success as marketing, an illustration of the ancient carnival tactic of telling the rubes anything to get them into the tent. "You won't believe what these girls take off!" a carny barker promised me and my horny pals one steamy night at the Champaign County Fair. He was close. We didn't believe what they left on.

The failure of *Thor* begins at the story level, with a screenplay that essentially links special effects. Some of the dialogue is mock-heroic ("You are unworthy of your title, and I'll take from you your power!") and some of it winks ironically ("You know, for a crazy homeless person, he's pretty cute"). It adapts the original Stan Lee strategy for Marvel, where characters sometimes spoke out of character.

The story might perhaps be adequate for an animated film for children, with Thor, Odin, and the others played by piglets. In the arena of movies about comic book superheroes, it is a desolate vastation. Nothing exciting happens, nothing of interest is said, and the special effects evoke not a place or a time but simply special effects.

Thor, to begin with, is not an interesting character. The gods of Greek, Roman, and Norse mythology share the same problem, which is that what you see is what you get. They're defined by their attributes, not their personalities. Odin is Odin and acts as Odin and cannot act as other than Odin, and so on. Thor is a particularly limited case. What does he do? He wields a hammer. That is what he does. You don't have to be especially intelligent to wield a hammer, which is just as well, because in the film, Thor (Chris Hemsworth) doesn't seem to be the brightest bulb in Asgard.

The land (sphere? state of mind? heaven?) known as Asgard is described in Norse mythology as being near Troy, or perhaps in Asia Minor. In the movie, as nearly as I can gather, it is not of this earth and must be elsewhere in the universe. It consists of towering spires and skyscrapers linked by bridges and buttresses and betraying no sign of a population, except when untold thousands of Asgardians are required to line up at attention like robotic Nazis to receive dictates from the throne of Odin (Anthony Hopkins).

Asgard's ancient enemies are the Frost Giants, whose home is Jotunheim. I believe, but cannot promise you, that Jotunheim and Asgard are linked by a bridge, although this bridge also seems to be the way Thor reaches Earth, so perhaps it's more of a gateway through time and space, which would explain why Asgardians hurtle across intergalactic light-years and land in New Mexico without a hair out of place.

Thor is the first to arrive, and encounters three human scientists. Whether he is human himself is a question the film sidesteps. We know from mythology that gods sometimes mated with humans, which is a hopeful sign. The humans are astrophysicist Jane Foster (Natalie Portman), her friend Darcy (Kat Dennings), and the distinguished Dr. Erik Selvig (Stellan Skarsgard). I mention she's an astrophysicist because she behaves more like a storm chaser, cruising the desert in a van and peering into the skies, which won't get you far in astrophysics. The van hits Thor after he unluckily lands in front of it. This is not a Meet Cute for the gods. Later there's a meteoric event in which Thor's hammer hurtles to Earth and becomes embedded so firmly that it can't be pulled loose by a pickup truck or even the federal government.

So now Thor is on Earth, his hammer is stuck, and I am underwhelmed. Thor luckily speaks English, and Jane and her friends take him to the local diner, where he eats lots of Pop-Tarts and, when he finishes his coffee, smashes the empty cup to the ground. "We don't do that," Jane explains as if to a child, and advises him to simply order another cup, after which he apparently absorbs human behavior and the movie drops the Taming of the Thor angle.

The three scientists are thin soup. Jane flirts demurely with Thor, Darcy stands next to her and does nothing very important, and Dr. Selvig regards them gravely and looms slightly above a low-angle camera while looking on with wise concern. There is also a government agent (Clark Gregg), whose every action is the remedy to an immediate requirement of the plot.

Superhero movies live and die on the quality of their villains. *Thor* has a shabby crew. The Frost Giants spend most of their time being frosty in their subzero sphere of Jotunheim and occasionally freezing their enemies. Thor's brother Loki (Tom Hiddleston) is dark-haired, skinny, shifty-eyed, and sadly lacking in charisma. He might as well be wearing a name tag: "Hi! I can't be trusted!" These villains lack adequate interest to supply a climactic battle, so the movie fabricates a Metal Giant, sends him to the New Mexico town, and has him blast fiery rays that blow up gas stations real good but always miss his targets. He is apparently killed by a sword through his spine, but why does he need a spine, since when his mask lifts we can see his head is an empty cavern?

And what about that town? It seems to be partly a set with two interiors (the diner and Jane's office) and partly CGI. It seems to go for a few blocks and then end abruptly in barren desert. Not even any suburbs or strip malls. I know aliens from other worlds are required to arrive in New Mexico, but why stay there? Why can't the Metal Giant attack the Golden Gate Bridge or scale a Trump Tower somewhere? Who cares if he turns a 7-Eleven into a fireball?

Here is a film that is scoring 79 percent on Rotten Tomatoes. For what? The standards for comic book superhero movies have been established by *Superman*, *The Dark Knight*, *Spider-Man 2*, and *Iron Man*. In that company *Thor* is pitiful. Consider even the comparable villains (Lex Luthor, the Joker, Doc Ock, and Obadiah Stane). Memories of all four come instantly to mind. Will you be thinking of Loki six minutes after this movie is over?

The director given this project, Kenneth Branagh, once obtained funding for a magnificent 70 mm version of *Hamlet*. Now he makes *Thor*. I wonder with a dread fear if someone in Hollywood, stuck with a movie about a Norse god, said, "Get Branagh. He deals with that Shakespeare crap."

## A Thousand Words ★ ½

PG-13, 91 m., 2012

Eddie Murphy (Jack McCall), Kerry Washington (Caroline McCall), Clark Duke (Aaron Wiseberger), Cliff Curtis (Dr. Sinja), Allison Janney (Samantha Davis), Ruby Dee (Annie McCall). Directed by Brian Robbins and produced by Robbins, Nicolas Cage, Alain Chabat, Stephanie Danan, Norman Golightly, and Sharla Sumpter. Screenplay by Steve Koren.

The poster art for *A Thousand Words* shows Eddie Murphy with duct tape over his mouth, which as a promotional idea ranks right up there with Fred Astaire in leg irons. The idea is that every time he says a word a leaf falls off the magical bodhi tree in his backyard, and when the last leaf falls, he dies.

Let's stop right there. Why did the bodhi tree magically spring out of the earth fully grown? I don't know. It must have something to do with a guru whose book he is trying to sell. Murphy plays Jack McCall, a literary agent who never reads books, and maybe this is karmic revenge. How is it determined that the tree began with one thousand leaves? I dunno. It looks healthy to begin with, and the average bodhi tree has about one hundred thousand leaves. How do I know that? I don't, but it seems likely.

Jack is a motormouth showboat who lives with his wife, Caroline (Kerry Washington), and their son in a vast glass-walled bachelor's pad. But Jack's most meaningful relationship is with Aaron Wiseberger (Clark Duke), his nerdish assistant. It's Aaron who tapes his mouth shut to save his life when he's down to a few hundred words. Some words he squanders on his cell phone, and even more get used up during visits with his mother, Annie (Ruby Dee), who has Alzheimer's and thinks he's his own father. You know with a dreadful certainty that sooner or later she will recognize him, and this will be intended as an uplifting turning point.

What *A Thousand Words* needs is some sort of a mystical scorecard to keep track of Jack's status in the universe. The guru who wrote the book, Dr. Sinja (Cliff Curtis), apparently knows something about this bodhi tree, but never explains the rules. When Jack finally apparently redeems himself, it seems to be by instinct or good luck. I say "apparently" because, as heaven is my witness, I'm not completely sure if Jack is alive, dead, or reincarnated at the end of the movie. You could build a case for all three.

The running gag is that Jack has to communicate without speaking, or talk himself to death. At one point this struggle is conducted by using several dozen talking dolls and action figures, which are conveniently scattered around the literary agency. Jack also does desperate pantomimes and gets so frustrated he seems ready to explode. He tries writing notes, but every word causes another leaf to fall.

I learn from Wikipedia that *A Thousand Words* was originally filmed in 2008. It was scheduled at one point to open in 2011, but was rescheduled until after the Oscars to take advantage of Murphy being named to host the ceremony. That didn't work out, either.

## 3 ★ ★ ½

NO MPAA RATING, 119 m., 2011

Sophie Rois (Hanna), Sebastian Schipper (Simon), Devid Striesow (Adam). Directed by Tom Tykwer and produced by Stefan Arndt. Screenplay by Tykwer.

Tom Tykwer's *3*, also known as *Three* or *Drei*, is an art film treatment of what in more vulgar genres would be called a threesome. It contains a good many sex scenes, but have you noticed recently how many orgasms in the movies are desperate, aggressive, or sad—anything but ecstatic? The most that can be said for the characters here is they all seem mighty pleased.

The movie involves a fortyish couple in Berlin who have a "committed relationship," but are not married because of all the usual weaselly reasons. Hanna (Sophie Rois) hosts a TV talk show about culture. Simon (Sebastian Schipper) runs a company that constructs large works of art for sculptors and suchlike. They get along warmly enough after twenty years together, but the excitement is fading. One night Hanna goes out for drinks after a show, and Simon learns from a doctor that he has testicular cancer. The doc says it's curable but surgery should be done quickly—like, now.

Simon can't get Sophie on her cell phone. She is preoccupied. The removal of one of Simon's precious spheres is required, and we learn along with Simon that this surgery is now done under local anesthetic; presumably just as a woman might want to be conscious during childbirth, a man wouldn't want to miss the halving of his family jewels. The guilty tumor is deposited in a steel pan with a little *clink*. I would have expected more of a little plop. This Simon, what a man.

Hanna has met a man named Adam (Devid Striesow). One thing leads to another, and without planning to they have intercourse. Neither one was hungering for sex, but it seemed like a good idea at the time, and if anything it makes Hanna friendlier with Simon after his inventory has been reduced. Not long after, in a modernistic and isolated swimming pool, Simon meets Adam in the locker room and somehow the conversation gets around to losing one of your testicles. Adam asks for a look, and before long they're having sex.

What you need to know about Adam is that he is not sex mad, not a predator, not aggressive. We sense he is a very nice man with a friendly smile. He isn't bisexual so much as accommodating. We learn a little more about the lives of Simon and Hanna, in visual displays by director Tom Tykwer (*Run, Lola, Run*) that use flashbacks, imaginings, and possibilities, mixed up with snatches of everyday life, bites of television, and a compressed edition of the two parallel love affairs as they develop.

What is crucial is that nice young Adam doesn't have the slightest idea that Hanna and Simon are a couple. He likes them both, they both like him, but it's an excellent question how they'd all feel if the cards were on the table. The movie is, in short, a melodrama that in other hands could easily become a farce. But Tykwer reins in the performances; his characters are intelligent, have gone into this situation with no desire to hurt anyone, and are involved in the kind of realignment that can happen in midlife.

The film is successful in an absorbing sort of way, but underwhelming. Devid Striesow's performance as Adam is important in its modulation. More affection is involved than lust, more curiosity than need. If he's not with the one he loves, he loves the one he's with.

## The Three Stooges ★ ★ ½

PG, 92 m., 2012

Chris Diamantopoulos (Moe), Will Sasso (Curly), Sean Hayes (Larry), Larry David (Sister Mary-Mengele), Jane Lynch (Mother Superior), Sofia Vergara (Lydia), Jennifer Hudson (Sister Rosemary), Craig Bierko (Mac). Directed by Bobby Farrelly and Peter Farrelly and produced by Bobby Farrelly, Peter Farrelly, Bradley Thomas, and Charles B. Wessler. Screenplay by Mike Cerrone, Bobby Farrelly, and Peter Farrelly.

The Farrelly brothers have made probably the best Three Stooges movie it's possible to make in 2012, and perhaps ever, since the Stooges stopped making them themselves. Much depends on whether that was what you were hoping to hear. The movie has the look and feel of a Stooges classic and possibly some of the same gags. So there's that.

I missed the whole Three Stooges thing. Either they weren't on the station in my hometown, or we hadn't bought a TV set yet, or they came to town too late for me. I'm pretty sure that at the right age I would have loved them. No doubt many parents will want to share their formative experience with their children.

For example, at the screening I attended, Mancow Muller was there with his twin daughters, Ava Grace and Isabella Sofia, who are sweethearts. No doubt he was grateful for the public service announcement at the end of the movie by two actors playing the Farrellys, who demonstrated to the audiences that the hammers and sledgehammers the Stooges hit each other on the head with were rubber props. They also used slow motion to show that no Stooge is *really* being poked in the eye, but at the eyebrows.

As much as anything else in the movie, this cautionary lecture evoked the era when the Stooges reigned at kiddie matinees and low-rent TV stations. "Warning—kids!" we were always being told. "Don't try this yourself!" Solemn stories were told about the kid who shot his eye out with a BB gun, or ate a lot of Kool-Aid powder and then drank an RC Cola and his stomach exploded. As nearly as I can recall, nobody was hit over the head with a sledgehammer.

The casting of the three leads is just about ideal. Larry, Curly, and Moe are played by Sean Hayes, Will Sasso, and Chris Diamantopoulos, who are made to look enough like the originals to justify no complaints. This movie has been in development hell for something like a decade, and survived the bankruptcy of MGM. Perhaps we should be grateful for the delay. Over the years Web sites breathlessly reported the casting of such as Benicio Del Toro, Sean Penn, Hank Azaria, Johnny Knoxville, and Jim Carrey, but it's better this way because it's less distracting. Sean Penn is an excellent actor, but I don't know if I could get into the spirit with him as Larry.

The film is wisely brief, ninety-two minutes, divided into three segments that are linked together with the Stooges being raised in an orphanage. They spent not only their childhoods there, but their entire lives until the present day—parents, for some reason, being reluctant to adopt them. Segments two and three center around the bankruptcy of the orphanage and the pledge by the Stooges to raise $830,000 almost overnight to keep it open.

The nuns running the orphanage are also well cast: Jane Lynch as the Mother Superior, Larry David (yes, Larry David) as the autocratic Sister Mary-Mengele, and Jennifer Hudson, slender and warm as Sister Rosemary.

As they forage the city in search of funds, the Stooges get involved in a murder plot against a millionaire, and Moe finds accidental stardom in the cast of a popular TV program that I will not reveal.

Having said all of these things, I must say one more: I didn't laugh much. I don't think the Stooges are funny, although perhaps I might once have. Some of the sight gags were clever, but meh. The three leads did an admirable job of impersonation. I think this might be pretty much the movie Stooges fans were looking for. I have no idea what their children will think about it. I guess what I'm wondering is, was it really necessary?

## Tim and Eric's Billion Dollar Movie ½ ★

R, 92 m., 2012

Tim Heidecker (Himself), Eric Wareheim (Himself), William Atherton (Earle Swinton), Robert Loggia (Tommy Schlaaang), Twink Caplan (Katie), Will Ferrell (Damien Weebs), Will Forte (Allen Bishopman), Jeff Goldblum (Chef Goldblum), John C. Reilly (Taquito), Zach Galifianakis (Jim Joe Kelly), Ronnie Rodriguez (Fake Johnny Depp). Directed by Tim Heidecker and Eric Wareheim and produced by Heidecker, Wareheim, Ben Cosgrove, Will Ferrell, Chris Henchy, Dave Kneebone, Adam McKay, Kevin J. Messick, Jon Mugar, and Todd Wagner. Screenplay by Heidecker and Wareheim.

I feel I've failed Tim and Eric. They've gathered a cult following by doing comedy sketches that are deliberately bad, and now they've made a movie that is more of the same for ninety-two minutes, and it must have taken them a great deal of work to maintain their low standard. By not finding even one moment of *Tim and Eric's Billion Dollar Movie* to be slightly funny, have I let down the side? There is a scene in this film where a character is defecated on by several people at the same time, and I dunno . . . I didn't enjoy it.

The purpose of a cult is exclusion. If you're not in the cult, you are by definition lacking some essential quality shared by its members. Those inside the cult can feel privileged, even gifted, by their ability to Get It. I was willing to Get It, I was sincerely prepared, but at the end of this experience, I concluded there was nothing to be Got.

The premise is that Tim and Eric have been given one billion dollars to make a movie. This money has come from Tommy Schlaaang (Robert Loggia) and Earle Swinton (William Atherton), who run the Schlaaang Corp. The corporation is in violation of Ebert's Law of Funny Names, which teaches us that a name intended to be funny in a movie will almost certainly not be funny. Not everybody can come up with Rufus T. Firefly or Elmer Prettywillie, and if Tommy Schlaaang is the best Tim and Eric can do, they shouldn't have tried.

Tim and Eric blew the fortune by making a short subject, which they believed starred Johnny Depp. Swinton and Schlaaang perceive that it is not Johnny Depp but an impostor. Worse, the fake Johnny Depp (Ronnie Rodriguez) actually looks a little like Johnny Depp. Even a non cult member like me knows that it would have been funnier if the Johnny Depp impersonator had been played by John C. Reilly, in character as Taquito, one of the most disturbed and disturbing characters I've seen in a while. To address Taquito as "snot nose" would not be an insult but the simple truth.

Taquito is a resident of the Swallow Valley Mall, where Tim and Eric hide out while on the run from the vengeful minions of the Schlaaang Corp. This mall is a dark and deserted place, inhabited by various failed life forms and certain actors (Jeff Goldblum, Will Ferrell) who in buying into Tim and Eric showed no better judgment than Swinton and Schlaaang.

I can't keep this up. Describing the movie is bringing down the level of my prose. As faithful readers will know, I have a few cult followers who enjoy my reviews of bad movies. These have been collected in the books *I Hated, Hated, HATED This Movie*, *Your Movie Sucks*, and *A Horrible Experience of Unbearable Length*. This movie is so bad it couldn't even inspire a review worthy of one of those books. I have my standards.

## Tinker Tailor Soldier Spy ★ ★ ★

R, 127 m., 2011

Gary Oldman (George Smiley), Kathy Burke (Connie Sachs), Benedict Cumberbatch (Peter Guillam), David Dencik (Toby Esterhase), Colin Firth (Bill Haydon), Stephen Graham (Jerry Westerby), Tom Hardy (Ricki Tarr), Ciaran Hinds (Roy Bland), John Hurt (Control), Toby Jones (Percy Alleline), Konstantin Khabensky (Polyakov), Svetlana Khodchenkova (Irina), Simon McBurney (Oliver Lacon), Mark Strong (Jim Prideaux). Directed by Tomas Alfredson and produced by Tim Bevan, Eric Fellner, and Robyn Slovo. Screenplay by Bridget O'Connor and Peter Straughan, based on the novel by John le Carre.

Yes, we imagine, international espionage is probably pretty much like this. No thrilling car chases and no big action sections, but rather a series of weary men, smoking and drinking tea or whiskey, in a series of conversations that circle an enigma. *Tinker Tailor Soldier Spy* is about the search for a high-level Soviet spy within MI6, the British intelligence service. This mole is not to be found in an exotic location, but seems more than likely to be one of the men in the room.

The movie is based on John le Carre's 1974 novel, which redefined modern spy fiction and inspired an ambitious 1979 BBC adaptation. There was reason to believe le Carre knew his subject. In the real world, where his real name is David Cornwell, he was one of the British spies who were betrayed by Kim Philby, the notorious MI6 operative who was a double agent for the Soviets. In the fictional version, MI6 is headed by Control (John Hurt), who studies a series of intelligence leaks and becomes convinced there's a mole in the agency; the nature of the intelligence suggests it must come from high up, and Control narrows his list of suspects to five men close to him.

The movie introduces them one by one, each played by a familiar face in a film cast with iconic British actors. "Tinker" is Percy Alleline (Toby Jones), "Tailor" is Bill Haydon (Colin Firth), "Soldier" is Roy Bland (Ciaran Hinds), "Poor Man" is Toby Esterhase (David Dencik), and "Beggarman" is George Smiley (Gary Oldman), Control's trusted lieutenant. If you're wondering what happened to "Spy," that would be whoever turns out to be the mole.

The film, set mostly in London in the early 1970s, is bathed in browns, shadows, and pale lighting. All of the men show a lot of wear, none more than Control; John Hurt's face is weary and deeply lined; his eyes set deep out of the way of cigarette smoke. But lest you think that is entirely because of aging, I interviewed him in 1984 while he was filming *Nineteen Eighty-Four*, and he looked much the same then.

As the film opens, he has learned that a Hungarian general who would know the mole's identity may be a possible defector. In a muted, serious conversation that will set the tone for the film, he assigns Jim Prideaux (Mark Strong) to go to Budapest and talk to this man. That mission goes wrong, and serves to alert the Soviets—although the mole would already know Control was engaged in sniffing him out. In the kerfuffle that follows, both Control and Smiley are dismissed from the service. Some time later, Control is dead from a heart attack and Smiley is recalled from "retirement" to continue the search for the mole.

Now follows a series of paranoid meetings in sealed rooms, snatched conversations in obscure corners of London, and flashbacks that may cast light on Smiley's investigation, although we cannot yet know for sure. All of this is superbly atmospheric in the hands of director Tomas Alfredson, who made the sober and effective vampire movie *Let the Right One In*. His camera is implacable, its moves sinister; the rooms are filled with smoke and fear, and the characters warily circle around—well, one another, really.

*Tinker Tailor Soldier Spy* looks, sounds, and feels exactly right. Alfredson's film is faithful to the tone set by the novel. But the screenplay, by Bridget O'Connor and Peter Straughan, is not a model of clarity. I confess I was confused some of the time and lost at other times; the viewer needs to hold in mind a large number of characters, a larger number of events, and an infinite number of possibilities.

More ordinary spy movies provide helpful scenes in which characters brief one another as a device to keep the audience oriented. I have every confidence that in this film every piece of information is there and flawlessly meshes, but I can't say so for sure, perhaps because I don't have a mind suitable for espionage. I enjoyed the look and feel of the film, the perfectly modulated performances, and the whole tawdry world of spy and counterspy, which must be among the world's most dispiriting occupations. But I became increasingly aware that I didn't always follow all the allusions and connections. On that level, it didn't work for me.

## Tiny Furniture ★ ★ ★

NO MPAA RATING, 98 m., 2010

Lena Dunham (Aura), Laurie Simmons (Siri), Grace Dunham (Nadine), Alex Karpovsky (Jed), Jemima Kirke (Charlotte), Rachel Howe (Candice), David Call (Keith), Amy Seimetz (Ashlynn), Sarah Sophie Flicker (Julia). Directed by Lena Dunham and produced by Kyle and Alicia Van Couvering. Screenplay by Dunham.

There is a strange space between when you leave school and when you begin work. You are idle as a painted ship upon a painted ocean. You grow restless. You cannot go back, and are uncertain how to proceed. *Tiny Furniture* is about Aura, who is becalmed on that sea.

She has graduated from college in Ohio and returned home to live in her mother's loft in TriBeCa. Her boyfriend called it quits; he had to return home to Colorado and see about the spirits of his ancestors, or something. Four years of education have left her with one video on YouTube and the ability to show approval when a guy says he's reading *The Road* by Cormac McCarthy. Her mother is a famous artist who makes a lot of money selling photographs of tiny furniture, sometimes in the same frame as the feet and legs of Nadine, Aura's sister, who is taller, thinner, and younger than Aura.

Aura (Lena Dunham) is discontented. She hates living at home but has no money to move out. She wants a good job but takes one taking reservations at a restaurant. She wants love and acceptance, and finds it much diluted by her distracted mother (Laurie Simmons) and her competitive sister (Grace Dunham). Of possible boyfriends there are: (1) Jed (Alex Karpovsky), a "big deal on YouTube," who rides a mechanical pony while reciting Nietzsche; and (2) Keith (David Call), who works at the restaurant and has a girlfriend, but asks her out and stands her up.

Aura's life unfolds without plot because there is none. The film seems deliberately motionless, although deep currents are stirring. We see Aura at home, with Jed and Keith, and with her new friend Charlotte (Jemima Kirke), who has a British accent, lends her clothes, and otherwise seems firmly one-up. None of these characters have what you might call chemistry, and that seems deliberate. This is a movie about people who are all passive-aggressive, including Aura. Nobody laughs or tries to say anything funny, and when Aura is happy sometimes, she doesn't trust it.

Aura is played by Lena Dunham, who wrote and directed the film. Her mother and her sister are played by her real mother and sister. The loft in TriBeCa is where her family lives. I have no idea if they're playing themselves, but they're certainly convincing. Dunham, indeed, plays one of the most real people I've seen outside of a documentary. She and the others are unaffected, behave as people we know actually do, live in familiar rhythms.

Visually, the film is simple and direct, as unadorned as the white cabinets that cover a wall of the loft. Dunham's cinematographer, Jody Lee Lipes, doesn't move the camera. It's locked down for a steady, flat gaze. This is correct. It sees like Aura sees. She regards with detached fascination as people behave as people will. Her personality doesn't suggest tracking shots.

Why do I feel such affection for *Tiny Furniture*? It's a well-crafted film, for one thing. For a first picture it shows a command of style and purpose; Dunham knows what she wants and how she needs to get it, and succeeds. Her character Aura is not charismatic or glowing or mercurial or seductive or any of those advertising adjectives, but she believes she deserves to be happy, and we do, too.

The movie has a scene in which sex is enacted. It isn't great sex. It calls into question Woody Allen's statement that the worst sex he'd had wasn't that bad. It happens unexpectedly between two people. It happens in the most depressing place for sex I can imagine. No, worse than whatever you're thinking. It is so desperately dutiful. Two people become seized with the urgent need to create an orgasm together, and succeed, and that exhausts the subject. The scene and what leads up to it define Aura and her partner in terms of what they will settle for. Sometimes that's better than nothing.

I know what the budget of this movie was, but never mind. Lena Dunham had every penny she required. She also had all the talent she needed, and I look forward to her work. It's hard enough for a director to work with actors, but if you're working with your own family in your own house and depicting passive-aggression, selfishness, and discontent, and you produce a film this good, you can direct just about anybody in just about anything.

## Titanic in 3-D ★ ★ ★ ★

PG-13, 194 m., 2012

Leonardo DiCaprio (Jack Dawson), Kate Winslet (Rose DeWitt Bukater), Billy Zane (Cal Hockley), Kathy Bates (Molly Brown), Bill Paxton (Brock Lovett), Gloria Stuart (Rose Calvert), Frances Fisher (Ruth DeWitt Bukater), Bernard Hill (Captain E. J. Smith), David Warner (Spicer Lovejoy), Victor Garber (Thomas Andrews), Jonathan Hyde (Bruce Ismay). Directed by James Cameron and produced by Cameron and Jon Landau. Screenplay by Cameron.

The new 3-D version of *Titanic*, like the original 1997 version, is a magnificent motion picture. The hour or more after the ship hits the iceberg remains spellbinding. The material leading up to that point is a combination of documentary footage from the ocean floor, romantic melodrama, and narration by a centenarian named Rose. The production brings to life the opulence of the great iron ship. Its passengers are a cross section of a way of life that would be ended forever by the First World War. In a way, the iceberg represented the twentieth century.

James Cameron's film is not perfect. It has some flaws, but I hate the way film critics employ that word "flaw," as if they are jewelers with loupes screwed into their eye sockets, performing a valuation. We can say there are elements that could have been handled differently. We can begin with some elements that are superb just as they stand.

To begin with, Cameron avoids the pitfalls of telling a story about which *everybody knows the ending*. Yes, the *Titanic* strikes an iceberg and sinks. That isn't the story he tells. He uses that as a backdrop for stories about hubris, greed, class conflict, romance, and a misplaced faith in technology. The *Titanic* was doomed the moment it was described as "unsinkable." There is a chilling conversation on the bridge between Bruce Ismay, the ship's owner, and Thomas Andrews, its architect.

Ismay: "But this ship can't sink!"

Andrews: "She's made of iron, sir. I assure you, she can. And she will. It is a mathematical certainty."

Its unsinkability perhaps explains why Captain Edward John Smith (Bernard Hill), despite being warned of icebergs, cranked the ship up to its top velocity and left it speeding blindly through the night. Would the captain of any other vessel have felt confident in doing that? In another sense, many of those on board thought of themselves as unsinkable, including the millionaires Benjamin Guggenheim (Michael Ensign) and the fictional villain Caledon Hockley (Billy Zane). Guggenheim called for a brandy and went down with the ship. Hockley would have thrown women and children overboard to preserve himself. Also on board was the Denver millionaire Molly Brown (Kathy Bates), who survived and is known to history as the Unsinkable Molly Brown. She's shown as one of the few arguing that her lifeboat turn back to rescue passengers freezing to death in the icy water.

Here already I have fallen prey to Cameron's storytelling and have become distracted from the ship's fate by the fates of those on board. Of greatest interest to us are Rose DeWitt Bukater (Kate Winslet), who is engaged to the snaky Caledon Hockley, and Jack Dawson (Leonardo DiCaprio), a steerage passenger who falls in love with her onboard and saves her life. She is the same Rose, known now as "Rose Dawson," who is the old lady, the sole living survivor, brought on board a salvage vessel near the beginning of the film (she's played by Gloria Stuart, who was eighty-six when the film was made, and topped one hundred before she died in 2010). This old woman, with such spirit and old, wise eyes, provides *Titanic* with what seems impossible: a happy ending. It is happy for her, at least, because she finds closure with the recovery of a drawing made by Jack and a final scene involving a famous diamond.

The Roses, young and old, provide a through line from the day the ship set sail until the present day. She creates the psychological illusion that she's the heroine throughout, rescuing the film from a chronological timeline and providing an eyewitness for the crew on the salvage and exploration vessel.

Cameron uses her as his excuse for an invaluable narrative device. He has the underwater explorers show her a little animated film that will "explain" to her how the ship sank, but actually explains it to us. This device is used all the time as a chalk talk or imaginary sequence in which the mastermind of a bank heist or prison escape explains the plan to those who will use it; he's really explaining it to us, so we'll understand it when we see it. As if there's not suspense enough when the ship is sinking, we're all the time wondering when it will break in half. Cameron is also not slow to bring the architect Andrews up to the bridge, so he can unroll his blueprints and explain to Captain Smith (and us) how the rushing flood waters will flow over one bulwark after the next.

The class differences onboard become a matter of life and death. The lifeboats are reserved for first-class passengers, and those in steerage are locked below behind sliding gates. Crew members enforce these distinctions, sometimes at gunpoint; so loyal are they to their employers that, even though they're going to die, they feel no sympathy for their lower-class comrades. In an early scene, it is by sneaking up to the first-class deck that Jack saves Rose from jumping off the ship. She has decided she prefers death to a life among affluent snobs like her fiancé; this shows she has more principle than imagination. Jack becomes the hero only because he flaunts all class distinctions, a decision that has its roots deep in nineteenth-century melodrama.

All of these matters take place in a ship created by art design, set construction, modeling, animation, and miniatures that are state of the art. James Cameron's films have always been distinguished by groundbreaking technical excellence.

Now to those *flaws.* Both of them involve the behavior of characters. There are several scenes involving Jack trying to help Rose escape the sinking ship, and then Rose helping free Jack after he's handcuffed to a pipe in a cabin, and then Jack again helping them to escape. Consider Rose. Of her own volition, she leaves the safety of a lifeboat and dashes back into the bowels of the ship to find Jack. She wades through water up to her waist, slugs an unhelpful crew member on the jaw, finds Jack, and then finds a fire ax to break the chain of his handcuffs.

Plucky, yes? But in all their other escape scenes, Jack pulls her behind him while desperately shouting, "Rose! Up here! Rose! Down there! Rose! Follow me!" et cetera. This grows monotonous and tiresome. It reminds me of one of the early definitions in Ebert's Little Movie Glossary, the Me Push-Pull You. That's an adaptation of a friend of Doctor Dolittle's, the Pushmi-pullyu. I define it as a male who treats a woman as a wee helpless creature who cannot save herself but must be pushed and pulled. Given Rose's behavior in finding her way through the flooding ship while saving Jack, she seems capable enough to be allowed the occasional "Jack! Up here!" (There is also the inconvenience that Rose and anyone else wading through the ice-cold water should quickly be dead of hypothermia.)

Another character I have questions about is Spicer Lovejoy, Caledon Hockley's pistol-packing bodyguard and dirty tricks man. Played by the superb actor David Warner, Lovejoy is a poker-faced tough guy entirely at the disposal of his boss. In the ship's desperate final moments, he is always at Hockley's side with helpful information, such as that a lifeboat on the other side of the ship is allowing men on board. Lovejoy is invaluable to the screenplay because he gives Hockley someone to speak and plot with. Otherwise the dastard would be reduced to dashing about madly on his own. Nevertheless, whatever Spicer is being paid is not enough.

Now for the final flaw. It is, of course, the 3-D process. Cameron has justly been praised for being one of the few directors to use 3-D usefully, in *Avatar.* But *Titanic* was not shot for 3-D, and just as you cannot gild a pig, you cannot make 2-D into 3-D. What you can do, and he tries to do it well, is find certain scenes that you can present as having planes of focus in foreground, middle and distance. So what? Did you miss any dimensions the first time you saw *Titanic*? No matter how long Cameron took to do it, no matter how much he spent, this is retrofitted 2-D. Case closed.

But not quite. There's more to it than that. 3-D causes a noticeable loss in the brightness coming from the screen. Some say as much as 20 percent. If you saw an ordinary film dimmed that much, you might complain to the management. Here you're supposed to be grateful you had the opportunity to pay a surcharge for this defacement. If you're alert to it, you'll notice that many shots and sequences in this version are not in 3-D at all, but remain in 2-D. If you take off your glasses, they'll pop off the screen with dramatically improved brightness. I know why the film is in 3-D. It's to justify the extra charge. That's a shabby way to treat a masterpiece.

## Today's Special ★ ★ ★

NO MPAA RATING, 99 m., 2010

Aasif Mandvi (Samir), Jess Weixler (Carrie), Madhur Jaffrey (Farrida), Harish Patel (Hakim), Naseeruddin Shah (Akbar). Directed by David Kaplan and produced by Lillian LaSalle and Nimitt Mankad. Screenplay by Aasif Mandvi and Jonathan Bines.

I love cooking and I love Indian food, and so I had a good time during *Today's Special.* That doesn't make it a great movie, but it made it a perfectly enjoyable entertainment for me. Sometimes when you feel strongly enough about certain elements in a movie, they redeem the rest. Nothing wrong with that.

Let's begin with this: India has produced one of the world's great cuisines. You may never have tasted it. Oh, you may have gone to a restaurant like the Tandoori Palace in *Today's Special*, which is a greasy spoon in Queens. The fact is, you may have enjoyed yourself there. I have been to many all-you-can-eat Indian buffets in Chicago, London, and elsewhere, and I knew I wasn't eating great cuisine, but I also knew I was enjoying myself and the price was right.

The movie stars Aasif Mandvi as Samir, a gifted sous chef in a high-falutin' Manhattan French restaurant. He doesn't get the promotion he's counting on, resigns on the spot, and claims he has a job offer in Paris. He never gets there, alas, because his father (Harish Patel) has a heart attack. It's up to Samir to run the Palace on an emergency basis, and he's so incompetent at Indian cooking that he orders out meals from another Indian restaurant.

Enter the enigmatic taxi driver Akbar (Naseeruddin Shah), whom he meets by accident. Akbar gives him an embossed card with only his name on it, nothing else. He claims to have been a great chef back in India. In desperation to find him again, Samir enlists three old-timers who play cards in the restaurant to phone their Indian friends. After a montage of one friend calling another, Akbar is tracked down and appears at the door. I believe this is possible.

Now the film moves into its Mr. Miyagi phase, with Akbar patiently teaching Samir the meaning of cooking and of life. Samir has lost his roots, and must reconnect his cooking with his heart, mind, and stomach. This particularly involves making his own garam masala. Now I'm on the edge of my seat, attentive. Do not make the mistake of so many Westerners in assuming that garam masala is some weird name for some esoteric component of exotic cuisine. No, it is the heart of south Asian cooking. Do not confuse it with "curry."

There is no mystery. It is a yellow spice mixture of various combinations of peppercorns, cloves, malabar leaves, long pepper, black cumin, cumin seeds, cinnamon, cardamom, nutmeg, star anise, and coriander seeds. Every region and every chef has a different recipe. That need not overly concern you. Go to the spice rack, buy a jar labeled "garam masala," and Bob's your uncle. It adds interest to just about everything this side of a wedding cake.

We learn that Samir, whose parents were born in India, who considers himself a great chef, has never mixed garam masala. This is like growing up in New Orleans and having to ask what a bean is. As his father recovers and Akbar teaches him about cooking and life, Samir also begins to fall in love with Carrie (Jess Weixler), a woman he met in the French restaurant's kitchen. Akbar's recipes transform the Tandoori Palace's cuisine, and crowds begin to form. And after an obligatory setback or two, there is a happy ending.

The movie's in-joke is that Samir's mother is played by Madhur Jaffrey. She is not only a considerable actress but a world-famous chef, whose cookbook taught me to seal a pot with flour paste to allow chicken and butter to bake in a sea of spices. Yum. Here she plays a typical Indian mother, despairing of her Westernized son and her impossible husband. It's like having Julia Child play the chef's mother-in-law.

So now you understand why I enjoyed the film. I know it is flawed. I know the story arc is as old as the hills. The romance is cut and dried. Akbar is well acted, but he is a story device. Aasif Mandvi is fun (he plays one of Jon Stewart's senior correspondents on *The Daily Show*). But as a movie, *Today's Special* is only just OK. What saves it, as it saves so very many things, is the garam masala.

## Tomboy ★ ★ ★ ½

NO MPAA RATING, 82 m., 2012

Zoe Heran (Laure/Mikael), Malonn Levana (Jeanne), Jeanne Disson (Lisa), Sophie Cattani (Laure's Mother), Mathieu Demy (Laure's Father). Directed by Celine Sciamma and produced by Benedicte Couvreur. Screenplay by Sciamma.

The first shot is disconcerting. The camera is close to a wind-swept head and shoulders floating through space and backdropped by sky, clouds, and trees. We're eventually shown that this is a child, standing up through a car's open sunroof. Because the title *Tomboy* gives it away, we know this person with the close-cropped hair is a girl. Otherwise there's no telling; she's ten, that preadolescent age when many children seem suspended between genders.

She has moved with her father, her little sister, and her pregnant mother into a new neighborhood where they know nobody. Not shy but certainly reticent, she hangs on the edge of a small group of kids about her age. A friendly girl named Lisa (Jeanne Disson) asks for her name—using the French pronoun suggesting she expects to hear a male name. "Mikael," says the newcomer. In a second she has become a boy, and will be one all summer.

Celine Sciamma's *Tomboy* would have been impossible without the casting of Zoe Heran in the title role. She isn't a masculine-looking girl or a feminine-looking boy. She is fresh, attractive, open-faced. If you think you're looking at a boy, you see one. If a girl, then that's what you see. The movie doesn't have a trace of gimmick to it; it's perfectly straightforward.

The heroine's real name is Laure. There is so much love and happiness in her home you can hardly believe it. She isn't a tortured or mistreated child; she and her little sister, Jeanne (Malonn Levana), adore each other. Her parents (Sophie Cattani and Mathieu Demy) are playfully in love, the unborn child is already a member of the family, and Laure whispers "secrets" to her. In this safe garden suburb, she spends her days outdoors, on playgrounds or in the woods or at a pond, hanging out with the others, who accept her. These aren't the mean and sadistic little creatures we sometimes find in the movies, but nice, cheerful kids. They like her. Him, I mean.

Much of this delicate movie involves our observation of Mikael in formation. She watches a soccer game, then joins it the next day, and only we would notice how she sometimes barely brushes her breasts to reassure herself they don't call attention through her T-shirt (they don't). When some boys walk to the edge of the woods to pee, she walks in a little farther. When they go swimming, she provides for a little bulge where one should be.

Does Lisa suspect? Yes and no. She is as observant as the movie is. What should we make of a scene where Mikael sits on Lisa's bed and she brings over cosmetics and announces she's going to apply makeup? And she does, tastefully: a hint of mascara, a touch of blush, a little lipstick. "You look good as a girl," Lisa tells Laure. "Mikael" leaves the makeup on when she goes home and her mother tells her the same thing.

The summer must end, and the deception must end as well. How this happens is not overly dramatic, and there is no tragedy. The world of these children is balanced at an age when identities are in constant formation. We're not dealing with *Boys Don't Cry* here.

*Tomboy* is tender and affectionate. It shows us Laure/Mikael in an adventure that may be forgotten in adulthood, or may form her adulthood. There is no conscious agenda in view. There is just a tomboy. Not everyone needs to be slammed into a category and locked there.

## Tooth Fairy ★ ★

PG, 101 m., 2010

Dwayne Johnson (Derek Thompson), Ashley Judd (Carly), Stephen Merchant (Tracy), Julie Andrews (Lily), Billy Crystal (Jerry), Destiny Whitlock (Tess), Chase Ellison (Randy). Directed by Michael Lemback and produced by Jason Blum, Mark Ciard, and Gordon Gray. Screenplay by Lowell Ganz, Babaloo Mandel, Joshua Sternin, Jeffrey Ventimilia, and Randi Mayem Singer.

In the pantheon of such legends as Santa Claus and the Bogeyman, the Tooth Fairy ranks down in the minor leagues, I'd say, with Jack Frost and the Easter Bunny. There is a scene in *Tooth Fairy* when the hero is screamed at by his girlfriend for even *beginning* to suggest to her six-year-old that there isn't a Tooth Fairy, but surely this is a trauma a child can survive. Don't kids simply humor their parents to get the dollar?

The film reveals that there's not one Tooth Fairy anyway, but a whole workforce, tightly scheduled and supervised by the strict head fairy (Julie Andrews). This comes as rather an astonishment to a rugged hockey player named Derek, played by Dwayne (The Rock) Johnson, who is sentenced to a term in Fairy Land for almost spoiling the young girl's faith. It happens so abruptly that he finds himself wearing a pink tutu. Oddly, a still photo of this sight is not included in the movie's press materials.

Derek's nickname in pro hockey is "The Tooth Fairy" because he is a specialist in body-slamming opponents so hard that you can fill in the rest. He hasn't scored a goal in ages. The coach puts him in just so he can take someone out. He spends so much time in the penalty box he has his own recliner installed.

The Rock plays this role straight, which is basically the way he plays every role. He's a pleasant, relaxed screen presence, but a Method Actor he's not. His idea of a tone for the Tooth Fairy is sincerity.

The movie's best scenes involve Fairy Land, where a brisk but very tall fairy social worker named Tracy (Stephen Merchant) adds some quirkiness. Merchant is a six-foot-seven British comedian, inheritor of the possibly genetic trait that populated Monty Python. His great regret in life is that he was never issued wings. Also in Fairy Land is Jerry (Billy Crystal), in charge of magic weapons, who issues Derek visibility sprays and suchlike.

Look, I hate to say this, but Billy Crystal has put on a few pounds. I say it not as a criticism but as an observation. Good for him. He seems more avuncular now, more confiding. Maybe he could start looking for dramatic roles as your favorite wise-guy uncle. Anyway, I've noticed in a lot of movies lately that the stars I've grown old with have, good lord, also grown old with me. There's a kind of fascination in how film so accurately records the passage of time. Julie Andrews, by still looking like Julie Andrews, seems to be swimming upstream.

Derek's girlfriend, mentioned above, is played by the divine Ashley Judd, thanklessly. I guess as an actor you know that in a movie named *Tooth Fairy* you're going to have a lot of scenes where you're tucking someone in. Fair enough, but where can you go with them dramatically?

The film is rated PG. I wondered why it didn't make Derek a husband instead of a boyfriend, but parents can relax: He seems to sleep on the couch. Uh, huh. The chemistry between the two suggests that they're together primarily because they work so well together at tucking time.

There's no way I can recommend this movie to anyone much beyond the Tooth Fairy Believement Age, but I must testify it's pleasant and inoffensive, although the violence in the hockey games seems out of place. It must be said in closing that given his nickname and reputation, it's a miracle the Tooth Fairy has been allowed to survive with such a dazzling row of pearlies.

## To Rome with Love ★ ★ ★

R, 111 m., 2012

Woody Allen (Jerry), Alec Baldwin (John), Roberto Benigni (Leopoldo), Penelope Cruz (Anna), Judy Davis (Phyllis), Jesse Eisenberg (Jack), Greta Gerwig (Sally), Ellen Page (Monica), Flavio Parenti (Michelangelo), Fabio Armiliato (Giancarlo), Alessandra Mastronardi (Milly), Alessandro Tiberi (Antonio), Antonio Albanese (Luca Salta). Directed by Woody Allen and produced by Letty Aronson and Stephen Tenenbaum. Screenplay by Allen.

Woody Allen's new film *To Rome with Love* generates no particular excitement or surprise, but it provides the sort of pleasure he seems able to generate almost on demand. The New Yorker who claims to be uneasy after a night away from home, here sets his fourth recent film in a European capital, treating Rome like a besotted tourist. He tells four stories that are intercut but not interlocking, and three of them are funny and charming.

Much of their appeal comes from the casting, made possible by Allen's apparent ability to persuade any actor to come and work with him for a week or two. Using a star saves a director from writing ten pages of screenplay, I've heard, because we think we already know a lot about the character. That helps in the way Allen skips lightly among his stories, which have the depth of sitcoms.

The best of the stories in *To Rome with Love* involves Allen himself, as Jerry, a self-doubting opera director visiting Rome with his wife (Judy Davis, in her fifth film with Woody). They're in Rome to meet the fiancé their daughter (Alison Pill) plans to marry. He is not particularly pleased with Michelangelo (Flavio Parenti), and seems to make a point of mispronouncing his name. But when he overhears the young man's father (Fabio Armiliato) singing in the shower, he knows a great tenor voice when he hears one.

His future in-law is an undertaker. Jerry begs to be allowed to record him on a demo tape. It doesn't work. The man can seem to sing only in the shower. This is the sort of zany shuffle that sidesteps the conventional setup.

In another story, Jesse Eisenberg plays Jack, a would-be architect based in Rome with his girlfriend, Sally (Greta Gerwig). When her friend Monica (Ellen Page) comes to Rome on a visit, Sally unwisely asks her to move in, since Jack would never have eyes for another woman. Untrue, since Monica, who seems drab on first sight, uncoils into a seductress.

Alec Baldwin costars in this segment in a rather ambivalent way. Able to materialize at will, he urgently warns Jack against Monica, and tries to head off a young man's romantic carelessness. This character requires the sort of magic realism that Allen is quite willing to allow himself.

Another episode: Antonio and Milly (Alessandro Tiberi and Alessandra Mastronardi) are newlyweds visiting Rome so his family can meet her. But they become separated one day, she has an encounter with her favorite movie star (Antonio Albanese), and he becomes the innocent recipient of a hooker (Penelope Cruz) sent as a gift to someone else. His relatives find them in a compromising situation, and he desperately tries to pass her off as his wife.

The fourth story begins with the notion that some people are famous for being famous. Roberto Benigni plays a guy who becomes the victim of overnight fame, is followed everywhere by paparazzi, can find no escape or peace, and then as suddenly becomes obscure again. As a premise this is past its shelf date, Allen never finds a way to pay it off, and Benigni quickly grows tiresome.

*To Rome with Love* isn't great Woody Allen, then. Here is a man who has made a feature every year since 1969, give or take a few, and if they cannot all be great Woody, it's churlish to complain if they're only good Woody. His previous film, *Midnight in Paris*, was magical. A few critics have said unkind things about his age, which strikes me as bad manners. So he's seventy-six. Good for him. Is his timing still good? Is he still funny? Aren't we happy to have another picture?

## The Tourist ★ ★

PG-13, 104 m., 2010

Angelina Jolie (Elise Clifton-Ward), Johnny Depp (Frank Tupelo), Paul Bettany (Acheson), Timothy Dalton (Jones), Steven Berkoff (Reginald Shaw), Rufus Sewell (The Englishman), Bruno Wolkowitch (French Sergeant). Directed by Florian Henckel von Donnersmarck and produced by Gary Barber, Roger Birnbaum, Jonathan Glickman, Tim Headington, and Graham King. Screenplay by Henckel von Donnersmarck, Christopher McQuarrie, and Julian Fellowes.

There's a way to make a movie like *The Tourist*, but Florian Henckel von Donnersmarck doesn't find that way. Here is a romantic comedy crossed with a crime thriller, shot in Paris and Venice, involving a glamorous mystery woman and a math teacher from Wisconsin. The plot is preposterous. So what you need is a movie that floats with bemusement above the cockamamie, and actors who tease one another.

Angelina Jolie does her darnedest. She gets the joke. Here is a movie in which she begins in a Paris cafe, eludes cops by dashing into the Metro, takes an overnight train to Venice, picks up a strange man (Johnny Depp), and checks them both into the Royal Danieli without one wrinkle on her dress or one hair out of place. And is sexy as hell. This is the Audrey Hepburn or Grace Kelly role, and she knows it.

Depp is in the Cary Grant role, of the obliging, love-struck straight man who falls in love and finds himself neck deep in somebody else's troubles. In theory these two should engage in witty flirtation and droll understatement. In practice, no one seems to have alerted Depp that the movie is a farce. I refer to "farce" in the dictionary sense, of course: *A comic dramatic work using buffoonery and horseplay and typically including crude characterization and ludicrously improbable situations.* Depp plays his math teacher seriously and with a touch of the morose.

The plot involves—oh, hell, you know, the usual mystery man who has stolen millions from a gangster and gone into hiding while meanwhile smuggling instructions to Jolie, his lover, instructing her to take the train to Venice, etc. And the cops from Scotland Yard who are tailing her in hopes of nailing the guy. And the gangster and his hit men who are also on the thief's trail. And chases over the rooftops of Venice, and dinner on a train, and a scene in a casino, and designer gowns, and a chase through the canals with Jolie at the controls of a motor taxi, and . . .

Well, there was really only one cliché left, and I was grateful when it arrived. You know how a man in a high place will look down and see a canvas awning that might break his fall, and he jumps into it? Yep. And it's shielding a fruit cart at the open-air market and he lands on the oranges and runs off leaving the cart owner shaking his fist. This is a rare example of the Vertical Fruit Cart Scene, in which the cart is struck not from the side but from the top.

The supporting roles are filled by excellent actors, and it's a sign of the movie's haplessness that none of them make a mark. You have Paul Bettany and Timothy Dalton as cops, Steven Berkoff as the gangster and Rufus Sewell as "The Englishman," who must be important because he hangs around without any apparent purpose. Once in London I saw Steven Berkoff play a cockroach in his adaptation of Kafka's *Metamorphosis.* It might have helped this role if he'd tried the cockroach again.

A depressing element is how much talent *The Tourist* has behind the camera. Florian Henckel von Donnersmarck, the director, made *The Lives of Others,* winner of the Oscar for best foreign film in 2007. The screenplay is by Henckel von Donnersmarck, Christopher McQuarrie (an Oscar for *The Usual Suspects*), and Julian Fellowes (an Oscar for *Gosford Park*). It's based on a French film written by Jerome Salle, which was nominated for a Cesar. All three winners seem to have used their awards as doorstops.

It doesn't matter that the plot is absurd. That goes with the territory. But if it's not going to be nonstop idiotic action, then the acting and dialog need a little style and grace and kidding around. Jolie plays her femme fatale with flat-out, drop-dead sexuality. Depp plays his Wisconsin math teacher as a man waiting for the school bell to ring so he can go bowling. The other actors are concealed in the shadows of their archetypes. Cary Grant would have known how to treat a lady.

## Tower Heist ★ ★ ½

PG-13, 104 m., 2011

Ben Stiller (Josh Kovacs), Eddie Murphy (Slide), Casey Affleck (Charlie Gibbs), Alan Alda (Arthur Shaw), Matthew Broderick (Mr. Fitzhugh), Stephen McKinley Henderson (Lester), Judd Hirsch (Mr. Simon), Tea Leoni (Special Agent Claire Denham), Michael Peña (Enrique Dev'Reaux), Gabourey Sidibe (Odessa). Directed by Brett Ratner and produced by Brian Grazer and Eddie Murphy. Screenplay by Ted Griffin and Jeff Nathanson.

If it had provided me with nothing else, *Tower Heist* would have afforded me the sight of a solid gold automobile being lowered from the penthouse of the Trump Tower with Matthew Broderick dangling from it. Sometimes you appreciate such simple human spectacles. To be sure, Trump Tower has been renamed "The Tower," and the man dangling from the car isn't the Donald, but this is an imperfect world.

This isn't a great heist movie for a lot of reasons, beginning with the stupidity of its heist plan and the impossibility of these characters ever being successful at anything more complex than standing in line. There is also the problem with Ben Stiller being cast as the hero: He was born to play the victim of heists, not the gang leader. You go against type. The victim here is played by Alan Alda, who is so loathsome he'd make a dartboard for Occupy Wall Street parties.

Quibble, quibble. The movie is broad and clumsy and the dialogue cannot be described as witty, but a kind of grandeur creeps into the screenplay by Ted Griffin and Jeff Nathanson. It's the kind of story where the executives at a pitch meeting feel they're being bludgeoned over the head with box office dollars. There is also the novelty that here is a comedy that doesn't go heavy on the excremental, the masturbatory, and symphonies of four-letter words. It's funny in an innocent, screwball kind of way.

The story: Josh Kovacs (Stiller) is the perfectionist building manager at the most luxurious condo skyscraper in New York, which providentially is located on Columbus Circle in the exact footprint of Trump Tower. His team works flawlessly, beginning with the beloved doorman Lester (Stephen Henderson). The penthouse is owned by Arthur Shaw (Alda), a financial wheeler-dealer, whose walls display priceless modern art. His most prized possession is a bright red 1953 Ferrari, once owned by Steve McQueen. It was taken apart piece by piece, he explains to FBI agent Claire Denham (Tea Leoni), and assembled there.

The FBI is on the job because Shaw has been running a Ponzi scheme, and among his loot are the pension plan and investments of the Tower's employees. So dear old Lester and all the others are penniless. Enraged, Kovacs recruits a team to break into the penthouse. They're looking for a wall safe, but then discover Shaw's Ferrari is solid gold—$65 million is hidden in plain sight. Obviously, this requires stealing the car from the penthouse, where no door or elevator can handle it.

The team: Lester, of course; Mr. Fitzhugh (Broderick), who is jobless, broke, has lost his family, and is being evicted from the building; and characters played by Casey Affleck, Michael Peña, Gabourey Sidibe (her second film since her Oscar) as a Jamaican whose father could crack safes, and—well, Kovacs decides they need someone more familiar with crime, and enlists Slide (Eddie Murphy), a loud-talking dude from the street in his neighborhood. Murphy, in his first role since 2009, is in full Eddie Murphy mode, with comic riffs and astonished double takes.

I won't describe how they plan to get the car out of the building, especially as the Macy's Thanksgiving Day Parade is passing directly below. But let me share with you that I suffer from a fear of heights, and the last thing you could get me to do is stand next to an open window on an upper floor of a high-rise and try to reach out and grab a Ferrari. The notion that no one would notice a bright red car being lowered from the Tower is preposterous, but realism is not the point. This movie would fall to pieces if it didn't hurtle headlong through its absurdist plot without ever pausing for explanations.

## The Town ★ ★ ★

R, 124 m., 2010

Ben Affleck (Doug MacRay), Rebecca Hall (Claire Keesey), Jon Hamm (Special Agent Adam Frawley), Jeremy Renner (Jem Coughlin), Blake Lively (Krista Coughlin), Titus Welliver (Dino Ciampa), Pete Postlethwaite (Fergie Colm), Chris Cooper (Stephen MacRay). Directed by Ben Affleck and produced by Basil Iwanyk and Graham King. Screenplay by Affleck, Peter Craig, and Aaron Stockard, based on the novel *Prince of Thieves* by Chuck Hogan.

There's a scene in Ben Affleck's *The Town* that expertly exploits the conversations we have with movie characters. In critical moments we urgently send mental instructions to the screen. Let me set up such a moment here. Doug cares for Claire. There's something she mustn't know about him. If she should see the tattoo on the back of Jem's neck, she would know everything. Jem unexpectedly joins Doug and Claire at a table. With hard looks and his whole manner, Doug signals him to get the hell away from the table. So do we. Jem is a dangerous goofball, and sadistically lingers. He doesn't know the tattoo is a giveaway.

If a film can bring us to this point and make us feel anxiety, it has done something right. *The Town*, Affleck's second film as a director, wants to do something more, to make a biographical and even philosophical statement about the culture of crime, but it doesn't do that as successfully. Here is a well-made crime procedural, and audiences are likely to enjoy it at that level, but perhaps the mechanics of movie crime got in the way of Affleck's higher ambitions.

There are two fairly extended scenes in the film, for example, during which bank robbers with machine guns exchange fire with a large number of cops. My opinion is that when automatic weapons are used by experienced shooters at less than a block's distance, a lot of people are going to get killed or wounded. It becomes clear in *The Town* that nobody will get shot until and/or unless the screenplay requires it, and that causes an audience letdown. We feel the story is no longer really happening, and we're being asked to settle yet once again for a standard chase-and-gunfight climax.

I believe Affleck, his writers, and their source (the novel *Prince of Thieves* by Chuck Hogan) know better, and their characters deserve better. But above a certain budget level, Hollywood films rarely allow complete follow-through for their characters. Consider the widespread public dislike for the year's best crime film, George Clooney's *The American*. People didn't want a look into the soul of an existential criminal. They wanted a formula to explain everything.

In *The Town*, Ben Affleck plays Doug MacRay, the next generation of a bank-robbing family in the Charlestown area of Boston. This square mile, we're told, contains more thieves and bank robbers than anyplace else in the country. It's a family trade, like cobbling or the law. Affleck heads a four-man crew most notably including Jem (a pudgy, loopy Jeremy Renner, miles different than in *The Hurt Locker*). They plan their jobs meticulously, going to lengths to eradicate DNA traces and confiscate security tapes. But Jem has a wild streak. He injures civilians when it's not necessary, and during one job does what is forbidden: He takes a hostage, Claire (Rebecca Hall). Kidnapping is a heavy-duty crime.

They release Claire unharmed. Turns out she lives in Charlestown. Jem gets paranoid. Doug trails her to a Laundromat, meets her by "accident," gets to know and quite unexpectedly gets to like her. This is what *The Town* is really about—how getting to know Claire opens Doug's mind to the fullness of a life his heritage has denied him. The film could have continued to grow in that direction, but instead pulls back and focuses on more crime. We meet Doug's hard-boiled father (Chris Cooper) in prison, and a local crime lord (Pete Postlethwaite, unrelenting). And we follow an FBI team led by Jon Hamm. They have a good idea whom they're looking for; you don't make a career out of bank robbery in Charlestown without the word getting around. But they lack evidence they can take to a jury.

The most intriguing character is Jem. As played by Renner, he's a twisted confusion of behavior, a loose cannon on a team that requires discipline. He's furious when he finds Doug friendly with the woman who could finger them, and the jumpy way he plays friendly is chilling. There's something interesting going on here: Doug is the central character and all interest should move to him, but at about the halfway point it becomes clear that his character has been deprived of impulse and committed to an acceptable ending. Jem, however, remains capable of anything. If you've seen a lot of Jeremy Renner before, you may need to look twice to recognize him; it's like the hero of *The Hurt Locker* moved to Boston and started on a diet of beer, brats, and fries.

*The Town* shows, as his first film *Gone Baby Gone* (2007) did, that Affleck has the stuff of a real director. Everything is here. It's an effective thriller, he works closely with the actors, he has a feel for pacing. Yet I persist in finding chases and gun battles curiously boring. I realize the characters have stopped making the decisions and the stunt and effects artists have taken over.

## A Town Called Panic ★ ★ ★ ½

NO MPAA RATING, 75 m., 2010

With the voices of: Stephane Aubier (Cowboy), Bruce Ellison (Indian), Vincent Patar (Horse), Jeanne Balibar (Madame Longray), Frederic Jannin (Policeman), Benoit Poelvoorde (Farmer). Directed by Stephane Aubier and Vincent Patar and produced by Philippe Kauffmann and Vincent Tavier. Screenplay by Aubier and Patar.

You know how kids play with little plastic action figures that balance their feet on their own little platforms? And how they're not on the same scale? And how kids move them around while doing their voices and making up adventures for them? And how literally anything is likely to happen in those adventures? Then you have a notion of the goofy charm generated by this new animated comedy from Belgium.

*A Town Called Panic* is well named because it takes place in a town where panic is a daily emotion. Here, in a house on a hill much larger inside than out, live the friendly roommates Cowboy, Indian, and Horse. Their neighbor is Farmer. Law is enforced by Policeman.

It is Horse's birthday, and Cowboy and Indian decide his gift must be a brick barbecue.

They go online to order fifty bricks, but order fifty million through a computer error, which causes no end of problems, especially when Cowboy and Indian stack them on top of the house, hoping to conceal their foolishness from Horse. I should explain that Horse seems to be the responsible adult.

Everybody talks like little kids. Indian and Horse are on the same scale, about twice as tall as Cowboy, although nobody notices this. They get around fine on their little platforms, even climbing stairs. Horse, who has four legs and can balance without a platform, takes Farmer's kids to Madame Longray's music lessons and falls in love with Madame, who is also a horse and plays the piano with her hooves, pretty well.

The most frequent line of dialogue in this enchanting world is *Oh, no!* One strange thing happens after another. You wouldn't believe me if I told you how Horse, Indian, and Cowboy all end up perched precariously on a rock slab above a volcano at the center of the earth, or how they get from there to the middle of an ocean and the North Pole, or how they happen upon a mad scientist and his robot, named Penguin, or the excuses Horse uses on his cell phone to explain to Madame Longray why he hasn't turned up for his piano lessons. Or why it rains cows.

*A Town Called Panic* is the work of Stephane Aubier and Vincent Patar, a Belgian team that first created this world in a group of short films that became enormously popular in 2003 on European television. I've never seen anything like this style. It's stop-action, but *really* stop-action, you understand, because that's the nature of plastic action figures. Cowboy and Indian can move their arms when they need to, but their platforms keep them upright.

I enjoyed this film so much I'm sorry to report it was finally too much of a muchness. You can only eat so much cake. But I don't think that's a problem. Like all animated family films, this one will find a long life and its greatest popularity on video. And because the plot is just one doggone thing after another without the slightest logic, there's no need to watch it all the way through at one sitting. If you watch it a chapter or two at a time, it should hold up nicely.

Now don't get me wrong. I'm glad I saw it on the big screen. It has an innocent, hallucinatory charm. The friendship of the three pals is sweet. I liked Horse's bashfulness when he's smitten with Madame Longray. And his patience with Indian and Cowboy, who get them into one fine fix after another.

## Toy Story 3 ★ ★ ★

G, 102 m., 2010

With the voices of: Tom Hanks (Woody), Tim Allen (Buzz Lightyear), Joan Cusack (Jessie), Ned Beatty (Lotso), Don Rickles (Mr. Potato Head), Michael Keaton (Ken), Wallace Shawn (Rex), John Ratzenberger (Hamm), Estelle Harris (Mrs. Potato Head), John Morris (Andy), Jodi Benson (Barbie), Blake Clark (Slinky Dog). Directed by Lee Unkrich and produced by Darla K. Anderson. Screenplay by Unkrich, Michael Arndt, John Lasseter, and Andrew Stanton.

The first two *Toy Story* movies centered on the relationship between a boy and his toys. In Pixar's *Toy Story 3*, young Andy has grown to college age and the story leaves the toys pretty much on their own. In a third act where they find themselves fighting for life on a conveyor belt to a garbage incinerator, we fear it could be renamed *Toy Story Triage.*

The problems all begin with that most dreaded of commands, "Clean out your room!" No mother in history understands that a boy's room has all of his stuff *exactly where he needs it,* even if he dumped it there ten years earlier. Andy's mom gives him three choices: (1) attic; (2) donation to a day care center; (3) trash. Examining his old toys, his gaze lingers fondly on Woody (voice by Tom Hanks), and he decides to take him along to college.

What with one thing and another the other toys find themselves at the day care center, which they think they'll like because there will be plenty of kids to play with them all day long. There seems to be relatively little grieving about the loss of Andy's affections; he did, after all, sentence them to a toy box for years, and toys by nature are self-centered and want to be played with.

Day care seems like a happy choice, until a dark underside of its toy society emerges in the person of an ominously hug-prone bear (Ned Beatty). They pick up, however, some additions to their little band, including Barbie and Ken dolls with extensive wardrobes. If you ask me, Barbie (Jodi Benson) is anorexic, and Ken (Michael Keaton) is gay, but nobody in the movie knows this, so I'm just sayin'.

Buzz Lightyear (Tim Allen) is back, still in hapless hero mode, but after a reboot he starts speaking Spanish and that leads to some funny stuff. I also enjoyed the dilemma of Mrs. Potato Head (Estelle Harris), whose missing eye continues to see independently of her head. This raises intriguing physiological questions, such as, if Mr. Potato Head lost an ear, would it continue to hear, or if he lost a mouth, would it continue to eat without a body? These are not academic questions; at one point, Mister becomes an uncooked taco shell. Mr. and Mrs. Potato Head must be old hands at such dilemmas, since children spend most of their time attaching their body parts in the wrong way, like malpracticing little Dr. Frankensteins.

Man, the toys have a dangerous time of it after they eventually find themselves at a garbage collection center. You have no idea what garbage has to go through before becoming landfill, and even an Indiana Jones toy would have trouble surviving the rotating blades. There is a happy ending, of course, but I suspect these toys may be traumatized for eternity.

This is a jolly, slapstick comedy, lacking the almost eerie humanity that infused the earlier *Toy Story* sagas, and happier with action and jokes than with characters and emotions. But hey, what can you expect from a movie named *Toy Story 3*, especially with the humans mostly offstage? I expect its target audience will love it, and at the box office it may take right up where *How to Train Your Dragon* left off. Just don't get me started about the 3-D.

## Transformers: Dark of the Moon ★

PG-13, 154 m., 2011

Shia LaBeouf (Sam Witwicky), Markiss McFadden ("Baby Face"), Rosie Huntington-Whiteley (Carly), Kenneth Sheard (Marc L), Josh Duhamel (Lennox), John Turturro (Simmons), Tyrese Gibson (Epps), Patrick Dempsey (Dylan), Frances McDormand (Mearing), John Malkovich (Bruce Brazos), Kevin Dunn (Ron Witwicky), Julie White (Judy Witwicky), Alan Tudyk (Dutch), Ken Jeong (Jerry Wang), Glenn Morshower (General Morshower). Directed by Michael Bay and produced by Ian Bryce, Tom DeSanto, Lorenzo di Bonaventura, and Don Murphy. Screenplay by Ehren Kruger.

Michael Bay's *Transformers: Dark of the Moon* is a visually ugly film with an incoherent plot, wooden characters, and inane dialogue. It provided me with one of the more unpleasant experiences I've had at the movies.

The series exists to show gigantic and hideous robots hammering one another. So it does. The last hour involves a battle for the universe that for some reason is held at the corner of Michigan Avenue and Wacker Drive in Chicago. This battle is protracted mercilessly beyond all reason, at an ear-shattering sound level, with incomprehensible Autobots and Decepticons sliced up into spurts of action with no sense of the space they occupy.

There is more of a plot in this third *Transformers*. It is a plot that cannot be described in terms of structure, more in terms of duration. When it stops, it's over. We learn that mankind's first mission to the moon was intended to investigate an alien spacecraft that crashed on the dark side. This ship, "the Arc," carried the robots to this solar system from their own, so that the good bots could continue their struggle for "freedom" against the bad bots. It is a bad omen when Lincoln's statue on the National Mall is decapitated.

Humans get involved. These include Sam Witwicky (Shia LaBeouf), who earlier saved the world but now has a job in a mail room, and Carly (Rosie Huntington-Whiteley), who is his sexy girlfriend because the movie requires a sexy girlfriend. There are also such characters as Mearing (Frances McDormand), a government official; Bruce Brazos (John Malkovich), Sam's anal-retentive boss; Carly's former boyfriend Dylan (Patrick Dempsey), whose classic-car collection upstages every robot in the movie; the FBI manipulator Simmons (John Turturro); the peculiar Jerry Wang (Ken Jeong); and the expert warriors Lennox (Josh Duhamel) and Epps (Tyrese Gibson). If you pause to consider for a second, not one of these characters is actually required in the conflict, which is, after all, pretty much between the bots.

Oh, but the humans are needed for us. They are required because bots have no personalities and little intrinsic interest apart from the banging noises they make. They speak in dubbed English that sounds oddly separate from the other voices in the film. And they are so many times larger than the humans that I was reminded of the scale used in *The Incredible Shrinking Man.* We also need people because I, for one, will never care for Optimus Prime any more than for an engine block.

There is no style or wit in the dialogue, except when Malkovich adds his own spin. This is one of those annoying pictures where disembodied voices are heard during chaotic action: "Class dismissed!" "Decepticon punk!" "We've got a Mexican standoff here!" "What do you think you're doing?" "Return what belongs to me!"

Shia LaBeouf is scarcely heroic, and his girlfriend has no particular function except to be in constant peril and (in two hilarious shots) stare thoughtfully into space as if realizing something. The only considerable dramatic scene LaBeouf has is when his mother (Julie White) brings the manic plot to a standstill long enough to urge a self-help book upon her son.

I hesitate to mention another problem with the film because in all fairness it may not be Bay's fault. The framing looks wrong. When you look at enough movies, you develop a sixth sense for what feels correct within the frame. This film seemed too close to its compositions. There was a paucity of headroom, feet were nearly cut off, the sides seemed to squeeze. This wasn't dramatic, but I could feel it.

Of course, I could be mistaken. If I'm correct, here's what may have happened. In the multiplex theater originally set for the screening, it was explained, technicians spent three hours programming the 3-D projector—and then their programming didn't "take." The multiplex resourcefully moved the film to another screen already configured for 3-D. I suspect, however, that the aspect ratio in that room was not quite correct.

Nothing, however, would have repaired the film's lack of narrative coherence. I have a quaint notion that one of the purposes of editing is to make it clear why one shot follows another, or why several shots occur in the order that they do. *Transformers 3* has long stretches involving careless and illogical assemblies of inelegant shots. One special effect happens, and then another special effect happens, and we are expected to be grateful that we have seen two special effects.

*Note: Bay is said to have tried to improve the characteristic light level of 3-D. In my screening, it was as dim as usual.*

## The Tree of Life ★ ★ ★ ★

PG-13, 138 m., 2011

Brad Pitt (Mr. O'Brien), Sean Penn (Jack), Jessica Chastain (Mrs. O'Brien), Fiona Shaw (Grandmother), Hunter McCracken (Young Jack). Directed by Terrence Malick and produced by Dede Gardner, Sarah Green, Grant Hill, Brad Pitt, and William Pohlad. Screenplay by Malick.

Terrence Malick's *The Tree of Life* is a film of vast ambition and deep humility, attempting no less than to encompass all of existence and view it through the prism of a few infinitesimal lives. The only other film I've seen with this boldness of vision is Kubrick's *2001: A Space Odyssey*, and it lacked Malick's fierce evocation of human feeling. There were once several directors who yearned to make no less than a masterpiece, but now there are only a few. Malick has stayed true to that hope ever since his first feature in 1973.

I don't know when a film has connected more immediately with my own personal experience. In uncanny ways, the central events of *The Tree of Life* reflect a time and place I lived in, and the young boys in it are me. If I set out to make an autobiographical film, and if I had Malick's gift, it would look so much like this. His scenes portray a childhood in a small town in the American midlands, where life flows in and out through open windows. There is a father who maintains discipline and a mother who exudes forgiveness, and long summer days of play and idleness and urgent, unsaid questions about the meaning of things. The three boys of the O'Brien family are browned by the sun, scuffed by play, disturbed by glimpses of adult secrets, filled with a great urgency to grow up and discover who they are.

I wrote earlier about the many ways this film evoked my own memories of such a time and place. About wide lawns. About a small town that somehow, in memory, is always seen with a wide-angle lens. About houses that are never locked. About mothers looking out windows to check on you. About the summer heat and ennui of church services, and the unpredictable theater of the dinner table, and the troubling sounds of an argument between your parents, half-heard through an open window.

Watching the film, I remembered Ray Bradbury's memory of a boy waking up to the sound of a Green Machine outside his window—a hand-pushed lawnmower. Perhaps you grew up in a big city, with the doors locked and everything air-conditioned. It doesn't matter. Most of us, unless we are unlucky, have something of the same childhood, because we are protected by innocence and naïveté.

As I mentioned the O'Brien family, I realized one detail the film has precisely right: The parents are named Mr. O'Brien and Mrs. O'Brien. Yes. Because the parents of other kids were never thought of by their first names, and the first names of your own parents were words used only by others. Your parents were Mother and Father and they defined your reality, and you were open to their emotions, both calming and alarming. And young Jack O'Brien is growing, and someday will become Mr. O'Brien, but will never seem to himself as real as his father did.

Rarely does a film seem more obviously a collaboration of love between a director and his production designer, Jack Fisk. Fisk is about my age and was born and raised in downstate Illinois, and so, of course, knows that in the 1940s tall aluminum drinking glasses were used for lemonade and iced tea. He has all the other details right, too, but his design fits seamlessly into the lives of his characters. What's uncanny is that Malick creates the O'Brien parents and their three boys without an obvious plot: The movie captures the unplanned unfolding of summer days and the overheard words of people almost talking to themselves.

The film's portrait of everyday life, inspired by Malick's memories of his hometown of Waco, Texas, is bounded by two immensities, one of space and time and the other of spirituality. *The Tree of Life* has awe-inspiring visuals, suggesting the birth and expansion of the universe, the appearance of life on a microscopic level, and the evolution of species. This process leads to the present moment, and to all of us. We were created in the Big Bang and over untold millions of years molecules formed themselves into, well, you and me.

And what comes after? In whispered words near the beginning, "nature" and "grace" are heard. We have seen nature as it gives and takes away; one of the family's boys dies. We also see how it works with time, as Jack O'Brien (Hunter McCracken) grows into a middle-age man (Sean Penn). And what then? The film's coda provides a vision of an afterlife, a desolate landscape on which quiet people solemnly recognize and greet one another, and all is understood in the fullness of time.

Some reviews have said Mr. O'Brien (Brad Pitt, crew-cut, never more of a regular guy) is too strict as a disciplinarian. I don't think so. He is doing what he thinks is right, as he has been raised. Mrs. O'Brien (the ethereal Jessica Chastain) is gentler and more understanding, but there is no indication she feels her husband is cruel. Of course children resent discipline, and of course a kid might sometimes get whacked at the dinner table circa 1950. But listen to an acute exchange of dialogue between Jack and his father. "I was a little hard on you sometimes," Mr. O'Brien says, and Jack replies: "It's your house. You can do what you want to." Jack is defending his father against himself. That's how you grow up. And it all happens in this blink of a lifetime, surrounded by the realms of unimaginable time and space.

## Trespass ★ ★

R, 90 m., 2011

Nicolas Cage (Kyle Miller), Nicole Kidman (Sarah Miller), Ben Mendelsohn (Elias), Cam Gigandet (Jonah), Liana Liberato (Avery Miller), Jordana Spiro (Petal), Dash Mihok (Ty), Emily

Meade (Kendra), Nico Tortorella (Jake). Directed by Joel Schumacher and produced by Rene Besson, Boaz Davidson, Danny Dimbort, Avi Lerner, Trevor Short, David Winkler, and Irwin Winkler. Screenplay by Karl Gajdusek.

*Trespass* is a home invasion thriller that may set a record for the number of times the characters point loaded pistols at one another's heads. First we're afraid somebody will get shot. Then we're afraid nobody will be. The suspense depends on the fact that the homeowners are smarter than the break-in artists.

The screenplay by Karl Gajdusek succeeds in devising enough dialogue to last ninety minutes in what increasingly seems like an exercise in overacting. We open with a key overhead shot, showing Kyle Miller (Nicolas Cage), a diamond dealer, speeding through what looks like a primeval forest on the way to his isolated modern home. I had some friends who lived in a modernist glass-walled house like this, and they finally sold it. They were in a wooded area, and my pal Marge said it made her feel creepy that there might be beady little eyes out there. "Probably only squirrels," I said. "That's even worse."

While he's driving, we hear Kyle on his cell phone, desperately negotiating to close a deal or raise some cash. He arrives home and is greeted by his architect wife, Sarah (Nicole Kidman), who apparently likes to expose herself to squirrels, and their teenage daughter, Avery (Liana Liberato), who is angry they won't let her go out to a party.

Barely enough time passes for Avery to sneak out of the house and Sarah and Kyle to make it clear their marriage Needs a Long Talk, when people dressed like cops ring at the security cam and force themselves inside. They are disguised with masks so inadequate that at one point I thought: "Hey! That's Ben Mendelsohn!" They know there's a safe in the house, and they demand $100,000. Kyle, afraid his family will be killed if he opens the safe, refuses.

So OK, they have a gun at his head. Only he knows the combination. They revise their demand: Now they want diamonds. Eventually they produce a hypodermic needle and say what they really need is his wife's kidney. "That's why I brought this knife," a crook snarls, brandishing a Bowie. If the movie had lasted a little longer perhaps they would have demanded being allowed to order pizza on their credit card.

Did I mention the house is isolated in a forest? Yes, and that's why the family has to deal with a dilemma I frequently notice in movies: There's no place to go. Not once but several times family members escape from the house and run into the woods, only to . . . yes, return. In a twist on this, Avery, the daughter, sneaks *back into* the house. She hears raised and threatening voices coming from downstairs. What does she do? Call the cops? Escape again? No, she calls out loudly, "Mom? Dad?"

The most fun in the movie is when Nick Cage, the world champion of Feverish Fast Talking, desperately explains why he has no (a) money, or (b) diamonds. This comes as news to his wife. Meanwhile, she recognizes one of the break-in guys as a guard who once put the make on her. He still believes she probably likes him more than her husband. The movie skillfully finds time to squeeze this crisis of infidelity into the plot, with more guns to the head.

At one point, I believe a family member holds a gun to the head of a gang member—but oh, no, we're not going to fall for that again. For variety, a little later a nail gun is pointed to a head. By then Nick Cage has already been wounded so often that it's a wonder he can keep on Feverishly Fast Talking. He's like a chicken that doesn't know it's dead.

The director of *Trespass* is Joel Schumacher, some of whose films have been good and others not so good. Do audiences demand plausibility in thrillers like this anyway? Schumacher throws in a teenage party, flashbacks to sensuous poolside scenes, *Rashomon*-like contrasting versions of key events, and footage from the security cams. Also a security system person having a conversation with someone at the home asks for the secret security code and is told, "I'll call you back."

## The Trip ★ ★ ★

NO MPAA RATING, 109 m., 2011

Steve Coogan (Himself), Rob Brydon (Himself), Claire Keelan (Emma), Margo Stilley (Mischa), Rebecca Johnson (Sally), Dolya Gavanski

(Magda), Kerry Shale (Steve's Agent). Directed by Michael Winterbottom and produced by Andrew Eaton and Melissa Parmenter.

After some movies, Gene Siskel liked to say, "I wish I'd seen a documentary about the same actors having lunch." A whimsical new movie named *The Trip* puts his theory to the test. We've seen Steve Coogan and Rob Brydon costarring in *Tristram Shandy: A Cock and Bull Story* (2005), and now here they are having lunch.

The pretense is that the *Observer* newspaper has assigned Coogan to do an article about dining in the north of England. His qualifications seem to be that he was born in Manchester and eats. When his girlfriend begs off the tour, he recruits his old friend Brydon to drive along, magnanimously offering to give him 45 percent of the fee. Brydon bids farewell to his wife and child, and the two set off in Coogan's Land Rover under gray winter skies.

The film, directed by Michael Winterbottom, consists of (1) Coogan and Brydon talking in the car; (2) Coogan and Brydon talking at breakfast, lunch, and dinner; (3) Coogan's luck at seducing hotel staff members; (4) Coogan standing alone in chilly but lovely landscapes trying to find a signal for his cell phone; (5) food being prepared and served; and (6) shots of the car on motorways and country lanes.

This is a great deal more entertaining than it sounds, in large part because the two actors are gifted mimics—Brydon the better one, although Coogan doesn't think so. They get into a sort of competition that allows them to compete with their versions of such as Michael Caine, Ian McKellen, Sean Connery, Woody Allen, and others. Brydon does a virtuoso impression of Caine's voice evolving from his early days in *The Ipcress File* through decades of whiskey and cigars into its present richness.

There's an undercurrent of rivalry throughout, based on what Coogan sees as his greater fame, success, and talent. What especially bugs him is that he's seen as a comic actor and denied a shot at the heavy-duty A-list material he feels he deserves. He also sees himself as more handsome, fit, and successful than Brydon, and from the way he considers his hair in a mirror, you'd think he wanted it to look that way.

Curiously, they give only perfunctory attention to the many meals they eat, although Winterbottom faithfully goes into the kitchens to show each one being prepared. Scallops are featured in at least half the meals. One breakfast centers on black pudding, which I believe is best eaten with the eyes closed.

Along the way they visit Lake District sites associated with Wordsworth and Coleridge, quote copiously, and speculate on Coleridge's use of opium. Coogan's reaction shot is priceless when one woman recognizes Brydon but not him. And there's an undercurrent: Brydon has a family to return to in a cozy home; Coogan has a son he's distant from and a barren modern apartment.

It's a good question how true to life any of this is. The movie lists no screenwriters, but although it looks like a documentary, it isn't one. Apparently this film is edited down from a longer BBC-TV series during which the food was possibly more discussed. At the end we're left with the intriguing question: Would we rather see the same two actors in a regular story?

## TrollHunter ★ ★ ½

PG-13, 99 m., 2011

Otto Jespersen (Hans), Glenn Erland Tosterud (Thomas), Tomas Alf Larsen (Kalle), Johanna Morck (Johanna), Hans Morten Hansen (Finn Haugen). Directed by Andre Ovredal and produced by Sveinung Golimo and John M. Jacobsen. Screenplay by Ovredal.

It is a misery to be a troll. You haunt the forests of Norway, live in clammy caves, and inhabit bodies incapable of processing vitamin D, so that the sun can cause you to crumble into stone. Your obsession is hunting Christians, but because you live in a Norwegian wilderness far from cities, there are few Christians to be found—and since some trolls are taller than trees, they can see you coming.

*TrollHunter* is a mockumentary allegedly edited from anonymous footage and certainly inspired by *The Blair Witch Project*. It has something going for it: We see a lot of trolls and we saw precious few witches. At first, the filmmakers aren't even looking for trolls; three young students are on the track of a man suspected of poaching bears without a license.

We meet Thomas (Glenn Erland Tosterud); his sound person, Johanna (Johanna Morck); and the cinematographer, Kalle (Tomas Alf Larsen); none of whom, of course, is especially competent because a requirement of the genre is a lot of queasy cam.

They're on the trail of a suspect, Hans (Otto Jespersen), who prowls the forest trails in a Land Rover with alarming scratches on its doors. Eventually Hans allows them to trail along, and they discover that the Norwegian government employs troll hunters in a secret program to stop the beasts, who are a threat to power pylons, the environment, and, of course, Christians. They sniff out Christians by their distinctive smell. That leads to some droll scenes in which Hans leads them in smearing their bodies with Troll Stench.

That's funny. A lot of *TrollHunter* (but not enough) is funny. I imagine the best way to see the movie would be the way it was presented at Sundance, at a "secret" midnight screening at which the capacity audience allegedly has no idea what it is about to see.

Trolls are very ugly, except to other trolls. There are various sorts, including mountain trolls and forest trolls. The shortage of Christians in their locales perhaps explains their ill humor. They spend a great deal of time roaring, bleating, squealing, and snorting at a very high volume, which is, after a point, too much of a muchness.

The fake-doc look nicely explains the partial glimpses and incomplete shots during the troll hunt, although we get a nice look at some of the beasts, who have amazingly ugly schnozzolas. There is a scene that seems like a loving tribute to monster movies since time immemorial, in which threatened humans huddle in a cave and monsters can be seen sniffling at the cave mouth. This solves the problem of incorporating effects (and miniatures?) into the shot.

At one point it's explained that trolls cannot be seen in satellite photos. That must be because of their coloration and not their size, because one in particular seems to stand fifty feet tall, easy. Why did I waste time thinking about satellite photos, however, when I was presented with a more pressing problem: If trolls can't stand sunlight, which creates vitamin D and helps with bone calcium, why do they possess so much calcium that a leading cause of death is instant calcification, which is not a pretty sight? Unfortunately, the film ends abruptly before the troll hunters can explain that. Of course, it's a requirement of the genre that all the children of *Blair Witch* end abruptly. But I digress.

## Tron: Legacy ★ ★ ★

PG-13, 125 m., 2010

Jeff Bridges (Kevin Flynn/Clu), Garrett Hedlund (Sam Flynn), Olivia Wilde (Quorra), Michael Sheen (Castor/Zuse), Bruce Boxleitner (Alan Bradley/Tron), Beau Garrett (Gem), James Frain (Jarvis). Directed by Joseph Kosinski and produced by Sean Bailey, Steven Lisberger, and Jeffrey Silver. Screenplay by Edward Kitsis and Adam Horowitz.

To the sad story of a father who was trapped inside a snowman for the winter (*Jack Frost*), we must now add *Tron: Legacy*, where the father has been trapped inside a software program for twenty years. Yes, young Sam Flynn has grown up an orphan because his dad was seduced and abducted by a video game. Now a call comes for the young hero to join his old dad in throwing virtual Frisbees at the evil programs threatening that digital world.

This is a movie well beyond the possibility of logical explanation. Since the Tron universe exists entirely within chips, don't bother yourself about where the physical body of Kevin Flynn (Jeff Bridges) has been for the last two decades; it must surely have been somewhere because we can see that it has aged. The solution, I suppose, is that this is a virtual world and it can do anything it feels like, but how exactly does a flesh-and-blood twenty-year-old get inside it? And what does he eat?

Joseph Kosinski's *Tron: Legacy* steps nimbly over such obstacles and hits the ground running, in a 3-D sound and light show that plays to the eyes and ears more than the mind. Among its real-world technology is a performance by Jeff Bridges as Kevin Flynn at two different ages—now, and twenty years ago. The original *Tron* was made twenty-eight years ago, but that would have made young Sam Flynn, his son, nearly thirty, which is too old for the hero in a story of this sort. The ideal age would be around twelve.

In a flashback we see Kevin, lord of a mighty software corporation, taking leave of his son as a child. At first you think Jeff Bridges looks younger in this scene because of makeup or Botox or something, and then you realize this is Bridges's body and voice, but his face has been rendered younger by special effects. They're uncanny. The use of profiles and backlighting makes the illusion adequate for this purpose. The real Bridges turns up later inside the program, whiskery and weathered, but the CGI version of younger Jeff sticks around to play Clu, a program he created, who now desires (you know this is coming) to control the world.

Kevin and Sam reconcile and bond. They join other cyberspace allies, notably including the beguiling Quorra (Olivia Wilde), whom cyber-Kevin has apparently been fathering instead of poor orphaned Sam. Does this symbolize the ways video games can destroy real-life relationships? Just asking. I'm thinking of Quorra and Sam as a possible romantic couple, but there's the pesky problem that she is virtual and he bleeds when he's cut—I think, although maybe not inside the program. This brings us back to a central question about *Avatar*: What or who, precisely, was Neytiri falling in love with?

I'm giving this more attention than the movie does, which is just as well. Isaac Asimov would have attempted some kind of scientific speculation on how this might all be possible, but *Tron* is more action-oriented. (Personal to sci-fi fans: If *2001* is Analog, *Tron: Legacy* is Thrilling Wonder Stories.)

The first *Tron* (1982) felt revolutionary at the time. I'd never seen anything like it. We showed it again at Ebertfest a few years ago. It was the first movie to create a digital world and embed human actors; earlier that had been done with special effects, matte shots, optical printers, blue screen, and so on. *Tron* found a freedom of movement within its virtual world that was exhilarating. The plot was impenetrable, but so what?

*Tron: Legacy,* a sequel made twenty-eight years after the original but with the same actor, is true to the first film: It also can't be understood but looks great. Both films, made so many years apart, can fairly lay claim to being state of the art. This time that includes the use of 3-D. Since so much of the action involves quick movement forward and backward in shots, the 3-D effect is useful, and not just a promiscuous use of the ping-pong effect. It is also well iterated. (A note at the top informs us that parts of the movie were deliberately filmed in 2-D, so of course I removed my glasses to note how much brighter it was. Dimness is the problem 3-D hasn't licked.)

A long time ago in 1984, Jeff Bridges appeared as an alien inhabiting a human body in John Carpenter's *Starman.* An article in the *New York Times Magazine* called him the perfect movie actor. He wasn't flashy; he was steadily, consistently good. Now that he has won an Oscar for *Crazy Heart* and appearing in *True Grit,* that is still true. Here is an actor expected to (1) play himself as a much younger man, (2) play himself now, and (3) play a computer program (or avatar?), and he does all three in a straightforward manner that is effective and convincing (given the preposterous nature of the material).

Sam, circa twenty (Garrett Hedlund), is well suited to his role, somewhat resembling Bridges. Olivia Wilde makes a fragrant Quorra. In some inexplicable way, these actors and Bruce Boxleitner (Tron) and Michael Sheen (Zuse) plausibly project human emotions in an environment devoid of organic life, including their own.

The artificial world is wonderfully well rendered, building on the earlier film's ability to bring visual excitement to what must in reality, after all, be slim pickings: invisible ones and zeroes. I soon topped off on the thrill of watching Frisbees of light being hurled, but some of the chases and architectural details are effective simply because they use sights and spaces never seen. And the soundtrack by Daft Punk has such urgent electronic force that the visuals sometimes almost play as *its* accompaniment. It might not be safe to play this in the car. The plot is another matter. It's a catastrophe, short-changing the characters and befuddling the audience. No doubt an online guru will produce a synopsis of everything that happens, but this isn't like an opera, where you can peek at the program notes.

I expect *Tron: Legacy* to be a phenomenon at the box office for a week or three. It may not have legs because its appeal is too one-dimensional for an audience much beyond immediate responders. When *2001* was in theaters, there were fans who got stoned and sneaked in during the intermission for the sound-and-light trip. I hesitate to suggest that for *Tron: Legacy*, but the plot won't suffer.

## True Grit ★ ★ ★ ½

PG-13, 110 m., 2010

Jeff Bridges (Rooster Cogburn), Matt Damon (LaBoeuf), Josh Brolin (Tom Chaney), Barry Pepper (Lucky Ned Pepper), Hailee Steinfeld (Mattie Ross). Directed by Joel Coen and Ethan Coen, and produced by Joel Coen, Ethan Coen, and Scott Rudin. Screenplay by Joel Coen and Ethan Coen, based on the novel by Charles Portis.

In the Coen brothers' *True Grit*, Jeff Bridges is not playing the John Wayne role. He's playing the Jeff Bridges role—or, more properly, the role created in the enduring novel by Charles Portis, much of whose original dialogue can be heard in this film. Bridges doesn't have the archetypal stature of the Duke. Few ever have. But he has here, I believe, an equal screen presence. We always knew we were looking at John Wayne. When we see Rooster Cogburn in this version, we're not thinking about Jeff Bridges.

Wayne wanted his tombstone to read *Feo, Fuerte y Formal* ("ugly, strong and dignified"). He was a handsome, weathered man when I met him in the 1960s and '70s, but not above a certain understandable vanity. Rooster might be an ornery gunslinger with an eye patch, but Wayne played him wearing a hairpiece and a corset. Jeff Bridges occupies the character like a homeless squatter. I found myself wondering how young Mattie Ross (Hailee Steinfeld) could endure his body odor.

Bridges's interpretation is no doubt closer to the reality of a lawman in those years of the West. How savory can a man be when he lives in saloons and on horseback? Not all riders on the range carried a change of clothes. Of course, he's a lawman with an office and a room somewhere in town, but for much of the movie he is on a quest through inauspicious territory to find the man who murdered Mattie's father.

As told in the novel, Mattie is a plucky young woman with a gaze as level as her hat brim. She hires Marshal Cogburn to track down that villain Tom Chaney (Josh Brolin). She means to kill him for what he done. If Bridges comfortably wears the Duke's shoes, Hailee Steinfeld is more effective than Kim Darby in the earlier film, and she was pretty darn good. Steinfeld was thirteen when she made the film, close to the right age. Darby was a little over twenty. The story hinges on the steel resolve of a young girl who has been raised in the eye-for-an-eye Old West, seen some bad sights, and picked up her values from the kind of old man who can go and get hisself shot.

What strikes me is that I'm describing the story and the film as if it were simply, if admirably, a good Western. That's a surprise to me, because this is a film by the Coen brothers, and this is the first straight genre exercise in their career. It's a loving one. Their craftsmanship is a wonder. Their casting is always inspired and exact. The cinematography by Roger Deakins reminds us of the glory that was, and can still be, the Western.

But this isn't a Coen brothers film in the sense that we use those words. It's not eccentric, quirky, wry, or flaky. It's as if these two men, who have devised some of the most original films of our time, reached a point where they decided to coast on the sheer pleasure of good old straightforward artistry. This is like Iggy Pop singing "My Funny Valentine," which he does very well. So let me praise it for what it is, a splendid Western. The Coens, having demonstrated their mastery of many notes, including many not heard before, now show they can play in tune.

Isn't Rooster Cogburn where Jeff Bridges started out forty years ago? The first time I was aware of him was in *The Last Picture Show* (1971), where he and his friends went to the local movie theater to see *Red River*, starring John Wayne. Since then that clean-faced young man has lived and rowdied and worked his way into being able to play Rooster with a savory nastiness that Wayne could not have equaled.

All the same, the star of this show is Hailee Steinfeld, and that's appropriate. This is her story, set in motion by her, narrated by her.

This is Steinfeld's first considerable role. She nails it. She sidesteps the opportunity to make Mattie adorable. Mattie doesn't live in an adorable world. Seeing the first *True Grit*, I got a little crush on Kim Darby. Seeing this one, few people would get a crush on Hailee Steinfeld. Maybe in another movie. But the way she plays it with the Coens, she's more the kind of person you'd want guarding your back.

Matt Damon, Josh Brolin, and Barry Pepper have weight and resonance in supporting roles. Damon is LaBoeuf, the Texas Ranger who comes along for a time to track Tom Chaney. Glen Campbell had the role earlier, and was right for the tone of that film. Damon plays on a more ominous note. His LaBoeuf isn't sidekick material. He and Cogburn have long-standing issues. Nor, we discover, is LaBoeuf a man of simple loyalty.

As Tom Chaney, Josh Brolin is a complete and unadulterated villain, a rattlesnake who would as soon shoot Mattie as Rooster. In the Western genre, evil can be less nuanced than in your modern movies with all their psychological insights. Barry Pepper plays Lucky Ned Pepper, leader of a gang Chaney ends up with and part of the four-man charge across the meadow into Rooster's gunfire, a charge as lucky for them as the Charge of the Light Brigade.

The 1969 film had glorious landscapes. The meadow and several other scenes were set in the San Juan mountains of Colorado, near Telluride. This film's landscapes are all in Texas, and although some are beautiful, many are as harsh and threatening as the badlands described by Cormac McCarthy or Larry McMurtry.

I expect Bridges and Steinfeld have good chances of winning Oscar nominations for this film. Steinfeld is good the whole way through, but the scene audiences love is the one where she bargains with a horse trader (Dakin Matthews) for the money she feels is owed her. Here the key is the dialogue by the Coen brothers, which never strains, indeed remains flat and commonsense, as Mattie reasons the thief out of his money by seeming to employ his own logic.

I'm surprised the Coens made this film, so unlike their other work except in quality. Instead of saying that now I hope they get back to making "Coen brothers films," I'm inclined to speculate on what other genres they might approach in this spirit. What about the musical? *Oklahoma!* is ready to be remade.

## Trust ★ ★ ★ ★

R, 104 m., 2011

Liana Liberato (Annie Cameron), Clive Owen (Will Cameron), Catherine Keener (Lynn Cameron), Viola Davis (Gail Friedman), Chris Henry Coffey (Charlie). Directed by David Schwimmer and produced by Schwimmer, Ed Cathell III, Dana Golomb, Robert Greenhut, Tom Hodges, Avi Lerner, and Heidi Jo Markel. Screenplay by Andy Bellin and Robert Festinger.

The bravest thing about David Schwimmer's *Trust* is that it doesn't try to simplify. It tells its story of a fourteen-year-old girl and a predatory pedophile as a series of repercussions in which rape is only the first, and possibly not the worst, tragedy to strike its naive and vulnerable victim. It's easy to imagine how this story could have been exploited and dumbed down. It works instead with intelligence and sympathy.

At its core is a remarkable performance by young Liana Liberato, who plays Annie Cameron, the happy child of a good home in upper-crust Wilmette, Illinois. The character could have been played in many ways, but Liberato evokes innocence, defiance, idealism, hurt—and trust—without ever seeming to be more aware than she should. We believe above all in her youth. We hear a lot about the premature sexualization of young teens; she creates a "good girl" who isn't advanced, who feels uncomfortable at a party where "popular girls" fake sophistication. She's . . . a nice kid.

She's never had a boyfriend when she meets Charlie online in a chat room. Schwimmer uses titles to show us their conversations. Charlie is in high school. Like her, he plays volleyball. He's a nice kid, too. He understands her. She grows closer to Charlie than any boy she's ever known. They talk for hours on the phone.

Charlie (Chris Henry Coffey) makes a confession. Actually, he's in college. Actually, he's a graduate student. Actually, he's twenty-five.

"Why do you keep lying?" she asks. But Charlie is comforting and persuasive. She agrees to meet him in a mall. She must have been warned about cases of online predators like him—but they couldn't have been talking about her Charlie. Yet when Charlie turns up, he's clearly well into his thirties. Annie is crushed. But he is persuasive and compelling, a smooth talker, pushing all the right buttons, exploiting her idealized fantasies about himself. Coffey is very good in the scene.

At this point in the film, I thought I had a pretty good idea where it was going. That's how it surprised me, by being fiercely respectful of Annie's feelings in all their complexities, and providing her with dialogue that reflects her confusion and vulnerability. Schwimmer is an activist in the field of rape awareness, and must have had knowledgeable collaborators, including his writers, Andy Bellin and Robert Festinger.

Rape is a cruel crime. For Annie, the loss of her virginity is not the worst of it. More important is her reputation, her world in New Trier High School, her self-esteem. She might almost have been better off not telling anyone what happened. She confides in a friend, who blabs to the school principal, and she's led away from school by two uniformed officers who come to investigate the crime. In this and countless details for the rest of the film, we realize a psychic rape is being added to the original one. Only a reserved but tactful psychiatrist (Viola Davis) completely understands what is happening.

Annie's parents are good people. Her British father, Will (Clive Owen), is a marketing executive—ironically, catering to the market for sexy teen fashions exploited by the notorious American Apparel. Her mother, Lynn (Catherine Keener), is sensible and loving. The marriage is healthy. What Annie desperately needs is privacy and space. What she gets is an intrusive FBI investigation, brutal gossip at high school, cruel jokes played on the Internet, and the destruction of the idealized vision of Charlie she clings to.

*Trust* is above all respectful of her feelings. It perhaps goes a shade too far in how it deals with her father's. He becomes obsessed with the FBI investigation, wants personal vengeance against the predator, gets involved in unwise ways. In a crushing scene where his anger leaps out of control, he has the effect of humiliating Annie before hundreds of her classmates.

*Trust* doesn't offer soothing solutions for Annie. Annie will survive, but has been damaged perhaps more by the aftermath than by the rape itself. The movie is merciless in depicting the methods by which pedophile predators operate. Charlie is the embodiment of evil. But society is lacking in instinctive sympathy and tact for Annie, and society isn't supposed to be evil. Catherine Keener does a warm, unobtrusive job of loving and comforting her daughter, but that's not enough—not when her husband grows more concerned with vengeance than with healing.

It is all too tortuous and complicated. Liana Liberato does such a poignant job of showing how and why. She has three scenes in particular where her wounded feelings spill out in words of anguish, and they are so well written and well acted that they're heartbreaking. David Schwimmer has made one of the year's best films: powerfully emotional, yes, but also very perceptive.

## Tucker and Dale vs. Evil ★ ★ ★

R, 89 m., 2011

Tyler Labine (Dale), Alan Tudyk (Tucker), Katrina Bowden (Allison), Jesse Moss (Chad), Brandon Jay McLaren (Jason), Christie Laing (Naomi), Chelan Simmons (Chloe). Directed by Eli Craig and produced by Morgan Jurgenson, Albert Klychak, Roseanne Milliken, and Deepak Nayer. Screenplay by Craig and Jurgenson.

If ever there was a movie that seems prepared to follow an ancient formula, that movie is *Tucker and Dale vs. Evil.* Consider. A van filled with college kids speeds heedlessly down the back roads of hillbilly country. A bearded redneck scowls at them from a pickup truck. They stop at a store with the ominous sign "last gas." The locals inside stare and snicker at them.

Arriving at their campsite in the woods, they pitch their tents, have beers and pot, and hear the story of the Memorial Day massacre, during which a group of kids just like them were murdered by mountain men on—

gasp!—that very spot! Twenty years ago today! So what do they decide to do? Go skinny-dipping, of course.

It probably won't be a spoiler to mention how the movie unfolds because the trailers have helpfully spelled it out for you. If you don't happen to know, stop reading now. Or perhaps not, because the movie doesn't continue down the same dreary road. In a clever if sensationally implausible twist, the only vicious character is one of the college kids, the two hillbillies are sweet and helpful guys, and one cliché after another is ticked off and upended.

Tucker and Dale, or Dumb and Dumber, are hoping only to enjoy a fishing trip at Tucker's new "vacation cottage," which looks haunted when they arrive and has a wall ominously covered with newspaper clippings describing murders in the region. They go fishing by moonlight, happen upon the skinny-dippers, and when nice, blond Allison is frightened by them and falls into the water, they rescue her and haul her unconscious into their boat.

This is interpreted by her friends as a kidnapping, and the basic misunderstanding between the two camps continues in the tradition of farce to lead to tragic misunderstandings. To describe the results would be cheating, but let's say fans of gruesome violence won't be disappointed.

There are a lot of actors in the movie, but only four who survive long enough to make a difference. Tyler Labine, as Dale, is a pudgy victim of low-self esteem, and Alan Tudyk, as Tucker, is his patient best pal, sometimes exasperated by him in the tradition of Laurel and Hardy. Katrina Bowden plays Allison, herself a farm girl and instinctively sympathetic with Dale. And Jesse Moss plays Chad, the leader of the college kids, who is a ferocious and hateful young man with a lifelong score to settle. The movie gives them not much more to do than fill their simple roles, which they do nicely. It's amusing when Allison tries to broker better communications between the two sides.

Students of the Little Movie Glossary may find it funny how carefully *Tucker and Dale* works its way through the upended clichés. I thought it had done a pretty complete job already, including the two or three chainsaws and the wood chipper, but I was much gratified at the end when a sawmill turned up.

## Twelve Thirty ★ ★ ½

NO MPAA RATING, 120 m., 2011

Reed Birney (Martin), Jonathan Groff (Jeff), Mamie Gummer (Maura), Portia Reiners (Mel), Karen Young (Vivien), Halley Feiffer (Irina), Barbara Barrie (Eve), Rebecca Schull (Katherine). Directed by Jeff Lipsky and produced by Daniel Sartorius. Screenplay by Lipsky.

Here is an unsuccessful movie with some surprisingly successful scenes. It has moments when it is electrifying and passages where it slows to a walk. Its dialogue is too "written" for the realism of film, but I can easily imagine it working well on the stage. It has more sex than any movie I've seen recently, and gives it much more thought. It doesn't work, but I doubt you'll regret seeing it.

Jeff Lipsky's *Twelve Thirty* involves a twenty-two-year-old named Jeff (Jonathan Groff) and all four members of the Langley family of Iowa City. Jeff claims at the outset he's a virgin and has never even kissed a girl. You're free to believe that if you choose. He's a young man with a lot of nuance behind his conversation, and in the opening scene he falls into conversation with Mel (Portia Reiners). She's his age and they work in the same restaurant. This scene eventually contains a self-contained play of its own. They join the table of two elderly British tourists (Barbara Barrie and Rebecca Schull), and the relationship and story of these two widows creates a lovely moment.

Mel is an intriguing take-charge woman who goes on a drive with Jeff and ends up taking him to bed after overcoming all his (pretended?) objections. But that's that. She enjoyed the sex but won't do it again. Later, we meet her sister, Maura (Mamie Gummer), in a girl-to-girl conversation with her best friend, Irina (Halley Feiffer). At that point we don't know Maura is Mel's sister. So yes, this is one of those interlinking plot movies where everyone (except the widows) ends up connected. But there's a difference: The movie doesn't cut between story lines with clever editing, but is told chronologically, so that we're allowed to make the connection for ourselves.

Jeff and Maura, urged by Irina, slip into a closet at a party, and what happens there you will see—or not see, because it's in the dark. Jeff flees weeping into the night, and goes to Mel's house the next day, where he meets her mother, Vivien (Karen Young). What happens then you will also discover, but let me say Young's acting, here and in an earlier scene with Mel, is quietly, touchingly exact, and her dialogue in various tones is particularly effective.

The father of the girls is Vivien's ex-husband, Martin (Reed Birney), a bisexual who now lives with Robert, never seen. Vivien tells a story about his kindness that is moving; elsewhere in the film, when she and Martin make love, Karen Young's smile of invitation feels uncannily genuine. Toward the end of the film, Martin presides over a discussion with his ex-wife, his daughters, and Jeff, and this is a scene that decidedly doesn't work, no matter how we take it.

So there you are. Ambition, precision, good acting, some acting that doesn't overcome the dialogue, and a scene in the dark that plays as a stunt. Also some distractingly cute repeating jokes about museums and lip balm. I wish all movies that don't work were this interesting.

## 21 Jump Street ★ ★ ★

R, 109 m., 2012

Jonah Hill (Schmidt), Channing Tatum (Jenko), Brie Larson (Molly Tracey), Dave Franco (Eric Molson), Rob Riggle (Mr. Walters), Ice Cube (Captain Dickson). Directed by Phil Lord and Christopher Miller and produced by Stephen J. Cannell and Neal H. Moritz. Screenplay by Michael Bacall, based on the television series.

*21 Jump Street* is the last movie I was expecting with that title. In other words, it's pretty good. There seemed to be little demand for a movie spin-off of the crime drama that ran on Fox from 1987 to 1991, and which had an early starring role for Johnny Depp. Perhaps realizing that, the filmmakers have abandoned any pretense of being faithful to the series, and turned to a mash-up of screwball comedy, action, and the *Odd Couple* formula.

The couple here are Schmidt and Jenko (Jonah Hill and Channing Tatum), who were opposites in high school and still are eight years later. In high school, Schmidt was a pudgy nerd who wore braces and couldn't get his mouth to work while trying to ask a girl to the prom. Jenko was a good-looking jock to whom all things came easily; unfortunately, he was the dim bulb in the chandelier.

In a brief prologue, the movie spares us the tiresome routine where the jock makes life miserable for the nerd; all he does is snicker with everyone else when poor Schmidt gets tongue-tied. They have no reason to be enemies because they're from different planets. When we meet them again, they're both in the police academy, where Schmidt aces all the exams and fails everything physical, and Jenko does the opposite. That makes them both misfits, and they feel a growing camaraderie.

After an unpromising start as bicycle-riding cops on park patrol, they're exiled to an undercover unit investigating a dangerous new drug infiltrating a local high school. The captain in charge (Ice Cube) is the typical police veteran who can't believe the incompetence of these losers. I should mention that his name is Dickson—inevitable in a movie papered with dick jokes. The male member, having gone unmentioned during most of the cinema's first 110 years, now costars in many comedies.

But back to the story. It often strikes me that the actors in high school movies look too old. But Schmidt and Jenko look *really* too old, and the movie isn't shy about pointing that out. Indeed, one of the pleasures of *21 Jump Street* is that the screenplay by Michael Bacall is happy to point out all of its improbabilities; the premise is preposterous to begin with, and they run with that.

Jonah Hill, nominated for an Oscar for *Moneyball*, has become a movie star by demonstrating that it's not so much how you look as how well you look it. He has an endearing appeal in early scenes where he uses close-cropped blond hair in a pathetic attempt to look cool. Hill lost a lot of weight to appear in this movie, but he's one of those guys who will never be described as thin. Channing Tatum, on the other hand, has a reverse handicap: He's improbably handsome, and has a (real) name that sounds manufactured by a press agent. Their attempt to pass themselves off as brothers supplies a running gag.

There might have been a temptation to write Schmidt and Jenko as rivals, but it's more effective here to develop them as friends who screw up together. They were pre-enrolled by Dickson in handpicked classes, but trouble starts when they can't remember their undercover names and each is assigned to the other's classes. That means Schmidt ends up playing Peter Pan in drama class, and Jenko is in advanced chemistry.

Apparently the conviction that we got high school all wrong is universal. Now Schmidt and Jenko get a fresh start, and Schmidt even gets another chance to ask a girl (sweet Brie Larson) to the prom. Meanwhile they're seeking the source of drugs in the school, which inevitably involves chase scenes and a motorcycle gang, including a fat, bald guy with high-rider handlebars. As usual, the chases and explosions are boring.

A disastrous party with drug abuse is funny, as the movie uses bizarre graphics to illustrate the various stages users go through while using the new mystery drug. What it all comes down to is a funnier and sweeter movie than I had any way of expecting, and the debut of Channing Tatum as an actor who can play comedy. He deadpans so well here he might start looking at Cary Grant movies for remake ideas.

## The Twilight Saga: Breaking Dawn: Part 1 ★ ★ ½

PG-13, 117 m., 2011

Kristen Stewart (Bella Swan), Robert Pattinson (Edward Cullen), Taylor Lautner (Jacob Black), Billy Burke (Charlie Swan), Peter Facinelli (Dr. Carlisle Cullen), Elizabeth Reaser (Esme Cullen), Kellan Lutz (Emmett Cullen), Nikki Reed (Rosalie Hale), Jackson Rathbone (Jasper Hale), Ashley Greene (Alice Cullen). Directed by Bill Condon and produced by Wyck Godfrey, Stephenie Meyer, and Karen Rosenfelt. Screenplay by Melissa Rosenberg, based on the novel *Breaking Dawn* by Meyer.

The *Twilight* movies have devoted three episodes to Bella Swan clinging to her virginity despite the compelling appeal of Edward Cullen, the vampire. Now comes *The Twilight Saga: Breaking Dawn: Part 1*, in which you have to give her credit: She holds out until after her wedding. Then she and Edward fly to Brazil and a luxurious honeymoon hideaway on the beach, where the morning after her wedding night she is black and blue with bruises, the frame of the bed is broken, all of the furniture is tossed around, and the draperies are shredded. Good gravy! What happened?

We have no idea. The movie doesn't show us! Yes, the most eagerly awaited deflowering in recent movie history takes place entirely off-screen. That something momentous took place is indicated fourteen days after the wedding ceremony, when Bella (Kristen Stewart) urps in the morning and discovers she is pregnant. Edward Cullen (Robert Pattinson) may have been dead for more than a century, but he's still producing industrial-strength sperm. Can humans and vampires mate? What's the blood chemistry on that? What will be in the wee one's bottle? Milk, or the unthinkable?

Despite these scientific conundrums, *Breaking Dawn: Part 1* is absorbing, if somewhat slow-paced, and has without doubt the most bloodcurdling scene of live childbirth in a PG-13 movie. Probably the sight of Bella and Edward demolishing the bedroom would have tipped it over into R territory.

The first half is slow and dreamy, as wedding preparations get under way. If you recall the lore from the earlier films, you'll know that marriage to Edward means Bella must become a vampire herself, which any groupie who has slept with Gene Simmons will understand. It's a lovely wedding, with blossom-laden trees framing a lakeside altar. Bella's father, Charlie (Billy Burke), is not entirely happy; his toast includes genial mention that should harm befall Bella he has a gun and knows how to use it. But he puts on a brave face while propelling Bella down the aisle. Edward awaits her, looking in pain as usual.

We get shots of the smiling guests. Many are familiar from the previous movies, but others on both sides of the aisle are new to us. They fascinated me. What were they thinking? How many knew Bella was marrying a vampire? Were they cool with that? Did anyone wonder why Edward apparently possessed not a single relative older than himself?

Back again is Bella's best friend, Jacob Black (Taylor Lautner), who you recall is now a shape-shifter who turns into a wolf. Enraged by Bella's pregnancy, he summons his pack. The wolves, it must be said, are underwhelming as a pack. They become huge, ferocious beasts with sharp fangs, and hurtle at top speed through the forest, and . . . well, that's about it. They're always hurtling somewhere. Hurtle, hurtle.

Given that he had months to prepare for the big event, I can't say Edward trained himself carefully for the home delivery. The sum of his medical training seems to have been a viewing of *Pulp Fiction* in which he learned about a real big needle you can plunge into someone's chest with great results.

Kristen Stewart is really pretty good here, although like almost all actresses, she believes pregnant women rub their baby bumps unceasingly. I would have liked more scenes developing her thoughts about married life. Although the possibility of an abortion is hinted at, we never learn her thinking on this question: Does a vampire baby have a soul? Does it have a right to life although, technically, it's half-dead? Luckily, we must wait only until November 16, 2012, when *The Twilight Saga: Breaking Dawn: Part 2* will open. It had better have the answers. If it doesn't, Charlie Swan has a gun and he knows how to use it.

## The Twilight Saga: Eclipse ★ ★

PG-13, 124 m., 2010

Kristen Stewart (Bella Swan), Robert Pattinson (Edward Cullen), Taylor Lautner (Jacob Black), Bryce Dallas Howard (Victoria), Billy Burke (Charlie Swan), Dakota Fanning (Jane), Peter Facinelli (Dr. Carlisle Cullen), Elizabeth Reaser (Esme Cullen), Jackson Rathbone (Jasper Hale), Kellan Lutz (Emmett Cullen), Ashley Greene (Alice Cullen), Nikki Reed (Rosalie Hale). Directed by David Slade and produced by Wyck Godfrey, Greg Mooradian, and Karen Rosefelt. Screenplay by Melissa Rosenberg, based on the novel *Eclipse* by Stephenie Meyer.

The price for surrendering your virginity is so high in *The Twilight Saga: Eclipse* that even Edward Cullen, the proposed tool of surrender, balks at it. Like him, you would become one of the undead. This is a price that Bella Swan, the virtuous heroine, must be willing to pay. Apparently when you marry a vampire, even such a well behaved one as Edward, he's required to bite you.

This romantic dilemma is developed in *Eclipse,* the third installment in this inexhaustible series, by adding a complication that has been building ever since the first. Jacob Black, the shape-shifting werewolf, is also in love with Bella (Kristin Stewart), and she perhaps with him. Jacob (Taylor Lautner) and his tribe are hot-blooded and never wear shirts, inspiring little coos and ripples of delight in the audience. Here is a fantasy to out-steam any romance novel: A sweet young girl is forced to choose between two improbably tall, dark, and handsome men who brood and smolder and yearn for her.

Nothing is perfect. There is a problem. The flame-tressed vampire Victoria (Bryce Dallas Howard) has been active in Seattle initiating new vampires, or Newbies, who in their youth are ravenous for blood and would have superhuman strength, if they were human. Victoria wants to destroy Bella in revenge for the murder of her boyfriend, James. Edward and Jacob both vow to protect the girl they love, and their fellow vampires and werewolves of course are prepared to fight to the death in this cause. This is true buddy love.

The movie contains violence and death, but not really very much. For most of its languorous running time, it listens to conversations between Bella and Edward, Bella and Jacob, Edward and Jacob, and Edward and Bella and Jacob. This would play better if any of them were clever conversationalists, but their ideas are limited to simplistic renderings of their desires. To be sure, there is a valedictory address, reminding us that these kids have skipped school for three movies now. And Edward has a noble speech when he tells Bella he doesn't want to have sex with her until after they're married. This is self-denial indeed for a 109-year-old vampire, who adds a piquant flavor to the category "confirmed bachelor."

Of Taylor Lautner's musculature, and particularly his abs, much has been written. Yes, he has a great build, but I remind you that an abdominal six-pack must be five seconds' work for a shape-shifter. More impressive is the ability of both Edward and Jacob to regard Bella with penetrating gazes from 'neath really heavy eyebrows. When my eyebrows get like Edward's, the barber trims them and never even asks me first.

There is a problem with the special effects. Many of the mountain ranges, which disappear into the far distance as increasingly pale peaks, look suspiciously like landscapes painted by that guy on TV who shows you how to paint stuff like that. The mountain forests and lakes are so pristine we should see Lewis and Clark just arriving. And the werewolves are inexplicable. They look snarly enough, have vicious fangs, and are larger than healthy ponies, but when they fall upon Newbies, they never quite seem to get the job done. One werewolf is nearly squeezed to death, and another, whose identity I will conceal, hears "he has broken bones on one whole side." Luckily, repairing the damage is only a night's work for Dr. Carlisle Cullen (Peter Facinelli). The problem with the effects is that the wolves don't seem to have physical weight and presence.

Much leads up to a scene in a tent on a mountaintop in the midst of a howling blizzard, when Bella's teeth start chattering. Obviously a job for the hot-blooded Jacob and not the cold-blooded Edward, and as Jacob embraces and warms her, he and Edward have a cloying cringe fest in which Edward admits that if Jacob were not a werewolf, he would probably like him, and then Jacob admits that if Edward were not a vampire—well, no, no, he couldn't. Come on, big guy. The two of you are making eye contact. Edward's been a confirmed bachelor for 109 years. Get in the brokeback spirit.

The audience watched this film with rapt attention. They obviously had a deep understanding of the story, which is just as well, because anyone not intimately familiar with the earlier installments could not make heads or tails of the opening scenes. The *Twilight* movies are chaste eroticism to fuel adolescent dreams, and are really about Bella being attracted and titillated and aroused and tempted up to the . . . very . . . BRINK! . . . of surrender, and then, well, no, no, she shouldn't.

## Tyrannosaur ★ ★ ★ ½

NO MPAA RATING, 91 m., 2011

Peter Mullan (Joseph), Olivia Colman (Hannah), Eddie Marsan (James), Ned Dennehy (Tommy), Sally Carman (Marie), Samuel Bottomley (Samuel), Paul Popplewell (Bod), Sian Breckin (Kelly). Directed by Paddy Considine and produced by Diarmid Scrimshaw. Screenplay by Considine.

Do you know the Scottish actor Peter Mullan? He's one of those "isn't he the guy?" actors you know you've seen before, but aren't sure where. It might have been in *Trainspotting*, *My Name Is Joe*, *The Magdalene Sisters*, *Young Adam*, or even playing a Death Eater in the latest Harry Potter. He's fit, compact, sharpened, and keeps his hair short, but if that makes him sound like an Identikit tough guy from an action picture, he isn't. This man projects lonely depths, deep sadness, and sometimes (but not in *Tyrannosaur*) a tenacious kindness. He concentrates our attention. He walks as if he expects a wall to accept defeat if he walks into it.

*Tyrannosaur* is the first film directed by another great actor, Paddy Considine, and it centers on two men trapped in a coil of drinking, violence, and nearly constant anger. Joseph (Mullan), in his fifties, lives alone after the death of his wife, and sits out the rest of his life in bars. In an opening scene, he gets pissed off in a Yorkshire pub, storms out, and kicks his dog so hard he has to carry the dog home. Carrying the dog is his kindness. Kicking it is his nature.

Sometimes a movie will devise a piece of business that tells you more than thirty minutes of dialogue. In this one, Joseph becomes involved in such a frightening situation that he runs away down streets and alleys, dashes into a charity thrift shop, and hides on the floor between two racks of used women's clothing. The shop is being run by Hannah (Olivia Colman), a sweet but weathered blonde in her forties, who addresses the clothes with concern: "Are you all right in there?" Joseph is not. Hannah offers to pray for him and suggests he might find help in Jesus.

Across the street from Joseph lives a

friendly young boy named Samuel (Samuel Bottomley), whose stepdad is the kind of man who patrols his deck with a bare chest, a can of beer in his hand, and a pit bull attached to a chain around his waist. You know the kind of man. These two men live in constant hostility, although Joseph likes Samuel. He also rather likes Hannah, because she is so endearing and helpless.

She is a sly alcoholic, in a movie where most everyone else is a bold drunk. Joseph sees her one day with a black eye. She got it from her husband, James (Eddie Marsan, another fine actor). James has seen them together, and is so threatened in his masculinity that his automatic response is to beat her. Joseph's automatic response is to defend her.

Joseph's situation now rotates to make him the protector of the abused boy and a woman. Not to suggest the movie shows him redeemed or reformed. The kind of man who starts out kicking his dog to death will probably not end up running an animal shelter. Perhaps *Tyrannosaur* is a dramatization of extreme situational ethics. Even in hell some demons must be better than others.

Peter Mullan's performance here is muscular and unrelenting. He knows he's weak and flawed, damaged by anger. He never lets himself off the hook. At one stage of his feud with the pit bull man, he picks up a sledge hammer and viciously pounds into pieces the tin shed in his own side yard. There is a logic at work. There's also great appeal in the character Samuel, who stands on the protection of his father's deck and shouts warnings at neighborhood bullies.

This isn't the kind of movie that even has hope enough to contain a message. There is no message. Only the reality of these wounded personalities. When I was young, the British angry young men had emerged on stage and screen, and I thought I got the message, which was that in the face of pitiless society, an angry young man must revolt. I think the message of *Tyrannosaur* is that some men are born angry, others experience something terrible to make them that way, and society's pity is wasted.

# U

## Uncle Boonmee Who Can Recall His Past Lives ★ ★ ★ ½

NO MPAA RATING, 113 m., 2011

Thanapat Saisaymar (Boonmee), Jenjira Pongpas (Jen), Sakda Kaewbuadee (Tong), Natthakarn Aphaiwonk (Huay), Geerasak Kulhong (Boonsong). Directed by Apichatpong Weerasethakul and produced by Weerasethakul, Simon Field, and Keith Griffiths. Screenplay by Weerasethakul.

Perhaps our conscious identities exist all the time and occasionally surface into the material world. If we were aware of that, it would make living within real time and space distracting; Wordsworth thought we remember heaven as babies. Later perhaps, if we live carefully and well, as we grow closer to death some tendrils from the other side reach out to greet us.

That is the possibility advanced by *Uncle Boonmee Who Can Recall His Past Lives*, which won the Palme d'Or at Cannes 2010. Don't be put off by its whimsical title, or by the name of its director, which looks strange to Western eyes: Apichatpong Weerasethakul. It's only a movie, and he's only a man. If you are open, even in fancy, to the idea of ghosts who visit the living, this is likely to be a curious but rather bemusing experience.

The movie is easy to understand. I discovered that on my second viewing. The first time through, at one of the morning press screenings at Cannes, I kept expecting for it to declare itself, to be about something. But a dying man like Boonmee is not much for plots, nor does he have an agenda for action. He is taking leave. What happens may seem very odd; the romantic scene with a catfish, for example, which you don't see every day. But to a mind accustomed to the idea of reincarnation, it must be good to meet spirits one has cared for, in whatever their present form.

Uncle Boonmee (Thanapat Saisaymar) spent his life as a farmer in a forested area of Thailand. It was not a perfect life. His nation went through upheaval in his lifetime, and we gather he saw more of that than he desired. Now he is dying of kidney failure, cared for by a male nurse from Laos and some of his family members. He stays in a house in the jungle, open to nature, and at his table is visited by ghosts, including his dead wife (beautiful as when he met her) and his son (who looks as if he got a good price on a gorilla suit with electric red eyes). But this isn't a ghost story, because these aren't ghosts as we understand them. They are as alive and aware as Boonmee.

There is a sequence here that may enthrall you. Boonmee makes a visit to a cave that seems to represent the womb for him. It contains sparkling lights and blind fish and is perhaps not an absolutely real cave. Well, if nature and man are one and interconnected, why would Earth not give birth? Or why would Boonmee in any event not visualize it that way?

At the film's end, there is a measured return to reality as we recognize it. The spirit world recedes. But does the real world have any more substance than visions and hallucinations—when we're having them? At any given moment, what's happening in our minds is all and everything that happens. Here is how Uncle Boonmee spent his final days, and how he recalled his past lives and those who shared them. Simple as that.

## Undefeated ★ ★ ★ ½

PG-13, 113 m., 2012

A documentary featuring Bill Courtney, O. C. Brown, Montrail "Money" Brown, and Chavis Daniels. Directed by Daniel Lindsay and T. J. Martin and produced by Ed Cunningham, Seth Gordon, Daniel Lindsay, Rich Middlemas, and Glen Zipper.

There have been football teams for 110 years in the history of Manassas High School in North Memphis, Tennessee. The school had never played in a single playoff game. At the beginning of the 2009 season, Coach Bill Courtney wonders aloud if the school may not have the worst football program in the entire state. The film follows him and three of his key players for the length of the season, at the end of which they are not undefeated but very nearly are. More important, they have won victories over personal demons.

These are poor black kids from a neighborhood bereft of opportunity. Once long ago Manassas was a prosperous working-class area with a big Firestone plant. But the plant closed up and moved away, and I just now realized that during the entire film I didn't glimpse a single retail establishment—not a supermarket, not a gas station, not even a bar. If I missed one, I hope so.

The film makes much of the fact that almost all of these young men are lacking fathers who are present and active in their lives. During a show of hands, we learn that not a single player has a parent who attended college. But every player has a parent who has been behind bars. For Coach Bill, fathers are also an issue. He grew up without a father present, and he shares a memory: After his own school football games, he'd see his teammates walking away with their fathers' arms draped over their shoulders. What was wrong with him? Why didn't he have a dad? His voice trembles with emotion.

Bill Courtney is a big guy who needs a haircut. This isn't his day job. He owns a company dealing in hardwood. At Manassas, he and his staff are volunteers, and yet this job threatens to consume his life. He not only teaches but counsels, deals with the lives, grades, and behavior of his players off the field, and depends on his self-improvement philosophy to shape their lives.

The three players the film focuses on all have a chance of going to college on football scholarships. That will be their ticket out of North Memphis—and no one wants to stay. This story is similar to *Hoop Dreams*, but this film centers on the coach, not the players. Sometimes they almost seem to be testing him, as when one walks away from a talk and seems to be challenging Courtney to see how far he will follow him. At the end of this scene, the coach has driven up off the road and is actually driving next to the player on the sidewalk.

We see highlights from several games, but football is the backdrop, not the subject. Again as in *Hoop Dreams*, a star player suffers a knee injury and his career may be cut short. Courtney takes his best star prospect, a very fast 230-pounder, and boards him with the family of an assistant coach, where he's given daily tutoring in the hopes of passing a college entrance exam. Is the possibility of a sports scholarship the best hope for these players? Maybe not, but what other possibilities are there? They have one marketable skill, playing football, and hope to trade it in as the down payment on a future.

Meanwhile, at home, Coach Courtney's own children don't get as much of their dad's time as his players do. There's a brief scene with his wife, who never quite levels about how she regards that situation. After six and a half years of volunteering, Courtney decides the time has come to leave football and focus on his family again. Bill Courtney is a good man. I'll take that away from this movie. In his circumstances, given his opportunities, he is doing what he can to make this a better world.

*Undefeated* won the Academy Award for best feature-length documentary. It is an emotional and effective film, and I'm happy for it. Yet I reflected that it was nominated and Steve James's great doc *The Interrupters* was not. You remember Steve James. He was also not nominated for his *Hoop Dreams*.

## Unknown ★ ★

PG-13, 113 m., 2010

Liam Neeson (Dr. Martin Harris), Diane Kruger (Gina), January Jones (Elizabeth Harris), Aidan Quinn (Martin B.), Bruno Ganz (Ernst Jurgen), Frank Langella (Rodney Cole). Directed by Jaume Collet-Serra and produced by Joel Silver, Leonard Goldberg, and Andrew Rona. Screenplay by Oliver Butcher and Stephen Cornwell.

Is there a term for the paradox of intended accidental consequences? That's when a movie shows something that must be an accident, and it turns out to be part of a plan. Since *Unknown* opens with examples of such events, it won't be a spoiler for me to discuss them. I'll bail out before the tricky stuff.

As the movie opens, we meet Dr. Martin Harris (Liam Neeson) and his wife, Elizabeth (January Jones), who are on a flight to a biotechnology conference in Berlin. I'm thinking all we need to know about biotechnology in a thriller is that it probably involves either genetically altered crops or dangerous plagues. Anyway, at the airport Dr. Harris lets a guy load his luggage and as the taxi leaves, we get a big shot of his briefcase, still on the luggage trolley.

So OK. Was this an accident? If I'm carrying a briefcase that contains a cure for world hunger or a formula of mass destruction, I'm not gonna leave it on the curb. That's like leaving a laptop sitting on the sink when you go into a stall at a public toilet. Anyway, Dr. Harris and his wife get to the hotel, she starts to check in, he realizes his briefcase was left behind, and *without telling her* he grabs another taxi to the airport. He tries to call her but can't get a signal. Ever had that happen to you in Berlin?

A container falls off the truck in front of them, the taxi swerves and plunges through a bridge rail. Dr. Harris is knocked unconscious, but his life is saved by the quick actions of the driver, Gina (Diane Kruger). He's in a coma for four days. He pulls himself together and races to the hotel, only to find that his wife says she has never seen him before and is happily married to the "real" Dr. Martin Harris (Aidan Quinn). Now his ordeal begins: How can he prove his real identity and understand the conspiracy that has taken control of his life?

As a veteran thriller watcher, you can think of several possibilities here. It was all a dream. He has been brainwashed. He only thinks he's Martin Harris. He only imagined he was on a plane with the real Mrs. Elizabeth Harris. The second taxi was waiting to pick him up. And on and on. Or possibly none of the above.

But let's do an instant rewind. Was it an accident he left the briefcase behind? If he hadn't, there would have been no need to return to the airport. Was the falling container an accident? Was it an accident that he got a (beautiful) undocumented Bosnian refugee taxi driver who performed a heroic rescue in icy winter waters? Was it planned that he would be able to walk into the biotechnology conference and find the (real or fake) Dr. Martin Harris?

I'm thinking, if I'm an operative for some sinister secret organization and I want that briefcase and the MacGuffin it contains, here's what I'll do: I'll knock off Liam Neeson, whoever he is, and steal the briefcase. Or break into his hotel room. Or drug him. Anything. Because, think: If he isn't the real Martin Harris, why does he possess the briefcase containing the MacGuffin in the first place? But if he's a fake Martin Harris, who is the real one?

The movie has answers of a sort to some, but not all, of these questions. All the same, it left me rerunning events in my mind and thinking, Wait! Are we dealing with the Paradox of the Intended Accidental Consequences here, or what? *Unknown* is a skillfully photographed and acted film, and few actors are better than Liam Neeson at playing a man who has had the rug pulled out from under him. I was reminded of Roman Polanski's *Frantic* (1988), in which Harrison Ford played a doctor attending a convention in Paris with his wife. In that movie, the wrong briefcase was picked up at the airport, Ford stepped into the hotel shower, and when he stepped out, he found his wife had vanished.

*Frantic* wasn't watertight, either. The basic situation (an innocent man trapped in a conspiracy he doesn't understand) was a favorite of Hitchcock's, but in his films every consequence is intended. I confess I felt involved in *Unknown* until it pulled one too many rabbits out of its hat. At some point a thriller has to play fair. We're not satisfied when characters find it necessary to come out of nowhere and explain to the hero the underlying reality of his situation. Why does he need to know? Just bump him off. Whenever I hear one of those underlying reality speeches, I think there should be a crawl across the bottom of the screen: "This is actually the voice of the screenwriter desperately trying to explain the plot to himself."

Anyway, maybe this is all just me talking. Maybe I've seen too many movies. *Unknown* isn't really a bad movie, just an absurd one. It has its qualities from moment to moment. It left me with this thought: It's a damn good thing Dr. Martin Harris got that blond Bosnian taxi driver. A lot of taxi drivers, you don't get service like that.

## Unstoppable ★ ★ ★ ½

PG-13, 98 m., 2010

Denzel Washington (Frank Barnes), Chris Pine (Will Colson), Rosario Dawson (Connie Hooper), Ethan Suplee (Dewey), Kevin Dunn (Galvin).

Directed by Tony Scott and produced by Scott, Eric McLeod, Mimi Rogers, Julie Yorn, and Alex Young. Screenplay by Mark Bomback.

The freight train pulls out of a siding with no engineer on board and accelerates to 70 mph, and you see how Tony Scott's *Unstoppable* gets its title. The movie is as relentless as the train, slowly gathering momentum before a relentless final hour of continuous suspense. In terms of sheer craftsmanship, this is a superb film.

The trouble begins when an engineer (Ethan Suplee) dismounts after thinking he'd brought the train to a full stop. He hadn't. When he sees the train slowly pulling away, the look on his face is adequate to fuel the next several minutes. At first it's assumed that the train is a "coaster," but no luck. It's under full throttle.

Scott tells the story from several points of view. In the cab of another train, a longtime engineer named Barnes (Denzel Washington) is breaking in a new man, Colson (Chris Pine). In the station yard, a yardmaster named Connie Hooper (Rosario Dawson) is in charge of dispatch and operations. In the railroad's corporate offices, an executive (Kevin Dunn) is concerned mostly about the cost of losing the train, which seems harsh since it is carrying hazardous materials and is rocketing toward the heart of Scranton, Pennsylvania.

Overhead, news choppers circle, providing a live TV feed, which Scott intercuts with the action. That allows him a plausible way to provide an overview and narrate the action; a similar device was used by his brother Ridley Scott to help us follow events in his *Black Hawk Down* (2001).

There isn't a lot of room here for personality development, but Washington and Pine provide convincing characters, the veteran driven by love of his job, the new guy more cynical. This conflict isn't ramped up for dramatic effect in the screenplay by Mark Bomback, but is allowed to play out as naturally as it can, under the circumstances. Rosario Dawson makes her dispatcher aggressively competent, and the hurtling train of course rumbles beneath everything.

Chase scenes involving trains have an unavoidable limitation: Trains require tracks, and can only go forward or in reverse. There are sidings, but getting onto one may not be very simple. Two other films that come to mind are Buster Keaton's *The General* (1926) and Andrei Konchalovsky's *Runaway Train* (1985), which won Oscar nominations for the two men in its locomotive, Jon Voight and Eric Roberts.

How Scott deals with his "chase" is not for me to reveal here, but although the possibilities of two trains on one track would seem to be limited, he and Bomback are truly ingenious. They employ a kind of logical lateral thinking: The trains can only move in certain ways, but those ways may not be as obvious as we assume.

Not that those are terms we're thinking of during the action. The photography and sound here are very effective in establishing that a train is an enormously heavy thing, and once in motion wants to continue. We knew that. But Scott all but crushes us with the weight of the juggernaut. We are spellbound. And we sure hope those little kids are saved.

## Urbanized ★ ★ ★

NO MPAA RATING, 85 m., 2011

A documentary directed by Gary Hustwit.

In 40 years, 75 percent of us will live in cities. These vast concentrations of population will provide a home, an environment, a world. To the degree that they're well designed, they will make their inhabitants happier or not. Living in Chicago has spoiled me; although the city has its problems, several key design decisions after the (perhaps providential) Chicago Fire preserved the lakeshore, suggested the pattern of radiating diagonal streets, inspired the rapid transit system, and preserved the central city as a vibrant core. In Millennium Park, a single striking piece of public sculpture, now fondly known as The Bean, has been the occasion for daily celebration. At evening rush hours on weekends, more cars are headed toward the city center than toward the suburbs.

But more cars are not altogether a good thing, as Gary Hustwit argues in his new documentary, *Urbanized*. This is his third film, after *Helvetica* (2007) and *Objectified* (2009), to consider the role of design in our daily lives.

The first two dealt with details, with the design of the most ubiquitous typeface of the century and with the packaging of consumer objects. *Urbanized* is a fast zoom out to the big picture: the colonies or hives in which we arrange, display, and support our lives.

Cities are a mixture of deliberate design, accident, history, geography, and countless small collective decisions by the citizens that impose themselves. For example, it is well known that in parks and public green spaces, people will walk where there should logically be a path, whether one is provided or not. On campus quadrangles, planners give up and pave the way.

The doc argues that the most disastrous city planning decisions have been marred by the grandiosity of the planners. From the air, Brasilia, the capital of Brazil, built from scratch in the jungle, looks like a magnificent grouping of sculptures. But for whose eyes? Aliens? On the ground, it is apparently not a very pleasant place to live. Robert Moses, the megalomaniac planning czar of New York City, saw organic neighborhoods as an impediment to his vast rebuilding schemes. Venice, by contrast, grew up island by island, structure by structure, in a shallow lagoon, with no coherent planning at all, and today is arguably the most agreeable city on Earth, despite its undeniable inconveniences.

In an undertaking on an impressive scale, Hustwit and his team travel the earth interviewing architects, city planners, officials, community leaders, and (perhaps not enough) ordinary people. He dramatizes how a stretch of abandoned rail tracks in New York was transformed into a green walkway, "the High Line," and how a majority of Copenhagen's residents travel by bicycle. He is silenced by the slums of Mumbai, where there is one toilet seat for every six hundred people, but there is this undeniable fact: For all of the misery and health problems of such areas, which are almost beyond fixing, they grew and operate by human decisions, and for the people who live there they have more life and soul than "projects" stacking them into cells.

Hustwit's heroine is Jane Jacobs, who famously praised mixed-use neighborhoods and "eyes on the street" as the heart of city life. What people like to do is stroll down a street where they know people and shops, there is variety and novelty, and there are things to look at. My own recent obsession has been with the invasion of soulless cookie-cutter branch bank offices, mobile phone stores, and other sterile pests that crowd out shops, restaurants, and ordinary human activities.

As architects draw, so men live. A New York writer observes happily that *Urbanized* closes on a shot of the magnificent Manhattan skyline. Yes, but there is nowhere in Manhattan where you can stand to see it. I recommend that he admire the Chicago skyline after walking out to the end of Navy Pier, or taking a stroll along twenty-six miles of our beach paths.

# V

## Valentine's Day ★ ★

PG-13, 124 m., 2010

Jessica Alba (Morley Clarkson), Kathy Bates (Susan), Jessica Biel (Kara Monahan), Bradley Cooper (Holden), Eric Dane (Sean Jackson), Patrick Dempsey (Dr. Harrison Copeland), Hector Elizondo (Edgar), Jamie Foxx (Kelvin Moore), Jennifer Garner (Julia Fitzpatrick), Topher Grace (Jason), Anne Hathaway (Liz), Carter Jenkins (Alex), Ashton Kutcher (Reed Bennett), Queen Latifah (Paula Thomas), Taylor Lautner (Willy), George Lopez (Alphonso), Shirley MacLaine (Estelle), Emma Roberts (Grace), Julia Roberts (Captain Kate Hazeltine), Bryce Robinson (Edison), Taylor Swift (Felicia). Directed by Garry Marshall and produced by Mike Karz, Wayne Allan Rice, and Josie Rosen. Screenplay by Katherine Fugate.

I've heard of all-star casts, but *Valentine's Day* has a *complete* star cast. What did other movies do for talent when this one was filming? It has twenty-one actors who can be considered stars, and some are very big stars indeed. It's like the famous poster for *It's a Mad Mad Mad Mad World,* with a traffic jam of famous faces.

That's the movie's problem. Gridlock. It needs somebody like that tough traffic warden who stands under the L at Wabash and Randolph and fiercely wags her finger at drivers who don't shape up. The actors in this movie could populate six romantic comedies with reasonable plots, and a couple of sitcoms. Of course you'd need scripts. *Valentine's Day* is so desperate to keep all the characters alive, it's like those Russian jugglers who run around trying to keep all their plates spinning on poles.

I won't even attempt to describe the plot. Nor will I tell you who the characters are and who plays them. Just the names would come to sixty-three words, and if I described each character in twenty words, I'd run out of space way before I got to Captain Kate Hazeltine (Julia Roberts). I will mention it was nice to see Shirley MacLaine and Hector Elizondo as an old married couple, and of interest that two Taylors (Swift and Lautner) had scenes together.

For the rest, words fail me. The structure of the film involves a large number of couples and additional characters who are not in couples. We wake up with them on the morning of February 14, and all of their stories are completed by midnight, and as Ricky told Lucy, there's a lot of 'splainin to do. Several ancient formulas are employed. (1) Best friends who don't realize they're really in love. (2) Guy who thinks she loves him but she doesn't. (3) Girl who thinks he loves her but he's married. (4) People sitting next to each other on an airplane strike up a conversation. (5) Guy misunderstands phone call, draws wrong conclusion. (6) Fifth-grader's first crush.

The most important characters are a florist named Reed (Ashton Kutcher) and his best friend, Julia (Jennifer Garner). They don't have enough screen time to create three-dimensional characters, but at least they get up to two, leaving everyone else stuck at one or below. They're both attractive, but then all twenty-one stars are attractive, especially if, like me, you think George Lopez is handsome, especially when he smiles.

There's one peculiarity. Usually in formula pictures with this huge a cast, maybe one couple will be African-American, one Latino, and one Asian. No such luck. There are no Asians at all. The black characters include a goofy TV sports reporter (Jamie Foxx) and a wise agent (Queen Latifah). Lopez, a Mexican-American, is relegated to the role of Kutcher's sidekick (i.e., the Tonto role). There are a lot of Indians in the movie, at the next table in an Indian restaurant, revealing that when Indians are out to dinner, they act just like Indians in a movie comedy.

The form of the movie may remind you wistfully of a much better one, *Love, Actually,* which created characters we cared a great deal about. None of the characters here ever get beyond the Look—There's (Name of Star) Threshold. You know, when your mind says, Look—There's Patrick Dempsey! Look—There's Anne Hathaway! Look—There's Topher Grace! Wow—That's Jessica Biel!

*Valentine's Day* is being marketed as a Date Movie. I think it's more of a First Date Movie. If your date likes it, do not date that person again. If you like it, there may not be a second date.

## A Very Harold and Kumar 3-D Christmas ★ ★ ½

R, 90 m., 2011

John Cho (Harold Lee), Kal Penn (Kumar Patel), Neil Patrick Harris (Himself), Amir Blumenfeld (Adrian), Paula Garces (Maria), Danneel Harris (Vanessa), Tom Lennon (Todd), Danny Trejo (Mr. Perez). Directed by Todd Strauss-Schulson and produced by Greg Shapiro. Screenplay by Jon Hurwtiz and Hayden Schlossberg.

With a title like *A Very Harold and Kumar 3-D Christmas*, here is a film that might be mistaken by the innocent for family entertainment. A better title might have been *A Very R-Rated Harold and Kumar 3-D Christmas.* The gang returns in their third comedy with F-rated language, nudity, excrement, pee, child endangerment, cheerfully offensive ethnic stereotyping, sacrilegious portrayals of Jesus and the Virgin Mary, a large (artificial) 3-D penis leaping from the screen, and so much pot smoking that the film could have been shot using a fog filter.

It's sort of inspiring, isn't it? Kal Penn, the son of immigrants from India, and John Cho, born in South Korea, find success in America as the stars of three big movies making jokes about Indians, Koreans, Chinese, blacks, Latinos, and Jews. We're not really melting in the melting pot if we're not making money from ethnic stereotyping. The rags-to-riches story is even richer; in order to costar in this movie, Kal Penn took a leave of absence as associate director of the White House Office of Public Engagement.

It's not that I was particularly offended; it's that I didn't laugh very much. Ethnic jokes are cutting edge among slack-jawed doper comedies, but sometimes (as in the first and still funny *Harold and Kumar Go to White Castle*) they had touches of wit and insight. Here the humor is intended to pound us over the head. When a white woman tells an Indian man, "I don't date black men," doesn't that rather make you curious to hear how he might respond? How about "most Indians are genetically Caucasian"? What would a dumb blonde say to that? (Sorry, I don't remember if the woman was a dumb blonde. I'm just assuming she was. See how this works?)

I have no idea if this movie was made stoned. Like its predecessors by Cheech and Chong, it might as well have been. One clue: It contains parodies of many film styles and genres. Although I saw it in 2-D, it was easy to tell the big 3-D moments, as in the giant phallus and gusts of smoke blown at the audience. What I wasn't expecting was a scene simulating Claymation. Or footage using the same style of blended motion-capture and animation as in action films.

The plot: Harold (Cho) has drifted away from Kumar (Penn) and become a successful Wall Street trader, where his office is under assault by protesters. Kumar has split up with Vanessa and lives in the ruins of a bachelor apartment. Santa delivers a package for Harold at Kumar's apartment. Kumar delivers it on Christmas Eve to Harold's suburban manse, loaded with Christmas decorations to impress his Mexican father-in-law, Mr. Perez (Danny Trejo), who hates Koreans.

Mr. Perez throws out Harold's gaudy artificial tree and replaces it with a perfect Douglas fir he has lovingly grown for twelve years. The Perez family (so numerous they arrive in a school bus) leave en masse for midnight Mass, the package from Santa contains a giant spliff of holiday weed, Harold throws it out the window, it blows back inside and sets the perfect tree on fire, and the two lads have only a few hours to find a replacement tree in Manhattan or face dire consequences.

That's only the setup. The movie is about the disastrous adventures of H&K as two treacherous African-American tree vendors sell Kumar's reserved tree to someone else, leading, of course, to a chase scene, an overturned SUV, etc. The nature of the slapstick owes a great deal to Cheech and Chong, but somehow the magic energy between Harold and Kumar has faded.

It's my suspicion that Penn and Cho have outgrown the characters, but are contractually sentenced to continue doing remakes as long as the movies make money. Both actors have moved on to other things, and we don't feel the delight of the original 2004 movie or perhaps the (unseen by me) *Harold and Kumar Escape from Guantanamo Bay* (2008). The movie seems a little tired. It's one thing to get a laugh with a lot of baby poo thrown at an SUV window. But when the poo is still there an hour later, you wonder how intensely anyone cares.

## Vidal Sassoon: The Movie ★ ★ ½

PG, 94 m., 2011

Vidal Sassoon, Michael Gordon, Mary Quant, John Frieda, Peggy Moffitt, Ronnie Sassoon, and Beverly Sassoon. A documentary directed by Craig Teper and produced by Gordon and Jackie Gilbert Bauer. Screenplay by Teper and Heather Campbell Gordon.

*Vidal Sassoon: The Movie* might as well be titled *Vidal Sassoon: The Infomercial* for all of the distance it maintains from its subject. Its best quality is that it made me like and admire Sassoon, although if there is anything unlikable and not admirable about him, I wouldn't have discovered it here. The movie is structured around a new book on Sassoon being published by Michael Gordon, who also produced this film and appears in it, and that will give you a notion of its objectivity.

Vidal at eighty-three is alert and superbly fit, a yoga practitioner who still bends into pretzel shapes and lifts weights. The world's most successful hairdresser is the very definition of a self-made man: Born in the Jewish ghetto of London's East End, he was abandoned by his father and placed by his mother in an orphanage for several years—not because she didn't love him, but because she was poor. "She came to see me every week," he says, and in his teens, she apprenticed him to a hairdresser who was a firm disciplinarian. To have unshined shoes or untidy fingernails was a grave offense.

Sassoon never particularly wanted to be a hairdresser. He wanted to be an architect, he tells us, although his spotty education might have put an end to that dream. He was ambitious, and he came to love cutting hair. He worked hard, he was a perfectionist, he soon had a chair in the West End and then his own shop on Bond Street. By then it was the Swinging Sixties, and Vidal Sassoon was at the very epicenter with his revolutionary, architectural haircuts and finally the "five-point cut."

Having never heard of this cut (my ignorances are manifold), I realized on seeing it in this film that I've been looking at it all of my life. To one degree or another, half the women alive must wear their hair differently today because of Vidal Sassoon's scissors. Then came the New York shop, the Vidal Sassoon Academies, the shampoo and hair products line, the daily TV show, the TV commercials for Sassooning, and millions and millions of dollars. Such circles did he move in that once in a health spa, because of a lamentable mix-up, he received an enema intended for Gore Vidal.

It wasn't easy. He was born with a Cockney accent (and demonstrates that very convincingly), and took elocution lessons from a voice coach at the Old Vic. He explained to women why he would not cut their hair the way they wanted it cut. He danced around his clients with a pair of scissors instead of an array of hairdressing hardware. He was married three times, had three children, lost one because of an overdose, is happily married today, and is dedicated to "progressive causes."

There must be more. We will not discover it here. What we will see is a good many classic haircuts and testimonials from current or former employees. There is also an affectionate chat with Mary Quant, who was doing with fashion what Sassoon was doing with hair in the 1960s. It has been a good life. If you know as little about hairdressing as I do, ask yourself two questions: Have you always known Vidal Sassoon was the name of a famous hairdresser? Can you name another one?

## Vincent: A Life in Color ★ ★ ★ ½

NO MPAA RATING, 96 m., 2010

Featuring Vincent P. Falk. A documentary directed and produced by Jennifer Burns.

You have never heard of Vincent P. Falk, but if you've been near Chicago's Marina City you may have seen him. He's the smiling middle-aged man with a limitless variety of spectacular suits. He stands on the Michigan or Wabash avenue bridges, showing off his latest stupefying suit. He flashes the flamboyant lining, takes the coat off, spins it in great circles above his head, and then does his "spin move," pivoting first left, then right, while whirling the coat in the air. Then he puts it on again and waves to the tourists on the boat, by now passing under the bridge.

You might be forgiven for suspecting that

Vincent is a few doughnuts short of a dozen. I know I did. Then I saw the remarkable documentary *Vincent: A Life in Color,* which unfolds into the mystery of a human personality. Would it surprise you to learn Vincent is a college graduate? A Cook County computer programmer? A former deejay in gay North Side discos? Paying his own rent in Marina City? Buying his own suits? Legally blind?

All of these things are true. I can believe he buys his own suits. What I can hardly believe is that they are sold. We accompany him on a visit to his customary clothing store, which perhaps caters otherwise to members of the world's second oldest profession.

Jennifer Burns, the producer and director of the film, says that like most Chicagoans, she'd seen Vincent and his colorful suits around for years. How could she not? Then one day she was looking out her office window, watching him performing for a tour boat, "and I was struck by the look of sheer joy I saw on his face. I thought to myself, whatever else you have to say about this guy, he has figured out what makes him happy and he does it, regardless of what anyone else thinks." She approached him, and he agreed to be the subject of a film—not surprising, since his pastime is drawing attention to himself. The subtext of the film is how differently life could have turned out for Vincent.

Vincent, whose surname comes from the last of his foster families, was an orphan abandoned by his mother and raised at St. Joseph's Home for the Friendless. There the nuns discovered that Vincent's problem wasn't intellectual but visual and taught him to read, along with the rest of the class, making sure he was always pushed up against the blackboard so he could see. In high school he was picked on relentlessly, and learned to respond with humor. He was a member of the National Honor Society, the chess club, the debate team, and the diving team, luckily never diving into a pool without water. We meet his diving coach, who was as surprised as we are.

Vincent reads with his good eye held less than an inch from a book or computer screen. Sometimes he uses a magnifying glass. He used a cane in high school, then threw it away and walks freely everywhere in Chicago. It is terrifying to think of him crossing a street.

Vincent, a bright student, was accepted at the University of Illinois, where he studied computer science. He eventually wound up at the Illinois Institute of Technology, studying aeronautical engineering. Yes. He became a popular deejay, first for the go-go boys at Stage 618, and then at the gay disco Cheeks. He didn't exactly fit the image, his old boss recalls, and he held the albums an inch from his face, but he was a great spinner. It was during this time he concluded he was gay. For the past twenty years, he's been a computer programmer for Cook County, helping to track billions of dollars in tax revenue. "He's one of the most brilliant programmers I've ever met," his current boss says.

All of which is admirable, but how does it explain the suits? He started wearing the suits in the 1990s, and says he gave his first bridge show in 2000, adding the "spin move" about a year later. He knows the times when every tour boat passes his bridges, and the guides know his name and point him out somewhere between the Wrigley Building and Marina City. To the guides on the Mercury boats, he is "Riverace" (rhymes with "Liberace"). The captain of one of the Wendella boats says you can set your watch by him. Both of his bridges and both of the TV studios are within a short walk of his home.

There is a great deal of discussion in the documentary about Vincent's motivation. It solves nothing. Vincent himself will say only that he likes to entertain people, to cheer them up a little. One expert in the doc speculates that Vincent has spent a lot of his life being stigmatized and isolated, and the suits are a way of breaking down barriers. I confess that the first time I saw him, I saw a man with unfocused squinting eyes and a weird suit, and leaped to conclusions. Having seen this film, I applaud Vincent. Here is a man who likes to buy Technicolor suits and wave them at tour boats. So why not? What are the people on the boats so busy doing that they don't have time for that?

*Note: This review is based on my earlier blog entry.*

## Vincere ★ ★ ★ ½

NO MPAA RATING, 128 m., 2010

Giovanna Mezzogiorno (Ida Dalser), Filippo Timi (Benito Mussolini), Fausto Russo Alesi

(Riccardo Paicher), Michela Cescon (Rachele Mussolini), Pier Giorgio Bellocchio (Pietro Fedele), Fabrizio Costella (Young Benito). Directed by Marco Bellocchio and produced by Mario Gianani. Screenplay by Bellocchio and Daniela Ceselli.

The image of Benito Mussolini has been shifted over the years toward one of a plump buffoon, the inept second fiddle to Hitler. We've seen the famous photo of his ignominious end, his body strung upside down. We may remember his enormous scowling visage trundled out on display in a scene from Fellini's *Amarcord.* What we don't envision is Mussolini as a fiery young man, able to inflame Italians with his charismatic leadership.

That's the man who fascinates Marco Bellocchio, and his *Vincere* explains how such a man could seize a young woman with uncontrollable erotomania that would destroy her life. She was Ida Dalser (Giovanna Mezzogiorno), at first his lover, later his worst nightmare. When she first saw him before World War I, he was a firebrand, dark and handsome, and she was thunderstruck. For Ida, there was one man, and that was Benito (Filippo Timi), and it would always be so.

Her feelings had little to do with his politics. *Vincere* might have been much the same film if Mussolini had been a Christian Democrat. Her feelings spring from a fierce love, which at first is mutual. That he is filled with ideas and ambition makes him all the more attractive, but does she even care what those ideas are? She supports them as a matter of course, selling all she has to support his party newspaper.

They have a son. He leaves to serve in the Italian army in the war. He is possibly lost in combat. She doesn't hear from him. It is an old story. When he reappears after the war, it is impossible for him to lie low; he is Mussolini, in his own mind the chosen one. They are reunited briefly, and the old passion is there. Then she discovers he has a wife. A mistress and a child are decidedly . . . inconvenient for him.

It is revealing how inconvenient Mussolini considers them, and how his values were shaped by bourgeois Catholicism despite his politics. As he makes a strategic alliance with the Vatican, he cannot imagine, and he doesn't believe the public can accept, a leader with a mistress. His wife, Rachele (Michela Cescon), certainly cannot. We might assume Ida could be hidden away or even kept in plain sight, like his friend Hitler's Eva Braun. But no.

If Ida had been capable of staying out of sight and staying quiet, some accommodation can be imagined. A discreet government pension. A home in a city distant from Rome. That is not to be. She considers Mussolini a demigod, and with all the passion of a woman defending her child, she wants her son—hers!—to be acknowledged before all the world as the great man's offspring and heir.

Bellocchio, once himself a fiery young artist (*Fists in the Pocket*), now a legend of the generation of Bertolucci, is concerned with Mussolini's fascism primarily as backdrop. His film is focused on Ida. The last time she sees him in the flesh is the last time we do. Thereafter he's seen only in newsreels—a convenient way for Bellocchio to age and fatten him.

We see Ida's marginal, scorned existence. We see her enacting life scenes that could be staged in opera: She bursts upon Mussolini during public appearances, dragging along the hapless boy as evidence of Benito's heartlessness. The boy himself is bewildered, less concerned with his purported father than with his daily existence with a mother consumed by her obsession.

Was she mad? The term is "erotomania," defined by the conviction that someone is in love with you. It can be a complete delusion, as in the case of celebrity stalkers. But it is not delusional if that person *was* in love with you, held you in his arms night after night, and gave you a son. The fascists instinctively protect Mussolini. When Ida appears in public places, she is surrounded and taken away without Benito even needing to request it. Finally, shamefully, she is consigned to an insane asylum and the boy locked up in an orphanage. She becomes a familiar type: the poor madwoman who is convinced the great man loves her and fathered her child. She writes letters to the press and the pope; such letters are received every day.

Bellocchio bases his film on the performance of Giovanna Mezzogiorno. She is one of those actresses, like Sophia Loren, who can combine passion with dignity. As Mussolini, Filippo Timi avoids any temptation to play with the benefit of hindsight. He is ambitious, hopeful, sometimes unwise of success. The film's title, which translates as "victory," reflects for much of the film a hope, not a certainty.

The film is beautifully well mounted. The locations, the sets, the costumes, everything conspire to re-create the Rome of the time. It provides a counterpoint to the usual caricature of Mussolini. They say that behind every great man there stands a great woman. In Mussolini's case, his treatment of her was a rehearsal for how he would treat Italy.

## Vision ★ ★ ★

NO MPAA RATING, 110 m., 2010

Barbara Sukowa (Hildegard von Bingen), Heino Ferch (Brother Volmar), Hannah Herzsprung (Richardis von Stade), Alexander Held (Abbot Kuno), Lena Stolze (Jutta), Sunnyi Melles (Richardis's Mother). Directed by Margarethe von Trotta and produced by Markus Zimmer. Screenplay by Trotta.

Tip O'Neill told us "politics is local," and I suppose that applies as well to a cloistered religious order as to a city. *Vision* is about a remarkable twelfth-century woman named Hildegard von Bingen, who was closed up with a Benedictine order at a young age and rose to become its leader, the author of spiritual books, a composer of music, and an expert in herbal medicine. Although beatified, she was never elevated to sainthood, but is a saint for many feminists and holistic practitioners.

As embodied here by the powerful presence of Barbara Sukowa, she was a considerable woman, and succeeded in gaining almost everything she desired despite a church hierarchy controlled by men. From the age of four she reported visions of God, and as these continued, they gave her authority and won her followers. Indeed, although in a cloister, she was permitted to go on speaking journeys and became quite widely known.

She also succeeded in moving her nuns from within the walls of the male monastery and building their own separate retreat, and then another. This she did despite the fierce objections of her superior, Abbot Kuno (Alexander Held), by appealing over his head to the local archbishop. Still refused permission, she apparently fell into a coma and was revived only by the presence of God. Or that is what she said.

What went on in the mind of this woman, essentially uneducated, who could not read Scripture but learned, wrote her books in her own modified alphabet, and composed one of the largest surviving groups of Gregorian chant? That's what fascinates the German writer-director, Margarethe von Trotta, who makes a choice to view Hildegard's life in its externals and reveal few of the thoughts behind her sometimes forbidding facade. We never know what she's thinking. That's tantalizing.

In the small, closed world where she was raised, she clung to Jutta (Lena Stolze), the child who accompanied her to the cloister. They were "given to the church" as a sort of tithe, their entire lives decided before puberty. It is important to Hildegard to be right, and to be seen as right, and Jutta is her satellite and idolater. A new novice, Richardis von Stade (Hannah Herzsprung), enters the convent and is favored by Hildegard, and an emotional triangle forms that is all the more desperate because none of the three recognize the lesbianism that may be at its core. In another time or place, their interdependent relationships would be recognized as romantic, but here all is sublimated in religion and a struggle for moral supremacy.

Was Hildegard faking her visions and comas? Yes, probably, but she didn't realize it. She seems to have been spellbound by her own legend, and if her deathlike state during one crisis is psychosomatic, it is no less deathlike. She seems to have been an entirely sincere woman, self-deceived to her core. And a good woman, too, whose gifts in so many areas suggest an intelligence that found all the expression it could behind the cloister walls. One of the monks, Brother Volmar (Heino Ferch), recognizes her gifts and helps her to realize them, and so her passion is released in words, music, and church politics rather than in madness.

Trotta is one of the most important feminist directors of recent years. See especially *The Lost Honor of Katharina Blum* (1975),

*Marianne and Juliane* (1981), and *Rosa Luxemburg* (1986). Here she declines to impose a set of feminist ideas. She's intrigued by the well-known story of Hildegard. The film is intense, measured, and too slow, but absorbing. What was life like for this brilliant woman in a world entirely without stature or recognition for women? How did she play the cards she was dealt as a child? How did she maneuver? How aware was she of her uniqueness?

Barbara Sukowa never quite lets us know. She carefully avoids modern body and facial language, and stays within the limits of the age. So does Trotta. We must enter these lives with our imaginations, and realize that no matter what rules society lays down for women—for anyone—ways can sometimes be found to prevail on one's own terms.

## Viva Riva! ★ ★ ★ ½

R, 98 m., 2011

Patsha Bay Mukana (Riva), Manie Malone (Nora), Marlene Longange (Commandante), Hoji Fortuna (Cesar), Diplome Amekindra (Azor). Directed, written, and produced by Djo Tunda Wa Munga.

*Viva Riva!* is the first feature I've seen from the Congo, and the last one I would have expected: a slick, exciting, well-made crime thriller, dripping with atmosphere. The plot would be at home in many countries, but the African locations are a gripping bonus here. You might learn more about Congo from this film than in a documentary, and you'd probably have more fun.

The hero is a good-bad guy named Riva (Patsha Bay Mukana), a charming, fast-thinking con man who has stolen a truckload of gasoline from some crooks in Angola and plans to resell it for a small fortune in Kinshasa. This detail is itself revealing. Some thrillers involve fortunes in gold or diamonds; the poverty and shortages in Congo make a truckload of fuel drums worth a fortune.

Riva is not a cautious thief. He's a partying ladies' man, whose objective in getting money is to spend it. He plans to hold the petrol off the market as gas prices grow higher, and in the meantime plunges headfirst into a shadow world of bars, brothels, conspirators, and gangsters. It is his fate to fall head over heels for Nora (Manie Malone), the mistress of a local crime lord, who only perhaps can be trusted. Oh, she likes him well enough. She also likes staying alive.

Soon Riva is being pursued by the gangster's men and also by some very angry Angolans who want their gasoline back. The writer-director, Djo Tunda Wa Munga, ingeniously entwines this generic plot with a riot of local atmosphere: street life, homes, dance clubs, whorehouses, warehouses, cops and robbers, connivers and stoolies, torture and mayhem. It is a true achievement, I suppose, to make a Congolese feature that is the rival or superior of any hard-boiled Western film.

I guess this is technically a film noir. By centering itself on the mean streets, a noir often records more about a time and place than a studio-centered mainstream drama. Consider that our images of postwar Vienna and London may largely be inspired by *The Third Man* and *Night and the City.* This film moves effortlessly through its locations. It knows its way around. It makes no particular point of poverty, corruption, and the seller's markets created by shortages. It doesn't even bother to point out the irony that the Congo needs fuel that exists in abundance in nearby Nigeria.

The actors all feel like seasoned professionals, assured and persuasive. This is in no sense a bargain-basement production; it's as if a Congolese cinema springs full-blown before our eyes; this is apparently Djo Tunda Wa Munga's first film, but he knows what he's doing.

Apart from its other qualities, *Viva Riva!* has an unconscious authenticity. When big Hollywood stars are surrounded by CGI effects, we're always thinking, "action movie." When new faces are filmed in real places, there is a persuasiveness that's impossible to contrive. The movie offers the rare pleasure of a film that creates its own world, unfamiliar to us but feeling real. It's like a shot in the arm for the action genre.

## The Vow ★ ★ ½

PG-13, 104 m., 2012

Rachel McAdams (Paige), Channing Tatum (Leo), Jessica Lange (Rita Thornton), Sam Neill

(Bill Thornton), Scott Speedman (Jeremy). Directed by Michael Sucsy and produced by Gary Barber, Roger Birnbaum, Jonathan Glickman, and Paul Taulieb. Screenplay by Abby Kohn, Marc Silverstein, Stuart Sender, and Jason Katims.

*The Vow* is a well-behaved, tenderhearted love story about impossibly nice people. It's not even about whether they'll get married. They've been happily married for four years. The problem is, she can't remember them. She can't even remember her husband.

Paige and Leo are a young Chicago couple. She's a Lake Forest blue blood who angered her parents by dropping out of Northwestern Law School, moving into the city, and enrolling at the School of the Art Institute, where she sculpts clay into such forms that Leo mistakes a pile of fresh clay for one of her artworks. Leo has opened an independent recording studio, arguing that although everyone may be able to produce songs on their laptops, he can aim higher—at the heights of an old Sun session, for example.

They live happily. They are in love. She is estranged from her parents. They look great together, and played by Rachel McAdams and Channing Tatum, why shouldn't they? The actors bring a dreamy warmth to the roles. Then one snowy night they're rear-ended by a truck. He wakes up in the hospital. She remains in a drug-induced coma to assist her brain in reducing its swelling. When she recovers, she has no memory of ever meeting or being married to Leo.

Indeed, she thinks she is the same person she was before her life changed. She thinks she still lives with her folks (Sam Neill and Jessica Lange) and is still engaged to Jeremy (Scott Speedman). Her parents, who approved of Jeremy but not of Leo, couldn't be happier, and expect to bring her home with them. Leo convinces her to come home with him and see if any memories return, but it's as if she's living with a stranger.

This film is based on the real-life story of Kim and Krickitt Carpenter; she never did regain her lost memories, but they're together today, with two children. Paige and Leo don't seem headed in that direction. Leo, it must be said, is a paragon of patience, taking her to their favorite date spots, reminding her she's a vegetarian, showing her the studio she has forgotten. But all of this is alien to the old Paige, and she's still attracted to Jeremy.

Scott Speedman is a good choice for the old fiancé. From some camera angles, he reminds us a little of Wile E. Coyote. From head on, he's friendly and handsome. He isn't necessarily a bad guy. Nor are her parents evil, although there is something snaky about the Sam Neill character. They connive to take advantage of her memory loss, which has so conveniently eradicated all of the changes they disapprove of.

This same story could be a fraught melodrama with pumped-up characters and dire consequences. *The Vow* is more of a sweet date movie for Valentine's Day; the women can identify with this poor Paige who belongs with the handsome Leo, and the guys can think that Rachel McAdams has just about the sweetest smile since Marisa Tomei. The more we discover about the story, indeed, the nicer a guy Leo turns out to be. The way the story resolves itself contains poetic justice.

But it's all too painless. One can imagine the anguish of the case in real life. How, really, do you approach the subject of having sex with your husband if you don't remember him? Especially when he is theoretically not the kind of man you would choose, and you believe you're engaged to a man you love? *The Vow* never really grapples with that. It's pleasant enough as a date movie, but that's all.

A footnote. The movie is said to be set in Chicago. It struck me as strange that it has such a large number of second unit shots of the city: skylines, elevated trains, the Music Box theater. Yet the couple themselves are rarely seen there. There is one nice shot of the newlyweds running from the Art Institute across a footbridge into Millennium Park and ending up under The Bean, but otherwise something fishy is going on. Yes, the movie was shot mostly in Toronto. Poor Toronto. Poor Chicago. Poor Paige and Leo. Poor Jeremy, even.

# W

## The Wages of Fear ★ ★ ★ ★

NO MPAA RATING, 148 m., 1953 (rereleased 2012)

Yves Montand (Mario), Charles Vanel (Jo). Directed by Henri-Georges Clouzot and produced by Clouzot and Raymond Borderie. Screenplay by Clouzot and Jerome Geronimi, based on the novel by Georges Arnaud.

When the great French thriller *The Wages of Fear* (1953) was first released in America, it was missing parts of several early scenes—because it was too long, the U.S. distributors said, and because they were anti-American, according to the Parisian critics.

Now that the movie is available for the first time in the original cut of director Henri-Georges Clouzot, it is possible to see that both sides have a point.

The film's extended suspense sequences deserve a place among the great stretches of cinema. Four desperate men, broke and stranded in a backwater of Latin America, sign up on a suicidal mission to drive two truckloads of nitroglycerin three hundred miles down a hazardous road. They could be blown to pieces at any instant, and in the film's most famous scene Clouzot requires them to turn their trucks around on a rickety, half-finished timber platform high above a mountain gorge.

Their journey also requires them to use some of the nitroglycerin to blow up a massive boulder in the road, and at the end, after a pipeline ruptures, a truck has to pass through a pool of oil that seems to tar them with the ignominy of their task. For these are not heroes, Clouzot seems to argue, but men who have valued themselves at the $2,000 a head that the oil company will pay them if they get the nitro to the wellhead where it is needed.

The company, which significantly has the same initials as Standard Oil, is an American firm that exploits workers in the unnamed nation where the film is set. The screenplay is specific about the motives of the American boss who hires the truck drivers: "They don't belong to a union, and they don't have any relatives, so if anything happens, no one will come around causing trouble." There are other moments when the Yankee capitalists are made out as the villains, and reportedly these were among the scenes that were trimmed before the film opened in this country.

The irony is that the trims have been restored at a time when they have lost much of their relevance, revealing that the movie works better as a thriller than as a political tract, anyway. The opening sequence, set in the dismal village where unemployed men fight for jobs, is similar to the opening of John Huston's *Treasure of the Sierra Madre* (1948), even down to the detail of visiting the local barber. But while Huston used his opening to establish his characters and work in some wry humor, Clouzot creates mostly aimless ennui.

Although eager to establish his anti-American subtext, he reveals himself as a reactionary in sexual politics with the inexplicable character of Linda (Vera Clouzot), who does menial jobs in the saloon. She is in love with one of the local layabouts (Yves Montand, in his first dramatic role), who slaps her around and tells her to get lost, and she spends most of her time sprawled on the ground, although always impeccably made up. There is no apparent purpose for this character, apart from the way she functions to set up such lines as, "Women are no good." If the opening sequences, now restored, have a tendency to drag, the movie is heart-stopping once the two trucks begin their torturous three-hundred-mile journey to a blazing oil well. The cinematographer, Armand Thirard, pins each team of men into its claustrophobic truck cab, where every jolt and bump in the road causes them to wince, waiting for a death that, if it comes, will happen so suddenly they will never know it.

Clouzot does an especially effective job of setting up the best sequence, where first one and then the other truck has to back up on the unstable wooden platform in order to get around a hairpin bend in the trail. The first truck is used to establish the situation, so we know exactly what Montand is up against when he arrives at the scene: Rotten timbers break, the truck begins to slide sideways, a steel support cable gets caught on the side of the truck, and we are watching great technical work as it creates great fiction.

When William Friedkin remade *The Wages*

*of Fear* as *Sorcerer* in 1977, he combined this scene with a later one in a jungle setting to create a sequence where a truck wavers on a vast, unstable suspension bridge. Friedkin had greater technical resources, and his sequence looks more impressive, but Clouzot's editing selects each moment so correctly that you can see where Friedkin, and a lot of other directors, got their inspiration.

One thing that establishes *The Wages of Fear* as a film from the early 1950s, and not from today, is its attitude toward happy endings. Modern Hollywood thrillers cannot end in tragedy for their heroes because the studios won't allow it. *The Wages of Fear* is completely free to let anything happen to any of its characters, and if all four are not dead when the nitro reaches the blazing oil well, it may be because Clouzot is even more deeply ironic than we expect. The last scene, where a homebound truck is intercut with a celebration while a Strauss waltz plays on the radio, is a reminder of how much Hollywood has traded away by insisting on the childishness of the obligatory happy ending.

## Waiting for "Superman" ★ ★ ★ ½

PG, 102 m., 2010

Geoffrey Canada, Michelle Rhee, Bill Strickland, David Levin, Mike Feinberg, Daisy Esparza, Bianca Hill, Anthony Black. A documentary directed by Davis Guggenheim and produced by Michael Birtel and Lesley Chilcott. Screenplay by Davis Guggenheim and Billy Kimball.

Toward the end of *Waiting for "Superman,"* there is a sequence that cuts between lottery drawings for five charter schools. Admission to the best of these schools dramatically improves school graduation and acceptance by a college. The applicants are not chosen for being gifted. They come from poor, disadvantaged neighborhoods. But the schools have astonishing track records.

We have met five of these students, talked to them and their parents, and hope they'll win. The cameras hold on their faces as numbers are drawn or names are called. The odds against them are twenty to one. Lucky students leap in joy. The other nineteen of the twenty will return to their neighborhood schools, which more or less guarantee a 50 percent drop-out rate. The key thing to keep in mind is that underprivileged inner-city kids at the magnet schools, such as Kipp LA Prep or the Harlem Success Academy, will do better academically than well-off suburban kids with fancy high school campuses, athletic programs, swimming pools, closed circuit TV, and lush landscaping.

*Waiting for "Superman,"* the new documentary by Davis Guggenheim, says the American educational system is failing, which we have been told before. He dramatizes this failure in a painfully direct way, says what is wrong, says what is right. One of his charts gets a laugh from the audience: Of students in a group of developed nations, Americans rank last in math skills. When the students are asked to guess their standing, Americans put themselves first. Meanwhile, jobs in Silicon Valley go without qualified Americans to fill them, and tech companies must import skilled employees from India and other poor countries.

Guggenheim focuses on an African-American educator named Geoffrey Canada, who deliberately chose the poorest area of Harlem to open his Harlem Success Academy. His formula: qualified teachers, highly motivated, better paid. Emphasis on college prep from day one. Tutoring for those behind in math or reading. There are also charter boarding schools with no TV, no video games. One kid says he wants in, but "my feelings are bittersweet."

One problem with most schools, Guggenheim says, is that after teachers gain tenure in two years it is almost impossible to fire them. In Illinois, for example, one out of 57 doctors loses his medical license, but only one in 2,500 teachers is fired. Some teachers flatly inform their students they have no intention of teaching. Guggenheim blames the powerful American Federation of Teachers, which is the top donor to national Democratic campaigns and state Republican campaigns. Any move to discipline incompetent teachers is met with fierce resistance. A union teacher is a teacher for life. That teachers themselves accept this is depressing.

The film demonstrates (1) that quality education is possible for even the most disadvantaged students; (2) the cost is low, considering that high school dropouts often turn to crime when they can't find good jobs. In ten years, there will be twice as many skilled, well-paid jobs in America as Americans qualified to fill them.

What struck me most of all was Geoffrey Canada's confidence that a charter school run on his model can make virtually *any* first-grader a high school graduate accepted by college. A good education, therefore, is not ruled out by poverty, uneducated parents, or crime- and drug-infested neighborhoods. In fact, those are the very areas where he has success. Consider this: Those lotteries are truly random, as by law they must be. Yet most of the winners will succeed, and half the losers (from the same human pool) will fail. This is an indictment: Our schools do not work.

Our nation is willing to spend trillions on war and billions to support the world's largest prison population rate. Here is a modest proposal: Spend less money on prisons, and more money on education. Reduce our military burden, and put that money into education. In twenty years you would have more useful citizens, less crime, and no less national security. It's so simple.

*Note: My review of a doc about a similar school in Chicago,* The Providence Effect, *is at http://j.mp/bkqXBZ.*

## Waking Sleeping Beauty ★ ★ ★ ½

PG, 86 m., 2010

Featuring Ron Clements, Roy Disney, Jeffrey Katzenberg, Peter Schneider, Rob Minkoff, Michael D. Eisner, Lisa Keene, George Scribner, Gary Trousdale. A documentary directed by Don Hahn and produced by Hahn and Peter Schneider. Screenplay by Patrick Pacheco.

In 1985, when Disney released *The Black Cauldron* to box office disappointment, the animation tradition at the studio was on life support. The studio that began a revolution with *Snow White and the Seven Dwarfs* seemingly no longer knew how to make an animated feature. Roy Disney, Walt's nephew and the largest single stockholder, masterminded an executive shakeup that brought in three men from Paramount: Michael Eisner, Frank Wells, and Jeffrey Katzenberg. That began a second golden age at Disney.

It is enough to name the animated films they made: *Who Framed Roger Rabbit, The Little Mermaid, Beauty and the Beast, Aladdin,* and *The Lion King.* These films proved beyond question that animation was a genre with great international appeal for moviegoers of all ages. Coupled with the home video revolution, they were responsible for literally billions pouring into the studio. Eisner, Katzenberg, and Roy Disney, however, had personal tensions (Michael and Roy thought Jeffrey was getting too much attention as the studio's boy wonder), and after the peacemaker Frank Wells died in a helicopter crash in 1994, the magical period ended.

*Waking Sleeping Beauty,* made by the studio after all but Disney had left (he died in 2009), is an extraordinary inside look at those ten years. It uses footage and taps into insights, memories, and home movies that only insiders would have access to. Its director and narrator is Don Hahn, who produced *Beauty and the Beast, The Lion King,* and *The Hunchback of Notre Dame,* among others. Another featured narrator is Peter Schneider, who became president of feature animation in 1985, head of Walt Disney Studios in 1999, and left in 2001.

*Siskel and Ebert* was produced by Disney during all of those years, and I had some contact with these men, and with Rich Frank, studio head before Schneider. Rich would amuse audiences by showing a reel of Siskel and me trashing some of his productions. Michael and Jeffrey insisted that everyone call them—and everyone else at the studio—by their first names. Peter Schneider came on board with a lower profile. One year at Rancho la Puerta, Chaz and I shared a dinner table with a smart, likable young couple from L.A. After a few days, *Siskel and Ebert* came up. "You know I work at Disney," the man said. Really? What do you do? "I'm the president."

It was like that then. I don't know what it's like now. There were rumors that Eisner and Katzenberg didn't get along, and countless articles analyzing why Jeffrey left and/or was pushed after Wells's death. A scene in this film goes a long way to explain the tension. When Jeffrey was in charge of all animation, Eisner announced at a studio meeting that a major new animation building would be constructed. It came as news to Katzenberg.

The most fascinating scenes in *Waking Sleep-*

*ing Beauty* involve the infamous Disney work ethic. Friends of mine at the studio said the unofficial motto was, "If you didn't come in on Saturday, don't even bother to come in on Sunday." Animators worked so hard they developed anxiety, migraines, carpal tunnel syndrome. The "family studio" required such long hours that some marriages failed. When Katzenberg held a no-holds-barred meeting with the animators, he actually teared up at their stories and relented. But he always came in on Sundays.

The film gives good screen time to the artists who created the films with their own minds and hands and worked in collaboration. There's even a glimpse of young Tim Burton, chained to a drafting board. A tension-breaking Mexican party in the animation department is recalled with the nostalgia of combat veterans given a week of R&R. Whatever happened, happened. The fact remains that those years were revolutionary, and if not for them, it's a good question whether Pixar, DreamWorks, and the other animation production sources—and Disney Animation itself—would still exist. Credit is due.

## Wall Street: Money Never Sleeps ★ ★ ★

PG-13, 130 m., 2010

Michael Douglas (Gordon Gekko), Shia LaBeouf (Jake Moore), Josh Brolin (Bretton James), Carey Mulligan (Winnie Gekko), Eli Wallach (Julie Steinhardt), Susan Sarandon (Jake's Mother), Frank Langella (Louis Zabel). Directed by Oliver Stone and produced by Stone, Eric Kopeloff, and Edward R. Pressman. Screenplay by Allan Loeb and Stephen Schiff, based on characters created by Stone and Stanley Weiser.

Oliver Stone's 1987 film *Wall Street* was a wake-up call about the financial train wreck the Street was headed for. Had we only listened. Or perhaps we listened too well, and Gordon ("Greed is good") Gekko became the role model for a generation of amoral financial pirates who put hundreds of millions into their pockets while bankrupting their firms and bringing the economy to its knees. Gekko has been able to cool his heels for many of the intervening years in a federal prison, which is the film's biggest fantasy; the thieves who plundered the financial system are still mostly in power, and congressional zealots resist efforts to regulate the system.

That's my point, however, and not Oliver Stone's. At a time when we've seen several lacerating documentaries about the economic meltdown, and Michael Lewis's *The Big Short* is on the best-seller lists, *Wall Street: Money Never Sleeps* isn't nearly as merciless as I expected. It's an entertaining story about ambition, romance, and predatory trading practices, but it seems more fascinated than angry. Is Stone suggesting this new reality has become embedded, and we're stuck with it?

In some ways Gordon Gekko himself (Michael Douglas) serves as a moral center for the film. Out from behind bars, author of *Is Greed Good?* and lecturer to business students, he at first seems to be a standard repentant sinner. Then he meets a young trader named Jake Moore (Shia LaBeouf) and finds himself edging back into play. Jake wants to marry Gekko's daughter, Winnie (Carey Mulligan), who hasn't spoken to her father for years. Maybe he can be the conduit for their reconciliation. He sincerely loves Winnie, who is a liberal blogger. Jake himself is ambitious, already has his first million, and wants more, but we see he has a good heart because he wants his firm to back alternative energy. Is this because he is green, or only likes it? A little of both, probably.

Jake works for an old-line Wall Street house named Keller Zabel, headed by his mentor and father figure Louis Zabel (Frank Langella). This firm is brought to its knees by a snake named Bretton James (Josh Brolin), who is instrumental in spreading rumors about its instability. Stone doesn't underline the irony that James's firm, and every Wall Street firm, is equally standing on a mountain of worthless debt. In a tense boardroom confrontation, Zabel is forced to sell out for a pittance. The next morning he rises, has his soft-boiled egg, and throws himself under a subway train. It is instructive that although tycoons hurled themselves from windows during the crash of 1929, the new generation simply continued to collect their paychecks, and Gekko expresses a certain respect for Zabel.

The death of his beloved mentor gives Jake a motive: He wants revenge on Bretton James, and suddenly all the parts come together: how he can hurt James, enlist Gekko, look good to

Winnie, gain self-respect, and maybe even make a nice pile of money along the way. It has taken an hour to get all the pieces in place, but Stone does it surely, and his casting choices are sound. Then the story hurries along as more melodrama than exposé.

Michael Douglas, of course, is returning in an iconic role, and it's interesting to observe how Gordon Gekko has changed: just as smart, just as crafty, still with cards up his sleeve, older, somewhat wiser, keenly feeling his estrangement from his daughter. Shia LaBeouf, having earlier apprenticed to Indiana Jones and at the beginning of this film with Louis Zabel, falls in step eagerly beside Gordon Gekko, but may discover not everyone in his field wants to be his mentor. Langella has little screen time as Zabel, but the character is crucial, and he is flawless in it. To the degree you can say this about any big player on Wall Street, Zabel is more sinned against than sinner. And then there's Carey Mulligan as Gekko's daughter, still blaming him for the death of her brother, still suspicious of the industry that shaped her father and now seems to be shaping Jake.

*Wall Street: Money Never Sleeps* is six minutes shorter than it was when I saw it at Cannes, and has a smoother conclusion. It is still, we might say, certainly long enough. But it's a smart, glossy, beautifully photographed film that knows its way around the Street (Stone's father was a stockbroker). I wish it had been angrier. I wish it had been outraged. Maybe Stone's instincts are correct and American audiences aren't ready for that. They haven't had enough of greed.

## War Horse ★ ★ ★ ½

PG-13, 146 m., 2011

Emily Watson (Rosie Narracott), David Thewlis (Lyons), Peter Mullan (Ted Narracott), Niels Arestrup (Grandfather), Jeremy Irvine (Albert Narracott), Tom Hiddleston (Captain Nichols), Benedict Cumberbatch (Major Jamie Stewart). Directed by Steven Spielberg and produced by Spielberg and Kathleen Kennedy. Screenplay by Lee Hall and Richard Curtis, based on the novel by Michael Morpurgo and the stage play by Nick Stafford.

The closing shots of Steven Spielberg's *War Horse* will stir emotions in every serious movie lover. The sky is painted with a deeply red-orange sunset. A lone rider is seen far away on the horizon. The rider approaches and dismounts. He embraces a woman and a man. They all embrace the horse's head. Music swells. This footage, with the rich colors and dramatic framing on what is either a sound stage or intended to look like one, could come directly from a John Ford Western.

It is Spielberg's homage, I believe, to Ford and to a Hollywood tradition of broad, uplifting movies intended for all audiences. The performances and production values throughout honor that tradition. *War Horse* is bold, not afraid of sentiment, and lets out all the stops in magnificently staged action sequences. Its characters are clearly defined and strongly played by charismatic actors. Its message is a universal one, about the horror of war in which men and animals suffer and die, but for the animals there is no reason: They have cast their lot with men who have betrayed them.

The movie, based on a best-selling novel and a long-running London and New York stage production, begins on a small family farm in the county of Devon. We meet young Albert Narracott (Jeremy Irvine), his usually drunken but not unkind father, Ted (Peter Mullan), and his hardworking, loving mother, Rosie (Emily Watson). Lyons (David Thewlis), the landowner, presses them for past-due rent.

There is a horse auction in the village. Ted's eye falls on a handsome horse named Joey and he determines to outbid Lyons for it, even if it means spending all the rent money. Rose is distraught: He was meant to bring home a plow horse at a low price and has purchased a sleek thoroughbred. But Albert and Joey bond, and Albert trains the horse to accept a collar and plow their stony fields. Then World War I breaks out. Drunk as usual, Ted sells the horse to the army. Albert vows he will see it again.

Now begins a series of self-contained chapters in Joey's life, as the horse passes from British to German hands, has a respite on a French farm, and then finds itself helping to drag a cannon much too big for the team. All of this is embedded in front-line battle footage as realistic as we saw in the landing at Normandy in Spielberg's *Saving Private Ryan.*

All wars are hell. Surely few were worse for private soldiers trapped in the muddy, cold desolation of the trenches. Horses thrown into this satanic chaos were confused, terrified, and sometimes driven mad.

Joey meets a series of masters, most of them on both sides men who respected horses. Yet war is no place for sentiment, and as an officer explains with brutal realism, a horse is a weapon and must either be used or destroyed. Surely some of the best footage Spielberg has ever directed involves Joey and other horses running wild outside the trenches, galloping in a panic through barbed wire lines and dragging wire and posts after them as their flesh is cruelly torn. There's one of those scenes of temporary truce when soldiers from both sides meet in No Man's Land to share wire cutters and set the horse free.

All of this is magnificent. But it reduces the center of the film to a series of set pieces. The narrative thread is supplied by Joey, who is such a helpless protagonist that watching his adventures becomes painful—especially, I suspect, for younger viewers. A famous film by Robert Bresson, *Au Hazard Balthazar*, follows a humble donkey through years of good and bad times, and shows all of the events as implacable chapters in the book of its life. Bresson makes no attempt to elevate the mule; its lot is the common lot of all dumb animals in a world of arbitrary cruelty.

Spielberg ennobles Joey and provides an ending for the film that is joyous, uplifting, and depends on a surely unbelievable set of coincidences. I suppose it must be that way for us to even bear watching such a story. I am reminded of *Schindler's List*. Six million Jews were exterminated in the Second World War, but in focusing on a few hundred who miraculously survived, Spielberg made his story bearable. Among the horses of World War I, it can only be said that Joey's good luck was extraordinary.

The film is made with superb artistry. Spielberg is the master of an awesome canvas. Most people will enjoy it, as I did. But not included in the picture is the level of sheer hopeless tragedy that is everywhere just out of frame. It is the same with life, and if you consider the big picture, all of us, men and beasts, have extraordinary good luck.

## Warrior ★ ★ ★

PG-13, 139 m., 2011

Joel Edgerton (Brendan Conlon), Tom Hardy (Tommy Conlon), Nick Nolte (Paddy Conlon), Jennifer Morrison (Tess Conlon), Frank Grillo (Frank Campana), Kevin Dunn (Principal Zito), Maximiliano Hernandez (Colt Boyd), Bryan Callen (Himself), Sam Sheridan (Himself), Vanessa Martinez (Pilar Fernandez), Kurt Angle (Koba), Erik Apple ("Mad Dog" Grimes). Directed by Gavin O'Connor and produced by Greg O'Connor. Screenplay by Gavin O'Connor, Anthony Tambakis, and Cliff Dorfman.

*Warrior* is a fight picture that arrives with perfect logic at a climax involving not one but three key bouts, and we forgive the coincidence that provides not one protagonist but two. The screenplay uses these devices to combine the structure of a rags-to-riches fighting story not unlike *Rocky* with the rich, seamy drama of a troubled family.

In an hour of scenes that establish them separately, we meet two brothers, Brendan and Tommy Conlon (Joel Edgerton and Tom Hardy). Brendan is a high school science teacher, married with children. Tommy is a Marine back from fighting in the Middle East. Both were high school wrestlers, trained by their father, Paddy (Nick Nolte). Now the circumstances of life bring them independently to the same decision: They need to fight to make a living.

Once this premise is clear, it is as certain as night follows day that Brendan and Tommy will meet in the ring for the championship. That accounts for the three climactic rounds, because each has to advance through a semifinal. What is intriguing is that *Warrior* doesn't have a favorite. We understand and like both characters, and so does the film. Director and cowriter Gavin O'Connor arrives at that standoff by playing fair: Both have motives, they are long estranged after an unhappy split in childhood, and in some ways they hate each other.

When their mother left their alcoholic father, it was Tommy who went with her to California and watched her die. It was Brendan who stayed with his dad. When we meet Paddy in the film, he is approaching Day 1,000 of sobriety after a lifetime of drinking, and embodies, as only Nick Nolte can, the shaggy, weathered heroism of a man who is trying one more time to pull himself together.

Tommy always blamed Paddy for abandoning his mother, although it wasn't that simple. Now he turns up in South Philadelphia after many years, fresh from the war, keeping a secret. He asks the old man to be his trainer for a mixed martial arts championship. Neither one has the slightest idea Brendan might be involved. Meanwhile, Brendan faces foreclosure on his house, but when he wins the purse at a low-level MMA fight in a tent in a parking lot, things get worse because he's fired from his job.

Mixed martial arts is a sport that perplexes me. I never quite understand how any of the fighters stay conscious for even one round. Hitting, butting, kicking, tripping, and slamming are all part of the game, and I may be naive but it all looks real to me. The punishment the fighters take is so severe that it strains credulity that the final matches are held during such a small time frame.

The fight scenes are choreographed and filmed with great energy and probably too much Queasy-Cam. Although the fighters must duck and weave, why must the camera? Various subplots involving Nolte, Brendan's wife (Jennifer Morrison), and his trainer (Frank Grillo) are intercut with the action, and although Gavin O'Connor is not shy about exploiting action, he uses the full force of strong characters to give it more meaning than action alone could supply.

This is a rare fight movie in which we don't want to see either fighter lose. That brings such complexity to the final showdown that hardly anything could top it—but something does, and *Warrior* earns it.

## Waste Land ★ ★ ★

NO MPAA RATING, 99 m., 2010

Vik Muniz, Fabio Ghivelder, Isis Rodrigues Garros, Jose Carlos da Silva Baia Lopes (Zumbi), Sebastiao Carlos dos Santos (Tiao), Valter dos Santos, Leide Laurentina da Silva (Irma), Magna de Franca Santos, Suelem Pereira Dias. A documentary directed by Lucy Walker, codirected by Joao Jardim and Karen Harley, and produced by Angus Aynsley and Hank Levine.

Across the world's largest garbage dump, near Rio de Janeiro, the pickers crawl with their bags and buckets, seeking treasures that can be recycled: plastics and metals, mostly, but anything of value. From the air they look like ants. You would assume they are the wretched of the earth, but those we meet in *Waste Land* seem surprisingly cheerful. They lead hard lives but understandable ones. They make twenty or twenty-five dollars a day. They live nearby. They feel pride in their labor, and talk of their service to the environment.

While the alleys of Chicago remain cluttered with ugly blue recycling bins that seem to be ignored and uncollected, these pickers rescue tons of recyclables from the dump and sell them to wholesalers, who sell them to manufacturers of car bumpers, cans, plastics, and papers. They raise their children without resorting to drugs and prostitution. They have a pickers' association that runs a clinic and demonstrates for their rights. From books rescued from the dump, one picker has assembled a community library. The head of the association says he learned much from a soggy copy of Machiavelli, once he had dried it out. He quotes from it, and you see that he did.

I do not mean to make their lives seem easy or pleasant. It is miserable work, even after they grow accustomed to the smell. But it is useful work, and I have been thinking much about the happiness to be found by work that is honest and valuable. If you set the working conditions aside (which of course you cannot), I suggest the work of a garbage picker is more satisfying than that of a derivatives broker. How does it feel to get rich selling worthless paper to people you have lied to?

*Waste Land*, the documentary by Lucy Walker that has been nominated for an Academy Award this year, takes as its entry point into the lives of the pickers the work of the Brazilian artist Vik Muniz. As a youth he had the good fortune to be shot in the leg by a rich kid, who paid him off; he used the money to buy a ticket to America, and now he is famous for art that turns garbage into giant constructions, which he exhibits and photographs.

Perhaps Walker intended to make the film

about Muniz. If so, her subject led her to a better one; as he returns to Rio to photograph pickers for a series of portraits, she begins to focus on their lives. We see where they live, we meet their families, we hear their stories, we learn of the society and economy they have constructed around Jardim Gramacho, "Gramacho Gardens." I was especially pleased by a woman named Zumbi, who stirs a huge cauldron of beef stew in her outdoor kitchen constructed at the site.

The workers bring her unspoiled meat and usable vegetables, she says, and that is easy to believe if you have ever been to one of the all-meat restaurants facing the Copacabana beach, where chefs wheel enormous pieces of beef, pork, lamb, and poultry from table to table to carve slices and pile them on your plate. The waste here must be considerable.

Muniz has the advantage of speaking the same language as the pickers, and having come from poverty. When he tells them his portraits will give them and their work recognition, they agree and are happy to cooperate—especially Tiao, who organized their association. Muniz intends to donate all the proceeds from his portraits to the pickers, which is simple enough, but then he and his wife, Janaina Tschape, have a discussion about whether he should invite Tiao to come along when his portrait is auctioned at Phillips.

Can you leave the life of a picker, fly to another country, stay in luxury, and then return to a garbage heap? How do you handle that? It is a matter for endless debate, but eventually Tiao does join Muniz at the auction, where his portrait follows an Andy Warhol, and wins a bid of $50,000. His reaction is to cry, as Muniz embraces him. He feels this is recognition for his life, for his determination to start the association, and for the dignity of his work.

If it makes it difficult for Tiao to return to the Garden, well, it was difficult to be there in the first place. Last year I saw a documentary named *Scrappers*, about the men who travel the alleys of Chicago seeking scrap metal. There is also Agnes Varda's great film *The Gleaners and I* (2000), about those who seek their livings in the discards of Paris. When we see men going through the cans in an alley, some of us tend to distrust and vilify them. They are earning a living. They are providing a service. Incredibly, they're sometimes called lazy. Documentaries like these three help us, perhaps, to more fully appreciate our roles as full-time creators of garbage.

## Water for Elephants ★ ★ ★

PG-13, 122 m., 2011

Reese Witherspoon (Marlena), Robert Pattinson (Jacob), Christoph Waltz (August), Paul Schneider (Charlie), Jim Norton (Camel), Hal Holbrook (Old Jacob), Mark Povinelli (Kinko/Walter), Richard Brake (Grady). Directed by Francis Lawrence and produced by Gil Netter, Erwin Stoff, and Andrew R. Tennebaum. Screenplay by Richard LaGravenese, based on the novel by Sara Gruen.

There's something endearingly old-fashioned about a love story involving a beautiful bareback rider and a kid who runs off to join the circus. What makes *Water for Elephants* more intriguing is a third character, reminding us why Christoph Waltz deserved his Academy Award. He plays the circus owner, who is married to the bareback rider and keeps her and everyone else in his iron grip.

The story, based on the best-seller by Sara Gruen, is told as a flashback by an old man named Jacob (Hal Holbrook), who lost his parents in 1931, dropped out of the Cornell veterinary school, hit the road, and hopped a train that happened, wouldn't you know, to be a circus train. Played by Robert Pattinson as a youth, he is naive and excited, and his eyes fill with wonder as he sees the beautiful Marlena (Reese Witherspoon) on her white show horse. The owner, August (Waltz), is prepared to throw him off the train until he learns young Jacob knows something about veterinary medicine.

In an age of prefabricated special effects and obviously phony spectacle, it's sort of old-fashioned (and a pleasure) to see a movie made of real people and plausible sets. The production designer, Jack Fisk, has created a believable one-ring circus here, and even the circus train itself has a personality. (August and Jacob spend an implausible amount of time walking or running on top of it, but never mind.)

The dynamic in the story depends on August's jealousy of Marlena and her stubborn loyalty to their marriage contract. This is where Waltz makes his contribution. Shorter than Pattinson, indeed hardly taller than Witherspoon, he rules everyone as a hard-bitten taskmaster whose easy charm conceals a cold inner core; it's the same dynamic he used as the merciless Nazi in *Inglourious Basterds.* He's much given to offering champagne toasts with a knife hidden inside.

In the early Depression, times are hard and jobs few. The circus is deep in debt, and August produces a new star attraction he thinks can save it. This is Rosie, a middle-age elephant he thinks Marlena can ride and Jacob can train and care for, although neither has worked with an elephant before. Scenes involving the personality and language comprehension of elephants create an intrinsic charm, and the movie surrounds them with a convincing portrait of circus life on the road.

The film's climax involves a series of dire events I will not describe, except to say it's a little unclear how they are started into motion. It's also unclear why Marlena continues to be such a dutiful wife long after August no longer deserves that privilege—but the fact that she does saves the character from dissolving entirely into melodrama.

*Water for Elephants* was directed by Francis Lawrence, whose *I Am Legend* and *Constantine* were not predictions of this relatively classic film. The screenplay is by Richard LaGravenese, whose *Horse Whisperer* also showed a sympathy for the personalities of animals. Rosie is not as charismatic as a horse, and as Jacob observes, she suffers from dry skin, but you have to concede that her timing is impeccable. This is good, sound family entertainment, a safe PG-13 but not a dumb one, and it's a refreshing interlude before we hurtle into the summer blockbusters.

## The Way ★ ★ ★

PG-13, 128 m., 2011

Martin Sheen (Tom), Emilio Estevez (Daniel), Deborah Kara Unger (Sarah), Yorick van Wageningen (Joost), James Nesbitt (Jack). Directed by Emilio Estevez and produced by Estevez, David Alexanian, and Julio Ferandez. Screenplay by Estevez.

Emilio Estevez's *The Way* was inspired by his son, stars his father, is dedicated to his grandfather, and is written and directed by him: a sweet and sincere family pilgrimage, even if a little too long and obvious. Audiences seeking uplift will find it here.

The story involves a California optician named Tom (Martin Sheen, Estevez's father), whose son Daniel dies while attempting to complete the Camino de Santiago, a centuries-old pilgrimage over high Spanish mountain country to the Cathedral de Santiago. Daniel was apparently religious. Tom is definitely not. He flies to Spain to identify his son's body, oversees its cremation, and decides on the spot to scatter the ashes along the way that Daniel planned to trek. In a nice touch, he even uses Daniel's backpack and hiking gear.

Daniel (played by Estevez) appears to Tom from time to time, in visions or imagination, as he rethinks their relationship. That adds a touching buried level to the story because in real life Estevez and his father are making the same journey in order to make this film. Their life relationship has been as loyal and healthy as possible, in contrast to the family outrider, Charlie Sheen, whom one cannot imagine walking three steps along this path.

A two-hour film of a surly man walking alone is not a promising idea. Although he prefers to keep his distance from others, Tom finds himself journeying with three other pilgrims. The most entertaining is Joost (Yorick van Wageningen), a cheerful Dutchman, whom Tom does his best to ditch but keeps turning up, undiscouraged. Then there is Sarah (Deborah Kara Unger), an unhappily divorced woman from Canada, who looks rich in a way that hasn't bought her happiness. And Jack (James Nesbitt), an Irish writer, who unfortunately embodies most of the garrulous jollity of the Irish and little of the wit and charm.

They are traversing beautiful country, which Estevez's camera employs without postcard excesses, and along the way they, of course, encounter colorful locals and fellow pilgrims, have some small adventures, and (inevitably) nearly lose the container with the ashes. At the end, Tom has arrived at some sort of reconciliation with his son and forgives him for having undertaken the damn fool pilgrimage in the first place.

That isn't a lot to happen in a full-length film, and after a point it begins to seem much of a muchness. Your response to it may depend on how receptive you are to the idea of the journey. Since both Sheen and Estevez are public about their Catholicism, I'm not sure what the point was of making Tom so firmly secular; perhaps so that even he, following so many centuries of footsteps, can sense some of their spirituality. *The Way* is a nice film. Not great, not urgent, but quietly positive.

## The Way Back ★ ★ ½

PG-13, 133 m., 2011

Jim Sturgess (Janusz), Ed Harris (Mr. Smith), Colin Farrell (Valka), Sebastian Urzendowsky (Kazik), Gustaf Skarsgard (Voss), Saoirse Ronan (Irena), Mark Strong (Khabarov). Directed by Peter Weir and produced by Joni Levin, Nigel Sinclair, and Duncan Henderson. Screenplay by Peter Weir and Keith R. Clarke, based on the book *The Long Walk: The True Story of a Trek to Freedom* by Slavomir Rawicz.

Not every incredible story makes a compelling movie. *The Way Back* is inspired by a four-thousand-mile foot journey that began with an escape from a Siberian prison camp in the dead of winter and continued across Mongolia and the Gobi Desert, ending finally months later in free India.

At every moment this is astonishing. Mongolia itself was said to be a prison because no one was thought able to walk out of it. Starvation is a daily possibility. So are injuries, disease, death by exposure, or capture by locals eager to collect a reward. Thirst and sun are nearly fatal in the desert. The travelers have only the clothes on their backs. We know some of them reached India, because the saga opens with that news.

But how did they possibly do that? Just as we're told: by walking. Walking and walking. And there lies the weakness of Peter Weir's film, which is nobly staged and has breathtaking cinematography, but frankly, not enough of a story in the vulgar populist sense. Desperation and exhaustion make it difficult for the trekkers to work up much in the way of characters or conflicts, and while that no doubt spares us many clichés, we are left, during their long walk, with too much of a muchness.

The group is often so bearded and weathered that members seem interchangeable. Two who stand out are Ed Harris, an American who claims his name is only "Mr. Smith," and Colin Farrell as Valka, a Russian. Has Harris ever given a bad performance? The group is led by Jim Sturgess as Janusz, who had the idea for the escape. Along the way they meet Irena (Saoirse Ronan), a young Polish woman. Her presence does not inspire romantic rivalries among the men. It's that kind of film.

Peter Weir is a master filmmaker (*Picnic at Hanging Rock, The Year of Living Dangerously, Master and Commander*). His cinematographer, Russell Boyd, works both in tight quarters and with astonishing vistas at the roof of the world. The film is a visual feast. I am far from sorry I saw it.

But there is one area in which it seems to be lacking. Details of survival. How exactly did they survive death by exposure in subzero Mongolia? Why didn't some of their meat spoil? Where did they find water in the desert? How did their footwear hold up—and why, as prisoners, did they have boots?

The answer, I fear, is that although *The Way Back* is described on its poster as "inspired by real events," it is fiction. The saga was first told in a best-selling book by Slavomir Rawicz, which was a European best-seller. But IMDb reports: "In 2006 the BBC unearthed records (including some written by Rawicz himself) that showed he had been released by the USSR in 1942."

There is an irony here. The film exhibits an admirable determination to do justice to a real story, but the story's not real. There's quite an op-ed debate going on right now between those (Neal Gabler) who say the cultural elite is finally being shouted down by populists and vulgarians, and others (A. O. Scott) who say such categories are meaningless. You like movies according to your own tastes.

Some people have bad taste and others have taste more like mine. Yet my taste is large. It contains multitudes. There is room for vulgarity, if it's well done. It's a shame to say so, but perhaps it would have helped *The Way Back* if Peter Weir had relaxed his standards slightly, slipped in some dramatic conflict, and made better use of that pretty Polish girl.

## W.E. ★ ★ ½

R, 119 m., 2012

Abbie Cornish (Wally Winthrop), Andrea Riseborough (Wallis Simpson), James D'Arcy (Edward), Oscar Isaac (Evgeni), David Harbour (Ernest), James Fox (King George V), Laurence Fox (Bertie), Natalie Dormer (Elizabeth). Directed by Madonna and produced by Kris Thykier and Colin Vaines. Screenplay by Madonna and Alek Keshishian.

There's dialogue in *W.E.* that probably holds some truth about the strange attraction the then-King Edward VIII felt for Wallis Simpson, the twice-divorced American he valued more than the British throne. Quoting from memory: "She absolutely possesses him. Not dominates. Possesses." There were tales that theirs was a sadomasochistic union, but as it's seen in *W.E.*, Madonna's new film, it seems based more on their mutual fascination with the awfulness of the thing they have done.

The movie indicates it was Edward who insisted they marry. Apparently so. He wanted to make a grotesque sacrifice in giving himself to this woman who, after all, was not that beautiful, not that young, and not that irresistible. As the Duke and Duchess of Windsor, their marriage lasted from 1937 to 1972, and they were known above all for maintaining a facade of high style, harmony, and no trace of regret. She was considered the epitome of chic and set a global standard with her clothes, her jewelry, her taste. What a shabby trade-off for the throne.

Madonna cowrote the film and has apparently been fascinated by the duchess for many years. That may explain why this is the story of two women, decades apart: Wallis Simpson (Andrea Riseborough) and Wally Winthrop (Abbie Cornish). Riseborough looks convincing with her white skin, red lips, severe hairstyle, and haute couture. I at least never found the duchess feminine, let alone sexy. Wally Winthrop is a fictional character, a rich, married Manhattanite whose thuggish husband slaps her around. She haunts the display at Sotheby's auction house of the Windsors' possessions: tablecloths, candlesticks, cigarette cases, crystal, silver. These totems are fetishes for her.

She's noticed by a smooth Sotheby's security guard named Evgeni (Oscar Isaac), and they feel an immediate sexual tension. I am not sure why the character or the tension exist. There are no expository scenes explaining how the stories of the two women are intended to connect; but obviously they must because Madonna bridges time and space to have them actually meet and discuss things they have found to be true.

This is an elegant, ambitious, and relentlessly monotonous film. Its period details seem authentic, its casting of historical figures (King George V, Queen Mary, Prime Minister Stanley Baldwin, and even Al Fayed) is convincing, and its visual style is mannered to project effortless continuity. But there is little human interest or excitement. It isn't written that way. The music and the dialogue seem curiously even and muted, and there aren't the kinds of drama we expect in a biopic. Everyone is too restrained and discreet to expose themselves. The movie's climax (and it is handled well) comes at a formal dinner party when Wallis calls King Edward "David," his semisecret family name; of course she shouldn't know it, and still less should a commoner use it on familiar terms in a reprimand. The king had ripped her dress by catching it under the leg of his chair, and what delicious irony that their great public scene should be inspired by her fashionable clothing.

I suppose the more you bring to *W.E.* the more you will take away from it. Unlike the popular movie *The King's Speech*, which involves Edward's brother George becoming King George VI, it doesn't make things clear as it goes along. When you walk in you'd better have all the characters straight in your mind. These are the kinds of people for whom so much goes without saying that there's hardly anything left to say. I suppose the monotonous tone of the spoken dialogue may be accurate; the duke and duchess don't seem to be demonstrative. Were they witty? Did they joke with each other? Did they say the things lovers say? Did they actually ever have sex? After seeing the film, I don't have a clue.

They seem to have existed for thirty-five years within a bubble, like creatures in a snow globe, he as the man who renounced the throne of the British Empire in order "to marry the woman I love," and she as that woman. He did it, they married, and were forever defined by that moment. If she possessed him, it is hard to see how she went about doing that. Something about her compelled him to need to be possessed. In a way, he may have forced the possession upon her. God, what an awful life it must have been, and how terrible that they may not have even known that.

## We Bought a Zoo ★ ★ ½

PG, 124 m., 2011

Matt Damon (Benjamin Mee), Scarlett Johansson (Kelly Foster), Thomas Haden Church (Duncan Mee), Patrick Fugit (Robin Jones), Elle Fanning (Lily Miska), Colin Ford (Dylan Mee), John Michael Higgins (Walter Ferris). Directed by Cameron Crowe and produced by Julie Yorn. Screenplay by Crowe and Aline Brosh McKenna, based on the book by Benjamin Mee.

There really is a Benjamin Mee, and he and his family really did buy a zoo. The Dartmoor Zoological Park in Devon, England, was opened in 1968, closed in 2006, and then was purchased by the Mee family. In adapting these facts into the movie *We Bought a Zoo*, all Cameron Crowe has done is move it to Southern California, supply it with a staff of character actors, and add two romances and a villain. The result is too much formula and not enough human interest.

Not that the film is without charms. Matt Damon makes a sturdy and likable Benjamin Mee, and Scarlett Johansson, as the head of the zoo's animal keepers, seems adamantly unaware that she's in a script that requires her to sooner or later kiss the hero. We even see Patrick Fugit, immortal as the hero of Crowe's *Almost Famous*, as a member of the zoo staff. He's never seen without a monkey on his shoulder, although that's his only point of interest. ("What do we do to make the Robin Jones character interesting?" "He always has a monkey on his shoulder").

At the outset, the movie's Benjamin Mee (Damon) is still in mourning after the death of his wife. He's raising their kids, Dylan (Colin Ford), in his midteens, and Rosie (Maggie Elizabeth Jones), who is seven. Dylan is nabbed for shoplifting and Benjamin, a journalist, decides it's time to leave the big city and raise them in the country. He finds an ideal house, which the real estate agent only gradually explains comes with its own menagerie. The place was once a private zoo, shut down for reasons involving money and regulations, and Kelly Foster (Johansson) minds the animals with the help of Peter MacCready (Angus MacFadyen), a pipe-puffing Scotsman, and Kelly's teenage cousin Lily (Elle Fanning), who seems not entirely unaware that she's in a script that may require her to sooner or later kiss Dylan.

Benjamin's brother Duncan (Thomas Haden Church) is an accountant who urgently advises Ben not to buy a zoo. Well, that's the function of a good accountant. How many times has my own accountant, John Foy, entreated me, "Roger, whatever you do, don't buy a zoo!"

Kelly is a great-looking woman (after all, she looks like Scarlett Johansson), but she's all business, dedicated to the welfare of the animals. She can see that Benjamin has a lot to learn. One of their first differences involves Spar, an old Bengal tiger who is in deep depression (so would we all be, if we had to live alone for sixteen years in an efficiency apartment). Should Spar be put down? Kelly and Ben have an emotional debate.

The villain is Walter Ferris (John Michael Higgins), an anal retentive animal control officer who enforces strict standards involving the care and housing of the animals. Walter is a nitpicker and a bit of a sadist, threatening to deny the place a license if fences don't comply within a fraction of an inch. He is invaluable to the writers, Aline Brosh McKenna and Crowe himself, providing them with a device to generate a series of crises and deadlines through which Benjamin and his staff, working together, begin to bond. Cute young Lily's love for the animals soon begins to inspire Dylan to dial down and begin to love the zoo.

You'd think a movie like this would be ideal for animal lovers. Not so much. The animals are mostly held at arm's length, like, well, animals in a zoo. Some snakes get closer; a sequence involving a crate of big poisonous snakes seems completely contrived. (Are snakes always shipped with dozens to the crate? Why do the snake crates inevitably break open in movies?)

*We Bought a Zoo* started me thinking about *The Descendants.* Both involve fathers faced with raising two kids (about the same ages) after the deaths of their wives. Both have big stars as their leads. Both involve making major life decisions. One has Hawaii as a supporting character, one has a zoo. *The Descendants* is getting some of the best reviews of the year. *We Bought a Zoo* not so much. Cameron Crowe has made wonderful films, but here the pieces go together too easily, the plot is too inevitable, and we feel little real energy between the players. It's pitched at a lower level of ambition.

## Weekend ★ ★ ★

NO MPAA RATING, 96 m., 2011

Tom Cullen (Russell), Chris New (Glen), Jonathan Race (Jamie), Laura Freeman (Jill), Jonathan Wright (Johnny), Loretto Murray (Cathy). Directed by Andrew Haigh and produced by Tristan Goligher. Screenplay by Haigh.

Remember the one about the dying actor's final words? "Dying is easy. Comedy is hard." The new British independent film *Weekend* suggests another truth: "Sex is easy. Love is hard." The movie involves two gay men who meet in a bar, wake up in bed the next morning, and begin a conversation that unexpectedly grows very deep. Some aspects involve homosexuality, but this isn't a "gay film." Most people can identify with Russell and Glen.

That's because some of us are more open and some of us are more guarded. Some of us trust easily, and others more slowly. Some of us have sexual feelings that are not open for discussion. Some of us pretend to be who we think we *ought* to be, and do it so well that even close friends don't know who we really are.

Russell (Tom Cullen) is a lifeguard for a swimming pool in Nottingham. This is a job on the way to other things. He's gay, and his friends, who are mostly straight, understand that in a general way. He goes to a straight party, relates well, and later goes cruising in a gay bar. We gather his sex life is conducted out of view of his friends. He ends up taking Glen (Chris New) home with him.

The next morning, Glen pulls out a recorder and begins to quiz him on sexual and personal topics. This is part of a vaguely explained "project." Glen, we learn, works in the art world. Their conversation is skillfully composed by the writer-director, Andrew Haigh, whose dialogue is never facile and moves sideways into more serious areas, such as whether Russell is completely comfortable with his sexuality and with specific practices. This conversation isn't forced, but friendly, and we sense that Russell is slowly opening up more than he usually does.

Time passes, Russell texts Glen, they meet up again, and an intimacy begins to develop that neither one was perhaps expecting. They like each other. Maybe very much. Maybe they're one of those rare couples "meant" for each other. Sometimes you meet someone, are intense for a while, never see each other again, and years later find yourself wondering if that time you missed the boat.

In some ways *Weekend* resembles the two Richard Linklater landmarks, *Before Sunrise* and *Before Sunset.* Years passed in the lives of the characters between those two films, but when they started talking again, the connection was still there. *Weekend* unveils its own sunset, or sunrise, as Glen reveals personal plans that suggest he and Russell may not have an indefinite future ahead of them.

The possibility of a deadline doesn't make them urgent or desperate, but more willing to reveal themselves—Russell in particular. Their meeting and brief relationship now take on a poignancy, a bittersweet value that makes it more special. This is a smart, sensitive, perceptive film, with actors well-suited to the dialogue. It underlines the difficulty of making connections outside our individual boxes of time and space.

## We Have a Pope ★ ★ ★ ½

NO MPAA RATING, 102 m., 2011

Michel Piccoli (Melville/Pope), Nanni Moretti (Professor Bruzzi), Renato Scarpa (Cardinal

**Gregori), Jerzy Stuhr (Spokesperson), Margherita Buy (Bruzzi's Wife), Franco Graziosi (Cardinal Bollati), Camillo Milli (Cardinal Pescardona), Roberto Nobile (Cardinal Cevasco), Ulrich von Dobschütz (Cardinal Brummer), Gianluca Gobbi (Swiss Guard). Directed by Nanni Moretti and produced by Moretti, Jean Labadie, and Domenico Procacci. Screenplay by Moretti, Francesco Piccolo, and Federica Pontremoli.**

What a terrible thing it would be to be the pope! What unthinkable responsibilities to fall on your shoulders at an advanced age! No privacy. No seclusion. No sin. There's a scene near the beginning of *We Have a Pope* when the College of Cardinals has been locked away from the world inside the Vatican. They cannot leave their quarters or communicate with the outside in any way until they elect the next pontiff and a puff of white smoke goes up from the little chimney atop the ancient building.

Nanni Moretti's camera studies the faces of these old men. They are white, black, Asian, wrinkled, spotty, apprehensive. We can read their minds. They're all thinking the same thing: "Not me, oh Lord! Don't choose me! I am not worthy!"

Several ballots are taken. We learn the faces and names of the leading candidates. The film has some fun with an ill-equipped TV reporter who mistakes gray smoke for white. There seems to be a stalemate. Finally a crucial vote is taken, and by some holy alchemy the cardinals all seem to be settled on the same man. "Melville . . . Melville . . . Melville," we hear, and the camera regards an old and frightened man who seems almost to shrink inside his vestments.

The actor is Michel Piccoli, eighty-six years old, winner of the best actor award at Cannes in 1980, a favorite actor of that noted atheist Luis Bunuel, with whom he made seven films, including *The Milky Way*, in which he played the Marquis de Sade. That alone would comprise a career, but he has worked with virtually every notable director and made more than two hundred features. This is one of his most endearing roles, and he brings great love to it.

It's clear Melville is a compromise choice—an old man, well liked, expected to leave the papacy vacant again before too many years have passed. The Swiss Guards take up their posts on a balcony overlooking St. Peter's Square, a Vatican spokesman and a senior cardinal appear, and the ancient words are intoned: "*Habemus Papam!* We have a pope!" Then we hear an unearthly scream. The announcement comes to a halt. All eyes are on Melville, quailing on his chair, his face buried in his hands.

He simply can't do it. He begs to be forgiven. Unfortunately, this is impossible. The will of God has spoken through the cardinals, and they are in no position to overrule Him. Vatican officials urge him to have a little rest, compose himself. It is even arranged for him to meet with Italy's best psychiatrist (the director Moretti himself), although he is baffled by the questions. Then he slips out of sight, runs through the Vatican City, and escapes onto the streets of Rome. Since his election hasn't been made public, he is just another old priest, and quickly enough he finds civilian clothes.

There are elements of comedy here, and some very low-key slapstick, but the film is respectful to the church and the papacy and takes no cheap shots. (A Vatican PR man does indeed use the F-word over the phone to Melville, but one imagines such things happen.) Melville wanders anonymously through the streets of Rome, meeting all sorts of people, enjoying simple everyday pleasures he hasn't experienced for years. As a young man, he always dreamed of being an actor, and he encounters a friendly theatrical troupe.

Piccoli brings warm humanity to those scenes. The film intercuts them with the action inside the Vatican, which has great entertainment value. The cardinals by law remain sealed from sight. They are joined by the psychiatrist, who also cannot be allowed to leave, and Moretti makes the shrink a catalyst for card games and even a volleyball tournament. There are arguments over the menus, and the rules of bridge, and the composition of the volleyball teams, and it's possible the cardinals haven't had so much fun in years.

Nanni Moretti is a much-loved Italian director whose films are usually warmly humanist. You may remember *The Son's Room* (2001), which won the Grand Prize at Cannes.

There's an inside joke in *We Have a Pope*, involving the enthusiasm with which his character organizes the volleyball tournament. In real life, Moretti has played water polo at the national level.

*We Have a Pope* is a film with great heart. Much of it comes from Michel Piccoli, who, let it be noted, may be eighty-six, but is not decrepit and is capable of outsmarting the Vatican posse on his trail. He approaches his role with seriousness, giving full weight to the frightening responsibilities it asks him to take on. A great deal of the plot involves Vatican tradition and politics, but this is not a cynical film. Quite the contrary. God has spoken, and it's up to the Vatican to make the best of it.

## Welcome to the Rileys ★ ★ ★

R, 110 m., 2010

James Gandolfini (Doug Riley), Kristen Stewart (Mallory), Melissa Leo (Lois Riley), Eisa Davis (Vivian). Directed by Jake Scott and produced by Giovanni Agnelli, Scott Bloom, Michael Costigan, Ridley Scott, and Tony Scott. Screenplay by Ken Hixon.

*Welcome to the Rileys* takes two old plots and makes a rather touching new plot out of them. What we've seen before is (1) the good man who hopes to redeem a prostitute, and (2) the frozen suburban couple who find new hope in their marriage. The film involves such characters in a story that is a little more real and involving than we expect.

James Gandolfini stars as Doug Riley, an Indianapolis plumbing supplies contractor. His wife, Lois (Melissa Leo), hasn't been able to leave their house in years. He's having an affair with Vivian (Eisa Davis), a black waitress at a pancake house, and their two brief scenes together show enormous warmth. He isn't ready to leave his wife, however, perhaps because he knows she would not survive alone. Their daughter was killed at fifteen in a car crash.

Doug goes to New Orleans for a convention, is depressed, wanders into a stripper bar, and finds himself through no desire of his own receiving a hard sell from Mallory (Kristen Stewart). He doesn't want sex. He wants to talk. She thinks he's crazy. She is worn and wounded, hostile and vulnerable. He drives her home and ends up fixing her plumbing, cleaning her shabby shotgun house, and offering her $100 a day to stop hooking.

We think we see where this will lead. That's not where it leads. Ken Hixon's screenplay deliberately avoids most of the obligatory dialogue in a situation like this, and throws some curves at us. One of the surprises involves Lois. Mired in deep depression, Doug decides with a jolt to sell his business and stay in New Orleans. When he informs Lois, she finds the courage to leave the house and drive herself down to New Orleans.

Now watch how she reacts to the reality of her husband's relationship with Mallory. This involves good writing and acting. She is a grown-up. She isn't jealous; she's more concerned that he's crazy. He isn't defensive; he's matter-of-fact. This is Mallory, she's a sixteen-year-old runaway, he's helping her, she doesn't want help. That's how it is.

It's such a relief to be spared the usual clichés here, and observe how Leo so convincingly channels a woman's mothering instinct. It's good, too, to see how director Jake Scott uses the physical presences of his well-cast actors. Stewart is far from the porcelain perfection of the *Twilight* movies, and it's a relief to see that it is, after all, physically possible for a teenager to have complexion problems in a movie. Leo is worn out by loss and worry, but is smart and kind.

And look at what Gandolfini does. He's a mountain of a man, but gentle, not threatening. In terms of body language, he establishes his character in a scene where he crawls into bed with his wife and the mattress sags and he burrows into his pillow and looks—comfortable. When he smokes, his huge hands dwarf his cigarette (there's a subtle tweak: He uses regular cigarettes, not king size, because they make his huge hands look even larger).

I was struck at once by the uncanny accuracy of his central Indiana-Illinois accent. I grew up in downstate Illinois hearing men speak exactly like him. A kind of firm, terse understatement, on a flat, factual note. I could close my eyes and imagine one lifelong friend in particular. Going online, I found that the coastal critics as a group thought he was using a Southern accent, "for some reason." They've never been to the Midwest, and possibly never to the South. We all sound the same to them. Gandolfini has the accent spot on, and it's certainly not one we've heard before from him.

*Welcome to the Rileys* does a convincing job of evoking its New Orleans locations. Mallory's house is messy and forlorn. Her street is depressing. The city at night seems a contrast between artificial merriment and loneliness, and more evocative than another city known for sin, Las Vegas.

What happens between the three people I will not say. The film introduces them, makes them plausible, and then what happens is pretty much what might happen. These people haven't studied up on their archetypes. Each one is doing the best possible, under the circumstances.

## We Need to Talk About Kevin ★ ★ ★ ★

R, 111 m., 2012

Tilda Swinton (Eva), John C. Reilly (Franklin), Ezra Miller (Kevin, Teenager), Jasper Newell (Kevin, Six to Eight Years), Rock Duer (Kevin, Toddler), Ashley Gerasimovich (Celia). Directed by Lynne Ramsay and produced by Jennifer Fox, Luc Roeg, and Robert Salerno. Screenplay by Ramsay and Rory Stewart Kinnear, based on a novel by Lionel Shriver.

It must be something like this to have a nervous breakdown. We find ourselves inside the mind of a woman whose psychopathic son has driven her over the edge. This is not entirely his fault. We gather she didn't want to get pregnant, isn't sure why she's married, was a mother who tried to mask hostility with superficial kindness. If she had her way, she would put her life on rewind and start all over again—maybe even as somebody else, since she's not very fond of herself.

*We Need to Talk About Kevin* is fragments of time, jagged and confusing, lurching around inside her mind. The film moves without any pattern between past, present, and who knows when. We cling to guidelines like the length of Tilda Swinton's hair to figure out when we are. For much of the film she lives with her husband, son, and daughter in an expensive suburban home, and when we realize they've lived there for several years, we begin to wonder, how can four people occupy a home for over a decade and not accumulate *anything*? The shelves and tabletops are as barren as those in a display home. What kind of a kitchen has empty counters? These people live there, but they've never moved in.

The mistake would be to take the film apart and try to reconnect the pieces in chronological order. The wife and mother, Eva (Swinton), has been so overwhelmed by despair that her life exists in her mind all at the same time. There is no pattern. Nothing makes sense. She isn't even really at the center of it; that position is occupied by her son, Kevin, who is an instinctive sadist with a gift for knowing exactly how to wound her, reject her, deceive her, and make her soul bleed. Kevin does things to Eva in this movie that are so cruel that an evil demon seems to be regarding her from his eyes.

That the film works so brilliantly is a tribute in large part to the actors. Kevin is seen at three ages. As a baby he is merely colicky and irritating and would try the patience of a saint. Between the ages of six and eight, played by Jasper Newell, he is a clever little monster who glares at her hurtfully, soils his pants deliberately, and drives her into such a fury that she breaks his arm. In any other movie, that would be child abuse. In this one, it is Kevin's triumph.

As a teenager, Kevin (now played by Ezra Miller) has started to cruelly resemble his mother in profile and hair. A demon seed. He is loving and affectionate with his father, Franklin (John C. Reilly), and has a way of making it clear that it's a deliberate charade designed only to hurt Eva. Franklin himself lives in a state of demented decency, deceiving himself that his family is living acceptable lives. He's positive, cheerful, disconnected, always behaves as nicely as he can, and in doing so suggests his profound cluelessness. Only the daughter, Celia (Ashley Gerasimovich), seems halfway normal.

An early scene shows Eva apparently participating in an orgy in a lake of blood. This turns out to be some sort of annual Italian tomato festival, but the image is disturbing. Eva apparently thought her early life was on the right track, and tells her screaming baby boy she would frankly rather be back in Paris than changing his diaper. He can't understand her, but don't you suppose he understands her dislike? Apparently even before he began to talk, Kevin made a vow to punish Eva for her feelings.

In an ordinary movie, there would be scenes in classrooms, meetings with counselors, heart-to-heart discussions between the parents. Not here. They never talk about Kevin. I have the feeling that Lynne Ramsay's film, by entering Eva's mind, sees only what has been battering her down for sixteen years. Ramsay regularly cuts to a scene where Eva is driving her car past flashing police lights toward the scene of some tragedy. Maybe everything else is intended to be a flashback, and the timeline begins when she finds out what Kevin did at his high school. Then she goes home. Does she ever.

Eva often looks in a state of shock. Her organism can't absorb more punishment. She is the wrong person in the wrong life with the wrong child. Is her husband as zoned out as he seems, or is that only her perception? As the portrait of a deteriorating state of mind, this is a masterful film. Swinton told me of a line in the script that wasn't used, wisely, I believe. After you see the film, think about it. She asks Kevin why he didn't kill her. "You don't want to kill your audience," he tells her.

## We the Party ★ ★ ★ ½

R, 104 m., 2012

Mandela Van Peebles (Hendrix Sutton), Simone Battle (Cheyenne Davis), Moises Arias (Quicktime), YG (Conscious Criminal), Mario Van Peebles (Mr. Sutton), Snoop Dogg (Big D), Patrick Cage II (Chowder), Ryan Vigil (Que), Makaylo Van Peebles (Obama), Morgana Van Peebles (Megan), Maya Van Peebles (Michelle Bailey), Salli Richardson-Whitfield (Principal), Michael Jai White (Officer Davis). Directed by Mario Van Peebles and produced by Michael Cohen, Dwjuan F. Fox, and Tal Vigderson. Screenplay by Van Peebles.

It's oversimplifying to compare *We the Party* to *The Breakfast Club* because both involve teenagers thrown together into a situation that tests them and helps them grow. A better comparison would be with *House Party* (1990), not least because it features so much music.

The movie's excuse for most of the music is a house party, thrown by the hero and involving a hip-hop contest with a cash prize, and a talent show connected to the high school prom. But the movie is about a lot more, and despite its flashy cinematography and colorful sets it contains a great deal that is serious about growing up in America today.

The movie was written and directed by Mario Van Peebles (*New Jack City*), who says he got the idea when some of his kids threw a party at their house. Mario, I should add, has five children, and four of them appear here, including Mandela Van Peebles, who plays Hendrix Sutton, a graduating senior who gets good grades—perhaps because of, or even in spite of, his father (played by Mario) being one of his teachers.

The movie takes place in a high school where many of the students come from affluent backgrounds. Hendrix is particularly aware of that, and his feeling of privilege inspires a dramatic event late in the film that's more effective because it's so unexpected.

*We the Party* accepts that teenagers are obsessed by the opposite sex, but it also realizes that many of them are more innocent than you might assume. This is a California high school where some of the kids are uptight about still being virgins on prom night. The movie walks a fine line, lacking scenes of specific sexuality but easily including enough scenes around a backyard Jacuzzi to explain the (soft) R rating.

Once again, as with *Bully*, the MPAA ratings board cleverly prevents admission to kids who might especially value this movie. That's despite the fact that Hendrix's big party bans booze, has a license, two paid chaperones, and cops dropping by because one of their kids is attending. Nobody in the movie even smokes—except for one ominous older brother who smokes a lot of pot and doesn't seem much improved by it.

Anyway, to get back to the central romance, Hendrix is besotted by a classmate named Cheyenne Davis (Simone Battle), whose willingness to skinny-dip in the Jacuzzi will certainly imprint itself on the book of his life.

This is a generation familiar with computers and social media, and that leads to a stupid bet that almost shipwrecks this budding romance.

Relations between the many races at this school are not fraught, and one of the most endearing characters is a not-real-tall white kid named Quicktime (TV star Moises Arias). He's a much-liked member of Hendrix's crowd who always knows what's happening and spreads the news; at his backstage computer he controls lights and effects during the big talent show.

All these kids are media-savvy. In the film's most powerful sequence, Hendrix and three friends collaborate on a video production as their senior class project. Of course they have a pro-level video camera, and of course they meet while driving two convertibles, a VW and a Mercedes. They begin on Skid Row, planning to pay homeless people five dollars to be interviewed. Three of them are scared to get out of the cars. Hendrix breaks the ice, and gets a priceless interview from a toothless bum. Then things take a turn when they meet two homeless white girls who are about their age with a tragic story of parental abandonment and homelessness. The filmmakers grow very solemn. I don't know why, but the inadequacy of their parting words to these girls seemed heartbreaking to me: "Well, good luck," they say.

Another major player is a student calling himself Conscious Criminal (played by the rapper YG). He's got two strikes against him, one thanks to a brother who made him take a rap. He's the only student in school who makes a point of skulking inside a black hoodie. His neck is completely tattooed, with a dollar sign on his Adam's apple. He is the poster child for your parents' definition of Bad Company. His whole attitude says, "Don't —— with me," but perhaps he is simply lonely and afraid. Hendrix knows him better than some, which leads to a climactic scene when the funds for the prom are stolen.

The way that scene is handled shows the instincts of a father in Mario. Hendrix gets mixed up in it, and so does his mother, the school principal (Salli Richardson-Whitfield). There is no way I can describe what happens without making it sound cornball, but it's not. It's a scene about morality and courage, and it leads to the movie's core message: Stay in school. Get an education. Don't let your life go down the drain.

Mario Van Peebles is a gifted filmmaker (his father, Melvin Van Peebles, all but invented Blaxploitation, and is glimpsed here in a cameo). Mario has a message and is ingenious in the way he embeds it in a display of wall-to-wall music, high-energy split-screen montages, and singularly attractive actors. One of his films is *Baadasssss!* (2003), about how his father made *Sweet Sweetback's Baadasssss Song* (1971). Now here's a film with four of his children. I find that heartening.

## What to Expect When You're Expecting ★ ★ ½

PG-13, 109 m., 2012

Cameron Diaz (Jules), Jennifer Lopez (Holly), Elizabeth Banks (Wendy), Chace Crawford (Marco), Brooklyn Decker (Skyler), Ben Falcone (Gary), Anna Kendrick (Rosie), Matthew Morrison (Evan), Dennis Quaid (Ramsey), Chris Rock (Vic), Rodrigo Santoro (Alex), Joe Manganiello (Davis). Directed by Kirk Jones and produced by Mike Medavoy, Arnold Messer, and David Thwaites. Screenplay by Shauna Cross and Heather Hach, inspired by the book by Heidi Murkoff.

Just what we needed. First *Friends with Kids* two months ago, about three couples who confront pregnancy, and now *What to Expect When You're Expecting*, about five couples so much in synch that deliveries and an adoption occur on the same day. I'd rather see a movie about one couple, treated in some depth, than these round-robins with the editor working up a sweat to keep all the interlocking stories in the air.

*What to Expect* is a cheerful comedy with just enough dark moments to create the illusion it's really about something. Cameron Diaz, Jennifer Lopez, Elizabeth Banks, Anna Kendrick, and Brooklyn Decker are prospective mothers, and as three live childbirths are intercut, Diaz wins the screaming contest as people shout "Push! Push!" at her. The girl's a trouper. Maybe we should be grateful that Lopez, in Ethiopia to meet her adoptive son, doesn't start screaming in sympathy.

But I'm being too snarky. This is a good-hearted movie with some winning performances, but it has so many characters (including a boys' club of new dads who stroll together in the park) that the plot nearly stalls with gridlock. It's clever, but the stories are thin soup, as they must be.

There seems to be an informal law that characters in a movie like this must have unusual and colorful occupations to provide easy markers as we move among stories. Diaz plays Jules, who is a TV weight-loss guru; we meet her and her boyfriend Evan (Matthew Morrison) just as they win a celebrity dance show on TV. When they're presented with a loving cup, Jules throws up into it. Gosh, maybe she's pregnant?

Wendy (Elizabeth Banks) is a best-selling advocate of breast-feeding, who despairs of ever getting a chance to practice it herself. She and her husband, Gary (Ben Falcone), have been tirelessly trying to conceive as slaves to an ovulation schedule that once sends them racing into the back room of a baby store for a quickie. Gary has spent years in the shadow of his father, Ramsey (Dennis Quaid), a millionaire NASCAR champion whose trophy wife, Skyler (Brooklyn Decker), is about forty years younger. When Gary and Wendy proudly announce, "We're pregnant!" Ramsey wins again—he and Skyler are having twins.

Jennifer Lopez plays a famous photographer, seen scuba-diving to shoot manta rays. After she and Alex (Rodrigo Santoro) cannot conceive, they adopt the little Ethiopian, who looks adorable enough to pose for Gerber ads. We're not out of cool jobs yet. Rosie (Anna Kendrick) and Marco (Chace Crawford) own competing food trucks, which vend fast food at events. She gets pregnant via a one-night stand, complaining at the hospital, "We never even went out on a real date."

Counterpoint for these stories, as if one was needed, is a quartet of new dads who meet weekly to wheel baby carriages through the park. They're led by Vic (Chris Rock), who is rich in one-liners. On every stroll they meet their mutual friend Davis (Joe Manganiello), a narcissistic fitness buff who would rather work out than impregnate anyone. In one gratuitous scene, he does pull-ups on a bar perfectly positioned to show off his six-pack abs, and then does one-armed pull-ups while using the other hand to check his cell phone. No call is that important.

Three of the stories synch in delivery rooms of the same hospital. The other two have happy endings. What the five couples have in common is that they're all in the same movie. The only interlocking stories are the NASCAR hero and his son. No, wait—the son is connected to Diaz because he was on her weight-loss show.

The movie is essentially a clothesline on which to display trigger-pushing moments. I grew weary of circling endlessly among the various stories. The actors are all good company, and I would have enjoyed seeing more of each role, something I suspect they would agree with me about. The movie is inspired by the longtime best-seller of the same title by Heidi Murkoff. It is nonfiction, which is just as well; there's no room here for anything more.

## Where Do We Go Now? ★ ★ ½

PG-13, 110 m., 2012

Claude Baz Moussawbaa (Takla), Layla Hakim (Afaf), Nadine Labaki (Amale), Yvonne Maalouf (Yvonne), Antoinette Noufaily (Saydeh), Julien Farhat (Rabih), Ali Haidar (Roukoz), Kevin Abboud (Nassim). Directed by Nadine Labaki and produced by Labaki and Anne-Dominique Toussaint. Screenplay by Labaki, Jihad Hojeily, and Rodney Al Haddad.

Here's a notion: Peace in the Middle East would come about more easily if it was governed by women. After relegating women to inferior or invisible roles in society, many of the region's nations are governed by men who want to prove how big their balls are. Even religious strife is largely fueled by testosterone, not theology. Although women are also flawed, in their natures they lean toward compromise and accommodation. They don't see everything as a test.

Nadine Labaki's *Where Do We Go Now?* is an intriguing comedy in which the women of a tiny, isolated Lebanese village conspire to bring about peace. The local Christians and Muslims have coexisted since time immemorial. Recently the men, inflamed by the introduction of TV and its outside news, have decided the two groups are enemies. When two crowds get into a shoving match, it's always the insecure hotheads who take the lead.

Members of the two religious groups are virtually identical in culture. They do the same jobs, eat the same food, like the same music, speak the same language.

So why do they fight? They're victims of ancient tribal instincts that evolved long before religion did. Men are bred to be warriors and defend the people in their caves. Now, even though they all live side by side, religious differences have put them in virtual cages. Sit them down and ask them to discuss their differences in belief, and they'd be at a loss for words.

The film opens with yet another procession of women dressed in black. They're going to the town cemetery, which has separate sections for Muslim and Christian corpses, as if it makes a difference. They clean tombstones, polish marble, pull weeds, plant flowers, and caress the faded photos of their loved ones that have been mounted in tacky frames. Too many of their men have died for stupid reasons. "Do you think we exist simply to mourn you?" one woman shouts at a group of men who are worked up for imaginary reasons.

Now these women decide to take steps to trick their men into calming down and living peacefully. Led by Amale (Labaki herself), who is secretly in love with a man from the other religion, they conspire to do what women have done for ages: manipulate their men, whose hungers and weaknesses they know so well.

That's where the movie's comedy comes in, since truth to tell, the opening scenes are funereal. They sabotage the television set. They stage-manage fake miracles. They get the men giggling together by feeding them hashish brownies.

And in their most inspired move, they enlist a drive in men that is stronger than religious devotion: sex. They import a busload of "exotic dancers" from the Ukraine, dreaming up an excuse about why they happen to find themselves here in the Lebanese boonies. This device reminded me of the wonderful film *The Band's Visit*, which was about an Egyptian police band that mistakenly found itself in a small Israeli village.

The Ukrainian performers turn out to be jolly good sports and inspire the men to realize how much they have in common. The local women are safe from detection because who would dream they could be capable of such a thing? Good feelings spread in the village, and tempers cool somewhat.

It's not really that simple, of course. There have been real tragedies here. One mother has lost her child. Emotions that can lead to death are not so easily defused by comedy, and that's the movie's problem. It's not so easy to alter our mood in response to the movie's prompts. The movie is never quite bold enough to point out the contradiction of Muslims and Christians hating one another even though they both in theory worship the same god.

Still, it's a brave try by Labaki. Lebanon was at one time known as a nation that rose above sectarian hatred; Beirut was known as the Paris of the Middle East. All of that was blown apart by senseless religious wars, financed and exploited in part by those who sought power and wealth. If women had been in charge, would they have been more sensible? It's a theory.

## The Whistleblower ★ ★ ★ ½

R, 112 m., 2011

Rachel Weisz (Kathryn Bolkovac), David Strathairn (Peter Ward), Nikolaj Lie Kaas (Jan Van Der Velde), Anna Anissimova (Zoe), Monica Bellucci (Laura Levin), Vanessa Redgrave (Madeleine Rees), David Hewlett (Fred Murray). Directed by Larysa Kondracki and produced by Amy Kaufman, Christina Piovesan, and Celine Rattray. Screenplay by Kondracki and Eilis Kirwan.

Here is a film to fill you with rage. It is based on the true story of Kathryn Bolkovac, a police officer from Lincoln, Nebraska, who accepted an offer to join the U.N. peacekeeping mission in Bosnia. While there, she uncovered direct evidence that underage girls were being held captive and bought and sold in a profitable sex trafficking operation. When she presented her evidence to her superiors, it was ignored. When she persisted, she was fired.

There is more. The American private security firm, DynCorp International, whose operatives committed these crimes and tried to cover them up, is still employed by the U.S. government in Iraq and Afghanistan, and was used in Louisiana after Katrina. Although its activities were at the center of Bolkovac's report, she found that local police and U.N. peacekeepers themselves were also deeply involved.

Although *The Whistleblower* is a fictional film, these facts were supported by a British employment tribunal that investigated her claim against DynCorp, finding the corporation's defense "completely unbelievable." That high officials in the U.N. Human Rights Commission were also aware of the sex traffic is unbelievable to me.

The movie, constructed as a relentless and frightening thriller, stars Rachel Weisz in one of her best performances, portraying Bolkovac as a quiet, intense woman who has heroism thrust upon her by the evidence of her own eyes. Investigating complaints of rape and forced prostitution, she visits private clubs where underage girls are exhibited and fondled, held captive, threatened with death, and actually sold to individuals to take and do with what they desire.

These young women were lured to Bosnia under false pretenses. Their passports were taken, so they could not escape across borders. Because of the curfews in effect in the area at the time, local citizens could not leave their homes at night, and so the customers at the clubs were, by definition, law-enforcement personnel not under curfew.

In her almost single-handed investigation, Bolkovac is often seen in scary nighttime situations; walking down a street or entering her apartment seems risky. The movie is not above employing images of female vulnerability to manipulate us, and it succeeds. What makes it so effective is that Weisz doesn't play her character as any species of action heroine, but simply as a competent, dutiful cop who is naive enough to believe her job should be performed by the book. After she comes to know some of the victims personally, after they trust her, the job becomes more of a mission.

David Strathairn costars as Peter Ward, one of Bolkovac's few colleagues who seem trustworthy. Vanessa Redgrave plays Madeleine Rees, a real-life official of the Human Rights Commission, who offers moral support and also warnings that the life of the young woman may be in danger. Monica Bellucci is Laura Levin, a bureaucrat who refuses to help repatriate the young women because, in cruel logic, they have no passports. And David Hewlett is Fred Murray, Bolkovac's superior officer, who is himself part of the cover-up.

The director, Larysa Kondracki, pervades the film with an atmosphere of male menace that, after all, is based on facts and court findings. In wartime, the rape of civilians is often considered one of the spoils, and no doubt it is a morale booster for troops who feel in danger. It is also a cruel blow against enemies—but these girls are not enemies. They are simply and pathetically victims.

The male world in which Bolkovac moves contains many men who regard her as a sex object and see sexual aggression as an expression of their masculinity. In this boys' club it is expected that members will go along, participate, or turn a blind eye. There is unspecified but clearly sensed danger if they don't. On one hand, they can party and enjoy sex. On the other, they can lose their jobs, their salaries, their pensions, and perhaps their lives.

For twenty years the news has reported from time to time on crimes alleged by employees of paid defense contractors. These cases rarely seem to result in change, and the stories continue. We can only guess what may be going unreported. *The Whistleblower* offers chilling evidence of why that seems to be so.

## White Material ★ ★ ★ ½

NO MPAA RATING, 105 m., 2010

Isabelle Huppert (Maria Vial), Isaach De Bankole (The Boxer), Christophe Lambert (Andre), Nicolas Duvauchelle (Manuel), William Nadylam (Mayor), Michel Subor (Henri). Directed by Claire Denis and produced by Pascal Caucheteux. Screenplay by Denis and Marie N'Diaye.

Isabelle Huppert is small and slender and embodies the strength of a fighter. In so many films she is an indomitable force, yet you can't see how she does it. She rarely acts broadly. The ferocity lives within. Sometimes she is mysteriously impassive; we see what she's determined to do, but she sends no signals with voice or eyes to explain it. There is a lack of concern about our opinion; she will do it, no matter what we think her reasons are.

In Claire Denis's *White Material,* she plays Maria Vial, a French woman running a coffee plantation in an unnamed African country. The land has fallen into war, both against the colonialists and among the insurgents. In an opening scene, a helicopter hovers above Maria, and French soldiers advise her to evacuate quickly. This she has no intention of doing. As it becomes clear that her life is in danger, she only grows more opaque. Huppert's approach is valuable here because any attempt at a rational explanation would seem illogical. I believe her attachment to the land has essentially driven her mad.

This isn't even her farm. It was owned by her former father-in-law and run by her ex-husband (Christophe Lambert). Now she is in day-to-day charge and moves with confidence. The way she dresses makes a statement: She likes simple sandals and thin print sundresses that make her seem more at home than durable clothing would. She doesn't even much like hats or sunglasses. She runs through fields like a child. She drives the truck, runs errands, goes into town to hire substitute labor when her workers walk away in fear of the war. There's a scene where she all but tries to physically restrain departing workers.

They try to be reasonable with her. Yes, it will be a good crop of coffee beans, but there will probably be no way to get it to market. Anarchy has taken the land. Child soldiers with rifles march around, makeshift army stripes on their shirts, seeking "The Boxer" (Isaach De Bankole), a onetime prizefighter and now the legendary, if hardly seen, leader of the rebellion. When Maria is held at gunpoint, she boldly tells the young gunmen she knows them and their families. Her danger doesn't seem real to her. There is no overt black-white racial tension; the characters all behave as the situation would suggest.

Claire Denis, a major French director, was born and raised in French colonial Africa, and is drawn to Africa as a subject; her first film, the great *Chocolat* (1988), was set there, and also starred the formidable Isaach De Bankole. Both it and this film draw from *The Grass Is Singing,* Doris Lessing's first novel, the idea of a woman more capable than her husband on an African farm. Her 2009 film *35 Shots of Rum* dealt with Africans in France. She doesn't sentimentalize Africa nor attempt to make a political statement. She knows it well and hopes to show it as she knows it. Huppert's impassivity perhaps suits her; the character never expresses an abstract idea about the farm or Africa, and the nearest she comes to explaining why she won't leave is asking, "How could I show courage in France?" No one asks her what that means.

We meet the ex-husband (Lambert) and his father (Michel Subor), but the other major figure in the film is her son, Manuel (Nicolas Duvauchelle). This boy, in his late teens, seems prepared to spend all of his life in his room. While his mother manages the farm, he projects indolence and total indifference. He cares not about her, the farm, or anything. Events cause him to undergo a scary transformation, but it's not one we were expecting. He doesn't move in a conventional narrative direction, but laterally, driven by inner turmoil.

This is a beautiful, puzzling film. The enigmatic quality of Huppert's performance draws us in. She will never leave, and we think she will probably die, but she seems oblivious to her risk. There is an early scene where she runs in her flimsy dress to catch a bus, and finds there are no seats. So she grabs onto the ladder leading to the roof. The bus is like Africa. It's filled with Africans, we're not sure where it's going, and she's hanging on.

## The White Ribbon ★ ★ ★ ★

R, 145 m., 2010

Ulrich Tukur (Baron), Susanne Lothar (Midwife), Christian Friedel (Schoolteacher), Burghart Klaussner (Pastor), Leonie Benesch (Eva), Josef Bierbichler (Steward), Rainer Bock (Doctor), Ernst Jacobi (Narrator). Directed by Michael Haneke and produced by Stefan Arndt, Veit Heiduschka, Michael Katz, Margaret Menegoz, and Andrea Occhipinti. Screenplay by Haneke.

Something is wrong in the village. Some malevolent force, some rot in the foundation. This wrongness is first sensed in a series of incidental "accidents." Then the murder of a child takes place. This forces the villagers, who all know one another, to look around more carefully. Is one of them guilty? How can that be? One person couldn't be responsible for all of these disturbing events. Have many been seized in an evil contagion?

After the first screening of Michael Haneke's *The White Ribbon* at Cannes, everybody had theories about who "did it." Well, we're trained to see such stories as whodunits. Haneke is never that simple. It all may have been "done," but what if there seems to be no doer? What if bad things happen to good people who are not as good as they think they are? In Haneke's *Caché* (2005), who shot the alarming videos spying on the family? Are you sure? Haneke's feeling is that we can never be sure.

This great film is set in rural Germany in the years before World War I. All has been stable in this village for generations. The baron owns the land. The farmer, the pastor, the doctor, the schoolteacher, the servants, even the children, play their assigned roles. It is a patriarchal, authoritarian society—in other words, the sort of society that seemed ordinary at that time throughout the world.

We are told the story many years after it took place by the schoolteacher (Ernst Jacobi). In the film, we see him young (Christian Friedel). The old man intends to narrate with objectivity and precision. He'll draw no conclusions. He doesn't have the answers. He'll stick to the facts. The first fact is this: While out riding one morning, the doctor was injured when his horse stumbled because of a trip wire. Someone put the wire there. Could they have even known the doctor (Rainer Bock) would be their victim?

Other incidents occur. A barn is burned. A child is found murdered. Someone did each of these things. The same person could not easily have done all of them. There is information about where various people were at various times. It's like an invitation to play Sherlock Holmes and deduce the criminal. But in *The White Ribbon* there are no barking hounds. The clues don't match. Who is to even say something is a clue? It may simply be a fact seen in the light of suspicion.

Life continues in an orderly fashion, as if a gyroscope tilts and then rights itself. The baron steadies his people. The doctor resumes his practice, but is unaccountably cruel toward his mistress. The teacher teaches and the students study, and they sing in the choir. Church services are attended. The white ribbon is worn by children who have been bad but will now try to be good. The crops are harvested. The teacher courts the comely village girl Eva (Leonie Benesch). And suspicion spreads.

I wonder if it's mostly a Western feeling that misfortune is intolerable and, to every degree possible, death must be prevented. I don't hear of such feelings from Asia or Africa. There is more resignation when terrible things happen. Yes, a man must not harm another. He should be punished. But after he causes harm, they don't think it possible to prevent any other man from ever doing the same thing.

In this German town there is a need to solve the puzzle. Random wicked acts create disorder and erode the people's faith that life makes sense. The suspicion that the known facts cannot be made to add up is as disturbing as if the earth gave way beneath our feet.

Haneke has a way of making the puzzle more interesting than its solution. If you saw *Caché,* you'll remember how, after a certain point, a simple shot by an unmoving camera became disturbing even when nothing happened. It wasn't about what we were seeing. It was about the fact that someone was looking, and we didn't know why.

It's too simple to say the film is about the origin of Nazism. If that were so, we would all be Nazis. It is possible to say that when the prevention of evil becomes more important than the preservation of freedom, authoritarianism grows. If we are to prevent evil, someone must be in charge. The job naturally goes to those concerned with enforcing order. Therefore, all disorder is evil and must be prevented, and that's how the interests of the state become more important than the interests of the people.

I wonder if Haneke's point is that we grow so disturbed by danger that we will surrender freedom—even demand to. Do we feel more secure in an orderly state? Many do. Then a tipping point arrives, and the Berlin Wall falls, or we see the Green Revolution in Iran. The problem, as philosophers have noted, is that revolutionaries grow obsessed with enforcing their revolution, and the whole process begins over.

Haneke's genius is to embed these possibilities in films rooted in the daily lives of ordinary people. He denies us the simple solutions of most films, in which everything is settled by the violent victory of our side. His films are like parables, teaching that bad things sometimes happen simply because . . . they happen. The universe laughs at man's laws and does what it will.

The film is visually masterful. It's in black and white, of course. Color would be fatal to its power. Perhaps because b&w film is hard to find, Haneke filmed in color and drained it away. If a color version is ever released, you'll see why it's wrong. Just as it is, *The White Ribbon* tells a simple story in a small village about little people and suggests that we must find a balance between fear and security.

## Who Do You Love? ★ ★ ½

NO MPAA RATING, 90 m., 2010

Alessandro Nivola (Leonard Chess), Jon Abrahams (Phil Chess), David Oyelowo (Muddy Waters), Chi McBride (Willie Dixon), Megalyn Echikunwoke (Ivy Mills), Marika Dominczyk (Revetta Chess), Keb' Mo (Jimmy Rogers), Robert Randolph (Bo Diddley). Directed by Jerry Zaks and produced by Les Alexander, Andrea Baynes, and Jonathan Mitchell. Screenplay by Peter Wortmann and Bob Conte.

The original studios of Chess Records on South Michigan in Chicago are as important to the development of rock 'n' roll as the Sun Records studios in Memphis. You could make a good case, in fact, that without Chess there might have been no Sun, and without Muddy Waters, Willie Dixon, Bo Diddley, and Chuck Berry, there might have been no Elvis Presley, Jerry Lee Lewis, or Carl Perkins. Rock 'n' roll flowed directly, sometimes almost note by note, from rhythm and blues.

*Who Do You Love?* is the second, and lesser, recent film about the brothers Chess, Leonard and Phil, and the label they founded. It tells the same improbable story of how two Jewish immigrant kids from Poland sold the family junkyard to start a music club on the black South Side, and helped launch the musical styles that have influenced everything since.

Both films are, of course, filled with music. The Chess catalog must have collected some nice royalties. The basic outlines of the films are roughly the same, although *Cadillac Records* (2008) didn't include Phil, the younger and quieter brother. Leonard (Alessandro Nivola) is hopelessly infatuated with black music, Phil (Jon Abrahams) more interested in the business.

It remains a little unclear exactly what Leonard feels about black people. Yes, he supports their rights. But he underpays them. He was fond of Etta James, called Ivy Mills here and played by Megalyn Echikunwoke. Her drug addiction is greatly fictionalized (she is still very much alive, for one thing) and her great hit "At Last" is shifted in time; the equivalent character in *Cadillac Records* is more moving. Leonard historically decided to back her with violins and a full orchestra.

In this movie's telling, Willie Dixon (Chi McBride, very good) was Leonard's scout in finding the best of a new generation of R&B artists. It's Dixon who introduces Chess to Muddy Waters (David Oyelowo) and lends him a guitar for his audition. But Leonard had a good ear and proved it with the stable he built.

He loved the music. In a no doubt exaggerated scene, his family is all packed up in the car and ready to leave on vacation when he explains he has to go on tour with Muddy instead. His wife, Revetta (Marika Dominczyk), is part long-suffering, part perhaps not fully aware from their suburban home of what's going on in the city.

The Chess Records story is part of modern folklore, and both films treat it too much that way: as a well-rehearsed saga. I think more edge is needed, more reality about the racial situation at the time, more insight into how and why R&B and R&R actually did forever transform societies in America and the world. Who had more to do with bringing down the Berlin Wall? Ronald Reagan or Muddy Waters?

## Wild Grass ★ ★ ★

PG, 113 m., 2010

Sabine Azema (Marguerite Muir), Andre Dussollier (Georges Palet), Anne Consigny (Suzanne), Emmanuelle Devos (Josepha),

Mathieu Amalric (Bernard de Bordeaux), Michel Vuillermoz (Lucien d'Orange), Edouard Baer (Narrator). Directed by Alain Resnais and produced by Jean-Louis Livi. Screenplay by Alex Reval and Laurent Herbiert, based on the novel *L'incident* by Christian Gailly.

*Wild Grass* is about an unlikely and fateful chain of events that to a young person might seem like coincidence, but to an older one illustrates the likelihood that most of what happens in our lives comes about by sheer accident. This is the new work by Alain Resnais, who may have learned this by experience: There's a springtime in your life when you think it should add up and make sense, and an autumn when you think, the hell with it, anything can happen.

Resnais has been making films since the dawn of the New Wave: *Hiroshima, Mon Amour* (1959), and *Last Year at Marienbad* (1961). Now he's eighty-eight. Preparing to write, I decided not to mention his age, in fear that some readers might think a director that age couldn't possibly be engaging. But praise must be given. *Wild Grass* is carefree and anarchic, takes bold risks, spins in unexpected directions.

It uses a narrator, which is just as well, because only from an all-knowing point of view can the labyrinth of connections be seen. The narrator begins by telling us that all the subsequent events will take place because the heroine, Marguerite (Sabine Azema), required a shoe size that was hard to find. Therefore on an impulse she went into a shoe store, found the right shoes, and walked out just in time to have her purse snatched by a thief.

Her billfold is later found discarded by Georges (Andre Dussollier), a married man. In the billfold he sees her photograph and learns she is single, a dentist, and a private pilot. He finds it necessary to meet her. This isn't so easy to arrange. Georges in the meantime is the subject of several oblique suggestions that Resnais is never all that clear about. Does he have fearsome secrets? Does he harbor fantasies? Is his mind coming apart?

As we meet these possibilities, we also get to know Marguerite better, with her jolly red hair and her best friend, Josepha (Emmanuelle Devos). You may not place these names, but if you go to French movies you've likely seen both many times; they're very likable, which means Resnais can enlist our sympathy without needing to recruit it. They're not quite sure what to make of this Georges character, and particularly his desire to go up in a plane with Marguerite at the controls.

From time to time we hear narration from characters. We find ourselves in unexpected situations. There are actions that seem objectively impossible. Resnais finds a tone allowing him to incorporate all these detours into the headlong flight of the film itself. Life is like that. In our minds it unfolds straight ahead of us because we remain oblivious to the pianos that didn't fall on our heads, the trucks that didn't hit us in the street, the plague we escaped, and, in this case, the incalculable odds against Marguerite going to that shoe store, and Georges finding her wallet, and her being a pilot, and so on.

I think Resnais's point is that life itself is utterly accidental (beginning with the odds against life arising in the universe, and the odds against our being born). When you look at it that way, everything that happens in *Wild Grass* makes perfect sense. The odds against any two people meeting in Paris almost seem small.

The film is a visual pleasure, using elegant techniques that don't call flashy attention to themselves. The camera is intended to be as omniscient as the narrator and can occupy the film's space as it pleases and move as it desires. Here is a young man's film made with a lifetime of experience.

## Windfall ★ ★ ★

NO MPAA RATING, 83 m., 2012

A documentary featuring Chuck Coggins. Directed by Laura Israel and produced by Israel and Autumn Tarleton. Screenplay by Israel.

Driving from Los Angeles to Palm Springs, you pass through a desert terrain in which a new species has taken hold. Wind turbines grow row upon row, their blades turning busily as they generate electricity and pump it into the veins of the national grid. This wind farm is a good thing, yes? I've always assumed so, and driven on without much thought.

A new documentary named *Windfall* has taken the wind out of my sails. Assuming it can be trusted (and many of its claims seem self-evident), wind turbines are a blight upon the land and yet another device by which energy corporations and Wall Street, led by the always reliable Goldman Sachs, are picking the pockets of those who can least afford it. There is even some question whether wind energy uses more power than it generates.

Laura Israel's film is set almost entirely in Meredith, New York, a farming area of some two thousand people in a beautiful Catskills landscape. A few dairy and beef farms still survive, but many of the residents are now retired people who have come here with their dreams. Most of them were once *of course* in favor of wind power, which offered the hope of clean, cheap energy. When an Irish corporation named Airtricity came around offering landowners $5,000, neighbors $500, and the town a 2 percent cut of the revenue, that was a win-win, right?

So it appeared. But some residents, including a former editor for an encyclopedia and the final photo editor of *Life* magazine, began doing some research. The town board set an energy advisory panel, and after a year of study it recommended the town refuse the Airtricity offer. The town board rejected the panel's finding. One of them recused himself because of his personal holdings in energy. The others saw no conflict.

This generated a furor in Meredith, and we meet people who were best friends for years and now are no longer on speaking terms. We watch board meetings and meet lots of locals; the film bypasses the usual expert talking heads and relies on the personal experiences of these individuals.

I learned that wind turbines are unimaginably larger than I thought. It's not a matter of having a cute little windmill in your backyard. A turbine is four hundred feet tall, weighs six hundred thousand pounds, and is rooted in tons and tons of poured concrete. If one is nearby (and given the necessary density, one is always nearby) it generates a relentless low-frequency thrum-thrum-thrum that seems to emanate from the very walls of your home. The dark, revolving shadows of its blades are cast for miles, and cause a rhythmic light-and-shade pulsing inside and outside your house. Living in an area with all that going on gives many people headaches, nausea, depression, and hypertension.

The effect on property values is devastating. The owner of a lovely restored nineteenth-century farmhouse asks—who will buy it now? People don't come to the Catskills to undergo nonstop mental torture. Nor do other living things like wind turbines. Their blades, revolving at 150 miles an hour, slice birds into pieces and create low-pressure areas that cause the lungs of bats to explode.

For the loss of its peace of mind, a community's cut of the profits may be enough to pay for a pickup truck. Tax revenue drops because many of those (who can afford to) flee. Turbines sometimes topple over or catch fire (all firemen can do is stand and watch). And of course the local taxing agencies have been required to copy sweetheart state and federal tax cuts, promoted by the industry's lobbyists.

*Windfall* left me disheartened. I thought wind energy was something I could believe in. This film suggests it's just another corporate flimflam game. Of course, the documentary could be mistaken, and there are no doubt platoons of lawyers, lobbyists, and publicists to say so. How many of them live on wind farms?

## Winnebago Man ★ ★ ★

NO MPAA RATING, 85 m., 2010

A documentary directed by Ben Steinbauer and produced by Steinbauer, Joel Heller, James Payne, and Malcolm Pullinger. Screenplay by Steinbauer and Pullinger.

There is a video on YouTube that has had millions and millions of hits and made its subject, a man named Jack Rebney, internationally known as Winnebago Man. He is perhaps even as famous as Trololo Man, and that's famous.

Rebney first attracted attention when an old VHS tape surfaced featuring the outtakes of a 1988 session when he was trying without much success to star in a promotional film for Winnebagos. Things were not going well. In take after take, Rebney blew lines, forgot lines, thought lines were stupid, was distracted by crew members moving around, was annoyed by stray sounds, was mad at himself for even doing the damn thing.

Every time the filming breaks down or Rebney calls a halt, he explodes in remarkable verbal fireworks. The only reason "Winnebago Man" doesn't consist of wall-to-wall f-words is that he separates them with other four-letter words. Once it made it onto YouTube, the video was found hilarious by countless viewers. But what were they laughing at really, and who *was* the real Winnebago Man?

A documentary maker named Ben Steinbauer decided to find out. He was curious about the reasons we like footage of real people subjecting themselves (usually unwillingly) to ridicule. Are we laughing at them, with them, or simply in relief that we aren't them? How does their viral fame affect them?

Jack Rebney seemed to have disappeared from the face of the earth. Using methods he shows in his film, Steinbauer finally tracks him down in northern California, where he lives alone in the woods, calls himself a hermit, and wants nothing to do with nobody—never. That's not because of the YouTube video, which he doesn't give a $#!+ about. It's because of the way he is.

Now around eighty, he works as a caretaker for a fishing resort that, it must be said, is never very evident in the film. He has an unlisted phone number and uses post office boxes, and his dog is all the company he wants. He does have a computer; I imagine figures like this feeding the endless comment streams on blogs.

Steinbauer visits him, chats with him, gets first one impression and then another. Rebney more or less agrees to be filmed. His YouTube fame is meaningless to him, but he figures it might be useful if he could parlay it into a way to air his views. Rebney, as you might suspect, has a great many views, including a roster of national figures he believes should be tried as war criminals.

Although we find out a lot about this virtual hermit and develop an admiration for his cantankerous principles, the movie leaves some questions unanswered. We learn that Rebney is threatened with blindness. We wonder how he will get along, at his age, living in a cabin in the woods. We might like to know a little more about Rebney as a young man. We suspect, but can't be sure, that much of his anger is not uncontrolled, but is aimed consciously at what he considers a stupid and corrupt world. He is not a comic character; he's dead serious.

Rebney is not touchy-feely. He is a hardened realist, whose only soft spot may be for his dog. He keeps up with events, feels the nation is going down the drain, and isn't sure why he was so angry while making the Winnebago promotional film. The crew he was cussing out were not good sports, and the outtakes made their way to Winnebago, which fired him. Then it went wide on YouTube.

Steinbauer takes Rebney wider still—all the way to the Jay Leno show, and to a fascinating personal appearance at a Found Film Festival, where he regards himself on the screen and then goes out to speak and proves himself the master of the situation. Steinbauer even sets him up with a Twitter account, but, typically, Rebney loathed it. His most recent Tweet, on March 28, 2009, was: "UP YOUR FERN."

## Winnie the Pooh ★ ★ ★

G, 69 m., 2011

With the voices of John Cleese (Narrator), Jim Cummings (Winnie the Pooh/Tigger), Bud Luckey (Eeyore), Craig Ferguson (Owl), Jack Boulter (Christopher Robin), Kristen Anderson-Lopez (Kanga), Travis Oates (Piglet), Wyatt Dean Hall (Roo), and Tom Kenny (Rabbit). Directed by Stephen Anderson and Don Hall and produced by Peter Del Vecho and Clark Spencer. Screenplay by Anderson, Hall, Clio Chiang, Don Dougherty, Kendelle Hoyer, Brian Kesinger, Nicole Mitchell, and Jeremy Spears, based on the *Winnie-the-Pooh* works by A. A. Milne and E. H. Shepard.

*Winnie the Pooh* is a sweet and innocuous children's movie based on the enduring tale of goings-on in Hundred Acre Wood. Although it's obviously intended for grade-schoolers and below, it may be appreciated by adults who grew up reading the A. A. Milne books with drawings by E. H. Shepard, which are so closely identified with it. This is that rare book that can hardly be thought of apart from its illustrations.

In a time of shock-value 3-D animation and special effects, the look of the film is gentle and pleasing. It was hand-animated, I'm told, and the backgrounds use a subtle and reassuring watercolor look. It's a nightmare-proof experience for even the youngest viewers.

The story you can probably guess. Pooh Bear craves honey, and many adventures result from his quest. An urgent subplot involves Eeyore the donkey, who has lost his tail. A possible clue can be found in the pin that is stuck where the tail was; do you suppose it was only pinned on all the time? As a result of his loss, Eeyore is more gloomy and lethargic than usual, and indeed in a grown-up movie we would suspect clinical depression.

This version, directed by Stephen Anderson and Don Hall, has a particularly engaging stylistic touch: The movie blends the typography and page design of the book (or an idealization of it) with the animation, so that words literally appear on the screen and seem to be as real as the characters, sometimes even landing in a heap at the bottom of the screen.

There are some jolly songs, performed fetchingly by Zooey Deschanel, Kristen Anderson-Lopez, and Robert Lopez, one of them involving a not really very scary monster named Backson, who I confess I do not remember from the books, although I have forgotten a great deal since I was six. (I do, come to think of it, remember Milne's book *Now We Are Six.*)

The voices include one nice surprise, Craig Ferguson playing Owl. There are also Jim Cummings as Winnie the Pooh and Tigger (who always makes me think of Frosted Flakes). John Cleese is the narrator. The dubbing talents otherwise seem to have been selected for their voices and not for their fame; we don't get such standbys as Angelina Jolie, Jack Black, and Johnny Depp. (When an animated movie advertises it *stars* Johnny Depp, what does that mean to people?)

The film is not long at sixty-nine minutes. It is preceded by an animated short about Nessie, the Loch Ness Monster, who we discover was displaced from her beloved pond by evil men constructing a golf course. Never has Nessie been so benign. The whole program could make a nice introduction to moviegoing for a small child.

## Winter's Bone ★ ★ ★ ★

R, 99 m., 2010

Jennifer Lawrence (Ree Dolly), John Hawkes (Teardrop), Kevin Breznahan (Little Arthur), Dale Dickey (Merab), Lauren Sweetser (Gail), Tate Taylor (Mike Satterfield), Garret Dillahunt (Sheriff Baskin), Sheryl Lee (April), Shelley Waggener (Sonya). Directed by Debra Granik and produced by Alix Madigan and Anne Rosellini. Screenplay by Granik and Rosellini, based on the novel by Daniel Woodrell.

The movie heroes who affect me most are not extroverted. They don't strut, speechify, and lead armies. They have no superpowers. They are ordinary people who are faced with a need and rise to the occasion. Ree Dolly is such a hero.

She is a girl of seventeen who acts as the homemaker for her younger brother and sister. This is in the backlands of the Ozarks. Her mother sits useless all day, mentally absent. Her father, who was jailed for cooking meth, is missing. She tries to raise the kids and feed them, scraping along on welfare and the kindness of neighbors. The children, like all children who are not beaten, are cheerful and energetic and love to play. They have not learned they are disadvantaged.

This world is established with bleak economy in the opening scenes of Debra Granik's *Winter's Bone,* which was a double prize winner at Sundance 2010. Unmistakably filmed on location, this is a society that has been left behind. It looks like Walker Evans's photographs of the rural Depression, brought forward to today. The unanswered question is how Ree Dolly grew up in this world and became strong, self-reliant, and proud. She didn't learn it from her parents.

The sheriff comes to call. Her father, Jessup, has skipped bail. To meet his bond, he put up the house—perhaps the only asset he had. If he doesn't turn himself in within a week, the family will be thrown out. Just like that. "I'll find him," Ree says quietly and firmly. And that's what she sets out to do.

Ree is played by Jennifer Lawrence, a nineteen-year-old newcomer who has already made Jodie Foster's new film. She embodies a fierce, still center that is the source of her heroism. She makes no boasts, issues no threats, depends on a dogged faith that people will do the right thing—even when no one we meet seems to deserve that faith. "Don't ask for what's not offered," she tells her little brother, although the lives of her parents seem to be an exercise in asking and not offering. Did she raise herself?

Everyone in the district knew that Jessup cooked methamphetamine. He is a modern moonshiner. What is obvious is that meth doesn't seem to have made him much money. Perhaps its illegality is its appeal, and its market is among people he feels comfortable with. Ree's travels in search of her father lead her to his brother, Teardrop (John Hawkes), whose existence inflicts a wound on the gift of being alive.

The screenplay, by Granik and Anne Rosellini, based on the novel by Daniel Woodrell, uses the ancient form of an odyssey. At its end will be Ree's father, dead or alive. Most likely dead, she begins to conclude, but unless there is a body her family will be homeless and torn apart. She treks through a landscape scarcely less ruined than the one in Cormac McCarthy's *The Road*. This land seems post-catastrophe. Although it has cars and electricity, running shoes and kitchens, cigarettes and televisions, these seem like relics of an earlier, prosperous time. If thrown-away possessions pile up around the houses of people, it is because they've reached the end of the line. There is no next stop.

There is a hazard of caricature here. Granik avoids it. Her film doesn't live above these people but among them. Ree herself has lived as one of them and doesn't see them as inferior, only ungiving and disappointing. In her father's world everyone is a criminal, depends on a criminal, or sells to criminals. That they are illegal makes them vulnerable to informers and plea-bargainers, so they are understandably suspicious. The cliché would be that they suspect outsiders. These characters suspect insiders, even family members.

As Ree's journey takes her to one character after another, Granik is able to focus on each one's humanity, usually damaged. They aren't attractions in a sideshow but survivors in a shared reality. Do they look at Ree and see a girl in need and a family threatened with eviction? I think they see the danger of their own need and eviction; it's safer to keep quiet and close off.

So the film rests on Ree, counterbalanced by Teardrop, who is aggressive with his hatefulness instead of passive in amorality. A story like this could become mired in despair, but Ree's hope and courage lock us in. How did she get to be the way she is? We are born optimistic, although life can be a great discouragement. In every bad situation, there are usually a few good people.

## Win Win ★ ★ ★

R, 106 m., 2011

Paul Giamatti (Mike Flaherty), Amy Ryan (Jackie Flaherty), Bobby Cannavale (Terry Delfino), Jeffrey Tambor (Stephen Vigman), Burt Young (Leo Poplar), Melanie Lynskey (Cindy), Alex Shaffer (Kyle). Directed by Tom McCarthy and produced by Lisa Maria Falcone, Michael London, and Mary Jane Skalski. Screenplay by McCarthy.

I was warming up to describe *Win Win* as a high-level sitcom, and then wondered what's so bad about it being a sitcom if it's high-level? You have a situation, and it's funny. That's a sitcom. You have a funny situation, and there's some truth in it and unexpected characters, well acted, and you may not have a great film, but you enjoy watching it.

*Win Win* centers on Paul Giamatti, an actor whose motivation often seems to be "I'm fed up and not going to take it anymore." He can play sweet, but he's most at home in a role like this: Mike Flaherty, a mediocre lawyer in a small New Jersey town, who can't make ends meet. He loves his kids and his wife, Jackie (Amy Ryan), but he doesn't like his work, he doesn't have the money to fix the boiler in the basement of his office, and he will happily wait until the dead tree in his front lawn falls on the house before he does anything about it.

Mike volunteers as the wrestling coach for the local high school team. You could not call this a passion. It is more of a task he has stubbornly set himself. Perhaps, years ago and in another body, he was a high school wrestler. He shares his office with an accountant named Stephen (Jeffrey Tambor), who is now also the assistant wrestling coach. It's a good thing the team usually loses because you cannot easily imagine Tambor smiling. Relieved satisfaction is about the limit of his capacity for elation. Joining them in a coaching triumvirate is Mike's best friend, Terry (Bobby Cannavale).

Mike has a client named Leo Poplar (Burt Young; remember him as Rocky's brother-in-law?). Leo is moving into Alzheimer's and refuses to leave his home of many years. When Mike discovers in court that Leo's estate will pay $1,500 a month to a legal guardian, he takes the job himself and immediately double-crosses his client by placing him in a nursing home. This is immoral and dishonest, but Leo will indeed probably be better off there, and Mike needs the money.

All of these scenes remind me of the detail and human qualities of McCarthy's two previous films, which involved sharply defined personalities in situations where their lives were interrupted by strangers. In *The Station Agent* (2003), a movie I would happily stop everything to watch again right now, Peter Dinklage played a dwarf obsessed with trains, who found his privacy invaded by a lonely woman (Patricia Clarkson) and a strange hot dog stand owner (Bobby Cannavale). In *The Visitor* (2007), Richard Jenkins played a withdrawn widower who finds a family of African immigrants has moved into his apartment.

Yes, those are technically sitcom situations. But both are more, and much deeper, than just comedies. He pushes that extra distance to find how his complex, plausible characters might respond. *Win Win* shows similar qualities, but takes fewer chances, and falls back on the ever-reliable Big Game/Match/Fight formula in its third act.

That employs a character who materializes well into the film. Kyle (Alex Shaffer) is old Leo's grandson, who has run away from home and hopes to live with the old man, but ends up living with Leo and Jackie. Mike finds no relatives for Kyle except for a druggie mother in rehab. Wouldn't you somehow know the kid is a champion wrestler? This is where the sitcom stuff clicks in. *Win Win* gathers all the strands (the illegal trusteeship, the wrestling team, the hazardous boiler, the wrestling, the rehabbing mother, Jackie finding out about her husband's misdeeds) and pays them off at the end.

Well, OK. It's too neat. Everything clicks into place. Life seldom has uncomplicated endings. But let it be said that Alex Shaffer, who was cast more for his wrestling than his acting, is effortlessly convincing. That Giamatti and Tambor are funny when they try to out-dour each other. That Amy Ryan does what she can with the loyal-wife-who's-had-enough role. That the ending has simple pleasures, although not those promised by the beginning or by McCarthy's earlier films. I'm happy I saw *Win Win*. It would have been possible to be happier.

## The Wise Kids ★ ★ ★

NO MPAA RATING, 95 m., 2011

Molly Kunz (Brea), Tyler Ross (Tim), Allison Torem (Laura), Sadieh Rifai (Elizabeth), Matt DeCaro (Jerry), Stephen Cone (Austin). Directed by Stephen Cone and produced by Cone, Laura Klein, and Sue Redman. Screenplay by Cone.

In the spring and summer of their senior year in high school, three best friends in Charleston, South Carolina, deal with their religious beliefs and sexuality. What kind of a film does that make you imagine? Possibly some kind of a melodrama, with big scenes of confrontation and truth-telling. Nothing could be more different from Stephen Cone's *The Wise Kids*, which is honest, observant, and subtle.

The film will be the opening night presentation of the thirtieth annual Reeling: The Chicago Gay and Lesbian Film Festival. I've seen only this single festival film, but I can predict that in many of the entries, homosexuality will be treated in a matter-of-fact way, as the norm in the lives of its characters. In the sweet musical comedy *Jamie and Jessie Are Not Together*, every woman in Chicago was apparently gay. Movies often create fantasy worlds. In the real world, not everyone is gay, and coming out can be difficult and painful.

*The Wise Kids* takes a refreshing approach to that reality. All of its characters are members of a Baptist church, but none of them is a religious zealot, and the most devout character is probably Tim (Tyler Ross), who during this summer will deal with the fact that he is gay. This will happen not with dramatic, pumped-up dialogue, but with understated, tentative conversations among friends, often on porch steps, walking down a street in the moonlight or at backyard parties. Cone is adept at body language, eye contact, nuance, and suggesting people's instinctive sympathy.

Tim's best friends are Brea (Molly Kunz), the red-tressed, open-minded preacher's daughter, and Laura (Allison Torem), who is fundamentalist and shocked by what she begins to realize about Tim. "It's wrong," she tells him. "I can quote you the verses from the Bible." But this is not in an argument, and Tim says he "prays on it," and now will pray for Laura. Brea, on the other hand, has a crisis of her own: She is beginning to question the foundations of her faith and contradictions in the Bible.

The film is cleanly, simply constructed of moments of communication. The word "gay" is hardly used. A fraught subplot involves Austin (Cone), the church musical director, and Elizabeth (Sadieh Rifai), his wife of eight years. He begins to realize he is gay, and Elizabeth perhaps realizes this sooner than he does. She observes that he's attracted to Tim, and there's a carefully written and photographed scene at a party where Austin and Tim share a moment of truth neither one of them expected.

Does Elizabeth scream at her husband? The movie spares us any such scenes, and we don't believe they're going on off-screen, either. The unusual quality of *The Wise Kids* is that the movie takes the faith of the characters seriously, and doesn't set anyone up as a caricature or a sitting duck. The moment I saw Tim's father (Matt DeCaro), for example, I thought he'd become a target: He's a good old boy with a beer belly. But he is also a loving parent, and note his tact and love in the conversation he has with Tim the first time the boy comes home for a visit after leaving for school. With a few words, he tells us of a lifetime.

There are no bad people in this movie. Only those who sincerely care for and about one another, and come to accept that, no matter what you think about it, some people are gay and always have been gay, and that's the way they are, and you can still love them. *The Wise Kids* may perhaps be one of the more unusual films in the festival.

## The Wolfman ★ ★ ½

R, 102 m., 2010

Benicio Del Toro (Lawrence Talbot), Emily Blunt (Gwen Conliffe), Anthony Hopkins (Sir John Talbot), Geraldine Chaplin (Maleva), Hugo Weaving (Inspector Aberline), Antony Sher (Dr. Hoenneger), Gemma Whelan (Gwen's Maid), David Schofield (Constable Nye), Roger Frost (Reverend Fisk), Clive Russell (MacQueen), Art Malik (Singh). Directed by Joe Johnston and produced by Sean Daniel, Benicio Del Toro, Scott Stuber, and Rick Yorn. Screenplay by Andrew Kevin Walker and David Self.

*The Wolfman* avoids what must have been the temptation to update its famous story. It plants itself securely in period, with a great-looking production set in 1891. Gothic horror stories seem more digestible when set in once-great British country houses and peopled with gloomy inverts, especially when the countryside involves foggy moorlands and a craggy waterfall. This is, after all, a story set before the advent of modern psychology, back when a man's fate could be sealed by ancestral depravity.

The film's opening and closing shots are of the full moon, which is correct. An early exterior shows Chatsworth in Derbyshire, perhaps the grandest of all English country houses, as a Gothic shriek. Inside it is derelict and unkempt, inhabited by the sinister old Sir John Talbot (Anthony Hopkins) and his faithful manservant Singh (Art Malik). Gas was well known as a means of illumination in 1891, and indeed electric lights were not uncommon, but Sir John makes do with flickering candles carried from room to room, the better to cast wicked shadows.

Sir John's son Ben and his fiancée, Gwen (Emily Blunt), were living there until recently, when Ben was savagely killed. Gwen writes to his brother Lawrence (Benicio Del Toro), an actor who is appearing in London in *Hamlet* and indeed is holding poor Yorick's skull when we first see him. Lawrence arrives in a foggy, chilly dusk, of course, and his voice echoes in the vast lonely mansion before his father emerges from the shadows.

I love stuff like this. The gloomier and more ominous the better. There is a silent classic named *The Fall of the House of Usher* that actually has dead leaves scuttling across a mansion's floor. Lawrence views his brother's body, which seems to have made a good meal, and then it's off to the obligatory local pub, where the conversations of the locals center on a strange beast marauding in the district. In the nineteenth century, a pub was the evening news.

More plot you do not require. What you might like to know is that *The Wolfman* has been made with care by Joe Johnston, and is well photographed by Shelly Johnson and designed by Rick Heinrichs. The music by Danny Elfman creeps around the edges. Del Toro makes Lawrence sad, worried, fearful, doomy. It's not just the loss of his brother. It's the earlier loss of his beloved mother. The family manse is haunted by his memories. His father, Sir John, however, is played by the bearded Anthony Hopkins as a man holding up perhaps better than you might expect. And he's well turned out for a man who lives almost in the dark.

The film has one flaw, and faithful readers will not be surprised to find it involves the special effects by CGI. No doubt there are whole scenes done so well in CGI I didn't even spot them; but when the wolf-creature bounds through the forest, he does so with too much speed. He'd be more convincing if he moved like a creature of considerable weight. In the first Spider-Man movie, you recall, Spidey swung around almost weightlessly. Adding weight and slowing him in the second film was one of the things that made it great. The wolfman moves so lightly here he almost cries out: Look! I'm animated!

I am not sure of the natural history of wolfmen. Is the condition passed through the blood? Apparently. How exactly does one morph from a man into a wolf? By special effects, obviously. The wolfman has much less pseudo-scientific documentation than the vampire. I understand why he sheds his clothes when he expands into a muscular predator. What I don't understand is how he always succeeds in redressing himself in the same clothes. Does he retrace his path back through the dark woods by moonlight, picking up after himself?

In any event, *The Wolfman* makes a satisfactory date movie for Valentine's Day, which is more than can be said for *Valentine's Day.* Truer love hath no woman, than the woman who loves a wolfman. And vice versa, ideally.

## The Woman in Black ★ ★ ★

PG-13, 95 m., 2012

Daniel Radcliffe (Arthur Kipps), Misha Handley (Joseph Kipps), Roger Allam (Mr. Bentley), Ciaran Hinds (Daily), Janet McTeer (Mrs. Daily), Shaun Dooley (Fisher), Mary Stockley (Mrs. Fisher), Tim McMullan (Mr. Jerome), Liz White (Jennet), Ashley Foster (Nathanial Drablow), Sophie Stuckey (Stella Kipps). Directed by James Watkins and produced by Richard Jackson, Simon Oakes, and Brian Oliver. Screenplay by Jane Goldman, based on the novel by Susan Hill.

Not since young Hutter arrived at Orlok's castle in *Nosferatu* has a journey to a dreaded house been more fearsome than the one in *The Woman in Black.* Both films (and all versions of *Dracula*) begin with the local townspeople terrified of a residence and the legends surrounding it. In this case, a green young attorney named Arthur Kipps (Daniel Radcliffe) is visiting a haunted house in the north of England, which can be reached only by a single-track road on a long, narrow causeway that lies so low in a brackish sea that the waters lap its edges.

Arthur's mission is to search a decrepit Gothic mansion for the papers of its late occupant. This woman is said to haunt the house in mourning for her dead child. Local legend has it that the ghost is responsible for the deaths of other local children, brought about in rage as her form of vengeance. No wonder, then, that the locals shun Arthur, refuse him room and board, and strongly suggest he take the next train back to town.

But Arthur must succeed because his job depends on it. His work at a firm of solicitors has been unsatisfactory, and he needs to support his son, Joseph (Misha Handley), because his wife died four years ago in childbirth. As in the Dracula legends, the carriage driver refuses to take him close to the mansion, but a stalwart resident named Daily (Ciaran Hinds, he of the portentous face) drives him there in his new motorcar.

The house is a masterpiece of production

design, crumbling, forlorn, filled with the faded and jumbled Victorian possessions of doomed lifetimes. It has a unique feature audiences will not fail to remark upon: its own sound effects crew. At every frightening moment, and there are many, the sound track paralyzes us with blasts of cacophonous noise. You wouldn't want to be in the theater next to this movie in a multiplex.

*The Woman in Black* is Daniel Radcliffe's first film since last year's *Harry Potter and the Deathly Hallows: Part 2*. With a few other diversions, the Potter series kept him working steadily for a decade, during which he has grown taller and sprouted a crop of sideburns, but at twenty-two still looks like a schoolboy—or a little young, anyway, to be the father of a four-year-old. Nor does he have much gravitas. The film might have had more effect if his character had possessed more screen presence, but *The Woman in Black* depends mostly on the decor, location, and supporting cast, some of them playing living people and some not.

The movie nevertheless is effective because director James Watkins knows it isn't a character study. His haunted house is the star. The illnesses of local children provide ominous portents. Daily's wife (Janet McTeer) balances precariously on the edge of madness. And there is a most satisfactory scene at a railroad station that might have had Daniel Radcliffe wondering if he will ever in his career take a routine rail journey.

## The Woman in the Fifth ★ ★ ★ ½

R, 83 m., 2012

Ethan Hawke (Tom Ricks), Kristin Scott Thomas (Margit), Joanna Kulig (Ania), Samir Guesmi (Sezer), Delphine Chuillot (Nathalie). Directed by Pawel Pawlikowski and produced by Caroline Benjo and Carole Scotta. Screenplay by Pawlikowski, based on the novel by Douglas Kennedy.

Tom tells the immigration agent he is visiting Paris to see his wife and daughter. He knocks on the door of her apartment and she tries to slam it. His daughter cries "Papa! Papa!" His wife calls the police. He runs away and gets on a bus. He falls asleep, and is shaken awake at the end of the line. His suitcase and most of his money have been stolen.

This is Ethan Hawke, wearing black horn rims and a long black overcoat. He is in a district of the city we have never seen before, a barren industrial district. Music comes from a bar, and he has enough change left to order a coffee. He's waited on by Ania (Joanna Kulig), a sweet young Polish girl; he asks her if a room is available and is pointed to the owner. This man examines his passport and assigns him a grotty space upstairs.

At this point Pawel Pawlikowski's film *The Woman in the Fifth* could go in many directions. I am alert because Ethan Hawke rarely accepts a bad movie, and the forlorn location declares the film will not be about "Paris" but about loneliness and desperation. In an English-language bookstore, Tom is recognized by the owner and we learn that he has published a novel, apparently a good one. He's invited to a literary soiree in a few days.

His situation continues to improve. Sezer (Samir Guesmi), the owner of the café, offers him a job, eight-hour shift, fifty euros a night. Using pass codes he will memorize, he will lock himself in a small room and watch a video monitor trained on the door. If anyone rings, he's to ask what they want. If they say they're looking for Mr. Monde, he's to buzz them in.

In this cell he is free to write, but all he can create is a long illustrated letter to his daughter. He sees her again at her playground. We learn that his wife has explained to her that he has been "sick" and has just been released from prison. At the soiree, he catches the eye of an elegant woman named Margit (Kristin Scott Thomas), who gives him her card and tells him to call. She lives in the Fifth Arrondissement.

Why do we feel so much more is happening in this film than is summarized by these facts? Pawlikowski's camera follows Tom obtrusively, with an intent and focused gaze. There's no attempt to pull back and allow him more than his immediate surroundings. His day falls into a pattern, illuminated by the friendliness of the waitress, Ania. She finds his novel and reads it. Is she too good to be true?

He visits Margit in her apartment. Without describing it, I will say there is something off about this scene. Her behavior seems preordained, almost scripted in the imagination. Is he fantasizing it? That's not what I'm suggesting. Something is going on, and as the movie continues we become more alert to signals from beneath the surface. *The Woman in the Fifth* is the kind of film you'd like to see with friends using the shot-by-shot approach. When do we first sense reality slipping away? Do we? Can the film be accepted on its own terms? Can the point of view be trusted?

And those shots that interrupt Tom's solitude in the locked room? The weathered bark of big old trees? The insects intent on their impenetrable tasks? An owl peering at us? Railroad tracks, converging, then parting? Where are they? Why are they?

So much depends here on the Ethan Hawke performance. This is a desperate man, faced with a series of crushing blows. At one point he howls in the street. He is a published novelist. Has he no resources? No one he can call? Why is Ania so sympathetic, and Margit so opaque? No answers could be as absorbing as the questions. Hawke has enlisted our identification and sympathy, but he seems hopelessly isolated within his own bubble of despair. How much of what happens is in his mind? Why does the busy cockroach crawl so intently across his manuscript pages?

## The Women on the 6th Floor ★ ★ ★

NO MPAA RATING, 104 m., 2011

Fabrice Luchini (Jean-Louis Joubert), Sandrine Kiberlain (Suzanne Joubert), Natalia Verbeke (Maria Gonzalez), Carmen Maura (Concepcion Ramirez), Lola Duenas (Carmen), Berta Ojea (Dolores Carbalan), Nuria Sole (Teresa), Concha Galan (Pilar), Michele Gleizer (Germaine). Directed by Philippe Le Guay and produced by Etienne Comar and Philippe Rousselet. Screenplay by Le Guay and Jerome Tonnerre.

Jean-Louis is the third generation of the Jouberts to occupy the same enormous flat in an ornate wedding cake of a Parisian apartment building. Our eyes are led up, up to rest on the mansard windows, each one opening from the small sixth-floor room of a Spanish maid who works in the building. It is 1962. The maids share a communal toilet and have no running water in their rooms, but they are happy to be in France and not Franco's fascist Spain. They keep one another jolly.

One floor down, on five, there is not cheer but much *tristesse.* Jean-Louis (Fabrice Luchini) was born in this building, has lived all of his life here, assumes he will die here, and plans for one of his sons to take over the family firm, move into the family flat, and follow his example. He has lived until recently under the thumb of his mother, and now that she has died the plans of his wife, Suzanne (Sandrine Kiberlain), to redecorate are met with outrage by the family's long-serving maid, Germaine (Michele Gleizer). She apparently believes the flat must be maintained as a memorial to her revered "Madame."

The two women raise their voices. Germaine threatens to resign. Suzanne says, don't bother—I'll fire you. The Jouberts are now helpless, being literally unable to boil an egg. Concepcion (Carmen Maura), another maid in the building, produces her pretty young niece Maria (Natalia Verbeke) as a job candidate, Maria is hired after one day's trial, and the lives of the Joubert family are changed forever.

You are suspecting that stodgy Jean-Louis will fall for the young woman. There is only a hint of truth in that. What happens is that he falls for the maids, all of them, and becomes infatuated with the working-class vitality of the women on six. Jean-Louis is firm and respectable, but timid, a captive of habit and tradition. His wife, Suzanne, is not the bourgeois caricature you might expect, but a pleasant-looking, carefully dressed and groomed woman who occupies her husband's staid milieu and plays a lot of bridge.

How it happens that Jean-Louis comes to live in his family's storage room on six I leave for you to discover. It happens after a lot of laughter in an innocent, sweet, and gentle comedy, which doesn't even ratchet up to the level of farce, with people running in and out of the wrong bedrooms. Bedrooms are hardly required. When his shocked sons come home from boarding school and visit him in exile on six, he requires only one line of dialogue to suggest his entire lifetime: "I've never been happier. This is the first time I've had a room of my own."

*The Women on the 6th Floor* is a pleasant movie, even-tempered, a romantic fantasy. It works because Fabrice Luchini makes a sympathetic hero, Sandrine Kiberlain makes a bewildered wife, Natalia Verbeke as Maria is warm and friendly, and the maids as a group believe in solidarity forever. There's some mild political and social satire as the lifestyle of the proletarian maids challenges the stodgy owner-managers, and as the Jouberts come to understand a marriage they seemed to accept unthinkingly. There are few reasons you must see this movie, but absolutely none that you should not.

## The World Is Big and Salvation Lurks Around the Corner ★ ★ ★

NO MPAA RATING, 105 m., 2011

Miki Manojlovic (Bai Dan), Carlo Ljubek (Alexander "Sashko"), Hristo Mutafchiev (Vasko), Ana Papadopulu (Yana). Directed by Stephan Komandarev and produced by Karl Baumgartner, Danijel Hocevar, Thanassis Karathanos, Stefan Kitanov, and Andras Muhi. Screenplay by Komandarev, Dusan Milic, Ilija Trojanow, and Yuri Dachev, based on a novel by Trojanow.

I don't suppose *The World Is Big and Salvation Lurks Around the Corner* can be described as plausible, but it's lovable in a way sometimes goofy, sometimes sad, always optimistic. The places are Bulgaria and Italy. The times are the Cold War and the present. The story shuttles between both times and both places.

In a village in today's Bulgaria, a small group of friends meet every day to gossip and play backgammon, a game they take very seriously. How seriously? As a matter of pride, they don't play for money. To be the winner of their never-ending tournament is to be the King of Backgammon, that is, the world. The reigning king is the immensely likable Bai Dan (Miki Manojlovic).

One day tragic news arrives. Bai Dan's son and daughter-in-law have been killed in an automobile crash. His grandson, Sashko (Carlo Ljubek), has survived. In flashbacks that continue through the film, we learn more of the story. Under the Communist regime, Bai Dan has not expressed the proper devotion to the authorities. You wouldn't call him a dissident, but he's feisty and sarcastic, and mocks a sullen man in a business suit who often sits in the café but refuses to join in a game.

This bureaucrat puts pressure on Bai Dan's son to inform on the old man. This suggests the young people, the wife pregnant, should leave the country quickly, and we follow them on a fraught odyssey through Yugoslavia to a refugee camp in Italy. Here they hope to get their papers to move on into Germany. In interlocking flashbacks, they're kept on indefinite hold by Italian authorities, who like collecting a per diem for their upkeep. Years pass. Then there is the crash.

Bai Dan travels immediately to his grandson's bedside, but Sashko has no idea who he is. He suffers total amnesia, a condition that is sad in life but invaluable to director Stephan Komandarev. As Sashko's physical health returns to normal, Bai Dan gradually wins the boy's trust, and decides the way to restore his memory is for the two of them to join in a journey back home to Bulgaria. In theory, the sights, sounds, smells, and language of his native land will restore the lad's memory. Sashko, robust, open-faced, apparently twentyish, after all has nothing better to do than go along.

It will not be a quick trip. Bai Dan obtains a bicycle built for two, and with Sashko, sets out to pedal halfway across the Balkans—where, the narration informs us, "Europe ends but never starts." Now we have the dependable mechanism of a road picture, including a stop at a hiker's camp where the young man meets a girl his age and has a skinny-dipping experience that will change his life.

Miki Manojlovic's performance as the grandfather is important to the film's success. There is a tendency in Eastern European movies for mustached salt-of-the-earth older men to become insufferable. Not here. Bai Dan is loving, stubborn, encouraging, and not wearing on our nerves. This is just as well, because Sashko is limited in the personality department, as well a man with amnesia might be.

Finally they arrive home, where grandfather and grandson face off in a backgammon game, cheered by the café's crowd of friends (still apparently around the same table in the same configuration after twenty years). I'm not sure if it matters, really, who wins their game, but I will observe that in Bulgaria, as in many, many other nations, the filmmakers find it handy to use a crowd of regulars in a café or bar as a sort of Greek chorus to bear witness and play a reliable audience.

## World on a Wire ★ ★ ★

NO MPAA RATING, 212 m., 1973 (rereleased 2011)

Klaus Lowitsch (Fred Stiller), Mascha Rabben (Eva Vollmer), Karl Heinz Vosgerau (Herbert Siskins), Adrian Hoven (Professor Henry Vollmer), Ivan Desny (Gunther Lause), Barbara Valentin (Gloria Fromm). Directed by Rainer Werner Fassbinder and produced by Peter Marthesheimer and Alexander Wesermann. Screenplay by Fassbinder and Fritz Muller-Scherz, based on the novel *Simulacron-3* by Daniel F. Galouye.

Late on the night of June 9, 1982, the West German film director Rainer Werner Fassbinder made a telephone call from Munich to Paris to tell his best friend he had flushed all his drugs down the toilet—everything except for one last line of cocaine. That was the line that killed him. He made his first film at the age of twenty-two, and forty films before dying at thirty-six. So there should be another fifty or sixty films. Could he have maintained his incredible output? We will never know. What is remarkable is what a high standard he maintained, what a stylistic vision he produced on such small budgets.

In the treasure of his work, it's not surprising that *World on a Wire* (1973), a two-part, 212-minute science fiction project for West German television, went unseen in the rest of the world for many years. Only now is it being shown in the United States. It involves a familiar sci-fi theme: the possibility that this entire world exists entirely inside another world, perhaps as a computer simulation.

I don't believe we're expected to be shocked by that possibility. The story centers on Stiller (Klaus Lowitsch), an engineer who works for a program named Simulacron, which fabricates complete identities for characters who don't know they're unreal. In the film, Stiller and others discuss the notion that reality is unreal, tracing it to Plato. The purpose of Simulacron is said to be the prediction of consumer trends twenty years into the future, although there may be a more sinister purpose. It's possible to imagine all the creatures inside Simulacron as living in a sort of SimCity controlled from a higher level. Or are perhaps the fabricators of Simulacron themselves manipulated by still higher puppet masters?

I'm not convinced Fassbinder really cared. The plot for him simply provides an occasion to demonstrate the way he imposed his visual and dramatic style on characters who were often played by the same actors, who spoke in the same mannered melodramatic manner, who inhabited worlds in which everyone seemed aware of artifice.

Stiller's dilemma is that his world, whatever it is, doesn't add up. He works for Henry Vollmer (Adrian Hoven), who has programmed Simulacron. Vollmer discovers something about his program before mysteriously disappearing, and Stiller believes he destroyed himself in despair. Then Lause (Ivan Desny), head of security for the firm, disappears. At one moment he's at a party, speaking with Stiller, and at another moment he's gone, his chair empty—and, more alarmingly, no one there realizes he was there or has even heard of Lause. Nor is there any record of him.

Fassbinder's camera massages his characters, gliding through elaborate spatial movements as if somehow their lives are connected in an occult way with the arrangement of their space and time. The dialogue is usually arch and ironic. The mannerisms—the smoking, the drinking, the sexual display—are affected. Recognizing such actors as Margit Carstensen (*The Bitter Tears of Petra Van Kant*), we realize we could be witnessing what they do, entirely arbitrarily, in this movie when they are not in that one. Fassbinder is their Vollmer. Perhaps Stiller represents all those fascinated by Fassbinder and how he lived and thought.

*World on a Wire* is slowed down compared to most Fassbinder. He usually evokes overwrought passions, sudden angers and jealousies, emotional explosions, people hiding turmoil beneath a surface of pose. Here there's less of that emotional energy. But if you know Fassbinder, you might want to see this as an exercise of his mind, a demonstration of how one of his stories might be transformed by the detachment of science fiction.

## Wrath of the Titans ★ ★

PG-13, 99 m., 2012

Sam Worthington (Perseus), Ralph Fiennes (Hades), Liam Neeson (Zeus), Rosamund Pike (Andromeda), Edgar Ramirez (Ares), Toby Kebbell (Agenor), Danny Huston (Poseidon), Bill Nighy (Hephaestus), John Bell (Helius). Directed by Jonathan Liebesman and produced by Basil Iwanyk and Polly Johnsen. Screenplay by Dan Mazeau and David Johnson.

Maybe it was the three exploding mountains too many. Or the dozen surplus fireballs. Or too much noise. *Wrath of the Titans* relentlessly wore me down with special effects so overscaled compared to the characters in the film that at times the only thing to do was grin. The characters, to be sure, are gods and not humans, but they are human-sized gods, and give it a moment's thought: What chance does your average muscular god have against the grinding stones of a labyrinth as large as a volcano?

But hold on a second. Why, you may be wondering, are the Titans feeling wrathful? The seeds of their present discontent can be traced back a decade (or two years in movie time) to the events related in *Clash of the Titans* (2010), where Perseus (Sam Worthington) defeated the Kraken and hopefully retired to raise his young son. Perseus, you may recall, is a demigod, the son of Zeus (Liam Neeson) and a human mother. Or maybe you don't recall. Anyway, Perseus's retirement is not meant to be because there is a crisis in the world of the gods. Humans are losing their faith in them, and the gods, no matter what you may have been led to believe, depend for their power on the faith of those who believe in them. I was reminded of Tinker Bell, and toyed with the notion of Perseus turning to the audience and asking, "Do you believe in gods?"

Perseus, in any event, is not very fond of Zeus, who did, after all, rape his mother. But the time has come to take a larger view. Zeus is being held prisoner by Hades (Ralph Fiennes), who hopes to usurp his power. Now Perseus must journey to the underworld to rescue his father, restore his power, and prevent Hades from ruling civilization. This he and his team must do by negotiating a labyrinth and descending to Tartarus.

The labyrinth scene isn't bad. This phenomenon was built from the outside in, we learn, leaving only one escape route. It consists of an unimaginably massive maze of enormous rocks, arranged like a clockwork mechanism so that its elements grind and shift and change forms. The stones indeed seem to be able to sense where the gods are, and toy with them. It is frankly impossible to see how the (human-sized) gods have half a chance in its bowels, especially since exits become dead ends, narrow corridors begin to crush in upon them, and so on. If you were to quiz me on how they escaped, I would be puzzled. They just . . . found their way out, I guess.

But never mind. *Wrath of the Titans* is obviously not concerned with plausibility. It lacks a comprehensible story and you won't need your CliffsNotes on the Greek myths. You get a rough idea of who the major players are, and then they spend a modest amount of time shouting laughable dialogue at one another while being all but forced off the screen by special effects.

That's where the fireballs and exploding mountains come in. No attempt is made to achieve a consistent physical scale in the movie, nor a comprehensible spatial plan. I was never quite sure where anybody or anything was in relationship to anything else, and eventually I gave up trying: This is a montage of sweaty, dirty, bloodied faces and figures assembled to fit between balls of fire.

I should have added that the movie is in 3-D. This is not a help. *Wrath of the Titans* is to begin with a dusty, murky pictorial confusion, not helped by dim underworld scenes, and although I'm sure the focus must be excellent, it had an imprecise feeling to me. Then the 3-D glasses did their bit to reduce the light level from the screen, and unlimited clouds of smoke, dust, and sand were generated by the explosions, and finally I found myself wondering, just for the heck of it, how the movie might have played with a more traditional approach. You know: Literate, concise dialogue. Characters we care about, with relationships that have meaning for us. Action set pieces within well-established spatial boundaries. Pacing that doesn't hurtle past us faster than the human ability to maintain interest. You know, that kind of stuff.

# X

## X-Men: First Class ★ ★ ★

PG-13, 130 m., 2011

James McAvoy (Charles Xavier/Professor X), Michael Fassbender (Erik Lehnsherr/Magneto), Rose Byrne (Moira MacTaggert), Jennifer Lawrence (Raven/Mystique), Kevin Bacon (Sebastian Shaw), January Jones (Emma Frost), Nicholas Hoult (Hank/Beast). Directed by Matthew Vaughn and produced by Gregory Goodman, Simon Kinberg, Lauren Shuler Donner, and Bryan Singer. Screenplay by Vaughn, Ashley Edward Miller, Zack Stentz, and Jane Goldman.

The best acting in *X Men: First Class* is by President John F. Kennedy, who in his Thanksgiving 1962 message to the nation expresses gratitude for the successful end of the Cuban Missile Crisis while suppressing what he surely must know, that U.S. and Soviet missiles spent a great deal of time flying back and forth while mentally controlled by the awesome powers of mutants. The movie's use of the missile crisis certainly serves the purpose of establishing this prequel in the early 1960s, and answers a question I've always had: Does the real world overlap with the histories of superheroes?

The movie is high-tech and well acted, with lots of action and noise as it portrays the origins of the X-Men, a group of about a dozen mutants (so far). It begins in a Nazi prison camp, where young Erik Lehnsherr is forced to witness a tragedy and finds he can control metals with his mind—but only when he's angry. He grows up to become Magneto, and is played by Michael Fassbender, the lean German actor who the buzzmeisters say will become a big star off of this film. Heaven help him. He was so good in *Fish Tank*, *Inglourious Basterds*, and *Jane Eyre*; must he play Magneto to become a star? For that matter, Raven/Mystique is played by Jennifer Lawrence, nominated for best actress earlier this year. Now a blue shape-shifter. The price of stardom.

Anyway, at Oxford, we meet the telepath Charles Xavier (James McAvoy) as a young man before he was paralyzed. He will eventually operate a school to shelter and train mutants, and he dreams they can help the world. His archenemy is Sebastian Shaw (Kevin Bacon), Magneto's cruel tormentor in the Nazi camp, now a man who recruits mutants to the dark side, where if they're good, maybe they'll be able to wear a helmet like his and look like a Roman charioteer. If anyone whacks him up alongside the head, he's gonna get a nasty cut from that pointy cheek protector.

Other mutants are gathered into one fold or the other. Each one has a specialty. There is a shape-shifter, a tempest-tosser, a screamer, a fire-blaster, a quick-adapter (named Darwin, of course), and so on. That each would develop a unique ability through simultaneous mutation is a tribute to the intelligent design of Stan Lee and his Marvel Comics crew. Still, it must be confining to have only one trick; you need to move with a crowd to cover all the bases.

The plot involves attempts by CIA agent Moira MacTaggert (Rose Byrne) to use Xavier to battle Shaw, who presents a threat to world peace. Exactly how the CIA discovered the mutants is a little unclear, and indeed the agency exists mostly as a convenience to the plot and the source of Moira, who seems to really like Xavier—and as a telepath, he should realize that if anyone does.

Anyway, the destinies of the good and bad mutants intersect with the Cuban Missile Crisis, which was not quite as we think of it. The scene where the mutants stand on a beach and mentally duel by causing both American and Soviet missiles to shuttle back and forth in the sky is . . . hilarious, I was going to say, but no, I should consider this scene more devoutly.

Director Matthew Vaughn in 2010 gave us *Kick-Ass*, in which an eleven-year-old girl was hammered almost to death for our entertainment. This movie lacks comparable violence, but is louder. At least all the X-Men are old enough to see an R-rated movie without adult supervision. Not that *X-Men* is R-rated; God forbid a comic book movie should turn away a single eager ticket buyer.

This is competent weekend entertainment. It is not a great comic book movie, like *Spider-Man II*, or a bad one, like *Thor*. It is not in 3-D, which is a mercy. The actors all embody their roles convincingly, if somewhat humorlessly, and the special effects cope admirably with those rockets changing directions. The battle scenes involve people having terrible things happen to them in somewhat incomprehensible ways, but they also create an intriguing texture for Raven the shape-shifter; Nicholas Hoult as Beast looks as if he's wearing a shag rug suit, but there you have it.

# Y

## The Yellow Handkerchief ★ ★ ★

PG-13, 102 m., 2010

William Hurt (Brett), Maria Bello (May), Kristen Stewart (Martine), Eddie Redmayne (Gordy). Directed by Udayan Prasad and produced by Arthur Cohn and Terence Rosemore. Screenplay by Erin Dignam, based on the story by Pete Hamill.

The action in *The Yellow Handkerchief* takes place within the characters, who don't much talk about it, so the faces of the actors replace dialogue. That's more interesting than movies that lay it all out. This is the story of three insecure drifters who improbably find themselves sharing a big convertible and driving to New Orleans not long after Hurricane Katrina.

The car's driver is a painfully insecure teenager named Gordy (Eddie Redmayne), who doubts most of what he does and seems to apologize just by standing there. At a rural convenience store he encounters Martine (Kristen Stewart), running away from her life. He says he's driving to New Orleans. No reason. She decides to come along. No reason. They meet a quiet, reserved man named Brett (William Hurt), and she thinks he should come along. No particular reason.

We now have the makings of a classic road picture. Three outsiders, a fabled destination, Louisiana back roads. and a big old convertible. It must be old because modern cars have no style; three strangers can't go On the Road in a Corolla. It must be a convertible because it makes it easier to light and see the characters and the landscape they pass through. They must be back roads because what kind of a movie is it when they drive at a steady seventy on the interstate?

The formula is obvious, but the story, curiously, turns out to be based on fact. It began as journalism by Pete Hamill, published in the early 1970s. In the movie's rendition, Brett fell in love with a woman named May (Maria Bello), then spent six years in prison for manslaughter, although his guilt is left in doubt. Martine slowly coaxes his story out of the secretive man.

You don't need an original story for a movie. You need original characters and living dialogue. *The Yellow Handkerchief,* written by Erin Dignam, directed by Udayan Prasad, has those, and evocative performances. William Hurt occupies the silent center of the film. In many movies we interpret his reticence as masking intelligence. Here we realize it's a blank slate and could be masking anything. Although his situation is an open temptation for an actor to signal his emotions, Hurt knows that the best movie emotions are intuited by the audience, not read from emotional billboards.

Kristen Stewart is, quite simply, a wonderful actress. I must not hold *Twilight* against her. She played the idiotic fall-girl written for her as well as that silly girl could be played, and now that the movie has passed a $200 million gross, she has her choice of screenplays for her next three films, as long as one of them is *The Twilight Saga: Eclipse.* In recent film after film, she shows a sure hand and an intrinsic power. I last saw her in *Welcome to the Rileys,* where she played a runaway working as a hooker in New Orleans. In both films she had many scenes with experienced older actors (Hurt, James Gandolfini). In both she was rock solid. Playing insecure and neurotic, yes, but rock solid.

The story of Eddie Redmayne, who plays Gordy, is unexpected. He fits effortlessly into the role of the scrawny, uncertain fifteen-year-old Louisiana kid. Yet I learn he is twenty-seven, a Brit who went to Eton, a veteran of Shakespeare and Edward Albee. Michael Caine explained to me long ago why it's easier for British actors to do American accents than the other way around. Whatever. You can't find a crack in his performance here.

These three embark on a road odyssey that feels like it takes longer than it might in real life. Their secrets are very slowly confided. They go through emotional relationships expected and not expected. They learn lessons about themselves, which is required in such films, but are so slowly and convincingly arrived at here that we forgive them. There is rarely a film where the characters are exactly the same at the end as they were at the beginning. (Note: Being triumphant is not a character change.)

The filmmaker, Udayan Prasad, made a wonderful British film in 1997, *My Son the*

*Fanatic.* I've seen none of his work since. Now this redneck slice of life. Since the characters are so far from the lives of the actors and the director, this is a creation of the imagination. As it must be. The ending is a shade melodramatic, but what the heck. In for one yellow handkerchief, in for a hundred.

## You Again ★ ★

PG, 118 m., 2010

Kristen Bell (Marni), Jamie Lee Curtis (Gail), Sigourney Weaver (Aunt Ramona), Odette Yustman (Joanna), Betty White (Grandma Bunny), Kristin Chenoweth (Georgia), Victor Garber (Mark), Jimmy Wolk (Will). Directed by Andy Fickman and produced by Fickman, John J. Strauss, and Eric Tannenbaum. Screenplay by Moe Jelline.

If only *You Again* understood that its story was suited for screwball comedy. It labors under the delusion that this assembly of half-baked ideas is destined for a higher comic calling, for example, in the warmhearted romantic weeper category. The movie is so laboriously contrived in every atom of its being that the only interest is in seeing if the characters can avoid the destinies decreed for them by ancient formulas.

No luck. Those who hate each other at the beginning will forgive each other at the end. Those who try to deceive will have their deceptions unmasked. Those destined for love will find it, but not without an obligatory setback at the 66 percent point. If there is a party, it will go wrong. If there is a tree house, it will fall out of the tree. If it is necessary to improvise a wedding at a hospital, a ward will be cleared to make space for a wedding so elaborate it would look unlikely in a church. I hope they save pieces of the wedding cake for the patients whose beds have been wheeled out into the hallway.

The actors are plucky. They're stuck in a movie that gives their characters not even a chance at a human characteristic. Benevolence, jealousy, resentment, charity, wisdom, disappointment, and love are turned on and off like water faucets, often with only a few lines of motivation. Occupations are like name tags: Wise old dad is revealed as a "doctor," mom runs a "bakery," daughter is "vice president of a national public relations firm" in her twenties, brother is a "lawyer," his fiancée is "working with the sick and underprivileged," the fiancée's mother "owns fourteen hotels" and a private jet. None of these jobs figures in any way in the plot, except that the hotelier knows how to say three words in each of six languages (she is played by Sigourney Weaver with such latent energy that I'm sure she would know more words if this movie were not rated PG).

The heroine is Marni (Kristen Bell). In high school she wore braces and glasses, was pimply, and was called "Moo" because her initials were M.O.O. (hint: Don't use your middle name). She is a blonde, of course, and was bullied by a brunette, of course. This was Joanna (Odette Yustman), who has now morphed into Florence Nightingale. Marni's mother is Gail (Jamie Lee Curtis), and wouldn't you know Gail went to high school with Joanna's Aunt Ramona (Sigourney Weaver), and they . . . oh, never mind.

Marni's grandmother Bunny is played by Betty White, whom I urgently advise to start playing against type, because the standard eighty-eight-year-old Betty White, although one hell of a woman, has grown a tad overfamiliar.

There were two parts of the movie I liked. The beginning, with a voice over by the then unpopular high school sophomore version of Marni, starts out funny before the plot settles in. And there is a moment when Aunt Ramona and mother Gail find out they were on the same cheerleader squad, and do an awesomely physical cheer together, and that is flat-out funny. Aside from that, the movie's pleasures are scant, apart from its observance of Gene Siskel's Rule of Swimming Pool Adjacency, which states that when well-dressed people are near a swimming pool, they will . . . yeah, you got it.

## Young Adult ★ ★ ★ ½

R, 93 m., 2011

Charlize Theron (Mavis Gary), Patton Oswalt (Matt Freehauf), Patrick Wilson (Buddy Slade), Elizabeth Reaser (Beth Slade), Jill Eikenberry (Hedda Gary), Richard Bekins (David Gary). Directed by Jason Reitman and produced by Reitman, Diablo Cody, Lianne Halfon, Mason

Novick, Russell Smith, and Charlize Theron. Screenplay by Cody.

They must have closed their eyes and crossed their fingers while they were making this film. It breaks with form, doesn't follow our expectations, and is about a heroine we like less at the end than at the beginning. There are countless movies about queen bitches in high school, but *Young Adult* has its revenge by showing how miserable they can be when they're pushing forty.

The movie stars Charlize Theron, one of the best actors now working, as Mavis, a character we thoroughly dislike. Not only is she drop-dead gorgeous, but we see how she makes herself look that way, and what happens when it comes undone. She plays the onetime high school beauty queen in Mercury, Minnesota, who moved to the big city (Minneapolis), got her own condo, and is sorta famous as the author of a series of a young adult novels about popular teens. Back home in Mercury they think of her as a glamorous success. Of course they haven't seen her in years.

They're about to. In real life, Mavis lives alone, her apartment is a pigpen, she chugs liters of Diet Coke and throws back shots of bourbon, and is likely to be single until the end of time. She receives an e-mail from Buddy Slade (Patrick Wilson), her high school boyfriend. Buddy and his wife, Beth (Elizabeth Reaser), have just had a baby, and here's a photo of the little darlin'. That does it. Mavis gets into her shiny black Mini, drives home to Mercury, and intends to attend the baby shower. In her mind, a tragic mistake has occurred. Buddy was intended to marry her, the baby should have been hers, and damn it all, it's not too late to set things straight.

*Young Adult* is the first collaboration between director Jason Reitman and screenwriter Diablo Cody since the success of their *Juno* (2007). Once again they center on a woman, but Juno was enormously likable, and Mavis seems unaware of her frightening effect on people. In the role of Buddy, Patrick Wilson faces one of an actor's trickiest challenges, portraying polite social embarrassment. When you have a wife and a new baby and are holding a breast milk pump in your hand, how do you respond when an old flame turns up at the door and expects you to drop everything and run off to Minneapolis with her?

The impossibilities of Mavis's behavior in *Young Adult* require some sort of cushioning, and the film wisely provides the character of Matt Freehauf, played by the comedian Patton Oswalt. Matt and Mavis had nothing to do with each other in high school. "I remember you!" Mavis now tells him. "You're the hate crime guy!" She is never the soul of tact. Yes, Matt was nearly killed in a gay-bashing incident in high school, despite the inconvenience that he is not gay. Now he still lives in Mercury with his sister, stuck on pause. His experience has given him insight into pariahs, and he immediately realizes Mavis is nose-diving into disaster. What Matt knows while Mavis remains clueless is that Buddy is perfectly happy with Beth and their baby, and shudders when he sees Mavis approaching.

Patton Oswalt is, in a way, the key to the film's success. Theron is flawless at playing a cringe-inducing monster and Wilson is touching as a nice guy who hates to offend her, but the audience needs a point of entry, a character we can identify with, and Oswalt's Matt is human, realistic, sardonic, and self-deprecating. He speaks truth to Mavis. Oswalt was wonderful a few years ago in *Big Fan*, the story of a loser who lived through his fantasy alter ego as a "regular caller" to sports talk radio. He is a very particular actor who is indispensable in the right role, and I suspect Reitman and his casting director saw him in *Big Fan* and made an inspired connection with the character of Matt.

As for Mavis, there's an elephant in the room: She's an alcoholic. "I think I may be an alcoholic," she tells her parents during an awkward dinner. Anyone who says that knows damn well they are. But civilians (and some of the critics writing about this film) are slow to recognize alcoholism. On the basis of what we see her drinking on the screen, she must be more or less drunk in every scene. She drinks a lot of bourbon neat. I've noticed a trend in recent movies: Few characters have mixed drinks anymore. It's always one or two fingers, or four or five, of straight booze in a glass.

Alcoholism explains a lot of things: her single status, her disheveled apartment, her current writer's block, her lack of self-knowledge, her denial, her inappropriate behavior. Diablo

Cody was wise to include it; without such a context, Mavis would simply be insane. As it is, even in the movie's last scene, she reminds me of what Boss Gettys says of Citizen Kane: "He's going to need more than one lesson. And he's going to get more than one lesson."

Leaving after *Young Adult*, my thoughts were mixed. After *Thank You for Smoking*, *Juno*, and *Up in the Air*, Jason Reitman has an incredible track record. Those films were all so rewarding. The character of Mavis makes *Young Adult* tricky to process. As I absorbed it, I realized what a fearless character study it is. The fact that sometimes it's funny doesn't hurt.

## Young Goethe in Love ★ ★ ★

NO MPAA RATING, 101 m., 2011

Alexander Fehling (Johann Goethe), Miriam Stein (Lotte Buff), Moritz Bleibtreu (Albert Kestner), Volker Bruch (Wilhelm Jerusalem), Burghart Klaussner (Lotte's Father), Henry Huebchen (Goethe's Father). Directed by Philipp Stoelzl and produced by Christoph Muller and Helge Sasse. Screenplay by Stoelzl, Muller, and Alexander Dydyna.

Knowledge about Goethe among many Chicagoans is limited to the old story about the proverbial driver of the Clark Street bus, who would shout out "Go-thee!" and then mutter under his breath, "Gher-ta." That is about as much as you need to know to enjoy *Young Goethe in Love*, just as you needed little knowledge of the bard to enjoy *Shakespeare in Love*. Here is a tempestuous romance involving a misbehaving young man who only at the end brings forth a literary masterpiece and becomes a great artist. You need know nothing about his work while watching this movie because it hadn't been written yet.

Why, then, make this movie? I imagine its primary target was the audience in Germany, where Goethe enjoys popularity second only to Shakespeare. I am reminded of a set of books I had as a child about the childhoods of famous Americans. Each book climaxed just as the hero was picking up steam. George Washington chopped down the cherry tree, and the rest was history. No matter, because *Young Goethe in Love* is a delight on its own terms even if it has little to do with the real Goethe; here is a randy young man not a million miles apart from Tom Jones.

Goethe is played by Alexander Fehling, a young actor who I suspect will cross over into international stardom. He's feckless, carefree, mischievous, and not a happy camper in law school. He fancies himself a poet. He fails his examination for his doctorate while providing an answer to an oral exam that proves only that he can speak. He lives in the provinces to begin with, but is banished by his angry father even more deeply into the sticks, where in the small town of Wetzlar he's placed in apprenticeship under Kestner (Moritz Bleibtreu), the stern local prosecutor.

Goethe is miserable in the practice of law and convinced he is doomed to obscurity. He is rescued from his blues by his new roommate Wilhelm Jerusalem (Volker Bruch), who convinces him to budge himself from gloom and attend a local dance, where the lad is enchanted by the saucy Lotte Buff (Miriam Stein). He pursues her with great ardor, and she returns his feelings. They engage in a great deal more rumpy-pumpy than you usually see in films about towering literary geniuses; passion overtakes them and they respond on the spot, disregarding rain, mud, and the risk of discovery.

Alas, the girl's father is respectable but poor, and hopes to marry her off to none other than Kestner, Goethe's boss. This Kestner is not a bad man, but he is no Goethe, although at the time Goethe wasn't either. The triangle leads to misery, a duel, and a great deal of trouble. The film's ending is happy only in a technical sense. What does it profit a man to gain the whole world but lose Lotte?

I learn that a great deal of *Young Goethe in Love* is fiction. It's a film with boundless energy, filmed in sunny, pastoral settings, gloomy interiors, and with authentic-looking sets and costumes. I imagine Goethe himself, an uber-romantic, would enjoy it immensely, although he might not realize it was about himself.

## Your Highness ★

R, 102 m., 2011

Danny McBride (Thadeous), James Franco (Fabious), Natalie Portman (Isabel), Zooey Deschanel (Belladonna), Justin Theroux (Leezar), Toby Jones (Julie), (Charles "Dance

King" Tallious), Damian Lewis (Boremont), Rasmus Hardiker (Courtney). Directed by David Gordon Green and produced by Scott Stuber. Screenplay by Danny McBride and Ben Best.

*Your Highness* is a juvenile excrescence that feels like the work of eleven-year-old boys in love with dungeons, dragons, warrior women, pot, boobs, and four-letter words. That this is the work of David Gordon Green beggars the imagination. One of its heroes wears the penis of a Minotaur on a string around his neck. I hate it when that happens.

This is the kind of farce Mel Brooks did ever so much better in *Robin Hood: Men in Tights*, and that was far from a good movie. It takes place in medieval days on a planet that looks like Earth except it has two moons—or maybe it only looks like two moons when the characters smoke that funny-looking pipe. I don't know how much money it cost, but I hope the money all went into sets, costumes, and special effects, because the screenplay cowritten by Danny McBride is so hopeless he doesn't even write himself a good role, and he plays the lead.

Can you believe the film also stars Natalie Portman, James Franco, Zooey Deschanel, Justin Theroux, and Charles Dance? Why did they do it? Maybe because David Gordon Green's previous film was a nice stoner comedy named *Pineapple Express* and they figured he could do it again? McBride, Green, and Deschanel worked before on a good movie named *All the Real Girls*, but that film came from a different time and a different David Gordon Green.

What calamity has befallen him? He carried my hopes. His first three features were *George Washington* (2000), *All the Real Girls* (2003), and *Undertow* (2004), and I gave all three four stars. I was in the hospital when he released *Snow Angels*, but it got good reviews. Then came *Pineapple Express*, produced by Judd Apatow, which was a pretty good Apatow-style movie, and I figured, all right, David wanted to see how it would feel to have a real budget and work with actors such as Seth Rogen, James Franco, Kevin Corrigan, Rosie Perez, and McBride (his buddy from college days). That was fair enough.

Now comes *Your Highness*. The movie is a perplexing collapse of judgment. Assume for the sake of argument that David thought the time had come for him to direct a farce. Fair enough. One with a severed cyclops head, an emasculated Minotaur, damsels in distress, crowds of witless extras, a castle, hydras, and . . . a mechanical bird? OK, they come with the territory. Not so much the bird. But why this screenplay? What did they think would be funny? They're satirizing a genre that nobody goes to see when it's played straight. It's sad when good actors dress funny and go through material more suitable for a campfire skit on the closing night of summer camp.

One strange thing about the movie is the relentless obscenity in the dialogue. I don't have the slightest difficulty with the f-word or most other words, as themselves. What I don't understand is why almost every single sentence has to be filled with them. Why is that funny? Was I supposed to be "shocked"? Was it intended as daring? It's puerile.

I mentioned boobs. Yes, there are a lot of boobs in this movie. But not much interest in women. Zooey Deschanel plays the intended bride of Franco, the son of the king. She's brought onstage, quickly kidnapped by an evil sorcerer, spends a good deal of time as a captive in his lair, is rescued, and lives happily ever after. She might as well be a mannequin, for all she's given to say and do. This intelligent, nuanced actress, standing there baffled. Used as a placeholder.

Natalie Portman is the Xena clone, a fierce warrior, laid on for anime fans who seem to regard such characters as masturbatory fantasies. She, too, has no personality, although she has more dialogue, all of it expressing clichés of steely determination.

Franco is likable. Likable? That's not good enough for a hero. McBride's character is pathetic, not in a good way. Rasmus Hardiker plays Courtney, the king's aide, who comes along on the quest so he can basically stand there and look at stuff. Oh, what a sad movie this is. David Gordon Green has made great films. He should remind himself of that.

## Your Sister's Sister ★ ★ ★

R, 90 m., 2012

Emily Blunt (Iris), Rosemarie DeWitt (Hannah), Mark Duplass (Jack). Directed by Lynn Shelton and produced by Steven Schardt. Screenplay by Shelton.

The title of *Your Sister's Sister* means, I think, that you have a sister and are a sister, in an endless loop. It opens with a memorial service a year after the death of Jack's brother. Everyone has good memories about him except Jack (Mark Duplass), who abruptly points out some of his brother's shortcomings. He leaves the room, and is followed by Iris (Emily Blunt), who we think may be his wife and, in fact, is his best friend. She tells Jack he should get away for a while, and offers her family's vacation cottage on an island off the coast of Washington state.

That sets up a spontaneous, engaging character study of three people alone in a cabin in the woods. Jack cycles out to the ferry stop with a huge backpack, discovering along the way he's getting a little old for such exertion, and arrives at the cabin around dusk. Trying to find the key, he suddenly realizes someone is already in the cabin and has just stepped out of a shower. This is Hannah (Rosemarie DeWitt), who hears Jack and comes after him with an oar before it becomes clear that Jack was invited, that Hannah is Iris's sister, and that she came out to the cabin on a moment's notice.

This series of scenes, semi-improvised like a lot of the movie, has a natural quality that gets everything said and yet doesn't feel like dialogue. It helps that both Hannah and Jack are friendly people with a sense of humor, which becomes only more clear when they sit down at the kitchen table and go to work on a bottle of tequila. If Jack has issues with his dead brother, Hannah has issues, too; she has just broken up with her girlfriend after a relationship of seven years. They negotiate around this development without going into details. Hannah knows of Jack as her sister's best friend, but it's unclear how much Jack knows about Hannah; that she's a lesbian, for example.

Here the onscreen presence of the two actors becomes useful. They get drunk but not Drunk, they are alert to their isolation in the woods, they like each other, and when Jack says that, you know, what the heck, maybe it wouldn't be the end of the world if we slept with each other, Hannah says, yeah, what the heck.

The next morning they are startled by the unexpected arrival of Iris and scramble to hide evidence from the night before. Jack implores Hannah not to say what happened. He sneaks out and returns, allegedly after a morning run, and an awkward situation is avoided. But why awkward? Iris is not Jack's girlfriend, and Hannah is not the first lesbian to ever sleep with a man. But, well, Jack got things a little out of sequence, didn't he, by sleeping with the sister of his best friend before having paid her that courtesy?

The way this unfolds is surprisingly engaging. I knew about the appeal of Emily Blunt and Rosemary DeWitt, but Mark Duplass has only recently started to register with me. He and his brother Jay began together directing such mumblecore as *The Puffy Chair* (2005), the underwhelming *Baghead* (2008), and the wonderful nonmumble *Cyrus* (2010). Mark also stars in *Safety Not Guaranteed* (2012). He's tall, comfortably built, shaggy, genial. He wears his testosterone lightly. He helps this film succeed because he doesn't push too hard in a tense situation.

DeWitt and Blunt are convincing as sisters, despite their different accents (that could happen to anybody). What occurs during these few days probably represents emotional gains for all three, although a surprise development near the end may not be necessary. It would be more in keeping with the film if it ended on a minor key. But maybe not. The development at least inspires some dialogue more heartfelt than Jack has had before.

## Youth in Revolt ★ ★ ★

R, 90 m., 2010

Michael Cera (Nick Twisp/Francois), Portia Doubleday (Sheeni Saunders), Zach Galifianakis (Jerry), Ray Liotta (Lance Wescott), Justin Long (Paul Saunders), Jean Smart (Estelle Twisp), Adhir Kalyan (Vuay Joshi), Fred Willard (Mr. Ferguson), Steve Buscemi (George Twisp). Directed by Miguel Arteta and produced by David Permut. Screenplay by Gustin Nash, based on the novel by C. D. Payne.

Michael Cera is not a sissy. It's more like he's unusually diffident. Laid back to a point approaching the horizontal. Yet he yearns. He's so filled with desire it slops over. I speak not of the real Cera, unknown to me, but of the persona he has perfected in such movies as *Superbad, Juno, Nick and Norah's Infinite Playlist,* and *Paper Heart.*

That was the comedy that pretended to be a documentary about his romance with Charlyne Yi, which was also going on in real life. That made for some ambivalent scenes, particularly since Ms. Yi herself is laid back so far the two could star in a movie based on *Flatland.*

*Youth in Revolt* gives Cera the twee name Nick Twisp, surrounds his aging virgin act with divorced parents who are both shacked up with lustful vulgarians, and then provides him with a dream come true in the person of Sheeni Saunders. She's played by Portia Doubleday, a new actress whose name will always be more melodious than those of her characters. They meet during family vacations at the sublimely named Restless Axles trailer park. For Sheeni, who speaks as if influenced by Juno, virginity is a once-touching affectation, and Nick Twisp is oh-so-eager to join her in this opinion. But there are many obstacles to their bliss, worst of all his family's tragic return home.

His family. His mother, Estelle (Jean Smart), lives with Jerry (Zach Galifianakis), a beer-swilling, belching lout who makes Nick's skin crawl. His father, George Twisp (Steve Buscemi), recently laid off, has robbed the cradle for his live-in, Lacey (Ari Graynor). Both parents all but flaunt their lovers before poor Nick; at Restless Axles, his mom asks Nick to clean up after dinner while she and Jerry (after his post-prandial burp) retire to the bedroom a few feet away for noisy rumpy-pumpy.

Sheeni's parents have much less screen time, so they're cast to make an immediate impression. Try to image M. Emmet Walsh and Mary Kay Place as your parents. OK. Nick is desperate to be reunited with Sheeni, tries to float reasons he needs to take a trip right away, and really inadvertently (honest) sets in motion an explosive, fiery chain of events.

Cera's style lends itself to one note, and the movie wisely gives him another character to play, an imaginary alter ego named Francois Dillinger, inspired by Jean-Paul Belmondo. Of course Nick would know who Belmondo is. I'd believe him if he were inspired by Jean Gabin. In this role, he has a mustache and smokes, but true to character, his mustache is wispy and he always smokes like it's his first cigarette.

It's often observed that comedy never works if an actor signals that he's just said something funny. I don't know if Michael Cera *can* do that. It requires such bold assertion. You'd get suicidal trying to get him to laugh at a joke. This passiveness is why he's funnier than Jack Black, for example, in their movie *Year One.* One of the secrets of *Youth in Revolt* is that Nick Twisp seems bewildered by his own desires and strategies. He knows how he feels, he knows what he wants, but he'd need a map to get from A to B. It's Nick's self-abashing modesty that makes the movie work. Here, you feel, is a movie character who would find more peace on the radio.

## You Will Meet a Tall Dark Stranger ★ ★ ½

R, 98 m., 2010

Antonio Banderas (Greg), Josh Brolin (Roy), Anthony Hopkins (Alfie), Gemma Jones (Helena), Freida Pinto (Dia), Naomi Watts (Sally), Lucy Punch (Charmaine). Directed by Woody Allen and produced by Letty Aronson, Jaume Roures, and Stephen Tenenbaum. Screenplay by Allen.

*You Will Meet a Tall Dark Stranger* is every frame a Woody Allen film, but it isn't very much more. Perhaps the title provides a clue. Its point of view is of an outsider—a fortune-teller, let's say, or the narrator of the film. This person knows about the problems of the characters, knows they hope, knows they lust, knows they dream, and knows that life is a tale told by an idiot, filled with sound and fury, signifying nothing.

That is not such an original observation as when first it was made, but it describes the action of the film well enough. We see several people worriedly scuttling about in search of happiness. These people lead enviable lives. They have money, professions, culture. At the end, for these fortunates and all of us, everything reduces to the hunger for love. It's not really sex they're after; it's to be reflected as valuable in the eyes of somebody new because they need reassurance. It can't all signify nothing, you see, if you're important to someone. This someone must be a new person because (1) you and your current lover know each other too well, and (2) you can project wonderful qualities on the new lover until you get to know that person too well. It is assumed all along, of course, that you are invaluable.

The time is the present. The city, London, where people seem to live in each other's pockets more than in American cities. We meet an old lady named Helena (Gemma Jones), whose husband, Alfie (Anthony Hopkins), has left her for a floozy blonde. She seeks consolation from a medium who sees her floating in clouds of glory and predicts she will meet a very special man.

Helena's daughter is Sally (Naomi Watts). Sally is married to Roy (Josh Brolin), whose first novel was a success and who has been living off her money ever since, while blaming her for writer's block. Meanwhile, the treacherous Alfie is spending a fortune on Charmaine (Lucy Punch), who is an *actress* and reminds me of Ben Hecht's definition of actress: "any woman under thirty who is not actively employed in a brothel, with many exceptions." (His definition of actor: "a waiter.")

Sally and Roy have fought about money and his unwritten second novel for so long they've lost interest in each other. Their eyes stray. Sally is drawn to her magnetic boss, Greg, who, as he is played by Antonio Banderas, makes it hard for us to blame her. Roy finds himself looking into the window of a flat across from his, where on display is the lovely Dia, who, as she is played by Freida Pinto from *Slumdog Millionaire*, makes it hard for us to blame him.

The way Woody Allen handles this is by a series of conversations in which paradoxes are illustrated by the search for happiness. Dia is remarkably sympathetic with Roy; it's not every subject of a Peeping Tom who introduces him to her parents. Charmaine is a floozy, but not entirely without a heart. The movie is forgiving. But the search for happiness is doomed by definition: You must be happy with what you have, not with what you desire, because the cost of the quest is too high. So consider old Helena. She doesn't meet a tall, dark stranger, but she meets a short, stout one. He owns an occult bookshop, and they determine it was meant for them to be together. What more can you ask? The others are all too smart for their own good.

# Z

## Zookeeper ★ ★ ★

PG, 104 m., 2011

Kevin James (Griffin), Rosario Dawson (Kate), Leslie Bibb (Stephanie). And the voices of Nick Nolte (Bernie the Gorilla), Adam Sandler (Donald the Monkey), Sylvester Stallone (Joe the Lion), Cher (Janet the Lioness), Judd Apatow (Barry the Elephant), Jon Favreau (Jerome the Bear), Faizon Love (Bruce the Bear), Maya Rudolph (Mollie the Giraffe), Bas Rutten (Sebastian the Wolf), and Don Rickles (Frog). Directed by Frank Coraci and produced by Todd Garner, Jack Giarraputo, Kevin James, and Adam Sandler. Screenplay by James, Nick Bakay, Rock Reuben, Jay Scherick, and David Ronn.

*Zookeeper* is a good-natured comedy about how the animals at the zoo coach Kevin James on his romantic life. Since he ends up with Rosario Dawson, they must know what they're talking about. What it comes down to is a buddy movie where the best buddy is a gorilla.

I confess to a sinking feeling when the first animal began to talk. I understand why animals talk in animated films, but in live-action films it usually just feels creepy. Studiously avoiding all contact with publicity for the movie, I naively expected a story about the profession of zookeeping—you know, some natural history, maybe some insights into animal psychology.

What I got instead were animals that speak perfectly in a variety of accents, ranging from Bernie the Gorilla (Nick Nolte), Donald the Monkey (Adam Sandler), Joe the Lion (Sylvester Stallone), and Janet the Lioness (Cher) down the evolutionary scale to Don Rickles doing Frog, who doesn't have a first name.

Kevin James stars as the socially inept Griffin, a zookeeper who deeply cares for his animals and discovers they like him just as much. He's sweet and goofy, and somehow once had the sexy Stephanie (Leslie Bibb) as his girlfriend. The story is, she broke up with him because of his low salary. But now it looks as if he'll get a job at his brother's luxury car dealership, and she's interested again. Problem is, he's paralyzed by shyness.

The animals team up to advise him, suggesting such tactics as aggression (the lions), marking his territory (the wolves), and puffing out his throat (Frog). He takes them so seriously that he marks his territory at his brother's rehearsal dinner by peeing in a potted plant.

Meanwhile, right there in plain view and sharing his love of animals is his fellow zookeeper Kate (Rosario Dawson), who has never looked more ravishing. Why would he prefer the shallow Stephanie? Because the plot requires him to, of course. That's the law in a romcom: The guy falls in love with the top-billed woman, but not before skirting romantic disaster.

It's not the romcom that's so entertaining, anyway; it's the slapstick. Griffin busts up his brother's wedding by swinging from long cloth strips that fortuitously hang from the ceiling, and later engages in a thrilling chase scene while assisted by Bernie the Gorilla. It is also funny when they go out to dinner together at T.G.I. Friday's, which Bernie has long eyed from over the top of the zoo walls.

Look, a great movie this is not. A pleasant summer entertainment it is. I think it can play for all ages in a family audience, it's clever to have the animals advising humans on their behavioral strategies, and besides, I'm getting a teensy bit exhausted by cute little animated animals. The creatures in this zoo all have the excellent taste to be in 2-D.

# The Best Films of 2011

Making lists is not my favorite occupation. They inevitably inspire only reader complaints. Not once have I ever heard from a reader that my list was just fine and they liked it. Yet an annual Best Ten List is apparently a statutory obligation for movie critics. Here's mine. It is actually a Best Eleven List because the editors think it would be clever in 2011 to pay tribute to *This Is Spinal Tap* and its guitarist Nigel Tufnel, who could crank his volume up to 11.

Therefore, I give you two lists, one with eleven movies and the other with nine. My best guess is that between six and ten of these movies won't be familiar. Those are the most useful titles for you, especially in these days when they are all available via on demand, or soon will be. The best use for Best Lists is to get viewing ideas.

## 1. *A Separation*

This Iranian film won the Golden Bear at Berlin and was named the year's Best Foreign Language Film by the New York Film Critics Circle. It is specifically Iranian, but I believe the more specific a film is about human experience, the more universal it is. On the other hand, movies "for everybody" seem to be for nobody in particular. This film combines a plot worthy of a great novel with the emotional impact of a great melodrama. It involves a struggle for child custody, the challenge of a parent with Alzheimer's, the intricacies of the law, and the enigma of discovering the truth. In its reconstruction of several versions of a significant event, it is as baffling as *Rashomon.*

A modern Iranian couple considers immigrating to Europe to find better opportunities for their daughter. The mother wants to leave quickly. The father delays because his father has Alzheimer's and needs care. "Your father no longer knows you!" his wife says during a hearing in divorce court. "But I know him!" says her husband. We can identify with both statements.

A caregiver is hired but cannot come, and his wife secretly substitutes for him. It's against her religious principles for her to touch any man not her husband, but her family needs the money. This leads to events that create a deep moral tangle. Asghar Farhadi's real subject is truth, when it is disagreed about by people we respect even though we know most of the facts. *A Separation* will become one of those enduring masterpieces watched decades from now.

## 2. *Shame*

Michael Fassbender's brave, uncompromising performance is at the center of Steve McQueen's merciless film about sex addiction. He's a loner with a good job who avoids relationships because of his obsession with sex. He is driven to experience multiple orgasms every day. His shame is masked in privacy. He wants no witnesses to his hookers, his pornography, his masturbation. Does he fear he is incapable of ordinary human contact?

There isn't the slightest suggestion he experiences pleasure. Sex is his cross to bear. The film opens with a close-up of Fassbender's face showing pain, grief, and anger. His character is having an orgasm. He is enduring a sexual function that has long since stopped giving him any pleasure and is self-abuse in the most profound way.

Carey Mulligan costars as his sister. She is as passionate and uninhibited as he is the opposite. She needs him desperately. He fears need. He flies at her in a rage, telling her to get out. She has nowhere to go. He doesn't care. Childhood has damaged them. *Shame* is a great act of filmmaking and acting. I don't believe I would be able to see it twice.

## 3. *The Tree of Life*

A film of vast ambition and deep humility, attempting no less than to encompass all of existence and view it through the prism of a few infinitesimal lives. Terrence Malick's film begins with the Big Bang that created our universe, and ends after the characters have left the realm of time. In between, it zooms in on a moment, surrounded by infinity.

Scenes portray a childhood in a town in the American midlands, where life flows in and out through open windows. There is a father who maintains discipline and a mother who exudes forgiveness, and long summer days of play and idleness and urgent unsaid questions about the meaning of things. Three boys in the 1950s American Midwest are browned by the sun, scuffed by play, disturbed by glimpses of adult secrets, filled with a great urgency to grow up and discover who they are.

Listen to an acute exchange of dialogue between the son Jack (Hunter McCracken) and his father (Brad Pitt). "I was a little hard on you sometimes," Mr. O'Brien says, and Jack replies: "It's your house. You can do what you want to." Jack is defending his father against himself. That's how you grow up. And it all happens in this blink of a lifetime, surrounded by the realms of unimaginable time and space.

## 4. *Hugo*

In the guise of a delightful 3-D family film, Martin Scorsese makes a love letter to the cinema. His hero, Hugo (Asa Butterfield), had an uncle who was in charge of the clocks at a Parisian train station. His father's dream was to complete an automated man he found in a museum. He died with it left unperfected. Rather than be treated as an orphan, the boy hides himself in the maze of ladders, catwalks, passages, and gears of the clockworks themselves, feeding himself with croissants snatched from station shops, and begins to sneak off to the movies.

His life in the station is complicated by a toyshop owner named Georges Melies. Yes, this grumpy old man, played by Ben Kingsley, is none other than the immortal French film pioneer, who was also the original inventor of the automaton. Hugo has no idea of this. The real Melies was a magician who made his first movies to play tricks on his audiences.

Without our quite realizing it, Hugo's changing relationship with the old man becomes the story of the invention of the movies, and the preservation of our film heritage. Could anyone but Scorsese have made this subject so magical and enchanting? Although I believe that 3-D is usually an unnecessary annoyance, the way Scorsese employs it here is quite successful; in calling attention to itself, 3-D subtly calls attention to film itself.

## 5. *Take Shelter*

Curtis LaForche (Michael Shannon) appears to be a stable husband and father with a good job in construction, but he also can evoke by his eyes and manner a deep unease. Curtis has what he needs to be happy. He fears he will lose it. His dreams are visited by unusually vivid nightmares: The family dog attacks him, or storms destroy his home. They live on the outskirts of town, in an area that is swept from time to time with tornadoes.

Director Jeff Nichols builds his suspense carefully. Curtis is tormented but intelligent. Fearing the family's history of mental illness, he visits his schizophrenic mother (Kathy Baker) to ask if she was ever troubled by bad dreams. He turns to the area's obviously inadequate public health facilities.

And he also acts as if his warnings should be taken seriously. He borrows money from the bank and equipment from work to greatly expand an old storm shelter in his backyard. His wife (Jessica Chastain) is frightened by his behavior. His job and health insurance are threatened. People begin to talk. And then a storm comes. It leads to a searing scene in which the man and his wife must confront their fears about the weather—and about each other.

## 6. *Kinyarwanda*

I was moved by *Hotel Rwanda* (2004), but not really shaken this deeply. After seeing *Kinyarwanda*, I have a different kind of feeling about the genocide that took place in Rwanda in 1994. The film approaches it not as a storyline but as a series of intense personal moments.

In an independent film of great emotional impact, the film's director, a Jamaican named Alrick Brown, establishes a vivid group of characters. A young couple from different tribes who are in love. The female head of a military unit trained in Uganda, hoping to bring peace. A Catholic priest. The mufti of

Rwanda. Most memorable, a small boy named Ishmael. Their personal stories are entangled in the ancient conflict between tribes, while the United Nations regards the genocide from afar. The title may put some people off. It is the name of the language both tribes speak, although the film is largely in English. I'm inviting *Kinyarwanda* to Ebertfest 2012.

## 7. *Drive*

The Driver drives for hire. He has no other name and no other life. When we meet him, he's the wheelman for a getaway car, who runs from police pursuit not by speed, but by coolly exploiting the street terrain and outsmarting his pursuers. By day, he's a stunt driver for action movies. The two jobs represent no conflict for him: He drives. He has no family, no history, and seemingly few emotions. Whatever happened to him drove any personality deep beneath the surface. Played by Ryan Gosling, he is an existential hero, defined entirely by his behavior.

The director, Nicolas Winding Refn, peoples his story with characters who bring lifetimes onto the screen—in contrast to the Driver, who brings as little as possible. Ron Perlman is a big-time operator working out of a pizzeria in a strip mall. Albert Brooks plays a producer of the kinds of B movies the Driver does stunt driving for; he also has a sideline in crime. These people are ruthless. *Drive* looks like one kind of thriller in the ads, and it is that kind of thriller, but also another and a rebuke to most of the movies it looks like.

## 8. *Midnight in Paris*

A fabulous daydream for American lit majors, Woody Allen's charming comedy opens with a couple on holiday in Paris. Gil (Owen Wilson) and Inez (Rachel McAdams) are officially in love, but what Gil really loves is Paris in the springtime. He's a hack screenwriter from Hollywood who still harbors the dream of someday writing a good novel and joining the pantheon of American writers whose ghosts seem to linger in the very air he breathes: Fitzgerald, Hemingway, and the other legends of Paris in the 1920s.

By (wisely) unexplained means, each midnight he finds himself magically transported back in time to the legendary salon presided over by Gertrude Stein. He meets Scott and Zelda, Ernest, Picasso, Dali, Cole Porter, Luis Bunuel, and, yes, "Tom Eliot." He even gives Bunuel the idea for his film *The Exterminating Angel.* Kathy Bates makes an authoritative Miss Stein, and Marion Cotillard plays Adriana, who has already been the mistress of Braque and Modigliani, is now Picasso's lover, and may soon—be still, my heart!—fall in love with Gil.

## 9. *Le Havre*

Aki Kaurismaki is a Finnish director who makes dour, deadpan comedies about people who shrug their way through misfortune. They have a hypnotic fascination for me. *Le Havre* is the sunniest film of his I've seen. Set in the French port city, it involves young Idrissa (Blondin Miguel), an illegal immigrant from Gabon, solemn, shy, appealing. The hero, Marcel Marx (Andre Wilms), fishing near a pier, sees the boy hiding waist-deep in the water. He leaves out some food and finds it gone the next day. And so, with no plan in mind, Marcel becomes in charge of protecting the boy from arrest.

The whole neighborhood gets involved in hiding the boy from the port inspector. This involves low-key comedy that occasionally shifts into high, as with a local rock singer named Little Bob (Roberto Piazza), whose act is unlike any you have ever seen. Young Idrissa finds himself in the center of a miraculous episode between Marcel and his wife, which may not be believable but is certainly satisfying.

## 10. *The Artist*

What audacity to make a silent film in black-and-white in 2011, and what a film Michel Hazanavicius has made!

Jean Dujardin won the best actor award at Cannes for his work as a silent star who is cast aside with the advent of the talkies. His career is rescued by a young dancer (Berenice Bejo) he was kind to when he was at the top. This wonderful film is many things: comedy, pathos, melodrama. For many people, this will be their introduction to silent movies and cause them to reconsider if they really dislike black-and-white. It's an audience pleaser, and many in the audience won't be expecting that. It was the first silent film to win an Oscar as Best Picture since *Wings* (1927).

## 11. *Melancholia*

This film about the end of the world is, Lars von Trier assured us, his first with a happy ending. I think I see what he means. At least his poor characters need suffer no longer. If I were choosing a director to make a film about the subject, von Trier the gloomy Dane might be my first choice. The only other name that comes to mind is Werner Herzog's. Both understand that at such a time, silly little romantic subplots take on a vast irrelevance.

That's even the case in *Melancholia*, which actually takes place at a wedding party for newlyweds. In the sky, another planet looms ever larger, but life carries on all the same here below. Kirsten Dunst is the new bride, and Charlotte Gainsbourg plays her sister. The two seem to exchange personalities. The details matter less than the grand overarching mood.

## 12. *Terri*

Tells the story the story of a fat kid who is mocked in high school. Terri (Jacob Wysocki) is smart, gentle, and instinctively wise. His decision to wear pajamas to school *because they fit* may be an indication that later in life he will amount to a great deal. He has character. He's been missing a lot of school and is called in by the assistant principal (John C. Reilly), a school administrator unlike those we usually see, offering kindness, anger, and hard-won lessons learned in his own difficult life. He and Terri slowly begin to communicate person to person.

Chad (Bridger Zadina) is another of the administrator's problem children, a morose, slouching outsider driven to pluck hairs from his head. Heather (Olivia Crocicchia) is a pretty young student who is threatened with expulsion; Terri steps up and defends her in a way that shows he respects her and empathizes. He may be a kid who is fat and weird, but he's much more than fat and weird. This film has also been invited to Ebertfest 2012.

## 13. *The Descendants*

George Clooney in one of his best performances as a descendant of one of Hawaii's first white landowning families, who must decide whether to open up a vast tract of virgin forest on Kauai to tourist and condo development. This decision comes at the same time his wife has a boating accident and is in a coma. Having devoted most of his attention to business, he now must learn to be a single parent of two daughters while also dealing with the King family's urgent desire to close the multimillion-dollar land deal.

Leading the push for the King family is Cousin Hugh (Beau Bridges). As affable as Bridges can be, he doesn't want to listen to any woo-woo green nonsense about not selling. The film follows Clooney's legal, family, and emotional troubles in careful detail, until director Alexander Payne shows us, without forcing it, that they are all coiled together. We get *vested* in the lives of the characters. We come to understand how they think, and care about what they decide about the substantial moral problems underlying the plot.

## 14. *Margaret*

Kenneth Lonergan's film begins with a young woman (Anna Paquin) thinking she may have contributed to a fatal bus accident through her own foolishness. She decides the bus driver (Mark Ruffalo) should also be held accountable, and makes it her business to see that he is. This story crosscuts with others, including Jean Reno and J. Smith-Cameron in a sweet midlife romance. The film inspired an online conspiracy theory when Fox Searchlight was accused of being shy about its 9/11 material. Actually, 9/11 figures only marginally; what's important is the conflict between the young woman's perfectionism and things as they are.

## 15. *Martha Marcy May Marlene*

Those are four names that apply at various times in the life of a young woman played by Elizabeth Olsen. "Martha" is her name. "Marcy May" is the name given to her by the leader of a cult group she falls into. "Marlene" is the name all the women in the group use to answer the telephone. The cult leader is an evil and mesmeric figure played with great effect by John Hawkes. Her experience in the cult causes her confusion about her identity after she escapes into the relative safety of the home of her sister (Sarah Paulson). Sean Durkin's film builds on the strong Elizabeth Olsen to show how easily groups can control their members.

## 16. *Harry Potter and the Deathly Hallows: Part 2*

The second installment in the last chapter of the legendary saga comes to a solid and satisfying conclusion, conjuring up enough awe and solemnity to serve as an appropriate finale and a dramatic contrast to the lighthearted (relative) innocence of *Harry Potter and the Sorcerer's Stone* all those magical years ago.

## 17. *Trust*

The bravest thing about David Schwimmer's *Trust* is that it doesn't try to simplify. It tells its story of a fourteen-year-old girl and a predatory pedophile as a series of repercussions in which rape is only the first, and possibly not the worst, tragedy to strike its naive and vulnerable victim. Liana Liberato stars as a "good girl" who isn't advanced, who feels uncomfortable at a party where "popular girls" fake sophistication. She's never had a boyfriend when she meets Charlie (Chris Henry Coffey) in an online chat room. Charlie is in high school. Like her, he plays volleyball. He's a nice kid, too. He understands her. She grows closer to Charlie than any boy she's ever known. They talk for hours on the phone. But Charlie is not what he seems.

## 18. *Life, Above All*

This South African feature centers on a twelve-year-old named Chanda (Khomotso Manyaka), who takes on the responsibility of holding her family together after her baby sister dies. Family members are suspected of having AIDS; the community ostracizes them, until a courageous neighbor finally steps in. An opening scene shows Chanda choosing a coffin for her baby sister. The seriousness and solemnity with which she performs this task is heartrending and heartwarming. Both director Oliver Schmitz and the gifted Miss Manyaka attended Ebertfest 2011.

## 19. *The Mill and the Cross*

Any description would be an injustice. It opens on a carefully composed landscape based on a famous painting, *The Way to Calvary* (1564), by the Flemish master Pieter Bruegel the Elder. Within the painting, a few figures move and walk. We might easily miss the figure of Christ among the five hundred in the vast landscape. Others are going about their everyday lives. The film is an extraordinary mixture of live action, special effects, green screen work, and even an actual copy of the painting itself (by Lech Majewski, the film's Polish director). Set not in the biblical lands but in Flanders, it uses Belgians as Jews and the Spanish as Romans, in an allegorical parallel that also breaks down into fragments of lives. It is a film before which words fall silent.

## 20. *Another Earth*

Joins *Melancholia* as a second 2011 film about a new planet hanging in our sky. This one doesn't presage the end of the world, but represents perhaps the very same Earth, in another universe that has now become visible. It stars Brit Marling as Rhoda, a young woman who has been accepted into the astrophysics program at MIT. She hears the news about Earth 2. Peering out her car window to search the sky, she crashes into another car, killing a mother and child and sending the father into a coma.

A few years pass. She's released from prison and learns that the father, a composer named John Burroughs (William Mapother), has emerged from his coma. Rhoda is devastated by the deaths she caused and wants to apologize or make amends or . . . what? She doesn't know. She presents herself at the shabby rural house where Burroughs lives as a depressed recluse. They grow closer. Did the accident not occur on Earth 2?

Those are my top 20, leaving out documentaries, which I will list later. To include them on the same list would be ranking oranges and apples. There were many other excellent films in 2011, some fully the equal of some of these. Alphabetically: *Beginners, Boy Wonder, Certified Copy, The Future, The Guard, Higher Ground, I Will Follow, J. Edgar, The Last Rites of Joe May, Le Quattro Volte, Margin Call, Meek's Cutoff, Moneyball, Mysteries of Lisbon, My Week with Marilyn, The Princess of Montpensier, Rango, Queen to Play, A Screaming Man, Silent Souls, 13 Assassins, Tyrannosaur, Sherlock Holmes: A Game of Shadows, The Whistleblower,* and *Young Adult.*

# The Best Documentaries of 2011

Why not fold documentaries into my list of the Best Films of 2011? After all, a movie is a movie, right? Yes, and some years I've thrown them all into the same mixture. But all of these year-end best lists serve one useful purpose: They tell you about good movies you may not have seen or heard about. The more films on my list that aren't on yours, the better job I've done.

That's particularly true were you to depend on the "short list" released by the Academy's documentary branch of fifteen films it deems eligible for nomination. The branch has been through turmoil in the past and its procedures were "reformed" at one point. But this year it has made a particularly scandalous choice. It includes *The Undefeated*, the Sarah Palin doc that drew a perfect zero rating from fifteen critics on the Tomatometer, but does not include *The Interrupters*, the most-mentioned doc in critics' year-end Best Ten Lists.

For Steve James of Kartemquin Films, who made *The Interrupters*, this is an old story. The documentary branch also failed to shortlist James's *Hoop Dreams* (1994), which is generally considered one of the greatest documentaries of all time. In a scandal at that time, it was revealed that the branch's volunteer screening committee turned off *Hoop Dreams* after watching only fifteen minutes.

The year's best documentaries:

## 1. *The Interrupters*

Steve James, who made the masterpiece *Hoop Dreams*, now makes his most important film, telling the story of ex-convicts who go daily into the streets of Chicago to try to talk gang members out of shooting at one another. All have done prison time. Some have murdered. They were young when they were seduced by the lure of street gangs. Today they see young people throwing their lives away and often killing bystanders by accident.

James's film follows members of CeaseFire, tough negotiators who monitor gang activity in their neighborhoods and try to anticipate developing warfare. They make it their business to know the gang leaders and members. They build trust. In some shots in this film, they are physically in the possible line of fire—and so are Steve James and his small crew. This film has true impact.

## 2. *Bill Cunningham New York*

A movie about a happy and nice man. Bill Cunningham was lucky to find what he loves to do, to win universal affection from all who know him, and to make a contribution to our lives and times. Doing what he loves is very nearly *all* he does, except to sleep and eat.

Bill celebrates his eightieth birthday in the movie. Every day of his life he still pedals around Manhattan on his bicycle, taking photographs of what people are wearing. You can find his work featured in big spreads in the *New York Times*. He's not a fashion photographer or a paparazzo. He's genuinely fascinated by what people wear, and will stop in the middle of the street if he spots an interesting hat.

## 3. *Into the Abyss: A Tale of Death, a Tale of Life*

Perhaps the saddest film Werner Herzog has ever made, centering on two young men in prison. Michael Perry is on death row in Huntsville, Texas, America's most productive assembly line for executions, and on the day Herzog spoke with him had eight days to live. Jason Burkett, his accomplice in the stupid murders of three people, is serving a forty-year sentence. They killed because they wanted to drive a friend's red Camaro.

Herzog became curious about the case, took a small crew to Huntsville and Conroe, Texas, where the murders took place, and spoke to the killers and members of their families and those of their victims. He obtains interviews of startling honesty and impact. We also meet Captain Fred Allen, who was for many years in charge of the guard detail on

Huntsville's death row. He starts talking with Herzog and is swept up by memory and emotion, explaining why one day, after overseeing more than one hundred executions, he simply walked away and decided he was opposed to the death penalty.

## 4. *Tabloid*

By Errol Morris, who says his subject, Joyce McKinney, is his favorite protagonist. In 1977 McKinney was involved in the infamous "Case of the Manacled Mormon," made to order for the British tabloids we read about during the *News of the World* scandal. A former Miss Wyoming, she was alleged to have kidnapped an American Mormon missionary in the United Kingdom, handcuffed him to a bed, and made him a sex slave. All lies, she says.

*Rashomon* will inevitably be evoked in discussions of this film. Many scenarios fit the facts. Morris presents officials with boundless reasons to think McKinney guilty of stalking, abduction, and possible rape. He also allows McKinney to offer a perky alternative perspective on the same events. Which version does Morris believe? With him, you never quite know for sure.

## 5. *Resurrect Dead: The Mystery of the Toynbee Tiles*

It's possible you've stepped on a Toynbee Tile yourself. These are hundreds of crudely lettered tiles stuck with tar to pavements and sidewalks in cities up and down the Eastern seaboard, as far west as Kansas City, and in three South American cities. They may have started appearing in 1983. What do they possibly mean? Who devises and places them?

Writer-director Jon Foy follows three tile sleuths: Justin Duerr, Steve Weinik, and Colin Smith. Starting with a small handful of meager clues, their detective work leads them to strange places: a paragraph in an old *Philadelphia Inquirer*, a play by David Mamet, addresses in South Philadelphia, a convention of ham radio operators. They find Web sites filled with tile photos and rumors. The film is confoundingly watchable.

## 6. *Cave of Forgotten Dreams*

The second film on my list by Werner Herzog, a master of both features and documentaries. He gains access to Chauvet Cave, above the Ardeche River in southern France. There humans created the oldest cave paintings known to exist. They spring from the walls with boldness and confidence, as if the artists were already sure what they wanted to paint and how to paint it. Perhaps twenty-five thousand years ago, a child visited the cave and left a footprint, the oldest human footprint that can be accurately dated.

The French archaeologists who discovered the cave in 1994 had to descend a narrow opening to the cave's floor, far below on the original entrance level. It is their entry route that Herzog follows in his spellbinding film. Herzog filmed in 3-D to better convey how the paintings follow and exploit the natural contours of the ancient walls. The process also helps him suggest how the humans of the Upper Paleolithic era might have seen the paintings themselves, in the flickering light of their torches. To the degree that it's possible for us to walk behind Herzog into that cave, we do so.

## 7. *Pina*

Wim Wenders's mesmerizing documentary presents the choreography of Pina Bausch, a German dancer and director. Watching the film, I didn't know she died in 2009, on the eve of principal photography. But I wasn't surprised when I learned that. It accounts for the elegiac tone of many of her colleagues and troupe members. They are reserved, introspective, solemn. Joining her troupe seems to have been more a life decision than a career move. They loved her.

Bausch's troupe shares a common understanding of time and space. There is a remarkable piece here called *Café Mueller*, which I'd earlier seen in Pedro Almodovar's *Talk to Her*, in which some dancers seem to wander blindly in a room where other dancers rearrange chairs and tables. The parallel with life itself is there to be seen. Wenders's use of 3-D is effective, helping him enter more fully into the performance space. There is usually no convention of a proscenium arch in the film. One piece uses water, and another sand, which the dancers cover the stage with and then crawl or roll through to leave marks of their movements. The entire film was, for me, meditative.

### 8. *Garbo the Spy*

He was called "Garbo" because an Allied spymaster thought he was the best actor in the world. Juan Pujol Garcia, a Spaniard based in Lisbon, fed the Nazis a stream of misleading information from a spy network that existed entirely in his imagination. Using invented facts and a spy network that didn't exist, he convinced the Nazis that the Allied landing at Normandy was a decoy operation to draw their troops away from the *real* landing site, at Calais. One man's imagination changed the course of the war.

Lacking period footage of Garcia (naturally), director Edmon Roch ingeniously cobbles together newsreel footage, scenes from old war movies, and modern talking heads to piece together his story of a startling deception.

### 9. *The Last Mountain*

Is there another state more cruelly defaced than West Virginia? Its mountains have been blown up, its forests ripped out, and the green land the settlers discovered now includes a wasteland of a million toxic acres. Nationally, one in one hundred thousand people get brain tumors. In a small West Virginia town surrounded by strip mining, six neighbors have developed brain tumors. What are the odds of that?

This is a blunt and enraged documentary about Coal River Mountain, the site of a last stand against Massey Energy, a company it says disregarded environmental concerns, compromised the political process, and poisoned great stretches of the state in the name of corporate profits. Now lakes of sludge loom above towns, rivers are dead and dying, and heavy metals invade the bloodstreams and brains of the inhabitants. Recent court findings against Massey provide a footnote to Bill Haney's film.

### 10. *Louder Than a Bomb*

Poetry slams began in Chicago in 1984 and have become an international phenomenon. They're poetry readings as a spectator sport. Individuals and teams are scored by judges on the Olympic ten-point scale. *Louder Than a Bomb* is about the 2008 Chicago-area slam of that name, the nation's largest. Teams and soloists from sixty high schools compete, and the finalists face off in a city-wide slam that fills a theater usually used for rock concerts. The suspense that year initially centered on Steinmetz, a troubled inner-city school that had never entered before it won the 2007 Bomb in a thrilling upset. Can Steinmetz and its coach, James Sloan, repeat?

The film was directed by Greg Jacobs and Jon Siskel (Gene's nephew), who followed several competitors for months and guessed well in choosing those they focused on. Like earlier docs about spelling bees and Scrabble tournaments, but with more showmanship and energy, it focuses on individuals and builds great suspense. Shown at Ebertfest 2011.

### 11. *Page One: Inside the New York Times*

One newspaper remains, as it has long been, the most essential source of news in this country. *Page One: Inside the New York Times* sets out to examine its stature in these hard times for print journalism, but ends up with more of the hand-wringing that dominates all such discussions. People who are serious about the news venerate the past, hope for the future, and don't have a clue about the present.

Much attention is given to the paper's role in digital media, but what happens is that a charismatic hero comes along and distracts from the big picture. That man here is David Carr, the paper's raspy-voiced star media reporter. He reminds me of the reporters I held in awe when I first went to work for newspapers. Like Mike Royko, Carr combines cynicism, idealism, and a canny understanding of how things *really* work. As we watch him meticulously report the story that exposed the lamentable "frat house" management of Sam Zell's *Chicago Tribune*, we see the reporter as a prosecutor, nailing down an air-tight case.

### 12. *One Lucky Elephant*

Tells the stories of Flora, an African elephant, and David Balding, who runs a St. Louis circus. Flora witnessed her mother killed, and was shipped in a crate to the United States at a tender age, where after training and bonding with Balding, she became the star performer and namesake of Circus Flora. This is a one-ring circus that was created as a commissioned work for the 1986 Spoleto Festival in Charleston and has performed annually in St. Louis since 1987.

Balding and his wife, Laura, decided Flora was reaching the end of her show business career and deserved a pleasant retirement. *One Lucky Elephant* follows their search for a home for Flora, which began in 2000 and became a great challenge. A larger question coils beneath the surface of the film. What happens to an elephant that is "trained"? Knowing humans all of its life, can it find happiness in an elephant sanctuary?

## 13. *Buck*

One of the big documentary hits of the year. Buck Brannaman was the original "horse whisperer," the character Nicholas Evans based his novel on and Robert Redford used as the on-set consultant for his film. He has a way with horses, and Cindy Meehl's documentary is moving as she shows them engaged in dances of understanding.

Buck was abused as a child, and that experience influenced his gentle approach to horse training. It involves empathy for the feelings of the horse. Buck understands how horses read humans, how they interpret gestures, and how they're "so sensitive they can feel a fly land." I was reminded of Temple Grandin, the autistic designer of cattle-handling chutes, whose secret was identifying the feelings of cattle with her own.

## 14. *Conan O'Brien Can't Stop*

The title has piercing accuracy. After NBC and Jay Leno pulled the rug out from under him, O'Brien went overnight from hosting the *Tonight Show* to being banned from television for six months. He became like Wile E. Coyote, chasing the Road Runner of his dreams off the edge of a cliff and afraid to look down. Enraged at Leno and NBC, he quickly undertook "The Legally Prohibited from Being Funny on Television Tour," which covered thirty-two cities, from Radio City Music Hall to the Bonnaroo Music Festival in Tennessee—where inside a tent in hundred-degree heat he was expected to introduce every act, and did.

Here is a man driven to assert himself. He waited five years for the *Tonight Show*, lost it in months, and needed to say to the universe, "Sir! I exist!" The film, directed by Rodman Flender, watches him before and after shows and en route between cities, seeing a man incapable of giving himself a break. Overworked, exhausted, assaulted by demands, he cannot say no to an autograph, patiently hosts waves of visitors in his dressing room, drums up work on his days off, and at times seems on the edge of madness. The man behind the image.

## 15. *Strongman*

A tantalizing example of the kind of documentary I find engrossing: a film about an unusual person that invites us into the mystery of a human life. Stanley Pleskun bills himself as "Stanless Steel, the Strongest Man Alive." Whether this is true is beside the point. Stanless, as I will call him, believes it absolutely. His girlfriend Barbara and his brother Michael agree, I gather, although they never actually say so.

How does the Strongest Man in the World support himself? He works as a freelancer in the scrap metal industry, collecting scrap and hauling it to a yard. We see him heaving heavy loads into the bed of his truck. Does this help him train? No, I learn from the film's notes, it tires him out and makes it harder to train. Although Zachary Levy, the filmmaker, followed him over a course of years and shot hundreds of hours of films, we see him actually training only twice: once squeezing a hand grip, and again staggering for several yards while carrying heavy concrete blocks.

His girlfriend Barbara introduces his act: "Ladies and gentlemen, boys and girls! Presenting Staaaaaanless Steeeel! The Strongest Man in the Woooorld!" He makes appearances at events in New Jersey and New York, bending steel bars, lifting trucks, and so on. He is paid $1,000 and expenses to appear on a British TV show. Is he really that strong? I have no idea.

## 16. *Project Nim*

Can a chimpanzee learn to speak by using sign language? Yes. But in what sense does it know what it is saying? *Project Nim*, a fascinating documentary, follows the life of a chimp named Nim Chimpsky as it's raised like a human baby and then shuttled from one set of "parents" and "homes" to another. The chimp emerges from this experience as a more admirable creature than many of its humans.

This is a new film by James Marsh, who made the Oscar-winning *Man on Wire.* Like Errol Morris on occasion, Marsh weaves dramatic re-creations into his film, so that sometimes we see actual documentary footage and at other times we see actors or even (although you won't notice it) animatronics. How this substitution fits with traditional documentary ethics I will set aside. It produces a very absorbing film.

### 17. *Waste Land*

Across the world's largest garbage dump, near Rio de Janeiro, the Pickers crawl with their bags and buckets, seeking treasures that can be recycled: plastics and metals, mostly, but anything of value. From the air they look like ants. You would assume they are the wretched of the Earth, but those we meet in *Waste Land* seem surprisingly cheerful. They lead hard lives but understandable ones. They make $20 or $25 a day. They live nearby. They feel pride in their labor, and talk of their service to the environment.

Directed by Lucy Walker, it takes as its entry point into the lives of the Pickers the work of the Brazilian artist Vik Muniz. As a youth he had the good fortune to be shot in the leg by a rich kid, who paid him off; he used the money to buy a ticket to America, and now he is famous for art that turns garbage into giant constructions, which he exhibits and photographs. Documentaries like these help us, perhaps, to more fully appreciate our roles as full-time creators of garbage.

### 18. *Phunny Business: A Black Comedy*

What Second City was for *Saturday Night Live,* a comedy club in Chicago was for virtually every black comedian who emerged in the 1990s. All Jokes Aside was a black-owned enterprise that seemed to have infallible taste in talent, perhaps because it was the only club in the country that didn't relegate blacks to "special nights" or "Chocolate Sundays." Its opening-night act was Jamie Foxx, then unknown. It introduced or showcased such as Bernie Mac, Cedric the Entertainer, Steve Harvey, D. L. Hughley, Carlos Mencia, A. J. Jamal, Sheryl Underwood, George Wallace, Bill Bellamy, Dave Chappelle, Adele Givens, and on and on, including the personnel of the touring Kings of Comedy and Queens of Comedy.

This is a film not so much about black comedians, although we see and hear a lot of them, but about black entrepreneurs. Raymond C. Lambert, who cofounded the club, began as a stock trader for the firm of the black Chicago millionaire Chris Gardner (who himself inspired the character played by Will Smith in *The Pursuit of Happyness*). After a visit to Budd Friedman's Improv in Los Angeles, he wondered why a club like that wouldn't work with black comics in Chicago. Turned out, it would.

### 19. *Make Believe*

A charming doc about the finalists in the Teenage Magician Contest at the annual World Magic Seminar in Las Vegas. From Malibu, Chicago, Colorado, Japan, and South Africa they come, dreaming of being presented with first place by the great Lance Burton. The documentary visits their homes, gets their stories, talks to their friends and parents, and follows them backstage in Vegas.

Not a single rabbit is pulled from a hat. Most of the tricks are small scale—locking rings, disappearing scarves, card production. A deck of cards in their hands seems to have a life of its own. One kid turns cards into iPhones while they're fanned between his fingers. We see him in his basement, building the props.

One thing we don't find out is how any of the tricks are done. The secrets in some cases are pretty widely known. Most of the people in the audience know in theory exactly how they're done, but are connoisseurs, judging how well they are performed. Magicians have a saying: "The trick is told when the trick is sold." These kids are sold on tricks.

### 20. *Being Elmo: A Puppeteer's Journey*

All Kevin Clash ever wanted to do was make puppets. That came even before he fixated on the Muppets. One day he had an inspiration so urgent that it required cutting up his father's coat. The result was a nice enough puppet, but when Kevin emerged from his creative frenzy, he realized his father might have stern words for him. Called in trembling to the old man, all he heard was: "Next time, ask."

*Being Elmo* is a documentary that follows him from his childhood through a series of good breaks that lead him into the universe of Jim Henson and *Sesame Street*, and we even hear an eyewitness to the day he "discovered" the Elmo character.

After another puppeteer grew frustrated and threw Elmo at Kevin saying, "Here, you try it," Kevin fooled around with a series of voices until Elmo, one of the most beloved of all Muppets, emerged. He also defined Elmo's central characteristic: All he wanted was to love and be loved, and hug you. What kid couldn't identify? The original Elmo craze led to buyer panics for the Tickle Me Elmo dolls, and Clash's life has been a happy one.

* * *

This list is based in part on my original reviews. Here is the Academy's complete short list of documentaries eligible for 2012 Oscar nomination: *Battle for Brooklyn, Bill Cunningham New York, Buck, Hell and Back Again, If a Tree Falls: A Story of the Earth Liberation Front, Jane's Journey, The Loving Story, Paradise Lost 3: Purgatory, Pina, Project Nim, Semper Fi: Always Faithful, Sing Your Song, The Undefeated, Under Fire: Journalists in Combat,* and *We Were Here.*

# Interviews

## Asghar Farhadi

January 27, 2012—In its own way, the success of the Iranian film *A Separation* is as remarkable as the success of *The Artist.* Neither one seems made for an American audience. One is silent and black-and-white. The other is from Iran, a nation not currently in official favor. Both just won Academy Award nominations, following their victories at the Golden Globes. *The Artist* had ten nominations, and *A Separation* was nominated not only for best picture but, in a surprise, for Asghar Farhadi's original screenplay.

The intriguing thing about his screenplay is that it gets us deeply involved, yet never tells us who it thinks is right or wrong. How do you choose between a husband and a daughter? Between a wife and a father?

There's an ancient ethical question, I mentioned to Farhadi in an online conversation. Your wife and your mother are both drowning—which would you rescue? Is there a correct answer to this question?

"I would want to save both of them or die trying," he said. "I know that's a cop-out, but the pain that comes along with choice is a result of real liberty, and the pain of choice is the result of being free to choose. Determinism and Authority exist side by side in this ancient example. In the film, I essentially try to ask this very question. Do we choose Termeh, the adolescent girl with a long future in front of her, or do we choose the old man with a past that is already behind? Do we sacrifice the future for the past? Having them both is the obvious ideal, but it is impossible here. This is the crossroads, and the choice is the important thing. The choice between Termeh and the grandfather, representatives of the past and the future, runs through the film on a greater level and through the struggle of two social groups. One looking toward the future and the other attached to the roots and the past. It is the struggle of the past and the future."

In a broader sense, we might expect the film to be critical of Iranian society. Although its events are embedded in the fabric of modern Iran, I'm unable to determine what its opinions are. All the important characters in the film are seen positively. There are no bad people here. Nothing that happens is the "fault" of anyone. They are good people facing impossible questions of the heart. In his Oscar-nominated screenplay, what is Farhadi's point of view?

"I've always felt that the filmmaker's point of view is secondary to the way that the film is accomplished," Farhadi said. "That's what really links the viewer to the film. The viewing public sees a series of images and either embraces it or lets it go. For me, the cinema has always been the most important thing—and features like being critical only come next. Being critical doesn't add value to a film, any more than a choice of genre does. It really comes down to precise and focused writing and structure.

"Instead of the expression 'critical cinema,' I prefer to use the term 'questioner cinema.' I like to put a question mark around the issues I'm concerned about. This is a way of inviting the viewer to critique, without my views getting in the way. I prefer to add numerous question marks to every issue. I think a cinema that asks questions is preferable to a cinema that is stylistically critical."

The great Iranian director Jafar Panahi is now in prison. Reuters reports: "He is accused of making a film without permission and inciting opposition protests after the 2009 Iranian election. He was jailed for six years and banned for 20 years from filmmaking, writing or any other form of artistic work." Now that *A Separation* has won the most international acclaim of any Iranian film, what has the popular and official reaction been like?

"Mostly people have liked the movie," he replied. "It has had a large audience and fortunately has evoked a lot of discussion, which is exactly what I hoped would happen. Seeing people gather in little groups after each screening to discuss the film: That's exactly what I wanted, and it gives me a nice feeling. It was also well received by the critics in Iran. But the official reaction was mixed. Being cautious toward commenting on the film was the common thing in all their reactions. Officials are used to judging the film and the filmmaker together. And they know that we don't agree on a lot of subjects. Well, let's just say that they can't make any comment without reservation. We have a proverb in Iran: 'A hit on the nail, a hit on the horseshoe.'"

Did the jailing of Panahi influence you in creating this work about a touchy area of religion and the law?

"If there was any influence, I was not aware of it while creating my work," Farhadi wrote me. "In general, these cases don't really have an immediate effect, but more of a long-term, discouraging influence on filmmakers. When I start writing a script, I try to keep these boundaries out of my mind in order to avoid limiting my thoughts. Sometimes I succeed, sometimes I don't.

"No doubt the situation and the atmosphere, consciously or unconsciously, have led me to this narrative style [the questioning cinema]. But now that I've reached this style, I feel that it's applicable in all social and cultural situations. As you see, this film was made and shown in Iran, using this very style. The same film was shown in countries with very different social situations and atmospheres. The viewers of other countries could relate to the film and to its style, a style that does not look at them from a superior level and does not treat them as passive viewers just like soccer spectators. So even without the boundaries, I like this style.

"Some watch it from a social angle, some from a moral angle, and some from a psychological or philosophical angle. The same thing happens with the characters: Some people will think the filmmaker is on Simin's side, some will think I'm on Nader's side, some will think my empathy lies with the maid. And everyone is right. I won't deny that in reality and outside the film I'm closer to some characters than others—but in the film, I've tried not to make any judgments and to write and direct in such a way as to show sympathy for each of the characters."

How, I asked, did the idea for the film come to you?

"I had an image in mind and later I figured that it must have come from something my brother once told me—the image of a middle-aged man giving a bath to his elderly father who is afflicted with Alzheimer's. This image was like a button that made me need to find the whole suite for it! I wanted to know: 'Who is this man? Where is his family? Why is he keeping his dad in the house? Why is he responsible for washing him? And does his father even recognize him?' And so many other questions. These really made different aspects of the story come to light for me."

The result is, I think, a great film, that steps outside Iran and poses questions for the whole world. More than any other recent film—at least among widely popular films—it does seem to inspire its audiences to step outside after the screening and continue the conversation.

## Tilda Swinton

January 22, 2012—When she was not yet five years old, Tilda Swinton told me, she saved the life of her brother. At least that's what everyone told her, and praised her for, and only little Tilda knew that soon after he was brought home from the hospital she intended to murder the baby.

This is not the sort of thing a person usually reveals, but it seemed relevant to our discussion of her harrowing new film, *We Need to Talk About Kevin.* Here is one of the best performances in the career of Swinton, a fearless actress who takes big risks in her films, but rarely one this big. *Kevin* is told entirely from Swinton's point of view, and she's on-screen almost every moment. She plays a suburban mother of two, the wife of a nice man (John C. Reilly), a woman deeply unhappy with motherhood.

It wouldn't be hard to blame her, if you had a son like Kevin. We see him at three stages of life, played by three actors. At the youngest age, what we feel about him is mostly projected: He has a colicky scream, he throws his baby food, she tells him that in all honesty she'd rather be in Paris than cleaning up after him. He's too young to understand her, but don't you suppose even very young children pick up the emotion in a statement like that?

*We Need to Talk About Kevin*, by the Scottish director Lynne Ramsay, has been called a monster movie. Everyone agrees Kevin is a monster, and some believe that Eva, Swinton's character, is one also. They have no love for each other. Even when he's six to eight (played by Jasper Newell), Kevin understands exactly what buttons to push. His dialogue is brutally cruel. As a teenager (played by Ezra Miller), he has a little trick of playing happily with his father, then catching his mother's eye and staring coldly at her.

You know it's wrong, you feel bad about your feelings, but you want to smack the little beast. Swinton told me the film reminded her of the childhood episode.

"When my third brother was born, I was so upset that it wasn't a girl. I so wanted a sister, and I had two other brothers. And I made the mistake of gunning for a girl and when it wasn't a girl and he was brought home from the hospital, I decided to kill him. And I went into his nursery to kill him and I didn't know what I was going to do. I hadn't thought it through. I wasn't a practiced murderer at this stage.

"And I noticed that he had a little sort of bonnet on with some ribbons going into his mouth and I started to pull them out. And then my nanny came from behind me and said, 'Ah, you clever girl! You're saving his life!' So I then had this legendary status in our family ever since as my brother-saver. But what nobody knew and what I had never really acknowledged to myself was that, you know, there but for the grace of a couple of ribbons I might have easily killed my brother; not necessarily in a vicious way, but in a way that felt natural to me."

There is a tendency to think of Kevin as Evil, with a capital E. He could have been named Damien, from *The Omen*. In our interview at Toronto 2012, Swinton said it's more complicated than that:

"I think there is a way in which society tries to push difficult things away from us, and we try and push them away ourselves and say that they are evil, we say that they are foreign, we say that they are not of us, that is not really useful to society. I'm not saying that one necessarily needs to embrace this darkness, but to know that it is of us, that it comes from us. That is really, really important because then we can look at responsibility."

Perhaps that's why, to a degree, Eva and Kevin understand each other so dreadfully well. Their mutual dislike is the substance of their relationship. Eva is patient, says kind things, and behaves in a solicitous way, but nobody is fooled. And what about Franklin, her husband, the John C. Reilly character? He maintains a steady, affable friendliness that is almost creepy. After he and Eva have a daughter, he lavishes love on both equally. Kevin goes through the motions of liking him, and he's deceived. Not Eva.

There's a point when she hurls Kevin against a wall. Child abuse, we would assume, but see the scene itself and decide what happened.

"When there's the 'accident,' when she throws him against the wall and breaks his arm," Swinton said, "he calls it the most honest thing she ever did. That's a tough moment, but I think that he appreciated that. He had her attention at that moment. I mean, it would be nice to think that it would be possible to get your mother's attention without getting her to break your arm, but I think that there's a way in which she really becomes a more functional mother only when he's incarcerated and everything else has gone."

Incarcerated. Yes, Kevin ends up in prison. I haven't described what he did to deserve that because that would make the movie too easy to categorize. I learn from another interview with Swinton that there was a line of dialogue in the script that didn't make it into the film. Eva asks Kevin why he killed who he did and spared who he did. "You don't want to kill your audience," he replies.

## Quvenzhane Wallis

June 19, 2012—If there is one 2012 movie that seems to have a lock on a best picture nomination, it is *Beasts of the Southern Wild*. And if there is a single reason its early viewers have loved it so much, it is an eight-year-old girl named Quvenzhane Wallis, who was six when she filmed it. Here is a case of a great role finding the perfect actress to play it.

My computer has trouble pronouncing names, I told Quvenzhane not long ago in my living room.

"That's OK," she said. We worked together on a phonetic spelling: kwa VAN ja nay. A beautiful name for this composed young woman, who deserves her own Oscar nomination, and whose nickname is Nazie.

The film is the feature debut of Benh Zeitlin, whose first short subject was made in the aftermath of Hurricane Katrina. It's set in the Bathtub, an isolated island area offshore from New Orleans, where the poorest of the poor scramble to survive. Shanties perch on stilts in the Delta marshlands. A boat is made from the bed of a pickup truck. The world of prosperity could be on a distant planet. We focus on a girl named Hushpuppy, whose mother has disappeared, whose father is loving but sometimes harsh, and whose determination is indomitable. The feeling is postapocalyptic, and there are rumors of another storm on the way, one that will flood the islands and their people.

At Sundance 2012, *Beasts* won the Grand Jury Prize. At Cannes, it won the Camera d'Or as best first film. At both, the small girl from Louisiana won hearts with her spunky, straightforward manner in the face of calamity.

As an actress, I asked Quvenzhane, what was the hardest thing for you to do?

"Doing all the lines because they are very hard and you have to remember all the lines—and sometimes they have long lines, so you've just gotta keep catching up."

How much of Hushpuppy is made up, and how much of her is like you?

"She has animals and she likes to explore the world and have adventures that she can always complete. But she's not really me because she doesn't wear her pants pretty much and she has more animals, likes to explore more and she can complete it anytime she wants to."

It comes out in a rush of enthusiasm. She's sitting next to her mother, Qulyndreia, and across from Zeitlin and Dwight Henry, a New Orleans baker who plays her father, Wink. But she doesn't look to them for guidance. This isn't her first interview.

Tell me about your audition, I said. They were looking for someone older. What do you think you did that impressed them?

"My audition turned out to be at the library, and my mom got a call from one of her friends and it was for a six- to nine-year-old. So my mom said I couldn't go 'cause I was only five. But we just went and we act like we're having nothin' to do; we had done nothin' wrong. And we just sneaked in because I was like one year younger so we just sneaked in and we walked out like we ain't done nothin'.

"So they called back and they said they were looking for Nazie. My mom says, 'Oh, you must be looking for Quvenzhane.' They were like, no, we must have called the wrong person and they almost hung up but my mom caught them. And she goes, 'She must have told you Nazie,' and they were like, 'Yes, that's who we're looking for.' And that's Quvenzhane. And they only found me because the character who is Hushpuppy, she does what is right and she is fearless and that's what I did at the audition."

Quvenzhane is in third grade at Honduras Elementary School in Houma, Louisiana, and has three siblings, Qunyquekya, Venjie Jr., and Vejon.

What did your family think about the movie?

"My siblings thought that it was a good thing to do, and my dad thought, 'Just let her go and see if she gets the part. She's young right now so I don't know if there is a talent that she thinks she can do.'"

Did anything turn out different than what you imagined while you were filming?

"Not really. Just that I missed a lot of school pretty much, but it helps because they gave me a tutor so there was nothin' to worry about."

Was it ever dangerous?

"Not really. It was all safe. All the fire things and all the fireworks, they wore safety things 'cause they have, like, safety fireworks. . . ."

You went to the Cannes Film Festival?

"Yes. It was awesome because we had a lot of standing ovations."

What was your impression of France?

She sighed. "I really didn't know that much French, so I was just like stay out of sight and wouldn't really talk that much. All I know is '*bonjour*,' '*merci beaucoup*,' and stuff like that."

In the film, Quvenzhane has an earsplitting scream that completely expresses her frustration at the difficult world she lives in, and after her father tells her that her mother swam away, she screams for her mother to return. No one will ever forget the power of that scream.

"I'm mostly a girl, so I really do these

things, but I scream and that came to me and I've been doing that since I was a little girl," she said, "and I would always scream for my brother so the other team can lose. That's not very girlie but it's something that I know how to do and always did."

Did they know about that when they put you in the movie?

"No. Well, the first day, the audition, I didn't tell them at all. So when I got the part and I first got to the set, I did it. So they didn't even know about it. Right in the middle or in the beginning or something. They didn't even know about it; they were kinda surprised."

What did they say?

"They said, 'Wow, you are very loud!' And I was just like, 'I know, that's why I didn't do it.' And when they came to the scene where I had to burp, I had to secretly act like I drank some water and I burped and then they asked me, 'How did you burp?' And I said, ''Cause I know how to do it on command,' and they said, 'Do it.' So, you know? I burped and they was like, 'Wow, you should have told us before.' So it was really funny to see them react to what I did and they didn't even know about it."

They learned more about you every day.

"Thank you. Anybody calls for 'Quvenzhane,' I know they're calling me, 'cause that's one of a kind."

# Ebert's Journal

## Sarah Palin Documentary

July 25, 2011—*The Undefeated* is a documentary about Sarah Palin made by and for the faithful, who may experience it in the way believers sit through a rather boring church service. At nearly two hours, it's a campaign advertisement in search of a campaign.

But that's not surprising. What astonished me is that the primary targets in the film are conservative Republicans. Yes, there are the usual vague references to liberals and elitists (although I heard the word "Democrat" only twice). But the film's favorite bad guys seem to be in the GOP establishment. Toward the end, the right-wing tub-thumper Andrew Breitbart opens up with both barrels on establishment Republicans, and is particularly angry about conservatives in Washington, whom he describes as eunuchs.

The filmmaker, Stephen K. Bannon, did a Q&A session at the Gene Siskel Film Center after its first Chicago screening. The screening was sponsored by the Chicago Web-based "firebrand humorous conservative" William J. Kelly.

The audience of about 180 was attentive but undemonstrative until more than an hour in, when CNBC's Rick Santelli drew applause for a rerun of his famous rant from the floor of the Chicago Board of Trade on Obama's mortgage bailout. Once the ice was broken, the audience applauded from time to time during fiery praise of the Tea Party and Palin speeches. Two audience members in front of me seemed unfamiliar with piracy laws, making no attempt to conceal their cell phones while making a video copy of some scenes.

*The Undefeated* contains no new footage of Sarah Palin, and indeed no new footage at all except for many running testimonials from Palin staff aides and friends, talk host Mark Levin, and the inexplicable Breitbart. The running commentaries, which seem to have been scripted for this film, are all filmed in faded color against a white background and get repetitious very quickly.

The rest of the film is cobbled together from TV and web clips and the kind of stock footage you cut to when you don't have new stuff to show. The TV clips include hostile attacks on Palin by such as Bill Maher, David Letterman, and news footage from cable news. There's a tiny glimpse of Tina Fey, and none of Palin's notable TV news interviews during the 2008 campaign are used.

A great deal of time is devoted to the state of Alaska, which is indeed nature's wonderland, and to Palin's early days, leading up to her election as mayor of Wasilla and governor of Alaska. Passages from her audiobook edition of *Going Rogue* are used as voice-overs. In those campaigns she focused on her Republican opponents as the bad guys.

Palin, according to the documentary, called out evildoers in her own party, did an exemplary job as Alaska governor, pushed reform, cut taxes, and brought the oil industry to its knees. When John McCain selected her as his running mate, we learn, she had an 80 percent statewide approval rating.

The film is surprisingly light on the 2008 election. There's extensive coverage of her acceptance speech at the Republican convention, no meaningful footage of John McCain, and the tale of the campaign is boiled down to three charts: McCain trails Obama, McCain leaps into the lead the day after Palin's big speech, and then the economy collapses and Obama takes the lead again. Blame for the collapse is not made specific, but there are several screen shots of George Bush.

The talking heads do a lot of talking about Palin's enemies. The cutaway footage here is inventive: the faces in an angry, jeering mob, which is not identified and isn't holding campaign signs; for all we know, these could be sports fans. Then snarling and apparently rabid dogs, whose politics are not disclosed. Gee, I was thinking, they've used everything but a mushroom cloud. Just then, hey, there it was, a mushroom cloud.

The film covers Palin's resignation as governor this way: After she returned to Alaska, everyone ganged up on her, and the attacks prevented her from governing. Here again, much blame is placed at the feet of the state's GOP establishment, which had never forgiven her for running against it.

*The Undefeated* takes opposition to the Democratic Party for granted and focuses on Republicans and establishment conservatives, who should apparently share the blame. It praises only the Tea Party and assigns credit to Palin for Tea Party victories in the 2010 elections. As Palin continues to prolong her entry into this year's GOP presidential primaries, one wonders if Stephen K. Bannon has his money on a third-party bid by Palin as a Tea Party candidate. I think that's where his heart is.

## The Enigma of Political Prayer

August 9, 2011—There are vertical prayers and horizontal prayers. Vertical prayers are directed heavenward. Horizontal prayers are directed sideways. It fills me with misgivings when a possible presidential candidate warms up by running a "prayer rally" in a Texas sports stadium.

A prayer "rally"? I can think of words like "gathering" and "meeting" that might more perfectly evoke the spirit. Prayer rallies make me think of pep rallies. Their purpose is to jack up the spirits of the home team and alarm the other side.

Of course, the other side has its own pep rallies, presumably leaving it to God to choose sides. That is why team prayers before a game strike me as somewhere between silly and sacrilegious. No infinite being can possibly care if Illinois beats Michigan. No God worthy of the description intervenes in the drift of a field goal kick.

It is sometimes said America was founded as a Christian nation. It was specifically not founded as a Christian nation, or the nation of any other religion. The founding European settlers were refugees from Christian nations, and had experienced quite enough at the hands of state religions. The separation of church and state is central to our democracy. It is impossible to conceive of any of the Founding Fathers approving of prayer rallies in connection with political campaigns. That is equally true of Fathers who were Catholic, Protestant, Jewish, atheist, deist, or agnostic.

The rally convened by Texas governor Rick Perry was, like many such meetings, a free concert featuring rock and C&W singers. If prayer and only prayer had been offered, the attendance, I suspect, would have been smaller. Its purpose was achieved not so much inside the stadium as outside—so that they could pray horizontally at us.

Such prayer strikes me as unseemly. Your religion is a matter between you and the god of your definition. The eagerness to convert outsiders strikes me as one of the aspects of a cult. I believe the low emphasis placed on conversion by Jews is admirable. If you want to become a Jew, you go to them. I believe religions should convert by attraction, not promotion. Respect for other beliefs, or the lack of beliefs, should be at the heart of religions.

The separation of church and state has rarely seemed more threatened. Many political leaders seem opposed to it. Some would translate their religious beliefs into the law of the land. Candidates are being asked to sign "pledges" designed primarily to embarrass those who do not sign them. A self-respecting candidate would explain that he will make his own pledges, for himself, by himself.

I have not taken a liberal or a conservative position. I have not spoken as a believer or a nonbeliever. What I've written is Civics 101. I wonder that no political leaders of either party have had the nerve to question the rally in Texas.

There are not two sides to the separation of church and state. There is only this: They must be separated for the health of our democracy. Americans are of many faiths and none. Our laws must apply equally to all. If your God doesn't agree, does that mean He accepts instructions from you? Are you content with such a God?

## A Shimmering Mirage

*Toronto,* September 15, 2011—The first time I attended the Toronto Film Festival, each day started with a press conference overlooking a hotel swimming pool, at which the directors peered at their clipboards and announced which films they would "probably" be showing later that day. That would have been in 1977.

Now here I am at the 2011 festival, one of more than a thousand accredited journalists. This has become the largest film festival in North America, far eclipsing any U.S. festival, and although Cannes is still the big kahuna, Toronto is probably number two globally. TIFF, as everyone in town calls it, now has its own headquarters building, the Bell Lightbox, which shows movies year-round in state-of-the-art facilities, and its selections sell out the vast Roy Thompson Hall and a dozen large, cavernous venues. If a ticket is left unsold, there is an impatient "rush line" frothing to get inside, even at eight-thirty on rainy weekend mornings for films you have never and will never hear of.

This is the ideal world for movie critics, when for eleven days in September it appears that our art form is glorious, urgent, and relevant. Here are the directors we value, the films we treasure, the moviegoers who care deeply. It is a fantasy, like a theme park for cineastes. In the real world, I see ominous signs that the movies are an endangered form. Good movies are still being made, but fewer theaters exist to cultivate audiences for them. Film societies have mostly disappeared. There are only a few repertory theaters. Independently booked art theaters are a dying breed. Films no longer have time to find their audiences before being pushed aside for the new models. Until recently they could do well on DVD, but now video on demand and cable are cannibalizing that audience, and without the first-run launches, they don't necessarily ever find their audiences.

Do most people know, even today, what "on demand" means? How many buy a film on cable? Netflix has found a large following, but now the studios are ending their sweetheart deals with the service. Blockbuster and other local video stores have largely disappeared. And besides, what does it mean, anyway, to "watch a movie"?

I am not a format snob. I enjoy movies on television and DVD. Yet it is fixed in my mind that a real moviegoing experience involves sitting in a large room with an audience and watching a movie on a big screen. On the second day of the festival, for example, I was one of 1,561 people in the Elgin Theater to see *The Artist*, by Michel Hazanavicius. This is a new French silent film. It is in black-and-white. It is not in widescreen but in the traditional 1:1.33 ratio, like your parents' TV set. It played to two other full houses here. Critics were turned away from the first press screening, in a theater holding 535 seats.

I loved it, but I'm sure I loved it more with the big, friendly audience at the Elgin, a classic movie palace, lovingly restored, with a proscenium arch, a stage, an orchestra pit, box seats, a balcony, and ornate decor. The audience laughed, applauded, cheered. It got all the jokes, including the way the movie played with being "silent." Of course there was music. But then toward the end a sound is heard on the track. Just a sort of "thunk." Within the logic of the film, we understood why this is, and it moves by small steps to a few additional sounds and just two words of spoken dialogue.

The film was made in France, is subtitled in English, and must have seemed a foolhardy and risky project for its backers. It was the surprise hit of Cannes in May, and won the best actor award for Jean Dujardin. He plays a global star of the silent era who is thrown out of work in Hollywood with the introduction of talkies. It was apparently unthinkable that a dashing swashbuckler would have a French accent.

We see his haughty disdain for sound, his progress into anonymity, his descent into poverty, his despair. Meanwhile, a sweet ingénue, whom he befriended in the old days, is turned into a star by talkies. In many respects, of course, this is a retread of *Singin' in the Rain*, and Dujardin even has something of Gene Kelly's toothy smile. Hazanavicius and his team master the silent language, and some audience members told me they were surprised at how absorbing the film was, partly because Dujardin is naturally likable (he has played 007 in a popular series of James Bond spoofs).

I don't know how the movie will fare in first-run release. I hope it will be a great success. But I fear some moviegoers will hear the words "black-and-white" and "silent" and close their minds to it. We live in a time when first-run screens are block-booked with noisy, mass-marketed mayhem; the models are the *Transformers* pictures, which are pounded into audiences conditioned to believe they are seeing real movies. Wit, charm, invention, and intelligence are not in demand these days, while these monstrosities suck the oxygen out of theaters on their way to becoming video games.

Of course there are respites. The Toronto festival is now known as the unofficial opening of Oscar season, and every year there's a good chance that many of the eventual Academy Award winners will premiere here. Discerning moviegoers no longer go to a movie a week, or even one a month. There are many films worth their time, but do they hear about them? How many people will pay for on demand to view virtually unknown films? How do most people ever discover the kinds of films Toronto plays every year? What kind of courage does it require to take a chance on an idea like *The Artist*? A festival like this is a beguiling mirage.

## Knocked Up At the Movies

October 22, 2011—Above all it was her personality. Pauline Kael had an overwhelming presence in a conversation. There will, no doubt, be many discussions of Kael's work and influence and with the publication of Brian Kellow's new biography *Pauline Kael: A Life in the Dark*, and the Library of America's forthcoming collection of her work.

She was the most powerful, loved, and hated film critic of her time, but her work cannot be discussed objectively by simply reading it. She challenged you on every page, she was always in your face, and she functioned as the arbiter of any social group she joined. She was quite a dame.

She might have liked that "quite a dame." She wrote with slangy, jazzy prose, always pepped up, spinning on the edge of a whirlpool. She never saw a movie twice, and wrote her reviews first-draft, in longhand on yellow legal pads. In her years at the *New Yorker*, she had no apparent restrictions on length. Reading her was like running into her right after a movie and having her start in on you. More than anybody else, she captured what those heady days of the 1970s were like, when the directors seemed to be running the Hollywood asylum and the cinema seemed to be shaping a generation.

The book tells me many things I didn't know, about her youth and spotty education and early experience among the bohemians, artists, and poets of Berkeley and San Francisco. She fell into the task of managing an art theater, and her program notes became locally famous. Usually poor, often living in uncertain circumstances, raising her daughter Gina, and presiding over an expanding coterie of creative outsiders, she made no substantial money until her early freelance pieces were collected in *I Lost It at the Movies*. That book sold 150,000 copies—surprising, since she lacked a national platform or reputation. It was the writing. It had a heady joy.

She responded strongly to movies, in love or hate. She didn't mince words. For her a movie was like a lover—good or bad in the sack. Her book titles hinted passion in the dark: *Kiss Kiss Bang Bang*, *Going Steady*, *Deeper into Movies*, *Reeling*, *When the Lights Go Down*, *Taking It All In*, *State of the Art*, *Hooked*, and her collection of her favorite work, *For Keeps*.

She became known in her early days for a feud with Andrew Sarris that became legendary in film criticism circles. Sarris was the critic of the *Village Voice*, was also given a great deal of space by his editors, and was said to be the man who brought the auteur theory to America.

That was the theory, shaped by French critics in the 1950s, arguing that chosen directors had a personal style that shaped all of their film, regardless of genre, and in that way their work was one extended exercise in that style. The French were particularly fond of American directors in such genres as war movies, Westerns, musicals, and others that were deliberately not highbrow art. They gave a name to "film noir," and by identifying its masters they helped form a new Hollywood Pantheon.

Sarris published a book, *The American Cinema*, which partitioned American directors into categories: In the pantheon were Chaplin, Flaherty, Ford, Griffith, Hawks, Hitchcock, Keaton, Lang, Lubitsch, Murnau, Ophuls, Renoir, von Sternberg, and Welles. Billy Wilder was later promoted to the pantheon, but Sarris relegated to lower levels such as Kubrick, Preminger, Wyler, DeMille, and other considerable names.

Setting aside those not in the Pantheon,

there is no denying the greatness of those included, and as a young critic with no formal film education, I seized upon his pantheon. To educate myself I began teaching in night school at the University of Chicago, and we worked through semesters of several of Sarris's choices. Just by making a list, whatever its worth, he gave me a place to start.

For Kael, such lists and hierarchies were worthless; they smelled of dogma, and for her lacked the thrill of the hunt for new and exciting directors. In reviews that sometimes bordered on ecstasy, she championed *Bonnie and Clyde*, *Nashville*, and *Last Tango in Paris*. She discovered new directors such as James Toback (*Fingers*) and Brian De Palma. In prose sometimes approaching hyperbole, she insisted on their greatness, and although she was often correct, for her the point was not their *objective* greatness in the pantheon sense, but her personal reaction to their work. In the lingo of her book titles, the films of such directors made her come.

My introduction to the New York film critics' world came in 1967, when I attended my first New York Film Festival. Pauline was the center of attention after every screening, especially of her beloved Godard, and in the back room of the Ginger Man, across Broadway from Lincoln Center, she held court over a big table jammed with friends and followers. She was not a snob. Despite my disreputable Chicago origins, I was welcomed to her group from the first, and she introduced me to such as De Palma, De Niro, and James Toback. Ironic that Pauline, so scornful of the auteur theory, essentially maintained her own pantheon of personal gods, to whom she was as worshipful as Sarris to his.

A post-movie dinner or drinks with Pauline was a tumult of words, laughter, cigarette smoke, conspiracy, and intrigue. Later it was said that her followers were "Paulettes," and followed the party line. Was I a Paulette? I've never seen myself listed, but then as a Chicagoan I must have been considered an agnostic. She would invite me to her apartment in the Dakota in gatherings of her friends, and I found it astonishing how minutely she followed promising new filmmakers, how many films she saw early, how much advice she gave, how many screenplays she read. If she only saw a movie once—well, maybe that was all the time she had.

We met often. There was a night of drinking during the festival in my hotel room, with Scorsese and me sitting on the floor at her feet. (It was circa 1970, and sitting on the floor was commonplace, I suppose as some kind of statement, just as wearing blue jeans everywhere had become.) When she was on the jury at Cannes, I was invited to a little bistro where she introduced Agnes Varda and Jacques Demy. When she briefly took leave of the *New Yorker* to accept a job offer from Warren Beatty at Paramount, she invited me to a dinner at an Italian restaurant with such as Ray Bradbury, Toback, and Robert Towne. "Honey," she confided, "I can't stay out here. They're all whores." Not including present company, it was implied.

In an obituary, I wrote, "Pauline Kael had a more positive influence on the climate for film in America than any other single person over the last three decades." What did I mean by that? Pauline had no theory, no rules, no guidelines, no objective standards. You couldn't apply her "approach" to a film. With her it was all personal. Faithful readers will know I am tiresome in how often I quote Robert Warshow, who in his book *The Immediate Experience* wrote: "A man goes to the movies. The critic must be honest enough to admit he is that man." Pauline Kael was that honest. She wrote about her immediate experience, about what she felt.

She's accused of being inconsistent and contradicting herself. Directors would fall in and out of favor. With her there was no possibility of inconsistency, because she always wrote about what she felt *right now*. What was the purpose of tilting that emotion to reflect something she wrote earlier? I sat next to her once in a New York screening room. She responded audibly. "Oh, oh, oh!" she'd say, in praise or disapproval. Talking like that would get her in trouble in Chicago. Pauline had—or took—license. You sensed something physical was happening as she watched.

That was her influence, and you can see it reflected all over the Web, probably by some critics who have never read her. It is all first person. Before the auteurists, when France was already the center of film criticism and theory, the critics of the important newspapers and magazines reflected the policies of the publication. In America, reviews were usually more sedate and removed (Manny Farber here being the exception, as he was to everything). Pauline Kael blew those attitudes out of the water. In my reviews and those of a great many others you are going to find, for better or worse, my "feelings." I feel a responsibility to provide some notion of what you're getting yourself in for, but after that it's all subjective.

A reader wrote me recently about a review where he sensed low energy and disinterest. He was right. The movie (*The Big Year*) was "good enough" in a humdrum way. But I didn't want to go steady with it. It didn't leave me reeling.

## The Sudden Death of Film

November 2, 2011—Who would have dreamed film would die so quickly? The victory of video was quick and merciless. Was it only a few years ago that I was patiently explaining how video would never win over the ancient and familiar method of light projected through celluloid? And now Eastman Kodak, which seemed invulnerable, is in financial difficulties.

Many of the nation's remaining mail order companies that process film from still cameras have closed, even though stills are having a resurgence in the serious market. New 35 mm movie projectors are no longer manufactured, for the simple reason that used projectors, some not very old, are flooding the market.

The reason for that is fairly disheartening. Some manufacturers of digital projectors required that existing film projectors be removed from projection booths before their equipment could be installed. Why? No doubt there was some concocted technical excuse for their underlying reason, to slash and burn the competition. (The distracting gimmick of 3-D was used to fuel this campaign.) A great many multiplexes are no longer capable of projecting the 35 mm format that has served faithfully since about 1895. One film festival, having received its opening night film from overseas, found no theater in town that could exhibit it.

I remember the first year video projection was demonstrated at Cannes. This would have been in the 1980s. A manufacturer arranged side-by-side screenings of the same material on film and videotape (I don't believe digital was operational yet). So limited was the interest, there were empty seats in the theater. The audience, mostly trade people and some movie critics, were unimpressed. We saw the usual shots of red roses and geisha girls. Film looked better, hands down.

But in 1990, in the white frame chapel of Kapiolani Community College on Oahu, the new Sony High Definition Software Center staged a demo of a thirty-six-inch Sony high-definition TV set at the Hawaii Film Festival. This was its official U.S. unveiling. The industry joke had been, "High-definition TV is five years in the future, and always will be." Shohachi Sakai, who accompanied the set from Tokyo, did not disappoint. "By 1995," he predicted, "these sets will be affordable enough for many consumers." What did "affordable" mean? A thirty-six-inch set is for sale today in Tokyo, he said, for about $40,000. "It is primarily for industrial use," he said—used, for example, as a monitor for technicians editing high-def television. "But the funny thing is, we are sold out," he added. "As many as we make, we sell. Japanese are eager to have the latest technology."

Well, it looked good. For $40,000 it should have. And then the technology moved into projection booths. You don't need me to tell you the rest of the story. Until fairly late in the game, however, I was a holdout. I persisted in preferring the look, the feel, the *vibe* of celluloid. Film had a wider range—whiter whites, blacker blacks, richer colors. Besides, I explained, satellite projection of theater-quality digital would involve a footprint containing every hacker and pirate in the world. Studios would never risk it, I promised. Yes, but why did I assume studios would use satellites to distribute first-run films?

And on and on. I insisted, like many other critics, that I always knew when I was not being shown a true celluloid print. The day came when I didn't. The day is here when most of the new movies I see are in digital. You and I both know how they look, and the fact is, they look pretty good. We've shown a lot of restored 70 mm prints at Ebertfest, and they look breathtaking. But 70 mm is no longer a viable format. (When any industry says a format is "no longer viable," that means "it may be better, but it costs too much.")

We live in a time few people could have foreseen on that day in Hawaii. I now view movies on Netflix and Fandor *over the Internet* on my big-screen high-def set, or with an overhead projector on a wall-sized screen, and the picture quality pleases me. The celluloid dream may live on in my hopes, but digital commands the field. I imagine there will always be 35 mm projectors at film festivals and various shrines of cinema. Most of the movies ever made have probably not yet been digitized, and in many cases there may be no money for that. But my war is over, my side lost, and it's important to consider this in the real world.

For me, seeing a movie in a real theater with a real audience is an inescapable part of the experience. I watch as many movies on TV as most people, and they're okay that way, but when a movie is on fire I want to sense the audience burning. To be carried along in the dark on a wave of laughter or tears is exhilarating. Therefore, anything that helps theaters against TV in their war of more than sixty-five years is a good thing.

Digital prints are cheaper to manufacture, distribute, and exhibit than film. They also make the distribution of non-blockbuster formats more practical—indies, art films, foreign films, documentaries, classics. Repertory theaters and their daily double features are mostly a thing of the past. The studios have long since stopped making and maintaining regional film exchanges. But today repertory has become thinkable again.

I wrote not long ago that with today's "consumer" high-def projectors, it is perfectly possible to rent a space and start a repertory theater, assuming you legally obtain the performance rights. Most distributors are happy to work with you—they like more venues. People have written me they run such cinema rooms in their towns or on their campuses. But why, you might ask, would audiences buy a ticket to see a movie they might be able to watch at home on TV? The best reason is a shared common interest. A movie is better with an audience, the ritual is more satisfying, and as new patterns of on demand form, such venues might get movies before they're available everywhere. They would be another tier in the distribution sequence.

I didn't see the death of film coming so quickly or so sweepingly, and I imagine the manufacturers of film stock didn't either. Yes, the usual gurus such as Scorsese and Spielberg still profess their undying love for celluloid. They both also praised black-and-white, and made *Raging Bull* and *Schindler's List*, and haven't made many black-and-white movies lately. They've also professed interest in Maxivision, my preference among all formats, which has a picture up to four times as good as anything you can see now. I fear they may have found it "not viable."

Speaking of my fears, I have a final one. Film on celluloid has proven remarkably resilient. Not long ago, invaluable missing footage from Lang's *Metropolis* was found surviving very nicely in Argentina. If we had the missing reel from *The Magnificent Ambersons*, we could watch it together tonight. How long will the digital file of a new movie survive and be readable? I have memory discs of pretty much everything I've ever written on a computer, but have no idea what format they were created in or how to read them. I also have carbon copies of everything I wrote for the *Sun-Times* from 1966 until around 1977, when we got computers in the newsroom. I made them on my typewriter. You remember those.

## Heteronormative Vampires

November 20, 2011—You read the word and without skipping a beat you know what it means. I am so clueless that I became aware of it for the first time in the past few days, in reviews of *The Twilight Saga: Breaking Dawn: Part 1*.

The observation is made that Stephenie Meyer's best-selling series of novels is profoundly heteronormative.

Her heroine, Bella Swan, holds to a conventional belief in chastity before marriage, and when she finally weds Edward Cullen in the fourth film of the series, she gets pregnant on her wedding night and produces a child with alarming promptness.

The word, I learn, was coined in 1991. It summarizes a worldview that creates a climate hostile to nontraditional sexuality. You have to give me credit. I may not have used the term, but I was right on top of the heteronormativeness of the first of the movies, *Twilight* (2008). What people don't always recall is that the person most in favor of chastity was Edward. As I wrote: "Come on now, what is *Twilight* really about? It's about a teenage boy trying to practice abstinence, and how, in the heat of the moment, it's really, really hard. And about a girl who wants to go all the way with him and doesn't care what might happen. He's so beautiful she would do anything for him. She is the embodiment of the sentiment 'I'd die for you.' She is, like many adolescents, a thanatophile."

Perhaps the reason so many young women love the novels and the movies is that, like many romance movies, they're about the deliciousness of temptation. For Bella to be tempted to make love with Edward is so exciting, especially because of the risks involved. For this couple, those risks become almost maddening, because Edward is a vampire. That's why he warns her they must stay far, far apart. He loves her too much to want her to become a vampire. Now there's a gentleman for you.

She, on the other, is all too willing to surrender. As I also wrote prophetically: "She's like, I don't especially want to die, but if that's what it takes, count me in. She is touched by his devotion. Think what a sacrifice he is making on her behalf. On prom night, on the stage of the not especially private gazebo in the public gardens, he teeters right on the brink of a fang job, and then brings all of her trembling to a dead standstill."

So many followers of the stories were eager to see Bella and Edward consummate their marriage that this latest film set box-office records. Yet, incredibly, we never see the events of the wedding night. The bridal chamber is a shambles on the morning after and Bella is black and blue with bruises, but we can only surmise what happened. Leaving out the main event was a wise decision by Bill Condon, the director. Imagine, if you will, Bella and Edward having passionate sex. The mind recoils. They are more ideals than real people: beautiful, perfect, young, idealistic. We have no desire to have the image besmirched by rumpy-pumpy.

Apparently at some point during the night Edward must indeed have employed his fangs, another event more thrilling to contemplate than to witness. That's the most obvious explanation for the result that their child is apparently a vampire, although perhaps it's a matter of simple genetics, the child inheriting the father's vampirism just as it might inherit his eye color.

We can't say. How *does* genetics theory work when one of the partners is dead? How dead *are* vampires? I've always assumed that all vampires started out alive and got that way by being bitten. Can they reproduce? Can two vampires reproduce together, or must half of the couple be human? That vampires recognize the distinction is clear because in the movie "humans" are clearly referred to as being in a separate category.

The argument is made in some studies of Stephenie Meyer's work that she embeds her own Mormon or Christian beliefs about heteronormative behavior. Chief among them is chastity before marriage. But doesn't *Breaking Dawn* make an equally compelling argument against sex *after* marriage? Edward was right that they should never have gotten married in the first place. The film, in fact, makes a good case for gay, lesbian, transsexual, and other vampires, in that they cannot be expected to reproduce. I don't know if Stephenie Meyer thought this through, but there you have it.

Still to come is *Breaking Dawn: Part 2*, a year from now. This will be quite a challenge for the filmmakers. If you've seen *Part 1* you know what I mean. This is one marriage in which the wisdom of Dr. Spock is not going to be of much use.

*Note: I continue to muse about the word "heteronormative." If you take it apart it seems to reduce to normal heterosexual. Somehow the scientific nomenclature transforms that into a negative. I understand the reasons why non-hetero minorities feel discriminated against, and sympathize with them. But doesn't "heteronormative" apply the same process of blanket discrimination?*

## Dissecting Declining Box Office Revenue

December 30, 2011—Box office revenue at movie theaters "lagged far behind 2010," an article by the AP's David Germain reports. Partly that was because the year lacked an *Avatar.* Partly because a solid summer slate fell off in the autumn. Germain talks to several Hollywood insiders who tried to account for the general decline of ticket sales; 2011 had "the smallest movie audience since 1995." I have some theories of my own, fueled by what people tell me:

1. Obviously, the absence of a must-see mass-market movie. When moviegoers hear about *Avatar* or *The Dark Knight,* they blast off from home base and land in a theater seat as quickly as they can.

2. Ticket prices are too high. People have always made that complaint, but historically the movies have been cheap compared to concerts, major league sports, and restaurants. Not so much any longer. No matter what your opinion is about 3-D, the charm of paying a hefty surcharge has worn off for the hypothetical family of four.

3. The theater experience. Moviegoers above thirty are weary of noisy fanboys and -girls. The annoyance of talkers has been joined by the plague of cell phone users, whose bright screens are a distraction. Worse, some texting addicts get mad when told they *can't* use their cell phones. A theater is reportedly opening that will allow and even bless cell phone usage, although that may be an apocryphal story.

4. Refreshment prices. It's an open secret that the actual cost of soft drinks and popcorn is very low. To justify their inflated prices, theaters serve portions that are grotesquely oversized, and no longer offer what used to be a "small popcorn." Today's bucket of popcorn would feed a thoroughbred.

5. Competition from other forms of delivery. Movies streaming over the Internet are no longer a sci-fi fantasy. TV screens are growing larger and cheaper. Consumers are finding devices that easily play Internet movies through TV sets. Netflix alone accounts for 30 percent of all Internet traffic in the evening. That represents millions of moviegoers. They're simply not in a theater. This could be seen as an argument for why newspapers and their readers need movie critics more than ever; the number of choices can be baffling.

6. Lack of choice. Box office tracking shows that the bright spot in 2011 was the performance of indie, foreign, or documentary films. On many weekends, one or more of those titles captures first place in per-screen average receipts. Yet most moviegoers outside large urban centers can't find those titles in their local gigantiplex. Instead, all the shopping center compounds seem to be showing the same few overhyped disappointments. Those films open with big ad campaigns, play a couple of weeks, and disappear.

The myth that small-town moviegoers don't like "art movies" is undercut by Netflix's viewing results; the third most popular movie on December 28, 2011, on Netflix was *Certified Copy,* by the Iranian director Abbas Kiarostami. You've heard of him? In fourth place—French director Alain Corneau's *Love Crime.* In fifth, *The Girl with the Dragon Tattoo*—but the subtitled Swedish version.

The message I get is that Americans love the movies as much as ever. It's the theaters that are losing their charm. Proof: Theaters thrive that police their audiences, show a variety of titles, and emphasize value-added features. The rest of the industry can't depend forever on blockbusters to bail it out.

## Think of Me as the Butler, Carson

January 20, 2012—For an hour before bedtime every night for a week, I've watched an episode of *Downton Abbey.* Last night the Earl of Grantham interrupted a garden party to announce the beginning of World War I, and I pulled up short. I was watching the first season via Netflix Instant, and inattentively failed to notice there were only seven episodes. I naturally expected ten.

I'm not one of those people who follows every series on Masterpiece Theater, HBO, or whatever. There's always a movie to be seen. The last series I watched completely was *Brideshead Revisited,* and before that all the way back to *Upstairs, Downstairs.* As you know, I'm an Anglophile. I seem particularly drawn to the era of English country houses before the first World War, and to a degree between the two wars.

Someone wrote that country house life in peacetime was the apogee of human civilization. Could have been Orwell. Or probably couldn't have. The point, as I recall, is that the upstairs and downstairs people were equally happy in their own ways. There was a stable hierarchy and everyone knew their place. "Knowing your place" is a term often used in connection with someone who tries to rise above it, but there's also such a thing as possessing and valuing your place. There is pride in doing one's job well, in being the epitome of a footman, a lady's maid, a butler, a valet, or an earl. In *Downton Abbey*, I think it possible that the happiest people may be Carson the butler and Patmore the cook—and upstairs, the earl and his wife, Lady Cora. They are happy because they do their jobs well and are loyal and helpful to those who depend on them.

The most admirable man, up or down, is Bates, the earl's valet, but he is far from being the happiest. He has too active a conscience. In early life he went to prison to protect his worthless wife. Now he would rather be fired than cost another man his job—even if that man is the vile Thomas Barrow, who has lied about him and tried to frame him. Bates adds considerably to the entertainment value of *Downton Abbey* by enlisting our deep sympathy, but there comes a time when defending your own honor ranks above protecting the job of a villain. Remember, too, that Bates has had to undergo alcoholism and being a "cripple," as everyone cheerfully describes him. Indeed, he almost got fired the first time because the loathsome O'Brien tripped him at an embarrassing moment.

There is nothing politically correct about *Downton Abbey*. Thomas is not only a liar and a thief, but a deceiver of young women, an aggressive homosexual, and a chain smoker. He teams up with her ladyship's maid, O'Brien, to share smokes and plot against Bates. Meanwhile, Daisy, the little scullery maid, lies for Thomas because, poor dear, she thinks she may have a chance with him. And it would make a nice match with Thomas as the lord's valet. The cook knows better about her hopes for romance: "He ain't a ladies' man." The view of homosexuality in the series is decidedly dated, but as a character, Thomas functions admirably. There is sly humor in the way the only two characters who smoke very much are the villains.

I gather there is more humor to come in Season Two, and that I will regret, because although my politics are liberal, my tastes in fiction respond to the conservative stability of the Downton world. The more seriously I can take it, the better I will like it. To be sure, there is monstrous unfairness in the British class system, and one of the series's themes is income inequality. What must be observed, however, is that all the players agree to play by the same rules. In modern America the rich jump through every loophole in the tax code. But look what happened in the first episode of *Downton Abbey.* The earl's presumptive heir went down with the *Titanic* and the title passed to a distant cousin, Mr. Matthew Crawley of Manchester, who now stands to inherit the title, the house, the land, and the money—including the personal fortune of Cora, the earl's wife. So deeply are the principles of inheritance embedded in the Crawley family that the earl seems staunchly prepared to give up their earthly possessions and be courteous in the process.

Of course the injustices of the class system work better in fiction than in life, because in fiction we all identify with the rich and powerful. Even in reports of reincarnation, people tend toward having been Henry V in an earlier life, and not a scabby footpad. In *Downton Abbey,* I identify with Carson. It is the liberal Mr. Crawley whose ideas are closest to my own, but the judicious and wise Carson whom I envy.

There is nothing in my own early life that explains why I'm such an Anglophile. Maybe it can be traced back to the day Mr. Willis, my mother's boss at the Allied Finance Co., went to England and brought me back the Coronation number of *Punch*, with its photos of the new queen and Buckingham Palace and Prince Charles, who was about my age. I could have been Prince Charles, if my mother had been the queen. Think about it. Then my Classics Illustrated comic books led to novels, until I was deep into Dickens and then Trollope and all the others. In London during the Blitz there was a sudden surge of popularity for Trollope's novels. There's nothing like Nazi buzz-bombs whistling overhead to focus your attention on the intrigues of Barsetshire.

Even my love of Indian fiction may be connected; at the Calcutta Film Festival, an Indian critic explained to me why P. G. Wodehouse is the most popular English-language novelist in India: "Both nations are class-conscious, love wearing the proper uniform at every moment, are obsessed with family, are devoted to ceremony, cultivate mustaches, and prize eccentricity." He may have had a point. Of all of Wodehouse's novels, my favorites are those about Blandings Castle, its Lord Emsworth, and the lord's trusted Pig Man, George Cyril Wellbeloved, to whom is entrusted the care of the Lord's prized pig, the Empress of Blandings. In Blandings, an enchanted world exists in which everyone is innocent, even a pig thief.

But I stray. Watching *Downton Abbey* gave me a sense of deep comfort. With the earl and his household I valued the great Yorkshire structure and its traditions. For an hour a night, it was mine. Yes, in the embrace of these ancient yellow stones and rich woods, the footsteps of countless ancestors had fallen. It mattered not if I swept the entrance or stood in it to welcome the queen, I was there through the generations.

I could understand why the earl had devoted his life to its maintenance. I could even understand why he was so determined to give up the title and his fortune on the sake of principle; if you live under laws by which you can lose everything when a ship goes down, then perhaps it's not quite so unfair that you have it in the first place. You didn't rob or steal to gain your possessions (although your ancestors may have). You were born into them. And with a blow from a lucky iceberg, a poor man in Manchester might find that he, too, was rich by the accident of birth.

In the meantime, life goes on at Downton. Marriages are arranged and rearranged. Kitchen maids get crushes. Lady's maids dream of mastering the typewriter and entering the prewar dot-com world. Grandmothers sternly defend ancient values and are willing to abandon them for benefit of family. A great machine like this country house can sail on through the centuries, its course not thrown off by the occasional discovery of a dead Turkish diplomat in the wrong bedroom. I am certain the snuff box will turn up eventually, and as confident as Carson is that Bates had nothing to do with it.

## The Oscar Losers: They Wuz Robbed

January 26, 2012—Of course, no nominee is really robbed of an Academy Award nomination. It's a gift; not a right. The balloting procedure is conducted honestly and reflects a collective opinion, which was demonstrated this year when the Academy voters had the curiosity to single out Demian Bichir for best actor for his deeply convincing performance as a Mexican gardener in Los Angeles in *A Better Life.* He wasn't on my mental list of possible candidates, but when I heard the name, I thought, "Of course! Good thinking!"

Does it therefore follow that in the best actor category, Bichir "robbed" Michael Shannon of *Take Shelter*, Ryan Gosling of *Drive*, or Michael Fassbender of *Shame*? It does not, even though those performances were so good. There were no unworthy nominees for best actor. But let me also point out that none of the five nominees was as electrifying as the three who were "robbed." That's not a fault. Their roles weren't of that nature.

In the best actress category, those who were "robbed" included Tilda Swinton in *We Need to Talk About Kevin*, Charlize Theron in *Young Adult*, and Vera Farmiga in *Higher Ground.* Here I will be bold and name two nominees I didn't feel were worthy: Meryl Streep and Glenn Close.

Streep, of course, is a paragon. Her impersonation of Margaret Thatcher in *The Iron Lady* was so uncanny she could have given a speech on the BBC and fooled a lot of people. But it wasn't a very good film and didn't make adequate use of her as a resource. In my review, I had a happy turn of phrase: She was all dressed up with nowhere to go. Nominating Ms. Streep seems to have become an annual ritual for the Academy, like bringing on the accountants with their briefcases. In the same category, if you are looking for performances as well-known people, consider Michelle Williams, who was uncanny as the ineffable Marilyn Monroe.

Vera Farmiga not only starred in *Higher Ground*, but also directed it. In both tasks she shows complete clarity about what she wants to accomplish. The film follows three stages in a woman's journey through religion: childhood belief, mainstream Protestant, fortyish evangelical. (She plays the third.) It never says she is making the right or wrong decision, only that what she does seems necessary at the time she does it. In a world where believers and agnostics are polarized and hold simplified ideas about each other, it takes a step back and sees faith as a series of choices that should be freely made. She is intensely human at every stage.

Glenn Close's performance in *Albert Nobbs* was too limited, I think. Her female-to-male transition evoked a character paralyzed with dread of discovery. Except for one lovely scene of brief liberation, there was no range, simply a woman who hopes that by keeping a frozen face and blending into the wallpaper she can pass. Her Albert Nobbs seems monumentally clueless if she believes it's plausible the cute little chambermaid yearns for a sexless marriage running a tobacco shop. Nobbs seems not merely frightened and shy, but lacking a basic working knowledge of life. That isn't inappropriate for the character, perhaps, but it does little to make the film more involving.

In her place I would rather have seen Tilda Swinton's devastating performance as the unwilling mother of a demonic son in *We Need to Talk About Kevin*, or Charlize Theron's self-destructive, vulnerable former prom queen in *Young Adult*. Yes, her character was as clueless as Albert Nobbs in thinking her high school boyfriend would drop his wife and new baby to marry her. But it's the kind of thinking an alcoholic can drift into.

In the same film, Patton Oswalt's performance as the legendary nerd in Theron's high school class deserved a nomination. So certainly did the work of Albert Brooks in *Drive*, as a gnarly old gangster a million miles distant from his previous characters. Both performers were *acting*. Who were they "robbed" by? Nick Nolte's work as the father in *Warrior*. I wrote in my review that "he embodies, as only Nick Nolte can, the shaggy, weathered heroism of a man who is trying one more time to pull himself together." Yes, but isn't that the role he's been playing routinely? To see him as the great actor he is, look again at his nominated leading performance in Paul Schrader's *Affliction* (1997). I hate to say it, but in *Warrior*, he's typecast.

Here's a question I hate to ask. Why was Max von Sydow nominated for *Extremely Loud and Incredibly Close*? It was not a great movie, and the role of a young boy's wise old companion was not original nor did it stretch. Does it strike you as ironic that at the age of eighty-two, with 145 IMDb credits since 1949, the iconic figure from so many of Ingmar Bergman's masterpieces should have been nominated for this? Brooks and Oswalt were taking chances and bringing forth from their experience characters who were original and new.

As best actor, I would have preferred seeing Ryan Gosling from *Drive* and Michael Fassbender from *Shame*. I'll get back to *Drive*. I think it goes without saying that Fassbender, playing a tortured, joyless, addicted masturbator, would not be nominated. To some degree, less perhaps in recent years, the Academy seems afraid the public will confuse the behavior of nominated characters with their own characters. They don't want to be seen as sympathizing with masturbators.

I have one complaint about the supporting actress category: It was not an actress but a film that was robbed. Jessica Chastain had an extraordinary year, but its highlight was the deeply believable mother in *The Tree of Life*. Her performance in *The Help* not only had less weight and dimension, but it served a character, the trophy wife, who was marginal compared to the other nominated actresses.

In the same category, the nomination of Melissa McCarthy for *Bridesmaids* was deserved. Her chubby, butch gal pal was an original, a woman whose authenticity stole every scene—and incidentally, a character we remember better than the leads.

Of course, this is all pure personal opinion. Most criticisms of the annual nominees can be translated as, "Here's who I would have nominated." I thought *The Tree of Life* was a masterpiece and was pleased that the Academy agreed. I know it had puzzled detractors, some of whom reportedly demanded their money back. You know my reservations about *The Help*, but it won great popularity and admiration. The best film nominee that puzzles me the most is *Extremely Loud and Incredibly Close*. It attached a 9/11 connection to the implausible story of a young boy wandering all over New York on a wild goose chase, but never mind: Did you meet anyone who really *loved* it?

The film that should have been named in this category is Nicolas Winding Refn's *Drive.* Transcending the crime genre, it stars Ryan Gosling as a man who lives primarily to drive. Sometimes he's a movie stunt driver, sometimes he drives getaway for crooks. He seems to have no family, no history, and seemingly few emotions. Whatever happened to him drove any personality deep beneath the surface. He is an existential hero, defined entirely by his behavior. Not depending on violence, not buttressed by chase scenes, this is a personality study. How often do we find the hero of an "action picture" to be deeply interesting?

I have saved the worst robbery for last, and of course it is the Academy's inexplicable decision to ignore Steve James and Alex Kotlowitz's *The Interrupters,* which I think by consensus was the best documentary of the year. Filmed on dangerous streets, it followed Chicago ex-cons and former gang members who formed CeaseFire, a group of "violence interrupters" who personally worked to talk gangs out of deadly shootings. This is the most discussed non-nomination since 1994, when James's masterpiece *Hoop Dreams* was not nominated.

It was later revealed that volunteers of the Academy's documentary branch turned off *Hoop Dreams* after watching only fifteen minutes. What their reasons were for passing over *The Interrupters* I cannot imagine. Which of the other nominees "stole" the nomination? I have nothing to say against any of them. So, tactfully, I will suggest it was a collective theft by all five.

## Indie Spirit Awards Join *The Artist* Bandwagon

*Santa Monica, California,* February 27, 2012—*The Artist,* a nearly silent film, made most of the noise here Saturday at the Independent Sprit Awards, winning for best picture, best actor, best director, and its cinematography. It was the last in a series of good omens for the surprise hit, as it headed for victory at the Academy Awards.

A no less significant award, for best documentary, was won by *The Interrupters,* made by Steve James and Alex Kotlowitz for Chicago's Kartemquin Films. The doc, about former gang members trying to keep the peace among street gangs, inspired an uproar when it failed to win an Oscar nomination. Many remember similar incredulity when James's *Hoop Dreams* (1994), widely considered the best documentary of recent decades, was snubbed by the Oscars.

Michel Hazanavicius, the French director of *The Artist,* arrived breathless onstage after racing from LAX with a police escort. He had flown in from Paris after his film won the Cesar Award, the "French Oscar," on Friday. He was named best director by both groups. His star, Jean Dujardin, won the Spirit Award for best actor, but not the Cesar. Cinematographer Guillaume Schiffman, whose distinctive black-and-white photography helped capture the spirit of a circa-1930 silent film, also won a Spirit.

*The Artist* steamroller has been so dramatic that it was necessary to take a breath and look around the Indie Spirits venue, a big tent on the beach, and reflect that this group, founded to support a new wave of American cinema, had joined in the applause for a throwback that was (almost) entirely silent, and (almost) entirely black-and-white.

"We created the best foreign film award to stop this s—t from happening," joked Seth Rogen, emcee of the high-spirited ceremony. "Did we learn nothing from Roberto Begnini?"

The Spirit Award for best actress was won by Michelle Williams, who played Marilyn Monroe in *My Week with Marilyn.* She recalled that at her first Indie Spirits she wore her own clothes and did her own hair, and they weren't so great. "Today," she smiled, "the only thing I'm wearing that I own is my dignity." She wore a tailored blue blazer and white shirt—conservative, except that the shorts under the blazer were cut as high as a pair of Daisy Dukes.

The most popular winner was veteran Christopher Plummer, who won for best supporting actor by playing an old man, long and happily married, who after his wife dies reveals to his son that he is gay. The best supporting actress was Shailene Woodley, who played George Clooney's troubled daughter in *The Descendants.*

*The Descendants* also won for best screenplay, by Alexander Payne, Nate Faxon, and Jim Rash. *Margin Call*, about unethical trading practices on Wall Street, won as best first feature for writer-director J. C. Chandor.

## Hey, Kids! Anybody Here Not Heard the F-Word?

March 15, 2012—Even as I write on Thursday night, a screening of *Bully* is taking place in Washington that may or may not result in the film's MPAA rating being changed from R to PG-13. Jen Chaney suggests in her *Washington Post* blog that a compromise might even be possible. The film is a documentary about how bullying affected five families and led to two suicides. It was slapped with an R because of its use of the F-word. Chaney asked Lee Hirsch, the film's director, "whether there was any chance he would consider bleeping out one or two of those expletives if that guaranteed a PG-13 designation for the movie, thereby allowing teen audiences to see it."

Hirsch replied he believes the F-word makes the bullying more real. Yes, and so no doubt it does. In its article on the MPAA ratings, Wikipedia tells us: "If a film uses one of the harsher sexually derived words (such as 'fuck') one to four times, it is routine today for the film to receive a PG-13 rating, provided that the word is used as an expletive and not with a sexual meaning." Apparently *Bully* either exceeds the count or refers to sexuality. I haven't seen the film, but let's say it uses the word more than four times. Then let's say Hirsch removes some of those uses so that it is employed only once. Would that earn him a PG-13? He tells Chaney he's willing to do whatever will help bullied kids. But he adds: "If you take that away, it's one more notch against that experience. It's one more big societal minimizing, or sort of negating, of the full extent of terror that comes with bullying."

Of course he is right. If a director wants to make a film against bullying, it is not for a committee of MPAA bean counters to tell him what words he can use. Not many years ago, the word "rape" was not used in newspapers, on television—or in the movies, for that matter. But there is a crime, and the name of the crime is rape, and if you remove the word you help make the crime invisible.

This is yet another example of the MPAA sidestepping ethical judgments by falling back on the technicalities of its guidelines. It is even more insidious because the MPAA never clearly spells out its guidelines, leaving it to filmmakers to guess—although they often judge by past experience. It seems to me that either the f-word is permissible, or it is not. If impermissible, nobody should use it at all in a PG-13 film. If permissible, nobody should count. Is it a magic word, a totemistic expression that dare not say its own name? Is it a vulgar equivalent of such a word as G-d?

The MPAA began to set this trap for itself when it got into the ratings business in the first place. It was intended at the time not to promote public decency in language, but to provide the motion picture industry with a plausible way to head off local censorship boards. When I started at the *Sun-Times*, the city had a board of censors made up of the widows of police captains, and their rulings were often inexplicable. There was also the question of whether censorship was even constitutional. Jack Valenti, in 1968 the new head of the MPAA, came up with the rather brilliant notion that a new code should be *voluntary*, and thus no test of the law. Studios and theaters would be asked for voluntary compliance.

With a few small tweaks over the years, such as the creation of the PG-13 rating, the code envisioned by Valenti remains more or less intact. It has become increasingly irrelevant, because so many films are now released with no MPAA rating at all. Since a theater showing an NC-17 film may have trouble with its landlord, or with the advertising standards of some newspapers or broadcast outlets, their distributors simply avoid the issue and don't submit it for a rating; the world looks the other way. The films where a rating makes a difference are usually big-studio wide-release productions.

The one thing the MPAA cannot ever do, Valenti argued, is get into the business of value judgments. It can advise parents that a film contains the f-word, for example, but not whether that use is appropriate. Now that twenty members of Congress have come forward to sign a petition protesting the R rating of *Bully*, we can assume that the film uses the word for justifiable reasons.

Over the years the MPAA's close ties with

the "business" of motion pictures has become clear in its hypocrisy involving sex and nudity. Films depicting much nudity and sex can usually count on an R rating. Yet it's fair to say that a film can contain a great deal of violence and still qualify for PG-13. Sometimes the MPAA seems to be slipping in a value judgment with odd wordings, such as "zombie violence," to signal that it's not all that serious, you see.

Now the defenders of *Bully* ask the MPAA to do something that makes it very uncomfortable: It wants the code and ratings administration to look at the film and say, "This film violates our standards for language in a PG-13 movie, but because it's a good film with a powerful and worthwhile message, we've decided to allow it a PG-13 anyway."

The pressure is mounting on the MPAA to do just that. The screening of opinion makers in Washington was hosted by Christopher Dodd, chairman of the association. When the movie was over, he must have had conversations with squirmy moments.

The MPAA has painted itself into a corner. It will be interesting to follow this case. I suspect that the MPAA will somehow devise a way to give *Bully* a PG-13 and yet make it appear that it upholds its standards. But the fact is, unless it sticks to its R rating it has exposed the entire code for the bean counting it is. It will be expected again in the future to allow value judgments to affect its ratings.

In a debate after the screening, according to a later *Post* story, Dodd pointed out that the film could be released "unrated," and almost seemed to suggest he hopes that will happen, and let the MPAA off the hook. Harvey Weinstein, also at the screening, suggested an unrated release might be a possibility. Thus he will once again have scored one of his famous publicity coups.

There was once a time when Valenti could make a reasonable-sounding argument in favor of his ratings. I wonder what he could possibly say today. Wikipedia recalls Hollywood's Hays Office and its code, which enforced strict guidelines for more that thirty years (it required even married couples, for example, to sleep in separate beds). The article continues: "Valenti, who had become president of the MPAA in May 1966, deemed the Hays Code—in place since 1930 and rigorously enforced since July 1, 1934—as hopelessly out of date and no longer appropriate for the current film and cultural environment." Yes. And in 2012, you can say the same thing about Valenti's code.

## *The Raid* and Why I Hated It

March 27, 2012—My negative review of *The Raid: Redemption* violated one of my oldest principles, and put me way out of step with other critics. In my review I gave it one star. The movie currently stands at 8.4 on the Internet Movie Database, 83 percent on the Tomatometer, 76 on MRQE.com, 73 on Metacritic, and 65.4 on Movie Review Intelligence. When my review appeared online at 12:01 a.m. Thursday, *The Raid* was hovering near 100 percent at Rotten Tomatoes. You need a 60 to be a "fresh" tomato.

These numbers, of course, are not drawn from the same pool of viewers. IMDb and Rotten Tomatoes are weighted toward a wide selection of mainstream reviewers. MRQE and Meta monitor more serious critics. MRI does an interesting thing: It surveys local and national markets and tries to estimate the actual box office effect reviews have had.

These numbers in themselves have no significance compared to the words in the reviews they reflect. But they tell me my review violated one of my oldest reviewing guidelines. When I began, I found the star rating system to be absurd. I still do. But I thought I'd found a way to work with it. I'd take a "generic approach." Instead of pretending a star rating reflected some kind of absolute truth, I'd give stars based on how well I thought a movie worked within its genre and for its intended audience. A four-star rating might indicate the movie transcended generic boundaries. For example, what genre does *The Tree of Life* or *Synecdoche, New York* belong to?

Most accounts agree *The Raid* is a superb martial arts film. Because it wasn't filmed in English, it found itself opening mostly in art or specialized theaters, where it did big numbers. In English, it might have done even better because it truly is full-bore wall-to-wall action. I suspect its first audiences knew exactly what they were in for, and found exactly what they wanted. The trade paper reviewers, whose job is to advise exhibitors what kinds of audiences a film is likely to draw, were ecstatic. It was "hard-driving, butt-kicking, pulse-pounding, bone-crunching, skull-smashing, blood-curdling" (*Hollywood Reporter*) and "a hand-to-hand, fist-to-face, foot-to-groin battle, with a few machetes and guns tossed in for good measure" (*Variety*). "Extraordinary stunt and fight work and nonstop excitement, but a warning . . . this may be the most violent movie I've ever seen" (Peter Rainer, *Christian Science Monitor*). "A slam-bang, knock-your-socks-off action bonanza with some of the most peerlessly shot, performed and choreographed fight sequences you're likely to see on screen" (Gary Goldstein, *Los Angeles Times*).

These reviews are accurate. I agree with them. According to my generic approach, I should have written a favorable review. Why didn't I?

Here's a paragraph from my review: "*The Raid: Redemption* is essentially a visualized video game that spares the audience the inconvenience of playing it. There are two teams, the police SWAT team and the gangsters. The gangsters have their headquarters on the top floor of a fifteen-story building, where they can spy on every room and corridor with video surveillance. The SWAT team enters on the ground floor. Its assignment: Fight its way to the top, floor by floor."

This will be dismissed by some readers as a manifestation of my lack of enthusiasm for video games. Perhaps so. I think it springs more from my affection for characters, plot, human nature, and other elements possible in movies. *The Raid* is monotonously single-tracked in showing one gruesome scene of hand-to-hand combat after another. Heads are destroyed like targets in a carnival sideshow booth. Bones are crunched as if Army Rangers are building a campfire. The corpses piling up in great numbers are disposed of, apparently, by invisible cleanup crews. Why are there no shots of the living stepping with difficulty over the bleeding mounds of the dead?

A plot? *The Raid* supplies only plot markers, which are handy signposts indicating, "There would be a subplot here if we had the time to stop for one." One marker says, "Brother." Another says, "Betrayal." The movie's first one says, "Pregnant Wife."

Fans of this genre are long accustomed to two brothers finding themselves on opposite sides of a conflict, eventually forced to meet each other in a brutal standoff. Good movies have been developed around this theme; consider Mark Wahlberg and Christian Bale in *The Fighter* (2010). In *The Raid*, we're being signaled, "We could take the time to plug in a back story here, but why bore people?"

In a movie involving a conflict between the police and criminal forces, we expect that one or more turncoats will be involved, a high-level operative will be working for the enemy, and so on. *The Raid* has characters indicating they have such a function, but doesn't go into much detail.

The Pregnant Wife is always effective. If the hero kisses his pregnant wife good-bye before setting out on his mission, that's an efficient substitute for fifteen pages of dialogue setting up the character. He's good, we like him, and let the killing begin. In some movies, the plot will find a way to hold the pregnant wife hostage, but do you have any idea how much time that can take?

So what am I saying? *The Raid: Redemption* failed as a generic success because it simplified its plot too much? Not really. It is a generic success. And yet my heart sank and I asked myself: Is this all they want? Are audiences satisfied with ceaseless violence, just so long as they can praise it for being "well choreographed"? Is there no appreciation for human dimension, meaning, and morality? Westerns were the first Hollywood morality plays, and it was always clear who was good and who was bad. Now it doesn't matter so much, and the cops and robbers in *The Raid* agree with Red Sanders: "Winning isn't everything; it's the only thing."

Another quote from my review: "There's obviously an audience for the film, probably a large one. They are content, even eager, to sit in a theater and watch one action figure after another pound and blast one another to death. Have you noticed how cats and dogs will look at a TV screen on which there are things jumping around? It is to that level of the brain's reptilian complex that the film appeals."

I can't take this much longer. I can't function like a butcher's scale. Is it enough to spend two hours determining if a film "achieves its generic purpose"? Shouldn't it do more than that? Perhaps provide some humor, humanity, romance, suspense, beauty, strategy, poetry? Not all of those qualities, but at least several of them? *The Raid* didn't even supply a single good-looking publicity still.

I've seen some incredibly brutal South Korean films recently, like *The Chaser*, that contain enough violence to stun any fan of *The Raid*, but also have the advantage of being very good films, with intriguing characters, puzzling plots, and ingenious situations. I watched spellbound. *The Raid: Redemption* is dead in the water. The butcher slams the raw slab on his scale and asks, "How many are you feeding?"

These thoughts, some readers inform me, are a function of my age. I'm too old to appreciate a movie like this any longer. That may be true. It doesn't mean I lack the ability. It means I have grown beyond that stage. I am not as easily satisfied. When I began as a film critic, the word "genre" suggested a type of film that had highly developed traditions, possibilities, and richness. Now it suggests a marketing decision.

These days, audiences enter a film like this with tunnel vision. They know what they want, and they'd better find it. A film surpasses the requirements of its genre only at hazard. One of the best recent crime films, *Drive*, was close to a masterpiece. Sarah Deming, a Michigan woman, filed a lawsuit against its distributors claiming its trailer was misleading. *Entertainment Weekly* summarized her complaints:

1. *Drive* was promoted as very similar to *Fast and Furious*, when in actuality, it wasn't.

2. *Drive* bore very little similarity to a chase, or race action film, for reasons including but not limited to *Drive* having very little driving in the motion picture.

In other words, she was offended that the film surpassed its genre. This news item got a good deal of publicity at the time. I wonder if it was a billboard on Hollywood's highway to hell.

## I Remember You

April 12, 2012—The e-mails have been arriving with depressing regularity. Often the subject line is only the name of a friend. With dread I know what the message will contain: That person has died. In recent weeks there have been seven such losses. Three came in a ten-day period, and I fell into sadness.

The first death that registered in my life was my Aunt Hulda, my father's sister, who was laid out in the front parlor and I was allowed to kneel at the coffin, cross myself, and say a prayer before this strange, pale, motionless body. More than ten years later, my grandmother died. I was in high school now, and this death was more real. When my father died at the beginning of my freshman year in college, that was a blow to my existence. He had been the towering figure in my life.

Later many others died, as is inevitable. The public death that had the greatest impact was the assassination of John F. Kennedy. He stood at the head of my idea of America, and I felt then and still feel that some kind of compact had been broken between history and myself.

In the 1980s, my best friend in Chicago died. He had given me my critic's job at the paper, but much more important than that, he had possessed such a huge personality that all of us in his circle were stunned. Not a day goes past when I don't think of him. Then my mentor as an undergraduate was killed by a car when crossing the road. All of my writing, whether he read it or not, had been instinctively done with him as my audience. In 1999 my partner Gene Siskel died, and it was almost unthinkable that such a presence had ended.

But let this not be a listing. I miss them all. But these recent deaths have seemed to threaten my idea of who I am and the life I have lived. They are contemporaries. They are reservoirs of memory, and in an important sense all that we are is how we are remembered.

Two cousins from downstate died recently. I attended both funerals. At the first funeral, the other cousin was not only there but uncanny in the way he still resembled the kid I'd grown up with. Oddly, many of my memories were of him playing his accordion on Christmas Eves in that selfsame parlor where Aunt Hulda had been waked.

A few weeks later, I received the unexpected news that he had been diagnosed with cancer.

Unthinkable. He had seemed so filled with life and spirit. Now I learned, in a phrase we've all heard, "They found the cancer had spread, and they closed him up again. . . ."

At that second funeral, they had a wonderful slide show of family photos on a big screen TV. Looking at one old photo, I was startled, and waited for it to come around again. I pointed at the screen and started to write a note to explain, but it was no use: Now that this cousin had died, there was no one in the room who would have understood—not even his own younger sister.

The photo showed a family gathering in front of a small house in North Champaign, on some land where there's now a shopping mall. In the second row, much taller than anyone else, was Uncle Ben. He was married to Aunt Mame, my father's oldest sister. He drove an oil truck, and when he passed our house he sometimes tooted his horn and I'd run out in front and wave.

He was high above me in the cab of the truck, a considerable figure. He smoked cigars, which I found odd and unusual. I remembered him being tall, but in childhood everyone seems tall. In the old photo, I realized how tall he really was.

I think there's a chance I was the only person in the room who knew it was Uncle Ben in the second row. There were probably a dozen who knew in general who the picture showed—ancestors on the mother's side—but does the name or an idea of Uncle Ben linger on earth outside my own mind? When I die, what will remain of him?

Memory. It makes us human. It creates our ideas of family, history, love, friendship. Within all our minds is a narrative of our own lives and all the people who were important to us. Who were eyewitnesses to the same times and events. Who could describe us to a stranger.

Last week the wife of that great Chicago friend died. That death struck me with particular force, because they were so much at the center of my earlier years in Chicago. It was her husband who was instrumental in convincing me to go in fifty-fifty with them on a little duplex in the woods in Union Pier, across the lake from Chicago in Michigan.

"You're not going to see these prices again," he told me. He was correct. For $25,000 we bought a two-family A-frame on a third of an acre with a path giving beach access. That would have been in about 1979.

They were people who others gathered around as if by instinct. We had a Chicago pal who had moved out there, a photographer and carpenter, and my friend ordered a big wooden deck. "How big? As big as the eye can see, around a fire pit. How big should that be? Big enough to roast an ox."

At that corner cabin in the Michigan woods a dozen friends, maybe two dozen, would gather for events at which we were essentially celebrating our friendship. "I'll light a candle in the window," he'd say, and he always would—to be our guide in the forests of the night.

In the same period of ten days, another friend of forty years died. He was a Chicago newspaperman, a tall, laughing man with a tall, laughing wife. In our crowd you had better laugh easily, even at the same old stories, repeated time and again. The couple who shared the house with me had a young son. This boy and the newspaperman instinctively bonded on occasions like the Fourth of July. They would drive over the state line into Indiana and bring back grocery sacks filled with fireworks, and prowl the far reaches of the lawn shrouded by smoke, setting off rockets that sometimes whizzed alarmingly low over the deck.

There would always be a fire in the pit, not for warmth or to roast an ox, but because since the invention of time humans have gathered in circles to gaze into the flames and ponder their mysteries. My friend said, "Every cabin in the woods needs an outdoor fire pit."

And now my friend's wife and the newspaperman have both passed away. Early one morning, unable to sleep, I roamed my memories of them. Of an endless series of dinners, and brunches, and poker games, and jokes, and gossip. On and on, year after year. I remember them. They exist in my mind—in countless minds. But in a century the human race will have forgotten them, and me as well. Nobody will be able to say how we sounded when we spoke. If they tell our old jokes, they won't know whose they were.

That is what death means. We exist in the

minds of other people, in thousands of memory clusters, and one by one those clusters fade and disappear. Some years from now, at a funeral with a slide show, only one person will be able to say who we were. Then no one will know.

## The Perfect Audience

May 1, 2012—In a back row of the Virginia Theater in Urbana-Champaign, Illinois, you will see a raised platform just the right size to hold a reclining chair. This is my throne at Ebertfest. Because of havoc wrought by surgery to my back and right shoulder, I cannot sit comfortably in an ordinary chair. Here I recline at the side of my bride, looking upon the packed houses.

I realized something this year that has been true before. Ebertfest draws perfect audiences. During a film that requires total silence, such as *Take Shelter*, the audience was totally absorbed. During a comedy, such as *Joe Versus the Volcano*, they laughed easily at the right places. They got wound up during *Kinyarwanda* and *Big Fan*, and were deeply moved by *A Separation*. They were in sympathy with *Terri*. They opened their hearts to the beautiful Indian family drama *Patang*. They negotiated the deep moral waters of *Higher Ground*. They felt joy and sympathy with our guest of honor, the Australian director Paul Cox, who has survived a liver transplant. There were countless intelligent questions, in Q&A sessions that lasted forty-five minutes. There were no clueless fan questions.

They were always in tune.

A friend who was sitting in the front row of the balcony, looking down on the ground floor, told me there was not one single little block of light betraying a cell phone. Most amazing of all was the audience's reception of the final film, *Citizen Kane*. We played my audio commentary track during the screening, so my voice could be heard one last time in the Virginia. Listening to a film critic talk all the way through a movie would inspire restlessness, even rebellion, from some audiences. Miraculously, once again, everyone was attentive. They actually cared about what I was saying. (Apart from one woman I heard in the lobby loudly demanding her money back because she paid to see a movie, and somebody talked all through it.)

Some of our guests, directors and actors, mentioned this. Not only had they never before seen their film on such a large screen before such a large audience, but they hadn't shared it with an audience like that—1,500 people. Today's audiences are often noisy and disrespectful, considering themselves part of the show. They complain to theaters that they aren't allowed to text during movies.

Can you really blame them? How many of today's films really hold your attention? When you see a film that does, it's a reminder of how most movies used to work. A new film such as *The Avengers* is a perfectly competent piece of work, delivering what the audience expects. It is also an assembly of absurd comic book caricatures with no human aspects, embedded not in a story but in a series of brief sensational moments of special effects action.

My friend Richard Corliss of *Time* magazine does a masterful job of exercising faint praise. He writes: "The movie guarantees fast-paced fun without forcing anyone to think about what it all means, which is nothing. 'A poem should not mean / but be,' Archibald MacLeish wrote. A pop-culture smash should not mean but do: break stuff, agitate the senses, keep the customer satisfied. *The Avengers* doesn't aim for transcendence, only for the juggler's skill of keeping the balls smoothly airborne, and in 3-D too (converted after production). At that it succeeds."

At that it succeeds. If that's what you want. I said sort of the same thing. It is not high praise. I have a feeling the audiences at Ebertfest would have been as restless and unruly during *The Avengers* as a crowd of fanboys at a Bergman. Who are the people in an Ebertfest audience? Some came from out of state, and others from all over Illinois. Many are locals, and University of Illinois students. There are always about fifty older people, block-booked by Road Scholar. As I thought about them, it occurred to me that they were the right age to have been members of the film generation in the early 1960s. They were lining up for Godard in their twenties, and now Road Scholar sells them a package tour to Ebertfest. God love them. Nobody signs up for nonstop movies from Wednesday night until Sunday afternoon without knowing why they go to the movies.

We had about fifteen audience members who write for my Web site. These were the Far-Flung Correspondents and the Demanders (who do on demand films). They were from Egypt, India, Poland, Brazil, Mexico, Canada, the United Kingdom—from all over. One of them wrote me, "Thank you for reminding me what a moviegoing experience can and should be. This is why I got into film criticism."

The great fim scholar David Bordwell, in introducing the Alloy Orchestra's program of silent films, said a few words about movie palaces like the Virginia, built in the 1920s. They ennobled and enshrined motion pictures. It seems to me that today's multiplexes slice movies into franchises like a mall with so many strip stores.

But as I sat on my throne in the Virginia Theater and joined a perfect audience, knowledgeable and attentive, watching good movies, I thought . . .

*Don't let it be forgot*
*That once there was a spot*
*For one brief shining moment that was known*
*As Camelot.*

## Movies Don't Stream Themselves

June 8, 2012—This will be the year that revenue from streaming passes revenue from DVD sales, according to a recent article in the *Hollywood Reporter.*

How do we feel about this? I ask as a movie watcher who subscribes to Netflix, Hulu, and Fandor, and also rents online from Amazon and Vudu. iTunes gets none of my business because the iTunes Store has been misbehaving on my computer. I average three streaming movies a week and three or four on DVD. I'm not an average consumer because a lot of my viewing is for work. But often of an evening I'll stream for pleasure. All of my streaming happens through a Roku player on HDTV.

Does anyone recall the time when HBO was first test-marketing movies on demand? There was much hilarity when it was learned that their Florida test market wasn't exactly a model of digital automation. Apparently actual employees were taking telephone orders and then scrambling around to push movies into playback machines—on videocassettes, because DVDs hadn't been introduced.

These days the video quality of most movies is acceptable to excellent, assuming the films themselves come from good prints. Netflix and Fandor deliver flawless service, although my Hulu has occasionally been freezing, presumably for buffering, in the high-use evening hours. On the whole I'm a happy camper. The first streaming movie I saw online was an old B Western from Republic, and the image was the size of a postage stamp.

I buy DVDs when I need to. Recently, for example, I purchased Bela Tarr's *Satantango* from Facets Multimedia because it absolutely is not available online. Many, many films are not. I find from instantwatcher.com, a site that monitors Netflix, that the most-watched titles are not likely to be by Bela Tarr. The top five titles at this moment are *The Rum Diary, Nude Nuns with Big Guns, Best Evidence: Top 10 UFO Sightings, The Patriot,* and *Absinthe.* Netflix has good depth, however, and every night before I turn in, I suggest a "daily streamer" on my Twitter and Facebook. Recent titles: *My Left Foot, What's Eating Gilbert Grape, Lost in Translation, Merci Pour le Chocolat, Still Walking, French Cancan, The Man Who Wasn't There,* and *Pi.* All of those are on Netflix Instant except for Renoir's *French Cancan*; it's part of the Criterion Collection on Hulu, which bought the Criterion rights.

Because I wanted to suggest films from several different sources, I asked my Facebook "friends" how they felt about Hulu and Fandor. Many said Hulu was fine with them. Many didn't know about Fandor. The Hulu supporters were fibbing. I can tell from click counts that the vast majority of my FB folks use Netflix Instant and that's it. Hulu draws barely 15 percent as many clicks, but of course most people use Hulu to stream TV, and by virtue of their excellence, Hulu's Criterion titles are less popular than *Nude Nuns with Big Guns.* Nothing alarms some moviegoers more than the news that a movie is a masterpiece.

What does this have to do with the watershed we're now passing, when streaming revenues pass DVD sales? A great deal, and a lot of it is bad news.

The companies that manufacture and distribute DVDs are in business to make a profit. They invest much of their income in the cost of restoring films, especially classics, so the DVD version usually has better visual quality than any 35 mm print you're lucky enough to see. If DVD sales decline, film restoration declines right along with them.

I was talking about this not long ago with an executive of a respected DVD label—never mind which one. He said Netflix was killing him. For years, when he released a new DVD title, he could count on a certain number of sales in three ways: (1) direct mail or Amazon, (2) video stores, and (3) a bulk order from Netflix. Judging by the predicted sales, he could judge his costs and cover his overhead.

"Now what's happened," he said, "is that video stores are closing because of streaming. Amazon sales are down because Amazon Instant streams a lot of titles. And people don't buy if they figure a movie will be streaming on Netflix. Previously, Netflix would buy a lot of titles to service their customers who got movies by mail. But with their price changes, they forced a lot of those customers to choose between mail and streaming. As a result, Netflix needs a lot fewer DVDs in order to be able to offer a title."

This is all obviously true. What does it mean for us? It means the day is coming when nonblockbuster titles will undergo a sudden income crisis. If you can sell between several hundred and a few thousand physical DVDs, you have a good chance of breaking even. If you have a Tiffany product like Criterion, you can afford the considerable costs of film restoration. When income dries up, those kinds of films become more challenging to manufacture and distribute.

Criterion seems to be fairly well situated for now, because its customers love the beautiful prints, value the extras like commentary tracks and booklets, and enjoy building a collection. Because Criterion has always had excellent taste, it has preserved and made available countless films that were long completely unavailable. Would you believe that Hulu (which doesn't yet have every Criterion title) offers 222 films from Japan and 201 from France—two of the world's three great cinemas?

But income from streaming is far lower than income from rentals and sales. Criterion's deal with Hulu helps them amortize the cost of their back catalog, but hardly pays for new restorations.

I know of a couple of companies that even now are releasing new DVDs of out-of-print movies. The Warner Archive regularly publishes back titles from its own catalog, in limited editions. And an enterprising company named Twilight Time buys the rights to publish three thousand copies of unavailable titles ("When they're gone, they're gone!"). Many studios just aren't interested in those kinds of DVD sales; Warner matches Disney as the most adept at marketing old films.

All of this leads us by a meandering path to my final destination, Fandor.com. This is a streaming outlet that specializes in independent films, classics, silent films, foreign films, documentaries, and shorts. Its site is rich with essays about directors, genres, and film history. The comments are invariably well written. And Fandor shares income fifty-fifty with independent filmmakers! That shows where its heart is.

You will not find *Prometheus* offered anytime soon on Fandor. It appeals to moviegoers who have *Prometheus* covered. Their customers seem to want to explore more deeply and widely than most streaming customers. I'm rummaging at their site right now, and seeing Mark Rappaport's *From the Journals of Jean Seberg* (1995); Andrei Tarkovsky's *The Sacrifice* (1986); Raoul Walsh's *Sea Devils* (1953); Mike Ott's *Littlerock*, which I favorably reviewed in 2010; Angelina Maccarone's *Charlotte Rampling: The Look* (2011); Curtis Harrington's *Ruby* (1977); Joseph Losey's *King and Country* (1964); George Hickenlooper's *Some Folks Call It a Sling Blade* (1999); and F. W. Murnau's *Phantom* (1922). Also a lot of Buster Keaton.

You haven't heard of some of these? That's sort of the idea. It's nice to know that a legendary figure like Mark Rappaport, whose films I reviewed in first run, can still share in his revenue.

Fandor has about the same monthly fee as Hulu or Netflix. I'm not saying you should drop everything and subscribe. Some people do a rotation from one service to another, to increase their variety. What I am saying is that sooner or later, streaming video is a bill that will come due. Independent films do not make themselves. DVDs are not self-manufactured. Income from streaming is not paying the rent and keeping the lights on. Sooner or later, one way or another, streaming will have to pay for the films it streams. That means us.

## A Few Calm Words About The List

August 1, 2012—The king is dead. Long live the king. Welles's *Citizen Kane* has been dethroned from the *Sight & Sound* magazine list of the greatest films of all time, and replaced by Hitchcock's *Vertigo.* It's not as if nobody saw this coming. The list first appeared in 1952, and *Vertigo* (1958) made the list for the first time only in 1982. Climbing slowly, it placed five votes behind *Kane* in 2002. Although many moviegoers would probably rank *Psycho* or maybe *North by Northwest* as Hitch's best, for *S&S* types his film to beat was *Notorious* (1946). That's the one I voted for until I went through *Vertigo* a shot at a time at the University of Virginia, became persuaded of its greatness, and put it on my 2002 list.

But let's remember that all movie lists, even this most-respected one, are ultimately meaningless. Their tangible value is to provide movie lovers with viewing ideas. In the era of DVD, all of the films on the list are available; in 1952, unless you had unusual resources, most of them could be found only in a few big cities.

What surprised me this year is how little I was surprised. I believed a generational shift was taking place, and that as the critics I grew up with faded away, young blood would add new names to the list. Kieslowski, perhaps. Herzog. Fassbinder. Scorsese. Lynch. Wong Kar-wai.

What has happened is the opposite. This year's 846 voters looked further into the past. The most recent film in the critics' top ten, as it has been for years, is Kubrick's *2001: A Space Odyssey* (1968). The two new films are silent: Vertov's *Man with a Movie Camera* (1929), and Dreyer's *The Passion of Joan of Arc* (1928). Murnau's great silent *Sunrise* (1927) is also on the list—three silents out of ten, and no Chaplin, Keaton, or Eisenstein.

Why not more recent directors? To make the list, a director is punished if too many of his films are voted for. He needs an "official masterpiece." With Buster Keaton that film used to be *The General*, but after the restoration of all of his films his votes have become scattered, I suspect, among *Sherlock Jr.*, *Steamboat Bill Jr.*, and other treasures.

It is a delicious irony that Ozu's *Tokyo Story* (1953) is in third place, in the very week it disappeared from IMDb's Top 250 after that site tweaked its rules. Jean Renoir made many great films, but *La Règle du jeu* (*The Rules of the Game*, 1939) has become the default choice. For years John Ford's *Grapes of Wrath* was called not only his best film but, by some, the greatest American film. His *Searchers* (1956) was widely disregarded on release, but is now in the pantheon. Fellini's *8½* is now his go-to film, although I prefer *La Dolce Vita.*

Then we have a separate list voted on only by film directors. They give first place to *Tokyo Story*, have a tie between *Citizen Kane* and *2001*, then go to *8½*, Scorsese's *Taxi Driver*, Coppola's *Apocalypse Now*, a tie between Coppola's *Godfather* and Hitchcock's *Vertigo*, and then Tarkovski's *Mirror* and De Sica's *Bicycle Thieves.* Four of these titles are from the 1970s, made since *2001: A Space Odyssey.*

The absence of two names surprises me—Ingmar Bergman and Akira Kurosawa. In a poll conducted by a British magazine, there are no British directors aside from Hitchcock. For all of the cheering for the French New Wave, no Godard, Truffaut, or their shipmates. Did anyone in Japan at the time foresee the ascendency of Ozu? It took an American critic, Donald Richie, to take his films to the Venice Film Festival and prove he was not "too Japanese" for export. Only Coppola has escaped the "official masterpiece" curse, with the directors giving *Apocalypse Now* the recognition it deserves.

In the new issue of *Sight & Sound*, the magazine will break the voting down further, telling us which directors had the most total votes. They will also release the actual ballots; reading who 358 film directors voted for can be revealing about their own work.

For years people have been telling me they just don't see what's so great about *Citizen Kane.* Now they tell me they just don't see what's so great about *Vertigo.* My answer will remain the same: "You're insufficiently evolved as a moviegoer." Or, more simply, "You're wrong."

Let's close by returning to *Vertigo*. Every time I've gone through any film a shot at a time over several days, someone in the audience has noticed something amazing. When I was at the University of Virginia, we got to the point when Scottie (James Stewart) rescues the unconscious Madeleine/Judy (Kim Novak) from San Francisco Bay and takes her unconscious back to his apartment. He gently undresses her and puts her into bed.

"His action is incredible," I said. "He's taking change of an unconscious stranger."

"She's not unconscious," said a voice in the dark.

"What?"

"She's pretending. That wasn't Madeleine attempting suicide, but Judy playing Madeleine. She's pretending to be unconscious."

And Scottie saved her, did not ravish her, treated her gently, and tucked her in. That may help explain why the next time we see her, coming into the living room and joining Scottie, she has a glow in her eyes. Madeleine went into the bedroom, and Judy came out. It's then she starts to love and pity him. Oh, this is an even deeper film than it seems.

**The Critics' Top Ten Greatest Films of All Time**

1. *Vertigo* (Hitchcock, 1958)
2. *Citizen Kane* (Welles, 1941)
3. *Tokyo Story* (Ozu, 1953)
4. *La Règle du jeu* (Renoir, 1939)
5. *Sunrise: A Song for Two Humans* (Murnau, 1927)
6. *2001: A Space Odyssey* (Kubrick, 1968)
7. *The Searchers* (Ford, 1956)
8. *Man with a Movie Camera* (Vertov, 1929)
9. *The Passion of Joan of Arc* (Dreyer, 1927)
10. *8½* (Fellini, 1963)

**The Directors' Top Ten Greatest Films of All Time**

1. *Tokyo Story* (Ozu, 1953)
2. (tie) *2001: A Space Odyssey* (Kubrick, 1968)
2. (tie) *Citizen Kane* (Welles, 1941)
4. *8½* (Fellini, 1963)
5. *Taxi Driver* (Scorsese, 1976)
6. *Apocalypse Now* (Coppola, 1979)
7. (tie) *The Godfather* (Coppola, 1972)
7. (tie) *Vertigo* (Hitchcock, 1958)
9. *Mirror* (Tarkovsky, 1975)
10. *Bicycle Thieves* (De Sica, 1948)

# In Memoriam

## Andrew Sarris

June 20, 2012—Andrew Sarris, who loved movies, is dead at eighty-three. He was the most influential American film critic of his time, and one of the jolliest. More than anyone else, he was responsible for introducing Americans to the auteur theory, the belief that the true author of a film is its director. Largely because of him, many moviegoers today think of films in terms of their directors.

Sarris died June 20, 2012, in Manhattan. His wife, Molly Haskell, herself a formidable film critic, said the cause of death was complications after a fall. He remained active until recent years, teaching film courses at Columbia University and writing for the *New York Observer*.

If Sarris didn't set out to be a film critic, he certainly didn't set out to become anything else. From an early age he was entranced by the movies, and after college and three years in the army, his career plans remained vague and he attended as many movies as he could. In the late 1950s he spent a memorable year in Paris, where a new generation of critics and directors was advocating the auteur theory in opposition to prevailing opinion that valued story and production values above direction. It was there that he met many of the founders of the magazine *Cahiers du Cinema*, some of whom were in the process of becoming directors, including Francois Truffaut, Claude Chabrol, and Jean-Luc Godard.

Returning home, still living in his mother's house in Queens, he persuaded the *Village Voice* to begin running his reviews, and from that pulpit he converted a generation of young cineastes to auteurism. The other great critical luminary of the 1960s was Pauline Kael, whose approach was more personal, rejecting schools or theories in favor of her immediate visceral experience.

Kael and Sarris had a celebrated feud during that time, played out in the pages of various film magazines, that had younger critics choosing sides and giving more thought to the philosophy that supported their own opinions. If I claim Sarris was the more influential, it was because he laid out his orthodoxy in objective terms, while Kael's was always more impressionist. Sarris's book *The American Cinema: Directors and Directions 1929–1968* suggested a pantheon of great directors who had made films in the United States, enthroning fourteen: Robert Flaherty, John Ford, D. W. Griffith, Howard Hawks, Buster Keaton, Orson Welles, Fritz Lang, Ernst Lubitsch, F. W. Murnau, Max Ophuls, Josef von Sternberg, Charles Chaplin, Alfred Hitchcock, and Jean Renoir. He later added a fifteenth name, Billy Wilder, while directing criticism at such well-regarded names as Otto Preminger, Stanley Kubrick, William Wyler, Stanley Kramer, and David Lean.

It is hard to believe that some of the names in Sarris's pantheon were ill regarded when Sarris began on the *Voice*. His first review was praise for Alfred Hitchcock's *Psycho* (1960), which had stirred up a firestorm of outrage. In my own first days as a film critic, Kael was my muse, but Sarris was my mapmaker.

In December 1967, my first year as a film critic, I read every word of Sarris's *Interviews with Film Directors*, which singled out those he found noteworthy. I underlined Sarris's observation: "Even art films have to make money and even commercial films have to make some statement. To put it another way, more and more critics are demanding that there should be more fun in art, and more art in fun. . . . In the process . . . it has become possible to speak of Alfred Hitchcock and Michelangelo Antonioni in the same breath and with the same critical terminology."

This, to me, was a signpost pointing the direction that a daily newspaper film critic might choose. One might also remember that for a nickel, then the price of the paper, the reader might reasonably expect to be entertained, since 95 percent of the readers would not go to 95 percent of the movies and yet might read the review.

I began to read Sarris regularly in the *Village Voice*, and found his voice to be clear and energetic, free of jargon and self-importance. Although he was famous as the leader of the auteurist critical school in America, he was not particularly theoretical or doctrinaire, and seemed in close touch with the actual experience of seeing the movie itself. The next year, his book *The American Cinema* was published and helped guide my frequent visits to the Clark Theater, a repertory house in the Loop that showed a different double feature every day.

In the 1970s I went to the Cannes Film Festival and met Sarris and Haskell. They were staying at the Hotel Splendid, which was then at the unfashionable end of town (although the new Palais was later built across the street). We'd met before at the New York Film Festival, but now Andy and Molly and I became friends, sitting late at night in the bar of the Hotel Majestic in a crowd that included the few other American critics who were then regularly at Cannes. Andy, already a legend, found festivals infinitely amusing and a great deal of fun. I cannot call up in my memory a picture of him discussing a film without smiling.

The last time I saw them at Cannes would have been in the early 1980s, when Billy (Silver Dollar) Baxter hosted a post-festival party at the Voile d'Or, a hotel down the coast at Saint Jean Cap Ferrat. They were in superb shape on the tennis courts. At some point after this Andrew contracted a rare disease that rendered him all but immobile for several months. Recreating this period in her 1990 memoir *Love and Other Infectious Diseases*, Haskell wrote: "My husband awoke one night with a fever of 105.9. I rushed him to the emergency room of a New York hospital, and there began a six-month drama in which doctors tried to figure out what was wrong with him, while I alternated between hope and despair. For the three months that Andrew remained critically ill and deranged, hallucinating most of the time, he was no longer the lover, friend, fellow critic and confidant I was used to."

But he recovered and their marriage endured, and he remained an inexhaustible force, going to the movies, writing, teaching, holding court.

I remember him the year *Apocalypse Now* was being premiered at Cannes. A half dozen American critics were invited to visit Francis Coppola on his yacht and talk about his film. That was the fateful night he expressed his doubts about its ending. Coppola told us he considered Cannes his "out-of-town tryout." Sarris asked, "Where's town?"

# Film Festival

## Toronto International Film Festival

### *Melancholia* Descends on Toronto

*Toronto*, September 13, 2011—More than in previous years, I'm noticing the laptops in the audiences here at the Toronto International Film Festival (TIFF). Some of the bloggers seem to be beginning their reviews as the end credits still play. Then you see them outside, sitting on a corridor floor, their computers tethered to an electric umbilical, as they type urgently. Of course many of them share their opinions in quick conversational bursts, and a consensus develops. Most films good enough for an important festival, I think, require a little more marinating.

Certainly that's the case with *Melancholia*, the new film by Lars von Trier. He seems to depart from every festival hobbling on whichever foot he's shot himself in this time, but can you deny he's one of the boldest and most original filmmakers of these days? I'm grateful that Magnolia Pictures screened it in Chicago before the festival began; as usual, TIFF seems to crowd the press screenings of all its films into the opening weekend.

Here is a film that requires additional time not to understand—it's quite transparent, for a von Trier—but to fully appreciate. Its subject is no less than the end of the world, as Earth collides with a vast planet named, yes, Melancholia. Von Trier explained that he had been going through an extended period of depression while making some of his previous films, *Antichrist* included. Now, having stopped drinking, he rebounded with this apocalyptic vision, which he cheerfully described as "my most optimistic film."

Alcohol is of course a depressant, and some people discover when they stop taking it that they bounce the other way, into inappropriate elation. That may somewhat explain von Trier's jolly statements about the Nazis, which got him declared persona non grata at Cannes last April. He thought everyone would know he was joking. "I'm no Nazi," he was forced to explain. Well, of course he isn't. But when you hear yourself having to say something like that, you know your mouth has raced heedlessly ahead of your mind.

This is not the time for my proper review of *Melancholia*, but let me just say a few words about its daring. Technically, it's science fiction, but this is a sci-fi movie like no other. As the new planet grows in the sky, there are no TV news updates, no cabinet meetings, no nuclear rockets fired at it, no surging mobs in the streets of Delhi, London, and San Francisco. Not even any supermarket riots—because with the world ending, how much bottled water do you need, really?

In fact, it is somewhat unclear in the early scenes what, exactly, the characters know about the phenomenon that first appears as the brightest of evening stars. It is noted with curiosity by Justine (Kirsten Dunst, never better), who with her new husband, Michael (Alexander Skarsgard), is on her way to a postnuptial party in the country. This party will involve not desperate world-ending drunkenness and sexuality, or prayer and meditation, or madness. Much of the time the impending calamity is not even the central subject of conversation. Von Trier has never made a more realistic domestic drama, depicting a family that is dysfunctional not in crazy ways, but in ways showing a defiant streak of intelligent individualism.

In any film involving the destruction of the globe, we know that, if it is not to be saved, there must be a "money shot" depicting the actual cataclysm. Assign a dozen other directors the challenge of creating a shot depicting such a catastrophe, and I doubt any could do better than von Trier does here. There are no tidal waves. No animals fleeing through burning forests. No skyscrapers falling. None of that easy stuff.

No, there is simply a character standing on a hill and staring straight at the impending doom, as von Trier shows it happening in what logically must be slow motion, with a fearsome preliminary merging of planetary atmospheres.

Violent death is often a shabby business in the movies. It happens in depressing bedrooms, bloody bathtubs, shattered cars, bleak alleys. Its victims are cast down, empty of life. Here is a character who says, I see it coming, I will face it, I will not turn away, I will observe it as long as my eyes and my mind still function.

Is it fair of me to speculate that von Trier himself regards death in that way? He tends to be grandiose, but if one cannot be grandiose in imagining one's own death, then when is grandiosity justified?

We arrived here last Wednesday, started seeing films Thursday, are booked up nearly wall-to-wall. This is not only one of the three or four major film festivals on earth, but one of the best run and most user-friendly. Wandering toward screenings, you encounter such filmmakers as Atom Egoyan and Jason Reitman, directors not here to do business but—what do you know!—to see movies. The public waits dutifully in queues, as if making a silent protest against the shoving matches before screenings at Cannes. The four local dailies (!) cover it like the *Washington Post* covers a presidential election.

Toronto announces the end of a summer of often disappointing and overinflated "blockbusters," and an autumn that feels like a springtime of the cinema. We'll be here until the end. More to follow.

## *The Artist* and the New Herzog

September 13, 2011—I have not quite become jaded. Sometimes I fear that I am so familiar with movie formulas that some films don't have a fair chance. Then I go to see Michel Hazanavicius's film *The Artist* and it tells a story that would have been familiar in the late 1920s, when it is set, and I begin by admiring its technique and am surprised to find, halfway through, that I actually care how it turns out.

This was the surprise hit of Cannes 2011, the winner of the best actor award for Jean Dujardin. It is a silent film—nearly. It is a black-and-white, in the classic screen ratio of 1:1.33, and has music, as all silent films did in one way or another. It is a loose retelling of *Singin' in the Rain*, another film about a silent star failing to make the transition to talkies. Dujardin plays a dashing Hollywood leading man named George Valentin, whose French accent might presumably make him unsuitable for sound movies.

Here you do not require the plot, which waits my actual review. What you may need to know is that silent films can weave a certain enchantment that isn't available with the greater realism of sound. During a good one, I fall into a reverie, an encompassing dreamy absorption that drops me out of time more than a talking picture. The actors do not speak to one another but embody what they would have said. They project emotions, and although they often do it broadly, the medium expands easily to encompass them.

The talkies make Valentin yesterday's star, and elevate a charming little starlet named Peppy Miller (Berenice Bejo) into fame. She's known for her little beauty mark, which Valentin penciled in with love and care. His new film is ignored, hers is a hit, he sinks into depression, she remains loyal, and . . .

There's a lot more, including a wonderful dog. But let me discuss Jean Dujardin. At age thirty-nine, he resembles young Sean Connery enough to qualify as the star of the OSS 117 films, the French 007 spoofs. The way he flashes his engaging smile here, however, reminded me more of Gene Kelly in *Singin' in the Rain*. He is confident, warm, friendly, and—unlike Kelly's character—not an egotist.

But there's something else. He would have made a great silent star. His face is perhaps too open and expressive for sound, except comedy. But it serves perfectly for the purposes here. More than many silent actors, he is subtle, and that allows him to negotiate the hazards of some unbridled melodrama at the end. I felt a great affection for him.

I had great admiration for the film as a whole, and so did the audience in the big Elgin Theater, which was possibly the warmest crowd I've been in at Toronto since the premiere of *Juno*. This would not seem a likely time for a silent movie, but *The Artist* ignores that and goes about its business. I wouldn't be at all surprised if it's a significant box-office success.

*Gazing into the Abyss: A Tale of Death, a Tale*

*of Life* is the saddest film Werner Herzog has ever made. It regards a group of miserable lives, and in finding a few faint glimmers of hope only underlines the sadness.

The documentary centers on two young men in Houston, one on death row, the other spared death but facing a life sentence. There is no reason to especially pity these two. They were responsible for murders distinguished by their stupidity. The film doesn't argue they were wrongly convicted.

Herzog keeps a lower profile than in many of his documentaries. He is not seen, and his off-camera voice quietly asks questions that are factual, understated, and simply curious. His subjects talk willingly. One speaks within days of his scheduled execution.

Why was one spared? We meet his father, also in prison for life. His testimony at his son's trial, at which he blamed himself for the boy's valueless upbringing, apparently influenced two women jurors to pity the boy—or perhaps even more the father.

Today this father seems a decent and reflective man. He bitterly regrets that he failed to take advantage of a college scholarship, dropped out of high school, and went wrong. He sees his mistake clearly now—too late.

The young men are uneducated, rootless, without personal resources. The father perhaps has benefited from prison, as his son may. We also meet their close relatives, a wife, relatives of their victims, a minister, and the remarkable Captain Fred Allen, who was long in charge of the guard detail on death row. What he has to say during a long introspective memory of one event in his life is one of the most profound statements I can imagine about the death penalty.

The people in this film, I think without exception, cite God as a force in their lives. The killers, the relatives of their victims, the police, everyone. God has a plan. It is all God's will. God will forgive. Their lives are in His hands. They must accept the will of the Lord. Condemned or bereft, they all apparently find comfort.

Opposition to the death penalty, I suppose, comes down to this: Although the convicted may not deserve to live, no one deserves to be given the task of executing them. I think that's what Herzog is saying, although he doesn't say it. In some of his films, he freely shares his philosophy and insights. In this film, he simply looks. He always seems to know where to look.

# Ebert's Little Movie Glossary

These are the year's new contributions to my glossary project. Hundreds of entries were collected in *Ebert's Bigger Little Movie Glossary,* published in 1999. Contributions are always welcome.

* * *

**The A.I. Voice Malfunction.** Almost all cinematic artificial intelligence will not shut down immediately. It will instead acquire a deep malfunctioning radio voice and will eventually fade out after the completion of a sentence. E.g., *2001: A Space Odyssey, I Robot.*

—R. Prashanth

**The Brilliant Checkmate.** Every time two movie characters are depicted playing chess, one of them will invariably find himself in the highly unlikely situation of being one genius-move away from checkmate (see the Kronsteen character in *From Russia with Love* and the replicant's creator in *Blade Runner*).

—Gerardo Valero, Mexico City, Mexico

**Deadly Efficiency Syndrome.** In a horror movie, someone always goes missing, usually permanently. The hero will suggest the idea that the group split into smaller groups of not more than two persons to search for that person; the reason is because the ship, house, woods, etc., is too big and it would seem more logical to break up into smaller groups to save time. This develops into the subplots of which the smaller groups meet their demise one by one.

—Jason Warren, San Francisco

**The Face-Sparing Punch.** Whenever the villain and hero face off and the former is disproportionately stronger than the latter, the bad guy won't throw a punch but instead will launch the protagonist into the air since a direct hit would surely destroy his face for future scenes. See Arnold throwing Nick Stahl and the Terminatrix-hurling Clare Danes in *Terminator 3*, Superman launching Lex Luthor in the original 1978 entry, and a cybernetic being discharging Colin Farrel in the new version of *Total Recall.*

—Gerardo Valero, Mexico City, Mexico

**Godzilla Geometry.** When a large crowd of terrified people flees a gigantic threat, they will run away in a perfectly straight line directly in front of the threat. It never seems to occur to anyone to turn left or right down a nice quiet street where the threat shows no apparent interest in going. (Examples: *Cloverfield, War of the Worlds,* every *Godzilla* movie ever made, etc.)

—A.J. Hamler

**The Half-Shave Equals Full-Shave Rule.** When a man is shaving in the movies and is interrupted mid-shave, when he wipes the remaining cream from his face, there's never any stubble left. He is later seen fully shaven even though he was interrupted.

—Zach Buchwald, New York

**The Law of Running Water.** No character who catches his reflection in the bathroom mirror will ever turn off a running faucet.

—James Garza

**The Mind-Changing Roar Rule.** Whenever we see a dog barking at another creature and the latter responds with a loud roar, the canine will invariably react by uttering a low-pitched howl and run and hide as quick as it possibly can. (See the dog barking at the Caesar chimpanzee in *Rise of the Planet of the Apes* and the one that confronts the T-Rex that's drinking water from a pool in *Lost World, Jurassic Park*).

—Gerardo Valero, Mexico City, Mexico

**Nameless Beer Rule.** When movie characters order a beer, they rarely specify the brand, nor does the waitress ask. They order "a beer"—not "a Heineken" or "a Coors" or "a Budweiser," just "a beer."

—David Cote

**News Flash Bracketing.** When any character turns on a TV or radio to find out about plot details, the pertinent details applying to the character's situation will always be prefaced with "This just in . . ." or "In a late development. . . ." Then, to let our characters know that the pertinent info is over and they can turn the TV off, it will be followed with either, "In other news . . ." or "And in sports. . . ."

—A.J. Hamler

**Obsolete Dial Tones.** Tense phone calls are ended with two outdated sound effects: the crackle of a plastic receiver being placed in its holder and a dial tone. This is done in films when both persons are on cell phones or wireless phones, which have not EVER had dial tones. I suppose it's because audiences are too dumb to know when a phone call has ended without those obsolete sounds.

—Jonathan Flanders

**The Pre-Cued Song Rule.** Whenever a CD or cassette is inserted into any player, there is no need for anyone to find the correct track, and not a moment of silence; instead we are instantly treated to the desired song (which usually begins somewhere in the middle).

—Damien Francoeur, Boston

**Retro Future Technology.** Every movie set in the future but filmed in years past will include one or several gadgets that will give away the real period when it was actually filmed (see the old-fashioned monitors and computers in futuristic movies like *Alien*, *Blade Runner*, and *Total Recall*).

—Gerardo Valero, Mexico City, Mexico

**Senseless Acrobatics Rule.** Named after the pointless habit by some movie characters of attacking another while performing elaborate somersaults which in reality would give any nemesis more than enough time to get out of the way (see Darryl Hannah's character in *Blade Runner*, the Bambi and Thumper villains in *Diamonds Are Forever*, and the penguin's henchmen in *Batman Returns*).

—Gerardo Valero, Mexico City, Mexico

**Soldiers Passing in the Fight.** The moment when a contingent of young soldiers about to go to the front crosses paths with wounded, forlorn soldiers coming back from the front. Invariably, the story's hero will exchange looks with a heavily-medicated victim.

—Alberto Diamante, Toronto, Ontario, Canada

**Superglue Girlfriends.** A mysterious connection binds women in movies to heroes that speak to them in monosyllabic grunts, come and go with no warning, show up with their faces beaten in, and hustle them out the door in a rush, insisting that they go stay with their mother where it's safe. Inevitably, these knockouts will stick around and wait for their man to finish "one last job," even though with minimal effort they could find someone just as attractive who would actually treat them well.

—Keith Nelson, Arlington, Va.

**Unlimited Arrows.** While movie gunmen are occasionally seen reloading their weapons, movie archers always have an unlimited supply of arrows. A prime example is Legolas, the Elven archer in *Lord of the Rings*. He spends the entire trilogy dispatching hundreds, if not thousands, of arrows, yet his supply never runs low.

—David Cote

**The Volvo Rule.** Many working class people in movies work in well-paying and interesting professions that require very little time spent actually working. They live in professionally decorated homes with spacious, manicured lawns. They always eat in upscale restaurants with soft lighting and exquisite menus. They drive Volvos or BMWs and are able to hop on cross-country or intercontinental flights at a moment's notice with no regard to the four-digit figure that such a flight would likely cost. The alternative lifestyle to this is the family living in chaotic blue collar squalor where the only employment options are working in a factory or waiting tables in a diner.

—Jim Mitchell, St. Louis

**Wolfganging.** When an individual or group, in order to show wealth, plays the music of Wolfgang Amadeus Mozart at an event. Wolfganging is most effective at fancy parties or weddings, using the song "Eine Kleine Nachtmusik."

—Nico Bellamy, San Francisco

# Index

## A

# B

# D

# E

# F

# G

# H

# L

# N

# Q



# R

# S

# T

# U



# V

# X



# Y